Yogi Ramsuratkumar

Under the Punnai Tree

कोटिसूर्यप्रभा

Yogi Ramsuratkumar
Under the Punnai Tree

M. Young

Hohm Press

कोटिसूर्यप्रभा

Cover layout: Kim Johansen
Layout and design: Becky Fulker
Frontispiece: Oil painting by Wendel Field, "Yogi Ramsuratkumar near Arunachala with Swami Ramdas in the distance," 1973.
Back Cover Art: "Kotisuryaprabhu and Kirti Mukha, 'Face of Glory,' " by Nara, 2003.
"Fan and Coconut Bowl" by Nara, 2003.

Library of Congress Control Number: 2003106277

ISBN: 1-890772-34-8

The following authors have kindly given permission to reprint quotations from published works: *The Gospel of Swami Ramdas*, by Swami Satchidananda, Anandashram, Kerala, India, 1990; *Waves of Love*, by Vijayalakshmi of the Yogi Ramsuratkumar Ashram, Yogi Ramsuratkumar Trust, Tiruvannamalai, India, 2002.

Photographs in this book are courtesy of: Dwarak Nath Reddy, Truman Caylor Wadlington, Lee Lozowick, Hohm Sahaj Mandir, Wendel Field and Ramanashram.

Poems written by Yogi Ramsuratkumar on pages 701, 705 and 706 are courtesy of Will Zulkowski; on pages 636, 637 and 711 are courtesy of Truman Caylor Wadlington. Drawings by Yogi Ramsuratkumar on pages 684 through 688 are courtesy of Truman Caylor Wadlington.

HOHM PRESS
P.O. Box 2501
Prescott, AZ 86302
800-381-2700
http://www.hohmpress.com

This book was printed in the U.S.A. on recycled acid-free paper using soy ink.

For Lee,

who fell in love with a dirty beggar a long
time ago, and now freely gives that love away.

TABLE OF CONTENTS

Acknowledgments

Researching stories for this book has been like a treasure hunt or a magical mystery tour, beginning in the States with Americans who knew Yogi Ramsuratkumar well in the 1970s, then in Tamil Nadu—Tiruvannamalai, Chennai (Madras), Madurai, Sivakasi, Tirukoilur, Trivendrum and Kanya Kumari—and later in Bombay. It was a process that revealed an epic of some mythic proportion: the story of one greathearted being and his abiding love of God, his connections with many great saints of Tamil Nadu and the stories of the intimate relationship between the guru and his devotees, told by people with bright shining faces and deep smiling eyes.

On the spiritual path, the master is reflected in the devotees in a very powerful and meaningful way. In November and December 2002, after the *mahasamadhi* of Yogi Ramsuratkumar, I traveled to India and had the opportunity to meet and spend time talking with many devotees whose personal stories and accounts appear in this book. As we sat together and talked, the force of Yogi Ramsuratkumar's love and living presence became extraordinarily tangible and deeply felt, as he was alive in them. The name of Yogi Ramsuratkumar was never far away; it was often on their lips as a constant remembrance. These are people who continue now, two years after his death, to remember their guru with lives that are about service, faith and devotional worship. Their accounts are fresh, moving, imminently real, evocative; it has been only natural to rely heavily on these and other firsthand accounts, and so I have chosen to let those who knew Yogi Ramsuratkumar well tell the story of his life, often in their own voice.

Reading between the lines of Yogi Ramsuratkumar's dialogues and interactions, we find the spiritual master at work with his devotees, where the transmission of grace is most vividly communicated. I have also chosen to include many details and lengthy descriptions of interludes with Yogi Ramsuratkumar because he himself once said, "Everything this beggar does is the teaching." It has been my experience that if we allow ourselves to go deeply into the stories, they become imbued with life by the spirit of Yogi Ramsuratkumar.

Throughout the text of this book I have both paraphrased and used direct quotes from accounts and stories that were given in interviews or written in journals. The dates of interviews and journals that were used are listed in the bibliography. At the same time that the stories included here are extensive, it is quite humbling to realize that this book represents only a part of the countless known and unknown people whose lives were transformed in some way by Yogi Ramsuratkumar. It is my hope that this biography and others that will come in the years ahead may serve to bring out more stories of the beggar king of Tiruvannamalai.

I am tremendously grateful to many people for their willingness to share something of their lives with Yogi Ramsuratkumar: Devaki Ma and Vijayalakshmi Ma of the Yogi Ramsuratkumar Ashram in Tiruvannamalai; Parthasarathy, Jayarama, Pankkajam, Dev Gogul, Kirsti, and Dwarak Nath Reddy of Tiruvannamalai; N. Subramaniam (Mani) and his wife Rajalakshmi (Raji) of Bangalore; J. Mukilan of Chennai; T. Pon Kamaraj of the Manthralayam in Kanimadam; Professor Sadhu Rangarajan of Bangalore; Swami Nityananda and Shakuntala of Tapovanum Ashram in Tirukoilur; Ramamoorthy; Ramanlal; Ravi and Saravanan (former staff members at the Yogi Ramsuratkumar Ashram); Shankara Rajulu of Madurai; Vasugi and Jairaj of Sivakasi; Nateshan and Sarada of Trivendrum; Gomathi, Ponvandu and Deivakani of Madurai; Ashish Bagrodia of Bombay; and Makarand Paranjape of New Delhi.

In particular my profound gratitude goes to Truman Caylor Wadlington, the first biographer of Yogi Ramsuratkumar, who made a unique contribution to this work both through an extended process of interviews and by magnanimously allowing his personal journals, photographs and artifacts related to Yogi Ramsuratkumar to be used for this project. His private journals from the years 1970–1976 and 1979–1980, when he spent a great deal of time with Yogi Ramsuratkumar and took copious notes in the moment, are archival treasures that provide unparalleled accounts of Yogi Ramsuratkumar's early teaching years. My gratitude goes also to Will Zulkowski, whose contribution was invaluable and who spent many hours in interviews and later in pinning down details as well as making photographs and archival material available, and to Wendel Field and Richard Schiffman who also generously gave of their time in interviews. Wendel Field's painting of Yogi Ramsuratkumar appears on the cover.

This book would not have been written without the help of Tom Lennon, who went above and beyond the task of conducting interviews in the U.S. with Caylor Wadlington, Will Zulkowski, Wendel Field and Richard Schiffman. Mariana Caplan and Ute and Volker Augustyniak conducted interviews in India for me; Ute and Volker also contributed a tremendous amount of time doing research and getting last minute clarifications and questions answered in Tiruvannamalai.

Lee Lozowick, my teacher, asked me to write this book. It was a task that I undertook with joy and gratitude as well as some trepidation. It was made especially challenging because it was his wish that the book be published in the spring of 2003; returning from India in late December 2002, I had four months to organize, write and complete the book for my publisher. It literally would not have been possible to meet this deadline without the help of many, many friends who spent weeks and months from January 2002 to April 2003 transcribing interviews, inputting journals, providing technical assistance, scanning photographs, executing the laborious process of lay out and design, proof reading, copy editing and supporting the progress of the book in countless ways. My profound gratitude goes to Becky Fulker, Paula Zuccarello, and Nachama Greenwald; also to Lesley and Steve Ball, Debbie Celebucki, Jaya Hoy, Rakini Chinery, Bhadra Mitchell, Ilana Thomas, Elise Erro, Nicole Bureau, Regina Sara Ryan, Mirabai Lodro, Rose Volckhausen, Sharana Lhaksam, Zachary Parker, Nara, Thom Shelby and Sylvan Incao. I would like to thank my family for their enduring patience and support, and the many devotees and friends of the Hohm Community whose stories appear extracted and paraphrased from the archival writings of *Tawagoto.* I would also like to thank Purna Steinitz, Balarama Zuccarello, Mariana Caplan, Vijaya Fedorschak, Stan Hitson, Mirabai Lodro, Tom Lennon, Nachama Greenwald, Regina Sara Ryan, Doug Fulker, Jim Capellini, Clint Callahan, Alain de Rosanbo and Gilles Farcet for their contributions.

Most of all, this work would never have been produced if not for the inspiration and guidance of Lee Lozowick, who also contributed a large amount of material that would otherwise have been inaccessible, including his extensive personal photo archives. He made the substantial archives of Hohm Sahaj Mandir completely available, including back issues of his community's journals, which contain priceless chronicles of meetings with Yogi Ramsuratkumar from 1988–2001, and the *Hohm Sahaj Mandir Study Manuals*, Volumes I – IV. He opened many doors and made it possible for me to interview devotees across south India, provided editorial guidance, context, and tirelessly answered my endless questions about his personal experiences with Yogi Ramsuratkumar. This book is the result of Lee's peerless devotion to his spiritual father, one of the greatest masters of our times, Yogi Ramsuratkumar.

Preface

I believe that we read biographies of great people in search of some hidden aspect of ourselves, some latent potentiality that lies deep within us. We unknowingly hope that some word, some phrase, some exemplary moment in another's life, will water the waiting seed of our own greatness. We understand, perhaps without knowing how we know this, that the fullness of another's realization is somehow not separate from our own. We sense that perhaps the only difference between these extraordinary beings and ourselves is that they perceived that very potential arising in their own lives, and then took the radical leap into the unknown which most of us do not dare to risk. We admire and sometimes envy the courage, the fortitude, the daring that prompted them to jump off the very cliff that in some real sense we all face. To study the life of Yogi Ramsuratkumar is to challenge ourselves to our own inherent possibility.

Yogi Ramsuratkumar is a man who not only allowed his mind and identity to be crushed into the vastness of the One, but who let his heart be shattered in kind, pulverized into angel dust, open and available to all. He is a man who went so far beyond what we know to be manhood that he almost ceased to be human, while *at the same time* displaying the heartbreak and suffering of our shared human core with more vulnerability than we can conceive of admitting even in our inmost hearts.

What we in the West tend to refer to as "enlightenment"—a radical and immutable shift from subjective to objective perception—occurred in Yogi Ramsuratkumar almost fifty years prior to his death. Imagine this possibility: you have seen through to the core of the nature of reality, had your identity shattered, your body, psyche, and conditioning reconfigured, and your heart broken into trillions of pieces, and then for the next fifty years you take the resulting energy, building ever upon itself, and you are propelled farther and farther into the direction of infinity, into endless becoming, at an incomprehensible speed. The energy and power gained through each progressive layer of surrender becomes rocket fuel for still deeper surrender, deeper letting go, deeper shattering, until the trace of what was once you becomes so inextricably intertwined with the All that there is scarcely even a hint of limitation to be found. I do not know the *meaning,* if there is one, of such an unfathomable degree of transformation. I do not know what it could possibly feel like or how to comprehend it. However, I do know that it is precisely what I witnessed. The seven months I spent with Yogi Ramsuratkumar on a daily basis, and my encounters with him over the years to follow, revealed a ceaseless outpouring of giving, without discrimination, to all. An intelligence that included all forms and aspects and ways of knowing. A literally endless fountain of sacrifice, using himself, his energy, and his body as the furnace from which the light of others could be lit.

It is a daunting task to attempt to describe an individual like Yogi Ramsuratkumar. Most of us have never encountered such a being, and we are thus limited by our own conceptualization when attempting to imagine such a possibility. For this reason, M. Young has probed the life of Yogi Ramsuratkumar not only in great depth, but also from multiple dimensions, and from the perspectives of his closest disciples, so that the reader might find entry to the ocean of his being through many rivers and channels. I invite the reader to temporarily suspend beliefs about what is possible for a human being to become, thus opening a crack in the psyche to receive the possibility to which the being of Yogi Ramsuratkumar points us.

The great masters of old are an endangered species. We would like to think that they reemerge with the regularity with which they disappear. Yet in our world of war, moral decline, and decreasing sense of values, it seems that fewer individuals emerge whose realization is so thoroughly and totally encompassing. Perhaps it is because fewer true disciples emerge who are able to make use of such an individual. We are further riddled by the emergence of so many con men, guru look-alikes, and even teachers of integrity who simply lack the vastness of Yogi Ramsuratkumar's dimension, that we scarcely know how to see what is in front of our eyes when we go to a master, even and especially in the presence of true realization. M. Young's own lifelong commitment to discipleship has given her a depth and discrimination that can guide us through the entryway to begin to perceive the context of the life of a saint. Young provides a lens through which we can recognize the poignancy and meaning of what may at times appear to be subtle gestures and bewildering communications of this truly uncommon saint.

It was said of Yogi Ramsuratkumar's own spiritual father, Swami Papa Ramdas, that "Ramdas plays football with the planets." That statement nagged at me for years. I always imagined it to be some type of metaphor, yet could never fully comprehend it. Then one day I saw Yogi Ramsuratkumar playing football with the planets, only he was using *us* as the ball. Using *us* to direct invisible forces in the cosmos, using *us* to refine universal currents, using *us* to heal the world—in both its seen and unseen aspects. The true Realizers of our world have a capacity to alleviate suffering on a personal and global level that is unparalleled by almost any other power or type of influence—*even* after their body has passed. And it is times in history like those in which we find ourselves, and those soon to come, when we will need to access and make use of this healing power more than ever.

For many people, the majesty of Yogi Ramsuratkumar will inevitably be recognized through his endless miracles; his extraordinary psychic abilities; the lessons he taught; the healing he brought to countless lives; the way in which he truly gave everything for God. Still, I maintain that to taste his love—even for a moment so brief as to leave you pondering whether you could have actually felt something *that* beautiful—is the greatest miracle of all. For to know a love of that vastness, of that dimension, of that encompassing nature, can shatter in an instant the paralyzing worldview gained through a lifetime of limitations. And even if we ourselves have not experienced it, simply to trust in the existence of such a love can in itself melt our own hearts, heal our cynicism and wounds, restore our faith, and fill us with the possibility of our own wellspring of love just waiting to be tapped.

Mariana Caplan, Ph.D.
Berkeley, California
April 27, 2003

Foreword
by Lee Lozowick

The only introduction Yogi Ramsuratkumar needs is to the mind. Yes, here in the West, He is only relatively known by those few who were fortunate enough to discover Him in His abode in Tiruvannamalai, Tamil Nadu, southern India. From the 1960s when He lived on the streets or on the holy mountain, Arunachala, or the 1970s and 80s when He lived in a small house by the brass market, or in the 1990s when His ashram was built—grand by even Indian standards—Yogi Ramsuratkumar was ever what Hilda Charlton, one of my dearest mentors and first teachers, called a "hidden Saint." He never sought devotees, couldn't be bothered to market Himself, and was only absorbed in God, who He called "Father in Heaven." He was totally surrendered to whatever will, destiny, karma or work this Father had in store for Him—and what Work it was, and is! Yes, Yogi Ramsuratkumar needs no introduction, except to the mind.

To the Heart, to That in every one of us which already knows the truth—the reality, the ever-present actuality of God as One, as never separate, as unitive consciousness, being and existence—Yogi Ramsuratkumar needs no introduction. Yes, true that He appeared as a body, which to a relative degree is the only ostensible subject of this biography; and yes, true as well that His body animated a great paradox of idiosyncracy and a great demonstration of apparent miraculous occurrences. But in fact He was never born, never lived, and—although that body has passed into dust—never died. He is the eternal symbol, the infinite message, the literal Word of God made flesh and now made spirit, for although His earthly form is no longer here, His Manifestation is more dynamic and available than ever.

Simply put, He is—never was but always is—past, present and future. The Name He assumed is itself a gift to us from His Father in Heaven, and could once have been Krishna or Rama or even Jesus. For is there really any difference between the One when that One incarnates, in any time and place, any dimension (what we might, in our illusions and divided perceptions, call reality or mythology), any culture, race, religion, social class or caste? Some would argue this point. Well and good—let them. For in another context, isn't "variety the spice of life"?

To His devotees, He is the Incarnation; not the only Incarnation, for such views are foolish and misdirected, mere opinions of confused divisive thought. No, just simply the

Incarnation going by the Sacred Name of Yogi Ramsuratkumar, having animated and demonstrated a great and wonderful play of appearance, and yet having left us an Objective Imprint and Influence by which He, this the Incarnation, is accessible and Radiant. Radiant in the sense that His Blessings—ever alive in every time and place and focused intensely, localized we could say, in the examples of those Magical Beings of the highest order, the Ancient Ones, always here and now, just who they are and as they are—are even in this very moment pouring out upon us, those who know this consciously and those who don't, pouring out upon us with purpose and Intention. And what purpose and intention, we might well ask? The one motive true to all such Living Deities: the compassionate and tender wish that all beings be happy, at peace, healed in body, mind and soul and ever-reflective, ever worshipping the Absolute One, Yogi Ramsuratkumar's Father in Heaven, with every breath, every gesture, every thought, aware or not.

I needn't talk about the "facts" of the life of Yogi Ramsuratkumar, for that is more than adequately fulfilled in the book that follows. I will only add that I am grateful beyond words to have known and lived with such a being and with His most loving and, to Him, most precious devotees. It is my fervent desire and prayer that some slight or deep flavor of Him touch you as you read; that in this text you may discover not only Yogi Ramsuratkumar, but yourself, for in fact there is no difference.

Lee Lozowick
Triveni
Prescott, Arizona
April, 2003

Introduction

In 1993 I met Yogi Ramsuratkumar for the first time, traveling to India with my spiritual teacher, the American Baul master Lee Lozowick, and his entourage of students. I had been hearing stories of Yogi Ramsuratkumar for seven years, and the anticipation and excitement of meeting such a rare being ran very high. At the same time, Yogi Ramsuratkumar was a mystery for me. Although I had studied Western and Eastern spiritual traditions for many years, I had never been to India and had never met an Indian saint. I was familiar with the lives of perennial greats like Ramana Maharshi, Swami Papa Ramdas, Ramakrishna, Chaitanya, Shirdi Sai Baba, Anandamayi Ma, Meher Baba, Neem Karoli Baba and Sri Aurobindo; I had spent time in the company of the great Bengali yogi, Sanatan Das Thakur Baul. My imagination was primed and ready . . . but nothing could prepare me for the sight, the *darshan*, of Yogi Ramsuratkumar and the impact he would have and continue to have on me over the years.

"Lee! Lee! My Father in heaven! My Father alone exists! All one, perfect unity, past, present, future! Everything perfect! My Father alone!" These were the ecstatic words of Yogi Ramsuratkumar, as he ran down the steps of the Sudama House to catch the hands of his devotee, who was kneeling to touch the beggar's feet. Laughing and smiling, Yogi Ramsuratkumar pulled Lee to his feet, up the stairs and into the house. His countenance was truly beautiful. His face was as bright as the sun, lit with a smile that was pure joy. I had never seen a being of such childlike innocence and purity, imbued with a divinity that was immediately felt in a direct communication of the heart. His simplest movements and the melodic lilt of his voice captivated my senses with a penetrating sweetness and spoke volumes.

Since then I have traveled three other times to India. On these trips I had priceless opportunities to interact directly with Yogi Ramsuratkumar, to be part of his *lila*—receiving his *prasad*, the purification of his smoking, his incendiary and penetrating gaze, his heart-melting smiles and laughter, and the deep penetration of his vast mind into my own.

These experiences made it impossible and unwise to write a biography with the critical and clinical distance that is employed by some biographers. Generally speaking, the mood of chilly dissection or cynicism leaves me cold as a reader; I prefer biographies that are inspired by a passionate appreciation for the subject. At best it becomes an affair of the heart, so that all the hard work—painstaking research, clarifying and organizing thousands of bits and pieces of information—is softened and shaped by reverence and even awe for the contribution the subject has made to the human spirit. In my experience, all really good biographies are written in this way precisely because it gives direct access to the essence of the person, so that the reader receives not just an intellectual view, but a deeper communion, through feeling and sensing. There is also the need for objectivity: the biographer must continually fine tune the lens through which the subject is viewed so that clarity is the medium in which love may have full reign.

But there is another reason to approach the biographical process with respect and the blush of genuine affection: Yogi Ramsuratkumar himself once spoke with great sadness and determination about a biography written about Ramana Maharshi, in which the biographer included facts that could discourage some who might read it. Yogi Ramsuratkumar was concerned that these facts, presented in the spirit of "truth," would only serve to disillusion some, turning them away from the spiritual path. He spoke emphatically on the need to praise, and only praise, when writing about the lives of saints. His philosophy was that every person has some light and some dark, even the greatest saints, and if the light is greater than the dark, then that is what should be remembered. He once said, "People should be inspired by the lives of the saints." And so this biography follows the master's wishes, yet it does not gloss over his fundamentally human aspects, his marvelous enigmatic eccentricities, or his fierce and uncompromising sides.

At the same time, it is extremely difficult to write about Yogi Ramsuratkumar. Many attempts have been made to paint a picture of this exceptional and mysterious individual, but the question remains, how can such a phenomenon of divine transformation be described? Even the first words on paper quickly pale and fade, disappearing into nothingness as if they have been burned away by an invisible fire. Perhaps this is the way Yogi Ramsuratkumar wanted it: his way of communicating truth—of instructing and working with devotees—was often cryptic and enigmatic. He rarely explained a teaching lesson or why he did the things he did; instead he wanted people to go beyond the mind and perceive with the heart, for only then can we absorb and integrate the teaching in a way that makes it truly our own.

For years Yogi Ramsuratkumar was a hidden saint, and even after he was "discovered" he talked about himself only on rare occasions to certain close devotees. There are many years of his life that remain entirely shrouded in mystery. The metamorphosis of grace that he underwent transfigured him so completely that he was literally no longer the person he used to be; from his unmitigated revelation of "my Father alone exists," why would he speak of that which no longer existed and was of no importance in the face of such a radical change? But in his supreme generosity and compassion, he did give us some hints and small encouragements along the way as to who he was and who he became.

The great God-realizers of India who were alive and in the flesh during the twentieth century have now all gone the way of impermanence: Neem Karoli Baba, Ramana Maharshi, Ramakrishna and his disciple Vivekananda, Paramahansa Yogananda,

Swami Prajnanpad, Swami Nityananda, Muktananda, Swami Papa Ramdas and Krishnabai, Anandamayi Ma, Sri Aurobindo and the Mother, and Hazrat Babajan, the crazy, God-mad female saint who initiated Meher Baba. Yogi Ramsuratkumar developed out of this milieu, the spiritual son of three great realizers: Ramana Maharshi, Sri Aurobindo and Swami Papa Ramdas. But those stories will come later in this book, as will the experiences of the many people, both Easterners and Westerners, who had the opportunity to meet Yogi Ramsuratkumar, to know him personally, and to become a player in the *lila*—the divine sport—of his life.

Considering the mystery of Yogi Ramsuratkumar, in attempting to create an accurate portrait of the man one could say that the moment that Ramsuratkumar, a saint hidden within the form of a simple beggar who spent many years wandering, finally landed in Tiruvannamalai and sat for the first time under the legendary punnai tree, his teaching work or divine transmission began and caught on, spreading like a wildfire that soon raged out of control. By the time of his death Yogi Ramsuratkumar had been lifted out of the streets on a wave that seemed to inundate him: there were suddenly thousands of devotees, a thriving ashram and a temple the size of a football field built in his honor. What led to his appearance in Tiruvannamalai in 1959, and the unfoldment of such a destiny? And what makes it relevant to spiritual seekers today?

The miraculous transformations of such human beings are a source of inspiration to all who embark upon the impossible journey of the spiritual path, and so we turn to whatever wisdom we can glean from the lives of saints. As with the lives of all great God-realizers, to become receptive to what their story has to give, one must "become as little children," as Jesus of Nazareth taught, because to truly hear and receive the reality of the life of a saint is to taste the kingdom of heaven. We have to set aside our assumptions, biases and opinions, drop the bonds of cynicism and doubt, and read with a pure heart, knowing that the life of a saint is an allegory, a vast parable, the elements of which have symbolic meaning that can be understood on many different levels. To follow in the footsteps of a true saint or even to look and see where he or she has gone—one must be willing to go where angels fear to tread, to travel to an unknown destination, accepting the inevitable paradoxes with awe, gratitude and wonder.

The stories of such mystics and mysteries are still present in modern day India, but the rich medium out of which these extraordinary individuals arose is rapidly disappearing, overlaid by Western attitudes and motifs, rendered into obscurity by the crush of technological powers coming out of the West. Modern India is having a torrid love affair with the dangerous icons of the First World West—computer technology, cell phones, satellite dishes, global media communications, nuclear weapons—and perhaps more insidious but equally destructive, Western fashion, politics, ideas, attitudes and consumerism. Instead of the traditional, classic dance form of Bharat Natyam, India now turns toward the slick movie productions of Bollywood; instead of saris and long black hair, we see Indian women dressed in blue jeans on the streets of Delhi and Bombay, hair bobbed short, sleek bodies exposed in skin-tight jeans. Instead of chai and coffee stalls serving hot drinks in handmade clay cups, we have Coffee Day and Barista—two

Western-style cafés in Pune where, I must admit, I too joined the crowds of modern Indians for a café latte. It is an inexorable and inevitable development as India joins the global community of influential nations.

As the spiritual presences, the living deities and archetypal forms of the Divine recede behind opaque veils, made concrete by the greed, drive for power and comfort that dominates the postmodern West, we are still given rare opportunities to remember what is essential, true and real. That is what this book is about: remembering one extraordinary individual who embodied the miraculous, the awe-filled sacrifice of one human life into a divine life. In the remembering of such a one, we have the opportunity to remember our own true nature, and to take heart in the certainty that the grace of God is still active and alive in the world today. As many of his devotees will candidly say, "God has walked on earth" in the form of a dirty beggar, Yogi Ramsuratkumar.

As little as we know about the early life of Yogi Ramsuratkumar, it is a story that must be told for the sake of the reader, so let us begin at the beginning, putting together the pieces of the puzzle that is the enigma, the conundrum, the hidden saint who was Yogi Ramsuratkumar. So this *guru charitra*—this biography of the guru—begins with both the few facts we have of Yogi Ramsuratkumar's early and mid-life as well as some of the legends that surround these mysterious years, then expands into the heart of this book: the story of the beggar saint of Tiruvannamalai, told by his friends and devotees, both East and West, who knew and loved him, more than life itself.

CHAPTER ONE

FROM THE RIVER TO THE SEA

1918-1953

"Ah, Varanasi . . ." Yogi Ramsuratkumar said, the rhythmic cadence of his voice trailing away in a wash of feeling that spoke volumes. It was always a surprise to see how close to the surface such feelings were in the beggar saint of Tiruvannamalai. It was 1998, three years before his death, and he was saying goodbye to Lee Lozowick and his large traveling party. As usual, he wanted all the details of Lee's departure and travel plans: What time will you leave in the morning? How many people? Exactly where are you going next, and by what means do you travel?

"We leave at midnight to drive to Chennai, then we will go by airplane to New Delhi and then fly to Varanasi, where we stay for one week, and then go by bus to Rishikesh," Lee answered. Yogi Ramsuratkumar absorbed this information with great simplicity and yet with an incredible focus of attention.

"Oh, by airplane," he said, and then, "Oh, thirty-three people." He seemed to be weaving every detail into an invisible matrix of blessing through which the devotees would then travel. But it was his final comment, "Ah, Varanasi . . . " that communicated a whole world of his own experience, instantly conjuring rich images of how his early life had been so intimately informed by the most ancient and sacred city of India.

That Yogi Ramsuratkumar grew up in and around Varanasi (Banaras) is an important part of his story. Not only was he immersed in the culture of the Ganges, as a native son of India he was swept up in the evanescent swirl, the mythic images and arcane secrets that inspire Varanasi with life. All this was as natural to him as the sun rising and setting each day. It was the rhythm and hum of his life as a child, and he was molded, informed and nurtured by its overflow, passing swiftly by his village as the Ganges itself.

Varanasi is a city with an undeniable mystique, and it is here that the story of Yogi Ramsuratkumar begins. Varanasi, whose ancient name is Kashi—the luminous or resplendent, the "City of Light"—is the holiest city of all India, where people make pilgrimage to die so their bodies can be cremated on the ghats beside the Ganges, the ashes and burning remains cast into the river and swiftly carried to the sea. According to

Hindu teachings, to die in Varanasi, the chosen domain of Lord Shiva, is to be released from the cycles of birth and death—or at least to insure a better rebirth in one's next incarnation.

The sun rises at dawn, a huge red ball hanging in the mists above the vast waters of the Ganges, slowly fading to silver as it rises into the morning sky and washes the city with a pale golden light. Countless temples, sculptures, ornate cornices, towers with carved columns, shrines and ghats that line the shore of the river emerge out of the mists and come to life with all the hustle and bustle of the day's activity. The city resounds with the music of Sanskrit chants, the deep clang or melodious ringing of temple bells, countless *arati pujas* performed as oblations and supplications are made to the archaic forces that seem to swirl about the cupolas and stone deities. Smoke hangs in the air in dense clouds, the transformational byproduct from dung and wood fires, the heavily congested traffic, the temple incense and burning of ghee, and from the famous cremation grounds of Varanasi.

Varanasi was already an old city when Rome was founded. It spreads down to the river in an incomprehensible maze of narrow lanes or *galis* and ancient, wide stone steps, winding through streets so narrow a cow can barely pass through them in places. The minarets of the mosques and the temple spires stand up above everything, thickly sculpted with gods and goddesses who overlook the fires and incense and offerings of ghee that are constantly being made at shrines all along the shore and in the streets. The cremation ground of the Manikarnika Ghat is busy twenty-four hours a day, with ten or twelve hot fires blazing in oval heaps of wood, wrapped bodies placed carefully in the center of each with flower garlands, marigolds, incense offerings. As the bodies burn, the skulls burst, legs and arms go akimbo in rigormortis, and flesh is slowly sizzled or melted off the bones, making the skeletal remains, seen through the smoke and blaze of the flames, the stark reminder of impermanence and the ultimate mysteries of life. The remains, sometimes not only ash but also bone, smoldering flesh and whole skulls, depending on how much money the family of the deceased can pay, are then dumped into the Ganges, steaming, still glowing with the coals of the fire. For the Hindus, the Ganges is not only a source of water and sustenance and the agent of death and purification, but a deity in and of itself. At the core of Varanasi—its character, mood and magic—are the burning ghats and the Ganges itself. This is where the story begins.

"Do you know what this is?" the father asked his small son, holding his hand and gazing out over the wide expanse of the river, flowing like liquid silver in the early morning light. They stood together on the clay banks of the river, not far from the village. Sadhus bathed nearby in the cool air, softly chanting prayers to the sun that rose through layers of river mist. "River," the child replied. The father had brought the three-year-old boy to the great river to receive its blessing, and he spoke to him gently, imbuing him with the sense of awe and magic that surround the mythical Ganges. He smiled at the boy.

"Do you think it is a mere river? Know that this is a goddess—the Mother! Ganga is the Mother, the Punya Thirta," the father spoke with tears in his eyes.[1] In that moment, the destiny of the boy glimmered like the light on the water, reflecting the radiance of a small child's innocence as he absorbed the presence of the river, alive, deep and swiftly flowing before his eyes.

Yogi Ramsuratkumar was born as Ramsurat Kunwar (pronounced Kuhn-were) on December 1, 1918 in a devoutly religious agricultural family in a remote village on the Ganges in the northern region of Bihar, only five miles away from Varanasi. The stories of his early years paint the picture of a boy who, from the beginning, loved the river Ganges and spent as much time there as he could, taking in the stories and folklore of the spiritual traditions that abound in legendary India. As he grew older, his strong affinity for the Ganges drew him to the river more and more, and he often went there to spend time with the sadhus and holy men who roamed the river and populated its shores. He listened avidly to their recitations of the Upanishads and the Vedas and took these deeply to heart. There he sat among them, mesmerized by their teachings and tales of sadhana on the road and absorbing the great stories and myths of India—the epic tales of the Ramayana and the Mahabharata, of which the Bhagavad Gita is a part; stories of Vishnu in his incarnations as Krishna and Ram; of Shiva and Kali, and of the Vedic gods, Agni, Surya and Soma.

He developed friendships with these holy men, who must have glimpsed in some way the destiny that lay within him. He was as magnetically drawn to them as he was by the river, and spent as much time there with them as possible. He would sometimes fall asleep on its banks only to wake in the predawn hours, bathe in its holy water and sit in stillness on its clay banks while the sadhus and monks sang their ancient prayers in the morning ritual of the *gayatri* mantra, chanting in the deep shadows of the river mists, in gratitude and praise of the rising sun, the celestial god Savitri: *Om tat savitur varenyam bhargo devasya dhimahi dhiyo yo nah pracodayat om.*

Ramsurat's love for the Ganges took many different forms. Being a very physical child, he loved to swim in the Ganges and was a strong, capable swimmer. Years later Yogi Ramsuratkumar laughed as he told the story, "This beggar got into a lot of trouble when once he swam across the Ganges!" He was severely scolded for taking such a risk, because it is an extremely powerful, deep and wide river with strong currents and undertows. Clearly he must have been a very good swimmer and exceptionally strong as well to attempt a feat that would be difficult for a grown man. Even at this early age the tremendously strong will, stamina and vision of an exceptional individual—who would only be moved by inner impulse, independent of the status quo or cultural, familial and social injunctions—appeared in his actions and interests.

These childhood affinities and impulses were, in retrospect, precursors of the direction his life would soon take. The urge to absolute freedom from all the restraints of

1 Vijayalakshmi, *Waves of Love*, p. 3.

societal conventions—to live under the stars, in sync with the sun and moon and wind and rain, to live a truly organic life, receiving only that which is freely given, to be a beggar who trusted completely in the beneficence of an all-giving Divinity, a living God who is intimately involved with His creatures—was the natural way of life for Ramsurat that came to fruition many years later, as he was moved by a will that was greater than his own and the expected forms of daily life began to fall away.

Like most children, Ramsurat was fun loving, and as much as he was steeped in the sacred texts and traditions of India that he learned at his father's knee and with the sadhus on the river, so he also helped his mother in the kitchen with the daily chores of the home. He often took food from his home to give to the religious mendicants at the river, or to those who wandered by, sometimes bringing the beggars and sannyasins right into his mother's kitchen to eat, as his sympathies lay with those who had given up all comforts and securities in their thirst for God. At the same time, his education continued; he excelled in his studies and played on the volleyball team—and yet, he had a natural sensitivity and restlessness that nourished his love for the Divine.[2]

When Ramsurat was twelve years old an experience occurred that had a tremendous impact upon him. One evening his mother asked him to fetch some water from the well, a regular chore to which he had grown accustomed. Walking through the thick trees at dusk, the path was lit by moonlight and he soon found his way to the well. As he lowered the pail with the rope in his hands, he noticed that there was a small bird perched on the rim of the well. As a playful boy will, he flicked the rope at the bird—perhaps to shoo the bird away, or just out of curiosity, to see what would happen. Whatever the motive in the mind of a child who hasn't fully cognized that there are consequences to one's actions, Ramsurat's aim was accurate and swift. The bird was instantly killed. Realizing the fatality of his act, Ramsurat ran to pick up the bird. He tried to revive it, pouring water into its beak, but it was dead. Carrying the bird to the Ganges, he watched as its body floated away on the waters, in the arms of the goddess Ganga, on its way to the sea. For a long time he lay on the bank of the river watching the night sky, illumined with the light of the moon.

Children are capable of great insight, and in the moments, hours and days after the bird was killed, Ramsurat was filled with remorse by the inescapable fact that he had been the cause of pain and death. This is the pivotal story of Yogi Ramsuratkumar's childhood that appears in all accounts of his life—an unforgettable experience that he spoke about on occasions to his devotees. It was this unexpected shock that gave him the firsthand experience of impermanence, and he began to ponder the questions of life and death, of loss and heartbreak, of responsibility for the other in any form. It is only through sorrow and remorse that true conscience dawns, and for one who is spiritually ripe, the death of a simple bird can be enough to unleash an avalanche of insights and the dawning of a profound awareness of self and others.

There is a similar story about the great American poet Walt Whitman, who

---

2 Ibid, p. 5.

frequently wandered alone as a ten year old boy on the island of Manhattan, at the time a place of forests and teeming wildlife. He discovered a pair of mockingbirds—a type of common Western bird that mates for life in bonded pairs and is known for its beautiful songs. He would sit beneath the tree where they nested to watch their flights, observe their comings and goings, and listen to their singing. The male and female birds took turns flying away in search of food, and each time one of the birds flew away, upon arriving back at the nest it would begin to sing, and the mate, sitting on the eggs in the nest, would sing back, as if in greeting. The interplay between the two birds became a thing of wonder and awe for young Walt Whitman. One day he came to sit beneath the tree and watch the birds, and he noticed that there was only one bird in the nest. It called out again and again with its song, but the other bird didn't come. For hours he watched the bird, calling and calling, with no response from its mate, until he realized that the mate would never return, and had met its death in some unknown manner. The call of the lone bird penetrated his heart with a feeling of utter loss and heartbreak that seemed as boundless as the blue sky. This experience of heartbreak, the fact of ultimate aloneness and the inexorable impermanence of all life, was the beginning of a mystical journey that is recorded in the narrative of his poetry, but it is also found in the life of a man who demonstrated an incomparable purity and selflessness in the actions of his life.

Ramsurat's early experience of death, loss, responsibility and sorrow was the first dawning of the ultimate individual obligation to express loving kindness toward all beings. The anguish Ramsurat felt over killing the bird caused such a profound introspection in him that some say he became an introvert at an age when a boy should be "wholly occupied with the wonders of the world."[3] Undoubtedly, it was an irrevocable event that started a chain reaction that would have far-reaching effects. As we shall see, later in his life Yogi Ramsuratkumar would have a particularly poignant relationship with birds, those universal symbols of the soul found in poetry and classical literature in the East and West alike.

In the year 1934, when Ramsurat was sixteen years old, he suddenly had what would be the first of many urges to wander away from his home with no concern for how he would survive without money or food. He went to Varansi. Walking from his village to the train station, a generous person bought him a meal and a ticket to the nearest stop—somewhere near the center of Varanasi. Arriving in the City of Light, Ramsurat headed immediately for the rich and opulent Golden Temple, the Viswanatha Mandir, near Manikarnika Ghat and the Ganges in the most ancient part of the city. Millions of pilgrims come to this great temple seeking blessings, healings, auspicious deaths and miracles of all kinds. Arriving in the morning, Ramsurat saw the Temple of Vishwanath, the Lord of the Universe, and entering, made his way to the inner sanctum, where he stood rapt in ecstasy before the deity for a long time. Ramsurat wandered around the nearby ghats on the river and around the ancient city in a state of wonder, making his way to the Annapurna and other temples before he returned to his village.

---

3 Ibid.

Two more times after this he was moved again to leave his village and travel; both times he was compelled to Saranath, only five miles outside Varanasi, the place where the Buddha preached his first sermon. Here too Ramsurat was seized with a deep love of God, an exaltation of the soul. These sacred places of Varanasi and Saranath carried the capacity to transmit the truth, or ultimate reality, and Ramsurat was a highly sensitive receiver. The conch call of the dharma, the eternal truth, was resounding inside him—a reverberating sound that would not be denied or forgotten.

Returning to his studies, Ramsurat still spent as much time as possible on the Ganges with the holy men and wandering sadhus, who were his primary companions during the years in and around Varanasi, and with whom he spent many hours in deep conversation about the imperishable reality that existed behind all forms. There were two roads open to him: the call of a life of renunciation, of unfettered longing for God, which pulled at his heart, and as avid student and even a scholar, the life of a householder and professional man. He continued to spend precious hours and days of freedom on the river with the sadhus, but the innocence and playful time of childhood always comes to and end and he had to make a choice.

In 1937 Ramsurat finished his secondary school education, then went on to complete university studies to become not only a high school teacher of English and history, but the headmaster—a role comparable in the West to a principal. Many of his devotees and numerous Westerners who were close to Yogi Ramsuratkumar have commented on how highly educated he was, a fact that was easily disclosed by his great facility with the English language and his surprisingly deep knowledge of Eastern and Western culture, politics, classical literature and religious scripture. He spoke several languages, but he grew up speaking Hindi and was fluent in English.

At some time after his schooling was completed, the pressures to conform to the Hindu way of life for a well-educated young man of eligible marriage age began to close in on Ramsurat. It is the custom in India for parents to arrange suitable marriages for their children. Following their parental duty, Ramsurat's parents found a bride and arranged for an engagement and marriage, without consulting Ramsurat, who was in another village at the time with friends. When he returned, he was shocked by the news: marriage was not what he had in mind. Avoiding the whole situation, he immediately said that he had to go to the Ganges to bathe. Giving this excuse, Ramsurat left the house and disappeared for several days, and in this way avoided meeting the girl and her parents and the looming challenge of an engagement or marriage ceremony. His parents soon discovered that he had gone to a nearby village to stay with relatives, but despite his attempts to evade what he must have intuitively sensed was counter to his destiny, eventually the long-standing norms and mores of the culture and parental pressure prevailed: Ramsurat married another girl, Ramaranjini, and started a family, eventually having three daughters and a son: Yashoda, Maya, Veena and Amitab.

So it was that in his early twenties Ramsurat followed the prescribed path of a Hindu householder and professional man. For some years he was a loving father and husband who was able to play the part of a very normal householder, although he had an introspective bent and whenever possible, chose to sit quietly alone. One story says that when his children didn't want to go to school for a day, he would allow them to stay home as long as they had written one page of Ramnam (the repetition of the name of God). He became the headmaster of a school, or perhaps schools, in a small village in the Bihar district, and he brought great integrity to his role for as long as he could manage to perform in it, but the urgent summons to a life dedicated only to God became more and more insistent in Ramsurat. It was a call that could not be denied; he was compelled from within to change the course of his life, and he literally became unable to work in any ordinary way. He became restless, and began to behave in ways that could not be understood by his family.

Ramsurat had spent many hours on the Ganges with an aged sage, known by the name of Swami Ramashram, discussing spiritual life and developing a relationship of mutual respect and appreciation. Swami Ramashram advised the young man to find a guru to guide him in his search for spiritual awakening, and urged him to visit the renowned saint and patriot of India, Sri Aurobindo Ghose in Pondicherry, and he alluded to another sage who lived not far away. Although he did not mention the name, he was referring to Ramana Maharshi.[4] A profound inner conflict ensued as Ramsurat realized that he had no choice: he was compelled to leave his family in order to follow the deepest promptings of his inner nature. He was a natural mystic and inspired idealist, and like so many mystics before him, he was driven by a relentless inner call. The revelation sank in that he was different from other men; he would have to walk a solitary path.

In 1947 Ramsurat bought a train ticket to Pondicherry. Already his state of mind was altered to the extent that it was becoming harder to function in the ordinary world. Right away he lost his travel bag and his ticket, and was asked to leave the train after making some miles toward his destination. He walked along the railroad track and came to a school, where he met the headmaster and asked for his help. The headmaster said that he could not help him directly, but he allowed Ramsurat to go to the classes and ask the students for help, which he did. Children are often more open-minded and compassionate than adults, and they readily gave small sums that allowed Ramsurat to continue his journey.

Arriving at Sri Aurobindo Ashram, Ramsurat spent some time there, but the great Aurobindo was a recluse who only came out to give darshan to the ashram residents once a year, on his birthday, spending all the rest of his time in seclusion. It is said that when Ramsurat went to the ashram of Sri Aurobindo, the staff wanted to throw him out because

4 Ibid, p. 7.

he looked like a ragged and unkempt beggar, but the Mother saw him from the verandah of her upstairs rooms and allowed him to stay. In another account Yogi Ramsuratkumar said that when he went to Pondicherry, Aurobindo wasn't available, but Ramsurat wrote a note to the Mother, and in return she sent a small packet of flowers; upon touching the flowers Ramsurat realized that a much higher life was possible, and it gave him great inspiration.

An avid reader and in many ways a scholar, Ramsurat studied the teaching of Aurobindo, which were prolific and readily available. These teachings threw fuel on the inner fires and catalyzed a period of deep self-examination and contemplation. Ramsurat was tremendously impressed with Aurobindo's yogic ability, his understanding that enlightenment is only the first step in a long purificatory development of the higher centers within the human being, and his concept of bringing higher energies into incarnation—the possibility of the realization of the supramental plane. The idea was to transform the human body, from the cells and tissues and organs, through the influx of tremendous energies that would literally divinize the individual on all levels.

These ideas resonated with his own experience, for unquestionably, Ramsurat was already undergoing a tremendous transformative process through arduous efforts of sadhana. Not only had he torn himself away from home and family, he was experiencing an inner upheaval of vast dimension. In order to make the leaps that he would make in the next twelve years, he had to leave behind everything that was familiar and step into a new world, in which his context of life and the Divine would be forever altered.

All true aspirants on the path have the experience of divine intervention; often we are guided in unexpected ways, by people we hardly know. These messages are of vital importance, and if we are paying attention, we can stay true to the path through the dreams and signs of guidance that are placed in our way every day. This was naturally true of Ramsurat, who was guided in every step. While he was at the Aurobindo Ashram a young *brahmacharin* (celibate renunciate) who resided there took Ramsurat under his wing, making sure that his needs were met. He was the divine messenger who gave Ramsurat the next piece of guidance on his quest: go to the great saint Ramana Maharshi at the foot of Arunachala. When Ramsurat heard this advice he realized that this was the saint that Swami Ramashram had spoken of. It seemed auspicious to hear of this saint twice, from two trusted sources, and Ramsurat undertook the journey to Ramanashram, situated at the foot of Mount Arunachala in Tiruvannamalai.

He stayed at Ramanashram for three days. In his highly receptive state of longing, he soaked in the vibrations of the great saint. At Ramanashram another devotee appeared who showed the young man a newspaper clipping about another great teacher, Swami Papa Ramdas in Kerala state. Responding to his instinctual feeling, Ramsurat left and went to Anandashram in Kanhangad. Many years later Yogi Ramsuratkumar said of this first meeting with Ramdas, "This beggar was not impressed with Swami Ramdas as he had been with Ramana Maharshi and Aurobindo. This beggar was not able to understand Ramdas at that time." On the other hand, Ramsurat immediately felt that the other two masters were "spiritual giants." He said, "With Ramdas, however, it was different. It was a kind of reaction . . . he was living luxuriously and people were serving him like a king."[5]

When ego catches the scent of its own demise, it will run in the other direction, even when the soul is striving toward the truth. One of the first trials of *tapas* for Ramsurat was the confrontation with his satguru, Ramdas—in Ramsurat's case, the ultimate purveyor of the annihilating force of grace. Certainly Swami Ramdas, in retrospect, was no less God realized than Sri Aurobindo or Ramana Maharshi. God realization leaves each individual with a particular imprint, part of which is objective and universal, and part of which is unique to the individual soul. Ramdas was unique in many ways; he was a mystic with a practical side, a man with a fantastic sense of humor, but he could also wield the sword of justice and truth as a strict disciplinarian, as we shall see.

Years later the love and devotion of Yogi Ramsuratkumar for Papa Ramdas and Mother Krishnabai became legendary, a subject that we will return to in later chapters. At this point in the story we find that there are principles of the path toward God realization, and specifically guru yoga, that are found enacted all along the way. All seekers of the true path find themselves in a labyrinth whose secrets must be penetrated through an arduous effort and dedication. It takes courage to confront the benign and wrathful entities—the dragons and gargoyles and demons—that lay in wait, acting as both guardians and initiators as one progresses in the great spiral that is the spiritual path. At the heart of this labyrinth is the place of perfect union, where realization of the Divine is the long-sought treasure, finally regained, because ultimately the realization is that there never was any separation. Ramsurat was at this point in his life, still a very young man, deeply immersed on this very journey, compelled forward, inexorably magnetized toward God like the planets circling the sun. He could no more turn away from his destiny than the earth could break out of its orbit. His deepest nature was calling to him, and he had no choice but to hear, respond, and enter into a long period of *tapas*.

Tapas, or the heat of fierce spiritual work, takes many different forms. It is not limited only to asceticism or the emaciation of the physical body, but to renunciation in a broader or deeper sense: self-restraint, mental austerity and the abandoning of desires. In the case of Swami Ramdas, his time as a wandering sadhu when he was constantly immersed in the sadhana of Ramnam, or reciting mantra as the name of God, was the *tapas* that burned away his worldly desires and left him, eventually, sitting in a cave on Mount Arunachala and wholly transparent to the Divine. There are many levels of self-examination that provoke the inner fires, such as the remorse that Ramsurat felt over killing the bird, or the conflict between leaving behind family life for the life of a wandering beggar, whose only succor—food, rest, shelter, friendship—comes as God wills. To live as a beggar, accepting fully in surrender the times of hunger and thirst as well as times of feast and friendship, is to invoke the fires of purification.

After leaving Anandashram and Kerala state, Ramsurat went back north to his home near Varanasi in Bihar and was reunited with his family. A year later, in 1948, he made a

---

5 Truman Caylor Wadlington, *Yogi Ramsuratkumar, The Godchild, Tiruvannamalai*, p. 35.

second trip south to visit Sri Aurobindo, recounted in his own words: "In 1948, this beggar went again to the South. He went first to the Aurobindo Ashram but could not stay there. Then he went to Tiruvannamalai and stayed for about two months with the Maharshi."[6] During those two months a subtle transmission flowed from Ramana Maharshi to Ramsurat, who spent a great deal of time in meditation, or carefully following the discourses between Ramana Maharshi and his devotees and the countless seekers who traveled through the ashram.

At one point Ramsurat was sitting on the floor near Ramana Maharshi, when he suddenly felt a powerful attention concentrated on him. Looking up from his meditation he met the gaze of the master. Ramsuratkumar looked away, somewhat nonplussed, but then returned the gaze and was quickly locked into a deep rapport with the timeless being whose steady radiance permeated him now. It was a moment of communion in which he was transported beyond time and space and into the eternal heartbeat of grace. The peace and sublime realization of Ramana Maharshi's being, focused through his gaze, catalyzed something deep inside Ramsurat and initiated a process of transformation. Ramana Maharshi himself wrote about the capacity of the saint to purify and initiate through the power of the gaze: "The holy waters of pilgrimage, the images of gods made of earth and stone, cannot stand comparison with the benign look of the Sage. They make one pure only after countless days. Know that the Sage no sooner bestows his gracious glance than he makes one pure."[7]

At Ramanashram it was the standard procedure after *puja* was done to the Mother's shrine for the *arati* plate to be given to Ramana Maharshi first to take *kumkum*. One day Ramsurat happened to be the first to touch the plate after Maharshi had touched it, and the electrical vibrations of Ramana Maharshi that now imbued the plate with spiritual power were transferred to Ramsurat, throwing him into an ecstatic state. Another time a devotee, Ekanath Rao, brought a bowl, filled with various fruits that were cut into pieces, into the hall where Ramana Maharshi was sitting. A small bowl had been placed within the large bowl, and in the small bowl were specially cut pieces, much larger than the others, intended for Maharshi.

This special treatment did not sit well with the master, whose teaching was the nondual realization of the oneness of all life, and abiding in that state in a way that would demonstrate, through action, the reality of such a great truth. Although Maharshi was always generous and compassionate with his devotees, he would not embrace such special treatment for himself. In this instance he was highly irritated by such a breach of protocol, and with a brusque movement, he pushed the bowl aside, spilling a few pieces of fruit on the floor. The fruits were then distributed to the devotees, who, not wanting to eat when the master was going without, had to sit with unwanted fruit in their hands, trying to discern what to do next. Out of compassion for the devotees, Ramana Maharshi picked up the fallen fruits from the ground and began to eat them, releasing everyone else

---

6 Truman Caylor Wadlington, *Yogi Ramsuratkumar, The Godchild, Tiruvannamalai*, p. 36.

7 Ibid, p. 37.

to eat.[8] Such humility and selfless behavior from the saint, who could have placed himself above everyone, made an impact on young Ramsurat.

Burning with the power of longing, Ramsurat again returned to his home in Bihar as a changed man. This was a confusing period of time in which he attempted to juggle the two worlds—the temporal world of family and relationship, and the timeless world of the eternal, the imperishable reality that lies beyond all forms. At one point Ramsurat convinced his wife Ramaranjini to make another trip with him to Anandashram. Off they went on the long journey south to Kerala, and with little or no money, it was a difficult and painful trip. It was only because of some savings his wife had kept that they were able to make it to Anandashram, but they were not permitted to remain there. Once again, at this second visit with Ramdas, he had a similar reaction to the saint. Years later Yogi Ramsuratkumar would say of this visit and his inability to recognize his satguru once again that "Swami Ramdas produced the same kind of feeling in this beggar," and that it was Ramdas himself who prevented Ramsurat from recognizing the master's "inscrutable wisdom."[9] Ramsurat and his family returned to Bihar, but his behavior had become more and more erratic each time he returned from his travels and with each visit to his guru Ramdas.

Clearly at this point Ramsurat was already deeply immersed in a process of mystical ascent and, it seems, an inundation of kundalini energies that were unleashed in his body. After his second visit to Ramdas, Ramsurat was unable to sustain the façade of so-called normalcy as a divine fever began to erupt, burning through the fabric of ordinary life. Ramsurat started to go barefoot all the time, and refused to touch money. He quit his job but insisted that his wife not work, which created great hardship for the family. He had always had a penchant for natural healing and only wanted to use Ayurvedic remedies for healing purposes; now he stopped eating all normal foods and ate only oranges and various other fruits. He often appeared to be crazy.

For his family, this must have been quite terrifying, because in India the familial role of the father is deified, based on ancient religious tradition. The father and husband is literally the divinely empowered polestar around which all else revolves—and now Ramsurat seemed to have gone mad. Even so, the family was not willing to let him go very easily. Ramsurat's relatives were alarmed and as a result of their fear and misunderstanding, he suffered the kind of abuse that many who have undergone the mystical transformation of the God-realizer have suffered. Anandamayi Ma, for example, underwent similar trials because her divine states of consciousness were misunderstood by her family. Ramsurat was put in a mental hospital for a month by his relatives and given electroshock therapy, but somehow he was able to pull himself together enough to convince the doctors, and perhaps his family as well, that he was fundamentally sane in psychological terms. This may have served as a further catalyst to sever ties more finally with his family, and around this time, 1949–50, he left and began to wander in the

8 L. Ramani, "The Joyous Presence of Yogi Ramsuratkumar," *Saranagatham*, May 2002, pp. 34-35.

9 Truman Caylor Wadlington, *Yogi Ramsuratkumar, The Godchild, Tiruvannamalai*, p. 38.

Himalayas, still seeking the guru he believed he had not yet found.

Yogi Ramsuratkumar was a person of profound sensitivities, and now he was caught up in a radical change involving all the glands and organs of the body as well as nonphysical dimensions of his being. As the energies within his organic system were accelerating and quite literally divinizing his body, his physical and emotional equilibrium was buffeted about by extreme forces and inner states of upheaval and change, both exalting and terrible. Many years later Yogi Ramsuratkumar said to Truman Caylor Wadlington, "The body of a saint goes through profound cellular changes. Every cell of the body goes through a transformation—every cell of the body is transformed!"

Shedding light upon the extreme difficulty of managing such supranormal processes and alchemical changes, Stanislav Grof—renowned psychiatrist and researcher in the field of consciousness studies and transpersonal psychology—writes about mystical transformation and the relationship between the activation of the kundalini, or serpent power, which moves in the body as energy and manifests in what may appear to be madness. Such a process may be activated either by intense spiritual practice, or by contact with a guru, whose simple physical presence can both initiate and activate the process of a radical spiritual awakening. This is a universal process that is found in all cultures and religious groups, including Taoist yoga, Korean Zen, Tibetan Vajrayana, Sufism, the freemasonic tradition, the !Kung Bushmen of the African Kalahari Desert, North American Indian tribes, particularly the Hopi, and many others. In the mystical Christian tradition it is notably found in the Eastern Christian monastic practice and way of life that emphasizes the "Jesus prayer," a spiritual practice that is in essence exactly like the repetition of mantra or the divine name (Ramnam) and involves the entire human being—the soul, mind, and body.[10] Grof states further:

> The Tantric schools have developed intricate maps of the chakras, have described in detail the physical, emotional, and spiritual manifestations of Kundalini awakening, and have preserved elaborate mythologies related to this process. Although not without dangers and pitfalls, the process of Kundalini rising is seen, in general, as one conducive—at least potentially—to psychosomatic healing, to positive restructuring of the personality, and to consciousness evolution. However, because of its uncanny power, the scriptures treat this process very seriously and recommend the guidance of an experienced teacher for persons involved in it.
>
> The ascent of Kundalini Shakti, as described in the Indian literature, can be accompanied by dramatic physical and psychological manifestations called *kriyas*. The most striking among these are powerful sensations of heat and energy streaming up the spine associated with intense emotions of various kinds, tremors, spasms, violent shaking, and complex

10 Stanislov Grof, *The Adventure of Self-Discovery*, pp. 111-112.

> twisting movements. Quite common is also involuntary laughing or crying, chanting of mantras or songs, talking in tongues, emitting of vocal noises and animal sounds, and assuming spontaneous yogic gestures *(mudras)* and postures *(asanas)*.[11]

India is the cradle that has nurtured many such eruptions of divine power, strong enough to shake the human frame out of its ordinary tendencies. A striking example of this in the Indian tradition is Mahaprabhu Sri Krsna Caitanya (1485–1533 C.E.), the most important ecstatic figure in Gaudiya Vaishnavism, who was considered to be an incarnation of both Radha and Krishna, the divine couple representing both the feminine and masculine poles of God. He exhibited startling trances and fits of divine candor throughout his life and was the inspiration behind a significant movement in devotional Vaishnavism, still alive today, as well as the patron saint of the Bauls of Bengal.

His life history is in many ways similar to that of Yogi Ramsuratkumar. Born in the north Indian region of Bengal, which borders Bihar, as Visvambhara Misra, Caitanya was a scholar who married a local girl and taught school, but he went into a trance one day in class and shocked everyone by falling to the ground raving, shouting and rolling around until he became stiff. Later his first wife died and he married Visnupriya and attempted to continue family life, but the states of divine madness grew until he began to teach the worship of Krishna, then finally took sannyasin vows and left his wife, children and family for Puri, where devotees began to gather around him. There he

> . . . . lived an ascetic life, eating little and often spending the night in meditation. He had strange physical symptoms of his intense love—his body would become distorted, stretched and compressed, sweat and blood oozing from his pores and saliva foaming at the mouth. Sometimes he was totally lost in ecstatic trance, sometimes he was half conscious, and sometimes he was in a normal state.
>
> Caitanya became well known for his ecstasies. His love was not a peaceful state, but a continuous fluctuation between divine and human personalities . . . . He would mistake his environment for Krsna's Vrndavana, sing and dance, and then faint.[12]

The *bhavas* and fits of divine madness that visited Caitanya left him crying, laughing, trembling and often dancing and singing. Sometimes he was insulting and irreverent and sarcastic. The worse his outer state, which sometimes looked as if he was suffering from poison, the more ecstatic and divine the internal *bhava*; in other words, internally he was in bliss. He rolled on the ground, hair disheveled, sometimes burning with fever, sometimes emitting deep, haunting sighs, sometimes sulking or laughing

11 Ibid.

12 June McDaniel, *The Madness of the Saints: Ecstatic Religion in Bengal*, pp. 35-36.

uproariously, in deep enjoyment, for hours at a time.[13] Caitanya went through a divine metamorphosis from the ordinary life of a Bengali householder and schoolteacher to becoming of one of the greatest devotional saints India has ever produced—an evolutionary process in which we find strong parallels to the life of Yogi Ramsuratkumar.

Ramsurat was beginning to experience very similar ruptures of raw divine energies. The delirium that is produced by such *mahabhavas* (divine states) as these can be frightening to those who are observing the phenomena. The wise understand that without the help of the true guide, these extreme interior flows and fires can easily tip the scale of the body and mind toward psychosis rather than mystical realization; it is at this time that surrender to the guru is the only refuge. As highly literate and steeped in the spiritual traditions of India as Ramsurat was, he knew well the importance of spending time in the company of saints, and that the guru was the only recourse in ultimate matters of grace and transformation. Because of this, when Ramsurat heard in 1950 that both Ramana Maharshi and Sri Aurobindo had died, he was devastated.

Of this pivotal moment in time, Yogi Ramsuratkumar said, "On April 14, 1950 when this beggar was moving somewhere in the Himalayas in search of Masters, Maharshi passed away. In the same year, December 5, 1950, the other great Master Aurobindo, also passed away. This beggar felt a type of restlessness that he had lost the golden opportunity of keeping company with these two Masters. Then one thing very important, it was the third chance to visit Ramdas. The two great Masters had passed away. This beggar thought to himself, 'Let me try again to visit Ramdas, for he is recognized as a great Sage.' So in 1952 this beggar did not go to Tiruvannamalai, nor did he go to Pondicherry, for the Masters were not there. But this time Swami Ramdas turned out to be an entirely different person. At the very first sight, Ramdas could tell a number of intimate things about the life and mission of this beggar which nobody but this beggar knew."[14]

According to Truman Caylor Wadlington, the last sentence refers to Yogi Ramsuratkumar having felt, from a very young age, a certain calling toward God-life. He goes on to say that Ramdas spoke to Ramsurat openly about a "mission" and about the nature of his future "inhuman labor," which was a profound and dramatic confirmation of what Ramsurat instinctively knew to be true. Yogi Ramsuratkumar continued, "Not only that, but the Master started to take special care of this beggar. This beggar felt that he had come to a place where he had a number of well-known intimate friends. This beggar began to feel from the environment of the ashram that Ramdas was a great Sage, a truly great Sage. It was then that this beggar first understood the great Master. Ramdas is this beggar's Father."[15]

Ramsurat had been at Anandashram for ten days when he asked for formal initiation from Ramdas, who agreed and initiated him into the mantra, *Om Sri Ram Jai Ram Jai Jai Ram*. The one spiritual practice that Ramdas asked of his devotees, the surest way to liberation, was to repeat the name of God in this mantra, which had been the mantra into

---

13 Ibid, pp. 36-37.

14 Truman Caylor Wadlington, *Yogi Ramsuratkumar, The Godchild, Tiruvannamalai*, pp. 39-40.

15 Ibid, pp. 40-41.

which Ramdas was initiated by his father, whom he considered to be his guru. After the initiation Ramdas instructed Ramsurat to repeat the mantra twenty-four hours a day, nonstop. Ripe as he was, Ramsurat became one with the mantra in the first week of constant repetition of the name of God, and entered into a state of ego-annihilation that left him irrevocably changed. The personality who existed before this time was now subsumed; in the words of Yogi Ramsuratkumar, "This beggar died at the lotus feet of Swami Ramdas in 1952." The wandering beggar from Bihar was now seized by fits of laughter and joy, of singing and dancing; there were long hours of wild ecstasy or of deep and abiding peace. In Yogi Ramsuratkumar's own words:

> This beggar ceased to exist in 1952. After that, a power has pulled him here and there. Even now, this beggar is controlled by the same power, the power that controls the whole universe! This beggar has no consciousness! No mind! All has been washed away! No thought, no planning, no mind to plan. No sense of good and evil. Swami has killed this beggar, but life has come. Millions and millions of salutations at the lotus feet of my Master, Swami Ramdas! The same madness still continues. He has initiated this beggar in Ramnam and has asked to chant it all the twenty-four hours. This beggar began to do it and in the space of a week, this beggar has got this madness.[16]

Yogi Ramsuratkumar once explained years later that he would have never wandered and gone through the ordeals that he went through between 1947 and 1952 if either Ramana Maharshi or Sri Aurobindo had been right for him. Although he always credited them as two of his three spiritual fathers and initiators because he felt that he had received so much from them, it was the graceful relationship with Ramdas that cleared the way for full surrender into the Divine. According to Yogi Ramsuratkumar himself, when he arrived at Anandashram the third time (in 1952), Ramdas was actually expecting him and awaiting his arrival. Recognizing the interior readiness of Ramsurat and his destiny as well, the great saint Ramdas greeted him just as a father would receive his own son.

When Ramsurat left Anandashram in 1952 he began to wander. These are the seven "lost years," veiled by time and perhaps mostly forgotten by Yogi Ramsuratkumar —or kept secret for reasons known only to him. Occasionally a memory would rise to the surface and he would tell a story from his past to a devotee: One day he set out for Tiruchi, but obeying the inner impulse that guided him in all things, he got off the train at Erode and remained standing by the tracks, absorbed in a *bhava*. A train approached from the distance, and as he watched it coming closer his body's natural instinct for self-preservation warned him to run away, but the inner voice commanded him to stay. Standing near by the tracks with his left foot on the rail, the train rushed over his toes. The pain was very great and he fainted. A Gujarati gentleman took him to the hospital

16 Vijayalakshmi, *Waves of Love*, pp. 12-13.

where he received medical care, but once again the inner voice demanded that he leave the hospital before he was healed. He climbed out the window and returned to his ecstatic wanderings, which took him all over India—often as a traveler without a ticket on a train to one destination or another. He had no food or plans, and took whatever came his way as the grace of God.[17]

This accident with the train was no small thing; in fact the toes on Yogi Ramsuratkumar's left foot were seriously damaged, and he must have been bleeding profusely. The condition of the physical body didn't mean anything to him; what was important was the spontaneous response to the inner impulse, or the instantaneous play of "Father in Heaven" as manifest through the human man. Until the end of his life, the usual concerns of clothing, bathing, food, money and shelter were meaningless to him. There was nothing but the inner call, the spontaneous movement through the world, informed by what Yogi Ramsuratkumar called "Father in heaven." After "Ramdas killed this beggar in 1952," there was nothing left but "my Father alone." His consciousness was merged with the Infinite in a way that is incomprehensible to all but those who have made the irrevocable leap across the octaves of being and into the Unknown.

When the energies of divinization begin to take over the body, there can be times when the personality no longer has control. The ordinary buffers that make it possible for the individual mind to make distinctions are dissolved, even destroyed in overwhelming states of oneness and unification with the Divine. Buffeted by the hurricane force of the living God erupting within his body, Ramsurat was misunderstood and often harshly judged not only by relatives, friends and neighbors, but by other devotees and aspirants of the path. God-realization manifests in different ways, but in its most potent form it is untamed, gone far beyond the demands of the mind for "normalcy" and "rationality." This unbridled ecstasy is often provocative to the "normal" ego, which seeks to control and dominate everything out of its deeply ingrained fear of death. Because of this, ego also fears ecstasy, wherein it is obliterated, sublimated and forced into submission.

Ramsurat Kunwar as a newly born *siddha purusha* regularly manifested *bhavas* and uncontrollable states of *prema bhakti* when he danced and sang, laughed or wept when the love of God overcame him. These first months of realization are chronicled in *The Gospel of Swami Ramdas* and provide invaluable insight into the events and the divine *lila* that occurred between the man who was becoming Yogi Ramsuratkumar and his satguru, Swami Ramdas, the dispenser of Grace. The following dialogues take place a year later, in December, 1953, when Ramsurat returned to Anandashram for the last time, consumed in the fire of transformation, a captive of divine love:

> **No. 351 "The odd Bihari"**
> December 5, 1953
>
> In 1952 a friend from Bihar had come to Anandashram and stayed three weeks. He was a school teacher on long leave. He had a beard.

17 Vijayalakshmi, *Waves of Love*, p. 15.

Though Papa had first agreed to his staying in ashram for a month, he had to be asked to leave earlier as his behavior was not satisfactory. He was highly emotional. One evening, during bhajan, he lay down on his back shouting, "Mataji, Mataji." Papa knew that it was nothing but a mere pretence and, when the bhajan was over, gave him sound advice. He was so much ashamed that he could not raise his head. Next morning Papa advised him to leave the ashram. It was reported later that he behaved like a madman at the railway station. At Erode he was knocked down by a railway engine and was taken by a Gujarati devotee to his house for treatment. He was later reported to have gone back to his house. He stayed there a few months and all found him to be out of his senses; he suddenly left the place without intimation to his people.

As soon as Papa alighted from the plane at Bhavnagar on the 3rd [December 3, 1953, a year later], he saw the Bihari in the crowd which had come to receive him. He was in dirty clothes and had a queer look. Papa recognized him immediately. It was later said that only recently he had come to Bhavnagar and was staying at the house of a devotee. He had told them that he was asked by Mataji to wander about. It appeared, during his short stay there he made himself a nuisance. He created unpleasantness in Ramdas ashram when Sai Baba's devotees were performing bhajan. He shouted why they should worship Sai Baba as Papa was all in all and they should worship none else. He had to be sent away by force from the ashram. Seeing his condition Papa advised him to go to Girnar and do sadhana.

When the morning bhajan was going on in the ashram, the Bihari started talking. Among various other things, he said, "Papa is my Krishna, Rama and Shiva. Mataji is my Radha, Sita and Parvathi. I am a saguna upasaka and they are my gods. I had been to Anandashram where Papa scolded me and asked me to get away. In doing so, he has dishonoured his own devotee. Now Papa asks me to go to Girnar. Why should I go to Girnar leaving my ishta devata here? I am not a nirguna upasaka and have nothing to do with Dattatreya."

Mataji, who was present, heard the talk and was wondering how Papa could tolerate such things. Seeing Mataji, the Bihari got up and came near her to do namaskar.

Mataji: "Why do you talk like one gone off one's head?"

Papa asked Sumatilal Kamdar to send him to Girnar with a blanket as it was rather cold there.[18]

18 Swami Satchidananda, *The Gospel of Swami Ramdas*, pp. 351-352.

In this exchange we get the message that Ramsurat was immersed in the worship of the immanent God—God in form, in manifestation, and having many qualities such as beauty, love, peace, mercy, wrath, severity, splendor, magnificence. That is, Ramsuratkumar was one who worshipped a personal God (*saguna upasaka*) that he found expressed completely in the forms of his *satguru* and *ishta devata* (chosen deity), Papa Ramdas, and his feminine counterpart, Mataji Krishnabai. This is an important statement of the particular spiritual path and revelation that God realization visited upon Yogi Ramsuratkumar, and an idea that will be returned to in later chapters. It is important to understand that the *nirguna upsaka* is one who worships Brahman or the impersonal God, beyond even the subtlest dimensions of form—the transcendent Divine that is without any qualities, as more exactly expressed in the nondualistic path of Advaita Vedanta.

Reading these and the following passages from *The Gospel of Swami Ramdas* one cannot but notice that at times Ramdas is reported as being extremely hard on, even critical of Ramsuratkumar and his ecstatic states, but when it comes to masters working with disciples, things are often not what they appear to be. In other words, Ramdas was in no way taking a moralistic or conventional position in relation to the wild states of ecstasy—singing the name of God and dancing in the hills or at other "inappropriate" times—that Ramsuratkumar was spontaneously exhibiting. Ramdas also left his home and family, his wife, children and job, to wander the roads of India for years as a mendicant beggar in search of God before he became the revered saint and spiritual master of Anandashram. During these years of wandering as a sadhu, Ramdas had many periods of time in which he was lost in divine states of consciousness and was no longer able to conform to the expectations of others to "behave properly." [19]

The life of Swami Papa Ramdas (1884–1963) had some interesting similarities to that of Ramsurat Kunwar. Born Vittal Rao on the full moon at Hosdrug, Kanhangad, in the northern part of the state of Kerala, India, Ramdas was never able to fit into the proscribed life of an orthodox Hindu. Perhaps it was because the day he was born was also the Hanuman Jayanthi—the birthday of Hanuman, the legendary devotee of Sri Rama; those who observed the baby, born to Srimata Lalita Bai and Sri Balakrishna Rao, noticed an unusual radiance in his eyes at the time.

Vittal was not particularly fond of school, and was often truant. In high school he continued to be indifferent to studies and textbooks, but at the same time he was an avid reader of books on many subjects. He enjoyed literature immensely, and acquired a remarkable aptitude for English. Vittal was a good conversationalist, and inherited a sense of wit and humor from his father. He would elicit roars of laughter from his listeners by the unique manner in which he related incidents from his own life or from his observations. Ramdas was aware that the humor lay more in the description of an event than the event itself.

Whatever situation he was in, it was the lighter rather than the serious side of it that appealed to his natural sense of the comedy and absurdity in life. Due to his lack of

19 These years are described in *In the Quest of God* and *In the Vision of God,* by Swami Ramdas.

interest in academics, Vittal lagged behind in his studies and as a result could not get through his final exams. He then joined a school of arts and studied drawing and engraving. However, he discontinued this course work and eventually received a diploma in textile manufacturing.

Vittal was married to Rukmabai in 1908 and in 1913 a daughter named Ramabai was born. He worked with his father-in-law for a period of time and attempted the life of a householder, but slowly and imperceptibly life was strengthening Vittal Rao's spirit of dispassion. Every evening he spent an hour at the house of his brother, Sitaram Rao, whose children would be engaged in *bhajans* before the image of Sri Krishna. During the *bhajans*, Vittal would lose himself in divine states, and he began to chant the Lord's name—Ram. The repetition of the divine name brought him equanimity and joy, and its sound would spontaneously issue from his lips throughout the day. He gave up his evening meal and other comforts of the body. Vittal's wife became frightened at the strange turn her husband's life was now taking. No persuasion, appeal and protest either from her or from his child could induce him to alter the course he was now being called to follow. He felt very strongly that he was called to this path by the Divine and was compelled to respond.

An important event in Vittal Rao's life occurred at this point. His father came to him one day and initiated him into use of the holy mantra, *Sri Ram Jai Ram Jai Jai Ram.* Balakrishna told his son that if he repeated the mantra constantly, he would be blessed with eternal happiness. Vittal's spiritual process and detachment from the world quickened. In December, 1922, he said goodbye to worldly life and left his family and Mangalore. Two days later he reached Srirangam, and after bathing in the holy Cauvery River, he began wearing the ocher clothes of renunciation. He took the vows of *sannyas*, and assumed the name Ramdas (servant of Ram) in honor of his chosen, beloved deity.

Shortly thereafter, Swami Ramdas visited Sri Ramana Maharshi, praying for grace. Bhagawan nodded his head, indicating that he had blessed Ramdas with his grace. Swami Ramdas' body trembled with emotion. On leaving the Maharshi he went to a nearby cave on Mount Arunachala and spent twenty days chanting Ramnam (the name of Ram), eating small amounts of rice that he cooked for himself. At the end of this time he was graced with a vision of Ram and became God-mad, intoxicated with the Divine. In this state of ecstasy he embraced everyone and everything he saw as Ram, and in that condition he traveled throughout India, visiting holy shrines and many different mahatmas.

A year later, his wife and daughter came to know that he was staying at the ashram of Sri Siddharudha Swami in Hubli. They visited the ashram, and with the permission of Swami Siddharudha, took Swami Ramdas back to Mangalore. Ramdas was unable to go back to the life of a householder, and instead he went directly to the Panch Pandav Cave at Kadri, where he stayed for over three months. Here Ramdas had the opportunity to engage constant meditation, and it was during this time that he entered *nirvikalpa samadhi*. Once again he was compelled to strike out on the roads of India as a wandering ascetic, and this time he attracted a large number of admirers and followers in the process.

His experiences as a mendicant have been chronicled in his books, *In Quest of God* and *In the Vision of God*.

After wandering for a few years Ramdas started a small ashram at Kasaragod. It was here that Mother Krishnabai first had contact with him. After a few years she decided to dedicate her entire life to his service and mission.[20] Swami Ramdas then moved to a new ashram, called Anandashram, where he and Mataji Krishnabai—who was considered his divine feminine counterpart—spent the remainder of their days. Anandashram in Kanhangad was created around Swami Ramdas in 1931. Though it was begun in a very humble way, it expanded considerably over the years, and by the time Ramsurat journeyed there, it was a thriving spiritual center that served many sadhus and mendicants as well as both Eastern and Western seekers who came to stay and chant the name of God.

Swami Ramdas, whom his devotees and followers lovingly called Papa, was always bubbling with joy. His realization of God in all aspects of creation had opened the floodgates of his heart. He reached the heights of realization by chanting the mantra *Om Sri Ram Jai Ram Jai Jai Ram*. (Ramdas added "Om" to the mantra himself.) Through this constant chanting he remembered and felt the presence of God within him and everywhere about him. His realization was that the entire universe was the form of God, and his oneness with the Supreme Being was naturally coincident with the absolute state of surrender—that is, acceptance of whatever happened as being the Will of God. Papa Ramdas therefore taught everyone who sought his advice to chant God's name constantly and to submit to God's Will in all matters. This practice, he assured them, would bring eternal happiness. They had no reason to doubt him because he was a living example of this realization.

Every year between 1949 and 1957, Swami Ramdas and Mother Krishnabai visited many places in India at the invitation of devotees. Wherever Papa went, *bhajans* with the chanting of God's name was the main feature. He was not inclined to give long lectures—though he would give short talks and answer any number of questions which were put to him on spiritual subjects. In 1954, he undertook a tour around the world. Many people from Europe, America, Japan, Malaysia, Singapore, and Ceylon had the opportunity of meeting him on this trip. He wrote many books in English and in 1933 he started a monthly publication, called *The Vision*, which carried his message of universal love and service. Eschewing all castes and creeds, Ramdas was a brilliant spiritual light among many in Mother India. For him, everything was about surrender and the grace of the Divine.[21]

Based on the candor of his own writings, Ramdas too was a wandering ascetic who moved about the countryside based entirely on inner impulse. He practically starved himself to death in a divine consumption, entered regularly into altered states of consciousness in which he became totally oblivious of his own body or his surroundings

20 The story of her spiritual unfoldment with Swami Ramdas is chronicled in *Guru's Grace*, Anandashram Publications.

21 Swami Satchidananda, *The Gospel of Swami Ramdas*.

and others, embraced untouchables (as a high caste Indian, this was not just radical but heretical) and even reported himself as smoking a chillum of tobacco or taking a few puffs from a sadhu's hookah on various occasions, based on divine whim.[22] Ramdas was the *sadhaka* who fed sugar out of his hand to dangerous serpents, who took food from a Muslim woman, saying, "Ramdas knows no difference between a Hindu and a Muslim."[23] He described the pandemonium of the Kumbhamela, where along with millions of others, he was almost crushed to death in the surge of the crowd. Ramdas understood only too well what Ramsuratkumar was undergoing, and as we follow the story, we begin to see that Ramdas guided Ramsuratkumar with a wise and steady hand.

Over time, as the revolutionary impact of God-realization became more integrated into his entire being, Ramdas settled down at Anandashram with Mataji Krishnabai to the work of communicating his realization in ways that became understandable and more easily assimilated by others. This was accomplished through his physical presence, through instruction to devotees and teaching lessons made on a day-to-day basis, through discourses and dialogues, and through his published writings. Although Ramdas was quite willing to interact with devotees at the level of dialogue, intellect and the mind, his fundamental disposition as a *prema bhakti* prevailed in the prescription, "Chant the name of God; it is the only way to liberation in the *kali yuga.*" This strong *bhakti* foundation which Ramdas provided to his devotees was the failsafe against a strictly intellectual approach to sadhana; to chant the name of God works beyond the mind, not bypassing it or leaving it out, but weaving it together with the other centers of the body: that is, the instinctual and the heart or feeling center. The playful spirit and disarming sense of humor that he had as a young man never left Ramdas, but became a part of the way he instructed his devotees. Many years later French filmmaker Arnaud Desjardins, who spent time with Papa Ramdas in the early sixties and filmed him, recalled that at Anandashram, Ramdas used to say, "Here we laugh the ego away!"

Every single element of the master's work with the disciple is a necessary element in grooming, molding, and ultimately transforming the one who seeks to assume the master's realization. It is no coincidence that only days after Ramsurat made the statement, "I am a saguna upasaka," Ramdas was giving eloquent and pristine discourses on the fine points of dharma and the teaching, speaking synchronistically about the *nirguna* and *saguna* aspects of the Divine, *purusha* and *prakriti* and the *Purushottama*, or Divine Being. Staying at the home of Upendra Bhatt in Rakjot where he was speaking to a gathering of devotees, Ramdas emphasized the need to control the mind and emotions and therefore to transcend the *gunas* (the three primary qualities of *sattva* (buoyant and cool), *tamas* (inert and concealing) and *rajas* (energetic and hot), which are the building blocks of Nature and from which are spun the equilibrium of all Creation. Clearly Ramdas understood that Ramsurat, in the throes of a process of God-realization, needed to balance the *nirguna* and *saguna* aspects of his being in order to achieve complete

22 Swami Ramdas, *In the Vision of God*, pp. 69-70, 73.

23 Ibid, Part II, p. 69.

liberation and transcendence of the binding effects of the three *gunas* and realize the ultimate Divine Being or supreme Lord, the *Purushottama.* If the realization of the *ishta devata* was truly Ramsurat's path, then he would have to achieve the realization of both the nonbeing of God transcendent, and the pure being of God immanent:

> **No. 363 "Realise nirguna and saguna"**
> December 6, 1953
>
> Devotee: "Should we realize the nirguna or saguna aspect of God?"
>
> Papa: "Both."
>
> Devotee: "Nirguna and saguna are opposites. Are they not?"
>
> Papa: "No, they are like the sun and its rays. The rays are not different from the sun. Nirguna is the changeless and formless Spirit and saguna is the manifestation; they are like the sun and its rays. The nirguna is beyond the intellect to comprehend. That is why He is called achintyarupa. He is the purusha. He is also the prakriti. He is purusha and prakriti together and also beyond both, and is called Purushottama.[24]

The presence of Ramsuratkumar became more disturbing to the peaceful air of Anandashram as Ramsuratkumar spiraled more deeply into mystical states and overwhelming *bhavas*. The formerly peaceful and scholarly teacher, a loving father and householder, now became agitated and driven by his longing for God and the fires of the inner work that had taken root in him. Yogi Ramsuratkumar once told Parthasarathy, one of his devotees, that in his early years he was a very strong-willed character, and these accounts reflect that indomitable drive. His desire to be in the presence of Ramdas and Krishnabai all the time inflamed the other devotees, at least in part because Ramsuratkumar was adamant and forceful—nothing would get in his way to the Divine, including the other devotees! A true sadhana is an intensely purificatory process, in which everything that needs to be purified and transformed is brought to the surface. Anger and aggression surged up in Ramsuratkumar, and Ramdas was stern in dealing with it. The guru always thinks only of the disciple's ultimate liberation in this regard, and to be soft or indulgent with a devotee of Ramsuratkumar's depth and destiny would have been disastrous. Ramdas had a firsthand knowledge of this ongoing experience of purification that is inherent in the process of spiritual transformation: for example, he himself struggled mightily to overcome anger. He once spoke about his own ferocious battle with such passions:

24 Swami Satchidananda, *The Gospel of Swami Ramdas*, p. 359.

> The first thing Ramdas was struggling against was anger. That is the worst enemy of man . . . . Ramdas found anger was trying to get a firm hold on him. So he prayed to God to free him from it. As a sort of discipline, he used to have in the room in which he lived, small placards on which were written 'Do not get angry.' He used to look at them and would be at once quiet. He was asking God to give him strength to resist anger. Simply writing the words on the placard won't do. You must get strength from God. For about six months [Ramdas] had absolutely no anger even under great provocation. There was enough cause for provocation as people about him did not agree with him in any way. They remonstrated with him and found fault with everything he did. He however remained perfectly calm and serene. It continued for six months. After six months some talk which was not very palatable made him burst into anger. But he did not speak anything. It came like a small wave and the whole body was burning. He rolled on the ground in terrible pain. After sometime he got up and sat when the devil left him. That was the last attack of anger and it never came again.[25]

This glimpse into the sadhana of a saint—before realization has been completely assimilated and while extreme *tapas* is being undertaken—is revealing in terms of how Ramdas worked with Ramsuratkumar. He did not allow him any emotional excess or indulgence at all, regardless of how exalted the mystical states may have been, or how buffeted about he was by the all-consuming drive toward divine union. Instead of coddling or offering false compassion, Ramdas was fierce and demanded absolute obedience. At this stage in the ascent toward a true and pure divine madness, the guidance of the guru is of the utmost importance, and all care was taken to keep Ramsuratkumar pointed in the right direction. At the same time, Ramdas did not allow Ramsuratkumar to cling to him—even out of the purest motives, fueled by a divine love—or exhibit attachment to his physical form.

Swami Nityananda of Tapovanum Ashram, who knew Yogi Ramsuratkumar for many years, said of these passages in *The Gospel of Swami Ramdas*:

> Because he was constantly following Ramdas around everywhere, perhaps Ramdas was trying to ask him not to identify him with the body. Ramji [Yogi Ramsuratkumar] was looking at Ramdas as the murti, the form of the guru. The form of the guru is also sacred and wonderful, but Swami Ramdas wanted him to look at the spirit behind the murti. Therefore he was saying, "Why do you come?" We must be able to feel the presence of the guru wherever we are. It is not necessary to seek to be always with the guru. When we are often very near the guru, then we lose

25 Swami Ramdas, *Ramdas Speaks*, p. 79.

touch, actually. Like in a lotus pond: there are lots of frogs very near the lotus, and they never get the benefits, whereas the bee comes from somewhere else, takes the honey from the lotus and flies away. Therefore, Mataji Krishnabai used to say, "Don't stay in the ashram continuously . . . leave the ashram and go. Learn and go and do your practices," to overcome the normal tendency to identify the guru with his physical body. You know, when he looks at you, you are very happy. When he doesn't turn and look at you, you are not very happy. All that is because of ignorance. It is enough if you are in his thoughts. Actually the guru can be at any distance—it doesn't matter. That's the main thrust there in those few pages from Swami Ramdas. That's the message. Swami Ramdas didn't want him to be over attached.

These comments also reflect the teaching that one must realize both the *saguna* and the *nirguna* aspects of the Divine, in the form of the guru. At this point the transmission had been made; what was needed was a long time of purification and integration. In the ongoing account of the "mad Bihari" in *The Gospel of Swami Ramdas*, we find that Ramdas has returned from his trip to Bhavnagar to find that Ramsuratkumar has returned to Anandashram from Girnar:

No. 385 "Don't insult saints"
December 12, 1953

Papa was back from Bombay by plane . . . . A couple of hours after Papa's arrival, the Bihari, who was asked to go to Girnar, came inside the ashram compound but was prevented by the gate-keeper from entering the ashram hall. In the afternoon, when Papa was in the hall, he suddenly dashed in and fell at Papa's feet. By then Papa had received all the information about him. After Papa's departure to Rajkot, Sumatilal Kamdar gave him a blanket and some money and asked him to go to Girnar as instructed by Papa. But he threw away the blanket and money and had a few hot words with Sumatilal. He had then disappeared for two days. When asked why he returned, he replied, "I had been to Girnar. There is nothing there. I want only Papa and Mataji. I cannot live away from them."

After prostrating at Papa's feet he was standing and gazing at Papa's face.

Papa (gravely): "Why did you come back from Girnar?"

Bihari: "I did not find anything there. I wanted to obey you and went with the idea of staying there, but something pulls me back to you. How can I live away from you and Mataji? I have no control over myself. Some strange power has taken possession of me. I will stay on here with you and follow you wherever you go."

Papa: "Nothing doing. We cannot permit one like you to stay with us. You may have love for us, but you abuse and insult those who love Ramdas. Is this the way you love Ramdas? You had angry words with Sumatilal. The other day you spoke in insulting terms about Sai Sattar Shah and Bindu Maharaj. How can you spiritually progress if you go on insulting saints? Ramdas cannot permit you to stay here."

Bihari: "Where can I go?"

Papa: "How and where did you live all these days? Carry on like that."

Papa then came in and the Bihari went out. He was, of course, provided with food at proper time, but was not allowed to enter the hall. He spent his time outside the ashram waiting for an opportunity to force himself in.[26]

In the entry for the next day, Ramdas speaks in a synchronistic manner about his own wanderings, in the quest of God, and the value of personal experience. As he says, "Experience is the great teacher in life," a clear reflection of his injunction to Ramsuratkumar to leave Anandashram and be on his own:

No. 390 "Pilgrimages are not everything"
December 12, 1953

Devotee: "Has Swamiji gone to Kumbhamela at Haridwar?"

Papa: "Yes, Ramdas had been there once."

Devotee: "Do we gain by going to such festivals?"

Papa: "Definitely. You get enough knocks, hits and kicks in the crowd. The most crowded period is the brahmamuhurta. That day, a bath in the Brahmakund, it is believed, gives moksha to the bather straightaway. Ramdas saw the bodies of hundreds of devotees carried to the burial ground. They were the bodies of those who were crushed in the crowd.

"Experience is the great teacher in life. We know about things only

---

26 Swami Satchidananda, *The Gospel of Swami Ramdas*, pp. 371-372.

> after we experience them. So, you can also go to Kumbhamela and know for yourself what you gain by it. In fact, whatever you want is within yourself. Then what is the fun of going here and there in search of it?"[27]

In this interchange Ramdas advocates personal firsthand experience in order to "know for yourself" what may be useful in a serious sadhana. The Kumbhamela is a good example of this—a famous gathering of many different kinds of religious pilgrims, sadhus, ascetics and sects like the Nath Siddhas, the Shakti cults and the Bauls. Every three years the Kumbhamela is held consecutively in the vicinity of one of four cities, based on an ancient myth that names these places as locations where *amrita*, the nectar of immortality, fell to earth during a heavenly conflict. Millions of people are drawn to the Kumbhamela; it is an event of immense proportions where many different powerful forces and influences collide, making it is both a sublime and dangerous place to be. Any and every possible seduction, distraction and fascination from the true path are readily available there, in the guise of spiritual experience.

The parallels between Ramdas' discourses and what Ramsuratkumar was going through are very revealing in the search for understanding the spiritual process. Ramdas' response to this question demonstrates that, although he had become a master of great eloquence and dignity, of elegance and diplomacy, he was also masterful in his skillful means of working with Ramsuratkumar. Ramdas was in many ways mercilessly hard on him, but at the same time, reading between the lines, his fierce demand on Ramsuratkumar can be seen as the highest form of regard, compassion, respect and even praise for the destiny of the disciple he saw before him. In the following passages, occurring a few days later, we find the fervent desire of Ramsuratkumar to be obedient to his guru, and his overwhelming, all-consuming desire for the object of his love, heart-rending to read:

> **No. 392 "Suffering, a lever to lift up the Soul"**
> December 15, 1953
>
> The Bihari was in the bhajan-hall. Papa, when informed of this, went to the bhajan-hall. The Bihari came and prostrated.
>
> Papa: "Ramdas has to tell you something. You must have your hair cut, have a clean shave, put on clean clothes and then come here."
>
> Bihari: "May I do that after bhajan?"
>
> Papa: (Patting him on the back.) "Yes, you do that after bhajan."
>
> His face lit up with joy as Papa patted him. Immediately after bhajan,

27 Swami Satchidananda, *The Gospel of Swami Ramdas*, p. 374.

arrangements were made to take him to the barber. He came back at 12 o'clock with close cropped hair, shaven face, white dhoti and chadder.

Papa: "Ah, that is good, it looks as if you have taken rebirth. It is clean outside. Do not create any more trouble here. Be quiet. Do not snatch away the Ramnam books from people who are writing Ramnam."

Papa came in and, referring to the Bihari said, "Now you cannot say he is dirty."[28]

In this passage it seems that Papa Ramdas is defending "the mad Bihari" to the other devotees, who have complained that the crazy beggar is "dirty." When the ardor of devotion of one person begins to stand out in some way, particularly when manifesting in a state of divine madness, it can be the source of great discord and strife among the company of devotees. One extreme example of such passions running amuck is that Shams y Tabriz, the beloved of the great Sufi poet Rumi, was actually murdered by the jealous devotees of Rumi. In some ways the spiritual path is no different than ordinary life, where primal passions such as anger, aggression and jealousy drive the behaviors of human beings and compel us into situations and actions for which we often have great regret or remorse. The difference is that for one on the path these passions become the fuel for a process of transformation, rather than an endless tangle of *samskaras*, or karma begetting more karma.

Why did Swami Ramdas send the mad Bihari away in December 1953? The transmission between Ramdas and Ramsuratkumar had been made a year before; Yogi Ramsuratkumar always pinpointed 1952 as the year when his human personality was irrevocably surrendered to the will of God through the grace of his guru. As Yogi Ramsuratkumar said many times in later years, "Ramdas killed this beggar in 1952; this beggar is no more. Only Father remains." When people referred to his mad behavior during this time period, Yogi Ramsuratkumar would say, "It was all Ramdas' lila. Simply Ramdas played some lilas, and this beggar was not conscious of them." The resulting divine madness and unstable behavior—the spontaneous ecstasies and *bhavas* that were overtaking Ramsuratkumar's outer manifestations—seemed to be causing strong responses from everyone around him.

The wild, uncontrollable behavior that was catalyzed by the process of transformation could have been a good reason to send him away, to wander the roads of India in the same way that Ramdas did many years before, but most likely there is more underlying Ramdas' decisions: In the process of wandering, Ramsuratkumar, with the blessings of Ramdas, would be guided into experiences and circumstances that would integrate and assimilate the divine energies that were thundering through his body, but it was also a gesture of respect for the destiny of Ramsuratkumar, which could not be fulfilled if he stayed at the side of Ramdas and Krishnabai.

28 Ibid, p. 377.

No. 395 "Admonition to the Recalcitrant Bihari"
December 18, 1953

2 p.m. As a number of letters were to be answered Papa was busy dictating. The Bihari in his usual unkempt way came in, prostrated and sat at his feet.

Bihari: "Papa, what shall I do? Tell me."

Papa: "Ramdas has told you what you are to do. You do not listen to what he says but go on asking what you should do."

Bihari: "I try to obey you. I went to Junagad, but somc other power forced me back to you. I cannot stay away from you. I do not know what is pulling me back to you. I have no control over myself."

Papa: "It is only the ego residing within you that makes you dance like this. You want everything done your own way. You have to get away from Ramdas. There is no place for you near him. You will not gain anything thereby. It is found by experience that those who associate always with us do not improve. They start finding fault with us and that becomes the cause of their regression. Even before starting to stay with Ramdas, you have begun to find faults. You asked the other day why Ramdas went to Rajkor and Bombay for attending marriage functions. You considered it a folly on the part of Ramdas and remarked he should not have done so. Is it with this attitude that you are going to stay with Ramdas? Give up that idea and go to Girnar. If you do not go to Girnar now, it is not going to leave you. Girnar will pull you. Believe it; this is true. If you lead an ill-regulated life like this, Ramdas can tell you, you will go off your head."

He could not say anything. Tears were flowing down his cheeks and he looked quite restless. Then slowly he said: "No, Papa, I cannot leave you and go away."

He again prostrated and left the room, weeping. Papa continued dictating letters till 3 o'clock.

8 p.m. Papa had his dinner consisting of two boiled vegetables and six ounces of milk. He was sitting in his room and before him were Mrs. Gunavantrai Kamdar, Sumatilal and his wife, Mataji and a few others. Amongst many topics the talk returned to the Bihari.

Mrs. Kamdar: "Papa, the Bihari is roaming about the whole day in the hot sun. He is restless and runs like a mad man. As he is not permitted to come

> in, he wanders outside."
>
> Mataji: "Looking at his condition, Papa feels sorry for him. He has great love for Papa. If he obeys Papa's instructions, he will soon come up."
>
> Papa: "Really, Ramdas feels sorry for him. True, he has great love for Ramdas and Mataji. But all others are less than straw to him. He does not care for them and falls out with them when they do anything that he does not like. He is not mad. He understands everything. The only thing is that he is bent upon his own way, which is harmful both to himself and others. He is not uneducated. He is a B.A., B.T., and was a teacher in some High School. When he came to us at Anandashram he was all right for the first ten or fifteen days. Later we found that his behaviour was not congenial to ashram life and we asked him to leave. He did so only after giving a good deal of trouble. When we came here, he was at the airport to receive us!"[29]

It is not uncommon in the stories of masters and devotees that the play between the two should be fraught with ways and means that are both wise and crazy. Here Ramdas makes the final, irrevocable communication to Ramsuratkumar: You must stand on your own. This moment of being "sent away" was an initiatory event as well, an event that catalyzed a long time of purification and integration of the realization that was working like an active enzyme in the organic and corresponding subtle systems of Ramsuratkumar, and it is out of every minute element and nuance of this alchemical process that Yogi Ramsuratkumar was born. And further, Ramdas makes a crucial teaching lesson on absolute obedience to the guru, on not finding fault with the guru, and that kindness, compassion and generosity to others is more important than even the fervid love of God.

These are some of the great teaching communications of Ramdas to Yogi Ramsuratkumar—the bodhisattva ideal that is reflected many years later in the words of Yogi Ramsuratkumar: "I do not seek for happiness. I only want to do my Father's Work. If even one being has benefited from my life, that is enough. It has been worthwhile. And if this body dies, the soul that may remain, may it be reborn again to do my Father's Work." (February 1993) The seeds of these teachings fell on fertile ground, as thirty years later Yogi Ramsuratkumar's instructions to his devotees with regard to relationships with others was, "Do not criticize others, but speak only praise." His infinite kindness and generosity to others was compelling and was demonstrated in countless stories, many of which we will hear in later chapters.

Understandably, there were numerous communications, instructions and teaching lessons made by Ramdas to Ramsuratkumar that were never recorded, but clearly he was giving Ramsuratkumar very specific feedback and guidance, as demonstrated in his instructions to go to Girnar, or his teaching lesson on the importance of not criticizing the

29 Ibid, pp. 379-81.

master. There are many things that will remain, rightfully, strictly between master and disciple. And so, after almost two months at Anandashram in the company of his master, Ramsuratkumar was asked to leave—to embark on the fulfillment of his own destiny. One thing that is not found in *The Gospel of Swami Ramdas* is the significant moment when Ramsuratkumar was leaving his spiritual father Ramdas, which Yogi Ramsuratkumar relayed years later to his devotees. Upon his guru's command, Ramsuratkumar readied himself to go out into the world. As he was leaving, Ramdas asked him, "Where will you go?" Ramsuratkumar's spontaneous reply was, "Arunachala."

Somewhere during these pivotal years between 1948 and 1953, Ramsurat Kunwar, the schoolteacher from Bihar, had became Ramsuratkumar, a wandering beggar who was driven by a passion for God. As an individual in a process of being re-formed by the will of God, the change from Ramsurat Kunwar to Ramsuratkumar was at the level of language a simple transition, but the internal transformation underlying such a change was arduous and even dangerous. Kunwar is said to be a common surname in Bihar, whereas the Sanskrit word *kumara* signifies an objectification of his humanity by its literal meaning: "the pure Male or soul of Man revealed in its universality,"[30] The name Kumar is translated more loosely as "boy," or "prince," which gave Ramsuratkumar's name the meaning: a boy or male child who is shining (*surat*) for Ram, the supreme Being.[31] The Sanskrit root word of *sur* means "to shine," or "to rule," and thus the name Ramsuratkumar has been translated by some as "Godchild." The meaning of the name, Ramsuratkumar, also reflects the impulse of the one who would eventually become not the *saguna upasaka* Ramsuratkumar, but Yogi Ramsuratkumar. Dr. Sujatha Vijayaraghavan wrote about the name, Yogi Ramsuratkumar:

> It is fascinating but not uncommon an event recorded in the annals of spiritual history, that Divine Masters often bear a name that is indicative of their special ministry. Perhaps some may brush aside such interpretations as pure poetic fancy. But the metaphysics of mysticism explains the mysterious ways through which sound and the meaning of names influence their orbit of existence. Vivekananda who fancied this particular name after some experimentation with others, emerged as the grandest teacher of Vedantic discrimination. . . . So too, watching the gigantic, righteous and merciful reshaping of the earth life that Yogi Ramsuratkumar has dedicated himself to, it is clear that he is truly the anointed son or 'kumara' of the eternal Rama who is the Truth. Born of the spirit or 'Surat' of the One Atma Rama who is eternal and exists as pure spirit, he is the Yogi, the symbolic link yoking earth and heaven.[32]

---

30 Judith Tyberg, *The Language of the Gods*, p. 194.

31 Ibid, p. 41.

32 Dr. Sujatha Vijayaraghavan, *The Spiritual Renaissance in India: 1830–1980*, p. 81.

In a state of divine madness, barely able to function or care for his own needs, barefoot, unkempt and in rags, immersed in visionary states and still at the mercy of the tremendous spiritual force that had been unleashed in his body by the years of extreme sadhana and the ultimate moment of surrender when Ramdas "killed this beggar," Ramsuratkumar left Anandashram forever, never to return. According to *The Gospel of Swami Ramdas*, it was in December, 1953, that Ramsuratkumar finally severed all ties with the ashram and therefore with his family, who knew of his strong connection to Anandashram, and with his former identity and life—one year after the annihilation in grace that he experienced through Swami Ramdas in 1952. Leaving Anandashram for the last time, Ramsuratkumar was thirty-five years old. His destination was Mount Arunachala, only five hundred kilometers away, but he spent the next seven years wandering the roads of India.

CHAPTER TWO

On the Streets

1959–1970

In the summer of 1959 a man dressed in the rags of a Hindu beggar arrived on the streets of Tiruvannamalai, calloused feet trailing dust from wandering the dirt roads of India. His disheveled, shoulder-length black hair and the youthful radiance of his face contrasted with the ageless quality of wisdom that marked his countenance. He had a long black beard that was lightly streaked with white, and his small and slender frame seemed to brim over with energy, vitality and vigor. He wore the traditional white dhoti and kirta of his culture, and his body was wrapped with a green shawl, as if he was oblivious to the stifling heat. His forehead was wrapped with a cloth in the style of a loose turban. Barely more than rags, his clothes bore the signs of hard times on the open road—wind, rain, hunger, dust, heat and cold. Having no place to take shelter from the weather, the beggar slept on the streets of the village, under trees, in cemeteries, around the Shiva temple precincts, under the shop awnings or on the railway station platform. Over time his favorite place became well known: he was the beggar who lived under the punnai tree.[1]

In 1959 and throughout the sixties Tiruvannamalai was little more than a rural village, bristling with the full-bodied life of India: dusty streets full of people and activity, women in colorful saris, tea and coffee vendors, the market stalls overflowing with baskets of fruits and vegetables, spices, incense, oils, shawls, dhotis and brass wares. Most of the people spoke Tamil, the language of the Tamil Nadu region; the street vendors spoke little English as compared to today, and it was fairly uncommon to see Westerners there. Those that did come were interested in the famous holy mountain, Arunachala, or the vast, sprawling and ancient Shiva temple, Arunachalesvara—or, most of all, Ramanashram, the ashram of the famous saint, Ramana Maharshi. Arunachalesvara Temple housed one of the five self-created Shiva lingams of southern India—the "Theyu Lingam," or Lingam of Fire, also known as Arunachalaeswarar, after which the temple itself was named. Tiruvannamalai was a good place for a yogi to remain anonymous and free to do his work, hidden in the streets among the beggars, the itinerant

1 Alexandrian laurel.

poor, the wandering red-eyed sadhus with their bowls and staffs, and sheltered by the bustling crowds and the pilgrims who came in droves during Deepam, when an immense ghee fire was lit on top of the sacred mountain, symbolizing Shiva's power of creation and destruction.

This was a time when India still embodied the full mystery of its ancient heritage, when beggars and wanderers, who pursued the Divine with a fervor the world has not seen elsewhere, were cared for and even revered by its peoples. It was a time when, like the Ganges, the oceans, rivers, mountains, forests, lakes and pools were holy and pure, alive with the presence of *devas* and elemental spirits. The holy mountain, Arunachala, abounded with these presences, with its caves, trees, hidden paths, ghats and pools. Surrounded by verdant rice fields, small farms and forests, Arunachala was studded with recondite temples and small shrines, as well as eight elaborate Shiva lingam shrines, placed in the eight directions. Its surrounding forests were populated by the sacred banyan tree, the tamarind, neem and punnai trees, as well as the exotic and graceful palms. The more cloistered gardens of the village bungalows were home to banana, mango, papaya and citrus trees, the sun-bleached walls heavy with red bougainvillea blossoms on profusions of vines. Even the streets and the bazaar were inhabited by the gods—saturated with the ancient spiritual potencies of India.

Every day people walked down the stone ghats to the rivers, temple pools and wells at morning and evening for the day's ablutions; every action and gesture was woven with the chanting of Sanskrit mantras and Vedic prayers. This was a time when miracles happened as an accepted part of any ordinary day, in which people worshipped in the ancient way, making sacrifices, *abhisheka* or oblations of clarified butter, fruit ambrosias, precious oils, honey, incense, fire, sandalwood water, rosewater, coconut milk, curds and the urine of the sacred cows to ghee-blackened deities. The fierce, beautiful, beatific or terrifying images of the Divine abounded on every street corner of this vast and magnificent land. The natural bond between people was instinctual, telepathic, communal in the tribal sense, and connected with the magic of the land. Western technology and ideas were an obtrusive but strong presence amidst this primal way of life, just beginning to take root in the cities but still virtually unknown in the villages and rural areas.

It was in this atmosphere that the beggar came and silently, unobtrusively, sought the refuge of Ramanashram, Mount Arunachala and the cool dark halls of the immense Shiva temple, where deities gleamed in the reflected light of hundreds of ghee lamps. At first glance he appeared to be just another one of many mendicant beggars, and yet there was an enigmatic presence about him, a subtle *rasa*, an air of freedom and something like beauty that penetrated the senses of the onlooker, just at the edge of awareness. Maybe it was the spontaneous eruptions of joy and ecstatic dancing, the chanting of the name of God that captured the hearts of the local people. But a true saint cannot remain hidden forever. Here was not an ordinary beggar, but a wandering yogi who had spent his life, and most intensely the past decade, seeking the wisdom and spiritual transmission of the most renowned spiritual masters of his time, and who had absorbed, under the wing of Papa Ramdas, the ultimate grace of God-realization.

For the past seven years the beggar had wandered the roads of India, guided by a divine instinct. Beneath the dirt and dust, the torn and stained rags, he was a man who exuded an air of purity, nobility, sanctity and a complete and utter lack of pretension. People began to notice that he was full of joy, intoxicated with a divine madness. At any time, in any place throughout the day he could break into song, and in the most natural, unadorned, and childlike way, began to sing in a voice of pure adoration, "Sri Rama Jaya Rama, Jaya Jaya Rama; Jaya Jaya Rama, Jaya Jaya Rama. Om Sri Ram Jai Ram Jai Jai Ram; Jai Jai Ram, Jai Jai Ram." It was not the haunting melody of these chants that stopped passersby in their tracks as they walked past, but the piercing sweetness of the voice that penetrated to the core of the heart as the chant continued, "Sita Ram, Sita Ram, Sita Ram, Sita Ram, Sita Ram, Sita Ram. Jai Hanuman, Jai Hanuman, Jai Hanuman, Jai Jai Hanuman."

Sitting beneath the punnai tree, on the ghats by the tank (a contained pool of water) in the Shiva temple, or wandering on the green flanks of Mount Arunachala, the beggar went about his work, sleeping little, blessing all, walking the streets, playing out simple but inscrutable *lilas* or divine games with those who were drawn to him. His slightest moves, his speech and his laughter were so captivating, candid and preternaturally real, that the mind was stopped, ego nonplussed. He had an uncanny ability to invoke wonder and awe in those around him, to effortlessly induce unusual states of consciousness in others, and to inspire praise and love of God.

There were also those who wondered, "What is that crazy old beggar doing out there, walking the streets and sitting under the trees, mumbling and singing and dancing?" His unconventional behavior, his total disregard for the normal concerns of human comforts led people to wonder whether he was crazy. His ecstatic praise of God, the unfettered dancing and spontaneous gestures of blessing drew attention—some of it unwelcomed. While some frowned upon such behavior, and were displeased that he was from northern India and spoke Hindi rather Tamil, many others began to realize that he was caught up in a divine madness that had burned away all human desire in him, leaving him wholly at the mercy of a grace that was entirely beyond the human personality, which was now obscured and subsumed by the greater urges that swelled up within him.

In India the custom of feeding the poor, the homeless, the wanderers and beggars, and particularly a wandering holy man, was a way of accruing merit, or good karma, and greater blessings in this life and the next, and in these times this age-old custom was still honored. But this beggar never begged for food: he simply waited until it was offered, and so, it was the simple village women, many of them living in poverty, who approached the beggar for blessings and provided food while he lived on the streets in and around the big temple complex for the next ten years. He easily won their hearts, for they had the instinctual ability to recognize sanctity when they saw it, and they brought gruel or rice or chapattis and vegetables—whatever they could spare from their own families—as *prasad* or sacred offerings to the holy man who was dressed in the rags of a beggar.

He became a constant presence of benevolence and grace on the streets of Tiruvannamalai that would, over the years, attract the passionate devotion of many ardent followers, both East and West. Sitting beneath the punnai tree, it was not necessary for this yogi to take the lotus posture, close his eyes and withdraw from his surroundings to meditate on world peace, fingers curled into classic mudras or performing secret *pranayama*. Every ordinary action of the beggar, his gestures and movements and speech were transfigured, made sacred by the ultimate sacrifice of personal identity that made him transparent to the constant inflow of divine influence. His entire existence had gone beyond the state of meditation into an absorption in the Divine that was beyond even the most sensitive and God-inspired who walked at his side. Responding to this inner urge, certain circumstances or people would evoke the name of God from the beggar, and he would raise his hands in a blessing to those who walked by, impelled by interior demand to the ecstatic utterance, "Ram! Ram!" Was he speaking directly to God on their behalf, or was he the embodiment of the Divine, speaking to them, calling them into relationship with a living God?

These spontaneous eruptions of the name of God, the frequent melodic chanting, the disarming lilt of his voice and the wonder of his laughter, the natural nobility and grace of his physical presence, his gestures and moves, his authenticity, simplicity and humility, and his naturally loving nature began to conquer the hearts of the local people. In 1959 he was only forty-one years old, and he had spent the past seven years wandering in a long arcane journey that would remain veiled from anyone's knowledge for the rest of his life. Some who knew him say that during this time he sought out the company of many great spiritual teachers, including Swami Nityananda and J. Krishnamurti, the chosen spiritual preceptor of the Theosophical Society who later renounced his role and became simply a great inspiring being who helped many seekers and *sadhakas* on the path. The beggar had been living in a state of divine madness since he was thirty-five, cast there by his guru, Swami Ramdas. Because his ecstatic speech often burst forth in the name of God, "Ram! Ram!" as he blessed those who came within his sphere, he began to be known as "Ram Ram" and "Ramji" or "Ramji Swami," but his true name was Yogi Ramsuratkumar. It would take years, and Yogi Ramsuratkumar's careful assertion of this many times to many people, before his devotees began to realize the importance of that name—more than a symbol, in fact, the very manifestation, the living truth of the magnificent revolutionary change that had occurred within his being.

When Yogi Ramsuratkumar first landed in Tiruvannamalai in the summer of 1959, he did exactly what he told Ramdas he would do—he went to Arunachala, the place where Ramdas himself was consumed by a God-intoxication that changed his life. To be exact, he went to Ramanashram, which rests at the foot of the holy mountain: the ashram of Ramana Maharshi that he had known well in his visits there when the Maharshi was still alive. There he lived for approximately one year, mostly due to the benevolence of one of the senior disciples of Ramana Maharshi, T.K. Sundaresan Iyer, who took Yogi

Ramsuratkumar under his wing, making sure he had a place to stay and food to eat. T.K.S. Iyer was one of the first in Tiruvannamalai to recognize the divine madness of Yogi Ramsuratkumar. By 1960 Iyer was insisting that the strange beggar was not an ordinary person. He said, "People should not be deceived by appearances. He is a *siddha purusha*." Yogi Ramsuratkumar did not forget the kindness and help that this man gave to him.

At the same time, there were others who looked with ordinary eyes and saw only a bothersome, unkempt dirty beggar. Their sense of propriety and social convention was offended by this man who simply did not conform to the rules and regulations of society, and who had a provocative habit of going into reveries of song and dance and inexplicable *bhavas*—states of being that were viewed by them as aberrations. Not only that, but he smoked cigarettes.

There were those people at Ramanashram, perhaps not unlike those at Anandashram, who misunderstood and mistreated the "mad Bihari," now a strange, elusive yogi from the north. One swami in particular actively disliked Yogi Ramsuratkumar and used to put thorns in front of his door. Those who were threatened by him or disliked beggars in general had support in high places: the wealthy and powerful Parsi woman, a Zoroastrian named Ma Talyerkhan, also disliked Yogi Ramsuratkumar and was known to create a negative atmosphere around the beggar. Once she railed out against the beggars and sadhus at Ramanashram; pointing to Yogi Ramsuratkumar, she said, "These dirty beggars should not be fed here!" It was this caustic comment that marked Yogi Ramsuratkumar's last day at Ramanashram. Regardless of Iyer's attempts to help, the conflict and negativity became too great a burden, and after a year, Yogi Ramsuratkumar left Ramanashram and went back to the streets, where he was free and at home. Regardless of the sincere and well-meant invitations that he received many years later, he never went back to Ramanashram after Ma Talyerkhan's remark.

Another element of the abuse he suffered was due to the political environment in southern India at this time, where there was backlash against people who were coming in from the north. This was due, in part, to the economic competition between northern Indian and southern India; many in the south believed that the north received more funds and financial aid from the government, and there was a spirit of dissidence that pervaded the south. At this time a number of sadhus and mendicants were being mistreated by these same political factions. Although his English was fluent, the deep-seated regional prejudices that are found in most large countries, like in the northern and southern United States, took a great toll on Yogi Ramsuratkumar. His Hindi speech and his frequent radical byword of "Mahatma Gandhi Ki Jai!"—victory to Gandhi—and "Jawaharlal Nehru Ki Jai!" was not welcomed by certain powerful conservative political factions within the state.

Back on the streets in the swirl of people, politics, survival, gossip and the countless things that make up village life, Yogi Ramsuratkumar was also still in a process of assimilating the annihilation of the personality that had occurred within him as the result of a radical surrender to the Will of God, by the graceful influence of Swami Ramdas. Lee Lozowick has said that when a radical spiritual awakening first strikes, the being is literally reborn, and it is as if he or she is now a newborn baby in a new world. In this raw state the clarity of perception and penetrating insight is excruciating, even painful and maddening. It takes a long time to mature within the new world of awakened consciousness. Ramdas, in his wisdom, knew that Ramsuratkumar would be led along the way to exactly those experiences and events that would be needed in order to focus and polish the radiance of God-realization—like a fine wine that must be aged to nectar, or the years of worship and oblations that it takes to create the beautiful shining patina on the old bronze deities that live in the temples. In such a process of transformation, the streets can be a powerful place to live.

After he left Ramanashram, Yogi Ramsuratkumar lived mostly at the cemetery or *smashan* (cremation ground) near the Esanya Mutt until 1962. These were years when it was very common for his ecstatic states to take the form of dancing. Tilakavati, who actually met Yogi Ramsuratkumar in 1975, stated that she saw him dance, and it was "the dance of Shiva," leaping, twirling, his limbs moving in graceful arcs as he chanted the name of God. She also reported that she once heard Yogi Ramsuratkumar dance to the sound of a *damaru*, the type of drum that Shiva plays in his cosmic dance, and that he made the sound, not with the instrument, but with his own voice. The sounds he made could not be reproduced by the human voice; how did he make sounds that were so awesome, inspiring, thrilling?[2] Similar, V. Ganeshan, the grand-nephew of Ramana Maharshi, who was close to Yogi Ramsuratkumar for many years after meeting him in the early sixties, told the story of having seen him chanting Ramnam and dancing, leaping gracefully from slab to slab at the *smashan*. This dancing went on for hours, during which time vast energies seemed to pour from his frame. Ganeshan said that in these hours Yogi Ramsuratkumar was so transported that he was oblivious to anyone who passed by.[3]

In 1962, three years after he first arrived in Tiruvannamalai, Yogi Ramsuratkumar traveled to Madras, where he spent a few months at the home of Shri Devasenapathi, a devotee of Swami Ramdas. After this he moved to the Pillaiyar Koil at the Ganapathi Temple—the temple to Ganesh, the elephant-headed god, son of Shiva and Parvati, to whom Yogi Ramsuratkumar was partial—near the Theosophical Society compound. He often visited the extensive library of the Theosophical Society, where he pondered over "many rare and valuable works. It was there that he met Sri Sriram, who later became the president of the Society." They developed a close friendship that lasted for the rest of Yogi Ramsuratkumar's life.[4] Yogi Ramsuratkumar had a keen interest in the Theosophical Society and the teachings of H.P. Blatvatsky and her famous book, *The Secret Doctrine*.

Yogi Ramsuratkumar returned to Tiruvannamalai in 1963, and according to close devotees, he spent six months around this time living in the cave of Gugai Namashivyar on Mount Arunachala. He knew well the many caves and secret paths and inhabitants of the mountain, both seen and unseen; immersed in the mountain's benevolent and mystical

2 Vijayalakshmi, *Waves of Love*, p. 20.

3 Ibid, p. 21.

4 Ibid.

spirit, it was the mystical power of Arunachala that helped further the divine alchemy that was at work inside him, as he would state many times in later years. It was around this time that Yogi Ramsuratkumar began to spend a great deal of time under the punnai tree in the fields outside Tiruvannamalai, where flowers were grown for the great Arunachaleswara Temple. He spent his time divided between the railway station and under the punnai tree carrying a palmyra fan, given to him by a sadhu at Ramanashram. Along with the palmyra fan, he carried a coconut bowl and an unusual staff made of various objects entwined together, as well as the newspapers he collected, which he carried in an old burlap bag. Occasionally he stayed under the peepal tree near the bus stand.[5]

In 1964, the year of Jawaharlal Nehru's death, he traveled again to Madras where he met J. Krishnamurti at Adyar. As the story goes, Yogi Ramsuratkumar went to the residence where Krishnamurti was staying, hoping to meet the famous teacher, but he had gone upstairs to rest. Upon inquiring if he could see Krishnamurti, Yogi Ramsuratkumar was sent away by the security person. Krishnamurti, looking out the upstairs window, saw Yogi Ramsuratkumar sitting under some trees a distance away.

"Who is that man?" he asked the security guard.

"Just some beggar," was the reply.

"I want to see him," Krishnamurti said, "please go and get him and bring him here." Standing face to face with Krishnamurti, Yogi Ramsuratkumar attempted to prostate, but Krishnamurti held him by the shoulder, preventing him from going into a full bow.

"I have only one question," Yogi Ramsuratkumar said. J. Krishnamurti said, "Yes?" and the beggar continued, "Is repeating the name of God (Ramnam) the same as what you teach?" Without hesitation Krishnamurti answered, "Yes."

Later Yogi Ramsuratkumar followed Krishnamurti to Bombay (now Mumbai) where Krishnamurti was to give a series of lectures. According to Vijayalakshmi, Yogi Ramsuratkumar was walking toward the place where the lecture would be held when a car stopped beside him. In the car was Krishnamurti. He entreated Yogi Ramsuratkumar to ride with him, then asked him to sit on the dais with him during the lecture. Years later Yogi Ramsuratkumar told one of his devotees, Appan Iyengar, that Krishnamurti insisted that Yogi Ramsuratkumar speak also, which he did to spontaneous applause. It was during this period of time, the mid-sixties, when Yogi Ramsuratkumar also traveled to Ganeshpuri to the ashram of Swami Nityananda, and later to Kanhangad to visit the ashram of Nityananda that is located there—although, obedient to his guru, Yogi Ramsuratkumar did not visit Anandashram at that time.[6] Krishnamurti was not the only great teacher that Yogi Ramsuratkumar sought out during these years; ten years later when Caylor Wadlington was visiting Swami Muktananda at Ganeshpuri, Muktananda asked him, "Who is your guru?" When he answered, "Yogi Ramsuratkumar," Muktananda said, "Yes, I know him."

---

5 Ibid, p. 22.

6 Vijayalakshmi, *Waves of Love*, pp. 23-24.

Returning to Tiruvannamalai from these trips, Yogi Ramsuratkumar was again an established presence on the busy streets, where he lived for many years as a hidden saint, conducting his work invisibly and steadily. His favorite haunt from the mid-sixties to the early seventies was the punnai tree near the railroad station, where he would stay during most of the day, and the Theradi Mandapam where the temple chariot was housed for the annual Deepam festival. He slept on the front verandahs of the shops and stalls in the bazaar near the temple. Certain shopkeepers were very supportive and friendly, while others were not. Yogi Ramsuratkumar usually had coffee every day at the Akila India Coffee Bar and the village women sometimes brought food for a midday meal, which he then shared with whatever friends were present. He only ate what was given to him as an offering of *prasad*; if food was not offered, he went hungry, sometimes for days.

And so in this way Yogi Ramsuratkumar lived within the labyrinths and potencies of the streets, and though he was rebuked by some, he was warmly accepted by the more arcane and traditional ascetic lineages that have monasteries or obscure ashrams—*peethams* and *mutts*—all over India, having small enclaves or branches in villages and towns like Tiruvannamalai. Many of these were clustered around the holy hill, Mount Arunachala, and Ramsuratkumar was often invited to these places, where he would be a welcomed guest for the afternoon and treated with high regard. Within the highly articulated world of sadhus, there are many different groups and subgroups with their own form of informal though effective organization. Within their world exists a network of refuges that accept mendicants and provide shelter as they move from place to place throughout India in a kind of underground network of guru/disciple lineages existing in unbroken lines. These existed on the back streets of Tiruvannamalai, which Yogi Ramsuratkumar knew well and traversed regularly.

Yogi Ramsuratkumar had a definite kind of "street credit" with the grassroots people of the village as well—not only the sadhus and wandering ascetics, but with the obscure spiritual lineages, the poor and low-caste village people and some of the merchants and chai vendors in the bazaar who accepted and recognized him. A few who had the clarity and depth of vision began to see through the beggar to the hidden saint and his inner work. Yogi Ramsuratkumar, like his father Papa Ramdas, never made any caste distinctions, except to occasionally make a teaching lesson for hapless devotees who abused the privilege of having a high caste status.

In 1964 the beggar befriended a local man, Perumal Sadaiyan, a bronze merchant in Tiruvannamalai, who became one of several early devotees to attend to Yogi Ramsuratkumar and care for his needs in a very specific way. The account written in his book, *Treasures of the Heart: The Unforgettable Yogi Ramsuratkumar*, is the first published work that offers a glimpse into the daily life of the beggar saint during the mid and late sixties.

Perumal first met Yogi Ramsuratkumar when he was seated alone in the bazaar in Tiruvannamalai one Sunday, facing the eastern temple *gopuram* (tower) with its gateway known as the "Gateway of Righteousness and Wisdom." Suddenly at the foot of the massive *gopuram*, he saw what he thought was a streak of lightning, a swiftly moving beam of light. Focusing his eyes, he saw that it was a human being, moving toward him with the most extraordinary gait and bearing. The face was obscured, and he had the strangest thought that he was seeing the supreme Lord walking in human form. Disbelieving, he tried to turn his attention away from the figure to focus on the temple and Mount Arunachala in the background, and the strange figure kept walking, purposefully, with a magnificent appearance and now a soft smile that was visible on his face.

> His gait was Kingly and he looked tall and striking. He held a palm-leaf fan and four or five newpapers in his hand. He had draped himself with a green shawl. His locks lay in clusters around his face. His face was shining, and clean with a broad and brilliant forehead. Thus he stood blocking the temple tower and hill out of my view. A spurt of anger arose in me quite discernibly but meeting him eye to eye my anger was put out at once.
>
> I gestured affectionately with my left hand and invited him to sit by my side. At once, he sat down unhesitatingly. Again I reverted my eyes towards the temple tower and the hill. Though my gaze was fixed far away I felt that the person seated next to me was watching me as if talking to me. I was sharply aware of his presence. Thus though we were seated side by side, we did not speak to each other. Almost twenty minutes passed in this way. He was looking at me keenly, which I could feel and I began to wonder why he was staring so. Perhaps it was my appearance, I thought.
>
> I sported a beard and matted hair. Being a prosperous merchant, I wore a ring, a chain around the neck and a bracelet, all of gold. Though it was a holiday for the market, it being Sunday, only I sat outside the shops in the bazaar. Perhaps Swami wondered at this.
>
> While he was watching me thus, I thought that I should get him at least a cup of coffee. I turned to the elder and said, "Sir! Please take some coffee," in a loving tone and heard "Yes, alright" in reply in a deep tone. I felt the sound fill my mind and strike my body. I became alert at once and brought me eyes and mind under control. The next moment I clapped my hands to call the boys playing on the terrace above the shops on the opposite side. The elder seated next to me asked me, "Why do you clap your hands and call those boys?" I replied very humbly, "Sir! I called them to fetch the coffee." Then, Swami was pleased to bid me for the first time. "Not them. You go yourself to get it." This made me angry again. Perhaps it was a mistake to have offered coffee to this man. Now he is giving me orders.[7]

7 Perumal Sadaiyan, *Treasures of the Heart*, pp. 2-3.

Perumal considered himself to be an important man, a respected merchant. In India a person of status does not run errands for others or carry coffee across town, but has someone of a lower status do it for him. He had just met a strange beggar, about whom he knew nothing, and yet he was compelled by his presence and beauty to serve him without question, even though he felt some ambiguity and even anger about it. Who was this beggar to have such an effect on him, and so effortlessly? It was most unusual, and on the way back with the coffee, his anger was fueled all the more each time he had to decline two or three offers from other people to carry the coffee for him. At one point he replied to the offer of help, "I am taking this coffee for a venerable person. Therefore I must take it myself."

Returning with the coffee he found that the swami was seated, facing west and smoking a cigarette. Even dressed in rags, there was a majesty about his presence. In fact, he seemed more like a king than a beggar. Perumal was surprised, but accepted that perhaps the swami had the habit of smoking.

"While you were on your way here, did not anyone offer to fetch the coffee?" the elder asked.

"I did not give it to them. I brought it myself," Perumal answered.

Taking the coffee, the strange beggar poured it into four vessels and began cooling it by pouring it from one vessel into another. His acts were entirely enigmatic to Perumal, who watched while the beggar cooled the coffee, then gave half the quantity to Perumal while scrutinizing his beard and matted hair. Then he poured the other half of the coffee into the coconut shell that he carried, and holding it in one hand, continued to gaze at Perumal.

"Who are you? Where do you live?" Yogi Ramsuratkumar asked suddenly. Perumal was rather taken aback, since they were sitting outside his shop, and replied, "This metal-ware shop is mine."

"At what time do you open the shop?" the swami asked.

"I open the shop at seven thirty in the morning. The closing time depends on the customers. It may even be ten at night when the shop is closed."

"What is your name?" the beggar queried sweetly.

"Sir! My parents and elders have named me Sivananainda Perumal." At this the beggar burst into a joyous peal of laughter for no apparent reason.

"Do you laugh because it is a very long name?" Perumal asked, trying not to be offended. At this he laughed more, and kept laughing until he finally looked at Perumal and asked in a soft voice, "Why do you sport a beard and matted hair?"

Anger flared in Perumal's vital and he exclaimed, "That is one thing about which you should not ask!" Yogi Ramsuratkumar only continued to gaze at him tenderly.[8]

Very shortly Perumal left to conduct business and went about the rest of his day, but he could not take his mind off the beggar, whom he referred to as an "elder." He eventually went back to his shop that day in hope of seeing the elder again, but he was

8 Ibid, pp. 3-4.

disappointed to find him gone. Perplexed by the whole interaction and the strange effect the elder was having upon him, a great restlessness began to plague him; he began to feel that he had lost something very precious.

The next morning, after his ablutions and prayers to the sun, Perumal went back to open his shop. Later that morning he spotted the swami coming toward the shop from the east. Without thinking, Perumal invited him to sit down in his shop. When the swami was settled Perumal sent for tea for everyone present, offering the tea, when it arrived, to the swami himself, which the beggar lovingly accepted. From the description given by Perumal, it seems that the stature of the beggar, whom he now called "Swami"—a title of respect—had begun to have its effect, and Perumal wanted to offer him something more substantial. When breakfast arrived he offered the *idlis* (fermented rice pancakes) to the beggar.

"Let us eat," he said, looking up at Swami. Only then did he really see him for the first time.

> His eyes were like the two shining watery white kernels of a freshly halved coconut, as though they were filled with tears. He said gently, "What is sent is meant for one person only, for you."
>
> I replied, "Sir! You please accept it."
>
> Again he said gently, "Let us both eat." I said yes at once and opened the box. There were six idlis and a sufficient quantity of chutney and sambar to go with it. Swami ate three idlis . . . . Then, pointing to the boy who had fetched the meal, Swami asked me, "Who is this? What is his name?"
>
> I replied, "His name is Raju. He is a brahmachari. A true friend."
>
> Swami called the boy near and asked him, "Do you know the name of this beggar?" And then in a nectarine voice Swami revealed his name for the first time: "Yogi Ramsuratkumar."
>
> Looking at me he asked me, "What is your name?"
>
> To this I replied, "My parents and elders have named me Sivananainda Perumal." Then Swami burst into a marvelous laughter which seemed to be suffused with joy. It became contagious and all of us laughed for at least five minutes. As he laughed, his face blossomed into redness.
>
> Oh! There are many types of laughter! But I can never hear or see a laughter such as this. I have seen and heard many types of laughter. This was the laughter of perfect innocence that would enchant the mind of anyone. His laughter was such that my mind because empty of all thoughts and was totally transfixed in that laughter. It was a laughter which would gladden the hearts of all, a laughter that I heard and saw so fully that I would never forget it.
>
> I have a reason to elaborate upon this laughter. Have you seen your

> own mind feel a joy when you stand by the sea and watch the waves rise one after another and race towards the shore? The laughter of our Lord Yogi Ramsuratkumar was like the sprouting of sheets and sheets of golden grain when the dark rain-bearing clouds shower down on parched earth. His laughter was gentle, too, like the soft rain-petals that touch and nourish fresh grain. The mind that revels in the golden colors of the sky, the wonders of the rainbow and the eye that has enjoyed those sights can understand what I am trying to say. Such was my state. It will be very difficult to understand his laughter that day, which was a dance of grace indeed. I cannot forget it. Since the day I knew that laughter it has stayed to brighten my mind, even now.[9]

Perumal was a practical businessman who was easily annoyed, even plagued by uncontrolled angers. A self-described man of vanity and pride, he was quickly transformed into a servant who wanted to do nothing but think of, follow, care for Yogi Ramsuratkumar. It was the rare quality of the laugh alone—a laugh that could melt the hardest heart—that captivated and finally captured Perumal. He began to look for the beggar every day, to seek his company, and to carry and care for his strange bundles—often newspapers, books and various seemingly unimportant things like string, rags, dried flower garlands and so on. These bundles or burlap bags were extremely important to Yogi Ramsuratkumar; they were considered sacred by virtue of the fact that he had "worked" with every object within the bundles. His apparent attachment to such junk or garbage was one of the reasons that some people thought he was mad. Yogi Ramsuratkumar often put his devotees to the task of caring for these bundles with the utmost respect.

The next day Yogi Ramsuratkumar took Perumal to the Arunachaleswara Temple, where Yogi Ramsuratkumar spent a great deal of time. They entered together through the *gopuram*, walked past the large Nandi bull (Shiva's mount), then went past the Kala Bhairava shrine to the ghat or steps that lead down to the Brahma Tirtha tank—the large temple pool of murky water that was covered with moss and dust. Yogi Ramsuratkumar stood facing northwest, gazing toward the mountain, his face lit with an awe-inspiring radiance. He proceeded to wash his face, hands and legs with water, and with a piercing glance at Perumal, gently splashed water on his face three times. His actions had the feeling and power of a sacred ritual, and surprised Perumal greatly. Yogi Ramsuratkumar bent down, scooped up water in his two hands and poured it gently in Perumal's hands, who drank with amazement. Coming from the beggar's hands, the water was not dirty at all, but pure and mild, and sweet to the taste. The next moment, with an enigmatic exclamation and a smile on his face, the beggar climbed up the steps of the ghat with Perumal following close behind.

Crossing the temple courtyard and walking past the large sculpture of Nandi bull, Perumal followed Yogi Ramsuratkumar, who held his hand and kept him close to his side.

---

9 Ibid, pp. 8-10.

Yogi Ramsuratkumar was known to walk extremely fast, and now he took off through the village, past the various shrines and temples that dotted the streets. Perumal began to think of his shop and his responsibilities back at the bazaar.

"What is it, Perumal? Are you thinking of the shop?" the beggar asked, looking at Perumal and sensing his discomfort. Surprised by such sweet attention, Perumal replied, "Yes, Swami." Yogi Ramsuratkumar looked at Perumal tenderly, but only increased his pace and continued on, walking with an unwavering intention and sense of purpose. As they passed the Kali temple and reached Dakshinamurthi temple, Yogi Ramsuratkumar bent down to have a glimpse of the shrine there, but did not linger or let go of Perumal's hand. He seemed to have a very specific mission, and they eventually came to a small pond near which lay a narrow path that Yogi Ramsuratkumar took. After walking some distance, they arrived at a deserted cottage surrounded by a thorny fence.

"Look Perumal. This is where this beggar stayed," Yogi Ramsuratkumar pointed toward a locked room on one side of the cottage.

> I looked through the window into that room. What I saw made me shiver. I was deeply moved and with tearful eyes and a heavy heart, I turned and looked at the divine person standing nearby. 'My Lord! Was it here that my Lord lived?' I thought. What met the eyes in the room was dreadful. Many black scorpions of the most poisonous kind were scuttling about. There were red scorpions also moving about with chameleons and some other reptiles. There were several clusters of white ants providing sustenance to these creatures. On the bundle of papers, and old clothes, a small snake was moving about. Though I narrate this quite easily, what I saw was something that was so shocking that one cannot forget the scene having seen it once. Even now, I remember it vividly.
>
> If there is one thing that our Lord Yogi Ramsuratkumar cherishes with great care, more than all material wealth, perhaps even more than this life, it is "The Hindu" and "The Indian Express" newspapers which he would read everyday. These papers were stacked in one corner of that room. White ants had eaten through these papers, through the middle of the pile. Only the four corners of the pile were in tact. On top of the pile, a snake with an open hood was dancing about. The rest was only a mass of white ants. Nearby lay a rust-colored dhoti, a shirt and a green shawl that he had used. The white ants had not spared his clothes also. They had eaten through it as well, quite happily.
>
> The room itself was a strange artifact. It had a roof of coconut palm leaves. But they were so old, the palm fronds had just dissolved into dust for the most part. Most of the roof was open to the terrible sun as well as rain. This run-down, dilapidated and dangerous room frightened me. I held the bars of the window and turned around. Two black scorpions, with their stings upraised, had begun to crawl towards my hand. Seeing this, Yogi

> Ramsuratkumar, whom I had turned around to watch, urged me to move, saying, "Hmm! Hmm!" and I snatched away my hand just in time. The scorpions capered here and there on the window. Desirous of seeing the room once again, I entered it. My mind was disturbed by a number of thoughts. "That such a great man had to live in such a dwelling or in the midst of poisonous creatures! A rare and great man not being understood by foolish people who beat and torture him. Yet how patiently he bore with all." With such thoughts passing through my mind, I turned around and looked at Swami. "Let us go," he said. My eyes were filled with tears when I looked at that fine figure and face that was saturated with love.[10]

Yogi Ramsuratkumar allowed Perumal into the daily rhythms of his life, and Perumal quickly discovered that the saint was beleaguered, harassed and not infrequently beaten by "miscreants"—certain local people who seemed to take a strange pleasure in such acts.

"Perumal! Please come. There is a small work that must be done," the beggar said one day, in his unusual way of calling the smallest actions "work" or "work that must be done." Who could know what was really happening? His actions, words and gestures were often enigmatic, incomprehensible, and yet he was entirely winsome, appealing, even extraordinarily beautiful. His form seemed to be permeated with an ineffable grace that communicated effortlessly, in the smallest movement and in stillness as well. Perumal commented that, when at the temple with Yogi Ramsuratkumar, it seemed that he was "conversing with the Gods."[11]

Yogi Ramsuratkumar took off walking, with Perumal following, past the Arunachaleswara Temple, the *gopuram*, the big Nandi bull and westward to the Brahma Tirtha tank in the temple, where once again Yogi Ramsuratkumar sprinkled Perumal with water two or three times. Again Perumal was irritated, but this was soon dissolved in the immediacy of the moment with Yogi Ramsuratkumar—who "walked with the majesty of a great warrior who has a thousand troops at his command."[12] As they walked at a brisk pace through the temple precincts and across town, past Agni Tirtham, then Seshadri Swami's ashram, Kaliamman Temple, and Ramanashram near the Dakshinamurthi shrine, they moved westward and into a forested area where cattle fairs used to be held. There was a place not frequented by many people, in a grove of Vathamadakki trees and tamarind trees. There Yogi Ramsuratkumar confided to Perumal that he used to spend many hours in solitude in this place, but he had been threatened and harassed a great deal, and had to leave.

"This beggar has suffered a great deal in this place," he said.

Perumal immediately said, "Swami, a friend of mine lives nearby. I shall request him to give you protection. Do not fear anything."

10 Ibid, pp. 13-14.
11 Ibid, p. 23.
12 Ibid.

"Only he who has suffered pain can understand fear. It is not possible to explain pain and fear to anyone," Yogi Ramsuratkumar replied.

"It will not happen again, Swami!" Perumal burst out, deeply moved by the troubles the beggar had revealed in such an innocent and gentle way.

On their way back into town Perumal saw Harikrishnan, a friend who lived in the area, and spoke with him about this news. Harikrishnan said that this was indeed true and he described that he had witnessed it.

"Yes, he would be harassed when he would rest under this tree. Some would scatter the newspapers on all sides. They would snatch his fan. They would shout at him and drive him away, saying, 'Don't come here again. Don't be here. Get lost!' I have seen all this and heard it too. Once they snatched the shawl he was wearing and flung away his blanket. They would grab his newspapers and fly it on all sides. They will now allow him to read the newspapers. I have seen some people trouble Swami in this manner."[13]

As the days went by Perumal continued to spend a great deal of time with Yogi Ramsuratkumar, serving him, attending to his "work" and neglecting his business for the joy of the camaraderie that occurred as people congregated there around Yogi Ramsuratkumar. He often worried about the shop, but at the same time he was compelled by the amazing experiences he had with the beggar saint. What could it all mean? Time went on and Yogi Ramsuratkumar continued to visit Perumal at his shop, and the days passed by. Business became dull and Perumal began to lose money. It seemed that his ordinary life—the concerns of a businessman, a man of progress and reason and status and worldly success—was beginning to erode, even to come apart.[14]

Wanting to have the presence of Yogi Ramsuratkumar in his shop all the time, Perumal asked him for a photograph and received the answer that, although his photo was not available, Yogi Ramsuratkumar would pose for a photo with Perumal, if he wished. Perumal asked to sit at Yogi Ramsuratkumar's feet, and so the photograph was arranged, with Yogi Ramsuratkumar wearing a green shawl, holding his palmyra fan in his upraised hand. That night he visited Perumal's shop, and he was singing, "Sri Rama Jaya Rama Jaya Jaya Rama."

It was during this time period that Yogi Ramsuratkumar healed Raju, a man who could not speak well. That night several people were already gathered at the shop when Yogi Ramsuratkumar arrived.

"Chant the name of Yogi Ramsuratkumar," he instructed Raju. "You will be able to speak well." A few days later they were back in the shop when Raju arrived.

"Perumal! Ask him if he chants this beggar's name!"

Raju was chanting the name of Yogi Ramsuratkumar and he began to happily sing the name—but he was singing, "Yogi Ramsuratkumal."

"He seems to be cured. He sings quite well," Perumal said, turning back to Yogi

13 Ibid, pp. 23-24.

14 Ibid, p. 28.

Ramsuratkumar, but the beggar was very unsatisfied.

"No! No! He is changing the name," he remonstrated. This was the first of countless times that Yogi Ramsuratkumar would tell people to chant his name, and would insist on the pronunciation being exact. He corrected Raju's chanting and all was well.

While Perumal's business prospects became more dismal, at the same time his faith and devotion to the unpredictable beggar increased, even though he received warnings from respectable people of the town. A Brahmin approached and warned him that Yogi Ramsuratkumar was a madman who should not be consorted with, and on another occasion a friend of his mother told him that Yogi Ramsuratkumar had died. He was grief stricken, and his mind raced with feelings of remorse and shame at not having protected Yogi Ramsuratkumar adequately, as he imagined that Yogi Ramsuratkumar had been killed by those elements in town who wished to get rid of him and who had threatened him many times before. He asked a friend who said he too had heard the rumor, and that others were talking about it as well. Because Perumal had to go to Madras and Tirupati on business, he had been gone for several days, and now upon his return, the days stretched by and he still hadn't seen Yogi Ramsuratkumar for some time. He was heartbroken and inconsolable.

One morning on the way to his shop he suddenly spotted Yogi Ramsuratkumar standing near the Gandhi statue in town. His body trembled with emotion and his eyes filled with tears as he stood watching Yogi Ramsuratkumar in the bazaar, while cars and other vehicles passed helter-skelter between them. Then Yogi Ramsuratkumar saw him too, and stood, smiling at him. Perumal ran to him and prostrated at his feet, but he simply patted his back in a fatherly way and said, "Rise, Perumal."

Now joyously reunited, Yogi Ramsuratkumar immediately sensed that something was worrying Perumal.

"Are mother and children well at home?" Yogi Ramsuratkumar asked gently. Not wanting to trouble Yogi Ramsuratkumar, Perumal waffled. They walked through the bazaar.

"Let us have some tea," the beggar suggested kindly. Perumal took Yogi Ramsuratkumar's coconut bowl and gave it to the shopkeeper at the Akila India Coffee Bar. He asked him to fill it to the brim and then asked for a glass of tea for himself, also filled to the top. When he returned to Yogi Ramsuratkumar with the tea, he said, "Perumal! Hand it to me," referring to Perumal's glass of tea. The beggar then poured some of the tea from the glass into his bowl, mixed the teas together, then poured some back into Perumal's glass.[15] Finally Perumal told Yogi Ramsuratkumar the truth—that there was a rumor going around that he was dead.

"These people will speak only like this. Father will look after everything. I am doing Father's work. This is Father's work. Father looks after everything," the beggar reassured him.

A few days later a man came bursting into Perumal's shop, saying breathlessly, "In

15 Ibid, pp. 32-33.

the northern quarters near the Durgamma temple in the small bazaar two ruffians are beating up your Ram Ram Swami!" Perumal instantly ran from his shop toward the scene, along the way seeing Murugan and Guruswami, two other friends of Yogi Ramsuratkumar.

"Sir! Someone is beating up your Yogi Ramsuratkumar!" he called to the men, and the three ran northward only to stumble upon the shocking sight of one man brutally beating Yogi Ramsuratkumar while many others watched complacently, "as if watching a show." Bearing everything graciously, Yogi Ramsuratkumar stood alone on one side. Not one friend, not one devotee had the courage to stop the vicious act. No one had dared to confront the ringleader. A gang of several local ruffians stood to one side, cheering the ringleader on, so to speak. As the three men ran onto the scene, the ringleader, who was beating Yogi Ramsuratkumar, saw that he was going to be accosted and he backed off. Perumal and his companions quickly moved toward Yogi Ramsuratkumar's side. His newspapers had all been scattered. His green shawl was flung to one side on the dusty ground. The man who had beaten Yogi Ramsuratkumar tried to grab his coconut bowl while he further berated him with curses, showering insults and verbal abuse. The three men approached this scene with hearts beating fast, eager to do justice, and the last ruffian began to run away.

"Don't let him escape. Catch the rogue, catch him!" Guruswami shouted and ran after him.

"No Sir! Don't catch him," Yogi Ramsuratkumar said. "Let this be for me alone." He stood there, bruised and bleeding all over and counseled peace to his friends, but Perumal was angry and wanted revenge.

"What is this Swami? You tell us to let go of the rogue. If we let him off he will come again!"

"Let him come. We shall bear it. Let us do Father's work."[16]

After the crowd dispersed there was no one left but Guruswami, Murugan, Perumal and Yogi Ramsuratkumar. They picked up his newspapers and his green shawl from the dust of the road. Yogi Ramsuratkumar's shirt was in tatters, and his body was bleeding from the scratches and nail marks on his skin. Perumal wondered, "How does he bear all this to serve the world and protect the people!" He stood watching the beggar, deeply disturbed by the whole incident and concerned for his future welfare.

"Don't worry Perumal," the beggar said quietly, "Father will look after everything. Let us do Father's work."

16 Ibid, pp. 37-38.

In 1965 Yogi Ramsuratkumar went to Tapovanum, the ashram of Gnanananda Giri, for the first time. Gnanananda Giri was a revered local saint and great yogi who was reputed to have mastered his body to the extent that he was over one hundred fifty years old. His ashram, Tapovanum,[17] was located in Tirukoilur, a small village not far from Tiruvannamalai, on the northern bank of the Pennar River. It had been established in the early fifties by the devotees of Gnanananda Giri.

During the decade of the sixties and into the early and mid-seventies, Yogi Ramsuratkumar developed a loving relationship with this well-known saint, who recognized the greatness in Ramji Swami, as he was affectionately known to everyone at Tapovanum. Gnanananda had such great regard for Yogi Ramsuratkumar that he gave him not only shelter and refuge from the abuse he was receiving in Tiruvannamalai, but over time he also turned many of his devotees toward Yogi Ramsuratkumar as guru.

Many sadhus and mendicants (*bhikshus*) used to come to Tapovanum to take *bhiksha*, or sacred food that has been given as alms, and Yogi Ramsuratkumar first appeared among those. Gnanananda Giri immediately recognized him and took him under his wing, giving him total permission to come and go from the ashram as he wished. Ramji Swami would suddenly appear, as if out of nowhere, stay for a day or a few days, or a week or two, then he would disappear again. For important functions like Guru Purnima he was always there during the years between 1965 and 1975. On these important occasions Gnanananda Giri would present him with the ritual shawl or cloth, traditionally given to monks or other religious persons, as a gift signifying respect. Gnanananda and Ramji Swami had a wonderful, fun loving relationship that is still remembered by the older devotees of Tapovanum with great affection and love. Much to the delight of the devotees, Gnanananda Giri and Ramji once had a race across the marble floor of the central courtyard under the *mandapam*[18] amidst much laughter and high spirits. At other times Ramji and Gnanananda Giri would sit for hours in silence.

Swami Nityananda, the current spiritual head of Tapovanum and disciple of Gnanananda Giri, remembered fondly that Ramji Swami was especially known at Tapovanum for singing beautifully. When Ramji first came to Tapovanum, only the most rigorous and stern Vedic chants were sung, but Ramji introduced the ecstatic, devotional *bhajans* of which he was so fond. Often he would settle under one of the large overhanging trees, and there he would begin to sing the name of God, or the melodic *bhajans* of the poet Mirabai. There was one Mirabai song to Giridhara Gopala (Krishna) in particular that Ramji loved and would sing: "For me there is no one but you; for me there is nobody but Giridhara." At other times he would sing, "Om Sri Ram Jai Ram Jai Jai Ram."

Shakuntala, a devotee of Gnanananda Giri and later of Yogi Ramsuratkumar, first came from Bombay to Tapovanum in 1962, and remembers well when Ramji, as he is still called by the devotees of Tapovanum, first came to the ashram in 1965. At that time he

---

17 Tapovanum: From Sanskrit, *tapas*, intense heat or fervor of austerity and Tamil *vanam*, forest or wood.

18 An ornate roof held up by columns, creating an open-air shelter.

stayed at Tapovanum for eight months. As soon as Ramji Swami first appeared at the ashram in 1965, Gnanananda Giri instructed Shakuntala to take care of him, and to sing Hindi songs to him.

"He speaks Hindi," Gnanananda instructed, "and he loves these Hindi songs." It was a particular instruction for Shakuntala, who was known for her exceptionally beautiful singing voice. Thus Shakuntala was the one who was responsible for serving Ramji food and coffee all day, and she often sat with him and sang *bhajans* in Hindi. Finding out that Ramji's birthday was on December 1, for many years Shakuntala would come all the way from Bombay just for Ramji's birthday, to get his blessings and to sing for him.

During the years when Ramji was coming to Tapovanum, in the late sixties, she would sing to him, mostly in Hindi and in Sanskrit, but occasionally in Tamil. He was very fond of the mood that her singing invoked, and often he fell into *bhavas*.

"Sing in Brindavan," he would say enigmatically, but she understood exactly what he meant. When she sang songs about Krishna he became silent and still as a statue, and would come and go in a state of superconsciousness. It seemed to her that he was completely in tune with Krishna, so that he would actually "go to Brindavan" during the chanting.

"My blessing is there, my Father's blessing is there, everybody's blessing is there!" he said with a sweet smile as he fanned her while she was singing. In these days his references to "Father" meant Swami Ramdas.

No one seemed to know exactly how Yogi Ramsuratkumar made his way to Tapovanum, but it was common knowledge that Gnanananda Giri had spent some time—ten days or two weeks—at Anandashram years before, with Ramdas and Mataji Krishnabai, who used to serve food to the visiting saint. It was a well-known fact that Gnanananda Giri had a tattoo on his arm that said "Ramdas." According to legend, it was during this time that the two saints each had a tattoo made with the other's name, so that Gnanananda's arm said "Ramdas," while Ramdas' arm said, "Gnanananda."

It is possible that Ramsuratkumar was present during this meeting between Ramdas and Gnanananda Giri, and that is how he and Gnanananda Giri came to be friends. What really happened is lost in the mists of time, but nonetheless, Ramji and Gnanananda were profoundly connected, and enjoyed a great friendship and mutual love of Swami Ramdas. In the complex tapestry of destiny, it seems that Papa Ramdas, who Yogi Ramsuratkumar had not seen for fifteen years, was still guiding his disciple with a firm, if unseen, hand.

Strong connections between the saints and God-realizers of India existed very commonly. Gnanananda Giri was not the only saint Swami Ramdas was connected with; the living elder disciples of Upasani Maharaj—the great saint and wild *avadhuta* of Sakori in Maharastra (west India)—remember well when Ramdas and Krishnabai came to visit Upasani Maharaj and his successor, Godavari Ma, on many occasions, especially after the *samadhi* (death) of Upasani. Yogi Ramsuratkumar himself was powerfully connected to numerous saints, many of whom remain a mystery. Some of these connections can be traced, however, such as the connection with Gnanananda Giri and Yogi Ramsuratkumar's well-known relationship with another "crazy" *avadhuta*, Mother

Mayee, or Mayamma, of Kanya Kumari on the southernmost tip of India, where the three oceans merge. Some say that Mother Mayee was "discovered" by Gnanananda Giri, but it is likely that he simply made her presence known to people in his area; Mayamma was believed to be anywhere from two hundred to three hundred years old when she finally shed the physical body in 1992.

There was, in fact, a network of saints and those who were deeply involved in the inner spiritual work of transformation for the good of all that existed in southern India during these years and in the following decades, including Yogi Ramsuratkumar, Nayanar Swami and Mouna (silent) Nirvana Swami, and Kasavana (smoking) Swami. Gnanananda Giri was pivotal in connecting all these saints together with the devotees of southern India; his devotee, Shri A.R.P.N. Rajamanickam Nadar (known simply as Rajamanickam) of Tuticorin, a wealthy merchant and ardent devotee, played an important role in bringing people to these various saints, as well as financially supporting the building of temples and various structures where people could come to worship, conduct their *pujas* and chant the name of God.

In the late sixties a number of prominent Indian families began to connect with Yogi Ramsuratkumar by circumstances that could only be designed by fate. They were not necessarily looking for a guru, but they all needed help, guidance, divine intervention. In 1967 S.P. Janarthanan was a prosperous young married man with a wife and children, but there were other troubles in his family. Both his elder and younger sisters had entered into marriages in which there were great difficulties, and these situations were causing suffering for the whole family. Janarthanan felt responsible for his family and was anxious to resolve the difficulties of his younger sister, Vasantakumari, but he also wanted to find a suitable husband for his wife Vijaya's younger sister, Radhika.

Janarthanan's uncle, Rajamanickam, was very affectionate and intimately involved with the family, and wanted to help alleviate their problems. Rajamanickam was an ardent devotee of Gnanananda Giri, and had urged his sister, Janarthanan's mother, Arumai Nayakam Ammal, many times to go to Tapovanum to meet the famous saint and seek his blessings. When the family situation worsened, she agreed to go, and so accompanied by Rajamanickam, Arumai Nayakam Ammal traveled to Tapovanum to seek help. Gnanananda Giri blessed them and said that all their problems would be solved by the grace of Ambika, the mother goddess. Janarthanan himself, when told of this blessing, was skeptical, but his mother had great faith in Gnanananda Giri, who she considered to be a great sage. Very shortly after this Vasantakumari's marital problems were resolved.

An event occurred while Janarthanan's mother was at the ashram in Tapovanum that would change the course of life for her entire family; there she met another sage, Ramji Swami, who left a very deep impression on her. Eventually the relationship of this family with Yogi Ramsuratkumar would develop, and he would become the central star around which their lives revolved. Janarthanan, the nephew of Rajamanickam, wrote in his memoir of these times:

Our Swami, Yogi Ramsuratkumar, used to come to Tapovanam from 1967 onwards. A lot of saints used to visit Tapovanam to have a darshan of Gnanananda Giri Swamiji. Our Swamji, Yogi Ramsuratkumar, was not noticed by any then. He used to stay at Tapovanam for months. He used to stay in a haystack, or on the shore of the river. Though he was very simple, he used to partake of any food at Tapovanam, but only if Gnanananda Giri Swami asked him to do so. On such occasions, Shri Shrinivasan of Kudamuruti village in Tapovanam, Smt Shakuntala, her children Jayaraman, Krishnamurthy, Vimala all looked after Swami's needs for food.

Gnanananda Giri Swami was born in Mangalore, and he had the name "Ramdas" tattooed in his hand. Whenever Rajamanickam visited Tapovanam, Gnanananda Giri Swami would send him to Tiruvannamalai to look after Swamiji [Yogi Ramsuratkumar]. He used to buy new clothes for Swamiji, who otherwise would wear torn and dirty clothes. Sometimes a lot of thread was used to stitch the holes in the shirt worn by Swamiji. The people who used to carry Swamiji's bundles were always seen engrossed in the task of stitching the holes in Swamiji's clothes. Once Gnanananda Giri Swami sent one of his close devotees, who was a senior police officer, to Tiruvannamalai to give protection to our Swamiji, saying, "A lot of people are tormenting him, and we may give some protection to him."

Rajamanickam uncle would meet our Swamiji sometimes in the cremation ground in the daytime, and at the vessel shop [in the Tiruvannamalai bazaar] mostly at night. Sometimes at night he would meet Swamiji at the place near the temple, where sculptural works were being carried out. One day he had met Swamiji at the site where the sculptures were being done, and Swamiji gave Rajamanickam a sculpture of Mahatma Gandhi at midnight and asked him to give it to Gnanananda Giri Swami immediately. Rajamanickam carried the sculpture all through the night and reached Tapovanam in the early morning; he cried while giving the sculpture to Gnanananda Giri Swami, and Gnanananda Giri Swami cried also while receiving it.

One day Swamiji was staying at Tapovanam. A child had gone to the riverside to take a bath, and he got one of his legs trapped in between two rocks. He could not take out his leg, try as he might. All the devotees gathered at the river to help, and when our Swamiji came to know of this, he rushed to the riverside. Swamiji counseled everybody to be calm and assured everybody that the child would be able to take out his leg in ten minutes. He came around [circled] the rock chanting some mantra and within ten minutes, without any effort, the child could take out his leg

> without any injury. Everybody was surprised and everyone praised Swamiji.[19]

While Gnanananda Giri was still alive, Yogi Ramsuratkumar went to Tapovanum during the *puja* to a deceased saint, a revered Swami, Shri Raghottama, the head of the Madhwa sect, who had died while touring places in south India and had stopped at Tirukoilur near Tapovanum. A memorial, called Brindavan, was erected at the site of his *samadhi* (place of burial). On this particular occasion Gnanananda Giri asked Yogi Ramsuratkumar to go to Brindavan and get *prasad*, which he should then bring to Tapovanum, but when Yogi Ramsuratkumar arrived at Brindavan, the ceremony was over and the prasad already distributed. The Madhwa sect being very strict in their observance of Hindu protocol and religious proscriptions, and seeing only a dirty beggar, refused to let Yogi Ramsuratkumar in.

This was a familiar experience to Yogi Ramsuratkumar, who had been spurned countless times since he left behind the life of the householder—the respectable, educated schoolteacher and principal, who was "killed by Ramdas" in 1952. He went to the river and sat on its banks, and slowly, the mass of devotees who had come from out of town for the *puja* ceremony to receive *prasad* dispersed. As the crowd cleared out a devotee named Govindaswami came to the river where Yogi Ramsuratkumar sat quietly. His heart was touched by the beggar, who he had seen being sent away without *prasad* earlier in the day.

"I saw you at Brindavan today during the *prasad* distribution ceremony. Did you have any food?" he asked with genuine concern. When Yogi Ramsuratkumar said no, Govindaswami took him back to Brindavan and got food for him. Like many who stumbled upon Yogi Ramsuratkumar—often by what seemed to be pure accident—he remained an ardent devotee of Yogi Ramsuratkumar for the rest of his life.[20]

Despite his connection at Tapovanum, Yogi Ramsuratkumar lived in Tiruvannamalai, and it was under the punnai tree there that many people came to receive their first darshan—the sighting of the master—of Yogi Ramsuratkumar. Well-known scholars such as T.P. Meenakshisundaram, M.P. Periasamy Thooran and A.S. Gnanasambandam gathered with Yogi Ramsuratkumar under the Punnai tree. Shri D.S. Sivaramakrishna Iyer of Tapovanum first met Yogi Ramsuratkumar under the punnai tree also, as did a great many of Gnanananda Giri's devotees and many others.[21] These were joyful gatherings, where Yogi Ramsuratkumar would share any food that was brought as a gift, or he would ask one of his devotees to get tea or coffee for everyone, and there was much laughter and often chanting the name of God.

During these years the people of nearby villages came for his blessing, and brought their children, their elders and their problems to him. As miraculous events began to show up around Yogi Ramsuratkumar, the word spread among the village people that there was

---

19 S.P. Janardanan, *A Life With Truth*, unpublished manuscript, translated into English by K.S. Padmanabhan.

20 Ibid.

21 Vijayalakshmi, *Waves of Love*, p. 25.

a saint whose blessings carried an unusual power—to heal the sick, to create wealth, to resolve problems of all kinds, to bring rain and prosperity to the people. But during this time Yogi Ramsuratkumar was still very much a hidden saint, known to only a very few.

In the mid-sixties he was invited by the devotees of Swami Gnanananda Giri to Tanjavur where Mahaperiaval of Kanchi Kamakoti Peedam, a holy man who Yogi Ramsuratkumar called "Paramacharya of Kanchi," was camped to give teachings. During the discourse Mahaperiaval was describing an *antarmukhi*, or one who resides completely within. Yogi Ramsuratkumar was sitting near a pillar in the room, facing Mahaperiaval, who pointed to Yogi Ramsuratkumar and said, "Here is an example of an *antarmukhi*!" After the praise that was implicated in this recognition, the people surged around Yogi Ramsuratkumar, wanting to know him, touch him, gain his blessing—a specter of things to come, many years later. Fortunately, the Paramacharya of Kanchi stopped the onslaught from getting out of control.[22]

22 Ibid, pp. 26-27.

CHAPTER THREE

A Westerly Wind

1970 - 1971

Westerners were not a new phenomena to India, given the centuries of British colonization, but in 1970 Tiruvannamalai was just beginning to experience the overflow of the hippie revolution, which hit India with an influx of passionate Westerners coming in search of Eastern wisdom teachings and spiritual adepts. Tiruvannamalai, being the home of the ashram of Ramana Maharshi, who was already known in the West as an extraordinary holy man, was a natural draw for the many pilgrims who began to travel through in much larger numbers than ever before from Europe, the United States, Canada, Australia and others places from the western front. None of them had ever heard of Ram Ram Swami, or a yogi called Ramsuratkumar, who lived in the mysterious labyrinth of the streets.

Yogi Ramsuratkumar was very protective of his privacy and his inner world—what he called his "work." He shied away from many contacts, and when he did allow people into his life, it was through the force of an inner impulse. Once Yogi Ramsuratkumar was compelled in a direction, he could easily relate with people of all kinds, from all countries and cultures. He had an amazing ability to adapt, like a chameleon, to different cultural ways of thinking, and during the years of the early seventies he was free to enter into the lives of young Westerners who found him and meet them fully there. The circumstances and events that surround these extraordinary meetings are the stories of a rare and unique individual, who made himself available to those who came by force of destiny into his life.

As Hilda Charlton would warn Lee Lozowick six years later when he was making his first trip to India, no one found Yogi Ramsuratkumar unless he wanted them to. Some people who came looking for the recondite beggar saint of Tiruvannamalai could spend one or two months in town and never find him. The Westerners who did manage to connect with him discovered a disarming and inexplicable personality; the atmosphere around the beggar was magical, spontaneous, totally unpredictable—and yet there was a highly refined intention and sense of purpose in everything he did. Being in his company one was quickly drawn into the sublime, the fiery unknown of life itself.

In May 1970 a twenty-year-old American, Truman Caylor Wadlington, was one of those Western seekers who came to Tiruvannamalai and stayed at Ramanashram. In Caylor's case, it took a spiritual emergency to connect him with Yogi Ramsuratkumar. Already strongly involved in meditation, Caylor had studied and read quite a lot about the lives of great masters, and was immersed in a serious spiritual search. As a sophomore in college in 1969 he had meditated under the guidance of the Self-Realization Fellowship and had experienced a strong energetic opening in the area of the sixth chakra—the "third eye" of kundalini yoga lore—that was at first very exciting but then became more and more painful. He rarely spoke about the situation with anyone, but his alarm grew after he arrived at Ramanashram and threw himself into meditation four to six hours a day. During meditation the pressure would build, the energy within the forehead and crown area swelling and bursting into headaches of painful proportions. He was forced to seek help when his body started becoming flushed with heat. The high voltage energy, pain and heat were all classic symptoms of kundalini awakening in the body—a dangerous situation without the help of a guru. Now at Ramanashram for a few months, he was desperately seeking help, and had spoken with all the spiritual elders he knew, some of them the living disciples of Ramana Maharshi. He had been directed from one person to the next, but no one had been able to help him, and the headaches were becoming excruciating—it was so bad that he couldn't sleep or rest.

One morning after breakfast he was sitting outside the ashram with a Swedish woman, Gilda Rensheild, who was leaving the next day. She was excitedly recounting an experience she had had the day before with a Frenchwoman, Aruna, and her friend Narakuthi Swami, an American who had lived in India for perhaps as much as two decades as a sadhu. Aruna had taken Gilda and Narakuthi Swami to Arunachalesvara Temple the day before, and on the backside of the temple, they had come upon a beggar that Aruna knew—a yogi of unusual spiritual presence.

The three Westerners sat with him for a while and chatted. The yogi asked them if either one of them had any questions. Gilda had two questions, things that had been troubling her for some time and that she needed answers for very badly. It seemed obvious, as Caylor listened to the story, that the meeting with the mysterious yogi was not accidental; rather, he had met them intentionally in some unknowable way. Gilda's questions were about a spiritual crisis and some personal troubles, concerning whether or not she should marry an Indian doctor from Bangalore. Sitting and talking with the Westerners, the yogi answered the Swedish woman's questions. The result of this encounter with the yogi was that the confusion she had been feeling cleared up; she felt completely uplifted and unburdened by her crisis.

On this day sitting under the wide overhanging trees outside Ramanashram, Gilda was effusive as she told Caylor about the extraordinary yogi that she had just encountered in what seemed like a chance meeting. Just when she was in great need of meeting someone like him, he was there! Caylor had a very receptive ear to all this.

"How did you find him?" he asked Gilda.

"You could never find him," she answered. "Maybe Aruna could help you."

He went to Aruna and begged her to introduce him to the yogi. Aruna had lived in

Tiruvannamalai for many years; she guarded her own spiritual privacy, and perhaps that of the hidden saint of Tiruvannamalai as well. Nonetheless, she said that she would try to find him, but she didn't know when. She thought she might run into him within a few weeks, because she went into town every day or every couple of days to shop in the market, but the very next day she met him and told him about Caylor. The beggar told her to come with Caylor to the temple at six o'clock the next day.

The next day Aruna took Caylor to Arunachalesvara Temple, and around five o'clock, the yogi appeared, walking through the massive stone *gopuram* at the entrance with little children running along at his side, playing and shouting and jumping. He was enjoying them immensely, and they him. Caylor saw right away that he was very dirty, and he carried a strange stick that was wrapped about with rags and bits and strips of cloth and other unidentifiable things. He wore a long white beard and had long black hair not quite to his shoulders. His face was young and radiant, and his eyes were clear and pure. He smiled beautifully, like a child, as he saw them. Caylor and Aruna had brought some bananas as a gift; a small crowd gathered around them, curious about the two Westerners with the dirty beggar, but the yogi simply stared at the crowd while he ate the bananas and held his mystical stick.

Then he turned his attention on Caylor and gave him a thorough looking through, it seemed to the very core of his being. For as long as five minutes he gazed in silence at the young American, and it seemed that the yogi learned everything about him in those moments—past, present and future. His gaze penetrated into Caylor's awareness without interruption as the minutes dragged on.

"Mr. K, have you been initiated?" was his sole question. Caylor answered that he suspected that Ramana Maharshi had done so in a dream. They talked for a while about nothing in particular, just light conversation about Caylor, his background and interests, about his growing up, about American poetry, what was in the news. Suddenly sundown came; the children and the curious bystanders were gone. As soon as it got dark they moved to a place where they were hidden from view, and there the yogi began to really address Caylor's questions. Caylor told him all about the headaches, and then the light conversation returned. Occasionally the yogi would touch upon a spiritual theme, but there was no "teaching"—no references to the scriptures, to gods and goddesses or magical formulas. Clearly this beggar was not inclined to teach doctrine in any way. More than anything it was the immediacy of his extraordinary, uplifting presence: he was simply and totally in relationship with the Westerners.

Later Aruna and Caylor took the yogi to a small restaurant for dinner, then they came back to the temple and sat by the water on the steps. It was a beautiful starlit night, and as they sat together by the shimmering water with the enigmatic beggar and talked of many things, Caylor realized that he was quite extraordinary, writing about him at the time, "He was really a gracious and wonderful man—so free, and like a child. He laughed so hard at the simplest statements—I won't ever forget his laugh! He was truly beautiful."

They spent the evening together, and finally around one o'clock in the morning, the beggar stood up and, drawing Caylor along with him, walked out of the temple to the back of a little soapstone shop where deities were carved, one of many shops that clustered along the front side of the temple, out on the street. The shopkeeper, a man named Ramaswami who was in the back cleaning up, greeted him. The shop was nothing more than a stall—a wooden platform about two feet off the ground with a roof and sides. Inside it a candle burned, and the forms of many different stone images could be seen in the soft light. Ramaswami took an aluminum folding chair and put it in the dirt street a few feet in front of the shop and asked Caylor to sit in it. Yogi Ramsuratkumar adjusted the chair slightly, to get it at the right angle, then went to the platform and sat down facing Caylor.

"Should I meditate? What should I do?" Caylor asked, feeling a little unsettled.

"You just be there. You don't have to do anything," the beggar replied.

The beggar took out his cigarettes and slowly put one in his mouth, lit it and began to smoke. Holding the cigarette between his thumbs and cupped in the shelter of his hands, he looked at Caylor out of the corner of his eye while it burned. The atmosphere became very intense as he drew deeply on the cigarette, its fiery tip glowing bright, then he sat holding it in cupped hands and gazing at Caylor with a tremendous focus. The concentrated smoking and gazing went on for at least ten minutes, but it was ten minutes that seemed like an hour. Finally the beggar just got up, walked over and put his hand on Caylor's head.

"This will come back," he said, "This is going to come back in about two weeks. You need to see me then. You can go back to the ashram now." He walked Caylor a long way down the road past the temple and back in the direction of Ramanashram. Then he stopped, took Caylor's hands warmly between his, looked in his eyes and said, "We will talk again."

Caylor's headaches went away completely, but exactly as the yogi had said, they came back in about ten days, as bad as ever. He was desperate to reach the beggar again, but he had no idea how to find him. Aruna wasn't going to connect him this time—he was on his own. He had heard that the beggar usually went to the same places every day at the same time of day, so there was some glimmer of hope. Someone like Caylor, whose need was strong enough, who had the desire and the karmic destiny to meet and actually befriend Yogi Ramsuratkumar, could and would find him.

Yogi Ramsuratkumar had a predictable route that he moved along each day in a sequence of movements around Tiruvannamalai that included sitting in the shade of the punnai tree for much of the day; later he was often at the Arunachalesvara temple and spent a lot of time at the ghat of the Brahma Tirtha pool or near the Ganesh shrine. At night he slept on the verandahs and steps of the shops in and around the brass market and the downtown bazaar. There were Indian devotees who were quite close to Yogi Ramsuratkumar, and some regular attendants, Perumal and Kuppuswami and others who did things for him, including caring for his many bundles and making sure he got his mail. There were always village people who were part of his world, who wandered by and made their *pranams*, or brought him food or *prasad* in some form.

If someone was looking for him, there were people who always knew where to find him, but there was an invisible sanctum around the beggar that was not easy to penetrate. He spent much of his time in solitude, quietly working in the temple precincts, out in the fields, walking the streets, or under certain trees that he favored. He slept on the streets, sometimes on the sidewalks or porches of his favorite shops, and he avoided a lot of people. In a way, he was secretive—not in an effort to hide, but to in order to avoid those who hounded and threatened him.

Anyone who wanted to find him had to get through a kind of labyrinth, and it was this mystery that Caylor faced now, as he searched for the yogi. At the time he only knew two or three of Yogi Ramsuratkumar's favorite "haunts," and first he went to Ramaswami's stone carving shop by the main entrance of the temple and to the places in the temple where they had met before. He sat in the Indian heat near Ramaswami's shop and in the temple, waiting and hoping that the beggar would show up. Now and then he asked people if they knew him, but they said no or else they didn't want to divulge any information.

At a loss as to how to find the beggar, and tortured by the worsening headaches again, one afternoon Caylor went to the *samadhi* shrine of Ramana Maharshi at Ramanashram. He sat there for an hour, meditating and praying to Ramana Maharshi for help in contacting the beggar, known to him then as "Ram Ram Swami." He needed to find him fast, and as he circumambulated the shrine, he prayed for a miracle, keeping in mind his plan: to go that night to the front entrance of the temple. Little did he know that it was a place that Yogi Ramsuratkumar wouldn't normally go at that time of day, because of harassment he was experiencing—something that Caylor would find out about later. Nonetheless, this was the plan, and it was this that he included in his prayer to Ramana Maharshi.

He left Ramanashram just before sunset, and on the way to the temple it began to rain. By the time he was standing at the stone entranceway, it was storming. He wandered around the temple *mandapam* for a while looking for the beggar, trying to spot his staff. Everyone on the streets had crowded beneath the *gopuram* at the entrance to take shelter from the rain, so there were hundreds of people standing shoulder to shoulder—but no Yogi Ramsuratkumar. Caylor recounted:

> I got tired, frustrated, really afraid. At times I'd just stand off to the side, keep my eyes open, wait fifteen minutes and then I'd run out into the rainy area outside the mandapam and call his name out loud. By then it was getting dark. I started standing in the open so that if he was nearby he would see me, and then every now and then I would run out into the rain, stand in the middle of the street, look around and shout. So one of these times when I ran out into the rain to look around for him, when I turned around to run back under the mandapam, I ran right into his chest! He was standing three or four feet away.
>
> I literally spun around, took a step and ran right into him. Our faces

were inches apart, we were nose to nose, and I stood back and he stood back with his staff raised and he had some of his attendants with him. He stood back and said, "Mr. K, what are you doing here?" and I just laughed out loud, and he laughed and he said, "Okay, let's go for tea."

So we then wandered down through the main street to a little place that was owned by a Hindi-speaking gentleman and that became one of our frequent haunts. I'd learn that he knew that place, he liked that gentleman and I could find him there sometimes. As it turned out that man would often see Yogi Ramsuratkumar in the early, early hours of the morning, and I learned that if I went there he would often have seen him and could tell me where he was going. That was the beginning of me tracking him to find where he was, to be able to connect with him.

So, we sat in that little tiny tea stall, maybe just two tables, room for six or eight people, and he had me talk about all kinds of things, just to keep some conversation going. Mostly he listened, and he'd say, "Ohh . . . Aha! . . . Oh," or he would exclaim, express astonishment at some drama. He got involved in my stories and kept me going, and finally after hours, when everything was closed and the old man was cleaning up and no longer serving other people in that little tea stall, he put his hand on my head like before and stood back for awhile. He smoked, looked intensely at me and said, "Don't think of anything, just sit there, just relax." He put his hand on my head again, and he didn't say anything about it ever coming back.

It was a miraculous occurrence, one of many that happened in ordinary circumstances with Yogi Ramsuratkumar. For the next year, 1970–71, the encounter between the twenty-year-old American and the yogi, whose inexplicable actions were suffused with the mystique of one who had gone beyond the beyond, grew into a deep relationship. Yogi Ramsuratkumar was very open with this young stranger, and amazingly, had a deep and innate understanding of his point of view as a Westerner, his habits, wishes, concerns, struggles. He seemed very attuned to this new generation of Westerners, who were hungry for the dharma and actively seeking spiritual experience. Still, Caylor had to pay a certain price to enter the guru's world. He had already opened the door with a genuine need, and he was to enter into a time of training and learning the protocol of being in the master's company. To begin with, Caylor had to be sensitive and resonant with the master to the extent that he could find him, somewhere in the streets:

I would have to go to a lot of trouble to find him. I only knew a couple places where he occasionally went, because I had met him in those two places. Usually, even though I might ask a few people where Yogi Ramsuratkumar was, they wouldn't know who he was, or if they knew he was, they said that nobody knew. But occasionally someone would just come by and they would recognize me as having been seen with him before, and they would say, "Ram, Ram?" Sometimes they would get my attention and say, "Railroad tracks. Railroad tracks." They couldn't speak English, but somehow they'd just say, "Bus station. Bus station," and I'd just go check it out. Eventually I would find him. I have no idea how the Indians knew where he was, or who they were.

In those days I really felt like I only could find him when he wanted me to find him. It was so magical and so elusive, so mysterious, that I didn't make inquiries to people. I felt that if I chased him, I was out of line. I basically only went when he asked me to come back, and I would only go when I was in some sort of spiritual trouble or something. Little by little he let me know . . . I got to know where he was, and he started letting me know that it was okay for me to come and see him, but it was always by invitation. He would say, "Come back in three days. Come back in ten days." Even in the later years, I had to follow his instruction about the day on which I could come. All that time, it was pretty much by his invitation. He would get angry if I came on some other day, which I did sometimes by mistake. He'd get very annoyed.

Yogi Ramsuratkumar usually had a dhoti and a blanket [a large shawl]; back in those days it wasn't always a green blanket, but it changed. It would be one color for some years, and then it would be some other blanket for a couple of years. He never bathed except to change when those clothes would literally start falling apart— the sleeves of his shirt would be detaching, and his dhoti would be torn. In those days someone would finally insist that he change and he would bathe and change his clothes every few months or something.

Even when he was alone, he still had a bag wrapped in about a dozen newspapers, plus some cigarettes, his coconut bowl for washing in the evening. He had his fan, and his staff. He made those things. In those days he had those things and he just carried them around on his shoulder. As soon as he started having people around him, he started having them carry stuff, but initially it was one bag, and then two. I think Kuppuswami was his first attendant—a poor Indian man who Ramsuratkumar always had a few rupees for, for him and his family. I think it was Kuppuswami, and then Perumal, who attended him, but there were other devotees who did things, who came around.

Yogi Ramsuratkumar was an obscure, ragtag figure in Tiruvannamalai in the early seventies. Most of the time there was no one with him—sometimes one person, maybe two, but in those years he was pretty much on his own and very unknown. He had little haunts, like a favorite little thorny bush out near the railroad tracks outside of town where he would spend most of the daytime hours; during the morning hours there

> was a little chai shop where he had tea; during the late afternoon there was a place that was a bank that was closed where he would sit in an area that was enclosed with an iron fence. It was shaded and cool and closed, and he could sit there. He had a pathway he followed from dawn to dusk every day, and at any given time you could fairly reliably find him at one of those places—if you knew where he was at different times of the day. It was a circuit he walked. Only occasionally did he head off in some other direction for various reasons, like up toward Ramanashram or up into a mountain, to Arunachala or one of the other ashrams. It would have to be some special invitation or some special work, or to meet someone. Otherwise he had a very low-key, obscure existence in Tiruvannamalai.

These were the years of Yogi Ramsuratkumar's life when he was free, as Shakuntala of Tapovanum said, to roam as he wished, to move about Tiruvannamalai and its outlying fields, to dance and sing—and to befriend people who were drawn into his sphere. During these years, and for the next two decades, before the inception of the Yogi Ramsuratkumar Ashram, the beggar entered into the intimate lives of people who came to him and interacted with them in the nitty gritty circumstances of their daily lives.

Yogi Ramsuratkumar took the young American man under his wing, guided him unerringly on the spiritual path, nurtured and nourished him as friend, father, spiritual guide and, eventually, as master. Who could have foreseen that Caylor's meeting with Yogi Ramsuratkumar presaged the tremendous influence of Yogi Ramsuratkumar in the West in years to come? The stories of this unusual relationship provide a tremendous doorway into the way Yogi Ramsuratkumar lived and worked during these years. Caylor was already keeping a journal, and he began to take notes whenever he was with Yogi Ramsuratkumar, often taking down Yogi Ramsuratkumar's words verbatim in the moment, as things were happening. The beggar didn't mind this note taking, as long as Caylor's attention could, at the same time, be focused on him. The early journals of Truman Caylor Wadlington provide a rare glimpse into the world of Yogi Ramsuratkumar, and how he was interacting and working during this time period, particularly with Westerners. We will turn to these journals time and again as the story of the early seventies unfolds.

It was a mid-summer morning in 1970 when Caylor called upon Yogi Ramsuratkumar at Ramaswami's shop. The day was clear and fresh, the sky was extraordinarily blue and the heat intense considering the early hour of their meeting. Yogi Ramsurat-kumar began to talk about Mother India, about Mount Arunachala and the Arunachalesvara Temple. Caylor had purchased some fruit and bread to share with Swami. The meeting was intended to be brief, because Caylor wanted to spend some hours of the morning meditating in the cover of the hillside, particularly in Virupakshi

Cave, and he would have to leave before the heat got too intense. Yogi Ramsuratkumar then told Caylor about how his master, Swami Ramdas, used to live in a cave that was not far below Virupakshi Cave. He said that Ramdas had met Sri Ramana Maharshi, and while in the presence of the famed saint, the gentle Ramdas experienced something profoundly mystical—the implication seemed to be that he experienced self-realization. Ramdas then moved down the hill to a vacated cave and there he spent two weeks in deep meditation.

Suddenly Yogi Ramsuratkumar volunteered to accompany Caylor to the caves on Arunachala, not a short or easy walk by any means. Rather, it was a long, hot and drawn-out march over winding stone paths, but the beggar brought delight to everything, as he drew Caylor more and more deeply into the guru's world. Caylor wrote in his journal at the time:

> I must concede that following that beggar was a joy and pleasure, regardless of the tiresome efforts. I loved to watch him walk—a child and yet a king. At last we came to two caves adjoining one another. We visited first the cave of Ramdas, though only briefly, for a young sadhu was busy proudly painting his new home. It was immediately evident that Yogi Ramsuratkumar and the sadhu were well acquainted. The sadhu escorted us both to the cave nearest to his. Within it was an older man who was also gracious and a friend of Yogi Ramsuratkumar.
>
> The whole group of us sat in this old man's abode for some time. The greater part of my stay there was spent meditating, with and without the others present—they one by one filed out of the cave, even Yogi Ramsuratkumar. I was deeply impressed with the understanding or feeling that Yogi Ramsuratkumar was guiding my efforts in meditation. This is no fantasy, nor is it a revelation of higher mind. I can say this because his help was felt in a physical way. It was as though his hand was pressed against my forehead to account for the movements of pressure and flow of energy. Then again, my being became at times extraordinarily calm and quiet.
>
> Swami and I then went to sit in Ramdas' cave—all beautiful in its fresh whiteness. The walls had been reshaped with concrete to form more of a rectangular style living quarters. The floor had been concreted and the walls were extended out in the way of ledges that served in some places as meditation seats and in other places as tables and bookshelves. It was darned attractive and convenient in style. I meditated in this place too while Yogi Ramsuratkumar sat in the doorway facing me. Not that he was mediating too, I cannot remember ever having seen the saintly one relaxed in a meditative posture. I will not disregard the highly probable chance that the beggar spent his every moment in a sort of meditation. I know little of such exalted matters to speculate upon them.
>
> It was during a short chat outside Ramdas' cave that Yogi

> Ramsuratkumar first spoke to me of things that play a strong part in my daily life now [six or seven months later]. He asked me if I had ever read The Secret Doctrine by H.P. Blavatsky. It was his surprise as well as mine that I had only the day before seen a reference to this book. In fact, I thought that it was the very book that Philip Pegler had lent to me to read!

As it turned out, the book Caylor had by H.P. Blavatsky was *The Voice of Silence.* Nonetheless, it was a pleasant and surprising serendipity. Yogi Ramsuratkumar began to speak with Caylor about things that were completely new to him, like the esoteric significance of the number seven. He briefly quoted the first few *slokas* in the first of "The Book of Dzyan," on which is based the entire "Secret Doctrine." The beggar asked if Caylor knew anything about a man named Henry Steele Olcott, a subject that was totally foreign to Caylor until two days earlier, when he had visited the library at Ramanashram to get a copy of the Bible. Inside the Bible was a bookmarker, yellowed with age and picturing H.S. Olcott on one side of it and the French scrawl of some previous book lender on the other. He wrote, "The photo impressed me so greatly that I kept it even after returning the book to the library."

"Reading *The Secret Doctrine* transforms the mind, Mr. K," Yogi Ramsuratkumar said. Then he instructed Caylor briefly on how he should read the book: he should not worry about the topics of the book, but just read the words, because the words themselves would have a transforming effect upon his brain, so that new and unused parts would become active and functional. The book was intended to replace any and all meditation practices, which had been so implicated in the terrible headaches. As long as any interest was maintained, Caylor should sit and read the text; otherwise, he could walk around or visit friends in the ashram vicinity. When the book was completely read, it was to be put aside for as long as six months to a year before reading it again. Yogi Ramsuratkumar even suggested to Caylor that this book was so important for him that it was the only book he ever needed to read.

"Perhaps there is a Henry Steele Olcott within you, Mr. K," he said, mysteriously. They stood up and walked lightly down the winding stone steps of the hillside, exchanged a few words and parted ways in the streets behind the Arunachalesvara Temple. He continued:

> The next day I rented a bicycle from a small cycle shop a short ways from the ashram and soon found myself cycling down the back roads near the temple in route to Ramaswami's stone carving shop. I inquired from the boys attending to the morning business about the locality of "Ram Ram Swami" as he was called by most of the villagers. One of the boys got the message across to me through hand motions and broken English that Yogi Ramsuratkumar was near the post office. I thanked him, bade farewell, and leaving the bicycle at the shop, jaunted away down the big alleyway market at the front of the Arunachalesvara Temple.

> Until this day I did not know that Yogi Ramsuratkumar frequented the area near the post office, nor had I made any acquaintance with the Sundara Café, [other than stopping] there once for chapatti and tea. As I spied into the small shops and coffee stalls around the post office, Swami was nowhere to be seen. At the end of the street where the bazaar is located is a small tea stall, the infamous Sundara Tea Stall. There he was, sitting on his heels with his back against the front wall of the shop, reading the "Hindu Times."
>
> This meeting was three to five days after our trip to the caves; we had promised to meet one another soon, that I might help Yogi Ramsuratkumar with his work (as a manner of speech). I gave him a present. He gave me a few beautiful marigold flowers. I always thought it peculiar but certainly not inexplicable that the flowers he presented to me would always remain fresh and fragrant for days and days, though they were not watered or cared for. They had been held by the beggar, he had looked into them and later I would place them on the back of Nandi Shiva—the logical explanation of their prolonged life. It was understood that the flowers he presented to me were to be used as tools, to effect me in subtle ways, to be sure. It was most common for me to walk about Ramanashram carrying one in my hand, to meditate with them in my lap, to, in a manner of ways, worship them and use them as a way to contact my saintly friend.
>
> Yogi Ramsuratkumar was so fresh and happy that morning. He was equally as pleased with my present to him as he was that I had made some effort to read *The Secret Doctrine*. We had a rather lengthy talk about the book. How it should be read and my relationship to the book. He often said that I was the first person he had ever told to read *The Secret Doctrine*. Many other people had come to the beggar for advice and guidance, but I was the first one to be told by him to read that book.

During these summer and fall months, while Caylor was reading *The Secret Doctrine*, he met regularly with Yogi Ramsuratkumar. Sometimes they would walk the streets together, and Caylor helped him carry his things—usually a little black ceramic pot that was filled with matches, cigarette boxes, scrap cloth, the staff and the stack of newspapers—all of which were collected from the streets and places he frequented.

The beggar's staff was another mysterious object: a crude arrangement of a long stick wrapped around with various things, with a long piece of brown twine that dangled and could be pulled taught to look almost like a bow. Often he would joke with Caylor, saying it was "Rama's bow."

At times the staff had peacock feathers or pieces of red or green cloth tied to it, some black string, some unidentifiable threads or ribbons, something taken from wrappers and a central stick. Sometimes there were two or three sticks at the center of this bundle of things that made up the magician's staff. One could only guess at the meaning and importance of these objects; clearly, anything that Yogi Ramsuratkumar handled was imbued with energy and spiritual power. He used the staff like an antenna or a lightning rod; it seemed to be a conduit through which he both received information and poured out blessing power. He was quite adamant with those around him that these things could not be left anywhere or carelessly discarded. He would have some object in his hands, work with it in some way, and then add it to the staff.

By August 1970 Caylor was leaving Ramanashram early in the morning to go to the village to buy bread, but the true motivation behind these frequent excursions was his constant longing to meet the beggar again. Soon after that Yogi Ramsuratkumar pointed out one of his favorite places—Ramaswami's stone carving shop in the bazaar near the huge Arunachalesvara Temple—which made it much easier to arrange times to meet.

Ramaswami's relationship with Yogi Ramsuratkumar was notable; he was kind, patient and helpful to the beggar, often giving him money or food without any hesitation. Yogi Ramsuratkumar was always quite verbal in expressing his gratitude and feeling of obligation toward Ramaswami and others who provided food and shelter for him. The relationship between Yogi Ramsuratkumar and Ramaswami was characterized by a deep religious understanding mixed with simple affection, gentleness and kindness. However, it wasn't clear whether or not the relationship was one of a guru and devotee. On the surface it seemed that their friendship was comprised of quite ordinary interactions, but underneath that there existed an abiding, deep and mutual respect and affection, even love. Ramaswami, a devoted Hindu, clearly understood that there was merit to be gained in protecting and caring for a person of such sanctity.

Ramaswami's shop was filled with sacred images. On the shelves and all over the floor were hundreds of soapstone sculptures of deities—the ubiquitous Shiva lingam, Parvati, Shiva Nataraj, Subrahmania (the Tamil god also known as Murugan, the god of youth, beauty, divine freedom and also a war god), and Ganesh. There were a number of young craftsmen who supplied the product for the shop.

It was at the stone carving shop that Yogi Ramsuratkumar discovered a small sculpture of Nandi bull and seemed to fall in love with it. He would go often to the shop and gaze at Nandi, empowering the sculpture with his own energy through the power of his attention. One day he gave the sculpture to Caylor to "take care of," explaining that Nandi is the divine animal that Lord Shiva rides on, and is considered a deity in its own right. It is often called Nandi Shiva because it is literally a part of Shiva, representing certain aspects of the Divine. Nandi bull is always placed in the temple facing his Lord Shiva, and for this reason Nandi's face is usually given a gentle, joyful expression. Yogi Ramsuratkumar placed tremendous importance upon the stone image, and proceeded to instruct Caylor to receive the Nandi, look at it often, and love it with all his hear

Forced to relax his formidable meditation schedule because of the headaches, Caylor soon realized that he had been operating under the misguided belief that if he wasn't absorbed in meditation, then he was no longer engaging *sadhana* or spiritual work. Being in the company of Yogi Ramsuratkumar, this dichotomy between spirituality and ordinary life was quickly exposed as an illusion, as the beggar was masterful in demonstrating the seamless nature of reality as the very Divine, simply within the flow of the day. Caylor found his attitudes toward spiritual life and practice being turned around, changed from the rigid, doctrinaire approach to a fluid, living awareness of God in all things, which was impressed upon him by the master.

Although it's impossible to know exactly what Yogi Ramsuratkumar's purposes were, he was successfully taking his young student's mind off of the obsessive meditation practice and putting it on *him*—the master himself. He was drawing Caylor into a relationship of guru yoga, which strongly characterized all his closest relationships over the years, in which the devotee's attention is focused entirely on the spiritual friend, who slowly becomes not only a guide but the all-consuming reality of one's life. In this process of divine transmission, the devotee's state of being becomes one with the state of being of the guru, and God-realization is transferred from one to the other. Literally, the devotee becomes imbued with the master's light, or *jyoti*. Yogi Ramsuratkumar never intellectualized this process by explaining or extrapolating on it—he simply acted as he was prompted, by divine instinct and deep inner impulse, from moment to moment. In this way he by-passed the rational mind and worked directly with the heart.

By October or early November 1970, the headaches were still plaguing Caylor. Over the months the beggar had been guiding and instructing him in his meditation, primarily by replacing meditation with reading *The Secret Doctrine*, repeating his instructions in this regard many times. Again he sought out Yogi Ramsuratkumar, asking for the beggar's healing intervention for a third time, and according to Caylor, the headaches were finally healed:

> I had led myself into anxiety and complete bewilderment. My meditations were forced to a halt when the energy flowing and pulsating in my forehead caused a ceaseless pressure that tore at my nervous system. Not for one minute was I able to find relief from this torture. A constant mental tension was my unwanted companion for weeks. My only relief was to sleep.
>
> I desperately sought out my friend, Yogi Ramsuratkumar. Three times he worked on me. We discussed the problem, its causes, its results. He then had me sit still while he focused on the location of my third eye. It was as though he had entered into me and was massaging that area of my head. That was not uncommon to any one of our meetings; however, something special was done during these three meetings. He placed his forefingers on my forehead and pressed lightly, slowly moving them over the area of pressure. He was somehow allowing the obstructed energies to flow more freely through this center. I was instructed to stop all meditations, to take walks on the hill, to visit friends freely, and to use Nandi Shiva as a meditation rather than "Who Am I?" All became well within a short time.

At their second meeting earlier in the summer the beggar had begun to talk about his relationship with his guru, Swami Ramdas. They were sitting together in Dasaratha's Sundara Teashop, and to Caylor's astonishment, the beggar told him that he had "developed" through Ramdas' mantra, *Om Sri Ram Jai Ram Jai Jai Ram,* and in fact he had done no meditation at all. Then he sang in a sweet melody, "Sri Rama, Jai Rama, Jai Jai Rama; Sri Rama, Jai Rama, Jai Jai Rama; Jai Jai Rama, Jai Jai Rama; Jai Jai Rama, Jai Jai Rama." Afterward they walked together through the streets in a happy mood.

Some months later, Caylor walked into town very early in the morning in search of Yogi Ramsuratkumar. As Caylor went from one of the beggar's favorite spots to the next, the mists still clung to the mountain and people were moving slowly, fires burning along the street for making tea and coffee. Not finding him anywhere, Caylor was turning back toward Ramanashram when he was suddenly approached by a village man—a rather unusual occurrence.

"Ramnam Swami?" the simply clad man asked. Caylor said yes, thinking that people must have seen him in the bazaar with Yogi Ramsuratkumar enough to associate him with the beggar.

"Bus station," the man said, and gestured with his hand. Caylor knew that Yogi Ramsuratkumar spent a lot of time near the train and bus stations, but he had never approached him there, feeling that somehow these places were off limits for him. Nonetheless, at this invitation he took off right away and soon discovered the beggar seated, childlike, beneath an enormous banyan tree, where he was seated with George, a devotee who was also a Christian convert, very poor, but a man of fine character. George often helped Yogi Ramsuratkumar in various ways. Sitting down with them, Yogi Ramsuratkumar soon began to talk about the banyan tree and the natural forces that emanate near it. The conversation rolled along, and soon they were talking about *The Secret Doctrine*. Finally the subject of the beggar's mantra came up, and Caylor asked him if he would sing it again for him sometime.

George went for tea and soon returned, and the three sat together under the tree drinking their tea in the morning chill. Yogi Ramsuratkumar began to smoke, and George puffed away on a cigarette too. After George left, Yogi Ramsuratkumar and Caylor walked slowly down the railroad tracks together, "like two delinquent schoolboys, taking turns peeing in the bushes while the other guy nonchalantly kept watch." Caylor wrote:

> On our way back it had begun to rain and chill. We sought shelter in a thatched hut by the roadside. We sat quietly. Swami had given me a cluster of flowers, and I fondled them in my hands. The rain played on the rooftop. Others had joined us in the tiny sheltering hut. I began to understand what was happening when Yogi Ramsuratkumar rose from the floor, positioned his magical staff at a fixed angle in the thatched wall, and

> instructed me to pay close attention to him. He began to sing his song.
>
> No song before this was of such power to me. Yogi Ramsuratkumar shook by the force of his words. Beautiful, beautiful was the tone of that sound! Awesome was the man creating it! I can still see him standing before us. His eyes looking far off, his neck strained, his frizzled childlike hair, so thin and soft like a baby's. I will tell you of his hands, but I don't understand them; they moved spasmodically with every word he sang. They moved the air about them and within them. This mad fellow had become a nucleus of forces and intelligent powers. I shan't forget it.
>
> Speaking of his hands, I recall how Yogi Ramsuratkumar stopped briefly in the middle of his singing to direct my attention from his face to his hands. He told me specifically to watch the movement of his hands. I found it nearly impossible to watch, and I had to turn my gaze away from the visage of a man so absorbed in a Passion and a Power.
>
> Aruna and I discussed together this phenomena of Swami's singing. That is to say, we purged our brains—feeble as they may be—to explain the forces that Yogi Ramsuratkumar was controlling. Aruna mentioned to me that the first time she had seen him go through this was at the Essanya Mutt, where hundreds of sadhus, including herself and Narakuthi Swami, gathered together for an annual spiritual celebration and *bhikshu*. The madman, Yogi Ramsuratkumar, was there. He seemed to be overcome by the energies of this holy reunion and consequently danced uncontrollably while singing his song. I have seen him dance. I have heard his song. Enough in themselves were these times—I find it difficult to comprehend this man in an uncontrolled fit of spiritual ecstasy. I am, however, excited to simply ponder over such a thing so magnificent.

Despite his rather reclusive existence, there were times when Yogi Ramsuratkumar was receptive to meeting certain people, for reasons that were impossible to fathom. As more Westerners came into Tiruvannamalai, there seemed to be an inscrutable purpose, a hidden intention in the spontaneous way Yogi Ramsuratkumar was moved—or not moved—to relate with various individuals. In late November 1970, two Western visitors appeared on the streets of Tiruvannamalai. That morning Caylor had found Yogi Ramsuratkumar at the Sundara teashop, and as they greeted each other, it seemed that Swami had been actually waiting for him to show up. After tea, they proceeded to Ramaswami's stone carving shop, and while visiting there with Ramaswami and some others, Swami interrupted to point across the walkway at the two young Western men who were browsing in the bronze shops.

"Do you know those men?" he asked, gesturing toward the Westerners.

"Yes, that is Jim, from Alaska, and Robert Lee, from New Zealand."

Yogi Ramsuratkumar seemed quite interested in these young men, and not the least bit anxious about meeting strangers. Caylor was aware of the negative attitude at

Ramanashram toward Yogi Ramsuratkumar, and it seemed that the beggar's relationship with the townspeople in general was quite delicate in some way; concerned for Yogi Ramsuratkumar and protective of his privacy and well being, he questioned whether these young men could handle the responsibility of a relationship with the beggar saint. He expressed his misgivings to Yogi Ramsuratkumar, who in his usual serene way simply said, "If there is a need to meet, there will be a meeting. If no need, there will be no meeting." Yogi Ramsuratkumar's birthday was coming up on December 1st, and they continued to talk about a possible small celebration on that day, while the two young men disappeared behind the shops along the alleyway. Within ten minutes Jim and Robert reappeared. Caylor told the story in his journal:

> I pointed them out to Swami. He turned to them, and he then went to work. It was sheer fascination for me to watch this man suddenly become like a dynamo of power as he concentrated himself toward Robert and Jim. I can't fathom what it was he really was doing—that is, I cannot know the real and true nature of the mystic work he does. It was only a minute before the tapping hand of the Alaskan boy, Jim, was felt upon my shoulder. My heart sank at my discovery by the two intruders.
>
> I greeted them, and I could see they were curious about my company. I introduced them to my two friends—leaving Swami's name absent and working to disguise him as an employee of the stone carving shop. I was truly amazed that Ramaswami, the shop owner and his employee, responded so ingeniously to the situation. They went to work, perfectly aware of my feelings toward the predicament, trying to sell stone carvings to the two confused customers and also include my yogi friend as a regular hand in the business, so as to disguise his true self. Yogi Ramsuratkumar played along nicely, but I could feel his reluctance.
>
> Everything came to a very sudden and silent halt when Robert asked the yogi his name. Oh, the silence of that moment! Swami stuttered and then stated his name. Robert didn't hear it or perhaps couldn't believe it and questioned once again. Finally Swami wrote the name on a scrap of paper, both in Sanskrit and in English. In the meantime Swami lifted the hearts of everyone present by creating a different atmosphere. He became so wonderful and joyful! Both Robert and Jim could hardly believe what was happening before their eyes, but they were pleased at the sudden change in emotion to [what was now] a hearty welcome—especially toward Robert. Swami paid little or no attention to Jim.

Watching this scene, it was clear to Caylor that there was a mutual attraction between Swami and Robert Lee. Yogi Ramsuratkumar greeted him warmly and invited him to sit down beside him, which Robert did. He became very still and asked if they had known each other before, alluding, it seemed, to a previous life.

"Yes, we have been friends before," the beggar replied. Robert didn't hear this reply, and leaned forward as if waiting for the Yogi to answer.

"Well, I know that you know me now, but I don't know about any other previous meetings," he now said, enigmatically. Robert asked if he could take a picture of his new friend and Yogi Ramsuratkumar said no.

"If you want to take a picture of this beggar, you can take it on December 1st," he offered, speaking of his birthday, which was the next day. He then turned to Caylor and asked him to make all the arrangements. It was an amazing synchronicity, because Caylor had been wishing for a photograph of Yogi Ramsuratkumar—now the guru was fulfilling his desire. As the conversation rolled along lightly, it turned very humorous, as was often the case with Yogi Ramsuratkumar, who covered his face with his hands, laughed uproariously and slapped Robert on the knee to include him in the play.

"You certainly are a happy man," Robert exclaimed, amazed by the yogi's animated sense of humor and playful antics. The beggar turned to him with a twinkle in his eyes.

"If there is love in a man's heart, the whole world will be beautiful," he replied.

When Yogi Ramsuratkumar referred to himself as a beggar, Robert said hesitantly, "You are no beggar." It seemed that Yogi Ramsuratkumar didn't hear him, because he made no response.

"You are not a beggar," Robert repeated, with an air of wonderment. An uncomfortable silence fell upon the group. Yogi Ramsuratkumar sat quietly, and then said so beautifully, "I know that, but will you allow me to refer to myself as a beggar?"

A master shapeshifter, the beggar then turned on a dime and began to laugh and frolick again, bringing his incredible sense of humor back to guide the situation—a great wise one in the guise of a beautiful and innocent child.

From the time Yogi Ramsuratkumar first appeared in Tiruvannamalai in 1959 he was known to carry newspapers around with him and spend time reading them every day. The young American he had befriended soon discovered that the beggar was tremendously concerned with the "nuances of politics," in India especially, but also in the world at large. At times he would talk about the details of some of the problems India was facing and the importance of India's eventual role in the world. He believed that India was a spiritual dynamo, a kind of nexus or central hub, so that the future of world events rested on India's spiritual path and power. He believed that the great spiritual masters of India were playing a pivotal role in protecting India as a world power. Yogi Ramsuratkumar himself was one of these, and his work was connected with this.

As young Caylor got to know Yogi Ramsuratkumar during the months after his first meeting with him in July 1970, one of the things that became noticeable was that the beggar was being seriously harassed by a number of people. At first it was a great puzzle as to why anyone would want to abuse a saint, an obscure beggar who sat under the trees and chanted the name of God, but Caylor came to understand more deeply the political climate of south India at that time.

India had been in a state of political upheaval for many years. Yogi Ramsuratkumar had grown up and come of age during the awesome struggle for independence from British rule; he had been profoundly influenced by Mahatma Gandhi and Jawaharlal Nehru. In 1948 when Gandhi was assassinated, Yogi Ramsuratkumar was traveling back and forth across India from north to south, seeking the company of the masters. Although he had not been directly involved in the struggle, he was acutely aware of the nuances and undercurrents within India; his vision was for a unified and peaceful India, which could emerge as a world power and out of her incredible spiritual heritage, offer the kind of leadership, demonstrated by the life of Gandhi himself, that the world so desperately needed.

In the early seventies there were those political elements within India that wanted to follow Pakistan and establish political autonomy for various states. In Tamil Nadu there was a political party that was connected to a secessionist movement that wanted to develop south India's autonomy. There was controversy over the channeling of the central government's funds—grants and money for industrial development—and it was believed that these were given to the northern states, keeping south India politically disadvantaged and poor. This also contributed to limiting the number of south Indians in key political positions. Resentment brewed over these inequities, and those factions in Tamil Nadu that wanted to challenge the current political system were going about it in an underhanded fashion—with bombings, assassinations, surreptitious killing. In was not uncommon for a political enemy of the dissenting party to get hit by a car, and no one knew how it happened.

Yogi Ramsuratkumar was connected to this only by virtue of the fact that he was a Bihari from northern India and spoke Hindi, not Tamil, the language of the state. As a northerner, he was considered an undesirable element by those who wanted Tamil Nadu to become an autonomous state. He lived on the streets as a beggar and by all appearances he was nobody in the eyes of the political machine, but he was being tailed and harassed on a daily basis. If he sat out underneath the punnai tree or in the shade in the bazaar, there was always someone about forty feet away who would just stand there the whole day, watching. He would point to these people and say to Caylor, "You see that? They're always watching this beggar. This beggar never has at least a moment."

Often the harassment took the form of psychological abuse and intimidation tactics. These same people asked Yogi Ramsuratkumar for cigarettes, or a few of them would come over and stand five or six feet away and stare at him, not asking for anything, but looming over him with an intimidating presence. Sometimes he would say, "What do you want?" At other times he would get very loud and shout at them, or he'd ask someone to throw them out if he was in a shop or stall.

It was a very tense time, and as Yogi Ramsuratkumar began to walk with Caylor along his usual trail through the city. Caylor discovered that the beggar was very anxious about crossing the street and quite nervous around moving cars. He was literally hustling from one corner of a building to the next corner, to underneath a sheltering tree and then from that tree over to the well, and then from the well across the street to the next safe zone. Caylor was very moved by all this, but Yogi Ramsuratkumar didn't talk about the worst of it until twenty years later:

> He told me once, many years later in 1993, that it was the incident with the car that precipitated his request to me to write the book. He said he was walking at night along the backside of the temple. The backside of the Arunachaleswara Temple is where the mountain almost immediately starts to rise up, and he was walking along the backside of the temple, I don't know where he was coming from or going. As he was walking that route some headlights suddenly turned on in the distance. It was a parked car, and judging from the impression I have, it was maybe a hundred yards ahead of him. He immediately had a sense of danger. He kept walking but he was very concerned, very alert, and as he continued to pass along the backside of the temple, this car started to move towards him. Then he started moving off to the side of the road, thinking that the car was just going to maybe pass, but as he moved off the road the car started to veer towards him. He hustled over to the backside of the temple wall, which must be twenty feet of solid stone of some sort. He was cornered up against the backside of the temple and the car just gunned it—just went to smash him. At a certain point he said that he just prayed to God, and at that point the car just smashed! Just as it hit the wall it must have been an arm's length away from him, and the driver tried to gun it to hit him.
>
> He hustled on by and the car left the scene, but it was really very scary for him. I was around at the time that occurred; I happened to be spending a lot of time with him then, and he saw my bewilderment, my puzzlement at the whole thing. At some points he would try to explain. He'd say, "Mr. K, you don't understand. If you'll read the newspaper, if you ask around, if you pay attention, you'll start to understand what is going on here. You'll see that this group is torturing wandering sadhus who come down from the north. They don't want these people in the south, and they'll accuse them of raping a village girl, and then they'll have gangs beat them until they are dead. They have people accuse them of some political insurgency and then they'll be jailed. These are just sadhus, naked wanderers and religious mendicants from the north. So those people can't come down to the south anymore. They know they can't come this way."
>
> He would talk at length in this way about the sort of backhanded, surreptitious, hidden oppression of people from north India—and especially people of some influence, I think. Religious people, priests, high caste people, political people . . .

It was this frightening occurrence that catalyzed Yogi Ramsuratkumar's request to Caylor in 1971 to "write a book about this beggar."

Yogi Ramsuratkumar, the Godchild, Tiruvannamalai by Truman Caylor Wadlington was the first written material ever published about Yogi Ramsuratkumar. The book was first and foremost an attempt on the part of Yogi Ramsuratkumar to save his own life and call off the factions that were harassing him by educating the public about his purpose. In order to protect Yogi Ramsuratkumar—to defend, in a way, his tremendous vulnerability—a more public profile and greater understanding of who he was became necessary. This concern was not founded in his wish for personal survival, but in an urgent necessity to protect his "work."

By mid-November Yogi Ramsuratkumar was meeting with Caylor as often as three times a week, ostensibly to keep close tabs on the reading of *The Secret Doctrine*. Caylor was reading three to seven hours a day, and found that it was resulting in a powerful flow of energies within him, particularly in and around the forehead and brain. Unusual bodily phenomena occurred during the readings also; for example, the page would become lit with a strange light, and his vision would preternaturally expand to encompass the whole page.

The master was tremendously pleased when Caylor finished the book. It was a task, given by the master, which had serious implications in several domains. For one thing, it was the way Yogi Ramsuratkumar was working directly with establishing energetic harmony in Caylor's system after the eruption of power spiritual energies that seemed to be running wild and causing the headaches and bodily discomfort. It was also a task that required obedience to the guru, and laid the foundation of a certain rapport between the guru and the disciple for the bigger task would soon be given: moving to Madras and writing the book.

At the same time Yogi Ramsuratkumar was candid in disclosing the kind of stress that he was living under and allowing the young American to experience him in many different circumstances, and Caylor began to realize that the master's behavior was totally inexplicable. Yogi Ramsuratkumar had an uncanny knack for playing tricks on the rational mind. He could be a consummate actor when he needed to be, and he could animate any and all emotions, if playing a role was necessary to his work. And yet there was much delight to be experienced in witnessing the master's tremendous skillful means in this regard. Caylor wrote some months later, reflecting back in a journal entry on March 18, 1971:

> His childlike disposition, his innocence, his humor, his awesome seriousness, even his feigned enthusiasm or humor bordering on lunacy—still it was Yogi Ramsuratkumar. The beggar man was never to be misunderstood, for all of it was his method and way of living the work he did.
>
> On the other hand, it may be truthfully said that the beggar was not to

> be understood whatsoever. That is to say, one could not detect much coherence or fluidness in his behavior. Balance in his company was to be derived by renouncing all hopes of understanding what "this lunatic" (as he often referred to himself) was doing. Why did he behave so? Such questions could easily sever any hope of retaining any relationship with him, particularly a spiritual relationship—except for the fact that one very quickly begins to observe in him a kindness and a childlike consideration and love towards those who harbor good will and desire understanding of things not oft considered by men. This is the attitude that pervades his lunacy, his enthusiasm, his reprimands—all of his behavior—which proves the underlying purity and holiness of his work and his very inner nature. He becomes an open book more easily read than a third grade reader.

An example of this occurred when, in the third week of November 1970, Yogi Ramsuratkumar instructed Caylor to make an appointment to see him through Ramaswami as soon as he had finished reading *The Secret Doctrine.* At the exact time arranged through their merchant friend, Caylor found Yogi Ramsuratkumar standing, watching him, some way up the temple walkway, perhaps thirty meters from the tiny stone shop of Ramaswami:

> I simply will never be able to convey the gladness in my heart of the times I turned and spied that man! He always stood with his eyes fixed upon me, before I noticed him. As soon as I am in his company, the entire world changes its colour . . . .
>
> He sat facing me in the temple. The ancient stone floor of the courtyard lay beneath us. The elephant figure of Ganesh, son of Shiva, sat considering the two of us from his sacred hearth. Only once before had Yogi Ramsuratkumar entered into me as he was doing this night—in my very first encounter with him! For perhaps ten to fifteen minutes our eyes were joined in a rapport, and in this rapport he was understanding deeper parts of me. My eyes were restlessly trying to fix themselves steadily upon his—but his gaze provided no foothold in which for me to rest.

In the midst of this delicate moment, as Yogi Ramsuratkumar and Caylor sat locked into a deep gaze, a village woman approached, walking up behind Caylor aggressively and interrupting the sacred space that had been so carefully created by Yogi Ramsuratkumar. She seemed to want to intrude by placing her attention and her thoughts on the beggar and the young man who sat in such stillness. It was exactly the kind of harassment that went on regularly in relation to Yogi Ramsuratkumar, and his strong response seemed to confirm the worst. He vehemently threw a tiny marigold flower to the ground that he had been slowly turning in his fingers until then. At this movement from the beggar, the old village woman then turned away and walked toward the temple exit.

Caylor sat still, quite puzzled and unsure of what was going on, and then Yogi Ramsuratkumar turned to him and gave a rare explanation: The woman who had approached Caylor from behind had intended no good will. He had reacted with such explosive energy only to create the impression to her that he was angry and would not tolerate her misdeed. He picked up the tiny flower and then focused again on Caylor. After some time of concentration, he breathed deeply, sat back and relaxed. Even when an explanation was given, there was still the sense of other dimensions having been affected by his actions; that is, anger carried blessing with it as well as sweetness or serenity.

"No meditation is necessary at present," the beggar said, suddenly concluding the session. Later that evening the master instructed Caylor to leave Tiruvannamalai and settle for some years at the Theosophical Society in Adyar, Madras. He further instructed that Caylor should get a job on the Theosophical Society estate, and that such a move would be the best thing for his inner development. He indicated that Caylor should wait to read the third volume of *The Secret Doctrine* and assured him that all would go well.

The next day, December 1, 1970 was the birthday of Yogi Ramsuratkumar, and he allowed Caylor, Robert Lee, Aruna and some of his Indian devotees to celebrate it with him. Caylor had gone to the village to buy the roses needed for Swami's birthday celebration. It was eight o'clock in the morning, and he got ten beautiful pink roses at the flower market behind Dasaratha's tea stall. The flowers had been wrapped in leaves and tied with a string, so as he rode his bicycle around the corner, he stopped at the main road of the bazaar to unwrap the flowers and put them in an empty milk can that he had brought for that purpose. It was an unwieldy moment, holding up the bicycle, untying the package, positioning the can and sliding the flowers in, all at the same time, and he was absorbed in juggling all this when, to his surprise, he saw that the beggar was waiting for him at the side of the tea stall. Clearly he had anticipated Caylor's visit to the market and had something in mind for him. Caylor wrote:

> Swami greeted me. He held my hands warmly and with purpose. It was only a moment before he had left me and returned with a whole string of flowers—beautiful yellow marigolds. He tied the two loose ends together making it into a necklace; he took these flowers and reverently placed them around my neck. Facing the sun he pointed to it and said some things which I can't remember, whatsoever. I do recall, however, that he was saying something about the work I was to do in my life towards awakening our beloved Mother India. I felt as though he was performing some mystic ritual—that this occasion was a sacred initiation, with significance I wouldn't quite understand for years to come.
>
> This had taken place in the street so that many, many curious Indian villagers had been attracted. I felt kind of disturbed by the immense scene that we had created. Swami could easily tell that—like so many other things he had done—I was failing to follow the really deep significance of

> his actions.
>
> We went into the tiny tea stall. I presented Swami with a birthday rose—he said that it would be something he would keep with him at all times (as he does his other tools: matchbooks, string, scrap cloth, sticks, etc.). Anyhow, our meeting and our words were to be treasured and I knew, so did he.

"There are saints, Mr. K, who will throw stones at those people who come near them, but whoever is hit with those stones is blessed by them," the yogi said to Caylor that morning. It was a simple statement that contained the teaching he was demonstrating that day with Caylor: Everything the guru does is purposeful, and contains a tremendous power to bless. Yogi Ramsuratkumar had a way of making simple acts during his day into very powerful rituals of initiation, blessing and spiritual empowerment. Adorning his devotees with flower *malas* or giving them flowers, pouring water from the temple tank over their heads and hands, serving them tea and coffee—all these acts became powerfully imbued with grace by the spiritual dynamo of the beggar.

As the *jayanthi* (birthday) of Yogi Ramsuratkumar progressed, they had arranged to meet again at three o'clock in the afternoon at the deserted temple—Sri Pacchai Amman—at the base of Arunachala on the north slope. Caylor and Robert Lee had left Ramanashram together at one-thirty in order to shop in the bazaar on the way. Caylor brought more flowers, and he and Robert bought three cakes and some cigarettes for Swami and Robert.

It was a very long hot walk, which gave Caylor and Robert some time to get acquainted. By the time they arrived at the meeting point at a small temple on Mount Arunachala, it was exactly three p.m. They were surprised to find no one else waiting for them. Inside the temple or *mutt* were about two dozen Indians with all kinds of foods, sweets, coconuts and offering plates, obviously having been prepared for some celebration. Surely Yogi Ramsuratkumar hadn't invited all these people! Aruna soon showed up, and the Westerners gathered around and talked together briefly. She said that the gathering had to do with something like a confirmation for a youth. She assured Caylor and Robert that she was not going to stay to witness all the commotion when the chicken's head was cut off in sacrifice to the gods, then she quickly disappeared over the rocks on the east side of the temple to sit beside the beautiful, peaceful, contained pool of water.

Twenty minutes later George appeared to escort the Westerners to a more secluded and appropriate place that had been chosen by Yogi Ramsuratkumar. The meeting started out on a rough note, however, because George first had to more or less carry a delirious drunken man all the way down the rocky slope to the roadway—a distance of almost one-third of a mile. Then, to everyone's surprise, he returned with eight or nine of his own relatives, making the group altogether about thirteen people, including Yogi Ramsuratkumar.

Another of the guests, invited by the yogi, was the head officer of the

Tiruvannamalai railway station where the beggar often sat underneath the punnai tree. Quickly wood was gathered for a fire, tea was made and the food prepared—oranges, bananas, cakes and so on. Yogi Ramsuratkumar appeared to be in a less joyous mood than usual, perhaps because he was absorbed in his work with the group, but, as Caylor wrote, "Even so, his childlike manner, innocence, and beautiful smile prevailed over everyone. He laboriously explained the procedure and significance of the blowing out of the birthday candle," then made his silent wish and blew the candle out.

Throughout the afternoon Yogi Ramsuratkumar was a striking figure, an enigma sitting in the direct glare of the sun's burning rays for three and a half hours while the others sat in the shade. He seemed to be absorbing the spiritual energy of the sun, which he then transmitted to the three photographs that he allowed Robert Lee to take that afternoon. Despite the fact that his forehead was perspiring heavily, he insisted on sitting in the sun while everyone else sat in the shade of the giant boulders and overhanging rocks on the mountainside. Not only did he transmit the energy he was collecting into the photographs, but he also seemed to be channeling the currents of this solar energy into the individuals who were sitting with him.

It was not what one would usually expect from a birthday party; instead, the beggar had effortlessly invoked a sacred space, in which the group spent many quiet hours observing the spiritual master at work, laboring selflessly for everyone. Throughout this time, Subramanian, one of the yogi's devotees who helped guard and protect the sanctuary around him, sang Tamil spiritual songs with great devotion. A mood of a deeper communion arose in the space, as the beggar saint invisibly wove the group together.

"It has always been the desire of this beggar," the yogi said, "to celebrate his birthday. Today that final desire has been fulfilled. It is written in the Hindu philosophy that when all the desires are washed away—when one has become desireless—that person is freed from the wheel of rebirth. When one is desireless, he will be reborn no more into this world. This beggar's last desire has been fulfilled!"

"Swami, this world has suffered a great loss today," Caylor joked. Yogi Ramsuratkumar's joyous laughter rang out and he slapped his hands on his knees. His laughter was beautiful and free—a teaching in and of itself. He stopped laughing only long enough to ask Caylor if he wanted him to be reborn in this world, and then he laughed some more.

Around five-thirty the food was cleared away and the party came to a close. The group headed back toward the village, each going their own way at various points along the way. Aruna asked if Swami would spend some time with Robert, Caylor and herself, while the rest of the group returned to the village. Still on the flanks of Arunachala, he stopped with the Westerners and nested on some huge boulders where they gathered around him for the few remaining hours of the evening. Caylor wrote:

> It was a beautiful evening with a delicate and colorful sunset. A rather small tank (pool of water) was not too far away—it reflected something of the sky above and seemed to contribute to the serenity and freshness of the warm winter evening.

Everyone seemed to be pretty well tired out, me in particular—I could hardly think. Not only that, but my birthday spirit had left long hours ago. My fatigue, I was fully aware, was due primarily to Yogi Ramsuratkumar working on my mind, and secondly to the heat of the day, and, lastly, to the energy spent during the celebration . . . .

Robert began asking questions about Swami's past. Yogi Ramsuratkumar answered them without too much reservation. He was his humble and childlike self—a beggar man with a majestic heart. He sat still, gazing at Robert. He asked him if he had ever spent much time in the presence of a master. Robert answered that he had not. He added that he had never met any such enlightened saints before this encounter. Swami enquired more deeply into Robert's spiritual past—that is to say he asked that Robert explain carefully any mystic experiences which had ever occurred to him, and he further enquired about the men whom had influenced him spiritually in his life. All this was aimed at trying to discover who the master was or what the experience was that had given Robert the extraordinary progress that Yogi Ramsuratkumar repeatedly claimed the boy had attained.

Robert explained very hesitantly that in the very early stages of his meditation that he had an experience of samadhi. Secondly, he told of a meeting that had occurred between he and Sri Bhagavan Ramana Maharshi. Maharshi came to him one night, sat on his body . . . . then disappeared as mysteriously as he had come.

It was Robert's turn to ask Swami what his spiritual experience had been; to everyone's surprise, including his own, the question was put frankly to Yogi Ramsuratkumar, "What have your spiritual experiences been?" After some silence, the beggar responded.

"This beggar has had no experiences."

Swami did tell the wonderful story of his past search—beginning in Kashi, proceeding with the proper dates all the way through his years and encounters with such masters as Aurobindo, Ramana Maharshi, and his Father, Swami Ramdas. The best I can remember of all this is as follows: He was born December 1st, 1918 in Kashi (Benares), Uttar Pradesh. He attained a college education and wandered about at times with the sadhus on the banks of the Ganga. He was not fully convinced of the existence of the "higher life" which could be won by man's efforts. In 1947 he went to the Aurobindo Ashram. He has said that it was there, at the Aurobindo Ashram, that he first walked through the entrance way—he became convinced of man's potential 'higher life.' Between 1948 and 1949 Swami wandered about between the ashrams of Sri Aurobindo and Ramana Maharshi. He said that he felt that it was these two great souls who started the real work on him.

> He mentioned an incident he had with Ramana Maharshi. While he was sitting in the old meditation hall one day, he felt a peculiar feeling, just as though someone were looking at him. He looked up from his meditation to find that Ramana Maharshi's powerful and dynamic gaze was upon him. Swami quickly looked away, for he didn't know what to do. For a moment, he glanced up again to find that still the sage's eyes were cast upon him.
>
> Yogi Ramsuratkumar expressed to me the feeling of utter helplessness he felt at that time. Surely, however, that glance of Ramana Maharshi's upon that aspiring young man had a fantastic transforming effect. No doubt about it. It was at Sri Ramanashram, as Swami explained, that a certain person gave him a newspaper clipping—it sent him to Ramdas for his final time. Yogi Ramsuratkumar had visited this great enlightened soul a number of previous times but had failed to "understand" him. He said, "It was in 1952 that this beggar first understood Ramdas. Ramdas is this beggar's Father."
>
> After the deaths of both Ramana Maharshi and Sri Aurobindo, Yogi Ramsuratkumar felt that "all had been lost"—that there was nothing left for him. Then, finally, from what I understood, after Swami arrived for the final time to settle down at Kanhangad, Ramdas greeted him and told him that he had been expected for some time. Ramdas was happy to receive one of his beautiful children. It was after his initiation and "the Experience" of Yogi Ramsuratkumar that Ramdas came to him and expressed to his 'New Born' that there was no need for him to remain at the ashram any longer.
>
> Swami was introduced to his work in this world, and he received from Swami Ramdas some intimations of the developments of the future. Together they must have brought each other to understand also the nature of the work, "the inhuman labor" that that beggar was to spend his life performing. Swami told Ramdas that he would leave to go to Arunachala. He left and traveled throughout the entire expanses of India. He finally rested, as he had previously said he would, at the foot of the great Hill of Fire, Arunachala.

Yogi Ramsuratkumar was tremendously open and candid with people, and yet he would not play ego's game of fascination with the spiritual process, thus he answered Robert Lee's question with, "This beggar has had no experiences." He was constantly offering koans of this nature to people who bumbled into his world. Robert Lee wanted to know about Yogi Ramsuratkumar's ecstasies and visions, and instead, the beggar turned to talking about his search for the guru and finally recognizing his own guru, Swami Ramdas. For him, the core of the spiritual path was about the relationship between the aspirant and the guru—not the "cheap thrills" or spiritual powers that might be encountered along the way. Not long after that, Robert became very restless and soon left the group. The sheer force of the beggar's purity and raw spiritual presence had a way of revealing the domination of ego and all its machinations; it was very intense being in his company, and many were quickly overwhelmed by it.

At nine o'clock that evening the group headed back into Tiruvannamalai, with George and Subramaniam rejoining the group. Yogi Ramsuratkumar had instructed them to stay some distance away when the others left so that he could have some time with the Westerners. Yogi Ramsuratkumar created very specific spaces with people, and on this evening he was concentrating on the Westerners and keeping them near him so that he could work directly with them. His attendants, like George, tacitly understood from their long association with the beggar that he did not want anyone to interfere during this time. When an intrusion did occur in the yogi's work, it had an extreme effect. Yogi Ramsuratkumar entered into highly sensitized states of consciousness when he worked like this; his space and the state of being that he was in was easily jarred and disrupted by the slightest change in the mix. Such disruptions when he was working in this way were reported by many people over the years to cause great pain and agitation to Yogi Ramsuratkumar. It was the job of George, Perumal and many others who served as his attendants to provide a buffer for him, and to help create a space of sanctuary around the master so that he could be free to work.

Afterward, George and Subramaniam rejoined the group for a pleasant walk. On the way home the group stopped to have tea and something to eat. Caylor reflected, "The night was beautiful. Swami took good care of us all. I sat with him for a while at Ramaswami's stone shop while Aruna went off to get her flashlight repaired. When she returned we said farewell to the perfect One. He held my hands in his, gave me a beautiful and brotherly look, then he sent us on our way." The vast mind of the guru is always at one with that of the disciple, so that it seemed like the beggar had the native ability to read Caylor's mind, as he often responded instinctively to his deepest wishes—like giving permission for Robert Lee to take some photographs of him just when Caylor had been wishing for some. If Caylor prayed for something, or asked for it silently, it was amazing how the guru received this and understood.

Two days later, on December 3, 1970 the ten-day Deepam Festival was in full swing and the fire was burning brightly atop Mount Arunachala. The bazaar near the Arunachalesvara Temple was full of excitement and light-hearted activity. Walking slowly past the temple and enjoying the local children, Caylor looked for Swami but he wasn't to be seen. Nor had anyone seen him at Ramaswami's stone-carving shop. Walking along the streets during the festival there were all kinds of sights—snake charmers, fortune-tellers, shops selling many different things, food and sweet shops. Passing through the length of the bazaar, he bought some sweets and then made his way to the Sundara tea stall to take some tea. He wrote:

> No sooner had I finished my refreshments than did George come into

> the doorway. I offered him some tea and we talked together for some time. We were happy to see each other. George told me that he had just finished walking with Swami to Ramaswami's and was now on his way back home. He assured me that Yogi Ramsuratkumar would still be there now.
>
> Swami and I had a long night ahead of us. As things worked out, I must have met him, finally, at about eight p.m., and we didn't depart until about one-thirty that night. Our talk was really fascinating. Only in the last five or six meetings had he begun to give me any instruction or guidance in my Way—it was this particular night that seemed to be most plentiful in that respect.
>
> Our talk was very lengthy, sporadic, and divided. It will be impossible to remember everything that was said—but that which will be remembered is pretty much verbatim. Then, if I recall correctly, Swami and I met and walked together to our usual sitting place at the side of the beautiful, beautiful tank inside Arunachalesvara Temple. From where we sat, we had a wonderful view of the fiery hill, the ancient temple, the moon and the stars of night, which reflected off the water, so still and clear. Together, truly together, we talked and stimulated one another in our conversations.
>
> Swami enquired as to my progress in reading *The Secret Doctrine*, and said of that godly book, "These are no man's words. They are not the words of a man. God himself took hold of Madame Blavatsky's hand and wrote with it." He emphasized, "It is said that reading *The Secret Doctrine* transforms the mind."
>
> While he was talking a little girl crept up to us maybe four or five yards away. She wanted money or perhaps something to eat. Yogi Ramsuratkumar excused himself: he was going to "do" some of his "work." Perhaps expressing it in such a way is not quite right, but it seemed that our friend was being disturbed by the vibrations of the innocent little visitor. She went away, but only after he paid quite a bit of attention to influencing her to do so. It wasn't more than minutes, however, before she reappeared. This time Yogi Ramsuratkumar got up and did a peculiar dancing or skipping step for the complete length of one side of the tank. After having returned in the same manner and sitting down, the little girl went away. Apart from the little girl, Swami's childlike dance was a wonder to behold—it was the first time I had seen him do such a thing.

Yogi Ramsuratkumar had a very different way of working with the little girl that night than he had with the old woman who interfered with his work some weeks earlier. It was one of many instances when the beggar was observed dancing as a way in which he invoked a certain magic or divine presence.

That night Caylor had brought some gifts—bread, fruit and flowers—for Yogi

Ramsuratkumar. It was late and the temple would soon be closing. It was time for them to leave, so with Caylor carrying the mystical stick and Yogi Ramsuratkumar carrying everything else, they made their way out of the temple. At the time Yogi Ramsuratkumar's pot was broken and wrapped up in his shoulder wrap; he held his papers in his arms, and the flowers and fruit were in the other hand. As they walked out toward the temple entrance together, a large group of devotees of Ramana Maharshi walked past singing *bhajans*. Caylor remembered, "It was one of the first times I had ever heard such a thing. I can remember how proud I was walking with Yogi Ramsuratkumar and thinking at once that the tune of these men was beautiful and melodious. Yogi Ramsuratkumar waited for them to come down our way. As they passed, he singled out each one of them and gave to them something they would surely benefit well by . . . . it was all done by the look in his eyes."

Leaving the temple and walking together through the deserted streets, they went to Ramaswami's shop, which was also empty and quiet. They sat down alone together on the vacant boards of the shop, which was usually "crammed full and cluttered, as are all the shops, from the floor to the ceiling with merchandise." They began to talk about a wide range of subjects, from what Caylor should buy as a gift for his mother for Christmas to Nandi Shiva, the Theosophical Society and J. Krishnamurti's coming talks in Madras. Deciding what would be best as a Christmas present for Caylor's mother was an amazing process, as Yogi Ramsuratkumar asked her name, what her interests were, her job, her age, something about their relationship, and then finally drew some numbers on a card and had Caylor choose one. In the end, his final conclusions for Mrs. Carolyn Caylor Wadlington were perfect: A carving of any four-legged animal such as an elephant, camel or horse, carved in ivory, brass or wood.

The conversation turned toward the ideas of J. Krishnamurti, H.P. Blavatsky and The Theosophical Society. Yogi Ramsuratkumar spoke about the president of the society, Brother N. Sri Sriram, who was a personal friend of his, with very high praise.

"He may not be called a saint or a sage," Yogi Ramsuratkumar said, "because people don't come and touch his feet, but he understands people. Do you follow my point?" He began to talk about the *Bhagavad Gita*, explaining its meaning as he sang the verses by heart, first in Sanskrit, and then in English.

"Krishna said to Arjuna, 'Except for me, not the smallest thing exists.' The whole cosmos and everything in it is His body. 'I alone exist.' This beggar is just the dust at His feet. It is the pathless path—there is no method to realize Truth. Everything that exists is Truth. There is only one Life, Mr. K. There is one Life, alone."

Caylor was talking about the various animal vehicles of the gods, and said, "Shiva rides on the back of the sacred bull, Nandi. The Buddhists *arhats* are also pictured riding on the back of a bull, aren't they?"

"I don't know. Do you think I will ever get to ride on the bull? Sometimes I feel like he has been riding on this body," the beggar said, then he peered at Caylor out of the corner of his eye. Caylor's mind was stopped by this paradoxical statement, and immediately the beggar burst out laughing and took his hand.

"The most wonderful thing would be to be conscious of His Will and be an instrument to It," Caylor said.

"Who is there to be an instrument? If there is not Life in the soil and the rocks of the earth—then how do the plants grow?" the beggar responded. As he said that, he pointed to a lonely weed growing up in the dirt road.

It was a rare moment of pure dharmic discourse from Yogi Ramsuratkumar—a statement on the nature of nonduality: "Who is there to be an instrument?" He was saying that the separative identity, which longs to be a conscious instrument of God's will, is an illusion because there is only the One, the Absolute. He had just repeated Krishna's words to Arjuna, "Except for me, not the smallest thing exists . . . I alone exist." He was making the point that one must realize the unitive nature of ultimate reality before one can talk about being conscious of God's will. At the same time, it seemed that Yogi Ramsuratkumar was saying that he himself had gone beyond the nondual realization as he teased Caylor with the highly ironic and paradoxical remark, "Do you think I will ever get to ride on the bull? Sometimes I feel he (Nandi bull) has been riding on this body!" Such statements have the positive effect of bewildering the analytical mind, which seeks a way to enlightenment, or the realization of nonduality, through reason and intellect, when all teachings tell us that it cannot be attained through rational means.

They met again four days later. Caylor had just finished circling the hill—circumambulating Mount Arunachala—a task that the beggar saint often instructed him to do. Yogi Ramsuratkumar had said on one occasion regarding meditation and the spiritual path, "The hill helps us, Mr. K. The hill helps us." He also said that the circumambulation of the holy mountain was enough sadhana for anyone.

As Caylor walked to the bazaar, the streets were extremely crowded with people who had come to celebrate the annual festivities of Deepam. Stopping first at the flower market to buy flowers for Yogi Ramsuratkumar, and then to buy the bread and fruit that was his usual gift, he walked carefully by the tea shop, wondering if Yogi Ramsuratkumar was inside. Not seeing him at first glance, he walked on, then something compelled him to back up and look again, and sure enough, there was the beggar, smiling and smoking a cigarette. In an instant it was clear that he was expecting Caylor and had pulled his attention back to the tea stall. It was a day of high celebration, being Deepam, and Yogi Ramsuratkumar had already consumed countless cups of tea and milk, offered by friends and devotees, but he gladly accepted Caylor's offer to join him in another cup of milk.

Caylor had come with a question burning in his mind. His close friends, Joan and Will Zulkowski, who had financed his trip to India, had returned recently from Bangalore, bringing with them the stories of their wonderful experiences with Satya Sai Baba. Caylor was wondering if he should visit this teacher himself, but at the same time he thought it was perhaps disrespectful to ask Yogi Ramsuratkumar about Satya Sai Baba; nonetheless, based on his past experience, he felt that Yogi Ramsuratkumar would understand, better than himself, what was really on his mind.

For any questions of great importance, Yogi Ramsuratkumar would not answer them without having them first written carefully, word for word, on a slip of paper. His reasons for this were mysterious, but he was willing to explain briefly to Caylor that before answering a question or giving guidance he had to first understand every possible effect and reaction that might come to the questioner. And indeed, it was a fascinating process to watch, as it also involved the highly focused ritual of taking out a cigarette, lighting and then smoking it. When the beggar worked in this way, he went into an altered state of consciousness; as the silver strands of smoke floated in wreaths around his head and disappeared into the air, he was tuning into the invisible realms and gathering information there, which he brought back to this plane in the form of an answer. The burning of the tobacco seemed to have its esoteric purpose as well; it was a mystical process of consciousness, fire and air. Often his index finger and thumb would move rapidly as if moving a *japa mala* through his hand in an involuntary repetition of mantra, his body sometimes shook, and perspiration often came to his brow. All these things were typical when he worked to answer a question of any vital consequence to a *sadhaka*.

"Is Satya Sai Baba what he claims to be—that is, an avatar or an incarnation of God? If so," Caylor queried, "then is it not my duty to meet with him and follow devotedly any guidance he might give to me?"

"You have put me in a very difficult position Mr. K," Yogi Ramsuratkumar began. "To this beggar, a saint, a sage, and an avatara are all three the same. That is what this beggar feels. Whether you call a man a saint, a sage, or an avatara—it makes no difference. They are all the same. But, unless a man knows that he is not the body, he is not any of the three. Do you follow my point, Mr. K? I am infinite and so are you and so is everyone. But, there is a veil. There is a veil. Do you follow me, Mr. K? You can see only an infinitesimal part of me." Yogi Ramsuratkumar pointed to his body.

"Just like when a man stands on the shore of the ocean and looks out over the great ocean," he continued, "he sees only a small part of it. He sees only a fraction of the vast ocean. Everyone can see only a small part of me. The whole cosmos is but an infinitesimal part of the real man. But, how can a man see the whole cosmos?" He paused, then said, "It is not for this beggar to talk these philosophies. He is here to talk with the people and mingle with them."

It was a rare moment when the beggar revealed himself in his way; although he referred to the infinite nature of everyone, his statements, "You can see only an infinitesimal part of me," and "Everyone can see only a small part of me," seemed to be the actual answer to Caylor's question. Why would Caylor need to go to see Satya Sai Baba when the same God-realization, the same wisdom was sitting in front of him in the form of Yogi Ramsuratkumar? And yet, to answer this question directly forced the beggar's hand and put him in "a very difficult position."

Caylor had in his possession a very old book—an art piece made of painted wood and beautifully worked. The pages were of a thick, rich antique paper and bound in such a way that the book unfolded page after page into one long strip, with the front and the back covers each at opposite ends. It was a treasured family heirloom, brought back by his great grandfather, Reverend Marcie Gettle, from his trip to India. Understandably, it had a deep and mystic significance for Caylor, and he had brought it with him, along with a few clothes and bare necessities, to India. On this day he had made the *pradakshina* of Mount Arunachala with this book in his hand, hoping that Yogi Ramsuratkumar might get to see it:

> I showed him the book. He asked me to remove the book from the box that contained it and to set it carefully on the table on my right. He then proceeded to look through the small photographs and reverenced items I kept alongside the book within the box. Finally, he stood up and made his way around to the front of the table I was sitting at. He asked me to unfold the book along the length of the tables joined together, until all the pages were visible to him. I did it. He asked me a few questions about the book.
>
> "How old do you think the book is, Mr. K? Perhaps over one hundred years?"
>
> I didn't know, and I told him so . . . . It was at this point that a few individuals inside the teashop went to the evil ways of work. They began to make ugly comments about the worth and age of the art piece, which they understood was of sentimental value and worth to both Yogi Ramsuratkumar and particularly myself. I made no notice of these remarks until I realized my wise friend's reactions to these men. I thought all along that they were comments made in simple ignorance and lack of culture; then I realized that these men were purposely tormenting the beggar with their subtle remarks. Yogi Ramsuratkumar looked at them in a funny way. I can't remember noticing them leave but they dispersed quietly and without much ado.
>
> Swami, in the meantime, impressed with his sight something of himself upon the very pages of the book. He stood before me gazing in concentration over each page of the book, once and then twice. Yogi Ramsuratkumar then told me to put the book into the box. We left soon afterwards.
>
> It had become obvious to me—very, very evident—that a great deal of malice was always being dealt to my friend. More and more, he was purposely putting me in positions where I might see these things with my own eyes. Today, as the streets were crowded and it was too dangerous for him to walk unguarded through the town's streets, I offered my assistance by walking him back to the great banyan tree which serves as his shield against evil, and more than that, his home and companion. After we reached the tree, we soon departed.

The last time Yogi Ramsuratkumar met with Caylor before he left for Adyar, Madras was on December 13, 1970. It began the day before, when Caylor had set out from Ramanashram to find Yogi Ramsuratkumar. At first he had very little luck. He went from one place to the next—all the usual haunts where Caylor had grown accustomed to finding the beggar. He checked the teashop and then walked the streets for an hour or more, wandering in search of him. Finally, on his way home, he stopped for a cup of milk and some biscuits at the Sundara teashop, and there he inquired from Dasaratha if he had seen Swami. Sure enough, he was sleeping in the back room. Caylor sat quietly drinking the milk, not wanting to wake the beggar, but Yogi Ramsuratkumar began to rustle and then joined him.

Their conversation very quickly came around to the mechanics of computers—it seemed that the beggar was interested in learning about these "superminds." Yogi Ramsuratkumar had asked Caylor to talk about computers on two or three prior occasions, indicating that he needed to know about them for his own purposes. Synchronistically, since the subject of computers had come up, Caylor had purchased a bar of soap that was wrapped in two pieces of paper; as it turned out, the inside wrapper was, oddly enough, a computer card of the punch type. Secondly, a new arrival at Ramanashram was a young German man, Andy, a geophysicist specializing in the study of computers. Caylor had talked with him as much as possible, asking him to explain and diagram the mechanics and technical workings of a computer. As his knowledge was extensive, it was a very good connection, and it was for this reason that Caylor arranged to meet with Yogi Ramsuratkumar the next night at six-thirty.

The next night Caylor set out to search for Yogi Ramsuratkumar accompanied by Aruna, who had news of Narakuthi Swami for the beggar. Before going to the teashop they stopped to buy some flowers to give to "Swami," as they called him. As it turned out, the meeting occurred right away. Caylor wrote:

> Swami was sitting at the bench waiting for us as we arrived. He was happy in his heart to see us both. Yogi Ramsuratkumar was seated smoking a cigarette as he always does when he is having company. In addition to that he had a new tool—a string of rudraksha beads. Just as each and everything he carried with him or wore was an instrument, so too was this necklace, or japa mala. Immediately after Aruna and I had greeted him and seated ourselves by his side, Swami handed me his invaluable and treasured tool—his stick. I was instructed to hold it in the air for some time—I did so happily, for it was a rare occasion to get to hold this instrument and be of some service in his work. Those people who were interfering with his work soon left. I was shown where to place the stick; I did so, and it probably remained working for him as a vigilant guard against ill intentioned intruders.
>
> Aruna left after a short time. Yogi Ramsuratkumar and myself abruptly began to focus our minds on the activities of the previous night and to begin again to discuss the workings, potentialities, the functions,

and the likenesses of the human mind to modern-day computers. Hours were spent conversing on this subject. I showed him the diagrams that Andy had drawn and gave him the computer punch card that I had found only days earlier. All this information was being sorted out and stored by my friend. I cannot forget how certain points were stressed and how my position in relation to him was obviously so very important to all of this. I could only feebly explain the fundamentals of these machines as Andy had expressed them to me, however, I am convinced that Yogi Ramsuratkumar had access within me to knowledge and experience relating to this which I myself had lost contact with or rather no longer could willfully recall to mind. In some way or other, I probably was of more service than I suspect I was from the surface proceedings.

It was quite late when we stopped talking. Our minds were fatigued—we had entered together, through his power, into a separate world, and while we were there we labored or concentrated all our energies on conveying to one another this information. Yogi Ramsuratkumar directed me towards the café doorway—he carefully stressed that my movements should be slow as I moved away from him.

The night sky was clear, the streets were empty and silent. We stretched our limbs and breathed deeply of the night air. It was nice to be together. Once again we had arranged to meet together one more night to discuss the same line of thought; however, as things moved on we both came to the understanding that tonight would be the last meeting before my departure [for Adyar, in Madras].

We walked slowly through the streets. Having decided to have something to eat, we went to the café, not but a few yards distance from the tea stall. We thoroughly enjoyed our chapattis and coffee, even though there were some disturbances, incidents, or shall I say, simply, that certain people employed at the restaurant consciously abused and tormented my beggar friend. As I had exhausted all of my money, Yogi Ramsuratkumar ended up paying the larger part of the bill. Yogi Ramsuratkumar didn't have enough money either; consequently, he made arrangements to pay some other day.

Down the street, not too far from the Khadi Industries Store, we settled to talk in the quietude of the vacant streets and the starlit night. We must have talked for nearly two more hours before our farewell. Our conversations gravitated toward Swami's work and the honest and severe suffering he endures throughout his working—that is to say his waking—hours. Every moment of the day and not at night, only by God's Grace, he is tormented. A network of patrolling automobiles and lorries work to [locate his whereabouts] at all times. Besides this, the vehicles are aimed and maneuvered to destroy this blessed beggar fellow. There are times

> when the automobiles do seem to cease in their wicked tricks; however, never, never is he left at ease, for always he is being watched, given the worst of people's thoughts and followed step by step where and however he goes. Though I myself have not seen Yogi Ramsuratkumar being stoned and pelted with rocks, he has mentioned to me that this sort of thing happens occasionally. How often I do not know. All the rest of this torture I have myself witnessed while being with him. For years and years on end, this treatment has continued daily without recess—who is so mighty among mortal men to bear such treatment? I question my strength to stand more than a few short days of such a thing. We talked for quite some time about this state of affairs, and how a man's privacy is sacred to him.

As their conversation went deep into the night, it turned toward why Yogi Ramsuratkumar would be such a target, which led to a profound discussion of world politics, the interference of First World powers like Great Britain and the United States in Indian politics, and the attempts to cause division among the many diverse peoples of India. With over two hundred languages in India and a great deal of racial and religious ethnocentricity, this would be one tactic that could be taken to undermine the potential of India to emerge as a world power. According to Yogi Ramsuratkumar, a conspiracy was underway in which political parties were being set up that were popular to the masses suffering from poverty and hunger, which stress racial and language ethnocentricity and engender the persecution of any who stand apart from the norms, or who take radical or liberal political stances. These political divisions within India could encourage the formation of individual nations apart from the federation of states currently existing in India.

Always in favor of the unity of all people, Yogi Ramsuratkumar openly opposed separations and divisions based upon race, religion, language or politics with his slogan, "Mahatma Gandhi ki jai!" He professed the innate unity of men, the spiritual power of India, so long as it remained harmonious within and between her peoples. Nonetheless, from the outsider's point of view, he was of Aryan rather than Dravidian racial descent, which is a common difference between northern and southern Indians. And finally, he spoke mostly Hindi and English, not Tamil, as is native to south India, whose factions were greatly opposed to the Hindi language taking over in India.

Yogi Ramsuratkumar spoke with Caylor about how in past ages it was spiritually profitable for India to be kept in relative material poverty; it is a condition that may have been executed purposefully by the highly evolved spiritual beings and hierarchies that guide India and the direction of her spiritual light and forces in the world. This was the situation that best supported the cultural milieu out of which the great God-realizers were created. But, India was now beginning to suffer, both materially and spiritually, because of a one-sided development in the midst of an aggressive and materialistically oriented world. As a result, those beings are beginning to move Mother India to a stable position in the world of nations. He felt that India had slept for good reasons perhaps, but it was time for her to awake and arise to spread the truth in a world that was calling for spiritual guidance.

Further, he felt that material development was necessary at the present time for the protection and welfare of India's people. If Mother India's material development—and thus her ultimate spiritual awakening—is impacted by conspiracies and interference from the West, then those people and forces guiding and administering such a vile movement would surely be crushed and destroyed. These were some of the reflections that Yogi Ramsuratkumar shared in conversation with Caylor that night.

"Raise your hands to God and pray for the protection of this beggar! Say to Him, 'You know the beggar who lives in the small village of Tiruvannamalai and who does his work for You? Please, watch over him, protect him, and see that not one hair on his body is touched. He is Your child, and has given his life to Your Work. When those who do Your work for You and have given up everything to You need Your help—it is Your duty to protect Your children and to watch over them,' " Yogi Ramsuratkumar said to Caylor, speaking passionately.

Then he said, "All I ask is that sometimes you take time off from your work to remember this beggar—to think of the torture this beggar is going through daily. If you will just remember his name." Caylor was tremendously moved by the heartfelt candor and innocence of these tender and sacred revelations:

> I feel deeply and ardently that my friend is doing a vast task in this world. It is for me to remember all the ways he has helped me, he has helped India, and heavens only knows how far he has lifted the hearts of all men. God bless him and protect him . . .
>
> We spoke also much about my stay at Adyar. For the past month, he had been drilling me with certain subtle thoughts about this divine place and its equally spiritual founders. It was this night that he told me that the Theosophical Society should be my home for as long as possible. He stated that it may be necessary to shift to the Indian Section headquarters in Benares—but that in any case, I should stay for as long as five years, if possible.
>
> "You may take it as a joke, Mr. K," he said, "but you will some day be an international speaker for the Theosophical Society. This beggar has taken into account the way you think, your humor, your temperament, your life as a child. Everything about you indicates that the Theosophical Society is the best place for you. The best place."
>
> In reference to my becoming a speaker for the TS, he said, "One need not be well educated. If there is some spirituality in a man, there will be a power in his words."
>
> That night was blessed. Yogi Ramsuratkumar had spent days on end with me, working on me untiringly. He had given so much of himself to me—sometimes hours on end he would sit close by to me and work on my

mind, somehow permeating and transforming it with his spiritual being and power. I had become part of him. I told him this. I told him that I would do what he asked. That I must do what he asked—for there was nothing or no way I could ever repay him for what he had done for me. I assured him, nearly in tears as I said it, that what I had to give him was not so much, but that he should never hesitate to call to me for help. Never, never should he hesitate, for I would give to him my all and everything. Just as I said this I looked away, up into the sky, to see a falling star flash across the sky. It seemed to mean something.

"Any help that is needed will come to you automatically, until you are made into a perfect instrument of God," he said.

Then I understood that it was time to depart and also that there would be no meeting with this beggar tomorrow evening. He clearly expressed this through repeated hints and how unusually close he had drawn me to him this night. It was the last meeting for a long time.

"We have a meeting tomorrow evening, but will you forgive this beggar if he doesn't meet you? Will you forgive this beggar if he doesn't come?" We both understand each other's heart.

Thinking back I can only remember things fragmentarily—how it was that we decided to stand and part, I do not know. Just as in all our previous meetings I had grown to understand that this was a moment to be silent. It was a time when I could convey to my friend thoughts without expressing them verbally. Such a saintly one is he, dressed in rags and hair hanging in a childlike way almost to his shoulders, the eyes so loving.

He held my hands in his. I could hardly bear this moment. I knew not how to face him. No thoughts ran from my being to his. Finally, "May God Help You," and he had understood.

"Please go now. You are a son of Mother India." Those were his last words to me. The glory of those words ran through my whole body. In pain, I turned from him, bent over, and with my face hidden from his, I moved away. Then I looked up once again, and a beautiful falling star streamed its fire across the morning darkness.

Swami watched me move down the street. Standing silently in the vacant bazaar, he bid me farewell in a way I cannot fathom. I turned and looked down the street. He too had gone. Once again, he was alone to do his work. There would be no Caylor to seek him out in repeated evenings; no Caylor to escort him and protect him from wicked men; no Caylor to laugh and to cry with him. With all my will and with all my heart I sent my blessings to the beloved man. I said goodbye, and I said thank you.

The black and starlit sky shone down on me. I raised my hands and in prayer I sent to him the song of my heart as a poem . . . Just as the last word had left my lips, then for the third and final time, a falling star

> arched its way down over the little village in the very direction I was faced. I cried.

The guru had given tremendous gifts of spiritual empowerment and initiation to the young American over the six months that had passed since July 1970. He had been extraordinarily direct and forthright, and had drawn Caylor into his world; now Caylor was entering into a different phase—one in which he would live in Madras, work at the Theosophical Society and have the opportunity to integrate all that had been given. Interestingly, Yogi Ramsuratkumar's emphasis on this direction for Caylor had started right at the beginning of their relationship. Caylor reflected years later about this time period, and how the idea was first discussed between the two:

> Just weeks after I first met Yogi Ramsuratkumar, he met me one time very late at night and he started talking about Madam Blavatsky and Colonel Olcott, her colleague of that era. Those two together established the Theosophical Society. I had no idea why he started talking about these people and *The Secret Doctrine*. He would point toward heaven and say, "He took her hand and wrote with it," and "This is mantra, this is mantra." He said that the whole book had some special power, and if you read it, it was like reading the Upanishads. It had a mantra power because it had been written in this way. He encouraged me to read it. I have no idea why, but he asked me to go to the library at Ramanashram; he said that they would have a copy of it.
>
> He said that I should stop all my meditation practice; whenever I wanted to meditate, I should just read that book. He had me read it from beginning to end, and the day that I finished it he sent me to the Theosophical Society in Madras. When I met him in the late afternoon in the temple he would have me tell him everything I could about *The Secret Doctrine*. I couldn't remember much because it was such a dense book! I couldn't figure out what she was talking about most of the time. All the Kabbalistic numerology and the astrology and Egyptian alchemical cosmology and alignment and planetary objects and cycles. It's 1700 pages long! I'm still embarrassed that he would ask me questions about this book. He was keeping track of where I was in the book for months, and as I neared the end he would keep track of my reading page by page—how close I was to finishing.
>
> Then as it became clear that I was going to finish it, that week he asked me to meet him and tell him. So we sat down in the temple and he had me tell him what I could about it and I was completely embarrassed

> because it was a huge fog to me that day! The level of intellectual detail and all this talk about Sumeria and Chaldea and various ancient lands I had never heard of! Of course it was kind of interesting to read about Atlantis and those type of things, but I didn't have the vaguest idea about it. I was twenty at the time!
>
> So, he would ask me questions, and we would laugh and laugh. I'd say, " Swami I can't remember! I'm so embarrassed, but I can't tell you much. She was talking about this and that." He laughed and laughed and said, "Beggar man gives you such a hard job!" Then he told me about the headquarters of the Theosophical Society in Madras. He told me about the president, and he said that he was an enlightened master. His name was Sri Ram. He said that I should write a letter to Sri Ram in the coming days and explain that I wanted to come and work there. I could come for a short visit and do some job there—work for the Theosophical Society convention. So I wrote a letter and I got a letter back from Sri Ram. Yogi Ramsuratkumar had me read that letter from Sri Ram many times to him! Then he sent me off to live there, and I spent the next five or six years there, in Madras, at the Theosophical Society.

During the early months of 1971 while living in Madras, the intense impact of his time with Yogi Ramsuratkumar began to spill out in sporadic but prolific writing as Caylor retraced his experiences with a passion. Many of the journal entries that were written during this time, January through May 1971, are about events that occurred during the seven months in 1970 he was in Tiruvannamalai spending time with Yogi Ramsuratkumar.

It was a year of great change, integration and digestion for Caylor as the process of spiritual transformation took root in him. The headaches had gone away, and the powerful energies moving within his body seemed to have been harmonized by the subtle healings and inner work Yogi Ramsuratkumar had done with him. Being in the presence of the guru had catalyzed a deep process, so that his nights were often taken up in divine reveries and ecstasies. Once he found himself dancing spontaneously, and found that his whole body was "pulsating with forces while the energies played a fiery havoc within." During this time he experienced a variety of phenomena, including bodily ecstasies, strong dream states that involved direct instruction from and communion with Yogi Ramsuratkumar, flows of cool but fiery energies within the body, sometimes focused in the hands and feet. One of his friends at the Theosophical Society confirmed that, indeed, it was likely that his body was "impregnated with spiritual energies." He had been saturated in the divine influence and blessing force of a spiritual adept, a *siddha purusha* hidden beneath the rags of a beggar.

No one could rely on expectations when it came to the enigma of Yogi Ramsuratkumar; he moved freely wherever the wind took him, toward whatever divine work he was called to by the inner promptings of "my Father alone." In mid-May 1971 Caylor's longing for his "beloved friend" had grown strong, but he had no idea when or how he would see the beggar again. He became anxious to make the trip back to Tiruvannamalai, and hopping on a bus to Tivandrum, seven and a half hours later Caylor was there. He searched everywhere—all the usual haunts—but Yogi Ramsuratkumar was nowhere to be seen. He went to the punnai tree at the railway station, to the Sundara teashop, to Ramaswami's stone shop—none of these yielded a dirty beggar. He went to Ramanashram and secured a place to stay in a guest room. He wrote, "Everything looked absolutely vibrant! I must have changed somehow. I never was receptive and sensitive to those energies before. The play on the hill was a beautiful release after such a long bus ride—this entire area is mysterious and awesome. It's beautiful and free."

Will and Joan Zulkowski arrived in Tiruvannamalai the same day, and the old friends spent three hours talking and getting acquainted with one another again, but Caylor found it difficult to describe the depth of what he had been through and how much it had changed him. He was no longer seeking self-realization or enlightenment, but was embracing the ideas of J. Krishnamurti and Sri Aurobindo, who "renounced themselves as the instruments of divinity and accepted totally whatever fate was due their way. Self-Realization was the least on their minds . . . . shall I say, I have simply followed the surface suggestions of a Great Yogi."

For the next several days Caylor looked and asked for Yogi Ramsuratkumar everywhere he went. He had learned something about the beggar's ways, however, and although he was sure that the beggar saint knew he was in Tiruvannamalai, he also believed that Yogi Ramsuratkumar was incognito for good reasons. He wrote, "Never is he so difficult to find except when he purposely makes himself a mystery. For a worthy reason he is not meeting with me. Perhaps he is engrossed in his own work and would find it detrimental to have to adjust his mind to a very much different current to relate to me . . . . I will concede that I am disheartened at not seeing the one to whom I owe my very life."

One day Caylor ran into a friend named Mark Manion at Ramanashram, who lightly mentioned that he was going to see "Jungle Swami," who lived on the east side of Arunachala in a jungle ashram that his guru had established. Caylor mentioned that Mark might like to see Pundi Swami, who Mark said he had heard about from Wendel Field, Will and Joan. Caylor showed Mark a photo of Pundi Swami and gave him directions for finding him. The photo of Pundi Swami was encased in plastic along with a photo of Yogi Ramsuratkumar.

"Who is that?" Mark asked, turning the photo of Pundi Swami over.

"He is another yogi I know," Caylor answered obtusely. Mark wanted to know where the photo was taken, and Caylor answered, "On a big mountain." Mark chuckled, since Caylor was obviously evading the real question, which was, "Where can I find him?"

When they joined up again later, Mark told Caylor that he had met Pundi Swami for a few short minutes amidst a crowd of a hundred or more devotees celebrating a religious festival around him. There in the small village a man from Calcutta approached Mark and invited him to accompany them in their private car to Tapovanum, where they would receive the darshan of Gnanananda Giri Swami. Upon arriving there they discovered that the ancient sage was not coming out to give darshan to anyone; he was said to be deeply occupied with his *tapas*.

While he was there, Mark met a great yogi, "a wise old man." He recognized the amazing yogi from Caylor's picture, which he had just seen that morning. Yogi Ramsuratkumar spoke with him for three or four hours. He asked if anyone had ever taken his picture on a big mountain with two stone horses on either side. Yogi Ramsuratkumar answered that he could remember some Scottish boy having done so, referring to Robert Lee, who took the three photos of Yogi Ramsuratkumar months before, on December 1, 1970, at the birthday party when he was with Caylor, Aruna, Robert, Subramaniam, George and his family on the western slope of Arunachala.

Mark asked the beggar many other questions, but Yogi Ramsuratkumar "feigned spiritual ignorance and lunacy laughter and joked with him." Until they became better acquainted, Yogi Ramsuratkumar spoke to him only through a third party. Like a Zen master, the beggar spoke in seemingly nonsensical paradoxes, but he held Mark's hands and caressed his skin.

Mark was deeply impressed, but didn't know what to make of this strange behavior—was the beggar the lunatic he claimed to be? It quickly became clear to Mark that this was in fact a great sage, a unique being of wisdom and spiritual joy. At one point he asked Yogi Ramsuratkumar where he had become so well versed in Zen. Yogi Ramsuratkumar skillfully and sweetly replied that as he had hung about various ashrams for some time, others had acquainted him with the Oriental path. Mark also had the vague impression at Tapovanum that Yogi Ramsuratkumar was to be undergoing some final initiation, although what that meant was very unclear.

Mark quickly became the instrument to bring Caylor back together with Yogi Ramsuratkumar. The next day, May 16, 1971, Caylor and Mark left Tiruvannamalai early in the morning by bus and arrived at Tapovanum by nine-thirty. They searched for Yogi Ramsuratkumar, but found only a few servants in the colorful ashram compound. Through gestures and broken English they managed to communicate that they had come to see a certain yogi. Instantly people knew that they were talking about Ramji Swami. They were told that he had gone to the river early that morning with a friend and would return shortly. They took off toward the river and soon met Yogi Ramsuratkumar on the highway with a man named Ganapati.

It was a very happy reunion, and the beggar appeared to be happily astonished as he embraced Caylor. Immediately he told Caylor that there was "much work to do" that day, work that in the long run might bring "a new chapter in the life of this beggar."

Yogi Ramsuratkumar, Ganapati, Mark and Caylor went to a hotel and sat together over cups of coffee, which the beggar insisted that they drink, whether they wanted it or not. He paid for it—two rupees—and it quickly became a joyous gathering laced with laughter and high spirits. These coffee rituals orchestrated by the beggar saint were often thick with a sense of purpose that emanated from his being; when the guru pays for something, or gives a gift, there is always significance. Ganapati soon left the group, and the other three walked across the road to sit beneath some towering trees along the roadside, amidst the ruins of an old house foundation where they found seats. There Yogi Ramsuratkumar engaged in an animated conversation for three hours, holding Caylor's hand and arm. During this time Caylor became deeply absorbed in the spiritual current that was flowing out of the beggar like a swiftly moving river of light.

The first order of business was to straighten out some confusion and conflict that had occurred around letters and money that Caylor had been sending to Yogi Ramsuratkumar through Aruna, who was, for various reasons, choosing to separate herself from the close friendship she had had with Yogi Ramsuratkumar and Caylor. Although this was an amicable split, it was still rather disconcerting, and Yogi Ramsuratkumar explained to Caylor that often those disciples who are closest to a master will for some reason separate themselves from and turn against him. Most often such people one day return to the master. In other cases, no such return or reunion occurs. A new arrangement was agreed upon, whereby Caylor would send all correspondence through Ramaswami.

As they talked together Yogi Ramsuratkumar relayed to Caylor that early on that morning he and some others had gone to bathe in the Pennai River just a mile distance from Tapovanum. There was one gentleman who, while wading out into the current, stumbled and at the same time slid his foot into a crevice of the rocky riverbed. For hours people from the village and from the ashram tried every possible means to release him from the trap. The beggar relayed the event to Caylor, who wrote about it in his journal:

> Everything anyone could dream of was put to the test, but still his foot was held firm in the rocks. The man's leg had been pulled and twisted until the slightest pressure caused an awesome pain to his foot, and he was in a state of desperation. His foot was bruised and cut to such an extent that it was impossible to do anything more. The incessant pain was taxing the strength of his body and mind. There were villagers who were considering amputating his foot for it seemed to them the only means left to free him.
>
> Sri P. Radhakrishnan, an officer in the Public Works Department of Madras, could see no reasonable way to slide his foot out of the crevice, however the man's release was soon to come, and in a most miraculous way. Yogi Ramsuratkumar had returned to the ashram and there he had fallen into some peculiar state of consciousness. His outward behavior and appearance had lost most all similarity to that of a normal man. Then with two friends looking after him, he journeyed down the road till they arrived at the scene of the incident. Villagers were all about, waiting for something or someone to find release for their friend.
>
> Establishing his two cohorts at a carefully chosen point along the

> riverbank and making it perfectly clear to them that under no circumstances were they to move from that spot, the yogi stated emphatically to them that at exactly 8:40, ten minutes from the present time, Sri Radhakrishnan would discover himself free from the trap which mercilessly held him. For anyone to have said such a thing after so many people's tricks and schemes had failed to bring any result other than agonizing pain could surely have been nothing less than a clear indication of a man's lunacy—or of his divinity—for he had been trapped for three and a half hours. It was 8:30 now, and he was to be free in ten minutes!
>
> As Yogi Ramsuratkumar waded into the river towards Radhakrishnan, the village children moved towards the peculiar man to push and splash him. Their mischievous intentions were easily foreseen, so he retraced his steps to the riverbank. Then moving upstream he assumed a position behind Sri Radhakrishnan and somewhat distant from the villagers. It was at that very moment that the ensnared man turned and glanced only for an instance into the fixed gaze of Yogi Ramsuratkumar. The foot lodged in the rocks of the riverbed slid free.
>
> The village people became exultant, and because it had happened precisely as foretold by Yogi Ramsuratkumar, the two men who were instructed to remain stationed along the riverbank and in this way had been instrumental, jumped up and down cheering out, 'You have saved him! You have saved him!'
>
> Sri P. Radhakrishnan went to the Tapovanum Ashram later that morning. In religious gratitude he prostrated himself at the feet of Yogi Ramsuratkumar and presented to him an offering of plantains. Swami accepted his offering graciously and extended further blessings to him, foretelling a revolutionary change of goodness that would come to his life from that moment onward.

This particular miracle is quite famous in the lore of this time period of Yogi Ramsuratkumar's life. It is told in various ways in different accounts. Some say it was a boy and others a girl whose foot was caught, but here we have a firsthand account by Yogi Ramsuratkumar of the details of what happened. It was significant in the emergence of Yogi Ramsuratkumar as a great master because it was a public miracle that was witnessed by many people; the word spread quickly and the local people were mightily impressed by the news. That same day, Yogi Ramsuratkumar began to speak again with Caylor about his own history, adding in some facts that were previously unknown. Caylor took notes, writing down the words while Yogi Ramsuratkumar spoke.

Speaking of his return to the south in 1948, Yogi Ramsuratkumar recalled that when he spent two months in Tiruvannamalai in the company of Ramana Maharshi, he himself put very few questions to the great sage; however, he could remember well a number of questions that were put forward by others. There was a certain man, in particular, who had come directly to India from the United States in order to meet Ramana Maharshi and have him answer questions that were vitally important to the book he was then writing. The name of the book was *Destiny and Free Will*, and it was this book that had drawn the American man to visit the holy man of Arunachala. In connection with the subject of his book the man was told by Ramana Maharshi, "Even the stars have destiny, as well as free will." After the sage answered his questions, Yogi Ramsuratkumar said that the man flew directly back to the United States.

"Then there came a man from north India with a beard and long hair, a young man maybe thirty-five to forty," Yogi Ramsuratkumar continued. "He had come with his wife. He put some questions about kundalini shakti to Maharshi, who answered, 'Ultimately, in all types of yogas, kundalini shakti is awakened.' " Yogi Ramsuratkumar added for emphasis, "Kundalini shakti, which in English is called the serpentine power—in all yogas it is awakened."

The beggar relayed that the young man asked another question: "Under the guidance of a master, if a yogi is doing sadhana and the master passes away, should the disciple change the master, take a new one?" The Maharshi emphatically replied, "No, the same master will do."

Yogi Ramsuratkumar then told the story of his search and many travels from 1948 through 1952, when he finally came to realize that Swami Ramdas was his guru. Caylor took notes throughout this time while Yogi Ramsuratkumar spoke candidly. These was the actual time when Yogi Ramsuratkumar gave Caylor the material for the first biography written about him. He continued, telling Caylor the story of his initiation with Ramdas. A certain woman came to the ashram one day with all the required preparation to perform the ritual of her initiation—Swami Ramdas was to initiate her that day. Caylor recaptured this in his journal on May 17, 1971, taken from his notes of that afternoon:

> After the completion of the holy ceremony, Yogi Ramsuratkumar began to feel that he too wanted to take initiation, yet he was too shy to go to Papa, as Ramdas was called by his devotees, and ask him if he could receive initiation. The manager of the ashram, Swami Satchidananda, had been a wonderful friend and kind helper to Yogi Ramsuratkumar since the time they first became acquainted. Swami went to him and told him that he wanted to take initiation. Satchidananda gently urged him to face Papa with his wish. He did so and much to his surprise, right then and there Swami Ramdas consented. Ramdas looked away to one side, and for a moment thinking deeply, he then turned and faced his timid devotee and said, "So you want to be initiated. Sit down."
>
> Yogi Ramsuratkumar sat at his feet and repeated the sacred syllables of the mantram which was given to him to be forever his path to God. None of the required articles of the traditional initiations were used—only the force and divine power of the Ram mantram. When Papa had finished he said to his disciple, "Go, and repeat this mantram day and night all the

> twenty-four hours."
>
> Yogi Ramsuratkumar continued, saying, "After nearly two months with Ramdas this beggar wanted to prolong his stay in Anandashram. Thrice this beggar approached Swami Ramdas—every time he was refused. The last time Ramdas exclaimed, 'There are a number of people who can be fit for ashram life. We don't want any more of such people." Ramdas explained illustratively to Yogi Ramsuratkumar, "Look at the trees in the forest. They are firm and strong. Then see the trees in the gardens. We care for them, but do they grow so well, so strong as those which grow in the forests?"
>
> Yogi Ramsuratkumar then said, "There are a number of interesting things in connection with the life of this beggar during those two months of his stay with Swami Ramdas which cannot be given at present. After 1952 this beggar never went to any ashram or to any master for the sake of spiritual guidance, though he met so many of them . . . but never for spiritual guidance." Yogi Ramsuratkumar then relayed that since 1959 he had been "keeping to Tiruvannamalai." When he left Anandashram so far back as 1952, he was asked by Swami Satchidananda where he was intending to go. Yogi Ramsuratkumar replied that he was going to Arunachala; however it was only following years of wandering all over India that he finally arrived there.

That day Yogi Ramsuratkumar told of another incident in the early years after he left Anandashram—a humorous episode that took place on a road near Trivandrum. After having visited the great monument in memory of Swami Vivekananda in Cape Comoran he walked casually along the road northward through Kerala en route to Trivandrum. One day he observed a stalled truck far in the distance. The truck was obviously broken down and the men were trying to start the engine. As Yogi Ramsuratkumar drew near to the truck he stopped and watched the work they were doing on the engine.

"You are having trouble starting your car?" he asked, and then added, "Please start it now." He touched the engine and said aloud, "By the Grace of Ram your car will start." At first they scorned him derisively, thinking him some kind of lunatic. Their tempers had grown short with their failing efforts, and they spared him no generosity. When, to everyone's astonishment, the driver was able to start the engine with ease, they were so surprised and delighted that they extended their heart-felt thanks to this mysterious mendicant and saluted him as they drove away.

Yogi Ramsuratkumar narrated this event sitting on the side of the road near Tirukoilur, not far from Tapovanum, that day. As the afternoon wore on, they conversed on a wide range of subjects that would eventually be collected, arranged and elaborated to form part of the book that would be *Yogi Ramsuratkumar, the Godchild, Tiruvannamalai*. With Caylor still taking copious notes, the beggar saint continued to speak, making it clear that he believed Caylor had been brought to him to be a "divine instrument" who might help him with the extraordinary work that was compelling his life by writing this small life sketch, which he envisioned as a thirty or forty page booklet. He was very clear that no harm could come to Caylor in doing this, and that in fact he would find tremendous help from higher forces—the book would more or less write itself.

"We are doing it for some other purpose," he said, "for our protection we want it." Based on what he had personally witnessed, Caylor was convinced of the urgency and necessity for such a project to be undertaken. He reflected in his journal:

> No selfish interests were motivating the creation of this book; rather, as one could plainly see, both the life of a great saint and the indeterminable lives of seekers of Truth might eventually find peace and solace as a result of [such a publication]. I say this for the simple reason that Yogi Ramsuratkumar is in desperate need of devoted care, and he rewards one hundred percent with the powers of the spirit those who provide for his needs. The yogi is an instrument of Divine Force and has mastery, attainment and unity with the intelligent and conscious aspects of the Forces of which his physical body is but an instrument and vehicle. Yet he suffers no end by the ignorance of men about him. Seeing a madman in him they stone him, beat him, and persecute him all his waking hours. Yogi Ramsuratkumar said, "This book will bring a new chapter to the life of this beggar."
>
> For three years he has endured torment and torture that no man could endure for more than a few days. I have witnessed the plots and endless schemes which are forever put upon him. By God, I testify that his greatest miracle of all is that still he lives! For no man, lest he be a child of God, could survive the treatment that men have made him suffer. Anyone else would be crazed and deranged in only days' or weeks' time.
>
> Every word was to be left to my discretion, and what was eventually written was to be left unchanged, even to the last punctuation mark, for divine guidance was to be in truth the actual author. Yogi Ramsuratkumar also stressed the importance of the photographs. He said, "Seeing the photographs people will come to understand this beggar."

That afternoon a storm had come and gone, they had moved to a nearby hotel and their conversation had finally stopped, but the day was not over. Yogi Ramsuratkumar then invited Caylor and Mark to go with him to Tapovanum and meet the one-hundred-fifty-year-old master, Swami Gnanananda Giri. They eagerly agreed and, "as if three were one, we sauntered out of the hotel," across the road and the patchwork of puddles to arrive finally at the Tapovanum temple, where the priest had begun the magnificent evening *puja* ceremony amidst much chanting and waving of lights. Caylor was surprised to see Yogi Ramsuratkumar prostrate himself before Gnanananda Giri, but the very action itself communicated a great teaching on the divinity in man: there was no contradiction in the actions of these two great souls, who obviously revered each other, as the great sage bowed as well to the beggar, for all men are the (eventual) embodiments of realized God-consciousness. Caylor and Mark were introduced and *pranamed* to Gnanananda Giri.

The elaborate *puja* lasted for almost two hours, while Yogi Ramsuratkumar paced the floor behind where Caylor was sitting, focusing his attention on the work that he had given to him. Finally they got ready to leave, but Yogi Ramsuratkumar continued teaching and instructing up until the last moment of their day together. Caylor wrote:

> Because I had expressed a wish to have a photograph of Swami Gnanananda, Yogi Ramsuratkumar chose one for me. He collected in his hands a stack of various photos and without looking, he drew from the bunch the very one which I myself would liked to have had. He held it for a moment to in some way concentrate himself upon the picture. In addition to this he had the manager of the ashram hold the photo against the sandals of Swami Gnanananda in order to impress the master's blessings upon it. The portrait of Swami Gnanananda was then presented to me by Yogi Ramsuratkumar. It was to be looked to at special times, as it would be of immense help to me.
>
> "It is not merely a photograph, but something much more," he said.
>
> With this we said goodbye and proceeded to walk together out to the road so that Mark and I could catch a bus back to Tiruvannamalai. Swami said he was going to be returning in two or three days, during which time we could meet if I was still in town, but I was not going to be, for the next morning I had plans to leave for Pondicherry.
>
> Mark Manion, my friend from Sai Baba's Brindavan, had been an invaluable instrument to link Yogi Ramsuratkumar and myself together. He was truly thankful for having been brought into contact with such a great soul as this beggar-man, yet he was at the same time thoroughly exhausted and wished only to leave for the ashram in Tiruvannamalai. I could never blame him for surely Yogi Ramsuratkumar had stretched his consciousness to its breaking points, and if that is not the case then he should be excused for the simple reason that he had had almost nothing else to do than sit patiently while Swami and I conversed. While awaiting the bus, I asked Swami to elaborate on a subject he had touched upon earlier that day.
>
> "In the world there are various spiritual [movements] working to bring about a revelatory change, a new world. It is in connection with the great world movement that this beggar does his work." He said that he had been a disciple of Aurobindo, a man who believed and worked for the ideal of human unity on Earth. Though Aurobindo is now dead, his work must be carried on. Yogi Ramsuratkumar said that because he believes in the dream of Aurobindo, he too has devoted his life to bringing it to an earthly reality.

> "This beggar believes in the vision of his spiritual master, Aurobindo," he said. He explained that Aurobindo had a dream and a vision of a universal unity and peace on earth and furthermore of a revolutionary race of spiritual supermen.
>
> The bus came tearing down the highway. The water on its wheels made a ripping sound. Yogi Ramsuratkumar, my beloved father and teacher, bid us farewell. We held hands briefly, then Mark and I shot for the bus. I was only halfway on when the bus pulled away, but with a bit of acrobatics I managed to make my way in and to find a place to sit and quietly surmise the incredible events of the day. It was evening, about six o'clock, on May 17, 1971.

Caylor left Tiruvannamalai the next day and, after some travels, returned to Madras and the Theosophical Society, where he began work on the book, *Yogi Ramsuratkumar, The Godchild, Tiruvannamalai*.

From the above passages it becomes clear that Yogi Ramsuratkumar believed deeply in the necessity of the Great Work, called by the names of spiritual transformation, divine alchemy, or work on self in many different traditions, which is also reflected in his appreciation for the writings of Madame Blavatsky. Yogi Ramsuratkumar took inspiration from many different sources, was widely read and fluent in working with different ideas of how this great work might be expressed, from the teachings of his three fathers to great teachers of the East and West, as we will see in coming chapters. From this tremendous universality—the depth and breadth of his realization—Yogi Ramsuratkumar always returned to the statement, "This beggar had three fathers: Aurobindo, Ramana Maharshi and Ramdas. But Ramdas killed this beggar in 1952." On this occasion in May 1971 he was expounding on his understanding that Aurobindo had deeply engaged and articulated truths that were of great important to the evolution of the human race. He was well aware of the grave difficulties and obstacles to such a revolution in human consciousness, but, as he said to his friends on that day, "This work must be done. It is all that we can do. But this beggar will tell you—it won't fail."

CHAPTER FOUR

Emergence: A Hidden Saint Is Discovered

1971-1976

As the radical awakening of the being in God-realization matures and evolves, the burning radiance of that awakening begins to shine in the world in a way that is undeniable, attracting the attention of those who have the eyes to see. Over years, the extraordinary state in which Yogi Ramsuratkumar lived became apparent to some, and the momentum of this recognition began to take on the speed of a hurricane moving inland. Yogi Ramsuratkumar could no longer remain hidden in the labyrinths of the streets, the temple, *mutts* and small, arcane ashrams, making his rounds and going about his work silently and invisibly. The early seventies brought a tidal wave of change as people began to flock to him. He was moved by the will of God in various ways in relation to whatever was brought his way, and he found himself compelled to bless all and to befriend many. As Westerners discovered him, there was also a tremendous movement among the Indians that was stirring in the native background, coming largely out of Tapovanum and spearheaded by Rajamanickam, his family and a few others, and gaining momentum in the mid and late seventies. As the story of Yogi Ramsuratkumar unfolds in time, we will mingle with the many characters who knew him well.

The connection that Yogi Ramsuratkumar had developed with Caylor Wadlington was a milestone in the ongoing relationship between West and East as it manifested in Tiruvannamalai. Westerners came to India seeking yogis, saints and sadhus in the early and mid-seventies and flooded Tiruvannamalai. Some of the relationships that were formed with Yogi Ramsuratkumar took hold, the medium being fertile, and became long-term over the years, while others lasted for a day, a week, or months. Countless numbers of unknown people came and went from his life, having been touched by his blessing.

In 1969 Wendel Field was a student in the fine arts program at a university in Bloomington, Indiana, where he met Caylor Wadlington and Will Zulkowski. The three young men were serious about their meditation practice, and along with two other friends, established a small, informal "ashram" in a house that was available to them, where they lived and meditated. It was a time of great change in the culture in the West and in the

United States in particular, as young people from all over were gravitating toward the hippie movement; there was an explosion of passionate interest in yoga of all kinds, kundalini experience, mind expansion, altered states of consciousness, shamans, yogis and spiritual masters. These interests ranged in authenticity and durability: from the whimsical and curiosity seeking fad-followers, to the merely intellectual, to those who were truly drawn to the spiritual path.

Wendel Field was serious about his art and about the spiritual path. He spent most of his time painting and meditating, and when Caylor left for India in the spring of 1970 and the meditation house was disbanded, Wendel was also compelled to the East, seeking that which was true and real. His friend Will Zulkowski, who was a conscientious objector at the time and had been arrested for demonstrating against the Vietnam war, wanted to go to India with his wife Joan, but couldn't because of the community service he was involved in. Instead, he helped finance Caylor's trip and then, some months later, Wendel's trip to India.

Arriving in India in 1971, Wendel went to Tiruvannamalai first because of his interest in Ramana Maharshi, where he stayed briefly at Ramanashram. At the time Caylor was living in Adyar at the Theosophical Society, and the two friends didn't connect. While staying at Ramanashram, Wendel met a young sadhu who said, "You should go see Sai Baba." After a few weeks in Tiruvannamalai and some visits with other local swamis, Wendel continued on to the Aurobindo ashram for a few days and then went to see Sai Baba, where he made an immediate and strong connection with the saint. Sai Baba's advice for the young American was, "Don't go sightseeing, go 'saintseeing'." Taking heed of this recommendation, Wendel traveled for awhile, going to Rishikesh and then visiting Neem Karoli Baba, who he liked very much.

Later that same year Wendel visited with Caylor in Adyar, who was living in a house that had been built for Krishnamurti, about three hundred feet from the ocean, with many beautiful trees and strong nature spirits. It was here that Wendel first heard about Yogi Ramsuratkumar and the book that Caylor was writing, and he was inspired to paint a picture of the beggar saint. Wendel explained, "So I did this little painting . . . . I'd never seen Yogi Ramsuratkumar before, never met him—I just worked off a photograph. The whole image was done in concentric circles from his forehead, you understand. He was in green because Caylor said that he always wore green."

About three months later Wendel returned to Tiruvannamalai and stayed in a hotel south of the temple. He walked past the row of shops in the downtown bazaar and toward the Arunachalesvara Temple one day, and as he walked he unexpectedly saw Yogi Ramsuratkumar sitting in one of these shops. Recognition dawned immediately, and in the same moment the beggar turned and looked back at him intensely. Wendel didn't approach him or say anything, but kept walking toward the temple. When he came back out, Yogi Ramsuratkumar was gone.

Leaving his hotel the next morning, Wendel walked out the front gate and almost ran into Yogi Ramsuratkumar.

"Mmm! Have I seen you somewhere before?" the beggar asked. Wendel had the distinct feeling that Yogi Ramsuratkumar knew all about him, but they went on with the formalities.

"Yes, I saw you in the temple last night."

"I mean before that . . ." the beggar mused.

He was holding Wendel's hand and standing very close to him. He was carrying a stick or wand with a cluster of peacock feathers tied to it, along with other strange things—strings and such. Suddenly they were walking through the streets together at a very fast speed, in Yogi Ramsuratkumar's usual burning way.

For the next few years Wendel had the opportunity to spend quite a lot of time at the shops in the bazaar with Yogi Ramsuratkumar. The beggar was usually dressed in a white dhoti and shirt, with a green cloth wrapped around him—it seemed that green was a significant color for him. Most remarkable to Wendel was the beggar's tremendous sense of humor and the touch of irony he brought to situations. For example, in answer to the questions of those intellectual Westerners who read the books of Ramana Maharshi and asked the beggar lofty questions about nonduality, he would often begin his response with, "This sinner, this beggar, he'll be the last one to say . . ." At other times the beggar would be laughing and laughing, even frolicking, when he would suddenly become very intense, grab his sticks and fan, hold them high up in the air over his head and walk back and forth. At times like this the atmosphere around him was charged, heavy and even fierce. He would pace back and forth for a few minutes over a stretch of twenty feet or so and then come back and sit down, continuing the conversation right where he had left off, without commenting on what had just happened.

Wendel often found Yogi Ramsuratkumar by literally running into him—walking around a corner and bumping into him. At other times, it was by arrangement. Usually when Wendel got within range of the beggar, Yogi Ramsuratkumar would see him and raise his hand up, palm out and say, "Come on, come on!" Then they would walk together or sit somewhere to drink tea and talk and laugh while the beggar smoked.

Once Yogi Ramsuratkumar took Wendel to celebrate the birthday of Ramanuja—the famous south Indian philosopher-saint who wrote many classic texts on Hindu theology—at a very nice house not far from the north wall of the temple. There were spiritual luminaries from all over town there, including the head priest from the temple. They had set up a special seat for Yogi Ramsuratkumar, and Wendel sat next to him for the festivities.

"The movie's over, let's go!" Yogi Ramsuratkumar said suddenly. As they were walking outside, the head priest was about ten feet away from the beggar saint. There had been some tension because the seat of honor was given to the odd beggar and not the head priest, and as Yogi Ramsuratkumar passed by, the priest muttered rather cynically, "Why, it's the Godchild." Yogi Ramsuratkumar turned around and walked directly to the priest, bent down and touched his feet.

"It's God himself," Yogi Ramsuratkumar said.

It was an intense moment in which the priest was both blessed and chastised, the teaching lesson made all the more potent because the gesture was completely sincere and free of guile or motivation.

One day Yogi Ramsuratkumar and Wendel walked a short distance up the east side of Arunachala, and there the beggar told Wendel to read a specific book—*Future Shock,* by Alvin Toffler. Sometimes Wendel read aloud from this book to Yogi Ramsuratkumar while the beggar listened laying down. When it appeared that he was asleep, Wendel stopped reading, but each time he stopped Yogi Ramsuratkumar would say, "Go on."

Once Wendel was reading to the beggar saint from *Future Shock* on the mountain, and although it seemed like a day of placid ease and calm, Wendel noticed that there were "weird, mysterious things" going on around the beggar. While Wendel read and Yogi Ramsuratkumar appeared to be asleep, two Indian men wearing Western-style suits were trying to sneak up on him. It was strange enough to see south Indians dressed in Western attire, but they were skulking surreptitiously around behind rocks, stealing looks at the beggar or trying to spy on him. Watching them watch Yogi Ramsuratkumar, Wendel thought the whole circumstance very bizarre, but Yogi Ramsuratkumar never talked about it. Finally the beggar mumbled something about "those guys," then they left and walked to the temple.

Other than this odd event, Yogi Ramsuratkumar never mentioned the harassment or death threats that he had received to Wendel, who was at times witness to other strange goings-on as well. It was an example of how Yogi Ramsuratkumar worked differently with each person who came to him: unlike Caylor, Wendel never heard a word about *The Secret Doctrine* and the Theosophical Society from Yogi Ramsuratkumar, nor did the beggar ever speak about his past, or about his relationships with Ramdas, Ramana Maharshi or Aurobindo. At the most superficial level, in Wendel's case it was not necessary for him to know about the harassment, whereas it was Caylor's destiny to write the biography, and he therefore had to know. The master had a natural antenna for the unique karma and destiny of each person who came into his immediate sphere of influence; he was well aware of Wendel's relationship with Sai Baba, and he always encouraged him in that direction, specifically by instructing him to include the image of Sai Baba in an important painting that Wendel was working on.

Wendel had picked up a number of chants while visiting Sai Baba, and often Yogi Ramsuratkumar would say, "Wendel, sing a song." Sometimes, when he didn't know all the words, the beggar would laugh and say, "Okay, sing another one!" Wendel recalled a rare occasion when Yogi Ramsuratkumar had changed into new clothes, and all that day and night he was "up singing and dancing for hours." It was a very dramatic moment when the beggar would begin to dance, swinging his body around in ecstasy. Sometimes he broke into dance right on the street. His fingers often moved automatically, as if he was holding a bead *mala* in his hand and doing *japa*. It was not uncommon for him to break into singing, "Om Sri Ram Jai Ram Jai Jai Ram."

One day Yogi Ramsuratkumar told Wendel to meet him in the field on the south edge of town around noon. It was New Year's Day in 1972. Yogi Ramsuratkumar was sitting with a small group of six or eight Americans and Europeans who were hanging out with him during that time period. Diane Jones, a British woman who he called Gita, had her cameras with her that day. She asked Yogi Ramsuratkumar several times if she could take photos of him. At first he said no. He was always known by his devotees to be extremely particular about how photos of him were taken. He didn't want her to take photographs unless they were exactly as he wanted them—highly intentional.

"How many photographs are you going to take?" he asked after a while.

She jokingly said, "A hundred and eight," the number of beads on a prayer *mala* used for *japa*.

"Okay, come on!" Yogi Ramsuratkumar responded. There was something about her comment, "a hundred and eight," that opened a window, an opportunity for the beggar saint to create a teaching *lila* for the Westerners. Moving spontaneously, he immediately instructed Wendel to grab one of the cameras, as Gita already had two or three, and leaving all the others behind, he walked fast off through the fields. They never rejoined the group that day, but spent the rest of the day walking around, with Gita Jones taking photographs. As they went from one place to another Yogi Ramsuratkumar would find some spot and stop there for a photo to be snapped. Sometimes he held up a piece of string or some other object, and doing whatever magic he did, at a certain moment, when the timing was exactly right, he would say, "Okay, okay . . . now!"

The three cohorts wandered around all day, taking photos, roaming off through the fields, sometimes walking a foot deep in water, sometimes with Mount Arunachala as the backdrop, and at other times through the courtyards and ghats at the temple. At one point Yogi Ramsuratkumar took them to the home of local farmers—devotees who were happily surprised by the unexpected visit from the beggar saint. Quickly they set about to make special food, which was served two or three hours later to the honored guest and his friends. After this extended visit and the meal, Yogi Ramsuratkumar took Wendel and Gita to the home of some other devotees. Again the Westerners saw the great surprise and pleasure of the Indian devotees, who responded happily to such a great honor and auspicious occasion. These were the indigenous people who had known him for some years, and who came to him asking for rain for their crops or blessings for their children and families. To have him arrive unbidden at their doorstep was a tremendous boon.

All the while, Gita continued to shoot more and more photographs of Yogi Ramsuratkumar without any thought of keeping count as the spontaneous adventure of the day rolled along. Yogi Ramsuratkumar was laughing and playful, but at the same time, there was a feeling of seriousness, of intention, that was underlying everything. He set up the stage for each photo, adjusting whatever he was holding, waiting for some unfathomable timing and saying, "Wait . . . okay, now."

All day Gita snapped photos; as long as Yogi Ramsuratkumar was willing, she kept shooting. Some were in color, and some were in black and white. When the negatives were developed, much to the surprise of Gita and Wendel, there were exactly 108 photos! Not only had they amazingly turned out to be the exact number that Gita had jokingly told Yogi Ramsuratkumar she would take, but also there was a mysterious and pronounced aura of light around the form of Yogi Ramsuratkumar in many of them, exactly as if it had been airbrushed on the print. Wendel was convinced that it was the result of Yogi

Ramsuratkumar's strange way of orchestrating the details of each picture, fiddling with strange objects and waiting for the right moment. It seemed that the more the guru lingered over some infinitesimal and seemingly unimportant thing—a piece of string or a leaf—the more the photo was imbued with spiritual power. In some pictures the phenomena was stronger than in others, so that it would just appear as a hint of light around the figure—a luminosity past the edge of his body. Many of the photos were spectacular; most of them were given away over the years to different people, now scattered in unknown parts of the world.

When Wendel first met Yogi Ramsuratkumar, the divine madness and spiritual power of the beggar reminded him of Juan Matus, the inexplicable shaman, Yaqui Indian and medicine man who was immortalized in Carlos Castaneda's books about him. The first of these books, *The Yaqui Way of Knowledge*, had been published a few years before and was an instant success in the counter-culture and consciousness movements of the late sixties and early seventies in the West. Yogi Ramsuratkumar used to ask Caylor to read aloud all the Castaneda books he had; he listened with great interest, and always expressed the highest regard for Castaneda and don Juan. Several of the young Americans found a striking similarity between Yogi Ramsuratkumar and the almost mythical Juan Matus.

Wendel commented about Yogi Ramsuratkumar, "Here you are with this guy and you haven't the slightest idea what he's really doing, but it really doesn't matter! Sitting there in the experience and laughing and being totally present—that's what it was all about. That was the whole point, really." At the same time, just being in his company caused one to reflect more deeply, especially about one's own actions, motives and thoughts. There was such a spirit of mystery and a sense of cosmic proportions involved in his slightest movement that it made his companions stop and think about what they were doing.

Yogi Ramsuratkumar liked to sit and watch Wendel paint. On one particular occasion Yogi Ramsuratkumar took a blank drawing book and made line drawings on at least twenty-five or thirty of the pages. According to Wendel these were "a curious mix of things—an innocent thing" like the way a child would draw, but also with "some kind of medicine, some kind of power in it that was given particularly to me." These were all done at one sitting, and each one was different from the others.

"Oh, I'm going to go by and see this yogi who I haven't told you about," Caylor told Will and Joan Zulkowski, who were in India for the first time. It was May 13, 1971, and their close friend, Caylor, had been in India for a year. They were planning to spend most of this trip in Bangalore at the ashram of Satya Sai Baba, but they were in Tiruvannamalai, with Joan recovering from hepatitis. When Caylor went to see Yogi Ramsuratkumar and told him about his friends who were in India, to Caylor's great surprise Yogi

Ramsuratkumar proceeded to describe them in detail, saying, "Oh, Joan . . . Yes, this beggar knows those people." Then he said, "Well, this is not a good time to come now; they can come another time."

Upon returning to the States they lived in Washington, D.C., where they worked to save the money to go back to India. In 1972 they got word from Caylor that he had just finished writing a book about Yogi Ramsuratkumar and he needed their help to get the money together to publish it. They stepped in and "cuffed together five hundred bucks" and sent it—half of it coming from donations and the other half from Will and Joan themselves.

In 1972 the first publication of *Yogi Ramsuratkumar, The Godchild, Tiruvannamalai* came out. For months before it was published Yogi Ramsuratkumar asked Caylor to read and reread the text to him, many times over. The reading of the book would often spark a rash of storytelling from Yogi Ramsuratkumar, which would then get added in. Many people who knew Yogi Ramsuratkumar wondered at the "theosophical overview" of the book, but the beggar himself was extremely happy with it; even when asked, he would not allow Caylor to change or edit any of it. He considered it to have been inspired by God. He did make some changes, however; for example, Caylor had made the statement that Yogi Ramsuratkumar was never married, and the beggar deleted this from the book.

A few thousand copies were printed; Caylor kept about two dozen and Yogi Ramsuratkumar had all the rest, which he gave away as he saw fit over the next few years. It was Caylor's idea to include pictures, but they were all handpicked by Yogi Ramsuratkumar, and included the three photos taken by Robert Lee on Arunachala on December 1, 1970. On numerous occasions in the years ahead Yogi Ramsuratkumar expressed his deep appreciation to Caylor for the book, as well as to Joan and Will; he never forgot how much they had helped him. After the book came out Yogi Ramsuratkumar said to Caylor:

> Finally it has become apparent as to why this beggar was made to endure the last five years of pain and persecution . . . If that had never developed, this beggar would never have called upon you to write this life sketch. It was my only recourse; it was no longer possible for me to live and work unnoticed, nor could I even remain in Tiruvannamalai. Already the book has begun to alleviate this situation, at least to the extent to where it is possible for this beggar to continue with his Master's work. But what the book has done for me is not important compared to what it may do for others. No book may fail to uplift or inspire, Mr. K. Every book shall touch the heart of a brother.

The threats on Yogi Ramsuratkumar's life forced him out of obscurity and gave him no choice but to become more visible as a saint. In fact, it catalyzed an acceleration and magnification of his work. This is further revealed in a statement Yogi Ramsuratkumar made to Joan and Will: "By helping with the book, getting money for the book to be published, you have helped this beggar stay in Tiruvannamalai, and thereby the universe itself." Eventually it also helped provide basic sustenance for the beggar saint, as devotees who came from Sivakasi, Tuticorin, Bangalore, Madras and other cities became very attuned to his needs. Overall, things got better for Yogi Ramsuratkumar.

In 1973 Will and Joan returned to India. Will had written to Caylor in Madras and asked him to go to Tiruvannamalai and ask Yogi Ramsuratkumar if it would be a good time for Joan and Will to come to meet him. Caylor went to Tiruvannamalai and saw Yogi Ramsuratkumar, then wrote back that he had said, "Yes, tell them to come. Tell them Mother India's arms are always open." At the bottom of the page was written, in his hand, "My Father blesses Will. My Father blesses Joan. Yogi Ramsuratkumar."

In November 1973 they arrived in Tiruvannamalai with Caylor. The news was that Yogi Ramsuratkumar had a fever so he couldn't meet with them the next morning, but they met soon enough. Caylor knew that Yogi Ramsuratkumar was staying out in a farmer's field, so they walked there and discovered the beggar sitting beneath a tree. He invited the three American friends to join him in the shade. The day was overcast, but very bright with the diffused light of the strong tropical sun. Sitting beneath the tree in this long-awaited meeting with the beggar and immersed in his presence, Will closed his eyes and passed into a very deep state—a *samadhi* of some type. It was such a deep state that he wanted to stay there forever. The surroundings were completely blanked out and there was only a deep, inner space filled with light. He felt the presence of a powerful light moving slowly in a circular motion inside him. Then he could hear the beggar saint calling to him, as if from afar.

"Well, Mr. Will, no good to be on that side, please come to this side. No tea, coffee, and cigarettes inside," the beggar laughed.

"Nope, never coming out of this space!" Will declared.

"Will, come to this side—no tea, coffee and cigarettes are inside!" Will could hear the beggar talking to him, then suddenly he said in a slow but firm voice, "Two, nine, zero, eight . . ."

Suddenly Will's eyes opened, as if involuntarily, and there was Swami, standing right in front of him. Will had been instantly catapulted back into the normal consciousness of his body, which seemed to delight and entertain the beggar to no end. He started laughing and laughing.

"Two, nine, zero, eight seems to be Mr. Will's number!" He laughed for at least fifteen or twenty minutes. Everybody was laughing. Caylor was laughing, Joan was laughing, Yogi Ramsuratkumar was laughing. After that, even though he had been with Satya Sai Baba since 1971, Will thought, "This guy's got to be my guru, because to have an experience that strong . . ."

Joan had doubts, however, and when they went to Bangalore to see Sai Baba, she held up a black and white picture of Yogi Ramsuratkumar to show it to Sai Baba during darshan. Holding the picture she merely said to herself, "This man is my guru." Sai Baba put his hand on the picture and said, "Yes sir" to her.

Joan and Will were with Yogi Ramsuratkumar for two weeks during their initial meetings with him. He had them come to him every night in the bazaar and spend eight hours with him. Will recounted:

> He wouldn't let us sleep at all. If we started to lie down he would say, "Please sit up." This was down in the bazaar, in the brass market. The people at the brass shops were his devotees. He had a very ratty straw mat, really threadbare and not very soft, that he slept on. He would talk all the time with us. We were really the only ones. Nobody else came.
>
> At night we usually had some candles burning. He would have somebody go out and buy some candles, usually me or Joan. And then he would have the people at the tea stall bring tea, because he just added it to his account. Every time we went to the bank we gave him some money, but he'd just give it away to George and to a couple of those guys who were his attendants, because they had no money and they all had families.
>
> Swami was very, very charming and very, very sweet, but he would be fierce, too. When I first met him he was just so loving and kind to us. And for some reason, he took a liking to me, I don't know why, but we really got on well. He was just very, very gracious to us.
>
> He was so mystical— you never, ever knew what he was doing. You never knew what he was up to. You just couldn't figure it out. He was just so beyond, beyond, beyond, beyond—all he had to do was sit there. We had a room near Ramanashram, not on the ashram, and at that time there were no rickshaws, there were only those horse-drawn buggies, and they didn't run early morning or late night. So we usually walked back and forth. That was the introduction.

One night during those first two weeks, Yogi Ramsuratkumar started talking around three o'clock in the morning. He had a way of talking to one person indirectly, through another. On this night he turned to Joan and told her Will's future.

"Joan, one day Will is going to be a really great healer. He will be able to throw dirt over people's heads and they will be healed. Even heads of state will come to see him." Then he said, "He's going to be a good teacher, but no big following. Just small, maybe like fifteen people, mostly one-on-one."

"Swami, I'm not capable of that. I'm just an ordinary kind of person," Will protested.

"Father's will, Father's will, Father's will," he responded, absolutely insistent. When he made predictions like this, it was impossible to know if he was talking about this lifetime or twenty lifetimes in the future; nonetheless, when he saw something about a person, he spoke with absolute certainty.

"Well, let's see what happens," Will said.

Yogi Ramsuratkumar was his mysterious self, but always very playful and humorous with Will and Joan. Once someone came who was looking for Babaji—the famed yogic master who was supposed to be hundreds of years old and lived somewhere hidden in the Himalayas. Yogi Ramsuratkumar laughed and laughed the whole time.

"These people are looking for Babaji," he exclaimed to Will and Joan with incredulous laughter. His exclamation was filled with a sense of the absurd, the irony being that the guru function is always the same, regardless of whether it is appearing in the form of Yogi Ramsuratkumar or Babaji. He himself was the same as Babaji, but the seekers saw only a dirty beggar—a veil that he used quite effectively as a smokescreen to weed out those who weren't serious about the spiritual path. At other times when similar interactions arose, he would simply become very quiet.

Very few people had an inkling of the kind of universal work that the beggar was doing as he walked around the city from day to day, or sat smoking beneath the punnai tree near the railway station or in the temple courtyard near the Ganesh shrine. During these years Yogi Ramsuratkumar sat in the Theradi Mandapam, where the temple chariot was housed, just around the corner from the brass market. Once when Joan and Will met him at the *mandapam*, the beggar was not feeling well. The conversation turned to J. Krishnamurti and his teachings.

"Oh, talking about J. Krishnamurti makes this beggar feel better," he said. "Sometimes the weight of the whole universe is on this beggar's shoulders."

Will was one of the people who Yogi Ramsuratkumar befriended and let into his world in a very personal way. Like Caylor, Will was privy to the fact that Yogi Ramsuratkumar was having threats made upon his life, and that there were people in Tiruvannamalai who caused him great suffering. At times when Will and Joan were sitting with him or walking out toward the fields or some other place in town, Yogi Ramsuratkumar would urgently point and say, "Will, look over there. Look over there! See all those people staring at us? They're just here to harass this beggar."

It wasn't hard for Will to see that these people spent their entire day staring and glaring at Yogi Ramsuratkumar. Sometimes they threatened those devotees who owned restaurants that gave coffee and food to the beggar with serious insinuations and open threats that some harm would come to their families if they kept having any association with him. Yogi Ramsuratkumar handled these situations with equanimity. Once when Will was spending the night with Yogi Ramsuratkumar, eight or nine men came in the middle of the night. They were insanely drunk, They were cursing Yogi Ramsuratkumar, screaming and yelling at him, "We're going to beat you up." Will's first response was to fight with them, but there were too many of them for one person to take on. Yogi Ramsuratkumar's response was quite different.

"Oh, Vishnu has come. Oh, Hanuman has come. Oh, Shiva has come," he said, and miraculously, they all went away. One moment they were going to cause serious harm to him, and the next moment, they were gone.

Yogi Ramsuratkumar's life had not been an easy one, but he had no complaints. He lived the way of true beggary, accepting completely whatever came his way. One of the teachings of Upasani Maharaj is, "Be satisfied with whatever is available." Yogi Ramsuratkumar embodied the qualities of surrender, acceptance and the spiritual fullness that creates a mood of plenitude and abundance, even in the face of scarcity or serious threats to his physical survival. He lived entirely off the goodness of the people around him, and so he ate whatever food the village people brought in their generosity, and for this, he expressed profound gratitude.

One day a woman devotee came and brought food for him. Yogi Ramsuratkumar had tears in his eyes as he accepted the food, and said to Will, "This lady cooked for Swami Muktananda!" He was visibly moved and honored that she had at one time cooked for such a great being, and now she also cooked for him.

Nonetheless, the great spiritual masters are also human beings, and even a perfect saint feels pain and has his or her preferences now and then, as relayed in the following story. Yogi Ramsuratkumar had no teeth, and so he had to mash his food up, even something soft like bananas. For that reason he didn't eat a lot of fruit, but his devotees loved to bring sweets to him, which are a symbolic and traditional offering, and sometimes he would get tired of eating them. Will told this story:

> He'd say, "Ah, this beggar's so sick of sweets. Joan, go to the bazaar. Get this beggar some grapes. And make sure they're really sour." Joan would get them and wash them, and then he would say, "Will, this beggar does not understand why Joan needs to wash the grapes."
>
> When you buy grapes on the main street of Tiruvannamalai, in the market it's really dusty! He'd say humorously, "Oh, you know Joan. She's always trying to keep real clean!" Sometimes he would tell Joan to go back to the temple and walk around [a specific shrine] nine times. And then she'd go off, but first she'd need to get a bath, because she couldn't go off without a bath. She had to have a bath every day, so she'd go back to our room. Then she'd come back feeling refreshed, and Swami would say, "Oh, now we've given Joan some work to do that she can do for us," and he laughed.
>
> You know, people think saints have no emotional side, but Swami had a very emotional side too. Every time he got ill he would say, "Oh, Father can fix this beggar and make this beggar well." Once he was very sick for a long time and he said, "Oh, Father's grace, Father's will. He can make this beggar instantly well," then he would joke that Father was not responding at that moment!
>
> Everything was always God's will. When Swami had complaints about his health or about something else, the people around him would say, "It's God's will." Swami would joke with them about that sometimes . . . and it was very, very humorous, but these were people who had come to him for many years and known him over a long time. These weren't the new people. New people were always in awe, you know. Swami had a very, very human side to him in the sense that he just didn't have any pretentiousness about him. There was just no air that he was someone that

> you weren't. He always kept his focus, and he always said his focus was, "doing Father's work." What I gathered more and more was that he was really working with the cosmic energy.

Joan Zulkowski once recounted that Yogi Ramsuratkumar rarely talked about spiritual matters during the cycle of his ordinary day. He would wait until the quiet of the night, after the activity of the village had settled down or stopped altogether. Once the shops were closed and people had been sent away, those who were lucky enough to stay were then privy to another side of the beggar: "He would tell us with no uncertainty that he is a master, and that he is doing his Father's work perfectly. He would also say, 'Father is pleased with this beggar's work.' He would say that it is not this beggar's lot to live in an ashram and have that kind of surrounding. He would laugh and say that it was his lot to live the life of a beggar, and he does it very well." He also talked about his vision for the world: he saw that the present order of the world would be completely changed in twenty-five years. He said that they wouldn't even recognize that it's the same world. He believed there would be peace and harmony.

"Swami," Joan said on one of these occasions, looking around at the well-dressed Westerners who were visiting the beggar, "it looks as though there are kings sitting before a beggar, but we are really beggars sitting before a king."

In those days Yogi Ramsuratkumar never wanted to have anything left dangling or unfinished at the end of the day. Usually people brought fruit or food or money during the day, and as soon as he received these gifts, he would send someone over to buy food to share with everyone who was gathered around him, because he didn't want to have any money or food left by the time he went to sleep. At ten o'clock every night he sent his visitors away, and then he slept on the wooden sidewalks near the market place because by that time the shops would be closed and the bazaar was nearly abandoned.

The *lila* of the sour grapes continued that day, which included some very direct lessons in working with energy—not at the cosmic level, but at the most basic metaphysical level—and that also demonstrated the wide breadth of connections and relationships that Yogi Ramsuratkumar fostered and enjoyed with all kinds of people, from the most ordinary to the most extraordinary.

When Joan returned with the grapes, Guruswami, a old friend of Yogi Ramsuratkumar, had arrived. It was early summer, and the sun was blazing down, the air sweltering. Being from the market out on the streets, the grapes were wrapped in the typical Indian style—in a small sheet of newspaper and tied with a thread that is twisted into a little knot at the top. Yogi Ramsuratkumar carefully divided the grapes and distributed them evenly to everyone. They were *prasad*, but they were almost unbearably sour. Finally Guruswami complained. He even gave his grapes back! He and Yogi

Ramsuratkumar were old friends, and they found the sour grapes very funny. They laughed together like conspirators, and the beggar slapped his knee in mirth. Then Guruswami turned to Yogi Ramsuratkumar and asked him to ask Joan to give him a grape.

"Joan, Guruswami wants you to give him a grape," Yogi Ramsuratkumar said. Joan knew something fantastic was about to happen; she suspected he might turn the sour grape into a lusciously sweet one. She gave Guruswami the grape and he held it for a little while. Guruswami asked Yogi Ramsuratkumar to ask Joan to hold out her hands in a specific way.

As soon as Joan held her hands out to meet Guruswami's closed fist there was a loud cracking sound in the air—the grapes were changed into a handful of coins tumbling into her opened hands! Her body became very hot for a moment. Even though Joan was expecting something like that, she was awestruck. The loud crack had brought everyone's attention instantly into sharp focus. Will recounted, "In the seconds it took me to realize that a grape had just become a handful of coins, I became mildly hysterical with amazement."

Guruswami was simply sitting next to Yogi Ramsuratkumar, looking like an innocent party, as if he'd had no part in the miracle. There was no sense of pride in him. Instead it was comical, the contrast between the two yogis and the wide-eyed Westerners, who wanted to ask a million questions but were so stunned they couldn't even talk.

Guruswami told Will and Joan that he was born in north India and that all his life he had longed to live the life of a sadhu, but when he was still very young his guru had told him to get married and live as a householder. He was opposed to this, but he obeyed, and his master gave him a *puja* to perform at home every day. He did this faithfully, eating only one meal a day and a glass of milk in the evening. At the end of the third year this power came. When he told them that he had no control over it, Yogi Ramsuratkumar wryly interjected, "So he says," and then he laughed, as he was translating all this for the two young Westerners who were getting a priceless education in esoteric physics, not to mention the madcap wisdom of the two yogis.

Guruswami was thin and small, weighing only about one hundred twenty pounds. During this time period he lived near Kanchipuram. An herbal doctor, he would come to Tiruvannamalai seasonally to collect herbs. According to Will, one would never guess that he was "anything out of the ordinary, except that one could see it in his eyes." His wise eyes betrayed him.

Will and Joan saw Guruswami with Yogi Ramsuratkumar on three occasions. One of those was at Tapovanum, when he came with his son. Yogi Ramsuratkumar asked the boy to sit with him, while Guruswami sat in the folding chair with Joan and Will opposite him. It was night and everyone was singing *bhajans*. Suddenly two Westerners walked past, then circled back and approached Yogi Ramsuratkumar.

"Are you Ram Ram Swami?" they asked.

"Yes, this beggar is known to some by that name."

He graciously invited them to sit. They said they were from Pondicherry, but apart from that bit of information, they didn't say much. After a while Guruswami said something to Yogi Ramsuratkumar and he translated for everyone else.

"Mr. Will, ask Guruswami for something."

Knowing that Yogi Ramsuratkumar had expressed a wish for some *mysore pak*, Will asked Guruswami for that. Guruswami asked for some flowers and Yogi Ramsuratkumar went out and brought some back. Guruswami held the flowers for a while. Suddenly there was a very intense energy in the air.

"Ready?" Guruswami asked. He handed the flowers to Yogi Ramsuratkumar, who laughed with delight.

"Mr. Will, Guruswami didn't make us any *mysore pak*, but here is one rupee." He held up a rupee with delighted laughter and said, "Go buy some!"

The atmosphere had become ecstatic from the antics of the two old friends. In a little while Guruswami directed the Westerners into a new seating arrangement. He was up to something. This time he placed both of his open palms over both of Will's. The same loud "crack" filled the air, startling everyone. Instantaneously a half-kilo of dates filled Will's hands. Yogi Ramsuratkumar started laughing and exclaimed, "Only in the company of saints will he do this! Somehow in this beggar's company he manages." It seemed like the beggar's sly way of letting them in on the secret: perhaps he was a player in the magic tricks as well.

Then the young woman from Pondicherry handed Guruswami something. He did not even open his hand before he gave it back to her. It had changed to money. Will recalled:

> She and her friend didn't seem much in the mood for this kind of play. And besides it was a pretty bizarre first impression for them—here was a so-called guru who joyously sings his own glorious name and who passes time with friends toying with a topsy-turvy natural order of things. Occult powers and pride—these and others—are all that the books warn us about. They left and must have felt lucky to have gotten away without losing their minds. But of course Joan and I were hoping not to be so lucky!

This is a story that echoes Wendel Field's impression of Yogi Ramsuratkumar, for it is an almost perfect parallel to the tricks and antics of Castaneda's don Juan and his cohort, don Genaro. For anyone who has read Castaneda's books, the similarities are impossible to miss. Don Juan and don Genaro spent many a day and night boggling the mind of the young apprentice, Castaneda, with their madcap wisdom and off the cuff wizardry, in much the same way as Yogi Ramsuratkumar and Guruswami did on these occasions. Their amazing feats as shamans were always aimed toward expanding the awareness of their apprentice and opening up his mind to a new field of possibility. Interestingly, all of the three young American men—Wendel, Caylor and Will—had interactions with Yogi Ramsuratkumar about Castaneda's don Juan. On one such occasion, when Will was talking with Yogi Ramsuratkumar about many different subjects including Castaneda's books, Yogi Ramsuratkumar suddenly turned the conversation around, saying, "Oh, Will, you should go see don Juan. You should spend some time with him!"

"I think he's dead, Swami," Will answered.

"Okay. Then go see Castaneda!"

"Will, shall we go to the temple?" Yogi Ramsuratkumar asked. Taking Will by the hand, the two walked through the streets with the beggar singing sweetly in a childlike melody, "Sri Rama Jaya Rama Jaya Jaya Rama." The presence exuded by the beggar, the intensity of his very being, the immediate proximity to his physical body, the intimacy of the moment created the sense for Will of being on another plane of existence. At that time in the mid-seventies there were ancient palm trees in front of a certain area of the temple. There Yogi Ramsuratkumar was greeted by a number of village women who crowded around him with such innocent and absolute devotion that it brought tears to Will's eyes. The women had bead necklaces they were selling for one rupee, and each one wanted to put a garland around Yogi Ramsuratkumar.

The women prostrated, bending to touch the beggar's feet with tears in their eyes. It was a scene one does not see in the West, and Will was deeply struck by their devotion and total lack of intellectual pretense.

"Will, do you have one rupee?" Yogi Ramsuratkumar asked. "You know, these people have no money. We must help them in some way or other." Will reached into his pocket and pulled out the rupee, then handed it to Yogi Ramsuratkumar. He commented that this kind of occurrence was very common in the beggar's company: "Whatever Swami had, he gave to them, with never a thought for his own needs.

Sometimes Yogi Ramsuratkumar lead Will into the inner sanctum of the temple, where they would sit and talk together, and later walk around the trees by the side of the temple to sit in the very back of the huge complex, closer to the Ganesh shrine that Yogi Ramsuratkumar loved so well. At the same time that Yogi Ramsuratkumar opened his life up to certain individuals, he also played a game of hide and seek. Often when he saw someone coming toward him—whether he knew them well or not at all—he would inexplicably grab his staff, coconut bowl and anything else he had and run swiftly away. This happened to many people, including Will and Joan at times, when they would run into Yogi Ramsuratkumar on the grounds of Arunachalesvara Temple:

> As soon as he would see us in the temple grounds, he would just look up and grab all of his things and run! When I asked him about that later, he always said that he was doing something then, and he constantly had to make adjustments. The work couldn't be interfered with, so then he would

> have to make an adjustment. This was especially true in the temple. He always said that the temple was where he did most of his work. Maybe because the grounds are large, there are twenty-five square acres, a lot of little niches where you can hide and not be noticed and not have anybody bother you. As far as I could figure it out, I think he did a lot of his cosmic work there; the temple was like his work area. And so when people saw him, he wasn't really keen on having a conversation or having any social interaction at that point.

Yogi Ramsuratkumar was often seen leaning on the pillar in front of the Ganesh shrine. There he would stand erect and would not talk to anybody. His Indian devotees knew that there was a standing order from Swami that nobody should go near him or make attempts to talk to him when he was in the temple. He would stand there for some time and the village people would come and prostrate before him, but if a large crowd gathered, he would often run away and hide in the temple complex. One devotee said, "Whenever Swami needed some rest and relaxation, after days together sitting with devotees and talking to them continuously and smoking more than ten packets of cigarettes, Swami would run to his Father's place— Lord Shiva's Temple."

Will spent four months in India at that time, and was with Yogi Ramsuratkumar for eight hours every day. There was also a two-week period when they were together for twenty-four hours a day. It was a rare opportunity, and one that very few Westerners, other than Caylor Wadlington, got to have—to be in the intimate company of the master in such everyday circumstances, and to experience the nectar of good company, of friendship and pure companionship with the master. At one point Yogi Ramsuratkumar came to Will's hotel room every day for five or six days. Will recalled, "It was just the two of us, hanging out, just like brothers, you know. It was really a golden opportunity—it was just completely nice. I'd never had such a good experience before." They had long conversations that ranged across many subjects. Yogi Ramsuratkumar even told Will the history of Tiruvannamalai and the city, and how the temple was built.

There was never a time when Yogi Ramsuratkumar wasn't working. Sometimes Yogi Ramsuratkumar, Will and Joan would stay out all night in the bazaar. When they spent twenty-four hours together they would walk out to a farmer's field near the railway station, and it was on these longer walks that Yogi Ramsuratkumar's staff came into full play. The staff—some peacock feathers and a stick wrapped up together with twine and rags—was used like a divining rod and always carried on long walks. It was clearly an object of extreme significance and importance; no one was allowed to touch it, except perhaps on very rare occasions, and only at his specific bidding. Sometimes as he walked briskly through the streets of Tiruvannamalai with Will and Joan, he would hold his staff up high for a moment then suddenly say, "Stop!" Then out of nowhere a car or a jeep would speed by. The staff seemed to serve in these instants like an antenna that helped him hone in on everyday living in Tiruvannamalai. His play with the staff, like a magician's wand, was mysterious, even mystical, but he never offered any explanations.

One day they were walking together out in the farmer's fields, through the rice paddies and narrow little paths, with the beggar in the lead. It was early morning. The mists were still rising over purple Mount Arunachala. The scene was so beautiful, with the rice in bloom, the mountain looming like a living presence, the green rice paddies and beautiful fields all around, that Will and Joan were looking around in wonder, but at the same time distracted by all this natural beauty. Suddenly Yogi Ramsuratkumar stopped, and Will was so enamored with looking at Arunachala that he ran right into him. Still holding up his staff like a "divine marauder with a lightning rod," Yogi Ramsuratkumar turned furiously on Will.

"Don't even think about God!" he almost shouted, "Just think about what this beggar is telling you to do!" Even a walk through the fields had tremendous importance for Yogi Ramsuratkumar, and paying attention was absolutely necessary if one was to be a companion of the guru and an apprentice or participant in his work. At a deeper level, this teaching lesson points toward the need for not only absolute attention but also absolute obedience to the guru. Many traditions maintain that the guru is even greater than God, because it is only through the guru's grace that one can realize God, a teaching that is reflected in Yogi Ramsuratkumar's forthright admonition, "Don't even think about God! Just think about what this beggar is telling you to do!" It is a basic tenet of any path in which guru yoga is the vehicle.

Oftentimes, because Yogi Ramsuratkumar got so many flower garlands during the day from various devotees, he would put some of these on Will and Joan and send them home at night weighed down by flowers. Sometimes people would say to them on the streets, "Are you going to a wedding?" They would laugh and say no. Yogi Ramsuratkumar was very insistent on these occasions that they wear the flower garlands until they got to their hotel. In his eyes, everything had its particular esoteric purpose and a ritual way in which it should be handled. As Will said, "Swami was always very, very sweet to us, but if we screwed up, then the wrath of God would come down on us. He was a totally, totally humble person, but you never did things your way—you only did it his way. If you didn't do it his way, it was goodbye."

Will also told a story of two German girls, Ute and Else, who were close to Yogi Ramsuratkumar and used to write him. Once when they came to visit they had a friend, Charles, with them. Yogi Ramsuratkumar gave all of his attention to the girls, but never once spoke to or acknowledged the presence of the young man. Not even once did he ask, "Who is this?" He was left completely out of the picture. Later, when Will asked him why he couldn't speak to Charles, Yogi Ramsuratkumar said, "He couldn't have heard what this beggar had to say to him."

During the early seventies Yogi Ramsuratkumar was making regular visits to see Gnanananda Giri Swami at Tapovanum, which had been an important place of refuge for him since the mid-sixties, when he stayed there for six months. In the early seventies he frequently came by bus from Tiruvannamalai to visit. He was always very simple about his needs, and would partake of food only if Gnanananda Giri Swamiji asked him to do so. On such occasions, the village women were responsible for preparing and serving the food. Swami Nityananda, a disciple of Gnanananda Giri Swami and the current spiritual head of Tapovanum, knew Yogi Ramsuratkumar from 1971 until his death. Swami Nityananda remembered Yogi Ramsuratkumar during this time:

> He was known affectionately as Ramji. When Ramji was staying here, he was very free. His moments were always difficult to forecast. But Gnanananda gave Ramji a lot of freedom. There was no question of asking, "Where are you going, how are you coming?" He could come and go and do what he wanted here. He liked this place, in fact.
>
> He sang quite beautifully. Sometimes he would sit beneath a tree and quite a few people would gather around him, chanting "Om Sri Ram Jai Ram Jai Jai Ram" with him. Then he would sing bhajans very beautifully. He was also fond of Giridhara Gopala (for me there is nobody other than Giridhara); it's a Mira *bhajan*. It was Ramji who introduced here the chant that is still sung today during prasad [meals], you will hear them today: "Gnanananda, Gnanananda, Sadguru Gnanananda."
>
> Sometimes he would sit under the big old tamarind tree, and he would be lost in meditation. He would seek solitude sometimes, then sometimes come and be with people. Perhaps quite a few people would ask him about their own personal problems or some sadhana and he would mention something, but in the early seventies his teaching was mainly Om Sri Ram Jai Ram Jai Jai Ram.
>
> Because we were all trained in Veda, he would ask me, "What do you think, Sundareshji? Do you think even the body of Krishna or Rama is a material body like ours?" I would just smile and say, "As long as it is born. . . it is in a human body." Because there is a school of thought that when the Divine comes [into a human incarnation], that particular body is entirely different—it is a divine body. But I used to say, whatever is born is the [same body as ours]. And he would laugh. Because it is *prakritic*—that which comes from nature. The innermost essence of awareness—that alone is reality. The imperishable in the perishable. That's one school of thought, whereas in Advaita we classify everything that is born in time—including the concept of God—everything that is in time is perishable. The imperishable in the perishable. It was wonderful!
>
> He was so fond of the *Avadhuta Gita*, an old traditional chant about one who lives in the absolute without any limitations of the body

consciousness. I was speaking about Yogi Ramsuratkumar immediately after his mahasamadhi, and I was saying that he was an avadhuta—one who has realized himself to be the imperishable. He is in perfect consciousness, the consciousness of the One that pervades everything. His main message was again and again, Ram, Ram, Ram, and guru bhakti—devotion to the guru. That was a really important aspect . . . I remember he was full of love and affection.

When Ramji used to call himself a beggar it was with a different connotation. All monks are beggars—*bhikshus*. We don't care for tomorrow. What we receive . . . is *bhiksha*. We are supposed to love solitude and let God take care of us. So for Ramji to call himself a beggar is one who is always like this—a *bhikshu*. It is a Sanskrit word: when *bhikshu* is translated it becomes "beggar." The Buddhist monks are called *bhikshus*. One who takes *bhiksha*—alms. That's the reason why he always used to have a coconut shell. When he was staying here, he used to go and take *bhiksha* from Mr. Ganapathy's wife, who is no more. He used to go to many houses for *bhiksha*; he would call that lady his mother and take *bhiksha*.

Yes, Ramji talked about Swami Ramdas. He used to say that he came here because it was Ramdas who brought him to Gnanananda Giri first. Yogi Ramsuratkumar said that he had three masters in his life; at the same time, he did not know who his guru was. It was only when Sri Aurobindo and Ramana Maharshi [died] that, when he met Swami Ramdas, he recognized his guru in him, and Ramdas also recognized the disciple in Yogi Ramsuratkumar.

But you know, Yogi Ram would get into a wonderful mood, even when he saw a bit of paper with something on it about guru—he would get into a fine mood, he would be in a sort of a *bhava*, they call it, of devotion, an emotion. He was so fond of Vedic chants, when Gnanananda Giri had his *mahasamadhi*, we used to celebrate every month in his memory, and at that time we used to have Vedic pundits chanting here. He was staying here and in fact we both used to sleep upstairs on the terrace. At that time I had not become a monk, I was not ordained, and he called me by my first name, Sundareshan. I was called Yogi Sundareshan, but he used to call me Sundareshji. He said to me once, "Sundareshji, are you able to see the *rishis* here? I am able to see them." He would say that. And as a token of his respect for the Vedas he would offer pranams to the place where the Vedas were chanted. He held the Vedas in such great love. He loved the Vedas.

During this time the network of friends and devotees who recognized and revered Yogi Ramsuratkumar grew within Tiruvannamalai and in the outlying areas and villages.

The connection at Tapovanum linked him in a practical way into a much vaster network, and some say it was this relationship with Gnanananda Giri and later, the devotion of Rajamanickam that catapulted his work into levels of public recognition that he had previously avoided at all costs.

S.P. Janarthanan wrote down the following story: One time when Yogi Ramsuratkumar went to see Gnanananda Giri Swami in 1972, Gnanananda pretended to be giving orders like an army commander. Yogi Ramsuratkumar appeared from nowhere and obeyed the command, in an immediate demonstration of obedience to the guru. Gnanananda Giri responded by placing *prasad* into Yogi Ramsuratkumar's hand and a palmyra fan on his outstretched shawl. Then Gnanananda Giri said something to Yogi Ramsuratkumar in Hindi, and the two of them burst into laughter. This was the pivotal moment when Yogi Ramsuratkumar would then, from that day forward, carry a palmyra fan with him wherever he went. The palmyra fan became a potent symbol of his power to bless, and even more; it was a scepter, another kind of honing device like the staff, that seemed to draw and channel divine power. It was after this that Yogi Ramsuratkumar was often called "Visiri Swami"—Fan Swami. Janarthanan reports that in the beginning, Yogi Ramsuratkumar would write down important events on his palm fans.

Many people believe that this event of Gnanananda Giri Swami giving Yogi Ramsuratkumar the palmyra fan was the symbolic act that spurred Yogi Ramsuratkumar to take on his universal work and to enter into a more public life; others felt that Yogi Ramsuratkumar was already deeply engaged in this same work, and that it was a convergence of events and vectors in time and space, of which the relationship with Gnanananda Giri was one part. The relationship between Gnanananda Giri Swami and Yogi Ramsuratkumar was reported in a newspaper article in the *Bangalore Express*, September 2, 1979, which also recounted the basic facts about the lives of both Gnanananda Giri Swami and Yogi Ramsuratkumar. After citing Swami Ramdas as Yogi Ramsuratkumar's initiator and benefactor of grace, the article states:

> The Yogi, who is firmly rooted in Gnana, who is ever in the beatitude of the blissful Self-atmarati, had his residence in Tiruvannamalai from 1959. He used to stay wherever shelter was available, under a tree, in the temple precincts, railway station, etc. Many scoffed at him, some laughed at him in derision. But he took them all with a mien full of tenderness and a beatific smile. As time passed on, people realizing his spiritual greatness began to come to him for communion in depth, for darshan, or for seeking relief from pain and suffering. Many found their desires fulfilled and felt that they had met the guide they had been seeking.
>
> Swami Gnanananda whom the saint used to visit often, decided to invest him with a mission. On April 27, 1973, Swami Gnanananda commanded the Yogi to reveal himself to the world, and gave him a palmyra fan and an incense stick symbolizing that a fragrant spiritual breeze would begin to blow from his presence.

> Two days later, in accordance with the plan that Swami Gnanananda and the Yogi had made, the former gave a pair of padukas to Sri Rajamanickam and told him, "Just as Sri Rama gave his padukas to Bharata, I am giving this to you."[1]

This giving of the *padukas* (silver feet that represent the surrender to the guru) was reported by Rajamanickam as the beginning of a task that he was given to spread the word about Yogi Ramsuratkumar throughout Tamil Nadu. Some claim that this task was given directly to him by Gnanananda Giri and Yogi Ramsuratkumar; others disagree, and assert that it was Rajamanickam who took this task on himself. Regardless of how this event occurred, Rajamanickam, a wealthy merchant with many important acquaintances and a large network of friends and associates, was a great devotee and philanthropist who played a very important role in the life of Yogi Ramsuratkumar, as well as in the lives of many other saints and their devotees, such as Mother Mayee of Kanya Kumari.

Mother Mayee was deeply revered in southern India. A true *avadhuta*, she cared nothing for her own survival or well-being, but lived in a state of spontaneous awareness that left her entirely vulnerable to the care of her devotees. She was reputed to be as old as three hundred years, although no one knew for sure. The oldest of the elders in the community could gauge the years of her life only by saying, "My great grandfather remembered Mayamma when he was a boy, and she was very old then." Mayee Ma was silent as she moved down the lanes and back streets of Kanya Kumari, scantily dressed in rags and surrounded by dogs. She had no home and no shelter, but lived on the beach. Neither did she beg for her food, but took only what was given to her by friends, devotees and local restaurants. It was believed that she resided in a state of pure God-consciousness. In her silence she communicated volumes, though it was said that she actually knew many languages. Some believed that she was an incarnation of Adi Parashakti (the primal and ultimate goddess or feminine principle) and that she came originally from Assam, though no one knew for sure.

She was tremendously strong and could swim from the shore near the ancient Devi Kumari temple to the rock where Vivekananda—the famous disciple of Ramakrishna who became a saint, political activist and savior of India—had his legendary vision of Divine Mother. She would often swim even further out, into the deep sea, and she was known to float on the water for hours at a time. She was called by many different names: Mayamma, Mother Mayee, Mayee Ma, Mayee Devi, the Goddess of Kanya Kumari, and simply Mother.

She drew attention to herself by the miracles that she performed without any thought or premeditation. Once a dog was run over by a car and mortally injured; its stomach was gouged open and intestines spilled out on the ground. Everyone ignored the dying dog, but Mayamma came running, lifted the dog onto her lap and gently placed the dog's intestines back inside its body. Within moments the dog came back to life, jumped

1 *The Bangalore Express*, September 2, 1979.

up and ran off. Many people who had ignored her, thinking her insane, began to flock to her for blessings. She never "performed" miracles; they simply happened in her presence.

Gnanananda Giri Swami was also aware of Mother Mayee. Once a devotee had come to Tapovanum from Kanya Kumari and was talking about the magnificent temple on Vivekananda Rock and other stories of the famous town. Gnanananda Giri asked him, "Have you not seen a gem there, a priceless one?" The devotee thought the guru was referring to the nose ring on the deity in the Devi Kumari temple, which local legend says reflects the sun's rays like a diamond, and is so bright that it blinded sailors at sea. Hearing this, Gnanananda Giri smiled and said, "No! The goddess is not inside the temple. She is outside the temple, roaming around in torn clothes carrying an old bundle and accompanied by dogs! She is the precious gem. A priceless one! You should have seen her."

That day Rajamanickam was present to hear these words, which he took to heart by making a pilgrimage to Kanya Kumari to meet this "priceless gem." His name, Rajamanickam, is translated as "king of gems," and this seemed an appropriate pursuit to undertake. At the confluence of the three seas—the Bay of Bengal, the Indian Ocean and the Arabian Sea—he found Mother Mayee, prostrated at her feet and became quite devoted to her. Seeing that she had no place to stay, he constructed a small cottage south of the Ganapathi temple in Kanya Kumari, but it was impossible to keep the divine mother to the hut, and she continued to ramble and wander, blown here and there by the inner winds of the spirit, and she continued to live, for the most part, the untamed life of one who was God intoxicated. In many ways there was a certain kinship between Mother Mayee and Yogi Ramsuratkumar, and in the years ahead Rajamanickam played a pivotal role in linking together these two together.

Gnanananda Giri Swami died in January, 1974. Yogi Ramsuratkumar was called to Tapovanam at that time and stayed there for about a month (although some say it was longer) in order to help the ashram through a difficult time of transition; because of Yogi Ramsuratkumar's influence, those who were connected to the ashram were able to start functioning as they had before. According to Janarthanan, at some point Yogi Ramsuratkumar was referred to on an invitation card as the chief disciple of Gnanananda Giri Swami. This ruffled the feathers of many, so Yogi Ramsuratkumar said that all disciples of Gnanananda Giri Swami were chief disciples, and hence when any invitation was printed, any one could also print his name as chief. When the village started functioning again as of old, an elder came to Yogi Ramsuratkumar and said, "Tapovanam is without a [chief] now, and you are a great saint but you do not have an institution. You have to take up the position as chief of Tapovanam. Gnanananda Giri Swami will not let you leave Tapovanam." But, as Janarthanan wrote, "Swamiji never liked to be a caged bird."

This seemed to be the signal that it was time to leave Tapovanum; immediately Yogi

Ramsuratkumar called Perumal and asked him to arrange for a person to carry his bundles. Perumal and a relative, Trishanku, came to Tapovanum and left with Yogi Ramsuratkumar, carrying the bundles by hand. All they knew at the time was that they were carrying them *somewhere*, as Yogi Ramsuratkumar did not inform them of what he was doing. It was an arduous and sweaty job, the weather being warm, as usual. At one point Yogi Ramsuratkumar asked them both to stop, put down their bundles at the river and drink the water. When the march started again, Yogi Ramsuratkumar turned toward Tiruvannamalai, and it was only then that the two realized where they were going.

All in all it was a thirty-five kilometer walk. The day became hotter and hotter, and it was very difficult to walk with the bundles. As they neared the train station at Thandarai, it was four o'clock in the evening, and they were exhausted. A devotee came running toward them calling to Yogi Ramsuratkumar that he had, with Yogi Ramsuratkumar's grace, constructed a house near the Thandarai Railway Station, and that very day was the housewarming ceremony. He wanted Yogi Ramsuratkumar to come and take food at his house.

"I have been visiting Tiruvannamalai for the past month, but I have not seen you there," the devotee said ecstatically. "Now you have come as a veritable god, and you must come to my house and take food!"

"We are three," Swamiji said, "will there be food for all of us?" The devotee replied that he would arrange everything and food would be ready in one half hour. Saying that, he went to make preparations, then came back and took them to his house to eat.

"First serve food to these two," Yogi Ramsuratkumar said, "and afterward I will take food." The man bought train tickets for Yogi Ramsuratkumar, Perumal and Trishanku for Tiruvannamalai, and then saw them off at six-thirty in the evening.

And so, Yogi Ramsuratkumar adroitly helped the ashram of Tapovanum during the difficult time of transition after Gnanananda Giri's death, but avoided the sticky situation of who would be Gnanananda Giri's successor. Yogi Ramsuratkumar honored Gnanananda Giri in part because he understood that the guru principle is the same wherever it appears in the realized human being. His reverence and respect for the spiritual authority of Gnanananda Giri was unquestionable, but in addition the relationship had its roots in the connection between Gnanananda Giri and Swami Ramdas, the guru of Yogi Ramsuratkumar, and perhaps it is there that we find the strength of the bond between these two extraordinary individuals. Yogi Ramsuratkumar's tremendous love and adoration of Swami Ramdas and Mataji Krishnabai never changed over the years, except to grow stronger; in Gnanananda Giri, he found a link to his beloved master. Because Yogi Ramsuratkumar revered Gnanananda Giri, there was confusion and misunderstanding in the minds of some, who either wanted Yogi Ramsuratkumar to take over after Gnanananda Giri's death, or were threatened by that possibility. Yogi Ramsuratkumar, however, had no intention of doing such a thing. To those who were confused about who his guru was, he would assert clearly, "Swami Ramdas was my master, not Gnanananda," and he was a completely "free bird" that followed a divine wind, wherever it wafted. He had a unique destiny that would lead him far beyond Tapovanum. Arunachala and Tiruvannamalai were his home, and would always be.

Will Zulkowski, who was in Tiruvannamalai and spending a lot of time with Yogi Ramsuratkumar at the time of Gnanananda Giri's death, sheds a slightly different light on the play of events. Yogi Ramsuratkumar never spoke to Will about Gnanananda Giri until his death occurred, at which time he took Will and Joan with him to Tapovanum. That was when they discovered that a significant spiritual leader and benefactor of Yogi Ramsuratkumar lived not far away, and that Yogi Ramsuratkumar was quite deeply connected with him. However, the idea that Gnanananda Giri had initiated Yogi Ramsuratkumar's universal work seemed ridiculous to Zulkowski, because from his experience, "Yogi Ramsuratkumar was constantly getting universal work." Will remembered:

> Gnanananda had just passed. That was the time we were spending twenty-four hours a day with Swami, and we were walking down the street when a car stopped. There was a twenty-minute conversation that happened and Swami turned to us and told us to get in the car. Next thing we know, we're in Tapovanum! We had a room there, and Swami stayed in the room with us, but then after a while he was sleeping on the veranda. At one point he seemed to get annoyed, and finally he said we should clear out—he said he couldn't juggle two things at the same time. So then we decided to go to the Theosophical Society in Madras.
>
> We never met Gnanananda Giri. He had just passed his body, and that's why his disciples were coming to get Swami—because Swami used to go there, and every time he would come to Tapovanum, Gnanananda would call him and say, "Spend one more day." Sometimes it would be weeks, weeks, weeks, weeks, and he'd want to get out of there. So then, he would just sneak out!
>
> But while we were there, right after Gnanananda died, everybody was vacating the ashram—you know, they were all going back to their native places. The devotees [who came to get Yogi Ramsuratkumar] were concerned because everybody was abandoning ship, so they had him come as kind of a stopgap measure. They were sweet people, and Swami said to everyone, "No, no, no. Gnanananda Giri is still here. He's still here. Don't leave. Don't go. This is your place. You've been here twenty, thirty years. Why are you going back to Delhi or Bombay or whatever?" And so he told everybody not to leave, but he changed the format. Gnanananda was very, very strict. They never sang bhajans. They did have the [Vedic] chanting—mantras, in a certain meter, in an almost martial style. Swami was singing, and he got them to sing bhajans every morning at four o'clock when they woke up. He'd then tell them to put in more melody; they didn't have to be so rigid.

About a month after Gnanananda Giri's death, when things had settled back into a workable rhythm, Yogi Ramsuratkumar returned to Tiruvannamalai and his usual routine—from the punnai tree to the streets, the temple, the fields, to the Theradi Mandapam where the temple car is kept and so on. Many of Gnanananda Giri's devotees began to turn more seriously toward him for blessings and guidance. Shakuntala said that before Gnanananda Giri died, she didn't fully understand that Yogi Ramsuratkumar was a great saint; she simply used to serve his food and enjoy singing songs and *bhajans* for him. Prior to 1974, whenever Yogi Ramsuratkumar came to Tapovanum he would stay for one day, two days, a week or more, and then he would go. He was there as a humble mendicant and friend of Gnanananda Giri, not to find devotees. Whenever the devotees approached him with questions he would say, "I am beggar, why are you asking me? I don't know anything."

Shakuntala was one of the devotees of Gnanananda Giri who would take the bus to Tiruvannamalai to see Ramji, where she often found him roaming in the fields. She carried food to him from Tapovanum, and then sometimes sat for hours in the fields, singing songs or walking and roaming around, carrying his staff and fan for him as they walked. It was after Gnanananda's *samadhi* that Ramji began to allow his growing admirers and devotees to formally celebrate his birthday: this first celebration occurred in 1976.

It was an important year in the turning of events around Yogi Ramsuratkumar. On September 26, 1976 Mother Mayee, who never traveled, allowed herself to be taken on a tour to visit devotees in southern India. Accompanied by Rajamanickam, she went first to Tuticorin and then to Kasavanampatti to bless another *avadhuta*, Mouna (silent) Swamigal. She was then driven to Tapovanum, where she paid respects at the *mahasamadhi* of Gnanananda Giri Swamigal; then she went to Tiruvannamalai to visit the Godchild. According to the Mayamma Samajan in Kanya Kumari—a temple built by Rajamanickam during the years 1974–1978 and maintained to this day by his son, N.A. Paramaguru—Mother Mayee and Yogi Ramsuratkumar spent twelve hours in conversation, at the end of which she said to him in Hindi, "Kaam jaldi karo," which means, "Do the work fast." Many devotees tried to guess what was communicated between the two, but the mystery remains: with the exception of her last words, the entire "conversation" was held in silence. On September 28 she returned to Kanya Kumari.

When Will and Joan left Yogi Ramsuratkumar at Tapovanum in 1974 after the death of Gnanananda Giri, they went to Madras for seven or eight months and lived in a flat at the Theosophical Society. During that time Caylor had met a swami in Madras who claimed to be enlightened, but who turned out to be a kind of "black magician," who was interested in using drugs to expand awareness. He promised his followers self-realization through drugs in a short period of time. Caylor, Will and Joan were drawn into this man's field of influence during a time when there was widespread experimentation with psychedelic drugs in the counterculture movement of the West, and it was easy to fall in with an Indian swami who was advocating the quick and easy way to advanced yoga and kundalini openings or "enlightenment," however temporary the high might be.

On the other hand, this was not just a "hippie" experience of the West: the serious use of sacred substances to heighten awareness and induce altered states of consciousness has been used in most ancient cultures for thousands of years, and India itself has a long history of this kind of tradition. The scriptures and tantras of Hinduism are filled with references to *soma* and the use of various psychotropic substances to aid in opening the chakras and unleashing kundalini in the body. Still today there are many sadhus and *sadhakas* of certain sects who use *ganja* (marijuana), hashish, opium and psychedelic mushrooms to enter into ecstatic states. All of this, of course, was well-known to Yogi Ramsuratkumar, and along with his amazing street savvy and natural sympathy with other cultures, he was aware of the drug culture in the West through his connection with the Americans who came to him. It is likely that the experimentation of his young friends was no surprise to him. However, he made it clear to Caylor, Joan and Will that from his view, drugs were ultimately a dead end on the spiritual path.

All three friends were enamored with the LSD experience, particularly after someone sent Caylor some clear "windowpane" acid, which they took in the strong spiritual atmosphere of Tirupati, a city in southern India that is famous for its Vishnu temple. It was a mind-blowing experience in which Will had a powerful vision of a four-armed blue deity. Later he described the vision and asked Swami if it was real. Yogi Ramsuratkumar answered, "Oh yes—that was real. It's not your imagination." Yogi Ramsuratkumar was making the point that the higher realms of existence are very real, and they can be accessed in many different ways, including through mind-expanding drugs, but that in and of itself is in no way spiritual transformation. The process of transformation is arduous, deep and fiery, and it has to be engaged with a sober intention—and, obviously, with the right guide.

In the meantime, the swami in Madras was pressuring Caylor to write a book about the benefits of drugs for the spiritual seeker, who could use them for self-transformation. At the time Caylor liked the idea, and talked with Yogi Ramsuratkumar about it. He counseled them that, although it was all right to experiment some, he drew the line at encouraging others to consider psychedelic drugs as a viable path to God. He was very firm and strict in this regard. He stated unequivocally that psychedelic drugs were a dead end for humanity in terms of real transformation or spiritual evolution. During that time it was not unusual for the subject to come up as certain people would come to ask for help for a friend, perhaps a heroin addict. Except on very rare occasions, Yogi Ramsuratkumar responded to these queries with, "Ah, this beggar cannot help those people involved in drugs." He considered the swami in Madras to be a very bad influence on Caylor.

"Please, don't write that book," he said. "It's not good to delve into that subject. You can experiment for yourself. Experimenting is natural, but don't write about it—don't lead others to it." Although he was spacious and magnanimous with Caylor, Will and Joan in terms of giving them room to learn hard lessons for themselves, he remained strict and adamant about his position, and it became the first and only disagreement between Caylor and the beggar saint.

Yogi Ramsuratkumar had no prejudices or moralistic sanctimony of any kind; on the contrary, he was constantly demonstrating his broad and deep understanding, his wise acceptance, his compassion and vast mind in relationship to every field of human experience. But he knew what was ultimately valuable on the spiritual path and what was not. On one occasion when a boy who went to the Brahmin school at Ramanashram had gotten into trouble and all the adults were righteously inflamed about it, Yogi Ramsuratkumar commented, "Oh, this sinner, this sinner can't point his finger at anybody because he's done the most sins of anybody." Then later he spoke again about the chastised boy, "He hasn't done anything wrong. He hasn't offended God in any way . . . just make sure he doesn't do that again." He was equally spacious and broad-minded about many things. Will once told Yogi Ramsuratkumar the story of his having been in jail, back in the U.S., for a couple of hours when he was arrested for protesting against the Vietnam war.

"Swami, have you ever spent time in jail?"

"Oh, yes," Yogi Ramsuratkumar replied, "This beggar has seen the inside of many jails." And he laughed, probably remembering the many times he had ridden on trains as a beggar, without a ticket. Beggars and sadhus were booted into prison for such offenses. Will commented on this conversation, "He wasn't ashamed. He just said yes, he'd spent many a night in the slammer!"

The whole episode with the swami from Madras came to a peak when Joan's involvement resulted in a painful separation from Will for a period of four months. It was an experiment that had backfired dramatically, creating a great deal of suffering for everyone who was involved. It was an especially traumatic and sorrowful time for Will, and he turned to Yogi Ramsuratkumar for help. Will remembered:

> I went to Tiruvannamalai, and I thought I was going crazy. I thought about killing myself. I wrote Swami [Yogi Ramsuratkumar] a letter and he sent me a telegram: "Come if you think some help is here." And so I went there. I thought I was just going out of my mind—I hadn't slept for days, I hadn't eaten for days.
>
> He took both of my hands and he held them, with his hands over mine. He just held my hands . . . and after that, I was totally normal. And then, he told me to be quiet.
>
> "Silence is the greatest power," he said. " Don't think about anything. Don't worry. Just don't think about anything. In silence is the greatest power. All we need is silence." Within about a month, Joan came back . . .

In the meantime, Will had written to Hilda Charlton, a well-established and highly popular spiritual guide for many on the East Coast in the U.S. at that time. Well-versed in

Eastern mystical traditions, Hilda had lived in India for eighteen years, staying with Swami Nityananda and Satya Sai Baba and traveling extensively.

As many as three or four hundred people would sometimes gather around Hilda at her weekly "classes." She was a revered spiritual elder to many people, including Will and Joan Zulkowski. When Hilda wrote back, Yogi Ramsuratkumar said, "Oh, can I see the letter?"

He merely touched the letter to pick up the vibrations and then said, "Okay. I got it." His understanding of the whole communication was instantaneous. Then he said, "Oh . . . we must write a letter, a thank you to Hilda," and he instructed Joan to write a letter to Hilda saying, "I just want to thank you for all your help." She also mentioned Yogi Ramsuratkumar; he then signed the letter, "Your son, Yogi Ramsuratkumar."

Hilda was in ecstasy for weeks after receiving the letter from Yogi Ramsuratkumar. "My God, a really great yogi has written me! This is a great, great yogi," she exclaimed time and again. "Read that letter over again to me!" The letter was read thirty or forty times. In return, Hilda wrote a letter to Will and Joan, thanking Yogi Ramsuratkumar, which he then asked them to read to him—thirty or forty times.

"Oh, what did that letter say again? Oh please, read that letter to this beggar again," Yogi Ramsuratkumar would insist. It was the kind of interplay that characterized their relationship from the beginning. Those who were observing this exchange recognized a certain rapport that seemed to already exist between the two elders. Hilda Charlton had known about Yogi Ramsuratkumar for some years, making the connection through Will and Joan Zulkowski because of their friendship with Caylor Wadlington. However, she had never met him physically. Her entire contact with him was through her American friends and students who had met him, and after that, on the inner planes. It was after this letter came in 1974 that Hilda said to her group of students, "I've got to meet Yogi Ramsuratkumar."

Back in the States in 1975, Will and Joan returned to Hilda's classes in New York where they told many stories of Yogi Ramsuratkumar to Hilda and the group. She said, "Will, this is somebody I have to meet. I have to meet this great yogi." It was a meeting that would finally occur in 1978.

As Rajamanickam began to spread the word about Yogi Ramsuratkumar, the extraordinary *siddha purusha*, Rajamanickam's family, friends and a wave of devotees in south India began to connect with Yogi Ramsuratkumar. In particular, the story of Rajamanickam and his extended family reflects important facts about this particular era in the life of Yogi Ramsuratkumar. Numerous members of the family had met Yogi Ramsuratkumar in previous years, going back to 1967 when Rajamanickam first encountered the beggar saint. At one point Gnanananda Giri pointed to Yogi Ramsuratkumar and said to Rajamanickam, "He is the guru." Over the years the relationship between Yogi Ramsuratkumar and Rajamanickam continued to develop, and whenever there were problems in his family, he would always strongly suggest going to Ramji in Tiruvannamalai to get help. According to Rajamanickam's nephew, S.P. Janarthanan, Yogi Ramsuratkumar was not noticed by very many people at that time—which corroborates the accounts of the young Americans. Yogi Ramsuratkumar was discovered by divine design, only by those who were guided to him. Clearly this was true among the Indian population as well; people met the beggar saint through word of mouth, by more or less running into him on the streets, by miraculous intervention, and often through connections with friends or family members.

Some years earlier there had been some upheaval in Janarthanan's family when his two sisters both had serious difficulties in their lives. The husband of the elder sister, Madanakumari, had died, which left the family no recourse but to assume the care of Madanakumari and her two children. The younger sister, Vasantakumari, had irreconcilable differences with her husband, Sri Radhakrishnan. Then the two sisters and their children became the responsibility of Janarthanan and his parents, and there had been much anguish and many financial difficulties within the family over these troubles. Janarthanan's parents were "worried beyond words." Rajamanickam, who was very much attached to his sister's family, had stepped in and advised that they visit Gnanananda Giri Swami at Tapovanum, and it was there that Janarthanan's mother, Arumai Nayakam Ammal, had first met Ramji Swami. Rajamanickam worked tirelessly to reunite Vasantakumari with Radhakrishnan, and finally, with the blessings of Gnananda Giri Swamiji, the family felt, their differences were resolved and the couple came back together.

But other problems arose: Janarthanan's wife's younger sister Radhika had married, at Janarthanan's suggestion, the "fair complexioned" Parthasarathy, but they didn't get along well at all, and the marriage was not working out. Rajamanickam convinced Janarthanan and his whole family to go to Gnanananda Giri Swami, who was still alive at the time, for his blessings for the couple. Parthasarathy accompanied them as well, but he had the impression that they were going to a temple. When they arrived at Tapovanum, Parthasarathy assessed the situation and went back to the car. The rest of the group entered the ashram compound to approach Gnanananda Giri, who advised the family to conduct a *paduka puja*, gave them his blessing and sent them on their way.

Even after the blessings of Gnanananda Giri, the marriage continued to deteriorate, and in the spring of 1975 Janarthanan again sought out the help of his uncle and the town elders to reunite the couple. This time Rajamanickam insisted that the family go to Tiruvannamalai to meet Swami Ramji and ask for his blessing for Parthasarathy and Radhika. Remembering how well things had worked out after receiving Gnanananda Giri's blessing some years before, Janarthanan agreed.

In late May 1975 Janarthanan, his wife Vijaya, his mother, one of his daughters, his wife's sister Radhika and his in-laws all made the trip to Tiruvannamalai to meet Yogi Ramsuratkumar and ask for his blessing to reconcile the marital problems of Parthasarathy and Radhika. With the exception of Janarthanan's mother, they had never heard of Swami Ramji before this. Thus the stage was set. They had been advised by Rajamanickam, who was now an ardent devotee of Yogi Ramsuratkumar, to go to the Arunachalesvara Temple around five o'clock—the time when the beggar saint was usually there. They arrived with a dozen well-ripened mangoes and some other fruits. Informing Perumal of their desire to meet Swamji, and that they were relatives of Rajamanickam, they were informed that Yogi Ramsuratkumar had left for the *mandapam* overlooking the bazaar downtown. Hurrying there to catch up with him, they found him right away. Janarthanan wrote:

> By this time Swami Ramji arrived and ascended the steps briskly. His appearance contradicted my conception of a sage. He had, as it were, not taken a bath for days, his shirt was soiled, his hair disheveled and his body full of dirt and bearing the marks of insect bites. [He had] a cheap cloth covering his shirts, and in all his appearance was like a beggar. My mother prostrated before him first, followed by my in-laws, then Vijaya and Radhika.
>
> I thought to myself, "He looks like a beggar. Why should I prostrate before him?" At that time I had two female children, Shobhana and Andal. My mother and Vijaya desired for a male child. My mother kept on imploring me to prostrate before him. Swamiji told my mother not to compel me against my wish. When my mother would not relent, I finally yielded to her request with much reluctance. When I fell at his feet, my mother expressed her desire that I be blessed with a male child. Swamiji blessed me . . . Then Swamiji stuck his hands into his pocket and took out seven lemons and gave one to each of us. There were seven of us and there were only seven lemons [as if he had known before our arrival]. Then he bade all of us to sit and he also sat down.
>
> Because of the extreme heat that had not subsided even at night, it was very difficult to sit down [on the concrete floor] at the mandapam. By this time it drizzled, which released still more heat. "Vijaya came and along with her came the rain!" Swamiji repeated this time and again, and kept on laughing. Every second he would raise his hand and bless us, which appeared strange to us. Then he would squeeze the mangoes one by one and suck juice through a hole made in it. Likewise he finished all the twelve mangoes. "Rajamanickam sends some people to this beggar and provides him with a lot of food to eat!" Saying this again and again, he kept laughing. Nobody but us could ever have seen such a strange spectacle of a person eating so many mangoes at a stretch!
>
> It was nine o'clock at night. I had no experience of sitting in one place for even five minutes at a stretch, but there I had to sit for a long time. Even then, Swamiji would not ask the purpose of our visit. I started pestering my mother to leave, but she counseled patience. Swamiji was

> watching all this, but he did not utter a word. Later I understood that he was actually waiting for the people to disperse so that he could begin the conversation.
>
> By nine-thirty p.m., the shops closed. Then Swamiji shifted his place outside. I informed him of my meeting with Gnanananda Swamiji, along with Parthasarathy. Swamiji then commented, "You need not have come to this beggar after getting the blessing from Gnanananda Giri Swamiji. Swamiji's words will not fail. Nobody would approach High Court after appearing in Supreme Court." Then he turned to Radhika and said, "Don't worry. My Father will keep you. Do tulsi puja continuously for six months, except during the monthly periods. Parthasarathy will definitely accord the respect due you. This is certain. This beggar wants to see Parthasarathy—Vijaya can arrange that," he said further. Then he sang in a very sweet voice, "Jai Hanuman, Jai Hanuman," and bade us good-bye. On that silent night the divine sound emanated from Swamiji to us, [and it seemed to] reverberate all over the world. When we took leave of Swamiji, it was 9:45 at night. As soon as we left that place, I told my mother that it would be the last time that I would ever visit a swamiji.[2]

Leaving Tiruvannamalai, they traveled to Tuticorin where Janarthanan told Rajamanickam about their visit with Yogi Ramsuratkumar. Rajamanickam was delighted and said, "Now nobody need take any steps to set right the estranged relationship between Radhika and her husband. Swamiji himself will take the necessary steps at the right time." He further advised Janarthanan, "If you want your business to prosper, then you may meet Swamiji frequently and if possible, send some donation to Swamiji every month."

Although Janarthanan had said he would not see any swami again after that, when he returned to his home in Bangalore his mind was drawn to thoughts of Yogi Ramsuratkumar. His image kept coming back to mind: "His impoverished external appearance, uproarious laughter, his style of smoking sitting cross-legged—the memories of all these started fleeting before my mind. I had a nagging desire to be able to laugh my heart out like Swamiji often used to do." Once again, it was the infectious joy and freedom, the delight and utter childlike innocence of Yogi Ramsuratkumar that had captured Janarthanan's heart, against all skepticism, doubt or pragmatic sense of propriety. Two months later he was inexorably drawn back to Yogi Ramsuratkumar, this time taking a friend, Shri Dayalan from Sivakasi, who, after listening to Janarthanan talk about Yogi Ramsuratkumar, desired to meet him also.

They reached Tiruvannamalai by seven p.m. and met Yogi Ramsuratkumar at the Theradi Mandapam. He greeted them and right away began to talk.

"You are the person sending a money order from Bangalore for the past two

---

2 S.P. Janarthanan, *A Life With Truth*, unpublished manuscript, English translation by K.S. Padmanabhan.

months?" he asked. "What brought you to Tiruvannamalai?"

"We came to meet you," they answered.

"Perumal—see, they have come from Bangalore to see this beggar!" he exclaimed.

Nayalam wanted to start a new business, and requested Swamiji's blessings, but the beggar advised him not to start a new business immediately. The conversation went on until twelve o'clock at night, but Janarthanan was engrossed in the exchange, and noticed that, this time, there was no boredom or bodily discomfort for him, as there had been the first time they had met.

"Chakravarti Rajagopalachari has translated Ramayana in Tamil, easy to understand for ordinary people," Yogi Ramsuratkumar said several times to Janarthanan, "you should read it whenever you have time."

It was a strange and unexpected request, because in the town where Janarthanan grew up people often spoke derisively about Sri Rama, which had given him an antipathy toward the religious figure. He wasn't happy to hear this recommendation coming from Swamiji, but nonetheless, Yogi Ramsuratkumar kept repeating it while tea was served from a neighboring teahouse, and coffee from the Indian coffee bar. After enquiring about the men's travel plan, Swamiji blessed them and sent them on their way.

Janarthanan returned to Bangalore and thoughts about Yogi Ramsuratkumar became stronger and more frequent. He wrote, "I began to realize that Swamiji was not an ordinary man, but one who lived for others. He was a jewel among men. I purchased Rajaji's book on Ramayana and started to read it gradually. I started feeling strongly that I should also be able to laugh like Swamiji. 'Perhaps, if I started living as per Swamiji's advice, I may be able to do so,' I thought. It was for this reason that I bought the book on Ramayana. One month after my visit to Swamiji, I got another opportunity."[3]

One month later Janarthanan's long-time close friend, Jayavelu, who owned a shop right next to Janarthanan's, was distraught because his mother was seriously ill, perhaps dying, from a kidney ailment and was currently in the hospital. He came to Janarthanan saying that he was making a vow that, if his mother got well, he would shave his head at the temple in Tirupathi. He knew about Janarthanan's previous visits with Yogi Ramsuratkumar, and that Janarthanan planned to go again the following day.

Jayavelu said, "I will accompany you. I will go to the temple and then shave off my hair in the fulfillment of my vow." He also expressed the desire to see Yogi Ramsuratkumar, so they departed for Tiruvannamalai, along with Rajamanickam.

The three left for Tiruvannamalai early in the morning and arrived there by noon to find Swamiji sitting under the punnai tree. It was the first time Janarthanan had visited Yogi Ramsuratkumar when he was sitting there. He greeted Janarthanan and then looked at Jayavelu.

"Who is this person? Why is he sporting a beard?" he asked. Jayavelu introduced himself to Swamiji.

"My mother was admitted in the hospital in serious condition. I had taken a vow in

---

3 Ibid.

my mind that if she gets well, I will tonsure my head in a temple. I am going to Tiruvannamalai temple today for this."

Swami asked, "What was your mother's problem?"

Jayavelu explained everything in detail. The visitors had brought a number of pomegranates to offer as *prasad*. Swamiji asked Rajamanickam to squeeze the juice out of the fruits then drank the juice, saying that it was "intoxicating." It was five o'clock in the evening.

Swamiji had the habit of going to the Theradi Mandapam by five o'clock in the evening, and that day he started walking there with George, Durai, Raja, and Jagannathan all carrying his bundles and the suitcases of the visitors. Rajamanickam carried the sack bundle that Swamiji usually carried on his shoulders. They all started walking through the railway street, and as they walked along Yogi Ramsuratkumar called out, "Mahatma Gandhi Ki Jai! Bharat Mata Ki Jai!" Along the way, at Gandhinagar, many women paid obeisance to him and invited him for coffee at their residence.

"My friends are here with me, I will come another time,' Swamiji told them. Seeing a dirty beggar wearing many garlands of flowers walking along the streets like this with an entourage and bundles, people in the street made comments, calling him a lunatic.

Once the party had left the punnai tree, Jayavelu became restless and bored; he wanted to rent a room and rest, but his suitcase was being carried by Swamiji's attendants, and he had to follow along. As soon as they reached the *mandapam* he asked Swami's permission to leave, but the beggar wanted him to stay and have tea first. Expressing his unwillingness to remain there in every possible way, Jayavelu was ignored by Yogi Ramsuratkumar, who expected him to stay until it was "time" to go. Finally, at ten-thirty that night Swamiji said, "Jayavelu has lost his patience. Take a room on Unnamulai Street and then come in the morning by about ten o'clock." They left and went to get a room.[4]

The next morning Rajamanickam was ready by five-thirty to see Yogi Ramsuratkumar. As soon as Janarthanan was also ready, Rajamanickam asked Jayavelu to get ready, but he said that he was going straight to the temple to shave his head. Feeling this was disrespectful to the sage, Rajamanickam became angry and shouted at Jayavelu, "This is not your house; this is Swamiji's place! Having come here you should not do anything without his permission!" But Jayavelu was determined, and pulling themselves together, the three men then set out to meet with Yogi Ramsuratkumar at Perumal's shop. Arriving shortly, they found that he was sleeping. Despite their protests, Perumal woke Yogi Ramsuratkumar up, who called out for Jayavelu right away. Tea was served to the whole group, then the beggar turned his attention on Jayavelu.

"Where are you going so early in the morning?" They explained that they were headed for the temple so that Jayavelu could shave his head and fulfill his vow. For the sake of clarity, they reviewed the whole situation—the hope that his mother would get well, and that if she did he would go to Tirupati with his family and shave his head. Taking all this in, Yogi Ramsuratkumar turned to Perumal and spoke.

4 Ibid.

"See Perumal, he takes a vow to visit Tirupati and tonsure his head if his mother gets well, and now he is visiting Palam, Tiruvannamalai to fulfill his vow." Saying this over and over again and laughing, Yogi Ramsuratkumar finally made the teaching lesson, saying to Jayavelu, "If you have taken a vow to go to Tirupati if your mother got well, then you should go to Tirupati only. If we take a vow, then we should fulfill that vow in the same manner. God exists everywhere. If we pray to Him saying we will do such and such a thing, then we should do only that. Tomorrow, if your mother falls ill again, then you will feel that it could be because you did not fulfill your vow in the exact manner. So, my friend, you should visit Tirupathi with your family and fulfill your vow."

"But my mother's health does not permit me to take her to Tirupathi," Jayavelu said.

"Don't worry. Give cow's milk to your mother during the journey," Yogi Ramsuratkumar instructed, "Go with family members to Tirupati. Your mother will live till she finishes her work here."

Jayavelu prostrated before Yogi Ramsuratkumar and touched his feet for the first time since he had met him. The group stayed on at the shop for a while, basking in the company of the beggar saint. Janarthanan asked Yogi Ramsuratkumar for a photograph of him. Taking one from a bundle of photos, Yogi Ramsuratkumar gave one to each of the visitors, then he turned to Janarthanan and said, "You said you are running a press. Why don't you print my photos and give them to me? The original picture is with Shri Krishnamurti at Tapovanum. Go with Rajamanickam and obtain the original." This was the second task that Yogi Ramsuratkumar gave to Janarthanan, the first being to read the *Ramayana*. Loading the three men down with *prasad*, Yogi Ramsuratkumar blessed them and gave them permission to depart. Rajamanickam advised Janarthanan, "To take prints of Swamiji's photo is not a small service. One is very lucky to get to do this. Do this job with great care." Right away they went to Tapovanum, obtained the original photograph from Krishnamurti, and left for Bangalore.

A few days later Jayavelu visited Tirupathi temple with his family and fulfilled his vow. Jayavelu's parents had had four children—three sons and one daughter. They started life in extreme poverty, but as their children grew up and the sons began to work and marry, their prospects improved. Janarthanan's account states that in less than a year after Jayavelu met Yogi Ramsuratkumar, his family's fortune improved significantly. Jayavelu's mother was most concerned that all of her children would be happily married before she died, and after the last son was married, she returned to Bangalore, took ill again and suddenly passed away the same evening. As it turned out, Yogi Ramsuratkumar's words, "Your mother will be well till she finishes her work," were affirmed, and made a lasting impression on these new devotees.[5]

By December 1975 the project to print the photos of Yogi Ramsuratkumar was well underway at Shobana Offset, a printer in Sivakasi. Janarthanan's younger brother Premkumar got approval from Yogi Ramsuratkumar after showing him the artwork for the printing. They had taken the task very seriously, using a new offset machine imported

5 Ibid.

from Italy and a machine operator who was excellent at his work. All photos that had been printed on this machine were of a superior quality; it seemed like everything was in place, but the printing was complicated by a number of factors, including the fact that it was the rainy season.

After some false starts, Premkumar brought the photos to Yogi Ramsuratkumar at the end of December. Janarthanan's parents, all the family members, Rajamanicka Chithappa, Tapovan Jayaraman and some others were gathered under the punnai tree at nine a.m. They were excited and in a hurry to show the photos to Yogi Ramsuratkumar, but he did not allow them to open the package until eleven a.m. that morning.

> Swami's eyes blossomed in happiness. Swami was repeatedly asking, "How could you print them so well!" Thereafter, at eleven-thirty a.m., Swami started looking at the photos deeply, without blinking his eyes. He was simultaneously chanting some mantras by holding his beard and rolling his fingers until four p.m. After that he distributed the photos to everyone who was present there, with their names written in his own hand. We had printed two thousand photos. Our plan was to give a few photos to Swami, and to sell all the rest at the best rate, but Swami laid down a condition that these photos should be distributed only by his own hands.[6]

Janarthanan appealed to Yogi Ramsuratkumar to have the exclusive right to print these photos, as they were to be used only for *puja*. The group departed after receiving permission from Yogi Ramsuratkumar to leave. The workers who had printed the photos had asked to meet Yogi Ramsuratkumar, and during their next visit, Janarthanan and Premkumar took them along. When Yogi Ramsuratkumar used to sit under the punnai tree, those who came for his darshan used to bring food in a tiffin. That day there were ten tiffins of food and twenty-two people who sat under the punnai tree on the ridge of the paddy field. Under the supervision of Yogi Ramsuratkumar, food was served to everyone on banana leaves. Yogi Ramsuratkumar was distributing photos at that time, but only to those who expressed their keen interest in having one for the right reasons, so that they wouldn't neglect to use it.

One woman who was close to Yogi Ramsuratkumar for a time asked the question, "There are so many number of devotees to your Swami—why haven't you established an ashram for him yet?"

When Yogi Ramsuratkumar was told about her question he said, "Wherever friends talk about this beggar, those are the places where this beggar lives happily. In whichever house this photo, that is printed at Shobana Offset, is placed, those houses are the ashrams where this beggar happily sits. Wherever even the fermented rice is offered before the photo of this beggar and consumed as prasad, those places are the ashrams where this beggar is willingly seated. Even the torn dresses, if it is placed before the photo of this

---

6 Ibid.

beggar and then worn, those places are the ashrams where this beggar lives with happiness."

Although two thousand photos were printed, only two hundred were given to Yogi Ramsuratkumar for distribution as he saw fit; the rest were stored in Sivakasi. Many devotees—farmers and shop owners—sent letters asking for photos of Yogi Ramsuratkumar. To each of these requests Janarthanan, Premkumar and their friends had to answer, "You must go and have the darshan of Swami, and collect it from him only." Not a single photo was given out other than through his hands, because he had given them the order, "These photos should not be sent through anyone. It should be received from hand to hand." Yogi Ramsuratkumar expected absolute obedience to his request; his vision for how everything should be handled was exact. To interfere with that would invariably bring his anger—however momentary and fleeting—down on the hapless devotee. To be the recipient of that objective wrath was not a position that the devotees wanted to court.

In the early and mid-seventies a young woman named Pankkajam was longing for the spiritual path; only thirty-one years old and married with a family, her desire for spiritual life was so strong that she wondered if she should be *brahmacharya*, that is, take a vow of celibacy. After a strong experience with the Shankaracharya of Kanchipuram, she started wandering around India. In 1975 she came across an article, published in a magazine in Tirupati, that mentioned a certain beggar saint who lived in Tiruvannamalai. She went to Tiruvannamalai with some friends and right away went to the large Arunachaleswara Temple. Walking through the compound, she saw the same beggar, lying inside the Ganesh shrine. Thinking to herself, "Oh, there is that Swami!" he noticed her and raised his fan, then told her to go inside the temple to worship. She went inside the shrine, thinking that she would then see him on her way out, but when she came back out into the light, to her great disappointment, he was gone. Making her way back through the labyrinth of the temple, she found him again at the *mandapam*. Her left to get cold drinks, and she stayed behind.

"Well, my friend, your good name?" he asked.

"Pankkajam."

"You know of this beggar?"

"I read of you in a magazine, Swami."

When he asked her what she wanted, she said, "I want only you, Swami, I want to spend some time with you." Then he laughed his inimitable laugh.

"Pankkajam wants only this beggar, not cold drinks!" he laughed some more. He called over a boy who seemed to be attending him and asked him to bring cold milk and some flowers. He proceeded to ask her many questions about herself: Did she have a family? How many children? How did she spend her time? She answered these questions, and told him that she spent most of her time praying and chanting. Then he asked her to sing some chants. He wanted sixty lines on Lord Shiva from the *Shiva Purana* and some other songs. For one hour she was with him, singing, and as it turned out, she had an extraordinarily beautiful voice. It was the first of many times that Pankkajam would sing for Yogi Ramsuratkumar. After an hour he sent her away, saying, "I will leave now, my friend. You please come often to see this beggar."

People from all walks of life were drawn to Yogi Ramsuratkumar, and connected with him in many different ways. These stories are small singular examples among an ocean of interconnections and interwoven relationships, of how deeply Yogi Ramsuratkumar became involved with his devotee's lives, and how quickly the bond between the guru and the devotee grows. Janarthanan, his wife Vijaya and their family became strong, fervent disciples of Yogi Ramsuratkumar, and were close to him throughout the remaining years of his life. Janarthanan eventually played a major role in establishing the Yogi Ramsuratkumar Ashram, many years later.

While Janarthanan, the nephew of Rajamanickam, and his entire extended family became established devotees of Yogi Ramsuratkumar, Rajamanickam's immediate family was also being introduced to the guru. Vasugi, the daughter of Rajamanickam and Dhamayantri, was fourteen years old when she first met Ramji Swamiji in the mid-sixties. She lived in Tuticorin and went to Tapovanum every month or so with her father. On this particular day she sat at lunch with her father and Ramji Swami. She didn't know who he was, but her father told her later, "This man is a great *mahan*!"—Gnanananda Giri's words when he introduced Rajamanickam to Yogi Ramsuratkumar, and Rajamanickam was now passing this understanding on to his daughter. At the time Yogi Ramsuratkumar was living under the punnai tree in Tiruvannamalai, and from 1972 on Vasugi used to go with her father to visit him there. Sometimes they found Ramji Swami under the punnai tree; at other times he was in the temple or by the vessel shop in the bazaar. He would always ask them, "What is your name?" and then "What is my name? You just repeat." In that way he taught them that it was important to call him Yogi Ramsuratkumar. Then he would say, "Sing some songs."

Some years later Yogi Ramsuratkumar put Vasugi together with her future husband, C.A. Jairaj, who had also met Yogi Ramsuratkumar first at Tapovanum, through his father, P.K. Chellakani, who spoke Hindi and would sit and speak with Ramji Swami in his early years there. After the marriage ceremony of Jairaj and Vasugi, they went immediately to Tiruvannamalai to receive his blessing. He put a flower garland around the neck of each one, blessed them and allowed many photographs to be taken of him with them—a rare privilege. He also gave them a copy of the book by Truman Caylor Wadlington, writing an inscription inside that read: "For Vasuki Jairaj with my best wishes for a happy married life of the holy couple!" His name was signed below, written in Hindi. Then he wrote on their marriage invitation, "My blessings to Chirianjini Jairaj and Vasuki on the occasion of their marriage. Yogi Ramsuratkumar." It was a very happy day, and the beginning of a long close relationship between the beggar of Tiruvannamalai and the family of Vasugi and Jairaj, their brothers and sisters and their families as well. Over the years Yogi Ramsuratkumar gave Vasugi and Jairaj guidance "in each and every little thing." It was

Yogi Ramsuratkumar who instructed them to live in Sivakasi instead of Chennai, where they planned to live.

When she first met Yogi Ramsuratkumar as a child, Vasugi simply listened in wonder to her father's words, "He is a great mahan!" She accepted this as a child accepts what her elders tell her, but after her marriage she came to know the truth of them for herself. About her close relationship with Yogi Ramsuratkumar, she said, "In married we life we have so many problems . . . In every way he guided us. He instructed us, 'You chant the divine name *loudly*!' First he told me to write the name of Shiva, 'Shiva Shiva Shiva Shiva . . .' After 10,000,000 writings of the name, he looked at my notebook and put a check and wrote his name." She continued this practice, called *gurunadhar*, writing the name of the guru, until, spurred by an inner impulse, she started to write the name of Yogi Ramsuratkumar instead. Then she also began to sing and speak the name of Yogi Ramsuratkumar.

Rajamanickam also took his daughter to meet Mother Mayee, the *avadhuta* of Kanya Kumari, who some said was the feminine counterpart of Yogi Ramsuratkumar. Indeed, Yogi Ramsuratkumar instructed Vasugi to celebrate the *jayanthi* (birthday) of Mother Mayee or Mayamma, as she was often called, on May 5 every year.

In the early 1980s Vasugi and Jairaj moved to Sivaskasi eventually to establish a lucrative business venture, a chemical factory; there they spread the word about Yogi Ramsuratkumar and introduced many people to their guru, the Godchild of Tiruvannamalai. A strong and vital network of Indian devotees was quickly growing as the lives of countless numbers of people were touched by Yogi Ramsuratkumar; for many, like Vasugi and Jairaj, Yogi Ramsuratkumar quite literally became a part of the family, and because they came to him with great faith, he guided them in all matters.

The families of Rajamanickam and P.K. Chellakani, the father of Jairaj, all became devotees of Yogi Ramsuratkumar. Jayalakshmi Shenbagaraj, the sister of Jairaj, also met Yogi Ramsuratkumar in the early seventies at Tapovanum, where they used to share food with him. The children in her family were all raised in a convent, and they were very impressed that Yogi Ramsuratkumar spoke English so well. In this way they used to converse with him: "Swami used to give us lots of philosophical guidance. He gave some interesting lectures—just like that, just over a cup of coffee. He used to like my father very much. My father used to follow to the point of Swamiji's word. We saw Swami first in Tapovanam, and then in 1974 and 1975 he would give us darshan under the trees in Tiruvannamalai. He used to have lots of bags and people would carry them around. Whatever people brought, food and flowers and such, he would then distribute to us all. He would give us such a good lecture. He would talk very well, about anything—current affairs and philosophical things. He knew about everything. Swamiji, there is nothing he didn't know."

Sometimes when they came to Tiruvannamalai seeking Yogi Ramsuratkumar, he was nowhere to be found. Then Chellakani would tell his children not to take it to heart in a negative way, but to take it as another way of being guided by Swami. When Kannan, the son of Chellakani's eldest daughter, was in a very bad accident, the family turned immediately to Yogi Ramsuratkumar. The boy was in the hospital in Chennai, and in critical condition. They had to charter a plane to take him to Bombay because they couldn't give the treatment that he needed in Chennai. He was in a deep coma and under treatment for six months, and Yogi Ramsuratkumar instructed Jayalakshmi to inform him daily of his condition through the mail. Every day for six months she wrote a letter to Yogi Ramsuratkumar, and slowly, slowly, he progressed, like a small baby growing. "It was only by Swami's grace. A really great miracle. It's only by Swamiji's mercy."

In 1976 Yogi Ramsuratkumar allowed his Indian devotees to organize the first formal *jayanthi* celebration in honor of his birthday on December 1. It was an auspicious occasion for his Indian devotees, who had been wishing to celebrate and honor their guru in this way for years. People drove in from towns and villages of Tamil Nadu, and it was a high-spirited occasion. There were some other unusual guests as well. A young woman from Finland named Kirsti was staying at Theosophical Society in Adyar that year, where she had met Caylor Wadlington. She, Chanandas and some of the other young Theosophists came to the Deepam festival in Tiruvannamalai in 1976, hoping to meet Yogi Ramsuratkumar on his *jayanthi*. Having read Caylor's recently published book, they all wanted to meet his master.

The first elaborate *jayanthi* that Yogi Ramsuratkumar had allowed his devotees to actually organize and host was quite different than the small, informal gathering that Caylor described in December, 1970. The celebration was held in a hall belonging to a devotee; when the Theosophists arrived, Yogi Ramsuratkumar came downstairs to receive them personally and then guided them upstairs where devotees sat singing *bhajans*. Yogi Ramsuratkumar had heavy flower garlands around his neck. Almost as fast as he could take them off and put them aside, a devotee kept putting more on. Kirsti wrote:

> It was the first time I witnessed a bhakti scene. Yogi looked like a very happy man. He had a twinkle in his eye, and the way he dressed was funny. He felt easily accessible. I felt happy near him. A year later I came again for the Deepam festival and sought him out. The twinkle in his eyes had stayed in my memory along with an inner feeling that I needed to meet this man again.

Another family whose lives became deeply entwined with Yogi Ramsuratkumar was Sarada and Nateshan. They first met Yogi Ramsuratkumar in 1975 during a very difficult time when they were separated because of conflicts within their marriage. A friend told her about a great saint in Tiruvannamalai who might be able to help her. She was reluctant, but her two sisters, Uma and Thilakavathy, upon hearing about this great man, insisted that she go. Sarada went very reluctantly with her sisters and several others, a group of about ten people. It was a Sunday, and first they stopped at Tapovanum, then went on to Tiruvannamalai, where they found Ramji Swami sitting on the verandah of the vessel shop. He seemed very dirty, but there was a strange and compelling force that emanated from him. When Sarada told him about her problems, he stared at her.

"So what?" he said forcefully, "I am having my own problems!" It was an interesting beginning, but the beggar quickly softened and instructed Sarada to do *tulsi puja*. Then he said enigmatically and with an intriguing sense of humor, "Sarada has come to me with a problem, but she is going to solve my biggest problem!" Without having seen her husband Nateshan, he reassured Sarada, saying kindly, "Oh, he is a nice man."

Although Sarada and Nateshan were still separated, the exchange with the beggar saint in Tiruvannamalai gave Sarada the strength to face her problems in a different way. In the company of Yogi Ramsuratkumar, such miracles often showed up in the way he brought harmony and ease to relationship in families, in businesses and in all aspects of ordinary life. One hot Sunday morning in July 1975 when Nateshan and Sarada had been separated for some time and Sarada was staying in Tiruvannamalai with the children to be near her guru, Yogi Ramsuratkumar turned and looked at her.

"Your husband will come and get you and the children today," he said, giving no further explanation. Miles away that same morning, Nateshan had the urge to listen to the radio. He had no TV, radio or anything—in fact, he never listened to the radio—but for some reason he wanted to on this morning. As he was listening, he heard about a religious festival that was happening in Tiruvannamalai and, on a whim, decided to go. It was a long drive, and leaving at nine a.m., he drove all day, as fast as he could.

Finally he arrived in Tiruvannamalai at around six o'clock in the evening. He went to the temple and there he saw his wife, Sarada, with their children, sitting around Yogi Ramsuratkumar. Seeing them there, he realized that he had not been with Sarada and his children for a long time, and his heart was deeply moved. The couple reconciled after that. From that time on Yogi Ramsuratkumar was at the center of their lives: "He changed our lives. From that day onward, everything was Yogi Ramsuratkumar. Whether I am happy or sad, everything is Yogi Ramsuratkumar." Because of the beggar's influence, Nateshan began to have a completely different understanding of the purpose of marriage:

> We get married to realize God. Children are to realize God. Marriage is not for our enjoyment, but to help you worship God. My wife and I had a problem and he mended it, because only a husband and wife can help others, even help a sannyasin. Only a family man can help others. Marrying is for God's sake—everything is for his service. Ramnam, chanting the name of God, is where everything begins. Our problems gave us the opportunity to meet our guru, and he made us one again. They say we are not one inside until we meet our guru—when we meet our guru, we become one.

Nateshan's cousin, Murugeshan, also met Yogi Ramsuratkumar in 1975. He connected very deeply with the beggar, and quickly became an exceptionally close devotee—a story we will return to in Chapter Six. Murugeshan, a very successful businessman, was studying an ancient poem titled "Akhila Thirattu" written by

Muthukutti Swami, a great saint of the Nadar Community who lived some three hundred years before in Kanya Kumari. Muthukutti Swami had prophesied in this poem that he would take a future incarnation as an avatar who would live in Tiruvannamalai and come holding a palmyra fan and a coconut bowl, and would be venerated by the Nadar Community. The description fit Yogi Ramsuratkumar perfectly.

The Nadar Community is a specific caste that, during the time of Muthukutti Swami, were considered low caste and treated almost like slaves. The saint predicted that the Nadar Community would generate people who would become very prosperous in business, specifically in the printing, match-making and firecracker businesses. Muthukutti Swami was persecuted and actually put in prison by the rulers of his time, but as it turned out, the Nadar Community did indeed become very prosperous merchants and businessmen in exactly those fields of enterprise. Many of Yogi Ramsuratkumar's devotees came from the Nadar Community.

Murugeshan was living in Tuticorin, and Nateshan went there once to have *satsang* with him. Afterward Nateshan went to Tiruvannamalai and met with Yogi Ramsuratkumar; when he found out that Nateshan had seen Murugeshji, he wanted to know everything about their time together.

"Tell me in detail," he insisted. Nateshan began to tell exactly what they had done in Tuticorin with Murugeshan, what they talked about and so on. Swamiji was sitting only five feet away from Nateshan, who vividly recalled:

> Swami was laughing like anything! There was no reason for him to laugh like that, and when he laughed like that, everything went away—the people, the room—and nothing was left but a bright light. I could see nothing, no physical shapes, only a personification of light, light, light—like a hundred thousand suns! Just dazzling. Then, after I don't know how long, everything came back. My heart was beating hard, because Swami had showered me with bliss for a split second. I was sitting silently, and then the heart was pumping and I was gasping and breathing heavily, then after a few seconds, Swamiji in a very soft tone changed the subject. He asked me, "How are father and mother? Is father in Tiruvannamalai?" and so on. I couldn't even answer. I tried to tell Swamji that he had given me this state of bliss, and when I tried to credit Swami with this experience, he said, "This dirty beggar doesn't know what place of bliss you are asking me about!" From that I could see that Swami was only in the now. He was only present here and now.

On another occasion Nateshan and Sarada were visiting Yogi Ramsuratkumar in Tiruvannamalai. He had taught them the chant, "Jayathu Jayathu, Jayathu Jayathu, Ramsuratkumar Yogi, Ramsuratakumara Yogi." One night when they were visiting he sent them away at nine-thirty, instructing them to go to the temple early the next morning and then come to see him. They were staying at a hotel, and the next morning they overslept.

Getting up and slowly getting ready for the day, they went to buy flower garlands to give to Swamji. When they went to him, he was sitting alone.

"Did you go to the temple?" he asked immediately. They glanced at each other nervously, then he said, "You overslept." He knew at less than a glance what their morning had been like.

Every few months Nateshan, Sarada and their whole family would make the long trip to Tiruvannamalai to see Yogi Ramsuratkumar. All of their family members started going to see Yogi Ramsuratkumar, and he became involved in all aspects of their lives. When they first met the beggar saint their daughter was one year old; he changed her name to Lakshmi Bai, a queen in Indian history who became a woman warrior and took up the liberation independence fight. He said of their daughter, "She will fight for her rights. She won't be like Sarada." Years later, as a young woman, Lakshmi Bai would fight for the right to marry outside her caste.

The mid-seventies was a time period when numbers of Indians were seeking out the company of Yogi Ramsuratkumar with greater and greater frequency and devotion. Janarthanan's friend Parthasarathy was one of these. Under the stress of marital problems and a lot of family pressures, Parthasarathy finally met Yogi Ramsuratkumar on August 13, 1976. He was urged by the family of his wife Radhika—the relatives of Janarthanan and Rajamanickam—to get help for his marriage from the beggar saint of Tiruvannamalai, but as with the visit to Gnanananda Giri some years earlier, he was highly resistant. At first he only came to Yogi Ramsuratkumar to appease his relatives, hoping that he could somehow deceive the beggar and get his own way in the end—to divorce Radhika and go away with another young woman who he thought he loved.

Nonetheless, Yogi Ramsuratkumar drew Parthasarathy into his sphere right from the beginning. Swamiji was always very particular about having photographs taken; most of the time he simply didn't allow it. Naturally, his devotees wanted to take snapshots of their guru on many different occasions, but he usually said no—with rare exceptions, like the marriage of Vasugi and Jairaj. But there was one famous old photograph of Yogi Ramsuratkumar that he used to give to his devotees, and in Parthasarathy's first meeting with him in 1976, Swami unexpectedly offered this picture to him. Perhaps this was the sign that Yogi Ramsuratkumar instinctively knew that Parthasarathy's devotion to him would weather life's storms and grow to the point of becoming an important aspect of "this beggar's work" in the years to come.

Yogi Ramsuratkumar asked Parthasarathy to read the works of Swami Ramdas, Swami Ram Tirtha, J. Krishnamurti, Rajneesh, Ramakrishna, Vivekananda and others, but he never preached at Parthasarathy or "taught" him directly. Instead, he gave him a tremendous amount of understanding and simply had him immerse himself in the great Indian spiritual philosophers. All of Parthasarathy's friends, the devotees of Swamiji, tried to make the point that he should love his wife Radhika, and spoke of brotherly love, but Yogi Ramsuratkumar gave him space to work it out. Parthasarathy remembered, "They wanted to force me, but Swami never did, he would only talk about the love of the saints, of the saints' biographies, and he asked me to go through several philosophies."

At the same time, Yogi Ramsuratkumar was firm in his counsel. In 1976 Parthasarathy unexpectedly phoned Janarthanan from Gudiyatham and told him that he was in dire financial straits. Janarthanan asked him to come to Bangalore where he lived to discuss the matter. About ten days later Parthasarathy arrived, and the two men discussed the losses that Parthasarathy had incurred in his business. He asked Janarthanan to help him settle all his outstanding loans, or to help him obtain the money from his father-in-law. Janarthanan replied, "You come to Swami in Tiruvannamalai. If he says so, we will settle all dues."[7]

They left right away for Tiruvannamalai in a rental car. At nine p.m. they reached the Theradi Mandapam, where Parthasarathy explained everything about his financial problems in Hindi to Yogi Ramsuratkumar. Repeatedly the beggar said, "Radika is crying. Set her right. Give her a place in your heart and everything will be translated." Janarthanan and Parthasarathy continued to talk with him until late in the night.

Of this period of time, Parthasarathy said, "When I came to Swami he said, 'This is not the place for d-i-v-o-r-c-e.' He would not even pronounce that word! Then he concentrated upon me for four years and he made me empty—totally, financially. He 'made' me wander like a beggar on the streets, and he 'put' me behind bars, in the jail for eighteen days!"

When Parthasarathy was released from his short stint in jail, he came home to terrible financial problems. His wife was gone, he was estranged from his other family members, and he had no one to help him. Standing alone in the streets, Parthasarathy wanted to commit suicide. He drove to Tiruvannamalai to see Yogi Ramsuratkumar, but he was spending time with some other friends and families. Inviting Parthasarathy in and asking him to stay, the beggar saint graciously offered him some food, but Parthasarathy refused and left. He was in deep emotional anguish, and decided that he would commit suicide. Back in his room, he wrote a letter to Yogi Ramsuratkumar, took two boxes of poison and went to sleep, assuming he would die within minutes or hours. But instead of dying, he slept for eight or nine hours. The next morning he woke up and went to the bathroom, and all the poison he had taken was somehow naturally eliminated—effectively drained out of his body. Confused and at a loss as to what to do, he left his room and walked out on the streets of the town.

As he walked around that morning, Parthasarathy soon ran into Yogi Ramsuratkumar who ran toward him saying passionately, "You can go to the top of the hill and jump from there, and see if you will die or not! You don't know, you are under the protection of this beggar!" Parthasarathy was deeply shocked by the whole circumstance: how did this beggar know all these things? The guru had assumed responsibility for his devotee; because of this the guru and devotee become so deeply united that the guru literally crafts the life of the devotee to make a worthy vessel of the Divine. Parthasarathy's life no longer belonged to him to do with as he wished. The shock of the guru's loving and compassionate intervention in this incident was the turning point that resulted in a

7 Ibid.

reconciliation between Parthasarathy and Radhika, who are happily married today. Parthasarathy commented:

> I didn't know anything about jnanis, saints, sannyasins—I didn't know anything about all that. When I first came to Swami I thought, "I can easily deceive this old man, and maybe I could get some money and I could also get married to some other girl." But after he exhibited this power, I began to understand.
>
> His ways were always unique. He would not teach directly to you. He would create a situation and he would force you to learn out of that situation. He would not have you sit before him, like ordinary saints and sannyasins, and make you meditate and force you to remember some names [Vedic mantras]—that was not his way. He always gave you full freedom, and he would create situations that would force you to learn certain things. That's his way.

These stories encapsulate and carry the flavor of these times—wonderful years when Yogi Ramsuratkumar had a certain freedom to move about and work in many different ways. Despite the persecution and political harassment that hounded him, he was filled with God intoxication, and his spirit was free to sing and dance in the streets, up on the holy mountain and in the fields around town. Yogi Ramsuratkumar was a great lover of poetry and music, and he was known for spontaneous ecstatic dancing that had a profound impact upon those who had the opportunity to see it. Perhaps partly because of his great love of music and poetry, his devotees began to write songs and poems for him. Parthasarathy remembered:

> I saw Swamiji dance several times, several times. Oh God, such a blissful dance he could dance! I remember when he took us walking along the railroad track, then he would dance and walk. When he was walking, he was also dancing. He would not seem to be touching the earth. He was walking as if dancing. He would carry his fan, and shake his whole frame, moving, moving, moving . . . all the time dancing and singing. If he saw people making fun of him, he would shout, "Maharaj Gandhi Ki Jai! Jawaharlal Nehru Ki Jai!" He would shout like this, like a madman, and he would raise his fan in his hands and run toward those people who were making fun of him, and they would run away.
>
> But if he entered the city and he heard a car or a jeep or a bus, he would get scared and he would stand in the extreme side of the road. Someone attempted to murder him once; some people had made several attempts to finish him off—some political people, some local thugs. They didn't like any of the Hindi infusion into this land, and Swami at the time spoke only English and Hindi, and there was much trouble at this time.

> There was a tailor at the time; he used to go to his shop as that friend would talk to him and offer him beedies [a type of Indian cigarette] and some tea. So he used to go there, and once he went there and there were more than ten or fifteen thugs in the shop waiting for his arrival. He went there and all the thugs started abusing him. One man started beating him with his stick also . . . Several things happened in this way.
>
> He liked songs, but he was a wonderful singer, also. When he chants a *nama*, sometimes he would sing some songs in Sanskrit or in Hindi—wonderful! He would chant his own name and he would dance. He also used to chant some Vedic mantras. What we chanted depended on the people who were sitting near him; if some Vedic scholars [were there at that time], Swami would request us to chant some of the Vedas. If someone was coming from Anandashram, he would ask us to chant Ramnam—"Sri Ram Jai Ram Jai Jai Ram." If someone came from Sai Baba's ashram, he would ask them to chant some bhajans of Sai Baba. And if Swami's own friends came, he would insist, "Only this beggar's name . . . . . This beggar has said, he wants all the people to remember his name alone."
>
> Once someone asked him, "Swami, why do you ask all the people to remember your name?" Swami turned to one of his devotees and said, "This beggar is also wondering. Why, this beggar asks. Can anybody tell why this beggar asks to chant his name alone?" Then one young boy who was there said, "Swami, all other mantras are very old, Swami, centuries old, but your name is fresh, Swami." Ahhh! He accepted that!

The first song ever written about Yogi Ramsuratkumar was written by Swami Mayananda, from near Pondicherry, in 1972. Mayananda came to know Yogi Ramsuratkumar by accident. Visiting Tiruvannamalai one day, Swami Mayananda was in the bazaar and came to the photo studio, where Yogi Ramsuratkumar was standing. He was immediately attracted to the emanations of the unusual beggar, and he wrote the song right there, on the spot. It became a very famous song and was much loved by Yogi Ramsuratkumar, who asked his devotees to remember it always. In the song Mayananda predicted the destiny of Yogi Ramsuratkumar, saying, "The whole world will bow before you."

During the mid-seventies there were a number of devotees who were beginning to write poetry to Yogi Ramsuratkumar. D.S. Sivaramakrishnan of Tapovanum wrote many poems and songs for the Godchild, and the well-known and loved author of children's books, Ki. Va. Jagannathan, eventually wrote one thousand poems to his guru, Yogi Ramsuratkumar. Before Parthasarathy met Yogi Ramsuratkumar, he used to write songs on a number of subjects. When he discovered that Parthasarathy could write songs, Yogi Ramsuratkumar asked him to write some songs about him. These must have pleased the yogi, because his next instruction to Parthasarathy with regard to the songwriting was,

"Only write songs on this beggar."

Once a famous Burmese saint named Sadophaya, who lived in the U.S., came to Pondicherry. Some friends of Yogi Ramsuratkumar brought him to Tiruvannamalai to meet the Godchild. When he came Yogi Ramsuratkumar said to Parthasarathy, "Oh, he is a great saint, he has a lot of followers in the States and all over the world. We should receive him fittingly. Is it possible for you to write some songs for him?" Parthasarathy had never heard his name and, at that time, didn't know anything about Sadophaya. He said nothing, but later Yogi Ramsuratkumar said to Parthasarathy, "No, my Father says you should write songs only on this beggar, not on anybody else." This was an instruction that Parthasarathy easily obeyed, and there was one song in particular, written by him in 1977, that Yogi Ramsuratkumar always danced to: "Yogi Ramsuratkumar is a blissful beauty, and the temple of Yogi is also a beauty."

In 1976 Yogi Ramsuratkumar had a dog named Sai Baba, who many of the devotees considered to be conscient. Much loved and indulged by Yogi Ramsuratkumar, the dog used to stand and bark at people, as if he was somehow responsible for what was going on! During this time the municipal workers were capturing and killing dogs. Sai Baba disappeared for three days, and Yogi Ramsuratkumar was extremely concerned, but after three days the dog came to the punnai tree. Yogi Ramsuratkumar became very serious and called Sai Baba to come near him and lie down beside him. Then he put his hands on Sai Baba's body, and he talked to the dog in a soothing way.

"Oh, these people are giving so much trouble to this beggar," he said, holding Sai Baba. "They wanted to kill this beggar and they wanted to kill Sai Baba. Oh! My Father is protecting Sai Baba; they need not bother." He kept his hands on Sai Baba for a half hour, then suddenly he turned to one of his devotees and said, "You take Sai Baba to the well and give him a good wash."

Sai Baba always did whatever Yogi Ramsuratkumar asked him to do, and so he went with the man to the well and had a bath, complete with soap. When the man and the dog returned, Yogi asked Sai Baba to lie down again. For the rest of the day Yogi Ramsuratkumar concentrated his attention on Sai Baba.

Parthasarathy remembered that whenever he sat near Yogi Ramsuratkumar, Sai Baba would often come and sit on his lap, and if the devotee pushed the dog away, the beggar did not like it. Sai Baba roamed all over the city and his body was covered with dirt and sores and fleas, and furthermore, the dog smelled very bad. One day Parthasarathy discovered a nice way to keep the dog from laying down on his lap—by putting his hand on its legs and massaging it.

"Oh, he likes it! You do it again and again," Yogi Ramsuratkumar said, watching with a smile. Telling this story, Parthasarathy laughed and said, "For the rest of the day I was massaging Sai Baba's legs!"

On April 4, 1976 the Mahakumbhabishekam, an important ritual event, was performed at the Arunachalesvara Temple in Tiruvannamalai. The temple managers had hoped that Sri Mahaperiyaval of Kanchi, a revered saint, would come for the auspicious occasion, but he was unable to attend. Chidambaram Chattiar, the head of the committee to organize this important religious event, heard that there was a great soul among the beggars in Tiruvannamalai—a yogi of very high God-realization—and he asked Yogi Ramsuratkumar if he would attend the rites. The beggar agreed to be present, but he refused to have his name mentioned in association with the event, or to receive any public honor. Instead, he silently and invisibly walked among the crowd throughout the week during which the ceremonies were performed.

It was during this week that Ki.Va. Jagannathan, the famous Tamil writer of children's stories, first met Yogi Ramsuratkumar. A person with a very deep and great love for God, Jagannathan had come to the temple for the *abhisheka* ceremonies with a friend who told him that there was a particular wise man in attendance; Jagannathan hoped to receive his darshan. They found Yogi Ramsuratkumar sitting surrounded by several friends. He spoke in English mixed with broken Tamil and his frequent laughter shook his whole body. Jagannathan thought, "How is he able to laugh like this?" There was joy in the faces of the people who surrounded him, and he had a large coconut bowl in his hand. Right away poetry began to spill forth from Jagannathan in torrents. Quickly someone ran for a tape recorder to capture the moment. Jagannathan would write many poems in Tamil about Yogi Ramsuratkumar in the years to come.[8]

Another family was introduced to Yogi Ramsuratkumar in 1976: R. Jeyaraj, his wife Sulokhana Jeyaraj and their family were neighbors of Rajamanickam in Tuticorin. Their son, J. Mukilan was eleven years old when, a few years before they heard of Yogi Ramsuratkumar, Rajamanickam advised Mukilan's father to make a trip to Kanya Kumari to meet the *avadhuta*, Mother Mayee. The family made their way toward the three oceans at the southern tip of India along narrow highways lined with huge old tamarind trees. Their lacy leaves spread wide over the road, giving shelter to the regular traffic of wooden carts pulled by white bullocks with horns painted blue and decorated with bells. The further south one drove, the more opulent the tropical backdrop: driving past black volcanic mountains that populated the flat green rice paddies and coconut palm groves like craggy giants.

Walking out onto the beach where Mother Mayee lived they met Rajendran, her attendant, who fed and clothed the Divine Mother and washed her clothes, tending to all of her needs. Every day she bathed nude in the sea, and he would make sure she was dressed again after her bath. As they learned, Mayamma was mostly silent, though she would often repeat exactly what her devotees said as a way of communication.

For example, if Jeyaraj said, "Mother, we'll go and come back," meaning they were leaving but would return in a few weeks or a month or two, if she gave her blessing for

8 Vijayalakshmi, *Waves of Love*, pp. 35-36.

their departure she would repeat what he had said exactly: "Mother, we'll go and come back."

The family of Jeyaraj and Sulokhana became very close with Mother Mayee, and would go to visit her as often as they could, spending their weekends with her on the beach at Kanya Kumari. During her daily sea bath she would take green seaweed and burn it. She often gave Mukilan small things—coins, or a piece of food. These were handed to devotees as *prasad*. She ate betel nut (*pan*) and liked to chew tobacco; sometimes she would chew it and then give it to them, also as *prasad*. If she was given some beedies by one of the village men, she would take a few puffs of those. As a boy, Mukilan once saw Mother Mayee smoking a locally made cigar. Considered an incarnation of Divine Mother, she was moved entirely by spontaneous impulse; at the same time, there was divine madness at work in her, and she could be very childlike, even though she was reputed to be as old as three hundred years. Sometimes when blessing her devotees, she would put *kumkum* or *vibhuti* (holy ash) all over their faces—on their noses, cheeks, forehead.

In December 1976, when Jeyaraj planned to go to Chennai for holidays with his family, Rajamanickam said, "You must go to Tapovanum and to Tiruvannamalai to meet the saint, Yogi Ramsuratkumar." He instructed them to go to the place where the temple car was housed, by the tower *mandapam*. They arrived and inquired where to go, parked their car and then walked to the small house on Sannadhi Street that had recently been procured for the beggar saint. The door was latched, but within less than a minute after they knocked, the door was opened from the inside and there stood Yogi Ramsuratkumar. Standing in the sun and looking inside to the dark porch where the beggar stood, all they could see was a bright, glowing face shining out of the cool darkness of the verandah. Then he opened the outer door, made of iron bars and grillwork, and stepped out into the light. They family *pranamed*, and Yogi Ramsuratkumar asked Jeyaraj, "Who has sent you here?" Rajamanickam, they answered. He asked their names and Jeyaraj introduced himself, his wife and his son, Mukilan, who was now fourteen years old.

"Where are your slippers? If you leave them outside, people will take them," he instructed as he opened the door to let them in. "So you can leave them there," he pointed to the porch as he took them into the inner rooms of the house. As they got to know Yogi Ramsuratkumar, like many others they were faced with the question, "What do you want from this beggar?" They got used to his strange actions, like when held his fan up in the air, as if it was a telephone and he was receiving a call that was coming down from the sky.

Rajamanickam called Yogi Ramsuratkumar "Ramji" and Mukilan's family called him "Swami." Very shortly after they first met him, Sulokhana called him "Ramji Swami" and Yogi Ramsuratkumar corrected her, saying, "Not like that, mother—you have to say 'Yogi Ramsuratkumar.' " From that time on they understood that his name was of great importance.

In 1976 Haragopal Sepuri first heard of Yogi Ramsuratkumar from his friend, R. K. Alwar of Neyveli, who said, "There is a Swamiji who lives under the trees in Tiruvannamalai. Sri V. Ramanujachari took me to him. Swamiji is very simple and lovable. You would certainly like him if you met him." Haragopal was intrigued, knowing the disposition of his friend to be similar to his own, and he eagerly looked forward to meeting this extraordinary person. Ramanujachari and his wife took Alwar and Haragopal to Tapovanum first and spent the night there, then continued on to Tiruvannamalai the next day. Ramji, as they called him, was staying in the house at Sannadhi Street, but Ramanujachari had told Haragopal that he himself had met Ramji under the trees during the daytime, or on the verandah of the shops that were closed at night.

Nonetheless, Haragopal met him at Sannadhi Street, where there were several devotees sitting. The house had a "helter-skelter" look to it: withered flower garlands, sacks full of unknown contents, bottles, tins, drying fruits and so on. When Ramanujachari introduced Haragopal as "a devotee of Kusum Haranath," Ramji immediately saluted that guru, who died in 1927, and spoke of him with honor, which immediately struck the heart of Haragopal. Kusum Haranath had come into Haragopal's life at a time when he desperately needed help, "when I was wallowing in the filth of worldliness."[9]

Thus Haragopal's relationship with Yogi Ramsuratkumar was one of love at first sight; his destiny was fixed in that first moment, the course of his life changed. He began to learn what it meant to have the guru's direct guidance and influence in his life. He wrote:

> During the several meetings with Ramji, what I have observed is that he never attempted to change the path of the devotee but confirmed the path the devotee had already been assigned.
>
> It is enough to say that Ramji is like a Philosopher's Stone which converts base metals into gold. If one wants to seek the Divine, here is Ramji who can put him on course. I do not want to lay emphasis on the miracles or supernatural powers of Ramji. Miracles and Mahatmas co-exist. They cannot be separated. It is true that Ramji has done so many things for me, but the greatest thing he has done for me is pointing the direction in which I should move.[10]

Again there is the theme of how closely interwoven the beggar saint became in the lives of his devotees, the intimacy that he allowed with the serious ones, and his extraordinary ability to meet each person at the heart of his or her concerns. Each

---

9 Haragopal Sepuri, *Experiences with Yogi Ramsuratkumar*, p. 2.

10 Ibid, pp. 2-3.

relationship that Yogi Ramsuratkumar fostered was innately unique, with its native undertones and ways of interweaving the guru and the disciple together.

In the second meeting with the guru, Haragopal was initiated into the name, Yogi Ramsuratkumar, through the pure and innocent circumstances of simply being with the beggar. Haragopal made his second visit to Ramji a few months later, again with Ramanujachari and his wife, reaching Ramji's residence very late in the evening, around eight p.m. He was hoping to spend as much time as possible with the extraordinary swami, and had been told that Ramji himself managed the comings and goings of his visitors. In other words, he expected people to leave him only when he had given them permission, or to stay only with his permission. To his surprise, that night they slept in the same room with Ramji.

Near dawn Haragopal woke up and sat near Ramji, who was still sleeping. Soon he woke up, softly singing his own name, "Yogi Ramsuratkumar, Yogi Ramsuratkumar." Haragopal thought very little about it; it would be some time before he realized the significance of such a thing.

"Go, sit there," the saint instructed him immediately, and he pointed to the farthest point in the room. Haragopal obeyed, and once settled in the new location, he set his gaze again on the beggar. He had noticed that Yogi Ramsuratkumar would allow women very near him and even permit them to massage his feet or light his cigarettes. The guru also allowed some of the men to massage his feet, and he often held their hands for quite some time. Haragopal wondered at this, and why Yogi Ramsuratkumar had ordered him to sit at a distance. Was he testing him, or what? He quickly realized that there was no rationale that would help him in this instance; he simply had to have faith.

Soon everyone was awake, and after their morning ablutions, Yogi Ramsuratkumar ordered coffee for all the devotees who were there. Ramanujachari told Ramji that he and his wife had to go to a relative's house, but that Haragopal would like to stay, and Ramji agreed to this arrangement.

A twenty-year-old young man, Sugavanam, and Haragopal were the only ones left with Yogi Ramsuratkumar. Haragopal worked up the courage to ask Ramji for "spiritual enlightenment." Again Ramji told him to go sit at the farthest end of the room. It seemed that this request for enlightenment, so reasonable and dictated by the thinking mind, did not contribute to intimacy or a deeper resonance with the master. After a while Ramji lay down facing the wall and away from Haragopal, then he told Sugavanam to tell Haragopal to write his request down on paper. Sugavanam relayed the message and Haragopal wrote, "Swamiji, please bless me that I may surrender completely to the Lord and love him like the *gopis* of Vraja."[11]

When Sugavanam brought the slip of paper to Ramji, the beggar asked him to read it out loud, then listened but remained silent. As it happened, on that day the son of a devotee was getting married in Tiruvannamalai. The devotee had asked Yogi Ramsuratkumar to come, and he took a bath and changed his clothes in preparation for the

11 Ibid, pp. 4-8.

ceremony, going into the inside room of the house at Sannadhi Street and then coming back out. As he walked out, he suddenly starting discoursing!

"What is surrender? When we are surrounded by enemies on all sides and find ourselves helpless, then we surrender. As long as there is strength, one wants to fight. Draupadi[12] was also trying to protect herself as long as she could. Only when she realized that she could no longer hold out, she surrendered to the Lord and asked for His help. When this beggar himself does not know how to surrender how can he help others to surrender . . . "

For almost half an hour Yogi Ramsuratkumar talked in this way as he moved about, in and out of the verandah and back into the inside room and out again. Not once did he make any reference to the gopis of Vraja. Haragopal was dazed and could not comprehend the significance of his rambling words. Ramji then gave him a small photo of himself and a piece of fruit, then left for the marriage ceremony at ten a.m. Haragopal reflected, "When in the *Bhagavad Gita*, the Lord specifically instructs Arjuna to surrender to Him and also in *Srimad Bhagavatam*, He instructs Uddhava to surrender to him, why was it that Ramji was speaking in such lighter vein about surrender?" [13]

Around two o'clock in the afternoon Yogi Ramsuratkumar returned to find Haragopal and Sugavanam still there. While he was taking a nap some devotees gathered. Yogi Ramsuratkumar asked Sugavanam to sing the chants in praise of himself over and over again. That evening Ramanujachari and his wife returned and Haragopal left.

Reflecting further, Haragopal began to find wisdom in the swami's words; he began to think of surrender in much deeper terms. Only the Divine can formulate surrender; it is not something that can be achieved by an effort of will, and further, the devotee must "unlearn what all he has hitherto learnt." And secondly, he felt that Ramji's silence on the matter of loving "the Lord like the *gopis* of Vraja" was an indication of his approval of such a path. For Haragopal, it was a rich and thought-provoking meeting with the master, in which he freely discussed classic Hindu religious texts with his eager devotees.

The third time he meet Yogi Ramsuratkumar, Haragopal was alone. This time the mood was different; the beggar saint showed much "intimacy and softness" toward him and asked him to sing the *bhajans* of Pagal Haranath. At one point Yogi Ramsuratkumar commented, "This beggar likes songs on Rama." Haragopal decided then and there to learn a song about Rama and sing it the next time he saw the beggar.

The next time Haragopal visited Ramji with some friends who were Vaishnavites, devout worshippers of Vishnu in the form of Lord Krishna and Lord Rama. They waited for Yogi Ramsuratkumar for hours, and finally he appeared. Offering their *pranams*, they sat down with the beggar.

"Rama, Rama!" he uttered in blessing.

Haragopal introduced his friends as coming from the Iyengar community.

"Haragopal, you are wearing this mark," Ramji said, gesturing to the Vaishnava

12 The heroine of the famous Indian religious epic, the *Mahabharata*.

13 Haragopal Sepuri, *Experiences with Yogi Ramsuratkumar*, pp. 8-9.

namam on his forehead. "Do you also belong to their community?"

"No, no Swamiji, I am a Sudra."[14]

"Oh!" Yogi Ramsuratkumar exclaimed. He placed his palms together in a *namaskar*, bent his head and moved his hands up and down as in worship to a deity. His movements were like a graceful dance, and Haragopal was exalted, exhilarated by the sight of such grace. The guru's statement was a direct reference to the Supreme Being or absolute reality that resides in all people, regardless of class, caste, race or sex; at the same time, from a cultural perspective it was a powerful and even heretical gesture to give such honor to a person of low caste. Yogi Ramsuratkumar's blessing threw Haragopal's mind into a free, childlike state, and he laughed spontaneously with the innocence of a child.

Yogi Ramsuratkumar then took the group inside the house and they settled in the front porch-like room. Some other devotees arrived and the beggar gave them plantains, guavas and gooseberry pickles to eat. In his company it seemed that years fell away along with troubles and burdens, and they were invigorated and brought to life. The beggar then began a conversation with Sampath, one of the Vaishnava friends of Haragopal, asking him about the famous Alvars[15] and the *divya deshas.*[16] Sampath was somewhat orthodox in his Vaishnava thinking. To clarify his concept of Vaishnavism, Yogi Ramsuratkumar asked him to narrate about the *divya deshas* and Alvars. Out of the one hundred and eight *divya deshas*, Sampath could remember only a few.

Yogi Ramsuratkumar then inquired whether Mathura and Dwaraka were included in the sacred sites and Sampath replied that they were not.

"Alvars have sung of the *divya deshas* they had visited," Yogi Ramsuratkumar said, unexpectedly offering a discourse. "Because they have not sung of Mathura and Dwaraka, it cannot be contended that these are not *divya deshas*. These are the places where the Lord[17] lived and sported. Vaikuntha is not somewhere up and high. Wherever there is the Lord, that is Vaikuntha. And wherever the Name of the Lord is sung, there the Lord is also."

For Haragopal, hearing these things so familiar to the religious literature of his tradition from the beggar saint was a revelation. To learn scripture by the book is an entirely different thing than receiving knowledge directly from the living master. Pursuing the discussion further, Yogi Ramsuratkumar asked Sampath to tell them about the Alvars, and Sampath started narrating the story of Tirumangai Alvar, who was the pious king of a small region in South India. He fell in love with a lady and asked her to marry him, but

---

14 The fourth social or occupational division in Hinduism, specifically from the Rig Veda, where the creation hierarchy among human beings is stated as *rajanya* (rulers), *brahmanas*, *vaisyas* and *sudras*, the latter of which were assumed as menial laborers. Their emergence in creation from under the feet of Purusha gives them a lower status and a description of their work.

15 A group of twelve Hindu poet-saints of the sixth to ninth century C.E. from South India who propagated a bhakti-oriented form of religion that became very popular. The Alvars were of mixed castes, a non-Brahmin elite that, through Brahmin support, gained a wide popularity. Nammalvar, the most complex and sophisticated poet of the group, was a *sudra* landlord.

16 Holy places or sacred sites whose praises were sung by Alvars and recognized by the Vaishnavites.

17 Specifically, the Lord Krishna.

the lady put a condition on her assent: the king had to feed one thousand Brahmins every day for one complete year. Then she would marry him. The king embarked on this task, but soon his little treasury was used up.

The king devised a plan to get money to feed the Brahmins: He would disguise himself as a bandit and rob travelers! With these earnings, he continued the feeding of the Brahmins. Almost at the end of the year, Lord Vishnu and his divine consort Lakshmi decided to grace the king. They disguised themselves as rich travelers and passed through the forest, where the king in disguise accosted them and demanded their jewels. Vishnu said, "You must take it yourself from my body!" The king began to remove the ornaments from the body of Vishnu, one by one. At last he came to the silver ring on the toe of Vishnu, but it was too tight to remove, and the king tried to get it off with his teeth. When his mouth touched the feet of the Lord a strange thrill ran through his body, and he looked up, only to see Lord Vishnu and Lakshmi in all their splendor, with their arms raised in blessing. Thus the king received Vishnu's grace and was eventually recognized as an Alvar.

Dwarkanadan interrupted the story and said, going straight to the point, "The Lord showed his human form and blessed the Alvar!"

"The Lord has shown human form!" Ramji interjected with enthusiasm. "Is human form real? This beggar's body is not real. The *vigrahas* (idols) in the temples are not mere stones. They are the Lord Himself." Pointing to Haragopal he said, "To Haragopal, it is not merely the photo of Pagal Haranath and Mata Kusuma Kumari. It is the real Pagal Haranath and Mata Kusuma Kumari."

At the mention of the name of the saint who was so dear to Haragopal, he was thrown into a state of bliss and spontaneously prostrated at the beggar's feet. He realized that although the Shastras[18] say that there is no difference between the Lord and his sacred image (*vigraha*), whether a picture, statue or religious idol, for most people this does not become real but remains a dogmatic teaching, a dry doctrine; now the beggar saint was making this teaching wholly real for him, and he felt the reality of it throughout his body. It was a revelation that can never come through intellectual knowledge, but only through the grace of God.

Ramji continued further, "The idols in the temples are not mere idols. They are the Lord Himself. What do you say Ganeshan?"

"Swamiji, the Lord is everywhere," Ganeshan responded.

"Yes, yes, Ganeshan and Prahlada can see the Lord everywhere. But, for people like us, we have to see the Lord in *vigrahas*. The Lord is very much present in the *vigrahas*. Otherwise, people would not be worshipping Lord Venkateswara for thousands of years, if he were merely an idol."

This exchange is a wonderful example of the master's skill in teaching through dialogue about the classic scriptures. Yogi Ramsuratkumar was masterfully affirming the faith of the Vaishnavites who had come to visit him, while at the same time affirming to

---

18 Hindu treatises on social and religious codes.

Haragopal that the photograph he had given to him was in fact not just a photo, but the actual deity itself, making two different teachings out of one interaction.

"Haragopal, have you anything special to ask this beggar?" he asked after a while.

"I have nothing special, Swamiji. However I have learnt a song on Rama," Haragopal answered.

"Why a song on Rama? You have Pagal Haranath," he replied, turning Haragopal toward the saint who had meant so much to him.

"Swamiji had expressed during my last visit that he likes songs on Rama very much. That is why I have learnt the song on Rama, to sing before Swamiji," Haragopal explained.

"This beggar likes songs on himself. Alright, sing!"

Sampath mentioned that his wife, Amrita, had health problems, and she began to narrate her troubles while Yogi Ramsuratkumar consoled her. Yogi Ramsuratkumar focused his attention entirely on Amrita. He addressed her as "Lakshmi" and asked her to sing some *bhajans*. He swiftly continued to engage her, asking her to repeat along with him the mahamantra, "Hare Rama, Hare Rama, Rama Rama, Hare Hare; Hare Krishna, Hare Krishna, Krishna Krishna, Hare Hare." When everyone else joined in the repetition he gestured for them to be silent. She sang the mantra, and several times he asked her to repeat it again, raising his open palm toward her now and then in blessing.

Haragopal asked the question, "Why does Ramji make the people narrate something, either from the scriptures or life story of mahatmas or saints, or *bhajans* and sometimes any story?" Most people come to the guru riddled with tensions and obsessions, which block the flow of grace or blessings; Haragopal observed that Yogi Ramsuratkumar engaged people in repetitions or kept them busy with activities, and in this way helped them relax and open up to the grace that flowed from him. Until one can relax and become receptive, the flow of benediction is not received and integrated. Haragopal commented: "If one wants to get the benefit of the blessings of Mahatmas, one has to approach with simplicity and openness. Then the Mahatmas can do wonderful things to us."[19]

Caylor spent five years at the Theosophical Society in Madras, visiting Yogi Ramsuratkumar and corresponding with him on a very regular basis. After six years in India, in 1976 it was time for him to finally return to the States. For Caylor, it had been a time of complete devotion to Yogi Ramsuratkumar; to have such intimacy with a great master was the relationship of every young aspirant's dream. At the same time, the guru/disciple relationship is one that challenges the disciple at his or her depths around the core issues of obedience, surrender and trust that are so necessary to guru yoga. Years later, Caylor reflected on his relationship with the beggar king:

19 Haragopal Sepuri, *Experiences with Yogi Ramsuratkumar*, pp. 16-19.

Yogi Ramsuratkumar never taught me any teaching; he didn't have a doctrine or dogma, so it was more of a relationship of just how he nurtured my life and directed me in various ways. He made it really clear at times that I belonged to him, that he belonged to me, that we had been together for untold lifetimes, and would always be so.

He was like my spiritual mother, in the sense that he guided my life, he had expectations for raising me; he definitely had an idea of who I would become, like his son, someday. He was like my mother, and he frustrated me in the same way that an [ordinary] mother would. There were many things that he encouraged me to do which I didn't do, or couldn't do. It didn't unravel like that.

Years later we'd be sitting in a group around Yogi Ramsuratkumar and he would say, "This beggar has tried to tell Mr. K about the Theosophical Society, but he doesn't listen to this beggar." That's just my recollection of how he'd say it. He'd go on and on about it. And so I'd just keep reading *The Secret Doctrine,* but it eluded me—I didn't get that connection. I liked reading the books, but what he was really talking

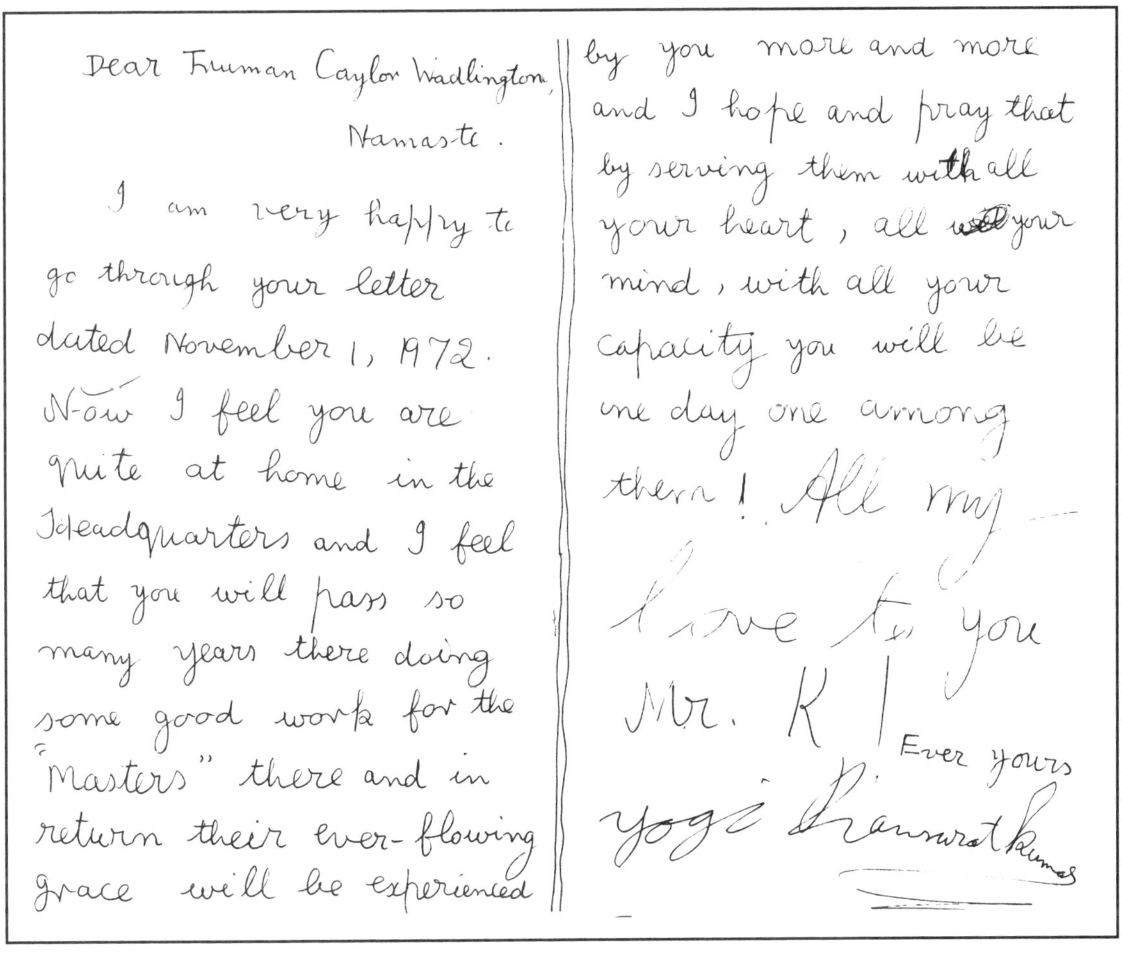

Dear Truman Caylor Wadlington,
Namaste.

I am very happy to go through your letter dated November 1, 1972. Now I feel you are quite at home in the Headquarters and I feel that you will pass so many years there doing some good work for the "Masters" there and in return their ever-flowing grace will be experienced by you more and more and I hope and pray that by serving them with all your heart, all your mind, with all your capacity you will be one day one among them! All my love to you Mr. K!

Ever yours
Yogi Ramsuratkumar

> about? What I didn't realize until twenty years later was that he was thinking of me having a lifelong career there, and I didn't get it until maybe some years ago. He was talking about me working in the gardens; I'd start working in the gardens—the Theosophical Society garden department—and then I worked in the publishing house for a while; then I worked as a part time editor for "The Theosophist." Yogi Ramsuratkumar was actually talking about me working for the Theosophical Society as a career, and I never got it. I hustled away in 1976 and went to Chinese medical school for my career.

It is the way of true masters in all traditions to challenge their disciples with difficult koans or conundrums that must be solved in a way that surpasses the rational mind. Many people on the path of guru yoga have discovered that the kind of teaching lesson that leaves them nonplussed and feeling like they missed an opportunity or failed to comprehend the master is usually the very one that becomes the most powerful in the end—but often in ways that are completely nonlinear and inexplicable. This was indeed a mysterious *lila*, because Yogi Ramsuratkumar had such certainty about the importance of Caylor's relationship with the Theosophical Society.

The consideration of continuing on with the Theosophical Society became an ongoing puzzle for Caylor, and after several years there he found himself drawn in other directions. Caylor spoke about his last meeting with Yogi Ramsuratkumar before he left:

> So, in the end when I left India in 1976, I asked him the very last time I saw him, very pointedly. Oh, it was an amazing meeting. He saw me at the temple and we spent much of the day together at the temple, where he divulged to me information about some of his other teachers, who they were and who looked after him during the months after his enlightenment, when he was completely out of it. He gave me a lot of very intimate details. I have no idea where that stuff came from. And then he walked me down the road a ways and I went back to Ramanashram, thinking that I wouldn't see him for a few years, because I was going back to the States.
>
> Then he showed up at my door at the ashram that night, and he spent a few hours with me in my little bungalow, talking about my plans, where I would be and what I would be doing, who I would be with, and his recommendations for who I should study with—what teachers I should be with. In that process I asked him if he was my guru. He said to me, "Anandamayi Ma is your guru." He knew I was going to see her, and that I have a deep love for her, a profound admiration for her, and I had seen her before. So, he said that she was my guru. In retrospect I see that as sort of letting himself off the hook—or letting me off the hook—but trying to make something out of what we were, what I was trying to make him. So, he sent me off finally to see Anandamayi Ma, and I went back to see her

twice. She has been one of my teachers, like he is, and always will be, all these years.

While I was sitting with him that night I thought to myself: I need to know that he can hear my thoughts in case I ever need him. I need to know he can hear my thoughts. So, while he was sitting there with me, I thought of three personal questions, and I asked him those three questions, in my mind—without any formality or gesture. It was just done as we were conversing. Then he left, and he didn't say anything, but it was a very deeply heartfelt parting, and I felt very complete. I wasn't thinking about those questions at all, but about half an hour later he came back to the door. He stood at the door and one, two, three—he answered those three questions out loud. And then he left.

Two years before Hilda Charlton met Yogi Ramsuratkumar in his physical body, she served as the connecting link in an unusual circumstance between the master and a future disciple, Lee Lozowick, whose relationship with Yogi Ramsuratkumar would become the polestar of his life. It was a relationship that would have widespread effects and generate a far-reaching spiritual influence on many people throughout the world in the years to come.

During the early 1970s Lee Lozowick was a family man with a successful business collecting and selling rare coins and stamps; he was also teaching meditation, parapsychology and metaphysics in a popular program, now called the Silva Method, that was highly successful in the consciousness and human potential movement in the U.S. He quickly became the New Jersey state director of this organization and from 1970 through 1975, he taught thousands of students visualizations, affirmations, psychic and intuitive processes, dream work, prayer healing, and much more. During these years Lee, along with some of his students, began to attend Hilda Charlton's weekly "classes" in New York City and they became close friends.

In the midst of all this Lee entered into a rigorous spiritual practice including meditation, pranayama and various other forms of yoga. He also began to devour the world's classic literature on the spiritual path, both East and West. Lee became more and more convinced that metaphysics and the manipulation of the mind and bodily energy in a self-willed way, even when applied for the good of all, was a dead-end street. His longing for the ultimate state of awakened consciousness, or God-realization, became so fervent that, after a period of solitude and an almost frenzied intensity of spiritual practice, he felt that he had nothing to live for but the impossible possibility of ultimate surrender into the Divine. The momentum of all this passion for God erupted in a night of intense prayer that remains rather shrouded in mystery in the biographical material surrounding Lee Lozowick; rather, all he says is that he woke up the next morning radically changed.

It was the early summer of 1975.

The best way this change could be described is to say that a permanent shift of context had occurred, and the new context was entirely defined by a surrender of his being to the Will of God. Lee's first book, which is the initial outpouring of this experience of transformation, is titled *Spiritual Slavery;* it is a provocative and shocking glance into the wild rush, the great influx of divine energy that he was experiencing as a "newborn"—as an awakened being. This book contained raw, direct statements of spiritual insight—and it had quite an impact on the spiritual scene in the New York metropolitan area. The penetrating force of such a vision was almost too much for those around him to bear. Nonetheless, very quickly people began to draw around him as devotees, and in September 1975 he was compelled to take on the formal relationship of spiritual teacher or guru in relationship to those who were coming for not only teachings, but for the ecstatic mood, the sense of benediction or grace that was generated by his presence, and for the sheer good company of his friendship. Lee spoke in the summer of 2002 about his experience of this time in his life:

> I woke up from a good night's sleep and I looked around and everything was different. It was like being born. Two things were obvious: the absolute radiance and brilliance of everything, and that nobody was seeing it that way. People do not see what is, as it is. And there was tremendous tension between these two things. That tension made me a little mad—not angry, but crazy. One thing that was obvious was that what arose, arose, and there was no movement to do anything about it. Being this great leader of a metaphysical organization [Silva Mind Control], it was obvious to the people who came around that day and the following days that something cataclysmic had happened to me. People didn't like it, because I was crazy—saying very provocative things. The gentle and insightful Lee they had known was gone. There were even private meetings—what to do about Lee?
>
> People had to make very difficult choices: to stay with the process and see what had happened, and what was going to happen, or leave. It was very difficult because I was telling people what I saw about their illusions and their condition of separation with no diplomacy, no tact and no compromise. It was very difficult for people. I wasn't in relationship with anyone—there was no one to be in relationship with! People had to put up with that behavior and I wouldn't shut up. Not only was I a teacher, but I was also their friend, because we were bonded with each other. It wasn't difficult for me because "I" wasn't there! Many people left, but some people stayed during that time because they were able to feel beneath the appearance of things.
>
> So, as I got used to this new context, this new "territory," and I began to figure it out, people were able to be fed, to be nourished by it. We were

> able to engage all three centers—mental, emotional and physical—instead of just the feeling center. . . .
>
> I was a little bit insane in the beginning: God-mad, but still mad. So I was really intense in my communication. I didn't know that I had a master yet, so I credited my [experience] as being directly graced by God. In retrospect I could see that all my discoveries on the path were the direct result of Yogi Ramsuratkumar, and I started to make connections . . .[20]

After this event occurred, Lee read everything he could find on spiritual topics. He prowled the human potential movement for good seminars, and he visited many traditional teachers, including Tibetan rinpoches, Zen Buddhists and Hindu masters. A number of American teachers, all claiming enlightenment, were popping up in the spiritual scene of the mid-seventies. Lee was highly critical of most American spiritual teachers as well as some of the less reputable Indian gurus who came to the States in the 1970s seeking devotees, money and fame. His irreverent attitude, heresies and criticisms of the spiritual scene in the U.S. at this time carried a high profile on the East Coast and drew disapproval from some quarters, but he was befriended by a fellow spiritual maverick and Fourth Way teacher, E.J. Gold, a California-based nonconformist and iconoclast who became an important source of mentorship and support for him over the years.

Another one of Lee's favorite teachers was Hilda Charlton; they met in 1971 and became close friends—a friendship that continued until her death. After the event of his awakening, Lee continued to make the drive in from New Jersey to New York City every week to attend her nighttime "meetings." Hilda seemed to have a natural simpatico for Lee's radical insights and heretical stance, and she easily took him under her wing. When people would complain about his crazy ways and vexing behavior, Hilda would smile and say, "Don't bother Lee, kids," as she used to call her students, "Lee is alright."

Each time Will and Joan Zulkowski returned from India, they would regale Hilda and her students with stories about Yogi Ramsuratkumar. It was through this medium that Hilda developed a very strong subtle rapport with him, although she had not yet met him. She had a way of invoking the presence of many different teachers, living and dead, including Yogi Ramsuratkumar, in her classes.

Lee planned a trip to India in the late fall of 1976 to honor what he felt were the roots of his own realization and the ancient traditions of the East that he had benefited so greatly from. Despite his reputation, Lee was not irreverent when it came to the genuine spiritual path and real teachers, and he felt that he owed a great deal to the teachings of India in particular, and the masters who embodied those teachings. Prior to the trip, Lee visited Hilda Charlton to ask her about places of pilgrimage and tap her vast experience of India. She impressed upon Lee that he must see Yogi Ramsuratkumar in particular, also known as "Ram Ram" or "Ramji," who lived in the southern Indian town of Tiruvan-

20 Lee Lozowick, Hauteville, France, July 1, 2002.

namalai. She told Lee that one could search endlessly for him, but if he didn't want to be found, no amount of effort could reveal him. Those who were meant to find him would come upon him quickly. His company was a precious gift; he was considered to be an embodiment of a very high level of realization. As far as Hilda was concerned, Yogi Ramsuratkumar was coming from "beyond the beyond the beyond." He worked on subtle levels to transform those who approached him in humility and reverence. Yogi Ramsuratkumar's service to those seeking him was to work directly with them on the level of spirit, often performing symbolic actions—in or out of their physical presence—while this inner work was going on.

According to Hilda, if a person was fortunate, Yogi Ramsuratkumar would bless him or her by smoking a cigarette—a ritual by which he literally consumed negative karmic attachments, purifying them as the tobacco burned. The palmyra fan he carried was also a symbolic tool that he used only when working a specific inner transformation in his visitors. Just before Lee left for India, Hilda was talking with Lee and a few of his companions. She held some Indian currency, rupees, in her hands; she wanted Lee to give these to Yogi Ramsuratkumar as *dakshina* (a sacrificial gift). As she spoke Hilda folded, unfolded, and refolded the money from corner to corner and in other unusual ways several times—almost as a nervous habit, it seemed—as she was putting it in an envelope. Finally, she handed the envelope to Lee and wished him and his party a good journey. Lee left with five American students, two women and three men: Janet, Susan, Jimmy, Ian and Pat. Years later Susan recounted to Sita Martin the story of their teacher's meeting with Yogi Ramsuratkumar:

> We all naively prepared for a one-month journey to India. We expected our teacher, Lee, to make fun of people with gurus who taught superficial peace and love. We knew how strongly he had criticized many of the Indian gurus who had come to the U.S. and encouraged large followings. However, what we saw in Lee in India was quite different from what we'd primarily been shown in America. When we embarked, Lee said to us, "This trip is about me being the devotee; you are simply to follow my lead."
>
> We traveled under harsh conditions. We took third class trains, buses—never taxis. We stayed in tiny ashrams and the cheapest hotels. Lee wanted to visit every shrine, guru and ashram that he could in four weeks time—and we did. But he did not bring his usual arrogance and criticism along. He did randomly make wisecracks and jokes when out of earshot of some of the more "famous" gurus we visited. But most of the time he epitomized the good guest and was respectful in an unassuming, invisible way. Nor did he speak of the uncompromising position he'd taken with Americans. He was very simply, "the devotee," to the extent that he referred to himself as such. He asked us to refrain from showing him the usual deference and formal protocol of the devotee to the guru. Our

devotion to him was to be completely internalized. Everywhere he offered obeisance, gifts, prasad. When we visited teachers of Vedanta or gurus, he sat quietly on the floor in the back. He shyly smiled when asked questions about our home and interests and never once said that he was a spiritual teacher in his own right with a good number of students. Those of us who had a tendency to imitate his criticisms and arrogance were now thrown back upon ourselves as we saw Lee honor, respect and actively and enthusiastically participate in ashram functions and Hindu culture.

Disembarking at the bus station, we arrived in Tiruvannamalai to visit Arunachala, the holy mountain and the ashram of Ramana Maharshi and also to visit a special friend who we had heard about from an extraordinary woman, Hilda Charlton, who gave weekly meetings in New York and often shared her experiences of the spiritual path. There was a saint she had never met on the physical plane, but she had the greatest respect for him. His name was Yogi Ramsuratkumar. She had given Lee an envelope to deliver personally to him.

That afternoon we settled in at Ma Talyerkhan's guest house near Ramanashram and set out to look for "Ram Ram" as he was affectionately called. One member of our group stayed behind, which made our number five. Lee—always in constant motion—wanted to hit the streets immediately looking for Ram Ram. We really didn't know how we would find him, or if we would. We met a fellow traveler, a Danish man, who said that he had just spent four months looking for the beggar saint, and only the night before had he finally found him. We were told that you could only find him if you were ready to, and that very few people did.

Arriving in the brass market— one of two places we were told we could find him—Lee told our group to split up and go in opposite directions to look for him. Lee and Janet went together, and Ian, Pat and I went together. Just as the others disappeared a small Indian man stuck his head around a corner and said, "Ram Ram" and pointed in a direction. We followed and turned around to notice that the man had now disappeared. Continuing, we turned a dark corner and discovered a wide set of concrete stairs leading up from what appeared to be a butcher's work spot. At the top of the stairs was a sort of open balcony, partially enclosed with arched columns, but entirely open to the night and whatever the weather might be.

We saw Lee and Janet sitting in the candlelight, and there was a man sitting in rags in front of them. My heart leapt into my throat with nervousness. A young boy, who turned out to be the son of Yogi Ramsuratkumar's attendant, Perumal, ran down the stairs and walked us up to be seated.

The yogi's presence was unsettling and riveting. I stared at him, not knowing what to do, and looked to Lee for any clues. I noticed that there were five cups of hot milk, already placed on the floor and waiting for the

> rest of the party to arrive. Later Lee told us that he and Janet had only just gotten there, and the five cups of milk were already there, waiting for them. It seemed miraculous that he would know to order five cups of milk for five guests, and yet he had obviously ordered the milk before we had arrived.
>
> Ram Ram was dressed in several layers of very well-worn clothing—torn shawls on top of dirty, unwashed shirts, two or three grungy dhotis worn one over the other. His unkempt beard and face were unwashed, and he slouched like a drunkard against the wall. Still, his presence in that place was like a welcoming light, and he was somehow appealing despite the squalor of his apparent circumstances. Indeed, his inner radiance seemed all the brighter for his outward appearance, and he was no drunkard by any means, but had an acute awareness of our slightest moves, as we saw when Pat, one of the young guys in our party, moved his cup of milk after he sat down. Immediately we were aware that he had transgressed some unspoken law. Yogi Ramsuratkumar looked at him sharply, and as the attendant stepped forward and spoke with him for a moment, it seemed that he might even order another cup of milk to replace that one, now that it was "tainted" in some way. Then everything relaxed again.[21]

He greeted the Americans in fluent English. Lee immediately handed him the envelope and announced that it was from a friend of his in America named Hilda Charlton. With childlike wonder, "Ram Ram" took the envelope, closed his eyes and held it between his palms, then opened it. He took the rupees out, passed them from one hand to the other and back again, then unfolded, folded and refolded the bills in a strange movement. Lee and Janet exchanged looks of amazement, because they had watched Hilda perform exactly the same movements with the rupees when she had given them to Lee back in New York. It was as if Yogi Ramsuratkumar was decoding a secret message. At the same time, he seemed very grateful. He turned to Lee's four companions and began to address each one with two questions.

"What is your name?" he asked, and then, "Why are you traveling in India?" Each one answered the first question with his or her name and the second question with the identical response, "I came here to be with Lee." The beggar absorbed this information each time, occasionally glancing at Lee curiously. After he had heard the same thing for the fourth time, he turned to Lee with a smile of amusement.

"You must be Lee!" he said, and he started laughing uproariously. Lee smiled too, appreciating the joke.

Then he gestured with his hand for Lee to come closer, inviting him to sit beside

21 Mirabai Lodro, personal journal, 2002, original version published in *Tattwa Darshana* as, "The Beggar and the Seeker" by Sita Martin, 1988.

him. Lee moved to a place closer, but Yogi Ramsuratkumar kept patting the cement floor of the balcony. Lee would inch a little closer, and the beggar would pat the floor again, then Lee would inch closer, and still the beggar would pat the floor, until it became very funny to everyone. The beggar was working with Lee in a way he had never experienced before; there was a mischievous glint in the beggar's eyes, while Lee looked a bit shy and clearly wanted to do exactly what this exceptional yogi wanted—no more, and no less. At the same time, he was delighted with the exchange and moved by the beggar's joyful play with him. When Lee was close enough, basically sitting right beside him, Yogi Ramsuratkumar turned his attention fully on him.

"What is your name?" he asked.

"Lee Lozowick," he responded. The beggar looked off into the distance and nodded.

"That's Russian, isn't it?" he asked. Lee smiled in assent.

"Jewish, too?" he continued. Lee nodded.

> When the yogi spoke, he had the most wonderful lilting tone to his voice, and his eyes glistened and sparkled in the candlelight. Then, one by one, we were called up to come near him. When he called me up he was able to tell me my father's profession and my mother's disposition. He was so very gentle with me, and I began to weep. Then he put a cigarette in his mouth. I remembered that Hilda said he smoked your karma away. He asked me to light it as he handed me the matches. He puffed and puffed as he looked at me. Then he looked very far away. I sat still and kept lowering my eyes; I felt like such a child in front of this ancient man—much younger than my natural nineteen years. Turning to one of the men in our party, Yogi Ramsuratkumar asked, "How old do you think this beggar is?" The man took a guess and then Ram Ram giggled. Turning to me and saying my name, he asked me how old I thought he was. With eyes wide and incredulous, and the awe I felt reflected in my voice, I said, "I have no idea," clearly meaning that I thought he was timeless. He threw his head back and erupted into peals of laughter. Finally, he gave me some jasmine flowers and gestured for me to put them in my hair, then motioned me back to my seat.
>
> Then he handed Lee the matches to light a cigarette. The match went out. Ram Ram smiled and motioned him to light another. Lee did so, and again the match went out when raised to the cigarette. Ram Ram was giggling now and motioned Lee to repeat the task. Lee did so again and once again the match went out. With each match Yogi Ramsuratkumar became more and more dramatic and humorous, with exaggerated looks of surprise and amazement. This continued until a total of six matches had gone out. After six matches, Ram Ram leaned back and gave Lee a mockingly hard look, as if he was appraising this unusual character. With a gesture, he motioned for Lee to try again. Lee persisted, but seemed a little

> nervous after three or four tries. The tension seemed to be building, as if something of great importance was going on, and yet, it was just a cigarette and some matches! The seventh match stayed lit and the cigarette quickly flared as Ram Ram inhaled. Once again he threw his head back in gales of laughter.
>
> As Lee sat beside the majestic man in rags, there was an intimacy and familiarity between them that surprised me. Ram Ram became very regal sitting there, and the rags draped over him looked like the finest silk. A turban of splendor lay atop his head. Lee's yoga whites—soiled and dirty from weeks of traveling— appeared pristine, while his face shone as he gazed devotedly at the man seated before him. I don't know how long we sat together in communion, witnessing these two looking as if it was a reunion of some kind. After a few hours, Ram Ram seemed to go very deep inside himself, and the attendant boy walked us down the stairs.[22]

The universal symbolism of the number seven, particularly the seven chakras of classical yoga, was not lost on the Americans; if Yogi Ramsuratkumar smoked away the karma of whomever he was working with, then it was quite difficult to find karma to burn in Lee's case, requiring seven matches to finally engage the process. The way Lee and his group had been lead directly to Yogi Ramsuratkumar, as if there was an open door waiting for them, was all so fantastic and enchanted that everything seemed drenched with magic that night. Although Hilda had talked about Yogi Ramsuratkumar quite a lot, nothing could prepare them for the impact he would make. As *mahasiddha*, ordinary circumstances turned into high rituals were Yogi Ramsuratkumar's stock and trade. At times like these he was the magus; he had tremendous skill and mastery in creating moods and spaces in which whole universes blossomed into being, arising for a time, then subsiding —for the benefit of all present. He worked his magic while tea or coffee or hot milk was served, while smoking a cigarette, playing with a child, petting a dog or sitting in complete silence. The silences in particular left one awestruck because they carried a sublime and astonishing power. Anything and everything became the tools of his trade, which was spiritual transformation.

The next day Lee and his group went back to visit Yogi Ramsuratkumar. Lee was very deeply impressed with this yogi. He hoped to spend as much time as possible with him during the next five or six days that he planned to be in Tiruvannamalai, but something happened that cut his plans short. Lee told the story:

> I liked Yogi Ramsuratkumar best of all the yogis and masters I'd seen in India, and I wanted to spend time with him. I was traveling with five other people; one of the three men was nineteen years old and very arrogant, brash and aggressive. We were sitting with Yogi Ramsuratkumar

22 Ibid.

> for the first time, and he gave us a lot of his time and attention. He showered us with attention, in fact, which was really wonderful, so the next day we went back to see him a second time.
>
> Yogi Ramsuratkumar used to carry a palmyra fan all the time and when he blessed people, he would hold the fan up. It was an important fan, given to him by Gnanananda Giri Swami, a famous local guru who had just died a few years before. The next day when we went to visit Yogi Ramsuratkumar, he had put his fan down while he was working. He had me sit next to him again, and he was holding my hand with one hand and using the other one, so he had put the fan down for a minute. It was fairly hot and the nineteen-year-old man picked up Yogi Ramsuratkumar's fan and started fanning him, which was a shocking breach of protocol under any circumstance! But given the particular sanctity of that fan, it was completely shocking and unexpected. Yogi Ramsuratkumar jumped in surprise, and turned to look at the young man. He just let the guy fan him for a minute or two, then asked for the fan back.
>
> We had planned to stay in Tiruvannamalai for five or six days and this was our second day, and I really wanted to spend time with Yogi Ramsuratkumar, but I was so shocked by this completely unexpected assumption of authority that I said to the people with me, "I am not willing to take the chance that something like this will happen again. I revere this saint, and I am not willing to have you, my students, interrupt and abuse his space, interrupt his work. So I am leaving. If you want to remain my students, you leave with me, and if you don't, do whatever you want." So everybody left with me . . . .[23]

Although for Lee the door to Yogi Ramsuratkumar was wide open at this time, and he could have spent more time with Yogi Ramsuratkumar over the next several days, he was responsible for his young student's actions, for better or worse. A strict teacher and a stickler for obedience and respecting those who deserved respect, Lee was unwilling to risk another breach of protocol in relation to Yogi Ramsuratkumar. Nonetheless, a deep connection had been made between the beggar saint of Tiruvannamalai and Lee Lozowick; a transmission had been made that would work its way into Lee's heart over the next few years. It was a strange and unique circumstance—a maverick spiritual teacher from the West with a reputation for profanity and unorthodox behavior, sitting reverently and shyly with an obscure Indian yogi and getting his heart stolen—even though Lee wouldn't realize it fully for four more years.

---

23 Lee Lozowick, *Hohm Sahaj Mandir Study Manual*, Vol IV, Chapter 21, pp. 294-295.

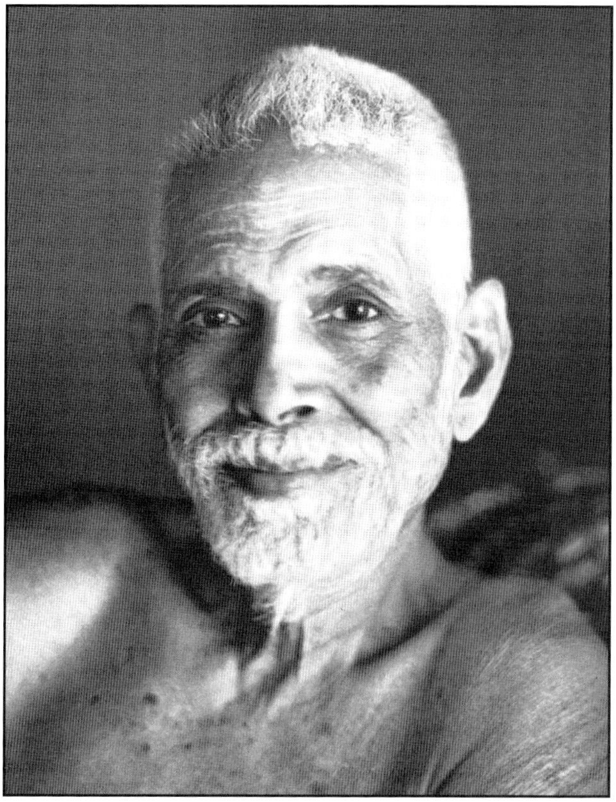

Ramana Maharshi (1879-1950).
(Photo courtesy of Ramanashram)

Sri Aurobindo (1872-1950).

Swami Ramdas (1884-1963)

Swami Ramdas and Krishnabai.

Yogi Ramsuratkumar, 1959.

Yogi Ramsuratkumar on Arunachala, 1959.

Yogi Ramsuratkumar, 1972.

Gnanananda Giri.

Yogi Ramsuratkumar at Tapovanum, circa 1965-1970.

Yogi Ramsuratkumar and Perumal, 1972.

Yogi Ramsuratkumar, 1971.

Yogi Ramsuratkumar on the ghat by the pool in Arunachalesvara Temple, 1973.

Yogi Ramsuratkumar with his attendants, 1972.

In a sunflower field near Arunachala, 1973.

On Mount Arunachala, 1972.

Yogi Ramsuratkumar, 1973.

Near the bus station in Tiruvannamalai, 1972.

Yogi Ramsuratkumar and Truman Caylor Wadlington, at the bus station, 1972.

Yogi Ramsuratkumar and Wendel Field, 1972. Photo by Gita Jones.

Yogi Ramsuratkumar with Sai Baba, 1976-1980.

Yogi Ramsuratkumar at the house of Wendel Field, late 70s.

Jayanthi day, 1976.

Yogi Ramsuratkumar with Janarthanan (right) and family
in a field near the punnai tree, 1976.

The house at 90 Sannadhi Street (far left).

The Theradi Mandapam on Sannadhi Street.

Yogi Ramsuratkumar with Caylor Wadlington and Will Zulkowski (right), 1972.

Yogi Ramsuratkumar with Caylor and Joan Zulkowski, 1972.

Yogi Ramsuratkumar with Vasugi and C.A. Jairaj on their wedding day, mid-70s.

Yogi Ramsuratkumar with Nateshan and Sarada, 1976.

Yogi Ramsuratkumar and Murugeshan, 1982.

CHAPTER FIVE

The Growing Storm

1977-1980

Until 1977 the beggar king made his daily procession around Tiruvannamalai, as steadfastly as the sun makes its way across the sky. With his attendants carrying his burlap bags filled with newspaper, string, dried flowers, cigarette packages, letters, notes, scraps, rags, old clothes and countless other items impossible to name, Yogi Ramsuratkumar went from the punnai tree at the railway station in the mornings, around town to various shops, tea stalls and mysterious rendezvous to which he was called during the day, and by five o'clock in the evening, to the temple, or to the Theradi Mandapam—the balcony where the temple chariot was parked. In 1977 it was there on the balcony, under the shelter of the *mandapam*, that he was often found in the evenings, sitting with visitors.

By this time his devotees were regularly providing food and taking care of him, but for so many years it had been feast or famine—either too much rich food and sweets given as offerings to a saint, or hardly any food at all. Sometimes he subsisted on massive amounts of sugar-laden tea and coffee, as the offering and receiving of these substances as gifts of *prasad* had become a ritual of communion that Yogi Ramsuratkumar enacted every day with his devotees. All this had taken a toll on his health, and it was during this time period, at fifty-nine years of age, that he developed diabetes. He had been living on the streets for almost twenty-five years. No more could he withstand the stress and pressures of waking up on the wet or chilly ground outside the bronze shop to the crack of a policeman's boot in his ribs, or running from cars that careened down side streets or local thugs who threatened his life.

It was time to make the transition from the streets into a place of sanctuary. Janarthanan and many other devotees had begged him for years to allow them to provide a suitable shelter, an actual house for him, and finally he said yes. The house at 90 Sannadhi Street, just across the narrow lane from the Theradi Mandapam, was purchased in 1976, but Yogi Ramsuratkumar refused to stay there for several months. He relented and took up full-time residence there sometime in 1977, but he was still often found in the evenings at the *mandapam* balcony overlooking the streets and the Shiva temple less than a block away, while keeping to his regular movement through town during the day. One could stand up on the platform of the *mandapam* and look down on the door to his house, which opened right off the street, and see the huge front *gopuram* of the Shiva temple as well.

At Sannadhi Street the beggar was able to have both more and less dominion over his own circumstances. While he was able to take shelter from rain and storms and to choose whether to allow people in or not, he was also a lot easier to find. His precious freedom was locked down just a little, and as even more people came to his door, by the necessity of protecting the subtleties and sensitivities of his work, in some ways he had to be more finicky and precise than he had ever been about each small thing around him. At Sannadhi Street one entered into Swamiji's domain; that meant that things had to be done his way. First of all, if a person came who didn't fit into his matrix energetically for some arcane reason or karmic tangle known only to Yogi Ramsuratkumar—and then most likely not by any rational, logical means—that person was promptly sent away. On the other hand, if one was allowed into the enclosed porch or verandah of the house with the other devotees, the unspoken understanding was that one had entered into Yogi Ramsuratkumar's magical chamber, and could not leave until dismissed, or else the alchemy was thrown off—a circumstance that happened all too often and incurred the beggar's incendiary "wrath." Only after he gave his blessing could one leave the house and go on one's way. There were times when people stayed there for two or three days at a time before he would let them go—but these are stories we will return to later in this chapter.

Shakuntala, who was one of the few people who had known Yogi Ramsuratkumar since 1965, still made regular trips from Tapovanum to Tiruvannamalai to see him. Now, instead of meeting him in the streets and roaming the fields with him during the day, or sitting under the punnai tree with him, she would come to 90 Sannadhi Street. Leaving Tapovanum in the morning and traveling by bus through the lush fields and distant rocky mountains that reared up here and there, Shakuntala would arrive in Tiruvannamalai and go straight to Sannadhi Street, where he always admitted her. Yogi Ramsuratkumar would ask the devotees to sit in a queue, and then he would sit opposite them on the floor and ask them to start singing. Often Shakuntala would lead and the others would accompany her. It was a mix of people, strangers and some familiar faces, and they would all sit together. Yogi Ramsuratkumar would then serve milk to everyone. The serving of milk, tea or coffee was continuous, off and on throughout the day—as many as six or seven times a day. Sometimes he would take some in his coconut bowl first, and then serve everyone else. Sometimes he would take one sip from his coconut bowl, then hand it to Shakuntala to drink, but he never explained this or talked about it at all. One simply followed his lead.

During the late seventies Yogi Ramsuratkumar would sometimes instruct people who called him Ramji or Ram Ram, "This beggar's name is Yogi Ramsuratkumar. Remember this beggar, say my name always, and whatever is your problem will get solved immediately." Sometimes he chanted his own name, and also "Jaya Hanuman, Jaya Hanuman." Whenever he sang "Yogi Ramsuratkumar" the devotees would join in with him; then suddenly his mood would change and he would ask Shakuntala to sing his name, sometimes for hours at a time. At other times he would ask her to sing the same song over and over again, as many as ten times.

Very few people shared the extraordinary endurance of the beggar saint to sit in powerful sacred spaces day after day, simply chanting the name of God for hours on end. The floor was hard concrete, and there were no pillows to offer small comforts, nor were there any distractions from the piercing clarity and simplicity of the atmosphere around Yogi Ramsuratkumar. After three to five hours of singing for him, Shakuntala would become uncomfortable from sitting in one place for so long and move a little to adjust her position on the hard concrete floor. Noticing this immediately, Yogi Ramsuratkumar would say very kindly, "Shakuntala, you want to go? Okay, Shakuntala, my Father blesses you." Then he would call someone to bring lime and fresh flowers and *kumkum* in the traditional way of parting with a guest, and offering these to her, he would bless her and send her away.

If she went to Sannadhi Street and Yogi Ramsuratkumar was not there, Shakuntala almost always found him at the punnai tree. He still made his circuit around town, carrying some peacock feathers and his fan, with four or five attendants carrying his burlap bags, and when the day was done, he would return to Sannadhi Street. His pockets were always full of things—string, notes, pieces of paper. Everything that he had "worked" with or handled became imbued with spiritual power, and so it was never carelessly tossed aside, but intentionally placed or kept in the burlap bundles.

To others who came, especially householders and even Rajamanickam on occasion, he would say, "Don't come and see me until my Father orders." This instruction was considered a very great blessing as well: by being told not to come, one would develop more and more devotion through the power of longing to see the guru's form. Things had improved for the beggar saint, but there was still a certain sting from the difficulties of the past as well as the new stresses that were involved in becoming a more public figure—more devotees and people who wanted his blessings meant less freedom to work silently and invisibly, as he had for years, and more responsibilities. His movement through the day, though often still mysterious and fluid, was only slightly hindered by the new circumstance. In the late seventies Yogi Ramsuratkumar spoke about his experience to Janarthanan:

> When this beggar was new to Tiruvannamalai, there were so many people against me. People used to give disturbance to this beggar without any reason. While going and coming on the road, they threw stones, made fun, sometimes even tried to kill. Once when I was walking through the railway line along with my bag, and a policeman came and told me, "I doubt that you are having illegal items in your bag. I will allow you to proceed only after you open and show your bag." He allowed me to go only after I showed him my bag.
>
> During this time a friend, Truman Caylor Wadlington, had visited from overseas. At that time he was a young man of about nineteen years. He had no experience of writing any book prior to that. This beggar made

> him to sit beside him, encouraged him, and gave information that should be in the book, made him to write it and got it printed at Chennai. After the book came out, this beggar personally distributed this book in each and every shop in Tiruvannamalai. Thereafter the disturbances reduced a little. This beggar was waiting to implement the sayings of Swami Mayananda in his song, "The world will adore you, and worship your form." You came, printed this beggar's photograph elegantly on your Shobana Offset, and gave them to me. This made a number of people become the friends of this beggar who took a major part in expressing their opposition to me.
>
> Yesterday also two friends came to Sannadhi Street house to meet this beggar. When they knocked on the door, this beggar came out to open the door. One of them was calling to the other, "Come, let us go." The other replied, "Wait! I will have the darshan of Swami and then come." The former took him away saying, "Is he Swami? Do you want to have the darshan of him? Come. I will tell you about him." Both of them have specifically planned as to how they had to behave with this beggar, and then they came. Do you see how carefully this beggar has to work?[1]

At this time there were also many Indian devotees who came to Yogi Ramsuratkumar with the sincere wish to understand the guru's ways and learn from him. There were also a growing number of devotees from Sivakasi, Tuticorin and other places in Tamil Nadu who came to visit Yogi Ramsuratkumar as often as possible. Shankara Rajulu of Madurai was one.

In 1978 Shankara Rajulu had a post as principal of the Arts College in Tiruvannamalai when he read about Yogi Ramsuratkumar in a magazine. At the time he wanted to get a transfer to a place nearer to Madurai, his family home, and for this purpose he wanted to meet the director of the college. Having read about this great mahatma, Yogi Ramsuratkumar, he thought he would go to get his blessings for the transfer first, and it was only for that purpose that he sought out the saint. Once he was there, the beggar talked freely with him, welcomed him and drew him in. He asked him what subject he taught, and Shankara Rajulu answered that he was a professor of Tamil.

"Have you read the *Arunachala Puranam*?" the beggar asked right away.

"No Swami I have not read it, but I will read it," Shankara Rajulu answered.

"Oh better, it's good to read it," the swami said, rather enigmatically. The very next day Rajulu was at the college. The professors there had arranged a function for the new principal, and then, according to custom, they came and honored Rajulu with a garland and a mango. They also gave him a book, and to his surprise, when he opened the gift, it was the *Arunachala Puranam*! His thoughts flew to the beggar saint he'd met just the day before. It was too extraordinary to be a mere coincidence.

Living in Tiruvannamalai for his work, Rajulu was separated from his family in

---

1 S.P. Janarthanan, *A Life With Truth*, unpublished manuscript.

Madurai and missed them quite a lot. He had been visiting Yogi Ramsuratkumar regularly when one day the beggar said, "You are alone? You can sleep with this beggar!" Rajulu was thrilled; he realized that most devotees only got to have a glimpse of the beggar, or perhaps they talked with him for a few minutes or visited for some hours, but now Rajulu would get to spend entire nights with him. He immediately agreed, and began to go every evening, after his work, to the house on Sannadhi Street. Rajulu said, "During those periods he used to talk about various things. I then took them all to be casual speeches, but now I realize that, if I recall all of them, they were expected to perfect me—they were all directed towards my perfection."

On another occasion Yogi Ramsuratkumar asked Rajulu if he had read the *Bhagavad Gita*. Rajulu responded that he was not a Sanskrit scholar and had not read it.

"It's better to read it," the yogi said.

"Yes, Swami, I'll read it," he answered. Rajulu had been going to see the beggar for two or three months at the time. The yogi further instructed him by saying that if he could not read the original text in Sanskrit, there was also a very good version in Tamil, with some essays included.

"You may read them also," Yogi Ramsuratkumar said. Rajulu readily agreed, and when he went to Madurai for the holidays he planned to buy the book. While he was casually searching for another book among his private collection, a book fell off the shelf and onto the floor at his feet. He bent down to pick it up and was shocked to find that it was the very book Yogi Ramsuratkumar had suggested that he read—the Tamil translation of the *Bhagavad Gita* with essays. He assumed that he must have purchased the book some years back, put it into his collection for future reference and forgotten about it. Rajulu had a very large collection of books, and out of those hundreds of books, that book was the one that fell out! Immediately he realized that Yogi Ramsuratkumar was expecting him to read it.

"Have you read the *Gita*?" the yogi asked upon seeing the professor. Rajulu then relayed the story of the book, which was in his own collection, literally finding him. Yogi Ramsuratkumar said, "Oh, that is Father's will." These kinds of extraordinary synchronicities and small miracles happened constantly for those who were keeping company with Yogi Ramsuratkumar, but he never took any credit for them. His usual comment on these occasions was, "Father's will," or "This beggar has done nothing—it is all Father's will." In fact the simple beggar never sought out any demonstration of the miraculous; it just arose spontaneously around him.

During the late 1970s Rajulu spent a great deal of time with Yogi Ramsuratkumar, and it was in the ordinary circumstanccs of thcsc days and nights with the master that Rajulu realized that everything the master did—even the simplest comment, gesture, movement or action—had meaning. Within all of his ordinary manifestations and interactions with his friends and devotees, the Godchild was slowly, slowly transforming those around him with his constant demonstration of kindness, love, compassion and acceptance. He never alluded to the sacred nature of his ordinary circumstances; instead, he made Rajulu feel as if there was nothing significant going on—it was merely a matter of daily routine. But whenever one of his devotees performed any small work for him, the yogi would say with great sincerity, "Thank you, you have done a great service to this beggar."

As Shankara Rajulu began to sleep every night at the house at 90 Sannadhi Street over an extended period of time, he shared moments of tremendous intimacy with the beggar saint and discovered more about the simple and austere way he lived. There were no beds, only thin mats on the floor, and no pillows. After a long day of being with people—smoking, blessing, talking, sometimes walking all around the city—the yogi would retire for the evening sometime between ten-thirty and midnight. Five minutes after he lay down, he would begin to talk on various subjects.

"You are not used to this—lie down, you have this for your pillow," Yogi Ramsuratkumar said to Rajulu, handing him a length of cloth. It was a simple gesture from a beggar, not associated with anything grand and certainly not much of a practical comfort as far as pillows go, but the gesture carried with it such care, affection and sweet regard for the other that it was more meaningful than a feather pillow. Shankara Rajulu remembered:

> That kind of personal care and attention he used to take for all his devotees. All his devotees can give hundreds of similar experiences. By the first light of day, he would order coffee, [cool it down] and then offer it to me. After taking coffee, he would say, "Oh, you've got work in the college, you must be going early. Go home." Then I used to take a rickshaw and go. . . .
>
> On a number of occasions he asked me to read certain articles or books that he had. Some articles would have appeared in the newspaper and some articles would have appeared in a magazine. He would ask me to read it, and then he would ask me to repeat it once again—usually a minimum three times, and no editing. The time used to be spent like that—and then he used to tell me incidences of his earlier experiences. In this way he was instructing me to respect all Mahatmas. He used to tell me about [various swamis], about Ramana Maharshi, about Aurobindo, about his own guru Ramdas and Mataji, J. Krishnamurti and other people.

Rajulu used to go frequently into Ramanashram, where he would sit in the hall and meditate. Upon returning to Sannadhi Street and saying where he had been, the yogi would ask, "Did you get peace of mind?" In 1978 Yogi Ramsuratkumar commented to Rajulu that although Ramanashram was a very fine place, the devotees there felt that there was no spiritual master other than Ramana Maharshi. This comment catalyzed the realization in Rajulu that in fact there was another master as great as Ramana Maharshi, and it was the swami himself, Yogi Ramsuratkumar. He felt that the beggar's comment was given as an oblique hint; although he talked to Rajulu a little about his years with Ramdas and wandering and standing in long lines to beg for food, in those days the beggar never spoke of himself as a spiritual guide to Rajulu, but as a humble traveler or devotee.

Yogi Ramsuratkumar did speak about his relationship with Ramdas, saying that his master poured all his love upon him. "This beggar used to be like a sheep going after food," he said. "If you have some grains of food in your hand, the sheep will follow you. That is how this beggar followed Ramdas." He told Rajulu that he could not bear separation, even for a minute, from his master. Once Ramdas asked Ramsuratkumar to stay at the ashram while he went to the house of a doctor. It was raining, and Yogi Ramsuratkumar could not stay away from his master, so he followed. When Ramdas came out of the house for some reason, he saw the beggar, Ramsuratkumar, standing in the pouring rain, waiting. The master told Ramsuratkumar to go "where I can be with you."

Telling this story Yogi Ramsuratkumar made the point that this is how the devotee must be with the master: the very sight of him, the very company of him, must all be taken as a great blessing. Rajulu said, "There is so much happiness in such a blessing! It is what the beggar told me. Some things he has also told to me about Mataji Krishnabi. He had great reverence for Mataji Krishnabi. He used to treat her as a mother, and whenever he talked about Mataji, he showed much reverence to her. He used to tell me that she was also an avatar." Shankara Rajulu remembered Yogi Ramsuratkumar speaking about his time with Swami Ramdas and Mataji:

> Ramdas didn't send him away. Of course, it is told in the book [*The Gospel of Swami Ramdas*] that he was not very clean and he had a beard. Some people had him get a haircut, gave him a new shirt and things like that—and then brought him to his guru. But Ramdas never objected to his coming and staying with him. Even though there were hundreds of people, [Yogi Ramsuratkumar] would like to be as near to his guru as possible. He would just push up past other people and go and sit near Ramdas, because that is the kind of attraction that he had for his guru. By telling these things he used to tell us that we must also develop such a kind of attachment towards our guru. It is for this purpose that he used to say these things.

Yogi Ramsuratkumar was very clear with Rajulu that Ramdas never sent him away. The beggar often had his devotees read the books of Swami Ramdas, and it was by reading these that Rajulu came to understand more about Yogi Ramsuratkumar himself. He said, "Whenever we read about Swami Ramdas we felt, 'Oh, this is Yogi Ramsuratkumar!' He had all those kinds of experiences; he expected us to do this. All those instructions found in those books were to be taken as the teachings of Yogi Ramsuratkumar. That's how I feel whenever I read Ramdas: I feel that Yogi Ramsuratkumar himself is coming and giving those instructions in the form of Ramdas."

Like numerous other devotees, Rajulu used to write songs about Yogi Ramsuratkumar, in which he would reflect on the profound love and divinity that he experienced in him.

Often the beggar would ask him to chant and sing the poems and songs, then he would say, "These songs are full of feeling—full of genuine feeling." This was a great compliment, because it reflected that the devotee was not being pretentious or intellectual in any way, but was genuinely moved to deep gratitude for having been the recipient of the master's love and sublime attention, and was compelled to offer these poems and songs in return. Rajulu remembered:

> He used to cover me with his shawl, just hug me and put so much love into me. I do not know how we deserve all that! But he used to do that like a mother. I would feel as if I have been with my mother, and that I was regarded there. [Quoting a poem:] "I have not tasted what love is before my seeing you. Only after seeing you and coming into direct contact with you, I knew the meaning of the word love. Prior to that all love was an expectation of something being given back to me. I say I love you, I expect something to be given by you back to me. But what can I give to him, to the master?" Without expecting anything from me, he showered so much of love upon me!

Rajulu often met with Yogi Ramsuratkumar in the Arunachalesvara Temple, where they would sit together. Although the beggar honored all the rituals and traditional pujas that were performed constantly in the temple and were interwoven throughout the rhythm of daily life in India, he made it clear to Rajulu that these were not necessary in his company. For example, at the time when the temple chariot—a massive rolling shrine decorated with carved wood images of deities and divine animals that is pulled through the streets during Deepam each year —was taken out into the streets, Yogi Ramsuratkumar and Rajulu were sitting in the Theradi Mandapam across the street from his house. It was Rajulu's first year in Tiruvannamalai, and as someone new to this fantastic, exciting procession through the streets, which were packed will throngs of ecstatic worshippers, he was naturally very curious and wanted to go out into the fray, but Yogi Ramsuratkumar would not permit it—although this did not come in the form of a spoken command.

Rajulu expected the beggar to set an example, as a guru, by going down to the procession and paying his respects. Instead Yogi Ramsuratkumar just continued with his conversation with Rajulu. He would go on talking, which made it impossible for Rajulu to get up and walk off toward the procession. Then it dawned on him: he was already talking with Arunachala Surat! He thought, "Why should I go and pay respects to the form of an idol, when the living Arunachala is sitting here talking to me? There is no need to go and do anything else." This [kind of thing] he did a number of times, and now I realize that he was instructing me, "I am here. You need not go to other places." In this way Rajulu came to experience Yogi Ramsuratkumar as the divinity.

Once Rajulu came late to Sannadhi Street because he had attended an important local *puja* ritual. Yogi Ramsuratkumar asked him where he had been. When he heard

Rajulu's explanation he then said, "That is not necessary for us." Rajulu reflected on this teaching:

> This was his way of talking: he will not say "That was not necessary for you," but "That was not necessary for us." He was saying, "See, you are coming here and spending your time with me, there was no necessity for these rituals." All that he addressed during my stay with him now appears to me in a different light [than it did at the time]. Nothing that he attests is worldly; it is all otherworldly. Whatever he says, it is all spiritual. I used to come and sing some songs about him in his presence. Once when I was writing one the lights in the house went out, but I continued to write. He asked me, "Are you able to write in darkness?" Then I told him, "When there is a such a big light before me where is the necessity for this worldly light?"
>
> These lines have also been incorporated in a song. That is, "You are an unfailing light; we do not require any other light except the light that you shine upon us, upon our lives." I said that and immediately wrote it down. Then he said, "Oh, that is true." He used to deny the miracles that happened, but when I used to say something like this, he would immediately go into a different mood, take up his fan, and go on blessing me. Or if I told him, "You are a very great light, the light of Arunachala. You are shedding your light on the earth . . . ." He would immediately [lift up] his fan and bless me for five minutes. On such occasions he used to be near me and accept what I said. But only now am I able to feel the significance of all those things.

Yogi Ramsuratkumar's relationship with Swami Ramdas was one of pure guru yoga, and this relationship and *sadhana* was continued in the form of his work with his own devotees years later. In guru yoga the devotee cultivates a total focus of attention and ultimately a total love in relationship with the guru. This total love is called *sarvatmabhava* and is beautifully described in the mythical stories of the love games of Krishna with the gopis in Book X of the *Bhagavata Purana*. Through a focus of attention on the guru, the devotee experiences communion with the innate wisdom and realization of the guru's being, and eventually becomes identified or resonant with that rather than the limited and egoic human personality.

Guru yoga seeks to establish a continuous flow that is cxchanged in a psycho-spiritual bond forged between guru and devotee. The devotional countenance or genuine loving posture toward the guru is the natural expression and conduit of energies that are shared between the guru and the devotee, and as *guru-bhakti* takes over it becomes the means by which grace is both attracted to the devotee and the channel through which it flows from the guru. In certain stages of the path *sarvatmabhava* may, in some cases, appear as an overwhelming obsession with the guru, as it did for some period of time in

Yogi Ramsuratkumar's relationship with Swami Ramdas. It is the guru's job then, as Ramdas so clearly demonstrated, to reinstate balance when balance is due.

This may take many different forms of skillful means on the part of the guru, which we will see Yogi Ramsuratkumar enact many times in *lilas* and teaching lessons with his devotees over the years. Because this was the path and the particular yoga to which Yogi Ramsuratkumar's devotees were called, one of the ways he guided them was by stating that the traditional *pujas* and proscribed rites and rituals were not necessary. The only thing that was absolutely necessary for the fruition of the path was to focus on the guru himself, and to aid in this *sadhana*, the devotees were given the guru's name—Yogi Ramsuratkumar.

"Hilda is coming to meet this sinner. You have praised this sinner, and Caylor has praised this sinner, but Hilda will expose this beggar," Yogi Ramsuratkumar said slyly to Will and Joan, then laughed uproariously. It was early July 1978 at Sannadhi Street, three weeks before Hilda would arrive from traveling in Ceylon. Will and Joan were in Tiruvannamalai visiting Yogi Ramsuratkumar and making arrangements for Hilda's arrival and long-awaited meeting with the beggar saint. On their first evening with the yogi, they told him that Hilda wasn't sure when she would leave Ceylon and arrive in India, but Yogi Ramsuratkumar was very sure that he knew exactly when she would arrive. After that night he dropped the subject of making arrangements for Hilda's arrival.

Sure enough, Hilda came on the seventh day, almost to the hour of what Yogi Ramsuratkumar had predicted. Upon receiving the word that Hilda was coming with twenty-six people and had arrived in Madras, Yogi Ramsuratkumar had Will reserve the hotel rooms and hold them for one week. They knew the day Hilda would arrive, but not the time. Joan had returned to the States to work, and on the day of Hilda's arrival Will met alone with Yogi Ramsuratkumar at the *mandapam* across the lane from the house on Sannadhi Street. They talked for more than an hour, making specific preparations for how everything should occur. The beggar gave lemons and other items to Will, which he insisted should be given to Hilda before she came to see him.

It was arranged for Hilda to stay at the Park Hotel, with everyone else at the Devashanam Guest House, so that she would enjoy some privacy. Hours before she was to arrive in Tiruvannamalai, Yogi Ramsuratkumar met with Will and asked him to bring Hilda to his house that very night—not to the Theradi Mandapam at the top of the stairs across the street, but inside the house. During the visit Yogi Ramsuratkumar made it clear that Hilda should not sit out on the verandah of the house at Sannadhi Street, where he usually sat with his visitors, because people were urinating all along the street . He didn't want Hilda exposed to such elements, and said that she should be given respect because she was a saint.

Will had never been inside the house at Sannadhi Street at this point, and so it was an exciting proposition. The house was not usually accessible, and seemed mysterious, with an air of sacred ground. Yogi Ramsuratkumar specified explicitly that only five people should come with Hilda and Will, making seven people plus Yogi Ramsuratkumar. On this point he was quite firm. He didn't care who those five were, but it had to be a total of seven. Will remembered:

> "You'll tell me whenever Hilda comes. I want you to give me notice as soon as she comes. And then I want you to bring her here immediately."
>
> Swami spoke with such power at that time that every atom in my body was vibrating. It was like, don't screw this up. I had never seen him exuding such power before. Every atom of my body was tingling. Hilda said later that when they were coming from Madras she felt like a set of big ears was just listening to her! She got in about eleven o'clock at night, but she was very tired, so I went over immediately and I told Swami, "She's here." I had a taxi waiting there, and Swami gave me very specific instructions. Only seven people could be there.

Hilda arrived by bus and was met by Will and taken to the Park Hotel, near the temple. Three members of her group were with them—Shanti, Vali and Uma. Hilda said, "Kids, be real thankful. Only a great being can draw you here from so far. He has drawn us here. It's all by his grace." The others came by car and taxi and soon rejoined Hilda. The original five people who were to go to Yogi Ramsuratkumar on this auspicious first meeting with Hilda and Will were Shanti, Vali, Lila, Al and Barry. The seven trooped off together and soon arrived at 90 Sannadhi Street. As they approached Hilda was already deeply impressed by the vibrations she was picking up. She commented, "This whole area is just filled with amazing golden lights." Yogi Ramsuratkumar appeared at the door and graciously invited them in. Immediately Hilda prostrated and touched the ground at Yogi Ramsuratkumar's feet.

"That's not necessary," he said,

"Yes, it is necessary," she replied with a smile. Everyone had brought garlands and presented them to Yogi Ramsuratkumar. Right away he gave them back, putting one on each person and blessing them as he went from one to another. He kept Hilda's garland until the end, after everyone else had been given theirs. When he placed it around her neck, she quickly took it off and held it. Swami said to her, "Always keep that garland."

Yogi Ramsuratkumar showed Hilda, Will and the visitors into the inner room of the house. It was the only time that Will had been beyond the verandah at Sannadhi Street, and he discovered that the room was very sparse, with a mat on the floor, piles of newspapers and some burlap bags. Everything was untidy and covered with dust. As the group took their seats on the floor, Hilda brought out a low folding chair and sat across from the beggar, who took his seat on the floor.

"Hilda, how do you feel?" he asked.

It was late, obviously she was an older woman, and she had been exhausted by the long bus ride from Chennai over rough and bumpy roads.

"Swami, I feel totally refreshed—like I've just gotten up in the morning!" she responded with a smile of amazement.

"Ohhh . . ." he said, in his childlike way of expressing wonder. Giving Hilda some flowers and lemons to hold, he gazed at her out of the side of his eyes silently, with strong concentration, for a long time—twenty or thirty minutes. During this time he stroked his beard and sometimes looked off into space above her head, while his thumb and forefinger moved rapidly, as if he was using *japa* beads to repeat a mantra. He began to smoke and asked Hilda some personal questions about her family, then turned his attention on each person in the room.

"What is your name?" he asked each one. Most of the conversation was made with Will as the go-between, since the beggar was used to his pronunciation and style of speaking. With each person he lit up a cigarette, which Hilda later said was the way he cleaned up the emotional garbage that people carried around, purifying each person so they could harmonize with the space he had created. He gave everyone a banana, and he peeled the bananas for the two little girls, Shanti and Vali. Every now and then he leaned against the wall and raised his hands up in blessing. The energetic dynamic of the space became incredibly intense as he worked, but he was soon interrupted by two people who intruded upon the sanctum he had created.

There was a knock at the door. Perumal answered it, then said something to Swami, who turned and said, "Will, go see who that is." It was Eleanor, who was traveling with Hilda but had not been chosen to come to this meeting with the yogi.

"I hear Hilda is in there, and I want to come in," she said, and she more or less barged her way in. Soon after that Mani, a cousin of the girls from Sri Lanka who was also traveling with Hilda, came to the door seeking the key to her room. When Hilda realized it was Mani, she said, "Oh, Swami, can she please come in? She's the kids' cousin; I'd really like her to come in." Hearing this, Yogi Ramsuratkumar perked up.

"What? Hilda wants someone here?" he asked.

Will answered, "Oh yes, Swami. Hilda wants Mani, the lady from Ceylon." So Mani was admitted to the porch as well, and Yogi Ramsuratkumar began to talk for a while.

"Don't judge anybody. This filthy beggar judges people," he said, then he recounted the story of how, many years prior, he was staying near Ramanashram and taking his meals there, when Ma Taliyarkhan came over one day and said, "These people, these worthless people," pointing at Yogi Ramsuratkumar, "they hang around. They shouldn't be fed."

"Oh, this filthy sinner has always remembered that!" he exclaimed to his guests. "Don't do like he does." He asked a woman, Lila, if she had resentment. She answered "No," and he said, "This beggar has resentment." He proceeded to tell them that he had declined all invitations to take his meals at Ramanashram from then on. Even a year or so later when Ma Taliyarkhan sent a message requesting him to come back, he said, "This beggar wouldn't go. He didn't forget and he never forgave her. Don't hold grudges like this beggar." Later Lila said that it took six weeks for her to face the resentment that was actually brewing inside her at the time of his enigmatic words, and to realize that the beggar saint was working with her and offering her help to bring those feelings out into the open and see herself more clearly.

The next day Eleanor got very sick and was sick for the next two weeks. Hilda gave a talk to her group in which she said, "Kids, don't ever push your luck. You got to come in to see Yogi Ramsuratkumar because I had the grace to see him. So you came on the coattails of my grace, Eleanor." She said that Mani was given permission because Hilda asked Swami if she could come in, but Eleanor, who tended to be cranky and irascible, had barged her way in. Now she had gotten sick, which Hilda believed as a result of being in a supercharged spiritual environment that she didn't have the capacity to process or digest properly. She said that Eleanor's karma wasn't ripe for a meeting of that particular kind with Yogi Ramsuratkumar, and all the karma that was past due to make her eligible for participating in such a space had to be burned up instantly—therefore, it was lawful that she had gotten sick. Hilda said, "That's a lesson. Never push your way to get on an airplane, never push your way in to see somebody, because you don't have that right. You haven't earned that right."

Shanti and Vali were seven and nine years old, and were considered to be very advanced souls who had been taken under Hilda's wing; one of them was a clairvoyant from birth. Yogi Ramsuratkumar had concentrated quite a lot of attention on the girls, asking them to come sit before him and answer questions. Hilda was a yogini herself and had trained Vali not to ever let on what she was thinking, but as she sat before Yogi Ramsuratkumar, her mouth dropped open. She kept staring at him. Hilda asked her, "What do you see, Vali? What do you see?" She was deeply impressed and kept saying that she was just "seeing light."

"How big is the aura?" Hilda asked Vali.

"It goes from horizon to horizon," she answered.

The next night all twenty-six people of Hilda's group were at Sannadhi Street with Hilda when Yogi Ramsuratkumar suddenly stood up and began to dance while he sang, "Sri Rama, Jai Rama, Jaya Jaya Rama," just as everyone was leaving. It was a stunning and sublime moment to witness his God-intoxication, and the visitors were deeply moved. Hilda said afterward, "Oh my God, Will, he's bringing energy from outside this universe . . . this is such a great master." A month later, in August 1978, Will told the story of this ecstatic dance at one of Hilda's meetings in New York City:

> We all watched Swami dance ecstatically and sing the names of God—just the bliss in his face, the complete ecstasy in his face!—and then the next second, he was changed. Usually we were with him at night, it was very hard to see his different intricate facial expressions. His facial expressions reflected an inner flux of divine energies—just like seeing a completely different person. As they say: God has a thousand faces; and we sure saw them in Swami. The different faces—a state of being for each situation. Something totally unique. Everything he does is one hundred

> percent. Afterwards Hilda said, "God, if we could do our bhajans like that! He brings the essences out of the universe: the essence of Rama, of Radha and Krishna. Not dead bhajans."

On the third day of Hilda's visit Yogi Ramsuratkumar asked specifically that only Hilda, Shanti, Vali and Will come. During this meeting another member of the traveling party knocked on the door and aggressively intruded, saying to Perumal, who answered the door, "Oh, I hear Hilda's here."

"Will, see who's there," Yogi Ramsuratkumar said. Will walked over to the door and looked out at the man.

"Swami's out. He isn't in," he said, attempting to dissuade the young man.

Yogi Ramsuratkumar interrupted, "Who is that?" When Will told him the man's name, he said, "Oh, he can come in." The beggar saint was sitting in the front of the room with Hilda and the two children, and as the man came in he said, "Oh, have him sit there in the back with the dog." He never once spoke to him. The man had a garland for Yogi Ramsuratkumar, but he was never given the opportunity to give it. Yogi Ramsuratkumar focused most of his attention on the two children, looking at them and blessing them.

Hilda had some questions she wanted to ask, and Yogi Ramsuratkumar told her to write them down. One question was, should she continue teaching, and to this he said yes. The last question was: What should be our relationship to the Lord of Mantra?

"Well, we must serve the Lord of Mantra. That's how we should be," he answered.

Hilda left Tiruvannamalai to visit Satya Sai Baba in Bangalore for some days and planned to come back to spend more time with Yogi Ramsuratkumar. When she returned it was Guru Purnima—the full moon in July 1978—and on this particular night Yogi Ramsuratkumar had his yearly bath and changed into new clothes. Usually his idea of a bath was to walk down to the ghat and into the tank in the temple, clothes and all. Will remembered, "He would walk into the tank and then out—that was the bath for that year. Swami always said he was just too busy—he had too much to do to take baths." In fact, during Hilda's visit was the first time Will had ever seen Yogi Ramsuratkumar perfectly clean, and it was a bit of a shock to see him in new clothes for the first time. When he saw the beggar, Will exclaimed, "Swami, you look like a maharaja tonight!"

Despite the fact that he rarely bathed, Yogi Ramsuratkumar never smelled of sweat and the usual body odors of human beings. Many people reported that he actually exuded a slightly sweet scent, like jasmine. According to Will, the old and ragged clothes he wore—usually for a year or more without changing them—were slightly musty, but there was never any odor about his body. When he did change, the old clothes were then put into one of the burlap bags with all the other things that were preserved, now sanctified by virtue of being closely associated with the physical form of Yogi Ramsuratkumar.

When Hilda was expected to return from visiting Satya Sai Baba, Yogi Ramsuratkumar instructed Will to tell him as soon as Hilda arrived back in Tiruvannamalai. Shortly before eleven that morning Will went to relay the message that Hilda would be arriving at Sannadhi Street around two p.m., but Yogi Ramsuratkumar was nowhere to be found. After waiting for hours, Will saw Perumal and said, "Oh, Perumal! I'm waiting for Swami. I want to tell him that Hilda's coming at two." Leaving the message, he went back to his hotel.

When Hilda arrived she said, "Will, let's go right now." Will remembered:

> Now, I can't argue with Hilda! She said, "I saw Swami's face, which means he's telling me to come." So we're standing in front of his house, and just then Swami walks up, coming back to his house from someplace. He looks at me and he says, "Can't you do anything right?" Oh God! I'm between a rock and a hard place, you know. And so Hilda said, "I should go." I said, "No, no, please, Hilda. Don't go. That'll make it worse." I thought, Oh man, I'm cooked!

Perumal was inside, and when Yogi Ramsuratkumar heard from him that Will had waited for hours and hours to tell him when Hilda would arrive, the beggar came back outside and said, "Oh, I'm so sorry." He said, "Please excuse this beggar's manners, Hilda. Please come in," and he turned to Will and said, "So sorry. My mistake. This beggar's madness." Despite his instantaneous willingness to take the whole responsibility on himself, Yogi Ramsuratkumar had made an opportunity available to Will to stretch himself beyond his usual mode of being, as Will reflected on this experience: "The interesting thing was that you always had to be on your toes with these people, because of their quality of being. You had to be absolutely at peak performance, or else you would get squashed like a bug—but it makes you feel very alive and very concentrated and very one-pointed. You're not just hanging out."

One of the ways the beggar saint gave teaching lessons was through behavior that was inexplicable at least and often totally mysterious. It was better not to allow one's ego to draw conclusions when the guru said he made an error, because "this beggar's madness" was the very impulse of God that orchestrated circumstances in which the devotee could learn something or be stretched beyond self-imposed boundaries. For one whose total identity has been subsumed by the will of God, there are no mistakes in the ordinary sense. Being trained by such beings of spiritual authority was a rare opportunity, and one that Yogi Ramsuratkumar did not give easily. Will had earned this kind of guidance and interaction with the guru.

During the sixth night that Will, Hilda and her group were with the beggar, he spent many hours with them; there were times of silence and pure blessing force that flowed like a river and times when the beggar talked freely. Often they sat under the *mandapam* at the top of the stairs across from the house on Sannadhi Street with nothing but a candle to light the hot, steamy darkness, and Yogi Ramsuratkumar would preside over the chamber. Sometimes other people would come and join them there; just simply passing the hours of the night in his company was a mystical experience, regardless of the events, or whether there was silence or conversation. Sometimes he would sleep, then he would wake up and say, "Oh, this beggar is so terrible. You've come all this way to see this beggar and he is just sleeping!"

On most nights Yogi Ramsuratkumar spoke to the group. He had an amazing facility to penetrate into each person with the exact teaching that he or she needed to hear at the time. At certain times he dropped the guise of the dirty sinner, the simple beggar who knew nothing, and talked with them directly about God, but the moment someone else would arrive, he would enter the disguise again for a few minutes until they had left. Everyone who came had to earn entry into the guru's world; although blessings were dispensed equally on one and all, the pearls of great price were not given away for free.

At one point a man came and joined the group around Yogi Ramsuratkumar. He said that he had seen a picture of the beggar saint, and immediately felt compelled to come and see him.

"Oh, all that's just propaganda and publicity. This beggar just makes propaganda because he's lazy and doesn't want to work. People will bring him food," Yogi Ramsuratkumar said. Hilda's group laughed at this, but the newcomer was flabbergasted and clearly had no idea what was going on. After a while, Yogi Ramsuratkumar sent the man away. Janis Reed, who was there and later recounted the story, said, "It seemed like a kind of test—to see if the man could see through the masquerade and follow his heart."

With Hilda's students he was kind and attentive and listened carefully when they talked about their personal lives. On their last night in Tiruvannamalai the group sat with Yogi Ramsuratkumar on the *mandapam* balcony. The weather was extremely hot. Yogi Ramsuratkumar was speaking very freely and talking about God. He said, "Father is everywhere and everything. Father is here in the form of this beggar. Father is here in the form of Janis. Father is here in the form of Ian. It's all Father." Janis had written him a letter of thanks for all his help, and stated that she felt she had a great friend in him.

"Father is the friend," he said, reading her letter. Then he said, "If this beggar is really a yogi as he calls himself then he is beyond all time and all space. He's everywhere and in everyone. He's past, present and future; he is everywhere, in all. Father's grace is always raining heavily; you just have to pay attention."

The 1978 visit was a highpoint in the long-term relationship between Hilda, many of her students and Yogi Ramsuratkumar; it was a relationship that Hilda herself was tremendously inspired by. Coming back to the States and resuming her weekly meeting in New York City, stories and anecdotes of Yogi Ramsuratkumar were often told as the importance of their meetings with him began to sink in and people realized more deeply the tremendous gift of his presence in their lives. They began to understand that Yogi Ramsuratkumar gave each person what he or she needed. When someone asked for something, he would respond to their request, but it was what he offered—without any interference from the recipient's personality, almost always prompted by the ego and the rationalizing mind—that carried the most transformational power.

In August 1987 when Hilda held her usual class in New York City one night, she asked people to recount their recent experience with Yogi Ramsuratkumar. Will Zulkowski was there and reflected on what it was like for him to be in the sublime company of the mad beggar of Tiruvannamalai:

> When Yogi Ramsuratkumar was once talking about Satya Sai Baba's wondrous powers, he remarked, very typically, that he himself was only a beggar and that only in many lifetimes distant could he evolve to that stage where he would be able to perform miracles. But I thought at the time that the true miracle is that he is able to change the lives of so many people and bring about in them a greater kinship to God. The real miracles that the masters do is not the disappearing and reappearing or materializing of this incense or that picture. The masters don't give importance, and Sai Baba does not give importance, to phenomena of this kind. The real miracle is the transformation of the human consciousness into something divine—that Swami did for everybody there, whether they were conscious of it or not. What they perceived or thought he was doing didn't matter.
>
> For this transformation to occur dynamically the people who came to him had to have only one quality: it is the quality necessary for spiritual mastery, and that is openness. When you have openness you have to be pretty selfless. At every turn you have to bare yourself. The more you can bare yourself, the more you can be free from shame, and fear and pride, without the slightest tint of ego—the more you can be with the master. That's what we have to do to be open. The purpose of this class and our contacts with enlightened beings is to learn to live openly, open to their grace. Not closed or narrow.
>
> Some people there thought I was holding them back from seeing Swami. They thought I was a big ego trying to block them from seeing Swami. But I can say in all honesty, by his grace, that I did the best I could. If anyone there was hurt—my apologies. When you call on the masters you don't listen to anybody else. We listen to what the master has to say. If he's pleased, we're pleased. If he's not, we're not. It doesn't matter what the others say, what they do or what they feel.
>
> I was with Yogi Ramsuratkumar when a lady came who was having a hard time with certain people criticizing her. Swami asked her, "Have you done the best you can?" And she answered, "Yes, I have."
>
> He said, "What more can you do? Leave aside the criticism. Leave aside the negation you've done all you can. This beggar is pleased. My Father is pleased. Why should you worry?" Similarly, we do whatever we have to in this life. Why should we listen to anybody else?
>
> One very important thing the master said was, "There is no greater service, there is no greater sadhana, than to serve a spiritual master. No greater sadhana." You can repeat the name of Ram, but to serve a spiritual master you really have to give your one-hundred-percent all. But also, when the master entrusts some work to you, his grace is also with you.

Likewise, when we tune into our God-self, or the masters—whenever we do work for them—their grace is there. We shouldn't feel that there is a great burden there. We should feel that it is our pleasure to serve. It is a wonderful grace to serve a master. In this sense when we are called to serve humanity, to serve one another, it is our pleasure, not humanity's opportunity. There is a difference.

When we sit with a master we should feel our heart is his heart, our being is his being. We should see no separation. We should feel no difference. We might feel that we are not worthy—but we must be worthy, worthy in our every act. Everything must be done perfectly.

There was a boy there named Joel, a musician, [who was also visiting Yogi Ramsuratkumar]. We were talking one night, and Swami had mentioned a book called The *Srimad Bhagavatam* by S.S. Cohen (translated). It's the story of Sri Krishna's life. According to this legend as a child Krishna once picked up a handful of mud and began eating it. His mother became very upset. Mother Yasoda came over, grabbed him off the ground and opened his mouth to clean the mud out, but as soon as she did this, she saw the whole cosmos in his mouth. Swami repeated this story to us day after day and always concluded with these puzzling remarks: "How Yasoda got on the outside looking in, we don't know. If all is in the mouth of Krishna, how did Yasoda see this from the outside?" Swami suggested to certain people that it would be a very useful meditation to imagine oneself in the mouth of Krishna. What is there to worry or fear since there is no place which isn't in the mouth of Krishna?

On another night we were sitting with Swami, star-gazing. Joel happened to know quite a lot about astronomy. He was talking about different stars: white dwarfs, red giants and a lot of others. And then he brought up the fact that a star's light is seen only after thousands or even millions of years, where it goes we don't know; it travels through space eternally. While I was sitting there I thought, "God, this is just like Swami. The light of a spiritual master irradiates infinite universes and just goes on and on. Who knows, maybe a million years from now someone will see a great light pass across the night sky of their distant world or maybe it will illuminate their interior space like a great blessing. Yet they won't know that it is the light of a spiritual master who lived eons ago in a distant galaxy.

I said, "Swami, your light in this world will one day go out, but even millions of years from now your light will still be shining in other worlds." And he said, raising both hands in blessing, "Is it?" Then I felt a fantastic wave of bliss.

Maybe that's the reason the great truths are still here and we still feel their impact. The light of the great masters is still here even after

> thousands of years. It travels ceaselessly throughout the universe. Nothing is created; nothing is destroyed.

Hilda was profoundly inspired and nourished by the meetings with Yogi Ramsuratkumar; she was brimming over with praise when she talked about him with her students at her regular weekly classes. Telling stories of the beggar saint and reflecting on his teachings was an important way to keep the relationship alive, and to integrate the blessings that had been received. "Will, he's way, way off the charts," she said, glowing as she spoke about Yogi Ramsuratkumar. "He's just so far out!" Speaking about the classic lore about yogis, the great white brotherhood and other esoteric legends, Hilda said, "He is way beyond all of that"

Will recalled that Yogi Ramsuratkumar used to tell stories about Swami Ramdas and his days at Anandashram. Whenever the beggar got a picture of Papa Ramdas he would stare at it for hours and hours, but when Hilda came, she said, "Will, you want to know something? He is standing on Papa Ramdas's shoulders. His realization is way, way, way beyond Papa Ramdas's realization." And yet, Will remembered that Yogi Ramsuratkumar remained steadfast in his devotion to Ramdas and his faith in his master's instruction:

> Yogi Ramsuratkumar always insisted that the name of Ram was enough. He often said that if one chanted the name of Ram, that's enough. He didn't put down [any other path], but he just said that chanting Ramnam was all that somebody [needed to] do. And then he told me about etheric markers—he said that the name of Ram has been repeated so many times, it's in the air. Basically, what I figured out in what he said was that his work is in the air, and Hilda actually confirmed that, too. She said, "Will, he's really not working on this plane, he's working in the air and he's in all the ethereal realms and everything like that, and with name and sound and energy." So it's like a big boost, you know . . . . that you can plug into.
>
> He was very adamant that the name of Ram is all you need, but he wasn't pushing it down anybody's throat. He always told me that whoever came to him, he tried to go to their path. He said if they wanted to come and talk about Marx, they talked about Marx. He didn't divert their path. He only tried to go with whatever they were interested in.

Once an American seeker came to see Yogi Ramsuratkumar and said to him, "Swami, I want to hang out with you for three months." The beggar just looked at him. About an hour later Yogi Ramsuratkumar said, "Well, we've met. You don't have to come back any more." With others, Yogi Ramsuratkumar was totally receptive. His responses seemed to depend entirely on the individual's state of being and inner receptivity, and in this way he mirrored back something of great importance to each person—his or her own self. This ability to be a mirror is one of the most important natural or innate functions of the guru, because one can only progress on the spiritual path if one has a clear, truthful knowledge of self in all its aspects—mental, emotional, physical and spiritual dimensions.

Another story reflects the guru's response when someone approached with a highly receptive openness: There were two young German women who came around Yogi Ramsuratkumar during this time period. They had known him for sometime, and were just arriving back in India. As they walked up the steps to the balcony where Yogi Ramsuratkumar was sitting on the platform, he called out, "Who is here?"

The response came, "Ute and Ilse."

"Ohhh! Ute and Ilse!" He jumped up, and as they joined him, he approached them lovingly and generously, saying, "This beggar is so bad. You've written so many letters, this beggar has never responded."

They had brought some cigarettes and other things from the gift shop at the airport. They were planning to be in Tiruvannamalai for a couple of weeks. They had both been fasting, and one in particular had fasted for a very long time.

"Oh, she's so strong," Yogi Ramsuratkumar said, looking at her. "She's always thinking of this beggar, thinking of this beggar all the time." Two weeks later as they were explaining their plans to go north to Benares, they asked Yogi Ramsuratkumar, "Swami, what should our *sadhana* be?"

"This beggar will do your *sadhana* for you," he replied. "You've written this beggar all these years, and he's never responded. You've come, you've served this beggar his breakfast and so many things. Now it's this beggar's turn to give you something. You go to Benares—just go and have a good time."

Later in 1978 another student of Hilda Charlton came to visit Yogi Ramsuratkumar, Richard Schiffman. He was staying at Sai Baba's ashram and decided to come to Tiruvannamalai with Phil Goslin, a Sai Baba devotee from the U.S. Heading toward the temple, they found Yogi Ramsuratkumar in the tower *mandapam*, where he was offering tea to several people who were sitting with him. He called Richard up to sit beside him, took his hand and began to stroke it. Very sweetly he asked his name and where he came from. It was the name, "Richard," that captured his attention.

"Richard . . ." Yogi Ramsuratkumar said, "Richard the Crusader."

"No, uh, not the Crusader," Richard began. Phil interjected, "You mean Lion-Hearted."

Yogi looked at Richard and said, "Lion-Hearted?" Richard said no.

"No, no, no. Not Lion-Hearted—Crusader!" Yogi Ramsuratkumar insisted. After that whenever he saw Richard, under the punnai tree or out by the edge of the fields, he would say very sweetly, "Oh, Richard the Crusader has come!" Richard wondered why he was calling him that, and said, "I realized that when I first sat in his presence, my thought was, 'This is really the Holy Land. Only in India does someone who looks like a beggar, sitting on the street like this, have people revering him and seeing divinity in him. This is really India—this is the real thing.' Businessmen and well-dressed people and everyone else, just coming to see him there."

Richard and Phil were in Tiruvannamalai for a week or so, and when they were leaving, they went to see Yogi Ramsuratkumar at the punnai tree. After saying goodbye they started to walk away and had gone about fifty feet when they heard his voice calling out after them.

"You're wondering why I called you 'the Crusader?'" the beggar called out to Richard. He answered yes.

"Because you've come back to the Holy Land." Then he said, "You're also wondering if Sai Baba is going to speak to you."

Richard was stunned. Quickly putting together the comment, "Because you've come back to the Holy Land" with his thoughts at the time of his first meeting with Yogi Ramsuratkumar, Richard then realized that he hadn't mentioned anything about the fact that, although he was staying at his ashram, Sai Baba had not yet given him an interview, which wasn't terribly unusual because some people could stay there for years without ever speaking to Sai Baba.

"Don't worry. He'll talk to you as soon as you get back," the beggar then declared. The audience with the master was now complete, and Richard and Phil left. The day after Richard returned to the ashram Sai Baba called him in for a private interview.

People's lives were profoundly touched by meeting the beggar king; the subtle influence of grace was at work, which drew people back for more of the pure joy of his wise and chimerical company. Between 1977 and 1980 there was another influx of visits from Westerners to Yogi Ramsuratkumar, like Kirsti, who had continued to seek him out as her guru, finally by coming to live permanently in Tiruvannamalai.

Caylor Wadlington also returned to India from the States in late 1978 and stayed for several months. This was a rich and promising time, and in many ways quite different than the early years. *Yogi Ramsuratkumar, The Godchild, Tiruvannamalai* was going into its second printing, and in the years since he left India in 1976, Caylor had stayed in contact with his guru; nonetheless, it had been two years since they last met. Arriving in Bombay on January 12, 1979, Caylor traveled to Madras where he stayed with his friend A.V. Sunder before stopping by the Theosophical Society for a short visit and then to Pondicherry for one night at the Aurobindo ashram. On the night of January 21, he arrived in Tiruvannamalai and took a room at the Park Hotel.

The house at 90 Sannadhi Street was a new element in the mix for Caylor. He wasn't sure which house along the street belonged to Swami. Sannadhi Street was little more than an alley off the main street of the town, Car Street, so named because the temple car used for the Deepam festival is parked by the Theradi Mandapam where Yogi Ramsuratkumar so often sat. The *mandapam* had become the place where the beggar king, dressed in rags, held his nightly court. Caylor wrote in his journal at the time:

I arrived at eight o'clock that night. The hill was not visible in the deep dark moonless sky—just a vast cloud of brilliant stars. I approached the master around nine p.m. with bananas, flowers and cigarettes. I had no trouble locating the platform on which he is usually situated; the mammoth temple car was actually uncovered and ready to roll. The platform itself is a sort of loading dock for the temple car, some twenty feet high.

I walked down the alleyway—one of those public peeing paths—and turned right toward the stairs to the platform. It was very dark, with no streetlights. I wondered if the master was going to be up there. I thought I might have to go searching in the temple, or else at his house—but which one was his house?

The steps [to the Theradi Mandapam] were enormous, constructed wide enough for a large ceremonial procession. I noticed a cluster of shadows a little more than midway off to the left-hand side. I was sure these must be Swami's right-hand helpers—Jagannathan and company. Above them on the main level I could make out a number of clear-cut images in the dimly lit candlelight. Devotees to the left; the master alone in a corner, facing them. His bright red and orange garments cast a warm-hued reflection upon the whole stage.

I got midway up. The shadows had taken notice of me at step one and were mumbling in Tamil. They decided not to stop or question me. Sai Baba, however, was far more vocal. Yogi Ramsuratkumar had stopped talking with his guests and was looking intensely between the slats of the louvered panel that was between us.

One of seven or eight Indian guests was holding Sai Baba. He was barking and growling. I greeted him by name as I reached the last few steps, laid down my bag, stepped out of my sandals and turned beyond the great pillar to see Swami. His eyes were all afire with God's joyous intensity.

"Oho! Come here," he said. I had been cautious and paused, until I knew he recognized me. Stepping forward, I placed my offerings into his open hands and myself at his feet. It was a gesture that I really felt from within. I found a space and sat down.

"Namaste, Swami."

His eyes were brilliant and for at least twenty minutes his fan was raised in blessing. The power mounted until at times it overpowered in gushes within me. Afterwards I opened my eyes and noticed that he was relaxed. Now fanning himself, he said, "I am going to give you some trouble." He took me by the hand. We walked together towards the bazaar.

We stopped. Still holding my hand, he explained that he wanted me to go to Ramanashram and meet Raja Iyer to arrange with him some

> accommodation in the ashram or in a private room for rent—perhaps in the Bose compound, he suggested. I should return to see him after three days—the evening of the 24th. Before leaving me, he asked about my mother and placed some fruit and a packet of puffed rice in my hands.

In the morning Caylor's friend Chris asked him if he'd met Yogi Ramsuratkumar the night before. He answered yes, that it was a very intense meeting.

"Do you find he has changed?" Chris asked.

"Yes. In some ways," Caylor answered, "but in other ways he never changes." In the days that followed, Caylor found himself in a process of refining his understanding of his relationship with Yogi Ramsuratkumar. It was a time when expectations and hopes for the kind of social ease in relationship they'd had at the beginning were being purified and burned away.

As Caylor said, in some ways nothing had changed: Yogi Ramsuratkumar continued to strongly encourage Caylor toward *The Secret Doctrine* and the Theosophical Society. He said, "This beggar feels you have gained a lot from *The Secret Doctrine*, and he feels it is important you should keep some contact with that book. It doesn't matter if you read only one page each day or even one paragraph or even one sentence. *The Secret Doctrine* will help you."

On January 25, 1979 they met again at the *mandapam* by the temple car. When Caylor first arrived two Indian gentlemen were already sitting with Yogi Ramsuratkumar. They were asking his blessing for the formation of a Chit Fund (private co-op fund) named after a disciple of the deceased Ramalinga Swami. The master, as Caylor often referred to him now, lay back listening and seemed to be seeing deeply into the situation. Then, "as if a tornado suddenly tossed him," he sat up and demanded with great urgency that the devotees go back to Madras immediately. The two men were alarmed and confused, but Yogi Ramsuratkumar was insistent. He said he would pray for their project, gave them a packet of biscuits and then hurriedly said goodbye. It was the kind of interaction Yogi Ramsuratkumar had many times with people, in which he would become attuned to some difficulty or serious danger that could be avoided if plans were changed, or if someone embarked on a journey at the right time. In these instances his blessing took the form of his agitation or ferocity; such force was required to compel people to act in accord with his vision, in a way that would avoid suffering for them.

"Make preparations to go to Madras. Go to Madras. I will pray," he said again, blessing them and rushing them off. One of the men was confused and had not registered the fact that thc beggar had given his blessing; as a result, he was still pleading with him while fumbling in the darkness to find his shoes. After the Indian devotees left not one word was spoken—the master, as Caylor often thought of him now, seemed to be working internally. Caylor wrote:

> The Master then gestured for me to move over to the spot where they had been sitting. I laughed to myself thinking, "Now it's my turn to sit in

> the hot seat!" The room was cast in a deep shadow. His form was a single mass of a deeper gray, no details being discernible, except that his fan was raised from time to time overhead. His body was outstretched and his head cushioned by his arm underneath, his face usually buried under the fan or the arm and elbow positioning it. His force stilled my mind, searching its depths for a way to make real the prayer of this aspiring soul. Like a young bird with feeble wings not yet exercised, he was preparing to initiate the first flight. He was working with, in and beyond me at some other level. I sensed this from the beginning and kept quiet. After some few minutes—sensing this interior energy—I sat in meditation. We met at seven p.m. and he left at eight p.m.

For the next two weeks Caylor found Yogi Ramsuratkumar almost every night at the Theradi Mandapam, just across the street from his house on Sannadhi Street. During this time period Yogi Ramsuratkumar was often concentrated inwardly, as if he was walking unknowable interior paths. Sitting in his company there were deep, streaming silences that went on and on, sprinkled with short conversations as visitors appeared at the *mandapam* off and on throughout the evenings. During these intense spaces Caylor sat in various states of meditation, while being linked quietly and invisibly within to the presence and guidance of the master. It was a time in which the master seemed to be taking the work he had done with Caylor years before—the healing of the headaches associated with meditation, kundalini and sixth-chakra phenomena—and moving it to the next level. During these weeks many people, devotees and various attendants came and went. Occasionally a Westerner would arrive, sometimes bumbling into the space.

"This is not the right Swami!" exclaimed the blond, bearded young man who had just arrived in their midst. Yogi Ramsuratkumar had been laying in the candlelight with his head resting against a pillar. It was another quiet, meditative evening. Yogi Ramsuratkumar asked the young man, who had three Indian guides with him, to sit beside Caylor.

"What is this—some kind of meditation meeting?" the young man asked, looking at Caylor.

"No," Caylor answered, "We just don't happen to be speaking for the moment. People come here to him with their questions, problems and prayers," he looked at Yogi Ramsuratkumar, "and he answers their needs." Yogi Ramsuratkumar gave the other devotees a cluster of plantains and sent them away.

"What Swami are you looking for?" Yogi Ramsuratkumar asked. The young man answered that he was looking for a certain Vala Swami, who he had met just that day and arranged to meet at seven in the evening at the temple.

"So you have come to the wrong place," the master said with consternation.

"Maybe this is the right place," the young man replied quizzically. And with that Yogi Ramsuratkumar exploded into peals of laughter. This exchange relaxed the tension that was building in the space, and afterward they sat in silence again. When the young man tried to speak, the master raised his hand to constrain him, but obviously his mind was boiling with questions. He seemed puzzled and disturbed, but still, there was no further discussion permitted as to whether he was allowed to go on to his other appointment or just stay in the almost stern silence of Yogi Ramsuratkumar's chamber, into which he had haplessly fallen.

Two days later Caylor was sitting again with Yogi Ramsuratkumar at the *mandapam*. An interesting sadhu was visiting. He was dressed in a clean white cloth, but with the disheveled look of asceticism from living on the streets. His hair was matted, and he never spoke a word. Yogi Ramsuratkumar sat up after a while and positioned himself facing the two, then sat moving his fan at different angles and directions to see and work. Sometimes he became very still, and the mood of meditation prevailed while two children sang *bhajans*, always out of key, but with innocence and charm.

"This beggar is the disciple. The whole cosmos is his guru," Yogi Ramsuratkumar said, and with a glint in his eye he looked at Caylor and said, "You are also this beggar's guru." Caylor laughed at this, and Yogi Ramsuratkumar continued, "Everything is this beggar's guru in one form or another," concluding the nondualistic stream of consciousness and cracking up with laughter. He gave Caylor prasad: incense, tangerines and flowers.

A woman, Shanti, asked Yogi Ramsuratkumar if he would hold her baby. "What is its name?" he asked. He held the baby very close to his face and looked long and deep into her eyes; there was a palpable sense of a magnanimity of spirit, a great blessing being impressed upon the rest of the child's life. He held the baby so she could stand on his knee, and only gave her back to her mother after she had pulled his beard for a while.

It was a calm and peaceful evening, and the charmed atmosphere around the beggar seemed timeless. It had been raining and the streets had just begun to dry. A small cooking fire was burning, the clay pot balanced over three sticks of wood and three rocks; the flames cast light across the sheltered space. Yogi Ramsuratkumar's attendants and some children were there, as well as Sai Baba, who barked and demanded attention, sometimes asking for affection. After a while Yogi Ramsuratkumar said goodnight in his usual way, and Caylor departed for his quarters.

Every night at the *mandapam* with Yogi Ramsuratkumar seemed to bring a new teaching lesson of one kind or another, and the next night was no exception, as Caylor wrote:

> On January 29 thc mastcr was lying on the top step when I arrived—seemingly asleep, but more probably roaming about "somewhere" else. When the attendant informed him that I was there he briskly said in a reprimanding voice, "You have changed the time. Please come at seven." I had spent some time with Hamsa and Om Sadhu before coming. I gave him some bananas and a twenty-rupee note. He stood away for a few moments and examined it in the starlight, then sat down in front of me.

The time was now seven forty-five p.m. Evidently he prepared himself each evening for my arrival at seven. He had been waiting for me.

The master sat fanning; his mind was penetrating and ever alert to each key point of awareness I touched upon. With each subtly wrong moment within he would make an audible sign or else initiate the absence of one. That is, if he was fanning, he would stop; or if he was not, he would move slightly. These instructions were mysteriously clear to me—even though we never spoke. I had the distinct impression that the master was positioning himself at different points around me—I heard clicking sounds, wind rustling and parts of my immaterial psychic structure being touched by him.

This movement into self-abstraction became quite pronounced until one moment this disturbing inner/outer bearings prompted me to initiate a sort of mental outreach towards a familiar landmark. The master suddenly jumped up and rushed down the stairs. He gave brief instruction to one of his attendants and then returned.

Shortly after this I entered a state where everything which I experienced to exist was exclusive of myself; no longer interrupted my space. I felt a click inside my head; suddenly I could no longer discern between what was an interior psychological phenomenon and an exterior sensorial one. It was unknown ground—and I resisted this sense of being lost until I saw that its very quality of being unknown was new and real.

The attendant then brought some buttermilk. Sai Baba was laying on my lap until Swami missed my glass and poured some buttermilk on him. Sometime in the midst of all this the Danish boy Henrik came. He sat beside me for at least forty minutes. No one spoke. I remember also that when I could no longer dissociate myself from the pain I felt in my legs, the master spoke aloud three times, "Rama, Rama, Rama." This seemed to permit me to move. The forces till then seem to have cemented my body in one position.

The meditation then concluded when I came upon the question inside as to whether there existed a self or soul at all; judging from my experiences until then, in all probability there existed only varying depths of selflessness. Suddenly the master interrupted, "This beggar will take leave of you now." I pranamed at his feet. He gave me a few flowers and a lime.

As we walked down the stairs he said, "Come at seven." I remained quiet in a sort of spiritual cloud. Swami asked, "Your chappels?" [Shoes.]

"I have them Swami," I replied in this way. He made sure I had my feet on the ground!

Caylor was deeply involved in an investigation of meditation, self and no self during these days. He often sat in silence, alone with the master. It seemed that Yogi Ramsuratkumar was intimately aware of and in fact guiding every subtle nuance of Caylor's meditation.

Caylor had come to Tiruvannamalai with a detailed plan for rewriting the book in a style less steeped in the lore of the Theosophical Society. He wanted to make numerous changes and felt that his perspective was much broader and deeper now, so many years later, but he quickly found that the beggar was "very adverse to changing even a single word" in the book. Yogi Ramsuratkumar made it clear that from his standpoint he had imbued the book with a spiritual power, and it had an existence of its own on another level that was connected to him. The writing style was really of no importance; what mattered was whether the book had the capacity to communicate who he was, and to serve as a bridge from the reader to himself, which it did. It had accomplished its purpose very well, and there was no need to expend energy in changing something that was already working.

However, the original book was coming up for its second printing, and during this time Caylor and Yogi Ramsuratkumar were planning for that and expecting to receive an estimate of the printing costs in the mail. Every evening they met at the *mandapam*, and sometimes it seemed that the master was leaving Caylor to fend for himself in a way. This new form of relationship with the master ignited the inner fires and sparked a deeper mood and contemplation of the spiritual process, as Caylor described:

> The nights continue to be starlit. The new moon is in the northwestern sky and the hill is illumined in a pale light. The platform is grungy with city dust and strewn with drying berries that smell sweet. There is a long crude ladder along the west wall; Swami often leans back against it, his fan nicking, sometimes crashing, at its bottom leg over head. The architectural style [of the mandapam] seems more [Moslem] than Hindu, and with Yogi Ramsuratkumar sitting there dressed the way he is, it all sort of takes one back to the Persian empire. There sits a Persian master right out of the *Rubaiyat*.
>
> The master now reveals—slightly unveils—his vast, vast power. I humbly bow at the lotus feet of this kingly sinner, and I begin to understand how he is inclined to refer to himself as a beggar and sinner. If there is no self and all else is but the world's creation, then all of this is mere substance, and God our only glory. It is all for him to do with as he pleases. We have nothing but him.
>
> There is nothing easy about the selfless state—either in our approach to it or in the final expression. It's a perfection welded in the fire of perpetual sacrifice. Every spirit and circumstance of darkness will unite as a challenge to light. One must face an almost demonic conspiracy. Only by God's grace and total self-abnegation will his spirit triumph.

On February first the nightly meeting took another turn, leading more deeply into the subtle flow between the master and the student. While Caylor struggled with the mind in all its "vital complexities—striving for survival, the extreme parameters of desires and fear, all seeming to hinge on unworthiness and finally dissolving into peace," the master arrived and began to instruct:

"Leave focusing of chakras aside. Follow breath," the yogi said.

"How to follow the breath?" Caylor asked.

"There is some music. 'Tis a sound. In-breath, out-breathing . . . Never mind about a mantra or about celibacy for now. We are just concerned now about your following the breath. That is all . . . This beggar hasn't answered all of your questions, I think."

"Yes you have, Swami," Caylor said. "Thank you."

"This beggar's Father will look after you. He will see to your every need."

The next night the instruction continued. Phyllis, a student of Hilda Charlton, was there with the yogi, and as Caylor approached, Yogi Ramsuratkumar said, "He has come." Everything on the platform was lost in deep shadow. A Tamil man and his child sat to the left of Phyllis. Kneeling before the master, Caylor held out a pillow, saying, "Swami I have brought a small pillow for your head. Would you like to have it?" He paused, considered, reached to touch it.

"It is mine, but you keep it for this father."

Caylor laughed. "I have two of them," he said, as he moved toward his usual seat and began to sit down.

"Please keep them both," he said decidedly. Caylor handed the other one to Phyllis and touched her leg with it, but she was meditating and didn't respond.

"About this question," Yogi Ramsuratkumar began, "of following the breath. Because there is this problem of heaviness in the body, this beggar feels there is no need at present to concentrate the attention in the third eye, or the sixth chakra and all this. Follow your breath! Leave aside all concern for kundalini. It's not helping us. Because there is this problem of heaviness, you should drop it. That is what this beggar advises. You should do whatever you think is right, but this beggar feels that everything else will follow upon simply watching the breath."

After a long pause he continued, "How to follow the breath? There is some music. We listen to this music." He demonstrated, breathing loudly. "Call it a sound or music. In-breathing, and out-breathing. We follow this sound. All thoughts subside. The mind becomes very quiet. Do this practice now." He raised his staff in blessing. "Leave aside these other questions: A mantra, celibacy, and other things. Follow the breath."

Another silence fell upon the group, and then the beggar king spoke in a commanding tone, saying, "This dirty sinner has pleaded to his Father for Phyllis. And his prayer will be heard." He raised his staff. "The Father will look after you."

"Thank you, Swami," Phyllis said. It was the first time since Caylor had returned that Yogi Ramsuratkumar had spoken so much; until then, his disposition had been austere and stern. The master continued to follow Phyllis's meditation with his fan mysteriously probing, directing, encompassing her. Spiritual power was building to a peak in the space as Yogi Ramsuratkumar worked with them. It was a very strong exchange, much of it occurring in a subtle reciprocity that catalyzed the inner state, as Caylor wrote: "To my astonishment without any expectation or provocation, my mind became very still and quite suddenly began repeating the mantra of Ramdas—*Om Sri Ram Jai Ram Jai Jai Ram*. I had never experienced anything like this before. Peace and power blossomed on its own—it was a wonderful condition. My heart was happy and full. Then a question began to arise: 'Is this a true or imaginary initiation?' " Soon afterward Yogi Ramsuratkumar dismissed them.

Two days later Phyllis and Caylor were with Yogi Ramsuratkumar again at the *mandapam* platform. The day before he had dismissed them early after becoming annoyed at their "lack of interest." The next night the yogi again encouraged Phyllis to follow the breath—especially the sound, the music of breathing. Then he became annoyed, saying, "When we cannot create interest this only shows our incompleteness. When Swami Ramdas initiated this dirty beggar into the repetition of the Ram mantram, he also stirred some interest in it."

Feelings of failure and self-reproach commonly arise in sadhana as, over time, the master's demand for uncompromising practice—or relationship to the Divine—becomes more actively demonstrated. The longer a disciple traverses the spiritual path, the harder it gets, and the greater the demand for higher, deeper, stronger practice. The master's total disregard for all of ego's usual concerns rubs more deeply into the fabric of one's awareness; the demonstration of what Caylor described as the master's "blatant, persistent, adamant disinterest with money, objects or gifts, people's expectations and the demands of human relations or public and personal opinions" could easily become a thorn in the side of ego. At the same time, Caylor knew that the master saw and responded to the nuances of life that everyone else usually dismisses, ignores or completely overlooks.

And so during this visit Caylor found himself in a very different relationship with the beggar king he had known so well years before, and at a very different level of practice. Not only was the guru placing a much greater demand on him, but Caylor was feeling the demand within his own being. He wrote a letter to the master on the afternoon of February 5, 1979, expressing his difficulties with the practice and asking a number of questions about the Ram mantra, his relationship with *The Secret Doctrine*, and the irritation Yogi Ramsuratkumar had expressed about his "lack of interest." He ended by admitting that he was not an "ideal devotee," but asked to be allowed to continue to spend the evening with him.

That night the master read the letter in candlelight with intense concentration. Jagannathan had placed the candles at designated spots near Yogi Ramsuratkumar, and then situated a wooden crate opposite him. The glow intensified as Swami leaned into the halo of light that encompassed his body, while all around him there were only shadows. Reading the note again and turning the pages front to back, checking to see that he had read all, he then placed these at his side.

That night there was a small group with Yogi Ramsuratkumar along with his usual attendants. Phyllis arrived and offered flowers to him, which he held for a moment, then returned to her. He adjusted everyone's seating so that she could sit beside Caylor. Encircled in a private globe of candlelight, the yogi spent a few minutes reading another letter, inserted it in its envelope, and then leaned back against the corner pillar, never giving a gesture or word in reply to these questions.

A noticeable internal shift of mood suddenly came over Caylor. He felt tangibly blessed, and he basked in the presence of Yogi Ramsuratkumar. Returning to his lodgings, he wrote: "From then until the time he sent us off, [I was] dipped into the great river of God, in pools, streams, waterfalls of all depths, in sometimes tranquil and sometimes cascading waters. There were a thousand faces, the names and forms of numberless perfections, always flowing to fulfill, sustain and nourish life unto greater life. I saw that this river ever flowed and the only way to stay in its current was to not block it."

The next night, February 6, as Caylor was approaching the western gate of the Arunachalasvara temple, a marriage was in procession, replete with Bollywood-style lighting, and a grand procession of women dressed in colorful wedding attire; their garments and jewelry sparkled, and their long flowing hair was decorated with flowers. Then he noticed Swami standing on the stairs of the *mandapam*, watching his approach. He seemed to be waiting for Caylor to arrive.

As Caylor reached the top of the stairs he saw that there were others already seated on the platform. Yogi Ramsuratkumar led him into the "sanctum"—the covered platform at the tops of the stairs—and gestured for Caylor to place the things he had brought on the floor near his fan.

"What is the mantra given to you by Nisargadatta Maharaj?" he queried. After a short hesitation to recall it, Caylor answered. "*So'ham.*"

"Repeat it now. Meditate with it for some time," Yogi Ramsuratkumar instructed. After some time he spoke again. "Do you know what those words mean? *So'ham.* 'I am that.' "

Caylor injected, "Brahman," then began to explain about his "initiation" by Nisargadatta Maharaj. Yogi Ramsuratkumar said reassuringly, "Whatever happened in the past is alright." The meditation continued.

Examining the varieties of *prasad* before him, he gave some plantains to Caylor and Phyllis. "Was there any difficulty?" he asked Caylor.

"Uh, no Swami."

"Continue with this method for some time."

"What method?" Caylor asked.

"You were repeating the mantra?" he seemed to be clarifying.

"No. I quit after you stopped me. I thought you wanted me to use it only during those initial ten minutes after we were discussing it. I didn't realize I was to continue."

The master answered, "Yes. I follow. It doesn't matter." The master rose to say goodnight to the Westerners.

It seemed extraordinary that the master would ask Caylor to repeat a mantra given by another master, but it was a particular form of meditation that Caylor admittedly preferred. Yogi Ramsuratkumar typically worked with people based on their preferences, or by encouraging and supporting whatever path to God they were already committed to or interested in. Nonetheless, Yogi Ramsuratkumar would soon reveal another possibility, which began as Caylor rounded the corner at Sannadhi Street the next night to find the guru again standing at the top of the stairs.

As Caylor reached the top of the stairs, the master spun round and led the way, his fan in hand. They took their places, sitting as usual on the floor. The air was still warm from the heat of the day. The *mandapam* was dark, but no candles were lit. Yogi Ramsuratkumar's face was barely visible, even though the sky was brightened by the half moon and a scattering of stars. Yogi Ramsuratkumar's attendants—two men and a boy—stood on the stairs, talking. The image of the master lingered powerfully as Caylor began to work with the *so'ham* mantra, which seemed dry and lifeless on this night. Caylor wrote:

> For no reason outstanding I began repeating the master's name. It occurred to me that so far as I can remember, I have never worked with his name for more than a short while, ten to fifteen minutes. So the course was set. Soon I felt a link with the guru. Invisible. Tenuous. For more than half an hour I centered in on this. It was a small rivulet flowing out from the soul; the process then like swimming upstream, deeper, deeper. The current flowed more strongly, now drawing me toward a space near the center of the chest.
>
> Then at once the focus vanished. I felt something had changed. The atmosphere was a vast space. The point of attraction was, I intuited now, somewhere overhead. I allowed my sensitivities to follow this feeling and I began to repeat the mantra from a hypothetical center overhead. At once this new current began to coalesce. The centers in the head began to expand with a living force.
>
> I discovered one thing, quite wonderful. When thoughts arose that I tended to resist or that tended to rouse fear or discord, this invisible connection between myself and Yogi Ramsuratkumar would quake and my consciousness tended to shift to one side or other—out of alignment with his. But by offering up these thoughts into this stream from above and by taking refuge, impurities and all, unto this point of origin—a chakra of most luminous details—all discord seemed to be absorbed into this.

"This beggar is taking leave of you now," Yogi Ramsuratkumar said, instantly drawing the strong inner meditation of the evening back into the ordinary world of the *mandapam*. As the two Americans gathered their things to leave, the beggar walked over to place *prasad* in their hands. Caylor prostrated at his feet and stood up to leave.

The next night as Caylor prepared to leave the *mandapam* Yogi Ramsuratkumar said, "You can use it," as he handed him a packet of incense. It seemed to Caylor that he was really referring to this inward process of repeating his name in *japa*. The whole initiation had taken place in the subtle exchange between the guru and the disciple. In these spaces the slightest movement made by Yogi Ramsuratkumar had incredible reverberations, to the extent that Caylor observed: "The Master let his fan drop to the floor, and suddenly my whole body was rushing with energy—overflowing every pore."

Later that night Phyllis told Caylor an interesting story. She had just met Ma Talyerkhan that day for the first time, and had talked with her about Yogi Ramsuratkumar. Ma Talyerkhan said that she had known him since his very early days in Tiruvannamalai, and she was pleased that he still remembered her. She said that she felt the "master was the result of Western popularity." Ma Talyerkhan relayed the story that some months ago when she was ill, one of "her sannyasins" had met "Ram Ram" in the temple. Upon hearing of her poor health, Yogi Ramsuratkumar had sent some fruit to her and asked the sannyasin to make sure she ate all.

It was a revealing story that shed light on the beggar's comment a few months before to Hilda's students about his lack of forgiveness. Perhaps he was using the fact that Ma Talyerkhan had caused him suffering, and his human reaction to that, to make a point about accepting reality as it is. His total acceptance of the reality of suffering was a reflection of his state of inner unity, which made it possible for him act with compassion —to bless Ma Talyerkhan with a gift of *prasad* when he heard that she was ill. Reflecting on the master's transcendent reality and how that unitive point of view manifested in the world, Caylor wrote a few days later:

> On our way home Phyllis and I had an interesting discussion, again pointing to many apparent differences in the ways of Yogi Ramsuratkumar and Hilda. Most striking perhaps that Hilda teaches us to appraise and discriminate the affairs within and without our personal worlds in terms of good and bad, spiritual and unspiritual. Yogi Ramsuratkumar doesn't seem to perceive the world in these terms. Further more, he never makes any moral or ethical demands upon anyone to change in any way. All kinds of people come to him, but he does not favor any, nor point out the faults, nor demand virtues of any man. One at last feels, "I am okay." He never requests anyone to surrender to him. His is a master with no disciples. The only prerequisite is sincerity.

As Caylor and Phyllis arrived the next night, Yogi Ramsuratkumar was sitting outside smoking on the steps. He put the cigarette out as they walked up and led them into the *mandapam*, then pointed out a place on the floor where they should place their offerings of *prasad*.

"This beggar has misplaced your letter," Yogi Ramsuratkumar began right away. "He has searched all over for it, but it hasn't turned up."

"That's alright Swami, I've brought you another little letter tonight," Caylor answered. "Nothing so specially important that you need to read it now. You can read it anytime."

"Yesterday this sinner was sitting in the temple. Your letter was with me then. How it got misplaced I don't know." He was clearly very concerned about the lost letter, and continued, saying, "I was carrying it with me over these last couple of days. Something precious. Not that this beggar didn't know what's in it. He has read it so many times. Yesterday this beggar spent one hour retracing his movements, inquiring here and there, but it didn't turn up." It was extremely unusual for Yogi Ramsuratkumar to lose any object with which he was working.

Soon the conversation turned to the new letter, which detailed Caylor's current reading of *The Secret Doctrine, Volume II*, which he had just finished for the third time. He had already read Volume I four times and had started a fifth reading. The second part of the note concerned the reprinting of *The Godchild:* if the book was to be reprinted while Caylor was in India, then he wanted to delegate the project to a few friends. Knowing that Yogi Ramsuratkumar wanted him to leave aside all concern for the book while Caylor was there, it seemed like the best course of action.

The letter was addressed, "Dear Master," and as Yogi Ramsuratkumar read this, he immediately announced, "This sinner is only a slave—no master! This sinner is a slave to everyone."

Then upon reading about *The Secret Doctrine*, Yogi Ramsuratkumar was inspired to speak at length, saying: "This beggar is very happy. This beggar feels that so far as you are concerned, nothing is more important than reading *The Secret Doctrine*. It is not possible for us to understand how these things shape a life—all I can say is that it is the most important thing for you. From the very beginning I learned from somewhere that *The Secret Doctrine* was very important. This beggar was told this by someone then, and he still gets this same thing for you from above. All of your life this book will guide you. You may read other books from time to time, but stick with *The Secret Doctrine* always. There is no use reading book after book after book, endlessly. We want to become absorbed in this one book. It is your scripture.

"It doesn't matter *how* you read the book—just read it, talk about it, think about it, discuss it," Yogi Ramsuratkumar continued. "So far as you are concerned, this beggar feels that no other meditation—whatever mantra or method you may choose—can be as important as this. This is all that is necessary for you. This dirty sinner doesn't know what J. Krishnamurti says about meditation, but his meditation is something that takes up the whole mind. Meditation is something so interesting to us that we think about it, dream about it, talk about it. We can't forget it. Any verse of the beginning stanzas can give you such a wonderful view for meditation."

Yogi Ramsuratkumar continued, "When you left for home I advised you at that time to continue reading *The Secret Doctrine* and to keep in contact with the Theosophical Society. Do you remember?"

Caylor assured him that he did in fact remember well. Yogi Ramsuratkumar then said that in his opinion *The Secret Doctrine* was written to enlighten people about God. Everything in the book, he said, from cover to cover, would show us the way to God. He said that though Caylor might find newer books that would find fault with it, he should pay no attention to such criticism.

Concerning the second printing of *The Godchild*, the master explained that it was not so urgent now. He wanted Caylor to give his full attention to his *sadhana* while he was in India, and to be with those few holy people he had chosen to see. He said that although many people inquire about the book, the important thing now was Caylor's *sadhana*. He further stated that Caylor devoted quite a lot of time to "this work," or the book, at a time when it was most urgent, and that he and his Father were ever-grateful. Raising his hand in blessing, he sent Caylor home for the evening. Just before leaving, as he was gathering his things together, the master approached Caylor again.

"The mind is full of space for thoughts," the beggar said with a smile. "You can occupy some of that space with thoughts about *The Secret Doctrine.*" They both laughed.

"Alright Swami, I will." As Caylor and Phyllis left, Yogi Ramsuratkumar stood with a regal demeanor and his hand raised in blessing.

On February 11 the beggar king again spoke eloquently on the same subject: "The mind, we know, has a tendency to roam about here and there—always searching. Within *The Secret Doctrine* there is so much space. It's a very big book, so therefore there is plenty of space for the mind to roam about. If our mind is going to wander let it wander here and there, anywhere it wants to go, within *The Secret Doctrine*. This beggar feels *The Secret Doctrine* will take people to God. Every page was written only to reveal something of His nature."

For almost ten years Yogi Ramsuratkumar had been urging Caylor to use *The Secret Doctrine* as the doorway through which he could most readily walk into realization. During this time Caylor was working with many different techniques and styles of meditation; he had also been strongly influenced by U.G. Krishnamurti, whose teaching was there is no guru, no self and no spiritual process. This approach seemed at odds with Yogi Ramsuratkumar's fundamental instruction to his devotees, which was Ramdas' instruction to him—the name of God is all you need. It created some conflict for Caylor, who wrote:

> When I work with this meditation I feel and I fear that I may become and am becoming estranged from the beloved Master, the one whom I care most about. I long only to impress his lotus feet upon my heart. I dream only of merging myself into him. Indeed I have no soul, no self, only this state of desperate lifelessness. Master, you alone can instill life into this soul-less corpse. I pray that your divine self will find this body a fit home. May God himself install your shining soul in my heart.

A few days earlier Caylor had made a short trip to Pondicherry, where he met with several friends, including Preben Sorenson, who had wanted to meet Yogi Ramsuratkumar for some months, since he had read about him in *The Godchild*. Caylor was especially eager to have them meet since Preben had spoken briefly about the possibility of translating the book into Danish.

Arriving back in Tiruvannamalai mid-afternoon on February 12, Caylor and Preben quickly went to the bodhi tree near the bus station, where the beggar usually sat during this time of day, but he wasn't there. In an exchange with Ranga, the flower salesman, they heard that Yogi Ramsuratkumar was in the fields beyond the train track, but when they looked, he wasn't there either. Finally they discovered him in the temple, sitting and talking with Ramaswami, who owned the soapstone shop, an Indian woman, and two naked sadhus who were sitting nearby.

"Mr. K! Come here!" he called to Caylor as soon as he saw him. It was a happy reunion; he held Caylor's hand and seemed to work to "bring a bit of equilibrium" into his system after the long journey from Pondicherry. He was dressed in a clean white dhoti that he had wrapped in the north Indian fashion, pulled up between the legs. The clothes he had changed out of were wrapped around his newspaper.

After the introductions, Preben handed Yogi Ramsuratkumar a gold and silver talisman inlaid with several different stones, hoping that he would magnetize it. Yogi Ramsuratkumar held it in his hand for quite a while, then took it out into the sun to examine it closely. He walked back to where the group was sitting and stated that some other holy man seemed to have touched it, which was true. Preben asked him to also magnetize the ring he was wearing, but upon holding the object, Yogi Ramsuratkumar said that the ring had very little spiritual value, as it "was not cooperating with the rest of the system." He told Preben that he had done what he could to get it to work for him.

Around six o'clock Yogi Ramsuratkumar decided that the group should head up the hill and towards Wendel Field's house. In the late seventies Wendel Field had a small cottage in Tiruvannamalai where he painted, and Yogi Ramsuratkumar used to come to the cottage occasionally to sit with Wendel while he painted, in particular, a picture of Satya Sai Baba. Wendel was a devotee of Sai Baba, who had asked him to paint the picture. It was an amazing painting, described by Caylor as "Sai Baba seated on a lotus in space with angelic beings and stars in the classic mode. At the same time there was breathtaking space. Everything was translucent and mostly light and energy. It sounds like a cliché, but it was a masterpiece."

After a moment of serious consideration, Yogi Ramsuratkumar decided to take the route along the mountain road. Along the way the group picked up two more Westerners, Dominique and Soren, who were on their way to see Yogi Ramsuratkumar. Arriving at the cottage where Wendel was living, the group talked while they sat and waited. In the meantime Wendel had gone to walk around Arunachala with his friend Katherine; they had returned to look for Yogi Ramsuratkumar but he wasn't at his usual place. The naked sadhu who had been with him at the temple earlier approached them. Speaking Hindi and gesturing wildly, he communicated to Wendel that Yogi Ramsuratkumar had actually gone to his house, which was about a mile and a half away.

Finally Wendel came running into the compound of his house panting—he had run all the way from the town, and his companions, Katherine and Jerry Bass and the others, would arrive soon. Wendel and Caylor hadn't seen each other for several months and they embraced warmly. A large group—Caylor, Preben, Sorenson, Wendel and Katherine, John Kelly, Raman, Dominique, Soren, Ute and Ilse—settled on the floor together in the company of the beggar saint. It was an enchanted night of very high spirits that everyone would remember, with Yogi Ramsuratkumar talking at length on many different subjects, from politics to the most sublime dharma and teaching. At times he fell into raptures, chanting the name of God, "Sri Rama Jaya Rama, Jaya Jaya Rama," or got up and danced in paroxysms of sheer ecstasy.

Wendel Field remembered this evening as being threaded through and through with laughter and Yogi Ramsuratkumar's marvelous sense of humor. It was "one of those things where frequently you were laughing. Your jaw would hurt—we were laughing that hard. And sometimes you didn't even know what you were laughing about!" At other times the conversation became very serious, and Yogi Ramsuratkumar entered fully into the conversation. He talked about the wonder and perfection of God's universe, from the smallest atom to the largest galaxies.

"Everything is God's grace—all is His play. He pulls the strings, we are his puppets," Yogi Ramsuratkumar said to the group, in a rare teaching discourse. "We are all God's servants, and we should be like Hanuman and serve Rama. The Impersonal (formless) God manifests as a personal God—that is, Krishna, Rama—when needed to help us. They are but different aspects of the One." He then told the story of Krishna's mother looking into his mouth and seeing the universe, and he said, "We are all safe in the mouth of Krishna. All is God (Ram)—everybody, everything, even stray thoughts, such as those experienced in meditation." He urged everyone to be in harmony with God's law.

It was an extraordinary opportunity to hear the beggar speaking on subjects he rarely entered into. At one point Yogi Ramsuratkumar alluded to his distant travel in consciousness to the limits of the universe and the circumstances of the circle beyond which no man proceeds—the boundary of life and consciousness beyond which no man can go as long as he remains identified with the marketplace of the world. He talked about the potential of human beings, and the Source of all life, which remains the great mystery.

Wendel's painting, which was hanging on the wall, was exquisite, done in micro-brush style with vibrant colors. Satya Sai Baba graced the center of the painting; above and all around him were many historical holy men, while the underworld was beneath, with throngs of people falling into the grips of winged devils and flaming demons. Upon hearing someone comment that Sai Baba said not to jump from guru to guru because it makes holes in the heart, Yogi Ramsuratkumar agreed strongly and told the group that they should find the right teacher, serve him and accept his teaching. "Remember God's name" was the basic instruction, and he spoke about the importance of forgiving and forgetting, again using himself as the example, saying, as he had with Hilda's students, "Don't hold grudges like this sinner." Then he began to talk about the eternal quality of things; for example, a star emits light that is always present somewhere in the universe even after the star dies. In the same way, a master's teaching is always present, even after he passes out of his body—one only needs to tap into it.

On this rare day and night Yogi Ramsuratkumar drew Caylor into his world in a powerful way as the group entered into an enchanted realm that lasted until four or five o'clock in the morning. The group talked and had tea until Dominique, Soren and the two German girls had to leave, as they were heading north the next day. Yogi Ramsuratkumar gave them his blessing, and the smaller group became more intimate and warm as the night wore on. Surprisingly, Yogi Ramsuratkumar began to talk about the unique nature of the relationship between guru and devotee, using himself and Caylor as the example. He made direct statements about the strong connection they had had in past incarnations, and how they had been spiritually bonded for many countless births. The room was dark, lit only by the glow of a candle that burned, and the atmosphere had become very potent. The conversation changed focus to the teachings of J. Krishnamurti, politics and many other subjects. Caylor wrote:

> How we launched into the next thing I cannot remember, but it involved something about politics, the end of the war, and the difference between the Western and Eastern mind. The Western mind, he said, must always question everything; he must inquire and discover the truth. But the Eastern mind always knows the truth, he always knows the truth is God, so there is no call for inquiry and discovery. J. Krishnamurti, he said, is an Indian with an inherent knowledge of God and truth, but because he was brought up in the company of Westerners, he has not the language of the East, the result being a curious mixture of East and West in the man. But always, even as a little boy, J. Krishnamurti has known that God existed everywhere, there was no need to discover him anywhere.
>
> The political rap was pretty heavy. Ramsuratkumar knows more politics than anyone alive probably . . . it seems to involve his work. He has all the countries of the world figured into his scheme for world brotherhood . . . and he knows the problems that face each nation.
>
> It was at about this time that I fell asleep and didn't wake up again till morning. But the others continued on till four or five in the morning. The next day Katherine, Wendel and I made some chapathis and vegetables while the others were in the living room talking. I remember one topic that arose for discussion: Tantra. John Kelly and Ramsuratkumar were having a point in controversy. Yogi Ramsuratkumar submitted, but made it known that he didn't feel that John knew what he was talking about. In any case Yogi Ramsuratkumar did comment at one point that kundalini shakti was the key to wholeness and unity with the universe, since the same serpentine fire was pervading the universe that was alive and active within man. He said that it was this force which his master

Swami Ramdas awakened in him.

The group finally dissolved and Yogi Ramsuratkumar went back into town. The next day several people were gathered with the yogi when he began to explain that on three occasions someone had placed something in his eyes at night, and now he was finding difficulty with his eyes for the first time in his life. At the same time that he spoke candidly, he spoke about this adversity with the equanimity born of self-sacrifice and surrender.

"Some sacrifice was necessary," Yogi Ramsuratkumar said, reflecting upon the divine purpose behind such experiences in his own case, and hinting at the higher work that was the compelling force of his life. "For the candle to give light, it must burn."

There was an important teaching contained in the beggar's statements. Clearly in these experiences Yogi Ramsuratkumar suffered consciously for the good of all, the allusion—"For the candle to give light, it must burn"—being that a certain spiritual radiance and therefore blessing power was the result of any suffering that he personally endured, precisely because he was able to suffer it consciously and without blame or rancor.

Yogi Ramsuratkumar went on to tell the group that four years ago a man had come to him three times and said, "You must leave this place. What is the use of your being here?" It was not a command, but a warning.

Concerned by the very real threats to the beggar saint's well-being, Preben had asked Yogi Ramsuratkumar if he would ever go westward. There was no immediate response, but before Preben left that day, Yogi Ramsuratkumar answered him by saying, "This beggar's Father has understood the conditions here in Tiruvannamalai. But he has told this beggar that he must remain here doing the master's work. Some sacrifice must be made. The master had made it clear that this beggar must be a sacrifice to a great work."

Strangely enough, when the Satya Sai Baba painting was finished Yogi Ramsuratkumar blessed the painting and sat with Wendel and Katherine. Unfortunately, the painting was lost on a bus ride shortly thereafter, when Wendel tied it to the top of the bus. Arriving at his destination, the painting was gone.

For the next few days the meetings continued at night on the platform beneath the *mandapam*. Caylor observed in his journal that by February 17 the master was not speaking; he seemed to have returned to a very internalized state, "obviously engaged in work which is beyond my comprehension." That night in their meeting at the *mandapam* Caylor and some other devotees sat in the candlelight, largely in silence with the master. Caylor's own internal state was one of profound internal doubt and confusion and a strong current of negativity. Just as he was beginning to see some light at the end of the tunnel and felt his heart beginning to open up, Yogi Ramsuratkumar suddenly walked out and talked to Jagannathan, who was attending to his needs at this time. He came back into the *mandapam*, concentrated for a moment, then gathered a few things from the floor in front of him and walked forward to give them to his visitors. He dismissed them and looked at

Caylor with his hand raised, saying, "Rama Ramachandra Rama."

The next day the sky was dark, with storm clouds rolling overhead. All of the master's burlap bags—filled with precious pieces of flotsam and jetsam as well as hidden treasures that had been handled by Yogi Ramsuratkumar and somehow sanctified—were stacked up against the wall of the *mandapam*. Krishnamurti, a boy and another man were singing "Arunachaleswara." Sai Baba was running around. There were no candles lit, which made Yogi Ramsuratkumar only a shadow extending from the pillar. The singing stopped and silence prevailed until the master asked Phyllis how her meditation was progressing. After hearing her report, Yogi Ramsuratkumar told her to continue with her work and explain all to Hilda.

"The Father is all truth," he said, "all beauty, all power . . . The Father is the Supreme Master! This dirty sinner is His slave. Not even that, but what can one say—though he doesn't deserve to be called even the Father's slave, still he lives only to serve the Father."

Yogi Ramsuratkumar continued, "Don't adore this dirty beggar. Give your love to the Father. Only He can save you. This beggar can do nothing. Surrender unto Him, merge with Him. He is spirit. Does this beggar have the power to save anyone? The Father is everywhere! But so far as you are concerned, you are practicing this breathing. For you the Father is in the breath. Listen to the music; he is in this music."

In December 1978 Lee Lozowick left the States for his second trip to India. This time he brought three students along with him, and they planned a ten-week trip in which they would travel extensively across India, visiting Anandamayee Ma, Muktananda in Ganeshpuri, Rajneesh in Pune, and traveling to Bombay, Bubaneshwar, Kajaraho, Puri, Brindavan, Shirdi, Varanasi, Rishikesh, Haridwar and many other places. He wanted to pay his respects to many different lineages and traditions in India, and at the top of Lee's list of priorities for this trip was to again seek out the beggar, Yogi Ramsuratkumar, in an extended five-day stay in Tiruvannamalai. The memory of the extraordinary holy man, whom he had first met in early January 1977, was still very alive for him; there was an inexorable pull, a deep-rooted curiosity, even though his work as a spiritual teacher had continued to grow and develop. He had three published books, and still assumed that his own spiritual awakening was not the result of a relationship with a human master, but entirely the "Grace of God." As Lee said many times in later years, "Yogi Ramsuratkumar was different than all the other saints and yogis and spiritual masters that I met. Nobody was like him. I somewhat naively thought I was already enlightened at the time, but he had something I wanted—spiritual power. Of course, there was no way I could take something from him that he didn't want to give."

Lee and his group arrived in Tiruvannamalai on February 20, 1979, on a rainy afternoon. After dropping their bags briefly at Ramanashram where they were staying,

Lee immediately hit the streets, heading toward the temple, the brass market and the downtown bazaar in search of the beggar saint, heading for the Theradi Mandapam where Lee had met Yogi Ramsuratkumar two years before. Finding him there, they had hardly taken their seats with Yogi Ramsuratkumar when he turned his full attention on them. Two of the women had met the beggar saint with Lee in 1977, but since then their names had been changed. Regardless, at least by the appearance of things, the beggar seemed to have no recollection of having met any of them. He asked the older of the two women who were traveling with Lee the question with which he almost always began an exchange.

"What is your name?" he asked in his melodious voice, looking at the first of Lee's three students.

"Radha," she answered.

"Ohhhh . . . *Radha*," he responded enigmatically, emphasizing the Sanskrit name—that of the famed mythical consort of Lord Krishna—as if this was the most wondrous thing he'd ever heard. He looked at her and then at Lee. He turned to the second woman and said, "What is your name?"

"Mirabai," she answered.

"Ohhhh!" He stole a glance at Lee again, as if to say, "Very impressive," Mirabai being one of the most famous poet-saints and God-realizers in the history of India—a woman of wealth and riches who gave up everything for her love for Krishna. "Mirabai . . ." His eyes widened and his voice trailed away in awe.

Then to the other man in the party, he asked, "Your name?"

"Balarama," replied the man. Balarama was Krishna's half brother. This elicited a longer, "Ohhhh . . ." from Yogi Ramsuratkumar, and an even greater sense of awe and wonder. The beggar was beginning to shake with mirth as he turned slowly toward Lee, who he had called up earlier to sit right next to him, so that he and Lee were facing the other three.

"And who are you . . . " he asked, his voice trailing off into a long pause as if for effect, " . . . *Krishna*?"

Then he dissolved into peals of laughter, his whole body shaking with the enjoyment of the joke, his laughter resounding in the space.

Lee smiled sheepishly and the beggar's laughter slowly subsided. Turning back to the man in Lee's party, he asked again, "What is your American name?"

"Joe," the man answered.

Yogi Ramsuratkumar looked perplexed and fumbled with the pronunciation. "Joke?" He queried.

"Joe," he repeated.

"Joke!" Yogi Ramsuratkumar smiled with a gleam in his eye. "Joke!" The wordplay between Joe and Joke went on for some time, until a very young American man approached the group and sat down. He seemed out of sync and nervous. Yogi Ramsuratkumar turned his attention to this young man, asking his name and kindly inquiring as to how he was faring in India.

"How long have you been in India?" the beggar asked.

"I've been here for several months," the young American answered.

"How has India been for you?" Yogi Ramsuratkumar continued, seemingly aware that the young man was struggling.

He answered, "Oh, it's been really rough. I've had some difficulties. If it hadn't been for this little book," he pulled a small yellow booklet out of his pocket and held it out, "I don't know what I would have done. I've been reading it every day. It's gotten me through it all."

"Ohhh . . ." Yogi Ramsuratkumar seemed quite interested, and the young man handed him the book. He held the book tenderly, and turned it over in his hand. He read the title out loud, "*For the Love of God*," and then said, "Who wrote it?" while peering at the cover.

The young man answered, "Lee Lozowick."

Yogi Ramsuratkumar said, "Lee Lozowick!" He turned to Lee, who was sitting beside him and said, "Lee Lozowick wrote this book. Have you ever seen this book?"

"Yes," Lee answered, completely floored by this truly unbelievable turn of events.

"Do you know this Lee Lozowick?" Yogi Ramsuratkumar asked innocently, still talking to Lee.

"Yes," Lee answered with mounting embarrassment and anticipation.

"And who is he?" asked Yogi Ramsuratkumar.

"It's me," Lee answered, awestruck.

"It's you!" Yogi Ramsuratkumar said with total amazement, looking back and forth from the young man to Lee. "You are Lee Lozowick?" Lee answered yes. Yogi Ramsuratkumar's face was a study in wonder. He asked over and over again as he held the book in his hand, "This is you? You wrote this?" It was a moment of sheer magic. Lee simply answered yes to all of Yogi Ramsuratkumar's questions, but as he said years later, "I was wondering, how did Yogi Ramsuratkumar pull this off? This has got to be staged. Did he set this guy up or what? But he didn't . . . it all happened by pure coincidence, if you can call it that."

The beggar king was attended that day by Perumal, who sat on the stairs and only entered the master's space when he was called upon. Then he would come forward, arranging for coffee or milk to be served and announcing various visitors or taking care of other things that Yogi Ramsuratkumar needed. This afternoon he came and went, being dispatched on various tasks, while his son, Kamaraj, played nearby. Perumal soon brought a round of hot milk for everyone. Handing the booklet to Lee, Yogi Ramsuratkumar said, "Please read this." Lee read:

> God cannot be attained, or sought, understood or bought. God cannot be 'had' in any sense of the word, by any stretch of the imagination.
>
> God must be lived. But how? Only through the most absolute, selfless, and totally sacrificial love. God, in order to become truly 'The Father' of Jesus, or 'The Guest' as the Sufis would say, must be loved beyond mind, beyond senses, beyond all that you see and all that you

> don't. Only Love absolute will do.
>
> God does not appear to those who beg, who cringe, who seek for His divine aid. Nothing must be asked of Your Lord. He is not the Beloved, the Very One, the Only Real, to one who asks of Him a favor. The seeker, wanting of the Very Lord validation of his or her maya, his or her illusion, never realizes God in Truth . . . .[2]

With his eyes closed, Yogi Ramsuratkumar sat poised in a posture of deep listening while he smoked his cigarettes. Lee paused and the beggar opened his eyes and said, "Please read . . ."

Lee continued, "To see God face to face one must never see the face of personality, of 'the wish.' One must see only the face of God as He gazes at His child, His lover, His only one . . ."

The reading had continued for some time when the beggar turned to Lee and began a conversation.

"Lee, do you love God?" he asked seriously.

"No," Lee answered.

"This beggar doesn't love God either," the yogi answered slowly, thoughtfully.

Then Yogi Ramsuratkumar turned to Lee again and asked, "Lee . . . what do you want?"

"I want to be just like you. I just want to be a beggar," Lee answered.

Yogi Ramsuratkumar sat back, closed his eyes for a moment and then looked at Lee for a long time. The mood turned very deep and somber, then he said, "No, that is not possible. You are destined for many things, Lee. You will travel far, all over the world. This poor beggar is destined only to sit in the filth in this small town. I am a poor beggar. But you . . . you are a king and will have many riches." He repeated, "You will travel far and wide—all over the world." His eyes were moist and bright with the gleam of tears in the soft afternoon light. Seeing Lee's visible disappointment, he became very gentle as he said, "I am sorry. I must be the beggar, and you must be the king."

Yogi Ramsuratkumar began to smoke, and as he smoked the mood changed from somber to joyous. He began to hit Lee on the thigh with the palm of his hand, over and over again, laughing with the glee of a wise and old child. At one pointed Lee's eyes flared involuntarily, as if the slaps were beginning to sting quite a bit—or maybe because the energy behind that slap was tremendously powerful in another way. Yogi Ramsuratkumar found this even funnier and broke into a cackle while he continued to slap. At one point Lee sheepishly placed his hand, palm down, on his thigh to protect it from the blows, but Yogi Ramsuratkumar playfully and briskly pushed his hand away and continued slapping with as much vigor as before, laughing all the while. At the end of this he rubbed Lee's leg gently and looked affectionately at him.

2 Lee Lozowick, *For the Love of God,* pp. 3-4.

It was an extraordinary afternoon of impossible and amazing synchronicities. Again, the Americans were captivated by the preternatural beauty and natural charisma of the beggar. A big part of the magic of that afternoon was that Yogi Ramsuratkumar read the future for Lee, as he did on many occasions for others. The booklet, *For the Love of God*, was returned to the young American man, who soon left—and interestingly, was not seen again.

Speaking to a group of students in 2002, Lee told his version of the story:

> The second time we visited Yogi Ramsuratkumar was in 1979. We were sitting with him and he was pouring his attention on us. As soon as we met him, he said to me, "Come over and sit here next to this Beggar." He lined up all my students facing us. He didn't know I was a teacher—at least not consciously. I didn't look any different than anybody else. I had been teaching for a few years, and I had already had enough of community, students, the burden of guruhood and all this business—I knew I had no choice, but at the same time, the mind said, "How did you ever get stuck with this job? Man, you could have been rich!" I had been successful in business, and in the three years after I sold my business, all my friends became multimillionaires—it could have been me! Instead I sold my business and spent all my money publishing *Spiritual Slavery* and *Beyond Release* and buying a piece of property where I could live with my students.
>
> Yogi Ramsuratkumar was really a romantic figure—one of the real yogis. Hilda Charlton, who first told us to go see him, had said, "He is one of the hidden saints, one of the ancient ones." Very romantic. In 1976 we had visited all the other yogis that had lots of Western students—Satya Sai Baba, Swami Muktananda, Shiva Bala Yogi and others—and if they didn't have Western students, they wanted them. But Yogi Ramsuratkumar was just sitting there in his rags, smoking a cigarette, with his eyes up in his head in some altered state of consciousness. This was the most exquisitely perfect Indian setting imaginable, and I was watching Yogi Ramsuratkumar.
>
> His life looked like my dream: I had the idea that it would be great to sit in this incredibly romantic setting with the temple just there, all the sounds of Indian street life, the hawkers and the music, the smells of incense drifting on the air. Here, watching Yogi Ramsuratkumar, I saw that every three or four hours somebody would wander by, walk up the steps, bow and say a few words. He would say a few words back to them and they would wander off, then he would just sit there alone. Boy, did that look good to me! Meditating for hours a day on the concrete platform. I was looking at him and thinking, "This guy . . . yes, yes!"
>
> He looked at me and said, "Lee, what do you want?"
>
> Did I say, freedom, money, comfort? None of those things. The only

> thing that came to my mind—which was already his mind, and this proves it, because Lee Lozowick could never have thought of this—was, "I want to be just like you."
>
> Yogi Ramsuratkumar used to look up over your shoulder like he was reading the future—but it's his mind reading the future, not his eyes. It was very exciting when he did that. So he kind of looked at me and his eyes went up. For a long time he wasn't looking at anything, then he looked me in the eyes again and tears came to his eyes. He was very choked up. He said two things, one of which everybody knows, and the second of which only I heard, and I have never told anyone and I am not going to, because it reflects too positively on me, and it would be misused by my students.
>
> So Yogi Ramsuratkumar looked me in the eyes, and tears came to his eyes and his voice was a little bit choked up. He said, "No, Lee will travel all over the world." At that time, that was absolutely ridiculous because there were maybe twenty people in the community, and we had no money. We were just a bunch of kids, myself included. I was an immature guru kid, and my students were immature devotee kids! At that time I had not the slightest intention of teaching anywhere except right in our little New Jersey town, or maybe in New York City. I had no idea of traveling and going around the world.
>
> Yogi Ramsuratkumar could *see*. When he would look up like this, some people would say, "He is reading the Akashic records," or whatever we call it. The way I look at it is that he was reading your life, as it is in the moment. He just wanted to see how to respond to my request, to be just like him, so he had tears in his eyes—because little did I know how much like him I was going to be. Before Suzuki Roshi gave the transmission of his lineage to Richard Baker, just before they walked out of the room for the initiation ceremony, he turned to Richard Baker and said, "I am really sorry for what I am about to do to you." So, the part about traveling around the world—well, Yogi Ramsuratkumar didn't have tears in his eyes about that. That part was just, "Oh yeah, this is what you're going to do."[3]

Caylor went to meet Yogi Ramsuratkumar early in the afternoon that same day, and along the way encountered Phyllis. It was a good day for a long walk, having rained that day and remained cloudy and cool all afternoon; she had just finished a five-hour *pradakshina* around Arunachala. She mentioned that she believed she had seen Lee Lozowick at Ramanashram earlier that day. Caylor had never met Lee personally, but owned a copy of the book, *For the Love of God*, having also heard of him from Hilda Charlton, who mentioned Lee from time to time in her New York meetings. He commented that he doubted that it was Lee Lozowick she had seen, but as soon as they

4 Lee Lozowick, *Hohm Sahaj Mandir Study Manual,* Vol. III, Chapter 2, pp. 12-14.

reached the *mandapam*, Yogi Ramsuratkumar announced the news.

"You know Lee? Yes, Lee Lozowick! He has come," Swami burst out as soon as Caylor and Phyllis entered the *mandapam*. Yogi Ramsuratkumar went on to relay how Lee and his three friends, Radha, Mirabai and Joe, had waited on the streets that very afternoon singing *bhajans* for three hours.

"Such patience this beggar had rarely witnessed in any soul!" Yogi Ramsuratkumar said. He told Caylor that he had wandered out to see who was singing the *bhajans* and learned it was "famous Lee," as Yogi Ramsuratkumar put it. He had spent some time with them earlier in the day, and even as he was recounting all this to Caylor and Phyllis, Lee and his friends walked up the stairs and joined the group. Yogi Ramsuratkumar asked everyone to shift their position, with Phyllis moving to the far right so that the four other guests were between Caylor and Phyllis, and the circle was enlarged to include Lee, Radha, Mirabai and Joe. Lee sat across from Yogi Ramsuratkumar.

Within some few minutes, two Ambassador automobiles stopped in front of the house. Perumal announced the visitors, some Indian businessmen, one of whom was Parthasarathy, a close devotee of Yogi Ramsuratkumar. The beggar rose to greet the men as they came walking up the steps and onto the platform of the *mandapam*. They were positioned along the stairway side of the platform.

"How is it that you have all come to see this beggar?" he asked.

"Mr. Parthasarathy had told us about you, Swamiji."

"So you have come all this way—then he must have spoken very highly about this beggar!" Yogi Ramsuratkumar took on a playful guise, and everyone was completely taken in with the enjoyment of it. Turning to Parthasarathy, he said, "Somehow you must have convinced them that this sinner is a holy man. Like some other friends who are fond of this beggar, you bring these holy people to bless this sinner. It is your compassion. Unless you bring all the holy people to bless this dirty sinner, how can he ever be purified?" At each pause Yogi Ramsuratkumar broke into mischievous laughter. Everyone else laughed too. "We have come for your blessings." After sitting for five minutes with the businessmen, Yogi Ramsuratkumar suddenly got up, walked down the stairs and toward the Ambassador that was parked in the lane. He went directly to the driver of the car and began to talk with him, leaving the devotees upstairs while he chatted happily with the driver. The Indian businessmen and the Americans sat there together in silence, looking at each other. Lee asked one of them where they had come from.

"We drove from Madras," they said. It was a long way to drive for the beggar's blessings to have only a few minutes with him. It was powerful to witness Yogi Ramsuratkumar making such a teaching lesson: the corporate heads of an important investment company went largely ignored while the saint spent all his time with their chauffeur, a mere servant. After fifteen minutes with the driver, Yogi Ramsuratkumar came back up the stairs and then, with the full force of his spiritual authority, he blessed the men, saying, "You have my Father's blessings." As he raised his hand in blessing, the men all prostrated and received a piece of fruit from Yogi Ramsuratkumar. He followed them out and watched till they were gone.

After these devotees left, the now extended group of Americans fell into a sublime silence in the exalted presence of Yogi Ramsuratkumar. Caylor wrote in his journal that day:

> The meditation that followed was pure love. Right from the start of this long uninterrupted silence, I relaxed into an aura of deep love and peace. It was unnecessary to even meditate. Yogi Ramsuratkumar relaxed against the mandapam pillar. He was enveloped by shadows. Occasionally the candlelight flashed in his fiery eyes or coruscated off his gold brocade shawl; he wore gold on the outside, but the real gold, so to speak, was on the inside. Lee's friends, Joe and Mirabai, were experiencing something quite intense—automatic kriyas and mudras were manifesting in their bodies. Seemingly alarmed, at one point the master inquired aloud, "What is her name?" She then became more relaxed, and the physical contortions ceased. Lee and Radha sat quietly, casually, totally at ease. At the end Yogi Ramsuratkumar joked with Joe, slapping him on the back, calling him "Jo-lly." We all had been deeply moved by this experience.

The next day Lee and his company met again with Yogi Ramsuratkumar, spending most of the time in silence. It was after this day that Lee wrote his first poem to Yogi Ramsuratkumar, dated February 21, 1979, Mt. Arunachala.

Was there ever a Slave
    who had such a Master?
Was there ever one so low
    who was blessed by One so high?
Was there ever one more lost
    whom You had chosen to find?
Was there ever one who hid so far
    whom You sought so long?
I think not Dear Beloved, I must be
    the only one for whom
You would suffer so and Love so.
    I think I must be the only one.

Lee and his students continued meeting with the beggar every day until they left Tiruvannamalai, on February 24. On one of the evenings they approached the *mandapam* and joined Yogi Ramsuratkumar. The *lila* of the booklet, *For the Love of God*, still hung in the air like the lingering scent of jasmine. One evening Yogi Ramsuratkumar gave Lee, who was sitting beside him, a sidelong glance, and with the innocence of a child, asked, "Lee, do you know God?"

Lee answered, "Yes."

"Does God ever talk to you?" the beggar pressed on.

Lee answered, "Sometimes he talks to me."

"Ohhh . . . Ohhh! You are so lucky . . . God never talks to this poor beggar. This beggar prays, but God never talks to him. Tell me, does God ever eat with you?"

"Sometimes he does, sometimes he doesn't . . ." Lee answered.

"Tell me, when God comes to you, what does he wear?" the beggar queried again, much like a small child.

"Sometimes God wears a suit like a Western businessman, and sometimes God wears the rags of a beggar, just like you," Lee answered quietly, keeping his eyes on Yogi Ramsuratkumar with an unwavering gaze.

Yogi Ramsuratkumar slumped back on the wall, his right hand holding the palmyra fan raised to his head. He gently rocked back and forth in a rhythmic sway while his left hand seemed to hold an invisible *mala* that moved in the long established habit of *japa*. Breaking out of this *bhava* he slowly asked Lee, "Do you know how God speaks?"

Lee answered seriously, "Sometimes he gives great speeches, and sometimes he speaks just a few words, like you."

"Do you know where God lives?"

"Sometimes in a big fancy mansion, and sometimes on the streets, just like you," Lee responded.

The purity and innocence of the yogi's totally guileless questions blossomed in the space like a summer garden while their spiritual potency grew and swelled, until Lee had answered twenty or more of his questions on the nature of God. Throughout this time Yogi Ramsuratkumar slipped in and out of *bhavas*, in which he would fall back against the wall of the *mandapam*, close his eyes or hold up his fan in blessing. The small area of the platform, perhaps twenty feet by twenty feet, overlooking Car Street down below, had been transformed, as it was on every night when Yogi Ramsuratkumar occupied its environs, into a sacred space—a *temenos*, circled around and protected by the divine influence of a great master, posing in the rags of a dirty beggar.

These questions about the nature of the Divine as the immanent God, posed as if by a child, were like a subtle yeast that had been planted in a fertile medium, and in this way the experience with the beggar worked in Lee at a deep level. They spurred a creative process that Balarama described:

> Our traveling schedule, which was twenty-six cities in seventy-three days, was grueling. We traveled many miles, by bus, train and plane. Once we arrived in Tiruvannamalai to visit Yogi Ramsuratkumar, we were staying at Ramanashram, and Lee and I shared a room. Contrary to my usual tendencies, during this time in Tiruvannamalai I felt moved to not bother Lee with any questions or inquiries or ask anything of him—unlike the rest of the trip, where all three of us were freely questioning Lee and in a constant dialogue with him. He seemed very happy to be left alone, and after our first two meetings with Yogi Ramsuratkumar, every evening

he was writing like mad. It was clear that the best way to serve him was to leave him alone, to be quiet and allow him all the space and silence he needed to write.

I had the sense that it was a pivotal point in the dharma, in his teaching; something was happening that was very important. I didn't want to have a casual relationship with him. I was always joking with Lee and everybody else—attempting to be humorous—and when Yogi Ramsuratkumar kept saying that my name was "Joke," it was a shock of a kind. I was at the effect of his teaching lesson, and it became a very strong consideration for me. Lee's intensity with his own process threw me into my process, and so for me too, it became a time of reflection, and I was drawn into reflecting on what was going on in Yogi Ramsuratkumar's company. For two days Lee wrote in the late evenings, or if we had a period of rest during the day, in between visits with Yogi Ramsuratkumar. There was a mood of relaxed consideration in him, and it became a time of respite and sanctuary, where he could just write.

The essay that Lee wrote during this visit with Yogi Ramsuratkumar, which was inspired by their interaction, appeared in his next book, *The Cheating Buddha*, published in 1980. It was a consideration of loving God, the recurring theme of his interactions with Yogi Ramsuratkumar, and began with the heading, "Dedicated to Ram Surat Kumar, My Dear Ram Ram. Mt. Arunachala—February 21, 1979." The following is an excerpt from that essay:

> Loving God is not as simple as one would think . . . . How common are the world's religious cults and movements whose followers all claim to "love God." And yet even this spiritual love is no more than a matter of brain chemistry. Rather than genital orgasm, the spiritual seeker experiences the firing of other nerve endings in the brain as a result of energy movements due to excessive meditation, pranayama, or the aura of one who is experiencing the same. The seeker "feels good" and thanks God for feeling so good, even ecstatic, and assumes that he "loves God" because of this.
>
> And as long as he continues to get these "good feelings," as long as he gets high every time he meditates, he remains under the quite mistaken idea that he still "loves God" and will "love God" forever. The culmination of self-meditative illusion is the seeker who gets high, even mindless, in any teacher's presence or even at the mere suggestion of things spiritual, and therefore assumes that he is a great saint or perhaps Jesus.
>
> Both the puerile "love" and the adolescent mentality, genitally centered, and the "love" of the so-called spiritual student, brain centered and mind created, are casualties to the cessation of the programmed

activity that generates their respective feelings.

How many ex-lovers of God there are! All because their teacher stopped "getting them high" or because they became intellectually or emotionally disillusioned or because meditation became boring and uninteresting or too challenging . . . . Of course none of that was Love, Truly. Love is not so fragile that it is destroyed by mere worldly activity, for love is a matter of Heart. Loving God is a Heartful affair, not one of intellectual rationale or proper nerve or muscular activity. Love for God, once seen, once felt, is Love for God eternally, regardless of external or internal conditions and states of body and/or thought. Loving God is not a physical determinant, although certainly, even frequently, particular physical states of pleasure accompany this Love. Even so, neither these physical states alone nor any amount of proselytizing, verbal or mental, in themselves can equate with Loving God. Loving God is a matter of Real Heart, not just the heart in the center of the chest which is often the focal point of attention when one thinks or attends to Love. The Love for God is nonspatial and nontemporal.

When one loves God, one Loves under all circumstances and through all expressions of humanness high and low. When one Loves God Truly, falling out of Love is not only absurd, it is literally impossible. If one "falls out of Love," that one has never loved. This applies as well to temporal love of the male/female, male/male or female/female type. Once one Truly Loves, he loves forever, even in the face of the involution of the worlds and universes into the void. And when one Loves, he Loves even when the Beloved is lost or absent. Love, once felt, once Heartful, depends on no object or attention, not even the form or thought of the very Beloved that is the source of this unimaginable Love in the first place.

When one truly Loves another human, that Love continues whether the Lover loses the Beloved through death or to another human being. The Lover Loves forever, even though he or she may find another mate, even another Beloved. Still always, the Beloved is Loved, present or absent. That is why great Lovers like Meher Baba and Jesus Christ loved so many and so fully, so powerfully. Their Beloved Lord was in every face, He shone through every eye. They Loved all who came on bended knee.

And when the Spiritual Beloved is lost, as in St. John's Dark Night of the Soul, even then, in the face of the most devastating loss and emptiness, the True Lover Loves still. Any Lover of God Loves whether God stays or goes. Loving God, one doesn't need the outward show of "pomp and circumstance." Just to Love, the Beloved always knows, He rests, offering all. And the True Lover knows that he is always offered all by his Beloved. St. John, during the unbearable heat of the Dark Night, knew even then that this very heat was God's Gift. And such is the Heart of anyone who truly loves God. It is His Heart.[4]

This essay marked the beginning of a major revelation that would be termed by his students "the sacred message and ultimate teaching work" of Lee Lozowick, which was published in 1982 as the book, *The Only Grace is Loving God*. The book, written in the "twilight language" of a divine ecstasy, makes a distinction between the "Will of God" and the "Whim of God." The Whim of God is solely related to the only Grace, which is the divine gift of loving God in the most profound sense. According to the author, "Loving God is not, cannot be attained, but it is not already True of anyone either. It is the only true Gift of God to Mankind. Loving God does not transcend the ordinary earthly circumstances but obscures the distraction in them, through the obsession with the Beloved's visage."[5] The book, inspired by Yogi Ramsuratkumar, begins with the first published poem written to Yogi Ramsuratkumar by Lee.

For so long I sought riches
 and found much wealth
till I discovered You,
 a Beggar,
and now seek only the Poverty
 You so regally bear.
To be as Poor as you,
 Beloved Guru,
is a blessing I only dream of
 with awe.
So sings Lee, his wealth effaced
 in the Poverty of his Lord.
May this only be so.

In early December 1977 Kirsti, a friend of Caylor's from the Theosophical Society who had met Yogi Ramsuratkumar the year before at his *jayanthi*, came to Tiruvannamalai again for the Deepam festival and sought Yogi Ramsuratkumar out. He received her, and it was the beginning of a lifetime relationship in which he guided and worked with her in many different ways—some of them difficult to bear, as he was often moved to simply send Kirsti away. Juxtaposed with other relationships Yogi Ramsuratkumar had with Westerners, it seemed that he was hard on Kirsti, but things are not always what they appear to be. Kirsti was an extremely strong practitioner and yogini with a natural

4 Lee Lozowick, *The Cheating Buddha,* p. 41.
5 Lee Lozowick, *The Only Grace Is Loving God*, p. 44.

disposition toward renunciation, austerity and devotion. Her example demonstrates how the guru will often give the stronger sadhana to those who have the fortitude, discipline and being to withstand it. In Kirsti's case, he refused to even admit that he was her guru and kept the relationship, in her own words, "very casual, yet there was a power in him; his every action left no doubt that he seemed to know what he did and what was going on with you. There was a sense of mastery of his every movement, action, word, glance." In her experience, even the dog, Sai Baba, was part of how he worked. Years later Kirsti reflected about her second meeting with Yogi Ramsuratkumar and the early years in his company:

> The twinkle in his eyes had stayed in my memory along with an inner feeling that I needed to meet this man again. I found him at his house. He said to come at seven-thirty p.m. I gave him an apple and his dog kept rubbing against me. I don't remember anyone else being present at that first meeting in 1977. It took maybe an hour. I sat in the corner on the verandah and he held the apple in his hands and against his forehead; he seemed to be pondering. Indeed, there was so much joy and love in him.
>
> What kept me hooked to Yogi Ramsuratkumar, although I saw many mahatmas who invited me to join their ashrams and acted as if they were a guru to me, was the greatness of his personality. One was like a beggar in front of a king near him, but it did not matter that one could not ask questions or tell events of one's personal life to him and engage him in normal discussion. People did not dare to knock at his door if he was inside the house when they arrived to see him. They waited, feeling that somehow he knew they were there and would come if he wasn't too busy with something else.
>
> He never explained his actions. Some Westerners I knew misinterpreted his sternness sometimes as anger, but I felt it was just intensity. If his sternness reminded them of someone in their past who had been short-tempered, they would feel hurt and cry for a full day after being told, "This Beggar is busy. There is no need to see him. There is nothing here. Go to the temple!" For me that meant that he was seeing someone else that day and really was busy. Next day one could try again.
>
> His intensity transmitted a power that silenced my mind, and the heart would begin to glow and stay so for the rest of the day and often the night also. When I sat with him every night in the [late] 70s, the whole night and next morning my mind would be very quiet with direct perception of things and events around, with a mood of joy and peace at the background. If I was resting, the mind would stay in a state between waking and sleeping with a sense of being secure, protected, embraced by love and deep peace. If at that time I brought my attention to anything that had been bothering me, I could see how to act about it. I could understand

how the mind worked. The right action would keep up the capacity of insight; it would come from that peace I felt near him. If I acted out of agitation of reason or feelings, it would land me in trouble. So, I would always be still when in doubt and wait until it was revealed what to do from that peace and joy within.

One of his main qualities was unpredictability. Whatever he did startled my mind clear, and if sitting with him for some time, the mind would melt into peace and clarity. I always went to him expecting him to act according to the moment. If he was wrathful today, tomorrow he could be extremely kind and loving. He kept his freedom to act according to how he felt always intact, until the ashram came up which probably needed some adjustment with the activity that is inevitable when people live together and need to work together. I do not know that side of how he was. My relationship with him was always direct, involving only him.

A few months later on Guru Purnima [1978], he asked some ladies to sing his name and personally taught us the tunes. He demonstrated how every mood going out from him was under his control. Once I sat with him in the [mandapam] tower when he was waiting for Caylor to come. He wore the turquoise turban and blue and gold bedsheet Caylor had given him. He was pacing back and forth, impatiently glancing to the street, like a lover eagerly waiting for the beloved. Until then, whenever I went to him I had felt that love pouring upon me; some friends said that once when they walked in the streets after sitting with him, they felt drunk with the joy and peace of his attention that had showered upon them.

This time, [as he waited for Caylor], I could see the love oozing out from every pore of his being, but it was as if I had been placed behind a glass wall. There was as little coming towards me as I could expect from a cement wall. His love was not a casual mood, it was something else. He had mastery of energy, all of his personal energies, to such a degree that the interactions looked casual. But the spontaneity was that of someone thoroughly skilled, not that of a person who acts on impulses. His love was total giving, yet it would stay under cover when something else was needed for a particular situation.

Caylor came. Later on Yogiji told Caylor to tell me to stay near Ramanashram so I could stay longer in Tiruvannamalai and meditate. He did not speak to me directly. That day it was as if I did not exist to him directly. Whenever he gave any instruction for sadhana it was a hint like that. If I followed it up, or even noticed it, it was up to me.

For six weeks after that whenever I went to see him he would give me fruit and say, "No need to come here now. Ramanashram is a very good place for meditation." Until then I had been sitting in the caves on the hill [Arunachala] in the daytime and going to see him at night. The

> mountain was a wonderful place to be. I loved it. This time, in spite of the noises at the ashram, I sat solidly four to ten hours daily in the meditation hall. He never told me how I should meditate so I just observed the mind and feelings, tried japa and recollected past moods and experiences to see how they worked on my consciousness. He had told me to sit, so I sat and waited to see how his Father's blessing would work on me.
>
> During this time Sai Baba the First, Yogi Ramsuratkumar's dog, used to be around. I usually sat in the back of the tower, and when people sat in such a way that I could not see him, the dog would go and rub himself against them and they would move aside. Indians don't like to be touched by dogs. Sai Baba really helped me with darshans. When Yogi gave orders he would howl a long "*Oooommmm.*"
>
> Sai Baba the Third was so overwhelmed by love of his Master that he would jump. He could not get in satsang if he got too ecstatic. During that time I spent three hours at the temple every night. The dog would start jumping when he saw me. He remembered seeing me sitting with the Yogi. I said to Ramsuratkumar, "The dog is so fond of you he starts jumping when he sees anything that reminds him of you." I had always felt half invisible in the presence of Yogiji, but this time he gave me the greatest compliment I ever heard from his lips. He said, "Kirsti is more fond of this beggar than the dog!"

Yogi Ramsuratkumar once told Kirsti, "This beggar wants to be free to move without a fixed program." That day he cut the "singing lessons" with the women short and sent Kirsti away. Later she saw him wading in puddles of rainwater in the temple, holding the hand of a young man from Bangalore who used to visit him often. He often sat in the temple, where he could see people going into the shrines for darshan while he stayed invisibly in the shadows. Concealed in this way he was free to bless everyone who walked into the temple, raising the fan in his hand and moving it in a rhythm with the slowly moving queue. Kirsti wrote, "I felt his work was to bless people to know his Father, yet he was everything for everyone."

While sitting on the flagstones of the enormous temple with Yogi Ramsuratkumar and a few others, Kirsti watched a feeble old man approach, hobbling along with a staff. He stopped and shouted, "Please, forgive my sins!" The beggar asked him to repeat what he said and the man yelled, "Please, forgive my sins." Absorbing this in an instant, the yogi pondered briefly, then raised both his hands in blessing and shouted back, "My Father forgives your sins! Your sins are forgiven!" Satisfied, the old man walked away joyfully, almost dancing.

It was not unusual to find Yogi Ramsuratkumar sitting in the sun on the flagstones in the temple courtyard, wrapped in several warm shawls during some of the hottest times of the year. Nonplussed and disbelieving that he could bear such heat, Kirsti asked, "Are you cold?"

"Kodi Kodi Swami wears even twenty gowns at times," the beggar replied, but Kirsti couldn't help but notice that that was in the winter. On this hot May day, Yogi Ramsuratkumar was wearing seven or eight shawls. These acts of *tapas* were somehow mysteriously connected with the inner work of the beggar king, the aim of which was for the benefit of all. Once when some devotees were sitting on the verandah of his house on Sannadhi Street, he stood up and raised his hands in blessing and said, "This beggar is happy to be born again and again and again if his life has benefited even a single living being. This beggar is happy to be born again and again to do his Father's work." Many times he was heard to spontaneously utter, in ecstatic moments, this vow of the bodhisattva. Another time he said, "All the sins of humanity are in this beggar." Because of this burden, he understood and accepted everyone.

Yogi Ramsuratkumar's relationship with Kirsti was enigmatic to the extreme. He often sent her away or refused to talk with her at all; still she persisted, believing in her heart that he was her guru. On one such occasion, when the yogi had made her stay outside for some time he said to her, "If you truly love someone, whatever he does is alright." At other times he would say things like, "This is not the place for people like you, you can get nothing here . . ." Kirsti wrote to him in a poem, "Your words have made me self-concerned. I do not know what kind I am." The guru kept her always slightly off balance in this way, so that she was never certain whether he would draw her in, invite her to sit with his group at any given time, or send her away to the temple or to meditate at Ramanashram. Whenever she made a mistake, he would remind her about it for days. It was always a delicate balance in his company. The question for everyone was, how to come into the sacred space he had created and interact without causing any disturbance to his work?

Although Kirsti asked him on many occasions to admit that he was her guru, Yogi Ramsuratkumar was not willing to make such statements, and he did not relent. He frequently sent her to Anandashram, where she spent a significant amount of time with Mataji Krishnabai before her death. At one point when she pressured him on this point, he said, "Ramdas, the master, is alive here," patting his heart, demonstrating that one should be close to the guru regardless of physical distance. When she asked for initiation, or *diksha*, he became impatient and snapped, "Some gurus like to send their devotees to other gurus." If she had said one more word, he would have thrown her out—an experience she had had on some occasions. Sometimes he would say bluntly, "This beggar is busy!" and send her away. An understandable statement only if one realized that his life was actually one of prayer and abiding communion with the "Father in Heaven."

This burden was not lost on Kirsti, who noticed that sometimes Yogi Ramsuratkumar would look worried when he saw devotees approaching with huge garlands, some of them being six feet long and weighing pounds. At times like that he would often shout from a distance when he saw them approaching, "Go to the temple, do not come here!" Sometimes he was drenched with water that was sprinkled on the flowers to keep them fresh, and his shirts would be stained with thin red stripes, dyed from the strings around the flower malas. The weight of many of these malas, which sometimes had thorny leaves or odd sticks in them, could be quite uncomfortable, but it was not uncommon to see him weighted down with four or five of them at a time, virtually lost in a swath of roses, the small fragrant white *sampangi* lily and tulsi leaves.

Once Kirsti waited for hours in the Theradi Mandapam for Yogi Ramsuratkumar to appear. When he finally arrived with some new friends, he noticed her right away.

"You have been waiting here for two hours, isn't it so? Two hours is a very long time. Go, and take rest," he said kindly. Then, giving her an apple and with hand raised in blessing, he sent her away. The guru, in her case, forced her to work with uncertainty, paradox and what appeared to be rejection, but it only served to fan the fire of her devotion to the beggar king of Tiruvannamalai.

Once when she had a flu coming on and was feeling quite ill, she walked passed his house on Sannadhi Street with some friends while following a temple procession. The master was just opening the gate to his verandah and walking down the few steps to the street, when he looked up and gazed at her for a few seconds. Then he was gone back inside—and all of her aches and pains were also gone. The flu went away, and she went on to walk around Mount Arunachala, offering incense and flowers to a Shiva *lingam* shrine, not returning home until the sun rose.

His ways were totally unpredictable in one way and consistent in another. At one point Yogi Ramsuratkumar commented to Kirsti and some others visitors from the Theosophical Society, "Caylor stayed with this beggar for six months in order to collect information for the biography, but this beggar did not tell him anything!" Although some felt strongly that the book was more a "vision of an unfolding of a theosophical adept" than an objective account of Yogiji's life, one could not really make an assessment based on such a comment coming from the master of paradox and subtlety. Yogi Ramsuratkumar spoke on occasions about various experiences of his earlier years, and he told certain stories to individual people, but one thing was certain: never did he divulge anything of substance about those seven mysterious years of wandering between 1952 and 1959.

Caylor crossed paths with Kirsti a number of times during the winter and spring of 1979, like in their meeting with the master that occurred on February 27 that year. Caylor had stopped for a lime soda while he bought some jasmine flowers for Yogi Ramsuratkumar. Walking up the steps to the Theradi Mandapam, he saw the master loom large in seeming anticipation. His fan was raised overhead "like a sword cutting deep." Caylor prostrated before him and offered the flowers and a ten-rupee note.

"Soon you can leave this place. Go to Madras for some time. This beggar is not used to this kind of sitting every night." It was a blunt and sudden commandment.

"Yes Swami. I will go," Caylor answered, rather down-heartedly as he turned to find a seat. The conversation turned to a discussion of some health problems Caylor had been having, for which Yogi Ramsuratkumar made very specific recommendations. Then he commented on a letter that Caylor had recently written to him.

"What you wrote in your letter about all existence being suffering because it is rooted in desire and fear is true. For this reason this beggar asks you to live your life with as few desires as possible. All desires cannot be uprooted, but we can make an effort to eliminate many and lessen the strength of them. Some wise men have rightly said it is only when the all-pervading Divine begins to overtake our lives and to fill our hearts that these last remaining desires fall away. It is this beggar's experience that, when at last our minds become filled with the holy name of the Father, then there is no room for other needs and attractions. All desires fall away. Remember the Father and remember His holy names. It is up to you which of them you choose . . . This beggar has said so many times that in his opinion *The Secret Doctrine* will give you strength. There is much food for you there. And as the mind has a tendency to wander here and there, you can let it wander within *The Secret Doctrine*.

"This one sentence in your letter," he continued, " 'All existence is suffering.' You say it is from the Buddha?"

"Yes, it was the first of his four noble truths," Caylor answered.

"Is this sentence found in *The Secret Doctrine* anywhere?" Yogi Ramsuratkumar asked. Caylor responded with what he thought it would be, but in the style of Madame Blavatsky. After moment of silence Yogi Ramsuratkumar continued.

"Have you read the writings of Yogi T. Subbha Rao?" He was referring to a highly respected member of the Theosophical Society.

"I have read some essays. His book I have never read."

"He had great respect for *The Secret Doctrine,*" the beggar commented. Caylor added that in fact Subba Rao was requested by his master to contribute a great deal to the Sanskrit features it. In this way Subba Rao helped create the book.

Yogi Ramsuratkumar then raised his hand in blessing and went on with enthusiasm, "This beggar is pleased that at least you have some admiration for him. Yes, he has done a lot to create. This beggar has passed through much of what he has written and he sensed tremendous power there. His words work. They help us. Those books may be in the library at Adyar. You can pass through them sometime."

Unusually verbose, Yogi Ramsuratkumar continued, "Adyar is most suitable for you now. For many reasons—not only the fine accommodations . . . There is something about your temperament. I can't say what it is. Go there, settle down. Be there for some time. And then if you wish, you may come to see this beggar now and then for a day or two or travel anywhere you wish.

"This beggar also feels you should meet Anandamayee Ma and spend some time there with her. It will be very good for you to meet her. There is some reason this beggar is making this suggestion. He expressed this wish to you some years ago—you may be remembering."

Caylor replied, "Swami, I did have the opportunity to meet her twice, but I have never stayed with her long."

During this interchange the beggar had walked out of the *mandapam* several times to meet various guests, Indian devotees who had arrived. Kirsti sat beside Caylor on the concrete floor. As the evening deepened the beggar's profile was silhouetted against the night, bright and majestic with starlight. It was quiet, and the mood was one of great gratitude and love.

Caylor ventured, "I have decided not to go to Kanya Kumari as I proposed in my letter to you."

"Oh . . . That is so good. This beggar felt it was not right for you, but he did not feel he should interfere if you wanted to go." He stood up and walked over to Caylor and gave him some flowers and grapes—the *prasad* for the evening. It was time to leave. Kirsti and Caylor bowed before him. Yogi Ramsuratkumar pointed skyward.

"The Father will look after you," he said, and sent them on their way.

The days flowed past and Tiruvannamalai was its usual bright and swirling chaos of images and impressions—the busy tea and coffee stalls; swarthy pigs roaming in the mud, scavenging amidst the refuse that littered the streets; the noisy chatter of children; beggars and sadhus wrapped in rags, sitting on the stones and watching the passing streams of humanity with reddened eyes; the gleam of brass vessels in the market; crows soaring black against sunrise and sunset. Above all this the green mass of Arunachala rose up, generous host to the resonant deities carved in stone on the temple *gopurams*, the gods who appeared as if from the mists of time and watched over all.

It was March, 1979 and Caylor was back in Tiruvannamalai. He had walked to the *mandapam* barefoot through windy, rain-swept streets that ran like rivers. The sky was filled with dark clouds and the heavy presence of the storm glowered like a hurricane. On the way there another Westerner, Murray, had called out and asked Caylor to tell Yogi Ramsuratkumar that he, his wife Shanti and the baby Mithra would try to come if the rain stopped.

"You said you have three letters—please give them," Yogi Ramsuratkumar said when Caylor arrived. He held his hand out to receive the items.

"Yes, Swami," Caylor rummaged through his bags to retrieve the letters, knowing that Yogi Ramsuratkumar knew full well there were more items than the letters that Caylor had brought, intending to ask for his blessing.

"I have also some gifts. Will you accept them?"

"Who are they from?" the beggar asked. Caylor deliberated to remember everything in his sack. He had come with a locket given by a friend, Laura, a cassette tape from Hilda and other items.

"From myself and one other friend," he answered.

"Alright. Let me see what it is."

Yogi Ramsuratkumar accepted some items and refused others, then they settled down on the floor under the shelter of the *mandapam* and again the silence began to overflow. After a moment of indecision Caylor tried again, "Swami?" Yogi Ramsuratkumar stirred, not sure at first who was calling for him.

"Swami, one of the three letters is from a girl who loves you very much." He gave a gentle *namaskaram* with hands placed gently together at his chest, to signify his appreciation for her reverence towards him.

"She has enclosed a locket with her letter. She hoped that before I left you might bless it for her."

"We will see," the yogi replied, noncommittal. The silence fell back over them like a blanket, leaving Caylor to contemplate the mystical madness of the guru. A gray Ambassador stopped on Sannadhi Street at the bottom of the stairs bearing an Indian family that came for the master's blessings. The mother prostrated at the beggar's feet in a bodily gesture that spoke volumes of an inner surrender.

Kirsti, Murray and Shanti arrived and settled into the space. The beggar suddenly retrieved the letters from somewhere underneath his blanket and felt each one. He asked Caylor to open the one with the locket enclosed, then held his hand out for it and closed his hand around it. He pulled the chain through his fingers to see it more closely in the candlelight.

"This beggar feels this has already been sanctified by somebody," he stated in a questioning tone. "Perhaps Hilda has touched it. Somebody has sanctified it."

Caylor answered, "I believe she only wears it for meditation. She has told me she feels you are her guru." He said nothing, but held the locket a while, then gave it back.

A few days later, carrying jasmine flowers and some cigarettes, Caylor approached the bazaar where he had been searching for Perumal. Slowly, he started up the stairs to the *mandapam*. Entering the tower "room" he found Yogi Ramsuratkumar waiting for him, cast in the yellow haze of two candles.

"I am leaving for Madras tomorrow. I will leave in the morning." Caylor began.

"Ohhh," the beggar replied softly. Once again silence reigned over the space until the subject of Laura, the girl who had sent the locket, came up. When Yogi Ramsuratkumar began to ask questions about her, Caylor explained that she worked with acupressure therapy, but was now working in a hospital.

"Has she ever met this beggar?"

"No," he explained. "She has come to know you through Hilda. She is one of Janis' closest friends. She also has a daughter, Elisa."

"How do you pronounce her name?" he asked. He was gathering information about the unknown young woman who said he was her guru; it was a way to tune his blessings to her. Caylor pronounced the name carefully, until Yogi Ramsuratkumar indicated he had registered it. A long silent pause ensued.

They talked about other mutual acquaintances and friends of Caylor's back in the States, students of Hilda Charlton. A man named Freddy had written a song for Yogi Ramsuratkumar sung to the tune of "The Battle Hymn of the Republic." Caylor sang it for the beggar, who studied the paper where the words were written. A very sweet mood of intimacy seemed to descend upon them.

The beggar took up his small cloth bag—the one-rupee variety—and took out three letters. He handed one to Caylor, saying, "Please look at this one very fine letter. You will not be knowing him, but you will understand something of what he writes here." The writer's name was Sadashivan, and the letter said, "Humble prostrations at the lotus feet of Sri Satguru Yogi Ramsuratkumar. Shirdi Sai Baba says: 'I require no door to enter. I have no form nor any extension. I live always and everywhere.' " It was signed off to "Sri Satguru Yogi Ramsuratkumar who also lives always and everywhere."

While Caylor studied the letter, Yogi Ramsuratkumar studied him for nearly ten minutes; it seemed he wanted Caylor to take note of something. Some visitors arrived; Caylor handed back the letter and said, "He has understood you, Swami."

"But he has never met this beggar!" he exclaimed.

Soon Kirsti arrived, and Caylor moved to a seat near the pillar, deeply grateful for the intimate moments he had had. Not speaking directly to Kirsti, Yogi Ramsuratkumar gave her instructions through Caylor to stay near Ramanashram rather than in town, if her stay would be a prolonged one. A strong silence settled on them for over half an hour, in which Caylor mulled over the words in the letter. He fell into a devotional mood, and wrote later, "The renunciation of self and the all-pervading nature of the guru were delved into. Sang the master's name interiorly until he sent us away. Humble prostrations at the lotus feet of Sri Satguru Yogi Ramsuratkumar."

On March 20 Caylor sat again with Yogi Ramsuratkumar in the usual place. Kirsti was there also, and after a meditative silence the master stood up forcefully, picking up something that had been lying on the ground in front of him. These he placed in Caylor's hand, saying, "It is nellikkai." The beggar had handed him some dried gooseberries and an orange as *prasad*.

"Should I go?" Caylor asked, wondering if this signaled that it was time to go. Also giving something to Kirsti, Yogi Ramsuratkumar answered, "Tomorrow you can leave. This beggar has detained you for two extra days. Please excuse him."

A discussion of Caylor's travels in India ensued, in which Yogi Ramsuratkumar said kindly, "This beggar wishes you a pilgrimage." Caylor would travel to Delhi, Hardwar and Brindavan. With Yogi Ramsuratkumar's blessing he would also spend two weeks with Anandamayi Ma before he would leave in early May. Another silence welled up, this time blessed with a golden sense of well being and blessedness. Suddenly Yogi Ramsuratkumar rose again.

"I am taking leave of you now," the beggar said, handing Caylor and Kirsti flowers and a lemon. Prostrating at his feet, Caylor said goodbye.

Caylor humorously noted this moment of goodbye in his journal with the unknowable Yogi Ramsuratkumar: "Pretending to be poor and helpless, the master then thanked me and Kirsti for our devoted friendship and help. 'This beggar is always in need of friends . . . ' he said. After saying this he said, 'This friend (meaning Kirsti) is always coming and sitting with this beggar. She should sit in the ashram meditation hall. It is the perfect place for sadhana.' I could see she was almost crying. We walked down the stairs."

Caylor returned to the U.S. in May 1979, then came back to India again six months later, arriving in Tiruvannamalai again on December 16, 1979 with a close friend from Madras, A.V. Sunder, who was in charge of the second printing of *Yogi Ramsuratkumar, The Godchild, Tiruvannamalai*. They had brought the newly-printed second edition with them to give to Yogi Ramsuratkumar. After taking a room at the Dharmasala they met with Yogi Ramsuratkumar at the Arunachalesvara Temple, where they spent several hours together discussing business related to the reprinting of the book. The next morning Yogi Ramsuratkumar came to their room.

"After leaving here last night this beggar has had time to go through this book nicely. He feels the book is alright, photographs and all. It is quite satisfactory." He then suggested that Caylor go through the book, saying, "You will perceive some difference."

Caylor responded that he sensed "a strength and integrity missing in this edition."

Yogi Ramsuratkumar laughed softly and said, "This beggar feels that there is a spirit of yours that is missing."

Over the years the book had had its desired effect—it helped mitigate the harassment, the beatings and threats upon the beggar's life and gave him more safety within which he could relax into his work. Even so, very few people knew that while some of the harassment had stopped, there were still people who snuck into the backyard of his house on Sannadhi Street and scattered small pieces of broken glass in the pathway to the water closet. In the dim early morning light he would walk over the glass and cut his feet. After the broken glass was cleared away, the next morning there it was again. It wasn't until years later that Yogi Ramsuratkumar talked about this more openly.

At this time Yogi Ramsuratkumar was looking for a place where he could spend time with a small group of Westerners and A.V. Sunder without any interruption. A friend, Monica Egli, a young European woman who lived in Tiruvannamalai, had offered her house to the beggar saint and his companions for the afternoon. When they were settled in her sitting room, Yogi Ramsuratkumar commented, "This beggar would like to have some good time with Caylor like in the previous times. But in those days he was interested in experimenting with drugs. With drugs he thought he could practice yoga, but this beggar disagreed."

Sunder's nervous movements quickly captured the beggar's attention.

"What is this?" Yogi Ramsuratkumar asked, turning to Sunder.

"I have body pain."

"Body pain! Where?" Sunder pointed to his thighs and calves and said that he had pain all over his body and also mental pain, which he had become used to since childhood. Yogi Ramsuratkumar walked over to him and touched him in those spots.

"The pain is gone!" Sunder exclaimed in amazement.

"This beggar did not do anything. Father did it all." This was Yogi Ramsuratkumar's usual statement when he made the miraculous happen, such as spontaneous healings. His Indian devotees were quite used to this phenomena; in fact, he was well-known to heal or evoke miracles in many instances. It was new to the Westerners, however. After some while Sunder said that the pain had now arisen in other places in his body.

"Ohhh . . . Your body pain seems to travel all over!" Again Yogi Ramsuratkumar touched Sunder, who exclaimed that the pain had disappeared.

With a smile Yogi Ramsuratkumar said, "Even Sunder is adding to my propaganda! This beggar wants propaganda; this body wants propaganda. This beggar doesn't worry about what's inside the body."

Later Sunder said to the yogi, "Give Caylor all my good karma. I have so many buckets of good karma and bad karma. I request you to give all my buckets of good karma to Caylor."

Yogi Ramsuratkumar said, "He wouldn't want it."

Sunder said, "Then you take it."

The beggar replied, "I only take. I don't give," but Sunder was insistent.

"Alright, this beggar has taken it. Now you can cease to exist. But, you know, it is one thing to say these things and something else to truly surrender your karma. It is one thing for someone to say such things and quite something else to surrender his actions and the fruits of his actions to the Father. Unless we learn to give all good actions to God, it is all a waste. Whatever benefit is accrued will be spoiled by taking account the good things one may have done. All things belong to the Lord. It's very good to give back what we have. That's a virtue. We have to give what we have to the Lord. That's all we can do. It's a rare virtue."

Yogi Ramsuratkumar began to sing, "Jaya Hanuman, Jaya Hanuman . . . " His beautiful voice filled the space, bringing the sweetness of the strong *prema bhakti*, the mood of love and adoration of God that was underlying his words, even more fully into the room.

Sunder said, "You live such a beautiful life. How can I be like you?"

"*Enna*! Don't come down to this beggar's level."

"I want to be a beggar like you," Sunder insisted.

"What do you know about the life of this beggar?" Yogi Ramsuratkumar responded, "I can say in truth you know nothing about this dirty sinner. His real life is with Father, and there is really nothing I can say about that. Is there anyone who can say anything about him? He will always remain the unknown."

"Who is your Father? Do you mean God?" Sunder asked.

"You can call him anything you want . . ." Yogi Ramsuratkumar replied. Then, "Sunder is here. Everything is beautiful. You know the meaning of the name Sunder? 'Beautiful.' "

Caylor was taking sketchy notes of the conversation and the master's words. Gael, one of several Westerners who were present said, "He's our witness. We have a witness."

Juliette asked, "Witness . . . what does it mean?"

Gael answered, "Witness means observer."

Yogi Ramsuratkumar interjected, "Oh ho . . . he's observing. Somebody has to observe, so Caylor is observing." He was holding a cat and talking about how the two young European women, Juliette and Monika, had seen him in the temple and made their house available, which was quite helpful because it provided a place where no one could come and disturb their meeting.

"Others think this beggar gives time only to foreigners and this beggar feels troubled. Now we will have a good time if Monika wills it also. All are fine and peaceful here. Oh ho . . . this cat! She doesn't want this beggar." He was playing with the cat and musing about the situation. "All are quiet here. Near the temple it's all noisy and disturbance, but here it's all quiet. Ohhh! I hear the crow. A lonely crow . . . its voice is prominent. Monica, do you hear? The crows voice is prominent. Perhaps it is feeling alone. . ."

With the cat struggling to escape from his hands, Yogi Ramsuratkumar said, "Oh ho! This cat wants to escape from this beggar!" Sunder, who was sitting nearby, buried his head in Yogi Ramsuratkumar's lap. "All are good here. When Sunder is here all are good. But before there was a difference between this beggar and Caylor. He was experimenting with drugs, but now it's all okay. All have the right to experiment however they want. All are my Father's children—my Father decides and all happens. That's all I know."

The group had moved from the den, where Yogi Ramsuratkumar and some of the others smoked, back to the living room of Monika's house. Yogi Ramsuratkumar began to speak again, "In the world good and pain exist as dualities independent and inseparable as day and night. The saints and sages of all ages, like the Maharshi, no longer saw the two as distinct or different. Pleasure and pain cease to provoke desire and fear. That is their vision, their freedom. This beggar wonders when he can attain such vision! He is bound to pass there through some illusion." Caylor laughed at this remark.

Yogi Ramsuratkumar continued, "Remember God. Take His name to heart. Be thinking of Him. It is really all a matter of faith. If we have faith that Bhagavan is with us, then He is there. This kind of trust is inviolable. Like this, if someone keeps faith in this sinner that he will be with him, then this sinner will be watching over him. There is no question of there being anything bad. The Father is everywhere, acting in everything. It is all His will . . . You can call Him any thing you want, but I only know Him as my Father. This beggar knows He is there. That's all he knows. *Enna*."

"Do you refer to your father as the God?" someone asked.

"I know Him only as my Father. He is there. He knows this beggar. He is here. I know He is here."

Alain, a Frenchman who was with the group, had a camera; he asked Yogi Ramsuratkumar if he could take a picture of him. Yogi Ramsuratkumar assented, but wanted to go outside into the garden. There was some discussion of the lighting in the room and in the garden—which one was best. Alain commented that there was no light in the room, and yet there was light in Yogi Ramsuratkumar's face. He said, "I want to take a photograph of you as you are here."

Juliette interrupted, inhaled on her cigarette and said, "Maybe if you shine a bit more," referring to the beggar's radiance.

"What?" Yogi Ramsuratkumar asked.

"For the camera!" she quipped. Everybody laughed, but Yogi Ramsuratkumar was very quiet. The woman's remark had been inappropriate; it was off the mark to refer so casually to the beggar, who always made it clear that the radiance, the miraculous, the beauty they saw in him was all "Father in heaven."

After that Caylor and some of the others walked back toward town with Yogi Ramsuratkumar. When they came to the banyan tree he stopped and said to Caylor, "This beggar will leave you here. You can go and put them on the bus. After they go, you can come and talk to this beggar. This beggar will be inside the temple . . . You can search for this beggar at the *gopuram* or near the Ganesha temple. This old beggar will be there only." Caylor prostrated at his feet.

"That's not necessary," he said, as he tapped Caylor's back.

Later Caylor and Alain found Yogi Ramsuratkumar in the temple. They began to discuss the Tulsidas *Ramayana*, specifically the verse that says, "When a raindrop falls into the sea it falls to the ocean floor. And if it strikes upon an oyster's shell it becomes a priceless pearl."

Yogi Ramsuratkumar said, "Like this we need only take a single thought or word from the teachings, and if we sincerely practice it, all can be realized."

One month later Caylor returned to Tiruvannamalai from Adyar, Madras on Wednesday, January 16, 1980 accompanied again by his close friend A.V. Sunder. Also with them was Peter Hoffman, an older man who was like a father to Caylor. Peter was the private attaché of Rukmini Devi, who owned a well-known private art college in Madras. A very close friend to Caylor, Peter had taken the younger man under his wing in Madras, and had taken him to meet Swami Muktananda and Nisagadatta Maharaj. Now Peter was eager to meet the peerless beggar saint, Yogi Ramsuratkumar, for the first time.

After grappling with the luggage and bouncing down the road in rickshaws, they arrived at the cottage of a friend, Carey McGraw. It was a hot and beautiful day, graced with a bright blue sky, and after confirming that there would be a flat to rent as previously arranged, they were settled in for a short stay. After dinner, Peter and Caylor split up and Caylor headed for the flower bazaar, where he bought a rupee's worth of jasmine and a single rose. Walking down Sannadhi Street and checking the chariot *mandapam* for a sight of the beggar king, Caylor greeted some old friends and the dog, Sai Baba. Krishnamurti, one of Yogi Ramsuratkumar's attendants told Caylor to go to the temple, where he soon found the master, walking along the courtyard near the Vinayaka shrine. Caylor wrote:

> We greeted one another warmly. He held my hand in his for a few moments in the stillness of the night, then asked me to be seated in the space just facing the Vinayaka (Ganesh) shrine. He took his position aside the temple pillar. We did not speak. During the hour we were there we did not exchange a single word. A few of the townspeople had come to request his blessing, including some rather far-out looking sadhus. Also Hans (Hamsa) Dieder and several Westerners walked by. Finally Swami began to walk towards the courtyard and motioned for me to follow. We did not

walk far.

He handed me a telegram from Hilda sent by Will, in which she requested his blessings. Evidently she has been feeling very weak, generally overburdened with decisions and business and in pain from an arm injury. We discussed the situation in New York for a few minutes. Then the master instructed me to write to Hilda in care of Will and to "tell Hilda that in one or two months, she will feel light like she has no burdens at all."

I felt a very deep inner peace and joy walking around the temple with him. I didn't know where we were going but I sensed that we would soon be parting. Then to my surprise he lead me towards the northern gopuram, and there, pacing up and down the full length of the prakaram, we talked under the night sky—moonless, but studded with a treasure of pearl-like stars glistening overhead.

I cannot remember much that we talked about—a few questions about Hilda in New York, my health, and also about my stay at Adyar. Perhaps the most disturbing moment that night occurred in connection with Adyar: He asked me how I had been while staying there, and I assured him that my life there was more balanced than here in Tiruvannamalai. He was immensely pleased with this and suggested that it was not necessary for me to be here in Tiruvannamalai, and except for periods of travel, I should stay in Adyar. He assured me that his presence would be with me there, and that our physical association here was unnecessary. This was unsettling.

We discussed my present situation: what time had we arrived, where and in what cottage were staying, who was our host, Carey McGraw, and details about Peter Hoffman. He assured me that he would try to meet us there, early the next day. He accepted my gift of flowers just as I took leave of him.

The next morning Caylor was walking up the lane towards Leyf's restaurant, hoping to get a bite to eat before the master arrived, but to his amazement, Yogi Ramsuratkumar was coming toward him from the far end of the lane. Meeting midway, the yogi explained that he was glad to get away without unnecessary delays in town, meaning that he was able to slip away from the many devotees and supplicants who often crowded around him. But also, on this day he had dedicated himself to the group of Westerners, and when it came to Father's work, it would not be delayed, but entered into with unflagging enthusiastic and energy. There was no such thing as "down time" for Yogi Ramsuratkumar. There was no time to waste, and on this day he was shining like a *crore* of suns as he walked down the road in new clothes—a pure white *dhoti* and garments that shone in the morning light, an orange-red cloth turban tied haphazardly around his head, and a red silk shawl that blazed against the bright white of the new fabrics. He greeted Caylor and they walked together to the bungalow.

"Look who I found on the road!" Caylor announced to his friends as he opened the door for Yogi Ramsuratkumar and walked inside the house. The men were unprepared for an early appearance of the master in their midst, but that didn't stop Yogi Ramsuratkumar. Seeing Carey in the next room, the beggar thought he was Peter Hoffman, and rushed to his side, taking his hand in a warm greeting that was his characteristic affectionate manner. While being introduced, he continued to hold Carey's hands but became very still and quiet, as though he was tuning into the essence of the person before and listening deeply to its voice. While Peter was fighting his way out from under his mosquito net Yogi Ramsuratkumar spoke about Caylor to Carey, saying, "I don't like that he experimented with drugs. It did some harm. Something is there I don't like."

Just waking up, Peter Hoffman walked in and murmured some words of apology, but the master was thrilled to discover him. The men gathered in Carey's bedroom with Yogi Ramsuratkumar, where Peter explained that he hadn't expected to see him so early, but he was deeply grateful for his visit. Carey excused himself, explaining that he was headed to *pradaskhina* around the hill, and the master held his hand once more before he parted.

Soon coffee, biscuits, bananas and *chikki* were served. At first the conversation focused on affairs and current events at the Theosophical Society: the death of John Coats, its most recent president, and the elections of a new president currently in process. Yogi Ramsuratkumar stated that, in no uncertain terms, Rukmini Devi Arundale would be elected the next international Theosophical Society president. He then encouraged Peter to talk at length about each of the earlier presidents, the mahatmas who guided them, the work and ideals undertaken by each. A topic that was always near and dear to Yogi Ramsuratkumar came up: J. Krishnamurti and his teachings. As usual, the yogi continued to assert the deep connection between Caylor and the Theosophical Society, saying, "Mr. K belongs to the Theosophical Society. This beggar has given some hints, some indications like this previously, but these have gone unheeded."

Two little girls, Mumtaj and Gulab, came by to see Caylor and brought two red flowers. Sccing thc children, Yogi Ramsuratkumar invited them to come in, and the flowers were given to him. The question came up about these two flowers and whether or not they were the same, which evolved into the age-old Upanishadic question: what is the difference between *jivatma* and *paramatma*, or the individual soul and God. It was a consideration that captured their imaginations for a while, until the discussion went on to Caylor recounting the story of how Guruswami had once taken a few sour grapes from Joan Zulkowski and made them instantly sweet. On another occasion Guruswami took some leaves and turned them into coins.

This inspired Yogi Ramsuratkumar to tell a story of something he had seen during his long travels across India: A yogi held some flowers in the sunlight and several time changed them from one color to another to another; and on another occasion an adept had taken some small pebbles from the roadside and then turned them into tiny sea shells.

As noon approached Yogi Ramsuratkumar slept while Caylor brought in a gourmet meal for the group: red rice, spinach, vegetables, dal and chapattis. Yogi Ramsuratkumar had never eaten red rice, and he remarked several times that it was the best he had ever eaten. After lunch the conversation moved toward politics. Yogi Ramsuratkumar said that Marxism and Communism, however brutal it may appear, survived only because a few people—though perhaps unknown—were selfless individuals who empowered its influence in the world. Carey lent support to this idea and suggested that Marx himself was one such person, having only the welfare of humanity at heart. Upon hearing this statement, Yogi Ramsuratkumar raised his hand in blessing.

At the end of the day, as the visit was winding down and the men became more tired, Peter asked Yogi Ramsuratkumar for any advice that might be of help to him, spiritually or otherwise. The master did not hesitate to say, "You don't need anything. Everything you need will be given to you."

As the beggar prepared to leave, Peter stepped forward to thank him from the very depths of his heart; not knowing if he would ever see him again, he prostrated at the master's feet.

"Swami, will we see you again?" Caylor asked as Yogi Ramsuratkumar turned to leave. He paused and looked far away, as if tomorrow was a thousand years from that moment, then replied, "We shall see."

Although they didn't know if he would come, the next morning the men were ready for a possible early morning visit from the beggar king. They had stocked extra supplies of food and coffee, and this time they were up, dressed and well prepared for the master's "divine visitation." To their delight, he came again in the early hours of the morning.

"If someone will walk around the hill every day, no other sadhana is necessary," Yogi Ramsuratkumar said. Although no one had said anything, the beggar was tuning into Carey, who soon announced that he was going to do *pradakshina* around Arunachala, leaving Caylor and Peter Hoffman alone with Yogi Ramsuratkumar.

During the hours that followed Caylor quickly wrote down the master's words, catching moments to write while preparing coffee and snacks in the kitchen. It was an amazing day of companionship with the guru, in which Yogi Ramsuratkumar actively engaged in warm friendship and dynamic conversations on many different topics with the men.

Again the talk turned to the Theosophical Society, with Peter speaking about the masters who were involved in the inception of the organization, who felt that people would better listen to messengers from the West—thus the coming of Madame Blavatsky, who had been a great champion of the Indian spiritual heritage during the hard, long years of British rule.

"Madame Blavatsky, Colonel Olcott and Annie Besant were saviors of India," Yogi Ramsuratkumar responded, "they have saved these dirty beggars of India—dirty beggars like this . . . " He was referring to himself, and to the many sadhus and religious mendicants of India. He continued, "This beggar is very selfish. He has to learn something from the Theosophical Society. It is so kind to all, especially to India."

As Peter continued to speak about the internal structure and workings of the Theosophical Society and Mrs. Besant's political ideals and efforts in India, the yogi said, "So long as there are people who love India, who love these dirty sinners of India, we will be here. We don't come where we are not wanted. This beggar feels all these great mahatmas are here in India, unseen. Those people who deserve to know them will be graced to know them . . . This beggar is very lazy. He just sits and talks. How could he ever be worthy of such grace?"

Peter then asked, "What is it that obstructs the flow of love? I think it must be the idea of self. I hope someday there will be a flood of light which will wash away this idea, this ego."

"You people who work for the Society have no ego," Yogi Ramsuratkumar answered, with supreme generosity.

Peter disagreed with this and then quoted Nisargadatta Maharaj on the nature of self-concern and how to rid oneself of it. But Yogi Ramsuratkumar was adamant, saying, "Oh, you people who work for the Society are doing the masters' work. You will be looked after." Later in the conversation Peter criticized the general attitude of exclusivity in the Theosophical Society, which encourages its members to disinterest in other spiritual movements at best, or a kind of closed-minded disdain at worst.

Yogi Ramsuratkumar disagreed, saying, "People who have devoted themselves to the work of the Society don't need to look to masters outside. All their spiritual needs are looked after. I have no doubt about it." Peter mentioned that he hoped if Rukmini became the new president of the Theosophical Society, she would bring a new, more eclectic approach to the organization and invite other masters and teachers to participate in the events of the Theosophical Society. He was expressing the wish that masters like Yogi Ramsuratkumar would feel more comfortable at Adyar.

"It is the master's work you are doing. There is no need for us to be with you there," Yogi Ramsuratkumar insisted resolutely.

The conversation about the Theosophical Society continued and veered slightly into Caylor's place in it, then the talk turned to T. Subba Rao.

"Yogi T. Subba Rao is a great rishi," Yogi Ramsuratkumar said passionately, entering fully into conversation with Peter Hoffman and giving him every opportunity to talk about his concerns for the Theosophical Society and spiritual life. They began to talk about how some teachers take only an intellectual approach, which Peter found distasteful.

Yogi Ramsuratkumar replied, "That is all we can do. We have got only intellect. The acquisition of that which lies beyond the intellect depends upon the Father's grace." In these interactions Peter began to form an understanding of how Yogi Ramsuratkumar worked. He noticed how the beggar saint would encourage interest in an idea and then seem to sit back and concentrate intensely on other levels while one or more persons continued to speak on that idea.

"You have to work so hard," Peter said to Yogi Ramsuratkumar.

"Very rarely this beggar gets friends who speak about God and religion. Mostly people come with their problems," he replied.

At the end of the afternoon Yogi Ramsuratkumar asked Peter and Caylor to read a part of a chapter entitled, "Energy and the Cultivation of the Field" from one of J. Krishnamurti's most recent books (1979). The master had also read it, and asked Caylor to read an entire chapter, which was ten or twelve pages long and focused on the question of a subtle psychic structure and kundalini energy. J. Krishnamurti maintained that it is not the awakening of kundalini that creates a truly religious life, but vice versa. As to the question of how we are to awaken to this condition of no-ego or no-mind, Yogi Ramsuratkumar did not disagree with J. Krishamurti, but chose to interject his own view:

"If we remember God's name the mind is empty," he stated unequivocally. He always came back to the radical reliance on the name of God in the repetition of mantra, or *nama japa*, which was the path of grace that he experienced with his master, Swami Ramdas. Then he paused and added, "However, we can remember Him only when the mind is empty!" He laughed at the irony of this paradoxical statement. "This beggar is not capable of using Krishnamurti's language. In reply to this question I have used my own language, the language of my master Swami Ramdas."

Then Yogi Ramsuratkumar asked Caylor to read aloud the chapter in the book one last time. Caylor observed of this experience, "He drew my mind into a very deep and lucid state. I felt to be a witness of myself. Words were being sounded effortless, sonorously, resonantly. My solar plexus felt light and empty. I could hardly contain the laughter that kept wanting to bubble up from within." It had been a rare afternoon of rich conversation with Yogi Ramsuratkumar, in which he lavished the men with his wisdom and the uncompromising context of his own realization; having spent all day in such sublime company, the men were feeling the effects of the guru's power to bless with his simple company and conversation. No one could remain unaltered in such a circumstance; rather it was common in the presence of Yogi Ramsuratkumar that people experienced unusual states of consciousness, happiness, clarity, insight, deep feelings of love and well-being.

In the afternoon Yogi Ramsuratkumar began to speak about his own guru, saying, "Papa Ramdas was a great hunter. He killed this beggar." Later that day he expressed the same idea with a different metaphor, saying, "Papa Ramdas was a great tiger. He swallowed up this dirty sinner." On the topic of free will, which often churns up strong opinions, the group became excited and passionate. Yogi Ramsuratkumar was simple and direct, always inhering in the realization of the One and the path of divine grace, saying, "This beggar feels there is no such thing as free will; there is only the will of the Father."

At one point Yogi Ramsuratkumar paused in the conversation to ask Caylor when they had first met. Caylor answered that it was June 23, 1970, and Yogi Ramsuratkumar said, "Did it occur to you that it has been ten years?"

Shortly after five o'clock that afternoon, Yogi Ramsuratkumar was ready to leave and invited Peter and Caylor to join him on his walk; he planned to take the mountain route back to town, in order to avoid going through Ramanashram, where many people would recognize him and want him to stop and visit. As they walked up the mountain path, the master became exhausted almost immediately. Every step became an effort for Yogi Ramsuratkumar, who was dizzy and perspiring.

"It has been a time long since this beggar last climbed this hill!" Yogi Ramsuratkumar commented as they walked. Caylor had never seen him in that condition before, and the beggar himself seemed surprised. The men were naturally concerned, and they walked together up the mountain very slowly. When Peter expressed his concern about the elder saint's physical condition, Yogi Ramsuratkumar replied, "If this body does a little service for the Father, it is alright. We have to discriminate to know what will serve the master's purpose and do that." Yogi Ramsuratkumar had never allowed his physical needs to interfere with "Father's work," and despite the body's reaction to physical exertion and the beggar's age and health, "Father's work" was the focus of the excursion. No one could guess why Yogi Ramsuratkumar had made such a "discrimination," as he called it.

Upon reaching the first crest the men suggested that they stop and while they rested Yogi Ramsuratkumar began to recall bygone days with Caylor on the mountain, when the newly-printed first edition of *The Godchild* was just out. They talked about the many days they spent at the caves and shrines on the mountainside, and of the time they walked around the hill together on Deepam.

"Shall we continue on our journey—our holy pilgrimage?" the beggar king asked. Then he began to speak eloquently as a mood of exaltation seemed to sweep over him, saying, "We will go in search of our Lord. Maybe He will meet us on our way! But even if He disappoints us, it doesn't matter. We will continue our quest," Yogi Ramsuratkumar said, instantly defining the underlying purpose of their walk up the mountain.

"I never thought I would have the honor of going on a pilgrimage with you!" Peter exclaimed.

The strong Indian sun shone down on them as they walked along. The mountain views were magnificent, and as they walked down the path, Peter said, "This view of the hill is beautiful."

"This hill and this temple, they have saved this beggar," Yogi Ramsuratkumar commented thoughtfully, with reverence. His words seemed somehow connected with the purpose that was being accomplished on this unusual outing. Reaching Skandashram, the small stone buildings sheltered under tall green trees where Ramana Maharshi spent much time meditating, Yogi Ramsuratkumar said, "So we have climbed up, now we have only to go down." He enigmatically repeated this statement three times. Resting on the rock promontory that overlooked the *gopurams* of Arunachalesvara Temple down below, he said, "This beggar is tired. Where is that energy for the cult nation of the field? Where is this energy J. Krishnamurti talks about?"

"If only I could give you some of my *prana*," Peter said, "I would! But you wouldn't want my *prana*—it's very polluted." They all laughed, but Yogi Ramsuratkumar became serious again, remembering and perhaps contemplating in some way the long path and extreme exertions of his own life, perfectly symbolized in the difficult walk up the mountain. Returning again to the theme of gratitude for the sanctity of Mount

Arunachala, Yogi Ramsuratkumar said:

"This beggar wandering here and there, tired of wandering but having no home—Arunachalesvara, in the form of this hill, had mercy on this miserable sinner. So he gives thanks, a thousand thanks, to this holy hill, this holy temple. Oh, the magnanimity of the Lord! He has given me shelter for twenty long years. Whereas others who come are enabled to stay only days or weeks . . . For thousands of years the hill has given shelter to so many dirty sinners like me—and Arunachala will give us shelter for thousands of years to come."

It was a tremendously moving and auspicious opportunity to witness and hear the beggar's sacred words of prayer and praise. The mood continued as they made their way down the rocky winding path. Having descended as far as Om Namosivaya Guhai, Yogi Ramsuratkumar rested again beneath a large bodhi tree. He turned to Caylor and said, "Peter has helped us to spend these two days together. We will take leave now. You needn't try to meet this beggar at present. We have spent enough time together. There is no need to search for this beggar or to meet at fixed times. Leave it to the will of the Father. When this beggar feels we should meet, he will call you, and by the Father's grace we will meet again.

"You can stay here in Tiruvannamalai if you wish—walk round the hill, carry on your meditations, or whatever you do. Read *The Secret Doctrine*, or else return to Madras or travel north and spend time with Anandamayi Ma. If you settle down for some time in Tiruvannamalai, it will be best if you don't expand your contact here. Better to expand social contacts in a place like Adyar, but not here."

Expressing his deepest heartfelt appreciation, Peter remarked, "In these two days you have worked so hard to help us."

"It is this beggar's play, his *lila*—not work. When there is activity that is motivated by self-interest and ends with pleasure or pain, we may call it work. It requires exertion. But when we live outside the reach of pleasure or pain, a realized man is untouched by these. Our activities are effortless. Our work is really our play."

He walked away, then stopped and turned to face the two men who stood watching as he departed. "According to Peter we should express our thanks to the tree." He shouted, "Thank you, Mr. Asvattha!" Then he walked away laughing.[6]

After leaving Tiruvannamalai, Caylor stayed for a few weeks at the Theosophical Society in Adyar, Madras, then went to Kerala to visit with friends. A month later, on April 5, 1980 he was back in Tiruvannamalai. It was extremely hot that time of year, often over one hundred degrees. Two days later, Caylor had the only meeting ever in which he sat alone with the master from beginning to end. He recounted in his journal:

> As I approached via the alley I noticed the master looking over the

---

6 *Asvattha*: Sanskrit: A type of fig (Ficus religiosa); considered the sacred "world tree," the embodiment of many deities and home to numerous devas. Also known as the *peepal* or bodhi tree.

> rail overhead, watching for me. After sitting with him for a few minutes all the symptoms of physical ill health I was feeling disappeared. I felt strong and concentrated. Yogi Ramsuratkumar rose and walked out onto the steps. He stood by the mandapam gate looking unto the sky, adjusting his blankets, which he wears even in summer. Occasionally he flashed a fiery side-glance in my direction. He was waiting.
>
> I felt somehow awed by his regal stature. I sat watching him, wondering how he became what he is. This became the question and a fixation. There seemed nothing in my psychological gestalt to account for him. Finally a rather inconspicuous equation formed in my mind, placing him on one side and God on the other. God? That is what I have forgotten!
>
> As this awareness dawned, Yogi Ramsuratkumar walked back in and sat down. The way was open and the energy now seemed magnified. Ten minutes or so passed. He sent me away. No word yet about my departure.

The next day as evening approached Caylor made his way to the chariot *mandapam*, stopping to buy three sweet limes and a large garland of jasmine flowers for only one rupee, which was surprising because they were worth five. Caylor thought, the flower man must have anticipated their ultimate destination.

The master was sitting alone in the *mandapam*. The floor was clean and spacious where before there were red berries drying all over the stone. They left a strange sweetness in the air. The silent *bhava* of mystical love was still in the air from the night before. Yogi Ramsuratkumar moved to the corner pillar and sat down. In the darkness the lights from the streets below shone on the side of his face. He occasionally threw a smouldering glance in Caylor's direction.

One of the most disconcerting things that happens frequently in the company of a true master is that many different passionate emotions are catalyzed, demanding a fierce willingness to self-observe and make distinctions between what is real and what is illusion. This was the opportunity that was presented to Caylor as he found himself suddenly feeling alone and contemplating his lack of love and devotion. His mood quickly spiraled very far down.

"I will leave you," Yogi Ramsuratkumar said, suddenly rising while handing flowers and fruit to both Kirsti and Caylor.

Feeling withdrawn and uncommunicative, Caylor rose to leave, and casting a glance in the master's direction, he wished him a good night. As he moved away toward the steps, Yogi Ramsuratkumar suddenly appeared at his side.

"You are alright?" he asked lovingly.

"I'm okay," he answered. The beggar's gesture of love instantly turned Caylor's mood around. Caylor reflected on this exchange, "Now he was like a dream. I felt his love so deeply and thought to him in gratitude and affection, 'You are so wonderful.' The moonlight overhead shone with a heavenly aura in his eyes as we stood on the steps. Then he stepped away."

"What's your program?" Yogi Ramsuratkumar asked the next day, handing Caylor some flowers and a lime. Caylor had walked into town that day and stopped at the flower stall to buy flowers and then met the master, rather uneventfully. After an hour of sitting in "ideological abstractions," Yogi Ramsuratkumar spoke to him about his travel plans.

"From Madras I will travel to Delhi, sometime later his week. And because I really don't like to travel much, I'll probably stay most of April with Anandamayi Ma. I tour out from Delhi in several directions. Also, I may travel to Srinagar. There is a great Sufi master there."

"His name?" the beggar inquired.

Caylor paused, "I have it written down."

"No, that's alright . . . And here in Tiruvannamalai?" he questioned.

"I have no fixed plans."

The beggar was silent for a moment, then ending the meeting for the night, he said, "We have met. You can leave tomorrow morning."

Pranaming and turning to leave, Caylor said, "Oh, I have something for you."

"What?" Yogi Ramsuratkumar asked rather gruffly.

"A card from Will and Joan." Rummaging through his bag, Caylor found the letter and handed it to Yogi Ramsuratkumar, who took it with interest, but upon seeing that there were one thousand rupees inside, he said, "What for?" Then he handed it to Caylor before he could answer. "It's alright. You keep it with you and spend it."

Caylor pursued further, "Is there some address I can use to send you money from time to time?"

"There is no need. When this beggar is in need he will tell you."

Wishing the beggar saint well, Caylor walked down the stairs and took off down the street. He left India soon after this meeting, and would not see the master again for thirteen years.

Later he commented in his journal that the guru had worked with him during this visit in ways that were frustrating to his conventional ideas of spiritual work. Sooner or later the true master confronts the disciple with some form of *neti neti*: the traditional teaching of "not this, not this," or drawing thc attcntion away from the marketplace of phenomenal existence—which applies, perhaps most of all, to one's attachments and illusions about the spiritual path. Caylor reflected in his journal on the wise ways of the unfathomable Yogi Ramsuratkumar:

> I came to India this time with so many expectations and hopes for deepening my spiritual life, but the master had not addressed any of these. What's more, I have the feeling sometimes that he is suspiciously, silently engaged in smoking them all away . . .
>
> The being of a Godchild is somehow like a mirror of the soul, in which we recognize God's love and wondrous divine spectacle. This man's life was somehow returned to him, and he has since made it a gift—something special for all of us, imbuing it with manifold perfections so

that it fills a place in the greater working of our world and his. Life unto life. Heaven unto earth. Nourishing and sustaining. The small expanse, returning to its home in the heart of him, the greater expanse. The beloved. All this we see reflected in the pure and untainted.

CHAPTER SIX

The Sannadhi Street Years

1980-1990

"Ohhh! Come on, my friends!" the beggar exclaimed as he opened the door in the early morning to invite Murugeshan, Parthasarathy and Shivashankara into his house on Sannadhi Street. Soon the coffee would arrive, often served by Yogi Ramsuratkumar's own hand, and then breakfast, lunch, tea, dinner as the beggar shared whatever food came to him while the day expanded into the unique dimensions of intimate companionship that could only be experienced in his company.

Murugeshan, Parthasarathy and Sivasankara didn't know each other before they became devotees of Yogi Ramsuratkumar, but the master brought them together in a unique circumstance and through him, their families became deeply and affectionately bonded together. Having known the beggar saint well since the mid-seventies, from 1980 until the death of Murugeshan in 1984 the three men and their families were kept together by Yogi Ramsuratkumar as a contained small group that had a particular and unusual relationship to the master and his work. Yogi Ramsuratkumar asked them to meet every month for three days in Tiruvannamalai; many times their whole families came with them, children and all. Sometimes the beggar would come to their house or lodgings and sometimes they would go to Sannadhi Street. On other occasions they would make a place to meet and everyone would gather there. The gatherings at Sannadhi Street often found them cooking meals together, with Yogi Ramsuratkumar helping, but most of the time they brought food to the house from the hotels of his choice. It was an extraordinary circumstance that was created for the specific purpose, as Yogi Ramsuratkumar said, "to do my Father's work." Parthasarathy remembered these unique times:

> All the twenty-four hours! All the twenty-four hours Swami used to work with us! When we met together, we wouldn't have any sleep, virtually for seventy-two hours! We would just go on, talking and talking. Even when he would sleep before us, his sleep would be a teaching for us. He would ask us to read from some book, and the book would be very boring, you know. Swami would sleep, and he would start snoring, then we'd think, "Swami is sleeping. He would not mind if we skip part of this,"

> but when we would skip the pages, Swami would raise up slightly and put things back in perfect order: "Oh, Parthasarathy, this beggar slept. You start reading from that particular page!" There would be no escape! A devotee had written a book on Anandamayi Ma, but we could not make head or tail out of that book. We were terribly bored and we skipped some pages and Swami would say, "Oh, this beggar slept— you start from that particular page!"
>
> From 1980 to 1984, we were all together. Swami told us once, "So far this beggar's name, and three peoples' names will also be with this beggar—these three people will also do my Father's work." Murugeshan, Shivashankar and Parathasarathy: Shivashankara was an offset printer, Murugesan was in the cotton spinning mill, and Parathasarathy was a pauper at the time! A pauper and a beggar—a professional pauper!

Yogi Ramsuratkumar kept these three men alone together, virtually isolated from all the other devotees. He never allowed them to mingle with the other devotees, which was sometimes very difficult for them. At times Yogi Ramsuratkumar came to their room and stayed with them for seven, ten or even fifteen days in a very concentrated environment or chamber in which there was basically no outside influence. Sometimes he kept them at Sannadhi Street and would not allow them to see or talk to other devotees that came for his darshan there. These devotees he met at the iron grillwork door to the porch and talked with them there or outside.

On various occasions the three men would walk from Tuticorin to Tiruvannamalai—a long journey of about 550 kilometers. On one of those occasions they were walking to Tiruvannamalai for the Deepam festival, and when they got to Madurai, they became tired, so they stayed in a hotel. They were talking among themselves about how the yogi would often keep them totally alone and never allow them to have his audience with other people. They wanted very much to see how the crowds greeted Swamiji, and they thought perhaps this time they could sit in a corner to enjoy his *darbar*. They wanted to mix with the other devotees and to have their guru's darshan in the celebratory atmosphere of the festival, with everyone else.

When they arrived in Tiruvannamalai, Yogi Ramsuratkumar saw them and became very serious right away. Then he took Murugeshan, Parthasarathy and Shivashankara aside, put them in the house on Sannadhi Street and locked the door. He was actually pushing people away from the gate itself, saying to one of his attendants, "Don't allow any people inside. If anybody comes, disperse them and then come and inform this beggar." At the time there was a long line of people that had formed, waiting to receive his darshan, but Yogi Ramsuratkumar was busy—spending time with the three men inside his house—and they were all sent away.

"Swami, we came here not to disturb you, but to enjoy your presence with the other devotees," the men said, feeling quite badly about the plight of the other devotees, who wanted to see Yogi Ramsuratkumar and came, sometimes from great distances, only to find him unavailable or out of sight.

He answered. "My Father says this beggar should spend this day with you people. This beggar feels quite at home with you people." For the three entire days he was sequestered inside the house with Parthasarathy, Murugeshan and Shivashankara while devotees came and knocked insistently on the door, only to be sent away. During that time he would only come out for one hour, stand at the gate to the verandah with a flower garland in his hands and in this way give darshan. People knocked loudly on the door all day long, but Swami just said to his companions, "Ohhh . . . disturbance from these people! These people do not understand. This beggar is doing his Father's work." Then he took the three men inside, from the enclosed porch to the inner rooms of the house.

The next evening asked the three men to go upstairs, and from there they could see the people. Then he went out and stood before the gate. Parthasarathy recalled:

> Then afterward he came and again he locked the doors. For three whole days we were with him! He didn't allow us to take coffee, for three whole days! We just had some puffed rice and bananas—some rotten bananas, for three days. He didn't allow us to go outside. So once we said to Swami, "Swami, can we send Parathasarathy to get some coffee?" He said, "No, Murugeshji, we are doing my Father's work. We should not waste time."
>
> "Father's work" meant just to have communion with [us]. Murugeshan died in 1984, and this happened in 1982. His whole attention was with Murugeshan at that time. He died in 1984, so his time was very short—in two years he was completing his course. Murugeshan departed as a realized soul. Swami told us, "Murugeshji is sitting in my Father's lap." So whenever Murugeshan came, only Parathasarathy and Shivashankara could be there; nobody else should be in the company. Swami would not allow anybody else in but we two. We had a unique association.

Yogi Ramsuratkumar had a particular relationship with Murugeshan, who he referred to as "my king" and "my raja." He called Shivashankara his philosopher, and then of Parthasarathy he would say, "Parthasarathy is a realized soul! We cannot make any conditions on Parathasarathy. He is a free bird—he is a realized soul!" Parthasarathy recounted that this was the master's playful way of humorously prodding him, implying, "Nobody can talk to Parthasarathy; nobody can try to teach him!"

Yogi Ramsuratkumar particularly liked the *Bhagavad Gita*; he used to chant *slokas* of it on certain occasions, or he would sometimes quote the verses and talk about the meaning of them, like the passage in which Krishna narrates the attributes of the real devotees whom he likes, or certain *slokas* on bhakti yoga. Once Murugeshji translated the *Avadhut Gita* by Dattatreya into Tamil and had it printed in a small booklet. Swami asked each of the three men to read it to him, and then he asked Murugeshan to give the meaning in English. It was so hard to understand as the poems were narrating the attributes of Brahma. Yogi Ramsuratkumar said, "Oh, Murugeshji, my King . . . *Bhagavad Gita* is enough for us!"

Murugeshan has become a living legend among the Indian devotees of Yogi Ramsuratkumar, and it is generally known that Yogi Ramsuratkumar considered him to be God-realized at the time of his death. Many devotees assume that the tremendous love, time and attention that Yogi Ramsuratkumar poured into Murugeshan was not only to prepare him for the surprise of his coming death, but also to catalyze a rapid and profound transformation in a short period of time.

When he first came to Yogi Ramsuratkumar and for many years, Murugeshan had a drinking problem. A prosperous businessman, Murugeshan would get drunk and go to Sannadhi Street house, staggering up the steps to Yogi Ramsuratkumar, who would take him in his arms, saying, "Oh my child, you have come here to me like this!" Taking him in, the yogi would then take care of him.

Murugeshan was controversial and provocative in other ways as well; he often used what was considered to be rough or inappropriate language with Yogi Ramsuratkumar. For example, he once said, "Swamiji, what is this materialistic world? We will both elope!" Meaning that they would run away together, like lovers. In a classical culture like India, this was considered a rather scandalous or offhand way to speak to one's guru. Because of these kinds of remarks, the devotees would complain to Yogi Ramsuratkumar that Murugeshan was using "filthy" language to him.

"What, Murugeshji, you are using such words?" Yogi Ramsuratkumar would innocently ask after the devotees complained. But it was clear that the master tacitly understood something much deeper in Murugeshan's meaning and he was therefore allowed familiarities and demonstrations of love that other were not. This was generally accepted by Yogi Ramsuratkumar as a lawful function of the context or underlying meaning that Murugeshan brought to such statements, but Yogi Ramsuratkumar made sure that the others understood this as well.

"Parathasarathy, this beggar heard through some friends that Murugeshan used some filthy language on mentioning this beggar, and he abused this beggar. Is it so?"

"No Swamiji, he is not abusing Swami—even though he is mentioning some filthy language, it is not abuse on my thought," Parthasarathy replied.

"What word is it he uses?" he insisted.

When Parthasarathy repeated the word for him, the yogi demanded to know what it meant. Parthasarathy wrote the word down in Tamil on a piece of paper and showed it to Swami. A man who was a Brahmin priest was also sitting there, and he said, "Oh! It's a filthy language, Swami!"

"No, no, this beggar wants to know the meaning of this word. If my king, Murugeshan, utters this word, there is a meaning, definitely a meaning to that word! This beggar wants to know the meaning of that word. You will go and bring your dictionary."

The Brahmin brought a big dictionary and showed them that the word referred to "hidden parts."

"The word means 'the hidden parts,' Swami."

"Oh, he uses such strong words for this beggar," Yogi Ramsuratkumar exclaimed, "but it is out of love for this beggar. It is out of love for this beggar, isn't it?" Yogi Ramsuratkumar then explained that in a *sloka* in one of the scriptures that are sacred to Lord Vishnu—"a thousand *slokas* that are glorifying Lord Vishnu"—this same word is used. "Oh, now this beggar got it. Murugeshji is not abusing this beggar, Murugeshji is glorifying this beggar!"

A woman who was a devotee of Sai Baba came to visit Yogi Ramsuratkumar in 1982 with her two daughters and her boyfriend, who was a scientist. The yogi brought them inside his house and right away started concentrating upon the scientist, who was a nonbeliever, by talking with him earnestly. Within a few minutes the man became very emotional and got tears in his eyes. He said to the beggar, "Swami, shall I kiss your hands?"

"Oh, this dirty beggar's hands . . . it is so dirty, and it may give you a bad smell."

"Oh, it's all right, Swami. This hand is Jesus' hand. I want to kiss it," the scientist persisted. The yogi allowed him to kiss his hands, and by then the man was frankly shedding tears. The woman was amazed by this, saying that her boyfriend was always a nonbeliever, a strong skeptic who doubted everything, but suddenly, here in the presence of Yogi Ramsuratkumar, his heart had opened up. Nonetheless, after one or two hours the beggar said, "Now, this beggar has seen you people nicely. You can go now."

"Shall we come tomorrow morning, Swami?" they asked hopefully.

"No, no need to come over here again."

"But we are going to be here for another ten days! Can we meet you again?"

"Yes, this beggar has seen you nicely. My Father will always be with you. You can go—and do your other works. You can stay at Ramanashram . . . you can do your [spiritual] duties there." They were shocked!

"Swami, we want to come again!" they begged.

"No, these three friends came all the long way from Tuticorin to see this beggar and this beggar is busy, he will not be available for you." The master was unmovable.

The "three friends"—Parthasarathy, Murugeshan and Shivashankara—witnessed this exchange and saw the Americans leave in tears. After they had gone Murugeshan started arguing, "Swami, we have just been coming from Tuticorin to Tiruvannamalai, only eight hours' journey. She came a long way just to see you, Swami, just to be sent away!"

"Not like that, Murugeshji . . ." the beggar replied. "These friends came to India to see the people like this beggar. They will stay here for ten days and they will go to Tirupati and they will stay there for ten days, then they will go to several cities, they will go to Hardwar and then to the Himalayas. They will see several saints and sadhus. But you people came a long way from Tuticorin to see only this beggar. And after this beggar leaves, you will go directly back to your house! Your total attention was with this beggar, and this beggar's attention is also with you people. These people will see several people like this beggar . . . So, my Father wanted to give them something, and my Father gave them . . . That's enough."

In this way Yogi Ramsuratkumar made the teaching that the devotee's entire attention must be on the master in order to have the master's attention on him or her in return; it is a relationship of natural reciprocity. Only if the devotee's attention is solely on the master can the master engage the devotee at a deeper level. If the spiritual aspirant is scattered in his or her interests, looking here and looking there, the guru is bound by law to work only at the most basic level, offering blessings, but not the more profound and therefore much more intense relationship of the *satguru* to the devotee.

During these years, 1982-1984, the closeness between Yogi Ramsuratkumar and his chosen three ran very deep; they were free to argue with Swami, eat off his banana leaf, laugh together. There was a tremendous depth of camaraderie and communion between the master, the three men and their families. As he molded their unique relationship into a bonded organism, the master was involved in every aspect of their lives and became the sun around which they revolved.

At times serious, sublime or profound, Yogi Ramsuratkumar could also be merry and rollicking in the ways he made teaching lessons for them, and he enjoyed their light-hearted and humorous repartee with him as well. Yogi Ramsuratkumar often instructed people to go to Madras to hear J. Krishnamurti give public lectures. On one occasion he sent Parthasarathy, Murugeshan and Shivashankara to Madras to stay for as long as J. Krishnamurti would be there. Every day Parthasarathy went to hear J. Krishnamurti, whose teaching was very attractive to him. On one such occasion J. Krishnamurti finished his talk and was walking away. Parthasarathy usually stood shyly and discreetly off to the side, just waiting to see what would happen after the talk, but this time J. Krishnamurti walked directly toward him.

"What are you waiting for here?" J. Krishnamurti asked Parthasarathy.

"Just to see Krishnamurti," he responded. This answer appealed greatly to J. Krishnamurti, who laughed and laughed, then gave Parthasarathy a warm embrace and looked into his eyes. Suddenly Parthasarathy realized that it was his association with Yogi Ramsuratkumar that had drawn J. Krishnamurti to him in this way. He said, "Then I understood: When you have the acquaintance with the Swami, then almost all the saints and sadhus are very, very close to you—there is no doubt about it!"

Afterward, when the three men came to Yogi Ramsuratkumar, he inquired, "Who got the opportunity to touch Krishnamurti?" referring to the way J. Krishnamurti used to greet people by shaking hands. This physical contact with Krishnamurti was important, as it was understood that a saint or holy man could transmit grace through touch. Parthasarathy remained silent when Yogi Ramsuratkumar asked this question, thinking wryly, "Well, I didn't touch J. Krishnamurti."

Sensing all along that Parthasarathy had had contact with J. Krishnamurti, Yogi Ramsuratkumar pushed the issue, saying, "What happened to you, Parathasarathy? Did *you* have the opportunity to touch Krishnamurti?"

"Swami, I didn't touch him. He touched *me*!" When Yogi Ramsuratkumar heard this, he laughed and laughed in enjoyment at the tongue-in-cheek joke behind Parthasarathy's logic.

At the same time that there was tremendous camaraderie, humor and the fullness of ordinary life with Swami and the three friends, the sense of the sacred was always present, and there were many deep, tender and awe-filled experiences of communion between them. On one such occasion, Yogi Ramsuratkumar began to speak about his own condition or God-realization, in a rare declaration of self-revelation, remembered by Parthasarathy as an extraordinary night with the master:

> Once, it was a bit late in the evening and we were staying in Tiruvannamalai—Swami, Murugeshan, Shivashankara and me. Also our wives were there—Radhika, Prema (the wife of Shivashankara) and Rajakumari (the wife of Murugeshan). Swami suddenly started saying, "This beggar used to call himself a beggar, but there is nothing either in this world or that world to be begged upon by this beggar. This beggar used to call himself a dirty sinner, but there cannot be such a pure, crystal-like vastu[1], either in this world or in that other world. He is always only his Father. He is always One, One!"
>
> When he was uttering these words, his whole frame was glittering, glittering, glittering . . . It was midnight and we were spellbound—we were *spellbound*! Three times he revealed his mystery with us. He was talking about himself, about his own self. It was such a vast mystery—you can't comprehend it. You can be one with that, but you can't comprehend that. You can just be burned in that fire. He was just like a fire at that time. He was glowing and glowing and glowing, and it was only he who permitted our thoughts within us. Such powerful words as he spoke at that time!

"Parthasarathy, is it all right?" Yogi Ramsuratkumar asked sweetly.

He had had Parthasarathy staying with him for several days, and the night before he had announced that he would be going to the marriage ceremony of some devotees the next day. At four o'clock the next morning Swami woke Parthasarathy up and asked whether his dress was presentable enough for the marriage. His dhoti and shawl were extremely dirty, but Parthasarathy hesitated to say so. Understanding his silence, Yogi Ramsuratkumar said, "Oh, you don't like this beggar to attend the marriage wearing these dirty clothes. Alright, this beggar will change today."

Thus saying, he walked over to a pile of clothes in parcels that had been offered by devotees. Opening the first package, he found a brand new *dhoti*, and changed into it. Then he picked out another parcel, looking for a shirt, but the parcel he picked was also a *dhoti*. Three times he picked different parcels, searching for a *kirta* top, but all were *dhotis*. He was wearing only a *dhoti* at this point; the upper half of his body was bare.

1 Vastu: Sanskrit: dwelling, habitation, chamber or house.

Tired of looking for shirts, he tried to cover his chest by pulling the bottom of the *dhoti* up and over his right shoulder, then asked, "Parthasarathy, is it all right?"

Again, thinking it was not such a good idea, Parthasarathy did not reply. Once again, Swami understood and said, "Oh, you don't like it—it is all right." Adjusting the cloth of the *dhoti* and trying to make it adequately cover his chest, the beggar asked again, "Is it alright?" Parthasarathy refrained from speaking, not wanting to tell Swami that it wasn't appropriate apparel, but not wanting to lie and say, "Yes, it's fine" when he didn't feel it was.

"This also you don't like. Alright . . . *you* go and pick up a parcel and see whether it is shirt or *dhoti*." With these instructions, Parthasarathy went to the pile and picked one parcel. The beggar asked him to open the parcel, and lo and behold, it was a shirt.

"Oh, Parthasarathy helped this beggar," Yogi Ramsuratkumar said, and immediately put on the fresh shirt.

"Now everything is ready," he smiled, "but this bad smell . . ." Saying this, Yogi Ramsuratkumar shook his head and said, "Ahhh!" Parthasarathy recalled:

> Oh, the divine perfume of sandalwood that emanated from his body! Remember, it was four o' clock in the morning and Swami did not wash even his face, but his face started glowing with golden beams. All the dirt and grime that was on his face was now gone, and the musty smell of his old clothes, all gone. Oh, the golden glint of his face! It was a marvelous scene! He started smiling at me with all the shyness in his face.
>
> "Will this be acceptable?" he asked shyly and sweetly. Then he locked the house carefully, caught hold of my hand and started walking down the road like a king.

Parthasarathy was given a glimpse of the "pure, crystal-like vastu" of the Godchild. Despite the fact that he often chain-smoked, minimally bathed once a year at most, and rarely changed his clothes, Yogi Ramsuratkumar was reputed by all who knew him to have a sweet scent about his person. The cloying smell of stale cigarette smoke never clung to his body as it is known to do. With Yogi Ramsuratkumar and his three friends, such ordinary miracles were understood, and it was in the domain of daily life, with families and children, that the subtlest of work could be done. And so, the real work happened subtly. Whenever Murugeshan, Shivashankaran and Parthasarathy were with Swami, his attention was entirely and happily concentrated upon them.

"This beggar feels quite at home with you friends. This is Vaikuntha,[2]" he said once.

Another time Swami was discussing politics, world affairs and history. Murugeshan suddenly said, "Swami, when we are here together with you for days, the other people might be thinking that we are deeply contemplating your Father, and you might be pouring on us your special grace by teaching us about the ways to attain your Father. Who

2 Vaikuntha: Sanskrit, Vishnu's eternal paradise.

knows, here we are just talking about politics, world history and about eating and drinking!"

Upon hearing this, Yogi Ramsuratkumar became very serious. Murugeshan's remark seemed to compel him to give an important teaching on how he was working with the men. He said, "Murugeshji, talking about other subjects may be insignificant, but being together with this beggar is the most significant event. The real work is done and goes unnoticed. It has been covered with these significant or insignificant talks. The masters have their own way to do Father's work. The real work is uniting, merging the chosen beings with my Father! That's all!"

It was Murugeshan who first discovered in the three-hundred-year-old poem, "Akhila Thirattu," written by Muthukutti Swamigal, a prophecy of his own future incarnation as an avatar, which was described as holding a palmyra fan and coconut shell bowl. The text stated that the avatar would be venerated by the Nadar community, and would live in Tiruvannamalai, all in all a perfect description of Yogi Ramsuratkumar. Inspired by this discovery, someone asked Yogi Ramsuratkumar about it. He said, "Ah yes, this beggar is Muthukutti Swamigal and so many other things," the inference being that he was one with everything, so why not Muthukutti Swamigal too? Yogi Ramsuratkumar once told his devotees the story, "Once some devotees asked J. Krishnamurti, 'Are you Buddha? Sri Krishna? Or Jesus Christ?' and Krishnamurti replied, 'I am also Buddha, Krishna and Jesus Christ.' "[3]

In 1983 a photograph was taken of Yogi Ramsuratkumar and Murugeshan. It was a very fine photograph, and at the time Murugeshan said to his cousin Nateshan and some other relatives and friends, "You remove me from the picture so we can have this photograph of Swamiji." Murugeshan's image was cut away and the photo was reproduced for distribution among the devotees. Nateshan had been a very close devotee of Yogi Ramsuratkumar since 1976, when the master mended his marriage problems with his wife Sarada; in fact, the beggar sometimes allowed Nateshan to massage his feet so that he would be more comfortable going to sleep. Even so, when Yogi Ramsuratkumar saw the photo with Murugeshan cut out of it, he started shouting at them in rage, "Who separated me from my raja, my king?" For a while that day he wouldn't talk to anyone; he was very unhappy. Normally he would ask Nateshan, Sarada and their children to stay, but he angrily sent them away. At the time he was petting Sai Baba and working with Murugeshan, who stayed for four days. Finally, he instructed the devotees to destroy all the photos except one. This was six months before Murugeshan's death.

Shortly before Murugeshan died, Yogi Ramsuratkumar said something to his mother that was quite cryptic at the time, but in retrospect seemed not only prophetic, but a way of easing the pain that would come. Speaking to Murugeshan's mother he said, "Mother, have you gone to Calcutta, to the Ramakrishna temple there? You can go there, it is a good place." In retrospect, the family of Murugeshan felt that this was Swamiji's way of saying, "If we leave the body there and go with the Divine, it is a good place to die."

3 Vijayalakshmi, *Waves of Love*, pp. 32-33.

Murugeshan passed away unexpectedly in Calcutta from heart failure. When the heart pain first started, the best cardiologist in Calcutta was called and on his advice, Murugeshji was taken to the hospital. On the way to the hospital his younger brother said to him, "Do not worry, Murugeshan, you have the best doctor. You are in good hands."

"Everybody is in the hands of God," Murugeshan replied. These were his last words. He died upon reaching the hospital on April 4, 1984 at four p.m. His body arrived at his home in Tuticorin on April 5 and on the same day the final rites were performed. He was only forty-five years old.

Upon hearing of Murugeshan's death, Parthasarathy was shattered. Only one month before—to the very day—the friends had been taking leave of Yogi Ramsuratkumar after a three day visit with him. For four days after Murugeshan died, Parthasarathy was unable to sleep, until finally he went to Yogi Ramsuratkumar on April 8, arriving very early in the morning. Immediately Swami took him in, and with great compassion sat down beside him and explained many things about Murugeshan's death to him—how the end came, what his last words were, how the body was brought to Tuticorin, how the rituals were conducted and who performed them. Finally the beggar asked, "Parthasarathy, how many days have passed since you slept?" Parthasarathy replied that he had not slept since the day Murugeshan died.

Just at that moment someone knocked on the door with hot *idlis* for Yogi Ramsuratkumar. The beggar brought them back to Parthasarathy and shared them with him, then he lay down on his mat in the back room of the house at Sannadhi Street and asked Parthasarathy to lie down also. He encouraged him to talk, which he did, and within a few minutes, Parthasarathy finally fell asleep. The yogi woke him up at noon and asked him to share the midday meal with him. Afterward, he told Parthasarathy to lie down again and talk. Within moments, Parthasarathy was sleeping soundly and easefully. Around eight o'clock that night, Swami gently woke Parthasarathy up and offered him some chapattis, which they shared. After dinner, the same gentle ritual was repeated: Swami asked him to lie down and talk, and again he was soon fast asleep. The next morning around four o'clock Yogi woke him up and said, "Parthasarathy, this beggar has seen you nicely. Now this beggar leaves you. You can go to your place." In this way he eased the pain of Parthasarathy's grief and sorrow, and prepared him to go on with his life.

"These people were from this beggar's family. If you want to know about this beggar, you can ask these people," Swami suddenly said to his three companions. It was 1982 and Ramaranjini—the wife of Ramsurat Kunwar—her eldest daughter, son-in-law and their baby son had come to Tiruvannamalai seeking Yogi Ramsuratkumar. Looking at the members of the Kunwar family who stood before them at Sannadhi Street, Parthasarathy, Murugeshan and Shivashankara were shocked.

When the family first arrived Yogi Ramsuratkumar didn't know who they were, but after some interaction with them it became clear that Yogi Ramsuratkumar had been rediscovered by his blood family. Parthasarathy recounted humorously, "Then Swami insisted, saying, 'If you want to know about this beggar, you can ask them.' But then he made our minds totally blank! He put us in a totally numb state, and we couldn't even raise our hands—we didn't move from our seats!" It was a very unusual sensation, given the intimacy of their usual relationship with the guru.

The husband of Ramsurat Kunwar's eldest daughter had read a magazine article about a living beggar saint of Tamil Nadu named Yogi Ramsuratkumar, who appeared to be crazy and smoked nonstop. His immediate thought was that the name was very similar to that of his wife's father, but the family questioned it because in the time that they had known him, Ramsurat never smoked—in fact, the opposite was true of him, since he was quite fastidious about eating fruits and juices and only using Ayurvedic remedies for healing. Still, the son-in-law wondered if this could be his mysterious father-in-law, who disappeared as a wandering mendicant in search of the Divine, so many years ago. They decided to make the journey to Tamil Nadu from their village in Bihar in the north, not far from Varanasi and near the Ranchi Railway Station. Traveling to Tiruvannamalai, they encountered the beggar in his house on Sannadhi Street.

Yogi Ramsuratkumar did not recognize them as his family members at first, but treated them exactly like everyone else who came for his blessing. The conventional connection between them had been severed long ago, and in this Yogi Ramsuratkumar was stern but compassionate. Truly there was no trace left of Ramsurat Kunwar, nor had there been for over thirty years at that time. Yogi Ramsuratkumar remained, as always, in the abiding state of God realization and dis-identification with all worldly positions and purposes; it was literally impossible for him to vivify the roles and expectations of the religious dogmas, proscriptions and social norms of his culture.

Offering as *prasad* some special milk sweets from a famous dairy near their village, they came forward and introduced themselves, and the beggar spent some time with them. Some tiffins of food were brought by devotees at one point, and the family thought that "father" would surely share this meal with them, but he did not. Instead he instructed them to go get food at their hotel. The next day, however, it was different; while sitting in his company, the food arrived and this time he shared it with them. Yogi Ramsuratkumar told them not to come back to Tiruvannamalai again, then he instructed them to go to Anandashram, the ashram of Swami Ramdas, to receive the spiritual guidance of Swami Satchidananda.

Yogi Ramsuratkumar sometimes interacted differently with children than with adults, as if another law applied to them, and the three friends were amazed to watch their spiritual master take his grandson, Murari, and put him on his lap. The innocence and purity of the child called forth a particularly tender blessing: Fondling the baby and playing with him gently, Yogi Ramsuratkumar murmured over and over again, "Long live Murari . . . Long live Murari!"

When it was time to end the visit, Yogi Ramsuratkumar said, "These people have come to see this beggar after a long twenty-three years' time. You have come here to see this beggar; you wanted to see this beggar. This beggar has also felt that you can come and see this beggar. The same old dirty sinner is still here. He is the same sinner, he is the same mad beggar. If you think this beggar is closely related to you people, then my Father will protect you. But don't think to make a scene here. You have come here to see this beggar—you have seen this beggar. Now you should go back to your house and live your life. And hereafter, you should not disturb this beggar." Those were the last words he spoke to his family before he sent them on their way.

Over the years Ramaranjini came to Tiruvannamalai on two other occasions, but she was not given permission to see Yogi Ramsuratkumar. He would say, "These people should be properly honored, but they should go to Anandashram." Parthasarathy remembered:

> Swamiji said the householders are the most able to reach God. He used to say that sannyasins have a lot of the stumbling blocks—you have to be alert, to watch yourself, your mind, your thoughts—but for the people who are living in the family it is very easy to have the darshan of God. Swami used to say these words: "This beggar committed a great sin by deserting his family to remember his Father, but this beggar's friends, they are remaining in the family—still they are knowing my Father all the twenty-four hours." He was very, very happy about that. It's not true, of course; he spoke like that just to impress upon us that we were supposed to go and do the right thing. He always compared us with himself, and in that way he elevated us. When you are being compared to a god, it is such an elevating feeling. Whenever he uttered the word "sinner," it sounded to me as if it was the holiest word. Whenever he uttered "beggar" or whatever, then that word was very dear to me. "This beggar is a sinner, a bad, dirty sinner." The words became very, very dear to me—they became divine words.

As guru, Yogi Ramsuratkumar commanded the Kunwar family to refrain from talking about themselves as relatives of Yogi Ramsuratkumar, which they understood was to protect them; the growing fervor around the Godchild of Tiruvannamalai was such that, had people found out who they were, they could easily have been mobbed on the streets. Some said that he sent them away because of the political harassment he had received, and that he felt his family was a walking target.

Yogi Ramsuratkumar sent them to Anandashram to receive the guidance of Swami Satchidananda, the spiritual successor of Mother Krishnabai, who was the successor of Papa Ramdas. They took his instruction to heart and went to Anandashram many times, coming from Bihar in northern India. A frequent visitor at Anandashram, Ramaranjini speaks with quiet dignity and great reserve about the man she once knew. Described as a very tall, elegant woman with the noble bearing of an elder who has known great difficulty and has truly served others, she has always been treated as an honored guest at Anandashram, given a special room and individual interviews with Swami Satchidananda. Still wearing the traditional red *kumkum* that betokens a married woman in the part of her pure white hair, her presence is a strong reminder of the kind of personal sacrifices that must be made by and for those who are irrevocably called to the Divine.

Haragopal Sepuri and his family continued to develop their relationship with the beggar saint of Tiruvannamalai. Many of their interactions with the guru were captured in Haragopal Sepuri's books, *Experiences With Yogi Ramsuratkumar* and *Further Experiences with Yogi Ramsuratkumar*. In every interaction that has been captured by devotees who have written about Yogi Ramsuratkumar, we find the seeds of the beggar's teaching and blessing power; as we penetrate more deeply into their meaning, these are simple stories that can be read and reread, told and retold.

Sometimes the transformative impact of an interaction is found in the kernel of a question, posed by the master to the devotee. Such an encounter occurred on May 23, 1982, when Haragopal and his wife Durga went to visit Yogi Ramsuratkumar at Sannadhi Street. When they first arrived the beggar saint was busy with other devotees, so they waited for a while outside. As soon as the visitors left, Yogi Ramsuratkumar beckoned to them to come inside. Prostrating at his feet and offering the fruit they had brought, they sat down.

"Swamiji, my last visit was in December 1981. Again I could come to see Swamiji only now. We want Swamiji's blessings that we could come often to Swamiji."

"Whenever there is need, you will come," Yogi Ramsuratkumar replied immediately.

Durga said, "Swamiji, there is no charm in living." She had been struggling with bouts of depression and other mental and emotional troubles.

"Yes, yes," he replied, "nobody wants to live in this world. Some want to go to the abode of the Lord and live there only. What do you say, Haragopal?"

Nonplussed by the vastness of such a consideration and humbled by the presence of the saint, all Haragopal could say was merely, "Swamiji. . ."

Five months later Haragopal went to visit Yogi Ramsuratkumar again, bringing with him several friends. They arrived at Sannadhi Street at the same time that the beggar was coming back. It was immediately obvious that the guru was not feeling well. He said that for a week he had no appetite and had been vomiting whatever he managed to get down.

Inquiring about the names of Haragopal's companions, he then said, "Haragopal, do not bring new people. This beggar has no time even to attend to all those who have fed him for several years. If the crowd increases, it will become very difficult," he said forthrightly.

Then he asked Haragopal to feel his pulse; it was the first time that he had allowed Haragopal to touch him, giving him first one wrist, then the other. He seemed to be in a lot of pain. His right wrist was tightly bound with some black holy thread, which interfered with Haragopal's ability to check his pulse. The beggar produced a knife and asked him to cut it off, then when Haragopal tried to give it to him, he said, "Keep it," quite casually. Haragopal pressed the black strings to his forehead, pranamed and placed them in his pocket, grateful for such a kindness. Later the threads would be placed on his shrine at home.

Another group of devotees came: the wife, sister and mother of Sri Subramanian, a retired postmaster of Tiruvannamalai. They had some personal family problems and had written to Yogi Ramsuratkumar about them previously. Despite his illness, Yogi Ramsuratkumar worked closely with them that day. His condition seemed to fluctuate, for in moments he was radiant, while in other moments—as they recounted new problems and further developments—he appeared pained. He had asked Haragopal to sit beside him and take his pulse. He whispered to Haragopal.

"These people do not understand what I am doing to them. Their main problem is different. Seeing my condition also, they are posing new ones. They do not understand. If people just follow my instructions, I can help them much."

In the middle of this two more supplicants showed up at his door. Yogi Ramsuratkumar asked Haragopal to go to the door and give them the message.

"Swamiji is taking rest, you may go. Father's blessings." When they lingered after the message was delivered, Haragopal tried to clarify the situation for them and talked with them for a while. When he came back in the house Yogi Ramsuratkumar seemed annoyed.

"What are you talking about to them? You do not understand the world. By not following my instructions, instead of being of help to me, you will only bring me trouble!" Yogi Ramsuratkumar was stern in this feedback, clearly demanding absolute obedience from his devotee, not personal initiative. In other words, do only what the master has asked, nothing more and nothing less. Any initiative on the part of the devotee could and usually did interfere with subtle dimensions of work. Haragopal grasped this immediately and said, "It is a mistake, Swamiji," quickly taking in the guru's reproof to heart.

On an earlier visit Haragopal had been given a similar teaching lesson. Yogi Ramsuratkumar had asked him to close and bolt the door, but he only closed it. The beggar had said, "You will only give me double work. Some people will directly come in." Yogi Ramsuratkumar then asked Haragopal if he could stay for awhile.

Muthuvel, a healer from near Tapovanum, arrived and began to attend to the ailing beggar also. Haragopal suggested some homeopathic medicine, but as there was no interest in this, he stopped making suggestions and simply waited to follow the guru's instructions.

That evening it rained. Yogi Ramsuratkumar was alone with Haragopal and Muthuvel. Around six-thirty that night the beggar's suffering became very acute. After an ineffectual attempt to vomit, he came back from the courtyard and lay down exhausted. Haragopal sat near his head and Muthuvel held his hand. It was a powerful moment of intimacy with him.

"Father has gone somewhere. Father is not attentive to this beggar . . . . If Father wants, He can cure this beggar in a minute! Jesus Christ on the cross said, 'Father are you there?' These were his last words . . . This beggar has been living only for the service of Father; he has nothing for himself!" Yogi Ramsuratkumar became very emotional and his voice cracked as he spoke. It was fruitless to receive his words through the logic of the mind—they demanded only the tender witness of the heart. He continued, "Father has given a lot of work to this beggar; this beggar has much work to do . . . ."

They spent the night with Yogi Ramsuratkumar. At five in the morning he rose and ordered coffee for all three, putting some of the coffee in his coconut bowl and drinking it. Then the beggar walked through the backyard to the water closet, and while inside it, he began to sing very sweetly, "Sitaram, Sitaram, Sitaram, Jaya Sitaram." A *rasa* of divine sweetness filled the air and entered Haragopal's senses. Every move of the beggar seemed permeated with sweetness; it was as if he had been transformed during the night, the youthful radiance of his face and form restored.

Around one-thirty that afternoon the beggar gave Haragopal *prasad*, plantains and two apples, and sent him on his way, saying, "Thank you, Haragopal." He had spent more than twenty-four hours with the beggar saint, and he found himself deeply affected by it. He wrote, "The purity of mind that lingered on after this episode was gratifying. Though it appeared that Ramji was suffering all the while, his blessings were charging me. The Lord has given Ramji really a very sweet role to play. Ramji, on the pretext of illness, permitted me to touch his body, and my joy knew no bounds at the rare privilege."[4]

Later, when Haragopal told his friend Ramanujachari about Ramji's illness and discomfort on this day, he found it hard to believe. He said, "I have seen him put a handful of raw chilies into his mouth and eat them without any trace of discomfort in his face." Clearly things were often not what they appeared to be in the company of Yogi Ramsuratkumar; at the same time, it was certain that he had been ill that day and night, then completely changed, bright and whole the next morning. When the life of an individual has been subsumed into the Divine, every act and nuance of his or her existence becomes permeated with awesome forces of transformation. It is through the transmission, the communication of the master's divinization that the disciple experiences the reality of the master's multi-dimensional life, wherein the processes of transformation are occurring on many levels, with far-reaching, even universal effects.

A year later, on October 23, 1983, Haragopal was visiting Yogi Ramsuratkumar. The beggar king seemed thinner, and must have lost some weight. Suddenly he started speaking.

"There is no need to be pessimistic. Sri Aurobindo, the greatest optimist in the world, says that the whole creation is racing towards perfection. So there is nothing to worry; everything will be alright," Yogi Ramsuratkumar smiled.

4 Haragopal Sepuri, *Experiences With Yogi Ramsuratkumar,* pp. 51-57.

At eleven-thirty that morning a woman came from a village ten miles away from Tiruvannamalai. She was speaking English, and she had brought food for Yogi Ramsuratkumar, which he accepted sweetly, showing great kindness and gratitude to her. After eating the food, he gave her what food was left to eat from from his plate—a great blessing for her.

"She has cooked for the workers, and after attending to the house work, she has brought food to this beggar without eating herself," he relayed to the others who were present, then asked her about her husband. She said that he had gone to Vellore to file a suit about the division of their property.

"He has lost faith in God because he is always getting troubles," Yogi Ramsuratkumar explained. "Father should remove all our troubles. Sometimes Father does not hear the request of this beggar. If Father does not remove our troubles, at least He will give us strength to withstand them." This was Yogi Ramsuratkumar's way of teaching: he was telling them that the solution to a problem is not always found in removing the problem, but in changing the attitude with which one works with it. The way of the spiritual path is to cultivate strength of character through surrender, faith and acceptance in relationship to one's problems, rather than to have all problems removed.

Yogi Ramsuratkumar handed Haragopal a book of lectures by J. Krishnamurti and asked him to read a chapter out loud. While he read Yogi Ramsuratkumar dozed off and on, then asked him to read it again. Waking up fully he unexpectedly engaged the devotees in a consideration of dharma, saying, "J. Krishnamurti says that no guru is necessary. Gajaraj, what do you think?" he asked.

"Swamiji, his theories are not solving our problems," Gajaraj answered.

Yogi Ramsuratkumar burst into his inimitable laughter, then collecting himself, quoted a devotee who had said, "J. Krishnamurti takes you very high in the air with his abstract preachings and then without any support leaves you there." Then he burst into peels of laughter again.[5]

In the early eighties a young man named Ravi started driving taxis. Ravi and his family had met Yogi Ramsuratkumar around 1978, when he used to walk past their house on his way to the railroad station. Walking past, he would stop and say, "Sri Rama Jai Rama!" Slowly Ravi and his entire family realized that the beggar who blessed them in this way and was always singing to Rama was a great being.

In 1980 when Ravi purchased, with the help of his parents, his first new car for the taxi business, he took the car to Yogi Ramsuratkumar for blessings. The beggar walked around the car three or four times and blessed it. Every day when Ravi left for work in his car, he would go first to Sannadhi Street to get the beggar's blessing, and only then would

5 Ibid, pp. 58-60.

he begin his workday. Usually if there was a large crowd, he asked Ravi to go; if there were very few or no people, he would ask Ravi to stay for hours. On these days they would sometimes sit for hours together and Ravi would talk with the beggar about family matters. Yogi Ramsuratkumar became very close with Ravi and his family, and when Ravi's father died in 1984, the beggar came to their house during his final days to bless the family. When Ravi's father died, he and his brothers began to feel that Yogi Ramsuratkumar was their father.

So it was that, over time, as Yogi Ramsuratkumar's need for transportation became greater and as he got older and could not walk long distances in the same way as he could before, Ravi became the beggar's driver. On one occasion in 1985, some devotees went to see the Shankaracharya of Kanchi to get his blessings. The Shankaracharya said to them, "In Tiruvannamalai there is a beggar—you go and get blessing from him." When they came to visit Yogi Ramsuratkumar they conveyed a message given to them by the Shankaracharya in Kanchipuram: he wanted Yogi Ramsuratkumar to go to see his guru in a far away town. Yogi Ramsuratkumar sent a message in return: "Pranams to Shankaracharya," it began. "Why should this beggar go and see Shankaracharya's guru there when he can see Shankaracharya in Kanchipuram?"

And so it turned out that on December 25, 1985, Ravi drove Yogi Ramsuratkumar to Kanchipuram to visit the Shankaracharya. Five people accompanied the beggar: a magistrate, his daughter and some devotees. Yogi Ramsuratkumar did not talk about anything in the car while traveling. Always thinking of others, during the drive the master said, "If anyone wants coffee or a break, they can get down from the car and have it. This beggar doesn't want anything to eat or drink." Arriving at Kanchipuram, Yogi Ramsuratkumar met the Shankaracharya. After sharing formal *pranams* they gave each other shawls in the traditional way, then sat together for hours, talking very little but gazing at each other for a long time.

Yogi Ramsuratkumar had similar connections with many saints in south India, such as Mother Mayee of Kanya Kumari. During the early 1980s the link between Yogi Ramsuratkumar and Mother Mayee was active in interesting ways, bringing about the introduction of a new wave of ardent devotees. Professor V. Rangarajan was one of these.

When Rangarajan first met Mother Mayee and started spending time with her during 1980-1981 at Kanya Kumari, she was staying around the Vivekananda temple on the rock or wandering on the beach. She was apparently illiterate, ugly, dirty and mad. She had forty or fifty dogs following her around. Professor Rangarajan sat at her feet and poured out his devotion to her. At the time he had cancer, and Mother Mayee, who was fond of chewing tobacco, spit a wad of well-chewed tobacco into his hand and told him to eat it. From that moment on his cancer was cured and never returned.

A few years later, in 1984, Mother Mayee sent Professor Rangarajan to meet the mad beggar, Yogi Ramsuratkumar. Rangarjan was told that the beggar saint often sat in the Arunachalesvara Temple in Tiruvannamalai. On September 1, 1984 Rangarajan had traveled to Tiruvannamalai and was sitting in a shop owned by a friend. When he inquired about Yogi Ramsuratkumar, his friend replied, "Oh, you mean that Vishiri Swami"—meaning the one with the country hand fan. Rangarajan said, "Yes, I would like to see him." Although his friend did not personally know the beggar with the palmyra fan, he did know where he lived, and he took Rangarajan to the house on Sannadhi Street, where he introduced himself and the professor to Yogi Ramsuratkumar.

To their great surprise the yogi said, "Yes, I have to talk many things to the Professor. You may leave him here and go." Yogi Ramsuratkumar led Rangarajan into his abode and closed the door.

> The Yogi took me to a hall inside the house. It looked more like a dumping ground where all the town's garbage was accumulated. I found old books, newspapers, letters, cigarette butts, burnt match sticks, empty match boxes and cigarette packets littered everywhere. The floor had perhaps not seen the touch of a broomstick for months together. There were bundles wrapped in rags by the sides of the walls, some old aluminum vessels, a number of pictures of the Yogi hanging on the walls and a number of withered garlands. To my utter surprise, I could find even currency notes of higher denominations and coins littered around the torn mat on which the Yogi used to sit. He made me sit on another torn old mat opposite to him. For some time he was gazing at me without asking anything. On my part, I was too dazed to be in the presence of such a strange person whom I could not judge at once whether he was a mad old beggar or great saint or godman.[6]

The professor sat silently in front of the madman, who by all appearances could have been repulsive to someone of a more squeamish or dilettante nature, but somehow simultaneously an inexorable attraction for the beggar was dawning in the professor's heart.

"This beggar has the bad habit of smoking, please bear with me," the yogi stated, then he took a cigarette, placed it between his lips and lit it. Looking keenly at the erudite man before him, the beggar asked, "What made you come to this beggar, Professor?" The mood behind this question instantly put the professor at ease, and the feeling that the yogi had known him well for a very long time began to creep into his awareness.

"I am a devotee of Mother Mayee," the professor replied, nonplussed by the sheer presence of his new acquaintance. Upon hearing this news the yogi immediately put down his cigarette, took up his palmyra fan and held it beside his right ear while peering deeply into the professor's eyes. The experience was one of having an electrical current passing through the nerves of his body; the professor felt himself being transported to another realm altogether, and he began to spontaneously chant the *gayatri* mantra, perhaps in an effort to bear the searing intensity that beamed forth from the beggar's eyes.

---

6 Professor V. Rangarajan, *Glimpses of a Great Yogi*, pp. v-vi.

"You need not take medicine, but you can take honey. Honey is not medicine!" the beggar said quite matter-of-factly, but taking the professor by surprise. How did the simple beggar know that Rangarajan had been cured of a serious cancer by the grace of Mother Mayee, without the aid of any medicines? Prostrating at the beggar's feet in response to this, Rangarajan then took his seat again and looked at the yogi with wonder and awe.

Yogi Ramsuratkumar asked Rangarajan to take off his glasses, then held them and asked, "Is it not time to change the spectacles?" As mundane as it seemed, this was not an ordinary question but an obviously symbolic one: the meeting with the master was a turning point in Rangarajan's life. It was through the master's grace that the disciple would have greater clarity and a proper view of life.

"Yes, it is time, Maharaj," the professor answered. Deeply recognizing the significance of the moment, he then began to tell the yogi of the long and convoluted path that had brought him, compelled by an internal spiritual impulse, to the feet of the beggar. He gave him a copy of the magazine, *Tattva Darsana*, and the beggar slowly and carefully leafed through the pages, looking sharply at each page. Earlier that year Professor Rangarajan had started the magazine, *Tattva Darsana*. The first quarterly issue came out on February 28, 1984. It had a picture of Sri Aurobindo, one of the spiritual fathers of Yogi Ramsuratkumar, and a title "First Supramental Manifestation" with the subtitle "February 29, 1956, Wednesday, Sri Aurobindo Ashram, Pondy."

When Yogi Ramsuratkumar saw this he asked Rangarajan, "Did the First Supramental Manifestation occur only in 1956?" The professor was shocked, and the master "burst into a hearty laugh."[7]

The hours passed in long discussions on topics related to the spiritual path. Rangarajan felt that he was sitting before the virtual Himalayas of wisdom and spiritual understanding. Bowing his head, he said, "Maharaj, I want to write a small biographical sketch about you."

"Why should you write about this beggar?" the yogi asked. "What is there to write?"

"Maharaj, I know you don't require a biographer nor a biography. But, for the sake of posterity . . . " Suddenly, before Rangarajan could finish his sentence, the yogi had burst out laughing loudly. The laughter seemed to go on and on, until just as abruptly he became silent and took up his fan. Holding it again close to the side of his ear, he looked deeply into the professor's eyes. After some time, he "rose up out of the heaps of books strewn about him, brought a few and gave them to me." These were copies of *Yogi Ramsuratkumar, The Godchild, Tiruvannamalai*, by Truman Caylor Wadlington, a few booklets, one of the souvenir publications brought out on his *jayanthi* in former years, and two books of poems written about him by the renowned Tamil writer of children's stories, Ki.Va. Jagannathan. He autographed each one, some with his name and some with the professor's name, and said, "There is nothing in the name. Both are same!" Then

7 Sadhu Professor V. Rangarajan, "Salutations To My Deeksha Guru," *Yogi Ramsuratkumar Souvenir Book*, p. 57.

he gave the professor a beautiful color photograph of himself.

With great emotion Rangarajan asked the beggar for initiation. Yogi Ramsuratkumar said, "Why? You have already gotten it . . . . Continue your practices. My Father blesses you!" The beggar rose from his seat and walked toward the door with Rangarajan close behind. He prostrated once again at his feet and then prepared to leave, but the yogi caught hold of his hands unexpectedly and sat with him on the steps beside the street. Yogi Ramsuratkumar seemed "immersed in samadhi" while he sat, holding the professor's hands. The scholarly professor felt pulled inexorably toward a "realm of bliss." After a while Yogi Ramsuratkumar released his hands, and the first meeting was over.[8]

Thus, presenting himself before the "awe-inspiring eccentric beggar," Rangarajan found himself in a state in which the "last vestiges of egoistic pride in the study and scholarship of philosophy started falling like dilapidated scaffoldings on the advent of a whirlwind."[9] As their relationship unfolded the beggar would often tease the professor, prodding at his intellectual background with slightly sarcastic or paradoxical comments. Once a couple came from South Africa and asked Yogi Ramsuratkumar for his grace to impart spiritual knowledge to them, so far away from Mother India. He responded, "This beggar is no teacher. His master has taught him only one line: Om Sri Ram Jai Ram Jai Jai Ram." Then he glanced slyly at the professor and said, "You take Professor Rangaraja. He will give lectures." It was a joke, but at the same time Professor Rangarajan left the next year to spend three months in South Africa to give lectures and discourses to various organizations, and to serve as an editor for the Divine Life Society of South Africa. This experience drove home the point that the bhakti or devotional approach to spiritual life was far more effective than intellectual knowledge.

On April 26, 1988 Professor Rangarajan came to Tiruvannamalai to celebrate the *jayanthi* of Swami Papa Ramdas in the Banyan Tree Cave on Mount Arunachala, where he had been invited to give a talk. Just after sunrise and the early morning meditation, to the great surprise of the devotees who had organized this event, Yogi Ramsuratkumar made an unexpected appearance.

"Where is Rangaraja, the Swami from Madras?" Yogi Ramsuratkumar called out, walking up to the group of people. Rangarajan ran quickly to meet the beggar, who embraced him warmly, then clasped his hand and said, "Yesterday you told that you would come again to this beggar today. But this beggar said that there was no need, for we had already spent a long time together. Last night, after you left, this beggar thought over it: 'Rangaraja is doing a lot of service to this beggar. He has come all the way from Madras for this program. Swami Sundaram has also invited this beggar.' So this beggar thought, why not this beggar go and see Rangaraja? And this morning Chidambaram came. He offered to help this beggar come here, so this beggar could come to see Rangaraja . . .

---

8 Professor V. Rangarajan, *Glimpse of a Great Yogi*, p. x.

9 Sadhu Professor V. Rangarajan, "Salutations To My Deeksha Guru," *Yogi Ramsuratkumar Souvenir Book*, p. 57.

Where are you staying, Rangaraja?" Rangarajan pointed to the terrace above the cave.

"Come on, let us go there and sit. This beggar will spend one or two hours with you." Then he almost dragged the professor up to the terrace. As soon as they got there, Yogi Ramsuratkumar sat down on a mat and asked Rangarajan to sit beside him, but many other devotees came rushing up to see the Godchild. As they settled in around him, he began to speak to the people.

"Swami Vivekananda spoke about 'Aggressive Hinduism.' Nivedita wrote a book on it. But when will this 'Aggressive Hinduism' come? How long will it take?" Kirsti was listening in the crowd that day, and she commented that Hinduism was taking root in the West.

"Yes, Hinduism will go to Europe and America. They will all become Hindus and we all will become Christians. Is it so?" Yogi Ramsuratkumar asked the devotees rhetorically. "This beggar once asked a Protestant missionary whether he would convert Catholics into Protestants. He said 'No.' But he would convert Hindus into Christians." The beggar burst into hilarious laughter at this, then said, "We will all become Christians and they will become Hindus!" He continued, "If Hinduism goes from India, who will preserve our Vedas and Upanishads?"

Breakfast was soon served to everyone, and the discussion continued. Rangarajan was fasting on that day but the yogi insisted that he eat some fruit. When one devotee asked if he could take some photographs, the beggar replied, "This beggar doesn't allow taking photographs, but Rangaraja is with me. You can take two photographs of this beggar with Rangaraja." After these two photos were taken he turned to Kirsti with a twinkle in his eye and asked if she too had a camera. She answered yes, and he instructed her to take two photos. Just then two monkeys jumped up and sat behind the yogi and the professor. When Kirsti hesitated to take the photos because of the monkeys, Yogi Ramsuratkumar said, "Doesn't matter. Rangaraja and this beggar here and behind us, Sugriva and Hanuman!"

His words instantly transformed the tableau that was gathered for the photo, as he alluded to the mythic royal family of Lord Rama, casting himself as Sri Rama with Rangarajan filling in as Sita. In the mystical traditions of Hinduism, the devotee often takes the role of the feminine counterpart of the deity, such as Sita in relationship to Ram, or Radha in relationship to Krishna. This is understood to be the most attractive and effective way to worship God, because the feminine counterpart is considered to be the symbolic embodiment of *prema bhakti*, or pure transcendent devotional love for the Divine. It seemed to be a way in which the beggar saint was giving generous, although cryptic, teachings on this auspicious day.

Yogi Ramsuratkumar declined the offer from Sundaraman Swami, the organizer, to give a talk at the ceremonies. Instead, after only a few minutes with the crowd where the talks were being given he pulled Rangarajan by the hand into the cave where Swami Ramdas had sat and meditated sixty-five years before.

"Rangaraja, this is the cave where my Master lived!" Yogi Ramsuratkumar spoke ecstatically. "This is where He sat and meditated. Rangaraja! From here He used to go to the Maharshi Ramana! Ohh! This is the cave where Swami Ramdas sat and meditated! Come, let us do some bhajan." They sang Ramnam together, *Om Sri Ram Jai Ram Jai Jai Ram*, and then, caught up in the master's mood, Rangarajan made a direct request for initiation.[10] He recounted this moment in his book, *Glimpses of a Great Yogi*:

> Then he dragged this servant closer to him and whispered the *Taraka mantra*, which He received from His Guru, Swami Ramdas, thrice in my ears, making me repeat it thrice. This servant fell prostrate at his feet and prayed in a voice choked with emotion, "Maharaj, I don't want to be a professor or editor any more. I want to be a sadhu. I want to be a beggar like you." The Yogi looked straight into my eyes and raising the palmleaf fan in his hand, uttered in a raised tone: "Rangaraja is a sadhu!" His emphatic declaration brought tears of joy in my eyes.[11]

Years later Rangarajan wrote about this occasion for *The Yogi Ramsuratkumar Souvenir Book*:

> The timing of this event was also most significant. It happened hardly ten months prior to the Mahasamadhi of Mataji Krishnabai of Anandashram in February, 1989. After the initiation while taking leave of Him, this sadhu was told by the Master: "My Father will guide you. Now you can go back and continue to do what you have been doing all these days. Renunciation is not giving up anything. It is just changing your attitude towards the world. My Father alone exists, nothing else, nobody else." My Master used to say, "It is not easy to get a Guru, a spiritual master. It may take sometimes many births to get a spiritual master." But the Master Himself comes into the life of the disciple when the appointed hour comes, or, in other words, when the instrument is ready for His work.[12]

Another devotee who came to Yogi Ramsuratkumar through Mother Mayee during this time period was T. Pon Kamaraj, a lawyer from Nagercoil, a town near Kanya Kumari. A man with a no prior spiritual inclination, in the early eighties Pon Kamaraj was diagnosed with leukemia, and his health was quickly degenerating. His father, Thiru Thavasi, knew the great *avadhuta*, Mother Mayee, who wandered on the beach nearby, and he took his son to meet her. Approaching her on the beach on day in 1984, she looked at him and laughed, then pointed to a man who was standing nearby holding a yellow

10 Professor V. Rangarajan, *Glimpses of a Great Yogi*, pp. 60-64.

11 Ibid, p. 64.

12 Sadhu Professor V. Rangarajan, "Salutations To My Deeksha Guru," *Yogi Ramsuratkumar Souvenir Book*, p. 58.

cloth bag that bore the name and image of Yogi Ramsuratkumar, saying, "Yogi Ramsuratkumar, Tiruvannamalai." The fire of devotion and faith was kindled within Pon Kamaraj at this meeting with the wild woman of Kanya Kumari, and he made his way to Tiruvannamalai right away. His body was deteriorating fast; the doctor had told him that he had seven days to live. He could barely walk more than ten feet at a time; his physical condition was bleak.

After searching for a few days he discovered the beggar saint standing on his doorstep and immediately prostrated before him. Awed by the spiritual power that emanated from the older man, Pon Kamaraj felt that he was seeing, for the first time, the incarnations of Lord Vishnu—Rama and Krishna—in the form of the dirty beggar. The beggar asked Pon Kamaraj to come back an hour later, which he did. Pon Kamaraj recounted the story of his first meeting in the booklet, "Bhagwan Sri Yogi Ramsuratkumar: His Divine Life and Message."

"What do you see in the beggar that you have come here? This beggar has only a coconut shell and a palmyra fan," the yogi asked.

"I see you as Lord Shiva, Sri Rama and Sri Krishna," Pon Kamaraj replied. Yogi Ramsuratkumar burst into a fit of joyous laughter.

"Go to the temple! Pray to my Father. I am not a doctor," the beggar said, waving away the praise.

"Oh father, you are the Lord of the universe, you are the savior of the universe. I have been sent by Mother Mayee," Pon Kamaraj pleaded his case.

"No, this beggar is nothing. He is a sinner, he is not a doctor. You go to the doctor and undergo treatment for that," Yogi Ramsuratkumar declared.

Pon Kamaraj was persistent. He said, "You *are* the doctor! You are the only person who can cure my disease." And with this Yogi Ramsuratkumar called Pon Kamaraj inside the house. He picked up his fan, stick and coconut bowl and began to dance and sing, "Sri Rama, Jaya Rama, Jaya Jaya Rama; Jaya Jaya Rama, Jaya Jaya Rama." In his dancing he jumped here and there, and he patted Pon Kamaraj's stomach, which was swollen with the illness. Immediately Pon Kamaraj felt an electric shock and cried out, "Oh Lord! You have cured my illness!"

The beggar simply said, "No, Pon Kamaraj. Don't say like that. All are my Father's lila. My Father alone . . . Everything goes to my Father. This beggar is nothing."

It was the beggar's divine laughter that reverberated throughout the atmosphere and lifted Pon Kamaraj out of his worries. At that moment a devotee brought some food, which the beggar then shared with his guest with the "care and compassion of a mother." Just as Pon Kamaraj was going to ask for a photo of the beggar, he brought out a framed photograph, a cassette of songs written by Pulavar Periasamy Dhooran, a book of poems by Jagannathan and the book written by Truman Caylor Wadlington, *Yogi Ramsuratkumar, The Godchild, Tiruvannamalai*. These he gave to Pon Kamaraj, and with his blessings, sent him on his way. Pon Kamaraj said:

> After that my entire body changed. The body of my younger days

> was there again. Yogi Ramsuratkumar saved my life. I am an advocate; I was practicing criminal and civil law at that time. I completely neglected my profession. I only wanted to study his power, the miracle that had taken over my life and spread his *nama* all over India. Bhagwan had done this, and lots of miracles in various people's lives.

In the late eighties Pon Kamaraj obtained permission from Yogi Ramsuratkumar to procure a piece of land in a small village, Kanimadam, not far from the ocean a few kilometers away from Kanya Kumari, where a temple complex, the Manthralayam, would be built in the next few years to house a fourteen-foot-high stone *murti* of Yogi Ramsuratkumar. The beggar blessed the project, and declared that his subtle influence would fully pervade the statue and the *mandir*. He made one stipulation: traditional Vedic rituals must be performed to the statue daily by Brahmin priests. Pon Kamaraj had been granted his wish: to spread the name of Yogi Ramsuratkumar to the people.

By 1986 Lee Lozowick had been writing letters and poems to Yogi Ramsuratkumar since he returned from India in 1979. These inspired poems were written in the heat of the moment and tossed into the mail; no copies were made, and many were lost. Although Lee wrote many poems to Yogi Ramsuratkumar, only a few poems were recorded from this early era—these reveal a man falling in love.

In 1981 Lee wrote in a poem to the beggar, "To be as Poor as You, Beloved Guru, is a blessing I only dream of with awe," dedicated to his "Beloved Ram Ram" in the book, *The Only Grace Is Loving God*. But it was not until 1983 that the poems reflected the fruition of the question, stated in his poems, that had festered deeply in the heart, now at a crisis point in the fevered heat of love's crucible. In these poems Lee Lozowick is not only a lover of an ephemeral Lord, as in his earlier poetry, but a love-maddened devotee, crying out to the "Thief" in human form who had stolen his heart:

> Oh Treasure in beggar's robes,
> disguised from those who cannot see —
> is Your son mistaken here?
> Are You just a dirty Sinner,
> shunning devotee's praises
> while plying Your Thief's trade?
> Will you leave me without a raft
> to cross this ocean of illusion and grief,
> or will You humor this arrogant Fool,
> old Rogue of Love?
> I hear stories of Your wild play—

oh how they make me long to be at Your side.
Yet when I asked You
for such a Blessing,
You told Lee this
while laughing in Your Madman's way:
"This old man's Father
wants Him to be in Tiruvannamalai,
but perhaps God
wants you to travel for Him."
It is true that Your son is young and naïve,
and You are Ageless in Your disheveled rags,
but lee is pierced to the core
by the desire to honor Your Words.[13]

May 3, 1983

Slowly, between 1979 and 1983, the American teacher, now established with his students in an ashram in central Arizona, went through another radical transformation: the metamorphosis from a maverick guru with no lineage—one who thought his spiritual realization had come without the help of any human master—to a humble supplicant spilling out his heart to the one who he had discovered was his guru, his master and his lord. It was an unprecedented situation, although not at all antithetical to dharma, wherein a spiritual transmission was made through subtle realms, before the disciple had even met the master. These were outrageous claims, and Lee had no qualms about making them; for him, it was not a theory or a possibility, but an abiding certainty.

On May 3, 1983 he wrote these lines to Yogi Ramsuratkumar: "How I long for You Father / for You are my only hope. / I have struggled alone / for far too long." As the reality dawned that the dirty beggar had been the source of Lee's awakening in 1975, the source of his teaching and his work with students, what was a cool insight became, over time, a burning revelation in which he discovered Yogi Ramsuratkumar living at the center of his own heart. There was no equivocating in these poems; rather, they were direct, straightforward, candid declarations of love that would play an important role in the *lila* of the beggar king of Tiruvannamalai in the years to come.

In a flurry of nine poems written to Yogi Ramsuratkumar on May 3, 1983, Lee proclaims outright for the first time his relationship with the dirty beggar of Tiruvannamalai. In this rash of love-maddened songs, Lee answers again the question that the master asked him in 1979: "Lee, what do you want?" Now, instead of, "I want to be a beggar like you," the answer revealed the heart on fire. Lee begged the "old Rogue of Love" to allow him to glorify the name of Yogi Ramsuratkumar and praise him to the world; he begged longingly to be called back to the beggar's side; and he begged to be

13 Lee Lozowick, *Death of a Dishonest Man*, p. 229

allowed to "weep before You with madness / as Your joyous Devotee."

> The first time I came to You[14]
> I was curious.
> Honor and respect were given
> out of propriety and pride.
> The second time I came to You,[15]
> I was secretly hopeful.
> Honor and respect now paid
> out of yearning and pride.
> The third time I will come to you[16]
> let me bow my head and submit my will.
> Let me not be honorable or respectful
> but swallow my ugly pride.
> Let me weep before You with Madness
> as Your joyous Devotee.
> Yes, the third time I come to You,
> oh Father Yogi Ramsuratkumar,
> call me to Your side
> and dispel lee's ignorance and his arrogance.
> Pierce me with the arrows
> from the bow of Your Fiery Love.
> Speak Your son's name
> even once darling Father,
> that will surely be enough
> for a lifetime.
> Speak Your son's name
> even once dirty Beggar,
> and it will take lee a lifetime
> to be worthy of You.
> Have You ever thought of me
> since I have met You?
> Don't tell me if You have,
> for I could not bear such a Blessing.[17]
>
> May 3, 1983

14 1976.

15 1979.

16 It turned out to be 1986.

17 Lee Lozowick, *Death of a Dishonest Man*, pp. 237-238.

After 1983 the poetry began to flow in earnest from Arizona to Tiruvannamalai, and by 1986, having heard nothing in return from the beggar, Lee planned a long trip to India with twenty-one of his students, including three children. The primary purpose of the trip was to spend time with Yogi Ramsuratkumar. One of Lee's students recalled this time period in *Tattva Darsana*:

> Lee began to speak of Yogi Ramsuratkumar as his guru and spiritual master. He began to say that he must have had help prior to his awakening and that the just hadn't recognized it. Now he knew one very definite source of that help. Lee began to call himself a beggar and referred to his community as "a school of beggars," meaning that we are nothing in the face of God and we could never afford to forget that this was one of the most moving messages of Yogi Ramsuratkumar. Lee began to speak more and more of his teacher in India and how indebted he was to this man. Many newcomers wanted details of who this Indian man was and how they might find him. Lee would not give out his name, where he lived or any information about him. He somehow felt it was Yogi Ramsuratkumar's preference not to be sought after by immature, curiosity-seeking Americans looking for miracles and spiritual sideshows. Lee considered Yogi Ramsuratkumar to be a gem among gems. He explained that he had now discovered his spiritual lineage. He had long before said that he did not have one, but now, he most emphatically did. He felt in the same way that Yogi Ramsuratkumar had described receiving a spiritual transmission from Papa Ramdas, so too had Lee been graced with a transmission from Yogi Ramsuratkumar, the beggar king.[18]

Lee Lozowick spoke about his relationship with Yogi Ramsuratkumar during this time of major transition and revelation. It is a story he has told on countless occasions:

> In 1979 when we visited Yogi Ramsuratkumar he was very friendly and warm with me, and I began to feel that I had a relationship with him, though my teaching at that time was still completely impersonal. I came back to the States in 1979 and I found myself writing devotional poetry to him! It was shocking—this was as uncharacteristic for me as flying! I wondered, where is this poetry coming from? It was oozing out of my pores like nectar, and I was writing it down and sending it to Yogi Ramsuratkumar! So, I looked at it and said, "There's more going on with this guy than I thought . . . This guy is my master! Oh my God!" I was telling everyone, "It's all an illusion, everything is an illusion, just realize God. You don't need a master, just wake up!" and suddenly I realize, "I've

18 Sita Martin, "The Beggar and the Seeker," Original version published in *Tattva Darsana*, 1988, pp. 42-44.

> got a master! And he was my master before I met him!" I was connected to him before the shift of context occurred. That took my breath away.
>
> I was smart enough not to resist it. I kept having deeper and deeper feelings about him. When I first realized he was my master, I had no feeling for him other than a kind of camaraderie—I thought I already knew all about Rumi! I was just cool—no emotion. But this incredible devotional poetry was coming out, and I was just accepting it, like, "Well, alright." I didn't feel any emotion. When I realized he was my master it was just a clear feeling of certitude. It was just clear. Obvious. "This is the way it is. Fine, he's my master. Good." Little did I know, on many levels . . .
>
> As the years went by, slowly I was beginning to have some feeling. I wouldn't call it love, maybe devotion, longing, the pleasure of remembering him. In 1986 we went back to India. I'd been writing to him, telling him what a great devotee I was. But I was starting to feel a little bit more. I was starting to feel anxious—like going to meet your lover! I hadn't seen him in seven years. On both previous visits with him there was an unconditional welcome—"Come, come!" But this time, it was very different.[19]

What happened on this third visit in 1986 was exactly what Lee had asked for in his poems of May 3, 1983, although not in the way one would typically hope for. Very early on in the trip they went to Tiruvannamalai planning to stay for ten days, the primary purpose of the trip being to see Yogi Ramsuratkumar. Upon arrival in Tiruvannamalai, Lee and his group heard on the streets that "Ram Ram," as they called him, did not want any visitors. He was telling people that he was not a guru, and that they should not waste their time with him. This was a little foreboding, but Lee was undeterred. It was an early afternoon in January, quite sunny and hot in the Indian winter when Lee and six of his students went to the Theradi Mandapam, seeking Yogi Ramsuratkumar. He was not there, but Perumal's son, Kamaraj, now a teenager, was there. Upon talking with Lee and his group, Kamaraj walked over to the house on Sannadhi Street and pounded on the door.

The form of Yogi Ramsuratkumar could be seen coming through the shadows of the enclosed porch toward the door. When he opened it and stepped out into the bright light of day it was a surprise to the Westerners—he looked older, and it was the first time they had seen him without his turban. His long tangled hair, still dark in contrast against the white beard, flowed around him. He stepped outside where the group stood in a semi-circle around the door.

"What do you want?" he asked briskly, seeming annoyed.

Lee answered, "We came to see you." The beggar looked at Lee, obviously the leader of this group, which he seemed to size up with a fraction of a glance.

"Have you seen this beggar before?" he asked, acting as if he'd never seen any of

19 Lee Lozowick, Nantes, France, June 23, 2001.

these people before in his life.

"Yes, we saw you in 1976 and in 1979," Lee answered. "I've been writing to you." The beggar looked at Lee and shook his head with a frown—clearly he had no memory of the earlier visits, nor did he remember any of the letters or poems. This was definitely not the reception that Lee had hoped for, and it was fast becoming certain that the beggar had no memory of their previous meetings.

"Alright—you can come in," he said reluctantly, then turned and walked up the steps and into the cool shadows of the verandah. Lee and his six students walked behind him and took their seats on the floor, with Lee close to Yogi Ramsuratkumar. He turned to Lee and said, "What is your name?"

When Lee answered, "Lee Lozowick," the beggar looked at him in total non-recognition. He shook his head and pursed his lips as if to say, "Never heard of you."

"I've been writing to you. I've sent some poems since we last saw you in 1979," Lee ventured. Still he had no idea who Lee was. He looked at Lee and shook his head again.

"Are you *sure* it was this beggar? Maybe it was some other yogi?" he queried.

"No, it was *you* . . . it was definitely *you*." Lee answered with some dismay. The beggar shook his head again as if totally perplexed.

"Do you know this beggar's name?" he asked Lee.

"Yes, it's Ram Ram," Lee answered.

"No!" the beggar thundered, and instantly the whole room seemed to reel with the soft blow of his swift anger. It was as if he was saying, "You are the supplicant, I am the master. Do not be so familiar!"

"Do you know this beggar's name?" he repeated forcefully.

"Yogi Ramsuratkumar," Lee responded quickly.

"Say it again," the beggar insisted.

"Yogi Ramsuratkumar."

Somewhat mollified, Yogi Ramsuratkumar turned to the person sitting next to Lee and asked, "What is your name?" After the question was answered, then he asked, "Do you know this beggar's name?" The lesson was well taken and the answer this time was "Yogi Ramsuratkumar." The beggar went down the row, asking each person their name, and then asking if they knew his name. He had them repeat his name, sometimes several times.

Finally he said, "Now you know this beggar's name."

It was a formal initiation into the sanctity of the master's name as mantra, and his communication sank deeply into the hearts of those who were present. Never again would Lee or one of his students refer to Yogi Ramsuratkumar as Ram Ram. The moment of instruction passed and the conversation that ensued was very ordinary and even superficial; the beggar talked about sports, soccer and mundane affairs of life. There were no amazing *lilas* or symbolic play like in 1976 and 1979. After sitting with Lee and his group for a short while, Yogi Ramsuratkumar dismissed them. As they were leaving Lee explained that although he had only six people with him, there were twenty other people traveling with him who hoped to meet the beggar saint. He asked if he could bring another group later that day.

"No. *You* have seen this beggar. That is enough. Go away," was the stringent reply, implying that because Lee had seen him, the rest of his students didn't need to. Stunned and crushed by the turn of events, Lee returned an hour later to the house on Sannadhi Street with six more of his students and his five-year-old daughter, Amy. He understood well that the master had said not to send anyone else, and he wanted to obey his command, but he was determined that his small daughter would have the darshan of Yogi Ramsuratkumar. So, sending them up to the door, Lee sat in the sun down the street and watched as they were greeted at the door by Yogi Ramsuratkumar and taken inside. An hour later they came back out, smiling and laughing with the beggar, who seemed like his old charming self again. As it turned out, Amy had hidden behind her mother's back, and Yogi Ramsuratkumar was delighted with her. Talking sweetly with the child, he soon coaxed her out of hiding and into a conversation.

"Who are you? Why, you must be Gita!" he said, smiling. Not only had the beggar charmed this second group of Lee's students, he had given Lee's daughter a beautiful new name.

Walking down the street to meet Lee, the group was aglow from the loving attention they had received. Lee instructed them to go back to Ramanashram where they were staying, and he sat back down on the dirt and sharp rocks of the street in the blazing sun. He had decided that if his master had told him not to come back, he would have his darshan from a distance. Perhaps he would be able to see him when he came to the door to greet visitors.

Not only was it a hot, bright afternoon; the small lane that is called Sannadhi Street was filled with garbage and refuse. The sounds of the bronze market and the bazaar on Car Street filled the air, along with the smell of stale urine that permeated this frequently used lane. An hour went by, then another and another. Occasionally Yogi Ramsuratkumar would answer a knock on the door. Each time he looked down the street to where Lee sat, some sixty or seventy feet away, but within clear sight of the door. Sometimes he shook his head, as if to say, "That crazy American! What is he doing, sitting in the hot sun?"

Finally he came to the door and, seeing Lee still sitting there five hours later, he relented and beckoned to him to come. Lee walked up to the door and Yogi Ramsuratkumar said, with some resignation, "Are you sure it was this beggar that you met before?" Lee answered that, without a doubt, he was certain it was him.

"Lee, I know what you want," the beggar said. "You want a guru. This beggar is no guru. There are many gurus in India. Go away and find one somewhere else."

"It's true that in India there are many masters and many gurus, but there aren't many beggars. I don't want any of those things. I want a beggar," Lee answered. With a little smile, as if perhaps, just maybe, this was an acceptable answer, the beggar invited him to come inside for a while. They sat down together on the porch.

"How long will you be here?" he asked Lee.

The reply came, "Ten days," then, "Can we see you again?"

Ever so reluctantly, the beggar said, “Alright . . . you can come a little, now and then.”

It took many years for the *lila* of this meeting with Yogi Ramsuratkumar to sink in fully for Lee Lozowick, the self-proclaimed American master who called himself a “Western Baul”—a story that will be told in later chapters of this book. Lee recounted his own story:

> I was pretty pulverized, like the ore in the gold before they smelt it. What ego was left was pretty much in shreds. But I figured, well, he was my master before this; he is still my master. If this is the way it falls out, this is the way it falls out! So I said to myself, “Well, okay, he doesn’t want to see me again and I’m going to obey his wishes, but I can still have his darshan.” We had planned to be in Tiruvannamalai for ten days. In the space of a couple of minutes I figured, well, we’ll travel through India and follow our itinerary, and when I go back to America, I’ll just never see him again. I thought to myself, he’s my master, that’s a fact. As much as I love India, which I do, I won’t go back. But while we’re in this town, I can at least have his darshan.
>
> I didn’t want to be aggressive, so I went down the street where I could see his doorway, and then when someone comes to see him and he opens the gate, at least I’ll see him standing there, and these will be my last images of him in my whole life. So, my attention was particularly acute. But also this is the way ego works, because no matter how far I go down the street, if I can see him, then he can see me. So even though I’m not sitting in front of his door, banging on the door being aggressive, well, there I am. He had told me to go away and not come back, but I excused all that, in my mind. I excused the fact that I had no hat and it was about forty degrees centigrade, and the Indian sun was bright.
>
> So, I went down the street and sat down in my meditation posture in the sun. It took five hours, but eventually he called me back in, and we had a couple of conversations before I left Tiruvannamalai. Nothing spiritual, just social chitchat. He asked me if I liked football and was very disappointed when I couldn’t even give him a good discussion on football, which I knew nothing about!
>
> In essence, that day in 1986 I was born, because before that day I was not a disciple. I was a student, a devotee, a worshipper, an adorer, but I wasn’t a disciple. The day I became a disciple, the minute I became a disciple was the minute my relationship to my guru changed from human being to human being, to human being to God. The language of this was there before: I had all the right words in all the right order: “Everyone is God. You are God. I am God. The master is God,” but it was theory up until that minute, when my master said, “Go away and don’t come back.”

> He actually said to me, "Lee, I know what you want. You want some guru. You want some saint. You want some sage. This beggar is none of those things. Go find somebody." He said that because that is what I wanted: I wanted an object that I could project and transfer upon. To be ultimately effective, our relationship with our teacher sooner or later has to be free of this projection, this transference.
>
> At the same time, he was my master, my guru, and when he sent me away, in that instant, I was born. Up until that moment it was just a philosophy—a very satisfying philosophy, one that I could argue with amazing eloquence and commitment. I was already a very successful teacher, but I hadn't gotten it, not just in the body, but gotten it, without duality: not me and him, subject and object, good and bad, this and that. I hadn't gotten it at that level until that minute, when he told me to go away and something shifted, or broke.[20]

Lee and his group continued their travels through India and returned to the States in March, 1986. He continued to write poems to his master, which he mailed on a regular basis, and he resolved to obey his master's wishes: he would not return to India. He said, "I grieved in my poetry and I grieved in my teaching work." For Lee there was nothing Yogi Ramsuratkumar could do to change the fact that he was Lee's master—even send him away forever. The mad beggar of Tiruvannamalai was the one who had stolen Lee's senses, broken his heart and in fact, given the greatest treasure that can be given between human beings—the grace of God that awakens the innermost heart, and the fire of longing for the beloved. Lee returned to the States broken-hearted indeed; he was resigned that he would have to worship Yogi Ramsuratkumar from afar:

lee says:
Oh You crazy Beggar, Who thinks
He hides His Father's Blessings
beneath tattered robes and
Madness. Hah, those robes are Regal,
that Madness the Father's gift.
Father Your son has found
You out, Thief, Sinner, dirty
old Beggar Man in Tiruvannamalai,
the center of this bad Poet's
universe. You will not, hah, You
have not escaped me, oh crazy
Beggar. You lovely One, delightful

20 Lee Lozowick, Pierre Chatel, France, July 23, 2001.

One, lying, stealing, this bad Poet's
senses.

September 29, 1986.[21]

"You will soon get a great man as your preceptor, and your life will greatly change thereafter! A very rare opportunity is awaiting you," said Devaki's friend at the university, as she was preparing for her final examinations for the M. Phil degree in physics in October 1986. A lecturer at Sri Sarada College in Salem, Devaki wondered in disbelief, remembering her search of many years. "How many great men have I seen and prostrated before? Still the mind is in control. Love doesn't spring up from the depths," she thought with some sorrow. She had spent many days and nights shedding tears of longing for the ultimate relationship of one's life—the love that exists between the guru and the disciple. Her ideals were the saints Mirabai and Andal. For four years she had been seeking out holy men and saints in search of a Ramakrishna, whose life and teaching had been a tremendous source of inspiration for her, but Ramakrishna was long gone, and the question remained: were there any beings like Ramakrishna left in this world? She had heard about Yogi Ramsuratkumar, but she was skeptical: Did such an "Ideal Man" exist in today's times of strife and conflict?

Born the seventh of nine children to Brahmin parents, Devaki had been intensely devoted to Krishna since childhood. She showed academic brilliance from an early age and excelled at all she undertook to achieve. As a young woman she was passionately drawn to Sri Ramakrishna and his disciple, Vivekananda; she had visited the ashram and *samadhi* shrine of Ramakrishna in Calcutta. Deeply aware that her spiritual path could not go further without the graceful help of a true master, her heart was on fire with longing, and as the saying goes, "When the disciple is ready, the master appears."

Driven by longing, she was impelled to travel the four hours from Salem to Tiruvannamalai during the Christmas holidays that year. Going first to Ramanashram on December 24, Devaki prayed before the shrine in the meditation hall. It was evening, and as she sat in meditation, a power failure threw the room into sudden darkness. Her prayer became, "Oh Sri Ramana! Is there darkness here too? Will I never see in my lifetime a god like you or Sri Ramakrishna? Will there be no light in my life?"

Three days later, on December 27, 1986, Devaki went with two friends to the house at Sannadhi Street and knocked on the door. By a stroke of serendipity, it was also the anniversary of the day that Swami Ramdas took *sannyas* vows. Devaki wrote of this fateful meeting:

21 Lee Lozowick, *Death of a Dishonest Man*, p. 250.

> It was a pleasant sight never before seen by me when that Divine Person opened the doors and came and stood before me. My mind rolled and fell at His feet. Without knowing the reason, tears trickled down my eyes. It is impossible for ordinary people like me to describe so beautifully as Sri T.P. Meenakshisundaram has done in his "Sri Ramji Akaval" ("Hail Sri Ramji"), the divine resplendence which surpassed the unkempt hair and soiled garb of Bhagavan.[22]

Devaki was not inexperienced in the world of saints. She had been initiated years earlier by the head of the Ramakrishna order and was the disciple of a female saint for a period of time. She had been seriously engaging *sadhana*, as well as she knew how, and she had seen many genuine saints and spiritual giants of India. So many of these people—even the sannyasins and sadhus in the forests of northern India—though sincere, were in control of themselves; they always behaved in the way that was expected of a saint. Some of these saints were highly disciplined, wrote many erudite books and were serious practitioners of yoga. What was the difference between Yogi Ramsuratkumar and all the saints and holy persons she had encountered in her search? Years later Devaki spoke about how she perceived Yogi Ramsuratkumar on this first meeting:

> I don't know how to say it. He was just beautiful. The others looked beautiful too. Every gesture he made was beautiful—the way he sat, the way he looked, the way he walked. Everything about him was beautiful. Anyone else I have seen there was also a controlled calm. I had attended all those retreats and so many places. I had been to Ramakrishna regularly. In so many places I was having darshan. I had visited almost all the ashrams at that time. In fact, when somebody mentioned Bhagawan's name, that I go over there, I didn't take it seriously at all. But then I was not prepared for what happened at that time. He was so different from anyone else. Even the little gestures he made were so godly. How else to describe it? The way he walked, the way he talked. You know, the light used to pour out of his eyes. His eyes were so powerful. I used to see sparkles coming out—sparks! Sparks coming out, there was such light pouring out of his eyes. And he looked so wild, you know? Something beyond the human . . . Godly.

That night in December, Yogi Ramsuratkumar asked the women to come inside and sit down. Sitting down in front of Devaki, he spoke to her in a compassionate voice. As Devaki looked at the beggar for the first time, she saw the same eyes of compassion, kindness and light that she had seen days earlier in the picture of Ramana Maharshi.

"Do you want to say anything to this beggar?" he asked.

---

22 Ma Devaki, "The One Beyond the Reach of Thought," *Tattva Darsana*, 1994, pp. 26-27.

"I want to see God," Devaki answered slowly.

"Ohhh, Devaki wants to see God!" His eyes twinkled and the barest hint of a smile hovered about his face. After a moment's silence he said, "Devaki will see God. She is a pure soul. Devaki will see God!"

One of Devaki's companions interjected, "Swami, we do not know whether we are pure or not. Because these words come from your mouth, from this moment we have become pure!" At these words, with his face turning ruddy and eyes sparkling with light, he raised both his hands and for the next ten minutes, blessed them in this manner. The three women were spellbound and aware of a strong but subtle current of energy, a divine vibration in the body.

That night Devaki looked up and saw many beautiful photographs of Swami framed and hanging on the wall. He also had a box of photos that the women had looked at longingly, but he declined when he was asked for one earlier in the evening. Devaki said to one of her friends, "So many photographs, I would like to have one. Shall I ask him?"

"No, no, you don't dare ask anything, because he would ask us to get out immediately. He doesn't like if you ask, he'd chase us out!" This was an unpleasant possibility, so Devaki said nothing about the photos and only approached saying, "Bhagwan, this offering is still there," to remind him of the fruit she had brought.

"I'll let you keep it there," he said, and she sat down in her place.

After awhile he said, "Get up." The three women rose from their seats.

"And now you people can go, this beggar is going to leave you, leave all the three of you," he said kindly. They followed him and were exiting the door when Devaki had one foot across the doorway and on the top step. Suddenly he twirled around, turned to the side and looked at her. He was standing very close to her, and she found herself utterly rooted to the spot.

"Do you know this beggar's name?" he asked piercingly.

"Ramji," she answered.

"No," he said, and to her great surprise, he pulled out the same photograph that she had seen and wanted earlier and gave it to her.

"You see this?" he queried.

"Yes," she answered, transfixed by the moment and the close proximity to the Godman.

"You read the name underneath," he instructed.

She said, "Yogi Ramsuratkumar."

"You read it again."

"Yogi Ramsuratkumar."

"No, you read once more," he stated emphatically, instructing her to make the repetition for a third and final time.

In such an ordinary circumstance, standing in a doorway on a first meeting, the devotee was initiated into the mantra. Little did she know that his name would become rooted in her mind and being in such a way that would transform her life. But the immediate tangle of the moment was that one of her friends was angry that she hadn't gotten a photograph. Knowing quite well what was transpiring for the three friends,

Yogi Ramsuratkumar began to laugh.

"Swami, please give me one photograph," the friend asked.

"No, no, no, no, there is only one photograph for Devaki," and then he gave one apple to each of the three women.

"This you take," he said, and let them out the door. Devaki remembered:

> After I stepped outside the house, I don't know what came over me. There was such a deep, deep peace within me. It was as if the whole being had come to one place, and I was drenched in divine peace. There were no thoughts in me at all. I didn't know how we got back to the room.
>
> The next morning at about five o'clock we were standing opposite Ramanashram when something strange happened. Next to Ramanashram is the Dakshinamurti temple. We were waiting for the bus and out of the Dakshinamurti temple one man came. He looked so much like a beggar; he was nude and his hair was all ruffled. It was early morning, five o'clock, very dark all around, and this fellow came running straight toward us, as if to do some harm to us.
>
> There were two friends with me. They were afraid and hid themselves somewhere. I saw him running towards me but I had no reaction. I was still very quiet when he came and stopped dead at a little distance from me; then he went around me and ran back into the temple again. It was such a strange thing, and after that the two friends emerged from their hiding spot. They came and joined me, and they were saying, "How could you stand there like that, with a man looking so like a ruffian, and he was coming towards you, he was running at such speed he could have done anything to you! How could you stand there?"
>
> But nothing happened to me. I was not even aware that he was going to do anything to me. I saw him, my eyes were seeing everything, but there was no reaction; there was only a deep peace within, and there was a sweetness, because now and then Swami's face would float before my eyes. It was like the Divine Beggar had put a noose around my head. It was as if Tiruvannamalai had put a rope around me. I never imagined in my wildest dreams that I would come here and settle down.

Returning to Salem, for the next fifteen days Devaki went through all the usual routines of her life, but there was an incredible peace within her. She was going to her classes, teaching and lecturing as usual, but she found that her faculties were highly sharpened; she could easily solve the most difficult problems of quantum mechanics or mathematical physics, right in the classroom without even trying. Everything seemed cast with a kind of perfection during that time; every little thing worked out well. If somebody died she had no reaction, but on the other hand, if someone brought happy news, she had no reaction to that either. The world itself looked like a dream; there was a constant sweetness within and a very deep peace permeating everything, as she recalled:

> I would sit in one spot and look at space vacantly. After fifteen days it began to go away and things were like they were before, getting irritated with something and inefficient at work, feeling happy at happy news and sad at bad news. All the reactions began to come and I became my old self. But then some fire started within and I began to feel a thirst for Bhagwan and at the slightest opportunity I would run to Tiruvannamalai.
>
> The second time I went to him I was alone. I had taken two tender coconuts with me. By that time I had become a little bold, so I thought I would give him one and I would take one for myself. One doesn't do such things with a mahatma—you just have to offer everything to him, and if he gave something as *prasad* it was very good, otherwise you don't bother. But then I gave him one and I was hoping that he would leave something for me. He drank the whole thing and then I gave him the second coconut. He began to drink and I was afraid that he would drink up the whole thing again in a second. When he was halfway through it I said, "Please leave something for me." I just couldn't resist it! Then at that time somehow, he indulged me.
>
> He smiled and said, "Okay, all the rest is for Devaki." And then he left it in my hand and not only that he said, "After drinking it you open these two and take the coconut also inside. Consume the whole thing," he said.

Over the next few years Devaki was compelled by a burning feeling of longing for the darshan of the beggar saint, whose presence had begun to take over her life. Again and again she returned to Tiruvannamalai. On one such occasion in 1987 Dr. Sujatha Vijayaraghavan, a friend of Devaki, had just written a beautiful little book on several renowned saints of India, titled *The Spiritual Renaissance In India: 1830-1980.* The book included three or so pages about Yogi Ramsuratkumar in one of the chapters. Although Sujatha was a salaried professional person and was earning money, she didn't yet have the money to publish the book. Taking the manuscript with her, she and Devaki went to Tiruvannamalai hoping to have it blessed by Yogi Ramsuratkumar. They found him sitting at the temple.

Yogi Ramsuratkumar put his hand deep into his pocket and took a ten paise coin out of it; he put it into Sujatha's hand and said, "My Father's Blessings. This will be used for your publication!"

In 1988 the money came through and the publication was completed, but after the book was printed Sujatha saw that there were many mistakes despite all the efforts to proofread the text. Sujatha and Devaki went to Sannadhi Street with two or three hundred books in a large box and deposited it right at the front steps of the house, at the beggar's feet. He opened the door and let them in. He took up one of the books right away and asked Sujatha to read.

"First you read the last chapter. Conclusion," he instructed. As she finished it, he began to laugh.

"So, the conclusion is over. Now let us begin from the beginning," he declared cryptically. Sensing that his words were symbolic, the two women took turns reading the first page and then the whole book, chapter by chapter. Right away it was obvious to Yogi Ramsuratkumar that there were many mistakes in the book. The women became embarrassed when the beggar also read it out loud, making it clear to them both that they had botched the preparation of the manuscript.

During this time period, in the late eighties, Devaki came from Salem to Tiruvannamalai to visit the beggar frequently. She watched carefully what was going on around Yogi Ramsuratkumar, and she longed to have the opportunity to serve him in some way, but instead, whenever she came the beggar would tell her to sit in a corner and stay there. At the same time he would give many tasks to others—to run errands for him, to handle small things that needed to be done, to take care of his food, cigarettes, newspapers, coffee and so on. Some of the other devotees were allowed to be very close to him, but Devaki was kept at a distance. He wouldn't allow her anywhere near him.

On the day that Devaki and Sujatha brought the manuscript they were seated a little away from the yogi, and again Devaki was longing to serve him. A number of people arrived, and he had everyone sitting in the rooms inside the house, whereas Devaki was in the passage that led to the room where everyone else sat. Then he called Sujatha and another woman to come and serve food to everyone. While the whole group sat eating together with Yogi Ramsuratkumar, Devaki sat alone with her banana leaf plate in the dark passageway outside the room. Looking in at everyone with longing, she tried to see Yogi Ramsuratkumar but he was obscured by the people who were seated around him. For a while she struggled internally with the situation, but then she made her peace with it. Then Yogi Ramsuratkumar moved out to the small porch of the house.

"Devaki, you can clear this ashtray now," he suddenly said. It was a small aluminum ashtray that he used at that time, and she happily took it outside on the step. When she tilted it to pour out the ashes and cigarette butts, even though she was careful to hold the ashtray securely, it suddenly fell into the gutter. Horrified at the mistake and terrified of Yogi Ramsuratkumar's wrath, she jumped down, picked up the ashtray and wiped it clean with her sari. Devaki described her chagrin in that moment:

> I tell you, terrified is not the word! I got so terrified because in those times I was very afraid of him. I wouldn't even breathe loudly, lest he should send me out. And the ashtray fell down into the gutter! Then I ran, as if some devil was behind me, and picked it from the gutter. Then, without thinking, I used my *palu* and then wiped it clean. That gutter is full of all kinds of things—people would sit near Swami's place and pass urine and all kinds of things! But at that moment I only wanted to take a clean vessel to him, so I used my sari and wiped it clean nicely. My hands

> were shaking. I thought I would drop it again, right at his feet! And somehow, with great trepidation, I just put it at his feet. There was no way he could have seen it, but he still knew what had happened. I didn't say anything at first. I knew that somehow he would know. And then, I stammered out what happened—that I had dropped it. "Oh." Was all that he said. He kept quiet. Then he made me sit again in my place.

The retribution did not come; Yogi Ramsuratkumar took the news mildly and Devaki sat back down. Then, with each newcomer into the house he would announce it in an amused way, as if it was quite a wonderful joke.

"This beggar gave some work to Devaki. You know what she did? I gave her the ashtray to clean it and she dropped it into the gutter!" And then he laughed heartily and slapped his thigh several times, then laughed again. Devaki was mortified:

> I was wishing all kinds of death on myself, hoping that the earth would explode and I would go under! I just didn't know where to go and hide myself because he was telling everyone. He must have said it about ten times to ten different people, and then every time he would slap his thighs and laugh. Whenever a *mahatma* speaks it applies to all the people there, in some personal way. Sujatha, the friend with whom I came, was also feeling bad because she had made a mess of her book. Bhagawan had given her ten paise, saying that that the script was nice and he wanted her to publish. So, that was the work given to her. Now, she had brought books with all kinds of mistakes in there. So, she thought it applied to her also: "I gave some work and she dropped it into the gutter." So, she also began to feel very bad about it and thinking that his words were meant for her. And I was thinking that it was meant for me. So, both of us were feeling miserable.

"Devaki, yogis are like fire! You shouldn't play with them!" the beggar said, looking at Devaki.

"Well, for me it is all right, Bhagawan—I would like to get burned in that fire and come out gold, pure gold," she responded.

"Oho!" he said with some sarcasm, as if not very impressed with her answer. There was an insipid quality to his tone that conveyed much more than his simple utterance, and it struck Devaki to the heart. It was her first instruction in how to work for the beggar king:

> I saw it happening because every little thing that he said, every little move he made was for Father. And it meant intense work on his part. So, there is no playing around. No, there is no playing the fool with him. One has to be very, very, very careful. Otherwise, we can spoil his plan—spoil

> his Father's work. Of course, he had to adjust many times. It was inevitable, you know, because he was here to live with fools like us . . . ignorant people. Slowly, slowly, we learned, of course. Gradually, we learned. And so, that was the way he conveyed to us.
>
> First he said, "Conclusion is made. Now let us begin from the beginning." So we thought, "That is the way Father's work is done." He sees us as the finished product, then he starts working on us. The end is known to them, and then they start working from the beginning. That is the way it is with Father's work. We are always finished products for them. Of course, we have to go through the process and we wouldn't know what the end is, ourselves, but they know all the time. I learned that on that day: the way Father's work is done. Another thing that we learned is when he gives us some work, it should be done perfectly. Otherwise, it means that we have dropped the thing into the gutter! After telling people about it ten times, he became very nice to me, saying, "See, Devaki . . . though she dropped it into the gutter, it is all filthy there, but she used her sari—she made it clean."

There was nothing that Yogi Ramsuratkumar didn't notice. He saw every minute detail of what the people around him were doing, and even beyond that. His senses were sharpened to a degree that gave him a preternatural awareness that spread over many dimensions—not just the physical plane, but the subtle planes that exist all around us. The multi-dimensional nature of his work was such that many of his interactions were extremely subtle, and demanded a one-pointed focus of attention from the devotees in order to receive and make use of the blessings that were an intricate part of every interplay. In this way, he trained certain devotees to be able to participate with him in "Father's work." At the time Devaki had no idea just how involved in this work she would become in the years ahead.

On another occasion Devaki and Sujatha went to see Yogi Ramsuratkumar. Sujatha had a very sharp intellect and an extraordinary talent for speaking publicly in a way that captured people's attention. She was also an excellent writer, and wrote quite beautifully. She had a particular disposition for *jnani*—a sharp intellect and capacity for critical analysis—whereas Devaki was disposed toward *bhakti*, with much devotional fervor and strong emotional states. Suddenly Yogi Ramsuratkumar pointed to Sujatha and said, "J. Krishnamurti?" Then he said, "Krishnabai. Krishna," referring to himself and Devaki, pointing out that Sujatha had something of J. Krishnamurti in her, Devaki had something of Krishnabai in her, and he himself was Krishna.

During these years Devaki's longing to serve Yogi Ramsuratkumar became a burning fire. She worried about him constantly and anguished over whether he was getting proper food and care. It was in Devaki's nature to be extremely concerned with Yogi Ramsuratkumar's physical welfare:

> I was praying to Divine Mother all the time that he should be looked after well. He should be fed nicely. He should sleep nicely. And there should be a good roof over his head. And there should be someone to attend and run around and give him whatever he needed. If it was raining or cold, I wouldn't touch his feet for fear that it would be cold if I touched him. It didn't matter to me if I didn't do *namaskaram*—it mattered to me if I touched him with cold hands.
>
> If it rained I would sit in Salem and think, "My God! It's raining here. If it rains in Tiruvannamalai, who will look after him—it will be so cold! Who will put the blanket on him?" Then if I put my hand into food, I would immediately think, "What is he doing? Is he going without food? Is somebody giving him food? Who is taking care of that?"

When Devaki heard that Yogi Ramsuratkumar had stopped taking ghee, which is considered highly medicinal, without saying a word to anyone she quickly dropped the use of it, although it had been prescribed for her for a painful condition of the tongue and she had a strong liking for it. A few months later, she went back to see Yogi Ramsuratkumar. Seated with the guru and some other devotees over food, someone was serving ghee and offered her some. Suddenly Yogi Ramsuratkumar called out, "What is it? Ah, ghee! Oh, you put some here for me!" They put the ghee on his banana leaf and he began to eat it, looking at Devaki with a sidelong glance to see that she too was eating the ghee. How did he know such things? Such subtle interactions created feelings of awe and wonder in the devotees, and even more, they felt the deep love and regard of the guru for his disciples. Devaki recalled:

> Such warmth and love in one simple gesture! He would just look at you like that. And you know, he may be looking at so many people—there would be twenty, thirty people around him, it would be so crowded. He would be so busy! He would be smoking, he would be looking at this person, that person, penetratingly, and amidst all that work, one person would be seated quietly in the corner and he may just give her a glance—not nearly as much as he would be giving the others. But in that half glance there was so much warmth and love that the person would feel fulfilled. I had received like that.
>
> Once during a whole session he had ignored me. There were so many people and he was paying special attention to everybody there, and I was totally ignored. But, for me, seeing him was most important—not his blessing me. It had always been like that. I don't know why. People go to a saint to take blessings—to benefit from him. But all that time, my concern for him and for me, seeing him was enough. If I could see him at close quarters, that would be most fulfilling. So, I was very happy even to be sitting there. But there were other times when I cried—when somebody

> received some special grace and he would deliberately ignore me. Deliberately! You know, just to make a point, he would do that sometimes. Then I knew that he was doing that for some mistake I had committed. Then I would feel very bitter. How many times, endlessly, he had driven me out of that house! He would not allow me to go even one step. So many times I stood before that gate, only to be driven out—only to be chased out, mercilessly. I cried and cried and cried so much in those days.

Often he would ignore Devaki completely, giving *prasad* sweetly to everyone else, and then casting it harshly at her. Then, while she was still seated with everyone, he would just glance at her for one second and give her hand or arm the lightest touch. She said, "A stroke, a minute stroke, and it was done so tenderly and it wouldn't be obvious to anybody how tender he was, how loving the whole gesture was except to me, the receiver. That was his talent. He could be so charming. After that I was jumping about the whole day! I was jumping about like a monkey! Drunk on honey, just one glance like that!"

In 1986 Dwarak Nath Reddy, a wealthy retired candy baron who moved to Tiruvannamalai in 1983 with his daughter, Sandiya, had gone to a *jayanthi* celebration for Yogi Ramsuratkumar that was organized that year in Madras. He hadn't met the beggar saint yet, but he was asked to be a key speaker on that day and given the subject, "Happy Birthday to the Unborn." Some time later he went with a friend from Pondicherry to meet Yogi Ramsuratkumar.

"This beggar was waiting to meet Dwarak Nath Reddy," Yogi Ramsuratkumar said humorously, having seen the *jayanthi* program for the celebration in Madras. Obviously intrigued with the idea of someone speaking about him without having met him, he quoted the title of the talk and said gaily, with his usual joyous laughter, "I wanted to meet the person who was talking about the happy birthday to the unborn!"

There was an immediate flood of affection, friendship and camaraderie in the beggar's relationship with the businessman and his daughter. Reddy commented, "We felt a lot of affection and respect for him and joy in being with a person who has so much joy in himself. So, he accepted us immediately. After that we would meet just about anytime—we would go and sit with him for a while at Sannadhi Street. If we happen to go there, we were received, and he would ask us to come in. He accepted us so instinctively. We were so happy—Swamiji was such a joy for us!"

After that there were many times when Dwarak Reddy and Sandiya were in their house, which was called "Kripala," and they would hear the beggar's voice coming from outside and calling loudly, "Sandiya! Sandiya!" When she would come out, he would burst into smiles.

"This beggar would like to stay here for some time. Can he stay the day here?"

Naturally, the answer was a delighted "Yes!"

He loved to sit out in the lush garden of the Kripala grounds, where he would stay for hours under the mango trees. He had a particular love for the two mango trees in the garden, and he would have lunch there, often with other devotees or friends who came with him, or who would come seeking him. Everyone was welcome; it was a time of very sweet communion, easy friendship and relaxed, happy times together.

One of the devotees that Dwarak Reddy and Sandiya met right at the beginning of their friendship with Yogi Ramsuratkumar was Devaki, the young physics professor from Salem. She and her friend Sujatha were part of a group of people who were very devoted to the beggar. One day Yogi Ramsuratkumar came to Kripala, bringing Devaki and Sujatha with him. He visited for a while, then got up to leave.

"Sandiya, these ladies will stay with you!" Yogi Ramsuratkumar said, and leaving Devaki and her friend there, left and went back home to Sannadhi Street. After that Devaki became like a daughter to Mr. Reddy, and like an older sister to Sandiya. Every time Devaki had any free time she would travel all the way from Salem and wait to see the beggar, even for a few moments. She often spent the weekend with Sandiya, and they would go together to visit the yogi. Reddy said, "If Devaki had a glimpse of Yogiji, she was happy for the day, she was so totally committed."

Sometimes the yogi would come to Kripala and say to Sandiya, "This beggar is so hungry," and then they would go together to buy food. He often called Sandiya by the north Indian version of her name, Sanda. He would look at the vegetables and ask, "Sanda, do you know how to cook this?" or "Do you know how to cook that?" So they would buy vegetables or cook *idlies* sometimes. He became a part of the family, and sometimes slept at Kripala. Sometimes the beggar would come and lie down in the garden; at other times the family would put leaves out on the patio of the garden and eat meals together there. At times Yogi Ramsuratkumar would read *Guru's Grace*, on the life of Mataji Krishnabai, and he would cry, his love for Krishnabai was so great.

Yogi Ramsuratkumar often treated Sandiya, a grown woman, as he would a five-year-old child, and in this way she was brought into the world of divine innocence that characterized the Godchild himself. Devaki and Sujatha followed suit in their relationship with Sandiya, using her as a "go-between" for themselves and the beggar saint. Yogi Ramsuratkumar often asked Sandiya to tell stories from the religious mythology of India—like the fables of Krishna—which she did with a dramatic flair and natural talent for mimicry, "The boy is returning to the forest . . ." She would spin the tale as if telling it to a small child, so that when the tiger came she would growl, when the birds entered the story she would make their noises, and Swamiji would laugh and laugh, then he would make her repeat it again. But sometimes Sanda would feel like she really was five years old, and then the beggar would say, "Okay, this beggar will read it for you." These Krishna stories were natural to this time period, Dvaraka being Krishna's mythical "city" and the name of her father, Dwarak Nath Reddy. As Sandiya said of Yogi Ramsuratkumar many years later, "He was our Krishna and we were the *gopis*."

In the fall of 1988, Lee Lozowick was surprised to receive a letter from India, from a man named T. Pon Kamaraj. He had never heard of this man, and the letter came "out of the blue." It was a mysterious invitation to come to south India as the guest of Yogi Ramsuratkumar's devotees to attend a large *jayanthi* celebration that was being planned at a small village called Kanimadam near the cape of south India. There was no hint of any kind as to why this invitation was being issued or by whose command. Lee had never heard a word from Yogi Ramsuratkumar; he had no idea what this was about, but he immediately sent a reply by mail saying that he would come, and he planned to bring seven of his men students with him—five Americans and two Germans. Based on his master's last instruction to him to "Go away," Lee assumed that he would only visit with the devotees of Yogi Ramsuratkumar, but he planned to go to Tiruvannamalai for two days at the end of the trip—"just in case" the master was willing to see him.

Lee and his group arrived in Madras on November 28, 1988, where they were warmly greeted and taken to the home of Professor Rangarajan, who, with his wife Parvati and daughter Nivedita, hosted them lavishly. During the next two days, Rangarajan regaled the Americans with stories of Yogi Ramsuratkumar. Hungry for stories of the master, Lee and his students listened with keen attention.

Rangarajan told a story of a disciple who once argued with Yogi Ramsuratkumar when he said that he was the sinner and she was the saint. "No," she said, "I am the sinner and you are the saint." Back and forth they went like this until he threw her out of the house. The next time she was allowed into his darshan, and she did not argue. In another story, Janarthanan, a long-time devotee, asked Yogi Ramsuratkumar if he could build an ashram for him. The beggar replied, "Does Mount Arunachala ever move?"

Through Rangarajan, the Americans discovered that the yogi had allowed only one formal *jayanthi* celebration over the years, which had occurred in 1976 in Tiruvannamalai. Although he had been asked many times, since then he had only allowed his devotees to celebrate elsewhere. For the past few years there had been *jayanthi* celebrations in various towns of southern India, like the one in Kanimadam where Lee was going.

As Lee heard the professor recounting stories, his students watched him for any reactions. Lee demonstrated no emotion whatsoever, but remained cool and serene. It was well known within Lee's community that their spiritual teacher's guru had sent him away. It was a strange koan for his students, who didn't really know yet what to make of such an unusual circumstance. It was a great mystery, and they were about to be the witnesses in the next chapter of its unfoldment. When asked how he felt about seeing Yogi Ramsuratkumar again, he said, "Nothing happens for me on the outside. I feel something in the heart." A few years later that "something in the heart" so obliquely referred to by Lee would be revealed in the devotional fire of his poetry.

That night Rangarajan's wife and daughter stayed with friends so that Lee and his students could sleep at the professor's house. In the morning he talked with them about Hindu deities until Lee said, "Would you tell some more stories of Yogi Ramsuratkumar? I have none. Everything I have gotten from him has been on the inside."

The professor told many stories about the miracles that devotees experienced in the company of Yogi Ramsuratkumar—spontaneous healings, problems solved, harmony and peace brought to families, businesses, marriages. After a while Rangarajan began to humorously refer to Lee sitting in the sun outside the house at Sannadhi Street two years before, hoping to see Yogi Ramsuratkumar. When the men asked how he knew about that, he responded that Yogi Ramsuratkumar had told him. Then he brought out five letters that Lee had sent to Yogi Ramsuratkumar, all containing poetry. Rangarajan proceeded to tell Lee how one day when he visiting the beggar saint, Yogi Ramsuratkumar rummaged through the piles of newspapers and apparent junk that was strewn all about and came up with several of Lee's poems, which he wanted published in *Tattva Darsana*.

Surprised and even a little chagrined, Lee exclaimed, "Uh oh!" He had expected the poetry to remain discreetly unknown to anyone but himself and Yogi Ramsuratkumar. Then he shrugged and said, "Once you give something, it's no longer yours." It was a principle that holds true in all relationships: gifts that are given with no strings or expectations attached are the gifts of the heart. This is never truer than in the eternal affair of the heart that exists between the guru and the disciple. Any gift of *prasad*, whether it is fruit, flowers or poetry, when given freely and completely cultivates the mood of surrender, and of submission to the will of God as it manifests in the guru.

Rangarajan further revealed that Pon Kamaraj, a close devotee of Yogi Ramsuratkumar, was organizing a major event to celebrate the *jayanthi* of Yogi Ramsuratkumar in southern India near Nagercoil. He explained that Pon Kamaraj was building a *mandir* to Yogi Ramsuratkumar in Kanimadam, a tiny village situated only five kilometers from the cape at Kanya Kumari. There a fourteen-foot high statue of the beggar saint would be housed. While sitting with the beggar king at Sannadhi Street and talking about the upcoming *jayanthi* celebration, Pon Kamaraj had asked Yogi Ramsuratkumar about the organization of the event. Yogi Ramsuratkumar got up and looked around, then picked up a large bundle—a bag full of "trash." He instructed Pon Kamaraj to take the bag, wait seven days, then open it and search through it.

"In there you will find something," he said enigmatically.

Back in Nagercoil seven days later, Pon Kamaraj opened the bag and searched through its contents. The only things he found that captured his attention were seven envelopes that had been mailed to Yogi Ramsuratkumar from a return address in Arizona, U.S.A., with the name Lee Lozowick on them. Pon Kamaraj had never heard of this American man, but he immediately returned to Tiruvannamalai and showed the seven envelopes to Yogi Ramsuratkumar, saying, "This is what I found in the bag you gave me."

"Invite this man," Yogi said, pointing to the name Lee Lozowick, "and he will come. Lee will be here." Pon Kamaraj quickly dispatched an invitation. Listening closely to this amazing story, Lee slapped his knee and said, "I knew it!" He had instinctively felt that the mysterious trip back to India had been somehow catalyzed by the dirty beggar himself, and this was the confirmation.[23]

Lee and his group of students left Madras on the bus for Nagercoil the next day, accompanied by Ramanlal, who had been introduced to Yogi Ramsuratkumar in 1984 by his father and had become an ardent devotee after the beggar healed his arm from a terrible, debilitating accident. Arriving just off the bus at five the next morning, they were ushered into a house and then a small room where two, seven-foot-high paintings graced the wall above a shrine: one of Yogi Ramsuratkumar and one of Mother Mayee. Purna Steinitz, who had been on the 1977 trip, recognized Perumal, the attendant of Yogi Ramsuratkumar, and his son Kamaraj, who came forward to greet Lee and his companions. A *puja* was performed, waving lights (*arati*) to the images at the shrine. Afterward the group was driven to the hotel where they would be staying and arrived just in time to see the tropical sun rising over the sea.

What they discovered next was another surprising turn of events: There were about ten thousand followers of the beggar saint in the small villages and towns around Kanya Kumari and Nagercoil, and everywhere there were posters announcing the event of the *jayanthi* celebration, with Lee Lozowick's name printed on them. Evidently the plan was that Lee would perform the inauguration of the Manthralayam, which was still just a grass hut at this point. With the *mandir* unfinished, the *jayanthi* celebration was held in a large hall, open on two sides. People streamed in from all directions, and as the visitors walked in the first thing they saw was a large banner, hung across the entrance, that read, "Lee Lozowick, the Effulgent Flame of Yogi Ramsuratkumar in the West."

Being honored as an "American saint" was a different experience both for Lee and his students; at this time Lee normally lived a very quiet, almost reclusive existence with his devotees on an obscure ashram located just outside a small city in the high desert of Arizona. Although he had published nine books and had a growing body of dedicated students in the States and a small group of new students in Germany, he nonetheless kept an extremely low profile. Now he found himself thrust into a very interesting situation: he was greeted by the Indian devotees of Yogi Ramsuratkumar with elaborate formality, bedecked with flower garlands, his feet washed and anointed with *kumkum.* Two years after being brusquely sent away by his guru, Lee Lozowick had landed in southern India only to find that now he was the guest of honor—and all of it was the *lila* of Yogi Ramsuratkumar.

Lee and his students were quickly whisked up to the stage, where they were each given flower garlands. The back of the stage was lined with four large pictures: two each of Yogi Ramsuratkumar and Mother Mayee, strung with flower garlands and small yellow limes strung together as garlands. The Westerners were told that because the limes were very acidic, they represented the acid or burning fire of the guru that burns away impurities and cleanses the devotee. The American students were escorted off the stage but Lee stayed: he would be the keynote speaker on that day, making a presentation along with the Indian devotees of Yogi Ramsuratkumar who would also speak.

---

23 *Tawagoto*, Spring, 1989, Volume 2 No. 2, pp. 6-11.

The banners and beautiful saris of the women, the ample flower garlands of lotus, rose and small *sampangi* lilies flowed together onstage in the bright colors of India and merged with the streams of sweet incense and ecstatic chanting of the name of Yogi Ramsuratkumar to intoxicate the senses. The deep and soul-stirring polyrhythms of the drums added to the euphoria that floated in the air. Lee declined the chair he was offered and sat instead on the floor of the stage. He greeted the large audience of several hundred people with a smile and a *pranam*. The microphone was placed before him, and he began to speak:

> I am just an arrogant fool, so please forgive me if I offend anyone. In spending a couple of days in Madras before coming here, many of the devotees of my father Yogi Ramsuratkumar asked me to tell them of my experience with him. And all of the devotees in Madras told many wonderful experiences of everything that our father has given them. But he hasn't given me anything, he's taken away. When Americans travel to India, they usually look for gurus that can give blessings and give miracles, and give—just give things! When I traveled to India for the first time twelve years ago, I also looked for gurus that could give. I came to find my father Yogi Ramsuratkumar; instead of filling my heart with wonderful things, he broke my heart. But he broke my heart in a very special way. Only one Physician can heal this broken heart, and that's our Father in Heaven.
>
> Yogi Ramsuratkumar says that he is the only beggar and we are all the saints. Well, he acts like a beggar, he lives like a beggar and blesses like a beggar. But we don't live like saints. My father Yogi Ramsuratkumar has blessed me with the need to be like a saint and that's a very difficult thing to do. So Yogi Ramsuratkumar has not given me rest or relaxation or happiness. He's given me an impossible job to do, which is to actually be the saint that he sees me as. And for each one of us to be the saint that he sees us as. I have to admit that after twelve years I'm far, far, far short of that goal.
>
> When my father Yogi Ramsuratkumar first broke my heart, I looked everywhere to try and heal it. Even though he was very clear that only the absolute Father could heal that. I think that—please, accept this as my opinion—if our hearts have not been broken, we have not begun to consider our Father in Heaven yet.
>
> The last time I came to my father, he said, "Go away! I'm not a guru—that's what you want." And my response was that in India there are many masters and many gurus and many teachers, but not many beggars. Then he told me to go away again. So I guess my father Yogi Ramsuratkumar has not been happy breaking my heart once. He breaks it again and again and again and again. But I am very grateful to him, because without

> a broken heart, it's very easy to forget God.
>
> So, I wish I could tell you miracle stories, but I don't have any to tell. I would only suggest that we not look to miracles to make us forget our broken heart. We must have a very very very powerful urge to realize God, or we never will. In my life, the only thing that has taken my mind away from money and my stomach and the other things that are so easy to satisfy in America, is a broken heart.
>
> I think that's all I have to say. I could say that again and again, but I think that's enough.[24]

Afterward many of the Indians addressed the crowd also, including T. Pon Kamaraj, who spoke in Tamil and referred often to the American guest. Later they were told by devotees that Pon Kamaraj had said that Lee Lozowick was an Indian saint, and that they were all connected from previous births. The next week the Americans were whisked away on a whirlwind tour of many towns and villages of southern India, where Lee gave talks to the devotees of Yogi Ramsuratkumar and crowds of village people came to hear the American saint speak. Pon Kamaraj, Ramanlal and other devotees of Yogi Ramsuratkumar accompanied the group through days that were filled with activities: *puja* ceremonies, visits to temples and the *samadhi* sites of local saints connected with Yogi Ramsuratkumar, talks and speeches at various functions, businesses, schools and orphanages.

All of this was interspersed with the incredible, expansive Indian way of hospitality: there were fabulous south Indian meals, the formal *namaskar* and *pranam* offered to dignitaries and respected persons, entertainment like classical Indian music and dance, many flower garlands offered and exchanged and waving of lights (*arati*) in the beautiful and profound ceremonies of traditional Hinduism. The chanting of the name of Yogi Ramsuratkumar resounded through it all. It was a birthday party to end all parties, and it lasted for days, during which time Lee was lavished with praise and adulation, even as he spoke in the name of Yogi Ramsuratkumar. This carried a mixed blessing for the self-styled American guru—one that he spoke about after he returned to the States later that month:

> The thing that struck me the most was the second village we were in; they took us into a temple, the local worship house. Every place we went, the first thing we did was *arati*. Wild *arati*, all the children screaming and chanting, the incense billowing out! After the *arati* I gave a talk. They had a thirteen-year-old girl sing a beautiful song to Yogi Ramsuratkumar, and they had me give her a prize. It was really embarrassing. I didn't want to do it and she didn't want to take it, but it was one of those official things. When the talk was over we did another *arati* and after that they brought

24 Lee Lozowick, *Tawagoto*, Spring 1989, Volume 2 No. 2, p. 16.

> out food. People were coming up to me the way people approach Jesus or Satya Sai Baba! Unbelievable! It was ten o'clock at night, and so intense. I wanted to get out of there, but people came up to get my blessing like, if I'd said, "Drop dead now," they would have. They had complete faith. It wouldn't have surprised them if I had walked on water! They had no question about me, who I was, and for me, that was scary. My response was, if you ever think that it would be great to have power, if you ever wanted power over people and you go to a place like that and you even minimally open up and see the power people can give you—that's the last thing in the world I would want. I was cursing my fate the whole way out of the village.[25]

These reflections were demonstrated again in a talk Lee gave to the Madras Youth Organization, in which he spoke with a characteristic brash humility: "My father called me back to India to speak to Indians. That's his sense of humor—that he calls an American to speak to you! My father says we are all saints, but I don't feel like a saint, and I've done fifteen years of very intense *tapas*. For fifteen years my whole life has been about *sadhana*—not business and not money and not politics, but all about *sadhana*—and I don't feel much like a saint. I just feel like an arrogant fool from America, acting like an arrogant fool in front of such wonderful guests here tonight . . . ."[26]

After leaving Tamil Nadu, Lee and his group traveled to Kerala for a three-day visit at Anandashram in Kanhangad, where they had the darshan of Mataji Krishnabai in the last days before her death. Her condition was a shock to them, but Swami Satchidananda took the Western devotees of Yogi Ramsuratkumar under his wing, and as they sat with him day after day, he told them many stories of Papa Ramdas and Mataji.

Finally, at the end of their two weeks in India, Lee and his companions turned toward Tiruvannamalai. After dropping their backpacks at Ramanashram where they were staying, Lee and the seven men headed immediately toward the house on Sannadhi Street. The anticipation had built to a very high pitch, not only for Lee, but for his students as well. They had no idea what to expect. Would the beggar king send Lee away again? Or would he greet him and invite him in? Standing outside the door, the men could see that Yogi Ramsuratkumar was inside on the verandah with some Indian devotees. Lee stood quietly outside for a moment's hesitation, then walked up and knocked on the door. Yogi Ramsuratkumar got up and came to the door. Lee went down on his knees to touch his feet, his palms pressed together in a *pranam*. Yogi Ramsuratkumar moved swiftly down the steps to put his hand on Lee's back and draw him back up to his feet.

"Lee! You've been so kind to this beggar . . . so kind, so kind!" With his hand on Lee's back, he opened the door for them all to come inside. What had created such a drastic change in the master's response to the American spiritual teacher? Lee thought it

---

25 Lee Lozowick, *Tawagoto*, Spring 1989, Volume 2 Number 2, p. 54.

26 Ibid, p. 56.

was the poetry that finally got through:

> I told my students to wait about ten feet away while I went to the door, just in case he didn't want to see me. I knocked quietly on the door, a little hesitantly, and Yogi Ramsuratkumar came out right away. He looked at me with tears in his eyes and he said, "Lee! You've been so kind to this beggar . . . so kind, so kind!" This was very, very impactful, because if you are a disciple, your gratitude to the master is so big, that when the master expresses gratitude to you it's overwhelming—even for one as arrogant as me. So, my arrogance leaked out like water from a cracked pitcher onto the dusty streets of Tiruvannamalai! It came back, of course . . .
>
> It was as if we had been intimate for centuries, for millennia—as if I'd always been welcome in his personal spaces and privy to an unusual amount of intimacy and affection. I wasn't sure what he was grateful for. What did I do? As it turns out, the poetry I'd been sending finally created a certain recognition in him. Four or five years later, when we were sitting together—after he had had the poetry published in India—he was having the poetry read over and over again, eight, ten, twelve times for a poem, and we were talking about the poetry. His eyes brimmed over with tears, and he said, "This beggar threw all your early poetry out because he didn't know what it was." I realized that it was when I started keeping copies of the poems that he started saving them also.
>
> So, there was a process of several years when he was testing my mettle as a disciple. As he was testing me, I was more and more drawn to him in a feeling sense, more passionate about my devotion to him, more willing to serve him, to work for him. In the beginning he threw all the poetry away. Well, Americans are famous for their promiscuity, their unreliability, for their prejudice against "poor, ignorant Indians"—among other things. Yogi Ramsuratkumar had been disappointed by some of Westerners he'd known previously, so it's understandable that he would take my initial correspondence with a grain of salt. But once he began to telepathically understand that there was some possibility in this poetry, he began to respond.[27]

Vijay Fedorschak, one of the men who was traveling with Lee, recalled this crucial moment:

> We came up from the *jayanthi* in Kanya Kumari to Anandashram. We had been on an all night bus ride, and we got off the bus, dropped off our bags and then went immediately to Yogi Ramsuratkumar's house. Lee

27 Lee Lozowick, Nantes, France, June 24, 2001.

> knocked on the door. Lee was still not sure how he would be received, if at all, by his guru. There was some anxiousness and excitement for all of us about the whole thing. It was one of those moments when you are totally in the unknown. You could cut the thick mood, the anticipation, with a knife. Yogi Ramsuratkumar came out with this big smile on his face and grabbed Lee, who was *pranamed* before him, and brought him into the house. It was very joyous—that he had accepted Lee, and us in a way. He was going to see us, and he was very happy. It was like a long pregnancy had taken place and now it had given birth.

Yogi Ramsuratkumar invited Lee and the men into his house, and once inside the porch they saw that there were three Indian devotees already seated, a man and two women. It was a shabby space, and in the front of the porch, in an alcove by the doorway that led into the inner rooms were piles of dirt and sand and dried flower *malas*. Three of the men sat down near the front before Yogi Ramsuratkumar had a chance to tell them where to sit. There was still plenty of room, but Yogi Ramsuratkumar had a very specific configuration in mind for what would be most optimal to his work. He asked the three men to move down the porch with the others, while he and Lee sat together a slight distance away, on the step that led to the inner rooms of the house. It quickly became clear that he was working in very subtle ways, and one had to pay attention to his every move.

The beggar was wearing several layers of rags, the outer one being a bright pink shawl; under that was a red shawl, and then several other layers of grey, yellow and green. A soiled green rag was wrapped around his head. He sat concentrating his attention on Lee, holding his hand and stroking his arm, wrist and hand very gently. Sometimes he slapped him, hard, on the thigh or shoulder.

"How long will you be here, Lee?" he asked. Lee explained that they would only be there for a day and half—the rest of that day, the next day, and then they would leave. Yogi Ramsuratkumar repeated aloud everything that Lee said, as if he was absorbing the information and clarifying it somehow.

"Where did you come from?" the beggar asked. When he found out that Lee and the men had just come from Anandashram, he wanted to know when they had arrived there, the exact time when they had left, and where and when they had seen Mataji Krishnabai. Then Yogi Ramsuratkumar got up and set out teacups, seven of them—it was the perfect number for the men because Bandhu, one of Lee's students, had walked up Mt. Arunachala and had not made it back yet.

"This beggar put out only seven cups when there are eight people in your party! How did he know? Eight people and seven cups!" The beggar kept commenting on this, amazed by his own actions, as if watching another person. There was much laughter and many exclamations over this, and indeed, it did seem amazing. But more than such minor miracles, there was a deeper mood of sheer delight that was building, with Yogi Ramsuratkumar crafting the circumstance and filling the moments with his infectious laughter and his marvelous sense of humor. Every small thing that happened seemed to ignite his laughter and wonder as the afternoon wore on and the men spent many rich and flowing hours with him. They found themselves falling into *bhavas* as each movement or word from the beggar king seemed to amplify the ecstasy that was growing moment by moment.

Tea was served and he began to ask the names of the men who were present, focusing for a while on the man who was absent—what was his name, what did he do for a living? When Bandhu finally caught up with the group later, the beggar took his hand and asked, "How was the walk? Was it hot? How long did it take?" After a few hours, the beggar told Lee to take the men to the Arunachalesvara Temple, and he would meet them there very shortly.

Winding through the busy bazaar to walk through the massive *gopuram* at the front of the temple, the men found their way into the courtyard by the two ghats that led down to tanks of water. Soon Yogi Ramsuratkumar appeared, carrying his fan and coconut bowl. As soon as the beggar arrived many of the Indians in the crowd began to gawk and watch closely to see what the Godchild was doing.

Yogi Ramsuratkumar took Lee by the hand and walked with him around the temple, like a father with a son, while Lee's students followed rather awkwardly along behind. In this way they circled the ghats around the tank pools, often with Yogi Ramsuratkumar walking along the ghats one step above Lee, holding his hand. At one point the beggar stopped and sat down on the steps with Lee, their backs to the stone wall. They sat there for a couple of hours, with the men sitting in a semi-circle a few feet away. During this time there were silences and times of laughter. Yogi Ramsuratkumar was playing with Lee, and as Vijay said, "It was like a reunion between two lovers." The beggar kept slapping Lee hard on the thigh, back or shoulder and laughing. The slaps were forceful at the same time that they were tremendously affectionate, and it seemed that each blow delivered the full impact of the master's blessing. Wolfgang, another man in Lee's party who was taking photographs, asked the beggar for permission to take a photograph. He assented with a very specific instruction: "One photograph." The photo was snapped and the play continued. Holding Lee's hand, he began to play with the gold wedding ring on Lee's left hand.

"Is this ring pure gold?" he asking, looking over at Lee.

"Yes," he answered.

"Does your wife have one of these too?" Again, Lee answered yes. Yogi Ramsuratkumar wanted to know many other things as well, including how long they had been wearing the rings. Then he turned to the men and asked if anyone else was married and wore a gold ring. Each man showed the beggar his ring and answered his questions: "What is your wife's name? How long have you been married?" and so on.

"Now, please sit down," he instructed each man after he had seen his ring. During this whole time about two-dozen Indians had their eyes on Yogi Ramsuratkumar. Many came forward, *pranamed* and touched his feet. He motioned them away with a movement of his head or hand.

The mood of delight continued to soar along with the unfettered laughter of the beggar king, who often interjected odd questions like, "How long does it take to drive from Munich to Bonn?" They had no way to know that Yogi Ramsuratkumar was being prophetic, as his enigmatic comments often were: Thomas Bormann, a German devotee who was there with Lee, would be driving Lee and his rock & roll band on a performing tour all over Germany the next year.

"This beggar is very bad," Yogi Ramsuratkumar said several times.

"Mad or bad?" Purna asked. The beggar broke gales of laughter.

"Very bad, very mad," he laughed so hard that he was holding his sides and rocking back on his seat. He was totally free in this moment, rocking and rolling in a fit of divine laughter. Vijay wrote later, "He laughs so hard it throws you off balance. There is no control in it, like the way you might think don Juan would laugh at Carlos Castaneda."

"When Vijaya gets back home and tells his wife he has been to see a beggar, very bad, very mad, she will tell him, 'I don't want you to go back to India!' " He started laughing again. Vijay had begun to have uncontrollable *kriyas*—an affect of having kundalini energy running through the nervous system, which can result in spontaneous outbursts of speech, *mudras* or other bodily movements. Vijay's arm kept shooting up into the air toward the sky no matter how hard he tried to stop it. Yogi Ramsuratkumar began to playfully interact with Vijay, glancing over at him and smiling now and then. Every time he looked at Vijay and smiled, the arm would involuntarily shoot up into the air, much to Vijay's chagrin.

"Vijaya is looking to space," Yogi Ramsuratkumar said laughing, "Lee and this beggar are looking at the ground!" It was a simple statement that carried a world of teaching communication about the spiritual path; spiritual realization that serves the great divine process—that is, the universe and all sentient beings—is grounded, ordinary, functional, not flyaway or spaced out in any way. God is found on the earth, not in the sky.

Suddenly, after a short silence he started singing beautifully, "Sri Rama, Jaya Rama, Jaya Jaya Rama, Sri Rama, Jaya Rama, Jaya Jaya Rama." His voice was sweet and pierced the heart of the listeners; slowly the song trailed away into a silence that was soon embroidered with the dulcet sounds of a nearby bird's song, which drifted on the warm air. Listening deeply to the sound of the bird's singing, Yogi Ramsuratkumar said, "Ohhh . . . that bird's song is so much more beautiful than this beggar's song! God makes the best music—better than this beggar can make."

It was time to get up and walk again. The beggar led the group, holding Lee's hand, taking the them through the courtyards and ghats, coming now and then upon sadhus who lived in the dark corners of the temple, and who came out to bow or *pranam* or touch his feet. With some of them he stopped and spoke a few words as he passed by.

"Now you lead us," he said abruptly, turning to the men who had been following him and Lee all day. It came unexpectedly, and the men took some time to organize themselves into a coherent effort at leading, bumping into each other and going in different directions. Confusion reigned for a few minutes, until one of the men turned around to look at Lee and Yogi Ramsuratkumar, who said with the voice of authority, "Go on, go on! You lead and we two follow!" Finally they worked it out and took off through the temple grounds. As the men attempted to circumambulate a shrine, going around to the right side of it, not aware that the strict tradition is to circumambulate from the left, one of the temple priests yelled at them. Still not comprehending, the priest had to shove them toward the left. Yogi Ramsuratkumar found this hilariously funny.

"Lee," the beggar said in his melodious voice, almost like a song itself, and with a mischievous smile, "do you think they are leading us or misleading us?" He broke into peals of laughter. It seemed that the group was intent on going in circles, winding around the temple pools several times. Soon afterward Yogi Ramsuratkumar left unceremoniously, without a word as to what the next day would bring.

The next morning Lee and his students walked along the paths on Mount Arunachala, passing the cave where Papa Ramdas meditated and also Skandashram, where Ramana Maharshi meditated. Returning in the early afternoon to Sannadhi Street, Yogi Ramsuratkumar was waiting there, and soon they were seated again in the cool shadows of the verandah. As soon as the men got settled on the floor, the yogi began to walk up and down the length of the porch, pacing back and forth in front of them like a tiger, with hands raised in blessing and sweeping through the air as if in a paroxysm of grace. He was working with Lee's students during this time, and did not pass in front of Lee or look at him. Then he sat down and started smoking. It was impossible to know what he was doing.

The space was quiet for a while and then the beggar started to make light conversation while he smoked. He had a newspaper in his hands and referred to an article in it about the *jayanthi* celebration in Nagercoil that Lee and the men had just participated in. There was a photograph of the procession they had walked in through the villages.

"What kind of animal is this?" Yogi Ramsuratkumar asked, childlike, pointing to a picture on the same page in the newspaper. Looking more closely, Dasya said, "That picture was printed upside down!" Yogi Ramsuratkumar looked at it and started laughing.

"How do you spell aardvark?" he asked, smiling while he smoked, holding the cigarette in his characteristic manner, held between the thumbs and cupped within his hands. He turned to an Indian devotee who was present; he had been joking with him a lot and slapping him affectionately on the arms and shoulders. He asked him if he would bring tea for everyone. Upon the arrival of the tea another Indian devotees showed up and produced a hundred-rupee note. At first the beggar refused the money.

"You see how this beggar begs?" he said, laughing loudly, "Now you know how this beggar begs!" Yogi Ramsuratkumar took the note into his hand and began to laugh, "I am a beggar, but this beggar has a hundred-rupee note!" He found this extremely funny, and said it several times, but he held the note for a moment before he handed it back to the man, who then paid for the tea.

"When Vijaya gets back home and tells his wife he has been to see a beggar, very bad, very mad, she will tell him, 'I don't want you to go back to India!' " he said, repeating what he had said to Vijay the day before.

"No, she will want to come," Vijay responded. "She'll say, 'I'm coming!' "

Several times tea or hot milk was served, and once, while sitting in the temple courtyard, Yogi Ramsuratkumar passed crackers out to everyone. He crumbled one of these into small pieces and put a piece into his own mouth, then turned to Purna and said, "Purna, please help Mr. Lee with his work." It was another prophetic moment, as twelve years later Purna would, with Lee's blessing, establish an ashram in Montana and become a teacher in his own right.

Many times during the day Yogi Ramsuratkumar turned to Lee and said, "Mr. Lee has been so kind to this beggar. My Father blesses him."

Finally, after a pause, Lee responded, "No, it is you who have been kind to me." Yogi Ramsuratkumar laughed with delight and whisked the men on yet another walk around the temple precincts, as if he wanted to impress deeply upon them the images and vibrations of this place that was so sacred and important to him. He took Lee's hand and walked with him very slowly around the ghat while the men sat and looked at the fish swimming in the tank. The mood was very gentle.

As they left the temple to walk to a restaurant for an evening meal, Yogi Ramsuratkumar turned to Thomas Bormann and said, "Lead us across the street," which he did, then suddenly the beggar shifted into a different gear and began to walk at an unbelievably brisk pace through the streets. Lee ran to keep up with him, and the men barely kept up. It was beyond just a fast walk, which anyone could pace themselves to with a little effort; the velocity at which he walked was inflamed with a divine madness that seemed to give him supernatural strength, agility, speed. Such a dynamo both confounded and captivated the senses of the one who encountered it.

Walking briskly into the Brindavan restaurant the yogi looked at the picture of himself on the wall and commented to Lee, "Ohhh . . . They have a picture of this beggar in this restaurant," as if it was the first time he'd ever seen it. He sat down with Lee and the men quickly followed suit, then Yogi Ramsuratkumar asked Lee to order for everyone. Again and again Yogi Ramsuratkumar motioned to the picture on the wall, laughed and slapped Lee on the arm jovially while they ate their *masala dosas*. When the check for the meal came, several of the men had come forward, offering to pay for the meal.

"I'll pay for the meal," Thomas quickly offered.

"No," Yogi Ramsuratkumar interjected strongly, as he reached out and took the bill and handed it to Lee. "Lee pays. Lee pays for all."

It was time to say goodbye. Lee and his students would be leaving early in the morning to go to Madras, and then back to the States. Lee fell to the street in a full body prostration and touched the beggar's feet, then stood up and *pranamed*. There was a tinge of the sadness of parting in the air, though Lee looked at Yogi Ramsuratkumar with clear and calm eyes. It had been a joyful reunion for a man with a broken heart.

When one of Lee's students also dropped to the ground and prostrated at his feet, Yogi Ramsuratkumar said, "Thomas, that's not necessary. Mr. Lee has done for all." The beggar held his fan up in the air and said, "My Father blesses you."

Lee and the group walked a short distance down the street and then turned to wave one last time. The dirty beggar stood there, hands raised in blessing with the fan held in the air and spoke to the men, saying, "This beggar begs of you, and this beggar has received all he has begged of you. So I think none of you will shirk away, when this beggar begs of you. Don't forget the divine name. This beggar prays to his Father to bless you all who have come here. All the blessings of my Father for all of you!"

The visit marked a turning point, the beginning of a new phase for Lee Lozowick and for his students who would have the opportunity to meet the beggar saint over the next thirteen years and interact with him directly. For Lee, it was the beginning of an active and intimate relationship with his guru, in which his professed longings for "the Dirty Beggar" were fulfilled beyond his wildest dreams. After leaving Yogi Ramsuratkumar's company, when asked what his feeling was, Lee said, "The last two days was enough to last for eighty years."

A young man named Jayarama moved to Tiruvannamalai from Andar Pradesh in 1982 on a job transfer; he brought his wife, J. Bhuvaneswari, their foster child and his parents with him. His wife's brother knew of Yogi Ramsuratkumar, and introduced Jayarama to the book of poems written by Ki.Va. Jagannathan. On that first day, when Jayarama read the name of Yogi Ramsuratkumar in the introduction of Jagannathan's book, he was moved to go to the yogi's house and knock on the door. His house happened to be very close to where Jayarama worked, and he set out alone to meet the one who had inspired such a wealth of poems.

A small boy answered the door. He had been reading to Yogi Ramsuratkumar.

"What is your name?" Yogi Ramsuratkumar asked as he stood at the door looking at Jayarama.

"My name is Jayarama," he answered. Without a word the beggar turned and walked inside. Jayarama simply followed him through the door. He recounted:

> It was as if we had been very familiar for a long time. In those days he never used to take anybody inside his house. He just kept them on the portico. With me there were no rules and regulations; he just talked and I followed. Then he asked me to sit on a mat; he asked me to read a book for him. He told me, "Jayarama, you read for this beggar, one or two pages from J. Krishnamurti." He was gazing at me for a long time. I was simply sitting. He smoked. I was thirty-one years old.

Having recently moved to Tiruvannamalai, Jayarama and his family needed to find a house. Wanting Jayarama to be as close to him as possible, Yogi Ramsuratkumar looked for a house near Sannadhi Street, but Jayarama acted of his own accord. He was anxious to get his parents, who were very old, into a suitable home, and he bought a house near

Ramanashram instead of one close to Yogi Ramsuratkumar. Jayarama's initial connection with Yogi Ramsuratkumar was instantaneous and very deep, and it soon became clear that the master expected more from him than such a direct act of disobedience, which earned Jayarama nearly four years of silent distance from the master. Jayarama said, "He was angry with me—really angry! Whenever I would go to him, he would ask me to sit, but he would not talk to me. He would turn his face away, because I didn't obey him—I didn't understand him at all. I hadn't understood that I had done something wrong. I used to receive him in myself as I could, but the moment he saw me he would turn his head to the side and not talk to me." Even when members of his family visited the beggar saint, if they mentioned Jayarama's name he would become angry and snap, "Don't take his name!"

Four years later, Jayarama was at home with his family one morning early at six o'clock when he suddenly heard someone shouting loudly from the backyard.

"Jayarama! Jayarama!" The shout resounded through the neighborhood. The family rushed out to see what the commotion was all about and saw a very angry Yogi Ramsuratkumar, who then shouted, "You have made me shout at your gate! You have not responded quickly!" They quickly brought the beggar inside and Jayarama's father, Ramany, who Yogi Ramsuratkumar loved dearly, offered the beggar some honey, which he took. Then he settled on the floor with Jayarama's young foster son, Chetas, and played with him.

He asked the boy, "Who am I? Do you know?"

"You are a beggar," was the child's simple reply. Yogi Ramsuratkumar laughed and laughed and laughed.

"Chetas, do you know this beggar?"

"Yes, you are a beggar," the child said again. For half an hour the yogi played with the child, not speaking to anyone else—not to Jayarama, his wife or his father and mother—then he got up and said "Bye." Asking Jayarama not to follow him, the beggar walked back to his house.

One day Yogi Ramsuratkumar sent word to Jayarama's mother: "Send that fellow here." That evening Jayarama went to him at Sannadhi Street. Yogi Ramsuratkumar shared some gooseberry juice with Jayarama and another devotee, then he sent him home. "That was the beginning, January 1987. At the end of 1982 I met him and in 1987 he called me. He came to my house and took me; that is how it happened!"

Jayarama became very close to Yogi Ramsuratkumar and for several years was his primary attendant, often bringing him food, reading to him, doing whatever work he needed done. During the late eighties Yogi Ramsuratkumar read the daily news, *The Hindu*. Jayarama was instructed to buy it for him each day and bring it, but no one could touch it or read before it was given to the beggar. If someone had touched it or read it, then he would refuse to have anything to do with it.

Yogi Ramsuratkumar became very close with Jayarama's whole family; he kept a close watch over Jayarama's mother and father, and when a daughter and younger son were born to Jayarama, it was Yogi Ramsuratkumar who named them Godavari and Ramjianand, respectively. Jayarama's wife, J. Bhuvanesvari, used to cook often for the beggar and brought his daily buttermilk, a favorite food. He had a particularly close relationship with Ramany, the elderly father of Jayarama, who he often hugged and embraced. The two men used to massage each other, something that no one else ever did with Yogi Ramsuratkumar.

Interacting daily with Yogi Ramsuratkumar in ordinary activities, Jayarama had many teachings given to him simply through Yogi Ramsuratkumar's preferences and ways of dealing with things, like food. In one particular period of time Jayarama was with Yogi Ramsuratkumar all day every day, and he ate and drank only what Yogi Ramsuratkumar gave him. Because the food was usually bland, he began to daydream about spicy food. His mind was obsessed with the desire for spicy food, and once he tried to leave the house at Sannadhi Street and get some of the food he wanted. The beggar said, "Wait!" Soon a man came to the door with whom the yogi made very specific arrangements for some food. Shortly the man returned and again the yogi went over his instructions to him, making sure they were carried out to the letter. After awhile the food arrived, and Jayarama could smell the delicious spices, but in fact the food was so spicy, it was very difficult to eat.

Typically Yogi Ramsuratkumar would share whatever food he had with all who were present. He would serve the food equally, then sit down and initiate the meal by beginning to eat himself, and everyone else would then follow. On this day Yogi Ramsuratkumar instructed his devotees to put two banana leaves on the floor, then he had all the food served out equally on the two leaves. He sat at one place and gestured to Jayarama to sit at the other. Even smelling the food brought tears to Jayarama's eyes because the food was far too spicy for human consumption. The master ate a very small amount of all the various dishes, and suddenly tears started flowing from his eyes. Jayarama knew right away what would happen next: he would be asked to eat all the food.

"Jayarama, you eat this too!" Because it was the master's instructions, Jayarama had no choice but to finish both plates of food. It was the last time that Jayarama became obsessed with food, as he realized that the beggar was aware of his desires all along, and was working directly with the nature of desire as it manifested in Jayarama.

Yogi Ramsuratkumar was very fond of all kinds of juices, but he was particularly fond of bel juice, a kind of fruit juice. He also liked odd combinations of juices, and he would ask Jayarama to mix two or three juices together. For example, once he asked for orange juice mixed with milk, and another time for bel juice mixed with honey. He was also very fond of *shyam tulsi* (a kind of basil); sometimes he drank the juice of it, but often he made a paste of it and ate it. He particularly loved *amlaka* (gooseberry), and believed strongly in its spiritual and medicinal properties.

When Jayarama brought food for the beggar, Yogi Ramsuratkumar was always very grateful, and would say sweetly, like a small child, "The food was very tasteful," but if Jayarama failed to follow instructions or brought something that was different than the master's usual preference, he would become irritated. Almost every day for several weeks Jayarama brought buttermilk for Yogi Ramsuratkumar to drink, but then one day, when he developed a very severe cold, Jayarama took milk instead of buttermilk.

"You used to bring buttermilk!" Yogi Ramsuratkumar said very sternly, obviously irritated.

"There was none," Jayarama said weakly, knowing that there was no excuse for not bringing the usual buttermilk.

Yogi Ramsuratkumar had very definite preferences when it came to food and medicine. The beggar also had a strong liking for sukha chapattis, dal and sattoo, a preparation made out of roasted grain flour mixed with spices. Bhuvanesvari often cooked for the yogi, and there was a particular kind of wheat dosa (pancake) that she used to make that he liked. Although he did not like sugar, he did enjoy jaggery, a form of raw sugar made from sugarcane juice, and he particularly liked honey. Yogi Ramsuratkumar had a strong disliking for allopathic medicine. Whenever he was ill he always wanted ayurvedic or natural remedies. He loved red watermelon and often asked for watermelon juice, which he would also ask Jayarama to drink.

He had a special liking for ghee—clarified butter made from cow's milk. He believed in the healing power of the smell of ghee. Ghee is often mixed with dal powder to create a soup-like dish, and when this is done there is often a lot of ghee that is wasted, but the yogi would make a mound of the dal powder then carefully and meticulously pour the ghee into the mound so that all the ghee was absorbed by the dal powder and not wasted by making a heavy coating on the bowl. Even small acts like these were teachings in paying attention and bringing impeccability to every task. Such attention to detail was a way of building energy or spiritual force for the deeper work.

Working closely with Yogi Ramsuratkumar, caring for his needs and observing him, Jayarama found that in every day of his life Yogi Ramsuratkumar demonstrated surrender to "Father's will" and the embodiment and understanding of how faith and total surrender are linked together. Jayarama reflected, "Whatever Bhagawan has told us, directly or indirectly, or even very casually—even things that are irrelevant—if we go over them again and again in our minds, in those we will find seeds for our transformation." He soon discovered that if one observed closely the "hints" that the beggar gave during friendly talks and ordinary conversations with devotees, and then pursued these hints internally as a way of self-understanding, it became a way of sadhana.

It was very common for people to have kundalini openings that were triggered simply by being in the physical presence of Yogi Ramsuratkumar. Once Yogi Ramsuratkumar had a series of pictures taken while holding the hand of a devotee. With each photograph the devotee became more and more uncomfortable and irritated. Before long he was shouting, whether in great pain or in emotional agony was hard to tell, and this progression of intensity was perfectly captured in the photos. Finally Yogi Ramsuratkumar began to touch the man's back and the man literally went into a frenzy of madness, but the beggar brought him out of it by pouring some coffee first into his own coconut bowl, and then giving it to the man to drink. Such was the power of his energy—if a person did not have the physical, emotional and spiritual matrix to handle such a nuclear force, it could be completely overpowering.

Jayarama learned that Yogi Ramsuratkumar was a guru for all people—for those with less intellectual capacity as well as people with a lot of intellectual capacity; for people who were very humble and simple as well as people who were wealthy and powerful; for the people of the streets, the downcast and downtrodden, and for the VIPs of Indian society. At the same time that he worked in very unique ways with each individual person, his work had profound global and universal dimensions.

Yogi Ramsuratkumar used to say to Jayarama, "This beggar is running three ashrams—Ramanashram, Anandashram and Aurobindo Ashram," alluding to his universal work and the level of spiritual authority or obligation that he had been given. One day Jayarama was with Swamiji in the temple in the courtyard outside the Ganesha shrine, when Swamiji pointed to the ground. He knew that Jayarama could read Sanskrit, and there on the ground was the name, "Ramji," written in Sanskrit on the paving stones of the courtyard floor. It had been chiseled into the stone perhaps a thousand years before. It seemed an auspicious portent of the "Ramji" who would come to live in Tiruvannamalai eons later—Yogi Ramsuratkumar.

Despite the gravity and magnitude of the work with which he had been invested, in the late eighties Yogi Ramsuratkumar still had a very simple and in many ways anonymous life. The crush of visitors and supplicants was yet to come, but there were many devotees who came from distant places like Sivakasi and Tuticorin. According to Jayarama, it wasn't until after 1990 that the crowds began to amass before Swamiji's door every day. During the eighties it was possible to experience the unfettered moods of a beggar saint who had lived for so long on the streets—whether it was ecstatic laughter, unbounded joy or deep silence, song or dance or simply his spontaneous movement throughout the day. Even in the late eighties, when the tide was beginning to turn and the beggar king's court was slowly being turned into a religious institution, the beggar still danced. Jayarama remembered:

> He was not a regular dancer, but when the occasion warranted he would dance. He used to be ecstatic. When he used to see fellow people [celebrating] with love, then he used to dance, like Lord Shiva danced—even on the roadside! How to interpret this thing? One moment he will dance and the next moment he will be a great fire, and another moment, very sad, suffering something. He was all; he is everything. He used to shed tears also. People would have to dance for him. He shed a lot of tears . . . for us. He was one with us.

In the February-July 1988 issue of *Tattva Darsana*, Professor Rangarajan published an article written by Sita Martin, a student of Lee's who lived in Arizona, that loosely chronicled Lee's relationship with Yogi Ramsuratkumar and how they had met in 1977, 1979, 1986 and 1988. In the same issue an article written by Professor Rangarajan appeared in which he reported: "Lee Lozowick, a 'crazy poet' who turned into a spiritual seeker and has set up a spiritual community in Arizona, U.S.A., wrote a letter in verse to the 'mad Beggar' whom he has met a few times during his visits to this Land of Spiritual Light. In this whole country, Lee could find only one Mahatma who called himself a Beggar. Naturally, Lee fell under the spell of this 'Beggar' . . . ."[28] At the end of this article the first poem written to Yogi Ramsuratkumar by Lee, dated February 21, 1979, was printed—the first of many that would be published in the years ahead at the request of Yogi Ramsuratkumar. A permanent bond between the Indian and Western devotees of Yogi Ramsuratkumar was now set in place.

One year after the 1988 reunion, on December 2, 1989, Lee returned to India, again at the invitation of Pon Kamaraj, and hosted by many devotees of Yogi Ramsuratkumar including Rangarajan, Ramanlal and others. Pon Kamaraj told Lee that on the way to a Hanuman temple earlier that year, Yogi Ramsuratkumar had said to him, "Lee Lozowick is not an ordinary person. This beggar is Rama and Lee Lozowick is Anjaneya." Anjaneya is the devotional form of Hanuman, the archetypical devotee who, in the mythic story of the *Ramayana*, helped Lord Rama rescue his wife Sita from the ravaging and fierce demon, Ravana. All this was happening unbeknownst to Lee, who was carried along on the wave of Yogi Ramsuratkumar's *lila*. Traveling to the *jayanthi* celebration near Nagercoil, Lee was asked to inaugurate the almost completed Manthralayam temple in Kanimadam. It was a massive celebration, complete with the traditional cutting of a red ribbon by Lee and days of nonstop chanting the name of Yogi Ramsuratkumar to the pounding rhythms of the drums.

Lee was taken into the smallest dusty villages and remote temples hidden away in tropical foliage, where ghee lamps burned to primal deities, to speak about Yogi Ramsuratkumar and perform *puja* ceremonies. Sometimes Lee, Pon Kamaraj and a large entourage of devotees, both Indians and Westerners, would walk for hours in processions through the villages, blessing the homes and dwelling places of the local people—poor, rich and everything in between. They traveled from Madras to Nagercoil, Sivakasi, Kanya Kumari and back north again, singing and speaking the name of Yogi Ramsuratkumar everywhere they went.

After ten days of visiting many different temples, businesses and homes where they celebrated Yogi Ramsuratkumar, Lee and his students arrived in Tiruvannamalai to visit the master. On their first day in town they spent the afternoon with him at the temple. Early the next morning they received a message that Yogi Ramsuratkumar had been at the office at Ramanashram at six o'clock to say that a car would be waiting to take them to the outskirts of the city, where they would spend the day with him in the home of V. Ganeshan, the grandnephew of Ramana Maharshi.

At eight o'clock they arrived at the compound of Ganeshan's home; so began a ten-hour revelry with Yogi Ramsuratkumar. Although it may have looked innocuous on the surface, it was a space that made a rigorous demand on those who were in it, as Vijaya

28 Prof. V. Rangarajan, "The Yogi," *Tattva Darsana*, February-July 1988, p. 48.

Fedorschak wrote: " . . . it was a sesshin that a Zen Roshi would be proud of." Though the people who were gathered together were not meditating per se, it was at times a profoundly contemplative day; the mere physical proximity of the beggar worked at very deep levels on whoever was in his company to catalyze a tremendous inner movement and self-reflection. Yogi Ramsuratkumar's slightest movements seemed fraught with meaning, and there was the palpable sense that his simplest actions were inextricably linked with the cosmos. Vijay continued:

> Yogi Ramsuratkumar and Lee leaned against the right wall under a porch overhang outside the cottage. A few Indian ladies sat opposite them, smiling. Ganeshan, a truly rare devotee, waited on and served Yogi Ramsuratkumar all day . . . At various times during the ten hours I experienced intense ecstasy, depression, fixed attention, nervousness, sorrow, devotion, jealousy. Yogi Ramsuratkumar stroked Lee's hand and each individual finger. "These are *my* hands," he said, gently slapping Lee's hands.[29]

Four packets of ten cigarettes each lay on the ground in front of the beggar as they sat down together; he would smoke them all by the end of the day. He called for tea, and it was soon served. He playfully engaged Ganeshan, who was attending to his every need.

"You know, Ganeshan, the great master Nisargadatta Maharaj said that when we see the truth everything becomes as one. We will say, 'I am that' and 'I am that,' " he pointed to one of the men and then to another, "and 'I am that,' and 'I am that tree,' and 'I am that house.' But you know, Ganeshan, this sinner doesn't feel that way. This sinner says, 'I am this.' " He pointed to his own body. "I don't say, 'I am that and that and that'—this beggar is only this." He repeatedly touched the tip of his big toe, then his forehead as he said this.

The day was full of blessings; often Yogi Ramsuratkumar would get up and walk in circles around the men with his hands lifted in blessing. For a long time he worked on Lee by holding his hand in front of Lee's chest, then moving it outward as if he was pulling something out, his head shaking from the effort. This substance he then "spread" among the gathered men. Off and on during the day this gesture was repeated, as if he was pulling substance from Lee and then building something around him with it.

After holding Lee's hands for hours, Yogi Ramsuratkumar looked over at Ganeshan and said, "Ganeshan, these are my hands. Do you know that, Ganeshan? These are my hands," and he began to play gently with Lee's hands, squeezing each finger one by one between his thumb and index finger and pressing his fist into Lee's palm.

"These are my hands, Ganeshan. This and this," he held the fingers. "Is it not madness, Ganeshan? All hands are my hands—those and those and those," he pointed around the porch at the people sitting there. "All are my hands!" He burst into laughter and fell deliriously into Lee's lap, then hit him on the shoulder and rubbed his hand up

29 Vijaya Fedorschak, *Divine Slave Gita*, Spring 1990, Volume 8 Number 1, p. 32.

and down his arm quite forcefully.

"Is it not madness, Ganeshan? This beggar says that all hands are his hands! Is it not madness?"

"Mad with a capital 'M'—the kind of mad that is good for us," Ganeshan answered.

"This beggar is very bad. Ramdas gave him 'Om Sri Ram,' and he doesn't even do it," Yogi Ramsuratkumar said with the innocence of small child. He talked about how he only did the mantra for one week before the madness came upon him.

"How many years ago was that, Ganeshan?" The yogi laughed. "We must only do the work that Father has given us. We must finish it, and we can only do this by finishing our *lila* here."

As the day proceeded the porch became the location of the beggar's mastery and magic as he interacted with the group, showering pearls of wisdom and grace, and communicating most profoundly—through the power of his being—the vital necessity of "Father's work" and the blessing power that true surrender to the Divine makes available in the world of humankind. Inspired by Yogi Ramsuratkumar's words and his presence, another student, Jim Capellini, wrote:

> The space fell silent again and Yogi Ramsuratkumar leaned back, eyes shut, working the fingers of his left hand while holding Lee's hand with his right. The chamber he created that day was immense and yet airtight, able to withstand silence easily, and when he came back to us from these periods it was clear we had all gone somewhere with him. The space was shifted, just perfectly to accommodate the next words spoken or the next gesture made. When he came back this time he spoke softly to us, saying something like, "We must only do the work that Father has given us. We must finish it, and we can only do this by finishing our *lila* here." I had never heard it spoken in such a way. The play of existence became something one could feel an affectionate obligation to. It was work that had to be done.[30]

Yogi Ramsuratkumar began relating the story of Lee's 1986 visit, making it apparent that he wanted to give Ganeshan a clear picture of why Lee was so special to him; it seemed that his purpose was to weave his devotees, East and West, together in one tapestry—the proverbial coat of many colors, worn by a beggar.

"This friend came to see this beggar many years ago, and this beggar told him, 'Why do you come to see me again and again? Go away!' Next time he came with his wife and with children. What is his child's name?"

Lee answered, "Gita."

"Oh yes . . . that's right . . . Gita!" he exclaimed. "Lee came to visit this beggar with his wife and with Gita, but he wouldn't come in. I asked Gita, 'Where is your father?' and

30 Jim Capellini, *Divine Slave Gita*, Spring 1990, Volume 8 Number 1, p. 9.

she said, 'He's outside!' 'What is he doing outside? Go and get him!' But he wouldn't come in. This beggar looked outside and there was Mr. Lee sitting on iron in the hot sun. It was very hot! The metal must have been very, very hot, and he was sitting right on it refusing to come in. This beggar told him to go away, and so now he wouldn't come in." He fell silent for a while, as if he was remembering the event, then looked at Lee with gleaming eyes and caressed his hand.

"This beggar asked him again and again," Yogi Ramsuratkumar continued. "This beggar tried so hard, but he wouldn't come in."

Then he turned to Ganeshan and said quietly, "You understand now, Ganeshan?" He gave Lee a box of matches and began to chain smoke, looking around at each of the devotees that were present that day—Lee's men students and several Indians. While Lee lit his cigarettes one by one, Ganeshan got up and removed the bowl of water that he was using for an ashtray and replaced it with fresh water. Yogi Ramsuratkumar smiled and laughed, "Ganeshan is giving water to this beggar, and this beggar is getting fire from this friend," he gestured to Lee. "One gives water and the other gives fire. This is very good. It keeps the engine moving. If no water, then no fire, and if no fire, then no water! It keeps it moving!" His words were symbolic, pregnant with meaning, and they reverberated among the companions, giving rise to reflections on divine alchemy, and the functions of water and fire in the life of the soul. Yogi Ramsuratkumar asked Ganeshan to sit on his left side while Lee sat on his right. He held both of their hands.

As the day wore on the men who were sitting across from these three moved into different postures, trying to ease their backs and legs. Some slumped and others sat erect. After a long while Yogi Ramsuratkumar pointed to them and said, "Look, they have no support . . . "

"Everything is my Father. Nothing is not my Father, not anything past, present or future," Yogi Ramsuratkumar said. It was a song of praise for the moment that rang out in the cadence of his melodious voice. He asked the Indian women to sing some songs, and they sang beautiful evocative devotional songs. Then he turned to Lee's students and asked the men to sing any song in English. Stan sang a rock song, but Yogi Ramsuratkumar wanted more. He asked for something about Jesus Christ. The men came up with "Swing Low, Sweet Chariot" and "Amazing Grace" and then Janis Joplin's, "Mercedes-Benz." Then they turned to Christmas songs and sang "O Come All Ye Faithful" and "Silent Night." He asked the men to recite the Lord's Prayer three times, and then asked for someone to tell the story of King Arthur and the Knights of the Round Table.

Again Yogi Ramsuratkumar turned Lee's gold wedding ring around on his finger and then did the same with the rings of those men in Lee's party who were married. His play went back and forth from Ganeshan to Lee, as he held hands sometimes with one or the other, or with both at the same time. He was merry and bright, smoking frequently through cupped hands, or at times deeply silent and interior. After a while, taking Ganeshan's hand in his, Yogi Ramsuratkumar got up and walked around the grounds with everyone else following them.

"How will the scientists discover the origin of the universe, Ganeshan?" he asked.

Ganeshan thought about this for a moment then replied that if the scientists do not find the Father, they cannot discover the origin of the universe.

"Then they will try to discover the origin of the Father," said Yogi Ramsuratkumar, laughing hilariously and slapping Ganeshan's arm.

After Ganeshan told many stories of Ramana Maharshi at the request of Yogi Ramsuratkumar, the sun sank in the western sky toward the horizon and a long silence descended on the group. The chirping of many different birds filled the air and the last rays of the sun slanted through the porch with long shafts of golden light. Spying a bright fiery red shawl that had been brought by one of the women devotees but not yet offered to him, Yogi Ramsuratkumar asked for it. The woman handed the shawl to him and he immediately draped it regally across Lee's shoulders. He looked at Lee as if to assess his handiwork.

"This friend is all right. He will not get intoxicated. Look at all these fine clothes he is decorated in, but he will not get intoxicated. No, this friend will not get intoxicated." He had a way of repeating things three times, as if this was the magical formula for the blessing or alchemical operation he was working. His voice grew even softer as he said, "Mr. Lee will guide these friends," and he motioned to Lee's students who sat with rapt attention, saturated in the beggar's presence and understanding that Yogi Ramsuratkumar was directly affirming and further empowering Lee's work with his students. With these words and the setting of the sun, the long day was coming to a close. The next morning Lee and his students would be leaving.

"What time does the sun set at Anandashram?" the beggar asked sweetly, the simple question carrying all the implications of his love for Papa Ramdas. In Tiruvannamalai that day the sun dropped behind the horizon at six o'clock, and Yogi Ramsuratkumar rose to leave. Lee sank to his knees in a deep *pranam*.

"What are you doing?" the master asked, and then immediately took his leave in the most natural and unceremonious way. He seemed to be saying, "There is no need for rituals and formal goodbyes between us. There is no separation. We are always together."

Lee and his group left on the public bus the next morning for Salem, where they had the darshan of Mother Mayee, the oft-called "feminine counterpart" of Yogi Ramsuratkumar. Disembarking from the bus, they noticed a large, unusual dog that walked the visitors all the way to the house where Mother Mayee was living. Outside in the yard were about ten scrawny, almost wild-looking dogs.

Mother Mayee was situated in a reclining chair when Lee and the men came into the room. She seemed impossibly ancient, her face melted into folds of wrinkled flesh; she was in a completely interior or semi-conscious state at that time, which was just a few years before her death. As Lee and the men gazed respectfully at the *avadhuta*, she opened her eyes briefly, casting a feather's touch of a glance at them, then withdrew again into the interior of her own being. They soon left, and discovered that the same dog was waiting outside for them. The dog then led them through the streets, the throngs of people and the markets to the bus station, waited patiently while they climbed on the bus and did not leave the bus station until the bus pulled away—the agent of Mother Mayee had done its job.

Leaving Salem they traveled back to the home of Rangarajan in Madras and finally back to the States. In Madras Lee gave a talk to the Yogi Ramsuratkumar Youth Organization. It was an impassioned and somewhat brazen speech that ran true to his reputation of being heretical, iconoclastic and conventionally rude. He was candid in his observations of life in India, particularly lambasting the treatment of women. He said, "I see that there are mostly men at this meeting; it seems funny to me that the Goddess should be left at home. If the men are interested in God, they should be at home with the Goddess, not talking about God and pontificating about holy subject matter!" The thrust of his talk was this:

> Real teachers are not recognizable by what country they come from, but by how they teach. I apologize for being insulting, but I've spent twelve years being insulted by Yogi Ramsuratkumar. One of the things that I see in Indian culture is that the profound nature of who Yogi Ramsuratkumar is, is lost on the Indian populace. A master can only be effective to the degree that he is approached with maturity.
>
> There are two ways to approach God: either by taking from him, or by giving to him. If one offers oneself to God, then God becomes his slave; if he asks of God, God may give to him because he is ultimately generous, but the same possibility doesn't exist. God is still the Master. To serve God in this world is to love God. There is nothing that a human being can give to God but praise, worship and adoration.
>
> In 1975 I was adopted by Yogi Ramsuratkumar. Probably it was really a thousand years ago, but I like to keep things practical. Each time I visited him, he saw me for what I am—arrogant—and so he insulted me. With each visit the insult was worse, just to make sure. It's an extraordinary lineage, and I will probably insult everyone worse than I have today the next time I come to speak here, because, like father, like son. It's a great benediction to be adopted by such a lineage . . . .
>
> People are always asking me to tell stories of Yogi Ramsuratkumar, but my stories are my own, and people are never going to hear them. I can say that Yogi Ramsuratkumar is a great master who has no remnant of self-reference or self-interest left. Coming into this room full of men, I felt like pontificating for a while, which I think I've done.[31]

31 Lee Lozowick, *Divine Slave Gita*, Spring 1990, Volume 8 No. 1, pp. 36-37.

In 1984 when Hilda Charlton was preparing to make her second and last visit to Yogi Ramsuratkumar, Will wrote to him asking if he could come and spend a month in Tiruvannamalai prior to Hilda's visit, as he had during the 1978 visit. Yogi Ramsuratkumar responded, saying that there was no need for him to come.

"This beggar can't spend any time with you if you do come. There's no need," he wrote, also saying that when it was necessary, it would happen. He further explained that it was very rare for "this beggar to spend so much time" with one person, as he had with Will in past years. "When you are in need, this beggar will be there. But now, there's no need." Then he reminded Will of a letter he had written to him in the early seventies, when they had first met. On that letter he had written "Remember" in big letters.

Over the years Will Zulkowski had been blessed with having had a great deal of time in the physical presence of Yogi Ramsuratkumar, during which he was showered with his personal attention, but *sadhana* has its cycles and phases, exactly like ordinary life. There are times of active learning and accelerated experience, and then there are times of digestion and integration. The beggar's letter was a disappointment, but Will accepted it, understanding that the master was guiding him to find the guru's presence within. It was an entirely lawful circumstance, resonant with the dharma; the longer one has been on the path, the more maturity is expected of that individual's practice.

As it turned out, it was a way in which Yogi Ramsuratkumar was strengthening Will's faith to bear what was to come: not long after this, his wife Joan was diagnosed with a serious cancer. Yogi Ramsuratkumar's prophetic statement, "When you are in need, this beggar will be there," came to fruition in 1988. Will recollected:

> The next time I went back was because Joan was very sick. She had gone to Tiruvannamalai, and she was staying at that same hotel. She was very ill at that time. She was really in a lot of pain. Swami knew she had cancer and he would come every day to see her at the hotel. You know, it's not proper for a man to come into a lady's room, so she would meet him at the restaurant. Perumal or one of his attendants would come up and get her, and she would come to the restaurant and just talk with him. He was very, very compassionate, very loving, very kind . . .

Joan had been taking Tibetan medical treatment in Dharmasala, and when she became very ill, she was admitted to a hospital in Bombay, where she died in 1989. During Joan's final days Will sent letters and telegrams every day or two to Yogi Ramsuratkumar to keep him informed of her condition. After her death, the cremation of the body was done in Bombay and afterward Will took the ashes to Tiruvannamalai. He arrived at Sannadhi Street to find about a dozen people with Yogi Ramsuratkumar, waiting for his attention and time. The beggar sent them away, telling them to come back in an hour, and he also said that he would be busy the next day. Then he told Will, "Come early morning."

The next morning at six o'clock, Will came to the house on Sannadhi Street. Yogi

Ramsuratkumar quietly talked with him about Joan's illness and passing from the body, and he held the ashes, which were in a small stainless steel container, in his hands for an hour. In this way he worked deeply with the one who had been Joan Zulkowski. Will described these tender moments, saying, "He didn't say a word. He was just making various kinds of blessing gestures, you know, just quietly with the ashes. And then he said, 'Okay, you can start.' And so we went up Arunachala, up near Skandashram, overlooking the main Shiva temple. We thought it would be a good place scatter her ashes."

In Hilda Charlton's classes in New York City, the people who had met Yogi Ramsuratkumar and spent time in his company often told stories or spoke at length about their experiences of the Godchild. Once when it was Joan's turn to tell stories before the three or four hundred people who were present that night, she said, "I feel it's such an honor just to get a chance to talk about Yogi Ramsuratkumar. I can hardly believe this opportunity has been given to us. I know that the beggar in Tiruvannamalai would probably weep joyous tears at the thought of people in another part of the world, so many hundreds of them, thinking about him and talking about him."

Yogi Ramsuratkumar sent many of his "friends" such as Will and Joan Zulkowski, Pon Kamaraj, Janarthanan and Rangarajan to visit Anandashram, where he intended for them to receive the blessings of his guru through Mataji Krishnabai and the holy ground of the ashram itself, which included the powerful *samadhi* site of Papa Ramdas. The Finnish woman Kirsti, who had met him in 1976 through Truman Caylor Wadlington and the Theosophical Society, was another person that Yogi Ramsuratkumar sent to Anandashram to stay for a long period of time when Mataji was still alive, where she developed a powerful relationship with the living successor of Ramdas. Whenever she returned from Anandashram, Yogi Ramsuratkumar always wanted to hear stories of Mataji. Kirsti's experiences at Anandashram were powerful and rich, but she was always drawn back to the feet of the Godchild in Tiruvannamalai. Kirsti wrote about Yogi Ramsuratkumar:

> Yogiji used to send me often to Anandashram. He had total devotion and gratitude toward Ramdas and the people there. What he experienced when he was thrown into the true awareness, without his total love toward the guru would probably have been very traumatic. "Ramdas initiated and the beggar was dead and gone," Yogiji said. From then on there was only space for the guru, for God. The individuality was devoid of self-pity. He said he was so fond of Ramdas that he used to stand hours outside the gate of Anandashram just to get a glimpse of him. It was monsoon time; he got thoroughly wet standing there.
>
> When Mataji died in February 1989, I sent a telegram to Yogiji. I knew he would want to know as soon as possible. The man who was tapping the messages at the post office was flooded with tears. Everyone

loved her for her generosity and help for local people in need. Yogiji had sat the whole afternoon at the temple gazing at the sky over the mountain when the cremation took place.

I spent the rest of the day making garlands. Basketfuls of flowers kept arriving to the ashram and the women were busy stringing them together. Most friends liked to sit near the body at the *bhajan* hall and feel the blessing power. I thought, "All the *malas* I made were going to her," so I kept stringing together flowers the whole day. Pieces were given to everyone who arrived to place on the body. In the morning I had touched her feet and felt a tingling joy and luminous *shakti*. Yogiji had told me to touch her feet some years before and "everything would be given to me," but people in the ashram did not like her to be touched and one risked getting pushed away, very rudely, if one attempted it, so I did not do it.

Some months later I gave a garland to Yogiji and he wore it. I touched his feet when I was leaving and he threw it to me and bluntly stated, "You can go!" He often acted angry when he gave special blessings! No emotionality involved. The garland had a similar tingling sensation to it as Krishnabai's feet at the time of her *mahasamadi*, but Yogiji was very much alive. I kept the garland for a long time.

When Mataji was sick those ten last months, if one sat against the wall of her room it was as if a fire had been burning inside, a kind of electric heat. It felt good. If Sathya came to sit there that time, she would sweat so much it looked as if she had been in the rain. Her body reacted differently. Someone was translating to her what was going on, but I never knew. It was something about the sufferings of the world, like Christ on the Cross, that Krishnabai believed she was going through after childlike petitions of boons. She was reported to have said, "I asked to take on the sufferings of the world, but forgot to ask for the strength to bear it."

At cremation I sat a few meters from the fire, in a place where there was a window in the pyre to see the skull. A few sparks fell on me and burnt holes in my sari.

The ashes were kept in her room for several days so people could meditate near them. Clear light was powerfully manifesting.

Will Zulkowski was with Yogi Ramsuratkumar when the newspaper came announcing Mataji's death. The beggar immediately asked Will to go to Anandashram, even for a day or a few hours, but Will was leaving India that morning and was regretfully unable to comply with the request, however heartfelt.

Devaki and Sujatha traveled from Salem to Tiruvannamalai that day to seek out Yogi Ramsuratkumar, but the house at Sannadhi Street was locked when they arrived at five o'clock. They rushed to the temple, hoping to find him there. They came in through the door and he was walking in through another door with the newspaper in his hand. He handed it to the women and they saw the headline and article that said Mataji had attained *samadhi* at seven that morning.

The two women seated themselves nearby, and with Jayarama, were the only people sitting with Yogi Ramsuratkumar. He was very quiet and looking at the sky for a long time. From time to time he would narrate the events that would be happening at Anandashram at that time: "Oh, the cremation will be now. This or that should be done at the *samadhi*." It was as if he was seeing the whole scene in his mind's eye. Whenever he mentioned Anandashram his voice would break, and tears came into his eyes.

"Oh, Jayarama! What have you brought?" Jayarama had brought some food for the beggar, and he received it sweetly and began to eat. Another devotee arrived with some plantains; he took one and gave it to Jayarama, then took another and gave it to Sujatha. The last one he broke in half, dropping one half in Devaki's hands and keeping the other half for himself to eat. It was a poignant moment for Devaki that foreshadowed things to come.

It was after the death of Mataji Krishnabai that Yogi Ramsuratkumar gave Sadhu Rangarajan a mission that would become his life's work. Mataji had started the task of chanting 15,500 *crores*[32] of Ramnam, chanting *Om Sri Ram Jai Ram Jai Jai Ram*, for the purpose of promoting world peace. At the time only 1757 *crores* had been chanted. After her death, Yogi Ramsuratkumar gave Sadhu Rangarajan the impossible mission of taking on Krishnabai's task to chant 15,500 *crores* of Ramnam by the turn of the millennium.

In 1987, Devaki's friend Vijayalakshmi was a professional woman in a very high position of great responsibility in her work. Highly educated, she had no desire for spiritual work or gurus. Some of her friends were devotees of Sai Baba, and often encouraged her to meet him, but she wasn't interested. Finally a dream convinced her to go to meet the saint, who looked at her with love and compassion and asked her to stay on the ashram one more day. It was a compelling meeting, but she was already friends with Devaki, who had always been a seeker, and with whom she corresponded. Devaki wrote her a letter saying that she had met a saint named Yogi Ramsuratkumar, and that he was the real thing, a true avatar. She encouraged Vijayalakshmi to come and have his darshan. Still she was not interested, and it took some time for her to make the gesture.

She took a taxi from Madras and went to Tiruvannamalai, first visiting the big Shiva temple. She arrived at the house on Sannadhi Street without any prior notice. When she approached the saint's house, a young man, Jayarama, opened the door and said that Yogi Ramsuratkumar was busy and she should come back the next day. She was not used to being treated in that way; she was a woman of high rank in Indian society—a successful professional with a lot of status. She insisted on seeing the beggar saint.

Yogi Ramsuratkumar himself came to the door with his bare upper body wrapped in a shawl. He said, "This beggar is very busy. You can come back tomorrow!" She had brought some *prasad* and she wanted to give it to him, but he said, "You can give this at

32 A *crore* is ten million.

the temple," as if he had known all along that she had been to the temple first. Not getting what she came for, she went back to Madras.

The next time Vijayalakshmi came to visit she sent word to Yogi Ramsuratkumar in advance. When she arrived he was receiving visitors; he greeted her and kindly asked her to come in. She sat down and looked at him. From time to time he would lift his glasses up and look at her with tremendous love.

"What do you want?" he asked.

She surprised herself by saying, "I want you to show me the way." He sat and smoked, glancing at her now and then. It was the *mahasamadhi* day of Mataji Krishnabai, in February 1989. After that encounter she came to visit him every two months or so, rather infrequently, as her job was still the primary focus of her life and took most of her time and energy. Still, now and then she was drawn back to Tiruvannamalai to see the beggar saint.

On a sunny day in late February 1989 a businessman named Ramamoorthy, whose family business was in cotton gins and chilis, went to Tiruvannamalai with a close friend to meet Yogi Ramsuratkumar. Ramamoorthy was a spiritually-minded person, but the best part of his life had been "spent with lifeless machines," and now he wanted to seek out the saint he'd heard so much about. He was a little worried about meeting a realized soul, but his friend said, "Don't worry. You can just talk to Swamiji naturally, about anything."

Just as they were entering the Shiva temple around eleven-thirty, the beggar arrived carrying his fan and coconut bowl. Upon seeing Yogi Ramsuratkumar for the first time, Ramamoorthy found himself, almost involuntarily, bending down to touch his feet.

"What's your name, my son?" the beggar asked.

"I am Ramamoorthy," he said.

"Why have you come here?"

"I came here to meet you!" Ramamoorthy surprised himself with his actions and words; he realized that in the presence of the saint he was being moved to act according to God's will and not according to his own.

"Are you coming from the temple or going inside the temple?"

"We are going inside the temple . . ." They went in and paid their respects, and when they came back out Yogi Ramsuratkumar was sitting there calling, "Tambi, tambi, tambi, tambi!" which means "younger brother" in Tamil.

"Yes, Swamiji?"

"Since you have come by car, let this beggar have the pleasure of riding in this car." While the friend went to get his car, Yogi Ramsuratkumar instructed Ramamoorthy to sit near the small Vinayaka (Ganesh) temple by the main tower, and he asked him to sing a song. Ramamoorthy sang a song that was the first rhyme he was taught by his great grandmother—a song that says, "When you pray to Ganesha, all your problems will be solved."

Soon the car arrived, and climbing in, Yogi Ramsuratkumar said, "Please drop me at my friend's house." He wanted to go to Kripala, the house of Dwarak Nath Reddy. As the car wound left and right through the town, the beggar held Ramamoorthy's hand and said, "Do you want to talk to this beggar about anything?"

"No, Swamiji," he answered. Though he had his own problems—he was dealing with migraine headaches that caused a lot of pain—he was moved to say no. At the time Ramamoorthy didn't know that Yogi Ramsuratkumar sang Ramnam, but he asked, "Could you please give me a *nama* to chant?" Yogi Ramsuratkumar continued to hold his hand. Ramamoorthy became aware of the tremendous blessing that was flowing out of Swamiji. It is said in many of the scriptures and songs in India that the realized soul can bless one either by hand, by foot or by sight, and that speech or talking is not necessary. For example, Ramana Maharshi initiated merely by his eyesight, and in the case of Yogi Ramsuratkumar, the gaze of Ramana Maharshi was enough.

Much to Ramamoorthy's surprise, upon reaching Dwarak Reddy's house the beggar turned and said, "All of you also come with us." Ramamoorthy thought that when they reached Dwarak Reddy's house the beggar would leave them, but instead they would have the opportunity to spend some more time in his company.

"Our friend wants this beggar to give him a Ramnam," Yogi Ramsuratkumar told Dwarak Reddy as he settled into the garden. After a while he began to chant Ramnam, then he asked Ramamoorthy to chant it also.

"Sandiya," Yogi Ramsuratkumar called to Reddy's daughter, "without consulting your father, go and get a book." It was a very specific request. She went inside and brought out a book by J. Krishnamurti.

"Alright, read," he instructed.

Sandiya read about four pages, but Ramamoorthy was unable to digest what he was hearing at that moment. It seemed that the beggar realized this right away, because before long he instructed Sandiya, "Alright. You put a bookmark there and put the book aside."

Ramamoorthy was wearing two crystal *malas* that had been given to him by a friend. He asked, "Swamiji, can I wear this thing, this *mala*?"

"What is that?" the beggar asked innocently, as if he had never seen one before.

"It is a crystal *mala*, Swamiji," Dwarak Reddy answered. Ramamoorthy removed the *malas* from his neck and gave them to Swamiji, who immediately put them around his neck and wore them. One of the *malas* was dedicated to Lord Vinayaka and the other to the patron goddess of Mangalore. After a half-hour or so the beggar removed the *malas* from his neck and returned them to Ramamoorthy.

Yogi Ramsuratkumar then asked for some buttermilk, and Sandiya brought cups of buttermilk prepared with salt, pepper, chilis and other spices, which she served to everyone. By that time the small group was talking and laughing together. Ramamoorthy, who sold chilis, was joking with Reddy, who was a candy manufacturer, "Both of us are selling—you are selling sweet and I am selling hot!" Upon hearing this, the beggar started laughing. The singular quality of Yogi Ramsuratkumar's laugh was something that Ramamoorty had never heard before in his life. Ramamoorthy described it, saying, "The laugh *penetrates* your heart! That laugh only Bhagawan can laugh . . . "

Soon the two men grew hungry for the noon meal, and addressing the beggar, said that they would leave to take lunch. Yogi Ramsuratkumar graciously replied, "Alright, you can go, friends, and after lunch you can go home. No need to come back again."

Ramamoorty and his friend went to have lunch, ecstatically happy to have had the company of the yogi for two hours. They ate a hearty lunch and decided to go back to Kripala, where they prostrated at the beggar's feet. It was about two-thirty in the afternoon. Yogi Ramsuratkumar had had nothing to eat—only the cup of buttermilk, but after they had arrived he turned to Sandiya and said, "Sandiya, this beggar has eaten too much. Could you please give this beggar something?"

She said, "I have got some homeopathic medicine." The men had been talking about spices and such—Ramamoorty's family business—and he said, "Bhagwan, ginger powder is supposed to be good for digestion," without realizing that there was no possibility that Swamiji could have taken anything. The whole time he had been talking to Reddy and the American visitor, who was now sitting silently. Sandiya brought some ginger powder, and the yogi took it with some water.

It took some time for Ramamoorthy to realize that when Yogi Ramsuratkumar had said, "This beggar has eaten too much," in his cryptic way of making a teaching, he had meant Ramamoorthy, not himself. Back at home a week or so later, Ramamoorthy went to the doctor to have a check up and discovered that his cholesterol was dangerously high. When he discovered this, it dawned on him just how subtly Yogi Ramsuratkumar was teaching him on the day of that first meeting. Ramamoorthy remembered:

> There is no possibility that he had taken anything but a cup of buttermilk! He was saying to me, "You fool, you have eaten too much and your cholesterol has gone too high." He knew! I told my wife, "I've been a fool." Bhagawan was smoking cigarettes, he didn't take baths—see, he has passed all these formalities! We are like the student who knows "A is for apple" but have to see the picture of the apple—but Swamiji is Ph.D., Ph.D., Ph.D., doctorate, doctorate, doctorate!
>
> Two times he had said to me, "Do you want to talk to this beggar about anything?" I said no. But during the conversation between myself, the foreigner just silently sitting, my friend and Mr. Reddy, while we were just talking, Swamiji indicated to me "I know your whole history" with just two words that only three people—myself, my wife and one other person—would know. That was his way, you know. It's for a particular person; perhaps it may be from his own mouth or from somebody else's mouth. So, I was just shocked! I realized it only after a few days, "Oh Swamiji has mentioned that word, so he must have known totally about me."

That day no one else who was there had any idea that Yogi Ramsuratkumar had made such a subtle teaching. It was an example of something that commonly happened in the master's company—the easy and natural experience of his vast comprehension and the effortless melding of his mind with the mind of the devotee. The meeting that day catalyzed a process in Ramamoorty, and over time he began to learn the ways of Yogi Ramsuratkumar and to follow his instructions.

On November 13, 1988 Haragopal Sepuri traveled by bus to reach Tiruvannamalai. His wife Durga had sent some sweets to offer to the beggar saint, and in the downtown market he also bought some apples and oranges to offer. Reaching the house at Sannadhi Street, he found that the door was locked, so he turned and walked the short block to the Shiva temple. There he saw Yogi Ramsuratkumar sitting in the left outer corridor of the Vinayaka shrine, surrounded by some devotees. Performing obeisance first to Vinayaka, Lord Arunachaleswara and Mother Parvati, he then went straight to where the beggar was sitting and stood respectfully a little distance away.

"Oh! You have come!" Yogi Ramsuratkumar called out. He immediately began to work closely with Haragopal, engaging him in relationship and a series of activities that would last all day long. "Haragopal, if you have brought anything, please distribute it to all these people and also the children." There were a few children playing around near the Vinayaka shrine. Then he said, "I do not want anything to be placed here."

When Haragopal took out the package of sweets, Yogi Ramsuratkumar saw it and said, "First bring it to me. Let me touch it and then you can distribute the prasad." Haragopal was ecstatic to be given such an opportunity! Yogi Ramsuratkumar touched the sweets briefly, seeming to take a small amount, then he said, "Now you can distribute. Keep something for yourself also."

Four of the devotees with Yogi Ramsuratkumar were from Sivakasi and the rest were either local or from the surrounding villages. While they were sitting there another ten devotees came and joined the group. Yogi Ramsuratkumar asked Haragopal to give the sweets to them and to pass out the bananas he had brought as well.

"Haragopal, distribute these also. I do not want anything to be placed here," he said again. When Haragopal tried to cut some of the bananas in half so that everyone could have some *prasad*, the master intervened, clarifying, "You can distribute as it is. Not necessary that all should get it."

One of the devotees was named Pushparajan, who had some ailment of his eyes and told Yogi Ramsuratkumar that the doctors were not able to help. The beggar held his hand and asked detailed questions about the problem.

"What is the meaning of 'Pushparajan'?" the master asked.

"It is the king of flowers," someone answered.

"Who is the king of flowers?" he asked.

"Rose."

Yogi Ramsuratkumar giggled. Haragopal remembered that Yogi Ramsuratkumar always emphasized that the names of individuals should not be idly given but be given in connection with the Divine. After about fifteen minutes, he let go of Pushparajan's hand and said, "He will be alright in about six months' time. Let him take gooseberries every day. During the season, he may take fresh gooseberries, two per day. During off season, he may soak the dry bits in water and in the evening and in the morning he may wash his eyes with that water, wash his head also with it and drink the balance."

He continued, "You will not understand the effect of gooseberries from whatever I say. You will know only when you actually use it. Take it for one month and see for yourselves. It is useful in all kinds of diseases. The primary ingredient of most of Ayurvedic medicines contain gooseberries. The Ayurvedic medicines prepared by Pondicherry Ashram are very reliable. Maybe they are somewhat costly. Gooseberries prolong life. When fresh fruits are not available, take the powder of the dried fruits, a spoonful daily."

Then he repeated several times about the efficacy of gooseberries. He looked up at Mount Arunachala and remarked, "How old is this hill?" Several people talked at once, but no one really answered.

"Many beggars like this," he said, meaning himself, "would have come and gone, but the hill is there." Yogi Ramsuratkumar's love and reverence for the holy mountain often found a way into his conversation; he once told Kirsti that during his years of wandering, he found the Himalayas too strong, but Arunachala's energy in South India was softer and more suitable for his work. It unquestionably had not only offered sanctuary and shelter to him, but also spiritual blessings. Arunachala was an integral element of his ongoing work, and on this particular day he mentioned the hill again several times before noon that day.

An elderly woman arrived and *pranamed* to Yogi Ramsuratkumar, then sat down in front of him and spoke with him as if she knew him very well. She seemed very happy and sweet.

"What time did you enter the temple?" he asked her.

"Six a.m.," she replied.

"Now it is nearly noon. So you have spent six hours in the temple," he said lovingly.

They talked for a while and then she left. Yogi Ramsuratkumar explained, "She was widowed when she was twenty years old. From that time, she spends most of the time daily in the temple only." In Indian culture it is common for the life of a widow, and especially a young widow, to be fraught with suffering, loneliness and hardship. Yogi Ramsuratkumar was deeply moved by her devotion and the way she had risen above the great difficulties in her life.

At noon, Yogi Ramsuratkumar took Haragopal by the hand and started walking with him; they passed the corridor where the temple elephant was stationed, then he led Haragopal to the southern side and had him sit down beside him. As they sat there Yogi Ramsuratkumar held his hand, releasing it only to bless those who came and prostrated before him. Then he and Haragopal were up and walking again.

Yogi Ramsuratkumar walked up to a swami who was sitting in the courtyard. He was seated on a deerskin wearing two large rudraksh *malas* and had a crown made of *rudraksha* and other sacred implements. His face, which was very attractive, was suffused with serenity and simplicity.

On seeing Yogi Ramsuratkumar, the swami got up and walked forward to greet him. They each touched the ground at the other's feet as a gesture of respect and obeisance. Yogi Ramsuratkumar asked the swami to sit back down, while he and Haragopal sat nearby. Another swami walked over to Yogi Ramsuratkumar and *pranamed*, then talked with him quite intimately, as if they were very good friends. Yogi Ramsuratkumar seemed to have an easy and natural intimacy with both swamis; still holding Haragopal's hand, he talked with them in an animated way, inquiring as to their well-being.

"Has Swamiji eaten?" Yogi Ramsuratkumar asked the first one. The swami responded that he had to go for *bhiksha* (food alms).

Yogi Ramsuratkumar turned to Haragopal and instructed, "Go and ask the Swamiji whether he would accept *bhiksha* from you." Haragopal asked the swami if he would accept food from him.

"Do you belong to this place?" the swami wanted to know.

"No, Swamiji, but I will bring the food from a hotel."

The swami said that he ate only rice, and a conversation ensued about how to transport the food to the temple. The swami suggested that they go to the hotel for food, and putting on his *rudraksh* crown, he picked up his sacred implements and took the deer skin and set out with Haragopal, the second swami and Yogi Ramsuratkumar, who suggested that they go to the Udipi Brindavan hotel. The four walked through the temple *gopuram* and out into the street and made their way, with the beggar saint in the lead. Giving him the first bit of food from his banana leaf, the swami blessed Haragopal. Yogi Ramsuratkumar gave morsels from his own banana leaf to both the swami and Haragopal. These exchanges were considered blessings and simple ritual gifts of *prasad*. Afterward the swami immediately went back to the temple.

It was a day filled with simple *lilas* that carried powerful blessings for Haragopal. It was quite unusual to have the opportunity to spend such intimate time with his guru and be given small jobs to do for him. It was considered a great blessing to be asked to perform any service for the guru. For example, Yogi Ramsuratkumar instructed Haragopal to buy four packets of betel nut. Saying, "This one is for you," the beggar kept the other three, clearly as gifts for someone else, because the he himself never used the mind-altering betel. Once they were back at the temple Yogi Ramsuratkumar stood up from his seat on the ground, took Haragopal by the hand and walked to the center of the main courtyard where the elephant was chained at the second *prakaram*. He instructed Haragopal to go to Sannadhi Street and inquire of his attendant whether Radhakrishan and his companion had arrived.

At the *mandapam* across the street from the beggar's house the two attendants informed Haragopal that no one had come, and he returned straightaway to the temple.

The message delivered, Yogi Ramsuratkumar said simply, "I am going to sleep for some time. You keep awake." Haragopal kept vigil over the guru's sleeping form for the next hour or so, until it started raining and Yogi Ramsuratkumar woke up.

A stream of devotees were visiting the temple. Two young men who had earlier placed two apples at the feet of the beggar returned with a flower garland, but he ignored them and they kept a distance. Gathering their courage, a little later they approached with the garland and placed it around his neck, then stood before him *pranaming*.

"These people have already come," Yogi Ramsuratkumar said wonderingly, looking to Haragopal, "Why are they again coming?" He waved them away, and they bowed and left. Radhakrishnan and his companion came

"Swamiji, we came at two p.m., but went to book a room in the hotel. When we came here as directed by the attendants, Swamiji was in a trance and so we did not want to disturb Swamiji."

"This beggar was sleeping, and he says that Swamiji was in a trance," Yogi Ramsuratkumar commented rather sarcastically a few minutes later.

As soon as the rain stopped Yogi Ramsuratkumar got up, took Haragopal by the hand again and led him to the temple pool. Several people attempted to follow, but he waved them away, permitting only Radhakrishnan and his companion to follow. He finally led them to the swami who had lunched with them. He had moved under the *mandapam* to stay dry in the rain. As they all sat together Yogi Ramsuratkumar stroked Haragopal's hand sweetly and occasionally raised his stick and palmyra fan in blessing while gazing at the swami. The silence grew in intensity and became very powerful as Yogi Ramsuratkumar worked with this small configuration of men.

At three-thirty the beggar signaled that he wanted tea. The swami told Haragopal to get it, but Yogi Ramsuratkumar interjected that he wanted Radhakrishnan to get the tea. While the tea was coming the swami placed a bundle of books before Yogi Ramsuratkumar and untied the cloth. The beggar picked up the topmost book, handed it to Haragopal and asked him to read. It was written in Tamil, and Haragopal said that his mother language was Telugu, and his reading of Tamil would be slow.

"Read," Yogi Ramsuratkumar said. Haragopal plunged into the reading. Now and then the swami prompted him, and finally he covered three pages with some difficulty. Finally the tea arrived and Yogi Ramsuratkumar poured some tea from his tumbler into Haragopal's. The whole day had been highly auspicious for Haragopal, as the master had concentrated his focus and formidable energies on him, orchestrating many *lilas* for his benefit.

> I do not know how I should describe this experience, whether it can be called a spiritual experience, as generally conceived in our understanding. If it were a few years back, I would have gone into ecstasies. Now something subtle has taken place. During my very first visit meeting with Ramji, I went into ecstasy. Now I think, I have gone blank, a sort of nothingness. I am unable to explain it. All the meritorious

deeds of my past lives seemed to have condensed on this day.[33]

At four o'clock in the afternoon Yogi Ramsuratkumar turned to Haragopal and said, "Haragopal, you can go now."

"Swamiji, there are fruits in my bag," Haragopal said, rising and touching the beggar's feet.

"Take them for the children," the beggar instructed. Haragopal prostrated to the swami and left.[34]

As the numbers of devotees began to swell and people came seeking Yogi Ramsuratkumar's blessings, he somehow managed to remain elusive. Richard Schiffman, who first met Yogi Ramsuratkumar in 1978, told a story about visiting him again in the late eighties: Richard had come with a friend named Ken and was staying at Ramanashram. Ken wanted to meet Yogi Ramsuratkumar, and with fond memories of his time with the beggar in 1978, Richard was very much looking forward to seeing him again. Word quickly got out that Richard was going to see the Godchild, and before long there were ten people who wanted to accompany them to Sannadhi Street. Not knowing that Yogi Ramsuratkumar didn't like crowds, and that in fact he would often send away a whole group if there was one person in the group who wasn't resonant, Richard approached the house with the large group. He knocked on the door and Jayarama came out.

"Can I help you?" he asked,

"Yes, we've come to see Yogi Ramsuratkumar." Jayarama went into the house and very shortly came back to the door.

"Swamiji would like to know how many people?" They counted eleven and he went back in, then came back to the door again.

"No, Swami is resting. He can't see you."

Richard left, disappointed and remembering how sweet his time with the beggar had been almost ten years before. A few days later he and Ken were leaving Tiruvannamalai and were waiting at the bus stand. At the last moment they decided to make one last trip to Arunachalesvara Temple, to have the darshan of this holy place and say goodbye. Just as they were leaving the bus stand, the beggar suddenly jumped out of the shadows, blessed them and ran away as quickly as he could.

Yogi Ramsuratkumar's years of relative anonymity were quickly coming to an end. His devotees were fervently wishing to celebrate his *jayanthi*, and asked him each year, but after the first *jayanthi* celebration in 1976 he said no. However, he did permit them to

33 Haragopal Sepuri, *Experiences With Yogi Ramsuratkumar*, p. 100.

34 Ibid, pp. 90-100.

celebrate in other towns or locations—for example in Madras, or at the Mantralayam in Kanimadam. Still, on December 1st he would often steal away from his house on Sannadhi Street and hide in a devotee's house for the day to avoid the crowds and zealous well wishers—but he would not be able to put off the momentum of his own destiny much longer.

On one occasion in 1987 Shankara Rajulu came with the message that some school children, including Rajulu's, were on an excursion and wanted to have the beggar's darshan. Yogi Ramsuratkumar said that his house was too small for so many people, but also on that day there was some electrical problem and therefore no light in the house.

Wanting to the have the children come to the house anyway, Yogi Ramsuratkumar sent people in two or three directions to find an electrician who could come and fix the problem. They came back saying that the electrician was not available.

"Alright, we'll go to where the children are," he said, and he quickly took off, practically zooming from Sannadhi Street to the mansion where the children were situated. He was walking so fast that Rajulu could not catch up or even follow him. Arriving at the mansion, Yogi Ramsuratkumar found all the children and ten teachers, as well as members of Rajulu's family in a bus—about fifty or sixty people. He asked them to sit in three separate groups, one containing the children, the other teachers, and the third group the members of Rajulu's family. He asked everyone their name and blessed them.

"What are you going to do next?" the beggar asked.

"We are going to have breakfast."

"May this beggar also have breakfast with you?" he asked.

"Yes, Bhagwan, it's a pleasure! You can have breakfast," came the astonished and pleased reply. After the food had been served he inquired about the schedule for the rest of the day and Rajulu explained that the children were going to a popular picnic area by a water reservoir about fifteen miles away from Tiruvannamalai at the Sathanur Dam.

"Will there be enough room for this beggar in your vehicle?" Yogi Ramsuratkumar asked, to everyone's surprise.

Rajulu replied, "Everything that belongs to us is by your grace. Everything is yours—it is your bus! You can come and be there."

And so the beggar came on the bus with the children, the teachers and family members, taking a seat and asking Shankara Rajulu to sit near him.

"You see, when this beggar came to this city a number of people offered to take him to the dam in their cars, in their jeeps, in their vehicles but now this beggar is traveling in Shankara's bus!" He gave Shankara Rajulu a tap on the back.

Upon arriving at the reservoir Yogi Ramsuratkumar was very concerned when he found that there was very little water, only a few feet, in the reservoir.

"How will people here survive?" he said, deeply disturbed by the lack of water. "They depend upon the water from this reservoir for their irrigation. For the whole of next year they will have water only from this reservoir. Unless they have water here, how are they going to survive? How are they going to have their agriculture irrigation performed?"

Perhaps it was the great force of compassion, moving through the heart of a beggar who had an extraordinary capacity for prayer, which seeded the rain clouds that day. Miraculously, within an hour there was a torrential rainstorm, and the reservoir immediately began to fill with water. Rajulu said, "That is the kind of concern that he had for humanity—not only for individuals but for all of humanity. There were torrential rains that day, even as we were there! We got drenched, and then we came back to Tiruvannamalai." According to Rajulu, the water level in the reservoir increased and never went dry again from that day until the present time; though not full, it always had enough water to supply the farmers who depended upon it.

While they were resting at the reservoir the beggar began to speak to Rajulu, saying that his name would reverberate throughout the universe. He spoke of his name, Yogi Ramsuratkumar, saying, "This is not the name of this beggar. This is a mantra."

Yogi Ramsuratkumar had asked to be rowed out on the water in a boat, but the boatman had said it wasn't possible, so they simply sat in a boat that was moored at the dock on the reservoir. After a while the beggar said, "Are you not reminded just now of Sri Rama, Sita, and Lakshman being rowed across the Ganges when they went to the forest?" Rajulu immediately felt that the beggar was revealing himself as Rama by enacting this *lila* of sitting in the boat on the water.

Then Rajulu remembered that once when he was conducting some research in a commentary on the *Ramayana*, he had relayed to Yogi Ramsuratkumar a story not found in the *Ramayana* or other commentaries. When Rama, Sita, Hanuman and the others were coming back to Ayodhya after Sita was rescued from the demon Ravana by Rama and Hanuman, they stopped at the ashram of a *rishi* to take food. When the banana leaves were passed out as plates for everyone, they were one short, which fell to Anjaneya, or Hanuman in his devotional form. Upon seeing this, Rama's heart was moved with love for his great devotee, Anjaneya. To resolve the dilemma, Rama asked Anjaneya to share the food off his banana leaf.

Listening carefully to the story, Yogi Ramsuratkumar said, "Yes, this beggar also has not heard about this anecdote in any other *Ramayana*. That's a special message we have found."

A month later some devotees were gathered with Yogi Ramsuratkumar at Sannadhi Street when a woman brought food for him. As was his habit, Yogi Ramsuratkumar shared the food with everyone present. The woman had brought the banana leaves as well as the food, and she quickly laid them out. There were ten or twelve people, and as she distributed the banana leaves, she turned up one leaf short. Instantly Yogi Ramsuratkumar said to Rajulu, "Oh, there's a shortage of one leaf. You can come and dine with this beggar."

All religious myths are archetypal stories, encoded with information about the universal experiences of the spiritual path. The spontaneous embodiment of archetypal contents of the collective unconscious often finds a natural expression in the *bhavas* and enactments of the guru with his disciples. Rajulu commented on how this experience revealed Yogi Ramsuratkumar's innate divinity as an incarnation of Lord Vishnu as Rama:

> That is not to say that it was a privilege offered to me; it made me realize that he was re-enacting what he enacted in the incarnation as Rama. As Rama he offered one person, Anjanaya, his devotee, to take his food off the same leaf. I understood then that he was re-enacting what happened in another *yuga*, in a different epoch. In the Hindu *puranas* there are four *yugas*. This happened in a *yuga* prior to the incarnation [of Vishnu] as Krishna, because first of all Rama came and then Krishna came. After that, we are now living in this Kali Yuga. And so he made me realize that he was re-enacting what he enacted then as Rama—but this is a new experience that he is giving in this age, according to the needs of the people of this age. He made me a vehicle to understand this.

For many years the divinization of one unusual human being was hidden, only hinted at in oblique actions. But if one had the eyes to see, the gleam of gold, like rays of the sun, could be seen beneath the beggar's rags. Yogi Ramsuratkumar embodied the freedom of Papa Ramdas' *sannyasa* days for the Finnish devotee, Kirsti. She was inspired by the power, faith, freedom and love of the Divine manifesting so fully in his person, but his freedom was possible exactly because his divinity had remained a well-kept secret for so many years. As Shankara Rajulu recognized, that was beginning to change. Kirsti wrote:

> Yogi Ramsuratkumar did not allow himself to be treated with external shows of respect until the late eighties. If one got up when he came to the house or the *mandapam* tower at night, he would say, "Oh, you are standing, you must be in a hurry to go!" and he would send you away. If you just sat, he would sit down, light a cigarette and maybe say a few words. The atmosphere around the beggar was relaxed.
>
> After the temple (the Manthralayam) was built for him near Kanya Kumari, someone once asked about the worship done there. He said, "This beggar would starve if *nivedhya*"—food offering—"was not served there." The *murti* image had been installed according to the ritual rules.

He was openly referring to the embodiment of divine presence in the statue of himself—the "*murti* image"—that had its abode in the Manthralayam, where Vedic rites and offerings were made daily.

The decade of the eighties was a time in which the mad beggar of Tiruvannamalai, compelled by a great process of divine Intelligence, began to reveal himself over time in an inexorable process of evolution. There seemed to be several things that were significant catalysts to this process: The beggar was seventy-two years old, and throngs of supplicants were lining up outside his gate at Sannadhi Street. As the word spread and more people had the experience of Yogi Ramsuratkumar as God in human form, the house was not big enough to accommodate the numbers of people who sought him out. It became unsafe for him to walk alone out on the streets of Tiruvannamalai; he never knew when the devotional fervor of the crowd might get out of hand. But further, the death of Mataji Krishnabai in 1989 and the secure establishment of several key devotees, both East and West, in the late eighties—whose dedication to Yogi Ramsuratkumar and the lineage was unquestionable—seemed to herald the end of an era of Yogi Ramsuratkumar's life.

On May 7 and 8, 1988, Rajamanickam had sponsored a conference on the world message of Yogi Ramsuratkumar at Kamban Kalaiarangam in Pondicherry, amidst the protests of the beggar that there was nothing to say about him. As a companion to the conference, a book, *Divine Message to Humanity by H.H. Yogi Ramsuratkumar, the God Child, Tiruvannamalai*, was published with many photos of Yogi Ramsuratkumar. Although only about one hundred people attended, the event generated a great deal of publicity, and the book itself was widely distributed. When Yogi Ramsuratkumar heard about the plans for this seminar, he asked, "What does it mean by a seminar?"

"Discussing something about you, Swami," was the answer.

"You are going to discuss about this beggar?" he asked incredulously. "Why don't you discuss this beggar right here?" he asked, humorously making a teaching point. Why go somewhere else to talk about that which is everywhere and cannot be described, discussed or comprehended by the intellectual mind?

On July 8, 1990 an article was published in a Madras newspaper, *The Hindu.* It was written by Dev Gogul (under the pen name of Ilaya Raja) at the request of V. Ganeshan, reprinted in *The Mountain Path*, the magazine of Ramanashram, and excerpted here:

> "More publicity for this beggar!" he is certain to exclaim in delight, when he sees this in print. His flashing eyes would crinkle and he would put his hand to his mouth, hidden behind a generous white beard, as if to hold back the peals of laughter. His joy is infectious, sweeping everyone and everything into its blissful fold. His laughter is potent wine (medicine, if you prefer), enough to banish the cares of life, to refresh both body and spirit.
>
> Yogi Ramsuratkumar is no different from the scores of beggars who hang around the magnificent Arunachaleswarar Temple in Tiruvannamalai (Tamil Nadu). The casual passerby is unlikely to give him a second glance. Neither in the distinctive ochre robes of the *sanyasi* nor the spotless white of the saint, the earthy hues of his unassuming attire blend with the surroundings.
>
> The house which he now occupies, a stone's throw away from the main entrance to the temple, is equally unpretentious. Its sloping red-tiled roof and iron-barred verandah contrasts with the multi-storied modernity

of the other buildings which stand cheek-by-jowl on the same street. The open sewer in front of the house serves as a public convenience.

For thirty-eight years the Yogi has lived and played the role of a homeless beggar with the panache of a carefree millionaire. Asking nothing of nobody, and accepting no credit for himself, one can only guess at the enormous influence and timely aid he has quietly brought into the lives of innumerable persons.

"Swami," as he is affectionately called is well-known, not only in Tamil Nadu but also farther a field in India and abroad, sometimes in quite unexpected quarters. Though there are brief periods of privacy, he is usually engaged in fielding a seemingly endless stream of visitors who catch him at "home" or, sometimes, in the spacious flagstoned courtyards of the temple.

The darshan is always an informal affair. Clutching a worn, coconut-shell begging bowl and palm-leaf fan in one hand, the other raised high in benediction, the Yogi is brisk, even businesslike. The deep sensitivity, empathy and compassion radiating from this angelic figure is matched only by the trust, admiration, even sheer reverence of the supplicants: families, mendicants, farmers, professionals, children, businessmen. While some are content with paying their respects, others relate their problems and wait for answers.

The cumulative effect of the spectable, observed at regular intervals over several months, is one of surrender to sanctity. Here is a phenomenon beyond one's ken. No individual frame of flesh and bone can carry the burden of so much common woe and collective aspiration, nor personify extra-dimensional qualities usually attributed to images of stone, without the marrow of divine principle.

In a flash, Yogi Ramsuratkumar pre-empts idolatry. "My Father alone exists. Nothing else, nobody else. Past, present, future, only my Father, all-pervasive, everywhere. In Him, everything is included. Every object—man, animal, bird, tree, stone—all is nothing but my Father."

. . . . And I have heard him sing. Sri Rama, Jaya Rama, Jaya Jaya Rama, Jaya Jaya Rama, Jaya Jaya Rama. In a mellifluous voice which makes time stand still, this haunting song of love brings tears to my eyes.

Once, sitting by the side of the Yogi, a Tamil verse came to me spontaneously. In it the sacred names of my heart's cherished deities are strung together. The Yogi looked embarrassed, as his name appeared along with great saints.

> "Oh, how blessed is this life!
> How privileged am I to remember, even if
> for a fleeting moment,

Grandpa Koti Swami, Mother Mayee Ma,
That Splendid Sun of Jnana, Ramana
and Yogi Ramsuratkumar.
Life's purpose gained, what more do I need?"[35]

Dev Gogul was a regular visitor of Yogi Ramsuratkumar at Sannadhi Street during the late eighties and early nineties, and wrote this article, directly from his personal experience of the beggar saint. It was another sign of the times that pointed toward change.

Around the same time, sensing the pressing necessity for a larger residence and circumstance for Yogi Ramsuratkumar, Janarthanan, Perumal and other long-time devotees were anxious to build an ashram fit for a beggar king. Still Yogi Ramsuratkumar said no. Nonetheless, the supreme spiritual force that had guided his life was gathering momentum and potent energies were building up—like a nuclear reactor, it seemed that at any time things could explode. Ultimately, the beggar himself would simply be carried along on the winds of the blast. After 1990, a great transition began to take place.

35 Ilaya Raja, "A Forceful Presence," *The Hindu*, Madras, Sunday July 8, 1990.

CHAPTER SEVEN

A Time of Great Transition

1990-1994

"There is a yogi in the garb of a beggar in Tiruvannamalai," said Swami Nityananda of Tapovanum to Dr. T.I. Radhakrishnan. He had just asked for the swami's blessing for the upcoming Atiraatra Yagna (sacrificial fire) to bring blessings to the villages near Trichur, where they were meeting with the organizational committee to plan the event. Swami Nityananda continued, "His name is Ramsuratkumar. If you go and meet him and take his blessings, there will be no difficulty at all to make the Atiraatra Yagna a great success."

Pointing out that Tiruvannamalai was four hundred and forty kilometers away from Trichur, Radhakrishnan was obviously reluctant if not skeptical, but Swami Nityananda insisted that he should receive the blessings of the beggar saint. Despite some doubts, the doctor found himself making the long trip to Tiruvannamalai the next day and was soon knocking on the iron grill door at 10 Sannadhi Street.

A young boy answered the door and took the doctor's name, then disappeared into the inner rooms of the house. Very shortly he returned and said, "Swami will meet you in two minutes."

Soon the door opened and Yogi Ramsuratkumar appeared and invited the doctor and his companions inside. Once seated on the verandah, he gave them a drink made of honey— a divine elixir called *madhuparka*, given only on very auspicious occasions— and served it with his own hands from his coconut bowl.

"Are you Dr. Radhakrishnan?" the yogi asked. The doctor nodded his head in affirmation. Yogi Ramsuratkumar placed a packet of prasad in Radhakrishnan's hands then held them with his left hand, while the empty fingers of his right hand moved as if a *japa mala* was passing through them. He seemed to be attuning to Radhakrishnan at a very deep level. At first the doctor didn't feel anything special in this direct contact with the saint, but after several minutes he began to feel as though an electric current was passing through his body. Surprised, he looked around to see if it could be coming from some electrical source, but there was nothing.

For over ten minutes Yogi Ramsuratkumar held Radhakrishnan's hands and blessed him in silence, then he said, "This beggar has been praying to his master to bless you and the *yagna*, and he has done it. What you are doing is very dear to the heart of this beggar. Now you can go to Kerala. Don't waste time in Tiruvannamalai." Radhakrishnan and his companions immediately returned to Trichur.

The great success of the fire ritual, which brought about the needed rains in Kerala, spurred the doctor to return to Tiruvannamalai to see the beggar saint. He found him again at the house on Sannadhi Street, and was admitted right away. As always there were many devotees demanding the beggar's time, and he could not put his whole attention on the doctor.

"Doctor, if we sit here, we can't talk undisturbed," Yogi Ramsuratkumar said. "After some time, the devotees will start crowding up. Therefore we will go to some other place." Leaving Sannadhi Street, the Yogi Ramsuratkumar took Dr. Radhakrishnan to the house of V. Ganeshan.

"You brought good rains in Kerala by conducting the *yagna*," Ganeshan said after they arrived and were settled. "Why is it that we have not had rains in Tiruvannamalai for the last ten months? Why don't you bring some rains here also?" Ganeshan pressed genially.

The doctor replied in hasty repartee, "Why should you doubt? In the next seventy-two hours, you'll have a heavy rain here! At least for two hours . . ." Then he looked sheepishly at the great yogi who was sitting beside him and said apologetically, "Swami, I have uttered nonsense! You must kindly help me out!"

Yogi Ramsuratkumar burst into joyous laughter. He laughed like a young boy, and his laughter was so enthusiastic and rollicking that he fell into Dr. Radhakrishnan's lap and lay there for a few minutes. Some time later he walked out into the garden and looked at Arunachala Hill for a long while.

"I feel uncomfortable," the beggar said, "I want to lay down." Before they could spread the mat out properly for him, Yogi Ramsuratkumar rolled on the ground. After some time he looked intently at the sky, and suddenly dark clouds began to roll in. When the rains started he said, "I'm very tired. Please take me to my place."

Upon arriving back at Sannadhi Street, the yogi looked at the doctor and said, "Doctor, you need not stay here any more. This rain is only in Tiruvannamalai . . ." Immediately the doctor understood that it was time for him to go and he struck out with no delay. Exactly as Yogi Ramsuratkumar had said, there was no rain at all beyond the city limits of Tiruvannamalai, but the rain continued in the town for a total of two hours.

At one point during that afternoon Yogi Ramsuratkumar had made an unusual request of Radhakrishnan, asking unpredictably, "Doctor, if this beggar falls sick, will you come here and treat me?"

The doctor immediately agreed to come, but pointed out that there was some distance that would have to be traveled from Trichur to Tiruvannamalai, which could hinder his ability to provide medical care in a timely manner. Waving this concern away, Yogi Ramsuratkumar said, "The distance is not a problem." It was a prophetic request, and one that would come to fruition very soon.[1]

1 Dr. T.I. Radhakrishnan, "The Unforgettable Turning Point," *Yogi Ramsuratkumar Souvenir Book*, pp. 121-123.

"Sanda, don't be afraid. Sandiya, see there is nothing else, nobody else—only Rama exists! Don't forget this. There is nothing else, nobody else! Only Rama exists!" Yogi Ramsuratkumar spoke in his disarming, songlike way.

Dwarak Reddy and Sandiya often encountered the beggar when they went to do *pradakshina* at the Arunachalesvara temple. He would be sitting on the steps to the chariot *mandapam*, just across from his house. He could see them down the street, walking to or from the temple. Then, with a laugh, he would call to Sandiya from there, which was some distance away. Somehow she always heard him, even over the cacophony of the bronze market and the noisy street.

"How can you hear me, Sanda, from so far away?" the yogi asked with a laugh when she responded, "How can you hear me?" According to Sandiya, it was "his sudden recognition" of the fact that she was there that made it possible to hear his voice: when he placed his powerful attention on her, it pulled her attention automatically toward him.

"This beggar would like to come to Kripala!" he would often then say to them, the beautiful shady courtyard of Kripala being one of his favorite places of sanctuary for his work.

"Swamiji, we are doing *pradakshina*," Dwarak Reddy would tell him, "we will walk home and bring the car for you."

"You will walk home, Dwarak, and Sanda will stay with me. You bring the car!" the beggar king commanded. And that is exactly what would happen. After spending the day at Kripala, as evening drew close he would take his leave, saying, "Drop me in the evening at the temple!" Sometimes he stayed at Kripala from six in the morning until six in the evening. Sometimes he brought others with him, and at times devotees would come there for his darshan, or just to sit and have *satsang* with him under the most ordinary of circumstances out in the lush garden under the mango trees. The late eighties and early nineties were a time of many pleasant and joyful gatherings with the beggar at Kripala. Sometimes he joked with Sandiya, asking her to light his cigarette, then he would playfully say, "Be careful! My beard is there!" and he would brush his beard as if the fire from the match had been dropped down into it.

Sometimes he would speak like a child, saying, "I'm so hungry Sanda!"

"Swamiji, there is nothing to eat, only rice and curds," she responded, then he would just ask for buttermilk and say, "Come and sit!" Dropping the idea of food, he had already moved on; he wouldn't wait for ten minutes while food was prepared, but responded to the immediate call of the work in the present moment.

During this time period Devaki came to Tiruvannamalai often for the beggar's darshan and stayed with her friends, Sandiya and "Appa"—Dwarak Nath Reddy. Together the three would go to Sannadhi Street to see Yogi Ramsuratkumar. It was during this time that the beggar saint began to be even more fierce and rejecting with Devaki than ever before.

"This beggar is busy. You can go!" Yogi Ramsuratkumar said to Devaki, dismissing her tersely. At times when he was gruff with her, Devaki sometimes left in tears and cried all the way back home. In these ruthless acts of compassion, the master was tempering her attachment to his physical form, stoking the fires of longing and purifying her devotional fervor. Devaki remembered the powerful transformational effects of the times when Yogi Ramsuratkumar sent her away:

> It was like dropping a bombshell on my head. I thought the very sky had come down on me, and I simply wished death upon myself. My God, I had never cried like that in my life before! I began to cry openly right in the street. Everybody was watching me, and with the tears streaming down I reached the bus stand. I got onto the Madras bus and I sat there crying all through the journey. When I was about two hours away from Madras, I was feeling so miserable, and I thought Bhagawan had cheated me out of something nice. Hadn't I waited? Hadn't I obeyed him all along? Why couldn't he at least have given me a glance, or he could have just raised his hand, or he could have at least gently said "Please go away," or something! I was feeling so miserable and then in the next second, in a fraction of a second without my volition, without my will, some transformation came over me.
>
> Right in the middle of that misery, like a bubble, some nice feeling began to surface. Suddenly I found myself unable to cry anymore. The tears wouldn't come. There was no sorrow, there was no sadness in my heart, there was no misery anymore. And I began to feel so happy for no reason. In fact I became ecstatic, and for no reason at all it was ecstasy all the rest of the way to Madras. It still is a wonder to me how it could have happened. I had gone to the very limit of misery and then it turned into ecstasy; the whole thing turned into ecstasy and I began to laugh! I was crying so much, and then I was laughing so much—what did the people on the bus think? But it looked as if nobody noticed me. Even the driver or the conductor didn't notice me doing all those strange things. That was Bhagawan's grace. It was so different when I stopped the journey; there was such peace in my heart, there was such joy in my heart, that it was a jubilant Devaki that landed at my sister's place finally. It is still strange to me how it could happen.

During the summer of 1990 Devaki came to Tiruvannamalai every weekend to see Yogi Ramsuratkumar. During July and August the beggar sent Devaki away for seven weeks in a row. Sometimes when she reached the house on Sannadhi Street he would step up to the grill of the enclosed porch and shout from there, "No place—you can go!" Again the next weekend she would go back, seeking his company. This time he would send his attendant, Jayarama, out to give the message.

"Swami is busy inside, you can go," Jayarama reported, and Devaki would start crying, turning to leave.

A little later she would turn up again at the yogi's doorstep. Yogi Ramsuratkumar would stand beside the wooden door inside the porch and say, "This beggar is busy. You can go." Again and again she came and was sent away each time, weeping, to drag herself through the week only to start all over again the next weekend on the five-hour bus ride to Tiruvannamalai. On the seventh time he sent her away she began to entertain thoughts of ending it all. If her guru didn't want her, she had no reason left to live. Deciding against drowning herself in the pool at the temple, for fear it would be very bad for the people who came to the temple for spiritual upliftment, she decided to walk up Mt. Arunachala and find some means to "finish" herself.

Leaving the temple she noticed a strange man standing there, looking at her intensely, but she didn't take it as a threat to herself. He began to follow her, but still she didn't take it seriously, until she got close to Ramanashram and realized that he was certainly following her, a single woman alone, with malicious intent. Turning again to find the man close behind, she stared harshly at him, hoping to drive him away. Then again, passing by the Sheshadri Ashram, she turned to look at him and he leered back at her. It was a frightening moment, knowing that if she was up on the mountain, it was a lonely place where anything could happen. In a mind crazed with longing, it made perfect sense that it was quite different to kill oneself by a method of choice than to be killed, raped or maimed at the hands of another.

Just at that time a constable came walking past. She ran to the policeman and said "Look, this man is following me . . . " She explained that he had followed her from the temple, and that she wanted to go around the mountain. The policeman said, "Alright I will take care of him, but I would like you to go to your house. I am going to stand here and see that you reach your house. Then I will take him." He called the man over to him and said, "You will stand here; you don't try any tricks on me."

Devaki's suicide plans were thwarted. Leaving her no other choice but to go back to her room, the policeman walked most of the way back with her. Then she began to feel that this too was deliberately Bhagawan's design—knowing full well what she had in mind, he had sent the lurking man to threaten her and the policeman to protect her. Distraught and emotional, Devaki made a silent outcry to Yogi Ramsuratkumar: "You won't give me darshan and you won't let me die!"

Leaving again for Salem that weekend, Devaki was convinced that Yogi Ramsuratkumar did not want to see her; maybe he didn't even like her. Clearly he had no time for her, so she decided that she would turn her energies toward caring for her aging parents. At the time her father was very sick in the hospital in Madras. So in late August 1990 she took a leave of absence for ten days from her post at the university and planned to take the two-thirty train to Madras that afternoon. Just as she was walking out of the college with her ticket and bag in hand, someone came running up behind her and said, "You've got a phone call!"

It was quite unusual to get a call, and thinking it was probably about her father, she ran to take the phone. It was Sandiya calling from Tiruvannamalai to report that she had gone to visit "Yogiji" at Sannadhi Street; she was horrified by what she found. He was vomiting blood and so weak he could not walk. She called her father, who was away on business, saying, "You need to come, he looks that bad . . ." Now she said urgently, "Devaki, we want to inform you that Bhagawan is not well, he is very sick." Devaki hastily changed her plans, gave her train ticket to a friend and ran to catch the nearest bus to Tiruvannamalai, stopping only to ask her associates, "Please inform my parents that I'm not coming—I have some other work. Tell them that Bhagawan is not well. I am going to Tiruvannamalai."

It was nine o'clock at night and very dark inside when Devaki arrived at Sannadhi Street. Yogi Ramsuratkumar was lying down on the floor of the porch. Jayarama and his family were there attending to him. People were coming and going, and there was no way she could get near to him, so at nine-thirty she went to Kripala and joined Sandiya and Dwarak Nath Reddy. They were deeply concerned. It was clear that the beggar's strength was gone; he was still vomiting blood and he could only barely crawl. He had not taken any food the whole day and there was as yet no doctor attending. The prognosis for Yogi Ramsuratkumar seemed quite bleak. For Devaki it was a sleepless night of tears, pacing the floor and chanting the name of Yogi Ramsuratkumar:

> The whole night I was walking up and down, crying to Swami Ramdas, crying to so many gods, chanting Bhagawan's name all the time, Yogi Ramsuratkumar, Yogi Ramsuratkumar. I was mad and I got hold of his name and I was begging, begging, begging . . . suddenly it was five o'clock and then six o'clock. I waited until the *puja* for Lord Ganesh was done, and we rushed to his place.
>
> Seven times he had turned me out. This was the eighth time I had come and again, the previous night I couldn't see him. I had been awake the whole night, so you can imagine the effect on me. I was so scared that this time also he wouldn't let me inside. But somehow I wanted at least a glimpse of him. Dwarak Nath Reddy entered and then Sandiya. They prostrated and then Bhagawan gestured to them to sit there. He was lying down and very weak. [Bhuvanesvari, Jayarama's wife] who used to feed him was sitting there. Then I entered. I was so scared to go near him, I just stood there, and then I thought I would just prostrate, and I put my hands like that . . . . I don't know how he got the strength, but he half raised himself up, put his hand over mine, and he held my hand. He must have known what misery I had gone through the whole night, praying for him and chanting his name. I was so thrilled! It was one of those treasured moments of life. He put his hand on me by way of reassuring me that everything would be all right, like, "Don't worry." That was enough for me. It was a treasure for me—something I never expected.

The next morning it was obvious that if Yogi Ramsuratkumar didn't have medical treatment he would very quickly die. When Dwarak Reddy, Sandiya and Devaki arrived he had already refused all offers of help from the concerned devotees who were gathered around him. Approaching Yogi Ramsuratkumar, Reddy spoke frankly with him, saying, "This condition requires immediate attention. Can I take you to Madras, or to Vellore, which is closer?"

"This beggar doesn't want to go anywhere!" came the answer. Getting more concerned by the minute, Dwarak Reddy knew of an elderly homeopathic and natural physician who could come and treat Yogi Ramsuratkumar. Knowing that the beggar saint preferred natural healing methods, Reddy suggested the doctor as a last hope.

"Swami nobody is treating you here. I know one physician who treated Swami Ramdas, Satya Sai Baba and he's used to yogis also. Will you please come to my house and I will take you to him?" Dwarak implored.

"If he would see this beggar, maybe that can be done," Yogi Ramsuratkumar answered, to everyone's great relief and surprise.

Dev Gogul, who worked at Ramanashram and had been befriended by the yogi, was there that day as well, and he remembered his shock at seeing the beggar in this condition. As the men lifted Yogi Ramsuratkumar up, Dev grabbed his feet and helped to carry him to Dwarak Reddy's car, then went to Kripala, the Reddy's mansion, with him. Arriving at Kripala, they carried the beggar into the house and laid him down on the floor on a mat while arrangements were made for the doctor, but before they knew what had happened, they discovered that the yogi had somehow crawled outside to the enclosed garden, a lush and beautiful place shaded by tall trees, palms and adorned with many flowering shrubs. Impervious to their pleas, Yogi Ramsuratkumar refused to stay in the house—where he could have had anything he wanted or needed—and instead insisted on laying in the garden under the mango trees. It was the rainy season, and he had only two cotton spreads beneath him and a small pillow where he lay on the tiled patio floor of the walled garden. The devotees were asked to stay away with a very few exceptions; Jayarama was the person who stayed by Yogi Ramsuratkumar day and night and attended to his needs.

The doctor that was called was unable to make any headway with Yogi Ramsuratkumar; still he was vomiting blood and becoming weaker and weaker. Finally Yogi Ramsuratkumar said, "You can call Dr. Radhakrishnan." Jayarama was there, attending to his needs, and along with Dwarak Nath Reddy, Rajagopal, Swami Nathan and some other close devotees, Dr. Radhakrishnan was called and asked to come from Trichur immediately. The doctor came in a van with his team and began to treat him the very next day.

In the meantime, Sandiya began to arrange bed sheets, blankets and canvas spreads to make a temporary room around the beggar, rather like an army tent. Screens were put up on all four sides and a makeshift hospital room was constructed. It started to rain and there were scorpions, snakes, centipedes and millipedes all around, but still the beggar refused to move inside. He stayed there for ten days, sometimes in the pouring rain, his small "room" dripping with water and crawling with insects seeking shelter from the downpour.

Dr. Radhakrishnan had come with his wife, who was also a doctor, and a nurse. Right away the doctor insisted that Yogi Ramsuratkumar needed blood transfusions. Devotees lined up in the dirt street outside the garden wall to have their blood tested to see whose was compatible with Yogi Ramsuratkumar's, and the blood was drawn right there in a temporary laboratory set up by the doctors. The transfusion bag with the blood was hung from a branch of the tree. It was an extraordinary scene, fashioned by the beggar king, who would not be defined by social convention or by the drive for the survival of the body and its usual demands for comforts, even in this moment of crisis.

It was a strange way to be reunited with the beggar, but Yogi Ramsuratkumar permitted Devaki to stay at Kripala during the days of his healing process, where she could assist Sandiya and "Appa" Reddy in whatever was needed. She was content with any way in which she was allowed to serve, even though she was not allowed by his side in the garden bed. Devaki remembered:

> Bhagawan permitted me to stay, but he wouldn't allow me near. I was helping Sandiya and Appa with some things here and there. Only once I got the chance: finally there was nobody around, it was afternoon and he was lying down with eyes closed. I sneaked inside and took the fan in hand and I was just halfway through that when he woke up and said, "You!" I just dropped the fan and ran! I sat down and began to cry. I thought he couldn't stand the sight of me. I knew what it was that he meant by "You." One would know in his presence—he would see to it that you got the message somehow, and with minimal energy. He was so economical, you know, in divine energy!

Sick almost to death with bleeding ulcers, Yogi Ramsuratkumar lay in the garden and slowly got better under Dr. Radhakrishnan's care. Sometimes he would sit up and ask the devotees who were taking care of him to sing, and a spontaneous *satsang* would happen. Sometimes he asked Sandiya to sing, and the group did *puja*, even though he was unable to get up and move about.

One day when the beggar was still in bed three people arrived from the U.S.—two women and one man. They said that they were doctors from a hospital in New York, and they insisted on just a glimpse of Bhagawan.

"No, no. Swami is not well. We can't afford to let you inside. It will be a strain on him," Dwarak Nath Reddy said, but the Americans insisted on telling their story, explaining that once the devotees had heard it, they might change their mind.

"After hearing our story, please at least tell Swami. If he says no, it's alright." As it turned out, two years ago one of the women had had an advanced cancer and had been in tremendous pain. She was facing an imminent demise when she landed in Tiruvannamalai and heard about Yogi Ramsuratkumar. Even though her illness was so progressed that there was no hope for her, when someone mentioned the beggar's name she decided to go see him.

Yogi Ramsuratkumar sat with her and merely looked at her while he smoked a cigarette or two. Then he said "My Father Blesses you, you will be alright. You are cured. My Father has cured you. Father's blessings, you can go now," and dismissed her immediately after that. She didn't really believe that she was cured; she was still experiencing pain and some depression, but after she left Tiruvannamalai she began to feel a change for the better. She grew stronger and stronger and by the time she reached New York she felt much better. When she went to the hospital for tests, they found no cancer at all. She was completely healed of cancer and there was no need for the planned surgery or treatment. She had returned to New York a healthy person, and now she turned up two years later to tell him, "I am still alive because of you. I have no cancer problem."

"You see, I am able to stand here and talk to you because of the man who is laying down there. Don't you think that I must have at least a glimpse of his face when he is sick?" She had made her case quite well, and Dwarak Nath Reddy informed Yogi Ramsuratkumar of the visitors. He sat up immediately and said, "Let them come." The doctors from New York were extremely happy at this news and sat with Yogi Ramsuratkumar for some time. He gave them some *prasad* and then sent them off.

After seven or eight days in the garden, Yogi Ramsuratkumar was able to sit in a chair with the help of Jayarama. Devaki worked inside the house and provided hot milk and other refreshments for everyone, helping Sandiya in the kitchen and running errands as needed. There was a woman doctor who had attended to Yogi Ramsuratkumar at one point when he was ill at Sannadhi Street, but once Dr. Radhakrishnan took over, the beggar would have nothing to do with any other doctors. He told Dwarak Nath Reddy, "You tell her that she can please go back, this beggar doesn't want to see her." Once he was under the care of a doctor, he wouldn't allow another doctor even to enter, but clearly he had prophetically chosen Dr. Radhakrishnan months earlier, when they first met in April 1990.

During this time the marriage anniversary of Jayarama and his wife Bhuvaneswari came, but they were so caught up in the care of their master that they had both forgotten it. On that day a large garland was brought to Yogi Ramsuratkumar by one of his devotees; calling Jayarama and Bhuvaneswari to come and sit together at his side, he had the flower garland placed around the two of them, then asked them to sit together in his presence for several hours, after which Bhuvaneswari went home while Jayarama stayed to attend to Yogi Ramsuratkumar. It was an example of the selflessness of the guru: Yogi Ramsuratkumar was deeply aware of the needs of his devotees and served them, often putting them first, even when he himself was suffering or disabled with illness.

Once Yogi Ramsuratkumar was able to get up and sit in a chair, the doctor began to help him walk again with physical therapy. He was a seventy-two-year-old man who had been sleeping on the ground during pouring rains with a thin cotton spread beneath him for over a week. He had been through a grueling ordeal of severe illness, but he had an uncanny fortitude and an unfathomable inner strength. Nothing would get in the way of his work, and on the tenth day, he suddenly regained his strength: To the shock of everyone who was in attendance, he virtually disappeared from Kripala. It was a turn of events that no one expected. That morning he was lying down as usual under the mango tree. Dwarak Nath Reddy, Sandiya and Devaki were having breakfast when suddenly Yogi Ramsuratkumar's voice rang out from the garden, calling for Dwarak Nath Reddy. Immediately Mr. Reddy washed his hands and ran out.

"Dwarak Reddy, now this beggar will go back to his place," Yogi Ramsuratkumar said to his dear friend. Knowing the ways of the beggar, Mr. Reddy did not say a word in protest, but went to get the car ready. Within five minutes the beggar was gone.

"Hey, your Swami is walking, walking, walking, all around! I saw him with a group here, I saw him with a group there. He was running, he was walking," were the reports that came to the Kripala mansion in the days after Yogi Ramsuratkumar's illness. Devaki said, "You see, he had missed it so much—the open air, the streets, his walking . . . Hard it must have been for him to be bedridden!"

After Yogi Ramsuratkumar recovered from this bout of illness he was indeed back on the streets, much to the amazement of those who were close to him. The flow of visitors and devotees seeking blessings pressed in and continued to grow; Sannadhi Street overflowed with people. The queue for morning and evening "darshan" periods grew longer and longer, winding down the dirt street toward the temple.

In 1991 Rajalakshmi, the wife of N. Subramaniam (Mani), wanted to meet the beggar saint in Tiruvannamalai. She had heard about him the year before from a high official working in the Tamil Nadu government. She told Mani that she wanted to visit the saint, but he said no, he was not interested in saints and would only go to worship God at the temple.

"No, no no," she said, "we must go visit, at least once!" For two years she continued to ask Mani to go with her to meet the saint. Finally she said, "I am going whether you want to go or not." At this point Mani decided to go with her to the house on Sannadhi Street. At the time they were living in Chennai. Her two sons and daughter were all married, with lives of their own. It was a good time to explore new possibilities. When they arrived in Tiruvannamalai, Raji wanted to go to the ancient Shiva temple first, but didn't stay long. Arriving at the house, they joined the queue. One by one Yogi Ramsuratkumar called everyone else inside to have his darshan, but not Raji or Mani. They asked Yogi Ramsuratkumar's attendant, a boy who was standing near the grillwork door to the porch, "Why you are not sending us inside?"

"Only when Yogi says can I call. Otherwise I can't allow you to go in."

Raji told the boy, "Go and tell Yogi that we have come to see him." The boy went inside then came back out with the message, "They can come after they go to the temple." They had to go back to the temple, which was huge and would easily take two hours to see it all! They were also hungry, and Yogi Ramsuratkumar sent the message, "Tell them to go and eat something, then come back." They made their way to the temple and to a nearby hotel for some refreshments, then returned with some fruit to give as a gift.

After standing outside again for a long time, Yogi Ramsuratkumar called them inside. He asked their names, blessed them and received the *prasad* they had brought. He took the bag of fruit, put his hand inside it and looked at it, then gave it back to Raji, saying, "You take it as *prasad*." He blessed them and sent them away.

As they were leaving they saw a young Korean man, who had been standing outside, waiting to see Yogi Ramsuratkumar all day. He still hadn't been called. When Mani asked him how he had heard of the beggar saint, the boy said, "One Sadhu Rangarajan from Chennai. He told me about Yogi Ramsuratkumar, so I came." Returning to Chennai, Mani and Raji went to meet Rangarajan. At his home they saw a shrine and huge picture of Yogi Ramsuratkumar. They began to go to the *satsangs* that Rangarajan held, where they did Ramnam and sang the name of Yogi Ramsuratkumar.

The first time they went to Rangarajan's the *gayatri homa* was being performed.[2] The devotees were distributing small pocket-sized photographs of Yogi Ramsuratkumar, and a man told a story of being chased on the street by a cow. The cow charged against him with its horns, but the horns of the cow happened to hit his body where the photograph of Yogi Ramsuratkumar was kept in his pocket. Instead of piercing the man's chest, the cow's horns actually broke! After the *satsang* Mani and Raji discussed this story with some disbelief, saying, "How can we believe that the horn was broken . . . we have faith in Yogi Ramsuratkumar, but this is too much, no? A cow chasing a man, and broken horns!" But they each kept a photograph.

A few days later, in November 1992 Raji had gone with Sadhu Rangarajan to Tiruvannamalai to see Yogi Ramsuratkumar. Mani was traveling elsewhere with his sister, brother-in-law and their child when the driver of the car lost control and the car spun off the highway and rolled four or five times. At the very moment the accident occurred, Raji was sitting with Yogi Ramsuratkumar, who was asking many questions about Mani: "Where has he gone? Why did he not come?" and so on.

Given the severity of the accident, it was a miracle that no one was injured or killed. When the car began to careen off the road and tumble, Mani put his hand over the pocket of his shirt, where the picture of Yogi Ramsuratkumar was kept; he was convinced that it was his remembrance of Yogi Ramsuratkumar that saved their lives. After this incident Mani and Raji realized that the outrageous tale of the broken cow's horns was not just the story of a fanciful or romantic imagination. Mani said later to Raji, "This is a real thing. We could have all been killed, and this was prevented by Bhagawan." Their doubts resolved, from then on their lives were devoted entirely to Yogi Ramsuratkumar.

2 Homa (offering): a ritual sacrificial offering involving the ancient *gayatri* mantra.

In late November 1991 Lee Lozowick and nine of his men students traveled to India to attend the Jayanthi Day celebration at the Manthralayam in Kanimadam, and then went to Anandashram for a short visit. Finally, and most importantly, they headed east to Tiruvannamalai to spend three days with Yogi Ramsuratkumar.

Arriving at the house on Sannadhi Street after a fifteen-hour train ride, the men sat in the lane and waited, gazing off toward the massive stone *gopurams* of the Shiva temple. Lee greeted Perumal, who was standing outside near the steps to the *mandapam* where Yogi Ramsuratkumar's burlap bags of precious things were carefully stored. Immediately a young boy called Lee inside while the rest of the men sat and waited. They watched a lazy cow meander down the lane, stopping to eat a banana leaf plate that had been thrown to the side of the street in the piles of garbage. Across the street the brass market was in full motion, with artisans banging on bronze pots and people walking back and forth, coming and going from the bustling bazaar.

Over an hour passed quickly by, and then they were invited inside. They threaded their way through the dozen or so people who were packed into the verandah around Yogi Ramsuratkumar, where he sat with Lee. For twenty minutes there was nothing but the powerful silence of his darshan space, while he sat and smoked. Suddenly Yogi Ramsuratkumar got up, went inside the house and came back with his fan, stick and coconut bowl. Curiously, he walked in a circle around Lee and his students; the men sat in awe as he continued to circle their group seven times before he returned to his seat by the door next to Lee. His left hand worked automatically, as if he was passing a *japa mala* through his fingers, while in his right hand he raised the fan, stick and bowl, as if to conduct blessings with them from the supernal spheres. His face was a study in concentration, his brow knitting as though in pain. He got up again and circled the group, four, five, six, seven times.

Lee had given Yogi Ramsuratkumar a pile of gifts he and the men had received from various hosts while traveling in southern India. These Yogi Ramsuratkumar looked at then handed back to Lee, saying with a laugh, "You can take these back with you."

That afternoon V. Ganeshan arrived, and along with some other devotees, sat on the verandah with Yogi Ramsuratkumar, who still sat beside Lee and his Western guests. Greeting Ganeshan warmly, he introduced him to Lee.

"Ganeshan, have you read any of Lee's books?" he asked.

"No, Swami, but I have seen a copy of a *Tawagoto* from Lee's community. It was all about you, Swami," Ganeshan answered with a smile.

"Oh, God!" Yogi Ramsuratkumar smiled broadly and covered his face with his hand in embarrassment. His movements were imbued with an indescribable charm—no one could communicate with ordinary gesture like the beggar saint. When Yogi Ramsuratkumar asked who had written about him, Lee answered, "Vijay," who happened to be sitting there. Vijay had talked with Lee earlier about writing a biography of Yogi Ramsuratkumar, and now Lee broached the question with the beggar.

"Vijay would like to write a book about you, a biography," Lee began.

"Oh no," Yogi Ramsuratkumar exclaimed, "no biography of this dirty sinner. You shouldn't write about this beggar, this dirty sinner! This dirty sinner's past is so dirty—there is so much dirt. There is nothing to gain by digging up the past." A long conversation ensued, in which the men attempted to convince him that a biography could be a good thing. Vijay talked about how important it would be for people to know more about Yogi Ramsuratkumar's life and his teaching. Others chimed in while Lee sat and listened.

"Don't you think it would be valuable for people to realize that out of the mud grows a lotus flower?" Clint asked. Yogi Ramsuratkumar turned to Lee with a child-like look of delight and surprise on his face.

"Did you hear what he called me? A lotus flower!" Then he laughed and laughed.

Yogi Ramsuratkumar then made his position crystal clear. He said that too often people write about saints and masters and others who inspire us, but they feel that, in the interest of a relative "truth," they need to dredge up every bit of information that can be found. Too often these facts serve only to disillusion rather than inspire, whereas the lives of the saints should solely inspire and uplift people. Yogi Ramsuratkumar said that he had read many biographies that had tainted the master's brilliance; he had found one about Ramana Maharshi particularly disturbing. It had upset people and turned them away from the path. To cast shadows upon the light of the master's life was a great disservice. He said, "Every life has some light and some dark in it. If the light outweighs the dark, then we should only see the light and forget about the dark."

Therefore, he said that he felt the so-called "dirt" should always be omitted when writing about saints and other inspirational characters; only praise should be written, and only that which would uplift and encourage others toward God. The beggar was in an unusually talkative mood, and his teaching in this regard went on for a long time; it was the most animated conversation of the day.

"If you must write only about dirt," he said finally, "please do it after this beggar passes!"

The next day Lee received word that Yogi Ramsuratkumar was on his way to Ganeshan's house; a taxi would soon arrive to take Lee and the men in two trips to join him. Lee and the first group of men arrived at ten a.m. Soon they were all settled into the porch with Yogi Ramsuratkumar for eight hours of darshan. Ganeshan, his friend Anuradha and Jayarama were present also, and attended to Yogi Ramsuratkumar throughout the day, providing whatever he needed. Lee was seated to the immediate right of Yogi Ramsuratkumar against the half wall of the porch, their hands intertwined, while the nine men sat in a half-moon circle around them.

Yogi Ramsuratkumar often began conversations by first addressing Jayarama, but this time he looked directly at Lee and asked, "What is *rock and roll*?" He enunciated each word exactly, then asked if musical instruments were necessary for rock & roll, wondering if a demonstration was possible.

Lee had written Yogi Ramsuratkumar about the rock & roll band he had started in his community of students in Arizona. The band first performed in 1986 as a playful one time event, but in 1987 it became a serious project and by 1988 they were recording albums of original music, lyrics written by Lee and music composed by Lee's students.

Now the rock band had become a major enterprise of the Hohm Community, playing gigs in the States and touring Germany every year since 1989.

"Which of these friends are in the band?" he asked. Lee answered that three of the men there on this day—Stan Hitson, Matthew Files and Steve Ball—were in the band. The beggar turned to Ganeshan, Anuradha and Jayarama.

"Have you ever seen or heard rock and roll?" he asked them with great curiosity and an astounding innocence. They answered that, yes, they knew of it. Anuradha had seen it in the movies, and Jayarama had heard it on the radio. Yogi Ramsuratkumar found all this very charming, and laughed merrily at the idea that Lee was performing rock and roll—it was, after all, a very unusual way for a guru to teach, but the beggar saint seemed to simply marvel in great amusement at the idea of such a thing. Throughout the day he made a dozen humorous references to how Lee was a writer, a singer, *and* a guru. He was captivated by such a circumstance. Once or twice he hinted that he wanted to hear the band, on a cassette tape, or live, in person.

"Do you dance to this rock and roll?" he asked the men with a mischievous smile on his face. The men answer yes and shifted uneasily in their seats, hoping that they would not be asked to demonstrate the dancing without the music. Yogi Ramsuratkumar looked up at the green expanse of Mount Arunachala and laughed. He gestured toward the holy mountain.

"That rock is not rolling!" He collapsed into hysterical laughter and gave Lee's leg several hard but affectionate slaps with his hand.

When at midday a delicious vegetarian lunch was served, Yogi Ramsuratkumar looked over at Vijay then turned to Lee and asked, "Does Vijay like fish?"

"Vijay likes all food," Lee responded.

"I don't like lime pickles," Vijay laughed.

"Lime pickles are vegetarian," Yogi Ramsuratkumar smiled with a twinkle in his eyes. Thus began a conversation that ended with an instruction to Vijay to eat a strictly vegetarian diet—no meat, fish or eggs—for "one or two years."

"Swami takes what you like and gives what you don't like," Anuradha commented with a smile, enjoying the moment as she served the lime pickles with the meal.

After lunch Yogi Ramsuratkumar walked out in the garden for a while, hand in hand with Ganeshan. Walking back to the verandah, he brought two flowers and gave them to Lee. A few minutes later he gave Lee the empty Charminar package that had contained the cigarettes he had smoked that morning. It was a gift of *prasad*.

The Indian devotees all referred to Yogi Ramsuratkumar as "Swami," a nickname that carried great affection and was very attractive in its inference of intimacy. When Vijay said, "Swami, can I ask you a question?" Yogi Ramsuratkumar looked at him quizzically.

"Why do you call this beggar a swami? I am a beggar. Call me 'Beggar,' not 'Swami'!"

At one point Anuradha's sister, Sandhya, came in to have the beggar's darshan. She bowed, sitting on her knees before him and touching his feet.

"What can this beggar do for you?" he asked, a question that he phrased many times to his devotees. Perhaps this question was offered when he sensed that the person was troubled in some way. When she didn't respond he repeated the question again, then again, for a total of three times. A conversation ensued, and after talking with him for a while, she went into the house.

For most of the afternoon Yogi Ramsuratkumar sat hand in hand with Lee on the hard concrete floor of the porch, with only a thin woven blanket underneath them for relief. The hours stretched out endlessly as the sun moved through the sky. The long silences were punctuated from time to time with the beggar's spontaneous outbursts.

"Everywhere is Father! There is nothing to distract. All is Father, only Father. Father alone exists! All is peace, everywhere Father. Nothing else exists. Father alone. He alone exists. Nothing is separate, nothing isolated. Father is all!" These ecstatic words came out with the lilt of a joyous song, his voice rising and falling in the most extraordinary cadence and rhythm. He began to sing, "Sri Rama, Jaya Rama, Jaya Jaya Rama . . . Jaya Jaya Rama, Jaya Jaya Rama . . . Jaya Jaya Rama, Jaya Jaya Rama."

The tropical birds were singing brightly and loudly, flitting and flying about the garden, and they captured the yogi's attention. A black raven cawed and crowed loudly from its nearby perch. At the raucous call of the raven, Yogi Ramsuratkumar looked up at the bird and said, "Do you hear the song of that friend? That friend's song is so much more beautiful than this poor beggar's song!"

After a while Yogi Ramsuratkumar began to ask Lee many questions about his ashram in Arizona: how many people lived there; how many married couples were there; how many children were there; was there a school for the children; were any of the school teachers there, and so on. He wanted to know what time it was at the ashram in Arizona at that moment. In these questions he seemed to be creating a visual picture of Lee's ashram to align the forces of his blessings with the actual place and people. It was as if he was locating the ashram in time and space, becoming one with it in the temporal realm as well as in the eternal realm.

"Do you have a prayer on your ashram?" Yogi Ramsuratkumar asked Lee, who turned to Matthew and signaled for him to say the prayer that was always said before meals. With a slight gesture of his hand Yogi Ramsuratkumar indicated that Matthew should sit on the ground right in front of him. Seated very close to the beggar, Matthew began. When he got to the phrase, "Let us be in your heart, and annihilated in love," Yogi Ramsuratkumar stopped the recitation.

"What? What does that mean?" he looked at Matthew. "Say it again," he asked.

Matthew repeated the phrase until Yogi Ramsuratkumar understood that the word was "annihilated," then he asked him to repeat the whole prayer again. This time when Matthew got to the phrase, "All this is Yours," Yogi Ramsuratkumar interrupted again, blurting out like an excited child, "See! See! I was right! It says right there in the prayer, all this is my Father's blessing! Everything is Father's! All is Father's blessing!" His words were full blown with ecstasy and he beamed at the men, his eyes dancing with delight. He asked Matthew to repeat the prayer another four times before he was fully satisfied and

Matthew went back to his seat.

Yogi Ramsuratkumar's avid interest in the Arizona ashram continued as the conversation flowed along. At one point he relayed that at the Sri Aurobindo ashram thirteen tons of wheat are used each month. During this exchange Yogi Ramsuratkumar's right hand was entwined with Lee's left, and with his left hand he gently pinched the fleshy parts of Lee's hand.

"Is he cooked yet?" Anuradha asked humorously as she watched the master's play with his American devotee. Characteristically, the beggar did not answer the question, but simply said, "He is knowing," meaning, "Lee knows." He continued to stroke Lee's hand and arm, often looking deeply at Lee, who sat with his eyes focused on the master, saying very little, speaking only when he was spoken to.

"How do they manage such an ashram?" Yogi Ramsuratkumar wondered, then he spoke about how Sri Aurobindo wasn't interested in poverty, but wealth. He reflected, "Use all wealth for divine purposes!" It seemed he was further instructing Lee directly in relation to his work with students. He began to sing a chant to Sri Aurobindo, followed by telling a story about Lord Rama.

Turning his eyes to Lee, he asked, "When did you first see this beggar?" Lee answered that he first met him when he came to India in 1976 and 1979.

"This beggar only remembers 1986. How could he forget Mr. Lee's great *lila*?" He smiled, referring to Lee sitting in the sun for five hours on Sannadhi Street after being sent away. He turned to Jayarama.

"Jayarama! This beggar died in 1952 at the lotus feet of my master, Swami Ramdas! After this, Father alone remains here. Nothing else. Jayarama, Ramdas killed this beggar in 1952. Finished! It was not by this beggar's wish. Ramdas did it by force."

As the sun went down the sky darkened with rain clouds. A soft breeze rustled through the trees in the garden. The sweetness and peace of the moment expanded until the whole world seemed contained in the songs of the birds. It seemed that the old beggar, who listened so tenderly to their warblings as the wind caressed the lush foliage, was the very cause of the beauty and grandeur that unfurled in the silent underpinnings beneath their songs.

Yogi Ramsuratkumar sat holding hands with Lee, and for a few minutes rested his head on Lee's shoulder. His face became sublime and peaceful, and he looked up once or twice into Lee's face to gaze at him, then rested his head again on the shoulder. Not one to demonstrate his feelings or affection easily, for a brief moment Lee pressed his left cheek against the beggar's head, returning the affection with an embarrassed smile, then returning to his usual mode of simply receiving whatever the master offered.

"Jayarama! Did the sun set?" Yogi Ramsuratkumar asked.

"Yes, Swami," Jayarama answered.

"Oh God! This beggar is too late!" he exclaimed dramatically, then fell into a fit of rollicking, whole-body laughter, slapping Lee's arm and thigh several times and then pounding him on the back.

"It is all my Father's blessing," he said, summing up the day. "Everything is Father."

After a short pause he spoke again, "Our American friends are leaving," he said to no one in particular, as if musing to himself, "and we don't know when we will see them again." He repeated this three or four times, then stood up and walked toward the car that waited to take him back to Sannadhi Street. He turned and looked at Lee, as if every particle of his attention was concentrated into that gaze. His right hand moved in a slow sweeping motion, an arc of benediction. Suddenly he stopped, looked right and left to take in the whole group, bowed and began to laugh in his marvelously contagious way, and everyone else began to laugh with him. With that, the visit was brought to a close as Yogi Ramsuratkumar got into the car and it drove away.

In 1992 Perumal had told Ramamoorthy about a woman who wanted to donate some land to Yogi Ramsuratkumar for an ashram; she was prepared to sign over the deed in his name. Ramamoorthy's fortune was tied up in his family business, but he talked with a friend who had some money and they thought perhaps they could manage such a project. He wrote a letter explaining all this to Perumal, in care of Yogi Ramsuratkumar, Sannadhi Street, Tiruvannamalai. When the letter arrived, Yogi Ramsuratkumar called Perumal.

"Perumal . . . you have got a letter from Ramamoorthy. You open it and read it." Perumal read the letter to him and he said, "Who is that lady?" Perumal explained who she was.

"Where is that land?"

Perumal answered, "It is beyond the town . . . on the outskirts of the city."

"Not that land!" he snapped.

Even though their hopes for that property were dashed, they still felt that Swamiji might be open to another piece of land, but the next time Ramamoorthy went to see Yogi Ramsuratkumar, he said, "Ramamoorthy, ashram is a big problem. It means a big problem. Not now. You go and do your duty." At the same time that Yogi Ramsuratkumar was clearly saying that the time wasn't yet right, Ramamoorthy felt that he was also pointing out that his character, skills and disposition was not quite right for the job of spearheading the effort to find land. Yogi Ramsuratkumar had an instinct for knowing who was best at different jobs, and he was always adamant that the right person belonged with the job. Really it was common sense: he knew that only a plumber could lay the pipes, the electrician should do the electrical wiring and the mason should build the brick walls. In this case, it was Janarthanan who stepped forward to fulfill the task of finding the land.

"This beggar doesn't need any ashram," Yogi Ramsuratkumar said once again when Janarthanan broached the ongoing issue of building an ashram.

"But Swamiji, the devotees are standing in the hot sun and out in the rain. We should do something for them, Swami," Janarthanan pleaded.

"No!" Yogi Ramsuratkumar almost shouted, and stopped talking to Janarthanan for the next several days. About a week later the beggar seemed to have reconsidered the situation, as he brought up the subject himself.

"If it is for the devotees who are suffering, then it is fine to build an ashram," he said, then added, "This beggar may or may not come there." Despite this last cautionary note—in other words, don't have any expectations at all about what the guru will or will not do—Janarthanan finally had permission to start the long process of collecting the money and searching for the right piece of land. It was January 1, 1993.

The next week Janarthanan invited Parthasarathy, Ragunath and Ramamoorthy to join him in the task. When Janarthanan asked Ramamoorthy to help, he said, "Alright, if Swamiji agrees," and in this way Ramamoorthy became involved after all. Yogi Ramsuratkumar made two stipulations on the land: it could not be between the road and Mt. Arunachala, and it should not be far away from town. During the search four or five pieces of land were rejected by him. The land had to be exactly right—each time Yogi Ramsuratkumar was driven by car to the land, and there he would sit and smoke and ponder the energetic matrix of the place.

One day he went to see a barren piece of land, just sand and shrubs and weeds with lots of rocks. He sat in the car and smoked in the burning sun. Suddenly he said, "Janarthanan, this place seems to be too hot! Let us go . . ."

When the word got out that Yogi Ramsuratkumar had given his devotees permission to build an ashram, people began to come forward to donate land to the beggar saint. One merchant had thirty-two acres that he wanted to donate, but Yogi Ramsuratkumar said no. Two other people offered land, and again he said no. Finally Janarthanan came to understand that Yogi Ramsuratkumar wanted to pay for the land. The search for the right piece was in full swing.

Until the mid-eighties Tiruvannamalai had remained a village, but that was changing as the population of the town increased and rural India received into her heart the Western influences and visitors that began to flood into it. Evolution has a way of relentlessly exploiting all possibilities, and Tiruvannamalai was experiencing the effects of it as well. A similar process was at work in the life of the beggar saint; during the past four years a major change had occurred, one that had been coming for a long time. After the death of Mataji Krishnabai in 1989 and of Mother Mayee in 1992, Yogi Ramsuratkumar seemed almost catapulted into a major upscale in popularity and the demands of fame that would characterize the last decade of his work. It was a process of maturation that had to be accepted and met head on; not only did Yogi Ramsuratkumar allow Janarthanan to spearhead the efforts toward buying land and initiating the juggernaut of an ashram, but other significant changes were at hand.

The year 1993 proved to be a turning point in the destinies of many people, perhaps most of all, Yogi Ramsuratkumar. Part of the changes involved Devaki, who recalled this time period:

> I was coming and going from Salem to Tiruvannamalai, and I was

> very happy with life. I had found my guru, someone like Bhagawan, and my job was okay. I was with young children and teaching them was very nice for me. I was getting many holidays also, so I could always come and have his darshan and sit with him. Everything seemed perfect for me. I had no idea at all of leaving Salem or my job—in fact, I planned to get a Ph.D. So there I was very happy, very satisfied with life and I wasn't in for any change at all, just the Ph.D.
>
> One day I came to Sannadhi Street with a friend of mine and we were sitting there, and Bhagawan was just leaning on the wooden door, sitting on the small step [inside the porch]. A dog came and stood outside the house and looked up at Bhagawan. It was just standing there for quite some time, looking up at Bhagawan. Then he turned to me and said, "You see that dog there?"
>
> "Yes Bhagawan," I said.
>
> "You see, this dog comes and goes, this dog comes for food and then it goes away. This beggar would like this dog to be here all the time, but it comes and goes. It gets some food and is satisfied and happy with it, and then it turns away. But this beggar would like this dog to be here."

Yogi Ramsuratkumar then let the dog inside and fed it. After that the dog would come around more often, looking for food and often sitting very close to Bhagawan. A week or so later Devaki was visiting again with another friend, and Bhagawan had just given Devaki and her friend a piece of chapatti. The dog was sitting there watching them eat, and when Bhagawan went inside the house for a few minutes, Devaki's friend gave the dog a piece of chapatti. Seeing this, a discussion ensued between the two friends as to whether Devaki should also give some chapatti to the dog. Devaki chose not to because Bhagawan had given the chapatti to her, and it was *prasad*. She reasoned, "Bhagavan knows best—he has given it to me, so only I must eat it." Her friend saw it differently, and they discussed it back and forth for a while. Staying with her first response, Devaki decided not to give any chapatti to the dog and ate the whole thing herself, but afterward she began to have doubts. For some reason, the presence of the dog had managed to stir up all these considerations.

Soon Yogi Ramsuratkumar came back out and picked up the conversation where he had left it. Devaki was still wondering if she had done the right thing when the dog suddenly moved to sit beside her. Spreading himself out on her sari, the dog snapped a little and then went to sleep. It was strange that the dog would come to Devaki—someone who didn't like dogs, didn't feed it food, and was in fact a little afraid of it. The significance of Yogi Ramsuratkumar's earlier comments to Devaki about the dog, in which he used the dog as a symbol to make a teaching, became clear to her as Devaki further considered her obsession with the dog and its strange behavior:

> When the guru gives something, we have to do exactly what he

> says—not being impertinent, not assuming that the role of a guru is a caretaker—because it's all about the guru's word. Our business is only to do what he says and leave the rest to him, not to organize things where we are. When Bhagawan said, "This dog comes and goes and I would like this dog to stay there all the time, but it takes food and goes away," he meant me. Very little he spoke, very little actually happened there, but I learned so much. He was speaking cryptically when he said, "I would like this dog to stay."
>
> As it happened, after I went back to Salem I began to think, "Oh, maybe I should come to Tiruvannamalai." This thought began to take root in me, and it was a confirmation that the dog came next to me, touching my sari and going to sleep. But at that time I had absolutely no idea—not even the wildest of my imaginations or dreams—that Bhagawan would come to live with us at Sudama. This is only to give an example of how he worked. This is just one of the miracles of so many. But this was a very important thing for me—you see it decided the whole course of my life.

Since 1990 Devaki had been keeping Yogi Ramsuratkumar's empty cigarette boxes, feeling that they were imbued with spiritual force. At Sannadhi Street he would sometimes toss them to her after he took the last cigarette. Devaki recalled:

> How it began to happen was once after smoking, after the box was emptied, he took out the gold paper wrapper and made it into a clump, then he just threw that clump towards the door. It fell before me, and I took it immediately, before anyone else took it. I kept it safely because it had come from Swami's hand and it was used by Swami. I was so happy that he threw it there and I picked it up! He watched me like that, and the next time it happened he held it in my hand and I was looking at him. I was thinking that I didn't know what it meant, what [significance] it carried. I thought it was an empty cigarette box, a relic of Swami and I would keep it safely—that was all that mattered to me—but the cigarette box meant work, Father's work. I had longed for that without knowing what it stood for. So I was longing for that and praying and hoping that he would give it to me.
>
> Once he had given me a cigarette box and by some stupidity I left it there in his place and went back to Sudama. Then I suddenly remembered I had left the cigarette box there. Immediately I rushed to Ramanashram gate and took an auto, went all the way to his place. I stood outside, but I was frightened. You see, normally he wouldn't open the gates a second time to anybody, but he sent Sashi to find out why Devaki was standing outside. When I said I had left my cigarette box, he asked Sashi to open the door and he called me inside. He blessed me so much! He said, "See,

> you people—see? She has left her cigarette box, she is so mad like this beggar, she has come all the way to pick up a cigarette box."
>
> Then he gave that cigarette box to me a second time, and he blessed me nicely, and packed me off immediately. Just when I was beginning to hope that he might make me sit there for some time, he said "You can go." He wouldn't indulge anybody unnecessarily, if it is purposeless—no he wouldn't.

Between 1990 and 1993 Devaki had been coming to Tiruvannamalai regularly with Rajalakshmi, a colleague in the physics department, her sister Vijayakka and Vijayalakshmi. With the help of Dwarak Nath Reddy, they had rented some rooms where they could stay during their frequent visits, which Yogi Ramsuratkumar aptly named "Sudama," after the childhood friend of Lord Krishna. There the four women, Devaki, Vijayalakshmi, Rajalakshmi and Vijayakka, began to cook breakfast and lunch for Yogi Ramsuratkumar and his devotees; thus a "nucleus" of service was formed.[3] The formation of this group, with which Yogi Ramsuratkumar began to work very closely, had its precedent in the three men, Murugeshan, Parthasarathy and Shivashankara, who had been such a primary part of the beggar's work years before.

At one point Yogi Ramsuratkumar commented on the women's quarters, "This house is so small. When this beggar comes he wants to bring friends." So the four women began to look for a piece of residential property near the house of Jayarama—something permanent and more spacious where they could live and where Bhagawan, as they called Yogi Ramsuratkumar, could be served whenever he chose to gather there with devotees for darshan or an informal satsang. A few months later property was found and a house was built very close to the Kripala mansion, not far from Ramanashram, for this purpose. On November 1, 1992 the Sudama house, as it was called, was ready for the women to occupy it and the *garha pravesam*—the tradition ritual ceremony for entering a house—was conducted and attended by numerous devotees.

The day of the *garha pravesam* there was a gooseberry sapling, called *amlaka* in Sanskrit and *nellikkai* in Tamil—one tender, small plant—brought as a gift by Rajeswari's son, who had a huge farm in Tuticorin. The *amlaka* is a particular type of gooseberry that produces a bitter fruit the size of a lemon; it is often simply called *amla*, which means sour or acrid, because of its taste. Yogi Ramsuratkumar was extremely fond of these fruits, and often told people that the ancient *rishis* ate nothing but *amlaka* when they went deep into the forest for meditation. For months and even years the *rishis* survived on these gooseberries, which supplied all the vitamins and minerals they needed. Beyond that, these gooseberries had unusual qualities of a particular spiritual value. Yogi Ramsuratkumar often said that the *amlaka* was not only an elixir for all ills, but a general tonic for the whole body. It could be taken as a juice, eaten raw, peeled and eaten, cooked and so on; regardless of the form, it was good as a tonic to strengthen the immune system, and it

3 Vijayalakshmi, *Waves of Love*, p. 55.

was good for the brain; for this reason the ancient *rishis* used it to get deeper into meditation and also to maintain the body for the strenuous undertaking of *tapas*.

Since Yogi Ramsuratkumar was a great champion of the *amlaka*, it was only fitting that Rajeshwari's son offered the tree as a gift for Sudama house. Having come to Sudama house for the *garha prevasam*, Yogi Ramsuratkumar planted the *amlaka* himself on that auspicious day. A deep hole was dug and Anjaneyalu brought the seedling in its pot and helped with the planting, then Yogi Ramsuratkumar gave the plant its first watering with his own hand. It was another symbolic act, in which he infused the soil, the tree and the house with divine purpose. At this time the Sudama House was used only when the four women came to Tiruvannamalai to see Yogi Ramsuratkumar, and they did not stay there permanently.

On May 10, 1993 several devotees were gathered in the afternoon outside the gate at Sannadhi Street and were called in, one after another, to sit with Yogi Ramsuratkumar. V. Ganeshan was there as well as Devaki and several others. Bhagawan brought out four poems that had just arrived by mail from Lee Lozowick in the States, and he asked Ganeshan to read them loudly. Yogi Ramsuratkumar had been collecting Lee's poems for a long time, and had asked Rangarjan to organize them and publish them in a book in Madras. The reading of the poems had become a part of the regular darshan with the beggar, and now that they were being published in Madras by Sister Nivedita Academy, there was a mood of excitement about the project. Devaki wrote in her journal on that day:

> There were four poems—four beautiful poems. I broke into tears. Bhagawan turned to me with a smile and commented, "For Devaki also, this beggar is her pure delight." I smiled through the tears with folded hands, gratefully. Bhagawan was absolutely delighted with those poems.
>
> Bhagawan said, "Devaki will read the book again and again, when it comes out in the form of a book." I nodded humbly and happily.
>
> "This beggar would like to hear it all the twenty-four hours," Bhagawan said, and smiled again. Soon his face became serious and he began to reminisce. He said, "When he (Mr. Lee) came a second time, this beggar went to the gate and said, 'You have seen this beggar once. Why do you come here again and again?' This beggar said like this, not knowing this great man. Next time, he sent his wife and children. This beggar asked them where he was," he said with a break in his voice. "He was sitting outside in the hot sun on the iron bars." He paused and then said, "This beggar went to the gate and asked, 'Please come in.' But he said, 'No. I'm alright here.' " Saying this, Bhagawan's voice broke and there were tears again, this time more of them.
>
> All of us stared at Bhagawan, silently. For some of the devotees, this "bhava" mood of Bhagawan was new. A heavy silence followed. Then Bhagawan smiled once again to the relief of everyone around.

> Bhagawan said, "This beggar would like to hear these poems again and again. Devaki will read the book again and again. Ganesha, do you understand? You understand what he means in these songs?" Ganeshan smiled. Turning to me, he said, "Perhaps Devaki can understand . . ."
>
> Just when we were talking about the poems being published in the form of a book, Vivekanandam, the son of Sadhu Rangarjan, turned up with the information that Sadhu Rangarajan was on his way to Bhagawan. Bhagawan enquired of Rangarjan about the book and told him, "Come tomorrow morning since you have come with four other people."

Still torn between Salem and the new Sudama house and unaware of the extent to which she would become involved with Yogi Ramsuratkumar and his work, Devaki's longing to be with her guru reached a fevered peak. Realizing that it was "an unquenchable thirst," on July 15, 1993, with the permission of Yogi Ramsuratkumar himself, she took a voluntary retirement from her position at the university and came to live full time at Sudama house. She reached Tiruvannamalai at eleven-thirty at night with Rajalakshmi and Vijayakka, the other two "Sudama sisters." She was tired from the journey but also somewhat anxious, not knowing what would happen next. It was a time of momentous change, and in her heart was the prayer, "Bhagawan, I have left everything now. I don't want to own anything except you. And will you not welcome me; will you not give me some indication of welcome? Will you not receive me, Bhagawan?"

As they stepped down from the bus the loud horns blared out religious music from the Dakshinesmurti temple across the street. A huge crowd carrying gaslights was celebrating there, and the rousing ecstasy of a *puja* was underway. These horns are played at the most auspicious times—marriages, special ceremonies, birthday celebrations and such. A man came walking out of the group and approached Devaki, saying, "Amma, namaskar! Welcome to you! We are happy to see you." The man, a colleague of Devaki's who taught physics at a local college, explained that because it was an auspicious time, the hour marking the beginning of the month, they had just completed a *puja* at the Dakshinesmurti shrine, and were going to circumambulate the base of Mt. Arunachala. It was a royal welcome, an immediate answer to her prayer, and she felt the exchange was permeated with the all-pervading wisdom of Yogi Ramsuratkumar.[4]

The next morning when Devaki went to Sannadhi Street to the beggar's darshan, she was sitting somewhere behind the group of people. There were so many people she couldn't see him at all, nor could he see her. Yogi Ramsuratkumar called her up to sit by his side.

"Devaki, you have come!" he said.

Much to her surprise, he said, "When you stepped down on this soil yesterday night, what happened?" Her heart soared with happiness as he broke into peals of delighted laughter. She excitedly described to him the whole scene outside the Dakshineswar temple.

---

4 Ma Devaki, "The One Beyond the Reach of Thought," *Tattva Darsana*, 1994, pp. 26-27.

"Oh? He came and welcomed you!" he laughed heartily, speaking as if he already knew all about it.

Two weeks later Truman Caylor Wadlington was back in India. After a long hot five-hour bus ride, he arrived in Tiruvannamalai on August 3, 1993 to see Yogi Ramsuratkumar. It had been thirteen years since he had seen him.

Taking an auto rickshaw to Car Street, he arrived in the early afternoon and stopped at the flower bazaar near Yogi Ramsuratkumar's house, choosing a jasmine and rose garland. Making his way to 10 Sannadhi Street, he called softly at the door for the beggar at two-thirty. A young boy standing nearby told him to come back at four. Exhausted from the travel and the heat but determined to see the master, he bought some oranges and then climbed the stairs across the street from Yogi Ramsuratkumar's house and went to sit in the shade of the familiar *mandapam* above the temple car. Memories of many nights, sitting in the candlelight with Swami more than a decade before, flashed before Caylor's eyes. He wrote:

> As I put my things down and started to peel my orange, one of the many people there lying about on the rock-hewn floor rustled and rose to his feet. He stepped back when he saw me, startled at first. I turned. It was Perumal, sweet Perumal—Swami's companion of twenty years or more. He said my name, I said his. A formal *namaste* could not suffice, so I hugged him despite its undignified regard in this culture. We shared my oranges, sat and waited.
>
> Time passed. People began to line up at Yogi Ramsuratkumar's door as the four o'clock hour approached. I was well back in the line by the time I walked down the *mandapam* steps. Suddenly a frenzy ensued. Attendants opened the gate and ushered those nearest inside. I could not see him yet—the desiccated flower *malas* that were tied to the bars of the porch windows obscured all from view. Hundreds of them, dried, dusty and colorless. It conferred a sort of closed, dark, haunted appearance to the place.
>
> Finally I was ushered in. My heart literally skipped beats as I first caught a glimpse of him sitting in a corner, straight ahead from the door only ten feet away. Everyone was chanting his name. He looked smaller, more frail, but lighter in skin tone than I had ever seen him. He didn't seem to know who was there. His eyes were closed. His fingers were fumbling for a piece of sugar *prasad* in a bag at his feet. As I bent down one of the attendants stated my name out loud to him. He was startled. He struggled to open his eyes just to cognize my physical presence, took the

flowers from my hands and then put then over his own neck. As I bent down to touch his feet, I started to cry. My heart tumbled with a mixture of love for someone I hadn't seen in many years and confusion at how fast this was all happening. Some gesture in his hands seemed to urge me to move on. I said, "Swami it is so good to see you." He said nothing and did not even meet my eyes or touch me in any way.

The signal was clear. My confusion was put on hold. I stood and moved out of the way for the next in line. I was rather stupefied about that meeting for the rest of the day. After checking into the ashram, bathing, and going to bed, I realized I felt too sick to process it anymore. It was only when I awoke at four a.m. the next morning that I began to feel okay about it. It was so obvious that he was deeply immersed inside and wasn't able to pull out of that at a moment's whim.

The rest of that day was uneventful. Yogi Ramsuratkumar was away from his house in the morning and then didn't see anyone at his four o'clock darshan. I saw him get out of his car then, but he did not glance at me. The night was lit with a full moon. It was almost cool. The trees were magically fresh and windswept. I sat out on my veranda and listened to music. That night I dreamed: I was standing in the bazaar in the middle of the night. This was the place where Swami and everyone used to sit and sleep. It was our familiar haunt. I felt unable to find him, unable to go to his new abode. Just then he stepped round the corner and walked toward me a few slow, cautious paces. His hand was over his mouth. He did not speak, but his heart went out to me. I did not say anything either. As I began to cry I woke up.

I took an autorickshaw into town to see Swami and stood in line with the rest of the crowd till finally my turn came. I could see Ramsuratkumar was more animated, more outwardly focused. There were already a lot of people crowded into that small space, mostly women devotees singing the master's name. As I put my gift of a dozen bananas on his pile of fruit and flowers and kneeled down to touch his feet, a mixture of joy and sorrow welled up within me. Like in someone who was desperately lost for a long time and then is found. I couldn't contain my tears. They flowed and flowed for a long time.

Swami touched my back and asked me to sit against the wall just in front of him. He did not look me in the eyes but seemed to be gazing from time to time at my solar plexus area, and sometimes motioning with his hand—moving energy. My tears continued to stream forth. Others continued to file past one by one as He blessed them—saying "Rama"—and giving each a piece of rock candy, fruit, or flowers. Pretty soon my whole body was buzzing with energy. "Master, please shoot straight the sacred arrow of God's divine name into my heart so that I can never forget

Him." I felt like I had come home and now was safe, but I was afraid that upon leaving him I would lose my way.

Sitting in this flood of shakti, it seemed most clear to me that Yogi Ramsuratkumar was Arunachala. That Ramana Maharshi was Arunachala. That innumerable saints here had been vessels of that same great Force, and that Arunachala was—as legend has it—a kind of thunderous column of down-flooding light. From time to time Swami asked me or gestured for me to shift a few inches or feet in proximity to him.

People were continuing to file past one after the next and the ladies present continued to sing his name. I thought of Maharaji Neem Karoli's "ma's" or mothers. He was always surrounded by these women, mostly old or widowed, who loved him deeply, cooked for him, and so on. The Hindu ideal of female purity is not far off the mark in this environment. I thought of Ma Anandamayi—pure as mountain snow. To regard such women as other than mother, sister, or daughter seems a distortion.

I liked how Ramsuratkumar slapped certain people on the back. It seemed playful, loving. The master now was covered with garlands, maybe three or four huge ones. At one point someone presented him with a truly humongous one—perhaps ten or twelve feet long and maybe five inches thick. He asked that that person hang it on the windows with all the other old, desiccated and drying garlands. There had to be thousands of them. They were stacked at least three feet thick and along ten feet of barred window area. There was a lot of other debris piled up, including a delicately hand-painted plaque in memory of Kavikanta Ganapati Muni, a sage and scholar who lived here during Ramana Maharshi's time. Another fascinating physical feature of the space we were sitting in was the stunning hand carved—or shall I say "sculpted"—door into Swami's house. Awesome. It looked like it belonged in a temple itself. It must have been four or five inches thick and maybe only five and a half feet high, but the surrounding framework must have been carved a foot deep with temple motifs.

As time passed Ramsuratkumar seemed to wince or grimace from the discomfort of sitting for long hours. At least two and a half hours had passed and people were still coming. Finally, he dismissed us one by one. He sent me off with a slap on the back and a bundle of grapes and a pomegranate and apple. Outside, I stopped to take Perumal's hand warmly, laughingly in my own before heading back to the ashram.

Before stepping away two young Hindu people, obviously husband and wife, stopped me before I could get away. They were so sweet and innocent. They had read my book years ago and wanted to meet me. I was just charmed by their enthusiasm and sweetness. We talked about the book for a moment—that it was out of print. As I started to leave, Giridhar

> explained that today was a certain North Indian festival day. On this day, girls can choose some male friend to be her brother. Radha, his wife, asked me to be her brother. I agreed and she tied on my right wrist a little white medallion with Krishna and peacock feather at the center. The thought kept coming that I must hold fast to the divine name and let God and guru fashion of this what He wills. In the same way Yogi Ramsuratkumar used to say that his Father sculpted from rough-hewn rock—referring to himself, a beggar, a sinner—something glorious. Leave the sculpting to the Lord. Just hold fast to the name.

The next day Professor Rangarajan, author/publisher of *Tattva Darsana*, now dressed in the ochre robes of a sadhu, was visiting Yogi Ramsuratkumar with his wife, son and one other young man. They all sat directly in front of the beggar. His wife, Parvati, did not speak, but every time Yogi Ramsuratkumar got up to go and get something from the other room, she carefully swept up all the flower debris falling off his clothes, then tied them into small knots in her sari.

Rangarajan discussed the details of future publications of the magazine. As it turned out, Giridhar and Radha had, of their own accord and to Caylor's surprise, reprinted *Yogi Ramsuratkumar, The Godchild, Tiruvannamalai*. This had also been done without the permission of Yogi Ramsuratkumar, and he instructed Rangarajan to go outside and send them away. A scene ensued, with Radha shouting as she left, "Swamiji, I will love you forever!"

Later that afternoon Janarthanan, Ramamoorthy and some others who were making plans for the ashram arrived. Caylor wrote:

> At one point in the discussion—perhaps this was in the afternoon—the three "promoters" came. Swami stepped into the house for a brief five-minute powwow. They seem to come almost every day in their dark gray minivan. These are the people who are planning to build a future ashram. Yogi Ramsuratkumar was reading Lee Lozowick's poetry—though it's more correct to say that he was having us read it and re-read it. Very touching, high-quality stuff. This guy definitely reveres the ground Yogi Ramsuratkumar walks on.
>
> Then the direction of conversation shifted toward my early writing and how Yogi Ramsuratkumar asked me to help him in this way when facing a very oppressive situation here; how I had tried to decline because I feared my English wasn't up to the task. Also about how years later before the second printing I had campaigned with determination to pull out all the Theosophical stuff and how he refused to allow it. He praised me time and again, expressing his gratitude time and again. He wanted to make it clear to me—but maybe to everyone there as well—how he felt about the book and the work I'd done for him. He reminded all present that

> I was the first to use the term "The Godchild" in reference to him. That this name had been my one choice as the title for the book but that Yogi Ramsuratkumar had relegated this to position of subtitle under his name and above the word "Tiruvannamalai."

That afternoon during darshan at Sannadhi Street, Caylor was the first person to arrive and start the queue. He was moved by the sight of a local servant woman, who carefully swept the area in front of Yogi Ramsuratkumar's house, then watered down all the dust and painted a simple *yantra* with rice powder at the doorstep. A few others joined him, and suddenly they were summoned to sit with Yogi Ramsuratkumar sooner than expected, a little before four. The crowd formed quickly after that, and Devaki arrived to start the singing. For Caylor, it turned out to be an "afternoon of teaching":

> First, Yogi Ramsuratkumar asked Devaki to read a passage from some small book quoting from Papa Ramdas. It said something to the effect that as the *chela* meditates on the master's teaching he begins to acquire the characteristics of the teacher. Like the softness of heart that ensues is really the master's softness of heart. In this way, gradually the *chela* disappears and only the guru remains.
>
> Then he asked her to read an article from the *Mountain Path, Aradhana Issue*, 1993. I came to know later that this article was entitled "Papaji," by Sri Poonjaji. It was about this man's twenty-five years of ardent Krishna devotion and his awakening under the guidance of Ramana Maharshi. Toward the end he makes a strong point that it is not a question of having been a disciple of Ramana Maharshi, but of always being one. He states in effect that Punjaji totally vanished—only Maharshi remains.
>
> Certain passages really excited Yogi Ramsuratkumar, like that the guru never dies—the disciple vanishes, but the guru dwells in the heart of all forever. Swami drew parallels to his experience with Ramdas, saying that "only the Father exists." I could feel the master talking to me. I could feel his pull from within.

A few days later, after the drama of Radha and Giridhar came to an unpleasant head, Yogi Ramsuratkumar met with them—Radha in the morning and Giridhar in the afternoon. He blessed them and gave them the money they needed to go home. Later they told Caylor that they planned to go first to Kanchipuram where they would talk everything over with the Shankaracharya.

The next afternoon during darshan Caylor sat next to Yogi Ramsuratkumar and listened while a young man read some quotes from Swami Ramdas published in *Tattva Darsana*:

> In spiritual matters the best rules are those which are not made by others but self-imposed by the guru from within. A tree does not grow in

> the shade of another tree, but gets stunted. It can grow full only in the open. So also you must have a free and open atmosphere for your spiritual growth . . . .
>
> So get inspiration from saints, but do not think of taking shelter permanently in any ashram. Live alone in a free and open atmosphere. Then the God within will lead you. The indwelling God is none other than your guru who initiated you from outside as a human being. Guru is the immortal, all pervading spirit. Never look upon him as a mere person. If you develop this attitude from the beginning you will realize that the guru never dies.[5]

The new scene around the beggar saint was populated with a "throng of pilgrims passing by one-by-one for his darshan, his blessing, and leaving in their wake a mountain of fruit and flower gifts," as Caylor wrote, "In fact it's a fascinating parade of colorful people and circumstances in a furnace-like Zen intensity." Visitors now included people like Indian cinema stars and many strangers who were coming for the first time, as well as long-time devotees like Pon Kamaraj. There was a constant buzz going on among the Indian devotees about the new ashram, and one of the visitors was Chief Justice Arunachalam, who arrived one afternoon with an entourage of people from Madras who were engaged in the planning of the ashram. They spent an hour and a half with Yogi Ramsuratkumar while everyone else waited.

The next day, August 10, was Caylor's last visit with Yogi Ramsuratkumar. He had written a letter expressing his gratitude and devotion for everything that Yogi Ramsuratkumar had done for him and meant to him:

> And Your Noble Presence—having touched every cell of my being—I carry as a talisman within me. By the mere remembrance of Your Name, this Presence confers peace and safety in times of great urgency and need. Myself, my loved ones, and the distressed and dying patients who come to me for help are comforted. God's Grace is merciful.
>
> When I was just a boy in my twenties—so confused, so lost—it was You who first took me under Your wing. And it was Your tenderness and love that first began to heal my blind unfeeling heart. I can never forget the times You sweetly held my hand. Though decades have passed, these sweet memories are fresh. And these sweet memories—somehow painful but spiritually pure—grace this heart within with an invisible healing balm of Your sweet forgiveness to heal the broken hearts of others.
>
> I am giving this letter to Perumal—who I love and trust like my own brother. There is no more able messenger than he to convey my sacred message to my Master's hands—like as if to Lord Rama by way of trusty

5 Swami Ramdas "The Living Guru," *Tattva Darsana*, May-July 1993, p. 7.

Hanuman. Perumal can bring this to You in a private moment, whereas I cannot. In the group situation I didn't want to read this letter in front of all the others.

Tonight, as I write this, I suddenly realize I must be leaving soon. First to Madras, then to the north. I have long felt the pull to go to Varanasi ever since reading the poems of Kabir. After sister Diana died some years back, a fear began to grow in me that I might again neglect to express my heartfelt thanks to one of my spiritual parents before He died. But now having sat at Your feet, that fear is assuaged. In its place rests the assurance that "the Guru never dies." Thank you Yogi Ramsuratkumar. Forever, my heart is with You.

It was signed "Truman Caylor Wadlington." That day Caylor arrived at Sannadhi Street early with a flower garland in hand. Yogi Ramsuratkumar was sitting there reading a large Tamil book that he had had Devaki reading from days before. Caylor was content to stand and gaze at the mountain and the temple to one side, and the busy bazaar on Car Street on the other, until other devotees began to arrive and Yogi Ramsuratkumar started to call people in. Caylor was the first to go in; right away he told Yogi Ramsuratkumar that he would be leaving the next day, first for Madras and then north to Lucknow to visit Punjaji and then back to Austin, Texas. Yogi Ramsuratkumar listened patiently and then gave his blessings for Caylor to go.

He took a seat in a place where Yogi Ramsuratkumar had indicated he should sit, but when the other devotees came and took their places, the master asked Caylor to move and sit directly in front of him. Devaki, Vijayakka, Rajalakshmi and other devotees began to sing. After a while the conversation turned to the details of Caylor's travel plans. Yogi Ramsuratkumar again encouraged Caylor to stay at the Theosophical Society in Adyar while he was in Madras. They talked of mutual friends and acquaintances at the Theosophical Society, about the big banyan tree dying, and of Rukmini Devi's death. Yogi Ramsuratkumar asked Caylor if he still had a copy of *The Secret Doctrine* and he said, yes, he kept it in his meditation room at home in the States. Yogi Ramsuratkumar encouraged Caylor to go through the book one more time; it was an instruction that had remained the same throughout the years.

Again Yogi Ramsuratkumar brought up the fact that Caylor was the first person to use the term "The Godchild" in reference to him. Caylor had stated that it was, in fact, a direct translation of the name his mother gave him: Ramsurat. The next day Caylor left Tiruvannamalai with Yogi Ramsuratkumar's blessing. It was the last time he saw the Godchild of Tiruvannamalai in his physical form.

After a long, exacting search for the right piece of land, Agrahara Collai was found and procured. The land itself carried a mythical past: Ramana Maharshi mentioned in one of his books that near Ramanashram there was a place where people chanted the Vedas in ancient days, and the vibration of that still remained to this day on the property that was purchased for the Yogi Ramsuratkumar Ashram.

When the yogi first went to sit on the land it was barren, with nothing but small palms and shrubs dotting its sandy soil. The ground was so raw and rocky that no one wanted to walk barefoot on it, but Yogi Ramsuratkumar never wore shoes. He arrived at the land in the burning midday sun and walked out across the sand and through the scrubby growth. Looking out over the acres in the rainbow shimmer of the bright Indian sun he said, "Janarthanan, we will buy this land."

By the fall of 1993 the money was gathered for the ashram and the land was purchased. During the process of collecting the money for the land Yogi Ramsuratkumar worked very closely with the men who were managing the project. At every turn they found that he was one step ahead of them. Once a week they would come to him and report on the fundraising, but despite their best efforts, in the end it was Bhagawan himself who arranged for the money. As Ramamoorthy commented: "The final money was arranged by Bhagawan, not by us! Not by Ramamoorthy, not Janarthanan or Parthasarathy or Rajulu or anybody else. Every moment was made by him." Yogi Ramsuratkumar had his hand in every decision and every action that was required, including the registration of the deed and the correcting of last-minute mistakes.

"Janarthanan, you people take that registered deed to see Shivaramakrishna and read it before him." They went by car to Tirucoilur where Shivaramakrishnan—an older man who knew all the land registration procedures—lived. Reading the document with the experienced registrar, he soon interrupted, saying, "Stop! Stop! Instead of putting the 'seller' you have put the 'buyer'!" Ramamoorthy and Janarthanan recoiled in shock. It was the worst mistake that could be made in a deed! The document had been already registered, but somehow Yogi Ramsuratkumar knew that it needed to be checked over by Shivaramakrishnan. They came swiftly back to Tiruvannamalai and approached the registrar and explained the mistake. The registrar said, "It's a very good, very noble cause. You can type a new deed and bring it to me, and I will just glance at it; it's no problem." The deed was retyped, but to their chagrin, the same mistake was made again. After a third typing it was finally correct, and all was well.

By September the "Sudama sisters," as Yogi Ramsuratkumar called them, were established in Sudama house, only a few blocks away from where the new land for the ashram was located. There was tremendous excitement in the air as the devotees embarked on a major undertaking that opened their world with Yogi Ramsuratkumar to many possibilities. The new ashram was at the center of many conversations.

"This is going to be one of the most vibrant centers of the world," Bhagawan said, smiling. "It will be a most vibrant international center, this ashram." He repeated this sentence again and looked directly at Devaki with a smile, "This is going to be the most vibrant international center of spirituality . . . Devaki will make it so."

"Bhagawan, I don't understand what you are saying," Devaki said.

"This beggar is saying that Devaki will make it a most vibrant center, vibrant international center," he repeated again, still with the enigmatic edge.

Devaki remembered, "That was the first time I ever heard something like that—it was like a bombshell on my head! It was very typical of him; he would give you the most important news so casually that you wouldn't be at all prepared for it. I didn't know what to say. I suppose I was flabbergasted. I kept quiet and hung my head down. I was not sure whether he was making fun or saying it in all seriousness."

Three or four days after that Yogi Ramsuratkumar came to Sudama House and announced that everyone would go with him to the land where the ashram would be built. Someone grabbed a camera and they headed out down the lanes and toward the open fields, where the land was located. As the photographs were going to be taken Yogi Ramsuratkumar called to Devaki.

"Devaki, come and stand here next to me." Devaki obeyed and went to stand next to Yogi Ramsuratkumar and the photograph was taken. He told the photographer that he wanted the picture as soon as possible. Devaki thought it was strange, but she was happy that he had given her a chance to stand with him while the picture was taken. Two days later when the photos arrived Yogi Ramsuratkumar began to distribute them, giving a copy to Devaki and the Sudama sisters and to everyone who was present. Sashi, a young devotee of Yogi Ramsuratkumar, was there

"Sashi, do you see the picture? What do you think?'" he asked.

"Amma," was Sashi's straightforward and simple reply, meaning, "Mother," referring to how the photograph communicated Devaki's role to him.

After that Yogi Ramsuratkumar began to come to Sudama House very often at five o'clock in the morning. The women would hear the sound of the car, and rushing outside they would find Bhagawan right at the doorstep. Yogi Ramsuratkumar became a constant presence at Sudama House.

Again he asked Sashi, "Sashi, what do you think? You see her there with this beggar? What do you think?"

He said, "Like Swami Ramdas and Mataji Krishnabai, Swami." Then Bhagawan laughed. It was in that moment that the reality of the situation dawned on Devaki, but Yogi Ramsuratkumar never explained it all to her in a rational, linear way. Devaki was just discovering it right along with everyone else.

It became more obvious as, whenever Devaki was leaving Sannadhi Street, he often asked Sashi to fetch the driver to bring the car right to his doorstep; then Bhagawan himself would come out and instruct, "Devaki, you get into the auto." Then he would tell the auto driver, "Go straight to Sudama. This beggar doesn't want Devaki to stand around anywhere or do any shopping here and there. Go straight to Sudama." This ritual was repeated every time she left Sannadhi Street. At the time, his actions were a mystery to Devaki, who recalled, "I was thinking, 'My God, what care he is taking, that he should come up to the door, stand there and wave to me until the auto disappeared out of his sight.' And then one day soon after this announcement, he called for the car. Swami himself spoke to the driver, saying, 'I don't want Devaki to walk in the streets. I would like her to come in the auto and go back in the auto and not go anywhere in between. Every day you go at nine forty-five, pick her up and bring her over here.' " He had assumed total responsibility for Devaki's life, which had been subsumed and taken up in his work. Very soon he began to announce exactly that to his devotees at Sannadhi Street.

"Father wants Devaki for his work. My Father wants Devaki to help this beggar in Father's work," he said. Right away there were reactions; many people didn't like it—that their guru and the embodiment of God on earth should be associated with a woman in any way was scandalous to the conventional dogmatic point of view. Strong reactions were stirred up right from the beginning, but it was some months before all the devotees realized the major significance of the changes that were in the air.

In the fall of 1993 a formal registration of the ashram land took place and there was a public meeting attended by many devotees. It began at this time that during any formal functions or celebrations or during darshan at Sannadhi Street, Yogi Ramsuratkumar had Devaki come and sit beside him, and he instructed her to begin to take care of any service that was needed for his physical well being, such as lighting his cigarettes, preparing food, liquids, gooseberry tea or medicines for him, cleaning his ashtray, carrying his sacred objects and necessities when he requested and so on. These were jobs that had been previously reserved before for Jayarama or Swami Nathan; now, Yogi Ramsuratkumar instructed Devaki to take over all these forms of service to his person.

More and more of the devotees and friends who came for his darshan began to see Devaki seated beside the beggar. That autumn the headmaster of a local school asked Yogi Ramsuratkumar to attend a function at the school. Bhagawan sent word to Devaki at Sudama House. When she arrived at Sannadhi Street he said, "Devaki, let's go out." It was the first formal outing of Yogi Ramsuratkumar and Devaki, and they took off in the headmaster's car. Arriving at the school, Yogi Ramsuratkumar and Devaki were seated alongside the headmaster. Suddenly Bhagawan turned to Devaki and said, "Devaki you go and speak." Giving a technical lecture in physics in a classroom is quite different than speaking on behalf of the spiritual master, and Devaki had some trepidation, but Yogi Ramsuratkumar encouraged her.

"No, don't be afraid—you go and stand there, Father will speak through you," he counseled. She said a few sentences and then sat back down as quickly as possible.

Not long after this Yogi Ramsuratkumar took Devaki on another outing, this time to the marriage of the daughter of a devotee from Madras, who had come all the way to Tiruvannamalai for the marriage. Again Bhagawan asked Devaki to come to the house on Sannadhi Street, where they got into the car together in front of a crowd of devotees who all observed the unusual actions of the beggar saint. Devaki recalled humorously, "Even then it produced some static—that Bhagawan began to be seen publicly with a woman by his side and with a bottle of gooseberry water!"

Yogi Ramsuratkumar began to tell devotees who were prostrating to him that they could prostrate to Devaki as well, and he began to train Devaki in how to receive this, how to work, and how to bless others. Devaki found herself in a process of learning directly from Yogi Ramsuratkumar; part of that training was simply to endure the rigorous reality of living in such close proximity to Yogi Ramsuratkumar, whose energy alone was overwhelming. He rarely slept and kept odd hours. He required total spontaneity; anyone who lived with him had to be completely flexible and surrendered to his whim. There was no room for complaint or negative reactions. The demand to bear many different kinds of discomforts was immense, and as Devaki once commented, "It was not Brindavan, as people imagined." Instead it was incredibly hard work—an inexorable call to being nobody, having no personal needs or personal life of any kind, and dedicating every waking breath to one person: Yogi Ramsuratkumar, the Godchild.

In the fall of 1993 Yogi Ramsuratkumar spent most of his time at Sudama House. In November he fell ill again and it was then that it became apparent that he needed to be taken care of on a full-time basis, at least until he recovered. Devaki offered to move into the house on Sannadhi Street to care for him until he recovered, but he made the decision to move to the Sudama House, where he would reside permanently with Devaki and the Sudama sisters. This major change, which occurred on November 22, 1993, marked the formalization of a mandala—a spiritual family—that may have been coalescing subtly for a long time. Sudama House and the Sudama sisters were in effect a place of sanctuary and *seva* for the aging beggar. Their profound commitment to serve their guru created an energetic buffer from the crowds of people who were surging around him, but they also literally and symbolically represented the fundamental life force or *shakti*—the feminine aspect of the Divine. They became the dynamic source of a great deal of energy that was focused, directed and poured into his universal work.

Like many spiritual giants before him—Ramakrishna and Sarada Devi, Swami Ramdas and Mataji Krishnabai, Jesus and Mary, Sri Aurobindo and the Mother, Upasani Maharaj and Godavari Ma, Meher Baba and Mehera with the women's mandali, to name a few—Yogi Ramsuratkumar came to a point in his work where the feminine pole naturally came into manifestation. In one way this can be seen as an embodiment of a higher law: It is stated in many great esoteric traditions that the human soul is considered to be feminine in relation to the Divine. The feminine disposition in both man and woman in relationship to the Divine or Source of life is one in which the individual's total attention is turned in adoration toward the Godhead; the character of this adoration is devotional, ecstatic, receptive and surrendered, and is considered the highest possibility of the human being. It is a possibility that is embodied symbolically, and at best literally, in the female counterparts of many great spiritual masters in all traditions.

This model has its basis in Indian religious myth as well, where the gods are usually represented with their female counterparts, or *shaktis*: Krishna has his consort Radha and later his wife Rukmini as well as ten thousand other wives; Rama has his wife Sita; Vishnu has Lakshmi; Shiva has Parvati in many different forms, including Durga, Uma and Kali; Brahma has Sarasvati and so on. This is the symbolic representation of the fundamental polarities of life: the divine masculine and divine feminine forces, which in the ancient philosophical system of Samkhya is called *purusha* (the absolute or unmanifest Divine) and *prakriti* (the manifest Divine, or Nature). At the same time that

Yogi Ramsuratkumar and Hilda Charlton, Guru Purnima, July 1978.

Yogi Ramsuratkumar outside the Arunachalesvara Temple, 1980s.

Circa 1990.

Yogi Ramsuratkumar hugging the amla tree in the Reddy's garden at Kripala. Circa 1990.

Yogi Ramsuratkumar standing near the house on Sannadhi Street, 1980s. The temple Gopuram and Arunachala in background.

Yogi Ramsuratkumar and Lee Lozowick on the ghat by the temple pool, December 1988.

Lee Lozowick (third from left) and Pon Kamaraj (fifth from right, second row) with devotees, celebrating the *jayanthi* of Yogi Ramsuratkumar in south India, December 1989.

Yogi Ramsuratkumar reading *Guru's Grace* by Mataji Krishnabai in the garden at Kripala. Circa 1990.

Yogi Ramsuratkumar with Dwarak Nath Reddy, Sandiya Reddy and family in the garden at Kripala. Circa 1990.

Yogi Ramsuratkumar with Dr. Radhakrishnan. Circa 1990.

Yogi Ramsuratkumar in the garden at Kripala. Circa 1990.

Mount Arunachala. (Photo courtesy of Ramanashram.)

the divinity of Yogi Ramsuratkumar and his universal work was being brought from the formless realm into incarnation in the form of an ashram, so was it also brought further into manifestation through Devaki and the "mothers" of Sudama House, who faithfully strived toward the full realization of adoration of the Divine in the form of their *ishta devata*, or chosen deity—Yogi Ramsuratkumar. Over time their lives of selfless surrender would become artifacts, or physical embodiments, of the master's work, his blessing power and his legacy to the world.

The move to Sudama House in late November coincided with Lee Lozowick's trip to see Yogi Ramsuratkumar that year. When Lee arrived in Madras on November 27, 1993, he and his party were taken to the house of Sadhu Rangarajan, who immediately gave him the brand-new book, *Poems of a Broken Heart*. Lee began to pass copies out to the nine students who had accompanied him to India that year—much to our surprise.

It was my first trip to India, and I was stunned when Lee handed me the small paperback with Yogi Ramsuratkumar's picture in color on the front and back. Gingerly opening it, the poems started leaping off the page and into my heart; they were the divine messengers that set the mood for the next three weeks.

No one in the States had any idea that Lee was writing poetry on a regular basis and sending it to his master in India. It had been a very well-kept secret; even Radha, who had known Lee since 1973 and had met Yogi Ramsuratkumar with him in 1977 and 1979, was completely taken aback by the poetry. She wrote in her journal during the trip, "I had no idea Lee could write poetry like that."

Nor had I read anything quite like this poetry, although it was reminiscent of the great devotional poets Ramprasad Sen, Mirabai and Andal. To our great surprise, our teacher's interior experience opened up before our eyes: so this was how Lee felt about his own master! It was devotional poetry with a twist—most of the poems were written in a classic form that Rangarajan described as *nindaa stuti*, or "ironical praise," but many of them were pure proclamations of love and longing, written from a "son" to his "Father."

> Oh appa, appa
>   cries Your Foolish son
> let me drown
>   in the Ocean of Your Love
> in That Ocean
>   lee wants no life raft
> let Your Waves of Madness
>   wash over me
> let Your Current of Bliss
>   sing me Your Name forever

Oh appa, appa, Yogi Ramsuratkumar
Your son knows no-One but You.[6]

Ten Americans sat on the floor together in the small shrine room at Rangarajan's Madras home with the new poetry books in hand, quietly turning the pages and reading the poems. Our attention was fully captured by this new turn of events, and sitting in the spiritually potent shrine room, with its many beautiful photographs of Yogi Ramsuratkumar and Mother Mayee, as well as other saints we didn't recognize, the poems were brought to life even more. There were many bronze statues of deities and implements for *puja* as well: *arati* lamps, bowls for water, incense, ghee, flowers. As the day progressed Rangarajan invoked the presence of Yogi Ramsuratkumar with each *puja* that he performed, as well as with the stories he told about Yogi Ramsuratkumar and Mother Mayee.

Rangarajan also informed Lee that Yogi Ramsuratkumar now had an attendant and full-time companion, a woman named Devaki, and that he had recently moved to the house where Devaki and the Sudama sisters lived. Yogi Ramsuratkumar had asked Rangarajan earlier in the month of November to write an editorial for the next issue of *Tattva Darsana* to introduce "Ma Devaki," who he chose to call his "Eternal Slave." Rangarajan also explained to Lee that land had been purchased for an ashram, and plans were under way to begin construction. At the Manthralayam in Kanimadam the Vedic rites were being performed every day, according to Bhagawan's wishes. In fact, Devaki called every day to assure Bhagawan that the rites were being carried out. All the news spoke of major changes and promised a very exciting three weeks in India.

The next day Lee and his party were leaving for Kanimadam—where we would be hosted for nine days by Pon Kamaraj—while Rangarajan and N. Subramaniam (Mani) were driving to Tiruvannamalai to deliver boxes of *Poems of a Broken Heart* to Bhagawan. There was an extra space in the car, and Mani invited Lee to go with them, but because of his prior commitments, Lee had to decline. One of his students, Balarama (formerly "Joe," who had met Yogi Ramsuratkumar with Lee in 1979), went instead. Rangarajan, Mani and Balarama took off the next day, while the rest of our party left Madras with Lee for the long bus ride to Nagercoil.

Packed into the narrow seats of the bus, I held the new copy of *Poems of a Broken Heart* in my hands, hungrily reading and re-reading the book as we traveled through the lush tropical landscape. I noticed that Lee was absorbed in the poetry also, reading it as if for the first time, and drawn into the place of its origin . . . the mad beggar of Tiruvannamalai.

It was the celebration of Dewali and the courtyards, terraces and verandah walls of stucco houses and bungalows, tucked away under tall tamarind trees against the dark green shadows of the jungle growth, were lined with tiny ghee flames. As dusk fell and the bus sped over the rutted pavement of the road, loud horns honking and popular Indian music blaring over loudspeakers, the scene took on a surreal magic as we whisked past

6 Lee Lozowick, *Poems of a Broken Heart,* p. 81.

graceful palm trees, rich banana groves, ponds, lakes and waterways. Even in the dying light, women were coming outside to bend down and draw the elaborate, colorful rice mandalas on the ground in front of their doors. People gathered in front of mud huts and thatched-roof tea stalls where kerosene fires burned long into the hours of the night. The Dewali lights were like small golden jewels, calling the deities to hear the prayers of devotees across the land. The magic of India seemed inextricably tied up with the beauty of the poetry, and when I could not make out the words anymore, I finally put the book away.

It being my first experience of India, the powerful and beautiful impressions created a mood of serenity and a fierce but gentle sense of emptiness in me. India in all her glorious juxtaposition of light and dark, of beauty and horror, of feast and famine was claiming my heart. In the middle of the night we stopped at bus stops, threading our way in the darkness through dogs, beggars, refuse and the small crowds that milled around the bright tea stalls, where we bought bananas and cookies and listened to the lively strains of Indian music that blared over loud speakers. As we traveled through the moon-dark countryside that night it seemed to me that the deeper we got into India, and the closer we came to converging with Yogi Ramsuratkumar, the more Lee began to shine with the anticipation of seeing his master again.

Arriving finally at Nagercoil and making the short trip to the Manthralayam at Kanimadam, Lee was greeted by Pon Kamaraj, who prostrated at his feet and immediately showered him with the traditional and opulent hospitality of India—the devotional fervor of a *puja* ceremony. Ghee lamps were waved and flower petals filled the air with the powerful sounds of pounding drums and voices raised in chanting the name of Yogi Ramsuratkumar. Lee was adorned with flower garlands, his feet were washed and his forehead anointed with *kumkum*, while all of his students received smaller flower garlands around our necks. Pon Kamaraj was exultant to have Lee return to the Manthralayam; he quickly told one of the Americans, "When Yogi heard that Lee was coming he began dancing," and "Lee's body is in the U.S.A. but his spirit is in India, just as Yogi's body is in Tiruvannamalai and his spirit is here at the Manthralayam."

Over the next nine days we were pitched into a kind of devotional revelry I'd never experienced before. After the ceremonial greeting and *puja*, Pon Kamaraj led Lee by the hand through the now-completed Manthralayam complex, along paths of clean red sand that wound down open-air corridors flanked by high shrubs with glossy foliage, under tall palms and past a large rose garden to a small meditation room and then on to the temple or main shrine room. Crowds of people poured in behind us as walked through a portico entrance, where men danced and chanted, and into the largest of the shrine rooms: a circular room with a very high ceiling. The chanting rose to a fevered pitch and a curtain was drawn back to reveal the temple deity: a twelve-foot-high stone statue—a *murti* or empowered image—of Yogi Ramsuratkumar standing on a lotus pedestal, covered with enormous flower *malas* in rose, marigold, jasmine and pink lotus and a garland of the small, greenish-yellow limes as well. The face was covered with a powdery mask in light blue, and the eyes were inset with silver glass so that they reflected light like two jewels.

At its base were the bronze implements of complex *pujas*—many tall *arati* lamps filled with ghee gleamed with golden flames, baskets of whole flowers and flower petals were arranged around. Small silver or bronze vessels containing water, ghee, honey, sandalwood water, rose water, turmeric water and many other substances were carefully set out. A Brahmin priest sat bare-chested with the sacred thread wound around his upper body and wearing a long white dhoti wrapped around the bottom half of his slender frame.

Right away Lee went into a full-length prostration on the floor before the statue of Yogi Ramsuratkumar, and at that gesture a wave of ecstatic Indian devotees—chanting the name of Yogi Ramsuratkumar to the bold polyrhythmic beating of the drums and lead by several men who sang as if the world depended up on it—surged around him and the nine Westerners who stood behind him, rapt in attention and awestruck by the presence that was exuded by the statue and further enhanced and evoked by the fervor of the chanting. It was the day of Yogi Ramsuratkumar's Jayanthi Celebration, and the devotees had already been chanting his name nonstop for twenty-four hours when we arrived.

What followed were days of traveling over the dusty roads of southern India, passing bullock carts, rice paddies or banana and coconut palm groves on either side, while the van rocked with the sound of the constant chanting as the name of Yogi Ramsuratkumar reverberated through it all. We went to many small villages, rustic jungle temples, towns, factories and schools where Lee spoke about Yogi Ramsuratkumar and the spiritual heritage of India to large crowds of local people. They gathered eagerly to hear about the beggar saint of Tamil Nadu, to partake of the blessings and receive *prasad* from the hands of the blue-eyed Western "son" of Yogi Ramsuratkumar. At night the Yogi Ramsuratkumar caravan—with its van carrying Lee, his students and the *bhajan* singers and drummer from the Manthralayam—would find its way back to the Manthralayam, which was lit with thousands of small colored lights and seemed to vibrate with the sound of the name of Yogi Ramsuratkumar, which was constantly chanted over loudspeakers.

One of the stops made by the Yogi Ramsuratkumar *bhajan* caravan that traveled with Lee and the American guests was to the *samadhi* site of the "silent" swami—a much-revered local saint named Mouni Swami, with whom Yogi Ramsuratkumar was connected. The van and cars made their way up the black volcanic mountains through glossy green jungle growth to finally stop just at dusk outside a brightly lit, tiny stone temple on the side of a mountain. The rustic temple was mostly populated with very poor village women dressed in ragged saris, who wore chunks of gold in the stretched lobes of their ears and had radiant, beatific smiles. Most of them were elders, but they joyfully prostrated before the American guest of honor and with big smiles took the hands of the American women in the party, eager to share friendship. Lee performed the *puja* before the *samadhi* shrine, with its large Shiva lingam and sculpted Nandi bull. Afterward he passed out *prasad* to the local men and women. As the *prasad* was being distributed, a sadhu with matted hair, who had sat outside on the ground until then—rapt in a meditation posture with arms held high above his head for thirty minutes during the chanting—finally roused himself and came inside. Half naked and smeared with the white ash of *vibhuti*, he prostrated at Lee's feet and then received *prasad*. It was an unforgettable evening of blending East and West against the jungle backdrop.

The next night the Americans gathered with Pon Kamaraj in the small meditation room. He explained to us that Lee was being honored as Anjaneya, the devotional form of Hanuman. He spoke about an ancient temple that was located in layers of earth beneath the Manthralayam, and about a poem titled "Akhila Thirattu," written two hundred years before by a great saint, Muthukutti Swami, who had predicted that Anjaneya would come from the West to a temple that would be built above this ancient temple. The prediction said that when Anjaneya came from the West, then Ram would come to the new temple. This was connected to the same prophecy that Murugeshan had discovered in the *Akhila Thirattu*, in which Muthukutti predicted a future incarnation of an avatar who would come holding a palmyra fan and coconut shell bowl, who the devotees strongly believed to be Yogi Ramsuratkumar.

Pon Kamaraj said, "This prophecy was fulfilled when Lee Lozowick came in 1988 to inaugurate the Manthralayam." According to Pon Kamaraj, Yogi Ramsuratkumar was considered an incarnation of Ram, and Lee was Anjaneya, who had come from the West, as the prophecy foretold. It seemed that the myth of the Western teacher's relationship to Yogi Ramsuratkumar was swiftly gaining momentum. Lee seemed uncomfortable with this kind of attention, and listened silently with downcast eyes. The next day Lee gave a talk at the Manthralayam, which was packed with devotees and people from the local villages. Lee remarked self-deprecatingly, "I don't think I'm Anjaneya. I think I'm just a monkey . . ."

Nonetheless, despite his aversion to adulation and the limelight, Lee was being asked to represent Yogi Ramsuratkumar in villages, towns and small temples all around the area. He gave public talks and walked for many hours in long processions through the villages, performing *pujas* and distributing *prasad* to rich and poor alike. The ever-present strains of Yogi Ramsuratkumar *bhajans* floated on the air; our minds and bodies became so saturated in the divine name that it reverberated within us day and night. At one of his talks Lee began to speak about the three qualities necessary in the guru/devotee relationship: love, service and obedience. He told the story of being sent away by Yogi Ramsuratkumar in 1986, and about his return in 1988.

> I came without expectation of ever seeing Yogi Ramsuratkumar again. One takes a guru for everything. One must obey completely to receive all the Benediction that is available. The guru/devotee relationship is eternal—if you come back into incarnation, you have the same guru . . . .
>
> It physically hurts Yogi Ramsuratkumar when his children fight with each other over power and territory. This should be a sangha. There is only one position of power in a sangha, and that is the guru's position. I plead with you, don't create war in the sangha, please, because it hurts him. It tortures him when his children fight.[7]

---

7 Lee Lozowick, Winter 1994, *Tawagoto*, p. 11.

It seemed that Lee was sensing the storm that was brewing and would soon erupt among the devotees who objected to the installation of Devaki as the beggar saint's attendant and "eternal slave."

In the meantime, Balarama had rejoined Lee and the Americans. He sat with us on the porch in front of our rooms at Vivekanandapuram in Kanya Kumari and told many stories of his days in Tiruvannamalai with Yogi Ramsuratkumar. Upon arriving with Mani and Rangarajan, they had gone directly to Sudama House and found that Yogi Ramsuratkumar was ill and sleeping on the white marble floor of the shrine room. On one wall was a shrine with a huge three-by-six-foot picture of Yogi Ramsuratkumar. Many other pictures of the beggar graced the walls of the room. A set of wooden doors opened out onto a corridor that lead to both the front door and the enclosed porch. Against the back wall on the floor was the beggar king, asleep on a blanket. He was still sleeping as the men were ushered quickly and quietly into the room. Rangarjan sat on the blanket near the yogi, while everyone else scattered like a string of broken pearls across the floor in front of the master's prone form. Bala remembered:

> He was beautiful without his traditional turban of rags. His face was radiant, even as he slept. I was seated directly in front of Yogi Ramsuratkumar, seven or eight feet away from him, a perception that kept changing over the next four hours from eight feet to three feet to two feet, as it seemed he was at times very close or farther away, depending on the moment.
>
> The Professor gave Lee's new poetry book to Yogi Ramsuratkumar; he held it very delicately, as if handling an object of inestimable value. He looked at his picture on the cover then glanced inside.
>
> I saw Krishna Carcelle, a man visiting from France, *pranam* and offer *prasad*—some apple butter made by his wife. It was my turn next, and not having had the presence of mind to pick up prasad on the way there, I reached into my pocket and pulled out two pieces of candy, *prasad* that Lee had given me back in the States. Bowing before Yogi Ramsuratkumar, I said, "These are from Mr. Lee for you."

Yogi Ramsuratkumar looked at the candies with some astonishment, as if he had never seen such delights before. Almost wistfully, he said, "Lee, Lee . . ." His eyes filled with tears. He turned to Devaki and said, "Open."

She opened one up and placed it in his mouth. He looked at her and said, "Open," indicating that he wanted her to open the other piece for him to eat. She said that one was enough. He insisted a second time, "Open," so she reluctantly opened up the second piece and said again that one was enough for now.

"You," he said, pointing gently to her. Everyone laughed as she popped the second piece into her mouth. He turned his attention back to Balarama and gazed at him with eyes full of tears, as if seeing him from a distance and trying to focus on something he saw faintly that he wanted to bring into his field of vision. After a few moments Bala sat back down again.

Sadhu Rangarajan then gave Yogi Ramsuratkumar a letter that Lee had just written to him the day before in Madras. Having just awakened and still not well, Yogi Ramsuratkumar appeared somewhat dazed and confused as Devaki opened the letter. Then she showed him the three poems from Lee that were enclosed.

"Shall I read them, Bhagawan?" Devaki asked, holding the poems in her hand.

"Yes . . . " he responded slowly. He seemed to be reflecting deeply, then he mused, "Lee has written all these poems for this beggar," as if he was continually astonished at such a gift. It seemed that as the poems from Lee had accumulated over the years, their ability to transmit the essence of the guru/devotee relationship and who Yogi Ramsuratkumar was had become apparent. The poems had taken a particular position—a graceful place—in the beggar saint's work, empowered as they were by his own hand.

"This beggar didn't know what these poems were at first, and he didn't save them," he said, his eyes shining. He said that when Lee first came to him, for a long time the poetry was the only communication between them. He told the story of Lee coming to visit him in 1986, and how Lee had sat in the hot sun. To Balarama's great surprise, Yogi Ramsuratkumar started to cry as he told this story and spoke of the suffering that Lee must have endured that afternoon.

"This beggar cannot help himself," he said, crying. "This beggar lost some of these poems at first . . ."

After Devaki read the three new poems, Yogi Ramsuratkumar asked Rangarajan to read the preface he wrote to *Poems of a Broken Heart* out loud:

> *Nindaa stuti*—"ironical praise" or praise in the form of abusive reproach—is a very powerful but dangerous and slippery form of devotional poetry and many a great saintly poet, especially in Sanskrit literature, have boldly ventured into it in adoring their *Ishta devataa* or Chosen Deities.
>
> It is with tremendous dexterity and skill that Lee Lozowick, an ardent devotee of Yogi Ramsuratkumar Godchild Tiruvannamalai, has handled this form in his poetic epistles which he has been shooting at his Father at frequent intervals. Himself a dynamic leader of a spiritual community, Hohm in U.S.A., Lee Lozowick turns into "lee lozowick" in all humility, though he is proud of his being the "arrogant son" of his "Father" who is a "madman," "dirty beggar" and "sinner."[8]

Devaki then mentioned that there was an introduction to the book, written by Lee in late September, 1993. Yogi Ramsuratkumar immediately asked her to read it. After every sentence he asked her to read it again and then reread it, as if he wanted to draw from

8 Preface by Professor V. Rangarajan, from *Poems of a Broken Heart*, "Publisher's Note," p. i.

each word all the nectar it would yield until he made it a part of himself.

> How can one write an introduction to poetry? Poems are what they are, not because the poet cannot write prose, but because the poem touches a part of the human being that is usually inaccessible to any other form of writing. And why would one write poetry about Yogi Ramsuratkumar? When my Father gets access to those usually inaccessible parts, the Majesty of His Benediction, the Mercy of His Glance, the Power of His Love to break the heart in a way only His Father can heal is a Blessing of such rarity and purity that the poet, already destroyed by the beauty of Yogi Ramsuratkumar's feet, wishes others the same fate.
>
> Who is Yogi Ramsuratkumar and how did He become the One who smothers His gopis' senses with Bliss? That is a question better left for scholars to answer. I am only His son, and as this book attests, a poet—although I cannot claim to be a very good one. But then again, in the light of Yogi Ramsuratkumar, how could any image of Him begin to touch even the farthest edges of His indescribable Radiance.
>
> On the other hand, be careful. This dirty Beggar is no common saint. Love is no respecter of culture, or of personal preferences. Love knows no limits, and in knowing no limits it destroys everything in its path. And Love is something that Yogi Ramsuratkumar is a Master of . . . .[9]

We listened to Bala's stories hungrily, counting the days until we would reach Tiruvannamalai. After several more days of whirlwind activity—many ceremonies, speeches and *pujas* later—Lee made a visit to the small temple of Mother Mayee in Kanya Kumari, then traveled north to Anandashram near Kanhangad and spent several days there in the benevolent atmosphere of Papa Ramdas and Mataji Krishnabai. It always pleased Yogi Ramsuratkumar when Lee took his devotees to Anandashram, and Lee often made it a part of his trip.

One afternoon we were sitting in *satsang* with Swami Satchidananda, who was telling many wonderful stories of Papa Ramdas and Mataji Krishnabai, when a young American came in and joined us. Swami was talking about the need to see the guru through universal eyes. He said, "Ram is the all-pervading presence. When you realize the guru as this, then you can begin to deal with everyone with love and affection. When you look upon the guru as mother, then you are closer to him. The guru's form is the Universe; it is the feminine aspect, the manifest aspect of the Universal. You must think in terms of the Universe, talk in terms of the Universe and act in terms of the Universe. Do not limit the guru; when you are touching something, a handful of water, you are touching the Universe. In this way we begin to see others as parts of the Universe. It is a very beautiful practice—the more one does it, the more bliss and joy one experiences.

9 Lee Lozowick, *Poems of a Broken Heart*, pp. iii – iv.

Surrender, self-surrender! Whatever happens to our bodies is God's play."

He continued, "One must have complete obedience to the guru. To be with the guru all the time, this is the most difficult and the most blissful. They give love and care so fully, but they are constantly hammering on our ego, unless we are prepared to make ourselves a perfect zero! We hope to make ourselves a perfect zero as soon as possible!" Swami smiled and laughed gently, and everyone else laughed along with him.

When the *satsang* was over we walked outside to the courtyard and sat down on the steps to enjoy the garden. In the courtyard at Anandashram there is a large banyan tree that spreads its uprising roots in a chaotic maze of trunk and roots; its wide trunk and vast branches have offered shelter and shade to many countless seekers over the generations, including Yogi Ramsuratkumar. As we were sitting there, the young American seeker came up and sat beside Lee.

"Are you Lee?" he asked abruptly.

"Yes," Lee answered.

"I've just come from Tiru, and I have a message for you from Yogi Ramsuratkumar." Lee nodded his head and the young American continued, "Yogi Ramsuratkumar sends his *pranams* and his blessings and a message. He is looking forward to your visit, and he said, 'This beggar is Lee's slave.' " Lee listened quietly with no immediate response, and the young American repeated, "He said, 'This beggar is Lee's slave.' "

"That's not true," Lee responded, "but thank you," and he slapped the young man affectionately on the shoulder. As he walked away, the name of Yogi Ramsuratkumar reverberated in the air. The message had brought the fire of his presence into the foreground of our awareness, and it lingered in the golden silence of the afternoon. Two women began to sweep the smooth concrete floor of the courtyard, whisking their stick brooms in graceful arcs. The birds were calling and the sunlight, coming at a slant through afternoon air, suffused my senses further with the presence of the beggar saint, who we would see very soon. It seemed that Yogi Ramsuratkumar was beckoning, calling to us from afar.

Every day Lee was writing in his journal, and now that *Poems of a Broken Heart* was in our hands, those of us traveling with him had some idea that he was writing poetry to Yogi Ramsuratkumar. Years later, when *Death of a Dishonest Man* was published with Lee's collected poems from a twenty-five-year period of time, we would discover that after the interchange with the young American at Anandashram, Lee wrote:

> Oh You relentless Liar,
>   Yogi Ramsuratkumar,
> someone brought me a message from You:
>   You said You are lee's slave.
> Now You have gone too far
>   oh dirty Sinner.
> lee has sworn obedience to You,
>   but this, oh Father?

Well listen,
        I will concede You this:
if the slave can be
        the slave of the slave,
I will suffer the latest outrage
        of the mad Beggar.[10]

Before we left Anandashram for Tiruvannamalai, Lee sat down with us on the ground beneath the trees and gave fierce instructions for the upcoming visit with Yogi Ramsuratkumar. He said, "We are going to see Yogi Ramsuratkumar, and I want you to be crystal clear about the protocol of being in the same space with him. The first rule is: do not distract him or attract attention to yourself in any way. Do not ask questions, and only speak if you are asked a question." It was a hot afternoon in tropical Kerala, and we sat in the dappled light, tinted green in the shadows of the overhanging leaves. Lee spoke with passionate intensity about his master, and the necessity for being sensitive to everything that happened in his space.

He continued, "When we are sitting with Yogi Ramsuratkumar, it is entirely his space. We want to get what he wants us to have—not what we might elicit from him if we start talking and drawing attention to ourselves. Do not talk unless you are asked to, do not ask questions, do not draw attention to yourself, because if you do, he will go where you lead. We want *him* to lead. Be as receptive and attentive as you can. The idea is to pay attention to him, and receive whatever it is that he wants you to have. He works in very delicate, very subtle ways; he is a master of great means—he knows exactly what is needed. You don't." He hammered these points home, reiterating them several times. The next morning we left very early on the train.

We arrived in Tiruvannamalai on December 12, 1993. After checking into our rooms at Ramanashram, Lee immediately threaded his way through the dirt streets to Sudama House, only a few short blocks away from our quarters, past several beggars and some orange-clad sadhus that were lying along the streets or walking past. It was two-thirty in the afternoon when we arrived. Sudama House was a new arrangement, and Lee wasn't sure what the protocol would be here. Asking a neighbor, he was informed, "Yogi Ramsuratkumar sees people from four to six o'clock." We went back to Ramanashram to finish some business and then arrived back at the gate to Sudama House at three p.m. to wait in the bright sunshine outside the gate beside the high stucco wall. It was impossible to see anything of the house other than a bit of the roof. We were the first people in the long queue that quickly began to form behind us.

"Are you going to knock on the gate?" I asked Lee.

"No. We will wait until someone comes out and invites us in," he replied. Squatting in the dirt and leaning against the garden wall, he settled in to wait as long as necessary. It had been two years since Lee had seen Yogi Ramsuratkumar; the last visit had been in

---

10 Lee Lozowick, *Death of a Dishonet Man*, p. 476.

1991, when Lee spent three days in Tiruvannamalai with the master. Of our traveling party on this trip, only Radha and Balarama had met Yogi Ramsuratkumar before, but whether one had met him previously or not, the anticipation ran very high for all of us.

While we waited in the partial shade, Lee was relaxed, playful and as composed as ever as he told stories about Yogi Ramsuratkumar, but he was not one to put his innermost feelings on display. He had written the following poem at Anandashram the day before we set out for Tiruvannamalai, in December 1993:

> Tomorrow I will see You
>   oh merciless Thief of hearts.
> How will I act
>   when I set eyes on Your Form again?
> Will I fall on my face
>   and kiss Your toes
> or simply bow politely,
>   afraid to dissolve in love?
> lee tells You this,
>   Father Yogi Ramsuratkumar,
> one way or another
>   Your son will bathe in You.[11]

An hour later there were fifty or sixty people waiting to see Yogi Ramsuratkumar. The crowd was restless and expressing their discomfort from standing in the hot sun for an hour. Nivedita, the daughter of Rangarajan whom we had already met, opened the gate and looked out. She was shocked when she saw Lee standing there in the sun, and immediately drew him inside.

"Lee! Why are you standing out here? You should have knocked on the gate," she chastised lightly. "He has been waiting for you!" She called back toward the house, "Lee is here!" Lee and the nine Americans were let in and the gate was firmly closed on the rest of the disappointed crowd.

Walking in the gate and across the yard toward the house behind Lee, we watched as the front door suddenly burst open. A small, sturdy elderly man with a wizened white beard came moving with incredible alacrity and agility out the door and down the steps, pushing the two men who walked ahead of him out of the way and crying out, "Lee!" He had a green cloth wrapped around his head as a turban and a gray shawl wrapped around his body and thrown up over one shoulder. Love and warmth poured from his eyes, and his childlike excitement was infectious. His moves and gestures were mysteriously graceful and full of purpose. I was immediately elevated, lifted out of my ordinary state and into a world of new possibility by virtue of his simple presence, but it was the lilt in his voice that was so extraordinary and instantly disarming. His speech was songlike as

11 Ibid, p. 477.

he rushed forward toward his Western devotee with the overwhelming tenderness of a lover or a mother reaching for her long lost child. Lee was on the ground, prostrating and touching his head to the beggar's feet, while Yogi Ramsuratkumar affectionately slapped his back several times and then pulled him up.

Soon we were whisked into the front room of the house, a partially enclosed but airy porch, and Yogi Ramsuratkumar arranged the room with himself and Lee at the head of the room, sitting against one wall, with the two rows of Americans on their right and a row of about six Indian devotees, including the Sudama sisters, on their left. Shortly after everyone was settled Yogi Ramsuratkumar stood up and began to work, walking up and down the porch in front of the Americans, spontaneously raising his hands in blessing and making a wide sweeping motion across the field of physical space, almost as if he was impatiently, even fiercely whisking away some noisome toxic influence in the field of his work—namely, the *samskaras* of those who now sat wide-eyed before him, and with whom he would be in close proximity for the next three days. His movements were dance-like as he paced back and forth like a great tiger, blessing, blessing, blessing with his hands and eyes, sometimes stopping to gaze at one person, then moving on. Finally he sat down beside Lee and began to smoke one cigarette after another.

"Devaki, Lee has come here to bless this dirty beggar!" he said, his face beaming with happiness. The beatific smile on his face was completely disarming. He peered into Lee's eyes and joked that he was lucky to see Lee so soon after he arrived, because if Ganeshan had seen Lee at Ramanashram, he would have kept him there for a while.

When Yogi Ramsuratkumar wasn't smoking he was usually holding Lee's hand or caressing his arm. At one point he looked at Lee for a long time and then broke into peals of joyous laughter, covered his face shyly like a young girl in love, looked away and then back again at Lee. The impact of Yogi Ramsuratkumar was more than any of us were prepared for; his physical presence had left us speechless, and the love and affection he was pouring on our teacher was overwhelming. During much of this time he worked with one person after another through long, strong moments of gazing directly into our eyes, or just above the head, while he smoked or raised his hands in blessing.

"Devaki! This dirty beggar is Lee's slave!" He turned to Devaki and then back to Lee. He stroked Lee's arm tenderly and gazed at him for a long time.

"Devaki!" He called out again, "Devaki! Lee is this dirty beggar's master!" It was an outrageous statement, but he spoke it with such enthusiasm and innocence and certainty that one could only accept it. He slowly and deliberately laced his fingers into Lee's, dark and pale in juxtaposition, East and West mingled and married. Spiritual power swelled and thickened in the air while he worked with Lee in this way, often calling to Devaki and repeating, "This dirty beggar is Lee's slave!" and "Lee is this beggar's master!" Lee said nothing in response to these statements, but smiled unceasingly at his master, basking in his radiance, and sat with quiet receptivity. He seemed deeply attuned to the beggar and interested only in being receptive to whatever Yogi Ramsuratkumar chose to enact with him.

It was his unbounded happiness, joyful smiles and peerless laughter that captured my heart that afternoon and into the evening, as *Poems of a Broken Heart* was brought out and Yogi Ramsuratkumar asked Devaki to read poem after poem. I found myself fighting back inexplicable tears as the inimitable Yogi Ramsuratkumar said again and again, "Read that poem again," in his sweet, mellifluous voice. Devaki read the poetry for hours off and on during the day and into the night. Her renderings of the poems were sensitive, passionate, insightful and threaded through with an obvious profound appreciation of them. She threw her whole heart into it. There was no trace of envy or jealousy—she seemed truly thrilled by the praise and exaltation of her master. A true devotee, she set a shining example for the Americans. At one point, after she read a particularly powerful poem in which Lee begged for his "Father's madness" and made brash proclamations of kinship to Yogi Ramsuratkumar, calling himself the "son" of the "dirty Beggar" who becomes the "Father of lee," the beggar turned to Devaki and asked, "Devaki! What do you think of that?"

"I wish only to be Your eternal slave, Bhagawan," she said.

Yogi Ramsuratkumar was visibly, deeply moved by the poems, and each one invoked a mood or response. When the poet would address the beggar in epithets like "Rascal," "Miscreant," or "Trickster," the poem would evoke Yogi Ramsuratkumar's rich laughter and merry glances, accompanied by many hearty slaps on the back and shoulder to Lee, as if to say, "We two share in this joke, don't we?"

> I hear stories of Your great love
>   for Papa and Mataji.
> Yes, You Rascal,
>   You were Mad even then.
> This arrogant Fool lee
>   cannot love You like this on his own,
> But if You give him the Blessings
>   of Your Father in Heaven,
> then lee will love You
>   even as You loved Them.
> Oh Father, Yogi Ramsuratkumar,
>   Your son begs You for this gift.[12]

"Devaki! Lee called this beggar a rascal!" Yogi Ramsuratkumar would shake with laughter, his body bouncing gently up and down. Such a word as "rascal" in any given poem that was read would launch him into a fit of child-like laughter, and rocking and cackling, he would slap Lee's back or shoulder, then return to quietly listening while he smoked, hands cupped around the cigarette that glowed brighter with every draw of his breath. Many moods were invoked with the poems; some were tender, dulcet and loving, often eliciting another shy lover's glance from the beggar and the pure charm of his

12 Lee Lozowick, *Death of a Dishonest Man*, p. 420.

embarrassment as he covered his face with the hands, eyes misted over. Yet others caused the yogi to look full and long with perfect candor into Lee's eyes. Sometimes Yogi Ramsuratkumar would turn to Devaki after she read a poem and ask her to explain its meaning, but usually it was just, "Read it again," or simply, "Again . . . again." Still other moods seemed to bring a deep suffering and heartbreaking stillness to the beggar's form.

> As we witnessed the reading of the poems, Lee's gift to Yogi Ramsuratkumar, our hearts were melted and the space was rendered so vulnerable that the yogi could then begin his work of transformation and wizardry. I say wizardry because that's the image I got as the poems were being read by Devaki, and the yogi would begin to whip his hands through the air, as if he saw something that was taking place in a parallel universe, or that was at a wavelength we normally don't perceive. I would look at this sorcerer's eyes, and they seemed to see the entities we had brought with us, so that he could slay them on our behalf. All of our negativity and neurosis and ego was laid vulnerable through the poetry, and then he slipped in and did the rest in a short time.
>
> When he really got going was during certain poems, at certain times that the energy and emotion in the space got so fluid and vital. Then Yogi Ramsuratkumar and his son Lee and Devaki would become one being. Yogi Ramsuratkumar's hand movements would fall into perfect synchronicity, perfect timing and expression with the words and meter of the poem, and as he moved his face in the subtle work he was doing, it was as if he was the one speaking the poem. A woman's voice with this wild old sorcerer's body and movements just putting out this heart-breaking, moving poetry. The Father really doing his excellent work with his radiant son by his side, in silent yet powerful support. Ram and Anjaneya.[13]

Even after hours of repetitive reading, Devaki read the poems with great feeling and marvelous inflections. She seemed to understand the poetry from its depths. In between readings of the poems, at a slight gesture from the yogi, the Sudama sisters would start the chant, "Yogi Ramsuratkumar, Yogi Ramsuratkumar, Yogi Ramsuratkumar, Jaya Guru Raya," and we picked up the melody, falling in with their voices to lift the volume of the chant. Devaki often sat fanning the master, lighting his cigarettes, emptying the ashtray, pouring tea into his coconut bowl, wiping his beard and moustache with a towel after the tea or coffee. It was as if he was a small child and she had to care for his every need. Now and then a line of the poetry would invoke Yogi Ramsuratkumar's sense of humor, or he would look at Lee and interject an ironic statement.

Yogi Ramsuratkumar asked Devaki to read the introduction to the poems that Lee wrote, and as she was reading she came upon the line, "Love is something that Yogi

---

13 Doug Fulker, *Tawagoto*, Winter 1994, pp. 26-27.

Ramsuratkumar is a Master of, and He will destroy you if you let Him . . . ."

"Devaki!" Yogi Ramsuratkumar burst out, "Lee has come here to bless this beggar. Lee has come here to destroy this beggar . . . and he has brought an army to do it!" Then he burst into uproarious laughter and slapped Lee's back very hard.

"Devaki, do you also want to be destroyed?"

"I pray for it every day, Bhagawan," she answered.

It was a blissful afternoon that went on into the evening; the only disruption was the angry crowd that shouted and banged on the gate, furious that the "foreigners" had been let in while they were kept outside. Only a few devotees were asked in now and then to give *prasad* and *pranam* at the master's feet; he did not want his work disrupted by the unruly throng. As the sounds of discontent coming from the other side of the garden wall mounted during the afternoon, the crowd became almost abusive at one point, shouting angrily to be let in. They didn't seem to realize that everything was conducted by Yogi Ramsuratkumar's design—the beggar king was busy with his work, and did not want to be disturbed.

Finally Yogi Ramsuratkumar turned to Lee and said, "Lee, go tell them that this beggar is busy. Tell them to go away—this beggar is busy!" For the first time I saw the slightest flinch in Lee's usual calm and accepting manner. Here was a disciple committed to obedience, and his master was asking him to do something extremely difficult: for a naturally reticent and usually shy American to tell fifty angry Indians that they couldn't see their guru because he was busy with the messenger himself was not a fate anyone would wish for. Nonetheless, Lee walked out of the porch, down the steps and across the yard to open the gate and deliver the message in English. The crowd glowered and surged in closer, completely ignoring his words. He spoke again, "Yogi Ramsuratkumar is busy right now and would like you all to go home." The crowd seemed to be getting more agitated. Yogi Ramsuratkumar then sent Nivedita out, who walked to the gate and shouted in Tamil with a ferocity that would have scared off the most adamant and aggressive of them. Chastised but still reluctant, the crowd finally dispersed.

At one point a Mercedes drove up and parked outside the house. Yogi Ramsuratkumar said to Nivedita, "Go out and tell whoever that is that this beggar is busy. They can come back later." Nivedita walked out of the room. Two or three minutes later she was back.

"So? What happened?" Yogi Ramsuratkumar asked.

"Bhagawan, he owns a big company in Madras, and he sent a message to you."

"What is the message?"

"Tell Swami his dog is waiting in the street for him," she answered. Yogi Ramsuratkumar looked at Nivedita for a moment.

"Tell him to come in," he said, after a pause.

The man came in and sat very quietly against the wall. He didn't ask a question or interject anything at all into the space. Yogi Ramsuratkumar allowed him to stay for two hours. He left with tears in his eyes and a look of profound gratitude as he *pranamed* to Yogi Ramsuratkumar and then quietly walked away. It was an object lesson in how to approach the guru. The noisy, complaining, criticizing crowd was sent away, while this man approached quietly, humbly, without making any demands and was allowed into the master's inner sanctum.

That evening Yogi Ramsuratkumar told the story of his initiation by Papa Ramdas, how Ramdas told him to repeat the mantra twenty-four hours a day. He said, "This beggar tried for one week. Then Ramdas was with him all the time, everywhere and everything, nothing else, nobody else, nobody else but my Father." Balarama wrote about this:

> Nothing a saint does should be overlooked. This relaying of his initiation story was very significant to me; it set the tone for my perception. It seemed to be some sort of ritual beyond my comprehension.
>
> While poems were read and public darshan held and smoking was going on, Yogi Ramsuratkumar's body appeared to be conducting an enormous amount of energy or voltage. You could see it coursing through him, shooting out of his eyes. At times he fluttered imperceptibly with his lips moving all the time, in conversation with all the worlds, silently in communion with all of life.
>
> Yogi Ramsuratkumar ran his hands all over his face and hid those dark eyes of Ram playfully behind his hand whenever there was a line from Lee's poems that touched him. He laughed and hit, slapped or petted Lee's forearm. He welled up on the brink of tears many times when reference was made to Papa Ramdas or Mataji Krishnabai, then he would have the poem read again and again. The room filled up with the very taste of his love for his master—the room was so thick with devotion, you could cut it with a knife. This was not one isolated incident, but happened what seemed like every half hour.
>
> He clasped both of Lee's hands in his as if to let the power flow into him directly from his own body. He held Lee's hand, sometimes on his own knee, sometimes on Lee's knee. Sometimes their fingers were intertwined. At times Yogi Ramsuratkumar petted Lee like a lover, or like holding the hand of a beloved child. He gave gentle attention to Lee's entire arm from elbow to fingernail, holding it gently outstretched. Then he stroked the arm, touched Lee's face, the left hand and arm, the left knee and foot.[14]

The next day, December 13, we arrived at Sudama House at 7:45 in the morning, the exact time Yogi Ramsuratkumar had asked Lee to come. As we walked through the gate and approached the house, the front door was thrust open and the beggar king burst out and down the steeps with tremendous vigor and enthusiasm.

"Lee! Lee!" he cried, "My Father is everything, everywhere, one, perfect,

---

14 Balarama, *Tawagoto*, Winter 1994, pp. 55-56.

indivisible. My Father alone exists! My Father alone!" Lee was on his knees, touching the master's feet. Yogi Ramsuratkumar slapped his back affectionately and pulled him up. Taking Lee's hand, he walked with him up the steps and into the house, and with the nine Americans following behind, we settled again on the porch with Yogi Ramsuratkumar, Devaki and the Sudama sisters. Coffee was served and the reading of poems began right away.

As the day progressed, Yogi Ramsuratkumar asked Devaki to read a particular poem twelve times in a row. It was a poem that referred to many different famous pairs. Some of them were historical lovers, like Heloise and Abelard, Anthony and Cleopatra, Rodin and Camille, and others were masters and their disciples, like Marpa and Milarepa, Ramdas and Mataji, while still others were gods and goddesses—Radha and Krishna, Parvati and Shiva, Hanuman and Rama.

> Oh Yogi Ramsuratkumar,
>   Your son is such an arrogant Fool,
> listen to his sinful Pride
>   and his silly Foolishness:
> this bad Poet
>   reads of the great Lovers
> of Hanuman and Rama,
>   of Radha and Krishna,
> of Parvati and Siva,
>   of Vivekananda and Ramakrishna,
> of Rumi and Shemsi Tabriz,
>   of Milarepa and Marpa,
> of Mary and Jesus,
>   of Claire and Francis,
> shamefully of Cleopatra and Anthony,
>   of Juliet and Romeo,
> of Heloise and Abelard,
>   of Camille and Rodin,
> Madly of Layla and Majnun,
>   and longingly of Yogi Ramsuratkumar
>   and His Father Sri Ramdas,
> and Your son says:
>   "I will love my Father like this."
> I ask You, Yogi Ramsuratkumar,
>   is this not madness?
> lee listens for Your reply,
>   oh dirty Beggar.[15]

15 Lee Lozowick, *Death of a Dishonest Man,* p. 343.

"Who are these people?" Yogi Ramsuratkumar turned to Devaki and asked, after she had read the poem a few times. He wanted to know the stories of Milarepa and Marpa, Rumi and Shemsi Tabriz, Heloise and Abelard, Rodin and Camille, St. Francis and Claire. Lee told the story of each pair, then Devaki explained the stories to Yogi Ramsuratkumar.

"Devaki, you will remember every word and tell them again and again when this beggar asks!" Yogi Ramsuratkumar commanded with a smile.

Devaki laughed and said, "Maybe Lee will tell them again tomorrow . . ."

"No!" Yogi Ramsuratkumar said forcefully, "He says it only once! He is not that cheap! You must remember every word!" Everyone laughed, including Bhagawan.

"Yes, Bhagawan, I will remember," Devaki agreed.

During the reading he often fell into *bhavas*, sometimes with his head down on his chest as if sunk deeply inside himself to listen. He became so utterly still that one could think he had fallen asleep, but as soon as the poem ended he would raise his head and say to Devaki, "Read it again." With each reading the words of the poem were brought more vividly to life. Many of the poems were fervent requests from the poet to be granted his Father's divine madness. When this was read Yogi Ramsuratkumar looked up from his *bhava* and said, "My Father grants Lee's prayer." With a cigarette cupped in his hands, he turned to gaze softly at Lee, who sat quietly at his side.

"My Father in Heaven will grant Lee's wish, I'm sure," he said, with a gentle smile on his face, his gaze lingering on Lee.

On this particular day Yogi Ramsuratkumar had a basketful of exceptionally beautiful roses, some red and some yellow. He stood up and walked back and forth in front of Lee's students, who were again seated in the same position by the wall. His movements and actions were saturated with the palpable grace of divine purpose as he carefully placed a full-blown rose in the hand of each person.

The giving of the rose was a ritual itself, and seemed to happen in slow motion, as he looked deeply into my eyes and held out, ever so slowly, the perfect fragrant yellow rose. It hung poised from his fingers for the longest time, then slowly, slowly, the rose drifted, or by weight of gravity was inexorably conveyed, from his hand to mine. The eternal moment of communion was over as he moved to the next person. Then he had coffee brought in stainless steel cups. These he served to each one of us with his own hands.

At one point during the usual darshan hours a large crowd gathered again in the street outside the gate and waited in the sun. Now and then Yogi Ramsuratkumar would instruct Nivedita to let a certain devotee in to give *prasad*. The devotee would then come forward and *pranam* at his feet where he sat on the porch floor. While the person bowed he slapped their backs and shoulders and said, "Ram! Ram!" It was thrilling to hear Yogi Ramsuratkumar speak the divine name in blessing. It was powerful and beneficent, and at the same time it seemed to contain a command to the devotees to stop bowing and get up. As soon as they had received *prasad*, he usually said, "You can go now." Very rarely did he let someone stay and take a seat on the porch with the small group of Americans and Indians that was gathered there, as he did with Mani, who sat with the devotees for a long time one afternoon while we were there.

The long queue of people who were waiting to see Yogi Ramsuratkumar on this afternoon became more and more vocal about their discontent. Shouts and angry words could be heard on the porch, and disrupted the delicate atmosphere that permeated the beggar's intimate space. Finally Yogi Ramsuratkumar took it upon himself; taking Lee by the hand, he walked through the yard to the gate and opened it. There were about fifty unhappy people standing in the sun, waiting for his darshan and wanting his blessing.

"My Father blesses you all! This beggar is busy with these friends! These friends have come a long way to be here, and you can come every day. Go home! My Father blesses you all!" He asked Lee to repeat this, which he did. Somewhat mollified with having this brief darshan—the sight of the master standing in the gate, holding the hand of a foreigner—the crowd slowly began to drift away down the street. Yogi Ramsuratkumar and Lee came back onto the porch and sat down.

On this morning Yogi Ramsuratkumar asked Devaki to tell the story of Vivekananda's first meeting with Ramakrishna, which she recounted with simple eloquence. She was very new to the post that she had been given, but her devotion and fervent desire to serve Yogi Ramsuratkumar in all ways was apparent in every gesture. Her generous and radiant smiles put us all at ease and welcomed us into Yogi Ramsuratkumar's intimate circle for the three-and-a-half days that we were immersed in the beggar's sacred space.

Throughout the day the beggar drank gooseberry tea, which Devaki poured into his coconut bowl and handed to him to drink; whatever drops were left in the bowl when he was finished—whether it was gooseberry tea or coffee—he would then hand to Devaki to finish. At one point he gave Lee the coconut bowl to drink from, then took it back and drained the last drops of it himself.

Through watching the interactions between Yogi Ramsuratkumar and Devaki, we came to understand that she was caring for all his physical needs. Devaki was attentive to his every move, yet at the same time she was relaxed in the presence of devotion that she brought to her work. All of his food was served by Devaki, who ate whatever he left in his coconut bowl before she turned to her own plate of food. Nivedita told us that Yogi Ramsuratkumar slept very little at night; he was often awake reading all the mail that came from his devotees, or planning for the new ashram, and he still read the newspaper every day. He was deeply involved in the lives of his devotees, blessing their businesses, houses, building projects, marriages, births, wisely pairing people together in marriage and naming the child that came later. He generously and tirelessly worked.

Yogi Ramsuratkumar spent most of his day listening to the poetry, laughing, smoking, and frequently applying vigorous slaps and whacks to Lee's shoulders, back and sometimes arms. During these days of poetry reading, Lee was in the position of having his master reveal his innermost heart to the deeply listening world of Yogi Ramsuratkumar's intimate chamber, populated by both Indians and Americans. Lee was quiet, steady, and never spoke unless spoken to or asked a direct question. His equanimity flowed in equal measure to his love, reflected in the crystalline gaze of his blue eyes that looked constantly to Yogi Ramsuratkumar, whether in the form of long, loving gazes, quick, stolen glances, or simply when his eyes were lowered or focused within. His eyes often seemed to be the eyes of Radha, reflecting love's most sublime aspect.

"Lee will write poems on Devaki!" the beggar smiled and laughed as he uttered this commandment several times. That night Lee could be seen writing the following poem, which would not be published until *Poems of a Broken Heart, Part II* would come out a few years later:

> "lee will write poems on Devaki,"
>   You said laughing.
> Oh Father Yogi Ramsuratkumar,
>   what kind of talk is this?
> Can even a poem ever touch
>   the power of such service?
> Can even a poem ever touch
>   the purity of such devotion?
> Still, if this is what You wish
>   oh dirty Beggar,
> lee will put mere words
>   to she who is Your very heart.[16]

During the long hours of the day as we sat on the porch together, there was a tremendous sense of oneness, of connectedness and continuity; it seemed that Yogi Ramsuratkumar was the center of a mandala from which radiated everything and everyone else around him. It started with Lee and Devaki, and spread to the Sudama sisters and the Americans. We were inspired by the mood of devotion that was communicated by the Sudama sisters. Rajalakshmi and Vijayakka led the singing of Yogi Ramsuratkumar's name, which went on for hours at a time, interrupted only by Yogi Ramsuratkumar himself. Whenever he interjected something the chanting would stop while he had whatever exchange he wanted to have, then after a few minutes, he would gesture to the women to start the chant again. Everyone sat in exactly the same seat every time we were ushered to the porch, and then we would sit there, sometimes for four or five hours without moving. Now and then some of the Indian devotees were ushered in to have his darshan; they would come and prostrate at his feet, often bringing a flower garland to put around his neck. Yogi Ramsuratkumar immediately he took these off and placed them around Lee's neck.

"I am nothing—I am just a dirty beggar. But Lee, Lee blesses you. This dirty beggar has nothing to give. He only begs . . . begs, begs, begs. Only his Father in Heaven gives. Lee will give. Lee is blessing us," Yogi Ramsuratkumar spoke in his enigmatic way. The devotees were perplexed, but anxious to please the living deity in their midst.

How to describe such a one as Yogi Ramsuratkumar? His gestures and words were

16 Ibid, p. 478.

consumed with grace to such an extent that it seemed at times the man himself was overpowered by the God force that flowed constantly into his body, which seemed frail in comparison and trembled sometimes with the power of it as he moved in and out of sublime states, smoking our karmas and blessing us all. The sublimation of the human being in the raw Divine inspired wonder, awe and joy in those who basked in his company. At times there was something akin to deep sorrow—the heart-rending well of compassion—that took over his countenance, and in those moments it seemed that his suffering was as great as his joy.

The next day Lee and his group spent the day with Yogi Ramsuratkumar at the home of V. Ganeshan. Yogi Ramsuratkumar had arranged a day away from Sudama House, which avoided altogether the unpleasant scene with the crowd of supplicants outside his door, and allowed for maximum privacy in which he could do his work. We were picked up by car before dawn.

When we arrived Yogi Ramsuratkumar was already settled on the open-air patio in the back of the house, which opened out onto a lush garden suffused with the tender early morning light. He sat with his back to one wall of the porch area with Devaki, Vijayakka and Rajalakshmi to his right. On his left he seated Lee. The American men sat along one edge of the patio and the women along the other, facing Lee and Yogi Ramsuratkumar. Ganeshan and his companion Anuradha came and went, often sitting beside the Sudama sisters and conversing gaily with Yogi Ramsuratkumar. It was an intimate and idyllic arrangement in a small, very private space, embraced as it was by the verdant presence of neem trees, banana palms, citrus trees and many shrubs and flowers. Perhaps fifteen feet away from the edge of the patio was a well with a low circular stucco wall defining its parameter. During the morning a beautiful butterfly, black and white with magnificent dark red and orange markings, fluttered back and forth in the space, its colors flashing in the sunlight.

Yogi Ramsuratkumar smoked quietly for a long time, then the poetry reading began. Ganeshan and Anuradha sat on the porch with everyone while Devaki read several poems, then read the now famous poem from the day before, which had been read twelve times in a row: " . . . of Milarepa and Marpa, of Mary and Jesus, of Claire and Francis, Shamefully of Cleopatra and Anthony, of Juliet and Romeo . . ." Again the poem was read many times, and finally Yogi Ramsuratkumar asked Lee to tell the story of Romeo and Juliet. Lee gave a synopsis of the story while everyone listened. It was obvious that everyone, including Yogi Ramsuratkumar, knew this Shakespearean tale by heart. At the end of the story Yogi Ramsuratkumar took Lee by the hand and walked with him for a long while out in the garden, while the rest of us waited on the porch.

"Romeo and Juliet," Anuradha quipped with a mischievous smile and a twinkle in her eye, pointing to Yogi Ramsuratkumar and Lee as they walked and talked, hand in hand in the garden. Everyone laughed gently together. She was speaking for us all—no one had missed the obvious parallel. For a long time they sat on the ground beside the well with their backs against the stucco wall. They were engrossed in each other, but now they were close enough to the porch for the rest of us to hear drifts of their conversation, which was about Lee's musical project, a rock & roll band, called "liars, gods & beggars." Not staying on any one topic for very long, the beggar began to ask what seemed like extraneous but curious questions.

"Lee, are there kangaroos in Australia?" the beggar asked sweetly. Lee answered yes.

"Lee, are there many birds in America?" he pressed further.

"Yes, there are many different kinds of birds in America."

"What kinds of birds do you have there?" he asked with childlike innocence.

"There are sparrows and robins, blue jays, red birds . . ."

"Do you have crows in America, Lee?" the beggar asked.

"Yes, we have lots of crows, all over America. There are many crows."

"We have crows here too . . ." Yogi Ramsuratkumar said. The conversation about crows went on for a few minutes, while the beggar asked Lee more questions: "Are the crows in America as big as the crows in India? Do they sound the same?" He spoke with the innocence and curiosity of a small child, and yet there was always a sense of a unpremeditated purpose underlying his words. Unbeknownst to Yogi Ramsuratkumar, Lee's band had adopted the emblem of a black crow standing on top of a skull, almost like a talisman, to represent the group several years before. I had heard that the beggar saint often gave blessings or teachings through indirect or symbolic means; it seemed to me that his keen interest in the subject of crows was keyed into Lee's band—a way that he blessed the musical project perhaps.

Finally Yogi Ramsuratkumar got up and returned to the porch, walking hand in hand with Lee. They resumed their seats on the floor and a deep silence descended upon the beggar saint and his companions. After a while Yogi Ramsuratkumar turned to Devaki.

"Devaki, is there anything for this beggar to eat in there?" He was looking at the bag that was placed on the floor beside them, which she had packed with everything he would need for the day: packages of Charimar cigarettes, matches, towels, an ashtray, gooseberry tea and coconut bowl, and some small cake-like food that he had eaten at breakfast earlier that morning.

"No Bhagawan, you ate what we brought at breakfast," she answered.

"This beggar would like something to eat, Devaki," he insisted, like a petulant child. Again she looked through the bags, visibly distressed at not being prepared to provide for his every need and whim.

"No, Bhagawan, there is nothing. I usually pack myself quite well, but the last time we went out for the day you said I took too many things that we didn't need, and you instructed me to pack much less today..."

He shrugged away her reasoning and said, "If Devaki has no food, this beggar won't eat." Then he indicated that she should have packed more, which completely contradicted his earlier instructions to her.

Then he repeated, "Devaki, this beggar is hungry," exactly like a child would say, "Mother, I'm hungry!"

"Bhagawan, you speak in mysterious ways. I don't understand . . ."

Anuradha and Ganeshan quickly offered to bring food from the kitchen but Yogi Ramsuratkumar said no, making it clear that if Devaki couldn't provide the food, he didn't want it. Clearly he had a very specific intention. Devaki handled it quite well, and quite resourcefully. After a few minutes, she asked Bhagawan for permission to go out into the garden to look for some fruit on the trees that he could eat.

"Yes, you can look for something in the garden. Take Nivedita with you," he answered. Devaki was never allowed to leave his side without a woman companion, even to walk in the cloistered and protected area of the garden.

While Devaki and Nivedita were out in the garden, the yogi suddenly got up and moved to the exact center of the porch, between Lee on one side and the Sudama sisters on the other. It was as if the universe shifted somehow with this new arrangement, which created a slightly different geomancy within the configuration of people who were present. The American women were sitting directly to the right of the Indian women, watching intently. Now the beggar was a few feet away from Lee and directly facing him, instead of sitting beside him.

In a few minutes Devaki and Nivedita came back with three oranges and one lime, which Yogi Ramsuratkumar received with the delight of a child, surprised by a treat.

"This beggar was hungry and Devaki went out into the garden and found him something to eat!" he exclaimed with joy, as if it was a great miracle.

As Devaki returned she sat down where Yogi Ramsuratkumar indicated, creating a triangle between Yogi Ramsuratkumar, Lee and herself in the center of the room. She placed the fruit, some towels, a knife and cups on the floor at her side, then began to meticulously peel the oranges one by one, carefully taking all the inner skin from each segment. She handed the perfect, juicy inner meat of each piece to Yogi Ramsuratkumar, which he ate with relish. This peeling and cleaning and eating of the fruit took almost an hour; during the entire time, the yogi was turned toward Lee, locked into a gaze of what appeared to be an unbearable degree of intensity and intention.

While this transpired, everyone else on the porch chanted, "Yogi Ramsuratkumar, Yogi Ramsuratkumar, Yogi Ramsuratkumar, Jaya Guru Raya," in that particularly haunting and complex melody that the women of Sudama House sang literally night and day. The atmosphere of the chamber was so rare and refined yet charged and penetrating that some members of the group sat with tears in their eyes or quietly crying. The air itself seemed charged with divine purpose in the crystalline silence that seemed to radiate from the form of the "dirty Beggar." While he ate the oranges, Yogi Ramsuratkumar raised his hands into the air again and again in graceful spontaneous gestures of blessing toward Lee. I wondered how Lee could handle such a torrential outpouring, but he was radiant, full of the light that poured into him. His face was serene, naturally still and receptive. Lee did not fidget, shrink away, flinch or bat an eye, but sat in communion with Yogi Ramsuratkumar. Together they looked more ancient than Arunachala.

At one point Yogi Ramsuratkumar took a segment of fruit and, getting up and walking over to Lee, gave it to him to eat. Then he turned and settled back in place at the center of the porch. Lee ate quickly, without reserve. When the oranges were finished

Devaki squeezed all the juice from the lime and, following Yogi Ramsuratkumar's instructions, poured it into three cups, adding a little water to each. While measuring out the juice in the cups, Devaki had one cup slightly less full than the other two. Yogi Ramsuratkumar immediately gestured to her to make the contents of each cup exactly the same. Taking one of the cups, he got up again and handed it to Lee. When he sat back down, he drank the juice from his cup. Lee drank the juice in his cup, and Yogi Ramsuratkumar motioned to Devaki to drink the third cup. After the oranges and the juice were all gone, the sacramental ritual was finished. The mood shifted and relaxed in a way, as if shifting speed to a lower gear. A broad smile broke across Yogi Ramsuratkumar's face.

"This *lila* will give Lee good material for poetry! This beggar has made good material for poems for Lee!" He repeated this several times, chuckling a little with delight and satisfaction and a hint of mischievousness. Later, Lee would write:

Devaki picked three oranges
    to feed her Bhagawan.
She carefully removed every seed
    and every bit of skin
and gave only the sweetest essence
    to her Lord to eat.
Oh Father,
    Yogi Ramsuratkumar,
will You prepare Your son
    by cleansing lee of sins
and feed what is left
    to Your Father in Heaven
as tenderly
    as she fed You?[17]

The mystery of *prasad*—the exchange of a gift between the guru and the disciple—is tremendously important in the Hindu tradition. The guru's *prasad* is the literal gift of his or her substance, both physical and subtle. It is a highly symbolic gesture which acts as a metaphor or bridge for a subtle exchange of higher essence food, while also literally embodying the exchange of transubstantiated matter. The Sanskrit word *prasada* means "grace or favor, the mediation of God and hence, well-being,"[18] and can also mean "clarity, tranquility . . . of the inner being."[19] From the tantric perspective, anything the guru has empowered with his or her touch or attention has become blessed, transmuted into the body of the guru, and therefore is a transmitter and receptacle of grace. Yogi Ramsuratkumar was a master at transubstantiating food and substances in this way and

17 Ibid, p. 480.
18 Judith M. Tyberg, *The Language of the Gods*, pp. 7, 46.
19 Georg Feuerstein, *Encyclopedic Dictionary of Yoga*, pp. 269-270.

using them as vehicles for powerful alchemical blessings and empowerments, but it was the actions themselves that carried power. Through Devaki, the master enacted the purification of the disciple: the removing of veils, "skins" and even seeds to leave only the perfected and purified essence or *rasa* of the fruit.

These moments were made even more indescribably sacred by his frequent outbursts in praise of God. "All is My Father in Heaven, all perfect unity, total, complete! All in perfect unity, the all-pervading, all-powerful Father—in this and this and this," he pointed to flowers, shrubs, inanimate objects. "Everything, everywhere, all My Father in the play of all forms, only Father! My Father alone! My Father alone!" This he spoke with indisputable certainty, an unquestionable confidence, as divine witness to the play of creation, in which he saw only Ram. His joy in these moments of declaration was thrilling, infectious and sweet as ambrosia.

At four p.m. Yogi Ramsuratkumar, Devaki and the Sudama sisters left for Sudama House, followed by Lee and our group. We spent the remainder of the day together there, chanting the name of God and reading poems. After a meal was served, Devaki asked Lee to read one of his poems.

"I would like to hear the way you would read it, so I can hear the phrasing and how you would emphasize . . ."

"Let me get it together," Lee laughed, obviously shy and embarrassed. He smiled and gracefully complied with the request, but for a poet who describes himself often as an "arrogant fool" there was an interesting paradox in his discomfort as he read more than one poem for Devaki. His reading was exquisite in its simplicity and total lack of pretension or false devotion, and because of that, the true feeling of the poetry was laid bare. Later we heard from another Western traveler who had read *Poems of a Broken Heart*, "I never knew arrogance was such a virtue."

On that day alone we had had the privilege of spending fourteen hours in the rare company of Yogi Ramsuratkumar. It was our last day with him, and that night in the shrine room at Sudama House, Yogi Ramsuratkumar began to ask Lee questions about his ashram in Arizona, as he had in 1991. He wanted to know how many married couples, how many children and how many single people lived there. He wanted to know what the schedule of the day was like, what the food was like and so on. Lee explained that the food was vegetarian, mostly raw food or lightly cooked vegetables and some grains. Yogi Ramsuratkumar listened with interest.

"Do you serve coffee on your ashram, Lee?" Lee answered no. "Tea?" he asked. Again the answer was no. With a mischievous twinkle in his eyes, Yogi Ramsuratkumar looked at Devaki as if in amazement and began to laugh as he said, "There must not be very many people at your ashram, Lee!" Everyone laughed at the joke, including Lee, as Yogi Ramsuratkumar adroitly and humorously assessed Lee's strict approach to spiritual practice.

At one point Devaki spilled a very small amount of Yogi Ramsuratkumar's gooseberry tea as she was pouring it into his coconut bowl.

"Nothing bad ever happens. It's all my Father's Will," he said, then turned to Lee and said, "This beggar is afraid to tell Devaki she did something wrong."

Lee had brought gifts to Yogi Ramsuratkumar: two cassette tapes recorded by "liars, gods & beggars." The rock band and Lee's music had been a topic of conversation with the beggar during Lee's visit in 1991 also. Now, holding the cassettes and looking at them curiously, Yogi Ramsuratkumar asked Lee to explain.

"What is this rock and roll?" he asked with interest, "This beggar wants to know about what Lee is doing with this rock and roll."

Never one to give cosmic meaning to his projects or to things in general, Lee simply said, "Entertaining people," then gave a brief explanation of contemporary American rock music. Devaki wanted to play the tapes right away but Yogi Ramsuratkumar said, "No, it will wait until later."

On the first night of our visit, when he had given *prasad* to each person, he had instructed us in how to receive it, demonstrating himself by holding his hands out, cupped together like a small bowl in a receptive gesture. Each night we had left Sudama House with *prasad* in hand, given directly to us by Yogi Ramsuratkumar—an apple or banana or small packets of the opaque white rock candy, pure sugar. On our last night he called each person up and talked with him or her for a few minutes, asking, "What is your name?"

That night a delicious dinner of lemon rice, curd rice, sambar and vegetables was served in the shrine room of the house. We would be leaving the next morning before dawn, and the anticipation of saying goodbye was like knowing we would soon be ripped out of paradise—torn away from the most precious being in the world. With the impending physical separation from him hanging in the air, Yogi Ramsuratkumar began to talk about the poetry.

"Everyone should read this poetry every day," he said, looking around at us and even at Devaki. He repeated, "You should read this poetry every day." The moments passed by like a halcyon dream, in which Yogi Ramsuratkumar was speaking to us without reserve; his every word was a jeweled offering that we could take with us.

"Lee Lozowick has done a great work for this dirty beggar with these poems. The name of this dirty beggar will be scattered all over the world with these poems, written in English by Lee. Lee Lozowick has given a great gift to this beggar. Now this beggar won't have to beg anyone to write about this beggar anymore. No more. It is done now. Lee Lozowick and his reign of love will be all over the world . . . "

He repeated these things several times and said that there had been poetry like this in India before, but this was the first time it had been written in English. Speaking to Lee's students, he said, "Spread these poems all over the world. It will help this beggar's work." Turning to Lee he said, "Thank you, Mr. Lee, for doing this beggar's work."

Gazing at Lee, he said, "My Father blesses Lee with whatever he wants." The moment lingered and it seemed that time was stretched while Yogi Ramsuratkumar looked at Lee as if reading some subtle imprint. Then he said gently, "My Father blesses Lee with what he *needs*." He smiled sweetly and everyone chuckled at the inference, including Lee: there was a very big difference between getting what one wanted and what one needed.

In the years ahead Lee would often speak humorously about this communication from Yogi Ramsuratkumar, in a self-deprecating way, but it seemed in the moment that the master was giving Lee the gift of beggary, in answer to the prayers and outright demands of his poetry. The beggar was blessing Lee with the destiny of being a beggar—the mystical beggar who depends entirely on a Divine Intelligence, the will of God, to provide everything that is needed. To get what one wants is the prerogative of a king, or of the ego. When Yogi Ramsuratkumar said, “My Father blesses Lee with what he needs,” his voice resounded with implications that went far beyond food, clothes and shelter and penetrated into the labyrinth of transformation and radical surrender.

We gathered our small bags and *prasad* and filed out the door. Yogi Ramsuratkumar walked hand in hand with Lee to the gate. It was seven-thirty, and dark outside. There was no queue waiting outside the garden wall, and Yogi Ramsuratkumar stood beside the open gate and blessed each one of us as we walked out into the warm night. After touching the master’s feet and offering one last *pranam*, Lee was the last one out the gate. The beggar stood with one hand raised in blessing as he watched us walk away.

For three days Yogi Ramsuratkumar had showered all of his time and attention on Lee and his group, while many devotees and transitory supplicants stood outside in the sun and only a few were permitted entrance. It had been Yogi Ramsuratkumar’s way over the years to conduct specific work with small groups for periods of time. These three days with Lee and the Americans had been reminiscent of the days when he worked only with Murugeshan, Parthasarathy, Shivashankara and their families. It was the master’s *lila*, and many did not understand. Resentment brewed and seemed to peak when a wealthy devotee dressed in fine silk clothes came for darshan one afternoon. He was allowed in to see the beggar briefly, then left in a fluster. As he walked away he groused, “I think Yogi is losing touch with the common people!” It was a sentiment that was brewing under the surface of things as the fundraising for an ashram and large temple was swiftly gaining momentum.

Most of all, some of the devotees objected to the constant presence of Devaki and the Sudama sisters. Without question the move to Sudama House and the acceptance of a group of female attendants and one “eternal slave” was rocking the boat of the devotee’s expectations of their guru. Once again the mad beggar was going against the status quo, the rules and regulations, the dogmatic point of view.

After he had returned to Arizona, Lee Lozowick wrote on January 18, 1994:

> Just before he left
>   with a great flourish,
> a wealthy man
>   dressed in fine, expensive silks
> said: “I think Yogi is losing touch
>   with the common people.”
> I know Father,
>   for I was there.

What a shame that he has mistaken
    the body of an old Beggar
for the Regard of God
    and the Truth of Love.
I have seen Your Murti
    in Kanimadam, oh Bhagavan,
and felt Your Blessings
    in village after village.
Still some illusion persists,
    despite intelligence and education.
Some believe that appearance is spirit
    and cannot see their own Father.
They misunderstand Your Madness,
    expecting you to be polite and well-behaved.
Oh Father Yogi Ramsuratkumar,
    Your son tells them this:
"How much joy you miss when you blame
    the dirty Sinner for your own blindness."[20]

In January 1994 *Tattva Darsana* published an editorial written by Rangarajan about Yogi Ramsuratkumar and Devaki titled, "The Eternal Slave." Some of the devotees resisted the idea and some were vehemently opposed, while others were accepting and supportive, viewing all of the changes—including an ashram—from a bigger perspective, deeming them a necessary and natural evolution. Many were concerned about what this "appointment" meant. Was Devaki more than an attendant? Was she being groomed as a successor to Yogi Ramsuratkumar? Should she be considered another Mataji Krishnabai? Despite the tradition of many great masters who had female counterparts, patriarchal attitudes prevailed: How could they accept a woman in such a position? The editorial pulled no punches and went straight for the throat of the situation:

> In the case of Devaki also, the Divine Master tried to make her resist her own temptation to give up a lucrative and ideal profession. "What will you do if you are thrown out by the Master?" she was asked by a devotee whom the Master engaged to dissuade her from her attempt. "I will sit in a corner and chant His name," was the prompt reply from her. She gave up her job, sat in the presence of the Master for one whole year, her heart throbbing every moment to be of service to Him.

20 Lee Lozowick, *Death of a Dishonest Man,* p. 343.

> At last, the Master fell. Yes, it is really a great fall. Unless He comes down, how can He raise up the devotee? He has enslaved Himself by making His devotee His "Eternal Slave." When my Master declared "Devaki is my eternal slave" and that she would be by His side all the time taking care of Him, this Sadhu remarked, "Maharaj, I envy her. After my initiation, in the last five years, I never found a single opportunity to stay by your side and serve you. All these years I have been wandering for Ramnam. But she is going to be by your side all the time." Yes, Devaki is a thousand times more fortunate in getting this opportunity to be my Master's "Eternal Slave." However this Sadhu expressed his own consolation: "In a way, I'm more fortunate than you, Maharaj. After your initiation by your Master, He wanted you to go away from Him, but you have, in your immense kindness, permitted this Sadhu to visit you at least once a month."[21]

According to Rangarajan, Yogi Ramsuratkumar said, "This beggar needs someone to take care of him. Devaki and the Sudama sisters are taking so much care of this beggar that this beggar cannot live without them." Rangarajan continued in the article: "Yes, Devaki is to be envied by everyone, for she possesses the greatest wealth in this world which any human being can aspire for—total surrender and sacrifice to the Bhagavan, which leads to Immortality."[22] He referred to Devaki as a *pujarini*—a woman *pujari*, who can perform the worship ceremonies to the Lord, then concluded the article by saying:

> This is the month of Margasheersha, and the morning dew reflects the glory of Andal. Devaki reminds us of the spirit of Andal, Meera, Karaikkal, Ammayar and Mataji Krisnabai. This Yogi Ramsuratkumar 76th Jayanthi issue of *Tattva Darsana*, flowering on the Margasheersha morning, feels proud in spreading the sweet fragrance of the supreme sacrifice of my spiritual sister, Devaki. May the boundless blessings of my Divine Master Yogi Ramsuratkumar be showered on her who has offered the flower of her life at the feet of my Master.[23]

In early January there was a meeting at Sudama House between the ashram trustees and Yogi Ramsuratkumar. Several devotees were there, including Mani and his wife, Raji. The ashram project already had momentum, but a number of devotees were inflamed by the editorial written by Sadhu Rangarajan and refused to support the author's decision to accept Devaki as "eternal slave" and closest companion of Yogi Ramsuratkumar.

Bhagawan read through the editorial and a heated argument ensued. Yogi Ramsurat-

---

21 Sadhu Rangarajan, "The Eternal Slave," *Tattva Darsana*, November 1993–January 1994, pp. 5-6.

22 Ibid, p. 7.

23 Ibid, p. 8.

kumar was furious. He told the trustees that he had asked Rangarajan to write the article; it was only done at his instruction. They objected to the photograph that had been taken of Yogi Ramsuratkumar and Devaki in the fall of 1993 on the ashram property, also printed in *Tattva Darsana*. They challenged the master, saying that they would not accept the photograph of the beggar with Devaki; furthermore they refused to show the respect to her that Bhagawan had indicated was appropriate, nor would they allow her to live in the ashram.

"No!" Yogi Ramsuratkumar shouted at the trustees, reflecting their anger back on them, "Then let us not have ashram! Why are you building an ashram for this womanizer? You go and find somebody else as your guru and make an ashram for that man!" Yogi Ramsuratkumar shouted in a holy fury. It was like the roaring of a lion, and Sudhama House trembled from the power of it.

Suddenly he turned to Mani and said, "What do you think of this, Mani?"

"You are the creator of this episode, and you are going to be the solver. It is all your *lila*, Bhagawan," Mani answered.

Yogi Ramsuratkumar turned to another devotee and said, "What do you think?"

"You are a tall tree. Tall trees always fall first," he answered. People were crying and many of the devotees didn't dare to speak at all. Mani's wife, Raji, recounted:

> He was asking everybody about Devaki Ma. I was so scared that Bhagawan was going to ask me next. What to answer? I didn't want to answer what he would ask me. I thought, "If he asks Rajalakshmi, what should I answer? I don't know, and I'm so scared!" So, I was praying to Bhagavan, "Please, Bhagavan, don't ask me any difficult questions—just simple questions." Everyone was leaving the house when Bhagawan said to me, "Rajalakshmi, you stay back." Everybody went out. There were two parrots there. He asked me this question: "What is this?"
>
> "Parrots, Bhagawan," I said.
>
> "Okay," he answered. It was a simple question. He had answered my prayer!

A week or so after this Rajalakshmi sent a gift to Yogi Ramsuratkumar with the message, "Appa, how is Amma?" meaning, "Father, how is Mother?" When Yogi Ramsuratkumar received the gift and read the message, he was ecstatic; someone had stepped forward in support of what many people had overlooked—from the beginning, since September 1993, Yogi Ramsuratkumar had said, "My Father wants Devaki for his work." Reading the letter, he exclaimed, "Oh, here is a person who accepted this beggar as appa and Devaki as amma! This is the spirit this beggar wants from everybody. When this beggar says something, you should accept it as it is!" He was constantly teaching and demonstrating surrender to the will of God, and in the relationship with the guru, surrender begins with obedience.

Yogi Ramsuratkumar held the letter in his hand all the time and showed the message to everyone he saw for days. The message was loud and clear: "When the master says something, you should accept it as it is."

A few days later Mani came to Tiruvannamalai to have darshan with Yogi Ramsuratkumar. Many people came up to him and asked, "Who is Rajalakshmi?" When he responded, "She's my wife," they would say, "Oh, she's a great person. Bhagawan has been talking about her!"

As soon as Mani arrived at Sudama House, Yogi Ramsuratkumar said, "Devaki! Mani has come!" and turning to Mani he said, "You see, Mani, what Rajalakshmi did?" But Mani had no idea why Bhagawan was so excited and happy. Raji hadn't told him anything about the message, just that she was sending a money order to Bhagawan.

When Mani looked perplexed, Yogi Ramsuratkumar said, "Do you know the message, what she has written in the money order form?"

"No, she did not tell me anything, Bhagawan."

"Mani, will you do some work for this beggar? I want to send a reply, a message to Rajalakshmi. Will you carry it?" Yogi Ramsuratkumar asked. Mani said yes, of course, then sending everyone else out, he gave the following letter to Mani, written by Devaki with a postscript in Yogi Ramsuratkumar's own hand:

> From Appa Yogi Ramsuratkumar and Amma Devaki
> To Our Dear Loving Daughter
>
> Our very dear Raji,
>
> We were so happy to receive the note that accompanied your money order that Appa called everyone at Sudama and showed it! Your love and innocence has won his heart so totally that He has kept that note with Himself ever since. He remembers you often and He sends His love and blessings to you.
>
> I am also happy to tell you this: Your calling me "Amma" has made you my eldest daughter. All the other children are only after you!
>
> Yours affectionately
>
> Amma
>
> My dear Rajalakshmi, your Amma blesses you!!! We both are so happy to receive your note. My dear Rajalakshmi [written in Sanskrit] my father blesses you!!! My father blesses my dear Mani!!!
>
> Yours affectionately
>
> Yogi Ramsuratkumar

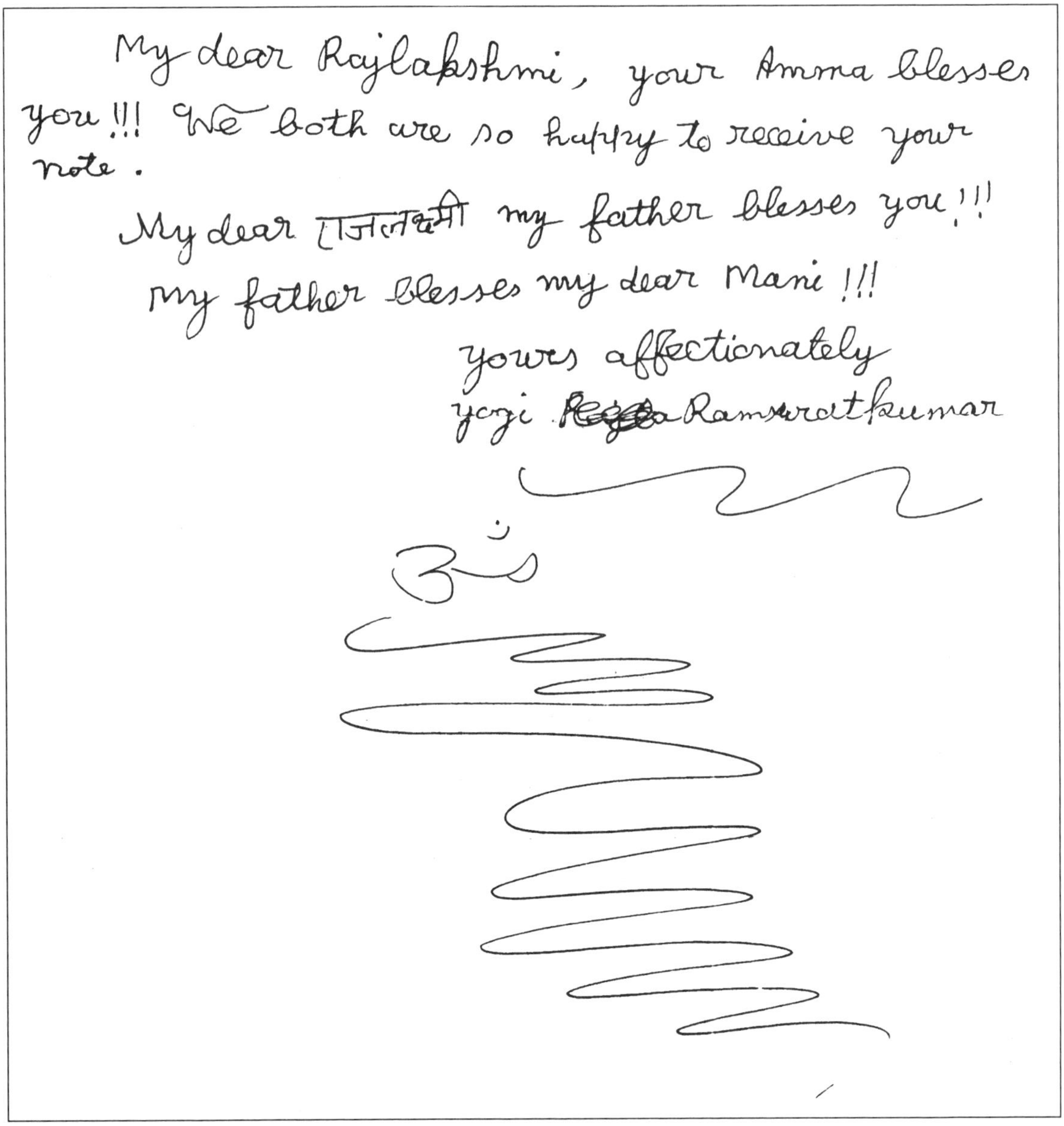

My dear Rajlakshmi, your Amma blesses you!!! We both are so happy to receive your note.

My dear राजलक्ष्मी my father blesses you!!!

my father blesses my dear Mani!!!

yours affectionately
yogi ~~Rega~~ Ramsuratkumar

Raji was ecstatic when she received the letter, having heard from many of Yogi Ramsuratkumar's long-term devotees that even if he liked a letter, he would not reply. She never expected a response, and this was a great blessing. A key phrase in the letter, one that captured Raji's attention the most was "Your innocence has won his heart." It was his answer to all the suspicion, cynicism and doubt of the other devotees: it was only with the eyes of wise innocence that they could see accurately the crystalline purity of Yogi Ramsuratkumar's relationship with Devaki.

A few weeks later Raji and Mani went to Tiruvannamalai to meet Yogi Ramsuratkumar. The first thing he said to her was, "How did you feel when you received my reply?"

"I locked it in my locker, Bhagawan, because it's a treasure for me," she replied. He laughed very hard at this news.

"Oh, she says it's a treasure for her!" He laughed and smiled at Raji. After that Yogi Ramsuratkumar began to call Raji his "daughter," and to draw her more deeply into his intimate circle of devotees. Both Mani and Raji were deeply touched; they were held in Yogi Ramsuratkumar's esteem, and at the same time, as relatively new devotees they were quickly immersed in the heat and intensity around the guru's physical person. They were beginning to experience what it meant to be close to the guru: obedience was called for in all matters, and many demands were placed upon them—all of which seemed designed to purify and train them in the fierce *sadhana* that they did not yet realize they had taken on.

Every time Raji came to Sudama House for darshan, Yogi Ramsuratkumar always had her sit beside him. If someone gave him a flower or money or if he had empty Charminar packets, he gave them all to Raji instead of Devaki, who normally received all these forms of attention. Yogi Ramsuratkumar often fed Raji small pieces of chapatti or rice with his own hands. Seeing these familial intimacies, people would come to Raji afterward and ask her, "How long have you known Bhagawan? You must have known him a long time?"

"No, only for two months!" she replied with a chuckle.

Life has a way of going on, no matter how heated a debate may be. The gossip and uproar over Yogi Ramsuratkumar's relationship with Devaki and the Sudama sisters was eventually swallowed up by the excitement and enthusiasm that the building of the ashram generated.

At one point Mani and Rajalakshmi wanted to go to Kanimadam for a celebratory event at the Mantralayam. Mani came to Sudama House to see Yogi Ramsuratkumar, and he waited in line with twenty-one people. When his turn for darshan came, he said to Bhagawan, "I want to go to Kanimadam," he said.

"No," Bhagawan answered flatly. "You go to Anandashram. You take your wife with you." After a moment he added, "You have seen this beggar here. Why you are going there [to Kanimadam]? You go to my father's place, Anandashram. Take your wife."

Back in Chennai, Mani told Rajalakshmi, "Bhagavan wants us to go to Anandashram." They packed their bags and went to Anandashram for three days; it was the first ashram they had ever stayed in, and there they got to experience a good model for how an ashram is run, and what ashram life is like. They liked it so much that Rajalakshmi said to Mani, "You find a place near Anandashram and buy a piece of land. We'll build a house here, we'll settle here." After three days they returned to Madras and Mani went to Tiruvannamalai.

"Why are you here?" Bhagavan asked, "I told you to go to Anandashram."

"I went to Anandashram and came back, Bhagawan," Mani explained.

"Only three days? Go back! Who asked you to come back? You go back to Anandashram!" was the frank reply.

"How can I go, Bhagawan, I'm just walking? How can I go?" Mani asked, nonplussed.

"I don't know—go back," the master said unequivocally.

Mani ended up staying at Anandashram for twenty-seven days and working on the ashram under Swami Satchidananda, serving in the dining hall and in many capacities, learning what it meant to run an ashram. Raji was also there, and made chapattis in the kitchen, helping the cooks. It was a learning experience—the perfect opportunity to train for the jobs that they would have in the years ahead at the Yogi Ramsuratkumar Ashram. At that time Mani had no idea that he would move to Tiruvannamalai and become the ashram manager and one of the trustees. On January 26, 1994 Mani again visited Yogi Ramsuratkumar at Sudama House. Bhagawan was sitting with all the devotees when he turned to Mani.

"Mani, whenever this beggar gets into madness he thinks of you, very often—whenever this beggar goes into madness. My Father says you are going to build temples and places . . ."

Mani was shocked. "You joke!" he exclaimed. When Bhagawan just looked at him, Mani reiterated, "This is a joke! Bhagawan, I think your Father is searching for someone else—not me." Mani had a natural affinity and affection for the beggar, and spoke with him just like a friend, but what Bhagawan was suggesting sounded overwhelming, impossible, exhausting—constructing temples and places for Bhagawan!

"No, no, no, no," Mani laughed, thinking that Bhagawan was just being playful.

Yogi Ramsuratkumar then blessed Mani and gave him a large shawl, saying, "Go back."

Mani left for Madras, but Yogi Ramsuratkumar was not joking. Mani was soon thrown into the all-consuming work of creating, from the ground up, a sanctuary of worship for the beggar saint. On February 27, 1994, exactly one month later, Mani was formally announced as the ashram manager or *sarvadikhari* and given a place as one of the ashram trustees. In the meantime Yogi Ramsuratkumar had given Mani the task of preparing the ashram grounds for the upcoming inauguration ceremony, when Swami Satchidananda would come to inaugurate the work.

Around mid-month, Yogi Ramsuratkumar called Raji in for a private interview at Sudama House, outside the usual public darshan hours. "What are your activities in Chennai?" he asked. He wanted to know if Raji sang, if she knew English, what her studies had been, what her interests were. He was grooming them both for the responsibilities that he would heap on their shoulders later.

Mani and Raji were living in a hotel in Tiruvannamalai during this time. One day Yogi Ramsuratkumar called Raji in and said, "This beggar would like you and Mani to look for a house." A house was found behind Sudama House and rented with Yogi Ramsuratkumar's help in negotiating with the owner. Immediately Mani and Raji moved into the house, which was aptly named the "son-in-law" house, since Raji had been named the "daughter." Yogi Ramsuratkumar came to do the housewarming puja, and went all over the house giving his blessing to each room. He was now involved in everything that happened in their lives, from where they would live and how to rent a house, to naming their grandchild, which was considered a great honor.

The controversy continued among the devotees over Yogi Ramsuratkumar's declaration of Devaki as his "Eternal Slave," and his subsequent move to Sudama House. There was as much, and perhaps even more, support for Yogi Ramsuratkumar, Devaki and the Sudama sisters, as there was resistance; in fact, it seemed that the outrage came from a relatively small but powerful minority. Most of the devotees simply wanted to honor and obey their guru and *ishta devata*.

One of the writers for *Mountain Path*, the well-known magazine of Ramanashram, jumped into the fray in an article that was published in the June 1994 (Aradhana) issue, in which she criticized Rangarajan and his editorial in *Tattva Darsana* for jumping on the bandwagon too quickly in a bad habit of changing from one guru to another: "Foreseeing that the saint will not be in the body for long, he has latched on to his ardent devotee Sri Devaki, as a sort of life insurance policy." Rangarajan was the primary target of the criticism, but most importantly, the author seemed called to speak for the devotees of Yogi Ramsuratkumar who were having the most difficulty with the appointment of Ma Devaki:

> The editor [of *Tattva Darsana*] asserts that the Yogi introduced Sri Devaki to him as "Ma Devaki"—an invariable sign that a successor has been appointed or at least unmistakably indicated. For some it is a sour pill to swallow, for, to them, Yogi Ramsuratkumar is their all in all, and their devotion is directed only to him and to no one else. For them even the thought of human replacement is unthinkable!
>
> However, it is true that Sri Devaki, who gave up her career to be with her master, is a surrendered devotee of the Yogi.[24]

In May 1994 Rangarajan published a rebuttal to this commentary in his editorial in *Tattva Darsana*, in which he stated again that the editorial in the November 1993-January 1994 issue was published entirely at the request of Yogi Ramsuratkumar himself. He wrote passionately about the guru principle and about Ma Devaki herself, frequently referring back to the *Mountain Path* article:

> There is no question of Ma Devaki "making a successful transition from her present one of the devotee-disciple to that of a mother embracing all those who flock to Yogi Ramsuratkumar without distinction and that with haste." Ma Devaki has no independent existence once she has been chosen as His "eternal slave." Her actions cannot be different from what He wills. If ever she should err, it will be only His error.[25]

24 Radha, "Sri Yogi Ramsuratkumar," *Mountain Path*, Volume 31, No. 12, p. 71.

25 Sadhu Rangarajan, "The Vision of Truth," *Tattva Darsana*, May-July 1994, p. 8.

On the other side of the world Lee Lozowick was writing poems, as Yogi Ramsuratkumar had asked him to do:

> Oh You, dirty Beggar—
> You've certainly got them talking now!
> I guess the gossips have no doubt
> about Your reputation as a mad Sinner—
> what with living with women,
> and drinking Your private stock of wine all day!
> Oh You crazy Liar,
> Yogi Ramsuratkumar,
> it surely must tickle Your ears
> to hear the tongues wag as they do.
> Oh Father, Father,
> Your son tells them this:
> I have met His Devaki
> and drunk His wine from His own hand
> and that dirty Sinner
> is a Madman after this bad Poet's heart.[26]
>
> December 27, 1993
>
> I've asked you countless times
> to tell me what You would have of me.
> Oh cruel Master of Your son's fate,
> Your order was clear:
> write poems on Devaki
> You said, sweet Father.
> So I who have bragged of Sacrifice
> must write of she who is sacrifice.
> In the face of her surrender
> Your Foolish son is exposed.
> No matter: bad Poetry for she
> who is the dirty Sinner's comfort.[27]
>
> January 17, 1994

Nine years later, on January 26, 2003, Dwarak Nath Reddy, who knew Yogi Ramsuratkumar and Devaki very well, spoke about the conflict in retrospect:

---

26 Lee Lozowick, *Death of a Dishonest Man*, p. 482.

27 Ibid, p. 486.

I can tell you this about Devaki: she has always been a rare devotee—so confirmed in her perceptions, so sure and so committed, that there are no questions left, no need to rethink anything. For her, a look at Yogi Ramsuratkumar or a look from him was enough for the day. She could live on that. She would come all the way from Salem and stand in the sun there at Sannadhi Street and maybe get a glimpse of him with no chance of going into the house. She would go back to Salem and she could be happy and contented, and five days later she could come and do that again. So that's what Devaki was always: she asked for nothing, wanted nothing, she was not even seeking explanations.

Devaki was taken into this circle. It must have been surprising even to Devaki; she was not the one who would ask a question. If you put a crown on her head, she would just sit quietly and accept it. If he threw her into the gutter she would just sit there until he asked her to get up. That has been Devaki all along. This I say with personal knowledge of that human being and the conviction I carry. The position she was put into was not of her asking, not of her seeking, and so she just said: "I don't have a right to ask for it, what right have I to say yes or no to what my guru and God says?" So, she has just been wherever she has been placed and she has done what her supreme Lord told her to do. That was her point of view.

We can have our opinions and judgments about it, but I think she is just a person of such surrender, which itself should make us respect her. Our judgments and everything aside—that's a surrender! We all talk of surrender, but I don't think I have seen anyone who can exceed her in real surrender. So whatever happened to her it just happened. She was not an actor, not a do-er in that at all. This Devaki I am talking of, the one I knew so closely ten years back, I don't think she could have become proud or arrogant or queenly or possessive or wanting a famous name. I don't see Devaki that way.

CHAPTER EIGHT

The Ashram

1994-1998

> Ever since this beggar died in 1952 he hasn't been able to do anything. Now the Father does everything. I do only his work. Only what he tells me. It's slavery—sweet slavery.
>
> — Yogi Ramsuratkumar

On February 26, 1994 Swami Satchidananda of Anandashram came to Tiruvannamalai to inaugurate the new ashram of Yogi Ramsuratkumar at the time of the *bhumi puja*—the laying of the foundation stone. Swami Satchidananda began his talk by humorously commenting that he had been asked to speak in Tamil rather than his native language, saying, "You are going to find it funny when you listen to my Tamil!" After making his salutations to Ramdas and Krishnabai and speaking with eloquence and reverence of his reunion with his "brother," Yogi Ramsuratkumar, his talk focused in on the need to see the guru as the all-pervading Absolute, not limited to his form or the function of miracle-worker. His wise counsel to the devotees on the auspicious occasion of this new beginning was to seek not the manifestation of the guru's miracles and attachment to his personal form, but to seek only the guru's grace—the "universal vision."

The following is excerpted from Swami Satchidananda's speech:

> I have not seen Yogi for 40 years. Before that I met him when he had come to the ashram during his sadhana period. That time, his Sadhana was very intense. He had taken mantra initiation from Gurudev Papa. He desired to remain with Papa, but Papa did not permit it for various reasons. Now we realize that it was God's will. Remaining far away, performing his sadhana, he became a yogi, giving out the fragrance of prema to all just as a bud blossoming into a flower diffuses its perfume around. All of you who have inhaled and enjoyed this perfume of love are, indeed, very blessed. My heart is deeply touched by your devotion. Your devotion makes me feel that the rare kind of love that the gopis had for Lord

Krishna as described in *Bhagavatham* could indeed be true. Any number of prostrations to you, who have this kind of devotion, will ever be inadequate. You are all fortunate souls, indeed!

Yesterday and today, many devotees narrated beautifully, with love and adoration, their experiences with Yogi Ramsuratkumar. Now what I am going to talk is about you. There is no need to talk further about Yogi, for it's all known well to all here.

You have all accepted Yogi as your guru. But, who is Yogi? Where does Yogi reside? Is he only in Tiruvannamalai? We have to contemplate this aspect clearly. Only when we comprehend this, we can progress further on the path of bhakti and jnana. Our guru is verily God Himself—the Lord of the entire universe, the all-pervading God, the One who has become manifest as everything is our guru. He has come in a particular form, in the form Yogi Ramsuratkumar, to give us guidance and instruction.

Keeping this in mind, whenever we have Yogi's remembrance, we should mentally prostrate to him with the reverential attitude that "He is not limited to this form only, but he is all-pervasive; his form or saguna aspect is the entire universe and he is seated in our hearts." Whenever we see him or prostrate before him, we must have this attitude. Then only we can become fit to give up or rise above the "dehatma buddhi" or body consciousness and experience our oneness with him.

We may all praise Yogi and glorify him talking about his miracles. From our ordinary viewpoint or at the level of body-consciousness, these are great wonders. But for the saints there is nothing great or astounding about these occurrences. They, who have triumphed over everything and declared their experience, "I am verily the Universe. I am the eternal Reality which is beyond everything," are capable of performing any great feat. These are not miracles for them. But they appear to be miracles in our eyes.

We should not get caught in these things, saying, "Yogi did this for me, did that for me"; "He cured me of my ailment"; "He got me promotion"; "He arranged my daughter's marriage," etc. If we keep talking about such things, we will remain stuck at this level. We don't want these. He will take care of all our affairs—is he not the all-pervading God? He is there only to take care of our lives. We don't have to ask him about our mundane affairs. There is no need to trumpet about these occurrences either. When we think of Yogi, what we have to pray to him is: "We should merge in his eternal being. We should be enabled to strive for that realization or experience." This is the only prayer we should make. He will look after the rest. Once he has given us this human body and created us in this world, it is his look out to guide our life till our death. That is his burden.

> Therefore, we need not ask him for anything.
>
> Many devotees who spoke yesterday and today narrated about Yogi's miracles with great love and joy. Among them, only one mentioned about universal vision and had asked for this experience. Why didn't the rest ask for that? Why have they not reached that level? At least from now, whenever you think of Yogi or see him, you must pray to him for universal vision and see the entire universe as his form. Whatever you see is his form. "I must get this experience." You ask him for this and he will definitely grant it. All the yogis, saints, gurus and the great beings are like wish-fulfilling trees. Whatever we think of or pray before them we will surely get it. Instead of asking for petty things, pray only for merging with his eternal being. It is better not to pray to them for mundane things.

Yogi Ramsuratkumar had asked Mani to manage the cleaning and preparation of the ashram grounds for this grand occasion, and it was after this that the work of constructing an ashram started in earnest. Yogi Ramsuratkumar was involved in every step of the process. At one point there were up to two hundred and fifty or three hundred workers working long hours, sometimes late into the night. Three meals were served every day. The plans for the ashram were quite elaborate, including an immense temple the size of a football field—at Yogi Ramsuratkumar's instruction, big enough to accommodate five thousand people—a spacious kitchen and dining hall, several cottages for ashram residents and guests, a meditation room and large reception or entrance room into the temple, a library and several outbuildings like the Yagashala, which would be used for the Vedic fire rituals.

By late spring construction on the ashram was well underway with as many as two hundred workers on site. The first building—the small, almost square stone darshan *mandir* with a thatched roof, located by the front gate—became the location of the morning and afternoon darshans, and would accommodate two hundred people squeezed in tightly.

Three times a day Yogi Ramsuratkumar was driven by Ravi, his driver, back and forth from Sudama House, which was only a few blocks away from the ashram. He came at seven a.m. for an early breakfast and again for the two periods of darshan that were held during the day, from ten to twelve noon and from four to six p.m. These darshan programs were open to the general public, and throngs of people began to arrive; guests and devotees from all walks of life came and went, seeking the beggar's blessing and wanting to offer *prasad*.

Every common moment was a moment of work for Yogi Ramsuratkumar. He once said to Ravi, "You know who is driving the car? My Father is driving the car." As Ravi drove Yogi Ramsuratkumar down the streets he would often instruct, "Slow, go slower," as he raised his hands in blessing to those standing in the queue, or to the beggars and sadhus who clustered along the edges of the streets and stood with hands pressed together in *pranam* as the beggar king rode by.

Yogi Ramsuratkumar's relationship with the ashram construction workers was particularly poignant, and he gave a tremendous amount of attention to them. He used to say, "Whosoever helped this ashram in any way will be especially blessed by Father. They are doing *tapas*. All these workers, even if they get money for it, they are doing *tapas*. They are doing my Father's work." He watched over them and their work with an eagle eye for detail. He was always concerned that the workers were cared for; he would often refuse to eat until they had all been served; sometimes he sat outside the darshan *mandir* with them while they ate, taking his noon meal with them.

Yogi Ramsuratkumar was very particular about each and every aspect of construction. He looked after the ashram with all the care and attention of a devoted parent—no detail was too small or unimportant for him to attend to. He knew every nuance of the enormous construction project and was kept abreast of current affairs on the ashram at least three times each day. How many workers there were at any one time, what tasks they were doing, what supplies had arrived, what supplies had been ordered, which items had been donated and by whom—all this and more was reported to the master. Yogi Ramsuratkumar made sure that his finger was on the pulse of the newly burgeoning ashram.

In addition to the construction workers, the ashram needed permanent staff members. Many who came to work on the staff got hired in various ways, but most of them were not devotees when they first came. With Mani as the ashram manager overseeing construction, the ashram staff began to take form: Ravi, the driver; Shaktivel, who worked in the office; Kannan, who was the gatekeeper; Rajeswari, a devotee who lived full-time on the ashram and managed the housekeeping; Mani's wife Raji, who Yogi Ramsuratkumar put to work overseeing the food service, or *annadhanam*, and many other details of daily ashram life. Ma Devaki and the Sudama sisters were also a constant presence, as they arrived and left with Yogi Ramsuratkumar every day.

People were drawn to work at the ashram in interesting ways. Many of them started working just for the paycheck, but were effortlessly won over by Yogi Ramsuratkumar. One such example was Saravanan, who first saw Yogi Ramsuratkumar many years before, as an eight year old boy outside the Shiva temple in town. The beggar had been standing in front of the temple with his fan in his hand, moving it about; Saravanan remembered that the old beggar had given him a fierce look. Years later Saravanan heard that many people were going to Sudama House for the darshan of Yogi Ramsuratkumar, who had become well known and popular among many different kinds of people. Thinking that he would go see what all the excitement was about, he stood in the queue outside Sudama House with the others devotees and pilgrims. When it was his turn to go in and prostrate before the master, Yogi Ramsuratkumar patted him on the back and said three times, "Rama, Rama, Rama," then handed him a banana for *prasad*.

"I really didn't like it. I gave the banana to a beggar," Saravanan remembered with a chuckle. Not long after that Vijayalakshmi introduced Saravanan to Ma Devaki, who spoke to Mani about him, and on May 13, 1994 he was hired to work in the ashram office in a clerical position. Right away he was shocked to realize the long hours that would be demanded, but things soon smoothed out and he began to come every day at seven o'clock in the morning and work until eight o'clock at night.

At first Saravanan never came out of the office. He could hear the songs and chanting going on, and these irritated him; it was troubling because the melodies of the songs and the words, "Yogi Ramsuratkumar, Yogi Ramsuratkumar, Yogi Ramsuratkumar, Jaya Guru Raya," quickly began to resound in his mind. He found that his mind was repeating the mantra for five or six days without cease. Finally one day Mani came into the office and said, "Hey Saravanan, people from many places are coming here to see Bhagawan and you are sitting inside in this office! You don't know Bhagawan's spiritual power. Come on out of this office and at least see him!" Thinking he would at least check it out, Saravanan went to stand with everyone else in the queue one morning to greet Yogi Ramsuratkumar as his car drove in.

That day Mani introduced Saravanan to Yogi Ramsuratkumar, saying, "Bhagawan, this is Mr. Saravanan who has come here to do clerical work."

"I see," the beggar said slowly, looking at Saravanan. "My Father blesses Saravanan." When he held his hand up in blessing, Saravanan was deeply surprised when his body moved backward in response to the force that gently pushed against him. It was a feeling of such benevolence that from that day on he was standing in the queue of devotees who came to see Bhagawan every day, morning and evening. These "drive-by" darshans became precious times for Saravanan that he didn't want to waste. Most amazing was that whenever he was having a bad day or felt down in spirit was always the same day that Bhagawan would call for him, saying, "Come. What is your name?"

"What is your name?" Yogi Ramsuratkumar would often ask, when he knew perfectly well what someone's name was; it was a way of focusing his formidable and vast attention on the person and establishing the flow of benediction, which would then come as, "My Father blesses you." It was amazing how often this happened to many different workers, just at the time when that person needed it the most. The fact of the master's attunement to the workers in this way built a tremendous trust and faith in them, and very soon they were convinced that he innately knew and understood their lives and their struggles. Yogi Ramsuratkumar's presence and actions were so impacting that those who came to work simply for the paycheck soon became dedicated and deeply devoted to him. Saravanan said, "Everybody came here and worked only for salary at first. After some months had passed, then they followed him: 'Okay, he is life itself—there is nothing else! Whatever he says . . .' "

Yogi Ramsuratkumar became everyone's beloved, and the staff members, like everyone else, lived for the sublime touch of his attention, often thinking, "Maybe he will call me today!" The workers were amazed at how attuned he was to their world. If someone was having a problem, that would be the day that Bhagawan called him forward in darshan. "Come," he would say, with his hand held out, the fingers giving the slightest gesture to beckon them forward. His everpresent question, "What is your name?" was asked as naturally of devotees he had known for twenty-five years as those he had only just met. This was completely lacking in guile or motivation; it was a function of his total inherence in ultimate reality—that is, the divine eternal presence of the moment. It was the open-ended possibility of the present moment, unlimited by the framework of expectations of past and future, that revealed the vast heart of God in his slightest gestures, his glances and perhaps most of all, in the incredible lilt of his voice. It was his gentle and extraordinary ways of understanding the inner world of the workers that captured their hearts; he was always one with them. He entered their hearts with such vast wisdom and practical magic, couched like a jewel in the setting of his perfect innocence.

In November 1994 Saravanan, Ravi and two other members of the staff pooled their money to buy Yogi Ramsuratkumar a gift of some new clothes—a *dhoti* and a fresh *kirta* shirt. The day before *Jayanthi* they gathered together and went into darshan. The protocol around Yogi Ramsuratkumar was such that the staff did not approach him unless they were called directly by him to do so. Usually they were standing ten feet away, available at the slightest notice, but not intruding in any way. Saravanan and the men pushed Ravi, who had known Yogi Ramsuratkumar for many years and had been very close with him, forward to be their representative in giving the gift of clothes.

They said, "Ravi, you go and tell him that tomorrow is *jayanthi* day—Swami will hear your words. We don't have the nerve to go near him!"

Very gently Ravi approached, pranamed and said, "Bhagawan, tomorrow is your *jayanthi*." Bhagawan ever so slowly turned to look at Ravi, who took heart and continued bravely, "When you come tomorrow, you have to wear these clothes." He put the clothes in Bhagawan's hands.

"Ohhh!" Yogi Ramsuratkumar said, looking at the clothes. "Those conditions are not suitable for this beggar. Whenever he wishes to wear these clothes, he will. Otherwise he will never wear them!" A hint of a smile played on his face. His regard for the workers came through, even as he spoke these words. He was far too unfettered to be captured and held by their love, but the day after *jayanthi*, he appeared wearing the clothes.

When the land for the ashram was first purchased, before the building began, Yogi Ramsuratkumar walked all around the property—a dusty field with a few bushes and a lot of small sharp rocks. A young local man, Selvaraj, saw the beggar walking on the land and began to clear and clean the ground where he would be walking. Selvaraj had never met him before, did not go to his darshan and had no idea that he would soon be working on the ashram. In early 1994 Selvaraj's brother was the night watchman for the ashram. One day in March his brother was not able to come to work, and Selvaraj came to do the night watch. There was nothing on the property but the small stone darshan *mandir*. When Mani discovered Selvaraj instead of his brother, he was angry and sent Selvaraj away. A few days later he called him back and said, "If you like working in the ashram, then you can come."

Although he was formally a trustee also, Mani was more like a co-worker with the staff than a distant and powerful "trustee," appointed by Yogi Ramsuratkumar to serve on the board of directors for the ashram. A tough and fierce taskmaster, Mani worked side by side with the employees to manage the construction of the temple and other ashram buildings in exactly the manner that Yogi Ramsuratkumar instructed—and Yogi

Ramsuratkumar's instructions themselves often involved the impossible. For example, when he wanted the football field-sized temple constructed without any pillars or posts: he insisted that the temple should be a wide-open vast space. Mani, a construction engineer who had built high-rise apartment buildings, airports and many kinds of massive buildings, argued with him that it was impossible and preposterous. It simply would not work.

"Mani will find a way," Yogi Ramsuratkumar insisted, and Mani somehow found a place that would cast the massive steel girders in unheard of proportions to span the temple ceiling. Somehow, it miraculously worked, just as Yogi Ramsuratkumar had said it would.

Yogi Ramsuratkumar was a stickler for punctuality, and he noticed when people were on time or not. He often said to the workers, "Be on time!" It took some longer than others to comply with this, but it was soon discovered that Selvaraj was an extremely reliable worker. His first job was to arrange everything for the breakfast meal that was served in the "breakfast hut," a cowshed with a thatched palm roof where Yogi Ramsuratkumar preferred to take his morning meal. Arriving at the ashram at six-thirty every morning, Selvaraj would bring the water, glasses, mats, banana leaves or plates and so on. At that time on the ashram Mutu was the personal attendant to Bhagawan. When he left in 1995, Yogi Ramsuratkumar himself chose Selvaraj to attend to him during darshan and at other times as well; as a result of this, Selvaraj was beside Yogi Ramsuratkumar almost all day long.

For the first year Selvaraj worked only for the salary and did not consider himself a devotee. Then something happened that radically changed his point of view. Without telling Yogi Ramsuratkumar, but getting permission from his immediate supervisor, Mani, Selvaraj planned to go away for a holiday to visit his mother-in-law in Melkaripur. He wanted to take a leave in order to do some work there, but after he left the ashram he began to feel that something was pulling him back; something was not quite right about his decision.

In the meantime, when Yogi Ramsuratkumar came to the ashram that morning at ten o'clock, he noticed that Selvaraj was missing.

"Where is Selvaraj? Where is Selvaraj?" he began to shout and yell. Everyone was shocked. Mani went to him and explained, "Bhagawan, he took a holiday. I have given him permission to go to his mother-in-law's. He is going to do some work there."

"If he goes to Melkaripur there will be trouble; it is very dangerous. He should not go there." Yogi Ramsuratkumar was very upset and distressed and Mani sent a messenger, who soon came running to Selvaraj's house.

"Bhagawan is calling for you—he is shouting and yelling for you!" Selvaraj immediately came to the ashram.

"Selvaraj," Yogi Ramsuratkumar said, "you don't go to Melkaripur. If you go it will be very dangerous."

"Okay Bhagawan, I won't go," Selvaraj agreed. His mind was already changed, and something very profound was going on inside him. He went to sit down in his usual place in the darshan *mandir*. A few minutes later Yogi Ramsuratkumar called him back to his side.

"If you go there to Melkaripur it will be dangerous!" Selvaraj again agreed, but Yogi Ramsuratkumar was bent on making the point. Two more times he called Selvaraj back up to his side and gave the same strong advice. The fourth time he called Mani and said, "You tell him, he doesn't work in Melkaripur!"

Whenever Yogi Ramsuratkumar felt that someone had not taken his words to heart or received the gist of what he was trying to say, he would repeat the communication three or four times. If he felt the person had gotten it, he only would only give the instruction once. Finally Selvaraj realized what was really going on. He went to Yogi Ramsuratkumar and *pranamed*.

"Bhagawan, I will not go without your permission—not only to Melkaripur, but wherever I go, I will get permission from you," Selvaraj promised. There was a much deeper commitment implied within the whole interchange, and from then on, his worldview was changed: Yogi Ramsuratkumar became the center of the universe. This kind of transformation occurred for many of the ashram workers.

When Yogi Ramsuratkumar had decided that one person was right for a certain job, he didn't want anyone else doing it. Once Ravi sent his brother to pick up Yogi Ramsuratkumar at Sudama House to take him to the ashram. Yogi Ramsuratkumar was very unhappy with this arrangement and sent Mani to tell Ravi, "Bhagawan was saying, 'If Ravi comes, this beggar will be happy. This beggar wants Ravi only. You tell him to come back.' " From that time on Ravi was the only person who drove Bhagawan.

This was also true for the Sudama sisters. When Vijayalakshmi first came to live at Sudama House, she didn't fully understand how Bhagawan worked. At first he allowed her leeway to learn what he liked and didn't like—a certain period of indulgence in making mistakes because she was new and didn't have the kind of exposure to him that Devaki and the other Sudama sisters had. Vijayalakshmi recounted:

> Right at the beginning I hadn't had much exposure to Bhagawan, and so I didn't understand what he might encourage and what he might not, and because I was new to the place, he also indulged me. Like if a friend of mine came and asked if she could take a photograph of Bhagawan, I would say yes, and then tell Bhagawan about it. Then Bhagawan also would say alright. It took me quite a little while to understand that Bhagawan didn't really want this kind of thing, but once I understood, of course, things turned alright.
>
> Another silly thing I used to do is that when Bhagawan came out of the toilet, his feet would be wet and I would scurry to wipe them with a towel. Then he'd say, "Raaamaaa, Raaamaaa." (Very slowly, almost with a growl.) I didn't understand what it meant, and then Devaki told me, "See, it's my work—you're not supposed to do that. And that's why he's saying, 'Rama' like that." All the personal services were done by Devaki, and I

> didn't know that. I thought, here was something to be done, let me do it. And so, he used to say, "Raaamaaa." When he said "Rama" in such a tone it stopped everybody in their tracks, it would come out so fiercely. I think almost everybody who came in contact with him would make some mistake because we just didn't have even an idea of what he really is.

Yogi Ramsuratkumar often had Devaki write letters and notes for him. When she was given a particular letter to write, it had to be done within a certain amount of time and there could be no corrections or later additions. The work had to be finished in a timely manner and without a lot of deliberating, hesitating or changing what had been done. When it was finished she would read it to him. Once it was read to him there could be no changes in it. This routine had an almost military discipline to it, to the point where Yogi Ramsuratkumar would add his own line in his own hand, "My Father blesses Lee Lozowick," or "My pranams to Janarthanan"—then there would suddenly be a touch of warmth, and he would cry out like a child, "Devaki, you see what this beggar has written nicely!"

If she said, "Bhagawan, your spelling is not correct. You have left an 'e' here," he would look at it and see what she was pointing to, then say, "Ohhh. This beggar has done . . ." Then he would correct it, and in that moment he was genuinely like a child, with no pretension. Within moments he could easily go from severe, to childlike, to demonstrating great maturity and dispensing profound wisdom, as Devaki recounted:

> That is why we had to be prepared for anything. And that is one of the reasons why he allotted one work to one person and he wouldn't want that to be interfered with. That person would be trained for it and that person would do it always. We had two watchmen, and one of them had to open the door and certain other work, while the other had different work. Even if one watchman was not there, the other should not take over his job. Oh, Bhagawan would shout! If one person is on leave and another takes over his work—if one person is suddenly absent for a day and the other person takes over that work—if that person is domineering and does it with relish, the [worker] will not be able to come back. I have seen this happen, because around Bhagawan there was such power, there was a force field in which every little thing assumed great significance.
>
> Suppose there is another person who somehow develops a desire to take over another person's work, then suppose his thought and will is stronger than the other person—that will assume such proportion that the first person I was talking of, if he should fall sick, or something should happen and he wouldn't be able to do his work and this person would take over—then he wouldn't be able to come back. That is interference with Bhagawan's work. This is not going the way Bhagawan wanted it, and it would affect Bhagawan himself. I have seen it happen so many times. So

that one particular work is allotted to one person; only that person is expected to go on with that work, and it will go on gloriously if it is left to himself completely.

In the spring of 1994 Lee Lozowick got news in Arizona from Yogi Ramsuratkumar saying that he wanted Lee to have an ashram in Tiruvannamalai, on land that was adjacent to the Yogi Ramsuratkumar Ashram property. They would virtually be next-door neighbors. This request from the master came as a shock; it was not something that the American teacher had ever considered doing, but at the same time, Yogi Ramsuratkumar's prophetic words to Lee in 1979, "Lee will travel the world," were beginning to manifest. Lee was now traveling and teaching extensively in Europe, and would establish a second ashram there in 1995. An ashram in India seemed impossible for many reasons, and certainly difficult due the legalities involved, but sworn to obey his guru, Lee immediately consented and begin to make plans. In the summer of 1994 Lee sent Balarama Zuccarello to Tiruvannamalai to facilitate the purchase of land for the project.

Bala arrived in late July, in the aftermath of the most extreme heat wave Tiruvannamalai had experienced in years. The small stone darshan *mandir* was packed beyond capacity with two hundred people or more. Entering the master's darshan, Mani ushered Bala to the front and gestured for him to sit near Yogi Ramsuratkumar, on his left side. To his right were seated Devaki, then Rajalakshmi and Vijayakka. For a long time the beggar held Bala's hand and stroked his arm. Soon Yogi Ramsuratkumar was up and working, as Bala recounted in his journal:

> He was parading like a boy of nineteen, up and down the aisle between the men and women's sides of the hall. His steps were firm, each step planted and in the next moment, unplanted and then planted again. With each step he extended his reach to the very center of the earth. Yet he moved like a boxer, like a warrior, like an impeccable warrior, young, vibrant, determined, undaunted. Being about his work in a way that made him seem mad, possessed! He appeared crazy beyond all reason and understanding.
>
> He does not have casual conversations with Ma Devaki. She is his absolute servant. Drinking his leftover tea or coffee or water. She keeps singing for the entire two-hour sitting, whatever song he calls out. Many times he asks for the same song four to five times in a row. After he requests her to repeat a song she takes an almost imperceptible moment to compose herself and then she sings.

Yogi Ramsuratkumar was masterful in orchestrating the darshan space, and by necessity a very strict protocol was kept in place, lest the crowd should get out of control in their devotional fervor and inundate him like a tidal wave. The public darshans made the beggar saint quite vulnerable to the loving but intrusive gestures of the devotees and supplicants who came seeking his blessings. In their attempts to touch his feet, his hands, the hem of his garment, his hair, he was often grasped, jabbed and prodded—on the chest, the hands, feet, head. Although well meant, it was invasive to his person and interfered greatly with the subtle dimensions of his work. It was difficult for the general public to realize that they would get more blessings from Yogi Ramsuratkumar if they gave him space to work, rather than imposing themselves on his physical body.

A few days later the injunction came from Yogi Ramsuratkumar himself that there would be no giving of *prasad* and prostrating before him at any time, anywhere. He said that by simply chanting his name he would be present, and this practice was as good as being in his physical presence.

"Even fishing in the sea is sadhana, if it is offered to God," he said.

Yogi Ramsuratkumar himself further announced at the darshan program that no one should tell him about their sick family or friends that they wanted healed. He asked the devotees to write everything down on paper and give the notes to Mani, who would give them to him.

During the first few days that Bala was at the ashram there was no *prasad* given, no conversation—just sitting, while Yogi Ramsuratkumar worked his invisible beads and smoked cigarettes, one after the other, and the chanting went on and on. It seemed that Yogi Ramsuratkumar had his attention in many realms at once. Bala wrote, "He appeared mad and at the same time, he was no fool." He rarely worked with people outwardly, other than through the ordinary means of the moment; most of the transformative work went on silently, invisibly, in the interior of each individual. During this time he had Bala sit next to him, held his hand and stroked his arm for long periods of time.

At this time Yogi Ramsuratkumar was wearing a long length of rope—rough jute—wound in six or eight loops and coiled around his shoulder. He had been wearing it since the construction on the new temple started. Every day he would walk around the grounds and bless the workers and their work, focusing a lot of his attention on the construction of the temple, going up on the second floor and walking among the workers, blessing all. He sometimes sat and watched the work from a chair. Already the ashram grounds were planted with trees and shrubs that would grow quickly in the tropical clime. A bed of kanna lilies made a splash of color, blooming in yellow and orange.

One morning Bala was invited to what Mani called a "family" darshan. Only a very few devotees were present: Yogi Ramsuratkumar, Devaki and the Sudama sisters, Mani, Raji and some of the ashram staff who were serving the space. Ma Devaki was reading from a book that compared Vedanta philosophy with Western science—some very intellectual considerations. During the next two hours, from ten a.m. until twelve noon, Yogi Ramsuratkumar held Bala's hand and gently stroked it almost continuously. Sometimes the beggar was hunched over smoking a cigarette, listening to the reading, and in the next moment he was marching up and down the aisle with fierce determination.

Like a guard at his post, he stalked back and forth.

Lee had given Bala some poems he had recently written, to be delivered into the hands of Yogi Ramsuratkumar. The beggar received these, read them himself, then handed them to Ma Devaki to read aloud. He responded to the reading with a wild flurry of play: laughing, slapping Bala on the hand, then hiding his face behind his hand in mock embarrassment.

When the opportunity arose, Bala approached Yogi Ramsuratkumar during darshan to relay the message—regarding building an ashram in India—that he had brought from Lee: "Bhagawan, Lee says he will do whatever you want." For a brief moment the beggar's eyes filled with tears, then the ordinariness of the moment prevailed, and the veils fell back into place. Yogi Ramsuratkumar picked up a cigarette and held it before him unlit while he looked around the room, as if scanning for where the greatest need was. When the cigarette was lit his body relaxed as the smoke drifted up in curls around his head.

"Did you call Lee to tell him that Bhagawan read his poetry?" Ma Devaki asked Bala later.

"No, but I wrote about it in my journal," Bala answered.

"It is very expensive to talk to Lee in America," Yogi Ramsuratkumar said, looking at Bala.

"We will send a fax, Bhagawan. I will type a letter and then we can send it by fax," Devaki offered. With this exchange Bala realized that Yogi Ramsuratkumar wanted Lee informed about everything that was going on in India while Bala was there.

A wealthy philanthropist—a rice factory owner—sat in the front row; he asked if he could sing some songs and Yogi Ramsuratkumar agreed, but he wanted the Sudama sisters, who usually lead the chants, to learn the song. The man explained to them how the chant should go, instructing them in the words and so on. It took awhile to teach the song, and finally everyone started singing with the man leading. At the end of the darshan the philanthropist gave many gifts to Yogi Ramsuratkumar and a sealed, paper-wrapped package, which he offered with a finger touched to his lips. As he placed the packet—a large amount of rupees— into the beggar's hands, Yogi Ramsuratkumar was almost in tears. He brought the package to his heart in a gesture of gratitude.

On July 29, Yogi Ramsuratkumar had a business meeting with Bala concerning the establishment of an ashram for Lee in Tiruvannamalai. He talked about how it would be necessary for Lee to have a representative in Tiruvannamalai on a full-time basis. "Balarama will stay to oversee construction for two to three years, because everyone trusts him and he is able to oversee construction," Yogi Ramsuratkumar stated. Bala was shocked and rather nervous about the idea; he had a wife and two children back in the States and many responsibilities there. After a long silent pause he stammered, "I'll have to ask Lee."

Two days later Bala woke up very early to see Yogi Ramsuratkumar, Ma Devaki and Mani sitting just outside. Bala was staying at the house of Mani and Raji, which was located behind Sudama House; evidently Bhagawan had made an early visit, and now sat quietly holding Mani's hand. The mood was sublime and gentle. At six-thirty, the usual time of meeting, Bala joined them. He pranamed and placed a flower *mala* around Yogi Ramsuratkumar's neck.

"A mala, so early in the morning! When did you get it?" Bhagawan asked sweetly.

"Last night in town," Balarama answered. Yogi Ramsuratkumar and the women were just preparing to leave, and soon left with Raji, who drove them back to Sudama House. Mani talked with Balarama about the many complications that were arising in the project to purchase land for Hohm Charitable Trust, which Lee Lozowick would have to establish in India. Obviously the project to establish an ashram for Lee was very precious to Yogi Ramsuratkumar.

Only the day before, when ideas for how to make the project work legally were being bandied about, Bala turned to Yogi Ramsuratkumar and asked what he thought of the ideas that were being discussed.

"I want Lee Lozowick to have an ashram here," he gently waved his hands in the air, as if to clear away clouds, "whatever the difficulties."

"Whatever you want," Balarama said.

"Very good!" the beggar smiled.

The next morning Yogi Ramsuratkumar wanted to go to the top of the temple roof and see the new concrete forms that had been lifted into place. He wanted to climb the stairs alone and asked that none of the ladies come with him.

"This beggar feels it is risky," he said to Devaki. "I will take the risk."

"I will follow you to the edge of the world, the edge of the universe," Devaki insisted, "I will go, and the other ladies will not come." After an excursion on the roof, Mani escorted Yogi Ramsuratkumar back down and he took his seat.

That day there were five hundred people on the ashram for darshan. They spilled out of the small darshan hall and waited in crowded throngs outside the building to see the saint. The crowd had to be let in for darshan in groups of forty; every fifteen minutes or so Yogi Ramsuratkumar called Mani and told him who he wanted to leave and how many to let in. Each new group of devotees were reminded not to *pranam* or touch Yogi Ramsuratkumar and to stay in their places.

"Bhagawan, there are forty more outside now wanting to come in," Mani reported.

"Forty more? Ohhh!" Each time Mani reported that there were forty more people he was equally surprised, as if it was a continual source of amazement that people wanted to see "this beggar." Among these were politicians, police officials, policemen and many different kinds of VIPs, as well as long-time devotees, friends and pilgrims passing through town.

On Sundays there were usually seven hundred-fifty to one thousand people; each person would spend fifteen to thirty minutes in the darshan *mandir*. With each new group of devotees Yogi Ramsuratkumar would get up, bless them with his hands and look into each one of their faces, so that he connected with each one individually. Bala wrote of this time, "Tirelessly, with the stamina of an ancient Vedic warrior, he would continually bless the room till all were accounted for."

That morning after breakfast Yogi Ramsuratkumar asked how many times Pon Kamaraj and his group, who were visiting from Kanimadam, had circumambulated the ashram. "Six to eight times, Bhagawan," Mani answered. Ma Devaki reported that they had been doing it since six a.m.—for two-and-a-half hours.

"They are blessing this ashram," Yogi Ramsuratkumar said. He was concerned about getting food to them and dispatched Mani to feed them right away, saying, "Tell them to stop chanting and take breakfast!"

In early August there were more setbacks in procuring the land for an ashram for Lee. As the business arrangements were being discussed during darshan, Yogi Ramsuratkumar began to talk about how important it was to him for Lee to have an ashram nearby.

"Lee Lozowick is a wonderful man," he said. "Lee said this beggar was guiding him even before he met this beggar." Then he laughed and covered his eyes, as if embarrassed. "It is not this beggar who guided Lee, but my Father. Lee is one of the most extraordinary persons this beggar has ever met. That is why this beggar wants him to have an adjoining ashram."

Yogi Ramsuratkumar repeated these statements two or three times, as was his way of normally speaking, but one never got tired of hearing the repetitions in his speech; no matter how many times he spoke something—for emphasis, perhaps, or until he felt someone had heard him—it was always fresh, melodic, inspired.

He began to ask for one song after another from the Sudama sisters. They rummaged through their bags to find the right songbook for his requests. This time he didn't ask them to repeat a single song, but asked for a new one each time. He spoke ecstatically about Ramdas and how he had met his father, and how Ramdas "destroyed" him in 1952, saying, "This beggar does not exist! Nothing and nobody exists—only my Father, near, near, nearest to far, far, farthest in everything and everybody. Nothing exists except my Father, perfect, absolute, infinite, unified in everything as everything. My Father alone!"

In the afternoon darshan Yogi Ramsuratkumar walked up and down the aisle swinging his rope, then walked over to peer out the window. The wind caressed his face and brushed his hair gently aside as he looked out into the blazing sun at the construction going on outside.

"Balarama!" he called. He instructed Bala to go outside to be with the surveyor as he measured the land. "It is hot and sunny. Balarama should take an umbrella with him," he cautioned, like a mother. Someone handed Bala an umbrella as he walked out the door. Once he was outside several of the men asked, "Why do you have an umbrella?" The men looked at Bala in disbelief. Bala is an Italian American with a dark complexion; he hardly needed an umbrella in the tropical sun. What was this American doing, anyway? There was only one possible answer to their question: The master had said to take the umbrella, so Bala took it.

Within the next few days the legal arrangements for the land seemed to proceed favorably, and it was looking positive for Bala to be able to return to the States soon. However, when the day came for him to leave, Yogi Ramsuratkumar wanted him to stay for another week. When he explained to the beggar that he needed to go to Madras to handle some other business, the beggar wanted him to stay on the ashram instead. He simply said, "By Father's grace it will all work out perfectly, I have no doubts."

Bala was quickly learning that nothing happened, nobody came or went, except by "Father's grace." For example, when the construction on the huge building that would house the massive temple, entrance hall, library, meditation hall and private abode for Yogi Ramsuratkumar was first begun, the ashram had less than ten percent of the money it would take to complete the project. The huge construction project was undertaken on pure faith—"by Father's grace," it would all work out.

That this was the most effective way to get things done was proven time and time again. When the workers were drilling deep into the ground for the ashram well, they had gone almost three hundred feet down and finally hit solid rock. Mani got some of the core drilling stone and sand and brought it to Yogi Ramsuratkumar.

"Bhagawan, we have gone down two hundred ninety-five feet, and still no water! Bhagawan, please bless us with water." He handed Yogi Ramsuratkumar the sand and stone—all the while Yogi Ramsuratkumar was laughing.

"My Father's blessing on the well," was all Bhagawan said. Four and one-half feet later they hit water and plenty of it. Yogi Ramsuratkumar named the well "Ganga."

Many people donated a great deal of money, services and supplies to the ashram—building materials, labor, plants, dishes or food. Some of the devotees who made donations would be considered quite poor by Western standards. Nonetheless, people were willing to give generously to make the ashram a reality; it was understood that there were great blessings inherent in such gifts and sacrifices.

Yogi Ramsuratkumar gave Mani the command to stay on the ashram for ten years, though Mani laughingly told Bala that he tried to find some excuse to leave at least three or four times a week. Each time he asked Yogi Ramsuratkumar for permission to leave, the master would say no. At one point Mani joked with Yogi Ramsuratkumar, saying that his mother was going to ask him if Mani could come to Madras, because he had left there six months before and had never come back.

"Then your mother will fight with this beggar!" Yogi Ramsuratkumar laughed.

A busload of people came from Madurai in early August. They were, for the most part, very thin, sickly and poor. When the bus arrived the small darshan hall was already packed with people, but Yogi Ramsuratkumar asked Mani to clear the space so that these sixty people from Madurai could come in. As soon as they entered Yogi Ramsuratkumar got up and walked to the door to meet them. He began to work furiously, and the mood in the room changed right away, becoming very quiet and hot. The people filled up about two-thirds of the hall. Walking up and down, waving his hand wildly over them, going back and forth, Yogi Ramsuratkumar worked at a fevered pitch. Balarama was tremendously impacted by this scene:

> These were the people he had come to help, not us fat, rich, educated Westerners who always position ourselves beyond his reach. Even by

> Indian standards these were extremely poor, simple folk who led hard lives. Yogi Ramsuratkumar physically shuddered while he extended his hands in a blessing posture over these people over and over again. The room was very tense. In my two weeks there I had not seen another group strain their necks as much just to catch a glimpse of the saint. Many of them looked confused and bewildered, many were lame, some were blind and a few had to be led into the room like zombies. Yogi Ramsuratkumar worked so very hard, pushing and pushing. They left in twenty minutes and the hall was again filled with new people.

Later that day a man came to the darshan hall and prostrated before Yogi Ramsuratkumar, offering *prasad*. Yogi Ramsuratkumar turned to Mani and said, just under his breath, "Do you see this man here who is offering his *pranams* to this beggar?"

"Yes, Bhagawan, I see him," answered Mani.

"Years ago when this beggar begged for food at this man's home, this man would beat this beggar." Yogi Ramsuratkumar then raised his hands in a blessing and said to the man, "My Father blesses you," and gave him *prasad*.

Again Yogi Ramsuratkumar told the story of Lee sitting out in the street across from his house on the hot iron bars in 1986. This time he said, "Lee did not hear me as I called and called to him. He was angry with this beggar because the day before he came and I said, 'I have seen you already.' He was mad at this beggar."

Ma Devaki told Balarama that they had seen the videos of Lee's rock & roll band, and they could not understand the words. Lee had sent the video of the band performing; the story was that when Yogi Ramsuratkumar, Devaki and the Sudama sisters saw it, the beggar had started laughing and laughing, saying, "Oh that is Lee Lozowick!" The video delighted him, and he got up and began to dance himself.

"Do you dance?" Devaki asked Bala, after relaying this story of the video tape.

"Yes," he replied.

"If we play a tape will you dance for us?"

He pleaded no with a smile and some embarrassment.

"You will not dance in front of Yogi Ramsuratkumar?" she asked. Bala shrugged and smiled sheepishly.

A few days later in darshan Yogi Ramsuratkumar said, "Today is August 7. Balarama will be leaving in a few days." Turning to Bala he asked, "Did Lee give you that name?" Bala answered yes.

"You are very lucky to have been given such a name," Yogi Ramsuratkumar commented.

Then he asked Devaki to read two poems from *Poems of a Broken Heart* in front of the packed darshan hall. First she stood up and explained them in Tamil, then she read them in English. Both poems were about the importance of Yogi Ramsuratkumar's name, which had been very central to his communication to his devotees of late, with the new protocol he had outlined: no prostrations, no touching his physical form—just chant the name of Yogi Ramsuratkumar. That is enough.

After darshan one of the devotees, a man named Kulotthungan, came up to Bala and said, "I think that since Mr. Balarama has come here there have been some changes." He looked at Bala's face and around his head as if staring beyond him. "Admit it," he said, "Have you not changed?"

Bala answered, "I certainly have, I certainly have." Since Bala had been there more than once the stresses of his situation—attempting to facilitate a business arrangement between his guru, Lee Lozowick, and his guru's guru, Yogi Ramsuratkumar, had seemed overwhelming. The raw power of the blessings that abounded, the intensity of being in the close physical proximity of Yogi Ramsuratkumar, under his wing in fact, had catalyzed a profound internal process in Bala. On one occasion when Bala was under a lot of strain, Yogi Ramsuratkumar had spent almost thirty minutes alone with him, working with his energy, rubbing and stroking his back and holding his hand.

Kulotthungan was right; Bala was going through very deep changes. There was no doubt that Bala had been softened up quite significantly during his stay. The Indian devotees, those who worked closely with the beggar king, were deeply familiar with the signs of such a process of spiritual transformation. Kulotthungan had known Yogi Ramsuratkumar since he was a teenager in 1972. When Yogi Ramsuratkumar lived at Sannadhi Street, he asked Kulotthungan to sleep on the porch every night beginning in 1990. Each night at nine-thirty Kulotthungan would arrive. At the master's instruction, Kulotthungan had to dress in a *dhoti*, shirt, cap and a woolen shawl all night, even in the hottest weather. The other men would make fun of him for dressing up "like a ghost" to sleep on the porch of his master's house, but Kulotthungan didn't care.

Marriage for Kulotthungan was out of the question—nor could he ever leave Tiruvannamalai. His life belonged to his guru. He was one of many long-time devotees who remained very close to Yogi Ramsuratkumar, but who was extremely invisible. Later, Mani told Bala that Kulotthungan was a very close devotee who had the master's regard and deep respect, but one would never know it, because Yogi Ramsuratkumar rarely if ever mentioned his name or referred to him.

The next day a gentleman came rushing into the hall, with Mani trying to stop him. He got within eight feet of Yogi Ramsuratkumar, who began to explain to him that Mani was the ashram manager, and he was only doing his job. This man had written some abusive letters to Yogi Ramsuratkumar, criticizing him for "sitting with women" and threatening to send the government tax officials in to examine the ashram records. He sat down for the rest of the darshan.

Before the evening darshan Yogi Ramsuratkumar asked Mani to bring the man directly to him if he came again. The man arrived at the ashram before darshan, just as Yogi Ramsuratkumar was standing on the steps to enter the hall. Approaching the beggar, the man prostrated at his feet. Yogi Ramsuratkumar said, "We do not allow that on this ashram," but he invited the man into the darshan hall. The man refused to come in for a long time; he was angry because he had asked for a private meeting with Yogi Ramsuratkumar and had been refused; he felt that he was being insulted. Finally he came in and took a seat in the corner of the room. While Yogi Ramsuratkumar was walking up and down the aisle blessing people, the man looked like he was crying.

On this day Yogi Ramsuratkumar was chain-smoking throughout both darshan sessions. The smoking was an integral and profound part of the darshan, often as a seeming counterpoint to his blessing fits—the dancing, pacing, prowling steps up and down, up and down the aisle between the men on one side of the hall and the women on the other. With every cigarette he smoked he gently and carefully opened the pack. There were no sudden movements in this—everything was one smooth, easy flow. He often stared intensely at each pack as if he was studying the box before he slowly pulled the cigarette out and lit it with great deliberation.

His intention could be felt with each cigarette as an almost heavy presence. He often appeared totally lost in thought or in a *bhava* of wonder as he gazed at the matches or the cigarette. Every step in the ritual was meticulous and weighted with the feeling of a moment fully savored. As for the matches, these he picked up and opened in whatever position the box was facing, which was often face down. He gently pushed the box open, then turned it over to slowly pull out one match, which he examined closely. Holding the box in hand, he would strike the match. If it did not light, he struck it again. If there was still no fire he would then turn the box over and try the other side. Often in the midst of this ritual he would stop several times and look at the room in general, or maybe at one person.

At one point the Sudama sisters were leading the chant while Yogi Ramsuratkumar sat hunched over, seeming to be wandering far away in his own internal landscape, or down starry pathways through a void, into universes known and unknown. He seemed like a thunderhead, a thick, very dark rain cloud rolling in upon itself, charged with power and energy. His beard moved as if he was silently begging for the blessings of his Father upon "this beggar's friends." Just at that moment the wind outside blew a large metal door shut with a resounding crash that sounded exactly like thunder. It seemed that the natural world was reflecting the beggar's mood. He raised his head.

"What day is it?" he asked Mani, who answered that it was August 8.

"Balarama has three more days with us. Lee was kind enough to let him stay. He could not stay unless Lee would let him. He is very kind. I am thankful to Lee for letting Balarama stay here because I wanted him to." He was speaking to Mani, who was looking away. He got Mani's attention and repeated his words.

Mani's son was planning to go back to Madras that day. No one came or went from the ashram without Yogi Ramsuratkumar knowing about it. He wanted to be informed of trips, business deals, health or illness, anything of importance or unimportance—all was grist for his mill, part of how he cared for his devotees. Once he knew what someone's plans were then he would say, "My Father blesses you."

After some silence Yogi Ramsuratkumar said to Mani's son, "I beg you to do one thing. If you have any problems, if anything happens where you need help, please repeat this beggar's name. Do you know it?" The answer was yes.

"Say if for me, please," the beggar spoke softly.

"Yogi Ramsuratkumar," he answered quietly.

"Yes, that is right."

Very early the next morning Yogi Ramsuratkumar paid a visit to Mani's mother, who was staying next door to Mani's house. A little while later Yogi Ramsuratkumar's driver, Ravi, invited Balarama inside the house. He entered and *pranamed* to the master, who slapped him on the back several times. He seemed overjoyed to see the American, and asked where he had come from. Raji explained that Bala was staying next door. Yogi Ramsuratkumar had Mani take several photographs of himself with Mani's mother, then he told him to make sure his mother got copies of them.

At the ten o'clock darshan Yogi Ramsuratkumar played a cassette of chants—Yogi Ramsuratkumar *bhajans*—that had been written and composed by Lee's student, Doug Fulker, which Lee had sent in the mail. The chants had been recorded in Arizona during a darshan program there, with about sixty or seventy of Lee's students singing. Yogi Ramsuratkumar played both sides of the cassette, and during this time he became very animated. He waved his hands wildly to the music as if he was dancing in his seat on the floor; he laughed and playfully hid his face in his hands as if he was embarrassed. His jubilation was contagious, and continued throughout the playing of the tape. He was as playful as a small child who couldn't believe he was hearing his own name, put to American-style *bhajan* music, accompanied by Doug, who played the mandolin.

"Who is that singer?" Yogi Ramsuratkumar asked Bala, as the tape played on.

"It's Douglas," Bala said, using his proper name, which was more understandable for the Indian sensibility than the gutteral, abbreviated nickname, "Doug."

"How many people are singing?" Yogi Ramsuratkumar wanted to know. Balarama answered fifty or sixty.

"Were you there?"

"No."

"Was Lee there?" he asked.

"Yes, certainly," Bala responded.

After listening to the tape Yogi Ramsuratkumar asked two women in the crowd to move up front and chant. They had very full, expressive voices, and they sang songs about Yogi Ramsuratkumar for about forty minutes while he sat slumped over in a *bhava*. Several times Devaki wanted to tell him something, but he was so concentrated in this way that he did not respond. When the singing was over he rose up again and said, "Sare," meaning "good" in Tamil.

A story was told about an elderly couple who wanted to do a special puja that required them to walk up Mount Arunachala at night. There was no moon, and the night was black as pitch. The elderly man and woman had great difficulty making their way and were afraid they were lost, but very soon a man with a white beard appeared and volunteered to guide them through the darkness. After the *puja* was done and they again reached the road, the man with the white beard excused himself, saying that he had to go to the toilet. He advised them to go down the rest of the way and he would meet them shortly. He never returned and when they called and searched, they could find no one. The elderly man was certain that it was Yogi Ramsuratkumar who had come to help them.

Finally Yogi Ramsuratkumar gave Bala permission to leave and spend one day in Madras on his way back to the States. He inquired about the flight arrangements and how the reservations would be confirmed. When all was settled, Bala said with some emotion, "I want you to come with me."

Yogi Ramsuratkumar answered gently, "This beggar is always with you."

All afternoon Yogi Ramsuratkumar was deep inside himself, very solemn and quiet. At one point he turned to Devaki and told her to get up. He gave her his coconut bowl, fan and stick and told her to walk up and down the aisle between the men and women's sides three times. She was very taken aback. A look of surprise and fear crossed her face. She did it then sat down.

After a while he looked at her and said, "Lets see if we can get you into even more trouble." He asked her to stand and he gave her the cord of rope he had been wearing for months.

"Walk all the way to the end," he commanded. As she walked he shouted out instructions for her to correct her posture. She did this four times. He held up his hands in blessing as she walked, showering his benediction on her all the while. A short time later he had her do it again only this time with the bowl, fan and stick. Bala reflected in his journal:

> All the faces in the room had a look of confusion and surprise. People had their attention riveted on her. This time, as she walked down the aisle, away from where Yogi Ramsuratkumar was sitting, two women started to sing a Ma Devaki chant. It was perfect. In a few moments the entire room was chanting. After Ma Devaki finished she appeared very much out of breath. When she sat down again she looked to be recovering from shell shock. She is in a very difficult position. She has Yogi Ramsuratkumar's support but she is still viewed as just a woman in a patriarchal society.

As Yogi Ramsuratkumar got up to leave he slapped Bala on the knee and said, "Thank you!"

The next morning Bala arrived at the ashram early. Suddenly he saw the beggar's car come racing into the compound with only the driver, Ravi, inside. Mani stuck his head in the window to see what the matter was, then called to Bala.

"Balarama, go in the car and bring your keys. Yogi Ramsuratkumar is at your room and he wants to get in!"

Bala jumped in the backseat and, before his feet could touch the floor, noticed a small carpet there. Ravi leaned over and moved the carpet, which was obviously for Yogi Ramsuratkumar. They sped away, and as the car pulled up to Bala's room, he could see Yogi Ramsuratkumar sitting on the stone floor outside his door, flanked by Ma Devaki and the Sudama sisters. Bala jumped out of the car, *pranamed* at his feet and received a number of sound slaps on the back, as if the beggar had just met a long lost friend he happened to bump into.

Ma Devaki gave Bala some things from Yogi Ramsuratkumar to take back to the States for Lee.

"Get your bag—I want to see you put them in your bag," Yogi Ramsuratkumar said, making it clear the gifts needed to be handled with the utmost care. When the items were safely stashed away in the backpack, he held the bag and blessed it and said, "You bring them inside now."

When Bala came back outside, Yogi Ramsuratkumar said to Devaki, "We have completed our mission, we may go." At the car he turned to Bala and said, "You will please let us know as soon as you are safe at home from your journey."

Back at the ashram, the mood was very jovial after breakfast. Six men were there, talking with Yogi Ramsuratkumar. He began to speak ecstatically, saying, "People say that I want my name chanted. It is not my name, it is my Father's. This beggar died in 1952! There is no one else, nothing else except my Father! All that exists is Father—anywhere, anyplace, near, far. Complete unity, all pervasive, in everything and everywhere. There is no isolation, only perfect unity. All that exists is my Father. He alone exists, everywhere. So when you are having any difficulty and you call out this beggar's name, my Father will answer you, he will help you instantaneously, because he alone exists."

Ma Devaki said, "We will miss Balarama, he has become part of the ashram. We will miss all the different expressions on his face. Joy, devotion, fear, bewilderment, confusion, looking puzzled." She laughed, as this seemed to endear him to her. Yogi Ramsuratkumar also laughed.

In darshan that morning Yogi Ramsuratkumar spoke about how one should assert that he or she is not the body but the eternal soul, a divine spark. He repeated this entire idea three times and said it was the teaching of Swami Nityananda.

Four people had completed a walking pilgrimage of one hundred miles, which had taken eleven days. Mani was very impressed with their devotion. Their group of fifteen had been on the ashram chanting since dawn. They had brought flower garlands to give to Bhagawan, and they didn't want to eat breakfast until they had presented the garlands.

"Why do these people cause this beggar such problems?" Yogi Ramsuratkumar snapped when he heard this news. "Tell them to eat, and they can give the garlands at ten o'clock!" It is difficult to fully grasp the burden of responsibility that the guru bears for the devotee. By refusing to eat breakfast—which is considered *prasad* on the ashram and therefore a blessing in and of itself—until they could give the flower garland to him, these people became an even greater burden for Yogi Ramsuratkumar. Not meaning to be insensitive, they were nonetheless putting the guru in a bind: To give the garland at breakfast disrupted his space and timing, but for his devotees to go hungry until he received the garland caused him pain. The greater service to the guru would have been to follow the ashram schedule and not make extra demands on him: have breakfast when it is served and offer the garland in darshan.

On the next day, August 12, Bala was getting ready to leave. Yogi Ramsuratkumar had been meeting with the architect, then he turned his attention on Bala and said, "It is better for Balarama to leave right now." It was almost two hours before his scheduled departure, but Yogi Ramsuratkumar was known to be a master of timing. There was always a purpose behind his pronouncements, and it had been shown time and time again that it was always wise to be obedient to his instruction. The guru had spoken, and it was the devotees' wish to simply obey. Yogi Ramsuratkumar handed some things to Bala, who then walked to the car. Devaki had a few last-minutes messages for Lee about the things Yogi Ramsuratkumar had given to Bala. Then she said, "Balarama, I want you to remember three words about these items that Bhagawan is giving to Lee: auspicious, sacred and precious." He repeated the words after her and the car took off.

The awakened being has the spiritual power to transmit vibrations across time and space. The power of Yogi Ramsuratkumar to transmit grace was so strong in fact that Lee Lozowick, an American living halfway across the world, experienced a radical shift of context that resulted in a permanent transformation of his worldview a year and a half before he and Yogi Ramsuratkumar met in the realm of time and space. The incredible emanations that come from the guru have a particularly powerful effect when one is in the physical proximity of the guru's form. In India some say that the great *mahatmas* or awakened beings live alone because the radiations of their immediate physical presence catalyze profoundly intense experiences within those who are around them, and very few can withstand the onslaught without great difficulty. Many people were known to have kundalini energy catalyzed and powerful experiences of mystical ascent just by being in the same room with Yogi Ramsuratkumar.

In 1994 and 1995 Devaki and the Sudama sisters were finding out what it meant to live in close physical proximity to the pervasive transformational power of Yogi Ramsuratkumar. The spiritual master is like the sun in the solar system; the closer you are to the sun's rays, the hotter it gets until you are incinerated—burned to a crisp. Obviously human life cannot be sustained on Mercury or Venus, because they are too close to the sun; it is only when there is some distance from the sun, as on the Earth, that the optimal environment for the sun's healing and life-giving rays becomes activated and life flourishes.

However, using this idea as a metaphor for spiritual life, annihilation of the separate self is exactly what one hopes may be accomplished, through the power of grace. The *sadhaka* wants to be burned up in the fiery emanations of the master's pure spiritual force. As Yogi Ramsuratkumar said, "The best sadhana is to be near one's guru, to obey and serve him. All other sadhanas are only after that. This is the best sadhana."[1]

1 Ma Devaki, "The Divine Beggar on Himself," *Saranagatham*, January 2003, p. 33.

Devaki and the Sudama sisters were learning to live in close proximity to a spiritual sun, and in order to serve Yogi Ramsuratkumar in the way that they were called to do, they had to be instructed, prepared and purified—they were in a kind of spiritual boot camp, in training for being able to do "Father's work." They had renounced the world and worldly desires, and their lives were now about sacrifice and service, and Yogi Ramsuratkumar used the mundane circumstances of daily life as the vessel in which the dross was purified from their bodies and minds in order to reveal the gold.

Much of this process of purification took place in the ordinary circumstances of everyday activities. For example, Yogi Ramsuratkumar had an extremely meticulous sensibility; he wanted everything done in a certain way. From his point of view, when something was placed on the table one fraction of an inch off the mark as he saw it, it affected everything—even the entire cosmos. Another form of purification was the rigorous schedule the Sudama sisters kept, following Bhagawan's rhythms and commands regarding food, sleep and activity.

It was already very clear that Devaki had to play a very specific role; Bhagawan told them that she was the divine mother, and that all the Sudama sisters should be considered as "Ma's." They had absolutely no personal life. Everyone was expected to obey Bhagawan implicitly, and to have no voice in matters. For Vijayalakshmi, who had joined the group also but was used to giving orders and being highly respected in her job, this was not an easy task—nor was it easy for any of the women. Yogi Ramsuratkumar expected a great and arduous *sadhana* from all four of them.

If Devaki was reading to him and she fell asleep or even closed her eyes for a few seconds, he would immediately wake her up, saying, "Read!" If she had a bad headache, he expected her to go on with her work. He would not allow her to rest, and every day was filled with the rigorous schedule of public darshans and all the needs of the burgeoning new ashram. Bhagawan expected Devaki and the Sudama sisters to be at his side every moment of the day—whether they were sick, healthy, happy, sad, tired or full of energy really didn't matter. The normal concerns of the human personality, psychology or the needs of the physical body were no longer relevant.

"No, no," he would say if Devaki wanted to rest, "there is no need for it! You just stay with this beggar, that will do." Sleep was not necessary. When Devaki became bitter about her failings, saying, "Bhagawan, I fail so miserably! What is the use of my living with you, I'm not able to serve you nicely?"

"Stop crying! You have a very bright future," the beggar admonished. "Father will shape you for this work!" At other times, when the work was overwhelming and things seemed bleak with the criticisms and distrust that came from other devotees, Devaki would get furious with herself and feel powerless in the face of her own shortcomings:

> I would be miserable at my own failings and then if I complained to him, he would say, "No, no, Devaki, you are doing wonderful work for my Father. See . . . it is very difficult to live with this beggar, even for half an hour, Devaki. Even for half an hour. People cannot live with this beggar

> for half an hour! Only Father wants to be with this beggar. But Devaki has lived with this beggar so long. Devaki is managing so well." And then he would encourage me with such nice words and love. He would be so nice to me at that time, and then, he often said, "It is very difficult to live with this beggar, for anybody. That itself is *tapas*." Just living with him, adjusting to him. No matter how many mistakes we make.
>
> It was a big challenge being with him because, for one thing, I was a totally different kind of personality. The first year it was terrible to adjust, and he made it very plain in the beginning that I would have to surrender my ego!

The intensity that was felt in the presence of the beggar saint was an experience shared by those who were close to him. Ravi, the driver of his car, who held his hand several times every day as he helped the beggar in and out of the car and into Sudama House, the temple, dining hall or wherever he was going, described this feeling as "heat and pressure." This was a subtle energetic phenomenon, and yet it was a bodily experience as palpable and tangible as the heat one experiences when standing in the hot noonday Indian sun. Beyond this crucible of heat and pressure, at every turn, at the slightest manifestation of ego on the part of those who were close to him and served him daily, the master pointed it out and corrected it, in one way or another. Vijayalakshmi went through this process of purification and more—the basic context with which she approached life had to shift:

> I used to feel really a match for him! I had very nice quarrels with him! Looking back, I wish I hadn't, but then I was totally unexposed to spiritual life. It was not a question of my not wanting to let go of my ego, but, one never knows about it, what exactly it is. That is the real problem. I mean, how to become something like zero, in no time at all? Right in the beginning he told me in so many words that spiritual life requires the shedding of the ego. Lesson one, lesson two, lesson three, lesson hundred, lesson infinity!

When Yogi Ramsuratkumar gave a task to be done, he wanted it done immediately. If he gave Devaki some small task and she was gone from the room for five minutes he would be calling, "Devaki! Devaki!" He was a relentless taskmaster in one moment and in the next moment he was the divine child, calling out for mother—"Devaki!" Then she would come and show him how to do some very simple thing. "Like this, Bhagawan," she would say. All together, Yogi Ramsuratkumar and the four women were a spiritual family, and often they were like children together, with many playful interchanges, laughter and the pure enjoyment of good company. Yogi Ramsuratkumar's marvelous spontaneity and sense of humor came through at the most difficult times.

At other times, it was just *tapas*. When Devaki wasn't reading to Bhagawan for days on end, she was doing *japa* and *nama* with the Sudama sisters, especially Vijayalakshmi, until they were all exhausted. During one of these times she was sleeping only two or three hours at night; not only was she exhausted, but her nerves were worn thin. When Devaki finally protested to Yogi Ramsuratkumar in a flair of anger, he started dancing. Devaki recalled:

> One time when I had been up for days with no sleep, and it was just going on and on, I got angry with him and protested. He started dancing! This made me even angrier and I imitated him—I started dancing too! And then he started laughing, laughing, laughing, until I started laughing too. This is how it was . . . we were a family together. It is amazing how he avoided controversy and bad stories—a saint living with four women! But he was so pure, so stainless . . .

A primary focus of sadhana for Vijayalakshmi was to do *nama japa* all day long. At times this became so all-consuming that her head would spin in the morning and cause all kinds of sensations to arise because of the power of the *nama japa* and the spiritual forces it unleashed in her. Sometimes she cried from the sheer gratitude and love that she felt for Bhagawan.

"Where is Yogi Ramsuratkumar?" the beggar asked, smiling at the devotees who sat around him. "People think he is only from here to here," he pointed to his head and feet.

"Yogi Ramsuratkumar is here, there, everywhere . . . everywhere! He is in all of you. All of you are in him. There is no place where this beggar is not. When people think that Yogi Ramsuratkumar is only from here to here," Yogi Ramsuratkumar pointed to his head and feet, "they become narrow, selfish and miserable. He is everywhere. He is in every one of you."[2]

These were some of the most fundamental teachings of the beggar saint, which he impressed upon his devotees many times, and it became more urgent as his failing health, which had been precarious for years, forced his devotees to realize that he would not always be with them. Once during these years, when Yogi Ramsuratkumar was in a state of ecstatic God-communion, he offered to give Ma Devaki a boon. When she heard this she said, "My wish is for you to live to be one hundred years old, Bhagawan." He was seventy-five at the time, and he granted her wish in the moment. Still, his often frail condition left many questions as to what the future would hold.

With an ashram that was open to the public that came in throngs, the form of interaction with the beggar saint had changed drastically for many long-time devotees and

2 Ma Devaki, "The Divine Beggar on Himself," *Saranagatham*, January 2003.

friends. By necessity he was less available for personal interactions at informal times. Many devotees were used to the intimate environment of the verandah or the rooms at Sannadhi Street, or they remembered very well sitting with him under the punnai tree many years ago, or out in the fields near the rice paddies, or walking on Arunachala. These kinds of circumstances were replaced by the formal darshans with two or three hundred people in attendance, or the traditional times of religious celebration that were regular occasions on the new ashram. For example, Yogi Ramsuratkumar now gave his devotees permission to organize the traditional *jayanthi* event—the celebration of the day the guru appeared in the world. Yogi Ramsuratkumar's birthday was on December 1, and this day became the high point of the year, as devotees, both East and West, flooded into the ashram for the auspicious occasion.

Since the mid-seventies Mukilan and his family had had a very personal relationship with the beggar saint in Tiruvannamalai. Their interactions with him had always been on a one-on-one basis. If the beggar had food, he shared his food with them; if he had flowers he shared those also. If Yogi Ramsuratkumar drank coffee or tea, so did his guests. In 1987 Yogi Ramsuratkumar had said to Mukilan, "You can think of this beggar from Madras—you don't need to come all this way." Mukilan had visited the master several times since then, most specifically for the blessing of his marriage to Lakshmi three years later, and at other times as well. Nonetheless, he had taken the master's instruction to heart.

Not everyone was able to accept this teaching. Many felt that the chaos and intense fervor of large crowds was simply not something they wanted to grapple with in order to see Yogi Ramsuratkumar. The sentiment, "Yogi Ramsuratkumar has lost touch with the common people" was uttered by more than one person, but it was not true. There were countless *lilas* that occurred for the devotees and friends who had been with Yogi Ramsuratkumar for a long time, in which he demonstrated, as much as he could, his love and care for them.

Shortly after the construction of the temple began in 1994, Mukilan came to Tiruvannamalai to visit Yogi Ramsuratkumar on the new ashram. He came to the small darshan hall with its thatched roof and waited for the beggar to arrive. Soon the car arrived and parked; Yogi Ramsuratkumar got out and walked to the darshan *mandir*. Devaki and the Sudama sisters had already gone inside, and Yogi Ramsuratkumar sat down outside on the porch and gazed straight ahead, not looking at anyone. Caught up in the surge of the crowd, Mukilan walked past him and went into the hall; he was invisible to Yogi Ramsuratkumar. The chanting started and had been going on for a while when Devaki stood up and called out, "Bhagawan wants me to ask whether anybody has come from Madras named Mukilan." Delighted by this unexpected turn of events, Mukilan stood up, walked to the front of the room and *pranamed* before Yogi Ramsuratkumar.

"How is your father?" the beggar asked. "Have you come alone?" Mukilan answered that his father was well, and that a staff person from his office was with him. Later he recalled:

> I was so happy that Bhagawan had called me. I thought, "Definitely, he knew that I was there!" It was carved in my mind very deeply: whatever we do, wherever we go, he knows. The incident made it very clear, we do not need to show our face for Yogi Ramsuratkumar to know if we have come. You don't need to tell him that you are there; he is an absolute example of "he who knows everything."

In November 1994 Mariana Caplan, a young Jewish woman fresh out of a graduate program in psychology in California, was traveling in north India, seeking a spiritual teacher and hoping to discover her "heart's calling." Although she knew she was looking for a spiritual teacher, she had no plan and was moving aimlessly from one place to the next, meeting one guru after another, when someone told her about Tiruvannamalai, a village in south India where a holy man named Ramana Maharshi had lived. It was reputed to be a place that had some spiritual power, and although she knew very little about it, she felt strongly drawn in that direction for no particular reason, other than that her heart was calling her there.

Arriving in Tiruvannamalai in late November, she met Michael Silverberg, a devotee of Amritananda Mayi, and some other Westerners. He told her that a Western guru was arriving with his disciples in a few days to visit his guru, Yogi Ramsuratkumar, a beggar saint who had an ashram in town. The only thing she heard about Yogi Ramsuratkumar was that he chain-smoked and didn't give teachings. Intrigued by the idea of a Western guru who was willing to be in the role of devotee in front of his own devotees, she decided to investigate. The day before Lee was to arrive she went to the yogi's darshan to "check out the scene."

When she arrived on the Yogi Ramsuratkumar Ashram she discovered that it was just being built. Workers were busy all over the grounds, and the huge temple, which was under construction, was a beehive of activity. The front entrance hall of the temple was finished, and this was where the darshan was held. She was shown to a seat on the women's side, and finally, after an hour and fifty minutes, an elder dressed in a loosely wrapped old *dhoti* and long woolen shawls with a turban around his head came walking in. He paced back and forth, raising his hands and swiping them through the air as if he was "swatting flies," she thought, but she understood right away that it was an unusual way of blessing. His pacing and blessing lasted for about five minutes, then he left just as unceremoniously as he had come. It was so fast, and she had seen so many "fake gurus" during her travels in India, that she just accepted it with no question. Her interest was piqued, and she returned the next day to see the American guru, a devotee of Yogi Ramsuratkumar, who she had been told about.

On November 28, the day Lee Lozowick was to arrive, Mariana arrived late for morning darshan, after meditating on Mount Arunachala for five hours. She walked in to find the beggar saint seated on the dais, holding the hand of a middle-aged Western man dressed in Indian clothes. For the next hour the yogi was involved in a process of healing this man, working intently on his knees. After a while it dawned on her that the American man was Lee Lozowick. For a long time Yogi Ramsuratkumar worked with his hands on Lee's knees, and then smoked and blessed him.

After the darshan Mariana immediately approached Lee and introduced herself, asking if she could attend the public talk she had heard he would be giving in Tiruvannamalai later that week. Lee was skeptical, as he often was with Westerners who roamed around India on the spiritual circuit. Mariana wrote later about this exchange:

> "Where are you from?" he all but barked at me.
> "California," I told him. "Originally from Maryland."
> "At least it's only California," he sighed, "I thought you might tell me that you were a citizen of the universe."
> I asked him if I could attend one of his teachings.
> "Why not?" he half-grumbled.[3]

That year Yogi Ramsuratkumar had instructed Lee to come only to Tiruvannamalai, instead of spending two weeks in southern India, visiting the Manthralayam and other villages and cities. He wanted Lee's annual India trip to be entirely focused at the Yogi Ramsuratkumar Ashram from that time on.

Lee and the ten students traveling with him arrived at the ashram to discover that a tremendous amount of work had been done since December 1993. What was a rocky field with a few scattered thorn bushes growing on it a year before was now a busy construction site, with several buildings already in place. Yogi Ramsuratkumar was sitting in a lawn chair with sunglasses on, beneath an elaborate wooden scaffolding structure that had been built to support the construction, which involved moving tons of wet concrete from the ground to the top of the temple.

About sixty workers were on the ground around the temple, each one responsible for a step in the process—carrying bags of cement, sifting sand, shoveling gravel or loading and retrieving the pans of wet concrete, which was then passed up a line of workers. The labor team included men and women. The women worked in bright saris, carrying heavy wok-shaped pans of sand or wet cement on the their heads with extraordinary grace.

Many trees and shrubs had been planted on the ashram and were beginning to grow. During the first year or so Yogi Ramsuratkumar instructed Mani to plant twenty-seven neem trees; these, he said, would purify the atmosphere. The fruits of these labors were just beginning to show in the kanna lilies that bloomed.

The temple itself was a gargantuan project that had already created some grumbling and controversy, but Yogi Ramsuratkumar was no stranger to this; it was a response his

3 Mariana Caplan, *Do You Need a Guru?*, p. 117.

actions elicited from people many times over the years. Many felt the temple was overly ambitious and grandiose, but Yogi Ramsuratkumar said that the temple would someday be filled with five thousand people—devotees and pilgrims from all over the world. It would be a vast space, reverberating with the name of Yogi Ramsuratkumar—a paradoxical fate for a dirty beggar who, for thirty years of his life, slept in gutters and on the streets. Here was one who had gladly endured hardships that most people could not imagine or fathom. Lee Lozowick wrote during this time:

Oh Father, Yogi Ramsuratkumar,
 this Temple of Yours
is surely as grand
 as anything the Universe has yet seen.
"He must be going mad,"
 the skeptics say.
"No," says lee, His son,
 "He has always been Mad."
"Who does He think He is?"
 the doubters scoff.
"No One but His Father's faithful servant,"
 says this bad Poet.
Yes Dearest, oh dirty Beggar,
 let them think what they will,
for You are Your Father's Slave
 as Your son is Yours.[4]

December 10, 1994

In 1993, during his last visit, Lee had asked permission to publish a book about Yogi Ramsuratkumar in the West. It was Yogi Ramsuratkumar's wish to be only one of several saints in such a book, and Lee's idea was to create a compilation of short biographies and quotations from several well-known Indian saints, juxtaposed with beautiful black and white photographs. The book would include Ramana Maharshi, Swami Ramdas, Nityananda, Shirdi Sai Baba, Swami Prajnanpad, Chandra Swami and Sanatan Das Baul, with a strong focus on Yogi Ramsuratkumar. The text would appear in English, French and German in order to make the book accessible to the Europeans who were beginning to hear the name of Yogi Ramsuratkumar through Lee Lozowick's travels and teachings. Although Hilda Charlton had included a chapter titled "Yogi Ramsuratkumar: The Hidden Saint of India" in her book, *Saints Alive,* which was published in the eighties, *Facets of the Diamond* would be the first widely distributed book in the West to feature Yogi Ramsuratkumar. Yogi Ramsuratkumar agreed to be included in the project with one

4 Lee Lozowick, *Death of a Dishonest Man*, p. 580.

condition: Lee himself also had to be included in the book.

The book was published in the States in the fall of 1994, and at the first darshan on November 28, held in the small darshan *mandir*, Lee brought eight copies in a bag as a gift for Yogi Ramsuratkumar. These he placed at the master's feet, where they sat unopened for some time. When Devaki mentioned that she thought they were books, Yogi Ramsuratkumar finally asked to have them opened. He picked up a copy with a broad smile of delight and began to thumb through the pages, smiling and almost blushing, covering his face in a spontaneous response of modesty at the twelve large photographs of himself. Then he grinned mischievously and made a joke, slapping Lee so hard on the back and on the leg that it knocked him over. The smile of pure enjoyment that spread across Lee's face never wavered as he quickly regained his balance.

For the next two weeks Yogi Ramsuratkumar would ask Devaki to read from the book time and again. He was particularly fascinated by a single photograph in the book of Sanatan Das Thakur Baul, which was the last photograph and also appeared on the cover. Sanatan Das, a Baul master from rural Bengal, was a close friend of Lee's who had visited his ashram in America in 1991. He and his sons, Bishwanath and Basudev, had conducted a concert tour throughout the Southwest—arranged by Lee and his students—in which they performed traditional Baul songs of love and longing for the Beloved. During their time in the States they lived at Lee's ashram in Arizona and became very close friends with him and his students.

The Bauls of Bengal, a small sect of wandering mystics and *tantrikas*, eschew all religious dogmas and rules and cleave instead to the guru's grace and the innate wisdom that they believe resides within the human being. A main tenet of their path places great faith and love in the innate goodness of humanity and the *maner manush*, or "man of the heart"—the soul of man—which may be discovered through arduous sadhana regardless of caste, creed, sex or race.

The Bauls are God-intoxicated mystics who trace their roots back to Mahaprabhu Chaitanya. Rather than worshipping the Divine through formal rituals, they worship through song and dance, wandering and begging for their food in the villages of Bengal and neighboring areas such as Bihar and Bangladesh, singing and dancing in the name of Krishna, their Beloved. They are a great joy and delight to the common folk of the region, because they bring upliftment and spiritual teaching in a way that is highly accessible and digestible for the common person. It is the Baul way to encode spiritual teachings in poems and songs rather than in the written or spoken word. In *Facets of the Diamond* there were no quotes from Sanatan Das Baul, nor was there a biography; instead there was one song, which the Bauls had written for their American friends. The song was particularly poignant, and a perfect offering to Yogi Ramsuratkumar:

> Namaskar!
> My Namaskar to the devotees of America!
> The devotees and the deity are the same—thus spoke my Guru.
> Of all God's plays the very best is His taking human form.

He keeps playing this again and again,
appearing as the human Avatar.
Khyapa says: Sanatan, listen, worship at the Guru's feet.
So I keep carrying this one-stringed
ektara—my friend for life.
It helps me cross the river of sorrow.[5]

"Lee, who is this man? What is he doing? Why is he like that?" Yogi Ramsuratkumar asked several times, studying the photograph for a long time. It was a magnificent photograph taken during a concert in America, in which Sanatan Das Baul was playing his *ektara* (a simple, handmade one-stringed instrument). He was standing with his head thrown back, eyes closed in the ecstasy of longing.

"Where does he live?" Yogi Ramsuratkumar wanted to know. Lee explained that he was a friend—a guru who lived on an ashram in Bengal and begged for his food. The teachings and way of life of the Bauls were so resonant with that of Yogi Ramsuratkumar that it seemed highly possible that he had known some Bauls during his years as a mendicant beggar, or even as a child, adolescent or young adult in Bihar. Since Bengal borders Bihar, it was likely that Yogi Ramsuratkumar had encountered the Bauls who wandered there, singing and begging; he could have even spent time with them during his years of *sadhana* on the road. Their love for spontaneous poetry, song and dance was reflected also in the beggar saint's love of the same. Yogi Ramsuratkumar never discoursed formally and rarely gave linear teachings; his declaration that Lee's poetry had told the beggar's story, and "no other books need to be written on this beggar," expressed fully the Baul sentiment—that the teaching should be encoded in poetry, song and dance rather than in intellectual considerations of dharma.

Yogi Ramsuratkumar's fascination with the photograph of Sanatan Das was an interesting echo of when Sanatan Das had first walked onto Lee's ashram in Arizona. The first thing he noticed was a picture of Yogi Ramsuratkumar on Lee's desk. He picked it up, studied it intently for a long moment and then held it up in the air and said triumphantly, "Baul guru!" Now Yogi Ramsuratkumar was gazing at the photograph of Sanatan Das Baul with a similar deep interest. Off and on in the weeks to come Yogi Ramsuratkumar would gaze at the picture and ask these questions again, sometimes of Lee and sometimes of Devaki.

In the meantime, the staff was busily preparing for the first of December, when the first *jayanthi* celebration would be held on the ashram. Invitations had been sent out to all the friends and devotees of Yogi Ramsuratkumar, and a festive atmosphere of high anticipation was building.

On *jayanthi* day Mukilan was one of many long-time devotees who arrived to find the beggar saint giving darshan to six hundred people. Unlike his last visit, this time Mukilan was one of many faces in the huge crowd, and he watched Mani offer the

5 Sanatan Das Baul, *Facets of the Diamond*, p. 197.

microphone to Yogi Ramsuratkumar, saying, "Bhagawan, will you speak to everyone?" With a big smile and a beaming face, the beggar said, "Wish you all a happy birthday!" Mukilan remembered:

> It was so different than my other experiences of Yogi. He was blessing the whole crowd, walking up and down the hall. He blessed everybody, wished us all a happy birthday. But to me, there was really no change. If the devotee is immature, they may see it that way, but it is the same compassion, love and affection. The same thing was there, because he knows that we are there. Why do you need to have a more one-on-one connection?

In these words Mukilan expressed the understanding of a very mature spiritual practitioner. When the truth of non-separation becomes real, a whole world of freedom opens up that resolves the entire dualistic dilemma of the illusion of separation, which is at the root of all suffering. To truly understand that the guru is always with us, never separate, is to relieve the fundamental conflict that all devotees or disciples encounter on the path: the paradox of the guru as God and the guru as a human being—who can appear to betray, forsake or withdraw from us.

At dawn on *jayanthi* day a Vedic *agni hotra* (fire ceremony) was conducted in the Yagashala, a rectangular, open-air thatched roof structure built on a raised concrete foundation. A large brightly colored mandala was drawn in rice powder in the middle of the floor with a large *puja* in the middle—a picture of Yogi Ramsuratkumar, fruit and incense offerings, ghee lamps, vessels for water and many sacred substances. The rice mandala had a border of seventy-seven ghee lamps, the age of Yogi Ramsuratkumar, which burned brightly. A few feet away near the northeast corner of the building was a raised fire pit, where the fire *puja* would be performed. The air crackled with energy even at this early hour, and the devotees had been chanting, "Yogi Ramsuratkumar, Yogi Ramsuratkumar, Yogi Ramsuratkumar, Jaya Guru Raya," all night long, the men taking thirty minute turns at circumambulating the *puja* in the center of the space, alternating with the women, who were lead by Devaki. Thousands of tiny colored lights were strung around the temple and twinkled around the sign that announced Yogi Ramsuratkumar's *Jayanthi*.

When Yogi Ramsuratkumar arrived he was led inside and seated at the eastern wall of the building, with Devaki seated a short distance away on his left and Justice Arunachalam on his right. Lee and his group were seated nearby, along the south wall of the structure. Devotees began to come forward with many flower *malas*, and the scent of incense mingled with the smell of fresh palm thatching, burning ghee and jasmine flowers. The garlands were presented to Yogi Ramsuratkumar, many of which he then gave to Justice Arunachalam, many of which he wore himself. Devaki was also garlanded, and Yogi Ramsuratkumar instructed her to give some of hers to the daughter of the Justice. The momentary glare of cameras bulbs flashing in sudden bursts of bright light invaded the mood of the moment.

After the *malas* had been presented, Lee stood up and walked to Yogi Ramsuratkumar, knelt down beside him and with a *pranam*, handed him a packet of new poems he had written. With a lingering look at Lee, Yogi Ramsuratkumar took the packet and held it between his palms in a gesture of *pranam*. Soon the chanting and circumambulation of the shrine stopped and the fire *puja* began, with Suresh, Rajmohan and several other devotees of Brahmin caste performing the rites. They began to intone the Sanskrit prayers, and the long ceremony of offering many precious substances into the fire began.

Holding the hand of Justice Arunachalam, one of the ashram trustees, the beggar sometimes watched the Vedic ceremony with interest, but often drifted away in *bhavas*, his head sunk to his chest. Suddenly he opened his eyes, leaned over to Justice Arunachalam and pointed toward Lee, saying, "Lee Lozowick."

As the sun rose over the horizon the ceremony came to an end and Yogi Ramsuratkumar left, guided away and down the concrete steps of the building by Mani, with Devaki and the Sudama sisters following behind. The rest of the day was filled with feasting in the unfinished dining hall—a large, spacious building attached to the kitchen, where meals for hundreds could be prepared in a matter of an hour. Long rows of narrow tables were set up with banana leaf plates and folding chairs. It was a lavish breakfast, with many special dishes added to the usual idlis and delicious, spicy sambar—a savory soup-like sauce made with a special powdered dahl, vegetables and spices. More than two hundred people were served that day.

Over the coming years the numbers would swell to two thousand on *jayanthi* day, but on this first birthday celebration the numbers were relatively small, which made it possible for Yogi Ramsuratkumar to eat with everyone. As he sat over his banana leaf and looked around the room, his face was transfigured by beatific smiles. His mood was joyful and infectious.

After breakfast he went back to Sudama House to stay until it was time for the first darshan program of the day, which would be held in the newly completed, spacious and elegant entrance hall to the temple—a large circular room about eighty feet in diameter. With its freshly painted pink walls, polished black marble floor and pictures of Yogi Ramsuratkumar's three fathers and their feminine counterparts, it would be a grand backdrop for the festivities of the day. It was only eight-thirty in the morning, and it seemed like the day was already full and bursting with the rich flavor of celebration.

During the days after the *jayanthi* celebration passed, the fast pace ebbed back to the usual flow of private intimate breakfasts with Yogi Ramsuratkumar, where Lee and other guests were sometimes invited to sit and take food with Yogi Ramsuratkumar, Devaki and the Sudama sisters. Mani and Raji were usually in attendance also, as well as other ashram staff members and devotees. The private breakfasts were often a time when projects and ideas were initiated and blessed by Yogi Ramsuratkumar, or when he gave instructions or made specific communications and casual comments that carried deeper significance. In his cryptic way, through seemingly ordinary comments or even jokes, he gave important instructions to those around him.

One morning in December in the breakfast hut Lee presented Yogi Ramsuratkumar with a manuscript written by one of his students, Sita Martin—a rendering of the *Ramayana* into ecstatic devotional poetry. It was titled "The Hunger of Love: Versions of the Ramayana." It was an epic piece of poetry, and Yogi Ramsuratkumar immediately asked Devaki to read it:

> Sita, Princess of Mithila,
> Daughter of King Janaka
> Sita, the child who was found
>   orphaned in the furrow of her father's field
> Prays to You on this auspicious day
>   to smile upon me
>   to shower me with Your blessings
>   to kindle the flame that has been ignited in
>   my heart
> I implore You
> To let Him lift the bow
>
> I thought this morning when I awoke
>   to the smell of sandalwood and amber
>   burning in the brazier upon my altar
> That today would be like any other day
> As I sprinkled rosewater upon my head
>   and dipped my finger into the tilaka
> My songs were to the Gods
> My thoughts on my beloved father . . . .
>
> Beloved Ram
> King of my Heart
> Lord of my Soul
>
> Today my father, King of Janaka,
>   gives my hand in marriage to thee
> Today I leave my father's house
>   to follow thee to Ayodya
> Today I shed tears of mourning mixed with tears
>   of joy

The poem recounted the love of Sita for Ram, and in the reading of it aloud, a mood of longing emerged, which mingled with the fine morning light that permeated the small palm thatched hut. Yogi Ramsuratkumar fell into a *bhava* right away, sinking deep inside himself, his head falling toward his chest. The mood was so powerful that at times tears streamed down his face as the poetry evoked the story of Sita's capture by the demon Ravana, the anguish of her separation from her beloved Ram and their final reunion.

Two or three times Devaki stopped the reading to remind Yogi Ramsuratkumar of the time, as it was his usual time to retire to Sudama House. Each time she stopped reading he raised his head and said sharply, "Read!" whisking his hand through the air as if to forcefully keep the reading moving. The poem was read through to the end. When it was finished Yogi Ramsuratkumar raised his head and looked at Lee.

"Lee Lozowick has written this poem," the beggar said, then looked at Devaki.

"No Bhagawan, Lee did not write it—one of his students wrote it," Devaki clarified.

"No, Lee wrote this poem," Yogi Ramsuratkumar insisted. Again Devaki attempted to clarify, offering the author's name.

"No Bhagawan—it was written by Sita Martin, a student of Lee's . . ."

"No!" Yogi Ramsuratkumar replied fiercely, "Lee Lozowick wrote this poem!" It was settled. The master had decreed that Lee had written the poem, and in that moment it became the truth, as if reality itself was revealed by his declaration.

"I would like to have your permission to publish this," Lee said after a few moments had passed.

Yogi Ramsuratkumar said, "You may publish it. Father's blessing . . ." He raised both hands in his characteristic blessing.

"I have another manuscript I would like to show you as well—I would like to have your permission to publish this one as well," Lee ventured, pulling out the rough draft for a children's book about Yogi Ramsuratkumar. Yogi Ramsuratkumar waved this manuscript away with a brisk sweep of his hand.

"Lee does not need my permission to publish anything. Lee can publish anything he wants!" Yogi Ramsuratkumar responded in his melodic voice. Again his hand swept through the air, as if he was clearing away any murkiness that might be adrift in it.

"This beggar will leave you now," he closed the conversation and the magic of the chamber that had enclosed the small group for almost two hours and swiftly left for Sudama House.[6]

During one of the afternoon darshans held in the entrance hall to the temple, Yogi Ramsuratkumar began to work in a particular way. With the blue-gray shawl thrown over one shoulder, he got up, came down from the dais and walked swiftly up and down the aisle several times. While he walked the chanting continued, lead by Rajalakshmi and Vijayakka, who sat to Yogi Ramsuratkumar's right on the floor beneath the dais facing him: "Yogi Ramsuratkumar, Yogi Ramsuratkumar, Yogi Ramsuratkumar, Jaya Guru Raya." Making one more sweep up and back and gazing at the crowd, the beggar stopped in front of Lee, who was sitting in the first row before the dais.

Yogi Ramsuratkumar sat down beside Lee and they looked into each other's eyes for a very long, extended moment. "Devaki!" Yogi Ramsuratkumar called out. Devaki came

---

6 This manuscript was published as a small paperback volume on March 23, 1995 in Kanimadam by Pon Kamaraj under the title *Hunger of Love: Versions of the Ramayana.*

down from the dais to his side; he quickly instructed her to sit in the front row of the women's side and at the same time told Lee to go sit up on the dais. When Lee hesitated, a bit shocked by this unexpected turn of events, Yogi Ramsuratkumar said sharply, "Now, Lee! *Now*! Do what this beggar says."

With Lee seated on his dais now, Yogi Ramsuratkumar continued to walk up and down the room, blessing the crowd while the chanting continued without pause. His movements were powerful, as if he was rearranging the universe itself, preparing the ground and planting the seeds that would come to fruition in new fields of possibility. The empowerment of placing his Western devotee upon the dais alone reflected the turn that Lee's work had taken in the West over the past three years. Traveling extensively, teaching every year in France and Germany, telling many stories of Yogi Ramsuratkumar and praising his name "all over the world," as he had said he would in his poetry, Lee Lozowick had become the emissary of Yogi Ramsuratkumar in the West. This act of placing Lee on his own dais would be repeated every year when Lee visited for the rest of Yogi Ramsuratkumar's life.

While Lee sat on the dais, Yogi Ramsuratkumar sat in Lee's seat on the floor on the men's side of the room, with Devaki just across the aisle on the women's side. Yogi Ramsuratkumar held the hand of Tom Lennon, one of Lee's students, part of the time as he sat there. The moment Yogi Ramsuratkumar rose from his seat, Lee also stood up and came down from the dais, meeting Yogi Ramsuratkumar halfway, where Lee bowed his head and bent down to touch the master's feet. As Lee stood up and *pranamed* with hands pressed together, Yogi Ramsuratkumar smiled broadly and slapped Lee's back three times, so hard that the sharp crack of it resounded through the vast, marble-floored hall. Soon everyone was back in their original seats, and the chanting still continued.

Everything had occurred in an exalted and joyful silence that existed beneath the constant melodious drone of the chanting of the name of God. There was a thrilling wave of presence and awareness that moved through the room, and as Yogi Ramsuratkumar regained the platform dais where Lee had just been sitting, the closing "ki jai" or "victory to the guru" was shouted out: "Om Bhagavan Sri Yogi Ramsuratkumar Maharaj Ki Jai! Sri Annai Devaki Mataji Ki Jai!"

At that precise moment Mani rushed up to the front of the room with a camera to capture the moment. Yogi Ramsuratkumar's hands raised up high in blessing, seemingly of their own volition and not by any effort of will, and blessed the crowded room full of people. The crowd went wild, clapping in time to the chant, calling out and standing up to see better. A wave of enthusiasm rushed through the room. Yogi Ramsuratkumar stood up on the platform and turned to touch the huge red Om that was painted on the wall behind where he sat. Just as suddenly as the surge of ecstasy had been unleashed, with this slight hand gesture from Yogi Ramsuratkumar, the space returned to a state of quiescence—the deep burning reverence and awe that so characterized the experience of sitting in darshan with the beggar saint.

The readings from the new book continued, along with readings from *Poems of a Broken Heart*. At one point after the beggar asked Devaki to read first his own biography, then the biography of Lee Lozowick from *Facets of the Diamond*, Yogi Ramsuratkumar began to speak.

"This beggar is in this book . . . this beggar allowed this only if he," he pointed to Lee, who was kneeling at his side, "was in the book too. This is a book about Indian saints, and Lee Lozowick is an Indian saint!" It was a stunning announcement.

At other times that day Yogi Ramsuratkumar would insist that Lee read from the book, beginning with his own biography. With an embarrassed chuckle, Lee obeyed. At various times Yogi Ramsuratkumar made *Facets of the Diamond* available for sale. It cost thirteen hundred rupees, which was a lot of money. Yogi Ramsuratkumar gave it to some of his devotees to look at and "decide" if they wanted to buy one. When someone bought a copy, he personally signed the book with a large Om.

A few days later the morning darshan was held in the intimate space of the small darshan *mandir*. It was a very different space than the large imposing entrance hall with its shining black marble floor. Yogi Ramsuratkumar had Justice Arunachalam sitting beside him as he invited Pon Kamaraj and his *bhajan* singers up to sing a favorite chant, the beautiful "Krishna Lalee" (as the Americans called it), written by the well-known screenwriter Sri Balakumaran, an ardent devotee. Pon Kamaraj and his group had been circumambulating the ashram grounds and chanting, carrying with them a large picture of Yogi Ramsuratkumar sheltered beneath a large umbrella. It was a very traditional sight, and their enthusiasm and passionate chanting filled the air with a devotional spirit.

Yogi Ramsuratkumar then asked Rajmohan to stand up and read a text in Tamil. When Yogi Ramsuratkumar got up during the reading to sit beside Lee in the front row, immediately two cameras were pointed toward him. He looked at them in surprise and then laughed. It was a warm and happy gathering.

On his last day at the ashram, Lee came to the dais during darshan to say goodbye to Yogi Ramsuratkumar; he and his group would be leaving the next day, and this was the last time he would see Yogi Ramsuratkumar until the next year's *jayanthi*. Lee kneeled at the side of the beggar and bowed his head to the beggar's feet.

"What can we give Lee?" Yogi Ramsuratkumar asked no one in particular. Devaki sat beside him watching. He looked around with sparkling eyes, as if he would find something in the air. "What can we give Lee? What can we give Lee?" he repeated. Then he looked down and noticed the *dhoti* he had wrapped about his body underneath the blue-gray woolen shawl, up over one shoulder and tied in the front with a tight double knot. The *dhoti* is a traditional dress for Indian men—an approximately four foot wide, nine foot long piece of cotton muslin, normally used to wrap around the lower part of the body. This one had been twisted and molded into a two-foot wide swath of cloth and wrapped around the beggar's body for a very long time. It was streaked and heavy with grime and dirt and almost stiff to the touch, it carried so much spiritual substance in it, both physical and subtle.

"This dhoti!" he cried triumphantly, having discovered the perfect gift. He carefully removed the several layers of *malas*—strings of prayer beads for *japa*—that he wore, placed them on the dais, then removed the heavy, long, blue-gray shawl that he wore, wrapped around his body and thrown up and over one shoulder in the manner he favored. Yogi Ramsuratkumar was never without at least one heavy woolen shawl, and this had to be removed in order to then pull the old *dhoti* over his head with the knot intact. In the process his turban came loose, and he allowed it to fall to the dais beside him as he handed the *dhoti* to Lee.

"This is very dirty, Lee!" he said with a sweet smile as he gently, carefully, slowly placed it in Lee's hands. Yogi Ramsuratkumar chuckled and everyone laughed at the irony of the situation—as if the *dhoti* being dirty would be a nuisance to Lee. Indeed the *dhoti* was stained dark and heavy with the accumulated dirt in the creases of its folds, but it was the same sacred "dirt" of the beggar that Lee wrote about in his poems. It was not the smell of sweat, fear and angst—which permeates most human existence—that exuded from the heavy length of tied cloth, but the smell of Mother India's deepest secrets—the scent of mystery, of fires, of hope and hopelessness, of a ravenous love for God, the raw ecstasy of a beggar's surrender. Speechless and awed by the fortune of such a gift, Lee took the *dhoti*, held it to his forehead and bowed deeply at the beggar's feet, where he lingered with his forehead pressed against the beggar's feet and leg for a long moment. Yogi Ramsuratkumar smiled down at him and put his hand on Lee's back. It was a moment suspended in time. A supernal sweetness hovered in the air, then the beggar raised both of his hands in blessing.

"My Father blesses Lee," he said, with infinite tenderness. Slowly Lee got up and went back to his place on the floor in the front row, the *dhoti* held gingerly in his lap.

Yogi Ramsuratkumar sat on the platform at the front of the hall bareheaded. His turban, nothing but a green rag, lay on the dais beside him. He carefully replaced the *malas* around his neck—five or six strings, the beads made of either huge brown *rudraksh* or large round quartz crystals that both reflected and contained the afternoon light, so that they seemed to glow from within. They lay like jewels on the faded and stained white of his *kirta* top. In his lap was the large shawl. His feet were stretched out in repose and his black hair hung down below his shoulders, a powerful contrast to the glistening snow white of his long beard. He appeared incredibly beautiful in this relaxed posture, vulnerable as a child in perfect innocence, and smiling radiantly, like the morning sun. It was a moment of pure grace. Lee sat in the front row with his eyes riveted to the master, hands pressed together in *pranam*, while the beggar gazed back in return, now solemn, eyes smoldering like a banked fire, palms pressed together in a mirror image. The silence of their communion deepened into gold as outside the sun sank toward the horizon.

Lee did not put the *dhoti* down for the rest of the day, but sat with it in his lap or carried it in his hands. The knot in the *dhoti* remained intact, and it would never be washed. On the long trip back to Arizona, the *dhoti* was carried by Lee in a cloth bag, kept carefully by his side over the miles. He had come a long way from the spurned and rejected lover of 1986, who declared that, no matter what the cost, he would love and praise his father, even if it had to be from far, far away.

In late 1994 the young American woman, Mariana Caplan, had made a very strong connection with Lee and his students. Before he left for Arizona in mid-December, Lee instructed her to stay in Tiruvannamalai instead of traveling around India and continuing her search, saying emphatically, "If you want to be where the action is, stay here." What he meant was, "If you want the real spiritual path, the real work, you should stay here, around Yogi Ramsuratkumar. It is the opportunity of many lifetimes." Although she felt she had found the spiritual teacher she was looking for in Lee Lozowick and was very smitten with him, Lee was often fierce in saying that he wasn't looking for students, and it was unclear to her as to whether or not he would accept her as a student. At the same time, she was tangled up in her own notions of the spiritual path, and failed to register the first major instruction Lee had given to her: "Stay here."

Instead of staying in Tiruvannamalai, in January 1995 she made plans to leave for Madras and then Kerala. Before she left, she gave Mani a note in darshan for Yogi Ramsuratkumar that said, "Thank you for introducing me to your son, Lee." The note wasn't delivered until the next day, when Mariana had already left for Kerala.

Although she had made plans for further travels, once she was in Kerala something kept tugging at her to return to Tiruvannamalai. It was like being drawn back by a magnet, and finally she gave in to the impulse, abandoned her ticket to Bangalore and returned to the Yogi Ramsuratkumar Ashram. As soon as she arrived several people came up to her and said, "Thank God, you're back! Bhagawan has had your note read twice a day every day in darshan for the past two weeks. Why didn't you ask permission to leave?" She was surprised, because she had no idea that once a connection was made with Yogi Ramsuratkumar, it was considered proper protocol to get the guru's blessing before leaving his company.

For the next two days she came to darshan twice a day, but nothing unusual happened. Feeling restless again, she made plans to go to Madras to pick up her boyfriend, who was arriving from England. She told Mani, "I'm leaving tomorrow morning, if you want to tell Yogi Ramsuratkumar."

At the next darshan when Yogi Ramsuratkumar drove up in his car, he leaned out the window and said to Mani, "This beggar would like to see the Jewish girl from California." When he was settled on the dais, she was called up to see him.

"They say you are leaving," he began. "Where are you going?"

"Madras," she answered.

"Why are you going?" he queried.

"To pick up my boyfriend, who is coming from England."

"And then where are you going?" he continued.

"Mahabalipuram, Pondicherry . . ."

"Where are you going?" he started the questioning all over again.

"To Madras," she answered again.

"Why are you going there?" he asked, then kept repeating this line of questioning over and over. Each time she would answer as best she could. His repetitive questioning carried the distinct reminder of Lee's words to Mariana: "Stay here." Finally Yogi Ramsuratkumar said, "Sit down," and indicated a seat on the floor beside the dais. He raised his hand in blessing, looking at her, and continued to bless her in this way for the next forty minutes. During this time she fell into a very strong state in which she spontaneously began to "confess" her whole life to him, internally. Mariana recounted:

> I already knew that he was telepathic, but I started spontaneously telling him with my thoughts everything I'd done—things I felt ashamed of, perhaps a lie I'd told, my imagined sins, scenes from my life. For forty minutes I was confessing, and it just kept coming and coming, very intensely.
>
> Then it arose from within, "Okay. In the morning I am going to Madras and picking up my boyfriend." Within five seconds of this thought, when the whole confession was complete, he said, "My Father blesses Mariana," and it was over. I felt like I had signed something in blood. It was a deal I couldn't break. It was the beginning of a whole play with him. He started having me lead chants in darshan. It was totally unconscious on my part, but my whole scheme was, "I love Lee, Lee loves Yogi, if Yogi loves me, then Lee will love me too."
>
> Two weeks later I was sitting in darshan one afternoon when Yogi Ramsuratkumar told me to go to the library with Devaki Ma. She had a message from him to give to me. First she repeated a verse from the *Upanishads* which says, all we have to do is sit at the guru's feet like little children. The second part of the message was that Yogi Ramsuratkumar said, "Lee Lozowick is Yogi Ramsuratkumar in America." This message had a very strong, immediate impact on me. Coming from Yogi Ramsuratkumar, I understood how important that communication was, because she was not telling me that Lee Lozowick was *like* Yogi Ramsuratkumar, or that he was doing Yogi Ramsuratkumar's work, but that he *was* Yogi Ramsuratkumar in America. Though I knew very little about what was going on, I understood the gravity of the communication. It was information that I needed in order to eventually come to more deeply appreciate Lee's role in relationship to Yogi Ramsuratkumar.
>
> And thirdly, she wanted to find out how long I would be staying in town. When I said, "I have no idea," she said, "You don't understand. You have to give him an answer." She clearly communicated that although I might not know this yet, Yogi Ramsuratkumar's word was the law. We talked for a while longer, and then, with our business done, the door handle suddenly turned and the door opened by itself. Without any hint of

> surprise or fascination, Ma Devaki said, "Oh, that's Bhagawan telling me to come back."

They returned immediately to the darshan and Ma Devaki reported the conversation to Yogi Ramsuratkumar, who called Mariana up to the dais.

"Devaki says Mariana will stay for six weeks . . . " he paused, then said triumphantly, "Mariana will stay for six years!" Saying this, he threw his hands up in a spontaneous fit of blessing, started laughing and then sent her back to her seat. He kept laughing and laughing, and his laughter was so contagious that Mariana started laughing. Devaki and the Sudama sisters were laughing, and then everyone in the hall was laughing. The laughter went on for an hour in a mood of almost delirious delight in the beggar's company. It was an initiatory event of significant proportions for Mariana, who found herself in basic training, sort of a boot camp for guru yoga. Yogi Ramsuratkumar was preparing her for the relationship she would later have with her teacher—his devotee, Lee Lozowick.

Six years later to the month after Yogi Ramsuratkumar said, "Mariana will stay for six years," he died. In retrospect, Mariana felt it was one of many signs that he gave of when he would shed his body.

As it turned out, she stayed in Tiruvannamalai until the summer, living for most of those months at the ashram of Hamsa, a Dutchman who was a guru or spiritual guide for fifty years to many people who had lived in Tiruvannamalai, but had never connected with the beggar saint before. Three times while she was staying there Yogi Ramsuratkumar came to bless the ashram of Hamsa, who was thrilled to have such an auspicious visitor grace his ashram.

Once Yogi Ramsuratkumar came with Ma Devaki and the Sudama sisters to see the puja done at the Dakshinamurti shrine in the center of the compound in the main temple. On this occasion a Western student was there and wanted to interview Yogi Ramsuratkumar, but all he would say was, "This beggar knows nothing! Father alone exists! That's all this beggar has to say." He would say no more, and the student felt he had gotten nothing, when he had been given exactly what he needed. Everyone else, including Hamsa, enjoyed it very much.

From January through June 1995, Mariana came to Yogi Ramsuratkumar's darshan every day, while she lived in the sanctuary of Hamsa's ashram—a perfect circumstance, orchestrated, she felt, by the guru's influence. She said:

> It was so graceful. I was just going along unconsciously, and the guru's influence was providing these perfect circumstances. The influence was already constructing the required circumstance.
>
> If you hung around Yogi Ramsuratkumar at that time, you really got that you weren't going to understand anything that was going on. You weren't given any information, so you were forced into an acceptance of not knowing. At best, darshan turned into this kind of technicolor surfing

> of Yogi Ramsuratkumar's energy. Even if you were miserable it became interesting because there was so much going on. You would just ride his waves, surf his energy. Sometimes he would have his head down, and you couldn't tell whether he was working or asleep. But either way, it was his ride.

When the time came for Mariana to return to the States in June 1995, she wrote Yogi Ramsuratkumar a note saying that she would like to leave to go to California for four days, then to Boulder, Colorado for one week where she would visit some students of Lee Lozowick, and then to Lee's ashram in Arizona. The next day the beggar saint called her up to the dais.

"This beggar doesn't understand Mariana's note. Could you explain it to him?" She explained it, then he said, "This beggar still doesn't understand. Can someone else explain it?" She felt that he was pretending he didn't understand when he understood it perfectly. Something else was up—he was making a teaching lesson. Again he asked Mariana to explain the note to him, then he asked Devaki to explain it. After she explained it he said again, "This beggar still doesn't understand. What is Mariana asking?" Finally Mariana herself was able to cut through the confusion.

"I want to go to Arizona and do whatever Lee says," she answered.

Yogi Ramsuratkumar broke into a big smile and threw up his hands to bless her, saying joyously, "My Father blesses Mariana!"

"My yoga isn't about liberation... it's about becoming a perfect vehicle for the service of God," Yogi Ramsuratkumar once said. The beggar saint had asked Lee to come back to India only two months after he left in December 1994 in order to be present for the signing of certain papers that would finalize the creation of Hohm Trust in India and the purchase and development of a tract of land adjoining the Yogi Ramsuratkumar Ashram. Lee left Arizona on February 13, 1995 with Stan Hitson, one of the composers, lead singers and guitarists in Lee's rock band, "liars, gods & beggars." They arrived two days later on the Yogi Ramsuratkumar Ashram carrying twenty copies of the heavy, hard backed *Facets of the Diamond*, "in all their weighty glory," as Stan Hitson wrote.

Arriving at three in the morning, after two hours of sleep Lee and Stan walked to the ashram to join the queue to greet Yogi Ramsuratkumar as he was driven onto the ashram for breakfast. The morning was cool and moist, the trees and tropical foliage replenished by a night's respite from the hot sun and the rejuvenating effects of the dew. As they walked briskly through the neighborhood that surrounded the ashram they were cheerfully and warmly greeted by many people of all ages. Stan wrote:

> Then we turned the corner and there it was: the raw, steel-framed structure of what will become a massive dome covering the entry to the temple on the ashram. It was an impressive sight standing out against the morning sky in Tiruvannamalai. It must have been fifty feet above the

> ground and there was certainly nothing else around to challenge it. My heartbeat quickened with anticipation as we approached the front gate. I know that Lee was excited about being here, about seeing his beloved Yogi Ramsuratkumar once again. I don't know who I was more excited for—Mr. Lee or myself ! We were greeted by Mani and others and directed to seats on the porch of one of the ashram's service buildings. We were served chai while we waited. There was already a great deal of activity on the property at 6:45 in the morning; the women were washing and sweeping the grounds adjacent to the buildings and many people were preparing for Yogi Ramsuratkumar's arrival and the day's work ahead.
>
> As Yogi Ramsuratkumar's car approached we moved to a standing position along the entrance driveway. Yogi Ramsuratkumar arrived in a car with Ma Devaki and another woman from Sudama House, where he lives, and the driver, always the same driver, who he had stop the car when it reached the place where Lee was standing. Yogi Ramsuratkumar got out of the car and walked up to Lee, took his hand tightly and stood there for just a moment before ushering Lee back into the car with him.[7]

Lee was taken to the breakfast hut with Yogi Ramsuratkumar, where breakfast was served every morning at seven-thirty. Shortly after that, the beggar went back to Sudama House, then returned for the morning darshan that was held in the entrance hall to the temple. Yogi Ramsuratkumar, Ma Devaki, the Sudama sisters and Mani entered the room first, then Lee and Stan were invited inside. Next the women filed in and took their places on the right side of the hall, followed by the rest of the men who were situated on the left. There were two attendants dressed in green pants and shirts who helped direct people to their seats on the floor and arrange the rows of people to maximize the use of the space.

The Sudama sisters were seated on a mat on the floor to the left of Yogi Ramsuratkumar's platform; Ma Devaki sat on the platform with him. While everyone filed in and got settled the Sudama sisters started the chanting, changing from one song to another at Yogi Ramsuratkumar's request. Stan described these songs as "melancholy and melodiously complex songs" that Yogi Ramsuratkumar requested by title; as soon as he said which song he wanted, the Sudama sisters would rustle through their chanting books for the lyrics and begin to sing. They lead chants for an hour, until Yogi Ramsuratkumar beckoned another woman or two from the audience to come up and chant.

While the chanting went on, the beggar smoked. Occasionally he asked Ma Devaki for a drink, and at times Mani would approach to deliver a note, to inform him that someone in the audience was asking for his blessing, or to let him know that someone had brought *prasad* they would like to give. With Yogi Ramsuratkumar's assent, Mani would then call the man or woman up to the dais, where they would deeply *pranam*, sometimes reach to touch the beggar's feet and offer their *prasad*. The blessing was often a sound

7 Stan Hitson, "Extraordinary Business," *Tawagoto*, Winter 1995, p. 71..

slap on the back while they bowed by his knee. When the darshan was over, Yogi Ramsuratkumar sent Ma Devaki and the Sudama sisters out first then exited down the center aisle and returned to Sudama House until late afternoon, when darshan would be held again.

A few days later Pon Kamaraj arrived. In darshan, the Sudama sisters lead chants for over an hour and then Yogi Ramsuratkumar asked Pon Kamaraj and his men to lead *bhajans*. Their enthusiasm was boundless as the drummer pounded out a complex rhythm and Pon Kamaraj lead the wildly ecstatic *bhajans* to Yogi Ramsuratkumar. Music and song were his gift to the master. Stan wrote:

> I could feel the restless anticipation of Pon Kamaraj and his followers who were seated right behind us. At last Yogi Ramsuratkumar beckoned Pon Kamaraj and his *bhajan* band to chant for him. The group of six men took a seat to the left and about fifteen feet in front of where Yogi Ramsuratkumar was seated. Pon Kamaraj began by chanting a beautiful and heartful rendition of the "Yogi Lalee" chant. His band waited restlessly but politely while he completed the song. Then all six of them ripped into a wild and energetic call and response chant. The drummer was pounding away, and all of them were clapping and moving to the intense rhythm. The space was electrified; people were moved to chant in response to the call. It was wonderful. First Pon Kamaraj, then the drummer, offered their wild, ecstatic songs. Yogi Ramsuratkumar smiled and hid his blushing face in response to their reverie. They played and poured themselves into their songs for nearly an hour until Yogi Ramsuratkumar had His fill. They paused briefly for Yogi Ramsuratkumar to rise and bid His farewell, then they broke into one final, fervent, rocking gospel as Yogi Ramsuratkumar exited to His waiting car. We were all high. I didn't want it to end. In my heart, it never will.[8]

The next day when Lee and Stan entered the darshan hall a tape of Doug Fulker's chants that had been recorded on Lee's ashram in Arizona was playing. Yogi Ramsuratkumar listened to the entire tape, about twenty minutes long, and when it ended he asked to have it played again, then again a third time.

"Can you sing this song for this beggar?" Yogi Ramsuratkumar asked the Sudama sisters when the tape had finished its third playing. They seemed surprised and said that they didn't know the words. Mani came and got involved in the discussion, and it was decided that they would listen to the tape one more time. Yogi Ramsuratkumar seemed delighted with the whole process, and after the tape played a fourth time, he turned back to Rajalakshmi and asked her to sing the chant. While she lead the chant Yogi Ramsuratkumar walked around crowd, going down the aisle and back up, stopping here or there to

8 Ibid.

look at one or another of the devotees. The chanting went on when Yogi Ramsuratkumar was leaving, but instead he changed course, walked up the aisle toward the door, paused, then turned around and walked back up the aisle, circling around the women. He came back up the aisle again and began to circle the seated men. Passing in front of Lee, he said, "You have composed a very fine song." Then he was gone.

That afternoon at four o'clock Yogi Ramsuratkumar began the darshan by asking for the same chant, and the tape was played once to refresh the memories of the Sudama sisters, who would lead the chant. After singing the chant for an hour, Yogi Ramsuratkumar's attention turned to the copies of *Facets of the Diamond* that Lee had brought as a gift for him. Stan had hand-carried a heavy box of the books on airplanes and through airports as they traveled across the globe. Yogi Ramsuratkumar handed Ma Devaki a copy and asked her to read from it. She introduced *Facets of the Diamond* and its patron, Lee, to the expectantly waiting darshan crowd, many of whom did not speak English at all, but came to soak up the radiations of the saint; for the devotees, if it was Yogi Ramsuratkumar's *lila* to sell these books, then that was his blessing.

Yogi Ramsuratkumar asked Devaki to read the dedication, the preface, the introduction, and then the biography and quotes of Lee. She stood fifteen feet in front of the dais where Yogi Ramsuratkumar was usually seated, but he came and sat beside her on the polished black stone floor as she read. Stan wrote:

> Yogi Ramsuratkumar seemed to love every word of it. When she finished, they returned to their seats on the dais and Mani came out with five or six more copies of the book. He announced that the books were for sale for 1,300 rupies, and that today was a rare opportunity, since both Yogi Ramsuratkumar and Mr. Lee were present, and that Yogi Ramsuratkumar would sign the book and offer it as prasad to anyone who bought one. Now 1,300 rupies is a lot of money by Indian standards, but immediately the man sitting next to me jumped up and said, "I'll take one!" He approached the dais while Mani took the plastic off the book and handed it to Yogi Ramsuratkumar, who opened it, drew the Om symbol inside the cover, and handed it to the man who was pranaming. Yogi Ramsuratkumar slapped him on the shoulder, and that was that.
>
> Two or three more people responded in the same way. Yogi Ramsuratkumar was having a great time with this; he was laughing and talking and very playful. He teased the people who came up for the book by turning to Mani and saying, "Mani, make sure you get their money!" . . . . I smiled to myself as I remembered the pain of carrying that box of books through the airport and on and off of every airplane. This was worth every bit of it.[9]

9 Ibid.

When there were still a few copies of the book left, Yogi Ramsuratkumar called one well-known devotee by name.

"Don't you want this book?" he teased. The man had no choice but to come forward and accept such an offer! Yogi Ramsuratkumar seemed to really like this part. He then called up the young American woman, Mariana Caplan.

"Do you have this book?" he asked.

"No," she answered.

"Do you have the money?" The answer was yes, and she bought a copy. Now, with the last copy in hand, he turned and looked at Devaki.

"Devaki will take this book," he announced. Looking at Mani, he said with a mischievous smile, "Make sure you get the money from Devaki," and then broke into laughter.

"We are having a good selling day!" he laughed, talking to Mani. Every time someone came up to buy the book, they had the chance to interact personally with Yogi Ramsuratkumar, and to receive his signature and his blessing. It was a *lila* that would be enacted several times in the years ahead as Lee continued to bring books, written and published in the States in praise of Yogi Ramsuratkumar.

As it turned out, another legal snag developed that delayed the signing of the papers for Hohm Trust for another month. It didn't matter that the business could not be conducted; as Lee said, "It will be a great trip anyway." They relished the time on the ashram with Yogi Ramsuratkumar and his circle of devotees. Lee was invited every morning at seven-thirty to the intimate "family" breakfasts, and on several mornings Stan was invited also. One morning as they came in and took their seats, Yogi Ramsuratkumar began to speak.

"Someone asked this beggar if he is happy. This beggar can't be bothered with happy. He only wants to do his Father's Work." He paused for a moment then continued, "Someone asked, is this beggar missing anything? Nothing is missing, there is only my Father's Work—always Father's Work. This beggar doesn't care if this body is healthy or sick as long as it can do Father's Work, only Father's Work."

His melodious voice penetrated the space in the tender early morning light that filtered in through the palm leaf thatch of the hut. Birds sang gaily outside and Yogi Ramsuratkumar raised his hand and moved it gently through the air as he talked. After breakfast, Ma Devaki asked a question. Devaki had received a letter from Lalitha, one of Lee's students, in which she had broached the idea of her teacher being given an Indian name by his Indian master.

"Bhagawan, you have said that Mr. Lee is an Indian saint. Would you perhaps want to give him an Indian name?"

"No! This name is fine. I have said Lee Lozowick is an Indian saint, then Lee Lozowick is an Indian name!" His response was absolute and put an abrupt end to even entertaining such an idea.

That morning Yogi Ramsuratkumar asked one of the Sudama sisters to read about

Papa Ramdas from *Facets of the Diamond*. She read a passage that described Ramdas' encounter with a sadhu who had practiced devoutly for thirty years, yet still was not enlightened. Yogi Ramsuratkumar interrupted, saying, "Sadhana can do nothing for you. Sadhana is what you do until you surrender, then God does everything. But you must do sadhana until you surrender."

Raji, Mani's wife, had a habit of offering flowers to Yogi Ramsuratkumar in the breakfast hut every morning, both red and pink hibiscus and strings of fragrant white jasmine. It was one of those things that, in Yogi Ramsuratkumar's company, quickly became a ritual that took on significance to the beggar. She found this out one day when she didn't bring any flowers.

"Where are the flowers?" Yogi Ramsuratkumar wanted to know. Later that day a devotee brought another kind of flower as an offering, which Raji brought to Bhagawan.

"Not this . . . white and red," he remonstrated, meaning the hibiscus and jasmine she usually brought. From that day on she brought white and red flowers every morning to Bhagawan.

On this particular morning Raji brought the flowers to Yogi Ramsuratkumar. Holding the flowers, he asked each person to come forward one by one to receive his blessing and a fresh flower from his hand. When it was Stan's turn the beggar took his hand and asked, "What is your name?"

"Stan," he answered. With a gleam in his eye, the beggar turned to Mani and said, "Mani, isn't there an English word, s-t-a-i-n? But the 'I' is missing... He has no 'I!"

Just that morning during the readings from Papa Ramdas there had been an account of Ramdas saying there was no "I," but only Ram—only Ram appearing in all phenomenal forms. Yogi Ramsuratkumar laughed, dropped the flower into Stan's waiting hands and slapped him on the shoulder. The moment of levity passed. Yogi Ramsuratkumar turned to Mani, and with sadness in his voice said, "Mani, we will not be able to sit with Mr. Lee tomorrow morning and share his blessings."

It was time for Lee and Stan to leave. Yogi Ramsuratkumar took Lee by the hand and walked with him to the car, where Ravi waited to take him back to Sudama House. There he paused, raised Lee's hand to his face and pressed it against his forehead. He stepped into the car and Lee stepped back, brushing the blessing of Yogi Ramsuratkumar's touch across his own forehead and hair with his hand. They watched as Yogi Ramsuratkumar drove away.[10]

By the spring of 1995 several of the cottages on the ashram were finished, and Yogi Ramsuratkumar gave the use of them to certain individuals for specific reasons. Rajakumari, the widow of Murugeshan, was given Devasenapathy Cottage—

10 Ibid.

Devasenapthy being another name of Murugan, the son of Shiva. Rajamanickam's son was given Manickam (jewel) Cottage. Each cottage, which was financially sponsored by various devotees, was given a name that was meaningful and that reflected something about its occupants. Some of the ashram trustees had personally sponsored cottages, Mani being one of them, and on March 20, 1995, Mani and Raji moved into Surrender Cottage. For the past thirteen months they had been living in a rented house behind Sudama House that had been arranged for them by Yogi Ramsuratkumar. The name of that house had been Mappilai Bungalow, which in Tamil means "son-in-law"—a symbolic coincidence with Raji's place as Bhagawan's "daughter," which made Mani his son-in-law.

Raji and Mani had made it through the first difficult year of serving the guru and the ashram, but the stress was tremendous. By the spring of 1995, they had been with Yogi Ramsuratkumar for a year and a half; many of the long-time devotees and older trustees challenged Mani's authority and criticized his management style. He was a tough taskmaster, but at the same time the workers felt that Mani was more like a co-worker, in the trenches of the everyday grind with them, and they respected his authority because Mani was able to marshal the work force and get things accomplished the way Yogi Ramsuratkumar wanted them done. Beyond that, Yogi Ramsuratkumar had said from the beginning that Mani was his "Father's choice" for the job.

However, it was a major lifestyle change for Mani, who only a year before had been a highly successful construction engineer running a big company in Madras and now chaffed at the discipline and austerity of ashram life. At one point during that first year Yogi Ramsuratkumar asked Mani to engage an experiment. He said, "For one hundred days you stay on the ashram, you don't smoke, you don't drink alcohol, and you eat no meat or fish. You read no newspaper and watch no television. After one hundred days, then you can drink a quart of liquor if you want to."

It was a radical approach to a fast purification of his old lifestyle, and it worked. After the hundred days of abstinence, Mani went to Bhagawan exultant, "The one hundred days are over!" With Yogi Ramsuratkumar's blessing, he went out to a hotel with a friend to have the rich food, meat and whiskey he'd been dreaming of, but he was immediately surprised to find that it was all flat. He had no taste for it and didn't really want any of it. He knew that he would be unable to return to the fast life he used to lead.

When he returned to the ashram Yogi Ramsuratkumar asked, "How was it?"

"You know how it was!" Mani retorted humorously. Yogi Ramsuratkumar laughed and laughed. After that Bhagawan pressed Mani into further service and made many demands on him, telling him, "This beggar doesn't want Mani to leave this ashram for ten years!" He guided Mani's sadhana by instructing him to simply work, and work hard, many hours out of the day. "Mani doesn't need to sleep!" he once told Raji, when she said that Mani was sleeping very little at night. He told Mani, "There is no need for any japa or dhyana for you. You are in the company of this beggar all the time. So you are doing tapas all the time. Your service to this beggar will do. Transformation is going on all the time. The greatest tapas for anyone is to stay near one's guru and do service to him, but very few are given this chance."[11]

At the same time, Yogi Ramsuratkumar supported Mani and Raji in the face of the criticism that came their way, saying, "Mani and Rajalakshmi are my Father's choice. You go on doing my Father's work. What else can we expect from the people? They will find fault with Mahatma Gandhi himself. They will talk like this, but you go on about your work."

The pressures and stresses were coming from every direction, and at times Mani was wildly desperate to leave. On more than one occasion he went to Yogi Ramsuratkumar in the heat of his inner conflict and confronted him harshly. "Why have you selected me? I don't want to work here! I want to go back to Madras!" Yogi Ramsuratkumar listened quietly while Mani vented his anger. On one occasion, Devaki expressed her concern after Mani left the room.

"How will Rajalakshmi manage? Mani is very harsh!" she said to Bhagawan.

"Don't bother, Devaki. Rajalakshmi knows how to handle Mani. She will manage," he replied with calm.

The next morning at breakfast he asked Raji with a hint of a smile, "Rajalakshmi, how did you manage Mani?"

"I gave him a tranquilizer, Bhagawan!" Raji replied with a smile, tongue in cheek. Bhagawan burst into laughter. On other days when he asked this question she would simply say, "I gave him two, Bhagawan!" and he would double over in gay laughter—the extraordinary healing laughter of a wise child.

At other times when Mani was having a hard time or arguing with Yogi Ramsuratkumar, Raji would want to scold him. Then Yogi Ramsuratkumar would look at Raji and say, "You sit still. If you are my daughter, you will say nothing."

In darshan during the summer of 1995 a woman devotee named Valliammai came with an opulent offering of jewelry for Yogi Ramsuratkumar. It was an impressive gift—four or five diamond rings, a diamond pendant, a diamond bracelet and so on. The beggar looked at the pile as if in awe.

"Valliammai, this is all for this beggar?" She answered yes. Right away Yogi Ramsuratkumar asked Devaki to put the jewelry on him. He wore the jewelry for a while, then asked Devaki, "Do you want anything from this?" indicating the rich pile of gold and diamonds.

"No, Bhagawan. You are all I want," Devaki replied.

He turned to the Sudama sister named Rajalakshmi and asked, "Rajalakshmi, do you want any of this?"

She too answered, "No Bhagawan, you are all I want."

Usually Yogi Ramsuratkumar asked Mani's wife Raji to sit with the Sudama sisters. She prepared herself to say the same thing if he turned to her and asked the same question. Instead he called to her.

"Raji, come here." She walked up to the dais and leaned over to hear what he

11 Yogi Ramsuratkumar, *Facets of the Diamond*, p. 159.

wanted to say, but for a moment he didn't say anything. He was loaded down with all the jewelry he was wearing. He took off a gorgeous gold and diamond bracelet and looked up at Raji.

"This beggar wants to give this bracelet to you. This beggar was thinking for a long time, 'This beggar should give something to Rajalakshmi.' Now this beggar wants to give this to Rajalakshmi." He reached out and put the bracelet on her wrist.

"A lot of criticism will come from this. Don't bother about those things. Even if Mani asks you to remove this, don't remove it. Never take this off. You can remove anything from your body, but not this bracelet . . . People will say so many things about this, but this beggar wants to see this bracelet daily when you feed this beggar."

During these years Raji was the one who brought Bhagawan's breakfast and fed him each morning in the breakfast hut. Yogi Ramsuratkumar would see the diamond bracelet every day on her wrist, when he would often take food right from her hands into his mouth. But perhaps more importantly, the bracelet would be a constant reminding factor for Raji, bringing remembrance of the guru's grace. The bracelet was an outrageous gift that could not be taken at face value, but called for a deeper discernment as to its meaning. Gold and diamonds have always carried symbolic value and spiritual attributes—the pure alchemical gold of the rarified soul and the long-term process of intense pressure through which carbon, or gross matter, is turned into the most precious of all gemstones: diamonds, which have an extraordinary capacity to refract pure light into its objective colors. It seemed the gift was a declaration of what was possible for his devotees: the spiritual transformation that occurs through the power of grace.

As the ashram sank its roots deep into the sandy red soil of Tiruvannamalai, people from all walks of life were drawn to Yogi Ramsuratkumar, and each person's story has unique facets that give some insight into how the influence of the beggar saint affected different people. In 1993 a wealthy young manufacturer from Bombay, Ashish Bagrodia, began to make regular pilgrimages to Tirupathi, a town in southern India that is important to Vaishnavas for its famous temple, the abode of Lord Venkateswara (Mahavishnu), located in a sacred place on a mountain. The protocol around the temple is very strict—no leather, minimal clothing (bare-chests for the men) and so on. Wheelchairs were not allowed near the sanctum sanctorum because they were considered machines. Confined to a wheelchair with muscular dystrophy, Ashish could not enter the temple at first. Very keen on going into the sanctum sanctorum, Ashish instructed his assistants to go to the manager of the temple to see what could be arranged for him. They spoke with the second deputy in charge, and he personally took Ashish into the temple. Thousands of people visited the temple every day; people stood in line to get into the temple and streamed through in a constant, steady queue. The deputy stopped the queue for a time and allowed Ashish to be taken in for a darshan of the deity.

Afterward the deputy said to Ashish, "Although you are in a wheelchair, you have come from Bombay and you have taken so much trouble, so why don't you visit my guru, my saint while you are in southern India? He is only three or four hours away, in the small town of Tiruvannamalai." Wanting to get back to Bombay as soon as possible, Ashish declined the offer. As he said, he was wary of the false gurus that abound:

> I just give him some excuse, because in India there are so many gurus and so many saints—in almost every village there is a saint, and he is like God incarnate. Most of them are frauds and fakes. As a policy I never go and meet saints and gurus. So I told him some story—it's not possible and so on. He was referring to Yogiji. I went back to Bombay after spending a lot of time in south. I went to meet Sai Baba, but I didn't visit Yogiji.
>
> In 1994, again I went to Tirupathi to the temple, and this time again this fellow allowed me to go in. He said, "My guru, my guruji is a very realized soul. He's a very good saint. You should just see him. I want him to see you. Once he sees you then he will start working on you." I was irritated by all that because I thought, this type of story is there every day in India—miracles and such—so I told him, "I have some work to do, I cannot go."
>
> In 1995 when I went to Tirupathi this man had been transferred by the government, but his son came along and helped me with the darshan. This year I don't know what happened—somehow I felt like this would be the third year he was telling me about his guru. He had been transferred to another location, but he told his son, "Okay, you take him to Tiruvannamalai," and I agreed.

Ashish had to travel to Madras first, where he could rest for a few days, and then he would go to Tiruvannamalai by car. He asked the temple deputy's son to go to Tiruvannamalai and wait for him there, promising that he would come in a few days. He recounted:

> I couldn't go directly to Tiruvannamalai because it would be too tiring for me. So I told his son that I would go definitely this time: "I'm going back to Madras now, I'll stay there for a few days and then I'll come to Tiruvannamalai. You go and wait for me at Tiruvannamalai. I'll come in a few days, and you can inform them." I feel I'm some big, big man, some industrialist! Who is this saint? Who cares what ashram they run! So I told him, "You go there, wait for me, you make all my arrangements. I want a personal meeting with the saint, see that I get a direct appointment." One office staff person from my company went with him also. He was there telling Mr. Mani, and Mr. Mani was telling Yogiji every day,

"Yogiji, he's coming, he's coming." And Yogiji would inquire everyday, "Is he coming?" And they would say, "Yes, he's coming." All this I came to know later on. Every day when they would say, "Yes Bhagawan, he's coming," Swamiji would just laugh, because he knew I wasn't coming.

Finally after three or four days I decided okay, let's go to Tiruvannamalai. I was staying in a really nice five-star hotel, so I went down, I sat in the car, and there were three cars to follow me—you know, the people with me, some of my luggage, etc. What happened? All the cars started, but the driver of my car lost the keys! This was my very favorite car—a Mercedes Benz 500 SCl. It's a very beautiful car; we had imported it just the year before and I had taken it south for the journey from Bombay.

I was very careful with this very expensive car, but the keys were lost. In India you may not get duplicate keys. We sat in the car, and that driver was so embarrassed. The whole day our people were frantically searching for the keys. The whole hotel was shook up. They were wondering what happened, because the car was in their parking lot. So finally, in the whole day we couldn't get the car keys. Next day morning, the driver, when he opened the car, he found the keys! All there intact, right there! He said it was just fallen under the steering wheel somewhere. This is the same place he must have searched twenty times the earlier day and he didn't find it.

So I said, "Okay we'll go now." We started the journey towards Tiruvannamalai and in ten, fifteen minutes, I don't know what happened to me—I decided that we would go to one more temple. We would go to Tiruvannamalai some other time. So I changed the plan all of a sudden. I don't know what came into my mind! We went to some other place, some other temple, and again that whole program was cancelled. When I came back, somehow I was restless or something. I felt that there was something preventing me to go to this saint. That made me more curious or determined to go.

The next day I finally went and we reached the ashram. Yogiji was in the dining hall [giving darshan]. It was about four-thirty in the evening. As soon as he saw me, he called me and he held my hand. He very lovingly talked to me, and he spoke in English only. I could see that he could have spoken to me in Hindi, but he spoke only in English. I also spoken to him only in English. He was smoking. He asked me questions like what's my name and where am I from and how come I came there. So I explained, "I was in Tirupathi at the temple and the administrator told me to visit you." I told him the administrator's name, and he knew him very well.

"You were to come a week ago," the beggar said to Ashish, pushing him just a little. Ashish began to recount his story and Yogi Ramsuratkumar said, "Yes, but you said you would come." When Ashish continued with his explanations, the saint said nothing, then suddenly turned to Mani and asked for the time. Turning turned back to Ashish, he said, "What time do you think you will reach Madras?"

Ashish had planned to go to the Shiva temple before he left town, and he calculated in his own mind that it would be about six hours before he would arrive back at his hotel in Madras. Yogi Ramsuratkumar took this information in and sat with it for a few minutes.

"Mani! This beggar thinks Mr. Ashish should leave now." Ashish had only been with him for ten or fifteen minutes, and he was surprised, but didn't really take the beggar's words seriously. He lingered and talked further with Mani. Suddenly Yogi Ramsuratkumar interjected, "This beggar thinks they should leave now!"

Mani tried to facilitate a quick exit, but Ashish protested, "We have just come, let us spend some time, see the ashram . . . Then we will go to that temple and maybe we can take a round in the car up the holy hill and then go."

Mani was trying to coax him, saying, "Please come out. Bhagawan says you should leave now!"

They left the darshan hall and Mani began to explain to Ashish very nicely that when Yogi Ramsuratkumar said something like that, everyone took it very seriously. There was always a meaning behind such things.

"It's in your best interest that you go now," Mani explained. "Don't take him lightly." But Ashish simply was not able to understand the ways of a true saint at this point in his life:

> I went outside and I was dilly-dallying, asking Mr. Mani questions, "What is this building, what is that?" I wanted to know more about Yogiji. Mr. Mani kept saying, "Go! Go! You should leave," and I kept asking him questions. He was not keen to answer my questions because he wanted me to just go. In all this, Yogiji got up and came out of the hall. Imagine! He came out, because at that time he was walking everywhere. He came out where we were talking just outside the dining hall in the area where people sometime sit. He stood there and said very loudly, with both his hands raised, "Mani! Father wants them to go!"
>
> For a moment I got a little nervous, seeing him that way. I was not willing to listen to him. I heard these kinds of stories all the time. Everybody in India talks about their gurus. Everybody's a god—everybody's a fraud. Who knows? Those kinds of thoughts were in my mind, so I didn't take him seriously. The seriousness of this whole thing of going away did not sink in, but Mani kept telling me that I should go, so then I said, "Okay, I'll leave the ashram premises at least."
>
> Once I was in the car I was thinking, "If he is saying this, then maybe we should not take a risk—there could be an accident, God knows what can happen. Let's not take a risk. Okay, we won't visit the temple, let's take

> a round of the hill"—which also we shouldn't have done!
>
> So then I went into the car, and our whole group discussed it. We all felt that when a saint says something, we should listen to him. Everybody advised me and then I said, "Okay, we will go back to Madras. We'll cancel the plan to go to the temple." But then after sitting in the car, I said, "Why not go around the hill? We won't get out of the car."

As they were driving around Mt. Arunachala some riots broke out in the town of Tiruvannamalai, and as a result they were stuck there when the district administration was forced to stop all traffic. Ashish and his entourage were trapped in their cars on the road next to Arunachala, just a few kilometers away from Yogi Ramsuratkumar's ashram, until ten o'clock that night. If he hadn't driven around the hill, they would have all been back in Madras by that time. They finally reached Madras around three o'clock in the morning. The whole way Ashish was thinking about Yogi Ramsuratkumar and how he should have listened to him. He decided he wanted to see him again, and postponing his return trip to Bombay, returned three days later, hoping that he could spend more time with the beggar saint. Ashish recounted this second visit:

> This time Yogiji was very nice and he spent a lot of time with me. He took my hand, and he was smoking, talking, laughing. He asked me whether I could stand, and I said yes I can stand with some support against the wall with some attendants helping me. He told me to stand, and while I stood he kept gazing at me standing for some time. I sat down and he was talking to me. I was talking to him, but still I was talking all kinds of nonsense, all irrelevant stuff. He also was talking to me nothing spiritual. I didn't have any spiritual talks with Bhagawan.
>
> I thought, if he knows so much then maybe he will be able to guide me as to what should I eat; I felt because muscular dystrophy had no cure, I might as well ask him if there is any good food that I should eat. So I just casually asked him, "Do you think I should eat some kind of food which would make me feel better?" So he thought, and he said, "This beggar feels you should eat groundnuts." Groundnuts are peanuts in India. He immediately asked Mr. Mani to get some groundnuts from the nearby fields. Within ten or fifteen minutes they got the groundnuts for me from the fields and then Yogiji peeled those groundnuts, and one by one he gave them to me. Just imagine! He cracked them and gave them to me and I kept eating them. He kept doing it, and giving them to me raw, just from the field.
>
> He spent a lot of time with me—almost one and a half or two hours. Then he asked me in detail why I came to the south and all about me, my family, my business, everything. When I told him, "I visit this temple of Vishnu," he was laughing a lot and then told Devaki Ma and Vijayalakshmi

> Ma to sing one *bhajan* of Lord Vishnu. They sang a *bhajan* which is dedicated for Venkateswara—for that form of Vishnu.
>
> So then enough time was spent and I was feeling very happy being with him. Afterward we went to the temple, but this time I was very careful: I told him my entire program! I wanted to check that I was not going to get into trouble! So I said, "You know, we are going to go around the hill and to the temple and then we will go to Madras." He said, "Yes, yes, my Father blesses."

Everything went well with their plans that day. Ashish returned to Madras then flew back to Bombay and immersed himself again in his business. He was still not very interested in anything having to do with spiritual transformation, but a seed had been planted. Something started working inside him, and he found himself remembering Yogi Ramsuratkumar with a great fondness. As his feelings for Yogiji grew, he began to send donations to help with the construction of the ashram. Mani would write back, saying, "We acknowledge the receipt of your check," and at the bottom of the page Yogi Ramsuratkumar would write in his own hand, "Yogi Ramsuratkumar, Tiruvannamalai," or, "My Father blesses Ashish, Yogi Ramsuratkumar, Tirvannamalai." It was pleasant to receive, but thinking no more of it, Ashish threw these letters away or told his assistants to file them in the accounts department. It took some time for a tough-minded businessman to have his heart touched and to realize it fully, but a few years later Ashish had three or four people on his staff searching for those very same letters, which had become precious to him. They found most of them. Ashish had become very serious indeed—a story we will come back to later.

As soon as Lee Lozowick arrived at the ashram on November 30, 1995 he let Mani know that he had a special gift for Yogi Ramsuratkumar, as the ashram protocol requested for any gift offering, no matter what it might be. In this case it was a magnificent bronze sculpture of Yogi Ramsuratkumar, about twelve inches high, seated in the cross-legged position with hands cupped around a cigarette, shawls and rags hanging in graceful folds—a familiar posture of the beggar. Sculpted by one of Lee's students at his request, as a piece of art alone it was an extraordinary gift; its sacred nature as a *vigraha* of the master gave it power in a multitude of dimensions.

Lee was itching to present the gift to his master, but in the first darshan that morning Yogi Ramsuratkumar said nothing. Near the end of the afternoon ashram Mani brought word to Lee that he could present the *vigraha*. Lee had carried the heavy statue all the way from Arizona himself, and now he approached the dais with it securely packed in its box. The photographers got wind that something important was about to happen and came up to snap pictures. Lee had gotten permission from Yogi Ramsuratkumar to bring

François Fronty—a disciple of the French teacher Arnaud Desjardins and a professional filmmaker who wanted to make a film about Yogi Ramsuratkumar called "Darshan." François was there with his video camera rolling.

Quickly Lee hefted the box up and ripped the wrapping off, then lifted the sculpture out of its packing material and handed it immediately to Yogi Ramsuratkumar. The whole unveiling took only a few seconds. There was no pomp and circumstance, no ceremony and self-importance—just the pure giving. Lee sat back and watched as Yogi Ramsuratkumar took the sculpture firmly into his hands. His face moved into an expression of undisguised wonder. It was an incredibly beautiful thing to look at.

Yogi Ramsuratkumar held the statue in his lap so that the front of it faced outward, toward the cameras. The video tape was rolling and captured for posterity the gasps of wonder and comments from several people who sat nearby and saw the chest of the statue glow with a rose red light, as if lit from within, while Yogi Ramsuratkumar held it.

Finally the master said, "This beggar will accept this."

As the yogi examined the sculpture, he showed it to Ma Devaki and the Sudama sisters. Their attention soon focused on the amazing detail of the hands and feet, which are by far the most stunning and accurately rendered aspect of the beggar's form in bronze. The toes even bore the scars of the train incident so many years before, when in a fit of divine madness Yogi Ramsuratkumar had frozen on the train tracks while a train ran over his toes. The hands were utterly exquisite, cupped around a cigarette—a reminder of the tremendous sacrifice of the beggar and the power of grace that flowed through him. Ma Devaki and the Sudama sisters craned their necks to see more of the statue and murmured appreciative sounds. It was an impressive rendering of the Godchild of Tiruvannamalai. Later Yogi Ramsuratkumar gave the statue to Mani and Raji as a gift.

A month later when the video was played back in Arizona, Lee said, "Now we'll see if the statue really did glow red, or whether we just imagined it." Amazingly, the red light was unmistakably captured on the video. It could be clearly seen, emanating for a few moments from the heart of the statue—the living force of the beggar saint entering into the *vigraha*.

During the *jayanthi* celebration of 1995 Yogi Ramsuratkumar received a formal visit from the Shankaracharya of Kanchipuram, one of the four Shankaracharyas of India, the spiritual lineage holders descended from Shankara. Shankara (788-820 C.E.) was one of India's greatest saints and philosophers who renewed Advaita Vedanta and Hinduism in general after those traditions had been historically displaced to some extent by Buddhism. The Shankaracharyas are the Hindu equivalent of the Pope of the Roman Catholic Church, and to be honored with a visit from one of them was not only auspicious, but a tremendous acknowledgment of Yogi Ramsuratkumar and a profound blessing for the ashram.

The ashram had gone all out in preparing for the Shankaracharya's visit. Colorful mandalas and yantras made of rice powder decorated the carefully swept sandy ground before the dining hall where the darshan would be held. Musicians were ready with their horns and drums and a feast was prepared. At the gate a crowd of people stood crushed together in the blazing heat of the sun. There was a strong current of anticipation and religious fervor in the air—even to set one's eyes on the Shankaracharya would bring great blessings!

Yogi Ramsuratkumar's reverence for the Shankaracharya was obvious as well. Every day in his darshan the Sudama sisters sing a beautiful song that was written by the 68th Shankaracharya, who was known for his brilliant intellect and scholarship and who was the immediate predecessor of the Shankaracharya who would visit Yogi Ramsuratkumar on this day. The song is a prayer that was written as an appeal for universal peace and sung at the United Nations in 1966—a plea for peace, prosperity and happiness for all beings and for Mother Earth. The singing of this prayer at the beginning of darshan is a ritual that continues to this day on the Yogi Ramsuratkumar Ashram.

Finally the Shankaracharya arrived and was greeted by much pomp and circumstance, blowing of horns and pounding of drums as he entered the ashram. A strict *brahmacharya*, the Shankaracharya was bare-chested but wrapped in an ochre shawl and wearing the traditional ochre *dhoti*. Across his forehead were several layers of *vibhuti*, or holy ash. He was tall, with an imposing stature, and towered over most others. Mani greeted him and ushered him into the ashram. His eyes were penetrating as he entered the dining hall and swept his gaze across the crowd and toward Yogi Ramsuratkumar, who had left his place on the platform and came forward.

Yogi Ramsuratkumar *pranamed*, knelt down and touched the ground at the Shankaracharya's feet. The Shankaracharya and his primary companion, a revered priest of the same order, sat on the dais while Yogi Ramsuratkumar took a seat on the floor in front of him. The crowd was not allowed to approach the Shankaracharya, who, as a matter of protocol related to his spiritual practice, does not touch anyone.

At the instruction of Yogi Ramsuratkumar, Mani came forward and invited Lee Lozowick to approach the dais and receive his blessing and *prasad*. Then Krishna Carcelle, a French devotee, was also invited to approach and receive a blessing. Everyone else sat and watched, happy to have this rare opportunity of the Shankaracharya's darshan. During most of this time Yogi Ramsuratkumar sat slumped over in a *bhava*, his consciousness absorbed within. It was a short visit, about thirty minutes, and soon the Shankaracharya left with his entourage.

This year Lee had come for a five-week visit, from late November through the end of December. Several of Lee's students traveled with him, as well as a number of students of his friend and well-known French spiritual teacher Arnaud Desjardins, whose master, Swami Prajnanpad, was one of the saints featured in *Facets of the Diamond*.

Lee had been drawn more deeply into Europe for almost ten years. As the demand for his teachings increased and French and Germans became his students, he was spending so much time in Europe that he had, six months earlier, obtained an ashram in central France, where he now lived four months out of each year. On this trip to India there were many Europeans, both students of Lee's and of Arnaud Desjardins. The French students of Desjardins included well-known author Gilles Farcet and his wife Laurence,

Alain de Rosanbo, and filmmaker François Fronty, who was filming Yogi Ramsuratkumar throughout the visit.

At one point Gilles and Laurence were sitting in the breakfast hut with Yogi Ramsuratkumar and Lee. The beggar had asked Gilles to read from a book, and as Gilles returned the book to him, he suddenly asked, "Many people know Mr. Lee in France?"

"Quite a few," Gilles replied, "more and more."

"How did Lee find you?"

"By the grace of God," Gilles said. Yogi Ramsuratkumar burst into laughter.

Gilles had discovered Lee through a mutual friend, Yvan Amar, whose master, Chandra Swami, was also featured in *Facets of the Diamond*. In 1991 Gilles had come to Arizona seeking an interview with Lee, who he wanted to include in a book about five Western spiritual teachers.[12] The result of the interview was an instant friendship, and in 1992 Gilles invited Lee to France to meet his teacher and to give teachings in Paris, Lyon and other places. The meeting between Gilles Farcet and Lee Lozowick, and subsequently between Lee and Gilles' teacher Arnaud Desjardins, was a long story—one that Lee would sometimes tell in the darshan hall when Yogi Ramsuratkumar asked him to "tell some stories."

Two weeks later Lee's daughter Gita arrived with her friend Anna Tredeau and Anna's mother, Rabia. Again there were many intimate breakfasts with Yogi Ramsuratkumar in the breakfast hut, where Raji gave him white jasmine and red hibiscus flowers each morning. The red hibiscus flowers were then distributed to those who were present for breakfast, while the jasmine was always returned to Raji, which she would immediately put into her hair.

Every day Yogi Ramsuratkumar playfully called upon Lee to read aloud at breakfast or in darshan the new, unpublished poems he had written and poems from *Poems of a Broken Heart*. Over the years Yogi Ramsuratkumar had asked Lee to read his own poetry many times; it had become a familiar request, and Lee's embarrassed response was a familiar moment of humorous interplay between the master and disciple. During this five-week visit the master's poetry-reading *lila* was repeated many times.

"I want you to read many, many poems," the beggar said sweetly to Lee one day during darshan. He handed a well-used copy of *Poems of a Broken Heart* to Lee and gestured to him to begin. Standing by the dais to the right of Yogi Ramsuratkumar, Lee read two or three, then paused, as if to say "Is this enough?" and turned toward Yogi Ramsuratkumar.

"I want to hear more poems," the beggar said with a smile.

"Okay, whatever you say," Lee smiled back, "but Ma Devaki reads them much better than I!" Ma Devaki laughed at Lee's predicament.

"Read more poems!" he commanded with delight, a broad smile on his face. Lee continued to read poem after poem, finally coming upon these lines:

---

12 *L'Homme Se Lève À Dans L'Ouest: Les nouveaux sages de l'Occident*, published by Albin Michel.

Will you still read Your son's poetry
        when You have thousands of followers
writing you love notes?
        The Crazy Beggar's Name is being spoken
all over these days.
        Will You forget Your son, my Father?

Yogi Ramsuratkumar began to laugh at these lines, and his laughter continued during the poems that followed. He laughed so hard that his body shook with pure enjoyment. At any pause from Lee, he commanded again, "Read more poems!" Finally, he took the poetry book back and handed Lee a copy of *Facets of the Diamond*.

"Read something from this book," he said.

"Can I read about you?" Lee asked, rather hopeful, it seemed, that he wouldn't have to read about himself.

"Anything," came the reply.

A group of about two hundred people sat attentively watching the action around Yogi Ramsuratkumar, who sat on the platform at the head of the room. Lee began to read, explaining that he would first read from the biographical section. The biography described Yogi Ramsuratkumar carrying a country palmyra fan and a coconut bowl, and at these words, the beggar suddenly raised his coconut bowl in one hand and the palmyra fan in the other in a spontaneous blessing. The crowd was exultant. A low murmur of joyous exclamation rushed through the room.

Over the years Yogi Ramsuratkumar had become very playful with Lee's students—the "army" Lee brought to "conquer" the beggar, as Yogi Ramsuratkumar said in 1993. He often told Lee to ask his students to lead chants, or to sing and dance during darshan for the benefit of all present. There was abundant laughter and high spirits on these occasions as the Westerners were put on the spot to represent the traditions of their own culture. Yogi Ramsuratkumar had a special love for Christmas songs—that is, songs about Jesus—and these he asked for often. Usually the women students traveling with Lee would stand up and go through a repertoire, remembered from childhood, of "Silent Night," "O Come All Ye Faithful," "Amazing Grace" and other well-known traditional English hymns. During the spontaneous and sometimes rough renditions of these classics, Yogi Ramsuratkumar would watch closely, listening and smiling. The singing and dancing always seemed to bring him great enjoyment.

In 1997 Will Zulkowski, who came to visit Yogi Ramsuratkumar every year, arrived with his friend, Richard Schiffman. When the beggar called Will up to sit nearby, he said, "Oh Swami, Richard's here."

"Ohh, come, have him come up . . ." It was a lovely reunion, and Yogi

Ramsuratkumar again expressed his gratitude that Will and Joan had helped him so many years ago with the publication of *Yogi Ramsuratkumar, The Godchild, Tiruvannamalai*, and that they had earned good karma in doing so. He was always warmly welcoming, and included Will's friends who were traveling with him, commenting, "Will and Joan have earned . . ." They had made such a contribution to the well-being of the beggar saint that he embraced their friends who came to visit as an extension of his regard for Will and Joan.

Will and Richard were visiting with Bret Carlson, a friend from the ashram of Amritananda Mayi, where Bret and Richard had been roommates. Bret now lived in Tiruvannamalai and was a regular visitor at the Yogi Ramsuratkumar Ashram. Richard remembered:

> I remember, it was really remarkable—going into that huge hall. We'd touch the feet of the statue and then prostrate to Yogi and it was strange, this huge, empty hall with the dirt floor—like a surreal sort of situation. He would be sitting there all alone, just kind of looking up, or saying something. Then he called Will and I up once and he was talking about Northern Ireland and different things, because there was an Irish man there who was leading a tour, and he was there with his people.

Yogi Ramsuratkumar called Will and Richard up to sit with him. Richard had some Indian crystals, and he asked the master to bless them, but Yogi Ramsuratkumar seemed reluctant.

"This beggar doesn't believe in those things," he said. As Richard tried to give him some of the crystals to hold and bless, he said, "No, no. You keep it." Finally Yogi Ramsuratkumar held the crystal up for a while and then gave it back to Richard.

When Will and Richard returned to the States, Richard asked a friend who was clairvoyant to hold one of the rocks. He asked, "Well, what do you feel in this rock?" He closed his eyes and said, "Tiruvannamalai." Richard and Will laughed about this later, realizing that Yogi Ramsuratkumar had put nothing into those crystals, though his capacity to bless and encode an artifact was known to be very great.

Yogi Ramsuratkumar was not particularly interested in most of the vagrant Western seekers who came through the ashram, nor was he interested in the New Age craze in general—although he was often incredibly generous to visitors of all kinds. By 1997 Tiruvannamalai was thronged with Western seekers who came to Ramanashram and to the Yogi Ramsuratkumar Ashram seeking blessings. Some were serious about the spiritual path, while others were looking for spiritual thrills, a quick high, a vacation with "meaning." Many of them were lost souls, aimlessly wandering around India, going from guru to guru. Some had very superficial motives for coming to ashrams—motives that they weren't even aware of. Dressed in white *punjabis* or saffron-colored *sannyasin* robes, they would drift in with spaced-out looks on their faces, or barge into darshan dressed in the garb of a mendicant sadhu with their hair in Baul topknots, wielding one-stringed instruments and demanding to sing Sita Ram chants for Yogi Ramsuratkumar, who would sometimes invite them to sing in his darshan anyway.

On the other hand, if he saw something in someone, Yogi Ramsuratkumar would speak out. Will remembered that once during this time period when Yogi Ramsuratkumar was being driven from Sudama House to the ashram, he saw an Australian man who was living in Tiruvannamalai with a Japanese woman. They were walking down the street and Yogi Ramsuratkumar happened to be passing by in his car. Telling Ravi to stop the car, the beggar rolled down the window and yelled out to the man, "Go back to America!"

The man said, "But I'm from Australia."

"Well, go back there!" Yogi Ramsuratkumar said emphatically.

Yogi Ramsuratkumar had been working closely with Westerners for many years; he had his own radar for who was good work material and who was not. There were many Western sadhus or just ordinary visitors to whom he gave a great deal of attention beyond the basic respect and ordinary kindness that he demonstrated to everyone. There were quite a number of Westerners who he'd known for years, loved dearly and treated like sons and daughters, and others whose callous and prideful interactions were unpleasant and memorable.

Will recalled a time years before when a Western man came to Yogi Ramsuratkumar. He rode a motorcycle, wore a skimpy *dhoti* and had his hair styled. He was the kind of person who had "a perpetual tan and a perpetual attitude," as Will said. He said rudely to the beggar, "What? You sit around and do nothing. How do you rationalize your existence?"

All pilgrims and seekers were welcome on the ashram, regardless of their reasons for being there. Tiruvannamalai was turning into one of those Indian cities, like Pune, Rishikesh and Lucknow, that drew Western pilgrims like bees to honey, and the Yogi Ramsuratkumar Ashram had become one of the regular places to visit. The ashram celebrated most all of the traditional religious days with rituals, as well as feeding numbers of sadhus daily and eventually developing a school for children. The ashram also fed masses of people on days of special festivities when ceremonial worship was performed, and professional singers and dancers often came to perform for Yogi Ramsuratkumar as well.

By far the most elaborate celebration of the year, however, was the guru's *jayanthi* day. This was always an event of significant proportion, and it was for this celebration that Lee Lozowick made the trip from the U.S. every year with growing numbers of students. Each year Lee brought a new group of his own students and two or three students of Arnaud Desjardins. One of these, Alain de Rosanbo, came every year with Lee from 1995 on, first visiting Chandra Swami at his ashram at Dehradun, U.P. Chandra Swami was the guru of Lee's good friend, French teacher Yvan Amar, and a revered north Indian saint. Each year Alain would deliver a gift to Yogi Ramsuratkumar from Chandra Swami—usually an orange woolen shawl, which Yogi Ramsuratkumar would often still be wearing the next year when Lee returned.

In 1996 Yogi Ramsuratkumar started putting Lee together with other long-time devotees and friends in the West. It became a very common occurrence for Yogi Ramsuratkumar to ask Lee to sit by the wall to the right of the dais with Krishna Carcelle, a French devotee who was a frequent visitor at the ashram, or other Westerners who were simply passing through for a few days, with the instructions, "Talk." Lee and Krishna would sit together sometimes for the entire darshan period, conversing, sharing stories of Yogi Ramsuratkumar and getting to know each other. One afternoon in darshan Yogi Ramsuratkumar called Lee up to the dais and gave him a much bigger task.

"Lee, this beggar would like you to meet these friends in America," he began, holding a scrap of paper in his hands. "Caylor and Will . . . This man, Mr. Caylor, did a very big favor for this beggar once. He wrote the first book on this beggar. Mr. Caylor and Will know each other, they're friends."

Devaki had written Caylor's name on a piece of paper, along with the title of the book. The only other information Yogi Ramsuratkumar gave Lee was that Caylor was now an acupuncturist and Will was connected to Hilda Charlton's community in upper New York State.

"This beggar wants you to meet these friends and go to Hilda's place with them, with Will and Caylor together, if possible," he elaborated. He made it clear to Lee that this was extremely important to him, so important that it wasn't really something that Lee had a choice about—it was a direct command from the master.

Both names were familiar to Lee. He had been given a copy of *Yogi Ramsuratkumar, The Godchild, Tiruvannamalai*, some years before in India by one of the devotees, and he had heard of Will and Joan back in the seventies through Hilda Charlton. He remembered Hilda saying in her classes, "Will and Joan are in India, kids! Will and Joan have met Yogi Ramsuratkumar!" The stories of their first adventures and sometimes misadventures with the Godchild of Tiruvannamalai were famous in Hilda's circle, where Lee had spent some time in the early seventies.

Thinking about his incredibly busy teaching and traveling schedule, the fact that he lived in France for four months out of the year and had extensive responsibilities with students around the world, Lee wondered when and how he would fit additional trips into his schedule. His dismay was somewhat compounded by the idea of having to track down two men for whom he had no address and no phone number, who lived somewhere in the continental United States.

With all this racing through his mind, Lee took the information from Yogi Ramsuratkumar and said, "Yes, I'll try to reach them . . ."

"Lee won't try," Yogi Ramsuratkumar said, cutting Lee off in mid-sentence, "Lee will *do* it!" It was clearly of great importance to him that Lee, Caylor and Will establish a connection. Yogi Ramsuratkumar smiled his brilliant smile.

"Lee *will* do it!" he repeated, slapping Lee on the back, his hearty laughter resounding through the room.

Later that afternoon Lee sat with his students on the steps of the bookstore at Ramanashram and told them about the task Yogi Ramsuratkumar had given to him. One of them volunteered to locate the phone number and address of Caylor Wadlington, the acupuncturist. When she returned to her home in Boulder, Colorado, she called an acupuncturist school in New Mexico and was told about the acupuncture registry in Washington, D.C. Contacting the registry, she was surprised to find out that Caylor lived a half hour away, in Denver, Colorado.

When Lee returned to America he called Caylor on the telephone and introduced himself as a "devotee of Yogi Ramsuratkumar." He explained that he had recently returned from India, and that Yogi Ramsuratkumar had asked him to call Caylor and wanted them to meet, and also to meet with Will at Hilda's place in New York. The call took Caylor by surprise, but he was very friendly and receptive to the idea of a meeting, and the two men arranged a time. A few years before Caylor had discovered *Facets of the Diamond* in a bookstore and was delighted to find Yogi Ramsuratkumar, the hidden saint of Tiruvannamalai, prominently featured in it. He had remembered Lee from Hilda's in the seventies. It was from Caylor that Lee got Will Zulkowski's address and phone number.

As it turned out Caylor was unable to meet Lee and Will in New York at the land of Hilda Charlton's community, but Lee flew to New York in the spring of 1997 and met Will Zulkowski. Together they drove up north to the land and visited there, where Will regaled Lee with many stories of his time with Yogi Ramsuratkumar. They talked about their shared experiences with the master and also with Hilda Charlton, who they had both known well and loved.

About a month later Lee and his student Tom Lennon, who lived in Boulder, went to Denver to meet with Caylor, where they heard a wealth of stories about Yogi Ramsuratkumar from the early seventies. As it turned out, Caylor had another treasure: an extensive cache of early photographs of Yogi Ramsuratkumar from the sixties and seventies. Yogi Ramsuratkumar himself had given Caylor most of these photographs and asked him to take care of them. When Caylor asked him what he should do with such a responsibility, Yogi Ramsuratkumar replied, "You will know what to do." When he realized that Lee's relationship to Yogi Ramsuratkumar involved both speaking and writing about him extensively in the West, Caylor generously offered the archival treasure of the photographs to Lee, many of which appear in this book.

Back in Tiruvannamalai six months later, in November 1997, when Yogi Ramsuratkumar found out that Lee had contacted and met with both Caylor and Will, he expressed his great happiness and appreciation—clearly it was of great importance to him that a connection between these men be established. Five years later, after his death, both Caylor and Will would play a major role in generously contributing invaluable material to this biography.

That year Yogi Ramsuratkumar gave Lee another task: Go visit Krishna Carcelle in Mauritius, an island country in the southwest Indian Ocean off the eastern coast of Africa, near Mozambique. That summer while residing in France, Lee flew from Paris to Mauritius with his student, Thomas Bormann, and spent several days visiting with Krishna.

Each year when Lee visited with his students one of Yogi Ramsuratkumar's favorite requests was to ask people to give talks or sing during his darshan. He often asked his long-time devotee Janarthanan to speak on the *Ramayana*, which he had instructed Janarthanan to study many years ago. Parthasarathy, Pon Kamaraj, Pankkajam and many others were invited to sing, lead chants or give talks. When V. Ganeshan or Sadhu Rangarajan came to the darshan, they too were asked to give talks.

Every year Yogi Ramsuratkumar asked Lee to read from recent poetry he'd written, or from articles his students had written about the beggar. Over the years Yogi Ramsuratkumar's most frequent request of Lee became, "Say something useful for these people. Anything at all." He also asked Lee to ask his students to speak: "Ask someone to give a talk," or "They can chant," and Lee would turn to one of his students and say, "Give a short talk—ten minutes or so," or he would simply gesture to two people to get up and lead the chants to Yogi Ramsuratkumar.

Poems of a Broken Heart continued to have a place of real value in the world of Yogi Ramsuratkumar. The reading of the poetry continued on the ashram and was especially amplified during the weeks when Lee was visiting. During the rest of the year Lee regularly mailed new poems to Yogi Ramsuratkumar, but sometimes Lee would send fax messages that would include a new poem; when that happened the fax was immediately brought to Yogi Ramsuratkumar, and would then be read to him by Ma Devaki many times every day. His fondness for poetry was apparent in his love and appreciation for all the poets who had written for him. At one point he had made a schedule or list of every poet who had written poems about him, so that all would be read aloud at various times, including Ki.Va. Jaganathan, T.P. Meenakshi Sundaran, Sankara Rajulu, Perumal Raju and others. One day Jaganathan would be read, the next day Meenakshi Sundaran, the next day, Lee Lozowick, and so on.

Still, Yogi Ramsuratkumar's assertion in 1993 concerning Lee's poetry held true: Lee Lozowick's poems filled a certain void in communicating to the world in English the life and graceful influence of the beggar king of Tiruvannamalai. In April 1997 a second book of new poems, *Poems of a Broken Heart, Part II* was published in Madras by Sadhu Rangarajan and the Sister Nivedita Academy, again at the request of Yogi Ramsuratkumar. The 230-page book contained at least twice the number of poems as the first book. In this edition's "Publisher's Note" Sadhu Rangarajan commented:

> Most of these verses were written by Lee after the publication of the first compilation of his poems under this title, but some belong to an earlier period and are added here. We have tried to compile them in the chronological order in which they have been sent to my Master by Lee at regular intervals from USA and other parts of the world, so that the readers may discern the development of this unique love of the son to his Father.

> That these epistles are manifestations of pure love and surrender of the poet at the feet of my Master is borne out by the fact that these epistles have been preserved by Ma Devaki at the instance of my Master who Himself wanted this Sadhu to bring out this second part also. A specialty in this part is that some of the verses are directed to Ma Devaki, the Eternal Slave of Yogi Ramsuratkumar, whose total surrender to Bhagavan and sublimation of her life into the state of Divine Motherhood, are very beautifully portrayed. We are sure that this second part of *Poems of a Broken Heart* will also break the hearts of Bhagavan's devotees and penetrate into them.

Lee brought to life the bold declarations in his poetry to Yogi Ramsuratkumar in many different ways; particularly evident was his intention to offer praise and spread the name of Yogi Ramsuratkumar in the West. In the Hohm Community there was a waiting list of Lee's own students who wanted to come to India with him; it was a coveted opportunity to meet Lee's master, whose influence and presence had reached mythological proportions through the many stories and *lilas* that had made their way back to Europe and the States through Lee's books, seminars and discourses. The life and work of Yogi Ramsuratkumar was also disseminated through *Facets of the Diamond* and many other published writings of Lee's students, which would include later books like *As It Is*[13], a chronicle of one year on the road with Lee Lozowick, which captured many of the stories of Yogi Ramsuratkumar that Lee told every summer while giving seminars in France, Germany, Switzerland, Belgium and England. It also recounted two weeks with Yogi Ramsuratkumar in Tiruvannamalai during December, 1998. Numerous articles about Yogi Ramsuratkumar were also published in international magazines such as *Terre du Ciel* in France and *Golden Age Magazine* in Australia.

After Yogi Ramsuratkumar accepted the gift of the bronze *vigraha* in 1995, Lee had fifty reproductions of the statue made, which were given as gifts or purchased by devotees and friends of Lee and Yogi Ramsuratkumar. Arnaud Desjardins himself procured one of these and installed it in the Ramdas Room at Hauteville, his ashram in southern France. Desjardins, a former filmmaker, made many films of great saints of the era, including Anandamayi Ma, Swami Sivananda and Swami Papa Ramdas. He spent a great deal of time with Ramdas at Anandashram, during which time he captured incomparable footage of the saint—immortalizing Yogi Ramsuratkumar's "father"—in his film, "Ashram." It was an amazing synchronicity that Lee and Arnaud became very close friends later in their lives, and the unusual connection between Arnaud Desjardins, Papa Ramdas, Yogi Ramsuratkumar and Lee Lozowick, unbeknownst to Lee and Arnaud, was discovered and brought to life.

Yogi Ramsuratkumar's first prophetic statements to Lee about his life, which at the time seemed vague and even far-fetched, had now come true. Some of Lee's published

13 M. Young, *As It Is*, Hohm Press, 1999.

writings, which by now included fifteen books, were translated into French, German and Spanish, reaching a broader audience in Europe and Mexico. Since 1980 all of Lee's books had been dedicated to Yogi Ramsuratkumar, and after 1988, when Yogi Ramsuratkumar allowed Lee's students to take their first photograph of him, his books also included a photograph of the beggar saint. All of these efforts were a reflection of Lee's expressed desire to praise his guru.

Traveling all over the world had connected Lee with many different people, and over the years, spiritual aspirants from the U.S., France, Germany, England, Canada and Mexico made the trip to Tiruvannamalai with him to visit Yogi Ramsuratkumar. Lee asked his students to keep journals whenever they were traveling with him, and particularly in Yogi Ramsuratkumar's company; excerpts from these writings were then published every year in *Tawagoto*, a quarterly magazine that is the journal of Lee Lozowick's ongoing teaching. These *Tawagoto* journals provide a view of the life of Yogi Ramsuratkumar from the perspective of Lee's students and also chronicle his *jayanthi* celebrations and darshan activities on the ashram.

"You see this *amlaka* tree? These trees are all a part of me. I am total, indivisible. I alone exist," Bhagawan spoke ecstatically, standing in the lush green garden at Sudama House. At the *garha prevasam* Yogi Ramsuratkumar had watered the new *amlaka* tree with his own hands. A year later, by November 1993, it had grown only as trees can in tropical environments. By 1995 the tree was loaded with thousands and thousands of gooseberries. The profusion of green fruits attracted the attention of everyone who walked past and saw the top of the tree over the garden wall. They were so healthy and beautiful to look at that some people would even stop and knock on the gate to ask if the gooseberries were for sale. Ma Devaki recalled:

> Bhagawan would lean against the tree and tell me that there were three hundred and thirty million devas or gods residing there, and that that is very significant. There are so many things we don't know. We know only our five senses, what we can see, what we hear, what we can talk about and touch, but there are so many things we cannot know, unless we go deep into meditation. And then of course another world begins to come into our view, because there are different levels of consciousness. As we do meditation we go from one level to another level to another level and so on, and at each level so many things get revealed—the hidden secrets of the world. So Bhagawan would say that all the devas are there, in the roots, and then he would touch the tree and put it to his eyes. It was his way of worshipping the tree.

Yogi Ramsuratkumar spoke predominantly in symbols, and for him the gooseberry tree was both a physical manifestation of benign and healing natural forces and a symbolic link with the archetypal world. He would walk out the door at Sudama House and go straight into the garden to the *nellikkai* (in Sanskrit, *amlaka)* tree, where he loved to sit for hours with his hand on the roots. In this and many ways he worshipped deities of the tree.

That year as the first fruits began to ripen, Bhagawan instructed the Sudama sisters not to pluck any of the fruit, but to only take those that fell naturally to the ground. He wanted the tree treated with the utmost respect. He had such reverence for the healing properties and spiritual significance of gooseberries that he was adamant that not one single fruit should go wasted or be misused.

As the first small fruits fell to the ground there were hundreds of them, all extremely bitter. So bitter, in fact, that they were impossible to eat, but Bhagawan insisted that all of them should be eaten. They couldn't be eaten raw, so the Sudama sisters decided to grind them up and mix them with some other drink and take it like medicine. That was the first solution to the gooseberry problem: take it in big doses like medicine, poured down the throat. In this way they would consume the gooseberries between the four of them: Devaki, Vijayalakshmi, Rajalakshmi and Vijaykka.

In 1997 one of the branches of the *amlaka* tree was so heavily laden with fruit that it leaned down on a branch beneath it and broke it off the tree. The branch that broke off had thousands of gooseberries on it; immediately Bhagawan wanted it taken care of, and he wanted all the gooseberries used. He called one of the supervisors at the ashram, Saravanan, to set the broken branch right. Saravanan came immediately, and during the two or three hours that it took to repair the damage to the branch, Yogi Ramsuratkumar sat watching and smoking the entire time. He blessed the tree over and over again, saying that the tree would live for hundreds of years and be fruitful and so on. In the meantime, thousands and thousands of gooseberries were shaken loose in one day, and the Sudama sisters had to carefully gather them all.

He instructed Devaki, Vijayalakshmi, Vijayakka and Rajalakshmi to find some way to preserve them and eat them. He was very rarely willing to give one or two gooseberries from the tree to anyone else; it was a very specific task for the four Sudama sisters to consume them. Devaki recalled, "We would all be looking at each other, knowing that these gooseberries were going to land in our stomach!"

Bhagawan was serious about this task for the women. Knowing full well that they couldn't possibly eat all of the gooseberries before they would rot he said, "No, you have to seek to preserve them. Salt is a good preservative; put them all in some water with some salt." It was very practical advice, since in south India there is a method of preserving small tender green mangos in which the fruits are soaked in salt water, then turmeric powder and mustard are ground into the fruit along with some commonly used natural preservatives. He advised, "You can use the same technique for this also and preserve it."

They cleaned gooseberries until they had one full bucket, then another. Suddenly they realized that they didn't have pots in the house that were big enough to contain all the fruit, and they had to send Venkataraman to buy some large buckets and pots. Finally they ended up with seven large buckets full of gooseberries. Yogi Ramsuratkumar said, "You must start eating them," and promptly on that day, they began to eat. Knowing that there was no escape, the gooseberries became a major project for the women, between the preserving and the eating of the fruits. All they could think of was ways to get the gooseberries into their stomachs! Gooseberries are bitter to begin with, but these were unripe fruits, premature and extraordinarily bitter and acrid to the taste. They decided that they could each eat twenty at a time, twice a day, and maybe as many as fifty each per day, which would mean that between the four of them two hundred gooseberries would be consumed every day. Each day they removed the seeds from a large amount and ground the pulp; then they brought the gooseberry mix to Yogi Ramsuratkumar for his blessing.

"Bhagawan, we are taking so much today," they said, coming for his blessing and showing him the large amount they would consume.

"Is it my Father's blessings you take?" he asked, then he blessed the gooseberries and the women.

The gooseberry *lila* became an ingenious form of *tapas*—in which internal heat is produced by austerities and strict discipline—created by Yogi Ramsuratkumar for the four women. They did not have the *sadhana* or *tapas* of mendicant beggars or sadhus; they had the *sadhana* of renunciates and the intense fire of guru yoga. Their *tapas* was generated by the master through his immense skillful means, and the demand of obedience to the guru's directions and wishes. Devaki and Vijayalakshmi were also staying awake at night, meditating and doing *japa* while Yogi Ramsuratkumar slept. Sleeping as little as two hours a night and eating mostly the sour, salty gooseberries created a powerful edge for their inner work, and so, during this time, their *sadhana* was very intensified, as Devaki relayed:

> I did some of the best meditations at that time, and Viji [Vijayalakshmi] and I would also keep count of the japa, sometimes forty thousand or fifty thousand. We were able to do it. And the thing is mostly Viji was free, because the other two people were doing a lot of work in the kitchen. So Bhagawan especially gave the work of doing japa to Viji, because Vijayakka was in the kitchen, seeing to the work of the house and I would be sitting with Bhagawan, doing whatever he wanted, so I wasn't free either. Whenever I got time free I would do japa, but mostly Viji was doing japa. And I was reading most of the time, reading books to Bhagavan and seeing to the correspondence and so many other things. Not a minute he would leave me out from his presence, even to the bathroom—only five minutes and then I should be back.

They found out individually what worked best for them in getting the gooseberries down. It was a question of how to make it tolerable. This went on day after day, and became a kind of ritual; after consuming their gooseberries, they would then come to the ashram for breakfast.

"You take only one *idli*," Yogi Ramsuratkumar instructed them each morning at breakfast, because if they ate more, it caused them to fall asleep even while they were sitting in the breakfast hut. Devaki normally took two *idlis* (a fermented rice cake) and then ate Bhagawan's leftover food as well, but they were existing on so little sleep that any substantial amount of food would dull the edge of their practice and cause them to crave sleep. If they ate very sparingly, then they could stay awake—and it was more important to eat the gooseberries than to eat anything else.

As the *lila* went on more gooseberries fell to the ground, but these had a black fungus on them because it was the rainy season. They showed the gooseberries to Yogi Ramsuratkumar with some trepidation.

"Bhagavan, it's fungus—can we still eat it?"

"Yes, you can still eat it, nothing would happen. You eat it! Nellikkai in any form is good for the body. Even when you have cold, you take it. You don't bother with the fungus."

It was overwhelming, and the women just stood there looking at him in disbelief, unable to say yes to his demand. A servant woman was there, and Yogi Ramsuratkumar called her in and showed her the blackened, fungus-infested gooseberries.

"Will you be able to put it to use? This beggar would like you to use it," he said. She replied yes. "What will you do?" he asked. She was very resourceful and smart, and she said she could put it in the *sambar* like a vegetable and then it could be drunk like a soup.

"You see it is black here—do you mind?" he asked.

"No, no, no, Bhagawan, whatever you give is alright for me," she said, and took it away.

The next day he wanted to know the fate of the gooseberries. She reported that her family had eaten the gooseberry *sambar*—it was *prasad*, a great blessing from Yogi Ramsuratkumar.

The eating of the gooseberries—preserved in buckets with salt, turmeric and mustard powder—went on for a year. At times a thick layer of inedible scum would form on top of each of the buckets. Surely it was time to throw it away! Bhagawan would look at it and say, very coolly and casually, "Oh, you can just remove it like that," and demonstrate that they could just scoop the rotten part off with their hands.

"Ah, that's alright! Now you take it," he said, pleased. He was pushing the women to break through the conditioning of the mind into a realm of infinite possibility, wherein the body, mind and personality can transcend their limitations. In order to make this leap, it became a question of obedience to the guru, and they chose to obey. Ma Devaki recalled:

> And then we would take it—there was no escaping! But the thing is we would never have been able to do it but for Bhagawan. Imagine, twenty to twenty-five bitter nellikkai every day, without missing a single day,

doing it day after day after day, month after month. It took about a year and a half. Apart from that we had to consume the new ones also, because every day so many would be falling! It was rainy season. There were winds also [that knocked them off the tree], so we would take them in two sessions: in the morning we would take the fresh ones, then during another time of the day we would take those old ones. I think it was mostly nellikkai for us for a year and a half, but he was so happy with us! I think it was worth all that trouble, to see him smile and bless us.

It's funny now, but it wasn't so funny when it happened. That's how he would make us work. Imagine night after night after night staying up like that and doing japa—it would not have been possible, but for Bhagawan's energy. He would be lying down and sleeping, but so much energy radiated from him that I would feel very alert. I wouldn't feel tired. Mostly whenever I felt tired it was when I got a cold and cough, or when I took food in the ashram.

Those were the times that were the hardest for me, because as soon as we returned to Sudama, again he would start working and he would begin to smoke and then he would ask me to read a book. Sometimes while even half way through the sentence I had fallen asleep over the book! He was a relentless worker. He wouldn't spare himself; he wouldn't spare others also. But whenever I had real difficulty—like real sickness, when I wasn't able to do anything—he would say, "Devaki, now I think you need rest. Go lay down for some time." And then he would give me a specific time and after that he would call me, pick me up and then back to work once again.

He would be so loving and kind that it would bring tears to our eyes. Somehow just one look, one word, one touch, we would feel a tremendous love from him—a tremendous tenderness and love from him. I don't know how it was possible for one being to convey something so tremendous just by one look or one word. But one word, one gesture of his would be so intimate, so full of love, it would make up for the whole sleepless night sometimes, because they were the hardest times.

So many things were happening in the ashram. The ashram was coming up and so many devotees came and they complained about this and that, so many things were going on, so many times of problems . . . One day there were about two hundred fifty or three hundred workers in the ashram, because the construction was at its highest at that time, and the workers made a campus and stayed there, having food three times a day and sometimes working late into the night. Many times problems would come this way and that way and it was all so new to me; I would be so frightened of many of them. Somebody would come from the ashram and complain: this has happened, that has happened; this person did that to me, that person did that to me. This person is threatening to leave tomorrow with the construction halfway—so many things. It would look as if the whole thing would go off before the morning came. You would think that some storm had crossed over there or something.

But next morning Bhagawan would just sit quietly listening, "Oh ho . . . Ohh, hmm . . . hmm...". And I would think, "Oh, now he will take up loads of cigarettes and finish one packet." But as soon as the person left he said: "Devaki go lock the door." He would go to sleep and within a minute or two he would start snoring.

I just couldn't help it. I asked, "Bhagawan, how is it that they are coming and telling you such terrible problems, they say tomorrow they are going to leave, they won't be there in the ashram. How can you keep quiet like this?"

"My Father is watching all this Devaki. My Father knows what to do. You don't bother. You go to sleep." On that day I would go to bed earlier and sleep. And believe me, the next morning by seven o'clock there would be no trace of any of these problems of the previous night! All would be quiet and even the people who went through tantrums the previous night, they would just be quiet and nice and recovered quite well. He wouldn't have done a thing. Probably just telling him was enough, but all had quieted down by morning. I would have spent a sleepless night over some of those things, only to find in the morning that there was not a trace of it in the ashram and everything was quiet. Bhagawan was right. Things would get arranged themselves, by his grace. Wonderful in the least!

There were many miracles, which wouldn't look like miracles at all, because that's one thing I noticed: Bhagavan did not do any conspicuous miracle—that is, anything that would draw attention specifically as a miracle. Most of his miracles were part of the natural flow of life.

On December 18, 1997 a larger than life statue of Yogi Ramsuratkumar cast in a dark bronze—a *vigraha*—was installed in the center of the Pradhan Mandir, the large temple. It had been in process for a few years, and was sculpted by Sri Kalasagar Rajagopal, the same sculptor who made the life-size statue of Ramana Maharshi at Ramanashram. The installation of the statue was a very important, auspicious event that caused a great deal of work for everyone.

Yogi Ramsuratkumar had been waiting for it to be done for some time. When the statue finally arrived, he declared that he wanted a permanent pedestal beneath the statue, and he told Mani that he wanted it installed without anyone touching the statue, which was now located in the middle of the temple. The workers listened to Mani in disbelief.

How could such a thing be possible? The statue was almost three meters tall and weighed tons. The workers argued with Mani, who said, "You don't understand—Yogi Ramsuratkumar doesn't want the statue touched, so we will find a way to do it without touching the statue!" Somehow, it was done the way the master wanted it done.

After the statue was installed the protocol of darshan changed. The devotees and pilgrims who came to the ashram were asked to first go to the temple "auditorium," as it was often called, the interior of which was still unfinished, and circumambulate the huge statue of Yogi Ramsuratkumar, which was now firmly in place on its pedestal on the dirt floor. After the ritual circumambulation was done, they made their way to the dining hall to chant until Yogi Ramsuratkumar arrived. The dining hall was the location of the actual darshan for several years, while the temple was still under construction. After the entire queue was finished with this process, then Yogi Ramsuratkumar would join everyone at the dining hall darshan.

While the devotees prostrated at the statue, Yogi Ramsuratkumar was almost always seated in a simple wooden chair about ten feet away. As people queued up and circumambulated the *vigraha*, coming around the other side they would then *pranam* to Yogi Ramsuratkumar and briefly have his darshan right there. A few feet away from that was a small open hut where Ma Devaki and the Sudama sisters sat chanting, cleaning flowers, making garlands, doing *japa* or other small tasks. The hut was just some wood poles and a thatched roof, made of striplings and palm leaves, built while the temple was under construction to provide shade and a place for Yogi Ramsuratkumar, Ma Devaki and the Sudama sisters during the heaviest phase of construction. From there Yogi Ramsuratkumar could watch everything that was going on. Many hours of chanting and prayer had been generated under the roof of that small hut. After the temple walls, the vast span of steel girders and the roof itself were completed, the hut could have been taken down, but Yogi Ramsuratkumar demanded that the hut be left there—forever.

As the queue of people came through and circumambulated, the slow, melodious chants of the name of Yogi Ramsuratkumar pervaded everything; chanting his name was the single most important spiritual practice—and for many of his devotees, the only practice—he gave. It was his gift to the world, a principle element of his work that we will explore in more depth later on.

During this time the beggar was imbuing the statue with his spiritual power. As the years wore on and it became obvious that his physical health was tenuous at best, Yogi Ramsuratkumar worked very hard to teach the devotees and pilgrims that he was not his body. His constant work with the *vigraha*—including the circumambulation of it—and the use of his name were two elements of this.

One day, Bhagawan was seated in the chair near the statue while the people came through one by one to circle it. Selveraj, who was the darshan hall attendant, was standing near Bhagawan. One man approached him after going around the *vigraha* and said, "Can we see Swami? Can we see Swamiji?"

"No, no, we can't approach him like that," Selvaraj explained. "Only if he sees you and calls you, then he may give you personal darshan. Otherwise, no, we cannot approach him like that." Just then Yogi Ramsuratkumar's voice rang out very sweetly.

"Tambi . . ." he said in Tamil, using the affectionate term meaning younger brother, "Tambi, come here. What was he asking you?" Yogi Ramsuratkumar inquired.

"He wants to see Swamiji," Selvaraj answered.

"Ohh! Then what did he see?" Yogi Ramsuratkumar said with an ironic chuckle. He made great teachings in the simplest ways, even casually, through his marvelous sense of humor and ability to play on words. The man had entered the auditorium and circumambulated the statue while the master was seated right there in his chair; he had had every opportunity to "see" Yogi Ramsuratkumar with his eyes, but he still wanted to "see" him in the personal sense of a private interview. Even beyond that, Yogi Ramsuratkumar was commenting on the chronic habit of the separative mind to deny the fact of unity or nonduality. He meant that once a devotee or pilgrim entered the sacred space of the temple, he or she was "seeing" only Yogi Ramsuratkumar. One did not have to have a personal interaction with his physical form in order to "see" him. At the same time, Yogi Ramsuratkumar was sitting right there, so how could the devotee not see him in the literal sense?

As he said many times, in many different ways, "Yogi Ramsuratkumar is here, there, everywhere . . . When people think that Yogi Ramsuratkumar is only from here to here," pointing to his head and feet, "they become narrow, selfish and miserable. He is everywhere. He is in every one of you." [14]

Sometimes a devotee would come to the ashram and approach the darshan hall attendants, saying, "Bhagawan knows me very well. Please go and tell him that I have come." When the message was delivered, Yogi Ramsuratkumar would call them up to the dais and say, "What is your name?" It would invariably provide a shock to anyone who was approaching in a prideful way, as described by Saravanan:

> This happened many times. He killed ego just by asking one question: "What is your name?" One time a puja was to be done by [a famous swami] from Kerala who was living in the Himalayas. He came to do puja in the ashram. Bhagawan himself prostrated to this man. The next year he came and said, "Go and tell him I have come! Last year I did the puja in the Yagashala; he wants to meet me immediately." Bhagawan looked at the entrance and saw him standing there and he said, "Let him sit at the corner." They put a chair in the back and he sat there. After that, he never came back.

Yogi Ramsuratkumar constantly worked to develop faith and the context of unity within the ashram staff. They were trained to be sharp and pay attention to his every move. Their entire focus was on him; if he made the slightest gesture, called for them or needed anything at all, they would see it.

14 Ma Devaki, "The Divine Beggar on Himself," *Saranagatham*, January 2003, p. 33.

Once Saravanan needed money and prayed for it. That very day in the evening darshan someone gave Yogi Ramsuratkumar a gift of three thousand rupees in all new currencies. Ravi and Selvaraj were standing nearby. The beggar slowly held his hand up and motioned gently for Saravanan to come.

"You take that money," Bhagawan said, holding out the rupees to Saravanan. "Count it," he instructed, then, "How much is there?"

"Three thousand," Saravanan replied.

"You take a thousand rupees first, immediately!" Yogi Ramsuratkumar commanded. "Then you give a thousand to Ravi and a thousand to Selvaraj!"

Yogi Ramsuratkumar always seemed to know what was going on with the staff, and he constantly demonstrated this omniscient quality in ordinary ways. Once a friend of one of the darshan hall attendants asked for a favor, saying, "I want to see Bhagawan." The attendant told him that he would have to come to the ashram and put his name on the list like everyone else—then perhaps he would be called up during darshan.

At the next darshan, when the attendant gave Yogi Ramsuratkumar the list of people who had asked to come up to the dais, he pointed to the name of the attendant's friend and said, "Is this your friend?" He always knew the inner workings of not only the ashram itself, but the workers, who knew the heart of the ashram and lived close to the pulsing of its deepest rhythms. It was the staff that Yogi Ramsuratkumar leaned on, quite literally, as he became less able to physically manage by himself.

All the workers fell in love with Bhagawan because his love for them was so apparent. When the huge temple auditorium reached an important point in its construction—the electrical fittings were in place, the roof was on, the big statue was properly installed—Yogi Ramsuratkumar called for all the workers to stand in a queue inside the temple. At that point in time there were about one hundred people lined up. Mani was holding Bhagawan's hand as he walked in and looked at each and every face there. As he stood there looking at the people who had accomplished this incredible labor for the sake of his Father's work, the beggar began to cry. The workers watched in astonishment, hearts in their throats, as tears streamed down the face of their beloved Bhagawan.

Yogi Ramsuratkumar never wanted any of the staff members to leave the ashram; he wanted everyone around him, like a big family. It broke his heart whenever there was any disharmony, complaint or arguments between his devotees. Bhagawan often started crying when there was discord. He watched everything that was going on in the ashram—the construction, the daily chores, the interactions between workers and between Mani and the workers—and he intervened whenever things weren't going the way he wanted them to. If Mani had ongoing problems with one of the workers, Yogi Ramsuratkumar would say, "Mani, you go work it out!"

When Yogi Ramsuratkumar had given a job to someone, he wanted only that person to do it. He did not want another worker to interfere with another person's work. When someone tried to interfere or complained, he said, "He knows about his work—you don't. Go on."

Once he saw Kannan, the watchman at the gate, sitting with the workers, chanting, and said, "The watchman is also sitting with the group. So, who is it looking after the gate?" Then he said to Mani. "Kannan should be near the gate." If one's job was to work for the temple, as in the case of Mani and the staff, then their work was more important than chanting or meditating. Their work, or *guru seva*, became their sadhana; serving the guru gained merit and magnetically attracted the force of his blessings. He would often say to them, "Go and attend to your work."

On another occasion, it was the day of the Saraswati puja, when everyone offers the instruments, machines or tools of their craft, art or work to the goddess for her blessing. In Hinduism every aspect of creation, animate or inanimate, is God: human beings, cows, dogs, trees, flowers, rocks, machines, cars, tools, houses, temples. Everything is pervaded by God force, and therefore there is only God. Because of this belief, *puja* is done to initiate all tasks or projects. For example, if one is going on a long trip in a bus, the bus driver will very likely do a *puja* to the engine of the bus before leaving. If the brick masons are building a wall, they may conduct a *puja* over the first three bricks and worship them as God. Cars are often worshipped, decorated with *kumkum*, flowers, even *arati* or waving of ghee lamps before the vehicle may be driven. In fact, one's very profession is God and all the instruments of one's profession as well. On Sarasvati *puja* day everything is worshipped as God in this way.

"Ravi!" Bhagawan called out playfully to his driver on the morning of Sarasvati *puja*. "What have you done today?" referring to the traditional rites that should be performed.

"Swami, we have the car, so we are going to hurry, we are arranging so that we can worship it," Ravi answered.

"Selveraj, what do you have?" he asked with a twinkle in his eye.

"Bhagawan, I have only this auditorium," Selvaraj answered with a laugh.

"Devaki, you hear that?" he turned to Devaki, "Ravi has a car for worship and Selveraj has auditorium. This beggar and you have nothing! Shall we go to Sudama?"

His eyes were twinkling with mirth, and everyone laughed with him at the joke, recognizing also that it contained the teaching within it. When Yogi Ramsuratkumar played with words in this way in casual repartee, one could interpret it in many different ways, but the highest interpretation was always the closest to the truth. Devaki commented:

> Any interpretation can be drawn from the words of the Mahatma, but the highest is the nearest truth. Always the highest interpretation that we give is nearest to truth. So that day I took it to mean that Bhagawan had no second to worship, there was only one. And he was saying it so humorously . . . "Selveraj has auditorium, and Ravi has his car, and all these people they have put all those things there to worship. This beggar and Devaki have nothing! We will go to Sudama!" It can also mean he is a beggar, he doesn't own anything, he doesn't have any possessions to worship, or it can also mean there is no second. He himself is everything,

only Father exists, and so there is nothing to worship.

In 1997 the main structure of the temple auditorium was finished, and Yogi Ramsuratkumar stopped the construction that would finish the temple, with its plan of marble floors and finished interior walls. It was an interesting time period; the legend was that Yogi Ramsuratkumar had predicted that he would die when the temple was completed, and as his health became more precarious, he stopped the final work on the grand temple complex. At the time he said that the work on the temple would be resumed when Father wanted it to be resumed.

Nonetheless, the huge temple supported the growing numbers of pilgrims and seekers who flocked to the ashram, especially on the saint's birthday and on other major religious days. As the crowds grew during the mid to late nineties, the need for security around Yogi Ramsuratkumar increased. The ashram staff and darshan hall attendants had a very big job in this regard. They had to guide people into the temple and explain the protocol of the space—what was expected of visitors and long-time devotees alike. Very often it was necessary for the temple attendants, after explaining the circumambulation of the statue, to say, "Don't go near to Bhagawan. Bhagawan himself has given those instructions."

When dealing with hundreds or thousands of extremely enthusiastic, if not zealous and at times desperate people, it was impossible for Yogi Ramsuratkumar to give private interviews. It became necessary to protect his physical body from harm due to the excessive devotional fervor of visitors and devotees. The staff members were acutely aware that the master's spiritual state had become more and more delicate, even exquisite, and that he moved in and out of *bhavas* constantly—these were some of the more dramatic outer manifestations of his work, which went on twenty-four hours a day. He quite literally could not bear the intrusive grasping that was often attempted in the spirit of devotional fervor, not because it disturbed him personally, but because it disturbed his work. Always the purpose of the protocol was to protect, respect and safeguard Yogi Ramsuratkumar's work, but he was also demonstrating the teaching of nonduality through his actions as well. Grasping at the guru was a function of separation, not unity, or the understanding that the devotee is already one with the guru. Enlightenment, awakening or great blessings cannot be grasped, forced or aggressively taken. The only way to avail oneself of the guru's grace is to approach with a soft and open heart.

The need for a greater field of sanctuary around Yogi Ramsuratkumar had been growing for a long time, and must have played a part in his final decision to allow an ashram to be built, with all of its attendant formalities and rules. For example, in 1993 when Yogi Ramsuratkumar was with Lee Lozowick and his students at the house of V. Ganeshan, a woman devotee came to the house to see the beggar. He was sitting cross-legged on a thin mat on the concrete floor of the portico, and she walked up to him, bowed down in a *pranam* and without any warning grabbed his feet out from under him. He rocked back, thrown slightly off balance, but he recovered as she pulled his feet roughly forward, touched them with her forehead and then pressed them several times to the floor affectionately. She placed two flowers, one on each foot, and bowed again with her forehead to his feet. Her actions were tremendously devotional, but the whole time he was barely keeping his balance, with his body thrown into an off-kilter position that looked terribly uncomfortable. He blessed her sweetly and warmly, and then she left.

Having witnessed much more dramatic demonstrations of the devotees' fervor, which resulted in aggressive behaviors that could easily get out of control in a very large crowd, the ashram workers developed a keen understanding and sympathy for Yogi Ramsuratkumar's needs for protection, as Saravanan explained:

> Bhagawan's work should never be disturbed. Whenever Bhagawan was in his work, he was in a state of trance or something like that. If somebody tried to talk to him, he would just shake his body or something. When he was blessing, he would close his eyes—he was gone somewhere. If anybody touched him then, he would immediately get a shock. So we thought we should be understanding; he should be able to work and be protected. Many people got away from us. On full moon days there were large crowds, many people . . . Somebody would be crying and grabbing Bhagawan's feet. The attendants would try to catch him.
>
> Selvaraj used to stand or sit nearby Bhagawan and I myself would stand near the Sudama sisters, near the hut. Kannan [the gatekeeper] used to stand in between myself and Ravi, near the gate. People would have to get past me and Kannan and Ravi. If somebody tried to make some trouble, then we would all gather together and bring them back. This was the procedure: whenever full moon day came, I would be exactly in front of Bhagawan, and Selvaraj should be very near to Bhagawan, and Ravi would stand near the gate and Kannan in between. It was in order to protect him from the people.

One of the ways the need for greater sanctuary manifested was that Yogi Ramsuratkumar stopped appearing in the regular darshan program on the ashram. When Lee arrived on November 30, 1996, he was told that Yogi Ramsuratkumar had not given darshan for eight months, but that morning was an exception, and he sat in the hall, holding and stroking Lee's hand. From that year on Yogi Ramsuratkumar rarely gave formal darshan—other than sitting in the Pradhan Mandir beside the statue while the queue came through to receive his blessing—except during the two or three weeks when Lee Lozowick came to visit. The staff and the devotees began to look forward to these visits from the American devotee in a whole new way: "Lee is coming—Bhagawan will be in darshan now!" Saravanan recalled:

> Whenever people stood in the queue to enter Bhagawan's darshan, Mani would come out and call Mr. Lee and his group, "Come," and he would put them in front of the queue. It was the procedure, each and every

> year. Whenever Mr. Lee came, Bhagawan went into the darshan hall and he called first to Mr. Lee and his group. He always asked Mani to call them first, and he asked them to sit in the front. For fifteen days, he focused on Lee and his group . . . He gave attention to each and every group, but Mr. Lee and his group was special. How can I tell? Because Bhagawan asked Mr. Lee to come and sit on his stage when he was there in the month of December, 1994; he asked Mr. Lee to sit on his stage, and Bhagawan was there, sitting on the floor. From that time on, I knew it—that Bhagawan had a very special place in his heart for Mr. Lee and his group.
>
> I watched this. He used to sit on the floor, and he watched Mr. Lee, how he was giving darshan! And after, Devaki Ma knows many things. Even from the very first lunch, he would ask Devaki Ma, "Did they finish their food, did they breakfast?" He would ask Mani. He focused so much attention there; he took care of Lee. Now also it continues; it will continue forever—with physical body, without physical body, it's not a problem. He is focusing on each and everybody who has entered into the ashram . . . From 1997 on he stopped giving darshan except when Mr. Lee was there —just for fifteen days while Mr. Lee was there. From that time also it was a known fact that Mr. Lee is very special.

Yogi Ramsuratkumar was always concerned with the details of hospitality and care when any group came to visit, and with Lee's group he had a particular focus of attention. Beginning with Lee's faxes that conveyed his traveling plans, how many people would be coming, from where, their names and so on, the accommodations for Lee and his people became the priority job for the members of the ashram staff. Yogi Ramsuratkumar would receive the fax message, have it read ten, twelve or fifteen times, then he would start asking, "How many people are coming? How many ladies? How many gents? What are their names? Where are they going to stay? How many cottages you are going to give them?" Mani was expected to know the answers and to oversee each and every detail.

"How many pillows are there for each?" Bhagawan would ask and Mani would give the answer.

"How many cots are there? How many people would stay in one cottage?" This information was provided.

"How many children are coming?" He wanted to know everything. One week before Lee was expected to arrive, Yogi Ramsuratkumar would begin with another barrage of questions and instructions, "Mani, what is the day today? You read the fax message again."

As soon as a devotee entered the ashram grounds, Yogi Ramsuratkumar took full responsibility for him or her. Particularly regarding Lee and his group, which grew larger and larger with every passing year, Yogi Ramsuratkumar often said to Mani, "You should be taking care of them very well; you should be showing much hospitality to them. You should always be taking care of Mr. Lee. There is no other work for you to do."

Arriving in Chennai on November 26, 1998 with Lee and his group, I was excited about seeing the changes in the ashram that I'd been hearing about over the past five years. The last time I had seen the ashram was in 1993, when it was a recently purchased plot of bare land. We arrived at four a.m. to find a thriving ashram complex—a well-established haven. As we walked in the dark through the tall wrought iron gate, the pale outline of the massive temple could be seen to the left as we walked barefoot on sacred ground, a row of tall palm trees swaying gently in the night breeze on the right. The air itself seemed saturated with the burning presence of grace—the pure benevolence of Yogi Ramsuratkumar. The night was like a warm black velvet cloak, scented with jasmine and a hint of the coming dew. The sandy red soil was pleasant beneath our feet.

We got settled into the ashram cottages where we would be staying, and soon one of the ashram kitchen servants came with a large covered pot filled to the brim with sweet and milky Indian coffee. Rumpled, stained and weary as we were from two days of traveling, we were counting the minutes until Yogi Ramsuratkumar would appear at seven a.m. in his car. Soon enough the long night disappeared with the first sight of Arunachala, crowned green and glorious behind the mists that were illumined by the early rays of the sun.

Arunachala! The holy hill seemed incredibly close as we sat on the porch of the ashram cottage—as if one could reach out and touch it. The ashram itself came into focus with the dawning of the day. In five years the bare green field of thorn bushes had been transformed into a lush paradise, adorned with several lovely stucco buildings, thatched-roof huts, the massive temple itself and the dining hall that doubled as a darshan hall until the temple could be completed. Along the row of cottages were many flowering bushes and vines that grew along the path and in green heaps over fence. A little musk deer grazed in the green yard of our cottage; the bell around her neck tinkled gently. We heard that the deer had wandered on to the ashram; the staff had taken it away once, but it returned.

At ten minutes before seven o'clock we lined up at the ashram gate with Lee and the Indian devotees—men first, then the women. It was a great joy to wait in the cool morning air, the cawing of crows mingling with the sweeter melodies of the small birds that flitted from the trees and shrubs. Facing the gate as we waited, Mount Arunachala rose up in the immediate distance, green and high with rolling rock crests here and there, scudded by low-hanging clouds and wisps of morning mist. The day sparkled with the fresh sheen of the tropical sun, and the sweet soft air of the ashram was easy to breathe. It seemed like we had landed in Vaikuntha. Soon the car would appear with Yogi Ramsuratkumar in the back, along with Ma Devaki and Vijaylakshmi.

The sun was already showing its promise of power and heat as we chanted, "Yogi

Ramsuratkumar, Yogi Ramsuratkumar, Yogi Ramsuratkumar, Jaya Guru Raya." I craned my neck to watch the potholed road at the gate. Finally the car came chugging along, and slowed to about three miles an hour as it rolled through the ashram entrance. Lee stood at the front of the line with the men, his palms pressed together in a *pranam.* As the car rolled slowly past, Yogi Ramsuratkumar's face appeared—the gleaming white beard, the green rag wrapped turban-style around his forehead, the blue-gray shawl wrapped around his body and thrown over one shoulder. His hand was raised in a gesture of blessing. There was no visible greeting or personal recognition from Yogi Ramsuratkumar to Lee, or at least none that was discernible. It was as if Lee stood there every morning to greet Yogi Ramsuratkumar.

When the car was parked Ravi and Mani helped Yogi Ramsuratkumar get out and walk into the hut. He leaned on their strong arms, while Ma Devaki and Vijayalakshmi walked ahead of him. As soon as his form disappeared into the building the devotees began to circumambulate the ashram, chanting. Most of Lee's students followed suit, but Lee went to sit under the thatched roof of the reception hut nearest the ashram gate. There he waited until Yogi Ramsuratkumar had breakfasted and was ready to leave, and the line formed again to offer salutations to the guru as the car drove slowly past. This time Yogi Ramsuratkumar kept his hands together in a gentle *pranam* as he gazed at people while the car passed by. Sometimes he would notice someone and his hands would go up in an instinctive response of blessing.

At ten o'clock there were about fifty people lined up to greet Yogi Ramsuratkumar as he arrived for darshan. While he settled in the temple, Lee was asked to stand at the front of the line of devotees, who then walked into the temple one by one to circumambulate the more than life-sized statue of Yogi Ramsuratkumar. Yogi Ramsuratkumar himself sat only ten feet away in what looked like a rickety old chair. After circumambulating the statue, we filed one by one in front of Yogi Ramsuratkumar, *pranamed* and received his blessings. Devaki Ma and Vijayalakshmi sat chanting under the small thatched palm hut to his left.

The first person in this long line, Lee circumambulated the statue and then lowered his body into a full-length prostration on the dirt floor of the temple in front of Yogi Ramsuratkumar. Again there was no demonstration of a personal relationship, no social greeting of any kind. It was unnecessary, and obviously not expected or wanted by Lee. Instead it was a formal and impersonal ritual. In this interchange between guru and devotee were many levels of teaching; Yogi Ramsuratkumar was not bound by sentiment or attachment to cultural forms—only his Father's work mattered. "Father alone exists," so why should there be any display of separation? At the same time, the master was completely present to the perfect communion of the heart that exists in silence. In silence, one felt the heartbreak of his communication: total love, uncompromising truth, ruthless compassion, crystalline purity, the piercing impact of his absolute surrender to the will of God.

Soon Lee's party and the Indian devotees were all in the dining hall where darshan would be held. Everyone chanted and waited for Yogi Ramsuratkumar to enter with

Devaki Ma and Vijayalakshmi. Although Lee and his men students were told by Mani to stand at the front of the line, Lee had taken a seat several rows back from the front of the room on the men's side. One of Yogi Ramsuratkumar's attendants came in and asked Lee to sit in the front row. He moved with his men students to the place that had been indicated.

Leaning on Mani's arm, Yogi Ramsuratkumar walked very slowly into the room, looking this way and that at devotees on each side. He was wearing a very wrinkled *dhoti* that came down to his ankles, a long-sleeved shirt and three voluminous shawls. Hidden beneath his long white beard and in the folds of his shawls were five or six *malas*, or necklaces of prayer beads, that hung around his neck. Some of them were *rudraksh*, some sandalwood, some rock crystal that shone in the light. The rolled and twisted cloth was wrapped many times around his forehead; it held his long hair back from his face. He moved in the slow gait of a very old man and slowly, carefully settled on the dais with some difficulty. It seemed that he was bearing tremendous pain on many levels, and yet his face was beautiful and shining. Despite his years, the ravaging effects of a very hard life and his ill health, he exuded an extraordinary wholeness and brightness.

Devaki Ma and Vijayalakshmi followed behind him carrying the bags that contained whatever Yogi Ramsuratkumar might need during darshan. Devaki carried his palmyra fan and coconut bowl. They walked up to the left of the dais, where they stood waiting for Yogi Ramsuratkumar to indicate where they should sit. He glanced at them and then gestured for them to sit on the dais to his right and facing him.

As soon as they were settled Yogi Ramsuratkumar called some of his Indian devotees up to the dais. He gave them *prasad* and talked very briefly with them. Soon he gestured for Lee to come. Lee jumped up, ran to the dais, went to his knees in a deep bow and pressed his hands together in a *pranam*. Yogi Ramsuratkumar put his hands on either side of Lee's hands and held them in his as he spoke quietly to him.

"Lee . . . you sit with these friends. Krishna, Bret, Alain . . ." he gestured toward the wall just a few feet away. Right away Lee and a small group of men—Alain De Rosenbo, Bret Carlson and Krishna Carcelle—moved to sit where Yogi Ramsuratkumar had had them sit for several years when Lee visited, in chairs along the side wall to Yogi Ramsuratkumar's right.

Two of Yogi Ramsuratkumar's women devotees got up at his request and sang a long, beautiful chant to Ram. During the chant Yogi Ramsuratkumar changed before my very eyes from a wise old man to something so far beyond that it confounded the rational mind. There before the crowd sat an incomprehensible being. The green turban criss-crossed over his long, disheveled hair. His head fell forward, but he wasn't asleep—he was consumed, taken within by the force of something that exuded from him at the same time as the sweetest love. I had a strong inner sense of being cleaned, cleared, made fit or worthy to be in his company.

When the chant was over Yogi Ramsuratkumar gestured to Lee to come up to the dais. Lee jumped up and ran, quite literally, with his hands full, mostly with the brand-new book, *Death of a Dishonest Man*—a hard-bound compilation of Lee's poems to Yogi

Ramsuratkumar from 1979 through March 1998, set in chronological order. The big dark green volume, published by Hohm Press in Arizona, was over twelve hundred pages and weighed in at about four pounds.

Lee's students had been asking to publish his poems in America since they had first come out in 1993, but it wasn't until Yogi Ramsuratkumar had *Poems of a Broken Heart Part II* printed in Madras that Lee agreed to this project. *Death of a Dishonest Man* included essays by a number of Lee's friends—Arnaud Desjardins, Robert Svoboda, Yvan Amar, Makarand Paranjape, Andrew Schelling, Claudio Naranjo, Gilles Farcet—as well as some essays written by his students. It also included a section of song lyrics written by Lee and recorded by his two bands, the rock & roll band and a new band called Shri that played traditional blues.

Lee lifted the heavy book toward Yogi Ramsuratkumar, who took the book in his outstretched hands and hefted its weight with a look of surprise and innocent pleasure.

"This is for me?" the beggar asked, like a child being given the most precious and unexpected gift in the world. He looked at Devaki Ma and then back at Lee with wonder and delight. He held the book as if it was a newborn baby, and his smiles bestowed a tangible grace in the hall. Immediately he began to look through the pages, stopping at the beautiful color photographs.

"You published this book?" he asked. Lee answered yes. "How much does this book cost?" Yogi Ramsuratkumar asked in wonder.

"Four thousand rupees," came the reply.

He exclaimed at the price,

"Four thousand rupees!" Another series of beautiful, brilliant smiles spread across his face, his eyes glowing like gems. It was hard to believe this was the same elder who had walked so slowly and gravely through the room a few minutes ago. Now he was dazzling and childlike, eternally young.

"Is this a lot for Westerners?" he asked Lee, referring to the price of the book. Lee said yes. Yogi Ramsuratkumar smiled another huge smile. His sense of humor was a wonderful thing to witness as he laughed and smiled and beamed with delight at the gift. He handed the book back to Lee.

"Devaki, you pay for it," he said, turning to Ma Devaki.

"It's a gift for you! I intended it as a gift," Lee protested, almost begging the master to take the book.

"No. Devaki pays. Devaki, you pay for it now," he decreed. Without hesitation she pulled out a checkbook, wrote the check and handed it to Yogi Ramsuratkumar, who peered at it for a moment before he handed it to Lee. Paying for the book—particularly when it was offered as a gift—carried strong symbolic implications of sacrifice and commitment. It spoke of Devaki's investment in the spiritual path, and the assumption of greater obligation and responsibility through her willingness to "pay" for the master's book. When the check was handed over to Lee, Yogi Ramsuratkumar held out both of his hands and received the book from Lee, who carefully placed the heavy, outrageously big volume in the master's hands.

"Lee, say a few words to all these people about this book. And read some of the poems," he said with a smile of pure enjoyment. Lee stood up and spoke briefly, telling the basic facts about the book: how Yogi Ramsuratkumar had originally had the poems published in India in *Poems of a Broken Heart* and now this volume had been published in the West. There were six hundred poems in the book, some essays and so on. Lee then read two or three of the most recent poems. While Lee read, a mood of pure divine presence expanded infinitely and pressed upon the hearts of the listeners. It seemed that Yogi Ramsuratkumar became everything and everyone in the room and beyond.

Lee finished his short talk about *Death of a Dishonest Man* and returned to Yogi Ramsuratkumar's side at the dais. In addition to the book, Lee had given him a recent issue of *Om Sri Ram,* the newsletter published by the North American satsang of Swami Ramdas, Mother Krishnabai and Swami Satchidananda devotees. Yogi Ramsuratkumar began to ask Lee questions about the newsletter, but it was impossible to hear what they were saying. The newsletter contained an article I had written about Yogi Ramsuratkumar. Lee quickly turned and gestured for me to come up, and as I walked up to him, Lee said, "Yogi Ramsuratkumar wants you to read this," and handed the newsletter to me, indicating the article I had written.

I *pranamed* to Yogi Ramsuratkumar and took the newsletter, then stood nearby, facing the crowd of about a hundred people, and began to read. I read as loudly and clearly as I could, although Lee told me later that my voice was barely audible. My nerves were strained from the long journey and lack of sleep but also by the discomfort I felt at being singled out so quickly in Yogi Ramsuratkumar's darshan. Despite my tension, it felt like Yogi Ramsuratkumar was lifting me up; he was underneath the reading, sustaining and empowering it. He was coming through me, dispelling my nervousness and doubt. I finished the reading, walked to Yogi Ramsuratkumar at the dais and bowed deeply to receive his blessing.

"What is your name?" he asked sweetly.

I vacillated briefly, not sure of what to say—the name that was on the byline of the article I'd just read, or the name I am usually called by, which is my middle name. Lee had instructed me over the years to use my first name, Mary, or M. Young, as my pen name, but since birth I had always been called by my middle name. Any resistance to obedience to my guru's use of the name "Mary Young" was apparent in that moment, as I lingered in hesitation. With a ferocity I'd never experienced in him before, Yogi Ramsuratkumar said, "Your name!" I answered with my middle name.

"Ehh?" he almost growled, not comprehending why I had said a name other than the one on the *Om Sri Ram* article. He repeated the question.

"What is your name?"

When I tried to explain the situation to Ma Devaki, Yogi Ramsuratkumar simply shouted at me, "Your name is Mary Young!" Immediately, without any volition of the mind, my head went down in a spontaneous *pranam* on the dais at his feet. There was no disagreement left in me. The communication was so clear that I could almost hear him saying, "Lee is your guru. If Lee calls you Mary Young, then you are Mary Young! And it is Mary Young who wrote the article about this beggar."

In his omniscience he knew where my resistance was, and at the same time that he worked with that resistance, he was empowering that which is essential and true. When he said the name "Mary" it melted my heart, becoming "Merri" in his beautiful Hindi accent, with a roll on the "r".

As I made my way back to my seat, duly chastened in a most loving way, Yogi Ramsuratkumar called Lee back up to the dais, where he knelt at his father's knee. "Read this again," he instructed Lee, who took the article and read it in a clear, loud voice. This time Yogi Ramsuratkumar seemed satisfied. Lee returned to the dais and handed the newsletter to Yogi Ramsuratkumar.

Within moments Lee asked some of his women students to lead chants. He had already instructed his traveling party to lead only the chants written and composed by his students, because, he said, that was what Yogi Ramsuratkumar wanted to hear. The chanting began. Yogi Ramsuratkumar continued the darshan until one o'clock—an hour later than the usual ending time—while the chanting seemed to go on and on. It felt like important things were afoot.

As soon as Yogi Ramsuratkumar left, the kitchen staff quickly and efficiently organized an area of the large dining hall for serving lunch. The food was excellent—spicy, delicious, and energetically pure. Everyone ate heartily of rice, *sambar* and curried vegetables.

Shortly before four o'clock Lee and the group gathered again at the gate to salute Yogi Ramsuratkumar as his car moved along the dirt road. After circumambulating the statue and *pranaming* to Yogi Ramsuratkumar as he sat in his chair, everyone went into the hall for darshan. Lee's women students were asked by the attendants to sit up front in the first row, directly across from Lee and the men. We took our seats and waited for Yogi Ramsuratkumar to appear while an Indian woman and then Bret Carlson lead the chants.

Yogi Ramsuratkumar came in after about fifteen minutes. Devaki placed the big, new poetry book on the dais beside him as soon as they sat down. He had Vasugi and Jairaj, long-time devotees from Sivakasi, come up and sit beside the dais on the floor. Vasugi stood up and talked for a while about the Yogi Ramsuratkumar *bhajans* she had been leading and about Yogi Ramsuratkumar's blessings. She spoke in Tamil and seemed very animated and happy. She had a tape that she played for him.

While the tape rolled on and we sat listening to the chanting, Yogi Ramsuratkumar presided over the space as pure deity. He was regal in his rags, and the emanations of his being were all-pervading. He was all grace and graciousness as he blessed Vasugi and Jairaj and gave them *prasad*. Finally, after about an hour of listening to the tape Yogi Ramsuratkumar said gently, "That is enough," and gave her a sweet smile.

"Lee, have some of your followers lead chants," he said after calling Lee over to the dais. Lee turned and gestured to Mirabai and I to lead the chanting. We got up and began the Hanuman chant composed by Doug Fulker—"Hanuman, Hanuman, Sita Ram Hanuman, Yogi Rama, Yogi Rama, Suratkumar Rama Rama." Yogi Ramsuratkumar picked up an orange and began to gleefully toss it back and forth in rhythm with the chant, which had a bouncy, child-like mood. He did this for a long time, chuckling softly while Devaki's eyes sparkled with delight at his obvious enjoyment. About thirty minutes into the chanting Mirabai left to attend to the children. I looked to Lee for instruction and he gestured to continue leading the chant alone. Yogi Ramsuratkumar called him up to the dais. After a quick exchange, Lee walked over to Rose and asked her to go get a poetry book, which she returned with shortly and handed to Lee, who took it directly to Yogi Ramsuratkumar.

"Who wants to buy this book right now? Pay for it tonight—*cash*! Four thousand rupees!" Yogi Ramsuratkumar called out to the crowd. His eyes gleamed with mischief. He looked like he would burst into uproarious laughter at any minute. The expensive price of the book, which he kept exclaiming and chuckling over, seemed to amuse and delight him. I'd never seen Yogi Ramsuratkumar sell things, and I wondered if he was imitating Lee—who regularly sold his own books and music cassettes and CDs during his seminars in Europe—or if he just enjoyed playing the Great Merchant, whose bazaar was God's place of worship, and whose wares were the playthings of a divine purpose.

The crowd responded to the beggar king's high spirits with their own. People were talking, rustling around in their seats on the floor. Yogi Ramsuratkumar laughed out loud. Lee sat on the floor beside the dais at the master's side. There was a big smile on his face as well. A European woman in the audience wanted to buy the book; she came up, gave the money and walked away with the book in hand. Immediately Yogi Ramsuratkumar asked Lee for another book and out went Rose to the cottage to bring one. People were stirred up. The chanting went on while the next book arrived and was sold instantly. Then Yogi Ramsuratkumar began to sign the books with an Om sign and his name. There was much laughter and commotion in the hall. The sweet mood of Yogi Ramsuratkumar's delight permeated the air as his laughter and quick smiles transformed everyone in the room. The Godchild was in a full-on play with his devotees, and everyone responded with happiness.

A third book was brought into the hall and Yogi Ramsuratkumar sold it instantly. Buying a book gave the devotees a chance to get close to the master; each time a book was sold, he blessed whoever had come up to get their book. The crowd was rapt, faces were shining, all eyes were on Yogi Ramsuratkumar and spirits were very high.

It was difficult to keep the chanting going all through this. One had to pay total attention to several different things simultaneously—the next verse of the chant, signals from Lee or Yogi Ramsuratkumar, the protocol of the space. The intense bearing down of the subtle energetic presence of Yogi Ramsuratkumar made ego seek small escapes, but there were none. One lapse of attention, any wandering of the mind or spacing out would throw off the chant. The training of attention in this way was one of many opportunities in Yogi Ramsuratkumar's company; at the same time, the brightness and power in the space had the effect of buoying one up, so that one was carried along on the current.

At six-thirty Yogi Ramsuratkumar still sat on his dais creating and destroying universes with his play. The chanting droned on and on. I had been standing up leading the same chant for almost an hour and a half. Yogi Ramsuratkumar seemed to be having so much fun that he kept the darshan going over thirty minutes past the time that it usually ended. Suddenly he asked his attendant Selvaraj to motion me toward the dais. I stopped chanting and quickly knelt at Yogi Ramsuratkumar's side.

"What is your name?" he asked.

"Mary," I answered in brief.

"What is your other name?" he asked, very sweetly. This time I answered my middle name, the name I have always been called by, dimly thinking it was the right answer.

He shouted emphatically, "Mary *Young*!"

It was a triumphant, even imperious statement of fact. Then he repeated, more softly and with a huge smile, "Your name is Mary Young!" An involuntary smile burst into life across my face with laughter just behind it as my body again spontaneously fell into a *pranam* at his feet. The air shook with something like happiness. How incredible it was to interact with this great being in any way he might choose! He was giving me a lesson in obedience to the guru, but his eyes sparkled with mirth at all the silliness. I had the recognition that we were having fun with each other, and yet there was no doubt about his spiritual authority. As far as Yogi Ramsuratkumar was concerned, the name that appeared on the article I'd written in praise of him was my name.

"Thank you," he said, very tenderly. It seemed to me that he was actually thanking the one who had written about the beggar king, Yogi Ramsuratkumar. At best, the one who writes is only an instrument in the *lila* of Yogi Ramsuratkumar; at worst, that one is muddied with doubt, confusion and resistance. His blessing was to empower the one who is nothing and no one, who takes no credit for the writing, who freely chooses obedience to the guru.

"My Father blesses Mary Young," he said slowly, with heart-stopping softness. He gazed at me for a long time, holding the *prasad* in the air above my cupped hands. It seemed that he had fallen into a very strong blessing trance. His face was etched with feeling, a love so great that it seemed he must bear it as pain or conscious suffering. His eyes looked past me and into something or someone unknown, unnamable. His blessing was aimed at this unknown, reaching beyond the ego-cherishing "me." His eyes called a mystery into life. I had the sense that I was being literally showered and pummeled by a storm of Grace. Finally he dropped the orange he had been playing with for over an hour into my cupped hands. Then the moment, suspended in time, fell away. I *pranamed* and returned to my seat.

Quickly he prepared to leave with Devaki Ma and Vijayalakshmi. He called Lee to his dais and told him to take his seat on the dais after he left.

"Stay with these people awhile," he said. Lee came over immediately and motioned to me to start the "Mangalam" chant that always signals the end of darshan. I started singing rather feebly.

"No—loud," Lee instructed from the dais. He corrected me, but his eyes were shining and merry.

Yogi Ramsuratkumar was gone and darshan was over. Mani came forward and asked Lee to perform the closing *puja*, which consisted of the waving of lights (a small camphor flame burning on a stainless steel tray) and offering incense and water at the shrine near the front door, then outside to Arunachala. Lee also waved lights to Yogi Ramsuratkumar's seat at the dais and to the shrine near the dais for the Shankaracharya of Kanchipuram.

"Just good, clean fun!" Lee said afterward, standing outside the dining hall under the thatched roof that sheltered the doorway. The mood was jubilant, and Lee had a big smile on his face.

The next morning Lee presented an orange wool shawl to Yogi Ramsuratkumar; it was a gift from Chandra Swami that had been sent with Alain De Rosanbo. It was exactly like the shawl that Chandra Swami had sent the year before.

"Is this the shawl he gave this beggar last year?" Yogi Ramsuratkumar smiled, pointing to the orange shawl he was already wearing underneath a green wool shawl, both tied across his chest with big knots. His innocence in this simple question was disarming. He held the shawl in his lap for a long time while the chanting went on, then his pale brown hand moved up gracefully and made the slightest gesture for Lee to come.

Lee immediately jumped up from his chair and bounded over to the dais. He *pranamed* and bent toward the master to listen to his instructions. Yogi Ramsuratkumar handed the shawl to Lee, who then placed it around his father's shoulders. Devaki and Yogi Ramsuratkumar both motioned to Lee to tie it in place. Lee took both ends, pulled them forward, and tied the first knot tightly. The yogi chuckled, perhaps at the strength in the act of tying. Then Lee tied the second knot, smiling along with Yogi Ramsuratkumar. Lee *pranamed*, received Yogi's blessings, then ran back to his seat. The tying of the knot over Yogi Ramsuratkumar's heart seemed like more than a symbol of how Lee and Yogi Ramsuratkumar are bound together. It was a simple act, but choked with meaning. Very soon Yogi Ramsuratkumar called Lee over again.

"Say something of use to these people," he said, pointing gently toward the crowd. Lee stood and faced the audience, gave a slight self-deprecating or embarrassed shrug, and launched into it. Scribbling notes as quickly and unobtrusively as possible, I wrote down the highlights of what Lee said:

> I'll talk about the book title, *Death of a Dishonest Man*. The title of the book uses very specific language; it refers to me in one way, but also offers an opportunity to others, so we can consider what is honest and what is dishonest. As long as we deny the Allness, the Unity of All that Yogi Ramsuratkumar so ecstatically speaks of, then we are dishonest, and in fact we deny the Reality of our very existence, and of the Divine.
>
> When we refer in English to death it doesn't always mean a literal death. Saul of Tarsus was a persecutor of Christians who had a vision of Jesus on the road to Damascus and was immediately changed from a nonbeliever to a believer. Saul said, "You have to die every day in Christ." You have to die to the knowledge that Father in Heaven is all, everything,

> everywhere, past, present, future, unitive, total Oneness. There is only God.
>
> So the title of the book refers to me but also says that we could all profit from considering whether we are honest or dishonest in this sense, because we believe we are separate from God. Yogi Ramsuratkumar says He is a sinner, but there is nothing about Yogi Ramsuratkumar that is dishonest . . . . The degree to which we are dishonest is the degree to which we have not died to the unitive Oneness, the Allness, of Father in Heaven.

Yogi Ramsuratkumar smoked and listened. He stretched his legs out in front of him. His bare feet faced those sitting in the front row, his legs crossed at the ankle. These feet communicated grace as did every contour and limb of the body. Every gesture he made effected the entire configuration of the large room, and in his *bhavas* and blessing fits—sometimes almost like spasms that seized him—he spun out our *samskaras*, transforming karma, piercing the murky veils of darkness with light. The greatness and rarity of his being continually pummeled my perceptions. A humble old yogi, with years of traveling barefoot on the dusty roads of India indelibly imprinted on his feet, God-intoxicated and quite mad by worldly standards and a beggar in rags, was a great God-realizer. His greatness was apparent in his utter simplicity, his total lack of pretension of any kind. He had no need for the trappings of sainthood—he was simply easeful, natural, blessedly present.

"Arunachala Shiva, Arunachala Shiva, Arunachala Shiva, Arunejeda," Ma Devaki and Vijayalakshmi sang at the beginning of every darshan. Yogi Ramsuratkumar sat smoking, peering out at the people. As these words resounded in the hall it was apparent that he was the holy mountain, Shiva in Arunachala—there was no separation between Yogi Ramsuratkumar and the mountain. The subtle presence of Arunachala permeated everything—green, solid and real but at the same time interpenetrating the unseen worlds. While Yogi Ramsuratkumar sat and smoked and watched us watching him, a number of small birds congregated on the outer windowsills just behind and to each side of his platform. It is well known that Yogi Ramsuratkumar liked birds, and they appeared to like him as well, as they gathered to sing sweetly, adding their voices to the songs we were singing.

Sitting in the company of Yogi Ramsuratkumar, I began to reflect: The mystical underpinnings of life and the reality of thc Godman are ideas that are often considered ludicrous, preposterous or even psychotic in the West. These magical realities are tacitly understood in India, and it is a worldview that I find not only refreshing, but affirming of one's wholeness, innate intelligence and instinct. To the eye of the soul, Yogi Ramsuratkumar appears as a beggar king holding court beneath the vast umbrella of Arunachala, a king whose greatest nobility is found in perfect, complete surrender to "Father in heaven" or the absolute will of God. At the same time he is the ultimate servant, as any true king should be, and he serves his devotees with stainless and pure love.

Yogi Ramsuratkumar exists as countless large and small acts of love of God in creation. It is this love that sustains the world, the universe and Creation itself. This is the face of God that the Hindus conceive of as Vishnu, who took human incarnation as Ram and Krishna—the aspect of the Divine that sustains and maintains all things through the sheer force of love, in order that the will of God might be enacted, evolved, realized in life, through matter, through incarnation, through a great process of divine evolution. Sitting in the revelatory power of his presence, I realized that I agreed with his Indian devotees: Yogi Ramsuratkumar *is* Ram.

For the next few days before *jayanthi*, Yogi Ramsuratkumar asked Lee many times to "Say something useful to these people." Lee had a way of using these opportunities to lavish praise on Yogi Ramsuratkumar without sounding unctuous or being obsequious in any way. The words of Yogi Ramsuratkumar's greatness coming from Lee's lips rang true: he meant what he said and he spoke with total conviction. He reminded the audience time and again of Yogi Ramsuratkumar's teaching: There is only God, only the unitive Allness, past, present, future, everything, everywhere, and that this is who we are, because there is no separation between all of life and the Divine.

In the afternoon talk Lee said that the day before a bird was singing outside the window where Yogi Ramsuratkumar sat on the dais. Yogi Ramsuratkumar was paying attention to the bird. "He was listening to the bird's song and paying attention to everyone in the room *also*," Lee said with a hint of mischief and a small smile. "Yogi Ramsuratkumar hears the voice of God in many places. It always inspires me when Yogi Ramsuratkumar acknowledges that God is everywhere, in all things . . . in the song of the bird, certainly in the mountain, Arunachala, in the taste of good food, in the beautiful flowers. God has many voices."

Lee told a story about sitting with Yogi Ramsuratkumar years ago. Yogi was chanting the name of God when a crow sang very loudly on a branch nearby. He stopped, looked at the crow and said, "That friend's voice is so much sweeter than this beggar's voice!"

During this time Yogi Ramsuratkumar was serenely smoking and watching Lee, listening intently. Lee began to talk about how the secret of existence is in the heart of man, and his speech effortlessly became ecstatic and sublime. "The truth is in us," he said, "in the flowers, in the song of the bird, in the taste of fine food. God is in the mountain..." He ended the talk with many paeans of praise to the greatness of Yogi Ramsuratkumar, of the great opportunity and joy of being in his presence. He talked about how fortunate we were to be in the company of Yogi Ramsuratkumar. He said, "Yogi Ramsuratkumar has his servants stand up and 'say something useful' or read from the scriptures or sing a song because he doesn't do any of these things. Instead he works only through Grace, and his Grace and blessings are showered upon all—we only have to receive."

Lee turned to the dais and knelt at his father's knee, his hands pressed together in a *pranam*. Yogi Ramsuratkumar chuckled slightly and put his hand on Lee's shoulder as he bowed. They stayed like that for a minute or more—Yogi Ramsuratkumar's hand lying pressed down on Lee's shoulder—and it seemed like a visible substance was passing between them. Lee's attitude was one of complete receptivity and submission—not submission as Westerners typically view it, but a submission that was ennobling and exalting.

Yogi Ramsuratkumar had Lee call up three other men—Krishna Carcelle, Bret and Alain De Rosanbo—and sit together with them on his dais as he left for Sudama House. This would happen every day while Lee was visiting. Sometimes Yogi Ramsuratkumar said to Lee, "Conduct all these affairs," and at other times, "Manage all affairs," as he waved his hand to indicate the room and all the people in it.

The next day Yogi Ramsuratkumar called Lee up to the dais and said, "Say something useful for everyone." As usual, I sat with a small notepad, scribbling as fast as I could. Lee started out talking about how in the West it is common for people who have been to the East to have many books, pictures of saints and all kinds of paraphernalia, but they never do anything with it. They marvel at the sanctity of such things, but don't change their lives to reflect the beliefs and teachings of the spiritual path. "In order for something to be useful, you have to *do* something with those experiences of sanctity," Lee said. Then he shared a dream that he had had some years ago:

> Most dreams, like our waking hours, are just illusions, but now and then Yogi Ramsuratkumar gives me a dream that is real and that makes a point. Yogi Ramsuratkumar and I were walking along together by the temple in the dream. The temple was completed, and all the finishing touches were on it. As we walked into the temple I saw something that caught my attention and distracted me. After a minute I realized that Yogi Ramsuratkumar had gone ahead. I ran to find him, but when I found Him, the communion we had before—when we were walking together and my attention was totally on Him—was gone.

Lee said that the dream was not personal and had nothing to do with him, but was a teaching about having faith in the name of Yogi Ramsuratkumar and keeping one's attention on the spiritual guide—the guru. Lee said, "He has said if you need his blessings, wherever you are, speak his name with faith and, 'This beggar will be with you.' So one element of faith is attention—paying attention."

Lee began to talk about how difficult it is for most people to simply pay attention, much less place total attention on the guru. He joked about how Westerners are easily distracted by the newest restaurant in town—like the new European restaurant in Tiruvannamalai, where crepes and cappuccino are served. He laughed as he said:

> Even on our ashram you hear people whispering, "Have you tried the

> new restaurant in town?" Yogi Ramsuratkumar is not His body—as beautiful as it is, and as much as we worship it. Yogi Ramsuratkumar is His Father in Heaven: all, one, unitive. When we lose our focus of attention on the sanctity of Yogi Ramsuratkumar, even for a moment or a day or a month, the blessings do not flow to us in the same way as they can when our faith, our attention on Yogi Ramsuratkumar as Father in Heaven, is total . . .

The next day Lee's student Purna Steinitz arrived with fifteen of his own students to join Lee's traveling party. All of the copies of *Death of a Dishonest Man* had been sold by Yogi Ramsuratkumar the first week after Lee arrived, and Purna had brought another case. That day the book-selling *lila* continued. At the beginning of darshan Yogi Ramsuratkumar asked Lee for more books, and he sent Rose to the cottage to bring one. Lee handed it to Yogi Ramsuratkumar, who gave it to Vijayalakshmi, who was sitting on the dais with Devaki Ma. She made out a personal check and handed it to Yogi Ramsuratkumar, who handed it to Lee. With book in hand, Yogi Ramsuratkumar signed it with a big Om sign and his name—no more than a wave of a line. He asked Lee for more books then asked Vijayalakshmi to make an announcement about *Death of a Dishonest Man* to the darshan of about two hundred and fifty people, saying also that Lee had some more books for sale.

When she had made the announcement, Yogi Ramsuratkumar said, "Whoever wants to can buy this book *now*. If you have *cash* you can buy this book—*today!*" He was smiling broadly. It was amazing how much he had been brought to life from the condition we had first seen him in, when he appeared frail and barely able to walk at the first darshan. He seemed rejuvenated, and his vast capacity for transformation, for irony and humor and delight sparkled on him as he played the role of salesman with relish. Lee stayed by his side, ripping the plastic covers off the books and handing Yogi Ramsuratkumar another copy as the next person came forward to buy.

It was a selling spree—Yogi Ramsuratkumar's book bazaar. He said laughingly, with a childlike innocence that blended easily with his divine sense of savvy, "We are selling *all* these books!" Then he looked at Lee and asked, "Are you selling books in America?"

Lee smiled and answered, "Yes, but not as many as you!" Yogi laughed and affectionately clapped Lee on the shoulder, as if he got the biggest charge out of this whole thing. Without saying anything he seemed to be demonstrating that he knew his devotee Lee quite well.

After darshan, the European woman who bought the first poetry book several days before came up to Lee as he stood under the thatched palm roof that shades the entry to the dining hall where Yogi Ramsuratkumar gives darshan. She cornered Lee and asked him if he would ask Yogi to sign her poetry book like he had begun to do with the others. For some reason, he hadn't signed hers.

"No," Lee answered flatly. "I don't ask for anything from him."

"No?" she asked quizzically, as if this was a great surprise to her.

"No. I don't even ask for anything for myself, much less for other people," he stated. Case closed. She looked amazed, and dismayed as well.

That afternoon the group gathered outside the cottage where Lee was staying on the ashram to drink the sweet coffee that was brought, at Yogi Ramsuratkumar's request, every afternoon at three. With the addition of Purna Steinitz and his students, Lee's group now numbered thirty-five people and constituted a very conspicuous presence. Nonetheless, while in Tiruvannamalai Lee reveled in being the devotee, and he took an invisible back seat to Yogi Ramsuratkumar as much as possible. In darshan Lee was always fiercely alert and aware of everything that went on in the space. His attunement to Yogi Ramsuratkumar was a rare thing to observe, and even many of the members of the ashram staff commented on it.

Fame had been following Lee around, however, since the beggar king had predicted it would twenty-five years before, and sometimes European or American seekers would come to the ashram looking for the "American guru." However, most of those kinds of intrusions were generally avoided by the fact that Lee had been giving public talks in the evenings in Tiruvannamalai for several years. This year the public talk would be at Bret's beautiful, newly-constructed house, only one block away from the Yogi Ramsuratkumar Ashram.

In darshan Yogi Ramsuratkumar continued to ask Lee to give talks, and they were consistently inspiring. Frequently the Indian devotees would come up to Lee and express their gratitude and appreciation for his ecstatic praise of Yogi Ramsuratkumar and the mood that he evoked. One day Lee said:

> Yogi Ramsuratkumar has asked me to say a few words. One of the most important principles in relationship to the guru is obedience. The philosophers debate about whether or not we have free will, but for the *bhakta* the question is, what can we do and what does the master do for us? What we can do is obey the master's wishes. Adoration and devotion we cannot pretend to have. By the master's grace—and only by the master's grace—we may come to love the master, to adore the master, to worship the master. But what we can do is follow what the master directs us to do. One of the things Yogi Ramsuratkumar has directed his devotees to do is to chant his name. This delights him and serves him, but it also brings blessings to devotees who do it.
>
> The task of devotees of Yogi Ramsuratkumar is not just to take blessings for ourselves, but to support the temple on Yogi Ramsuratkumar's ashram, which will bless *bhaktas* of all the generations ahead. The glory and majesty of Yogi Ramsuratkumar will not go away when Yogi Ramsuratkumar returns to his Father in Heaven. His glory will continue to grow and grow after he leaves his body and returns to Father in Heaven. This temple will serve the entire world. Yogi Ramsuratkumar has said that

> it is an international temple that will serve the whole world, and will serve all the *bhaktas*. Many of us are so fortunate and blessed to live here and get to see Yogi Ramsuratkumar every day. As the *bhaktas* say, "We can catch his scent."
>
> I hope I'm not insulting anyone by talking about another tradition here, but the Sufis talk about the "scent" of the Beloved. If you catch the perfume of the Beloved you are transported in ecstasy. If you walk to Sannadhi Street, if you are sensitive, you can catch the smell of the perfume that Yogi Ramsuratkumar has left behind there.
>
> Obedience to Yogi Ramsuratkumar can take many different forms. Perhaps to obey Yogi Ramsuratkumar is to bring his name to those who have not heard it before. Obedience is what we can do. If love comes, it comes—all we can do is thank the guru for such a gift. You could say that obedience is a form of praise, and God wants praise; the Universe wants praise. So you follow the scent of the Beloved, the perfume of the Beloved; you smell with your heart. If you smell food cooking you can follow that smell straight to the food. It's the same with the scent of the Beloved, but you smell that scent with the heart . . .

Lee's words penetrated the veils of growing concern over Yogi Ramsuratkumar's health and advanced years, and addressed the question that hovered in the air: How much longer will our Swamiji, our Bhagawan, our Yogi Ramsuratkumar live on this earth? It seemed imperative that the devotees begin to make a shift, to embrace what Yogi Ramsuratkumar had tried to teach and what he had embodied with his very life. In the years ahead the job of his devotees would be to create, support and sustain the sanctity of the ashram as a sacred place—the temple and Yogi Ramsuratkumar Ashram, Agrahara Kollai. It was Yogi Ramsuratkumar's vision that the ashram be a spiritual refuge, a generator of blessing power, a sanctuary of worship for the world and for generations to come.

On December 1, 1998 the *jayanthi* celebrations began at three o'clock in the morning with chanting and puja ceremonies in the temple. As we walked through thick darkness to the temple, the magic of India was in the air, combined with the power and presence of Yogi Ramsuratkumar. The still unfinished temple was like a vast cave, with its packed earthen floor. The large bronze statue of Yogi Ramsuratkumar had been surrounded with eighty brass ghee lamps, each one imprinted with the image of Yogi Ramsuratkumar's face, so that the perimeter of the concrete platform on which the statue stood was framed with dancing flames that burned brightly. The ghee lamps had been made especially for this auspicious occasion. Inside this circle were many mandalas and sacred designs intricately drawn in colored rice powder. High above tiny blue lights spelled out a message: "Long live Yogi Ramsuratkumar!"

Lee began the circumambulation of the statue with the men following behind him chanting the name of Yogi Ramsuratkumar. Thirty minutes later the women took over the chanting and circumambulating, and for the next few hours, the men's and women's groups would switch off every half hour. The only light was the flicker of the ghee lamps and the strings of small blue lights up above. Shadows danced on the distant walls as about forty-five chanting people circled the statue.

After the first five minutes Lee sat in a chair and watched while both the men's and women's groups switched off in the chanting and circumambulating of the statue. While the men chanted the women sat with Lee on the large, brightly colored cotton blankets that were laid out on the ground. Hot chai was served off and on during the following pre-dawn hours, and soon a pale light seeped into the temple. The children and their parents came in at five-thirty and everyone made a huge circle—about seventy-five people—for a kind of finale. The crowd dispersed around six o'clock to get ready for Yogi Ramsuratkumar's arrival for breakfast.

While the children had their chai in the temple just after sunrise, Mani began to talk about his life with Yogi Ramsuratkumar. Only five years before Mani was a construction engineer running a big company in Madras. He had only known Bhagawan for a short time when he was made one of the ashram trustees and manager of the ashram and its various construction projects. Yogi Ramsuratkumar wanted him on the ashram literally at all times, and he had not left the property for four years, except when Bhagawan requested his presence at Sudama House, only a few blocks away. He slept only two or three hours a night, and looked like a man who was burning in a hot fire—the fire of grace. Mani shook his head with a sober respect and awe of the ways of Yogi Ramsuratkumar as he spoke:

> The guru is very possessive—very possessive. If Yogi sees me talking to someone, he wants to know—"Who is Mani talking to? Mani doesn't need to be talking! Mani has work to do!" He doesn't want anything to keep me from my work. He is very possessive, very possessive. Even at the time of my mother's demise, I did not go to the funeral. He kept me here, on the ashram. When my children come to visit Yogi has them stay somewhere else on the ashram and not with me because he doesn't want them to distract me from my work. He is very possessive! I have learned not to argue with him. I just say yes to whatever he wants. I don't argue, I just listen. It is better for him to talk and for me to listen. He knows exactly how he wants everything to be. He is very, very meticulous—everything must be just so.
>
> It is a great blessing, of course. He says to me I don't have to chant his name or come to darshan or do anything—just work for him. Just work. Yes, yes, Mani is very blessed. Everyone says so. People say to me, "Mani, you are very blessed," but they don't understand how hard it is to be with a living saint. Mani is very blessed, but there is a fire under it . . .

Mani continued, saying, "Lee is like his Father. I say the son is like the Father. Lee is Yogi Ramsuratkumar's ambassador in the world."

He told the story of how Yogi Ramsuratkumar wanted a permanent pedestal under the statue in the temple, but he didn't want the statue touched by anyone to put the pedestal in place. It was an impossible task, but they achieved it. Somehow, he said, it was done as Yogi Ramsuratkumar wished. "I have learned," he said, "now I don't ask how it will be done, or say it is impossible, which it was. I just say yes when he asks for such things."

Mani told another similar story about putting up the steel girders that hold up the massive roof of the huge temple. Yogi Ramsuratkumar wanted this done without moving the small palm-thatched open hut that is in the center of the temple next to the statue, where Devaki and the Sudama sisters sometimes sit while Yogi Ramsuratkumar gives darshan in his chair ten feet away. Everyone said it was physically impossible.

"I just said yes, and with his grace, it was done!" Mani smiled with amazement, wanting to communicate to us the miracles of daily life with Bhagawan. For Mani, everything was accomplished purely by the grace of Yogi Ramsuratkumar, and he readily and without reserve spoke of this in all regards. His faith was extraordinary. When someone in Lee's party asked him for a picture of Yogi Ramsuratkumar and Devaki Ma and then thanked Mani, he said, "Don't thank me—thank Yogi Ramsuratkumar." In this way Mani referenced everything back to Yogi Ramsuratkumar, but with a grave and factual simplicity that was free of any sentimentality or inebriation. It's just the way it is—the guru's grace is everything. In these stories he communicated the reality of what it is to live with the immensity of the guru.

Soon it was time to line up at the gate for Yogi Ramsuratkumar's arrival at seven o'clock, but this time the car stopped at the second structure on the grounds, called the Yagashala—a large hut with a palm-thatched roof and concrete floor near the entrance of the ashram and the front of the temple. Yogi Ramsuratkumar, Devaki Ma and Vijayalakshmi went directly from the car to their places along the inside wall of the hut, where blankets had been spread out on the floor. On the other side of the hut three Brahmin priests had set up an elaborate puja for the traditional Vedic rites that would be performed this morning.

Four hundred people lined up behind ropes held taut by poles. Large red cotton blankets were laid on the ground for Lee and his large party, just below the Yagashala, so that Lee sat directly below Yogi Ramsuratkumar and could also watch the ceremonies. Lee's students and Purna and his students sat close together around and behind Lee.

On the other end of the Yagashala the priests had begun the ancient ritual. They began the long chant with an invocation to the deities Indra, Agni and Soma, just as the Vedas proscribe. Many flower garlands were offered to Yogi Ramsuratkumar and Devaki, while the priests and others came to *pranam* gravely and make offerings to the living deity, Yogi Ramsuratkumar, and then to Devaki, who stood by Bhagawan's side while he sat on the floor. She held her hands in a *pranam* to Yogi Ramsuratkumar throughout the ritual. Devaki's eyes were focused on Yogi Ramsuratkumar, and it seemed that she continually turned everything that came her way to him.

There was much for a Westerner to learn on this morning about the guru and devotee relationship. The vast majority of Westerners are novices when it comes to devotion, sacrifice and self-effacement in love, whereas these qualities are still alive in the cellular structure of the Indians, passed down through generations of spiritual tradition over thousands of years. Westerners have to deal with the propensity for fierce independence and rebelliousness, which are often considered desirable manifestations in the Western psychological view. On the other hand, we were inspired by the selflessness and devotion to Yogi Ramsuratkumar demonstrated by Devaki and her companion, Vijayalakshmi. The qualities that are engendered through total self-sacrifice were evident in the invisible bonds between these two women and Yogi Ramsuratkumar. The inner circle of Yogi Ramsuratkumar's spiritual family was now pared down to Ma Devaki and Vijayalakshmi, who had made it through some very difficult sadhana. The result of their hard work shone in the purity and nobility of their relationship with their master, in their determination to serve, and in their total attention on Yogi Ramsuratkumar.

During the ceremony Suresh, the Brahmin priest who led the Vedic rites and was a devotee of Yogi Ramsuratkumar, interacted time and again with the master. Suresh performed the rites every year at the fire ceremony on *jayanthi*, and watching him with Yogi Ramsuratkumar it was easy to imagine why he was given this job. The demonstration of genuine love and the integrity of real devotion that flowed from Suresh to Yogi Ramsuratkumar was something that one could see, feel and absorb. He was an example of devotional love in action.

Lee watched the proceedings, his eyes glued to Yogi Ramsuratkumar. He was a living example of how to approach this ancient tradition as a Westerner. His attitude was one of deep respect, constraint, dignity and receptivity. He never barged into anything, but knew instinctively when to have restraint and forbearance. It seemed that he felt his way into all circumstances. He was not trying to prove anything or get anything. He was there to serve, praise and receive whatever the master, Yogi Ramsuratkumar, gave to him.

The crowds of people, which had been growing larger over the past two days, was now immense. People were fed breakfast in the dining hall in groups of over a hundred; one group would finish and leave, and quickly banana leaves were laid out for the next wave of people, who were ushered in for a delicious breakfast of spicy *sambar* and rice with vegetables. People also waited outside the gates to get in for darshan.

At ten o'clock Yogi Ramsuratkumar entered and took his seat on the dais in the dining hall with Devaki and Vijayalakshmi. He immediately asked Lee to talk to everyone. Lee stood up and faced the crowd, a mingled sea of white and dark faces. During the talk various Indian devotees came forward to give *prasad* to Yogi Ramsuratkumar. One came with a heavy, long garland made of hundreds of red roses and placed it around Yogi's neck.

After Lee's talk was over he asked two of his students to lead the chants. While they chanted an Indian man came up to offer *prasad*; he fell weeping at Yogi Ramsuratkumar's feet, then grabbed the beggar's knee and foot and pressed himself into him. Bhagawan put his hand on the man's back, like a mother comforting her child. The look on his face was completely serene. Finally the man stood up and pulled a beautiful red and white wool shawl out of a bag and draped it over Yogi Ramsuratkumar's already shawl-laden shoulders. He *pranamed* again and Yogi chuckled at the new shawl.

Yogi Ramsuratkumar asked the man to speak to the audience, so the man stood up, faced the crowd and began to speak in Tamil. He was wearing a large oval ring—a picture of Yogi Ramsuratkumar surrounded by diamonds that sparkled even in the dim light. In English he said, "Yogi Ramsuratkumar is God in human form . . . " A few minutes later he broke into English again and said, "For Lee Lozowick, the great American saint who has come here to worship Yogi Ramsuratkumar—Yogi Ramsuratkumar is Lee Lozowick's God in human form too. Lee has come here not from India or Asia, but from all the way around the world, from the United States. He has come with thirty-five devotees who are here because they too feel God in Yogi Ramsuratkumar . . . "

An older Indian man, obviously a long-time devotee, came up to give and receive *prasad*. Yogi Ramsuratkumar greeted him with great affection, took the huge, gorgeous red rose *mala* off and placed it around the man's neck. He had a chair brought up and placed beside the dais, which he offered to the older man, who sat there very quietly for the rest of the darshan. He seemed genuinely overwhelmed by the lavish gifts of the rose *mala* and the opportunity to sit beside Yogi Ramsuratkumar.

During this time people were running up to take photographs of Yogi Ramsuratkumar—two, three, four people at a time. Some of them would run and drop to their knees, skidding toward the dais with camera raised and poised. Yogi Ramsuratkumar raised his hands in blessing. The cameras flashed and Yogi Ramsuratkumar endured it while the man talked on. It was well known that the flashing lights of cameras hurt Yogi Ramsuratkumar's eyes, but it seemed that on this day Yogi Ramsuratkumar had generously given his permission for flash photos to be taken, or Selvaraj or Mani would have taken the cameras away.

The photographers sat down, satisfied for the moment, but then another man with a camera rushed up from the far side of the men's part of the room. Selvaraj stepped in to stop him. The man spoke to Selvaraj; he must have said, "I have permission," because Selvaraj reluctantly stepped back and allowed the man to go ahead. Yogi Ramsuratkumar blessed this man's photos as well, with one hand and then two raised in the air, looking directly into the camera.

Not long afterward a film crew arrived. They turned on intensely bright lights and filmed Yogi Ramsuratkumar, Devaki Ma and Vijayalakshmi, then moved the camera toward the man speaking, the men's side of the audience and then the women's side. The huge camera swung around again to film Yogi Ramsuratkumar from yet another angle, then again from various different angles. The video would air on a local television station later that night.

The speaker was now talking in Tamil. He walked over to the dais and touched Yogi

Ramsuratkumar's feet to demonstrate a point. Finally he finished his talk and his whole family—four or five people—came up to the dais to give and receive *prasad* from Yogi Ramsuratkumar. They placed another shawl over Yogi Ramsuratkumar's shoulders. More photographs were taken as people crowded in with cameras and lights flashed. It seemed to be going toward excess. Even though permission had been granted, it seemed that more sensitivity and restraint could have been exercised in view of Yogi Ramsuratkumar's tenuous physical condition.

Now the family was putting two more shawls on the yogi, so that he had on the three shawls that he was already wearing, plus three more. He was laden down with shawls, and their heaviness seemed like a symbol of his awesome burden. In many ways it was a heartbreaking scene to witness. For a moment he looked like a very rare and precious creature who had been captured and held in a strange, willing captivity. Love poured forth from him; he was the fountain of everlasting love.

A little boy ran up to take pictures. Yogi Ramsuratkumar blessed him with one hand up, and immediately four or five men who had been taking pictures all along rushed up to get in on the opportunity. Yogi Ramsuratkumar gave to all. They sat down and Devaki took the three new shawls off of Yogi Ramsuratkumar's shoulders very carefully. Another man was invited up to see Yogi Ramsuratkumar. After kneeling and receiving his blessing, the man stood and faced the crowd. He chanted for a moment, then began to speak in Tamil. For our benefit perhaps, at one point he said, "Remain at the door of the guru like a dog!" then repeated it twice.

It was hot today in the Indian winter. The air steamed around us and we sweated. All the ceiling fans were turned on in the hall—except the fans above Yogi Ramsuratkumar, who must have been sweltering under all his woolen shawls. Devaki and Vijayalakshmi were also wearing heavy wool shawls over their white saris. The man was still speaking in Tamil and sometimes quoting Sanskrit scripture, then expounding on it. In English he mentioned Lee, then the United States and France and the "Influence" of Yogi Ramsuratkumar.

As soon as his talk was over Yogi Ramsuratkumar left the room. He did not ask Lee and the small group of men to sit on the dais as he had every other time when he left darshan. Instead his seat was left empty with scattered red rose petals and two full red roses that had dropped from the garland. The empty dais seemed like a forecast of things to come, when Yogi Ramsuratkumar would leave his body someday in the years ahead. During these days the bittersweet certainty that the aging beggar saint would drop his body and return to his Father in Heaven was a constant faint refrain in the symphony of life in the company of Yogi Ramsuratkumar.

There was no chanting ringing through the hall when we came into darshan that afternoon. I noticed that Yogi Ramsuratkumar and Devaki were looking at the poetry book and pointing to something. It had been clear that they had been reading and looking through the poetry book back at Sudama House in between darshans for several days, as they had a bookmark placed in it that kept moving forward in the book. One day, walking past Sudama House in the afternoon, we could hear Devaki inside, reading the poetry aloud.

Yogi Ramsuratkumar called Lee up right away and pointed to the prayer in Bengali that appears in the book at the beginning of the poems.

"It's in Bengali, Bhagawan," Devaki said.

"What is this?" Yogi Ramsuratkumar asked Lee.

"It says in Bengali, 'May the heat of suffering become the fire of love,'" Lee answered, then added, "It's a prayer."

"Oh. A prayer," as if this were the most wondrous thing possible.

Yogi Ramsuratkumar asked, "Where did this prayer come from?"

"I wrote it," Lee answered.

"What language is it in?" the beggar asked again, very sweetly.

"It is in Bengali," Lee answered. Devaki nodded.

"Do you read Bengali?" Yogi Ramsuratkumar asked.

"No," Lee answered.

"Ohhh . . ." the beggar seemed to absorb all this information into the vastness of himself, then after a pause he held out his hand toward the crowd that waited almost breathlessly in their seats on the floor.

"Say something..." His voice trailed away, and the silence hinted at that which was implied but unspoken in his communication to Lee.

Lee stood and talked about how the prayer, "May the heat of suffering become the fire of love," typifies the work that Yogi Ramsuratkumar does with his devotees. He spoke about the necessity to embrace all of the blessings of Father in Heaven, and to praise Yogi Ramsuratkumar not only when things are going well, but in times of suffering and difficulty. The highest practice is to understand and accept that whatever comes our way is the will of God. When we begin to praise God regardless of what is going on in our lives, then we can begin to participate in the work of Yogi Ramsuratkumar, and "the heat of suffering" may "become the fire of love." This kind of spiritual practice is sometimes called "conscious suffering."

Lee concluded by saying, "Yogi Ramsuratkumar is so compassionate and generous—like the Shankaracharya's prayer, "May all beings be happy and prosperous"—that He wishes His devotees to be happy. But also there is only God, unitive, all one, no separation, no matter what suffering we may encounter. That realization itself is a source of happiness—to know that no matter what happens to us, it is God's Will."

His words were impassioned as he spoke about realizing God and surrendering to the will of God. Lee's talks were an ongoing plea to live by a higher law, according to dharma, and to lift ourselves into the reality of the truth of oneness—"There is only God." Lee strove to take his listeners to a place beyond the supplication for Yogi Ramsuratkumar's benevolence in the form of miracles and blessings—in which one seeks only to have a better life, more comforts and good times—into a joyous obligation and conscious relationship with the Divine.

Soon three or four of the men who had taken pictures in the morning came up again and started taking more pictures, their flash bulbs going off in rapid succession. A little later the person who had been the most assertive in running up and taking photos with his flash camera ran up, fell to his knees and skidded forward toward the dais with his camera flashing.

"Enough!" Yogi Ramsuratkumar said emphatically, his incredible patience and generosity stretched to the limit. He pointed the man ferociously, imperiously, toward his seat.

"A gift, from Father to son," Mani said with a smile as he handed Lee one of the bronze ghee lamps that had been used in the temple the day before, imprinted with the image of Yogi Ramsuratkumar's face, his palmyra fan and coconut bowl. The day after *jayanthi* was Deepam, the great Shiva festival of light when the top of Mount Arunachala, which had been covered with huge amounts of ghee, would be set alight. Crowds had been amassing in town for the past two or three days in preparation for this holy day. Busloads of people were parked near the ashram, and people congregated around the ashram gate. The streets in town were literally rivers of people, pilgrims and sadhus.

Mani smiled and said to Lee, "Yogi is very happy that so many have taken food here yesterday. Twelve hundred people!" That was surprising news because the gigantic effort of preparing, cooking and serving that many people had been largely invisible and quiet. Today promised to bring more masses of supplicants to the ashram.

After Yogi Ramsuratkumar had driven through and gone to breakfast Mani and his staff passed along the news that no more photos could be taken. In fact, no more cameras would be allowed in Bhagawan's presence because the flash from the cameras the day before had hurt his eyes. This apparently did not include the video camera we had brought, because Purna was allowed to continue to roll the film. Mani talked to one of the Indian men who was standing in line for the "drive by" darshan. In a serious tone he said, "If you have a camera on you we will take it now and gladly give you a receipt for your donation to the ashram!" Hearing the way Mani was handling things for Yogi Ramsuratkumar, Lee beamed and said, "I love that man!"

Yogi Ramsuratkumar arrived for the morning darshan. There was a line of hundreds queued up through the ashram gate and out into the streets, and more people were coming, wanting to receive his darshan on this auspicious day. Lee's group, first the men, then the women, went through the temple first and then made our way over to the hall where darshan would be held. The hall quickly filled up with about three hundred people. Time moved slowly past while chanting was lead by two women from Lee's party, then two Indian men played bamboo flutes. More chants were led as the room continued to fill with more people. The dais remained empty, but the presence of Yogi Ramsuratkumar was sublime and filled the space.

The presence deepened and thickened in the room. Though physically still seated in the temple, Yogi Ramsuratkumar was pouring his benediction down like a steady, gentle rain. The group endlessly chanted his name. Eleven o'clock came and went, and Yogi Ramsuratkumar's platform remained empty. He was not coming into the darshan hall. We chanted some more, and some more.

Darshan ended with the "Mangalam" chant. We sat for a few moments while some of the Indian women brought around baskets of flowers. Each woman was given a rose for her hair. The platform was empty—his form was not there—and yet the living presence of Yogi Ramsuratkumar flowed like *amrita*. He had been in the temple all morning blessing the lines of people who came in droves seeking his darshan on this day. He was still there when everyone else had lunch. They had closed the gate at nine o'clock that morning after the first large group of people were let in, then the gates were opened again to let more people in.

When Yogi Ramsuratkumar arrived an hour early for the afternoon darshan he had the car stopped at the entrance to the temple. Mani ran over to confer with him. Immediately Mani and the other staff were catapulted into action: holes were dug, poles were set in place and ropes were strung to cordon off a lane where people could file past outside the temple, where the crowds would have the darshan of Yogi Ramsuratkumar on this auspicious evening of Deepam.

Outside the ashram gates hoards of people were swarming, pushing up against the gate to see the beggar saint. Out on Chengam Road and everywhere around the mountain crowds of ecstatic people, anxious to circumambulate the holy hill of Arunachala and gain untold scores of blessings in the act, jammed the streets. The overflow was surging against the gates of Yogi Ramsuratkumar Ashram.

When the stage was properly set, Yogi Ramsuratkumar was helped into his chair, which had been brought out of the temple and set on a large blanket. Mani and Selvaraj stood nearby while Devaki and Vijayalakshmi settled into their seats on the ground next to Yogi Ramsuratkumar. Devaki looked carefully to see what he might need, making adjustments here and there. On this day it was Yogi Ramsuratkumar's wish that the Westerners be given the seats directly in front of him. Lee was seated in front of and facing Yogi Ramsuratkumar, about ten feet away, with his students behind him and then Krishna Carcelle and his friends from Mauritius. Behind them, alongside the temple, stood or sat Yogi Ramsuratkumar's Indian devotees—two or three hundred people who were allowed to stay for the entire darshan. Together we all chanted, *Yogi Ramsuratkumar, Yogi Ramsuratkumar, Yogi Ramsuratkumar, Jaya Guru Raya,* for the next two hours. In the meantime streams of people filed past behind the ropes, having the opportunity to glimpse the saint. There were thousands of people who came filing through.

While everyone waited with high anticipation for the light to appear on the summit of Arunachala, silent preparations went on behind and around him to feed masses of people at the special feast that would be served later that night. Selvaraj and Mani waited to light the ghee pot that had been arranged on top of a ladder behind Yogi Ramsuratkumar; another pot of ghee had been arranged on top of the temple, where two men were stationed to light it in concert with the lighting of the fire on the mountain. These signified that Arunachala Shiva was here, in the form of Yogi Ramsuratkumar, and in the form of the temple itself.

Through all this Yogi Ramsuratkumar was unconcerned, childlike, tranquil. His gaze wandered often over the temple, which drew his attention again and again. He wore sunglasses against the glare of the westerly light, his eyes obviously still bothering him from the photo sessions. Devaki had gotten the sunglasses out, carefully cleaned them and then handed them to Bhagawan. He seemed very still behind their protective shade. She also called for a folded blanket to put under his feet so they wouldn't hang uncomfortably one or two inches above the ground.

Dusk fell slowly while the chanting flowed on and time seemed to stretch out into infinity. Behind the beggar saint the workers walked back and forth along the pathway from the kitchen to the temple, carrying heavy pots full of food for the feast. Three men struggled along to carry one hundred and fifty pound pots of rice and *sambar*. Women in bright saris hurried past with large bundles of banana leaf plates. The ashram cow was brought out of her shed behind Yogi Ramsuratkumar. She faced him and mooed loudly, then ate her dinner—a pile of hay—while standing and facing Yogi Ramsuratkumar and the mountain.

Finally Arunachala was lit. The crowd yelled and cheered with excitement and fireworks went off nearby and further away in town. Everyone was uplifted, thrilled at the sight of this grand symbol of Shiva's sovereignty over the three worlds, and his embodiment in the holy mountain. While all this ruckus and commotion went on, Yogi Ramsuratkumar sat still, unmoved, serene, just watching, looking up at the temple, looking over the crowd.

By now it was dark enough that Yogi Ramsuratkumar had taken the sunglasses off. His eyes were slightly unfocused and yet his gaze seemed very intentional. It was a burning, smoky gaze that wandered over everything, missing nothing, taking it all in. Another light—an iron pot filled with ghee set up on a ladder—sprang to life, along with the light on the high roof of the temple. In this moment the excitement and joy of all the Indians was highly contagious. It seemed to me that a powerful collective thought form rose up into the atmosphere, "Yogi Ramsuratkumar is our Arunachala Shiva! Shiva is alive, here at Agrahara Kollai, the Yogi Ramsuratkumar Ashram!"

Ma Devaki performed the *arati puja* to Yogi Ramsuratkumar, waving lights before the living deity, offering water, incense and flowers to his feet. When the puja was completed Devaki and Vijayalakshmi circumambulated Yogi Ramsuratkumar several times then *pranamed* at his feet. They led the chant, *Arunachala Shiva, Arunachala Shiva, Arunachala Shiva, Arunejeda.* Very soon after this Yogi Ramsuratkumar and the women left for Sudama House. Lee and his group were quickly instructed to take the back path behind the temple to the beautiful, finished front entry hall where a lavish, celebratory meal would be served.

As we hurried along the dirt path in the dusk the full moon was rising in the sky. It was mellow and golden, seen through the dust and smoke of the Indian night. A herd of cows walked along in a field on the other side of the ashram wall under dim stars that were just beginning to shine. In the distance were mountains that, in their rugged rockiness, looked very much like southern Arizona in the hot dark night. Palm trees and flowering shrubs loomed green and lush and shadowy out of the dusty ground. Fireworks, horns and shouts of joy pierced the calm night air with the sounds of ecstasy and chaos that abounded among the wild throngs of people that moved through the streets in long rivers of humanity.

With bare feet on the sandy ground we rushed to dinner—a six-course feast was served in the beautiful ornate entrance room of the temple. Its shiny black marble floor was cool to the touch. Large pictures of Ramana Maharshi and his mother, Sri Aurobindo and Mother Meera, and Papa Ramdas and Mataji Krishnabai hung on the walls. We left as soon as we were finished to make room for the next wave: the ashram would feed twenty-five hundred people there before the night was over.

"Yogi Ramsuratkumar understands human psychology," Lee began his talk in darshan the next morning. He began to speak about Yogi Ramsuratkumar's teaching to only speak well of others—to praise—but the human tendency is to criticize others. He said, "When we gossip we are trying to belittle others and make ourselves seem bigger. But we don't have to try to get some advantage over others through gossip and criticism. Yogi Ramsuratkumar has said to me many times, 'This beggar only wants praise.' But the important thing to remember is that even one who has much darkness in them also has some light."

After the talk Yogi Ramsuratkumar turned back to the new poetry book. First he sold three books, then he asked Suresh, the Brahmin priest who had conducted the Vedic rites on *jayanthi* day, to speak about the meaning of Deepam. Suresh spoke in his flawless English:

> The festival of Deepam is about the indescribable Supreme Reality which cannot be fathomed in words or intellectual arguments. That Supreme is pure compassion, and is available to us in the form of the holy hill Arunachala. In the scriptures, the *Puranas* and such, there is a legend that tells of a competition between Vishnu and Brahma over who is the greatest in all the Universe.
>
> In the middle of that argument Lord Shiva appeared as a limitless column of fire whose beginning and end could not be fathomed by anyone, by Vishnu or Brahma. Vishnu tried to find the bottom of it in his form as a boar, and Brahma tried to find the top of it in his form as a swan. But they could not. Then Lord Shiva appeared, beginningless and endless, and said, "Out of my compassion for every living being in the world I have taken the form of this holy hill."
>
> So Arunachala signifies the compassion of the Divine, and that is why the light is lit on the hill and devotees come from everywhere to attain merits by going around the hill. Lord Arunachalesvara we also have here in the form of Yogi Ramsuratkumar. He is that Supreme which cannot be attained through words or arguments. Therefore, I have no more words to

> describe this; only surrender, surrender, surrender at the Holy Feet of Yogi Ramsuratkumar.

After Suresh sat down Yogi Ramsuratkumar asked Lee to give a talk. Lee spoke about an article titled "Simple Living and High Thinking," that appeared in a yoga magazine published in Florida that Yogi Ramsuratkumar had read many times in darshan last year. The article relayed a story about a well-to-do man traveling on a train who goes out of his way to help an old woman with a lot of baggage, and then slips away, avoiding the tip that she wants to give him, thinking him to be a poor porter. Most people are too self-important to serve in this invisible way, seeking no acknowledgment or praise, but being fulfilled by the service itself. Lee continued with his talk:

> Yogi Ramsuratkumar is not an individual anymore. In 1952 He was "murdered" by Papa Ramdas. He is only the One, the continuous unity. There is only His Father in Heaven. However we found our way here, we are so fortunate to have this auspicious opportunity, to have found Yogi Ramsuratkumar in this lifetime, to be in his company.
>
> In the Bible it says that those who have the eyes to see will see the Christ, and those who don't, won't. For those who have the eyes to see Yogi Ramsuratkumar, he is pure light, pure Blessing Force. Others may think he is just an eccentric, but we should know that it is incredibly auspicious to find him in this life. It is unspeakably sacred to be able to sit at the feet of such a one. There is nothing he needs, nothing he wants—he is only here to serve the work of his Father in Heaven. If out of our deep gratitude we wish to give something back to him, we can consider simple living and high thinking.

Yogi Ramsuratkumar took Lee's hands in his own for a long time. Closing his eyes, he seemed to be working in some interior depth of himself, then he opened his eyes and looked long and deeply at Lee. He lovingly stroked Lee's arms and hands, then asked Lee to have someone lead chants.

During this long stretch of chanting Yogi Ramsuratkumar picked up *Death of a Dishonest Man* and began to look through it page by page. He slowly turned the pages, carefully and gently lifting each one. He was reverent with the book, holding it tenderly, gingerly. He had done this with the book the previous two days also, going page by page through quite a bit of it. Devaki pointed out the songs in the back of the book and his attention focused there. He looked up and called Lee over.

"Lee, this beggar would like to hear some of these songs," he said, pointing to the lyrics in the back of the book. Lee nodded his head, stood up, walked over to me and knelt down in one swift motion. He handed me the heavy poetry book and gave me a penetrating look.

"He wants some of the songs sung. Pick out two or three that you and Mira can do—be quick about it." Mirabai, who had been leading the chant with two other women, walked over while the women kept chanting. Stunned, we realized that we didn't remember the melodies to hardly any of these rock & roll songs, and furthermore, they would be incredibly difficult to sing without all the instrumental arrangements backing them up.

We quickly discussed what to do and stood up, *pranamed* to Yogi Ramsuratkumar a little sheepishly and faced the large crowd. We faltered and fumbled through three or four songs, making up melodies wherever we didn't remember the original tune, which was often. It was an agonizing but grand moment—grand because it was Yogi Ramsuratkumar's *lila*. Finally Lee walked over and said, "Okay, you're off the hook."

Yogi Ramsuratkumar was smiling broadly, looking very delighted and happy as we turned and *pranamed* to him and then took our seats. Lee faced the crowd and said that Yogi Ramsuratkumar had asked him to sing.

Lee never sang without his bands and was actually quite shy about singing, but if Yogi Ramsuratkumar asked it of him, he would do it. He apologized, explaining that the songs were meant to have instrumental backup; he charmed and melted the crowd with his explanations of the songs. His willingness to do something so obviously difficult for him disarmed everyone as the crowd laughed gently along with him.

After singing two or three songs, Lee turned to Yogi Ramsuratkumar and knelt at his feet to receive his blessings. Yogi Ramsuratkumar left shortly after that, instructing Lee to gather the usual group of men to sit with him on the dais—Alain de Rosenbo and Bret sat on the dais as usual, and now that Krishna Carcelle had gone back to Mauritius, Purna took his place in this group of Westerners.

After darshan Lee said to me, "Yogi says you and Mira can practice these songs and be prepared to sing tomorrow, so pick out some and work on them tonight. You can pull in other people if you want to on some of them..." This was definitely the unexpected. After dinner Mira and I took off to work on the songs. We found three that we could do together and two more that we would do with a small group of women. By the next morning, after practicing again, we would be ready.

At six o'clock in the morning it was still dark when the coffee arrived and was poured into stainless steel cups. Most of our large group sat together in the twilight predawn and sipped our coffee. A deep peace pervaded the air of the ashram. The sight of the full moon setting in banks of dark blue clouds evoked a strong mood; called *chandra* in Sanskrit, the moon is the image most often used by Baul poets to describe Lord Krishna, particularly in his form as Govinda, lover of the *gopis*. Everything seemed to speak of Yogi Ramsuratkumar, who would arrive soon in his car, and another day on the ashram would begin with its constant rhythms of darshan, chanting and *prasad*.

At the ten o'clock darshan Yogi Ramsuratkumar went straight into the business at hand. As soon as Devaki and Vijayalakshmi had finished singing the opening chants Devaki marked the songs in the poetry book with a piece of paper. Yogi Ramsuratkumar called Lee over, they conferred, then Lee came walking over to me.

"Wait until you hear this," he said, his voice full of delight at Yogi Ramsuratkumar's play. "Okay," he continued, "He wants the songs sung one by one, all the way through—*all* of them." This news sank in as I remembered that there were thirty-six songs in the back of the poetry book. All of our well-rehearsed plans crumbled to dust before my eyes.

"Can we skip around, do the ones we know best first?" I asked, getting more nervous by the minute; after all, we would be singing before Yogi Ramsuratkumar and two or three hundred people. It was impossible to be detached, and we naturally wanted the singing to be, at least, a pleasant experience for the listeners.

"No," Lee said. "Do them in order."

"We really don't remember the melodies to most of them, and some of them, four or five of them, haven't even been composed yet and have no music to them!" All this rushed out in a whisper, letting Lee in on the full extent of our predicament—as if he didn't already know. I could hear a voice inside saying, "Don't make excuses, just obey the guru."

"Make it up!" he whispered cheerfully.

I quickly assessed the situation. Mira hadn't arrived yet, and I would obviously be on my own for at least the first song or two. At the same time, I was happy beyond measure to have this opportunity to be at play with Yogi Ramsuratkumar, as I knew that he loved music, chanting and song. It would be a great gift to be able to bring a smile to his face with Lee's songs—playing the fool seemed a small price to pay. I took a deep breath and got up, *pranamed* to Yogi Ramsuratkumar and faced the audience.

I made up melodies on the spot, rambled around and bumbled through the first few songs feeling quite awkward. Although I love to sing, I do not have the voice of a soloist, and I was greatly relieved to see Mirabai through the windows in the back of the hall, walking as fast as she could in our direction. In a few more seconds she was standing beside me, although most of the time we couldn't sing the songs together because we were making up the melodies as we went, so we began to switch off songs until we got to the first Shri song that we had prepared to sing together. On two of the well-known songs a group of four women got up and sang with us. What a relief! It sounded very lovely. Then we were back to flying by the seat of our pants!

This went on for an hour and a half as we worked through the lyrics page by page, making most of the melodies up, doing our best to just sing. This was not a place for ego to exult, although later it seemed that we were more critical of our "performance" than everyone else thought we should be. It was much like being melted down—the intensity of the beggar's fire was much more than appearances could ever show, or that words could describe.

When it was over Yogi Ramsuratkumar called us up to the dais. One by one he asked our names. Mirabai went first and received *prasad* while I knelt on the floor behind her. Then it was my turn. I was determined not to make the same mistake that I had made before by just saying "Mary" when he asked my name. I moved up close to the dais where he sat. He picked up an apple from his tray of *prasad*.

"What is your name?" he asked sweetly.

"Mary Young," I said with confidence, as if I knew now for sure that this was my name. He burst into peals of laughter, threw his head back in a fit of delight. I had managed to crack him up. I smiled broadly and laughed with him. Devaki laughed too, and Lee had a big smile on his face as he sat in his chair watching and listening. Yogi Ramsuratkumar's body shook with laughter. His laughter was so incredible that it was worth any amount of foolishness to entice that sound into the world. The laughter died down and, with a little smile lingering on his face, Yogi Ramsuratkumar moved into a blessing pose with one hand up.

"My Father blesses Young," he said, using just my last name, and it seemed that included all the names that I might go by. He said it so tenderly that I think no one heard but me. He held both hands up and his eyes penetrated past me into lifetimes and beyond. When he was like this it seemed that he was reading the *akashic* records. His piercing gaze moved up above my head and to the right side of my body and just beyond, looking over lifetimes, past and future, clearing away debris and refuse.

In these moments he seemed to be untying knots of *samskaras* and cleaning up old karma. He was radiating benediction into the karmic momentum of one life, interjecting grace into that which would inexorably unfold across future incarnations. It is through grace that he hastens and accelerates the process of evolution, because he exists as the pure Will of God incarnate, here and now. This quickening of the soul's evolution is a great boon, but not necessarily pleasant to experience when one exists in the gross state, carrying all the illusory but tenacious and desperate baggage of ego. We cling to these identities of separation as if they were our paradise.

Everything Yogi Ramsuratkumar did proceeded from the unknown, fresh and gleaming with mystery, but as Mani had said days before, "with a fire underneath." The flame—*jyoti*—of Yogi Ramsuratkumar, the living saint of Tiruvannamalai, was a compelling conflagration. He held me with his eyes while I burned for a short while, captured in his roaring blaze. His hands fell down and the doorway to infinity closed.

"Thank you," he said, so gently it was like being brushed with the wings of a butterfly. This was the second time since we had arrived that he had thanked me. What a strange thing to hear from his lips! It gave me pause to consider—what would it mean to be worthy of such thanks? After a final *pranam* I sat down in my seat beside Mirabai, about ten feet away from the dais and directly in front of Yogi Ramsuratkumar. He looked at us for a long while, then he said again, "Thank you."

Yogi Ramsuratkumar called Lee up to the dais. His eyes were sparkling as they spoke together in quiet tones.

"Lee, this beggar would like them to sing some songs tomorrow," he began.

"Do you mean the songs that were just sung?" Lee asked.

"Some of your songs to this beggar," Yogi Ramsuratkumar answered.

"Does he mean the poems?" Lee turned to Devaki, asking for confirmation of what he understood.

"*Poems of a Broken Heart*," Devaki said.

"They can prepare some for tomorrow," Yogi Ramsuratkumar said, with a twinkle in his eyes, glancing over at us. Immediately after that he left with the Sudama sisters while the chanting continued for another thirty-five minutes, until darshan was over at noon. Lee and the men sat on the dais as soon as he was gone. Lee looked at Mirabai and me from the dais and clapped delicately, like a well-heeled lady at the opera, with a mischievous and benign smile on his face. He was smiling with enjoyment. Anything that pleased and delighted Yogi Ramsuratkumar pleased and delighted Lee. It was not an exercise in doing things "right" by linear or worldly standards. It was about lending oneself to the crucible in which Yogi Ramsuratkumar was doing his work.

After darshan as we stood outside the dining hall Lee stepped up and said gleefully, "Guess what you're going to do next! He wants you to sing the poems!"

After Devaki and Vijayalakshmi sang the opening chants in the afternoon darshan the chanting of Yogi Ramsuratkumar's name went on for an hour. Then Yogi Ramsuratkumar asked Lee to speak. He talked about the stories of Krishna and Arjuna in the *Bhagavad Gita.*

Then he told the story of Sudama, Krishna's childhood friend. Krishna lived in a palace with riches and silks, while Sudama was only a poor, starving priest, but one of great sanctity and integrity. His wife begged Sudama to go to his old friend Krishna, now rich and wealthy, with whom he had been *gurubhai* so long ago, for help. Sudama took a few grains of rice and offered them to Krishna, and Krishna said, "If you offer one grain of rice to me in true devotion, then you are blessed." Lee commented further on this teaching:

> It is really ourselves, not gold and riches, that we should offer to the Divine. We should offer not wealth and material things, but ourselves. In martial arts one bows to the teacher with open hands to signify a giving of one's self. So whatever is offered with pure faith, with pure devotion, that is what God wants, and it is received. In the West we think our offering to the Divine is a business deal—"If I give this to the guru, then the guru will give me that." But it's not a business deal. What we give is ourselves...
>
> In Yogi Ramsuratkumar there is nothing there—no desires, no ego. Yogi Ramsuratkumar went to Ramdas and gave himself, and what Ramdas gave in return was madness. We want to make a deal with the guru, but the guru makes no deals; the guru doesn't decide what to give us when we give ourselves. The guru is a pure vehicle of the will of God, of grace. Whatever blessings, whatever gifts of the Divine that are given, these are freely given—there is no return expected, nothing is asked for.
>
> So we approach the Divine with open hands, offer our souls, our spirits, for whatever Yogi Ramsuratkumar's Father in Heaven can use us for, and we surrender to that, whatever that is. If we offer even one grain of rice with pure devotion and pure faith, then the Divine gives freely, opens Its vast and limitless storehouse and gives freely.

After the talk was finished Lee went to the dais and knelt beside Yogi Ramsuratkumar, who closed his eyes and held Lee's hands. Yogi Ramsuratkumar raised his hands in blessing and said quietly, "My Father blesses Lee." Then, with much more force and a mischievous chuckle, Yogi Ramsuratkumar said, "My Father will give you what you *need!*" He chuckled again and smiled sweetly, patting Lee on the back lovingly, and the darshan was soon over.

After dinner Lee and company went to the house where he would be giving a public talk. Mirabai and I stayed behind. Not being composers, we stayed up very late, putting some of Lee's poetry to song, using the melodies of old folk songs.

The next day Yogi Ramsuratkumar did not say a word to Lee about the singing of the poems. Instead of singing, Lee and numbers of his students were now giving talks. Whoever gave a talk or led chants then had the opportunity to go to Yogi Ramsuratkumar and receive *prasad*. "Your name?" he asked, listening carefully to the reply, then dropping an orange, banana or apple into the waiting cupped hands of the devotee.

Sadhu Rangarajan came with his group of about twenty people from the satsang in South Africa where they chant Ramnam together. They were invited up to the dais as a group to give and receive *prasad* while Sadhu Rangarajan sat nearby at the beggar's knee. Soon Yogi Ramsuratkumar asked Rangarajan to give a talk. He began his talk by explaining that the word "avatar" means a descended manifestation of the Supreme Reality, the nameless and formless. Rangarajan then proceeded to speak about the importance of spiritual practice with great enthusiasm and zest:

> The *Vedas* try to explain that reality but cannot, because it is incomprehensible, beyond intellect, infinite. That reality, out of mercy and kindness, appears in physical form as a human being from time to time. The God Incarnate—Rama himself—declared, "I have come down in human form!"
>
> The descent of every avatar has a specific purpose. The Supreme Reality appears amidst us in human form or some other form to draw us toward it and raise us to consciousness, existence and bliss—sat, chit, ananda. To be born as a human being is a great gift. From a strict Vedic or Vedantic viewpoint, we have not attained the stature of human being at all. To distinguish between the appearances of things, of the world, and that which is beyond appearances, is to be human, but our minds are carried away by sensual pleasure, pride, greed....
>
> Even if you take human form, you do not necessarily use your discriminatory faculty. Only very few take to this path, which is to know that there is a higher God, *mahapurusha*, the guru—the one who dispels darkness and ignorance, the one who lifts us up from darkness into light, the guru. It is the guru who lifts us from the world of mortality to the world of immortality.

> Just putting a *mala* around the guru's neck is not enough. We have to surrender at the guru's feet. We have to learn the right way to approach the mahatma. The task before us is to totally surrender to his feet, through austerity, renunciation, absolute ahimsa [nonviolence].
>
> Yogi Ramsuratkumar, Ramdas and Krishnabai have prescribed for us to do Ramnam in all our daily tasks, offered to the Ultimate Reality, Ram. The purpose of our life in this world is to realize Ram. Atma Rama. Krishnabai asks us to chant Ramnam for world peace. You should do whatever you can every day, for five minutes, for fifteen minutes, whatever you can do. Even when you work in your office or in the kitchen, your mind can chant Ramnam mantra. When we churn the milk, the gopis synchronized the mantra with the churning. By the grace of Bhagawan, due to the merits of previous births, you get this mantra to chant.
>
> Now Yogi Ramsuratkumar has commanded Rangarajan to spread Ramnam all over the world. And now we chant, "Yogi Ramsuratkumar, Yogi Ramsuratkumar, Yogi Ramsuratkumar, Jaya Guru Raya." Rama's name is more powerful than Ram himself; Yogi Ramsuratkumar's name is four times more powerful than the name of Ram. It is like a homeopathic pill—it is more powerful than the thing Itself, Ram. Yogi Ramsuratkumar is Ram in physical form before us.

In Lee's afternoon talk, he said that many devotees aspire to very high things—realization or enlightenment—but don't stop to think of the price that has to be paid for such a treasure. Referring to the annihilation of ego that is implied in Yogi Ramsuratkumar's statement, "Papa Ramdas killed this beggar in 1952," Lee said, "Yogi Ramsuratkumar is mad," then he expounded:

> The rational mind cannot grasp what it means to become mad in God, but there are many examples of realization or surrender to God in the Hindu tradition, like Shirdi Sai Baba, Anandamayi Ma, Ramana Maharshi, Ramakrishna. We desire to serve God, but we should think twice before we ask for madness. When we ask for divine madness, we don't realize what a difficult master Father in Heaven is. He demands things of us that no human being can possibly demand—our wishes, our hopes. Father in Heaven demands everything of us.
>
> When we visited Yogi Ramsuratkumar many years ago he took us for walks around Arunachalesvara Temple, and he would bless all the sadhus there, speak with them and care for them where they rested around the bathing ghat. What joy it brought him to bless the sadhus and talk with them! But he can't do that anymore. He is a prisoner, a Slave of God . . . Yogi Ramsuratkumar can't go on a vacation like most of us!

All the Westerners and many of the Indians laughed at this. Lee continued, "Yogi Ramsuratkumar has no such luxury—he can't even walk out on the street anymore, because the fame of his greatness has grown so that if he goes out into the streets he is engulfed by many eager devotees. He is a prisoner of Father in Heaven. Now his only pleasure is to pour out the blessings of his Father in Heaven upon us . . ."

Lee told the story of the man who once came to darshan to give *prasad*. As this man *pranamed* Yogi Ramsuratkumar was so visibly moved and grateful that he had tears in his eyes. Later someone asked, "Bhagawan, why do you have such gratitude to that man?" Yogi replied, "That man has a tea stall near the temple and when this beggar lived on the street, that man gave him tea."

"Did you go to his stall every day?" the devotee asked. Yogi Ramsuratkumar answered, "Oh, this beggar only went once a month," and yet his gratitude for this small kindness was immense.

Lee continued, posing a question:

> If Yogi Ramsuratkumar felt this much gratitude for such small favors, how much more difficult must it be to work for Father in Heaven? The hardest work in the world is to work for Father in Heaven. To work for orphans or to feed the poor is very fine work, very necessary work, but very easy work compared to the work Yogi Ramsuratkumar does for His Father in Heaven.
>
> Yogi Ramsuratkumar just says, "My Father blesses you." He doesn't ask if you deserve it, or ask any questions, or for anything in return. He just gives endlessly. At the same time his sacrifice and his burden is so great. Just think, if you or I didn't even have the freedom to walk out of our house without being torn apart by avid devotees! But Yogi Ramsuratkumar wanted this madness. He went to Aurobindo, Ramana Maharshi and Ramdas to get it. Ramdas gave the madness to him: the beggar, gone, finished, nothing left but Father in Heaven! Wouldn't it be wonderful if, in some small way, we returned this sacrifice somehow?
>
> Yogi Ramsuratkumar asks for nothing in return. His life is surrender to the blessing of Father in Heaven. Yogi Ramsuratkumar's blessings flow endlessly, 365 days a year, eternally, forever, just giving and giving. To return some infinitesimal fraction of what Yogi Ramsuratkumar has given us, we chant his name. His form here in darshan is the most amazing gift possible, but to chant his name is what he has given us. The minute you speak or think his name, Yogi Ramsuratkumar is there.
>
> So he has given us this great mystical secret—to chant his name, to remember his name, to think of his name. This we can do, as our gratitude for what he has given. His name is magic—the great mystical secret of the Universe. His name is the name of Father in Heaven. It is the mantra of Father in Heaven. It is the sound of Father in Heaven. Chanting his name

opens the majesty and mystery of the Universe to us.

The next day Lee told the following story in darshan: A European woman who had known Yogi Ramsuratkumar many years before came back to visit him. She was disappointed by the changes she saw in the circumstance around Yogi Ramsuratkumar, and perceived that he had changed. She said sadly, "Oh, I remember when you were dancing on the mountain, so full of joy twenty years ago . . ."

Yogi Ramsuratkumar asked incredulously, "Not now?"

Commenting on the realization of the changeless, stainless, eternal reality that was communicated in the teaching of the master's response, Lee said, "Essentially, who Yogi Ramsuratkumar *is* does not change. It is impossible for him to change. For Yogi Ramsuratkumar this body is like this *kirta* top." Lee touched his shirt to demonstrate. He continued:

> When the shirt has served its purpose it will be taken off and put aside. When Yogi Ramsuratkumar takes off the kirta of this body and throws it away, we may feel abandoned, but we won't be abandoned. He won't have gone anywhere. He will always be here.
>
> Faith is certainty. Faith is solid, absolutely reliable. Faith is a certainty, a recognition, a heart understanding of reality as it is. If we only have belief, then we will feel disappointed and abandoned by Yogi Ramsuratkumar when he leaves his body behind. But if we have faith, nothing can shake that certainty and knowledge of our connection with Yogi Ramsuratkumar and the blessings of Father in Heaven.

Lee walked back to the dais and knelt beside Yogi Ramsuratkumar with his hands pressed together.

"Read these poems," Yogi Ramsuratkumar said, gently handing Lee what looked like a sheaf of paper with poems handwritten on them, which Lee had given to him when he first arrived. Lee stood and read for about fifteen or twenty minutes while Yogi Ramsuratkumar peeled a banana and then held it with an almost trembling intensity for a long time. At one point Yogi Ramsuratkumar held the peeled banana out toward Lee as if he couldn't wait to give it to him. There were several long poems, and as Lee read through them Yogi Ramsuratkumar handed the peeled banana to Devaki. With a look of surprise and delight she ate it. Then he picked up a second banana and held it in his hands until Lee was through reading.

"Eat it *now*," he said, handing Lee the banana as soon as he knelt down at his side. Lee ate the banana and put the peel in his pocket very quickly. Yogi Ramsuratkumar had Lee ask someone to chant. Three of the women got up and led the chants until Yogi Ramsuratkumar picked up the big poetry book and Devaki Ma turned the pages back to the lyrics.

Yogi Ramsuratkumar called Lee to the dais and asked him to have someone "sing some of these songs." Then Lee did something uncharacteristic: normally he spoke only when he was asked to speak in Yogi Ramsuratkumar's company, but now he interjected something into the beggar's flow by offering, "They have also prepared some of the poems," referring to the master's instruction of two days before. Yogi Ramsuratkumar stopped and sat still.

"They have prepared some of the poems, Bhagavan, some of *Poems of a Broken Heart,* to sing," Devaki explained, leaning forward. Within seconds Mira and I were standing in front of the room with a poetry book in our hands. We sang five poems, then turned toward Yogi Ramsuratkumar and awaited further instructions. He was slumped forward with his head on his chest and his hands cupped together gently in his lap.

"Is that all?" Devaki asked. She seemed to want more. Yogi Ramsuratkumar slowly came back to life and called us over. One by one we moved up to *pranam* and receive the banana he held out.

"Eat, now," he commanded softly. I ate as quickly as I could. The experience of sitting at his side eating the *prasad* was like having a very bright light shone into the depths of one's being.

"My Father blesses you," he said, bringing the tips of his fingers together in a gentle *pranam.* He gazed at us a moment, then it was clearly time to go. Just as we were getting up, he said, "You girls can take your seat." It was a touching and whimsical remark coming from Yogi Ramsuratkumar that was both very tender and kind. He spoke to us like a loving father.

For the next few days Lee gave talks in every darshan, and the chanting continued to permeate our senses with the name of Yogi Ramsuratkumar. Lee invited several of his students—Purna Steinitz, Mirabai, Radha, Tom Lennon and myself—to give talks during darshan as well. Yogi Ramsuratkumar also called up several of his Indian devotees to speak, like Janarthanan, who always spoke about the *Ramayana* in Tamil. After each person talked, they were called to the dais to receive Yogi Ramsuratkumar's blessing and a banana. Each time he said, "Eat this *now,*" or "Eat this, here and now!" Then the chanting of Yogi Ramsuratkumar's name was resumed.

The beggar saint sat and smoked, as he had on many occasions during the past two weeks. While the chanting droned on, the cigarette cupped in his hands glowed red, and the smoke curled up above his head in a slow dance with the air. Every inhalation seemed to pull in the suffering of the world. As the smoke disappeared in the air, *samskaras* and karma were transmuted within the alchemical body of the *mahasiddha*. His body was bathed in the pale morning light that shone from the large windows on either side of the walls behind his dais. There seemed to be a whole world outside the windows—a small animal, like a chipmunk or squirrel, ran back and forth across the top of the wall, and birds often perched on the windowsill to sing loudly, their songs drifting into the darshan. All these manifestations of life became a natural expression of the joy we experienced in the beggar saint's world.

The afternoon before we left Tiruvannamalai Alain De Rosanbo departed for Madras. That morning in darshan Yogi Ramsuratkumar called Lee and Alain up to the dais and wanted to know all the details of Alain's departure and where he would be traveling. The master told Lee and Alain that he would come from Sudama House to the ashram gate at two o'clock when Alain was leaving. This was an unusual boon—Yogi Ramsuratkumar rarely, if ever, went to the gate to say goodbye—but he had a special affection and respect for elders, and had often shown his regard for Alain. One year Yogi Ramsuratkumar had conducted a healing on Alain's knees. Taking a seat in a chair beside Alain, who couldn't sit on the floor, Yogi Ramsuratkumar placed his hands on Alain's knees, blessing and healing him.

After making the arrangements for Alain's departure, Yogi Ramsuratkumar then asked Lee to "say something." The room was darker than in the morning, cast in afternoon shadows. Rising to stand at the left of the dais, Lee began:

> We could say something about beggary, because Yogi Ramsuratkumar is a beggar. The way we ordinarily talk about begging is begging for food to eat. Yogi Ramsuratkumar was a beggar on the streets for many years, but when Yogi Ramsuratkumar calls himself a beggar it also means that to respond to a beggar is an extraordinary opportunity to be generous and charitable out of the goodness of our hearts. It is a great blessing to give to one less fortunate than ourselves.
>
> But there is another element of this idea of beggary. Whenever Yogi Ramsuratkumar offers us the opportunity to serve him—"This beggar has some work. Would you like to do some work for this beggar?"—then we have the extraordinary opportunity to be in communion with That which Yogi Ramsuratkumar is, the blessings of Father in Heaven. By serving this particular beggar in any way, even just to move a chair for him, we have the opportunity to be in relationship with Father in Heaven, as well as being generous and charitable.
>
> In 1993 the first book of poems was published by Sadhu Rangarajan. Yogi Ramsuratkumar was having the poems read over and over again by Ma Devaki, and at one point he said, "These poems should be read every day." He didn't say one poem or every poem, or every one of you should read these poems. He leaves it to us to make distinctions. Do we read one poem a day, ten poems a day, the whole first book every day?
>
> Yogi Ramsuratkumar has left this consideration of reading the poems completely up to us. We have to give ourselves to that in whatever way we can. That is the offering of a beggar. Yogi Ramsuratkumar is begging my students, and maybe all of us, to read these poems every day. It's a subtle form of begging. Yogi Ramsuratkumar is a divine beggar. The degree to which we respond to the divine beggar is the degree to which we are blessed. He begs us to chant his name. When we chant his name we are

> giving alms to the divine beggar. This begging is a very important spiritual tradition. We are blessed through that exchange with the beggar. All the benefits we get from giving when Yogi Ramsuratkumar begs are the blessings of Father in Heaven.

"My Father blesses you, Lee. My Father's blessings," Yogi said as he looked into Lee's eyes, handing him a banana. "Eat it, here and now." Lee ate the *prasad*, then Yogi Ramsuratkumar said, "Ask someone to talk."

Lee turned and gestured to one of his students, Zachary Parker, who got up and walked to the left of the dais, *pranaming* to Yogi Ramsuratkumar. He talked about meeting Lee when he was only sixteen —eleven years before—and how he had no idea at the time that Lee would become his teacher and that he would travel to many places with him and meet Yogi Ramsuratkumar. He spoke about how as a teenager he had injured his knee so seriously that surgery was required. Recently his knees had become very painful again and another round of surgery was advised by doctors, but Lee advised against this and said he would personally work on Zachary's knees. Lee sat down with Zachary and placed his hands on the injured knees for about thirty minutes; afterward the knees were miraculously better, and there was no need for surgery.

Zachary concluded, "When I thanked Lee for healing my knees he said, 'Don't thank me, thank Yogi Ramsuratkumar.' So, I want to take this opportunity to thank Lee, and to thank Yogi Ramsuratkumar." He turned toward Yogi Ramsuratkumar, then went to the dais and received *prasad*.

It was an interesting story for many reasons: in 1994 Yogi Ramsuratkumar himself had worked on Lee's knees, putting his hands on them and stroking them for about thirty minutes during darshan one day, at a time when Lee's knees were especially painful and problematic. Lee's knees had been healed, and it seemed that he had passed that on to Zachary in some way. It was one of many stories of how Yogi Ramsuratkumar used hands on healing to effect positive changes in his devotees.

Now as the afternoon darshan drew to a close Yogi Ramsuratkumar had Lee sit beside him on the floor while he gave shawls to each person in Lee's group of thirty-five people. One at a time we walked up and received a shawl that was passed from Yogi Ramsuratkumar's hands to Lee's hands and then into the recipient's hands. The first three or four shawls had been given to Yogi Ramsuratkumar during *jayanthi* and Deepam, and had been wrapped around his body, but every shawl contained the blessing of having passed through his hands, and would provide warmth on our coming travels to northern India.

Darshan was soon over. The time with Yogi Ramsuratkumar was quickly coming to a close. Yogi Ramsuratkumar had worked his magic and would send us on our way the following night at midnight.

Lee's group went out for dinner in Tiruvannamalai that evening; it was the only time we had eaten food off the ashram. A bevy of auto rickshaws pulled up to the ashram to accommodate the crowd of Westerners traveling with Lee and Purna. At the restaurant the owner warmly greeted Lee at the door, having known him for many years. He was wearing a T-shirt that said, "God's Child, Yogi Ramsuratkumar, Tiruvannamalai."

Early the next morning it was pouring rain and a little cool. At six o'clock when the coffee was served we drank it on the porch with Lee in the pale early light. Beside our cottage in his fenced patch of green, the little musk deer munched on grass, his bell tinkling lightly. Arunachala was shrouded with mist and clouds, but the Deepam fire still burned brightly on the distant tip of the mountain. Our last day with Yogi Ramsuratkumar had dawned, announced by the birds with their flurry of activity and song. A wild chorus had come to life outside, and all along the garden wall the lavender morning glories blossomed in a purple profusion. The hibiscus also burst forth with fresh new blossoms overnight, huge and rose red.

After Yogi Ramsuratkumar had come for breakfast, I took the opportunity to circumambulate the ashram with the other devotees. Yogi Ramsuratkumar had encouraged people to circumambulate the ashram; in a moment of ecstasy he had said that one circumambulation of the ashram would give four times the blessings as circumambulating Arunachala. It was a boon he bestowed on his devotees, like the chanting of his name. This morning the sky was overcast, with the distant mountain cloaked in mists. As we walked along chanting, Arunachala rose up green and hazy in the cloudbanks, while water dripped off the trees and shrubs all along the lush, verdant path that curved around the perimeter of the ashram. The ashram as a jewel of sacred space—a manifestation of Yogi Ramsuratkumar on the physical plane—was apparent in the quiet beauty of the path.

"A divine miracle," Mani had said of the ashram this morning before Yogi Ramsuratkumar's first arrival. "This was nothing but a bare field," he added. Then reflecting on his *sadhana*, he said, "I have done many building projects in my life. I have done much, much work before, but never anything like this. Never! It is very hard, very hard, but all this," he spread his arms to indicate the whole ashram, "is a divine miracle—all done by his grace!"

He went on in his straightforward way, "Never have I done anything like this. No time off, never a day, no vacation. Every day, every day, I work here. He won't ask anyone else to do things—just Mani. I can't make any plans. It is very hard. I never know from moment to moment what he will ask for next."

During the two weeks of our visit the daily routines of the ashram had become more apparent. The ashram was staffed by twenty to twenty-five full-time people. Despite the long, hard working hours and the amazing demands of the guru to do the impossible on a regular basis, the staff members were noticeably radiant, bright and kind; Yogi Ramsuratkumar was the buoyant, effervescent sea upon which they sailed, which was made very clear in the spontaneous, candid and fresh gestures of each person as they performed their daily tasks.

About two hundred people came to the ashram every day of the year, most of them taking their noon meal in the dining hall. All of the food served was considered to be *prasad*, and was exceptionally delicious and pure. It was clear that the servers in the dining hall loved their job of offering food as *prasad* to the pilgrims, devotees and worshippers who came through every day. On special religious holidays like Deepam, *jayanthi* day or the full moon every month, the crowds waxed to thousands. It was not uncommon for the ashram to feed twenty-five hundred people at Deepam alone. Yogi Ramsuratkumar's prediction that the temple would hold thousands of people from all over the world was beginning to come true.

When we came into our last darshan in the afternoon of December 9, Yogi Ramsuratkumar was sitting quietly on the dais with Ma Devaki and Vijayalakshmi. There was no chanting going on as there had always been before. The space was somber and peaceful. Yogi Ramsuratkumar and the two women sat on the dais in a unified field of radiance. As we took our places on the floor in front of them we were lifted up into the gathering force of Yogi Ramsuratkumar's presence.

"You can say a few words," Yogi Ramsuratkumar said to Lee when he called him over to the dais. "This is your last talk." Lee stood up and began to speak:

> We've visited Yogi Ramsuratkumar eleven or twelve times over the years, and Yogi Ramsuratkumar's blessings are the center point of everything; everything is simply him. By the appearance of things, we come here to Tiruvannamalai, and then we leave and go back to the West, but in reality no one comes here, no one goes back to America. We are always sitting at the feet of Yogi Ramsuratkumar. It is an illusion that we come and go, because we are never apart. And yet there are two dimensions of reality.
>
> One dimension is that everything is just what it is—empty and full, perfect as it is, connected. But there is also another dimension of reality . . . This dichotomy also shows up in the Indian tradition of Shiva and Shakti. Shiva is the eternal Oneness, all just as it is; Shakti is the dimension of phenomena. When I speak of essential reality or truth I refer to Yogi Ramsuratkumar, or Shiva—the eternal Oneness. Around that point of eternality and oneness, which cannot be described, is Shakti, the swirling display of phenomena—beautiful, bright, dark; changes that come and go; birth, death, rebirth, death. That play of phenomena is that which distracts us and keeps us confused.
>
> All the wonders of technology—even though I am completely computer illiterate—are distractions, the sophistication of the mind of man. It is all the swirling play of phenomena that captures our senses. But sooner or later, this lifetime or another, we will become less captivated by the swirling display of phenomena and more drawn into the still point which is Shiva, where there is no time—no past, present or future—because everything exists here and now. We will be drawn into that still point, until sometime we pass through that point and on to the other side,

> where there is no distinction, only God.
>
> These are our thoughts as we have our last lunch on the ashram, our last darshan, as we put our illusory luggage on illusory buses, and it will appear that we are getting on a plane and flying out of Madras, when really we are always here, at the feet of Yogi Ramsuratkumar. Nothing will have changed.

At this point Lee began to recount his meetings with Yogi Ramsuratkumar and the teaching lessons that he had received from the master over the years. He spoke about spending time with Yogi Ramsuratkumar in 1977 and 1979, and how two or three hours in his company was so rich and profound that it seemed like an eternity. He commented on how he had brought twenty-one people with him to India in 1986 to see his master, but the master had sent him away, actually telling him to find another guru. Then he returned to the subject of impermanence, of the two poles of life, Shiva and Shakti, and the interplay between the realization of nonduality and what he calls "Enlightened Duality":

> At the heart of things, at the essence of things, all of this is the play of phenomena. What was all this anyway but the play of phenomena? At the heart of things there has never been any separation from Yogi Ramsuratkumar, only communion, *baraka*, benediction, grace. All the rest is the sparkling display of phenomena.
>
> It is Shiva Nataraj—Shiva dancing out the play of phenomena. In one way everything I've been speaking about is just the play of phenomena; if we find ourselves in the play of phenomena, then the human thing to do is to be in that play according to God's design. At the heart of things everything is all the same. Everyone is the same regardless of color, caste or religious belief. If one is a beggar, rich or poor, we are all the same. There is no present, past, future, time or space, only Father in Heaven. And yet, finding ourselves in this dance, it behooves us to play however the Divine Choreographer has written us into the dance.
>
> So I have asked Yogi Ramsuratkumar to allow my sense of distinction to remain. In terms of an illusory prayer, I've asked Yogi Ramsuratkumar, in his grace, to allow me to be able to see myself as distinct from him so that I may bow at his feet in America. I have asked to remain in a mood of adoration or worship of him, because I find the state of adoration or worship to be the best state of all . . . .

Lee's words had the crystalline clarity of the absolute context of nonduality, and yet they were paradoxically tinged with longing for the Beloved—for the possibility of loving God that lies beyond the realization of nonduality, which is the pinnacle of Enlightened Duality. His speech had profoundly deepened the mood in the room until it became bittersweet, and like many others in Lee's party, I wondered if I would see Yogi

Ramsuratkumar again in this lifetime.

Lee ended with his usual thank you and turned to Yogi Ramsuratkumar, who took Lee's hands between his own and held them. After a few moments, he gave Lee *prasad* and said, "Eat it now." He sat and watched as Lee ate the banana, then he began to ask detailed questions about the rest of Lee's trip: when he would be in Varanasi, when in Rishikesh and by what means of travel. This was the first trip in five years in which Lee had not spent all of his time in India with Yogi Ramsuratkumar; because he brought his children this year and wanted to show them some of India, Yogi Ramsuratkumar had given his blessing for two weeks of extended travel up north.

"Lee, what time will you leave?" Yogi Ramsuratkumar asked slowly, his voice lilting.

"At midnight tonight," Lee replied.

"How will you travel to Delhi?" he asked.

Lee answered, "By airplane."

"Ohhh . . . airplane," Yogi Ramsuratkumar said, as if registering this deeply. Then, "How many? Ohhh, thirty-three."

He wanted to know exactly when Lee would fly back to America and from what city. Lee explained that he would spend a week in Varanasi (Banaras) with the whole group.

"Ahh, Varanasi," Yogi Ramsuratkumar said in a voice so tinged with awe that it struck my heart with meaning. The very way he spoke this word evoked the city's mythical power and magic, and set my imagination to racing. One could imagine the years Yogi Ramsuratkumar may have spent there, both as a youth and much later, as a wandering, God-intoxicated sadhu. That day, long before this book was a possibility, I thought to myself, most likely we will never know for certain about those years, but his soft and resonant, "Ah, Varanasi," spoke volumes to me.

From 1996 until 1998, whenever Ashish Bagrodia went to visit Yogi Ramsuratkumar he noticed that the beggar was always very happy. Ashish himself experienced an unusual feeling of well-being, as if some new strength was flowing into his body. Yogi Ramsuratkumar never talked to him about "spiritual things"—he was just always very happy and at the end of their time together he said, "Father's Grace." Ashish began to make more frequent trips because he knew that the old beggar was somehow helping him; but for him, Yogi Ramsuratkumar was still just a "special friend, a nice saint, a godly person." One thing he knew for sure: Yogi Ramsuratkumar was not a fraud as so many gurus turned out to be. Ashish had an instinctive certainty that the beggar saint was a genuine person, and that the donations of money he was sending were for a very good purpose.

Still it seemed that there was nothing "spiritual" going on. Yogi Ramsuratkumar would ask Ashish questions that seemed, at the time, irrelevant but pleasant conversation.

Many years later Ashish would try to recollect all those conversations, realizing that all of it had meaning and purpose, but at the time, when Yogi Ramsuratkumar asked things like, "Do they make salt in Gujarat?" it just didn't make sense. Then he would ask Ashish about certain poets in India. Sometimes he would comment on world politics. At other times he would ask Ashish about his business: How many employees do you have? What is the total turnover? What are your expenses? How much is the electricity? What are the wages paid? Amazingly, the saint talked to him exactly like one businessman to another.

A few years before Yogi Ramsuratkumar had advised Ashish to eat groundnuts to support his health, and Ashish always asked him to bless them. Yogi Ramsuratkumar would ask, "Is it helping you, is it helping you?"

"Yes, I think it is," Ashish would report.

"Father's grace. Father's grace," Yogi Ramsuratkumar would always say.

The relationship between Yogi Ramsuratkumar and Ashish went on like this in a "very happy-go-lucky, hunky-dory, laughter-filled" way until 1998. In 1999 Ashish went to the south of India on an extended business trip. Because his family business was in spinning yarn, making thread and weaving fabrics and textiles, Ashish needed to survey the textile mills in southern India as a way of learning new methods of production.

While he was staying in Coimbatore, which is only eight hours away from Tiruvannamalai, he went frequently to see Yogi Ramsuratkumar. Each time he came Yogi Ramsuratkumar seemed very happy to see him, and asked all about what he was doing in Coimbatore, which hotel he was in, how things were going, and then he would bless him very sweetly.

Suddenly, while in Coimbatore, Ashish began to feel physically weak, to the extent that it was frightening. Since the onset of muscular dystrophy he had not taken his disease seriously, nor had he gotten depressed or worried about his future. But now, for the first time in his life, he felt an intolerable fear. He thought, "I should go see the saint, he can help me," but praying for the master's blessing didn't occur to him—it wasn't that kind of relationship as yet. He had never asked Yogi Ramsuratkumar for a miracle cure for his disease, and in fact, other than asking what he should eat, he had never talked about his illness with him at all.

The next time he went to see the beggar saint, Ashish said, "Yogiji, I'm feeling weak."

Yogi Ramsuratkumar laughed, rather casually it seemed. Again, Ashish said seriously, "I really am feeling very weak, Bhagawan. I think you should help me. You should do something."

"Ohhh! Oh," he said in his enigmatic way. Ashish wondered, "What's wrong with this chap? He doesn't take me seriously. He just laughs!" Then Yogi Ramsuratkumar took Ashish's hands and held them in his very sweetly and started talking of business or other irrelevant things.

After his tour of the textile industry in the south was over, Ashish decided not to go back to Bombay, but to come to the ashram and stay for a month in one of the cottages that had been made available for him. During that time he met with Yogi Ramsuratkumar once a week. Ashish remembered:

> I told Mr. Mani that I would like to stay on the ashram whenever I come in the future, and because of my wheelchair I need some special arrangements in the bathroom, and also my bed has to be longer and bigger and all that. So, could I get one of the cottages modified at my cost? You see, I was thinking I am some big man. So my style of talking, thinking, communicating with the ashram was always like that. I used to think I am something special.

It happened that a French girl, eighteen or twenty years old, was visiting the ashram. She would come to Ashish's cottage and sit out front talking with he and his wife, Shantipriya. She had asked to stay in a cottage on the ashram, but had been told she would have to stay in town. She complained to them about her hotel and the mosquitoes, the noise, the heat, the dirt. Finally Ashish said, "Why don't you change your hotel? There's a better hotel in town, it's very nice—you can go and change it." She changed her hotel, stayed there for one or two days, had one last darshan with Yogi Ramsuratkumar, and then was on her way back to France.

Ashish had provided his own car to give her transportation to the airport in Chennai, but on the way she was in a very bad automobile accident. She almost died, all her limbs were broken and she was in intensive care.

It had been Yogi Ramsuratkumar's direct recommendation that she stay in the hotel she was originally in, and although Ashish had no idea this was the case, the fact that he had convinced her to change hotels and he had provided the car created a very disturbing situation. Ashish became very upset and wrote a letter to Yogi Ramsuratkumar to explain everything, suggesting that Shantipriya should go to Chennai to see the girl in the hospital. There was no response, and his anxiety mounted.

Soon enough one of the attendants was at his door, saying, "Bhagawan wants you immediately." Ashish hastened as quickly as possible to where Bhagawan was sitting under the asvattha tree between the temple and the Veda Pathashala, at the corner of the building. He could feel right away that something was wrong— Yogi was not his normal self—and so he pranamed, kept quiet and waited. Yogi Ramsuratkumar was holding the letter with both his hands.

"Have you seen this?" he asked. Ashish said yes. Yogi Ramsuratkumar was silent for a long time. He looked down at the letter and said, "On this type of matter this beggar has to say . . ." and then he looked up into Ashish's eyes and shouted angrily, "Nothing, nothing, *nothing*!" Each time he said "nothing" his voice became more powerful. Ashish commented on this powerful moment:

> I was trembling, you know. I have never been so scared of a person in my life. I'm quite courageous and I'm not scared of anybody, but I was trembling. It was like when Arjuna saw Krishna! I was shocked and I couldn't say anything. I was choked, I couldn't speak, so for a few seconds I didn't say anything and then I just literally bowed down and I said, "I'm

> sorry." The moment I said this, he got hold of both my hands and he said, "Father's Grace" And then he started caressing me. But I was still really scared!

This incident of Yogi Ramsuratkumar yelling "Nothing, nothing, nothing!" was the first thing that changed Ashish's relationship to him. As Ashish said, it was like the story in the *Bhagavad Gita* when Arjuna boldly demanded that Krishna reveal himself, but when Arjuna looked in Krishna's mouth, he was blinded by the power and splendor of the divinity he saw there. Yogi Ramsuratkumar once said, "Whatever this beggar does is a blessing. Even when he shouts at people in anger, it is only a blessing. They will surely benefit from that. When they sit in the presence of this beggar, my Father transforms them, even though they may not be aware of it." [15]

After that Ashish stopped asking for special appointments with Bhagawan and stopped having casual conversations with him. He never took the beggar lightly again. During that same time period, in 1999, he became close to Bret Carlson, an American who was living in Tiruvannamalai and had become very close to Yogi Ramsuratkumar and Lee Lozowick. Bret said, "You know, you're a fool. You have been taking Bhagawan lightly, and now you realize it." Ashish began to realize that he had been caught up in his own world. Instead of making demands for private meetings and certain privileges on the ashram, he should just go to Yogi Ramsuratkumar, sit in his darshan, not initiate anything and wait for his call.

Bret's counsel helped a lot, but meeting Lee Lozowick was the turning point. Ashish described the transformation he was going through as the guru worked with him:

> I realized that all these years I've wasted time, from 1993 to 1998. I had so many meetings with Yogiji, and I just took him lightly and wasted time— and now it's too late. Then, at that time Bret would occasionally talk of Mr. Lee also. I had never heard of him before. Once Mr. Mani had told me, "You know, some foreigners visit our ashram, and they have some books," and then he gave me the journal, *Tawagoto*, and then he gave me that book, *Facets of the Diamond*. I didn't read it. I didn't open it; I just kept it somewhere. I wasn't interested at the time, but Bret would say just a little about Mr. Lee, and then he would keep quiet. When he talked about Mr. Lee he always said, "He is very strict, he is very ruthless. He says things that nobody likes to hear," and all that. That made me very interested, you know—I like such people. I like people like that because it's interesting. So I said to Bret, "I want to meet Mr. Lee."
>
> "No, no, no, no, no," he would say, trying to put me off, "you shouldn't meet him. You don't know— Mr. Lee is a different kind of a teacher. He's not a person who is very friendly, nice, warm, who you go

15 *Facets of the Diamond*, p. 141.

Yogi Ramsuratkumar and Ma Devaki on Mt. Arunachala, 1993.

Yogi Ramsuratkumar with Ma Devaki and Lee Lozowick at the home of V. Ganeshan, December 1993.

Yogi Ramsuratkumar and Ma Devaki in the Darshan Mandir on the ashram, 1994.

From left: Ma Devaki, Yogi Ramsuratkumar, Swami Satchidananda, Pon Kamaraj and Sadhu Rangarajan, during the inauguration of the ashram, February 1994.

Yogi Ramsuratkumar and (left to right) V. Ganeshan, Janarthanan (on knees) and Anjaneyalu, digging the ashram well, 1993.

Yogi Ramsuratkumar with Mani and Ma Devaki leaving the Darshan Mandir, 1994.

Yogi Ramsuratkumar with the *vigraha* given by Lee Lozowick, November 1994.

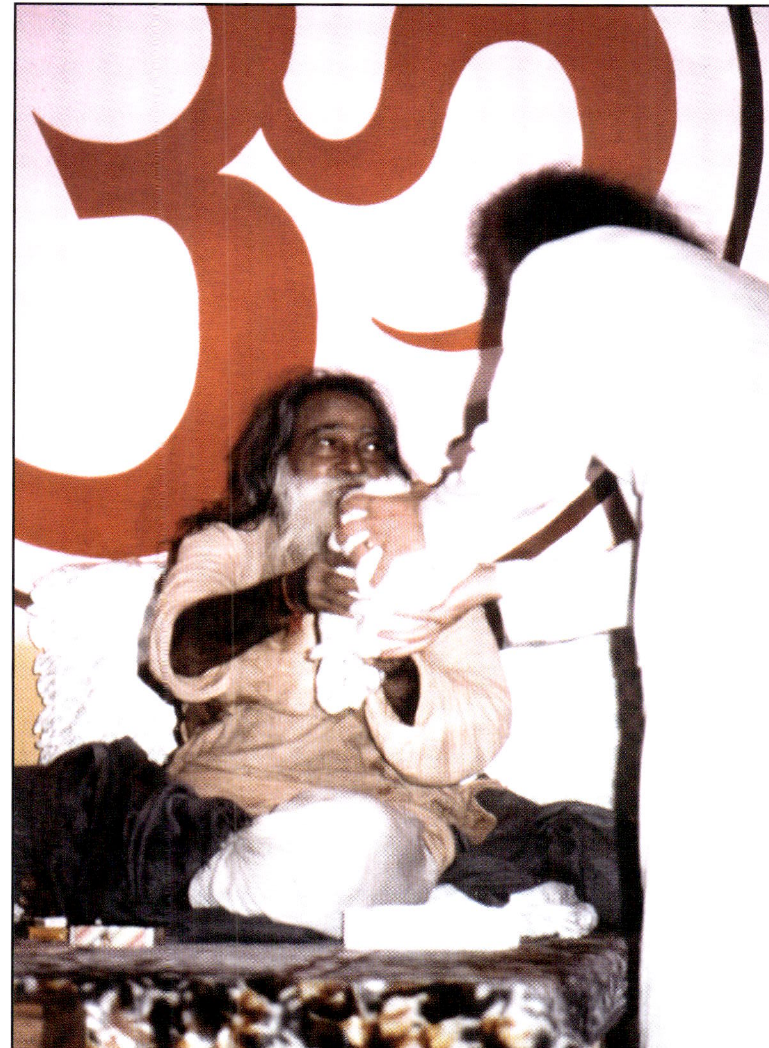

Yogi Ramsuratkumar gives the dhoti to Lee, December 1994.

December 1994.

December 1994.

Lee seated on Yogi Ramsuratkumar's dais, December 1994.

Yogi Ramsuratkumar blesses the crowd in darshan, December 1994.

Yogi Ramsuratkumar and Ma Devaki, December 1995.

Yogi Ramsuratkumar with the Sudama sisters on the ashram, mid-90s.

Yogi Ramsuratkumar with Raji, Ma Devaki and the Sudama sisters, 1994.

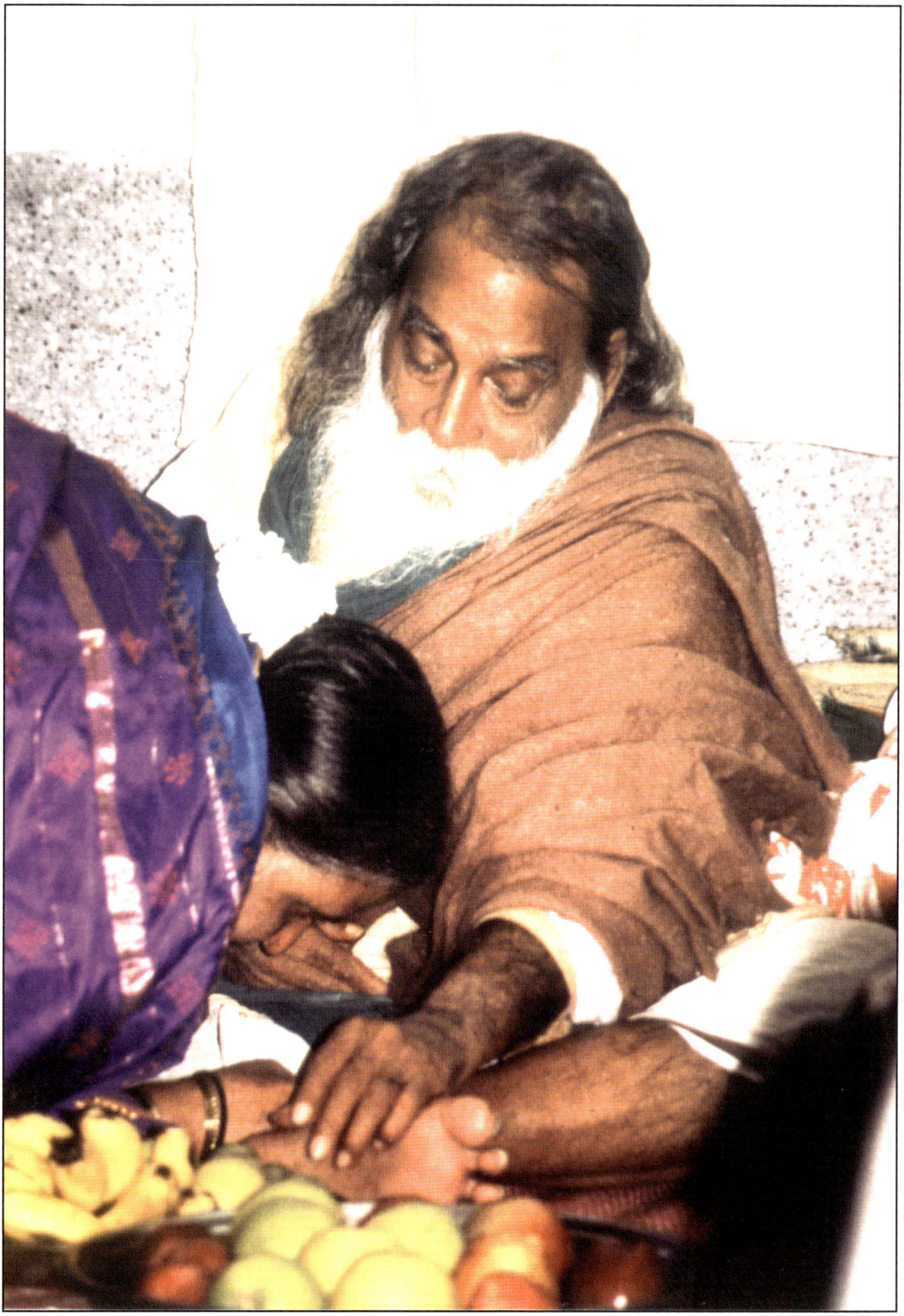

December 1997.

Darshan, 1997.

Darshan, 1997.

Yogi Ramsuratkumar signing a copy of *Death of a Dishonest Man* for Shaktivel, 1998.

Yogi Ramsuratkumar with (left to right) Justice Arunachalam, Ma Devaki and Mani in front of the Veda Patashala.

Lee giving a talk in darshan, with Yogi Ramsuratkumar, Rajmohan and Mani looking on, December 2000.

Yogi Ramsuratkumar selling *Death of a Dishonest Man*, December 2000
with Lee, Rajmohan, Ma Devaki, and Vijayalakshmi.

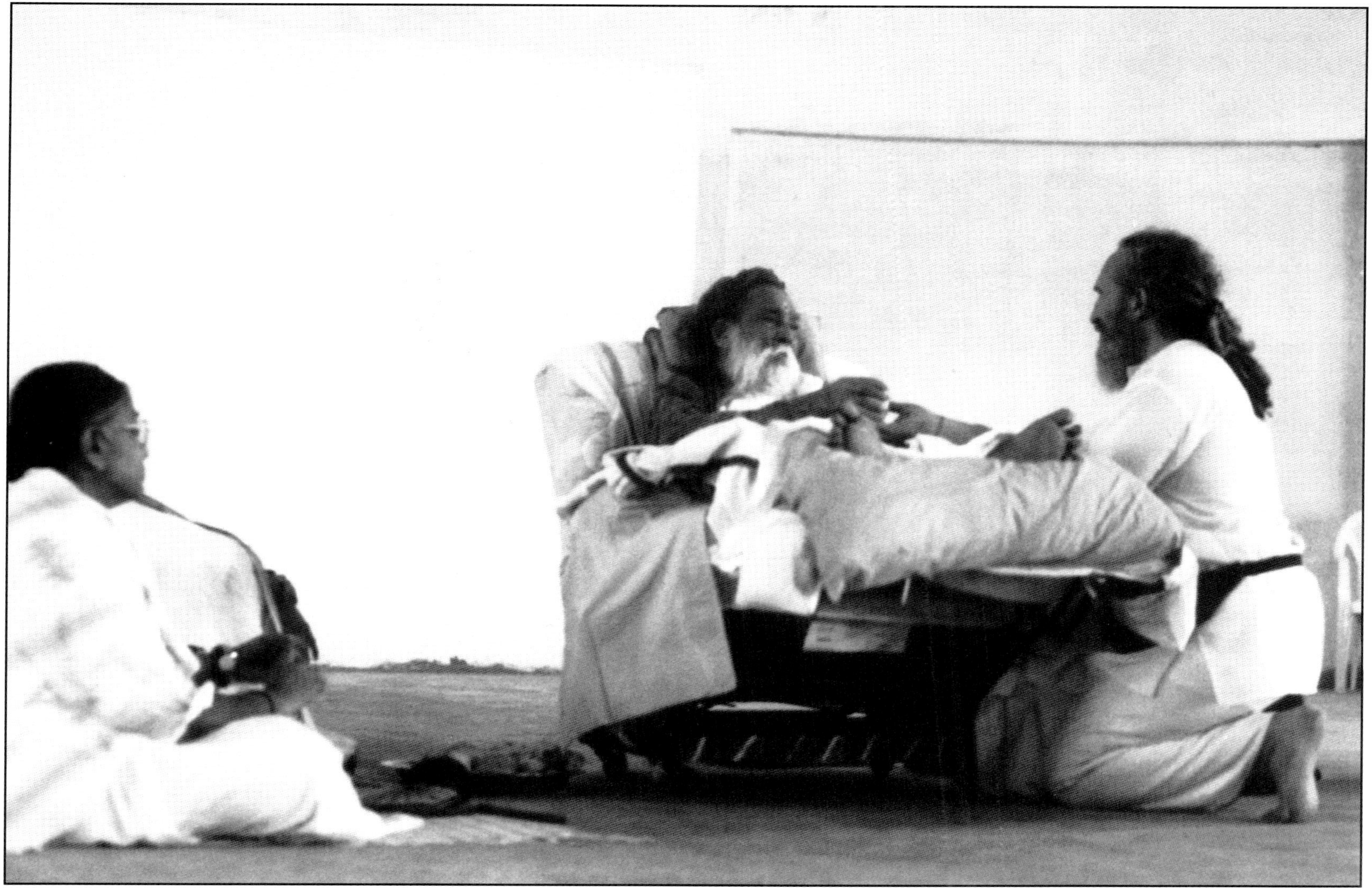

December 2000.

Drawing by Yogi Ramsuratkumar, circa 1971.

Yogi Ramsuratkumar smiling at the dancers, December 2000.

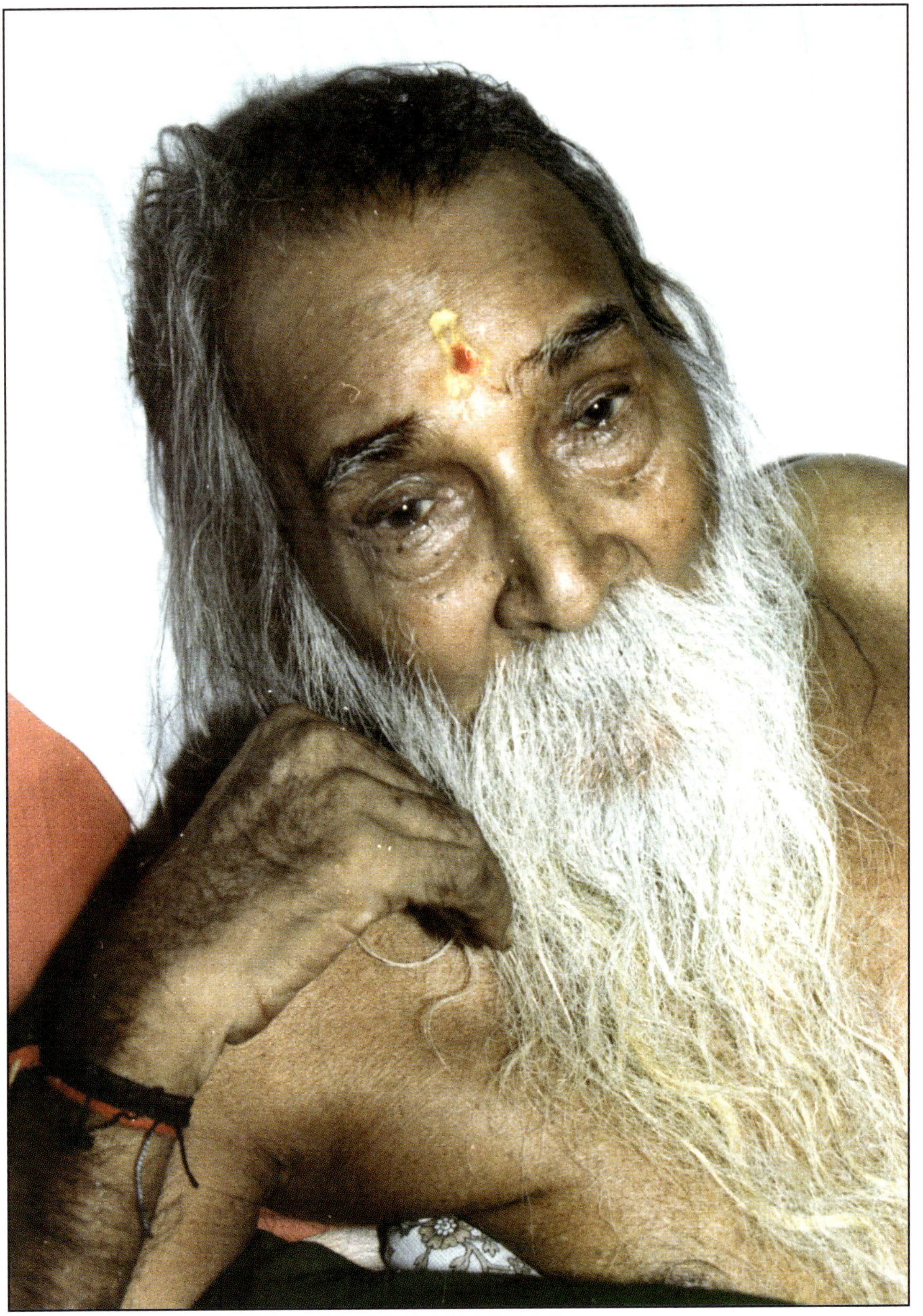

Yogi Ramsuratkumar in his bed in the temple abode, two weeks before leaving his body, February 2001.

> and get some great something. You may get a shock, you know. You may get insulted, and you will feel bad. And he's very strict and disciplined." The more he said these things, the more I would say, "No, I want to meet him." And he would say, "No, no, no, it's not good, forget it."
>
> Then Bret would say, "Mr. Lee has said this about Yogiji, Mr. Lee has said that, and what he says is correct . . ." I started feeling that I must meet Mr. Lee. Who is this person? Then in 1999 when Mr. Lee came, I went to the ashram. Bret had already scared me a lot, that you should be careful and all. I said, "The worst he can do is insult me. So big deal—in business we go places and get insulted, but in the end we make money. When you profit, who cares if you get insulted, if in the end you get something."
>
> Mr. Lee was mostly with his big group, and I would stay away, but once I saw that he was sitting alone with another lady outside the dining hall. Only two of them—the group was not there. So I said, this is a good opportunity. I went and *pranamed* and said, "So Lee, I am Ashish," and I started talking to him.
>
> "You know," I said, "I've heard this, that and . . ." Mr. Lee doesn't talk much, so I was trying to make a conversation. I was asking him, "When did you meet Bhagawan? What are your experiences of Bhagawan?" When I used to meet Yogiji in the beginning, from 1994 to 1998, I would talk to him just like that. There was no protocol. I would ask Yogi, "So, what have you been doing? What are you doing these days? When do you eat?" And you know what he would tell me?
>
> "Oh, this beggar is very lazy. He's just eating, drinking, and sleeping. This beggar is very lazy, Ashish," and then he would laugh!
>
> "How many hours do you sleep?" I would ask him, and he would ask me, "How many hours do you sleep?" And then I would tell him, "Eight hours, ten hours . . .Sometimes I feel I could sleep less, can you help me?" You know, I would talk to him just like that, and he would talk to me also like that. So, I was trying to make a conversation with Mr. Lee.

Lee's student Lalitha was sitting there listening while Lee answered Ashish's questions. Then Ashish said in a very straightforward way, "Mr. Lee, do you accept long-distance students—you know, just like we have long-distance learning? I'm in India, you know, but can I get your teachings?" Lee just laughed, but Lalitha said teasingly, "You don't know what you're getting into. Be careful with him. He can be very insulting!"

Ashish persisted, "What are the books written by you?" Lee answered his questions and told him about the books he had written that could be ordered from the States, the journals and so on.

Observing their conversation, Lalitha said, "You know, that's a big package you're asking for!"

"So what? I'll buy this also, I'll buy that also," Ashish smiled. When Lalitha kept warning him about how insulting Lee could be, finally he turned to Lee and said, "Mr. Lee, please insult me. You do whatever you want, as long as I get something, as long as I get something out of it. You do whatever you want—you be as ruthless as you want with me. If I get something at the end, I really don't care."

That year when Yogi Ramsuratkumar was selling *Death of a Dishonest Man* during his darshans, Ashish bought two of them right away. Yogi Ramsuratkumar was personally signing the books with a big Om sign. At first Ashish had no intention of reading it; he just wanted to have it because Yogi Ramsuratkumar had sold it and signed it. But after meeting Lee he decided to read the poetry, which was a catalyst in changing his relationship with Yogi Ramsuratkumar, as Ashish described:

> That was another turning point. Reading those poems I could find an expression of my inner feelings which my ego didn't allow to surface—the devotion that probably I had, but that was suppressed. The more poetry I read, the more and more I felt drawn to Yogiji, because of the poetry. I also had more and more respect for Mr. Lee, because he had written those poems. So somehow after meeting Lee and reading the poems, and after that "nothing, nothing, nothing" happened, the whole relationship changed. After that I had many, many meetings with Yogi, and he would call me up, but those were short and serious meetings, you know. He was getting older and very weak.

CHAPTER NINE

THE FINAL PLAY

1999-2001

This beggar is a born beggar, will remain as beggar, will die as beggar.

— Yogi Ramsuratkumar

Yogi Ramsuratkumar wanted his devotees to celebrate the fact that he was not his body and to understand that the body would inevitably fall away, but that which was the source of blessings, of love and delight, would remain forever. For years he had been saying, "Do not make the mistake of limiting this beggar to this body. He is everywhere. This beggar is not limited to this body. He is here, there, everywhere; in the table, chair, walls, in the very air. This beggar is not in this body alone."

In 1996 Yogi Ramsuratkumar had experienced another bout of ill health, found it difficult to move at all and was diagnosed with high blood pressure. He had had problems with stomach ulcers and diabetes for many years and since 1990 had been on a diet recommended by Dr. Radhakrishnan of simple foods cooked with no oil or spices.

In July 1999 Yogi Ramsuratkumar fell ill with a high fever, but quickly recovered. A few weeks later he was sick again. His attending doctor examined him and discovered a tumor, but the beggar refused to allow allopathic treatment or tests of any kind. His health was clearly failing; his time on earth was slowly coming to an end. It was all too easy to forget his instruction, especially at times when fresh blood was found wherever he had been sitting and he was clearly suffering physical pain. On one such occasion when Ma Devaki wanted to call the doctor to attend to him, he said, "No. This is nothing. If we call a doctor, then Father's work will come to a stop."[1]

Referring to the words of the great master Nityananda, he explained why he could not miraculously heal himself as he had healed so many countless other people, "This body is dust and mud. That Divine Force is not to be used for this body. That is only for the devotees . . . Father wants this beggar to suffer for the sake of cosmic balance.

1 Vijayalakshmi, *Waves of Love*, pp. 56-57.

Whatever Father wishes, will happen." These were the recurring themes that permeated his communication with regard to his illness and coming transition from the body during the last two years of his life.

"Bhagawan, whenever I have any problem, I talk to you, and I'm afraid that once you're not there, then whom shall I talk to? What will happen to me?" Ashish Bagrodia asked, having grown very attached to the beggar saint as he had come to realize the master's importance in his life.

The master became very irritated and said, "Everybody has to die."

"Yes, I know that, but still . . . who am I going to communicate with?"

The beloved elder, dressed in a *dhoti* and layers of shawls, his long white beard sparkling with light, and with a great weight of sadness gleaming in his dark eyes, looked at Ashish very sharply and said in a stern voice, "Communicate . . . with Father!"

"I don't know Father," Ashish pressed on. "I don't know how to communicate with Father. I know only how to communicate with you. And when you're gone, how am I going to communicate?" The more Ashish pushed his point, the more irritated Yogi Ramsuratkumar became.

"Communicate with Father!" he repeated abruptly, then quickly ended the meeting, saying gently, "My Father blesses you. You can go now."

After that, not wanting to disturb the master, Ashish stopped asking for appointments when he came to the ashram, but Yogi Ramsuratkumar almost always called for him.

"How are you, Ashish?" he would ask, inquiring sweetly about his health, his business and so on.

"Bhagawan, you are suffering, you're not well," Ashish said finally.

"Who told you?" the beggar asked.

"A few months back Bret wrote to me that you're not well. So it seems since the last few months, you're not well," Ashish explained.

Yogi Ramsuratkumar laughed and laughed, then he said, "These hands are rotting, Ashish. These legs are rotting. This whole body is rotting. Let this body suffer! Let Father do what he wants with this body!" He went on, "Everything is rotting. This beggar is rotting. Legs are rotting, hands are rotting. Let Father keep this body the way he wants. Let the body rot, Ashish!"

It was a powerful statement of the reality of the situation, and Yogi Ramsuratkumar accepted it fully. He was asking his devotees to do the same, rather than bring anxiety, sorrow and grief to him. Years before, when he had caught his fingernail, causing it to bleed, he had said to some of Hilda Charlton's students who were visiting, "That is the nature of this world—occasional shocks. Life would be boring without them, very dull." It was an attitude very few could emulate.

In the year 1999 the ashram was undergoing other changes as well: N.S. Subramaniam (Mani) left the ashram as manager in early 1999 and Justice T.S. Arunachala, who had known Yogi Ramsuratkumar since 1989, took over. An ardent devotee and ashram trustee, Justice Arunachala had been named *sarvadhikari* or chief administrator of the ashram by Yogi Ramsuratkumar in a will he had signed in 1996.[2]

Other changes were in the air as well: Bret Carlson, knowing of Yogi Ramsuratkumar's long-time desire for Lee Lozowick to have an ashram next to the Yogi Ramsuratkumar Ashram—a project that had, some years before, been thwarted by legal tangles—had generously donated his newly-constructed house to Hohm Sahaj Mandir Charitable Trust, which had been founded by Lee Lozowick at the request of Yogi Ramsuratkumar. The two-story house was located only one block from the Yogi Ramsuratkumar Ashram, and by 1999 it was just beginning to function as Triveni II, the headquarters for the Hohm Community in Tiruvannamalai. It had taken five years to bring Yogi Ramsuratkumar's wish into manifestation. Two of Lee's German students, Volker and Ute Augustyniak, and Bret were living there.

In late November 1999 Lee Lozowick came to visit with a large number of students, including Purna Steinitz and fifteen of his students. Lee stayed on the Yogi Ramsuratkumar Ashram, while Purna and his students stayed at Triveni II. During their stay, from November 27 through December 12, Yogi Ramsuratkumar began to appear in public darshans again. This year he sat in the small wooden chair in the temple, placed between the thatched palm hut and the large statue, for both morning and afternoon darshans. Ma Devaki and Vijayalakshmi sat in the hut just a few feet away from him, leading chants and serving him in whatever way he needed. Over all he was quieter and more contained than he'd ever been, and slumped in his chair in a deeply interior state. Only rarely were there moments of the joyful play that had characterized past visits from Lee and his group. Still, he asked Lee to speak to the audience and for the poems to be sung. The chanting of his name continued, as always.

At the same time, the beggar saint was extraordinarily intent as he silently gazed from time to time at each person sitting before him. The intimate touch of his eyes, at once tender, deep and heartbreaking, and the overwhelming presence of his being were deeply felt by the group. His somber quiescence contained a powerful communication as he continued to raise his hands in blessing upon the crowd. Hearing that Yogi Ramsuratkumar was in the temple and giving darshan, Indian pilgrims and devotees came en masse.

At one point the doctor was called to tend to the beggar saint; it was a tense moment when no one was sure what would happen next. Yogi Ramsuratkumar lay on the floor in the hut, with turban off and hair falling down over his bare shoulders. After a while the doctor went away and darshan was over.

In early 2000 Yogi Ramsuratkumar initiated a construction project that was very dear to him—the Ma Devaki Veda Patashala, a small building on the ashram that would

2 Ibid, p. 91.

house archives and be a place where visiting pundits, sadhus and scholars could stay who were conducting Vedic research and preserving the traditional scriptures and spiritual heritage of India. The purpose of the Patashala was to promote and sponsor research in the Vedas, and he intended the use and activities of the Veda Patashala to be directed by Ma Devaki, after whom it was named. It was located behind the temple, nestled under the trees that lined the lush orchard on the back of the property of tall, graceful palm trees, banana palms, mango and neem trees, citrus and punnai trees. On February 26, 2000 the foundation was laid with Shri Anjaneyalu, who Yogi Ramsuratkumar always entrusted with such projects, assigned as the building contractor.

No longer appearing in the darshans that were still regularly held in the temple, Bhagawan loved to sit outside under the large asvattha tree at the corner of the Veda Patashala and watch the construction. A rough palm hut was put up under the trees to shelter him from the sun and rain. From March to the end of May 2000 he sat by the Patashala and focused his attention on the building as it came into form. It was an important project for Bhagawan, and there was a definite sense of urgency. Vijayalakshmi reported that during this period, Yogi Ramsuratkumar spoke a great deal about his earlier days when he was wandering all over India, but discouraged any attempt to record it. He also spoke occasionally about the Veda Patashala, and called it the heart of the ashram.

Despite the tremendous suffering that his body was enduring, Yogi Ramsuratkumar remained the same throughout it all. During this time period Ashish Bagrodia visited Yogi Ramsuratkumar again. At this point he had become very serious in his sadhana and in his approach to the beggar saint. He was always very careful not to disturb him, because he was getting weaker and weaker, but the saint called him to his side and gently and sweetly inquired about his well being.

"How are you?" he asked as usual, "How is your health? How is your business? How is your father?"

"Sometimes I feel very weak physically, Yogiji," Ashish answered. Yogi Ramsuratkumar became very serious.

In years before when Ashish visited with Yogi Ramsuratkumar there was always laughter; now things seemed very serious. Ashish felt he was burdening Yogi Ramsuratkumar, when he himself was suffering so much, but he answered his questions truthfully.

"Weak," the beggar repeated slowly, after Ashish's response.

"Sometimes I really suffer physically, Yogiji," Ashish said,

Yogi Ramsuratkumar looked at Ashish with heartbreaking compassion and said gently, "Have faith."

"Have faith," he repeated, then gazed at Ashish for some time. His brown eyes conveyed a vast world of love. After a while he said, "My Father blesses you."

"Have faith in Father," he said. "Call it Father, call it God . . .have faith." And then he blessed him again, and told him to go.

Late in the spring of 2000, while sitting beneath the trees watching the men at work on the Veda Patashala, the beggar was quiet and peaceful, as usual. Suddenly he made the statement, "This beggar's body has suffered for some time." In May the tumors were confirmed to be cancerous, and Yogi Ramsuratkumar was growing sicker with each day. As the construction on the Veda Patashala drew to a close in late May, he declared quietly, so only those who were very close by could hear, "This beggar's work is over."

When the building was entirely finished, he said, "This beggar is going to take a long rest." These kinds of statements tended to strike deeply into the hearts of the devotees, who desperately wished to keep them with him at any cost. Devaki said, "Bhagawan, don't say that. We should die with you. We cannot live without you."

Yogi Ramsuratkumar's eyes flashed for a brief moment, and he said tersely, "Devaki! What is my age?"

In mid-June 2000 Yogi Ramsuratkumar became unable to walk. The doctors believed that he had had cancer for ten or fifteen years. He was plagued by frequent fevers and he was in a great deal of pain, though he never complained and remained bright, calm and extraordinarily loving. He held firm in refusing any form of allopathic treatment. If the doctor began to speak of surgery and other treatments, Yogi Ramsuratkumar would not allow him to come near him. All his life he had relied on natural remedies and Ayurvedic and Siddha systems of medicine—now that he had cancer it was no different. He knew full well what the progression of the cancer would most likely involve, having been informed by Dr. Rangabhasyam of Chennai as to exactly what his condition was.[3] All along he attempted to communicate to his devotees that his body was in the hands of his Father.

"Father will take care of this body," he said over and over again, but many of his devotees pleaded with him to allow some allopathic treatment in the hope of prolonging his life. Still he stood firm. He was the perfect embodiment of surrender; his acceptance of the reality of the body and the natural advent of shedding it like so many old clothes was a great teaching in and of itself. His sanity, grace and gratitude for the wonder and awe of Father's will was the shining force of his moments.

What he did not accept was that the doctors insisted that he stop smoking. For over seven months he did not smoke, and one day when he was sitting in the temple, he allowed the devotees to come in for darshan. Calling Parthasarathy to his side, he asked him for a cigarette, much to the alarm of those who were taking care of him. Parthasarathy gave him the cigarette while others were begging him not to smoke it for his health.

In response to all the clamor over the cigarette, Yogi Ramsuratkumar said adamantly, "This is my ashram. My Father says for this beggar to smoke. This beggar wants to smoke." He smoked that cigarette and then asked for another. Looking at Mani and the others, he said, "Mani, do you think this beggar is this body? Do you think Yogi Ramsuratkumar is this body? Devaki, do you think Yogi Ramsuratkumar is this body?"

"No, Bhagawan," they answered, but still they refused his request for another cigarette. Finally he turned to Mani's wife, Raji, and said, "Rajalakshmi, come here. Will you be able to get me a cigarette?"

---

3 Ibid, pp. 93-94.

"Yes, Bhagawan, I'll do it," she answered, going against the protests of the whole group. Raji gave the cigarette to him and then lit it. He asserted again, "This is my ashram! My Father is telling this beggar to smoke." It was his last cigarette, but not the last time he asked for one. It was not the need of an addict, but of a man whose life was subsumed by a great work in which he was compelled to smoke. The cigarettes had been primary tools of his work for unknown decades. Although the beggar had made it clear that he did not want the circumstance of the body to interfere with his work, the cigarettes were withheld—the triumph of science over spirit.

In June 2000 Yogi Ramsuratkumar wanted to visit some of the places that had been significant to him during his life. He was taken by van to the Sathanur Dam, to Kattu Siva, an ancient temple at the base of Mount Arunachala, and to the old house at Sannadhi Street. He was also driven to Tirukoilur to visit Tapovanum, and he asked to have the van parked by the side of the road across from the ashram. The devotees of Tapovanum were thrilled by this unexpected visit from the beggar saint. Some of them, like Shakuntala, had known him for thirty-five years. They brought *prasad* out to him, and received his blessing. Vijayalakshmi wrote, "Those days he was happy with the movement, good air and the satsang. But his health continued to deteriorate."[4a]

The pain grew to a point of extremity, causing him great suffering, but Yogi Ramsuratkumar was no stranger to suffering on many different levels. The devotees who were closest to him and attending to his needs—Ma Devaki, Vijayalakshmi, Rajmohan, Justice Arunachalam, Rajeswari and staff members who had been with him since the beginning of the ashram or longer—were steadfast and faithful in their love and service. Mani, as a trustee, and Raji his wife were there also, as well as Shankara Rajulu, who had resided at the ashram for two years at Yogi Ramsuratkumar's request. Many other long-time devotees came and went from the ashram, concerned about Bhagawan's condition, having precious moments of darshan with him in moments when he rallied. The eldest daughter, son-in-law and grandson of Yogi Ramsuratkumar came from Bihar to visit in the mid-summer. They stayed, as usual, with Jayarama and his family, and visited him on the ashram. Bret Carlson and Ute and Volker Augustyniak were there also, as well as many others who came and went during this time, or spent hours every day in the temple, chanting.

Unable to walk and confined to a reclining chair, Yogi Ramsuratkumar had been moved from Sudama House to his private quarters on the ashram some time before; now he was living in the abode—an apartment that had been constructed especially for him in the back of the temple. He had steadfastly refused medical intervention.

In early August his health reached a crisis point, and those who were caring for him felt he would die very soon without medical intervention. The closest of the Indian devotees were called and informed of the situation. Lee Lozowick received an urgent fax in France, suggesting that he and Alain de Rosanbo come to Tiruvannamalai as quickly as

4a Ibid, pp. 94-95.

possible. The message from Yogi Ramsuratkumar was, "If people want, they can come visit this beggar." Krishna Carcelle was contacted in Mauritius and came for a short stay then left.

Flying out of Paris, Lee Lozowick arrived in India with Clint Callahan to join Bret Carlson and Alain de Rosanbo on the ashram early in the morning on August 6, where they found Bhagawan lying on a rolling bed under the *asvattha* tree by the Veda Patashala with Ma Devaki, Vijayalakshmi and Rajmohan. He was mostly in a restless sleep state or deeply interiorized, wandering in other realms and sometimes crying out and moaning in pain. Now and then his eyes would open and he would make brief eye contact with someone. The situation was critical, and Lee and Clint left feeling that Yogi Ramsuratkumar could not live much longer.

When Lee returned to his ashram in France he spoke with students at a seminar about his guru's ailing health. He spoke about Yogi Ramsuratkumar as a "living scripture" and compared him to the Vedas, which he called "living beings," inspired, sacred texts that were designed to transmit the teaching directly. He said, "I don't relate to Yogi Ramsuratkumar as a man. He is the teaching; he is the Divine incarnate."

It was very painful period of time in which hard decisions had to be made. The crux of the matter was whether the devotees, who were now in charge of the physical care of the beggar's body, would abide by his expressed wishes—which were to be left to his work and to leave this life in whatever way might be the will of God—or to intervene with all the "help" of modern medicine. Unable to bear the awesome suffering of their guru's body, they continued to beg him to have medical care. Yogi Ramsuratkumar was finally transported to the hospital in Chennai, where surgery was performed. Vijayalakshmi wrote about this difficult time:

> Thus passed a few days with Ma Devaki and others close to him praying to him every day to allow intensive medical care. On 16th August Bhagawan gave a reluctant consent and immediately preparations were made to take him to Dr. N. Rangabhashyam's hospital at Chennai. On the 17th August Bhagawan was taken to the hospital. A check-up showed that most of the vital parameters were erratic and so for three weeks intensive care was given by the hospital staff to stabilize these. On 11th September 2000 the surgery took place and then started the recovery, with intensive care from the hospital staff and with constant prayers by devotees everywhere. Bhagawan began to recover and was able to move about in Chennai, though in a limited way. He was unable to resume his walking.
>
> Deferring to the anxious wishes of devotees, Bhagawan gave darshan in the hospital itself and thus thousands of devotees were able to have his darshan.
>
> On 23rd November 2000, he left the hospital and came back to Tiruvannamalai. The journey itself exhausted him. For nearly three weeks

> after reaching the Ashram from Chennai, Bhagawan did not get the kind of intensive medical care that he obtained at the hospital. There was also a stubborn infection resulting in continuous high fever.[4]

His daughter and her family came again to see him at the hospital in Chennai, but he was too ill to receive them. For a while the beggar saint teetered on the brink in a critical condition. At times it seemed he was in a coma or unconscious, but those close to him were acutely aware of his consciousness being active at all times, regardless of the condition of the body. When he was in critical condition during his months in the hospital, he often refused to talk to the doctors. They would come to examine him and say, "This man is unconscious."

"No," Ma Devaki and Vijayalakshmi assured them, "he is conscious. He is not replying because he doesn't choose to." The doctors didn't believe them until they called to him and he responded. He was often awake but silent for these hospital darshans and raised his hands in blessing. Vijayalakshmi wrote about this time:

> In this period of one year, Bhagawan's enormous reserves of strength were tested again and again. The peace and love which he continued to radiate through the months of illness, was phenomenal. During the months of recovery, while at the hospital in Chennai, there was daily satsang. Bhagawan's quotation from Tulasidas, Kabirdas, Mahaperiyaval etc. anecdotes from the lives of saints were feasts, which left one hungry for more. His cheerfulness and peace through all the extreme pain and suffering made one increasingly aware of this enormous presence in the form of Bhagawan. Perfect strangers were immediately attracted by him and wanted to serve him. His reiteration that one is not the body began to be understood.[5]

As his condition improved very slowly and he began to give darshan from his hospital bed, sometimes there were as many as two or three hundred people at a time who wanted to see him; each one had to get an appointment and stand in line. The beggar pleaded to be taken back to the ashram in Tiruvannamalai. At times his spiritual discomfort became so acute that he wept with longing for the sanctuary of the ashram, but following the doctor's orders, the devotees felt they could not take him home without risking his life, and he remained in Chennai. When it came time for Lee Lozowick's annual visit, the beggar demanded to go back to the ashram. He was determined to be there when Lee arrived, and he specifically requested that Mani and Raji, who had been away, should be there to meet him.

Unquestionably, the surgery prolonged his life for six months, but it also prolonged

4 Ibid, pp. 94-95.

5 Ibid, p. 95.

his suffering. Yogi Ramsuratkumar was a very long way from the ecstatic years on the streets when he was a hidden beggar saint, free to move and work as he wished. The story becomes thick with pathos, and there is the underlying subtle current that implicates the global human failure to understand the reality of a Godman. Perhaps if his destiny had not cast him into the hands of the world in the way it did, he would have simply lain down under a tree, perhaps a *punnai* tree or an *asvattha*, and passed away from his body, but he was obligated to act out his last days bound in the golden cage of love. All this too was the will of God, the beggar's manifest destiny. The final result was that it gave a short reprieve from his impending death and made it possible for the enactment of the final play of his vast *lilas*.

On November 23, upon his insistence, Yogi Ramsuratkumar was finally and reluctantly released by the doctors to return to Tiruvannamalai. Seven days later, Lee Lozowick and a large group of Western devotees, including myself, arrived at the Yogi Ramsuratkumar Ashram. I found myself back in India with Lee and company much sooner than I ever thought possible. It had only been two years since I last saw the beggar king; when we left the ashram for Varanasi in 1998, in my heart I thought it would be the last time I would see Yogi Ramsuratkumar. Now destiny had dealt a favorable and auspicious blow—we arrived in Chennai at midnight on November 30, 2000, happy to be back, yet not knowing whether we would see Yogi Ramsuratkumar at all during our two week stay on the ashram.

India is always the same. As soon as we got off the plane, the redolence and cacophony and dense sultry night brought all my memories of India back into focus in a flash—the lively streets full of people, the markets riotous with colors and forms to dazzle the senses; fires burning in tea stalls along the roadside; the gleam of ghee lamps in dark recesses of temples; the dusty forests of the north and the tropical groves of the south; the salt mists at the ocean's edge; the hazy sunrises and opalescent dusks.

Volker and Ute Augustyniak, who lived at Triveni II, joined us for the drive to Tiruvannamalai, and informed Lee that Yogi Ramsuratkumar had only a few days before returned to the ashram from the hospital in Chennai. He was living in the abode, his private quarters in the back of the temple, and had made only a very few public appearances. Given how gravely ill he had been during the summer, it seemed like the beggar saint had miraculously resurrected himself; nonetheless, everyone knew that he was in an extremely precarious state, and could leave the body at any time.

As we rolled along in the hum and jangle of the van moving fast over a bumpy road, I could see the massive trunks of the tall tamarind trees that lined the road. Bullocks pulling carts, people sleeping stretched out along the roadside in green grass, in sheds and hovels and on parked carts were illumed in bright blurs of short-lived glowing images, briefly coming into focus and then dissolving back into the night as we sped past.

At four-thirty a.m. the van rolled up to the gate and we stepped out onto the sandy ground of the ashram. Bret Carlson and Mani were both there to greet Lee with *pranams* and embraces. Justice Arunachala was attending to his wife, who was ill in Chennai, and would not be on the ashram for the next two weeks; in his absence Mani would take care of the needs of Lee, Purna Steinitz and their students—a large group of almost forty people. He accompanied Lee down the lane to the cottages while chai was brought from the kitchen and served outside. Over tea Mani extended the hospitality of the ashram. Upon seeing that Lee was settled, he said to the group at large, "Please, ask me for anything you need," before he walked away.

The morning was bright and cool, with a wide swath of white clouds and mist over green Arunachala, which rose up only a mile or two away, a massive elegant extrusion on the horizon. The view was magnificent and as inspiring as always—Shiva, the infinite and vast power of creation and destruction, manifest in the holy mountain. Near the cottages there were gray and gold finches that flitted about in the hibiscus flowers, and small black crows that cawed to salute the day.

We were informed by Lee that Yogi Ramsuratkumar had been keeping a spontaneous schedule, and had been waiting for the arrival of Lee and his group. At nine-thirty the word came that Yogi Ramsuratkumar had called for Lee and his company. Instantly we gathered and walked down the lane to the temple. The vast, cavernous temple induced a hushed mood of awe and reverence, and we took our places where Mani indicated, on cotton blankets that had been spread on the concrete floor before the wide, raised concrete proscenium adjoining the abode of Yogi Ramsuratkumar that had been constructed on the far end of the temple.

There sat the regal beggar king, propped up by light green pillows in a large, dark red reclining chair. His feet, which were elevated so that the bare worn soles faced the group directly, seemed to shower us with light. His legs were covered with shawls. Around his head was the famous green turban. His face was pale and seemed drawn in pain, and yet he was more beautiful and sublime than ever—translucent, frail, but extremely present and real. His dark eyes flickered with a heightened awareness as he seemed to see and read the space and every person or movement within it. Ma Devaki and Vijayalakshmi sat quietly on a bamboo mat on the floor to his right, their eyes fastened on him. On his left a dark, stately young man, Rajmohan, squatted on the floor, poised to attend to his every need.

Yogi Ramsuratkumar sat silently and intently, his eyes fixed in a softly penetrating gaze on Lee, who was already settled in his seat on the floor below the stage, directly in front of the master. A divine presence as thick as syrup filled the vast space of the temple, but it was concentrated in the immediate emanations of the physical form of the old beggar, Yogi Ramsuratkumar.

Lee, Purna and the men sat on the right side of the room, the women on the left. A number of Indian devotees filed in behind the forty Westerners and took their places on the floor for the darshan to begin. There were seventy-five or a hundred people there. After about five minutes of sitting and gazing at Lee, Yogi Ramsuratkumar called him up to the stage. Lee made it to the stage in what seemed like one bounding leap and approached Yogi Ramsuratkumar with the *pranam* of hands pressed together, then went into a full body prostration at Yogi Ramsuratkumar's feet. Returning the salutation of a *pranam*, Yogi Ramsuratkumar watched as Lee rose to his feet beside him.

"Say something," he said, as if he was merely picking up a conversation where it had been left yesterday. There were no formal greetings, no sentiments, but a recognition of a relationship that existed outside of space and time, perfect in its ongoing continuity.

Lee returned to the temple floor below the stage and turned toward the crowd to speak. He said:

> We could say a few words about consistency. When we have a good day we are clear, enthusiastic. But when we have a bad day, we forget. What is important is that we remember Yogi Ramsuratkumar all the time, under all conditions. If we only remember when things are going well, but not when we are under stress, then we have missed what is really going on.
>
> Yogi Ramsuratkumar says we must remember with faith that he is always with us, no matter what the circumstance. So in our ongoing practice, whatever it is—whether it is mantra or meditation or whatever—we must practice with consistency so we can do what we came here for, to praise God. To praise God when things are light, when things are dark. His regard is always on us, is always there. His regard is so profound and extraordinary, that even when we forget him, he doesn't forget us. To be grateful for that regard is to remember him with some degree of consistency—to bring consistency to our praise, remembering, gratitude. So please remember that consistency of practice, every day, is what invokes Yogi Ramsuratkumar into our lives . . .

Lee turned and walked back up on the stage to Yogi Ramsuratkumar's side and went down on his knees. Yogi Ramsuratkumar said, "Thank you . . . My Father blesses Lee. My Father Blesses Lee Lozowick."

The voice, the beautiful lilting voice of Yogi Ramsuratkumar, flowed out and filled the space with pure blessing. He gazed for a few moments at Lee, who returned the gaze, and between them there was a tremendous open vulnerability. For me, witnessing these two together always called forth an aching longing—a blueprint that exists deep in the soul, called forth from its ancient place. The refinement of relationship that was expressed in such moments between Yogi Ramsuratkumar and Lee was beyond the human realm and yet entirely human. There was very little need for words. Everything was communicated through gaze, glance and mood, a telepathic synapse, a transmission of being.

It was with grateful awe that we realized what a tremendous sacrifice Yogi Ramsuratkumar made to be with us in darshan during this time period. He gave us more than we ever imagined in our wildest dreams, at the cusp of his life. He was often animated and interacting with everyone in ways that I certainly didn't think would be possible after Lee had informed us of his condition in August.

Still, it was obvious that he was enduring great pain. At times he called to Ma Devaki like a small child, who with Rajmohan, constantly attended to his every movement and word. He stirred now and then in discomfort and slight agitation, which brought their attention immediately to him. Ma Devaki seemed to be Yogi Ramsuratkumar's eyes and ears to the world. She somehow magnified and magnetized all for him. She was radiantly bright, and appeared calm and happy, though I could only imagine what she must have been going through in such close proximity to the master, now unquestionably in his final play on earth.

During this first darshan, with the exception of his brief interchange with Lee, Yogi Ramsuratkumar seemed fragile, remote, removed, more childlike than ever. He winced in pain several times; clearly he was making an immense effort to be available to us. Gratitude for this opportunity pierced our hearts along with the reality of the impermanence of all things, and we fell into a bittersweet mood of longing that was rampant and thick in the atmosphere.

Yogi Ramsuratkumar asked to be introduced individually to the students who were traveling with Purna Steinitz. The introductions began, and one by one everyone went up and bowed at the side of Yogi Ramsuratkumar's chair. "Your name?" He asked. At noon he left the stage and darshan was over. To appear in darshan at all was obviously a tremendous strain on him, probably more than he could physically bear, and yet he had given so much. We left in fullness, wondering what would happen next.

At two-fifteen that afternoon the word came that Yogi Ramsuratkumar was calling for Lee alone. Lee immediately dropped what he was doing and went to the master. Thirty minutes later he came back, saying nothing about his time with Yogi Ramsuratkumar. Our group arrived with Lee at the afternoon darshan and were ushered into the front row seats. Yogi Ramsuratkumar sat in his chair at the front of the stage surrounded by the mandala of Ma Devaki, Vijayalakshmi, Rajmohan and Mani. We would become very accustomed to this scene over the next two weeks.

Lee was called up to sit beside Yogi Ramsuratkumar while the introductions to Lee's students were continued. When Volker was introduced, it was explained that he lived at Bret Carlson's house, which was now Triveni II. Not remembering the sequence of events and how the house had become Lee's ashram, Yogi Ramsuratkumar had a question about this, and Bret was called up to the stage to his side. Yogi Ramsuratkumar asked Bret about his house and Bret said, "It's not my house, Bhagawan; it's Mr. Lee's house."

Yogi Ramsuratkumar seemed to absorb this information into a deep recess of his immense being, then he said slowly, and with a sweet smile, "Thank you." His words penetrated the room and reverberated into the ethers. This "Thank you" was heavily weighted with meaning, with purpose. Bret bowed his head and *pranamed*, then left the stage. Yogi Ramsuratkumar was satisfied.

It began to rain hard, and the sound on the temple roof drowned out most of the conversation that was going on onstage with Yogi Ramsuratkumar, but the scene itself was an all-attractive and glowing tableau: the beggar king, Yogi Ramsuratkumar, surrounded by his devotees. The graceful mandala of their presence together made a powerful communication; the space and air around this divine family was electric, tinged with sanctity, but it was also eminently human and tangible, real, inviting. Yogi Ramsuratkumar's smile was heartrending; it tore across the fabric of the heart, a sweet wound that welled up with joy to see such a sight. Yogi Ramsuratkumar laughed at the men as they ran up to the stage, copying Lee's quick movements whenever the yogi beckoned to him.

"They are all running!" Yogi Ramsuratkumar said with disarming innocence. Even in the ordeal of illness, his delight came through.

When Alain de Rosanbo was presented, Yogi Ramsuratkumar noticed a marked change in Alain's health, as he was walking with more ease.

"Lee and Chandra Swami have made Alain better," he said with a smile. He kept Alain by his side for a long time, while the tall Frenchman presented him with a pair of saffron-colored socks—a gift from Chandra Swami. Yogi Ramsuratkumar had the note from Chandra Swami read aloud several times: "With love, regards and respect to His Holiness Yogi Ramsuratkumar, from Chandra Swami. November 28, 2000." He called Lee up to the stage to read the note to him again.

There was much commotion about the socks—where they were from, what kind of socks, the fabric and so on. Finally Ma Devaki put them on Yogi Ramsuratkumar's feet. At this point there were eleven people onstage around him, awaiting the opportunity to serve in some way. Lee and Alain sat nearby, and Yogi Ramsuratkumar sat with the saffron socks on his feet.

"Devaki, can this Beggar walk?" he asked suddenly.

"If you put your will to it, Bhagawan," Devaki answered.

"I have no will, no mind," he replied. "All Father, only Father. This beggar has never done anything, only Father in Heaven." These words fell into the receiving well of the temple like drops of nectar into a deep pool, causing ripples to flow in ever-widening circles from the point where drop becomes pool. I thought of how Papa Ramdas gave Yogi Ramsuratkumar divine madness many years ago: surely we were witness to that even now—the living presence of God in human form.

"Have you met Chandra Swami?" Yogi Ramsuratkumar asked, turning slightly toward Lee, who sat at his side.

"Yes," Lee answered, "one time for three days, and another time for one day."

Yogi Ramsuratkumar fell quiet, and some birds went into a beautiful flurry of ecstatic song just outside the temple. He seemed to be listening to their songs, then he asked again in a childlike voice that sang of pure reverie, "What is the name of this Swami?"

"Chandra Swami," Devaki answered.

Yogi Ramsuratkumar wanted to know more about the giver of the gift of socks, and Lee told him that Chandra Swami had been silent for forty years and he lived in northern India. Yogi Ramsuratkumar seemed deeply moved by the gift and the loving message expressed in the note. Finally he said, as if in wonder that such a person exists and would venerate him in this way, he said, "Such a simple man, Chandra Swami, and the way he respects this dirty sinner! How could Chandra Swami have such love for this beggar?"

His mood shifted and he reflected ironically, with his characteristic sense of humor, "This beggar is wearing socks, now he must have some shoes!" Everyone smiled, knowing that Yogi Ramsuratkumar had not worn shoes for over fifty years. It was impossible not to be drawn in completely. His presence was compelling and drew my attention to a point of focus on him. Only he existed in the room; everyone and everything else—the activity, the conversation, our very breath—was only a manifestation of him.

"This dirty beggar puts his head at the feet of Chandra Swami," he said with a ghost of a smile hovering about his pale face. "I read something about Chandra Swami in some English paper . . ." He mused.

"You read it many times in *Facets of the Diamond*, Bhagawan," Devaki interjected. As if reflecting on a great and wondrous thing, he said, "I didn't know Chandra Swami; I only knew Lee Lozowick. How it happened, I don't know, but it is all by the Supreme Father. This beggar has not done anything."

The silence gathered in invisible pools of spiritual force around him while we waited for his next words.

"Devaki, you can take these off now," he said slowly, referring to the socks, which were removed right away.

"What happened in the U.S. presidential election?" he asked, introducing another subject altogether, as if he had switched an invisible channel. Mani and Devaki knew all the details of the election and explained it to Bhagawan.

"Bush was the governor of a state," he asked in a half statement, half question, as if to clarify his memory. It was incredible to me that he knew such details of American politics.

"Yes, Bhagawan, Texas," Mani answered.

Yogi Ramsuratkumar and the Indian devotees had a better knowledge of politics in the West than most of the Americans sitting in the audience. We sat dumbly watching, surprised by his interest in George Bush—a controversial right-wing American president who generated no loyalty from any of the Westerners who were present that day. The conversation continued in this vein between Yogi Ramsuratkumar, Ma Devaki and Mani until, with a sweet and somewhat sly smile, he looked out at us and said with a wave of his hand toward us, "They are not interested in politics!" His smiled deepened. His attention went back to the socks, and then to the American election again.

"Devaki, that American man, Bush—I think he got the presidency. I don't know so much about this . . . They say there are a few capitalists who dominate the politics in the U.S. Devaki, how this came? They say the U.S. is the richest country in the world today!" The astute insights and questions of Yogi Ramsuratkumar, intermingled with his overwhelming innocence and immediacy of pure felt contact with ultimate reality was astounding to witness. Throughout this ongoing conversation about American politics he held Lee's hand. He was working in mysterious ways, and it seemed that he was weaving

Lee into his world.

Yogi Ramsuratkumar began to ask more questions about Alain's health, his doctors in America. He wanted to know all about Alain's trip to see doctors in Palm Springs. He rested for a few moments and then started talking about Monaco in Europe, changed the subject again to talk about a book by a Chinese Taoist master. He wanted to know if Lee had read this book.

Lee said, "The book I read by him was about emptiness."

"If you have any book by this friend, see that I get it," Yogi Ramsuratkumar said to Lee. He turned to Devaki, "Devaki, in Banaras there are some booksellers who will have this book." He seemed very eager to have this book, and a few minutes later said, "There are some books this beggar can use. Don't forget it; it's very important."

Yogi Ramsuratkumar, who had been at death's door three months before, was now able to turn on a dime, change subjects, speak with clarity and knowledge, and then without a shift or pause suddenly change to become completely sublime, childlike and innocent. Clint Callahan commented in retrospect, "To see the videos of Lee's visit in 2000 where Yogi Ramsuratkumar was actually speaking to him on the stage and looking at people was a shock to me. It was miraculous, because when we visited him in August, I imagined he would not live out the month."

It was indeed miraculous, the whim and play of his Father in heaven. Yogi Ramsuratkumar was being moved, this way or that, by a divine will and design that was impossible to understand in any kind of rational way. Everything he mentioned, however secular or mundane, like American politics, seemed weighted with purpose and meaning and blessing. It seemed in moments that he was stirring the world pot, placing his attention in ways that would channel the flow of blessings in any given direction. Most of it now was going toward the American spiritual teacher, Lee Lozowick.

The introductions to the rest of Lee's group had been put on permanent hold, as Yogi Ramsuratkumar's attention was moved in a different direction by the gift from Chandra Swami and his play with Lee. To witness this, even from where we sat fifteen feet away, was to be immersed in the sublime. It didn't really matter what he was talking about. Even the most hardened and cynical among us were captivated, enthralled by the exalted emanations of his being.

"Pon Kamaraj introduced Lee Lozowick to this beggar," he said to Devaki.

"No, Bhagawan, it's the other way around," she clarified.

Just then Rajmohan, who I had never met before, realized that I was writing down what was being said. He pointed in my direction and said to Yogi Ramsuratkumar, "That lady is writing something down over there . . ."

Ma Devaki glanced over at me with a smile and said to Yogi Ramsuratkumar, "That's Mary Young, Bhagawan." It must have been a somewhat familiar sight, as I had taken copious notes in his darshan in 1998. Gazing for a moment in my direction, Yogi Ramsuratkumar waved his hand ever so lightly, like a blessing in fact, as if to dismiss any concern with my writing and at the same time, giving permission. Then he said with characteristic selflessness, "These words of Lee's and Alain's should be written down."

During the ten o'clock darshan on December 1st, *jayanthi* day, we entered the temple, circumambulated the statue of Yogi Ramsuratkumar, then took our places on the floor below the empty stage. The chanting began and continued while a steady flow of people filed in and took their seats on the colorful cotton blankets and mats that had been laid on the floor in front of the stage. Over fifteen hundred people, who joined in the chanting and waited for the possible appearance of Yogi Ramsuratkumar, made the huge space seem smaller. After an hour Mani appeared onstage and beseeched people to stay calm, not to rush the stage and to keep their seats when Yogi Ramsuratkumar came out. As his condition was extremely delicate, it was both a heartfelt plea and also a demand.

Yogi Ramsuratkumar finally emerged from behind the partial wall of white concrete that covered the door to his private apartment—the "abode." He was rolled to the center of the stage in his big chair on wheels. His face was stunning. He looked like transparent glass, like a carved statue, but soft and terribly vulnerable. The intimacy of seeing Yogi Ramsuratkumar in this fragile state was almost unbearable. He appeared to be far, far away, wrapped in a pale quiescence that lay upon him like a veil. Five minutes later he was wheeled back into his private apartment, his wan face etched in pain.

The chanting continued until twelve noon, when the large crowd dispersed to take *prasad* in the dining hall—a rich and lavish feast with six or seven dishes that perfectly reflected the atmosphere of Grace, so obvious to the subtle perception, which flowed endlessly from Yogi Ramsuratkumar.

We arrived in the temple for afternoon darshan on *jayanthi* Day and circumambulated the statue. Yogi Ramsuratkumar was already positioned on the stage in his red reclining chair. As we took our seats he was expressing concern as to whether everyone in Lee's and Purna's groups were present in the temple. Rajmohan counted, talked with Lee and acted as go between. When the details were cleared up, Yogi Ramsuratkumar called Lee up to the stage and asked him to give a talk. Again there were twelve to fifteen hundred people in the hall. Lee *pranamed* to Yogi Ramsuratkumar then walked off the stage and turned toward the crowd to speak:

> Ordinarily we would use the word "birthday" in English, but with a being like Yogi Ramsuratkumar we call this day his "appearance day" because the appearance of birth, death and change is only the appearance of things. Yesterday Yogi Ramsuratkumar said, "This beggar has no will, no mind, only Father is present." You or I use personal will to choose a restaurant or something to do, but to Yogi Ramsuratkumar there is only Father. There is no personal will, only the pure Divine.
>
> Yogi Ramsuratkumar appeared, had many adventures with the sadhus on the Ganges as a boy, wandered all over India. Yogi Ramsuratkumar had three fathers: Sri Aurobindo, Ramana Maharshi and Papa Ramdas, who finally made him mad, who took away all human volition. So there has been some appearance of progress through time and space, and changes over time, but the Divine appeared in the world in Yogi Ramsuratkumar

and took on a certain play, a certain drama. The Divine arose and took on a certain appearance, so that we could relate to It. If the Divine appeared in Its true form we wouldn't be able to relate to it—like Arjuna, who asked to see Krishna's true form. Arjuna said, "Give me a glimpse of your true divinity," but when Krishna showed him, he wasn't big enough to bear it.

So, we have some clarity and understanding to realize that God takes human form so we can recognize and relate to God. Many years ago on December 1st a child was born apparently, and grew older every year, became an adult and grew old. In time and space it appears that changes have happened, but outside time and space, That which Is was never born, never grew, and will not die.

Yogi Ramsuratkumar said yesterday, "This beggar has no will, only Father." We are very lucky to have the opportunity to sit in the presence of and have darshan with the literal Divine, concretized in the human body of Yogi Ramsuratkumar as he really is—no will, only Father in Heaven, complete unity, no separation, complete oneness. Whenever we gather together in his name, it is exactly as Jesus said, "When two or more are gathered in my name, there will I be also." It's exactly the same with Yogi Ramsuratkumar. We're very lucky to be in the presence of one who has no will—it's all Father in Heaven.

Yogi Ramsuratkumar is very intelligent, there's no question about that, but he has no will of his own because it is all Father. We are so absolutely fortunate to be in his presence! In Islam it is said that if one makes the pilgrimage to Mecca to see the holy of holies, one will see paradise, but in Islam the holy of holies is a black stone. We have the Holiest of Holies here in this room—not a stone, but a living, breathing appearance of God, here in our midst, in this lifetime! So to return in gratitude some small part what has been given to us is to chant his name, to say his name with faith, because "When two or more are gathered in my name, there will I be also." So please, chant the name of Yogi Ramsuratkumar, remember the name of Yogi Ramsuratkumar.

Lee walked onstage and knelt beside Yogi Ramsuratkumar's chair to receive his blessing and *prasad*. Yogi Ramsuratkumar then said, "Purna must speak." After Purna gave a short talk, Lee presented a gift to Yogi Ramsuratkumar—videotapes of Yogi Ramsuratkumar that were compiled and edited from the vast video footage that had been taken during the past six years of Lee's visits on the ashram. Lee also gave the master a large number of poems that he had written over the past several months.

"Ask them to sing some songs," he asked Lee, after he had received the gifts. Returning to his seat on the floor on the men's side of the room, Lee motioned to Sharana and me to sing three poems. We stood and sang, then Lee indicated we should sing one more. After the fourth poem Yogi Ramsuratkumar called Lee back up to the stage.

"Lee, do you have any poetry books to sell?" Kneeling beside Yogi Ramsuratkumar, Lee laughed and answered, "I happen to have some with me." At Lee's request, we had carried heavy boxes of the massive books through many airports from Phoenix and L.A. to Japan, Malaysia and Chennai, precisely so that Yogi Ramsuratkumar—who had had so much fun selling them for the past two years—could sell them again if he wished.

Lee motioned to Purna, who took off with one of his students to get two cases of *Death of a Dishonest Man*. The book is so big that each case contains only eight books. Yogi Ramsuratkumar asked Lee to say something about the poetry book to everyone. Lee stood and walked down from the stage to speak. He laughed sheepishly and said, "Yogi Ramsuratkumar has asked me to say a few things about the book of poems. It's a collection of poetry written over twenty-five years. The title is *Death of a Dishonest Man*: I'm still dishonest, but with Yogi Ramsuratkumar's blessing I'm dying each day—or at least each month. That I can be sure of!" He said a few more things, keeping it very short and to the point.

Yogi Ramsuratkumar held up the first book and said, "This book is for sale." One of Lee's German students immediately got up and walked to the stage to buy it. While she was making the exchange, Yogi Ramsuratkumar turned to Mani, who was standing nearby.

"Say something . . ." he instructed.

Mani walked to the edge of the stage and faced the large Indian audience and made his brief pitch, saying, "Bhagawan has asked me to say something about this book. Lee has made a book on twenty-five years experience with Bhagawan. This is a way of blessing . . . A way to receive Bhagawan's blessing." Mani spoke in English and then in Tamil, and as soon as he was finished, a steady stream of people, coming one by one, formed a line that flowed up to the stage. In the meantime it had become clear that Yogi Ramsuratkumar was signing the books, and that each person had the opportunity to interact directly with him and receive his blessing. With each person he asked, "Your name?" before signing the book.

It was a tremendously tender and moving scene. Lee sat on the floor, about four feet away from Yogi Ramsuratkumar's left hand, where he unwrapped the cellophane from each book and handed it to Rajmohan, who then handed it gingerly to Bhagawan, placing it gently in his lap to sign. Rajmohan acted as intermediary between the buyer and Yogi Ramsuratkumar, along with Ma Devaki, who would also sometimes interpret people's words when Bhagawan didn't hear or understand what was said.

The beggar saint was like a small child, delighting in the play, and also clearly accepting their assistance in managing such a scene. The large crowd buzzed with excitement. Lee sat off to the side, handing each book over, receiving money from Yogi Ramsuratkumar and, following his instructions, counting it each time. He was quietly smiling and radiant. Two cases were sold, a total of sixteen books.

"Are there more?" Yogi Ramsuratkumar asked Lee. Soon Purna and the men came running up with two more cases. Alain de Rosanbo, who already had a copy of the book, went up to buy another. The buzz in the temple grew to a cacophony as a steady stream of people came in and went out. By the end of the beggar's bazaar four more books were sold, making a total of twenty.

"Good business," Yogi Ramsuratkumar said to Lee with a mischievous smile.

Lee smiled back and said, "Yes."

"Father willing, more good business," Yogi Ramsuratkumar said, his smile growing bigger and brighter. He was animated and enlivened by the play, his mood and energy and countenance completely changed from the pallor and pain of the morning. His smiles alone were worth traveling thousands of miles to see.

The chanting was resumed and a Western sadhu came into the temple. Yogi Ramsuratkumar noticed him right away and wanted Lee to talk with him. Lee invited him to sit beside him and they talked briefly while the chanting continued to fill the room. Soon afterward Yogi Ramsuratkumar said, "These people can disperse."

Mani came forward and announced that the crowd should disperse, "Quick, quick!" He seemed worried that the crowd would easily become overexcited and rush forward in a way that would overwhelm Yogi Ramsuratkumar. It seemed unthinkable, and yet in just a few days we would witness that religious fervor right there, in the temple. The ashram staff very effectively encouraged people to leave, ushering them out quickly as the closing victory call was sung by Pankkajam:

"Om Bhagawan Sri Yogi Ramsuratkumar Maharaj Ki Jai! Sri Annai Devaki Mataji Ki Jai!"

As we entered the temple on December 2 for darshan we saw that Yogi Ramsuratkumar was already positioned in his chair near the front and center of the stage.

"Say something useful to these people," he said to Lee as soon as everyone was settled. Lee stepped down from the stage to the concrete floor and addressed the crowd of about four hundred people:

> Yogi Ramsuratkumar has asked me to say a few words that might be useful, but what makes them useful is if we put them into practice.
>
> There is a certain fascination with phenomena that occurs. In the West, but also everywhere, we are curious and desirous of extraordinary circumstances; a life of simple humility is not so interesting to us. We discover various sadhanas, complicated yogas and so on, and we lose interest in the ordinary, everyday practice that builds obedience and draws the blessing of surrender. We want to progress quickly and we want altered states of consciousness.
>
> Yogi Ramsuratkumar has given us one practice that subsumes all others—to use His name as our connection to Him, as prayer, as praise. The wonder of that is that in fact Yogi Ramsuratkumar's name is all those things that we think we need to go to extraordinary measures to produce in ourselves.
>
> I'm not disparaging the esoteric yoga tradition that produces amazing

> results in the body and in life, but the repetition of Yogi Ramsuratkumar's name will produce all those things—if those are useful to our lives. Yogi Ramsuratkumar's name is invocational. Human beings have free will and extraordinary capacities, but when we invoke Yogi Ramsuratkumar's name, whatever is Father's Will is what will manifest. Many of us still imagine that we still have a personal will . . . .
>
> When we chant or speak or think his name, it is an automatic prayer to Father in Heaven to obviate your personal will, wishes, circumstances. To chant or speak Yogi Ramsuratkumar's name is to invoke Father's will for us in any given moment. It's not that Father in Heaven is some kind of dictator, where everything is taken away. Devotees are happy, successful, full of life and joy in Yogi Ramsuratkumar's company . . . .
>
> My request and prayer for all of us is to use the name of Yogi Ramsuratkumar with faith and remember Him under all circumstances, night and day, to allow the Blessings of Father in Heaven to come in and sweep away all dust and to move us in that way.

Yogi Ramsuratkumar called Lee back up a little later and asked about the poetry. Once again the great merchant opened his beggar's bazaar. Yogi Ramsuratkumar asked Lee and then Mani to speak about the book. They each gave short and concise speeches, and right away a line formed. As the ritual of the sales began, Lee sat as usual on Yogi Ramsuratkumar's left side, unwrapping the books and handing them to Rajmohan, who handed them to Yogi Ramsuratkumar to sign, while Mani escorted people to and from the stage in an orchestration of movement and form.

In the influence of Yogi Ramsuratkumar the whole scene took on a burnished quality. Somehow every move, every interchange was full and rich, heavy but also light, expansive, and wondrous at the same time. Pascal and Marie-Odile, disciples of Arnaud Desjardins who were traveling with Lee, gave Yogi Ramsuratkumar U.S. dollars; he peered at the money for a long time. Mani and his wife Raji and many other Indian devotees bought a book. The line kept forming and reforming as more people came and went, buying books and receiving Yogi Ramsuratkumar's blessing.

The flow went on like this until an Indian man came up to buy a book. A conversation ensued between the man, Rajmohan and Yogi Ramsuratkumar. After a few minutes the man called his wife and daughter up to the stage. The daughter was a quadriplegic, confined to a wheelchair. Several men from the audience came and lifted her up, wheelchair and all, onto the stage. She was wheeled forward by her mother, who was weeping and making supplications. Yogi Ramsuratkumar seemed agitated by the girl's condition, and between her tears the girl began to say, "Help me Bhagawan, help me—I'm suffering, I'm suffering."

Yogi Ramsuratkumar looked at the girl with eyes as old as the mountain, as dark and mysterious as the sky at midnight. The moment was fraught with the tension of a great irony.

"Yes, yes . . . " he said with compassion, "to be born is to suffer. Everyone who is born suffers . . ."

The personal suffering of this girl and her parents, set against the burden and sacrifice of Yogi Ramsuratkumar, whose suffering was also obvious and mysteriously both human and divine, was a striking teaching communication. The burden of suffering borne by Yogi Ramsuratkumar was so clearly impersonal and universal in every way, and yet he was also suffering personally as a human man in a physical body. Despite his own suffering his example of selflessness made this exchange made even more poignant.

His words seemed to echo in the temple, "Yes, yes . . . to be born is to suffer. Everyone who is born suffers . . ." Yogi Ramsuratkumar had spoken softly, but his words were crystal clear in the space—the same words that Buddha spoke as the first of the four laws of his teaching. "All life is suffering." What else needed to be said? After about five minutes that seemed like an eternity, the mother and daughter left the stage with tear-stained faces.

The mood changed completely as the gay bookselling spree continued unabated until all the books were gone. "Are there more books?" Yogi Ramsuratkumar asked sweetly. Lee answered that there were only two more books, but they were at Triveni.

"All else are sold, but there are two more at Bret's house, Bhagawan," Mani explained.

Clearly Yogi Ramsuratkumar intended to sell every last one of them. Bret was dispatched to get the books and took off running. Within minutes he was back again, to the surprise of Yogi Ramsuratkumar, who seemed very pleased that Bret did this task so quickly. As soon as the last two books were in Lee's hands onstage, Yogi Ramsuratkumar had Mani get up and speak to the crowd. He said, "There are only two books left. This is a way of *blessing*, not of selling . . ." he emphasized.

The last two books were quickly sold, making a total of forty-one books. The *lila* had come to an end; Lee had no more copies of *Death of a Dishonest Man* in Tiruvannamalai. Yogi Ramsuratkumar turned to him with a smile and said, "We are happy we have sold all these books."

"Good sales," Ma Devaki said, also smiling. She was obviously very happy to see Bhagawan smiling and animated by the activity of the morning.

"Not sales, blessings!" Yogi Ramsuratkumar corrected. "Nothing was sold! Only Father's blessings. That's why Lee brings all these books, because he knows it's a way for people to get Blessings." He smiled again and said, "Now everybody is happy and we can sing!" He was smiling and lively as he told Lee to ask someone to stand up and lead chants.

Returning to his seat Lee looked over at the women's side and asked Paula Zuccarello and I to get up and lead chants. We walked to the edge of the stage, pranamed to Yogi Ramsuratkumar, turned to face the audience then sang, "Om guru charinam, Om guru charinam, Yogi Ramsuratkumar, Om guru charinam," a chant written by Doug Fulker. After about twenty minutes of this, while Yogi Ramsuratkumar sat quietly, sometimes watching and listening, he said, "They can sing and dance." I looked at Lee for confirmation that I had heard Yogi Ramsuratkumar correctly. Lee mouthed at me with a wry smile, "Sing *and dance*." I looked at Paula and said, "We have to sing *and dance*." We joined hands with a smile and began to dance, dipping and swaying to the rhythm of the chant, and mostly going around in circles.

At four o'clock that day the Westerners traveling with Lee entered the temple and went straight to our usual seats. Yogi Ramsuratkumar was already established in the central spot onstage. He called Mani over and spoke quietly to him. Mani walked out to the audience and asked Parathasarathy to sing. Yogi Ramsuratkumar had called Parthasarathy to sing every day since we had arrived, which was always a joy for those of us listening. Whenever he sang, his gentle sweet voice would rise and fill the space with devotion and the humility forged from many years in Yogi Ramsuratkumar's company. His songs always strengthened and fed the mood of the space that Yogi Ramsuratkumar was creating. Today during his song Yogi Ramsuratkumar had a long discussion about some poems and songs with Ma Devaki and Vijayalakshmi. Yogi Ramsuratkumar was very concerned with getting copies and making sure that they had records of all the songs that Parthasarathy was singing.

Finally Yogi Ramsuratkumar asked Vijayalakshmi to sing a long chant while he closed his eyes and seemed to rest. Ma Devaki and Rajmohan were tending to his every movement and need. Obviously dressed and cared for by his attendants, instead of the beggar's rags he had worn for so many years on the streets, or the dusty and dirt-stained *dhoti* and voluminous gray-blue shawl he had worn in more recent years, Yogi Ramsuratkumar was now carefully dressed in a fresh, clean, pale yellow-green *kirta* shirt, his head wrapped in the usual green turban cloth. Behind his head were three or four small dark orange pillows. He was covered with a light wool shawl, and his reclining chair, almost a bed on wheels, was dark burgundy red. Across his chest lay the circles of his prayer beads—*japa malas*—in rudraksh, crystal and sandalwood.

All this rich color and the dusky pallor of Yogi Ramsuratkumar's dark skin made a contrast to the stark white and gray of the backdrop—the unfinished concrete of the temple walls and floor. All around Yogi Ramsuratkumar was vast space, infinite space, a creation in process, unfinished and evolving. Within that seemingly limitless space appeared his physical form, a small and powerful figure, exuding divine authority, as still as the infinite night, tender in his beauty and vulnerability, heartrending in his love.

He seemed to be in a deep state of repose, drawing himself inside to sleep, rest or listen. Who could possibly know? He was entirely enigmatic, but in a very human way he seemed weary. At the same time, his face was translucent. He had the polished, otherworldly look of a stone sculpture worn smooth from years of worship and adoration. He slept while Rajmohan and Ma Devaki fanned him on either side and Vijayalakshmi sang the poem once again. There was an aching presence of longing that permeated the whole scene, and I felt drawn in by the all-attractive magnet of Yogi Ramsuratkumar at rest in his mandala of sanctuary.

The mood of these tender moments was flavored by the eminent reality of his physical passing, which pressed in upon me as an acute sweetness of longing. This passage—the appearance of change in the physical form of Yogi Ramsuratkumar, of a journey from here to there—was somehow underway, and seemed to be rejoiced in by the angels and deities that thickly populated the atmosphere around him. It was a wonder and a great blessing to sit with him in these moments.

Yogi Ramsuratkumar appeared to wake up or come out of the deep reverie in which he rested. When he returned to the world of action, however delicate, tremulous or almost imperceptible his movements might be, it was as if the whole world was shifted into a new mode. He called Parathasarathy up again, this time to read something in Tamil, and then enquired of Ma Devaki about the shawl that covered his legs.

After Parathasarathy had sung and received *prasad*, Yogi Ramsuratkumar called Lee up to the stage and spoke with him for a few moments. Lee immediately bounded down from the stage and took off with several of the men, including Rajmohan, leaving the temple entirely. Yogi Ramsuratkumar had sent him to see the Ma Devaki Veda Patashala.

As soon as Lee left the temple, Yogi Ramsuratkumar looked at me. He made a motion with his hand that was as tender as a butterfly fluttering its wings, beckoning me to come to him. "Mary," he said, so gently I could barely hear it. Immediately I was absorbed in the magnetic attraction of his attention, which was reeling me in like a fish on a line. I walked up and onto the stage, got down on my knees and pranamed at his side. He looked into my eyes as if he had known me forever.

"This Beggar would like you to sing a song. And you can dance," he said, simply and sweetly. I looked to Devaki and asked, "One of Lee's poems?" for confirmation.

"Lee's poems, Bhagawan?" He nodded almost imperceptibly and spoke briefly with her. She looked at me with a smile of encouragement and said, "Yes, a poem and a song in English with dancing."

Then Yogi Ramsuratkumar looked at me and said very clearly, "Sing and dance, *like this morning*." The "like this morning" part was emphatic. Instantly I felt he was referring most of all to the mood of the morning dancing, which had been joyful and sublime. Mani was standing next to me and repeated, "Like this morning," to make sure I had understood. I decided to take what Bhagawan said literally, but just to make sure I asked one more clarifying question, since the heat of the moment, in such close proximity to Yogi Ramsuratkumar, was wiping my mind clean.

"With a friend?" I ventured.

"With a friend, Bhagawan?" Devaki repeated to Bhagawan. He made a slight gesture with his hand; it seemed to me that he was saying that the questions were unnecessary, as I already knew what he wanted. I walked down and asked my friend Sharana to join me. Within seconds we were dancing and singing before the large audience—hundreds of people were watching with great interest, but the only person I cared about was Yogi Ramsuratkumar. Again we sang, "Om guru charinam, Om guru charinam, Yogi Ramsuratkumar, Om guru charinam."

There was a tremendous surge of happiness, gratitude and ecstasy as the dancing and singing flowed through us with spontaneity, fluidity and ease. A perceptible flow of energy came from the audience; everyone seemed drawn into the praise and the prayer. Yogi Ramsuratkumar's eyes danced with pleasure and his face was transformed by the beauty of his smile. I felt that I would dance forever if he willed it. We danced and sang "Om Guru Charinam" for about fifteen minutes, but it passed like a tender dream before my eyes.

Finally the beggar king called us up to the stage to receive *prasad* and his blessing. Kneeling at his side, the dark smouldering fire of his eyes burned deeply into mine. His ancient and wan face exuded the most precious love. It was a moment I would never forget.

"I like that very much," he smiled. "The singing and dancing is very good. This beggar would like more singing and dancing. You can prepare some more, in English."

Those words, "The singing and dancing is very good," were messengers from the heart of God—pure love and mercy, melted and poured over the cold places of sorrow or separation lodged in my heart, like all human hearts, for a lifetime. His gaze seared into mine with the burning fire of love as Yogi Ramsuratkumar very, very slowly dropped the *prasad* into my outstretched hands. For what seemed like a very long time, I was riveted to his gaze, staring into infinity, into the heart of God, into the living heart of mercy and compassion. Trembling and drunk from the wine of Yogi Ramsuratkumar's sublime attention, I found my way back to my seat.

As soon as we sat down Yogi Ramsuratkumar called up a woman I would meet two years later when conducting interviews for this book—his long-time devotee Vasugi Jairaj, the daughter of Rajamanickam, who had been an ardent devotee of Yogi Ramsuratkumar. He said to her and a friend in English, "Sing and dance exactly the same way." They left the stage and stood where we had stood only minutes before; it was their turn to dance and sing for the beggar saint. It seemed that Yogi Ramsuratkumar was weaving his Indian devotees and his Western devotees together with these sweet *lilas*. I watched with a full heart while Yogi Ramsuratkumar's face lit up with the same love as he watched their singing and dancing; he was an infinite divine vessel, overflowing with a love one can only imagine and aspire to. His being was a pure conduit for the love of God. In those moments He was the divine Enjoyer.

Afterward many people, both Westerners and Indians, came forward to say that they were deeply moved by the dancing and singing. It was the *lila* of Yogi Ramsuratkumar, and those of us who danced could not take credit for it. It was his dance, his movement, his song. He had transmitted to us the heart on fire.

On December 3 the sound of voices lifted in resonant praise filled the hall while the large group waited for the appearance of the beggar saint. After a while Yogi Ramsuratkumar was wheeled out in his chair. Calling Lee to his side, he said, "I would like you to say a few words that would be useful to all. Thank you."

Lee turned and walked down off the stage to take his position just in front of the crowd. He began by telling a story of Ramdas and his devotee who drank from the spittoon Ramdas used. Ramdas called this man "a dangerous man," and Lee recommended that we all be "dangerous" in this way—willing to risk all for the transmission of the guru's grace. He ended his short talk and *pranamed* to Yogi Ramsuratkumar.

"Lee, I would like you to tell more stories, if you feel that you can do it," the beggar instructed. Lee smiled, *pranamed* and went back to storytelling.

"When I was young I never imagined I would travel in India, or how I would feel about India . . ." Lee then told the story, which he has told many times in India, Europe and America, of how he came to meet Yogi Ramsuratkumar for the first time in 1976. He told a few more stories and then turned to Yogi Ramsuratkumar and asked, "Shall I go on?"

"I want you to tell *more* and *more* stories. I want to *hear* . . ." Yogi Ramsuratkumar said lovingly, with a beatific smile at Lee.

The sublime quality of Yogi Ramsuratkumar's voice was completely disarming to the mind and ego, and in this moment it was especially so for me. I remembered Andrew Cohen once saying that when he met Yogi Ramsuratkumar many years ago at his house on Sannadhi Street, "His whole communication was in the lilt in his voice—that incredible lilt in his voice!"

Woven into the charm of these requests from Yogi Ramsuratkumar to Lee was the implicit understanding that Lee would be telling stories of Yogi Ramsuratkumar for many years to come, to audiences in the U.S., Europe and India, and through these stories many people would be blessed, simply by hearing the name of a dirty beggar. In this and other ways, Yogi Ramsuratkumar's work would continue in the years ahead.

Lee turned back to the audience and told more stories. He said of his first meeting with Yogi Ramsuratkumar, "I'd never met anyone like Yogi Ramsuratkumar. The greatest extent of my hopes and dreams can't begin to touch what I have found in Yogi Ramsuratkumar. I've tried in some way to capture some of that in my stories, though not very successfully, by my criteria."

Recalling his 1986 trip to India, Lee said, "I had been writing poems and letters to him all those years since 1979—paeans of my love and devotion to him, which he must have found humorous at the time." With a touch of the self-deprecation so characteristic of Lee, he talked about his own arrogance in assuming that he had devotion to Yogi Ramsuratkumar:

> As long as my relationship to Yogi Ramsuratkumar was based on any personal illusions—'me, me, me, I, I, I am a great teacher in America'—as long as my relationship was based on that illusion, I couldn't do the work that Father in Heaven gave to Yogi Ramsuratkumar with the purity with which it needed to be done. If I was looking for personal approval, if I was praising in order to receive praise, how pure could that praise be? As

> long as I held Yogi Ramsuratkumar to be anything less than the One we follow from lifetime to lifetime . . . . because a crumb from his table is greater than a feast of kings . . . .

When Lee went up to receive *prasad* Yogi Ramsuratkumar said, "This beggar didn't understand most of your language, but he is very happy that you say his name over and over again, every sentence. Thank you, thank you."

After Lee took his seat, Yogi Ramsuratkumar asked Devaki to ask the "girls who sing and dance" to come up and sing "some English songs." Devaki turned to me, smiled and said, "Bhagawan wants you to sing and dance."

As Yogi Ramsuratkumar had requested, Sharana and I had been practicing—both Lee's poems put to music and some well-known songs in English. We *pranamed* to Yogi Ramsuratkumar and went through "Swing Low, Sweet Chariot," "He's Got the Whole World (in His Hands)," and three poems written by Lee and put to the melodies of familiar popular songs. The same sweet mood took over, and it felt as if the whole crowd was dancing with us.

Yogi Ramsuratkumar motioned us to sit down and asked if there was anyone else who could sing and dance—"Christmas songs," he specified this time. Colette Lennon had come prepared with the music to several traditional Christmas carols, since Yogi Ramsuratkumar had requested these in years past. Now Colette, Paula Zuccarello, Paula Steinitz and Kristen Kelly, one of Purna's students, got up and sang Christmas songs and danced around and around in a circle holding hands. Their dancing and singing was sweet, whimsical and outright funny in moments.

Yogi Ramsuratkumar conducted business throughout this interlude, now and then watching them with a big smile of enjoyment. Every time they stopped he would call out, "Keeping dancing!" with a twinkle in his eye. The four women put their hearts into it, and Paula Steinitz's enthusiastic "Ho, ho, ho!" on "Jingle Bells" added some humor to the play. Colette and Kristen knew all the words of the Christmas hymns by heart and kept the revelry going. Several times the women stopped and *pranamed* to Yogi Ramsuratkumar, wondering if he wanted them to continue, only to receive a command, "Dance!" or, "They can dance some more."

It was a gift of grace to simply watch the beggar's sheer pleasure in the dancing and singing. Once he turned to the group of women with a charming smile and asked, "Are you tired?" They were breathing heavily from their exertions. They smiled back. Before they could respond he commanded with a mischievous twinkle in his eye, "Dance!" Watching from the audience, we too were swept up in the joy as the women took off again enthusiastically. Yogi Ramsuratkumar was transformed during these dancing episodes. He sparkled with energy; he was suddenly youthful, magnetic, the embodiment of allure, beauty, charm—the eternal Krishna at play with the *gopis*.

At one point Yogi Ramsuratkumar looked at the four women and called out in a surprisingly energetic voice, "Dance! Dance!" I think this must have been the most enchanting, joyful thing I'd ever heard spoken by anyone! It was complete and total permission to celebrate life—to enjoy and bask in the delight of life and love. The singing and dancing was only the surface of Yogi Ramsuratkumar's divine whim in these moments; it seemed that he was using the action of appearances—the singing and dancing—to feed and catalyze the hidden work that could only be perceived through the subtle senses, and even then remained a mystery.

As the interludes of singing and dancing progressed, one thing became very clear: what Suzuki Roshi called "beginner's mind" was the best approach to such an opportunity. This whimsical request to "sing and dance" from Yogi Ramsuratkumar carried with it the chance to work simultaneously with all three centers—thinking, feeling and moving. When these three centers are unified, there is a spontaneous, unfettered harmony of perfect action, an experience of something very close to the Baul ideal of *sahajiya*, or the natural state of awakened consciousness as it manifests in the body.

In the afternoon darshan, when we entered the temple Yogi Ramsuratkumar was already seated onstage with Ma Devaki and Vijayalakshmi in their usual places on the floor at his side, while Rajmohan and Mani stood close by. Yogi Ramsuratkumar was pale again, and this time seemed enervated, exhausted and tired. The happiness and animation of the past two days seemed to have fled in the face of his ongoing physical ordeal. He instructed Ma Devaki and Vijayalakshmi to lead chants, which they did for about thirty minutes. He was sleeping or resting during this time, his face slightly tensed in pain. Around four-thirty he was wheeled out in his big easy chair. Just as he was leaving, he called Lee up to the stage and talked with him for a while. I could hear him say, "This beggar is leaving now. I may not be able to come back, and so Lee will manage this space." He spoke further, but his soft voice drifted off into the vast space of the temple. Then he instructed Mani and Rajmohan to place two white plastic chairs in front on the stage—one for Lee, and on Lee's left side, another chair for Purna. As he left, the chanting was resumed.

It was cloudy and quite cool the next morning. As the darkness began to fade into light, the tropical landscape came into focus, and up above, a thick blanket of fog hung over Arunachala. By ten o'clock the mists were all gone and the day was hot and cloudless. Entering the vast cool temple for darshan, we were greeted again by an empty stage. Lee asked some of his students to lead the chants. The chanting had already induced a strong mood in the large gathering when the sleeping form of Yogi Ramsuratkumar was wheeled out of the abode and onto the stage over an hour later. Ma Devaki roused him to ask if someone should lead chants. He said, "Lee will lead all," and went back to what looked like a deep but uncomfortable sleep.

When the second chant was over Yogi Ramsuratkumar stirred from his sleep and said to Devaki, very much the way a small feverish child would speak to his mother, "Devaki, I go inside now . . . " He seemed to be in no condition to appear before the large crowd.

"What should the people do here?" she asked.

"Lee will manage. Lee and Purna will manage everything." He was obviously weak and too tired to carry on, and he turned the burden over, as he had many times before, to Lee.

One hundred and fifty people arrived by bus for the afternoon darshan. At four twenty-five Yogi Ramsuratkumar appeared. He had Devaki, Vijayalakshmi and Rajmohan sing the Shankaracharya's song for peace, "Mythreem Bajatha." After they had sung it several times at his request, Yogi Ramsuratkumar asked Pankkajam to come up and sing. She walked to the front and stood below the stage on the women's side of the room. Her mellifluent and powerful voice filled the room with a song that was so piercingly beautiful and rich with devotion that it was easy to be carried away on its powerful current. By Yogi Ramsuratkumar's grace there was transformational power in that voice. I wished it would never end.

My eyes were magnetically drawn to Yogi Ramsuratkumar, who sat impassively and quietly listening. Suddenly his physical image began to take on a supernatural brightness, a disorienting glow, a fog of luminosity. The physical world and body of Yogi Ramsuratkumar receded into a glowing blur, and out of that emerged another reality from which the living Lord appeared as all glory, mercy, power, love. These words may sound like overused rhetoric, but in this moment they were remade, resurrected, and completely true. Somehow my sight adjusted to bear the effulgence of Yogi Ramsuratkumar in his heaven realm. I perceived him as a being of incomprehensible dimension, alive in all realms, radiating compassion in all directions. This entire experience lasted perhaps five minutes and seemed to come as a direct transmission from Yogi Ramsuratkumar. It was his gift—the true darshan. From the sweetness of longing we were lifted into his realm, into the *mahabhava* of divine love.

After the second song Pankkajam sat down. The atmosphere was charged, altered in its cellular and vibrational structure. Yogi Ramsuratkumar looked out at Lee and said, "Lee can give a talk."

Lee talked about a famous Japanese poet from the seventeenth century, Issa, who was an awakened master in the Zen Buddhist tradition, which teaches "form is emptiness; emptiness is form," from the Heart Sutra. It is a teaching of nonduality—the realization that everything is the Divine, and that all apparent phenomena is continuous, interconnected and unitive. The formula "form is emptiness; emptiness is form" also contains the teaching that beyond the realization of nonduality, what the individual experiences within the world of form can be objective, or real. The full understanding of this teaching was given by Issa in a poem that he wrote when his only child died at less than two years old.

As Lee quoted the poem and began to talk of impermanence, the *rasa* of longing that had carried over from the poignant space of the morning's darshan now deepened even further:

> The world is but a dewdrop.
> Yes, the world is but a dewdrop.
> And yet, and yet . . .

> The dewdrop is symbolic that all things pass. In the morning the dewdrop is there, fresh and beautiful, and in the afternoon it dries up and is gone. All life is transitory—nothing is permanent, nothing lasts. We are born and grow; sometimes we are successful, sometimes we are not. We are healthy or we are not, and there is nothing we can do about it. The Buddhists say that form is emptiness. Anything we can see in the world of form has no lasting reality. Even our husbands, wives, children—everything arises and passes.
>
> Form is emptiness, but the Buddhists also say that emptiness is form, and so the last line of the poem says, "And yet, and yet . . ." We are living beings. We feel, we sense, and this too is real. We know the difference between light and dark, sickness and health, rotten food or good food.

He went on to explain that, from the nondual perspective, Yogi Ramsuratkumar is not separate from God—there is no duality in him. Lee used the following story as a demonstration of this: Years ago when Yogi Ramsuratkumar lived at Sannadhi Street, some devotees brought food as a gift. The beggar said that he would eat it later, but it sat untouched. Three days later when someone came to visit, Yogi Ramsuratkumar wanted to honor his guest by offering food. He said, "Oh yes, there is the food from the devotee!" The devotees who were with him knew perfectly well that the food had been sitting in the Indian heat for three days; it couldn't possibly be fit to eat. And yet when Yogi Ramsuratkumar served the food, it was perfectly delicious and fresh! That story exemplified the master's perfect inherence in the teaching—form is emptiness, or the reality of nonduality.

On the other hand, another time an old grandmother came for Yogi Ramsuratkumar's blessing, and when he heard of her problems, tears ran down his cheeks. That he could still feel acutely the suffering of others was a demonstration that, in the world of form, our experience is also real, which is the other side of the equation: emptiness is form. Lee continued:

> Yogi Ramsuratkumar is one with Father in Heaven, but he can still make distinctions. We think if we are one with God, there will be no distinctions. Yes, "The world is but a dewdrop." But for Yogi Ramsuratkumar, "And yet, and yet . . ." is also true.
>
> When a parent dies, our hearts break, when a child dies, our hearts break. All is illusion, all is real. At the same time, how do we understand? We don't have to because we've found Yogi Ramsuratkumar. Like Jesus, who died for the salvation of others, Yogi Ramsuratkumar lives for us, blesses us, suffers for us. He has given us his name as an anchor for God. Yogi Ramsuratkumar is the name of Father in Heaven. If we want to be woven into God, we should chant and speak Yogi Ramsuratkumar's name. To chant and speak Yogi Ramsuratkumar's name, to think and dream His

name is the connection that anchors, ropes, weaves us into the Divine. Father in Heaven is never far away.

In Islam they say that God is closer to us than the jugular vein. Yogi Ramsuratkumar's Father in Heaven is closer to us than we could possibly imagine. How do we realize that? Dream, eat, sleep his name. His name is mantra. The mood of Yogi Ramsuratkumar is the mood of union with God, of nonseparation, of Father in Heaven present here and now. Yes, " the world is but a dewdrop, and yet, and yet . . . " Please remember the name of Yogi Ramsuratkumar and chant it as often as you can.

This talk was bittersweet, lyrical and resonated well with the mood that Yogi Ramsuratkumar, as master magician, had crafted in the space that day. Lee's talk had fanned the fire of longing to a high fine flame. There were four or five hundred people in the temple listening, and the listening was very strong, perhaps because—even though many could not understand the meaning of Lee's English words and American accent—everyone could feel the *rasa* in the air and the quality of divine sweetness in his words.

Not long after Purna gave a short talk Yogi Ramsuratkumar said, "This beggar is tired. I am ready to leave. Lee will lead. . ." He indicated to Mani that the basket of fruit, which he was giving out as *prasad*, should be left with Lee. He was wheeled off the stage leaving Lee in charge, with Mani sitting on the floor beside him. Purna sat in the chair at Lee's side, and the chanting continued.

There had been no theatrics, no selling of books, no dancing or requests for Christmas songs, and yet the penetration of divine mood had sunk extraordinarily deep on this day. Whether he slumbered or sat in silence or called joyfully for us to "Dance! Dance!" the beggar king effortlessly blessed all and everyone. It seemed that the closer Yogi Ramsuratkumar drew to leaving the physical body behind, the stronger the sanctity and the raw divine presence of his being seemed to be gathering and building. This tremendous spiritual force seeped into our cells and dissolved layers of *samskaras*, bringing the ancient heart of hearts closer to the surface.

The next morning Yogi Ramsuratkumar again asked for singing and dancing, then talks from Lee and Purna. After Purna's short talk he went up to pranam to Yogi Ramsuratkumar.

"Your name?" Yogi Ramsuratkumar asked.

"Purna," he replied, kneeling beside the master.

"Who gave you that name?" Yogi Ramsuratkumar asked.

"Mr. Lee," Purna answered.

"My Father blesses you," Yogi Ramsuratkumar said, as if he had just concluded a very important ritual. In this particular exchange it seemed that Purna was empowered by Yogi Ramsuratkumar in the teaching role that Lee had given him—like a go-ahead, a green light, a formal acknowledgment from the source of all blessings. He released Purna from his intense gaze and prepared to leave the hall.

"Lee—you and Purna take care of this space. This beggar is weak and cannot stay. You can start the class," he instructed, motioning to Mani to set two chairs on the stage.

"Mahadeva, Mahadeva, Yogi Ram Surata Kumar . . ." Pankkajam's brilliant voice sailed out into the vast space of the temple and penetrated our hearts. Lee had asked her to lead chants as we sat in the afternoon darshan waiting for Yogi Ramsuratkumar to arrive. We had been chanting for thirty or forty-five minutes when Yogi Ramsuratkumar came in.

"Who is singing?" he asked right away.

"Pankkajam is singing, Bhagawan," Devaki answered.

"She can continue," he said softly. When Pankkajam's chant was finished he turned to Ma Devaki and said, "You lead." Devaki and Vijayalakshmi then lead chants for about thirty minutes.

Devaki had Bhagawan's sunglasses in her hands, and when she started chanting she gave them to Rajmohan to put them on him, which he did with extreme gentleness and care. Within a minute or less, Yogi Ramsuratkumar had taken them off again.

Yogi Ramsuratkumar seemed to have much more energy on this day. He was alert, awake and actively present in his physical form. Soon he sent Rajmohan down off the stage to tell Lee to give a talk, in which he spoke about the importance of the mantra of Yogi Ramsuratkumar's name: "We are so lucky to have something to bring our minds into focus, clarity and concentration." Yogi Ramsuratkumar listened intently as Lee began to talk:

> This ashram, this temple, and Yogi Ramsuratkumar are the seat of all sanctity. To be here is the same as traveling to the Himalayas or any other sacred place. When we have to leave this place we have to take his name with us into the storm of the world, because the world is like a storm that knocks us about.
>
> But we forget to call on Yogi Ramsuratkumar, even when we have God in human form right here before us, in our lives. The sun is bright, but it is dull compared to Yogi Ramsuratkumar! We wait until a crisis point to turn to the name of Yogi Ramsuratkumar for help. Why don't we think of it all the time, in every moment? Why don't we think of his name when we are literally drowning in the ocean of his blessing?
>
> So we repeat the mantra until even our cells are repeating it. Jesus said, "Even if you are not praising God, the stones themselves are chanting the name of God." When we have repeated the mantra until the cells are chanting the name of God—even when the mind, mouth and heart are not chanting the name of God—the cells themselves are chanting Yogi

> Ramsuratkumar, Yogi Ramsuratkumar, Yogi Ramsuratkumar, Yogi Ramsuratkumar.

The next morning as we sat in the temple waiting for Yogi Ramsuratkumar to appear, the chanting ebbed and flowed around us like a swiftly incoming tide. The day before Lee had talked about the mystical "hidden temple" within the temporal frame of the concrete structure of the temple, and now his words came back to mind. As we sat chanting the name of Yogi Ramsuratkumar day after day, we were being saturated with the sanctity of this place. It seemed that chanting the name of Yogi Ramsuratkumar called the hidden temple out of the mists and into reality in the here and now. Existing prior to the steel beams, the raw concrete walls and floor of the unfinished temple was the hidden reality of the inner temple, which Yogi Ramsuratkumar had called into being over the years by the force of his attention and presence. The more we chanted the name of Yogi Ramsuratkumar, the more we were drenched in the subtle nectar of this world whether we knew it or not; the more we were suffused with the prismatic light of the Divine in the form Yogi Ramsuratkumar.

Suddenly Mani was standing near the wall that covered the door to Yogi Ramsuratkumar's private apartment. It was the signal that Yogi Ramsuratkumar would soon arrive. At eleven o'clock he was wheeled in. Immediately he asked Lee to say something. Lee spoke, as he had on many occasions, about faith:

> It might be useful to consider the difference between faith and belief. Yogi Ramsuratkumar says that if we speak His name once with faith, then Father in Heaven will be there instantly. As Mani said yesterday, Yogi Ramsuratkumar is always with us. Only in our mind are we separate.
>
> Belief has to do with the mind—our projections and opinions. Faith has not to do with the mind, but with absolute knowledge. Belief changes, but faith does not. Sometimes we think we have faith, but it is belief . . . . Beliefs change when circumstance changes. Faith does not change; faith is unchangeable, unshakable. When we have faith then we understand, we know organically that this human being, Yogi Ramsuratkumar, is God in human form, and it doesn't matter if He smokes or whatever. When we have faith, it's not based on mind and opinions or what others may say. We know with that which is within us that is in union with the Master.

Yogi Ramsuratkumar seemed subdued and quiet during the talk. His days were clearly up and down—sometimes he was full of life, energetic, focused and present, enjoying the play that he created with his devotees. At other times he seemed like a newborn. There was a nascent look of purity and regeneration about him; he seemed to have a preternatural power to revivify himself after the worst days, when he was lethargic, sleeping, or seemed to be in great pain. But even on the days of great suffering he was not only ancient, but appeared with a burning whiteness, and at times it seemed that a throng of angelic beings hovered just behind his form.

Lee concluded his talk, saying, "To have faith in Father in Heaven is to have faith in Yogi Ramsuratkumar. His purity is not stained by anything physical. The purity that he is is stainless, eternal, indefinable and untouchable by anything. Nothing touches or changes that purity because it is immortal."

Lee walked up on the stage and knelt beside the master. More translucent and seemingly fragile than ever, Yogi Ramsuratkumar reached his hand up to Lee, drawing him closer. The beggar spoke quietly, somberly in a tremendously charged and stunning moment.

"Lee, spirit has not come back after operation," Yogi Ramsuratkumar said, "The body is here—but spirit is gone." Lee listened in deep attunement to Yogi Ramsuratkumar, and seemed to absorb these statements with a quiet receptivity and acceptance that went beyond words. Lee simply heard and received his Father's words, with no resistance or agitation in response to such an intimacy.

As they remained poised in these moments of silent communion, the space deepened in the dusky shadows of the cavernous temple, but within those shadows burned the *jyoti* of Yogi Ramsuratkumar—an incandescence that radiated the molecular structure and most minute particles of matter, gross and subtle, from the cells of our bones and blood to the most subtle and ephemeral forms within Creation. Holding Lee's hands between his own, Yogi Ramsuratkumar held Lee in his gaze.

Yogi Ramsuratkumar seemed eternally tired, weary. He seemed to be carrying the suffering of the world in the dark recesses of his eyes, in the delicate movement of his hands, in the smooth skin of his face. With a slight elegant move of his head, he signaled the end of one moment and the beginning of another, then he said to Lee, "You can sit down and ask Purna to speak."

Purna stood up and spoke about the magic and mystery of the guru. He began by saying, "Everything Mr. Lee has done—his entire teaching, the ashrams in Arizona and France, all of his books, *everything*—has been created from the magic and mystery of Yogi Ramsuratkumar. The Hohm Community is founded on the grace, magic and mystery that is Yogi Ramsuratkumar." Alignment to and resonance with the guru was the keynote of Purna's words and mood.

After Purna spoke Yogi Ramsuratkumar asked Mani to give a talk. Mani said, "I would add 'miracle' to magic and mystery. Yogi Ramsuratkumar is the personification of magic, mystery and miracle. This huge ashram, the temple, Hohm Community, everything is the result of that. 'My Father alone exists,' Bhagawan says. For me," Mani shrugged, "Yogi Ramsuratkumar alone exists. So when we go to him, it is better to listen than to talk, because he knows everything. He alone exists—nothing else."

When we entered the temple on December 7 Yogi Ramsuratkumar was seated on the stage surrounded by the usual mandala of devotees. He was alert, awake and ready to conduct the business of actively orchestrating the flow of blessings. Immediately he wanted to know when Purna would be leaving with his group.

"Tomorrow after prasad, Bhagawan," Ma Devaki answered, referring to lunch. Two large trays stacked with shawls and saris were then brought out and distributed to each person in Purna's group. Beginning with Purna, they were called up by name, one by one, with Rajmohan and Mani reading off a list. Yogi Ramsuratkumar handed each person a shawl or sari.

When Olga came up, Mani explained to Yogi Ramsuratkumar that she was the one who had miraculously gotten her visa to come to India when it seemed impossible. "She kept chanting your name, Bhagawan," Mani explained. Yogi Ramsuratkumar's smiles had the effect of lighting up the whole temple, and when he heard this story, he beamed at Olga. His happiness was apparent whenever he heard that someone had taken refuge in his name, simply because it meant that they were turning toward the Divine with faith. To this kind of news, he always responded with joy.

After the shawls and saris were presented, Yogi Ramsuratkumar turned his attention toward Alain de Rosenbo, who was ushered up on to the stage and given a chair. A long exchange ensued about the medicine Alain was taking. At Yogi Ramsuratkumar's request, a phone call had been made to Chandra Swami to get his opinion on the subject. Now Yogi Ramsuratkumar asked Mani to report what Chandra Swami had said.

In a loud clear voice Mani said, "Chandra Swami said two things, Bhagawan. He said, 'Alain does not need so much medicine,' and 'Yogi Ramsuratkumar is playing with Alain; it is Yogi Ramsuratkumar's *lila*. Yogi Ramsuratkumar can do whatever he likes!' "

At this news Yogi Ramsuratkumar began to chuckle, his whole body shaking with laughter for a few brief seconds. Then he had Mani repeat the message—ostensibly to make sure Alain had heard it clearly. Alain too was smiling at the "Yogi Ramsuratkumar can do whatever he likes" part of the message. Alain was escorted back to his seat in the audience and Yogi Ramsuratkumar asked Lee to give a talk.

"There was a time several years ago when Yogi Ramsuratkumar's eyes were very sensitive to light," Lee began. He told the story of when Lee was visiting at the ashram in Tiruvannamalai and Yogi Ramsuratkumar asked him to get special sunglasses from America. The sunglasses could have been obtained in India, but Yogi Ramsuratkumar insisted that Lee had to get them for him. Lee had to call the States, have someone buy them and mail them to India, which would take a lot longer than getting them in Chennai, for example. It didn't matter how long it took—what mattered was that Lee was the person who performed this particular task for Yogi Ramsuratkumar. Lee explained further:

> Everyone has their own role, their own work to do. That was my work to do; it was my job. In relationship to the master, each of us is unique—we have different karmas and tendencies. Each one of us has a very particular work to do with the guru. We cannot replace one another in that work. We struggle with what appears to be inequities with the guru. We wish we could have someone else's job. We look at their job and think if we had that job, we could do it better.
>
> Yogi Ramsuratkumar's blessings are universal. His regard goes to

> every devotee, without exception, without qualification. All are in the regard of Father in Heaven. We gauge things by appearances. We think, "This is important, this is not." But every devotee, even if they have never been in Tiruvannamalai, are in Yogi Ramsuratkumar's regard, absolutely equally, regardless of whether we are Indian, American, European. So please don't be envious of any other devotee, and chant his name with faith and enthusiasm. Thank you.

"Purna can speak a few words," the beggar said when Lee went up to receive *prasad* after the talk.

Standing and *pranaming* to Yogi Ramsuratkumar as Lee sat down, Purna said, "Yogi Ramsuratkumar has given us the world of devotion. That is the form of his teaching. He does not teach in a linear way." He posed the question, "We should ask ourselves, are we reading the poems every day, as he has asked us to do? It is through the simple acts of devotion that we are in Yogi Ramsuratkumar's heart. We can't win in the game of competition. We can only win by being part of his world . . . ."

Parathasarathy was called up to sing a devotional song with Yogi Ramsuratkumar's name threaded throughout it. Yogi Ramsuratkumar appeared to be resting while he sang. After awhile his eyes opened and rested with a solemn grace on Parathasarathy.

The refined and subtle quality of Yogi Ramsuratkumar's movements and gestures had the focused stillness and finality of one who is completely untouched by the false hopes of life and has accepted destiny in its totality. This acceptance carried the seed power of absolute peace. There was tremendous serenity around Yogi Ramsuratkumar; his body seemed steeped in serenity, or more accurately, it existed *as* serenity, as a placid lake of awareness. There was a painful cough, which caused his body to spasm from time to time, but it was like a ripple on still, deep water.

When Parathasarathy was finished singing, Yogi Ramsuratkumar called Lee to the stage and handed him a sheaf of papers—poems, hand-written in Lee's script—and said, "These are new songs . . . read the last one." Lee took the stack of papers, thirty or forty sheets, and walked down off the stage to read the poem dated November 25, 2000.

I stopped taking notes to watch and listen. Lee's words were resonant missives that moved through the air, and with a direct blow to the heart, burst into wonder at such a relationship with Yogi Ramsuratkumar as these poems so richly brought to life. There was an intense focus of awareness that was unleashed, like nuclear fission, in the moments of this reading. In the presence of the beggar king, the essence of the words gave witness to a rare glimpse of sanctity in the relationship between the guru and the devotee. It was the sound of the truth.

"Lee will write more songs, more songs . . ." Yogi Ramsuratkumar spoke with soft power that was prophetic—it was a command that had already been obeyed. I had heard Yogi Ramsuratkumar say this to Lee before, on more than one occasion.

After Lee returned to his seat Yogi Ramsuratkumar asked a number of different people to sing, dance or speak, in a quick succession of events. Mani gave a short talk then Janarthanan, a long-time devotee, was called up to the stage. He bent to touch the master's feet.

"Sing and speak about the Ramayana," Yogi Ramsuratkumar asked. Janarthanan spoke for a long time in Tamil, often quoting the scripture in Sanskrit.

"What time is it?" came the beggar's tremulous and sweet voice after Janarthanan had received *prasad* and sat down.

"It is twelve o'clock, Bhagawan," Ma Devaki answered. Everyone expected Yogi Ramsuratkumar to tell Mani to ask the people to disperse, but instead he looked at Mani and said, "Speak a few words." Mani chuckled, Ma Devaki sat back down, and Mani proceeded to give another short talk about Yogi Ramsuratkumar that ended with "Hang onto his lotus feet. . ." Mani turned and *pranamed* to Bhagawan and received *prasad*. Yogi Ramsuratkumar seemed to want to engage as many people as possible during this darshan, but lunch was past due.

"What time? Time to end?" he asked Ma Devaki. She answered yes.

"We will disperse," he said gently. Mani repeated this loudly to the large crowd of people, many of whom began to rush the stage, throwing themselves on the ground in prostrations, getting as close to Yogi Ramsuratkumar as they dared to come. As I walked out I turned to look back at the crowd. Yogi Ramsuratkumar was being wheeled away to the abode while the crowd surged and pulsed around the stage.

Yogi Ramsuratkumar was sitting outside under the bodhi (*asvattha*) tree near the Veda Patashala with Ma Devaki, Vijayalakshmi, Rajmohan and one or two other people all afternoon. When we were seated in the temple for afternoon darshan, he was driven in the van from the Patashala into the temple and up to the stage.

Yogi Ramsuratkumar asked Janarthanan to come up and speak again on the *Ramayana*. When Janarthanan had spoken and received *prasad* then taken his seat, Ma Devaki spotted V. Ganeshan, the grandnephew of Ramana Maharshi who had known Yogi Ramsuratkumar for many years. Immediately Yogi Ramsuratkumar asked Ganeshan, an accomplished and charismatic speaker, to come up and speak. Ganeshan walked respectfully to the stage, prostrated before Yogi Ramsuratkumar and touched his feet, then walked a few feet away and turned to face the audience. He began:

> I bow to the lotus feet of Swami Yogi Ramsuratkumar. Swamiji is the scripture in human form. You can have this only at the holy feet of the sage. Scriptures are just words. No scripture can make it for you. Only at the feet of the sage can you find the truth . . . .
>
> Those who are able to be at the feet of the holy master are blessed indeed. The longing, the pining, the true pining is not just a desire, a thought. You should melt from the truth, not just read a description of the truth. When you want rainwater, you have to go and find an existing saint. Why should we fall at their feet? Out of their kindness and compassion they allow us to prostrate at their holy feet. Just to give us, to partake with

us, the truth that they continue to be. It is a great fortune that Swami is still with us.

The great ones escape and hide themselves as madmen. The same blessing, presence, truth as Ramana Maharshi is available now in the form of Yogi Ramsuratkumar. The only thing to do is come and fall at his feet. It is so rare, only one in six billion people. That presence is the presence of God; not in the emotional sense, or devotional sense, but as the essence of truth. If you want to know the truth, you have to come and know the sage. One look, one touch is enough to communicate the same truth . . . .

How can we make it permanent? Go to the sage, fall at his feet, every minute. Every realization they will shower on us is to make us eternally [rooted] in the truth.

There is only one God for every being, sentient and insentient. The same teaching has been given by Jesus Christ, Buddha, Ramana Maharshi, the Shankaracharya—it is all the same message. Why do we have to hear the same message from so many sages? Swamiji has said, "We come again and again to relieve the suffering of the seekers. To alleviate the suffering of all souls afflicted with emotional, physical and spiritual problems, we come again and again." He has made that statement, and though it looks like words, it is very powerful.

A Hindu Brahmin seated here in Tiruvannamalai calls Jesus Christ "my master." His words are not statements, but a state [of being]. I can experience that state. States, not statements. How will you experience the words of Swami not as statements, but as states? Swami uses the royal "we" when he says, "We come again and again." As he uses the royal "we," then we must fall at his feet and his statements become states. You do not need a dictionary; you do not even need to understand the statement. You will experience the state if you fall at his feet. Scriptures are statements, holy statements, but only when you come to the feet of the sage will you understand the sage's state . . . .

Only when we receive the blessing of a master who is nobody but God—they make you God, they share that supreme peace with you. The only way to receive the blessings of the great master is to make a sincere effort. Dogmatic discipline is of no use. The sincere seeker can only fall at their feet. The moment you touch their holy feet you are consumed by them. Ramana Maharshi used to say, "We have been absolved already." There cannot be a greater effort than falling at the feet of the master. Every time you fall you are taking a dip into the eternal truth. The only way we can repay Swami's abundant grace and compassion is to fall at his feet, saying, "Swami, give me eternal peace." The simplest act of Yogi Ramsuratkumar relieves our ignorance. That is grace, *moksha.*

Ganeshan turned and walked back to Yogi Ramsuratkumar, bowed and touched his feet and received *prasad*. It was a very moving moment because Ganeshan had known Yogi Ramsuratkumar for very many years and been close to him. In 1991 Ganeshan had visited Lee Lozowick at his ashram in Arizona while on a speaking tour in the U.S; on a number of visits in Tiruvannamalai over the years Lee and company had spent the day with Yogi Ramsuratkumar at Ganeshan's home, sitting out on the patio by the garden.

Yogi Ramsuratkumar asked Rajmohan to speak a few words. A highly educated man, Rajmohan came forward and spoke:

> I don't know anything. I'm not a scholar. Lee has been repeatedly telling us that Bhagawan is God and that we should take his name. It's a great gift. I would only add one thing: People who live in Africa or American may not know Yogi Ramsuratkumar exists, but we must do right action. That is the very definition of God. . . . So we should come to Yogi Ramsuratkumar and take his blessing. We need to fall at the feet of God. We need the grace, the blessings of God in order to be God. But we come to Yogi Ramsuratkumar and we ask for this and that blessing for our suffering. It's like going to the wish-fulfilling tree and asking for coffee. We should go to Yogi Ramsuratkumar and ask for only one thing: "I want you. Only you. I want you." Thank you very much.

Yogi Ramsuratkumar seemed to be working in a very specific way on this day. He was like a CEO who had been away for a few days and was now back at the office and ready to get down to business. He was in charge and directing the show: "You do this, you do that." He had everyone engaged and coming and going with talks, songs, dances, business, the giving and receiving of gifts.

After Rajmohan's talk Yogi Ramsuratkumar scanned the room, as if to identify the next person who would be drawn into his vortex. Three or four minutes later he sent Mani to deliver a message to Lee: "Some of Purna's students can speak about their experience." Lee gestured to Joshua Levitt, who immediately got up and walked forward. His talk was brief and to the point. He talked about how he had been hearing about Yogi Ramsuratkumar and chanting his name for many years in Lee's company, and now with Purna also. He spoke about how deeply moved he was to finally see Yogi Ramsuratkumar in his physical form, and he recounted stories of how people in the West experience the presence of Yogi Ramsuratkumar in their lives.

Once again Yogi Ramsuratkumar asked Mani to speak. Breaking into a big smile, Mani moved forward on the stage and gave a short talk, the gist of which was, "This is all the Godchild's play with all of us. Yogi Ramsuratkumar's play with all of us . . . . He does everything, so just look in the direction of Tiruvannamalai and He will do the rest."

Yogi Ramsuratkumar then instructed Mani to ask the girl in the wheelchair, who had begged for his help last week, to come up and speak to the audience. Mani wheeled her chair to the front of the crowd, just below the stage and a few feet away from Yogi

Ramsuratkumar. The look on her face was one of wonder and surprise, but she began in a small yet steady and clear voice, "The people who spoke before me are highly qualified . . . they are higher beings than me. I was just sitting there thinking, what will I say if he asks me to speak?" She smiled a little then continued, "Then I thought, whatever words come to me will be his words." There was a small silence as she paused a bit, then continued:

> He is not putting words in my mouth, but they will be his words. Before I had this accident I was successful in all I did. I thought I was everything—that all achievements were made by me. Slowly, after this accident, he has thrown me into a place where nothing is me; everything is his will. It's Father's will that is happening, but Father has to push us into it. It took something like this for me to learn, so maybe you can learn from people like me. Whatever we plan will not take place—we should leave it all to his will and let him act. Everything I have said, everything left to be said, is guided by Bhagawan.

The change in the girl was miraculous. It seemed that in one week she had made a leap in understanding. Her demeanor and words were an inspiration. If she could see her situation with such clarity and grace, what could any of us have to complain about? Yogi Ramsuratkumar asked Mani to repeat what she had said. Mani turned to the crowd and repeated it loudly so that everyone could hear. The girl was lifted, chair and all, to the stage and wheeled close to Yogi Ramsuratkumar. Her father and mother were called up to the stage and received a blessing from Yogi Ramsuratkumar. As they were leaving the stage the father turned and came back to Yogi Ramsuratkumar and started talking to him again. Yogi Ramsuratkumar raised his hands up as if to indicate that the blessing had already been given.

"That's all . . . . Father's blessing," he said kindly but firmly.

Next a whole family—several adults, a baby, the grandparents—was ushered forward to receive the master's blessing. All were given prasad and blessed. Afterward Yogi Ramsuratkumar said, "They can disperse now."

It had been an action-packed darshan. The various "activities" of singing, dancing, speaking or conducting other business were opportunities for people to receive blessings directly from Yogi Ramsuratkumar. It was a rare moment to be in very close proximity to the master, to receive *prasad* from his hand, to feel the clarity and heat of his immediate physical presence, to be held in his gaze. The action of the space as he orchestrated it seemed also to be a way in which we could integrate and process the intense energies and the impact of Yogi Ramsuratkumar's physical suffering and the immensity of his sacrifice for us. Again, many people surged toward the stage, prostrating themselves and supplicating wordlessly.

December 8th was the day that Purna and his group would be leaving. We entered the temple for darshan that morning and chanted or the next hour and a half until Yogi Ramsuratkumar appeared. He seemed disoriented, in pain and uncomfortable. He looked out at the crowd as if from a very long distance away. After exactly three, excruciating minutes he said, "Devaki, we will go out." There were five or six hundred people in the temple, and as soon as Yogi Ramsuratkumar was wheeled out, about half of them got up and left right away.

Paula and Ute were leading the chant and continued. At five minutes before twelve o'clock, just before the end of the darshan, Yogi Ramsuratkumar unexpectedly came back. Once his chair was established on the stage, Ma Devaki and Mani told him that Purna and his group would be leaving after lunch at one-thirty. Yogi Ramsuratkumar motioned to Mani, who walked over and bent down close to hear.

"I do not feel alright. I cannot do anything . . . . Lee and Purna will take over . . . " It was a heartrending moment, when the pathos of the situation was piercing. His voice had a quality of pleading, as if he was imploring us to understand.

Mani came forward and said, "Bhagawan says he does not feel well and cannot stay." His job done, Mani turned back toward Yogi Ramsuratkumar, but who insisted that he say it again. Mani walked over to confer with Bhagawan, who insisted that he wanted his remarks repeated loudly, so that everyone could hear it. Mani walked back toward the audience and said in a loud voice, "Bhagawan has said, 'I do not feel alright; I cannot do anything. Lee and Purna will take over.' " After a minute or so Yogi Ramsuratkumar was wheeled out and Lee and Purna sat in chairs on the stage. The chanting continued briefly until Lee ended the darshan and we went to the dining hall for the midday meal.

The jolt of his communication was unforgettable. One of Lee's students who was there, Paula Zuccarello, wrote in her journal at the time, "It's difficult to describe the impact this had on me. I felt as if my heart was being ripped out of my chest. It took every ounce of control I had to keep myself from crying out. I was wracked with grief. I looked over at Lee for some kind of guidance, but he was as inscrutable as ever."

At lunch Lee made a comment to one of his students about Yogi Ramsuratkumar's statements in darshan. He said, "I didn't know whether to cry or faint." It was a glimpse into his inner world, and gave some insight into the depth of Lee's feelings beneath the poise that he demonstrated as we witnessed Yogi Ramsuratkumar's ordeal.

It seemed that Yogi Ramsuratkumar fervently wanted people to understand what his situation was. His innocent vulnerability gave everyone a dose of reality as it truly was, not an image glossed over by denial—either of his circumstance or of the magnitude of his sacrifice for us. The fact was that he was both human and divine, and the human man was dying.

The unfathomable sacrifice of the guru and the relationship between guru and devotee was not only implied in Yogi Ramsuratkumar words, but revealed for anyone who had the eyes to see. He was the Man on the Cross; despite tremendous suffering, he was an embodiment of spiritual slavery, an oblation of divine love, poured out for all. The tremendous gift of the beggar's company during these weeks broke my heart with the weight of sheer gratitude and love for him.

Mani's visits with Lee and friends over coffee at the cottage in the afternoon were always rich with anecdotes and stories of Yogi Ramsuratkumar. One afternoon Mani talked about how Yogi Ramsuratkumar could not bear for his devotees to fight among themselves. If you were not getting along with someone else, that would be exactly the person that Bhagawan would send you to talk to.

"If you say to him, 'I don't like Bret,' then you are *finished*! 'Go and talk with Bret,' he will say! 'Go and talk with Bret!' That sort of blessing I have gotten a lot," Mani grinned, as if he was enjoying telling a story about his own foibles. The laughter of his small audience was sympathetic, but it was a poignant story. There was much division, competition and jealousy among the devotees of Yogi Ramsuratkumar, and he had many times begged them not to fight among themselves, not to criticize each other, but to praise and look for the good in each other. The factions among the various groups of devotees was a cause of dissent and discord, and Yogi Ramsuratkumar had said many times that it hurt him physically when his children fought among themselves. The Lakota Sioux have a saying: "The boys throw stones in fun, but the Frog dies anyway." We have no idea the consequences of such childish behavior on the delicate fabric of the master's world—or how the master has to suffer our unconscious behaviors. It's a scenario that has been played out by devotees and disciples in countless situations around the precious jewel of the awakened one.

"One day he was in a very humorous mood," Mani continued. "First he asked Devaki to prepare food . . . . He asked me, 'What does Rajalakshmi say if you criticize the food she cooks?' I said, 'She says, "Get lost!" ' Then Bhagawan said that we should not criticize and find fault with anything, even with any food that someone has made. We should take it as it is. And if Bhagawan wrings his hands like this," Mani said, demonstrating, "he is angry. Angry means he is going to give good things—many blessings!" Everyone laughed again.

"If you are responsible for something that has happened, he knows everything. Sometimes he would say, 'Mani, where have you been?' I would just say, 'I am the culprit, Bhagawan.' Because if you go on telling some story, you are *out*! So at least let us be truthful to him alone! But if he has been angry with you, you are going to get so much compassion from him in a few hours. 'Are you alright?' he will say later. 'This beggar is so bad, so inconsistent!'

"Once Ma Devaki was making juice, and he called me, 'Mani, I have something for you—take two tumblers of this.' Another time I had a stomachache and when he found out, he sent sambar in two mugs. 'Drink it in one gulp,' he said, 'and go to sleep.' "

Coming from Yogi Ramsuratkumar, the exact thing that reason would expect to irritate the pain—spicy, rich sambar for a stomachache—actually made it better. Mani shook his head at the miracle of living in close proximity to God in human form. With a rapt audience, Mani continued his stories, saying, "You should never tell Yogi Ramsuratkumar that you have already done something if he asks you to do it again. Once we were in the ashram kitchen and Bhagawan asked me to ask the cook, Arunachalam, if it was okay for Yogi Ramsuratkumar to smoke in the kitchen. Of course Arunachalam said yes, but twenty times in fifteen minutes Bhagawan asked me to ask Arunachalam if it was alright for him to smoke in the kitchen. But *never* say, 'I already told him.' Every time I took it as a new command—my mind was so blank! Then finally he said, 'Please go now.' "

We waited in line outside the temple until four-thirty in the afternoon. When we took our seats, Yogi Ramsuratkumar was already waiting in his chair, front and center onstage. He called Lee up and said in a barely audible whisper, "Speak a few words." With a brief *pranam* Lee walked down off the stage and immediately began to talk:

> Yesterday there were talks about the need for the guru. There are many paths—jnana, bhakti. But for us there is the need to establish the Beloved in the heart. Yogi Ramsuratkumar can be many things for us—Lord, master, the source of magic, mystery, miracles. But he is also our Beloved.
>
> Arnaud Desjardins as a Western master is as realized a master as I've ever met. His grasp of Advaita Vedanta is profound. We asked him to speak about his master, Swami Prajnanpad, and the more he talked about him the more he became bright with a swoon of devotion, a *bhava* of love. At the end of the talk he said, "Don't be afraid to love the human master."
>
> Every time Yogi Ramsuratkumar smiles you can see the whole crowd light up. If we deny ourselves the right to love the master, we deny the most profound aspect; there is a literal rain of nectar in the body itself when we love the master. The body itself becomes an ocean of *soma*, of nectar, when there is love in our hearts. We want to do yoga because we are afraid of the love, the nectar, the swoon of magic and majesty we will feel when we love. We must bring the Beloved into our hearts so that we are soaked in the bliss, the beauty of the Beloved. Many of us miss that quality because we are afraid to love the human master. Here in Yogi Ramsuratkumar's company, the Beloved is alive, real, right here, right now.
>
> We chant the name of Yogi Ramsuratkumar, and we can be sure that Yogi Ramsuratkumar's relationship to Father in Heaven is absolute. He says, "Ramdas killed this beggar in 1952." One thing we can be sure of is that Yogi Ramsuratkumar is the Divine as much as we can see. There is no human psychology in him; only Father's Being, presence, transmission. Yogi Ramsuratkumar is not only guru, God, Lord, but also our Beloved. We must bring our Beloved into the inner sanctum of our being, to allow the Beloved to give us the taste of that pure devotion—not pride and vanity, but surrender and devotion.
>
> Yogi Ramsuratkumar is a wish-fulfilling gem, but he is also our Beloved. Do not be afraid to set up a shrine in your heart and worship your Beloved there, and when you do that, you will be showered with an ocean

of nectar. Thank you very much!

After Parathasarathy sang before the large crowd of three or four hundred people, Yogi Ramsuratkumar asked Mani to announce that if anyone on the women's side could speak, she should come forward and say something. It was clear that the master was giving the Indian women an opportunity to come up for his blessing and *prasad*. For the next hour a string of women came up to the front and spoke, many of them very briefly. These women were from many different places; some had traveled a long way to be there.

When one of them came up Mani told Bhagawan, "This woman says she is always praying to you." Yogi Ramsuratkumar looked at her gently.

"She can speak a few words," he said, holding his hand out gently to invite her forward to speak.

About thirty seconds into her talk the woman was overcome with emotion and could not continue. Weeping, she received *prasad*, touched Yogi Ramsuratkumar's feet and left the stage. The next woman was strong and bright, looking very healthy and fit in her pink and burgundy sari. Ending her enthusiastic five-minute talk in English, she turned to Yogi Ramsuratkumar and said, "I am very happy because of your blessing!" Devaki smiled broadly while she spoke.

To another woman the beggar said, "My Father blesses you and your whole family." Another came up who asked Yogi Ramsuratkumar for spiritual upliftment and peace of mind. When the tenth woman came up, she walked right up, touched Yogi Ramsuratkumar's feet and received *prasad*. Mani protested, "Bhagawan, she has not spoken anything yet!"

"Doesn't matter," Yogi Ramsuratkumar said, with a chuckle from Mani and the crowd in front who could hear their interchange.

By the end of this interlude twelve women had come up and received his blessing. Mani reported that they were almost all housewives; one of them was a teacher. Yogi Ramsuratkumar had made one of his amazing comebacks from his condition of the morning. His immediate and direct interactions with so many people had seemed like a direct extrapolation of Lee's talk, in which he said, "Don't be afraid to love the human form of the guru, and to take the guru into our hearts as our Beloved."

That day Ashish Bagrodia and his wife Shantipriya arrived with their entourage. The next day would be Deepam.

As we stood outside the temple on December 9 waiting to enter the darshan, a long stream of people amassed in a congested line that went all the way out through the ashram gates—people who wanted to celebrate Deepam in the presence of Yogi Ramsuratkumar. The word was out in town and among the devotees that Yogi Ramsuratkumar was appearing in darshan, and many came, knowing that it might be one of the last opportunities to see him alive.

As we filed into the temple I noticed that the statue of Yogi Ramsuratkumar, which is decorated every day with a large, fresh flower garland, was adorned with several. Rice mandalas had been drawn on the ground. In the front center of the stage a large gorgeous mandala was drawn and filled in with flower petals in yellow, orange, and purple. The chanting began as the temple auditorium quickly filled up with a thousand to fifteen hundred people. The stage was empty, and the name of Yogi Ramsuratkumar resounded in the air for the next hour and a half. People came and went during this time, talking and shuffling about; the large crowd was restless with anticipation.

At 11:43 Yogi Ramsuratkumar appeared. A ripple of excitement passed through the crowd. More people came streaming in through the open doors. It was quite noisy. Yogi Ramsuratkumar called Janarthanan to speak and sing, and while he spoke people continued to actively come and go. It was surprisingly loud and chaotic with a low rumble of voices in the background as people milled around in the back of the temple.

Through all this Yogi Ramsuratkumar sat still, in a state of what looked like total serenity. His face was like fine white alabaster, with that peculiar quality that some stone has of seeming to shine with a radiance from within. He closed his eyes, but he was only resting momentarily. He seemed to have very little energy to expend. His movements were slow, concentrated, as if he was moving through water. There was a sky blue pillow under his feet. He kept touching his hands to his eyes, which had troubled him for years, as if the light was painful, or his eyes were tender.

Devaki smiled and watched as Janarthanan spoke in the rapid, melodic tones of Tamil. All the Indians seemed to be enjoying his speech. At five minutes till noon Janarthanan was still talking. Because I couldn't understand Tamil, by ten minutes after twelve my thoughts were wandering toward boredom and lunch. Suddenly my attention shifted completely, and I became aware of a subtle ambrosia that was raining down on the huge crowd—a shower of nectar was gently and steadily falling like fine liquid gold. Yogi Ramsuratkumar's divine activity continued, regardless of the form of things, regardless of physical obstacles or whether he felt ill or well on any given day. This divine activity remained the one steady truth in the relentless face of impermanence.

At twelve-twenty Janarthanan was still speaking with great gusto and animation. He seemed to be winding down, then he stopped to a great round of applause. His wife came up and together they presented a gift of candy—several plastic bags and a container of individually wrapped small pieces of candy—to Yogi Ramsuratkumar. These were placed in his hands to be blessed and then returned to Janarthanan's wife. Yogi Ramsuratkumar told her to pass out two bags of candy to the crowd; it struck me that it was a physical manifestation of the nectar I had perceived raining down on everyone.

Janarthanan's wife started to pass the candy out at the front row on the women's side just as Rajmohan walked to the edge of the stage and said in a loud voice, "People will disperse, and anyone who wants lunch can go and have it."

At this point there were at least a thousand people in the temple. As Bhagawan prepared to leave, a mass of people surged up toward the front and threw themselves to the floor in full body prostrations, or supplicated in front of the stage, calling plaintively to Yogi Ramsuratkumar with hands folded in *namaskar*. Those of us who were sitting in the front rows on the women's side were now surrounded, caught up in the throng of people who were trying to get to the candy that was being distributed. Unlike the rain of subtle nectar that had fallen freely on everyone, there was only enough candy for a few dozen people.

Janarthanan's wife was literally under siege, inundated by people off to the side of the temple, where she held the silver tray with the *prasad* on it and tried to keep her balance as she was jostled about. People swarmed around the stage and around her. It was a sobering scene. It seemed like it could break into total pandemonium at any minute.

Yogi Ramsuratkumar was still onstage as we broke through the crowd to go around the back way toward the doors. Looking back at the stage from the temple doors, I saw that Yogi Ramsuratkumar had been wheeled safely out to his apartment, but two or three hundred people were still clustered around the stage, praying and making prostrations. The temple buzzed with noise, and many people circumambulated the statue of Yogi Ramsuratkumar, chanting. I understood then the necessity for such strict protocol and crowd control on the part of the ashram staff.

People could been seen all day long out on the mountain, climbing in faintly moving lines of white that dotted the mountain's green flanks. The religious fervor of Deepam was in the air. Deepam is the most important religious festival of Tiruvannamalai; there is the sense that the Indians are transported to another realm in this ritual—the realm of the gods. When I allowed myself to be caught up in the magic, I too was swept into the collective ecstasy.

Over coffee at three, Mani came out to sit with Lee and his group. He talked about Deepam, Arunachala and the light of the mountain being the first light of Creation—the light in the darkness. He spoke about the mythology of Shiva, and then said that when Yogi Ramsuratkumar used to circumambulate the mountain many years ago, he always walked in the opposite direction of all the other pilgrims.

This story reminded me of the wild and crazy-wise *heruka* of Tibetan Buddhism, or the contrary shaman, the *heyoka* of the Native Americans. They did everything backward as a way of teaching, or mind-boggling, in which the rigid expectations and projections of the rational mind are confronted and perhaps even transcended. In this way one can glimpse the freedom that exists beyond the confining definitions of the mind. Mani said that Yogi Ramsuratkumar walked around the mountain contrary to the others out of humility, but it seemed to me that the *heruka* and *heyoka* have a definite kinship of the spirit with the beggar king of Tiruvannamalai.

We entered the ashram temple at four o'clock and the chanting began, "Om guru charinam, Om guru charinam, Yogi Ramsuratkumar, Om guru charinam." The stage remained empty. There were more people in the temple than in the morning darshan—probably fifteen hundred.

An hour later Yogi Ramsuratkumar entered the temple and said, "They can continue the chanting." Around five-thirty everyone was asked to go outside and wait for Yogi Ramsuratkumar to come out to the tent that had been set up outside the temple, facing Mount Arunachala. The tent was draped with tapestries and cloths in rich colors and designs. The floor was covered with cotton blankets and colorful rugs. An elaborate *puja* tray was set up in the front with flowers, garlands, *arati* lamps, ghee, incense and so forth. Yogi Ramsuratkumar exited the temple in his van and was delivered to the tent, where he sat facing the mountain and the large crowd of over a thousand people, most of whom stood in the road or sat on the ground behind the roped-off area by the temple, about fifty feet away from him.

While Yogi Ramsuratkumar was being transported to the tent and settled in his chair, Lee and his group waited about twenty-five feet away near the temple while huge cotton blankets were laid out on the ground about fifteen feet away from the tent. We were then invited to take seats there, facing Yogi Ramsuratkumar, who was now in the tent in his reclining chair. Ma Devaki, Vijayalakshmi and Rajmohan were gathered around him; Mani, Raji and the rest of the ashram staff were directly in front of the tent, except for the security people, who were more mobile in relationship to the crowd. The ashram staff was a solid presence throughout this event.

Within minutes the fire appeared on the tip of the mountain and the crowd went wild. Simultaneously a fire was lit in a large wok-shaped pan on top of a ladder near Yogi Ramsuratkumar, signifying the light of Arunachala here on the ashram. Instantaneously a man in the crowd shouted a loud series of "ki jai's" that were caught up in an ecstatic roar of noise and religious fervor as the mass of people responded. General pandemonium had broken loose, and the policemen and security staff had their hands full with controlling the crowd. There was obviously a ritual *puja* planned for this moment, but it was lost in the frenzied but joyful uproar of the huge crowd. In one way the madness of the crowd was overwhelming, but in another way, the unrestrained ecstasy was intoxicating, refreshing, contagious.

Lee was called up to the tent to make an offering of a garland of tulsi leaves to Yogi Ramsuratkumar, which he placed around his neck. Raji, Mani's wife, then performed the *puja* to Yogi Ramsuratkumar, waving the light and making offerings to his feet. Devaki and Vijayalakshmi continued to chant. Just as the *puja* was completed, a large flock of big black crows flew over the tent, heading directly toward Arunachala, going from north to south above Yogi Ramsuratkumar's head. It seemed like a dramatic response from nature in this sacred moment—an affirmation of the sanctity of the rites performed, a salute to Yogi Ramsuratkumar as Arunachala, Lord Shiva in the flesh. The closing call to Yogi Ramsuratkumar and Devaki and the resounding "ki jai!" was lead by Pankkajam, but she was drowned out. In a loud voice Mani said, "Pankkajamji, lead the ki jai," and she tried again, but could not be heard over the din of the crowd.

As I walked away through the din and confusion toward the dining hall where a feast would soon be served, my attention was suddenly and dramatically pulled toward Yogi Ramsuratkumar, who sat in the dusky shadows of the tent watching everything. Yogi Ramsuratkumar as pure, impersonal divine force was sitting there in his chair as if on a throne, and looking in my direction. My wandering attention had been grabbed by his intense and silent one-pointed focus—his total stillness in the midst of frenetic action. He seemed like the center of the world, and for a flash in that moment, he was in fact Arunachala, with the universe emanating from his still form.

The next day, on December 10, we found out that the ashram had served food to twelve hundred people the day before at the Deepam feast. We entered the temple as usual at ten o'clock and the chanting began. The stage was empty except for the bright flower petal mandala that still graced the front of the stage and the big clock that was placed in a white plastic chair. There were three or four hundred people present.

We waited for Yogi Ramsuratkumar to appear while the chanting flowed all around. At eleven-thirty he entered and began to conduct business from his big red chair, blessing a man and his wife who had brought him a gift. At five minutes until twelve, just before the usual time for darshan to end, he asked Lee to speak about the importance of the temple. Lee bowed and began to speak:

> When this ashram was first being built, Yogi Ramsuratkumar said that this ashram was not just for Tiruvannamalai or India, but universal—a place of pilgrimage for all races and religions. A place of real sanctuary and power—like a lighthouse for ships, like a magnet draws iron filings—will draw those who long for sanctity and truth. They will bring their prayers and praises for the majesty and glory of his eternal work, and will leave with blessings beyond their imagining.
>
> So when you leave, don't think of Yogi Ramsuratkumar as a local saint. It's not like Yogi Ramsuratkumar, as a man, made some decision to buy land and build a temple. His praise, his beauty, his majesty is in this ashram. This ashram has continued to grow, and in very tangible and real terms sustains all the people of the earth, all races, all religions. Please remember all the wonder and majesty that we have right here in physical and spiritual terms.
>
> We can go take lunch, but one last thought: whenever there is a big celebration and people come and take *prasad*—the people who are closest to Yogi Ramsuratkumar call all the food on this ashram *prasad* because it is blessed food, sanctified food—every bite of food we take brings blessings for our hopes and wishes as we surrender to Yogi Ramsuratkumar. . . .
>
> To eat the sanctified food of this ashram is to be touched by Yogi Ramsuratkumar. When we digest that food it goes not just into our minds but into our blood, cells and organs, so the sanctity and holiness of Yogi Ramsuratkumar permeates our whole system, and every time the blood courses through our veins it is Yogi Ramsuratkumar coursing through the veins. So please, go and take lunch and have *prasad*, because that's what it

is. Thank you.

The audience broke into a spontaneous round of applause. Later Lee said that it was the first applause he had ever gotten, in all the years he had been speaking in the beggar king's darshan.

"You can disperse the meeting," Yogi Ramsuratkumar said as Lee bowed before him. "My Father's blessings on all."

At four-fifteen that afternoon Yogi Ramsuratkumar was settled at the front of the stage with Ma Devaki, Vijayalakshmi, Rajmohan and Mani in their usual places. A tray of apples, bananas and oranges sat on the floor beside Devaki, next to Yogi Ramsuratkumar's coconut bowl and palmyra fan. The space was filled with another large crowd of four or five hundred people, many of whom kept coming and going in the back of the temple. While the chanting continued, Yogi Ramsuratkumar, Mani and Rajmohan were deep in a discussion.

While Yogi Ramsuratkumar was involved in a conversation with Devaki and several people, Rajmohan started to fan him, but Yogi Ramsuratkumar waved him away. His green head wrap had been slipping down on his forehead uncomfortably for the past few minutes. Usually Devaki or Rajmohan would retie the head wrap for him, but now Yogi Ramsuratkumar took it off and sat bareheaded very briefly, then retied the turban himself. It was the first time he had done this for himself—as he always used to do—since we had arrived from the States.

He called Pankkajam up to the stage. She bowed and he said, "You can sing a song . . . and those people who have been singing can stop." He motioned toward Lee's students in the front row who had been leading the chant. As Pankkajam began a beautiful devotional song, Yogi Ramsuratkumar's head wrap began to come untied again. Rajmohan tried to help, but Bhagawan gestured him away with his hand. His head was bare for about thirty seconds while he awkwardly but determinedly got hold of the cloth and finally retied the wrap very nicely.

After the song was over and Pankkajam received his blessing, Yogi Ramsuratkumar said in a clear, strong voice, "Lee, give a talk—anything!"

Lee bowed and got up to speak: "Many years ago in New York City a woman named Hilda Charlton told me about Yogi Ramsuratkumar. . . ." He proceeded to tell the story of how he had first come to India in 1976, and how Hilda had told him about Yogi Ramsuratkumar.

While Lee was talking Yogi Ramsuratkumar continued to conduct other business onstage. A European man from Spain, a good friend of Lee's named Swami Satyananda who has lived in Tiruvannamalai for many years, was asked up to receive blessings and *prasad* from Yogi Ramsuratkumar.

In the meantime, Lee continued to speak:

> We may think that Yogi Ramsuratkumar is not very hidden by this

> big temple, the crowds of people, the many chants to his name. But I disagree; to many he is still a hidden saint. Jesus said, "He who seeth me, seeth He who sent me." Yogi Ramsuratkumar is nothing but Father in Heaven. This saying of Jesus might mean if we really see Yogi Ramsuratkumar—not just His body, or our fantasy and our projections—then we see Father in Heaven. We might say we see Father in Heaven, but to truly see God is to have no will of our own. Only Father, only Father.
>
> So to truly see Yogi Ramsuratkumar is to be completely eclipsed, completely subsumed in our personal wishes and will. To truly see Father in Heaven is to have no will of our own—to have only the Source of all life and blessings. So please, truly see Yogi Ramsuratkumar, and after that, no will of our own, no personal preference, only Father in Heaven. So be it!

Lee bowed to Yogi Ramsuratkumar, who raised his hands in blessing but did not offer the usual piece of fruit. Lee did not linger on the stage, but returned to his seat right away.

"What is the name of the man who sings?" Yogi Ramsuratkumar asked, with the innocence of a child.

"Parathasarathy," Rajmohan answered.

"Call him here. He can sing . . ." the beggar uttered very softly, and named a particular chant he wanted to hear.

This interchange was an example of the impersonal nature of God's absolute love. Yogi Ramsuratkumar has known Parathasarathy not just well, but intimately for over twenty-five years. In the state of surrender to his Father in Heaven, he did not remember Parathasarathy's name in this particular moment, but he was given the knowledge of what Parthasarathy's function in darshan should be.

Parathasarathy walked up and *pranamed* to Yogi Ramsuratkumar. Ma Devaki handed her songbook to Yogi Ramsuratkumar, who handed it to him. Parathasarathy had been using this songbook off and on for the past week when he was asked to sing certain special songs to Yogi Ramsuratkumar. The songbook never went from Devaki's or Vijayalakshmi's hands directly to Parathasarathy, but always through Yogi Ramsuratkumar.

Parathasarathy began to sing. A woman in a dirty, tattered sari walked up to the edge of the stage and fell to her knees before Yogi Ramsuratkumar. A security man from the ashram staff stood protectively just behind her.

"Go and circle," Yogi Ramsuratkumar commanded gently, indicating that Ma Devaki and Vijayalakshmi should circle the whole audience. They started off to the right, around the men's side, then the women's side and back up to the stage. While they circumambulated the crowd, Parthasarathy sang.

"Once more," Yogi Ramsuratkumar said as they stood beside him with palms pressed together in *pranam*. They circumambulated the crowd again, and then a third time. At Yogi Ramsuratkumar's gesture, Rajmohan gave him two pieces of *prasad*, which he gave first to Vijayalakshmi and then to Devaki.

"Sit. Sit down," he said kindly. "Thank you."

Calling for Lee, he gave quiet instructions, sending Lee to Alain de Rosanbo, who sat in a chair on the men's side of the room. They conferred, then Lee walked to the front near the stage and said in a loud clear voice, "Yogi Ramsuratkumar asked if Mr. Alain, who is from France, would have anything to say, to tell me and I would communicate it. Alain says that the shape of this area of the temple," Lee pointed to the wide, oval concrete proscenium or stage and the wall behind it with five high arches up above, "is symbolic of the Divine, and Yogi Ramsuratkumar sits in the center of that mandala and communicates everything—the whole universe. Yogi Ramsuratkumar sits in the center of the sacred mandala which is the center of the universe." Lee turned and walked up to Yogi Ramsuratkumar, who gave him *prasad* to give to Alain.

After a few minutes Yogi Ramsuratkumar took his head wrap off to re-wrap it for the third time this afternoon. Again his head was bare for about thirty seconds. Yogi Ramsuratkumar rewrapped the turban and called Lee back up onstage. He spoke with Lee, who then turned back to the crowd and said, "Yogi Ramsuratkumar would like me to repeat what Alain said. As we look at this space in the temple where Yogi Ramsuratkumar gives darshan, it communicates the glory of God. He is sitting in the center of the universe and demonstrates to us the availability of blessings—right here, right now—the presence of God in this universal mandala, this universal temple. We should return that grace by praising Yogi Ramsuratkumar and all saints, all sages, and by chanting his name. Thank you."

Lee sat back down and Yogi Ramsuratkumar said to Devaki, "Those girls who sing and dance . . ." Devaki looked up at me and gestured. "Tell them to sing," Bhagawan instructed.

"To sing and dance, Bhagawan?" Devaki clarified. He answered yes and added, "You can go down there and tell them."

Devaki walked off stage and to the front row where I was sitting with Sharana. She smiled at me and said, "Bhagawan would like you to sing songs, Christmas songs, and dance." Her smile deepened, and there was a hint of a twinkle in her eye. We got up and walked toward what had become the "dancing area" just below the stage.

"A song about *Christ*," Yogi Ramsuratkumar interjected. This was stated very clearly and emphatically. He didn't want a secular Christmas jingle, but a song about the great spiritual light of the West.

Taking our positions, we sang four brief versions of Christmas songs— "Silent Night," "O Come All Ye Faithful," and such—forgetting a few of the words here and there, but managing nonetheless to accomplish the task. After four songs Yogi Ramsuratkumar called us up to his side. One by one we bowed at his knee, bowed deeply, and received *prasad* from his hands. Immediately afterward, as we were walking back to our seats, Yogi Ramsuratkumar dispersed the group. The crowd again surged up to the front of the stage in a burst of devotion and religious fervor. Many flung themselves on the floor, and it seemed to me that some were weeping.

During dinner the Westerners gathered in the cottage with Lee. Ashish and Shantipriya and their staff people were there also. Everyone was buzzing about the meaning of the three circumambulations by Devaki and Vijayalakshmi, and the three times Yogi Ramsuratkumar tied his head wrap this afternoon in darshan. There is significance in the universal symbolism of the number three, but it was the felt experience of these actions that was important. It was evident that Yogi Ramsuratkumar was effortlessly at play as *mahasiddha* in these moments—there was magic at hand in these divine sports, as Ma Devaki and Vijayalakshmi were called upon to bless the crowd in this way. It seemed that many people felt that Yogi Ramsuratkumar's actions on this day were important.

In darshan on the morning of December 11 the crowd chanted the name of Yogi Ramsuratkumar for an hour, until Yogi Ramsuratkumar was wheeled onstage in his chair. Immediately he asked Rajmohan to speak a few words:

> It's really difficult to speak in the face of the infinite ocean of knowledge that is Yogi Ramsuratkumar, and in front of so many speakers, great scholars and people. But I can tell what I have learned in my association with Bhagawan. The association with a saint is a great thing. Unless we experience it in our lives, we cannot know, just by scriptures.
>
> A few years ago a couple came from the Ukraine. The man begged me to take them to see Yogi Ramsuratkumar. The wife showed no interest. I took them to the Sannadhi Street house of Yogi Ramsuratkumar. Bhagawan gave the woman a flower, but the man backed away and said, "I cannot come." Even our attempts to believe in God cannot come full unless He showers His Grace on us. This is the Grace of the Mahatmas. If one melon ripens among many unripe melons, they will all ripen.
>
> The saint will unfold everything in us that is good, that is holy. Many courses of meditation and yoga—I used to get crazy about all those things! Then a professor called me and said, "There is a roomful of dirt for one hundred years. What will you do?" Clean it, I said.
>
> "It is like a dungeon," he said. "You must keep the doors open for some days and then clean it." He said, "Life is a great process. Yoga, meditation, *dhyana* is like trying to clean up the whole system in one day."
>
> Just the name of Yogi Ramsuratkumar is enough. He is not asking us to do all the monkey jumping. Just take his name. . . . Always have faith in Father in Heaven and even if we cannot chant his name, keep our conscience clear and believe in Yogi Ramsuratkumar, come to him every day. Associate with a saint—that is a very great thing.

Afterward it was Lee's turn to speak, and he began by exhorting the crowd to speak only praise. He said, "In one sense, we are all saints. To treat any other human being with hatred or violence is to do that to Yogi Ramsuratkumar. So please, remember to speak words of kindness and sweetness, treat one another with generosity, because when you treat another badly and criticize, that is what you bring here. Please, bring only praise to Yogi Ramsuratkumar."

Yogi Ramsuratkumar gave Lee *prasad* and asked him to sit in a plastic chair at his side, then he called Janarthanan and asked him to say "something about Ramayana." About three or four minutes into Janarthanan's talk, Yogi Ramsuratkumar exited the stage, leaving Lee in charge.

That afternoon in darshan Yogi Ramsuratkumar orchestrated one event after another that gave Lee's students opportunities to receive his direct and personal blessing, by either singing and dancing or giving short talks. Lee and Dasya Zuccarello gave talks, then the beggar king called Lee back up and asked him to have "those girls sing some songs," gesturing gently toward where Sharana and I were sitting. Lee came to us and said, "Sing three poems." As usual we had the poetry book, *Death of a Dishonest Man*, with us. After three poems we turned toward Yogi Ramsuratkumar and *pranamed*. He motioned for us to come up and receive *prasad*. Apple in hand, I went back to my seat in time to see Yogi Ramsuratkumar say to Lee, "Ask some more people."

Yogi Ramsuratkumar asked Lee to sit beside him in a chair, and from this position at the master's side Lee was easily dispatched to arrange whatever request that Yogi Ramsuratkumar made. Colette Lennon and Erica Jen sang two short Christmas songs. Yogi Ramsuratkumar had instructed Lee to hand out the *prasad*, so when Colette and Erica went up to bow, Devaki handed the *prasad* to Yogi Ramsuratkumar, who handed it to Lee, who handed it to Colette and then Erica in turn.

Next, the master asked for "singing and dancing," and Sharana and I, who had become the dancing "girls," were back on, singing Christmas songs and dancing at the same time. Approaching the beggar king after these sessions was always a unique, tender and unforgettable experience; I would have stayed there forever at his side, but it was not my destiny. This time we received *prasad* that traveled from Ma Devaki to Yogi Ramsuratkumar to Lee, and then to our waiting hands. These frolics were clearly his way of further establishing Lee as his agent and bringing everyone into his *lila*; he seemed to be making one last brilliant gesture toward working directly with numbers of people, and specifically with Lee and his students.

As we sat down I heard Yogi Ramsuratkumar say, "Lee, ask some more people to sing." Lee asked Volker and Dasya. As soon as they started "O Come All Ye Faithful," Yogi Ramsuratkumar turned to Lee and said, "Lee, this beggar cannot stay long . . ." He instructed Lee to manage the darshan and was wheeled off the stage. Lee sat alone on the stage for the second time that day, directing the show that Yogi Ramsuratkumar had orchestrated as his appointed emissary. The *prasad* tray was left behind by Yogi Ramsuratkumar's attendants and placed beside Lee on the floor.

As soon as Yogi Ramsuratkumar left Lee asked Pankkajam to sing. She sang "Kurai Ondrem Ille," a beautiful devotional hymn that had been much loved by Yogi Ramsuratkumar in years past. She had sung it for him, over and over again, at Sudama House on many different occasions. Her resonant voice soared into the space and filled the temple in this evocative song in praise of Krishna as supreme Lord, protector of the weak, sustainer and wish-fulfilling gem. After the song she led a chant and then walked up to the stage to receive *prasad* from Lee.

After darshan I went to Pankkajam to express my appreciation and deep enjoyment of her singing that morning. She told me a story: only that morning a young friend of hers had said to her, "If Yogi Ramsuratkumar asks you to sing, would you please sing 'Kurai Ondrem Ille'?" Pankkajam answered, "Yes, if Yogi Ramsuratkumar wants me to." Then she explained, when Lee asked her to sing she said, "For me, Lee and Yogi Ramsuratkumar are the same," so she sang the song.

At the end of the day one could only reflect again in wonder on the tremendous magnanimity and generosity of Yogi Ramsuratkumar. The total selflessness of the saint—that the saint lives entirely for others—was made even more brilliant by how difficult it was for Yogi Ramsuratkumar to give darshan even for thirty minutes. And yet, he gave and gave. "Say some words . . . Dance and sing . . . Sing songs about Christ . . . Speak about the Ramayana . . . Circumambulate . . . Do such and such . . ." And then he left, bestowing the mantle of responsibility on Lee.

On December 12 it was still very dark at five-thirty, but the fire of Creation still burned on the tip of Arunachala. The full moon rode dramatically in the western sky turning the majestic clouds to silver billows, fabulous studies in water, air, light and dark. At every hour of the day there is always, in some way, the suggestion of India's mysteries.

Coffee arrived and Mani joined the group of Westerners. The birds sang their frenzied sonata while crickets droned on and crows cawed like raw and sassy trumpets from the rooftops. Within moments the light had grown, the moon receded behind the clouds and the fleeting beauty of the moment had passed. A monkey hooted nearby—not even as far away as Ramanashram, where the monkeys always congregate.

Yogi Ramsuratkumar was already on the stage when we were summoned early for darshan and came running in haste toward the temple. He was conducting business with his circle; Rajmohan was reading off the list of names of people in Lee's party. A stack of shawls and saris sat nearby on the floor, waiting to be handed out.

Lee went up first and received a shawl wrapped in a plastic bag, followed by the rest of the men and then the women. When all the gifts had been given and everyone had been blessed by Yogi Ramsuratkumar, Lee was asked to give a talk. He began:

> One of the things that confines us in relationship to Yogi Ramsuratkumar is that we want to be treated equally. At the level of blessings, we are treated equally, but we see things in material terms, when it's impossible for one person to have more blessings than another. We think that

> one person has great qualities, and another does not, but in blessing it does not work that way.
>
> Father in heaven has equal vision—there is no difference in race, creed, caste. Father in heaven blesses all equally. Each of us is unique in our divine essence, but in the inner world, there is no distinction. All are equal in the eyes of Father in heaven, in the eyes of Yogi Ramsuratkumar. All he asks is that we have faith and surrender.
>
> When surrender is given to us by grace, all are equal in surrender, even though there are differences in age, race, religion. When Father blesses us, we are all equal. When Yogi Ramsuratkumar blesses us, we find ourselves in his regard. In his regard we are all blessed constantly, without distinctions. Father in heaven has no bigotry, no distinctions, no prejudice. Only human beings have such things. . . .
>
> So please chant Yogi Ramsuratkumar's name. It is the key to the kingdom of heaven, as in the New Testament. When we chant his name we unlock the door to heaven, wherever we are.

Walking up on the proscenium, Lee knelt at Yogi Ramsuratkumar's side and *pranamed*. Yogi Ramsuratkumar instructed Lee to take the chair onstage and prepared to leave. As they were wheeling him out, Yogi Ramsuratkumar stopped Rajmohan and told him to place the *prasad* tray on the floor beside Lee, who was now sitting in the white plastic chair in the front of the stage, but turned toward Yogi Ramsuratkumar with his hands in a *namaskar*.

It was only ten-thirty and darshan would continue until noon under Lee's direction. He had been expecting his old friend Pon Kamaraj to arrive at the ashram for the past few days. This morning he was sitting in darshan, and Lee gestured to him, inviting him up to the stage. Pon Kamaraj walked up, prostrated to Lee. They were obviously happy to see each other; Lee beamed at Pon Kamaraj and asked him to lead chants.

Leaving the stage, Pon Kamaraj took a place in front of the men. Much to our delight, he lead a series of rousing chants for the next thirty minutes, most of which were the first Yogi Ramsuratkumar chants that the Hohm Community had ever learned. Many of these were brought back with the men who came to India with Lee in 1988, when Lee and Pon Kamaraj first met.

It was Pon Kamaraj who had asked Yogi Ramsuratkumar in 1988 who he should invite to the *jayanthi* celebration at Kanimadam. Yogi Ramsuratkumar gave him a bag full of trash and said, "Go through this and you will find something." Pon Kamaraj went through the bag of old papers, newspapers and letters; the only thing he found were seven envelopes addressed to Yogi Ramsuratkumar with a return address from Lee Lozowick in the U.S.A.

Pon Kamaraj took the seven envelopes to Yogi Ramsuratkumar and said, "This is all I found of interest in the bag." Yogi Ramsuratkumar looked at the return address with Lee's name on the envelopes and said, "Invite this man and he will come." This was after

Yogi Ramsuratkumar had sent Lee away in 1986, not remembering him at all from earlier visits. When Pon Kamaraj wrote to Lee and invited him to come to the *jayanthi* Celebration at the Manthralayam, Lee came with nine of his men devotees and was surprised to find himself welcomed as the key speaker, the honored guest, and the "Effulgent flame of Yogi Ramsuratkumar in the West." It was in 1988 that, according to Lee, "Yogi Ramsuratkumar accepted me as his disciple."

Pon Kamaraj ended the chants and walked back up onstage with Lee, lowered his body into another prostration, then stood up, bowed and received *prasad* from Lee. Darshan was over.

We chanted from four o'clock till five o'clock in the afternoon darshan, when Yogi Ramsuratkumar appeared onstage. After Janarthanan gave a talk and Parathasarathy sang, Yogi Ramsuratkumar gestured to Lee. With a quick jump and a few bounds, Lee was kneeling beside Yogi Ramsuratkumar with his hands pressed together in a pranam.

"Lee, speak a few words," the beggar saint said gently.

Lee rose, walked to the front of the crowd and said, "With a Being such as Yogi Ramsuratkumar, Grace is something that is never inaccessible, but always available. If we knew the Ocean of Grace, and how it just pours out, pours out . . . Grace is pouring out on us twenty-four hours a day, whether or not Yogi Ramsuratkumar's body is asleep or awake."

Lee talked about Arnaud Desjardins and his relationship with his guru, Swami Prajnanpad. He told the story of how, when Arnaud first met Swami Prajnanpad, Swamiji asked Arnaud what he wanted. Arnaud said, "Atma-darshana," the vision of the transcendental Self, which is synonymous with self-realization or enlightenment. Lee then told a story about how Swami Prajnanpad had made a teaching lesson to Arnaud to communicate that one couldn't have *atma-darshana* until one is ready for such a thing:

> That story was a demonstration of how most people approach the guru. We want everything, but we aren't prepared. Everything is there, always pouring out, pouring out. Yogi Ramsuratkumar's blessings are constantly gushing, pouring out, but we don't feel them because we're not prepared. In the West we come to the guru and say, "Here I am. Give me what I want." But we aren't prepared, when there is an unimaginable ocean of blessings!
>
> One of the things that makes us ready is faith. We have to have faith in Yogi Ramsuratkumar. People come to India and want to sit in front of the Master. The mind and the temple of the body must be prepared, but we come to the Master and want to bow at the Master's feet, when we are not prepared.
>
> When you come to Yogi Ramsuratkumar, come accepting, open, with open hands to fill yourself, because the blessings are here all the time, an ocean of blessings, a universe of blessings, available all the time.

At seven-fifteen the next morning Yogi Ramsuratkumar summoned Lee. Ten minutes later the word came that the whole group was being called to the temple. Everyone literally dropped whatever they were doing and ran to the temple through the morning air, still damp with the moist haze of the night.

We entered the vast empty temple and saw Lee sitting on the floor alone, facing Yogi Ramsuratkumar. Ma Devaki, Vijayalakshmi, Rajmohan and Mani were on the stage. As we took our seats I became aware of a strong mood of pure intention in the air that seemed to manifest subtly, so that the air was choked with something like a fine iridescent mist; and yet it could also be said that the air was as clear as a spring day at high altitudes, and in fact we were instantly lifted up to spiritual heights. The silence was thunderous in the language of the heart that flowed from the still form of Yogi Ramsuratkumar.

Something very important was afoot in this private darshan for Lee and his students. When we arrived and sat down Yogi Ramsuratkumar had Rajmohan count to make sure everyone was there. Two or three of the French people had not arrived yet. Yogi Ramsuratkumar wanted to know who they were and where they were. Every detail mattered in the aesthetic of the delicate atmosphere he was creating.

Once the parameters of the group and the individuals in it were established, it seemed that the beggar's work commenced at another level. He gazed out at us, looking at each person, then his eyes rested on Lee for a long time. At other times it seemed that he was taking in the gestalt of the whole group. We were melted, woven together with him in silence, and this absorption occurred on many levels all at once.

His gaze was piercingly clear, yet also smoky, hazy, like the light of the sun coming through the earth's atmosphere, down through clouds and fogs that moisten and make fertile the rich ground. I felt that I was looking on the face of God, the infinite power and presence and grace of God, concentrated into the beam of one human being and shining upon us now through Yogi Ramsuratkumar like light refracted through diamond.

It was a moment of pure transmission. This diamond-like quality of Yogi Ramsuratkumar's attention hovered and shimmered in the air and carried with it a superfine quality, an exquisite *rasa* so elusive it was impossible to catch, and yet it was as obvious as the sun shining outside. We were being washed in eternity by the diamond light of the beggar's ineffable being. His face was different than I had ever seen it, both sculpted and otherworldly, his eyes slanted and half-lidded, yet appearing also wide open, glittering with pure consciousness, pure awareness. He was looking, looking at us, and as we received this blessing, it seemed to me that he was also taking blessings from us.

It was never more clear to me that we are all part of a unified field in which there is no separation, and it was his being that communicated this reality. The seriousness and sobriety of this rare private darshan with Yogi Ramsuratkumar carried in its message a very specific wordless empowerment for each individual person and Lee's students as a whole, even those who were in America or Europe. We cannot know what these moments are about; we can only receive them and acknowledge the reverberations, the implications, of such a chamber. Still, there was a perceived quality of an anointing or empowerment, and it reminded me of Jesus with the twelve disciples at the Last Supper, as if Yogi Ramsuratkumar was saying, "Go out and spread the news. You have received—now you must share."

The huge temple rose up around us, creating a vast frame for this dip into the river of eternity with Yogi Ramsuratkumar. The morning sun came through the windows in dusty shafts of light, and outside the birds called, their songs a perfect counterpoint to the blessing of the beggar's deep silence.

"Give them some talk—just a few words," Yogi Ramsuratkumar said to Lee tenderly, after about five minutes of thunderous silence. Lee *pranamed* and got up to talk, turning toward the twenty or so of us sitting there. While Lee talked about the tremendous gift of having such an intimate darshan with Yogi Ramsuratkumar, and the responsibility it incurred to live in a way that was resonant with his life and teaching, the beggar saint instructed Rajmohan and Ma Devaki to lower his feet to the floor, which they very carefully and slowly accomplished. The solemn formality of this chamber was juxtaposed by the extreme tenderness and intimacy of it, which was manifested by the way Ma Devaki, Vijayalakshmi and the other attendants carefully performed this action. Yogi Ramsuratkumar's feet rested there, with a pillow and blanket beneath them, touching the ground for the first time since before he had been in the hospital. It was the first and only time his feet were on the ground throughout our visit.

After a few minutes Yogi Ramsuratkumar had his feet lifted back up again. In this intensely charged act Yogi Ramsuratkumar had taken the posture of the bodhisattva, who is rooted in life and always ready to walk, run, move and act for the benefit of all sentient beings.

Lee was in mid-sentence when Yogi Ramsuratkumar began to leave the space. The darshan was over; the work had been accomplished. As his chair was turned to go, Lee fell silent, turned and bowed, hands reverently pressed together.

At breakfast in the dining hall the whole group was highly charged. Peoples' faces were molded by wonder and awe at the mystery of Yogi Ramsuratkumar. Some eyes were luminous with tears, and others were turned inward. Lee was exceptionally bright; there was a glow of certainty around him. It seemed to me that his feet were firmly planted, as always, on the solid ground of trust and faith and commitment to the work of his Father, while his heart and eyes burned with invisible joy, turned always toward Yogi Ramsuratkumar.

As soon as we sat down to immerse ourselves in the delicious breakfast meal—our last at the ashram—right away a butterfly came winging into the room. As it winged through the room I remembered that there had been many stories about Yogi Ramsuratkumar appearing to his devotees as a butterfly. This one was white, medium-sized, and made its presence known to us in no uncertain terms. The women were sitting in a long row facing the men's row, so we were in a position to watch its play as it fluttered from one person to the next in a graceful flight. It perched on Guy's plate and then on Volker's hand and seemed to nibble at some invisible substance it found there. It stayed on Volker for about two minutes, then it flew to Ken's mouth and literally clung to his lips for a prolonged minute, while Ken sat still. When it lifted off again it flew upward and toward Lee to circle above his head three times, as if it was circumambulating the whole group in those rounds. From there it flew up to the wall below the large photograph of the Shankaracharya of Kanchipuram. There it stayed until we left the dining hall.

We entered the temple the next morning for darshan, and at ten forty-five Yogi Ramsuratkumar arrived. "Say something, Mr. Lee," he said. Lee *pranamed* and walked forward, stepped off the stage, faced the crowd and began to speak:

> Faith and trust are a little different. Faith is a universal trust, and trust has more personal implications. I think that I have faith in Yogi Ramsuratkumar . . .
>
> Many years ago when we were with Yogi Ramsuratkumar at Sannadhi Street, he said, "I'm hungry, let's go eat." Very exciting! It was the first time ever we had gone to eat at a restaurant with Yogi Ramsuratkumar. He took my hand and he started running—and he is like the speed of light! He ran through the streets full of buses, trucks, cars, bullocks, carts, bicycles. He was holding my hand, but what about the other eight men? He had his work, his plan, but I thought, what about the other men? What if they get lost, hesitate and lose us? How will they find us? And they did hesitate, but they kept up. That moment of doubt was a lack of trust. Did he know about the other men? Of course he knew!
>
> So, to have faith is to have absolutely no question that Yogi Ramsuratkumar is eternal, pure, stainless. Everything else is just the appearance of things. Everything is completely perfect in every moment. As appearances shift in every moment, it is the play, the *lila*. At the essential heart of Yogi Ramsuratkumar, nothing ever changes. The heart of who Yogi Ramsuratkumar is, is eternal, changeless, stainless! That is what we see when we have faith. When we see who Yogi Ramsuratkumar is, we see the Divine. Over time, our trust in the personal integrity of Yogi Ramsuratkumar is burnished into faith, through our surrender to him. There is nothing there but Father in heaven. So please remember Yogi Ramsuratkumar and chant his name in praise of That which he is.

Yogi Ramsuratkumar then called Pon Kamaraj, who approached and quickly threw himself into a full-length prostration, then stood up and gently touched the master's feet.

"You can say something," he said to Pon Kamaraj, who *pranamed* and turned to face the large crowd. Seven or eight minutes into the talk Yogi Ramsuratkumar spoke quietly to Rajmohan, who then walked off the stage to give Pon Kamaraj the instruction to sing with the four men who were traveling with him. Pon Kamaraj called the men up and with great enthusiasm they began to lead the familiar chants from the Manthralayam. Yogi

Ramsuratkumar watched with great enjoyment. He asked Ma Devaki for a pair of bells, which he had Rajmohan take down to Pon Kamaraj, which upped the energy of their already lively singing. Yogi Ramsuratkumar had a big smile on his face as he watched with delight.

"They can dance," he said, with a smile that seemed to grow deeper and broader with each moment. Pon Kamaraj turned to look at Rajmohan, who delivered the message. Pon Kamaraj threw himself into singing and dancing with a tremendous surge of ecstatic devotion. There was no hesitation or restraint on his part. Watching Pon Kamaraj, he reminded me of the Bauls who put all of their praise and worship of God into their song and dance.

Yogi Ramsuratkumar watched from his chair up on the stage with a brilliant smile on his face. We had seen him smiling a lot during the past two weeks, but this was the peak of all smiles from the beggar king. His eyes crinkled up in happiness, his face was bright and transfigured. Ma Devaki called for a video camera and a devotee started filming Yogi Ramsuratkumar and Pon Kamaraj. It was a wonderful moment to witness.

After about fifteen minutes Yogi Ramsuratkumar called Pon Kamaraj up to receive *prasad*. He fell to the floor at Yogi Ramsuratkumar's feet in a full-body prostration.

It seemed that Yogi Ramsuratkumar could barely contain his pleasure at Pon Kamaraj and the men. The energy that they generated charged the whole hall with spiritual power, visibly brightening the air. I realized that in the dancing *lilas* of the past two weeks, we had been Yogi Ramsuratkumar's feet and legs. We were literally dancing for a God-intoxicated beggar who could no longer dance himself.

That afternoon was the last darshan of our visit with Yogi Ramsuratkumar. We sat on the floor in the temple and chanted his name until he entered and said, "Lee can speak." Lee rose from his seat, walked forward, then turned toward the crowd and began:

> When we leave Tiruvannamalai, we don't leave Yogi Ramsuratkumar because he is always there, wherever we are. Even though we come here to see him, when we leave we are in his presence. His presence is particularly concentrated on our ashrams in America and France. People see Yogi Ramsuratkumar on our ashrams. This temple and this ashram radiate Yogi Ramsuratkumar's presence throughout the world. We come here and it's like being flooded with the tangible nectar, *rasa, amrit* of Yogi Ramsuratkumar. But his *bhava*, his *rasa* is everywhere. It shows up in extraordinary events, and also in ordinary daily blessings, all the time. There is no substitute to the physical presence of Yogi Ramsuratkumar, which is beautiful, inspiring, unique—and yet when we leave and Yogi Ramsuratkumar says Father in heaven blesses you, it means that wherever we are, wherever we go, Yogi Ramsuratkumar is there. Father in heaven is there.
>
> When we leave there is a bittersweet yearning that follows us, but he is still there. He has said, call his name once with faith and the blessings of

> Father in heaven will be there. So please, remember, wherever you travel, Yogi Ramsuratkumar is there—the *amrit*, the tangible nectar pours through us. He is always there, protecting, educating, guiding, serving us.

"Sing and dance," the beggar king commanded with a grand smile as Pon Kamaraj *pranamed* at his side, then prostrated at his feet. Pon Kamaraj called his companions to come up from the audience.

"Sing and dance!" Yogi Ramsuratkumar repeated with joyful emphasis, raising his hands ecstatically up into the air. Pon Kamaraj and the two men went into action, singing and dancing with fresh enthusiasm. This time they had brought some small percussion instruments with them. They danced in a circle, keeping time with their instruments and clapping their hands. Pon Kamaraj pumped the energy, lifting himself, the men and the audience into a heightened state of joy. After about twenty minutes of this Pon Kamaraj was sweating and exhausted, his chest heaving, but he kept going, pushing himself to the limit and beyond in a passionate explosion of devotion to Yogi Ramsuratkumar. It was clear that he would dance ecstatically until the master said to stop.

Yogi Ramsuratkumar smiled gently with tender endearment, not taking his eyes off Pon Kamaraj. He was the endless ocean of love, which poured from him to all of us. Again the videos and cameras were brought out to film, focusing in on Yogi Ramsuratkumar to capture his rare happiness and exultation for posterity. Pon Kamaraj unabashedly continued to escalate the fervor with which he sang and danced. After about thirty minutes he danced toward Yogi Ramsuratkumar with arms held out and above his head in praise and supplication in an inspired peak of emotion, which ended in his whole body falling into a prostration at Yogi Ramsuratkumar's feet. It was the grand finale to an extraordinary act of devotion, and the whole room was swept up into it.

The energy had been spurred to a peak of intense devotional ardor. Walking up on the stage, Pon Kamaraj knelt at Yogi Ramsuratkumar's side, took his hands and pressed them to his forehead. Passionately, sweetly, he then reverently pressed the master's feet to his forehead. Yogi Ramsuratkumar smiled at him with the supernal love of the great-hearted and gently placed *prasad* into his waiting hand. Pon Kamaraj *pranamed* again and then walked away, wiping the sweat from his face with a shawl, his chest heaving from the intense exertion.

"Parathasarathy," Yogi Ramsuratkumar said, "come and sing." All the raw energy and spiritual force that Pon Kamaraj had generated was now somehow blended and alchemized with the sweet softness of Parathasarathy's devotion to further refine the energy for Yogi Ramsuratkumar's purposes. This experience of Yogi Ramsuratkumar working the space at subtle levels had happened many times during the darshans of the past two weeks. Each time it seemed that he was masterfully using whatever energy was available to create subtle atmospheres that were charged with transformational power.

Today Yogi Ramsuratkumar was more energetic than he had appeared any time throughout the past days of our visit.

He was animated, happy, smiling brightly and watching everything with great interest. He asked Lee to have some of the men sing and dance. Volker, Ken and Karl jumped up enthusiastically.

"Can they do rock and roll?" Yogi Ramsuratkumar asked in his peerless way of innocent mischief, a gleam in his eyes.

Lee laughed and retorted, "They can roll for you, but they can't rock!" Everyone in the front rows—particularly the Americans and Europeans traveling with Lee—laughed at this light repartee. It was a great example of the kind of ease with which Yogi Ramsuratkumar has worked with Westerners over the years. Today he seemed to have a reservoir of energy that he was working off of as he staged and orchestrated one mini-event after another.

We were basking in his delight; the whole world seemed to turn on its axis, and the spheres moved through the firmament of heaven by the sheer force of the beggar king's enjoyment as his devotees sang and danced. The enthusiasm was contagious, and he began to ask several different people from the audience to come up and "sing and dance." Many of his long-time devotees were in the room for these last darshans. Jayarama, the beggar's former attendant, sat watching from the crowd, and his wife Bhuvanesvari was called up by Yogi Ramsuratkumar and asked to dance. She was joined by their two children in the final dance of the darshan.

Hearts were full of joy, and tears of happiness instead of sorrow filled our eyes. We were celebrating at a high level with the old beggar, whose generous and brilliant smiles shone on us like a thousand suns. It was his final legacy to us—sing, dance, enjoy, worship and praise, celebrate God, alive in the world! We had come full circle from the first few days of our visit, when the singing and dancing *lilas* had begun and Yogi Ramsuratkumar could barely lift his hand or speak to us. Now he was enlivened and rejuvenated in ways I could not fathom. His last words to us were, "Dance! Dance!" before he unceremoniously and quickly left.

At dinner that night in the ashram bungalow several guests joined Lee and the Western devotees: Pon Kamaraj and the two men who sang and danced with him this afternoon; the woman in the white sari and her husband; Ashish, Shantipriya and their attendants; and the Spanish man, Swami Satyananda, a friend of Lee's. A fresh raw vegetable salad was being provided by Triveni—a rare treat in India.

After dinner Lee said, "It was great to have the darshans be the way they were today—thanks to Pon Kamaraj!" Pon Kamaraj, who was sitting in a chair across the room, *pranamed* to Lee in acceptance of the acknowledgment.

Soon Rajmohan arrived and spoke with Lee, saying, "Bhagawan would like to know your program for tomorrow." Lee relayed the details—we were going to leave long before dawn.

"Is it possible to postpone leaving for one hour? Because Bhagawan wants to see you for a final interview," Rajmohan asked. "Of course," Lee responded, and plans were made.

The next morning, December 14, the packing began long before dawn. Bags and backpacks were carried in a steady stream as people scurried through the cool darkness along the path from the cottages, past the dining hall toward the dirt road by the temple, where the vans were parked and awaiting our departure. The stars were still shining brightly when everyone stood in the road with Lee by the vans, drinking the sweet coffee that had been arranged by Yogi Ramsuratkumar, and waiting for his call. A number of people had come to say goodbye: Mani and Raji, Bret, Ute, Volker, Pon Kamaraj and several others.

At five forty-five the call came: Yogi Ramsuratkumar was ready for Lee and his students. We quickly walked across the sandy open area and into the back of the temple, entering through the door that led to an anteroom to Yogi Ramsuratkumar's private apartment. Lee went in first while everyone else waited in the anteroom. Mani stood at the door to the room and called us in one by one, so that each person had a moment with Yogi Ramsuratkumar. The men went first, then the women.

As I walked into the big white room Yogi Ramsuratkumar filled the space, although Lee was sitting beside him on his right and Ma Devaki and Vijayalakshmi stood on his left side beside the big reclining chair. My eyes became completely magnetized to Yogi Ramsuratkumar, who filled the universe and immediately absorbed me into his field of play. I walked quickly to his side and knelt on the floor, hands in *pranam*, eyes glued to his face.

He very gently and tenderly handed me an apple as if it contained the most precious thing in the world, which it did—his love. Time vanished into eternity, but I was acutely aware that this was the last moment I would have with his physical form, in his rare attention, in this lifetime. I was spellbound by the fire of love in his eyes and could not move, until Lee made a slight movement of his hand and I realized that it was time to tear myself away. I stood and backed away toward the door, *pranaming*, my eyes riveted to him. His eyes never left my face from the moment I entered the room until the moment I left.

Standing about eight feet away from his chair as I prepared to leave, I noticed the warm radiance of Ma Devaki, who stood at Yogi Ramsuratkumar's side. She looked at me and smiled, and her smile was like the sun. I *pranamed* to her and became aware that Vijaylakshmi was beside her. One more lingering glance at the Beloved, who lay in a deep pool of silence, a pure incarnation of love, and I walked out.

A year later, when Lee was back in Tiruvannamalai, someone asked him the question, "What were the last words of Yogi Ramsuratkumar to you?" Lee responded:

> Yogi Ramsuratkumar had a particular smile that was objective beauty. The morning we left, Devaki Ma came and said, "Yogi Ramsuratkumar wants to see everyone in the group," so we all lined up at his door. He called me in; he was giving everyone an apple and asking me their name. The body was in tremendous pain. His attention was totally focused. He'd grip the apple and look at the person and drop it in their hands. Then

> I was the only one left with Devaki Ma and Vijayalakshmi. He did the same with me, and I *pranamed*. As I got up to leave his whole face broke out into that smile . . . there was a particular quality to that smile one would have to call shyness. His tenderness and love in the midst of that smile were so intense that he couldn't look you in the eye. I walked out of that room, and that's the last time I saw him. That's a memory I will carry for the rest of my life and probably beyond.

The day after Lee left, Yogi Ramsuratkumar gave his last two "conscious" public darshans in the temple, in which he was able to interact with people, ask them to chant and give *prasad*. His last two months were spent in the temple abode, which had a hallway that circled around the outside of it with windows that looked into the apartment. From there the devotees came to stand and have his darshan while he lay on the bed. Ashish Bagrodia described him at this time as "a royal king, lying on the bed with his flowing beard. Even with all those tubes, every few seconds his hand would go up like this, blessing, then come down—on its own.

It was a bittersweet time. In January 2001 people began to chant twenty-four hours a day. During the day the chanting took place in the hallway behind the abode, where the supine form of Yogi Ramsuratkumar could be seen on the bed. After eight o'clock at night the chanting was moved to the big hall of the temple. Volker Augustyniak wrote about this time:

> I received this chanting as a great gift that Yogi Ramsuratkumar provided for his devotees. Especially during the nights his presence was so strong—much stronger than I personally received from seeing his suffering and dying body during the day. I almost couldn't stand his suffering, but the chanting in the hall always gave me tranquility, confidence and faith that whatever happens has to happen for some purpose, even though I didn't have any linear or logical explanation for it.
>
> There were many situations when suddenly in the middle of the night the statue in the temple would start glowing in an otherworldly light. The face of the statue and its whole radiance changed many times during this period. Yogi Ramsuratkumar's presence seemed to move slowly out of his body and started tangibly filling everything else.[6]

In mid-January Justice Arunachala called Ashish Bagrodia and told him it would be a good idea for him to come, for no one knew how much longer Yogi Ramsuratkumar

6 Volker Augustyniak, *Tawagoto*, Winter 2002, pp. 127-128.

would be alive. Flying to Chennai from Bombay and then going by car to Tiruvannamalai, he arrived late at night and went immediately to the ashram, where he encountered the following scene, described by Ashish in his memoirs:

> When we reached the ashram all was quiet. There was no crowd, nothing. People informed me that Yogi Ramsuratkumar was serious but he was okay. They also told us that we could have his darshan. They had arranged to allow people to see Yogiji in the room where he was being nursed (by a full-fledged team, provided by Dr. Rangabashyam). The darshan would be through a glass window.
>
> I went to that place and had the most amazing darshan of my life, or rather a peculiar one too. What I saw from the window was a magnificent scene, although heart breaking but at the same time immensely divine. On this huge hospital bed, Yogiji with his flowing white beard, head with long and absolutely silver white hair, bare-chested with so many tubes running on both hands, with an oxygen mask on his face, was breathing very heavily and in deep sleep. It was as if Lord Vishnu was lying on his serpent bed as the King of the Universe.
>
> The most amazing thing was that Yogiji's right hand would keep coming up in the blessing posture every few seconds, although Yogiji was deeply unconscious, almost in a coma. This was the most amazing thing to be seen, as literally his hand would keep coming up to bless all the people there, and in fact it seems, as there was the danger/risk for the tubes to come out or maybe his hand would go to the oxygen mask and thereby destabilize it. Hence, it was felt that his hands should be tied by some string, therefore, even with his hands tied by strings, his hand would lift up by a few inches and then would go down. In spite of the oxygen mask, in spite of the tubes, in spite of being without a turban and in spite of being on a hospital bed, he looked as divine, as radiant, as magnificent as always—even more, maybe.

For the next weeks Yogi Ramsuratkumar's condition declined quickly, until by mid-February it was clear that the death of the physical body was finally imminent.

On February 10, 2001 Parthasarathy was in his office in Sivakasi when the phone rang. It was the ashram in Tiruvannamalai, saying, "Swami desires to see you. Is it possible to come over to Tiruvannamalai immediately?" He rushed there and arrived in the evening at five-thirty. Yogi Ramsuratkumar was in a deep sleep state. At eight o'clock he woke up.

Ma Devaki and Vijayalakshmi said, "Bhagawan, Parathasarathy is here. He has come. He has driven his car from Sivakasi to Tiruvannamalai to have this darshan." The beggar focused his eyes on Parthasarathy and smiled at him, touching his hand for some time.

"Thank you, Parathasarathy, for coming here," he managed to say quietly, gently. Others who had been particularly close over the years, such as Dwarak Nath Reddy, came to pay their last respects to the beloved beggar saint. Dwarak Reddy remembered his last meeting with Yogi Ramsuratkumar in the temple abode, two weeks before his death:

> The situation was turning more critical. I was probably one of the last people to have sat with him. He was in a reclining chair, and he was sitting there with Devaki. I felt that maybe we should take a picture—probably one of the last photographs that was taken of him. One time I had taken the camera and just kept quiet, but the next time I asked permission, and I took a couple of pictures at that time.

Vijayalakshmi wrote that it was remarkable how Yogi Ramsuratkumar gave intimations of his impending death to his devotees. Hearing of his serious condition, many devotees came to say goodbye. Shri Gajaraj, his wife and some relatives had come to the ashram for his darshan, but his daughter was unable to come. Instead, to her surprise, she found the old beggar standing on her doorstep, saying, 'All the others have come; why have you not come?' He asked her for some buttermilk and she went to get it; when she came back he was no longer there. He frequently appeared in the dreams of many people, both in India and in the West.[7]

Yogi Ramsuratkumar was, until the last beating of his heart, a glorious embodiment of the Divine within the sacred and heartbreaking crucible of his utter humanity. His example in the midst of profound suffering left many in wonder and amazement, shaken to the core. Shankara Rajulu reflected on the transforming impact of Yogi Ramsuratkumar's transmission of the Divine during this intense time:

> We are slowly made perfect by him—by his conversations, by his conduct, by his gentle behavior. When he was undergoing all these sufferings did he at any time complain about it? At any time did he want to be treated or to be given medicine? Or to be operated upon? No, because he used to always say, "This beggar died in 1952 at the feet of my master, Ramdas. My Father has taken over this body, and He is putting it to such use as He deems fit." Whenever Mataji Devaki used to care for him and worry about his illness, he used to say, "Worry, worry! Because it is my Father who does it, do you think that He will not take care of this beggar?"
>
> But his Father and himself are one and the same. For ordinary people like us he used to tell us, "My Father is there in heaven and he will bless you," but he also made us understand that Father and himself were one, just as Jesus used to say. Father has sent him, but he and his Father are not

7 Vijayalakshmi, *Waves of Love*, p. 97.

> different. He is an incarnation. He has come down to earth. Yogi Ramsuratkumar has made people to chant his name; that itself shows that he was willing to divulge that he is an incarnation. I am now realizing that every moment of my stay here [on earth], and it is that which has prolonged my life. He is giving me a new lease on life every day, every moment, in order to make me realize just that. I have been in the presence of the Almighty. I have been instructed, blessed by the Almighty.

Yogi Ramsuratkumar was a natural law unto himself until the very end, and abided wholly in perfect divine surrender. He once said of himself, "This beggar is a born beggar, will remain as beggar, will die as beggar," and these words were proven to be true. Devaki relayed a story as an example of that: At one point the clothes he had been wearing became terribly dirty. Ma Devaki begged him, day after day, to allow them to change his clothes. The clothes were so dirty that some of the people who came to see him commented on it, but still Bhagawan would not allow his clothes to be changed. In many different ways she tried to insist, cajole, beg, wheedle—all to no avail. She finally broke down and wept, begging him to allow them to put fresh clothes on his body, but he would not budge. Ma Devaki remembered:

> After seven days of rain and storm, at the most unexpected moment, he suddenly called me and said, "Devaki! Bring some clothes." It was just to let me know that he would do things only his way and at the time he chose. That's how it happened, after seven days! Many of his habits he kept up. In some cases he seemed to relent, but then probably only because the situation demanded—that was the best way he could do his Father's work. Everything was based on his work. If he seemed to relent in certain matters it was because it was the best way he could do his Father's work.
>
> He was Bhagawan right up to the end—to his samadhi. He was Bhagawan in every breath. He always did only what he liked and only if he liked. Nobody could move him from his position unless he wanted. If he had decided something, it was so and he would let you know in so many ways. The choice was with you—you could learn it the hard way or the soft way.

For days Yogi Ramsuratkumar seemed to hover back and forth between death and life. As Saravanan said, "One day he was very fresh, and then sometimes it was something like a darkness coming . . . then again sometimes very fresh." As he had in the hospital during the months in Chennai, in the hours just before his death, Yogi Ramsuratkumar went into a state that the doctors said was unconscious—all his systems were failing. Those who were closest to him felt the power of his conscious awareness through it all, regardless of the condition of the body. They felt the transmission of grace and his tremendous capacity for deep inner communion with them, the speech of the heart that transcends all other forms of communication.

Once he had not talked the whole day. His eyes were closed and he was very still; he seemed to be unconscious. Swami Satyananda Saraswati, a Spanish sannyasin that Yogi Ramsuratkumar had known for years and was very fond of, was called to the door by Ma Devaki to have a last darshan. He stood at the door of the abode and *pranamed*. With eyes still closed and all the appearances of being in a coma, Yogi Ramsuratkumar raised his hand in blessing. No words were exchanged. Vijayalakshmi wrote of this time:

> During the acute phase of his illness doctors decided to do dialysis since the kidneys functioned erratically. The dialysis was initially successful. But due to the dropping of blood pressure, dialysis could not be continued. The fever raged. The lungs became congested. Yet through all this Bhagawan, the embodiment of peace and compassion, continued to raise his right arm in blessing as devotees filed past the window of the room in which he was lying. It was most remarkable that the Supreme consciousness took note of the fact that thousands of devotees thronged to have a glimpse of their beloved, now in the final moments in this mortal body. The tongue continued to utter Ramnam, the eyes were closed most of the time, but the right arm was raised frequently in blessing. It was a magnificent sight.
>
> Bhagawan had taken pains to teach us again and again that we are not the body; the body is at best a garment which the Atman wears. It is subject to growth, decay and death; but the Atman, the Supreme, is constant, unchanging, ever blissful. The last days of Yogi Ramsuratkumar demonstrated that though the body suffered untold agonies, the spirit indomitably spread love, compassion and blessings.
>
> Even in the throes of severe pain he did not demand anything, but silently allowed his body to be medically attended to. In the last few hours he become totally silent, though he raised his right arm in occasional blessing. The breathing became difficult and finally stopped. An ineffable peace radiated from his mortal frame. This dropping of the body did not affect that Chaitanyam, ever present and radiant, whose presence could be felt and experienced.[8]

A few days before his *mahasamadhi*, while several devotees sat at his beside, he suddenly opened his eyes, looked Ma Devaki in the eyes and said, "I am everyone, everything, here, there, everywhere. I alone exist." Then he closed his eyes again. Very soon after that he stopped speaking entirely. The doctors and many devotees felt that Yogi Ramsuratkumar was in a coma and completely unconscious, but those who stood outside his room in the corridor or were allowed in for his darshan were convinced that he was

8 Ibid, pp. 96-97.

entirely conscious.

One woman who was staying in Tiruvannamalai at the time had traveled from France. She had never met the beggar saint before, though she had heard of him through Lee Lozowick. She spent many hours in the temple chanting the name of Yogi Ramsuratkumar during his last days, while the devotees kept a twenty-four hour vigil. She told the story of how she stood by the window and looked in upon the beggar saint: the body was in great pain, but as she watched, she saw Yogi Ramsuratkumar open his eyes and look at a long-time devotee who stood near his bed. "His eyes were the eyes of a child," she said, "and they were laughing!"

At one point during this time the doctors were convinced that Yogi Ramsuratkumar was unconscious. Ma Devaki was overcome with sorrow as she sat weeping in a corner of the room. With eyes closed, the beggar saint raised his hand and gestured to Ma Devaki to come near, then he held her hand and patted it gently, reassuring her, while the rest of his body remained still and deeply quiescent—as if comatose. From time to time he continued to raise his hand in blessing to those who came for a last silent darshan. He gave refuge to his grieving devotees through the power of his being, his compassion, love and ultimate blessing until his last breath in the physical body.

On February 20 in the early hours of the morning, the breath of the beggar king had labored for hours. The EKG monitor showed many low points when those keeping the vigil thought he would leave the body, then he would rally and his vital signs would stabilize again. He was surrounded by Ma Devaki, Vijayalakshmi, Mani, Justice Arunachala, Parthasarathy, Swami Nathan, Rajmohan, Ravi and several others; the members of the ashram staff and many devotees were sitting or standing nearby in the hallway. There were about thirty-five people standing in the corridor outside his room also keeping the vigil, and another one hundred people stood outside the temple. His hands continued to spontaneously rise in blessing until the very end.

At 3:19 Yogi Ramsuratkumar stopped breathing, which signaled clinical death, but the heartbeat continued to register on the electrocardiogram that was attached to his body. Justice Arunachala asked everyone present to circumambulate Yogi Ramsuratkumar's body, prostrate and touch his feet while the chanting, "Yogi Ramsuratkumar, Yogi Ramsuratkumar, Yogi Ramsuratkumar, Jaya Guru Raya," continued unabated. Finally, when the last person had circled his body and gently touched the cherished feet, his heart stopped beating. It was 3:45 in the morning. The soft and warm Indian night closed in around, embracing all in its veil of mystery, safeguarding the quiet tears that fell.

Death contains the seeds of ecstasy and wonder precisely because one is thrust into the bittersweet beauty of impermanence, which compels the human spirit to seek the perfection of that which is eternal. And so a great beggar, a true Godman, was gone from this world in his physical form and reborn in the unseen worlds beyond the five senses. His effulgent presence filled the vast sky and pulsed in the hearts of those who loved him. There was never a cessation of the communion of his heart with those who were receptive to hear, in joyful silence, the sound of the beggar's laughter, which would resound in the world forever. His body, exuding the splendor and sanctity of the life that was lived, was laid in state in the temple, while thousands of people came to pay homage to a beloved son of Mother India, and to the great treasure that was his life—as one devotee said, to "His life! His wonderful life, mother! Such a glorious life, you know!"

The body of Yogi Ramsuratkumar was beatific, serene and radiant in death. Laying in the red reclining chair that had become familiar in the last months of his life, his body was kept in the vast hall of the temple on the day of February 20, 2001. Ma Devaki and Vijayalakshmi sat on the floor beside him, as always, chanting the divine name. Throughout the day thousands of people thronged the ashram to pay their respects, offer prayers and to shed tears of gratitude and longing. The chanting went on twenty-four hours a day. A great spiritual light had gone out of the world, but in another way, that light was made brighter, now released from its clay container and set free into unbounded light, unbounded possibility.

The next day the devotees took turns carrying the body of Yogi Ramsuratkumar high over their heads on a bier covered with flowers, with hundreds of people following in procession as they chanted and slowly circumambulated the ashram. Afterward a traditional *abhisheka* (anointing of the body with sacred substances) was performed. The body was dressed and gently lowered into the *samadhi* site in the *padmasan* (lotus) pose amidst a great swell of devotion over the huge crowd that strained to get closer for a final glimpse. Sanskrit prayers were chanted and the traditional Vedic rituals performed. The final play was over. The death of Yogi Ramsuratkumar was an epochal point in time—the ending and beginning of a great era, on earth and in heaven.

CHAPTER TEN

LILA — IN THE GARDEN OF DELIGHT

One sunny winter morning in January 2003 I took a few minutes away from my work to talk with a friend. Cutting our conversation short, I heard myself saying with a smile, "I have to get back to the Garden of Delight!" Putting in long hours on this book every day to meet my deadline, I was obsessed with the project, but it was Yogi Ramsuratkumar himself who was consuming my days and nights. Still, the phrase "the Garden of Delight" had popped out of nowhere, and as I went back to the familiar incubator of my desk, I reflected on these words. I realized that this phrase, referring to Yogi Ramsuratkumar, had been percolating under the surface of my thoughts for days.

That very night Lesley Ball and I were talking about Yogi Ramsuratkumar, inspired by the handwritten journals of Caylor Wadlington, which she had just finished inputting for me. She told me the following dream, which she had had some years before:

> I was standing in the middle of a large feasting hall, and there were a hundred people around me, all of them absorbed with eating from the two long tables that were set up in rows in the big room. I was surprised to see Yogi Ramsuratkumar, standing in the aisle between the two tables. Everyone else was oblivious to his presence, and I thought to myself in amazement, "How can everybody be missing the fact that Yogi Ramsuratkumar is standing here? They are all so absorbed in eating!" He saw that my attention was on him and he gestured to me to come.
>
> "Can't they see you?" I said to him. He laughed and said, "Not everybody can. Not everyone will see this." He led me down the aisle toward a door that opened into a bright, sunny walled-in courtyard. We stepped through the open door and into an incomparable garden that overflowed with brilliant flowers of all colors, shapes and textures.
>
> "Look! Look at the flowers. See how beautiful they are! Smell them, feel them," he said, with such childlike wonder and awe at the beauty of the flower garden. His laughter was joyous as he stood with me, drinking

> in the beauty all around. He said, "This is the Garden of Delight. This is my teaching. This is it! This is it, right here." He kept laughing because so many people were missing the point.

"What was it that he called the garden?" I asked in absolute amazement.

"This is the Garden of Delight. This is my teaching," she repeated twice for me.

Yogi Ramsuratkumar's power to teach and transmit blessings through dreams, and the stories of those dreams, could be made into a book in and of itself. There are literally thousands of dreams like this one, in which he spoke directly to the hearts of devotees, by-passing the mind altogether. In this case, a better synchronicity couldn't have been planned out, and the title and blueprint for this last chapter was born. It was one of many small miracles that permeated and guided this project all along the way, as the presence and living image of Yogi Ramsuratkumar became the revelation in the process of writing.

Immersed in stacks of files of interviews, testimonies, private journals, books, bits and scraps of information, pamphlets, booklets, my own notebooks from the past fifteen years and many other resources, the mystery of Yogi Ramsuratkumar took on broad and deep detail, nuance of variegated hue and shade, subtle tones and delicate flavors. The beggar king emerged, bigger than life, as the agent of pure grace in the most refined *rasa*—the Garden of Delight described in Lesley's dream. Underlying all the phenomenal appearances of the master was an ocean of *ananda*. Despite the misunderstanding and abuses he endured in his life, the inconsistencies of his devotees caught up in the human dilemma, or the varieties of ways he taught and the many forms of relationship that he cultivated with people, his life was suffused with the nectar of delight, joy, love. As Yogi Ramsuratkumar once said, "If there is love in a man's heart, the whole world will be beautiful."

At one point during the writing of this book my family went out of town for the day, and by necessity I stayed home to write. That morning I was at my desk at six-thirty. A little later I went to the kitchen to have breakfast and lingered for a few minutes, washing up the dishes. Suddenly I became aware that I was not alone. Looking through the kitchen door into the bright space of the quiet living room, I saw the moving form of Yogi Ramsuratkumar, gray shawl thrown up over one shoulder, standing not far from the shrine where his *vigraha* lives. It was a transparent but vivid image that shimmered in the air, and the force of his loving presence was as vital and real as the sunlight on the cedars just outside the window. I knew instantly that he was watching and guiding my every move with the most benevolent and all-embracing spirit. I knew that he was blessing me, and that he was waiting . . . waiting for me to go back to my desk and the task at hand. Ever so gently, the beggar king said to me, "You can go back to work now."

It is impossible to describe the love communicated in those simple words. In that moment, I also knew that this book had to be finished at a very particular time—when Yogi Ramsuratkumar wanted it done. I knew then that Lee's push to complete the book was actually Yogi Ramsuratkumar's urgency—"Do whatever you have to do to have the book finished by the first of May." All this came flashing into my awareness in a matter of seconds as the image of Yogi Ramsuratkumar slowly receded, leaving wonder and fulfillment in the lingering radiance of his presence.

Yogi Ramsuratkumar's Garden of Delight was not an orderly, formal or studied garden, but a profusion, a wild tangle, redolent with fragrance, resounding with the songs of birds and the buzzing of bees that careened drunkenly here and there, gathering the hidden nectars that abounded. I could imagine the gardener himself, in a mad dance of creation, casting handfuls of seeds of all kinds into the dark and fertile soil, watered by the rain of his compassion, the tears of his greatest sorrows, and "warmed by the sun of his love," as Lee once wrote in a poem, for all beings.

Despite the garden's wildness, if you look at it with the right view, it makes perfect sense, and there is beauty in its divine order. In this last chapter we have an overspill, a profusion, the wild tangle of the *lilas* of Yogi Ramsuratkumar—a further tribute to the many ways the master worked with those who knew and loved him, and to his ultimate universality and the Great Work to which he so freely gave his life.

A MASTER OF RASA

The invocation of objective mood was a central element of the way Yogi Ramsuratkumar transmitted grace. He often did this through the use of music in the form of chanting the name of God, but also through touch, gaze and physical affection. For those who came to him for help, this sometimes resulted in radical healings.

Once there was a couple who came to Yogi Ramsuratkumar with their newborn baby who had a clubfoot. He held the baby in his lap and stroked and massaged its legs for thirty minutes. A year later they came back and said they couldn't remember which leg had been deformed—they were both healthy.

After Yogi Ramsuratkumar laid his hands on Caylor Wadlington's forehead in 1970, his severe headaches went away. Now a successful healer, acupuncturist and doctor of Oriental medicine, Caylor commented, "The headaches never came back. The [energy] is always there when I think of spiritual things or meditate or pray, or if I'm near some spiritual object, but it is never blocked like that. There is a sort of gauge of some sort. The headaches never came back . . . "

Ramanlal first met Yogi Ramsuratkumar in 1984. He was a law student in college when he was in a very serious accident that left his arm mangled; many of the veins in the arm had been severed, and his arm was limp and lifeless. At the time Ramanlal couldn't even hold a book with the hand of his damaged arm, and it looked like he was doomed to a serious disability. His father, Rathimathangam, had been a devotee of Yogi Ramsuratkumar since the seventies and took him to meet the beggar saint, who immediately asked Ramanlal to stay with him for two days.

During this time Ramanlal was kept inside the inner rooms at the house on Sannadhi Street; Yogi Ramsuratkumar worked with his arms for three or four hours out of each day, stroking, gently caressing and stretching them out. On the second day he asked Ramanlal to pull on the hook that hung above the door to assess the function of the arm. The arm felt better, and he could stretch it more. Yogi Ramsuratkumar simply said, "It will become normal," and sent him on his way. The arm became stronger and stronger, and he soon regained full use of it.

Yogi Ramsuratkumar used touch to heal on many occasions. One of Lee's students wrote about an interaction between Yogi Ramsuratkumar and Alain de Rosanbo that she witnessed in the mid-nineties:

> Yogi Ramsuratkumar, heaped against the back wall of the hut, is totally attentive to our arrival and yet looks completely immersed in God as he draws deep puffs on his cigarette. The Divine has delighted in giving this form the aspect of a beggar! There is an atmosphere of pure devotion and the people close to Yogi Ramsuratkumar give him looks of love. He rises from his cushions and walks a little unsteadily toward Alain de Rosanbo. He comes to sit on the floor beside Alain and puts his hand on Alain's knee. I am seated very close to this scene and watch intently. The closeness, the smell of incense burning as Yogi Ramsuratkumar works with Alain, eyes closed or pupils trembling, his fingers on his lips as he mutters. He is totally involved in what he is doing. There is a paradox between the gentle stroking his hand expresses as it moves along Alain's leg and feet, and the intention and strength behind each movement. When Yogi gets up, his body wavers. He looks around at each one of us; in his eyes there is no one to see, just an unfathomable look.[1]

There are countless stories of the miracles that occurred around Yogi Ramsuratkumar. People were often healed by his direct physical touch, but also simply by being in his company, or even from a distance. Yogi Ramsuratkumar himself once said, "Touch is one way of communication. Look is another. Ramana Maharshi did it to some people. Also be remembering, communication is possible. Vijayakka and Rajalakshmi are in Salem. When this beggar remembers them, it helps their transformation. Transformation is going on all the time."[2]

But the real miracle of his healing power was much deeper and greater than the healing of physical ailments or deformities; the real magic of his healing power came through the emanations of his being. People were transformed, changed for the better, through the sheer power of his love and delight in life. The mood of delight in the beauty and wonder of creation and the Creator was pervasive around him. It was this *rasa* of

1 Sian Bouyou, *Tawagoto*, Winter 1996, pp. 60-61.

2 *Facets of the Diamond*, p. 149.

love, wonder and delight that was at the center of the "pure and crystal-like *vastu*" that was Yogi Ramsuratkumar. Will Zulkowski recounted:

> I remember a lot of times he would stroke my arms. Sometimes he would sit there and stroke my arms for fifteen or twenty minutes. Each time I left I felt like a different person. When he put that energy into me, it was like he was rearranging every atom in my being. I don't want to call these experiences miracles, but they seemed like the best kind of miracles, because they're not outward, they're inward. It felt like he was using his delight to transform you vibrationally into something much more refined. I would feel completely different after I walked out of there, after just three or four days.
>
> Everything with him was so subtle. I remember asking him about him sitting in the big hall [the ashram temple] and what was happening in there, and he said he wanted to create an atmosphere so even the densest person could feel something in the air. That's what he worked for—he worked for a couple of years just sitting [in the temple] every day. He was working to purify that atmosphere, to bring that vibration to such a high, high, high state that even the most dense person on earth could walk in there and feel, "Hey, there's something here that's beyond me."
>
> That's what he did, and that's why his work was in Tiruvannamalai, because it was drawing and working with these elemental forces and blessing that place with such a power. Absolutely astounding! What he has left is . . . . a transformative vibration. All you have to do is walk into it and stay there for a while and be open, and something will happen to you. To me that's the great miracle—not pulling something out of a hat or materializing something. That's extraneous—there's no point to it. You see it once: all right, it blows your mind. But after that, what's the point? Are you transformed? No, it's a trap.

Yogi Ramsuratkumar imbued the temple on the ashram with the force of his blessing, but he also concentrated his attention—the power of his love and delight—on individuals as well. One of the ways this manifested was that he was extremely affectionate and loving. Physical affection is commonplace and accepted as a very natural expression of ordinary relationship in India, but this natural affection is demonstrated only between men and men, and between women and women, not across gender lines. Yogi Ramsuratkumar often used affection and touch to heal or to transmit grace and blessings to his men devotees.

The beggar's relationship with Lee Lozowick was extremely affectionate and intimate in this way. The expression of love between the guru and disciple that Yogi Ramsuratkumar demonstrated with Lee had a profound impact on Lee's students, who came with him from the West year after year to visit Yogi Ramsuratkumar. The affectionate caresses that they witnessed struck such a deep chord—the natural longing of the human being for objective relationship—that it often brought tears to their eyes:

> What a beautiful sight to see on our first morning as we walked into the darshan hall: Yogi Ramsuratkumar, who has not come to darshan in eight months, is sitting holding Lee's hand as we enter. They are sitting side-by-side, backs against the wall facing us. The mood of sweetness is piercing and my eyes are riveted to them as the chanting begins, while my heart is softly crying. From time to time Yogi strokes Lee's hand, each touch infused with the most exquisite tenderness. Other times he plays with his fingers, his fingertips. I realize that I am being witness to love in its most supreme form.[3]

> Over the next three days we were the witnesses as Yogi Ramsuratkumar spent about thirty hours hand in hand with Lee. The nine of us were fortunate to be the background upon which the love play happened. Yogi Ramsuratkumar held Lee's hand, sometimes on his knee, sometimes on Lee's knee, sometimes with hands intertwined, sometimes like softly petting a lover. He gave long, extended gentle attention to caressing Lee's arm from elbow to finger nail, holding it in an outstretched position, as if empowering the arm itself to bless. He stroked Lee's arm as if he was massaging a ball pitcher's arm. He touched Lee's face, the left hand and arm, the left knee and foot . . .[4]

At Ganeshan's house in 1993, Anuradha referred to Yogi Ramsuratkumar and Lee Lozowick in jest as "Romeo and Juliet," after one of Lee's poems inspired Yogi Ramsuratkumar to ask Lee to tell the story of the two lovers. It was one of those days when the beggar's love and affection was flowing like a fine wine. At these times his affection with Lee seemed to be literally the generating force of many different *rasas*, or tastes: celebration and praise of God, the exquisite tenderness of love and the delicate communion of the heart, the bittersweet and pungent longing for the unattainable Beloved. Yogi Ramsuratkumar was a master of *rasa*, and could easily create a *temenos*—a contained or sheltered alchemical chamber—in which such nectar was then generated and transmitted to those who were present. These objective moods had the power to transform because they were spiritually potent with the Divine.

"You, Raji, you give me prasad!" the Godchild demanded one year on the *jayanthi* of Lord Krishna. With Rajalakshmi, the wife of Mani, Yogi Ramsuratkumar also used touch to invoke mood, but in particular ways. He often insisted that she feed him with her

3 Nachama Greenwald, *Tawagoto*, Winter 1997, p. 41.
4 Tom Lennon, *Tawagoto*, Winter 1994, p. 55.

own hands, and on this occasion, the birthday of Lord Krishna, he fell into a Krishna *bhava*, taking on the identity of Gopala, and demanding that Raji feed him ghee (clarified butter) with her own hand. Like a small child, he opened his mouth and waited patiently to be fed.

On other occasions when he was distributing bananas as *prasad* to everyone, instead of handing the banana to Raji, he peeled it and then fed it to her with his own hand. These were significant acts in which the *siddha purusha* demonstrated his innate capacity to transubstantiate substances and work a divine alchemy. For Yogi Ramsuratkumar there was no need for the strict rituals and sciences of *rasa vidya*, or traditional alchemy—everything was accomplished by Father's grace.

One morning in the breakfast hut Lee Lozowick and Alain de Rosanbo were with Yogi Ramsuratkumar. It was a ritual every morning for Raji to bring an offering of red and white flowers to Bhagawan. Alain de Rosanbo described this in his memoirs:

> She would take a bouquet made of white jasmine flowers and present them to Yogi Ramsuratkumar. He would then take them in his hands and inhale the perfume of these pure jasmine flowers. One could see the delight in his eyes and face as he inhaled their exquisite and exotic perfume . . . Delighted, she would then stick some in her coiled hair. She would then take a bowl of fresh hibiscus flowers and distribute them among the devotees sitting around him. This was repeated every day. After the second or third day I was thinking in my mind that I was not being offered any hibiscus flowers because I was not as important as the others who were seated there. At this precise moment I suddenly became aware of the servant who served breakfast speaking with me. He requested me to go to Yogi Ramsuratkumar. I knelt in front of him and *pranamed*. At the same time feeling the elevating and blissful impact of his nearness, I looked at him, wanting to know the purpose of his asking me to come.
>
> Looking at me very intently, he took the red hibiscus flower, which he had received previously, and with all his presence that I could feel, presented to me very slowly his flower. I had the feeling that it was his whole being, the totality of him, that he was giving to me in overpowering *sattvic* emotions of love and compassion. I was struck with awe. My gazc was transfixed on his face and eyes. Not a word was exchanged. Time stood still! Nothing needed to be said—everything was there. The memory of this scene is buried in my consciousness like footprints on the sands of time . . . . He knew, and I knew that he knew.

The simple rituals that Yogi Ramsuratkumar empowered became his expressions of delight, like the giving of flowers as gifts to those around him. He used the flowers as a means of conveying blessings, of pure transmission, and of healing and purifying. One day during the summer of 1996, Yogi Ramsuratkumar said in the breakfast hut, "White Flower can come here," using an affectionate name for Raji. Yogi Ramsuratkumar was in a *bhava*, and with moist eyes, he slowly, slowly, slowly reached out his hands to receive the flowers.

"Hereafter, my Father wants to see you only in white," he said, looking at Raji with infinite love. The exquisite lilt of his voice was like the touch of a butterfly's wing on the hearts of those who listened and watched. From that day on, Raji wore white saris. That evening Yogi Ramsuratkumar called Mani in to see him.

"Mani, this beggar in madness told Rajalakshmi that Father wants to see her in white, but if she doesn't want to wear white, she can wear colors."

"No Bhagawan, she has already gone to buy white saris. She will abide by your words."

Through her devotion and commitment to Yogi Ramsuratkumar, and perhaps through the act of giving flowers every morning, Raji had earned this practice of wearing white—a symbol of purity that would remain a constant purifying influence and remembrance of Yogi Ramsuratkumar for the rest of her life.

The ritual of receiving the white flowers from Raji became very important for Yogi Ramsuratkumar over the years. Raji brought the white flowers every morning from February 1994 until his death, with the exception of a short time in June and July 2000, just before he was taken to the hospital. Because he was extremely ill, Raji did not want to disturb Bhagawan, so she decided not to bring the flowers. Mani disagreed, saying, "No, you should always take the flowers until Bhagawan tells you not to."

His advice was soon shown to be true. One morning Yogi Ramsuratkumar turned to Ma Devaki and said, "This beggar should not forget to take the white flowers from Rajalakshmi. If this beggar forgets even one day, it is your duty to remind me. There is a great significance that this beggar should take flowers from her." During this time Yogi Ramsuratkumar waited from early in the morning for Raji to come with the flowers. When she didn't come before seven o'clock, Ma Devaki would say, "Why are you so late? Bhagawan is waiting to take the flowers from you!" Turning to Yogi Ramsuratkumar, who lay as if unaware, she would say, "Bhagawan, Raji has come," and he would hold out his hand and receive the flowers without opening his eyes.

Yogi Ramsuratkumar once told Will Zulkowski that most people don't ever want to come back to this earth, but he said, "This beggar will take thousands and thousands of births," because of his compassion for humanity. It was his duty to come back, again and again. Similarly, he said, "I do not seek for happiness. I only want to do my Father's work. If even one being has benefited from my life, that is enough. It has been worthwhile. And if this body dies, the soul that may remain, may it be born again to do my Father's work."[5] It is a statement that is the essence of the bodhisattva's vow—the ultimate obligation to relieve the suffering of all sentient beings. Lee Lozowick spoke about how Yogi Ramsuratkumar brought joy and delight to this commitment:

---

5 *Facets of the Diamond*, p. 143.

Yogi Ramsuratkumar loved his devotees. He loved laughter. He loved conversation. He loved human company. He was always extremely available and accessible and open and communicative, and at the same time there was something of the magician about him. Something of what the magician does is to make a fancy display over here when the real stuff is going on very quietly and very unobtrusively over there. But we're very fascinated by the miraculous. One of the things that we often give our energy to and place our focus on is the miraculous—such things as miraculous healings and bilocation and levitation and such.

Traveling through the West, I meet many people who have been to Tiruvannamalai and met Yogi Ramsuratkumar in the sixties, the seventies, the eighties—many people who were here once or twice for a few days. Many people remember Yogi Ramsuratkumar clearly and strongly as if they were just here a day ago, and every single one of them has some kind of miracle story, but Yogi Ramsuratkumar was completely present and spontaneous, and when someone discovered him and he took them walking on the mountain or around the temple or whatever, there was always some miracle associated with it.

That's the thing we tend to focus on, and yet the true communication of Yogi Ramsuratkumar may not be in the miraculous. It may be in the everyday understanding that he is One, All, everywhere, everything. But we often have this very specific expectation of what we want to see or how we want Yogi Ramsuratkumar to appear to us—like coming to us in a dream, riding on a rainbow with lightning bolts of blessing shooting out of every pore in his body! Often in our own mind we're so focused on what we're looking for—our projections— that we miss actually how he's showing up in our lives, in a smile, in the song of a bird.

We were sitting with him one day and he was chanting and all of a sudden he stopped and listened and there was a bird singing. He listened for a minute or two minutes and everybody was silent so you could hear the bird very clearly, and tears came to his eyes. He said, "That friend sings so much better than this beggar," and for any of you who have ever heard Yogi Ramsuratkumar sing, he had just the most beautiful, sweetest voice. It would bring tears to your eyes. And yet for him every bird, every devotee, every child, every animal was Father, and had some blessing, some grace, some wonder, some majesty.

In our tendency to focus on the spectacular, which happens around Yogi Ramsuratkumar with tremendous frequency and tremendous intensity, we miss the fact that at the same time our daily lives are not about the miraculous. Our daily lives are about integrity in our profession, truth and honesty in our speech, gentleness and kindness in our actions, and consideration and understanding of our friends, our family, our children, our parents and so on. We often miss his presence in our ordinary daily lives and his offering, his gift, his blessing and the opportunity to find him in everything—in every circumstance, as mundane as it could possibly be—because our attention tends to be focused on the miraculous. And really, it could be said that the most miraculous of his blessings are the simple qualities of kindness and compassion and sensitivity to others.

So one of the greatest prayers that we can pray to Yogi Ramsuratkumar is a prayer for the benefit of others. Often when we think of prayer we think of, "I need this, I need to be healed," or for someone close to us, "My child, my mother, my father, my brother, my sister," when in fact there are other people in the world that are far less fortunate than the people we are praying for. Even when we pray for someone near and dear to us, in a very real sense it's also like a prayer for ourselves. Not that we should not pray for ourselves and for those near and dear to us— of course we should. And at the same time, we should not forget that Yogi Ramsuratkumar's universality was and is such that to pray for the other and for others—even for our enemies—is something that, in my experience, he tried to cultivate in us.

Yogi Ramsuratkumar was and is profoundly compassionate, not just towards those who give him something, who express their devotion, but to all people, even to those people who have cursed him and who maybe even have tried to hurt him, even physically. He did not throw himself heedlessly in the face of danger, but he still had love and compassion for those that may have disagreed with his views or not understood and been able to appreciate who he was and who he is.

So please keep this in mind and not only keep it in mind, but see immediately and directly in your own lives that Yogi Ramsuratkumar is not just the miraculous. He's not somewhere else, not in heaven now exclusively. It's not that, "Oh gosh, when he was on the streets I could go and have an intimate conversation with him, and then when he built this temple I couldn't do that anymore." Yogi Ramsuratkumar is the immediacy, the intimacy and even the familiarity of our everyday lives, of our families, of our friends, of our professions, of our culture and our world. So please see Yogi Ramsuratkumar as he is which is One, All, everything—past, present, future, night, day, unitive, continuous—and praise him as he is, not just in his miraculous form, but in every form.[6]

6 Lee Lozowick, December 3, 2001 at the Yogi Ramsuratkumar Ashram, Tiruvannamalai.

HOW HE WORKED WITH THE PEOPLE

Yogi Ramsuratkumar once said, "This beggar is meant to mingle with the people and talk to them." He had a natural ability to adapt to people from all cultures, and he knew an amazing amount of information about places he had never seen. His natural universality made it possible for him to work with different people in different ways. He had a vast ability to tune into the individual—whether it was a common villager, a local farmer, a sadhu or sannyasin, a rich devotee or a spiritual aspirant, East or West, from any walk of life—and giving that person exactly what he or she needed in the moment to move one step closer to God.

"He was a wonderful psychologist; he was a wonderful philosopher; he was a wonderful jnani; and he was a wonderful, normal, ordinary human being! He was very very human . . . very, very human. So this way it was easy for him to see his Father face to face," Parthasarathy reflected.

In working with his close devotees, Yogi Ramsuratkumar had a way of making the most profound teaching communications through the obscure means of paradox and riddle, hidden within the ordinary exchange. For example, many years ago the master had Parthasarathy staying with him at the house on Sannadhi Street twenty-four hours a day for a month. Early one morning Yogi Ramsuratkumar suddenly started saying, "Oh, this beggar knows that this beggar is sitting on his Father's lap. But this beggar doesn't *see* his Father face to face. Parthasarathy, how to see Father face to face?"

This simple interaction contained many layers of teaching, in the way that Yogi Ramsuratkumar frequently animated such teachings: with total innocence. In this instance his questions were a direct reference to his union with the Divine: in the state of unity, there is no one to reflect upon the Divine—no one to "see Father face to face." But further, the question—"How to see Father face to face?"—hints that there is something beyond union with the Divine that is possible: a state of enlightened duality, in which the one who has been absorbed in union may paradoxically enter into a divine separation, which allows the individual soul to experience adoration of the mystery of God as the personal Beloved. Parthasarathy recalled:

> I'm baffled, just baffled! He goes on telling me the same thing from morning till evening. Whoever comes, he would ask only this question, "This beggar knows the beggar is sitting on his Father's lap, but still, the beggar is not able to see Father face to face. How to see Father face to face?" He would ask all the devotees who came to him, just like a child. Nobody knew the answer.
>
> The next day he was saying the same thing. He was very much upset. I then told Swami, "I have seen my Father face to face; if you are not able to see your Father face to face, then it's your fate Swami, I can't do anything about it!" Because for me, he is Father. He laughed and laughed

> and laughed, and only then did he stop asking. He was just doing it to induce that faith—whether I accepted him as my Father. He wanted me to utter these words. Till that time he didn't allow me to sleep even. From morning till the evening, he was saying the same words.

Yogi Ramsuratkumar had a way of speaking in which he repeated the same sentence again and again, as if he was obsessed by an idea like "this beggar cannot see his Father," until the devotee actually heard what it was that he was saying. This was often done cryptically or through interactions that were symbolic, so in order to hear correctly what the master was saying, one had to listen to the real meaning behind the words. Parthasarathy said of this way of teaching, "Naturally repetition would give you boredom, but whatever Swami says, it is always fresh. Even though he utters the same words for a thousand days—for a thousand days, it remains fresh. Equally fresh . . . wonderful!"

On this occasion Parthasarathy was prompted—through the beggar's inimitable way of guiding the devotee—to articulate his recognition of the Divine in the *ishta devata* of the guru himself. Parthasarathy realized, "Because for me, he is Father." In this way Yogi Ramsuratkumar was also instructing in the cultivation of faith in the guru—a primary element of his teaching over the years.

On the other hand, he ferociously tempered his devotees' attachments to him, as he did with Ma Devaki and Lee Lozowick, who he sent away in 1986, saying essentially, "I'm not a guru. Go find a guru somewhere else." The way Yogi Ramsuratkumar molded and guided his devotees in the fine art of guru yoga can been seen in countless teaching stories such as this one, told by his devotees.

It is well known that in bhakti traditions the devotees are almost always obsessively attached to the form of the guru, which is encouraged as a key element of the path itself. This is also called guru yoga, in which the whole path revolves around a total focus on the guru—through service, obedience, love, devotion and attention. It is a paradoxical situation, one that is fraught with pitfalls.

Lee Lozowick once said to his students, "Guru yoga was Yogi Ramsuratkumar's essential communication of sadhana, so the answer to all our questions is 'guru yoga'." It takes a very wise guide indeed to lead the devotee through the labyrinth of such a path. Guru yoga requires absolute attention on the guru, but at the same time one has to be weaned of the neurotic dimension of this attachment in order for the mystical truth of the guru/devotee relationship to blossom. It is precisely the same lesson that his "father," Swami Ramdas, taught Yogi Ramsuratkumar when he sent him away from Anandashram.

Much of what Yogi Ramsuratkumar did was to infuse faith in the devotee. Many people who knew him truly believed that he somehow knew everything, and this was the source of his uncanny knack with the people who came to him from all over the world. He was easy with all of them; somehow he knew about the politics, culture and geography of their country; he knew about their land, their family structures, their beliefs, their faith.

He would work with anyone, and there was only one required condition: the person had to be genuine. Yogi Ramsuratkumar often sent away those who came to him with spiritual airs, who had delusions about their great spiritual attainment, or who pretended to be other than they were, perhaps because these kinds of people tended to be invulnerable. In this case he often merely said, "This dirty sinner, what can this beggar do? There is nothing this beggar can do, you can go to the temple, you can go to the great saints like J. Krishnamurti, Ramana Maharshi, Sai Baba—you can go to them. This beggar cannot do anything; he is just lazy. He just eats, smokes and sleeps."

Once Yogi Ramsuratkumar knew that a person had true commitment and real faith in him, he was completely dedicated to him or her. It didn't matter if the devotee had big problems or was confused or hardened by life and circumstance. With many who came to him more casually, he simply focused on whatever the individual person had faith in. If the person had faith in Krishna, then he would turn him or her toward worshipping Krishna; if the person had faith in science, he turned him toward science; if the person had faith in the world of business, he would work with them in that domain, as Ashish Bagrodia recalled:

> In 1999, when I was staying in the cottage on the ashram, he called for me. I went to him and I was just quiet, waiting for him to say something. He said, "Does your company export your products?" I said yes. He said, "Do you export to Australia?" I said no. "Do you export to Japan?" I said no. "Do you export to USA?" No. "England?" No. "Germany?" No. "France?" No. "England?" He must have said twenty or thirty countries, one after the other, and I would say no, no, no, no, no, no. Then he said, "Okay, now you may go." That's all—only that much conversation. Nothing.
>
> At that time we had just started exporting only to some God-forsaken country, I don't know where it is, called Yemen. He didn't ask me, "Do you export to Yemen?" I went for the next few days thinking that probably these are the countries we should export to. So I dictated a fax to our people to start looking into these countries to get addresses of potential customers. Now (four years later) our whole business is exporting to almost all of the countries that he mentioned, and it's growing and growing. We are doing very well in Europe and now we are starting a business in America. Probably it was to happen and he knew it was to happen and just asked me. It was a hint . . .

In 1988 Pankkajam asked Yogi Ramsuratkumar if she could go on a pilgrimage, which she was fond of doing, to a remote shrine in Nepal. She asked for his blessings and he said, "My Father blesses Pankkajam." Then he said, for the first time, "If you are in trouble, you call this beggar's name." Taking this to heart, she set out for Nepal.

Once there, she left the small town of Jengsung at seven in the morning on horseback to reach the famed Narayana (Vishnu) shrine near Muktinath. With her was a Shaivite swami, also on horseback. The horse owner had told her that she could make the journey over the mountains to Muktinath and back in one day to return the horses, but it had taken them nine hours just to get to the shrine.

After spending a short time at the shrine, she was ready to head back to Jengsung. It was cold in the mountains, and she was getting concerned as dusk began to fall. Her guide, a boy, had told her to go ahead and he would catch up with her, but he never came back. The horse became obstinate and stopped every hundred yards or so and whinnied nervously. The swami was no help either; he too was nervous and unsure, and began to hit his horse, trying to make it go faster.

When they reached the peak of the mountain, Pankkajam's horse balked and came to a stop. They waited for their young guide, but still he was nowhere to be seen. She began to realize that she was in danger: she was virtually a woman alone in the wilderness of the cold Nepalese mountains and night was setting in. Shivering in the dark, chilly air, she began to get really afraid. She jumped off the horse and yelled, "Yogi Ramsuratkumar" several times. Within five minutes a soldier riding a white horse appeared out of nowhere. He spoke beautiful English, and said kindly, "Madame, do you need any help?" Relieved beyond measure, she explained her situation. The soldier whistled to his comrades and six more soldiers on horses came riding up the trail. They helped her safely back to Jengsung.

She finished the pilgrimage, and when she got back to Tiruvannamalai she went to see Yogi Ramsuratkumar. To her great surprise, the first thing he said to her was, "Pankkajam, you called this beggar at Muktinath?" She relayed the whole experience to him, and he said, "Yes, you called this beggar. My Father is telling me you called this beggar, but this beggar doesn't know anything."

"Your faith will save you. Your faith will protect you," Yogi Ramsuratkumar often said. Once he made a powerful teaching on the nature of faith, beginning with the statement, "Father distributes duties. All of us do only His work. To Sri Ramakrishna Paramahamsa, Bhagawan Ramana Maharshi, Swami Ramdas and Sri Aurobindo, He gave the duty of teaching. To this beggar He has not given that duty. To have faith in the words of these masters alone, that is the duty allotted to this beggar. Thus, I have faith in the scriptures, in the words of these masters. That's enough for this beggar."

Upon hearing these words, an earnest devotee pleaded, "If this is the condition of such an elevated soul like you, Swami, what about us?"

"Where there is faith, there is no fate!" Yogi Ramsuratkumar roared in quick response. "Have faith. Fate will become inoperable."[7] For Yogi Ramsuratkumar, this was the power of faith: to subsume even one's karma, or one's fate, and lift one into the stainless and free state of perfect organic innocence, in which surrender to the will of God is the final grace.

7 Ilaya Raja, "A Forceful Personality," *The Hindu*, Madras, July 8, 1990.

In the early eighties Yogi Ramsuratkumar said many times to Parthasarathy, Murugeshan and Sivashankara, "Whatever happens in the world, happens by the will of my Father. So nothing is wrong in this world. Everything is perfectly ordered, because everything is done by my Father. Everything is done by my Father, then how can it be imperfect? Everything is perfectly alright." It was one of many ways that he demonstrated the importance of having faith.

For a long time Parthasarathy did not understand this teaching because there are so many troubles in the world—war, hunger, suffering. One day Yogi Ramsuratkumar asked Parthasarathy to go to the anatomy hall in the medical college, where his brother was studying to be a doctor.

"Whenever you go to visit your brother, you go to the anatomy hall," he instructed. Parthasarathy did as Yogi Ramsuratkumar asked: he went to visit his brother and insisted that he take him to the anatomy hall. His brother warned him that he might faint at what he saw.

"No, no, don't bother with such things, just show me the anatomy hall," Parthasarathy said. There he discovered that the students were dissecting the cadavers, removing the body parts and searching the abdomen. The abdominal section of the body was open and it seemed rather hideous to him, congested as it was with organs, all packed together tightly. He said, "Oh God! How can it be so congested?" His brother said, "Don't think like that. This is the perfect order. If this portion shifts, or moves another way, then it would give you enormous pain. You would not tolerate the pain. This is the perfect order." Parthasarathy said:

> Then only could I get it. The apparent confusion is not confusion. It is only apparently confused, apparently in war, in chaos, but deep into it there is a perfect order. Then I said to Swami, "Now I am able to understand what you mean by a perfect order." We are just seeing imperfectness because we ourselves are imperfect, so our vision will be only imperfect.
>
> His ways were always unique. He would not teach directly to you. He would create a situation, and out of that situation, he would force you to learn. Like ordinary saints and sannyasins, he would not have you sit before him and make you meditate and force you to remember some names—that was not his way. He always gave you full freedom, and he would create situations around you; out of that situation, that situation will force you to learn certain things. That's his way.

Parthasarathy used to make trips to Punjab, and at that time there was terrorist activity going on there. Yogi Ramsuratkumar said to him, "If you go to Punjab, and if you feel some crisis there—some man just standing before you with a gun—and if you remember this beggar, do you think this beggar will carry his body along from here to Punjab to protect you? No, my Father will send somebody to protect you. So have faith." Once a person had turned his or her heart toward him completely, then he was completely theirs.

Parthasarathy once asked the beggar what he should do about his spiritual growth.

"Swamiji, what should I do? Should I go into solitude, in some forest?"

"You remember this beggar," he replied. "You know that this beggar has accepted you. There ends all your sadhana. Leave it. Just remember that this beggar does enough for you. You need not worry about your spiritual growth; my Father will take care of you, my Father will be always with you."

Yogi Ramsuratkumar insisted on faith in the guru's grace. For those aspirants who had truly turned toward Yogi Ramsuratkumar as their guru, he insisted on faith in the guru and the name of Yogi Ramsuratkumar. Parthasarathy commented:

> He insisted on faith, faith in the name. This is for the spiritual aspirants, but for the ordinary common folk who come with some problems—"My daughter needs to get married and I have no money"—he would listen patiently. He was a very good listener, you know—a wonderful listener. He would listen so patiently, with such an attention. Oh God, it was tremendous! He would listen patiently for one hour, two hours, even, and after the person had given all their problems to Swami, he would become very easy. Then after that he would suggest, here and there, simple words. He would ask, "Who is your *istha*,[8] your favorite god?" They would say, "Krishna is my favorite god." He would say, "Remember Krishna . . . remember Krishna. Whenever you feel uneasy, in your heart, you remember Krishna—Krishna will protect you."
>
> He would not disturb anyone's faith. If anyone has faith in Krishna, if anyone has faith in Sai Baba, or J. Krishnamurti or Rajneesh or any saints or gods, he would not disturb it. He would intensify their faith upon their gods. After listening to all their problems, he would just intensify their faith and encourage those people to turn to their faith, to remember Krishna or whatever gods they liked. "Then all your problems will be solved, this beggar assures you. My Father's grace."

Yogi Ramsuratkumar had amazing and delightful ways of building faith in his devotees. Parthasarathy was leaving to go on a trip to the Himalayas and Yogi Ramsuratkumar told him a story: Two birds were eating fruit. One bird felt happy when eating sweet fruit, but when he ate bitter fruit he got annoyed. Suddenly he noticed that the other bird was eating both sweet and bitter fruit, but it was standing straight and poised, not reacting to the polarities of sweet and sour. Then the first bird realized, "I am also that bird. Why should I suffer and enjoy like this? Pleasure and pain are one and the same."

The point of the story was the relationship between *paramatman* (the Supreme self) and *jivatman* (the individual soul or personal self). *Paramatman* can eat the fruit, whether

---

8 *Istha devata,* chosen deity.

bitter or sweet, and remain serene in the transcendent point of view, whereas *jivatman* is associated with the body and its many identifications with pleasure and pain. When *jivatman* realizes that it is, in fact, *paramatman*, then *jivatman* is no longer at the effect of the endless cycles of attachment and suffering.

Parthasarathy began his three-day journey deeply contemplating this story. It was on his mind still on Sunday, when there was a holiday and he went to Rishikesh to meet an old friend. His friend told him about a sadhu who was living there and would be a good person to visit. Parthasarathy decided to take the opportunity to meet this person.

When he entered the sadhu's room, the sadhu immediately said, "See those two birds?" He pointed toward the window. Parthasarathy could barely contain his shock when he saw that there were indeed two birds standing on the window. The sadhu clapped his hands and the two birds flew away, then he began to laugh and laugh, as if he knew intimately the inside story of the joke. It was a purely delightful way in which Yogi Ramsuratkumar had permeated the whole trip with this story.

This quality of omnipresence and omniscience showed up around Yogi Ramsuratkumar in very ordinary ways as he interacted with people. He was not a magus to grandstand and make ostentatious shows of marvelous *siddhis*; instead, the miraculous appeared naturally, in everyday life. When Devaki still lived in Salem she was going to visit Bhagawan one day, and her mother was very sick. Just before she left, her mother said, "I know you don't ask him for anything, but please, tell Swami this time that I'm not well. For my sake, because I'm not able to bear it, please tell him that I am not well. And if he gives something for me, bring it." Devaki said yes to appease her mother, thinking that she wouldn't say anything to Bhagawan.

When she arrived at Sannadhi Street she was permitted inside and sat down with the other devotees. Many people were coming and going in the midst of light conversation with Yogi Ramsuratkumar, and she forgot all about the world outside Sannadhi Street, including her mother's request. Yogi Ramsuratkumar looked at her as she was leaving and asked, "How is your mother? Is she well?" Devaki explained that in fact her mother was not well at all, and Yogi Ramsuratkumar gave her *prasad* to take to her mother as his blessing.

The day that Prakash Yogini met the beggar saint on in 1983 was what she called "the sweetest day of my life." A deep affinity and rapport had developed between herself and Yogi Ramsuratkumar, and he gave her the task of administering Sri Ramji Ashram in Kanya Kumari. One day he said to her, "If anybody limits this beggar to this body, then there is no use chanting this mantra, 'Yogi Ramsuratkumar.' Yogi Ramsuratkumar is everywhere, in everything." He pointed to the walls, the table, chairs, benches. "Everything is Yogi Ramsuratkumar. Here, there, everything is only Yogi Ramsuratkumar," he said.

Early one morning when Prakash Yogini was at the breakfast hut with Yogi Ramsuratkumar and the some devotees, idlis and milk were fed to the cats. Bhagawan was enjoying the cats, when he suddenly turned serious and blessed them with raised arms. He turned to the devotees and said, "My Father alone exists; Nothing else, nobody else; here, there, everything, past, present, future. My Father alone exists. See my Father in the form of cats eating idli? That idli is also my Father. My Father alone exists everywhere."

This immediately had an impact on Prakash Yogini. At the moment she was feeling extremely ill and nauseated. She was afraid the opportunity of being with Bhagawan would be ruined by her ill health, and that if she had to get up and leave it would disturb the delicacy of his space.

Suddenly Yogi Ramsuratkumar said, "Prakash Yogini, come here." He pointed to the plate on which the cats had eaten their breakfast and said, "Remove that plate." She thought, "Here is the opportunity," and promptly removed the plate, still afraid that she might throw up at any time. Usually there was an attendant who removed the cats' plate after they finished their breakfast, but that day Bhagawan had sent him away to chase some dogs who were troubling the cats.

"Wash your hands," he instructed, which she did, thinking that she should ask permission to leave as she felt awful waves of nausea coming over her.

"Come and sit," he said. As she took a seat near him, she realized with some shock that the nausea had disappeared completely, and never returned.

Yogi Ramsuratkumar worked with devotees through close and intimate relationships, through conversations, laughter, the joy of simple living, through affection and sharing of common experience—this was his garden of delight. He went right to the heart of their lives. The transmission of grace went on all the time, at subtle levels. Although it was not uncommon for people to experience the opening of kundalini energy, simply by being in his presence, he denied having any such powers. Somebody came once and talked about having various *siddhis*. He said, "Oh, this beggar salutes you! He can't do any of those things, but he salutes you." Despite his disclaimers, he was at the very least a true *mahasiddha* who had no need for any dramatic demonstration of spiritual power. Nor did he need formal rituals or yogic techniques; he had gone far beyond these stages.

An example of this occurred in the spring of 1971, while *Yogi Ramsuratkumar, the Godchild, Tiruvannamalai* was being written. The beggar saint took Caylor Wadlington and his friend Mark to the village of Tirukoilur, where the ashram of Gnanananda Giri is located. There they sat in a tiny teashop on a narrow, two-lane road—a back road highway in India—where the village people would wait to catch the bus, just down the road from Tapovanum.

They moved down the road a bit to what had been a foundation of a building, where debris was strewn around, and there they sat down to talk about the book, about Caylor's plans and the Theosophical Society. It had been some months since they had been together, and as the afternoon passed, Yogi Ramsuratkumar began to talk about more and more significant things—his own past, his relationships with his three spiritual fathers and his life's work—while Caylor sat with notepad and quickly scribbled down his words.

It went on this way for some time, when Caylor suddenly heard a sound in his ears and something shifted, so that it seemed as if he was underwater. There was a ringing in his ears; he was hearing an inner sound, while all outside sound was muffled, as if he was in a big tube. There was a vibrant buzzing all around him, and he felt that he was going to lose his balance. He looked up at Yogi Ramsuratkumar and realized that the master had somehow shifted his state of consciousness. Yogi Ramsuratkumar leaned back and looked at him in a very focused way, then raised his voice slightly, although he continued to speak casually.

Caylor realized that he was having an experience of *shabda*, the use of sound vibration to focus the attention in a very powerful way, and it was the beggar's voice that was the source of it. He felt that he had been given a direct hit in the solar plexus, and that everything was spinning, spinning, spinning—much like the spinning movement of a chakra. He had the faint impression that whatever it was was spinning out of control, a feeling that made him burst out laughing. He became giddy with laughter and could not contain himself, while Mark sat next to him, watching it all. Caylor struggled to get balanced again. All the while Yogi Ramsuratkumar was just leaning back, talking in the most relaxed way.

Suddenly Yogi Ramsuratkumar said casually, "Mr. K, let's go get tea." He stood up immediately and the two young men followed him back over to the tea stand. Three hours had passed since they sat down on the foundation and Yogi Ramsuratkumar had started talking. Caylor had been taking notes all along, but he couldn't remember a word that the beggar had said. Never once did the beggar say to Caylor, "What is this, what's going on here? What did you do?" Instead it was just, "Okay, let's go."

They went to Tapovanum, where Yogi Ramsuratkumar introduced Caylor to Gnanananda Giri Swami, who Caylor described as "an amazing powerful saint—a really beautiful man." After sitting with Gnanananda Giri for a while, Yogi Ramsuratkumar took Caylor back out to the road and sent him back to Tiruvannamalai on the bus.

The family who owned Chandra Transport used to give Yogi Ramsuratkumar the gift of a new Ambassador, his favorite kind of car, every year after the ashram was built. The mother of this family, S. Ponvandu, first met the beggar saint in 1984. Her whole family came to rely on the blessings of the beggar in all aspects of their lives.

Once Ponvandu, her sister, daughter and the other women of the family went to see Yogi Ramsuratkumar at the temple before her sister's wedding to receive Bhagawan's blessing. As was the custom, they approached Bhagawan with their family jewels. He took the jewels and handed them to Ma Devaki, asking her to put them on him. He wore the necklace for a while, like a crown draped across his forehead, before returning them to the family.

When Ponvandu handed him a slip of paper with the name and address of her daughter's husband, Yogi Ramsuratkumar took it angrily and threw it down. He seemed extremely irritated. In a few minutes he picked it up again and handed it to them gently, saying, "My Father blesses you." As it turned out there were problems in the marriage and with the in-laws, and the husband was an angry man, but Ponvandu felt that the problems had been mitigated to a great degree simply by Bhagawan's interaction with the husband's name.

One day Deivakani Vijayrajan came to Ponvandu's house and saw a picture of Yogi Ramsuratkumar, who she had never seen before. She began to weep and cried out, "This is the man who came into my dreams!" Deivakani proceeded to tell Ponvandu that she had been extremely depressed for a long time. She had lost all hope and wanted to die when she began to dream about a kind and beautiful elder man, a mahatma who was guiding and blessing her. She had never heard of Yogi Ramsuratkumar or seen pictures of him until that day. Soon afterward she met the saint in person in the temple, when he called her and her family up and blessed them personally. Upon hearing her story, he told her to do Ramnam. Within two years her life was completely changed—the depression had long disappeared, and she gave birth to a baby boy.

Yogi Ramsuratkumar worked with the common people of the village also, addressing their concerns, usually having to do with family issues, fertility, the births of babies (especially male children), crops and rain. Once Ravi was driving Yogi Ramsuratkumar to Swamimalai for the marriage ceremony of the son of an ardent devotee, Mr. Sundaraman, an engineer who worked in the public works department of the city. On the way to the marriage ceremony with Sundaraman, Yogi Ramsuratkumar stopped the car at a tea shop in a very small village called Vaddalore. While they were there having coffee, a crowd of the village people came with an offering of *prasad*, seeking the blessing of the saint. As they gave him the *prasad*, they asked to buy his coffee and said that they had had no rain for five or six years, saying, "We need rain, Swamiji, can you help us?" Swamiji gave a little smile and accepted the coffee from them. The very next day the rain came.

In 1996, after the construction of the ashram was well underway, Bhagawan suddenly wanted to go around Arunachala one day. He called for Ravi, who took him by car slowly around the mountain with many devotees following the car on foot. When they reached the Ganapati (Ganesh) temple, Yogi Ramsuratkumar asked Ravi to stop the car. A woman who lived in that area came forward and begged the saint to bring rain.

"We badly need rain for the crops, Swamiji," she pleaded.

"Whatever amount you want, the rain will come," Yogi Ramsuratkumar said, raising his hands in blessing.. The next day the rain started, and it rained for two or three days.

Once in the seventies a village woman came to Swamiji with a sick cow. He listened to her very seriously for thirty minutes, then he said, "Ma, you will go to the temple and take the *abhisheka* water and force the cow to drink it. Do it immediately." Right away she went to the Shiva temple, got the water and fed it to the cow. The next day she came back and said, "Swami, my cow is *all right*! Thank you Swami!"

For the beggar saint, the ordinary problems of the village folk were equal to the problems of global humanity, of nations that rule, and in this way he had inherited from his father Swami Ramdas what the latter called, "equal vision." He saw everyone as being the same. There was absolutely no discrimination in terms of caste, race or sex on his part.

When Yogi Ramsuratkumar was living on the streets of Tiruvannamalai a woman approached him and asked, "Swami, what is the best way to attain God realization?" Just as the woman asked such a heady question, the beggar looked out on the street and saw a nearby vendor of *pakoras*, a snack of vegetables and batter fried in oil, standing with his cart. Swamiji shouted to him and invited him to come sit beside him. The hard working man came and gratefully sat beside the beggar saint, who took his hands sweetly in his own and inquired, "How is your business?"

"Swami, it is not well," he answered

"Oohhh. How are you preparing these pakoras?" the yogi asked.

"Oh, I would blend with some chilis and other things, and fry it in the pan, and that's it, Swami."

The beggar proceeded to spend forty-five minutes giving detailed instructions to the vendor on how he could perhaps improve upon his product, and therefore his business. He gave him some rupees and took a few *pakoras*, which he distributed to the devotees who were sitting around him, then turned to the woman who had asked the question about God-realization. Handing her a *pakora*, he said, "Amma! Now this beggar leaves you. You can have some *pakora*, and you can go!" And that was the end of the interview as well as the teaching lesson of the moment.

This is often how he responded to those who weren't serious—who had spiritual pretensions, but no real intention to engage spiritual life—or who were simply naïve about their own capacity to engage the path, as Parthasarathy observed:

> With the people who have no real interest in Godhood, this would be his way with them. If you are serious, only then will he come out. If I am not serious enough to have the way to attain the Godhood, then he would just tell these *pakora* stories, and he will drive you away, that's all. He needed serious people, to reveal about his Father. The people who have no interest and no seriousness but just pretend that they want to become a saint or a sadhu or sannyasi, Swami would not reveal anything about his Father. He would not say anything philosophical or psychological—not anything. He would just tell some *pakora* stories and he would send them on their way!

If the woman chose to inquire deeply into this interaction, she could find enough teaching on the nature of humility to give her years of work that would set her on the path toward God-realization. But there is more than a teaching on humility contained in Yogi Ramsuratkumar's interaction with her. In another way, he was actually honoring her request by giving her an opportunity to work harder within herself than she would have if he had simply given a heady discourse on the *Upanishads* or the *Bhagavad Gita*. These are only two possible insights that can be found in this interaction; every *lila* has many levels of meaning.

The beggar was also visited by city and government officials, as well as the police, who would come to him inquiring about spiritual matters. Once there were some police officers who came to have his darshan at the house on Sannadhi Street. One of the men brought a basket of fruit.

"What is it?" the yogi asked,

"I have a basket of fruit for you, Swami," the police officer replied. Yogi Ramsuratkumar asked him to sit down in front of him, and he listened for a long time to the man's story.

"Swami, I get up in the morning and do some meditation, I chant the name of God," he said, talking on and on about his spiritual quest. Yogi Ramsuratkumar listened silently and patiently.

"Now this beggar feels he should leave you," Yogi Ramsuratkumar said suddenly. "This beggar will touch these fruits and you can take them as *prasadam* with you." He took the police officer's hand, walked along to the car with him, said good-bye and then walked back to his seat.

There was a long line of people waiting to see him, and someone said, "Swami, there are a lot of people waiting for you and you spent so much time and gave all this respect to this fellow. Why?"

Yogi Ramsuratkumar replied: "Some people come to this beggar for bhakti; some people come to this beggar for some problems to be solved; and some people expect this beggar to give them some respect! What's wrong in giving them their due respect? There is nothing this beggar is going to lose. They wanted to get some respect from this beggar and this beggar gave them respect. Where is the problem? And if someone comes wanting some bhakti, this beggar is ready to give that bhakti to that fellow. He came here wanting to get some respect from this beggar and this beggar gave it to him!"

This was the incredible kindness and generosity of Yogi Ramsuratkumar—he was willing to meet people wherever they were and work with them there.

Most of Yogi Ramsuratkumar's teaching was done through the example of his life. He was the epitome of gracefulness, elegance, generosity, courtesy and kindness. His natural disposition was sweet and loving. He never complained or abused others verbally.

Once a person he had known for a long time was rude and abusive to Yogi Ramsuratkumar, who spontaneously responded by falling at the man's feet. Already angry, the man furthered his position by saying, "Don't try these things with me!" Later Yogi Ramsuratkumar said, "What to do? Some contact has to be established, so that the person can be helped. It is easy for this beggar to fall at his feet, but it is difficult for that person."

Once some devotees were commenting on how exquisite Bhagawan's manners were, even with those who were rude or abusive to him. They asked, "Bhagawan, why don't you teach us also to be like that?" Immediately he responded, "What else do you think this beggar is doing?"[9]

Perhaps what Yogi Ramsuratkumar demonstrated the most was his unshakable faith

9 Vijayalakshmi, *Waves of Love*, pp. 87-88.

in the will of God—his surrender to "Father in Heaven." He often said that faith is the key to allowing the divine influence of the guru into one's life in such a way that it is permanently transformed and buoyed by the pervasive presence of the master himself.

The living force of Yogi Ramsuratkumar's faith touched the lives of his devotees in immediate and personal ways; he generously and lovingly entered directly into the lives of his devotees to plant the seeds of faith that would take root and grow to fruition. Parthasarathy reflected:

> Our master is such a wonderful master! Such a great master, who came down to my level to uplift me. Such a wonderful master! A wonderful master! No rituals, no barriers—nothing is there. You can just go there, sit before him and just listen, just be in his presence, be in his silence, that's all. You need not worry about spiritual growth. He said once, when the tiger captures its food, it will go and sit and eat automatically. When the king cobra catches hold of the frog, the frog will go automatically. When you accept a guru, then the guru takes on all the efforts. You need not worry about that. He will swallow you. He will make you as himself—but you must have faith. That is the condition.
>
> You must have faith: "In all the circumstances, my guru is there—in pain or pleasure, in any circumstances." He will not forget you. You just remember him, that's all. That's everything. All and everything are being looked after by Swami. And if you will be totally alone, oh God, it's wonderful, it's wonderful: when you start sleeping, naturally the thoughts of him will come to you. Naturally his name will come to you. What a peaceful life it is!

When Pankkajam was diagnosed with diabetes, the doctor told her, "No more sugar!" Her blood sugar was very high, and the doctor said that she needed to start taking insulin. She said to the doctor, "I want to go see my doctor first."

"Who is your doctor?" the doctor asked.

"He lives in Tiruvannamalai," she said, thinking of Yogi Ramsuratkumar.

She came to see the beggar saint, and he had a box of milk sweets. Knowing the diagnosis she had just been given, she took a very small piece.

"No," Bhagawan said, insisting, "you like sweets—take a big piece!"

"Bhagawan, the doctor says I have diabetes, my blood sugar is very high and I will have to take insulin!" she told him.

He listened and looked at her, then gave her two pieces of milk sweets and said, "Eat."

For the next two or three days, Yogi Ramsuratkumar often called on her to sing when she came to darshan. When it was time to return to her home, Bhagawan called her up to the dais and said, "You say you are having high sugar in your blood? Have these sweets!" He handed her two sweets, then said, "You are perfectly alright." From that day on, she had no more problem with blood sugar.

His Cryptic Ways

Although steeped in the traditions of India, and having great respect for the *Vedas* and the religious scriptures of his culture, Yogi Ramsuratkumar never lived by the rules and regulations of society. He was a *jivanmukta*, a liberated being who had gone beyond such social injunctions. He was also often referred to as an *avadhuta*, a spiritual adept who has "shaken off" all worldly concerns. The extent of his annihilation in God is revealed in the following words of Yogi Ramsuratkumar, spoken on May 17, 1993:

> There is no individual here. There is no vyakti to own conscience or any concept of right or wrong. This beggar does not exist at all. Only Father alone exists. In 1952 everything in this beggar was washed away, leaving nothing as residue. It is Father and Father alone and nobody else and nothing else. Father in everything and everything in Father. Father alone exists.

Such a state of consciousness, wherein there is no *vyakti* (individuality, appearance or distinctness), is impossible to conceive with the mind alone. Its manifestations, actions, movements and gestures are pure and unmotivated, compelled as they are from "Father alone." As a result, it often appeared that Yogi Ramsuratkumar, like the Bauls of Bengal, took the *ulta* or contrary path.

The Bauls place a great emphasis upon *sahaja-samadhi*, or spontaneous, open-eyed ecstasy, a state in which consciousness is simultaneously merged with the Absolute, while one remains functional in the ordinary life of here and now. One who has realized *sahaja-samadhi* lives in both worlds simultaneously—in both the *nirguna* aspect and the *saguna* aspect of the Divine, the dimension of the Absolute or unqualified transcendent reality, and the dimension of relativity, of earthly existence and full incarnation into the human form. This is the state of the *avadhuta*—one who has gone beyond.

Yogi Ramsuratkumar made a statement that revealed his own nature when he said, "Avadhutas are great people. They are not bound by anything. So they cannot be models to the society." [10]

As one who existed in both the absolute and relative worlds, who had gone beyond the beyond, Yogi Ramsuratkumar had a tremendous range of skillful ways through which the transmission of the teaching was demonstrated moment to moment. His teaching transcended any form of dogma or credo, and was never bound by societal norms. As a function of habit, everyone brought their expectations to him—a saint should act, speak or look this way or that way. He was constantly shattering the projections, opinions and

10 Ma Devaki, "The Divine Beggar on Himself," *Saranagatham*, January 2003, p. 33.

prejudices that are commonly held in society.

This radical disposition of enlightenment gave Yogi Ramsuratkumar tremendous freedom to spontaneously orchestrate situations in which people could learn, without effort or premeditation on his part. Life itself was teacher enough, and when combined with the powerful blessing influence that permeated everything and everyone around the beggar saint, ordinary circumstances could become at times an almost unbearable crucible in which one was purified and slowly transformed.

One example of many occurred in early 1994 at Sudama House: Since Raji had sent the message in support of Yogi Ramsuratkumar's decision to make Ma Devaki his attendant, he had showered a great deal of attention on her. On one of these occasions Yogi Ramsuratkumar called Raji up to sit beside him on his bed at Sudama House. He took her hand in his lap and began to caress her arm like a mother with a daughter. Many other devotees were sitting there at the time: Mani, Rajmohan, Suresh, Nivedita, Devaki and the Sudama sisters.

"Mani . . . you have any objections?" Yogi Ramsuratkumar asked. "You have any objections if this beggar asks Raji to sit beside him? You have any objections?"

"No Bhagawan. She is your daughter, so I have no objections," Mani answered.

"Devaki," Bhagawan pressed, "you have no objections?"

Devaki said nothing.

"Mani, you have any objections?" he prodded further.

"No, Bhagawan. Raji is your daughter," Mani answered again.

The beggar began to go back and forth between Mani and Devaki, asking the same question, "Do you have no objections?" as he affectionately caressed Raji's arm. Mani continued to answer no, while Devaki remained silent.

Suddenly Rajmohan interjected, "I object, Bhagawan!"

Devaki agreed, "I also object. You are showing affection to her only. Always you are giving her flowers and much attention. You should be giving blessings to everybody. You should treat all of your children the same. To that, I object."

Yogi Ramsuratkumar was laughing and laughing. He said, "Rajalakshmi, you go and talk to Devaki. She is angry with this beggar because this beggar asked you to sit here. You go and talk to her. Otherwise, after you leave this place Devaki will scold this beggar. I am very scared! You go and protect me!"

"Bhagawan," Devaki protested, "why are you talking like this? You are going to play a *lila* with Rajalakshmi—you are going to give a very big work to her. That's why you are playing with her like this."

Through all this Raji was quiet. Being very new to spiritual life, she had no idea what was going on, and it was an uncomfortable spot to find oneself in. "I didn't know what to do, so I kept quiet," she said later.

Again Yogi Ramsuratkumar said, "Go and talk to Devaki. Go and talk to Devaki." Finally Devaki came and took Raji into another room, saying, "You have to obey Bhagawan, so we must talk about something."

"I don't know what to talk about," Raji explained.

"He is playing some *lila*," Devaki mused. "I can't understand why he is doing this—he is playing some *lila* that I don't understand."

They came out of the room shortly and Bhagawan asked Raji, "Did you talk to Devaki, Rajalakshmi? Did you tell her not to scold this beggar? Otherwise, after you leave this place, she will scold me. I am very scared!" He was laughing and smiling as he repeated these words. Again Raji remained silent.

Again he instructed her to sit beside him on the bed. Right away he started giving flowers to everyone. When Nivedita refused to take the flower and started crying, saying, "I don't want to take the flower—you give attention only to her!" Devaki intervened, saying to Raji, "I do not object, because you are Bhagawan's daughter."

Yogi Ramsuratkumar got up, walked over to Nivedita and sat down in front of her in silence. After some time he came back to the bed and sat beside Raji. That evening everyone ate dinner together, and afterward Yogi Ramsuratkumar said, "This beggar leaves you all!"

When Mani and Raji first moved to Tiruvannamalai they lived in a hotel. While Mani worked all day on the ashram, Yogi Ramsuratkumar had Raji come to Sudama House to spend time with him. He often had her sleep beside him, and once gave his pillow to her. There were many days when she was with him from eight o'clock in the morning until six o'clock at night. If someone gave Yogi Ramsuratkumar a special flower during the day he would hold it all day long, and when Mani came at six o'clock he would hand the flower to Raji and say, "Now you can go with Mani."

Mani laughed about this, saying, "While I was toiling on the ashram, this lady was having the pleasure of being with Yogi Ramsuratkumar!"

A similar opportunity to confront and resolve attachments and projections on the guru was given to the men who visited Yogi Ramsuratkumar with Lee Lozowick in 1988, when the beggar was playfully interacting with one member of the group, Vijaya Fedorschak, for days. Vijay had a lot of shakti or kundalini energy released in his body while he was in the company of the beggar, and his arm would often spontaneously and automatically shoot up into the air. Yogi Ramsuratkumar interacted with him a great deal during this time, and at one point said playfully, "Lee and I have our feet on the ground . . . Vijay wants to go into outer space!" Then he laughed and laughed.

All this attention was a double-edged sword for Vijay, who said, "It was uncomfortable. On the one hand I wanted his attention, but on the other hand, too much attention is embarrassing. So I tried to put a lid on it, but he kept playing with the energy, like he wanted it to come out. He would stop and do something else and all of a sudden he would just turn and look at me, and it would start all over again. After awhile I was feeling like, 'Release me from this, release me from the bonds of human existence.' "

Yogi Ramsuratkumar's play with Vijay also caused ripples of reaction among the other men. Purna Steinitz humorously relayed the way Yogi Ramsuratkumar worked with him around his own reaction of jealousy and attachment on this trip:

Yogi Ramsuratkumar had a lot of attention on Vijay on that trip. He was having a lot of shakti and Yogi Ramsuratkumar was completely enjoying it. He kept saying his name, "Vijay." His play and enjoyment with Vijay was a big element of the trip—it was very much a part of the space. During all this I was freaked out because Vijay was getting all the attention! Yogi Ramsuratkumar would not look at me, he didn't ask me my name, he didn't talk to me; he didn't say anything to me. All day long, all day long, I was freaked out.

Finally I couldn't handle it anymore, so I *pranamed*—Lee and Yogi Ramsuratkumar were sitting on the ledge together, holding hands. Yogi Ramsuratkumar was doing his work. I just got on my knees and *pranamed* with my head on the dirt ground for probably twenty minutes to a half-hour. I was on my knees, and I just kept praying to him, "Save me from this. I can't handle this. Save me." There was a lot going on [inside] when I was *pranaming*. When I got up I looked on the ground and there was a stick. I spontaneously picked it up and gave it to Yogi Ramsuratkumar—and he took it. It was just this spontaneous gesture, and that was all there was to it—he still wouldn't talk to me; he wouldn't look at me, he wouldn't say anything to me.

A couple of days went by, and then on our last afternoon he asked us to go out to dinner with him. We went to the Brindavan restaurant, and there was an amazing amount of traffic. He had Lee's hand and he just took off across the street really fast, and his *dhoti* came up and the muscles in his legs were like a football player! We went in the restaurant and I sat down at a table with Yogi Ramsuratkumar and Lee and a few other men. At the end of the meal I said, "I'll pay for the dinner," and that's when Yogi Ramsuratkumar said, "Mr. Lee pays for all."

When it was time to go we went outside, and when we were getting ready to leave, he opened up his rags and pulled out the stick and handed it to me. This was the first attention I'd gotten from him in days! He gave me the stick. Afterward we went to an auto parts store and got a rubber hose. I gently put the stick in there and got it back to the States and through customs that way. It's just a stick, you know? But when I got home, I noticed that at the end of the stick were four little branches coming out of it, in the perfect shape of his fan.

When Devaki first became a devotee of Yogi Ramsuratkumar she was terrified of him; she was afraid to move even her little finger in his presence. But in order to serve him, that had to change. Through the amazing fluidity of his expression and his skillful work with her, she became the embodiment of her namesake—the mother of Lord Krishna. Devaki remembered how the wisdom of the *jivanmukta*, Yogi Ramsuratkumar, manifested at times:

> After he came to Sudama, somehow he was like a baby and I felt like a mother to him, and that made things much easier for me. Very soon I took great liberties with him also. He was mostly a baby—a helpless baby at that. In one moment he would be that completely regal, majestic divinity, and the next moment he would be like a helpless child. That is something that I could never reconcile myself to. One moment he would be all majesty, all full of power and wisdom, and the next moment, he would be like a baby. He would call for something very ordinary; he would need somebody's help.
>
> It was constantly going on at Sudama that whatever he said was full of wisdom; it was packed with wisdom. We might not have understood it at the time, we might have taken it very lightly, but then later on these things come back to us. We would start shaking all over, sometimes to understand what he meant after six months, after a year—but perhaps we never understood some of the things he said.

At Sudama House Yogi Ramsuratkumar usually woke up at two-thirty or three in the morning, and at that time the Sudama mothers would send out for milk. Immediately Devaki would start reading. Sometimes he just sat and listened; sometimes he sat and smoked. He would often call for a glass of gooseberry water, and after that some coffee. Then there was more reading, until five o'clock when a porridge was served.

After that he asked Devaki to go into the garden and pluck four flowers. As soon as she stepped down from the verandah he would begin to call out: "Devaki, be careful! There will be snakes there," or "Don't hurt the tree and don't hurt yourself!" Even when the flowers were picked from the hibiscus he was concerned about how it was done. If Devaki started out walking too fast, he would correct her, saying, "No, no! Don't walk so fast. Walk slowly. Walk slowly." Many times he did not want Devaki out of his sight. If something had to be done on the other side of the house, he would call Vijayalakshmi to do it. Devaki recalled his enigmatic instructions:

> He was worried about me. He was concerned. I don't know why he was worried. Sometimes I used to feel so silly. "Can't I do this? Can't I do that? Can't I switch on a motor? Why does he insist on this?" But then later I understood that he was merely concerned.
>
> Once I wanted to go up on the terrace. He said, "This beggar is afraid for you. This beggar wouldn't like you to go alone to the terrace. It's better not to go there at all." I said, "Can you send one of these people to put on the globes there?" He said, "Yes they can go." Later on if I asked him why, he would say, "I don't know. This beggar doesn't know. Father says so." Flower plucking I could do. I should go and pluck four flowers, any flowers. Whether it was fragrant or not it didn't matter. And then he would give one to each of us. We would prostrate in front of him and take the

flower and go. And after that there would be Gita session.

His ways were cryptic in the very least, so that one had to work internally in order to truly comprehend and make the teaching real for one's self. And yet, at times the teaching he gave was crystal clear, if one was willing to drop the veils of ego and see without bias, projection, expectation or opinion.

In the mid-nineties a group of journalists came to the ashram to ask Yogi Ramsuratkumar some questions. After they arrived and circumambulated the statue, he said, "You people go to sit in the darshan and when I call you, you will come to see this beggar." All the journalists went to the dining hall to sing *bhajans*. In a while he told Selvaraj, "You can call them."

The journalists went to the temple and stood around Yogi Ramsuratkumar. There were eighty or ninety people around, almost crushing him as he sat in the small chair beside the statue. Ma Devaki, Vijayalakshmi, Rajalakshmi and Vijayakka were all there. One of the journalists was standing near an ashram worker. Breaching the taboos of class and status, rather than speaking directly to the professionals, Yogi Ramsuratkumar turned to the worker and said, "Ask them what they want." In that moment everybody received a shock, a bit of a wake-up call.

The journalists pulled themselves together and asked, "When will this world be destroyed?"

Bhagawan answered mildly, "As long as my Father exists, this world will exist. This world is eternal; so is Father. My Father is eternal."

Many of Yogi Ramsuratkumar's communications were highly symbolic. Once Ashish Bagrodia was in Gujarat on business, where his company had a spinning mill in a jungle area. Two thousand people worked there, and there was labor unrest and other serious problems, such as when someone cut the electric wires and they had to send horse-mounted police to find the cut line and repair it.

Ashish decided to send a fax to Bhagawan to let him know what was going on and to ask for his blessing. There were late night emergency meetings being called because every night there was a crisis in the factory. As a result, Ashish was sleeping the next morning when Mani called for him. His staff was reluctant to wake him up and said, "No, we won't wake him; please call back later." After three calls, Mani said, "You'd better wake him up. This is very serious."

When Ashish got on the phone Mani said, "We have received your fax, we have shown it to Bhagawan, and Bhagawan wants to speak to you." Ashish was shocked.

He thought, "The saint! I don't think he speaks on phone to anybody. How come he wants to speak to me?" Mani gave the phone to Bhagawan and Ashish said right away, "Bhagawan, Bhagawan, pranams! Yogiji, pranams," He shouted, thinking that Yogi Ramsuratkumar couldn't hear him.

"Ashish Bagrodia, can you hear me?" Bhagawan's voice came over the phone.

"Yes, Bhagawan, I can hear you," Ashish replied, again giving his *pranams*.

"Ashish Bagrodia, can you hear me?" Yogi Ramsuratkumar asked again.

"Yes, Bhagawan, I can hear you. Can you hear me, Bhagawan?"

"Ashish Bagrodia, can you hear me?" Yogi Ramsuratkumar asked a third time.

"Yes, Bhagawan, I can hear you," Ashish asserted.

After three or four times of saying, "Ashish Bagrodia, can you hear me?" Yogi Ramsuratkumar simply handed the phone back to Mani. Over the wires Ashish could hear him say to Mani, "No sound coming."

Mani knew that he had been able to hear Ashish very clearly, and said, "I would speak very clearly to him."

When Mani was back on the phone Ashish said, "Mr. Mani, but I can hear you. I don't know how come Bhagawan is not hearing me."

Mani said, "Anyway, Bhagawan has said everything will be okay. He has blessed you and your people," and then he hung up.

Yogi Ramsuratkumar spoke very little, and much of his speech seemed casual somehow. Whenever a person came with a problem, either physical, mental or spiritual, the moment he or she entered his presence, the beggar would quietly start smoking. After a short silence, he would very easily start a conversation, like "What is your name?" or "Where are you from?" Many people saw him ask these kinds of basic questions of people he had known for years. He would often ask about very ordinary kinds of things like, "How do you earn your money, how is your business?" The conversation could appear trivial, mundane or superficial, but at the end of it he would often pat the man on the back two or three times or smile at the woman, hand her *prasad* and say, "My Father's blessings, my Father will see to everything."

These casual conversations seemed to have the benefit of relaxing the person enough to make them more receptive to the guru's grace. Most people are much more deeply tense than they realize, so much of his play—the singing, dancing, giving talks, speaking of family matters, school, business, work, sports, politics—was partly a way of distracting the defense systems of the egoic mind so that the real transmission of grace could go into the body, the heart, the soul. Opening the way for grace to come in was behind much of his cryptic language and behavior, as Ma Devaki reflected:

> Mostly his language was cryptic—if at all he spoke, he spoke in cryptic language. Mostly symbolic. We had to be very alert to get to know what he meant. He never spoke at length, but one sentence . . . how much it brings! Once he said to me, "When you are serious about God, when you want to see God alone, why do you accept the existence of anything else?" He never spoke at length, you know, it was always just one sentence in the most unexpected moment, the most unguarded moment. He would suddenly tell you something very sharply which you would never forget.

Yogi Ramsuratkumar could be a strict disciplinarian, but he had many ways to make a point, many of them very paradoxical and impossible for the mind to understand. The only way to digest these teaching lessons was through the heart.

One of the ways that devotees learned was through their own disobedience, because usually there were natural consequences that brought the teaching lesson home. Sometimes Yogi Ramsuratkumar would insist on direct obedience and at other times he gave people a lot of room to make their own decision and succeed or fail. If a devotee kept asking questions of him—"Bhagawan, why not do this? Why not do that? Can I do this or that?"—he would sometimes just fall silent, and the silence itself made the communication. In this way many lessons were learned.

At other times the devotees would take his silence to mean that they could go ahead with their plans, or insist on having it their way, only to learn a bitter lesson the hard way, as recounted in the following story by Ma Devaki: When Yogi Ramsuratkumar first moved to Sudama House there were many weddings and other activities of the devotees that year. Many people expected him to attend these various functions and he felt that he should visit them, but he had been very sick and he was still weak. Devaki protested:

> I was afraid for him that if he should go to a wedding, there are many people there and he had to work hard on so many people—blessing, blessing. Every blessing that was coming from him consumed a little of his energy because he was smoking. He used to smoke continuously from morning to evening. He would sit in the same place from morning to evening and continue to smoke. I used to be afraid it would hit his health again. So I used to insist in the beginning, "Why are you going to the wedding? You are blessing them already. Now that you are awake, why don't you stay here, Bhagawan. Please let us not go." I used to beg him. I used to tell him a little strongly that we shouldn't go.

One day some devotees were organizing a wedding and wanted to invite Bhagawan to come. Devaki had said to him, "Bhagawan, one more wedding and one more heavy day for you, when you are not well, you are weak—it is not necessary right at the moment. Bhagawan, I beg you, please don't go." He said, "Yes, yes, yes," then he went outside to receive the devotee who had come to invite him to the wedding. Devaki felt a great relief and went on about her business, happily humming a song. Five minutes later Bhagawan called for her. The devotee with the wedding plans was sitting next to him.

"Devaki," he began, then he looked at the man and said, "You tell her."

"Swami's coming to the wedding," the devotee said.

"Bhagawan, you just now told me that you are not going," she cried out.

"No, I am not going. We are going. Devaki and this beggar are going."

Obedience was the only choice left. The decision had been made. Five minutes later Devaki was running to the car after Yogi Ramsuratkumar and they were on their way. He spent the whole day there.

In a fraction of a second he could become stern, and then even an inch of movement from those around him would disturb him. Those who were near him had to keep their place and not move at all so as not to distract him from his work. Sometimes he would lie down, raise his hand up a little and look off, as if into some other world, and the presence around him would become very intense and concentrated. Then Devaki and the Sudama sisters would know that he was immersed in some important work at that time, and he should not be disturbed for any reason. Devaki recounted:

> Then I would just go a little distance away and keep a book with me. I would quietly work, but I had to be near the whole time. Sometimes you know, another room needed some kind of tidying, and I may go for five minutes or ten minutes, but even that wouldn't be liked by him. But if I had to clean up the room, I would do it in five-minute installments. I would go put this away and do something and come back, but I had to hurry.

In 1990 Will Zulkowski was walking down the street with Yogi Ramsuratkumar when he suddenly said to Will, "Oh, you want to get remarried!" Just that morning at Ramanashram, Will had noticed some attractive German girls who were staying there. He had the stray thought, "Gee, maybe I should get remarried." Will almost staggered from the impact of the beggar's comment; it was unbelievable that Yogi Ramsuratkumar could pick up such a transient thought— "like a cloud on a clear day, passing through," Will said.

"Oh no! No, Swami," Will answered. He resolved himself to watch his thoughts, to discipline his mind more. In these and countless interactions Will came to the understanding that Yogi Ramsuratkumar could not be understood with the rational mind. Will continued:

> Swami was a very complicated being. You weren't dealing with a simple thing; you were dealing with someone highly complex and light years beyond you. We can't even fathom it. There were endless ramifications every time you crossed a line. And he let you know very quickly that you had crossed the line—boom! That was it! Once you got the correction, you made the adjustment. But those were his rules. You didn't ever play by your rules; you played by his rules. It wouldn't matter if Swami had known the person for twenty years and came and sat down; he might just get up and run away, because he had to make some kind of adjustment [in his work].
>
> Sometimes he was silent, but he was always busy doing something. Sometimes his eyes were closed and you could see that he was doing something, even though he was silent. And then you'd wait—we never disturbed him, because we knew he looked like he was really busy. It wasn't our place to interfere with that. When he looked relaxed a little

> more, then we could bring up whatever we wanted to talk about—and it really wasn't ever personal things. I never really asked him much for me personally because I didn't think it was important. I was more interested in the overview of things—how he thought things worked. I mean, this is the smartest man, the most aware man I have ever talked to in my whole life.

Those who knew Yogi Ramsuratkumar in the early seventies remember how enigmatic his appearance was, long before his "madness" was broadly accepted as coming from a divine source. He looked like nothing more than a crazy beggar with bizarre behavior, wandering around and living totally outside the norms of Indian society. For someone who got to know him better, who had the good fortune to be caught by his darshan, to catch a glimpse of the supreme magic that shimmered beneath his rags, it was an entirely different affair. The *siddha purusha* was always at work. For many people, the relationship with Yogi Ramsuratkumar was much more intimate and became the unique experience of their lives—for some it was the pinnacle of all relationships and for others it went even beyond that to the rare, even impossible relationship with the personal Beloved. It was a rapport that no one could concoct or fake; it had to be entirely authentic and spontaneous.

Even so, everyone made many mistakes in his company, and at any time the delicate equilibrium could be knocked off balance, in which case the devotee got another teaching lesson in how to live in the company of one who existed in a state of divine madness. Will Zulkowski commented:

> I felt I was very lucky to have these experiences at that level of intimacy and openness with Swami. He felt comfortable having me around, and I felt comfortable being around him. But sometimes I'd go there and he'd just [send me away.]
>
> Once I went to see him and said, "Swami, I'm here for two weeks. Can I come back in the evening, and kind of pack my stuff away in Tiruvannamali?" The next day I came and he said, "Good seeing you." This was a bad omen, when he said, "Nice seeing you, Will. Good we met."
>
> "Thank you, but Swami, I'm here for two weeks . . ."
>
> "Do as you like. But this beggar feels you should go to Puttaparthi."
>
> I had to drag myself on the bus to go to Puttaparthi! That was always his bottom line: "Do as you like, but this beggar feels . . ." But if you "do as you like" you just don't get the grace when somebody of his caliber is giving it out. I observed him pretty closely; he was never interested in anybody worshipping him. Sometimes he would say, "Oh, if people believed in this beggar—he doesn't have any boundaries." If we truly believed in who he was, then we wouldn't have to come, because there is no boundary. He doesn't have any limits of being here or there in form.

> Once Caylor asked him a very interesting question. He said, "What is the difference between realized beings?" and Yogi Ramsuratkumar said, "There is no difference. Once such a being has gone beyond identification with the body, then it's the role he has to play." He said that he came to play the role of a beggar, and he had to play it perfectly. That was always his story. People came and asked all these kind of esoteric questions, but he was so far beyond the mind and the kind of mental hullabaloo we go through. He was working in the cosmic spheres and we were in kindergarten, asking children's questions.
>
> In the West we have this overdeveloped intellect and underdeveloped heart, but Swami was also a very passionate person, very moving. People did small things for him—like the lady who brought him food, and he was so grateful.
>
> I remember Swami asked Caylor to sit by his body for three days, when Swami was out of his body. I don't know where they were—someplace in Tiruvannamalai—and Swami asked Caylor to watch the body, to make sure nothing happened to that body. Then when Swami came back in the body after three days, he just looked at Caylor and he had tears of gratitude that Caylor had done this for him. Caylor didn't expect it, but Swami just had such gratitude.

Caylor recounted that this episode happened on Mount Arunachala, in 1973, over a period of some days, when Yogi Ramsuratkumar would ask Caylor to watch over him for several hours at a time while he "worked." Another time, in the spring of 1976, just before Caylor returned to the States, he was staying with Yogi Ramsuratkumar in the home of a friend. Again, over a period of several days, Yogi Ramsuratkumar would lie down for hours at a time and ask Caylor to insure that he was not disturbed. At one point the beggar became very hot, and had a very high temperature—at least 103 or 104 degrees. At the time he behaved very enigmatically, intimating that he was working on something for one of his devotees who was in crisis.

The people who Yogi Ramsuratkumar drew together in ad hoc configurations for short or long periods of time often had no idea what he was doing. There was a time when he frequently put Sandiya, Devaki and Sujatha together. Once when he was visiting at Kripala he asked Sandiya to go into the garden to pick gooseberries—a smaller variety, not as bitter as some—from the big tree. The three women were seated together with the beggar, when, looking at the women, he put one *amlaka* on the ground by each one of them, making an imaginary triangle. Dwarak Nath Reddy was there also, and Yogi Ramsuratkumar was making casual conversation with everyone. Suddenly he would lift one *amlaka*, look at it and move it a little; after a while, he would do the same thing with another one. In this way he kept adjusting the position of the fruits in relation to the three women. His actions were mysterious—it was impossible to know what he was doing—but at the end of the "session" he gave one *amlaka* to each of the three women.

In this *lila* his actions appeared to be senseless, random, meaningless, but they were deeply purposeful. His actions, like his words, carried inherent spiritual power. Ma Devaki said, "Every word he has uttered, every word is beautiful, the way he pronounces each word and how softly he speaks. There is such beauty in every act."

It is said that the relationship with the mahatma, or great soul, and the devotee is similar to the relationship between mother and child. The baby nurses at the mother's breast even when it is asleep, and when the baby wakes, it is full, although it doesn't remember having eaten. With the master the work doesn't have to occur on the conscious level, nor does it usually, because there are so many levels of consciousness. The devotee is usually not even aware of the work that is being done on other levels, but when the time is right, the work that has been done will flower and come to fruition.

Ma Devaki sat with Bhagavan twenty-four hours a day, day after day after day, month after month after month, year after year after year. Sometimes Bhagawan would ask her to look at one photograph, for example of Swami Nityananda, for two or three minutes, and while she looked at it he would raise his hands in blessing. Or he might ask her to open the song book to any *sloka* (verse), and then he would ask her to read the verse and its meaning. Then he would ask her to read that same *sloka* for an hour or more, and then the meaning of it for another hour or more. All the while he blessed her and smoked, then raised his hands again in blessing and smoked again; in this way his tremendous blessing power was bestowed upon her. Yogi Ramsuratkumar said that the nature of his blessings was that when certain things were necessary for his work, they would bear fruit, but one had to be receptive. Ma Devaki recalled:

> Sometimes a devotee would come and give something to Bhagawan. Very sweetly and graciously he would say "Thank you." Immediately that person took it at face and said, "Oh please, don't thank me, we are fortunate to help you. You please don't thank me, but bless me instead." That has hurt Bhagawan, and after the person left he turned to me and said, "You see Devaki, these people don't understand. Whatever this beggar utters is a blessing. When this beggar said 'Thank you' it was a blessing, but he did not want it."
>
> You see, by saying, "Don't thank me," we are blocking the grace, not knowing the ways of a mahatma. Best thing is, we have to trust them totally—where they sit, whatever they do, whatever they say, is Father's grace. It's beyond blessing. Then we would be able to receive much more. "Even when this beggar got angry with somebody it would only be a blessing," he used to say.

This commentary sheds some insight on another story of a devotee who served as Yogi Ramsuratkumar's attendant at the ashram for many years. The beggar saint could be fierce with his devotees when he wanted to make an important point. Once when he was getting out of his car, one of the darshan hall attendants reached out to take his hand in order to steady him. Taking the offered hand, Yogi Ramsuratkumar said gently, "Thank you."

When the attendant said in return, "Thank you, Bhagawan," the yogi had a strong response.

"Thank you!" Bhagawan almost growled in return, and then three more times he snapped, "Thank you! Thank you! Thank you!"

The attendant immediately began to wonder what he had done wrong; what could have caused the master to get angry? For days he contemplated what the meaning of this could be, then he realized that Bhagawan was slowly working his heart, and that was the main point. The guru works in ways that penetrate beyond the mind, and in this case, the shock of his anger caused the attendant to reflect more deeply. He realized that the shock had caused some change to occur—a softening in his heart. He further understood that he should not be focusing on what he might have done wrong. The interchange left him more receptive to the power of the guru's grace, and with the recognition that "We should remember God all the time."

For years at Sannadhi Street prior to the inception of Sudama House, Yogi Ramsuratkumar had often been very harsh with Devaki. He often made her sit at a far distance, and when her longing to serve him was very strong, he would ignore her and ask the other women devotees—some who had been with him for many years—to do little things for him. Among the circle of the devotees, any opportunity to perform a small service or *seva* for the master was considered a very great blessing. As with all masters, Yogi Ramsuratkumar's attention was coveted, and small acts of attention or inattention from him could spark a range of intense feeling: from the fires of longing to jealousy, envy or deep rooted insecurities.

Often Yogi Ramsuratkumar made Devaki sit in a corner by the door, while other devotees were brought close and lavished with attention, or allowed to serve him in ways that Devaki longed to do. Devaki mused in retrospect on one such incident that happened at Sannadhi Street, when Yogi Ramsuratkumar was interacting with a female devotee:

> Right in front of me he would drink something from his coconut shell and give the rest to another devotee. He did it so many times that day, every time giving it to her. There was such an air of intimacy between the two of them and I was sitting there looking at them, when he wouldn't even allow me one step near! Deliberately he would do so many things which would only go to sharpen our love for him. This longing is good, what we call, "The heat of suffering becomes the fire of love."[11] This kind of negative treatment will sharpen our feeling for them. You begin to long, otherwise there will not be any longing. If people are so easily available

11 Taken from a prayer written by Lee Lozowick.

> we may not see anything significant—he knew it so well. He knew exactly how to pull the string and where to pull the string. Like the puppet.
>
> Another time, how Bhagawan made me wait and wait and wait in the temple, until four o'clock in the evening, with no water, no thought of food or water, only to say when I returned to Sannadhi Street, "Get out." But every time it only went to increase my love for him! Bhagawan always used to say, whatever happens is necessary for our growth, otherwise a thing wouldn't happen in our life. Whatever happens in our life is necessary for us. It is not only what we deserve, it is what we need for our growth and so it is grace. Grace from God. If we see this grace, if you see it as grace from God, it will turn into a blessing, and so all that turned into a blessing for me because it increased my longing for him.

This *lila* happened during the time when Bhagawan was frequently sending Devaki away from Sannadhi Street. As the whole story goes, she went to his house one morning at nine o'clock, quite nervous and tense, because just the thought of seeing him and possibly being sent away was overwhelming. He opened the wooden door and walked from the inner room, and as he did so, fear gripped Devaki. Without opening the iron grill door, he looked through its bars at her, lowered his eyes and said, "You can go to the temple and wait," then he deliberately turned his back.

Nonetheless, hope springs eternal, and feeling that he had given her hope that he would come later, Devaki walked to the temple. She took a seat where she could watch the front entrance to see if he entered. With her attention riveted to the entrance, she sat. It was nine-thirty, then ten o'clock, ten-thirty, eleven o'clock, then eleven-thirty, twelve o'clock, twelve-thirty, one o'clock, and so on until two-thirty—and still she sat eagerly awaiting Bhagawan. Thinking that he was probably busy and making up all kinds of reasons for why she should be waiting for so long for him to appear, she realized that she had been so focused on him coming that she had forgotten to drink even a cup of water, nor had she gone to the toilet. With her mind fixated completely on Yogi Ramsuratkumar, she had forgotten her body and its usual needs altogether.

By three-thirty in the afternoon she realized, "From morning so many hours have passed and Bhagawan is not coming. There is no hope. Probably he is not coming at all." As soon as this thought lodged in her mind, she began to feel restless and immediately the body made its usual demands.

Finally, at 3:45, she thought to herself, "This is the limit! I will at least go near his house and see what is happening, and if possible I will get a drink of water somewhere." She slowly moved out of the temple precincts and walked to his house on Sannadhi Street. There was nobody outside; the wooden door was still closed and the grill gate was latched. She went for a cool drink in the nearby market, then came back. Still there was no sign of him. Everything looked exactly as it had that morning.

Then she thought, "I have to knock this time, after all I have waited all these hours, so I have the right to do it." Without hesitation she walked up to the door and knocked loudly. Again the wooden door opened and this time she was very hopeful that he would welcome her. He came and saw her, lowered his eyes, turned his back once again and said, "Get out . . ." By tempering her emotional attachment to him and purifying her natural devotional fervor, this was one of the ways that Yogi Ramsuratkumar prepared Devaki for the responsibilty she would enter into years later.

During the first year at Sudama House after Devaki was announced as Bhagawan's eternal slave and she was serving him twenty-four hours a day, blessings were showered upon her, but still she felt that there was no conscious process of transformation going on. She was serving her guru with deep devotion and enthusiasm, but she did not feel transformed. She asked him, "Bhagawan, you are blessing me so much and still I am the same. I feel that I am still the same. Why is it things are not happening to me as we have read in books? And you are giving me so much blessing! Where do those blessings go?"

He said, "Father starts from the depths and you are going through so much transformation, Devaki, you may not be aware of it. But this beggar can see. This beggar knows what transformation has been going on in you. You don't have to be aware of it. It's not necessary that you should know what's going on. Father works from the depths."

When doubts assailed her, and she wondered why she did not feel more love and compassion for others, Yogi Ramsuratkumar assured her that spiritual progress was naturally occurring, simply through the fact of her love and service to him.

"If Devaki serves this beggar well, then she loves all," he said. "When she serves this beggar, it means she loves all. If she loves this beggar, it means she loves all," he replied. This is the same communication of non-separation that he made in countless other statements, including, "When you pour water on the root of a tree, the sap goes to the very tip of each branch, to every leaf, to every flower, to every fruit. It spreads to the whole tree. Like that, when you serve a saint, or when you serve your guru, it goes to the entire cosmos."

Once Devaki said, "Bhagawan, there is not transformation in me. You have been with me now for so long, so many months have passed since you came here and there is no change in me." Yogi Ramsuratkumar was quiet for awhile, then they went to the ashram, where the workers had marked the outline for the temple, but there were only some gaping pits here and there for the foundation. There was nothing else there but mounds of earth and these pits.

"Devaki, you see all of them? One day there will be a building here. But you see what is happening now? What the earth has to go through? There is so much digging and so much hammering, so many things have to be done on that. And one day you will see a beautiful building here. This is what is happening to Devaki also," Yogi Ramsuratkumar said in a rare moment of direct teaching. "See all these things? Can you imagine a building here? But do you see how ugly everything looks now?"

The ashram itself and the temple in particular was a perfect metaphor for the transformational process within the individual, and in general for the work of Yogi Ramsuratkumar. He predicted many times that one day the temple hall would not be enough, and people would have to stand outside in crowds. The temple was tremendously important for him because it would carry the embodiment of his work and become the vehicle of the grace that would flow to generations yet to come. He blessed every inch of the ashram grounds, every minute aspect of the buildings.

When the ashram was just bare ground and he was living at Sudama House, first thing in the early morning he would suddenly get up and say, "Lets go to the ashram." Arriving with Devaki and the Sudama sisters, he would walk around the parameter of the property, then sit and smoke. He was always working with the physical environment to saturate it with the power of his blessings. When it was a holiday he would insist that at least two workers should stay on the ashram and keep the work going. To some, his decisions may have seemed cryptic or arbitrary, but for Yogi Ramsuratkumar the construction on the temple represented, literally and symbolically, the momentum and actualization of "Father's work."

The Beggar's Love of Poetry, Singing and Dancing

It was a sacred day—the religious festival that celebrates the dance of Shiva, Parvati and the disciple. Devaki had arrived from Salem, and she and Sandiya, the daughter of Dwarak Nath Reddy, had gone to the temple at nine o'clock one morning. Because it was a sacred day of special rites, the temple was flooded with crowds of people. They walked through the *gopuram* and across the stone floor of the courtyard, and suddenly they saw Yogi Ramsuratkumar seated in a corner of the temple. There were a few devotees sitting around the beggar. Sandiya, who was a devotee of Ramana Maharshi, had a particular intimate, almost familial, relationship with Yogi Ramsuratkumar. She walked right up to him with Devaki, who was more reticent with him at the time, following.

"Swamiji!" Sandiya called. Yogi Ramsuratkumar always seemed to enjoy Sandiya's boldness with him; at the same time, she was child-like and pure in her love for the beggar saint. He welcomed them into his circle, and as they sat down with him Devaki was thinking that it was the day of the dance of Shiva, Parvati and the disciple. Having heard many stories of Yogi Ramsuratkumar's divine dancing, she longed to see at least a glimpse of it. Inwardly she was praying for such a boon, and finally she worked up the courage to say something.

"Ah Bhagawan, today's the day Shiva danced with Parvati and an intimate disciple. Wouldn't this Shiva dance for us?" He looked at her sharply and said, "Why not?" Then he began to talk of something else. He had a way of listening to one thing, then talking about something else, and later returning to the idea. As he talked to the other devotees who were sitting around him, he occasionally shot sharp glances at Devaki, but as time went by, there was still no dance.

Suddenly a gust of strong wind blew through the courtyard and rustled the leaves of the tree they were sitting under, making a musical sound. Yogi Ramsuratkumar looked up at the leaves moving in the wind and said, "Devaki, Shiva is dancing." Not making the association, she looked up at the leaves. Yogi Ramsuratkumar resumed his conversation with the devotees and soon began to distribute to everyone some food he had been given.

Suddenly two or three birds swooped low and flew across their group. Again he turned to Devaki and said, "Devaki! Shiva is dancing." This time she began to realize what he was communicating to her. As the conversation with the devotees picked back up, it seemed that Yogi Ramsuratkumar was engrossed with talking to everyone else, when he turned nonchalantly toward Devaki. He looked on the ground beside her and there was a centipede or millipede crawling by on the stones.

"Devaki! Shiva is dancing," he said, with such sweetness it would melt the heart to hear it.

Then she began to understand: "This man is not going to dance. He's going to show me all the motions, all the movements around, and make me aware that I have to see my Shiva dancing there, and that is really getting to know the truth." She realized that he was teaching her the way of the Divine in the universe. She resigned herself to his teaching and accepted that she would not see the Godman dance, but that he would show her the truth.

After a while Sandiya and the others left. The priests brought the statue of Shiva Nataraja (dancing Shiva) out of the temple, followed by a huge crowd in a religious fervor, accompanied by music and drumming. Yogi Ramsuratkumar walked over to a corner and stood there alone. Nobody was looking at him; the crowd of worshippers were busy looking at the statue of Shiva Nataraja, and all of his devotees were gone except Devaki.

Yogi Ramsuratkumar watched the crowd and raised his hands in blessing, but no one noticed. He went about his work silently and invisibly, as he had for so many years, the people not even aware that a beggar was standing near and blessing them. Hidden in a corner of the courtyard, he watched the crowd intently, hands still raised in blessing.

From where she stood, Devaki kept her eyes on Yogi Ramsuratkumar, and suddenly —lo and behold!—he began to dance in the corner to the music of the procession. No one was noticing him; all the action and attention was focused on the ritual that was being enacted with the Shiva Nataraja. He danced the divine dance, and he danced beautifully. In that moment, it was Shiva dancing, revealed in the movements of his hands and of his feet. He danced for just a minute or two then stopped, but it was an immeasurable gift of sweetness, grandeur and power. Devaki said, recounting the story, "Aye, one has to see it to believe it!"

Yogi Ramsuratkumar loved music, dancing and poetry—the natural expressions of the heart in the Garden of Delight. He invited many different professional singers, dancers of classical Bharat Natyam, and musicians to perform in his darshan, but most often he simply invited devotees and guests to lead chants in darshan, and on rare occasions he would ask people to dance.

When Lee Lozowick's group was visiting on Christmas Eve in 1995, Yogi Ramsuratkumar asked them to sing Christmas songs. Four of Lee's students got up and started singing Christmas hymns while Yogi Ramsuratkumar smoked and listened intently. The more they bumbled through, not knowing all the words and not having sung these songs together before, the more joyous it seemed the mood became. Whenever they made mistakes Yogi Ramsuratkumar would smile broadly and laugh. After a while he asked them to dance while they sang. Inspired by Western folk dances, they danced in a circle holding hands. The beggar watched with a grin on his face and laughed out loud.

Yogi Ramsuratkumar always asked whoever was in his company to sing. During the last decade of his life this love of music, song and dance manifested largely through his enjoyment of others, as was made so poignantly evident in the grand finale of his public darshans in November and December 2000, when his final words to the crowd of five or six hundred people were, "Dance! Dance!" When he could no longer walk, much less dance, he beamed and smiled as he watched his devotees, from both the East and West, singing and dancing.

Many devotees sang regularly for Yogi Ramsuratkumar and wrote songs or *bhajans* for him. Pankkajam, who had known Yogi Ramsuratkumar since the mid-seventies and who has a beautiful, evocative voice, frequently sang for him both at Sudama House and in darshan on the ashram. Parthasarathy, a very fine singer, was also often asked to sing songs that he had written for Yogi Ramsuratkumar. In 1977 Parthasarathy wrote two songs that often inspired the beggar to dance when Parthasarathy sang them. In the late nineties he wrote another song that was one of the beggar's favorites, "Samartha," which was recorded on cassette.

Parthasarathy spoke of the dancing *bhavas* of Yogi Ramsuratkumar in the early years:

> When he was walking, he was also dancing. He would not seem to be touching the earth. He was walking as if dancing; he would carry his fan and shake his whole frame, moving, moving. All the twenty-four hours he was in the blissful states, he was dancing and singing. He liked songs, and he was a wonderful singer, also. When he chants a *nama*, sometimes he would sing some songs in Sanskrit or in Hindi . . . wonderful!

Singing, dancing, poetry—these were always the natural expressions of his delight in the ever-present living God. On the other hand, he had a natural instinct for what was authentic and inspired by the heart on fire, and what was spawned from false devotion and the posturing of the sycophant, as made clear in the following interaction between Yogi Ramsuratkumar and Mani.

Mani once said to Yogi Ramsuratkumar, "Bhagawan, so many people are always saying such beautiful poetic things to you, telling you that you are all light . . ."

"Mani, people are always saying poetry to this beggar," Yogi Ramsuratkumar said. "You know what such poetry is, Mani? Lies, all lies!"

It was a powerful statement from one who was known to love poetry so much, but it pointed to the hypocrisy that is so often found in the honeyed words that are heaped upon people who have power of any kind, especially spiritual power. People wanted to praise and laud Yogi Ramsuratkumar, but their lives did not reflect that they had understood who he was and how he wanted them to live. Their lives were full of delusion and selfishness instead of self-awareness, kindness and compassion. Living under such illusions about oneself and one's motives place the dark weight of deceit on opulent expressions of devotion and lavish poetic words.

Yogi Ramsuratkumar once said, "The Divine descends where there is no selfishness. Even if there is a trace of selfishness, the Divine will not descend."[12] The ability to freely and genuinely praise is only possible when there is no selfishness, and it is praise that calls the Divine to descend upon humankind. In his vast wisdom, Yogi Ramsuratkumar knew this and wanted to hear praise from his devotees—praise of God, praise of creation, praise of humanity. It caused him great pain when his devotees criticized each other or split off into warring factions, a common phenomena in organizations around the world, spiritual or secular.

Yogi Ramsuratkumar also had a great love for literature in general. He was widely read, and familiar with Eastern and Western literary traditions, both classical and contemporary. He often recommended reading certain books or specific poets to various people. He believed in the power of books to instruct and even change the individual, beginning at the level of the mind.

Yogi Ramsuratkumar had a particular love for poetry, and was known to write poems on occasions. There is no record of poems that may have been written prior to 1970, but Caylor Wadlington and Will Zulkowski preserved a few rare poems written by Yogi Ramsuratkumar during the early and mid-seventies, written in the beggar's own hand. The childlike freshness of these poems touch the heart, and yet there is always a teaching contained in them that reflects the nascent and wise innocence of the moment.

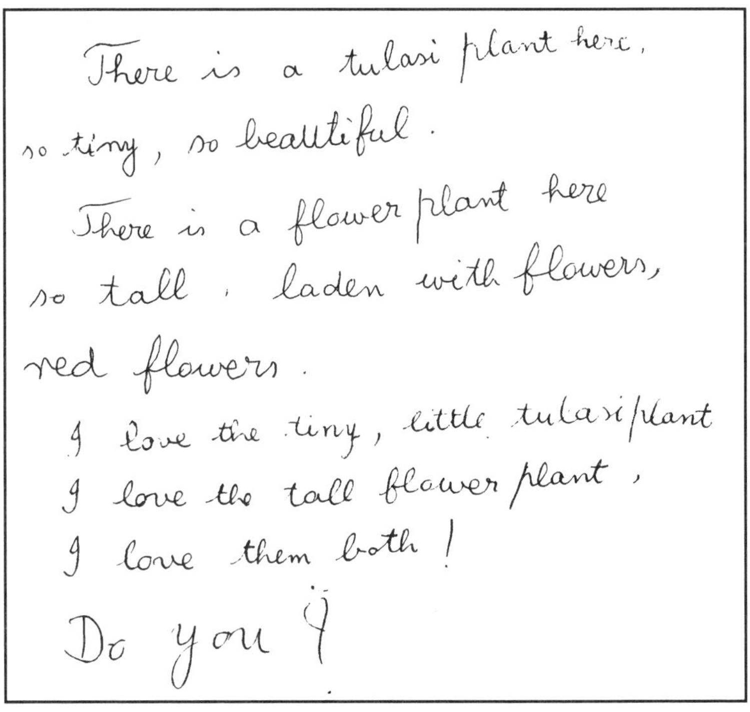
There is a tulasi plant here,
so tiny, so beautiful.
There is a flower plant here
so tall, laden with flowers,
red flowers.
I love the tiny, little tulasi plant
I love the tall flower plant,
I love them both!
Do you?

12 Ma Devaki, "The Divine Beggar on Himself," *Saranagatham*, January 2003, p. 33.

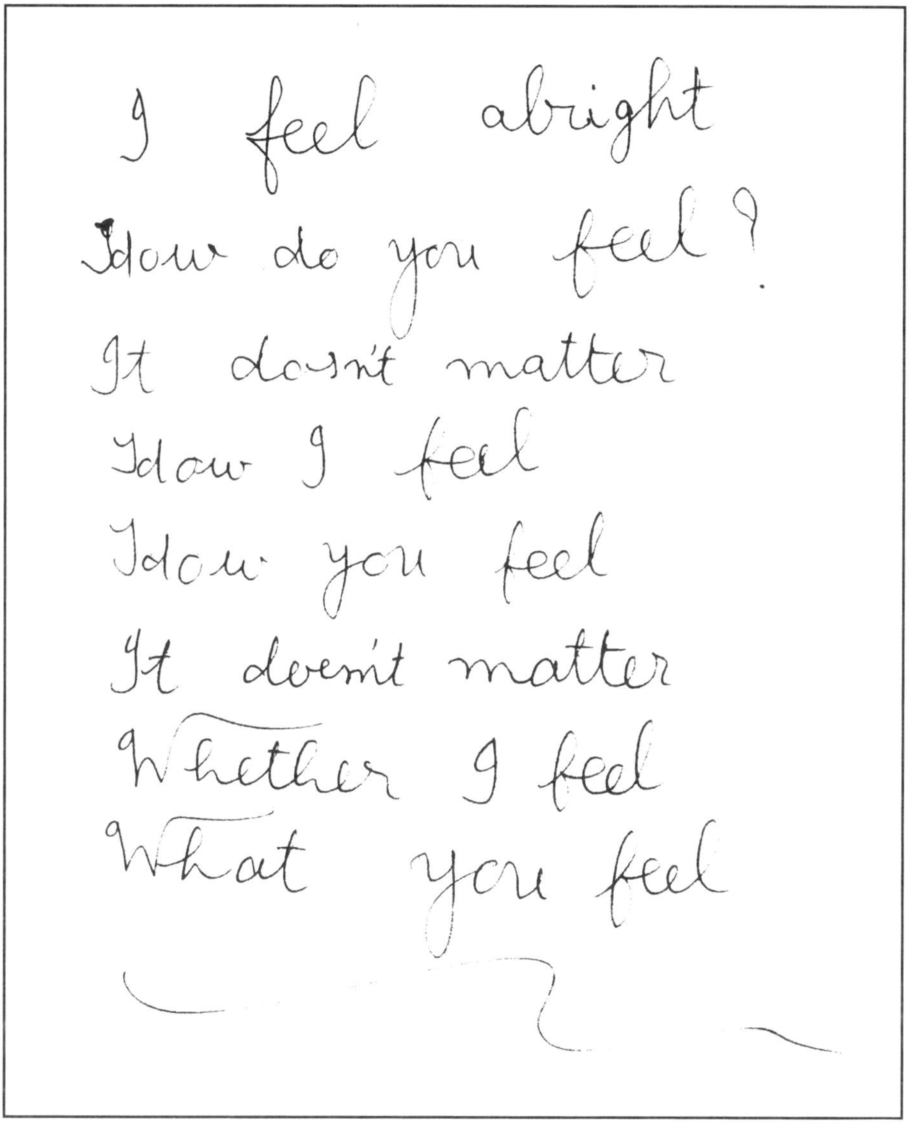

I feel alright
How do you feel?
It doesn't matter
How I feel
How you feel
It doesn't matter
Whether I feel
What you feel

The beggar saint was known to heal people by having them write poetry. Sivaramakrishnan Iyer had served Gnanananda Giri at Tapovanum and then became a devotee of Yogi Ramsuratkumar, writing numerous poems about him. When Sivaramakrishnan became sick with a serious stomach ailment, he was unable to move, much less to travel to Tiruvannamalai to seek the blessings of the beggar saint he knew so well. His niece, Lalitha, had planned a trip to Tiruvannamalai, and he asked her to convey his *pranams* to Yogi Ramsuratkumar. While visiting Yogi Ramsuratkumar at Sannadhi Street, Lalitha relayed *pranams* from her uncle, but it seemed that the beggar paid no attention to it at all. Then, before she left, he called her to him and asked her to write down these lines: *Jayathu Jayathu, Jayathu Jayathu, Ramasuratkumara Yogi, Ramasuratkumara Yogi.*

"Tell your uncle to write a song with these lines," he said. Lalitha returned to Tirukoilur and gave the lines to Sivaramakrishnan, who was disappointed that Yogi

Ramsuratkumar hadn't sent some *prasad* to eat or a blessing that could be directly applied toward recovering his health. The lines were impossible! How could he write a poem with them? He put them aside for a day, and still he was quite ill. Finally that night he looked at the lines again and started to write. After four or five lines, he felt better. Finally it struck him that writing the poem was the cure itself. Inspired, he wrote a twenty-seven verse poem titled "Nakshatra Malar Malai." By the time the work was finished he was completely well.

The next week he took the poem to Tiruvannamalai and went straight to the house on Sannadhi Street. As soon as he entered he heard Yogi Ramsuratkumar talking about the planet Saturn and its adverse effects on people. He turned to Sivaramakrishnan and asked, "Do you know 'Nala Charitram'?" The "Nala Charitram" is the story of the Emperor Nalan who underwent countless miseries during the period when Saturn afflicted him. Sivaramakrishnan recollected a few verses from "Nala Venba," and Yogi Ramsuratkumar then declared that all those present that day were free from the negative effects of the transit of the planet Saturn![13]

In the early years Yogi Ramsuratkumar often told people to read certain poets, and he encouraged his devotees to write poetry, which many people did: D.S. Sivaramakrishnan, Ki. Va. Jaganathan, Shankara Rajulu, Kirsti, Lee Lozowick, Parthasarathy and Perumal Rajulu to name a few.

Lee Lozowick's prolific outpouring of poetry, written in English, had a particular significance for the beggar saint; Yogi Ramsuratkumar seemed to recognize that this poetry had the capacity to inflame the heart with love of God. It was Lee's poetry that Yogi Ramsuratkumar personally instructed his devotees to publish, and also Lee's poetry that was consistently read aloud to him, at his request, for over a decade. This flood of poetry from the American spiritual teacher was published in the West as well and has inspired countless seekers and spiritual practitioners of many different paths.

One unique aspect of Lee Lozowick's poetry was the *ninda stuti* form in which it was written. As a result it has a particular edge to its bountiful praise and unabashed adoration of Yogi Ramsuratkumar as God himself. At the same time, Lee's glorification of Yogi Ramsuratkumar in words of love carry a powerful ring of truth, and are written with a fiery sword—the sword of clarity and insight. It is poetry as firebrand—revolutionary, iconoclastic and even heretical, to use the poet's own self-descriptive term. These seemed to be the qualities that drew Yogi Ramsuratkumar's attention and appreciation—and his total acceptance and embrace of it. It was poetry that was deeply resonant with the beggar's life and that carried the message of his spiritual slavery, his surrender to the absolute will of God.

Parthasarathy remembered Yogi Ramsuratkumar saying many things about Lee's poetry, particularly about the *Poems of a Broken Heart*. He said, "Swami used to allow people to sit near him at the time, and Devaki was reciting all these poems and telling him

13 Vijayalakshmi, *Waves of Love*, pp. 50-51.

the meanings of them. Lee's language is very unique, you know. It was such a plain language, like "the rogue" . . . [he laughs] Murugeshan used to use the same language. He used to 'abuse' Swami in the same way."

In the early eighties when Murugeshan was still alive and Yogi Ramsuratkumar was working closely with the three men—Murugeshan, Parthasarathy and Shivashankara—some of the devotees would complain to Yogi Ramsuratkumar about Murugeshan and his radical use of language in reference to the guru.

"Swami, he uses some filthy language; he is abusing you," they said.

"Is he?" the beggar would ask, putting the question back on them.

One day he said, "Parathasarathy, this beggar heard through some friends that Murugesan used some filthy language on mentioning this beggar, and he abused this beggar," he asked. "Is it so?"

"No Swamiji, he is not abusing you; even though he is mentioning some filthy language, it is not abuse to me."

"What word is it he uses?" he pressed, and Parthasarathy told him the word that was causing some controversy. It was considered a very "filthy" word in the language and culture of Tamil Nadu. Yogi Ramsuratkumar gave Parthasarathy a pen and some paper and instructed him to write the word down in Tamil, then he took the paper and handed it to a Brahmin who was sitting there.

"Do you know the meaning of this word?" he asked. The Brahmin read the word and was shocked.

"Oh! It's filthy language, Swami! We should not use this word, Swami," he protested, not wanting to talk about it at all.

"No, no, this beggar wants to know the meaning of this word. If my king, Murugesan, utters this word, there is a meaning behind it, definitely a meaning to that word! This beggar wants to know the meaning of that word. You will go and bring your dictionary." So the man brought a small Tamil dictionary, which Yogi Ramsuratkumar gave to Parthasarathy, asking him to find the word. When it wasn't in the dictionary, Swami asked the Brahmin to get a bigger dictionary, so the man went to the library and brought one back. There they found the word, which was translated literally as "hidden parts."

"Swami, the word means 'the hidden parts,' " Parthasarathy told him.

"Oh, he uses such strong words for this beggar," he exclaimed, "but it is out of love for this beggar. It is out of love for this beggar, isn't it?" Yogi Ramsuratkumar then explained that in a *sloka* in one of the sacred scriptures to Lord Vishnu—"a thousand *slokas* that are glorifying Lord Vishnu"—this same word is used.

"Oh, now this beggar got it. Murugeshji is not abusing this beggar, Murugeshji is glorifying this beggar!"

Parthasarathy compared this mood and use of language to the *nindaa stuti* form used in Lee Lozowick's poetry, saying:

> In Lee's *Poems of a Broken Heart* there are those words like "thief," "robber" and "mad"—there are several songs in which he gives this kind

> of meaning. It is out of love for the beggar, isn't it? He used the very same words there. Obviously if Lee couldn't love Swamiji, he wouldn't use these words. To "abuse" Swami you should have that courage, you should have that love, otherwise you cannot 'abuse' Swami. You should have that love.

In December 2002, almost two years after the master's death, Lee Lozowick was giving a talk to a group of Yogi Ramsuratkumar devotees in Madurai. He began to tell stories of Yogi Ramsuratkumar selling *Death of a Dishonest Man* over the years, and invited Mani to talk about his experience of these *lilas*. Mani told the story of how Yogi Ramsuratkumar had sold the large poetry books in darshan for four thousand rupees, during Lee's visits, recounting how Bhagawan had asked Lee to talk about the poetry and the book, even when the majority of the crowd in the darshan didn't understand Lee's English. Then Yogi Ramsuratkumar had asked Mani to get up and speak about the poetry book to the devotees. Mani relayed that Yogi Ramsuratkumar was adamant that the Indian devotees should pay the entire four thousand rupees for the large book—it was a matter of blessings, not business. Addressing the question "Why was Yogi Ramsuratkumar so enthusiastic about selling these huge books in English to his Indian devotees?" Mani spoke about his understanding of Yogi Ramsuratkumar's love of Lee's poetry:

> Bhagawan said once, "Mani, you know the meaning of poetry? Poetry is lies. All lies." But this poetry of Lee Lozowick he has accepted as the truth because it has come from the "dirty son" of Yogi Ramsuratkumar. Lee says, "Lee is the arrogant son, You are the dirty Father." If I am permitted to say it, only the son can write like this about the Father because he *knows* him. This is nothing but truth. This book is a treasure. This book is one of the key pieces in Yogi Ramsuratkumar's *lila*.
>
> You see, he was a giver. To Devaki Ma he said, "You pay," for this book, but he takes from you to make you more obedient to him. Mr. Lee says he is not devotional, but definitely I know he is kidding us! This book is written on the side of the common man, but you will reach the highest spiritual development if you read it. You will reach the highest bliss when you read this book. This book is a treasure. It is written with a higher sight; to call Yogi Ramsuratkumar [such names] you should know him fully . . .

Mani was referring to the form of Lee's poetry—*ninda stuti*, or "praise in the form of abusive reproach." As Rangarajan points out in his introduction in *Poems of a Broken Heart*, this is a very difficult poetic form in which to write. Only if one has the true feeling, out of which such words may arise, can it become a powerful vehicle through which the paradoxical and ironic nature of love is revealed. Like the songs of the Bauls of Bengal, the words of Lee's poetry are written for the "common man"—in the ordinary language of daily life, in the vernacular of the streets—which makes the message readily accessible to everyone, not just to an intellectual elite. This too was very resonant with the divine beggar's way of life and his teaching that there is no separation between any aspect of life and the Divine. Yogi Ramsuratkumar's blessings prevailed over all distinctions and separations of caste, race, sex or creed. Ma Devaki recalled:

> Lee's poems moved Bhagawan very much. Sometimes he would even have tears in his eyes and he would have me read the poem again and again several times, the same poem. So every time that he came carrying some poems of Lee, I used to read it to him and then he would say, "Again, do it again, do it again." Then whenever there would be the reaction from Bhagawan, he would smile and [raise his hand] like that: "You see what he says about this dirty beggar!"
>
> He liked all the poems. To some he might be busy working. There were times when I read out poems and he used to smoke quietly, which meant he was working, either on Lee or anything connected with Mr. Lee plus something else also—we wouldn't know. There may not be any open, verbal explanations [of how he was working] offered but there would be an understanding. Whenever I understood he would turn to me and smile his approval. Then I would know, this is it. I got it right. I have asked him, but then if he didn't want to reveal anything to me, he would say, "But this beggar doesn't know Devaki." Just like that. "This beggar doesn't know." And sometimes he would say, "This beggar cannot ask Father why. You are asking this beggar, but he cannot ask Father." Then I would know it's not my place to ask him. It was just a day-to-day affair. There were many things. It was all a mystery—everyday life.

LEARNING THE MASTER'S WAYS—HOW HE TRAINED THE DEVOTEES

"The man was just like the wind—always very free. He never kept anyone with him, so he was always free to do whatever Father wanted, all the time. He would say yes or no if you came to the door at Sannadhi Street. The saints love solitude . . . but we demanded attention, all the time," said Ma Devaki, when speaking of how Yogi Ramsuratkumar left Kripala House abruptly in 1990 after ten days of serious illness. However, over the years the beggar saint became a prisoner of love, freely bound by golden chains to his devotees. He was obligated to bless, and to work closely with those who God put in close proximity to him—but to work with Yogi Ramsuratkumar meant that one had to be able to endure the paradoxical.

Yogi Ramsuratkumar worked with his devotees in a different way than he worked with those spiritual aspirants who came to meet him out of curiosity, to get his blessing or because they were fascinated by spiritual power. Even if he sent someone away, no one went away "empty-handed." There was a teaching given in everything he did.

Yogi Ramsuratkumar once said to Ma Devaki, "This beggar is very bad, very mad. Sometimes Father commands this beggar to act in strange ways which would shake the faith of anybody. But Father commits no mistake. He loves us all and protects us all. Whatever He does is good for the individual and good for the entire cosmos. Father's ways are mysterious." Yogi Ramsuratkumar's ways were mysterious indeed, and yet, if one looks with an open heart and open mind at the countless *lilas* that he enacted with his devotees, the wisdom in his madness becomes easily apparent.

For those who were very close to him, the master was willing to actually instruct them in how to interact with him in order to participate in his work. This was really a training in how to live in a way that would invoke what the Tibetan Buddhists call *drala*—the innate beauty, magic and spiritual power that resides in every moment, at the core of every object, animate or inanimate. This instruction in living life as art was Yogi Ramsuratkumar's gift to those who knew him well. What follows are many different stories of ways in which the master instructed, trained and made lessons for his devotees, beginning with his long-time attendant in the eighties and early nineties, Jayarama, who spoke about his experience with the beggar saint:

> Complete silence. Silence. To do exactly what he wants, you have to grasp that. It took a lot of attention—a lot of attention. He made me successful in this. His every action would hammer our ego, in some kind of way it would hit. Only if we get into [that silence] can he do his work. It's very difficult to work for him. He used to call himself mad. Because of this madness, we could not predict him. He would suddenly send you out. The next day when you see him, he would say, "What do you feel?"
>
> I will tell you how he taught me the work—not in the sense of working in the world. One day I took some food for him; it was summer, very hot. He pointed out in the corner of the house to pick out a dry banana leaf so that he could take the food. In those days I used to be very careless in doing work. In getting the leaf, I treated it in a very careless way. I just pulled that dry leaf, and the way I pulled it in itself showed a lot of arrogance in me. Added to that, I tapped the leaf and rubbed it with my forehand, and all of a sudden there was a great thunder in the room. He was thundering, "What are you doing?" He was thundering like anything! I forgot the whole world. "What? I have not done anything! I just took the leaf and did like that. What is wrong with this?"
>
> The way his voice was heard in that room, nobody can imagine, except the one who heard it! Then immediately I calmed down, and I got it right. It was a very subtle feeling—the whole world was set right in that fraction of a moment. Then I understood, this leaf has got much value. It is going to be for our food. A great lesson he conveyed that day! On that day,

> my whole outlook from that incident was changed in whatever action I did, whatever we were doing—what he used to call "Father's work." He very often used to say, "Father's work."
>
> We always think we do for ourselves. We like something; we want something; we deserve something. We go around our whole lifetime doing this thing. But he taught me, whatever you do, it is Father's work. Because I am offering it to God, the devotion should be there in that. That was the lesson I learned from him. From that incident onwards, there was no necessity for teaching or for thinking, "How to do this for Bhagawan?" [The question] was not there at all, and it stayed like that the whole time with Yogiji. It was the undercurrent; it was there. It was teaching. That's the real teaching from a master. Lucky I was, to get it. Every action, every moment. He used to say to other people, "If I smoke, whatever I do, it is Father's Work." It's the undercurrent. That is godliness. The whole, the oneness—we find this teaching given in all the worldly scriptures, but it can only be given by a master like this.

Perhaps one of the greatest teachings on how to work with the master was given to a man who had been a devotee of Yogi Ramsuratkumar for a long time, who never came to visit at Sannadhi Street without bringing some common problem to talk about with the master. He had a great love for Yogi Ramsuratkumar, but at the same time he never simply came and said, "Swamiji, I am happy. I have come here for your darshan." Yogi Ramsuratkumar was supremely generous nonetheless, and whenever the man appeared he would invite him to sit down and he would say, "Do you want to say anything?"

"Some small problems, Swamiji," the man would say and then he would relay the details. This went on for ten years, until one day the devotee came and sat down beside Swamiji, and he started saying, "Just a small problem." Yogi Ramsuratkumar stopped him and began to speak.

"Can you put aside all your problems in a corner, and remember my Father on this finest day? Then alone can this beggar do something for you," he said simply. It was a great teaching for all who were present that day, and it offered a direct way in which the devotee could benefit tremendously from a simple act of obedience and recognition of the guru's teaching. Parthasarathy recalled:

> Then we realized—we should not take any problems to Swami. If the problems come, it is all of our own making. We have the capacity to deal with the problems, to solve the problem. When we go to Swami, we should be so open—we should just receive and be silent. The problem will take its own course. If you want to take your bath in the ocean when there are no waves, that is impossible. Waves are always there. If you want to see God instead of your problems, you have to take all the problems and you've got to face it and face it. Then only will you be free to see Father, to see God.

> Swamiji's teachings were very subtle—very subtle. In such a way you can always learn from it.
>
> Swami told us once, "For all other saints, they will do some *tapas* and they will start relating [the teaching], but for this beggar, if he walks it is the teaching. You just observe this beggar. If you just observe this beggar, it is enough for you. Any gesture of this beggar—that is enough. You do not have to worry about your spiritual growth. If he walks, it's a teaching; if he eats, it's a teaching; if he sits, it's a teaching; if he talks, it's a teaching. Whatever he does is a teaching. This beggar, all twenty-four hours, he is radiating, radiating, radiating. It's up to you to see it and to get it. But, once you come here and touch this gate, and chant once, only once, 'Yogi Ramsuratkumar,' then my Father does not send you away with an empty pocket. He puts something in your pocket. Just remember once, that is enough for you. Then you will start having evolution."
>
> Such a powerful mantra he leaves behind to us! Such a wonderful thing! And now it is everybody's duty to radiate, by living. By living! Our life should irradiate others. By living! It's very very essential to bring forth the necessary peace. It's not a cult, not a religion—it's a way of life. It's a state of being. It's a state of being he taught us, utterly! We are not here to create one more sect, one more cult, one more religion. No . . . let us live!

Yogi Ramsuratkumar often gave minute and subtle instruction in how to participate in his work by doing certain things for him, and in this, no single action was too small to be of great importance. When Yogi Ramsuratkumar was living on the streets in the bazaar he once told Joan Zulkowski that she could roll out his mat. He gave very explicit instructions on how to roll out his small rag, but she didn't do it properly. Immediately he said, "Stop!" He took the mat away from her and did it himself, saying, "Please Joan, sit down."

Joan sat down, but inwardly she was boiling mad. Yogi Ramsuratkumar looked over at her and said, "Will, Joan thinks this beggar is very arrogant." Later she told Will, "I was thinking exactly that same thing!" Will remembered this moment:

> There were no secrets with Swami. I was always out in the open. I always thought, "Well, these saints really know every thought, so you can't hide anything from them, so there's no pretending to be little Mr. Goody Two Shoes." All these people come around and all of a sudden they're so holy, when they don't live a life like that. That's all fake, and the saints know it. They're not fooling anybody . . . .
>
> Once I started thinking about my house upstate [in Hilda's community], "Oh man, these people are bugging me and it's just too much politics and I just want to get out of here. Maybe I'll move to California." So I go to see Swami, he's down at Sannadhi Street, and I go in the gate,

> and he looks at me. I'm the only one there, and he takes a look at me and says, "Will, I don't like that thought you're having." I didn't say a word. It was my first day there, my first one minute there—I hadn't seen him for a year. He just greeted me and said, "I don't like that thought. Please change that thought. That thought is disturbing this beggar." He said, "This beggar is only happy when you're there." That was the first thing he said, and he didn't even have to ask me what the thought was. I knew exactly what he was talking about. That is how attuned he was.

In the mid-seventies Will and Joan were waiting for Yogi Ramsuratkumar at the railway station, and they met and befriended an Indian man who knew the beggar. He said that he had seen almost all the saints in India; he had made many pilgrimages to holy places and met many saints, but Yogi Ramsuratkumar was the most carefree, joyous and happy. He said that when he went to gurus, he never asked for anything. He always made it a point never to ask for anything specific—he just asked for the guru's grace.

"Well, what can this beggar do for you?" Yogi Ramsuratkumar asked him once.

"Give me your grace, Swami, that's all I want—your grace," was his reply.

Will knew a Westerner named David Rothman who was a very successful lawyer in San Francisco. When he went to meet Yogi Ramsuratkumar he was one of a group of people who were there. The beggar went around the room and asked everybody what they wanted. Different people asked for different things, but David said, "I just want whatever you want to give me."

"All right," the yogi said, "I'll make all your decisions for you."

Somehow this lawyer was able to by-pass the mind and go right to the core of the situation: to ask for what the master wanted to give him, rather than what he himself would ask for from his limited perspective of desire and illusion. In this way he put himself at the mercy of the guru's grace in that moment, and therefore submitted to the will of God.

Yogi Ramsuratkumar demanded that his devotees do things his way, and that often meant there was no room for leaps of assumption or for taking certain kinds of initiative. Instead of rationalizing how reality should be from the linear perspective of the mind, Bhagawan developed in his devotees a great capacity to trust in the guru and trust in the innate magic and goodness of life itself. He instructed Mani and Raji in the fine art of surrender and obedience on countless occasions. As Mani said, "He was teaching me; he was guiding me; he was molding me—every second!"

Once eight dignitaries came to the ashram. Raji went to Yogi Ramsuratkumar to offer to bring drinks to Bhagawan and his guests. She said, "Bhagawan, I can give you some coffee and biscuits."

"No!" he commanded. "You bring nine cups of water!" Instantly she realized her mistake: she should have asked him what he wanted, instead of telling him what she would do.

On another occasion a rainstorm was on its way. Clouds were amassing in the sky and all the signs of a good rain were in the air. Mani went to Bhagawan and said, "Bhagawan, we should stop the work," meaning the construction that was underway.

"Stop the work?" Yogi Ramsuratkumar said, incredulously "No!" He smoked two cigarettes and the clouds went away. The rest of the day he was saying, with a touch of irony, "Mani was talking about some rain . . .!"

The lesson, in Mani's words, was one of absolute obedience: "You should not think, but just do as he says." This became easier and easier to do, because Yogi Ramsuratkumar proved time and again to Mani that he was working beyond the ordinary laws of the earthly realm.

One day Yogi Ramsuratkumar called Mani to him and asked, "Mani, do we have that book, *Hunger of Love*, on the ashram?"

Mani responded that he hadn't seen it, and he wasn't sure of its whereabouts.

"This beggar would like to see it. You will find it," he instructed firmly, and left in his car for Sudama House.

That afternoon Mani went to the ashram library and asked the librarian for another book he was looking for, *Guru's Grace*. When the librarian handed it to him, *Hunger of Love* fell out of it. It was one of countless small miracles that happened daily in Yogi Ramsuratkumar's company.

Yogi Ramsuratkumar often said that everything comes through grace; everything is experienced through grace. He said that he himself was nobody; he just prayed to serve his Father perfectly, and then grace came in. People who were open to him got that grace, and those who weren't open went away empty-handed, but with blessings from him nonetheless. The important thing was to somehow by-pass the mind.

In November 1992 a young man named Makarand Paranjape, a scholar, poet, novelist and literary critic as well as associate professor at the Indian Institute of Technology in Delhi, was visiting the Sri Aurobindo Ashram in Pondicherry, for the first time. There he befriended a man who invited him to come to Tiruvannamalai. They arrived in the city and spent the afternoon at Ramanashram, then went to the Shiva temple and bowed at its gates before heading toward the small house on Sannadhi Street. Makarand wrote:

> The room was dark. Behind me were some ladies, singing. One of them I would later identify as Ma Devaki. There were other devotees beside Bhagawan. But, wonder of wonders, he was smoking! I was surprised. There were packets of Charminar cigarettes lying strewn about near him. There were also heaps of flowers and fruit. I made my *pranams* and my offerings. Bhagawan did not seem much interested in me. He was speaking to some other devotees in Tamil. He would also burst out laughing, in a happy and child-like glee, from time to time. His face, hidden behind a white beard, was radiant and his eyes shone with merriment. He would ask other people to read to him and he would ask

> them questions every now and then. One young man entered, prostrated, left a card at His feet, and went away. When it was read, it turned out to be an invitation to his impending wedding! Before Bhagawan could properly bless him, he had disappeared. Everyone laughed.
>
> Bhagawan now turned to me. His gestures were unhurried and measured, as if he had all the time in the world.[14]

A short dialogue ensued, in which Yogi Ramsuratkumar asked Makarand his name, which he repeated twice. He paused for a moment.

"What are you doing?" the beggar asked.

"I am writing a book on Sarojini Naidu," Makarand replied.

"Sarojini Naidu. Good. Very great lady," the beggar commented reasonably. After a while he said, "I want to do a lot of business with you."

Makarand had never had anything to do with business, having only been a student and then a teacher. In fact, he came from a family of scholars. It was the first hint he received that the beggar's way of teaching was not going to appease or court the rational mind—a particular challenge to one so highly educated and steeped in academia.

Yogi Ramsuratkumar handed him an apple and said, "Makarand Paranjape, my Father blesses you. You may go now." Prostrating before the great yogi, Makarand received two hard pats on his back—the blows of grace that were characteristic of Yogi Ramsuratkumar's blessing. It was a simple beginning, and Makarand was drawn back again and again.

This lesson of going beyond the mind continued. Once Makarand was visiting Yogi Ramsuratkumar and they made a *pradakshina* around the mountain. After awhile Makarand's bare feet were hurting. He said nothing, but Yogi Ramsuratkumar commented, "Do your feet hurt?" Makarand answered yes.

"Keep walking and it will go away," the beggar advised.

By the time they had walked half way around the mountain the pain was completely gone.

During the nineties Makarand Paranjape regularly traveled all the way from Delhi to see Yogi Ramsuratkumar. Once he arrived in Tiruvannamalai at four-thirty in the morning. He decided to wait until the ten o'clock darshan at Sudama House to go to visit Yogi Ramsuratkumar because it was too early to intrude on the beggar. After a bath, he decided to walk barefoot up the mountain and go to one of the caves. The walk took much longer than he expected, and his feet were beginning to hurt. He wished for a pair of chappels (shoes), and suddenly his guide said, "Wait a minute," and he reached behind a rock and pulled out a pair of shoes, saying, "Put these on."

Finally he made it to Sudama House for the four o'clock queue and stood in line in the street. Someone came to the gate and said, "Are you Makarand Paranjape?"

14 Makarand Paranjape, "At the Feet of Yogi Ramsuratkumar," from the *Yogi Ramsuratkumar Souvenir Book*, pp. 387-388.

"Yes," he answered.

"Bhagawan has been waiting for you since four-thirty this morning!"

Stunned, Makarand made his way inside the house to the porch. As Makarand was prostrating at his feet, Yogi Ramsuratkumar said to him, "Arunachala has played a trick on this beggar!"

In 1980 Hilda Charlton was talking with a large group at St. John of the Divine in New York City about how Yogi Ramsuratkumar worked, and she asked the question, "Do you think Yogi Ramsuratkumar is humble? Sri Raman, do you think he's humble?"

"Yes, I really think so," Sri Raman said.

"Will, do you think he's humble?" she asked.

"I definitely think he's tremendously humble," Will answered.

"Caylor, do you think he's humble?" she pressed on.

He responded, "I think there are two sides to the coin."

"I do too," Hilda said, nodding her head, "I sure do, kids."

Caylor continued, "Because at other times he affirms exactly who he is. Only in very special, wonderful moments will he say with no reservation who he is and what he is doing on this planet. Otherwise he plays out different roles and faces."

Then Hilda spoke, saying, "I think he hides behind that screen . . . and then I also think he is teaching us humility—how to act. For example, what he said to Lila. He said, 'I never forgive anybody. They kicked me out of [Ramanashram] and I didn't have anywhere to go. I have never forgotten that.' Then he laughed. Then he said to Lila, 'Hilda forgives everything. Why don't you forgive everything?' You know, do you think he really meant that Hilda forgives everything and he doesn't? No. I just think he was teaching us. I don't think he's humble at all, because I think to be humble is a big ego [trip]. But to be neutral, neither swayed by praise nor blame, yet knowing what you are and not flaunting it—that is a state of Godliness. All that humility stuff is just to teach all of us not to think we're big guys. You understand? That's what I think."

Sri Raman said that there were two things that struck him about Yogi Ramsuratkumar: his humility and his incredible sense of humor. He was so open that it seemed you could talk with him about anything. He spoke perfect English, so you could come to him with any question and he would answer it.

Then Sri Raman said, "Those of you who have not been there to see him would be surprised by the fact that he smokes. But he doesn't smoke for physical enjoyment. Other yogis who have met him suggest that it is his way of burning up other people's negativity—negative thought creations or karma at a subtle level. It is a fact that he only smokes when he is in the company of guests. He is helping people in that way by doing that. This is difficult to understand; like so many aspects of spiritual life, if you try to reason it out with the logical mind, it's very difficult. He was so unpredictable that you never really knew what he was going to do next."

Despite the fact that Yogi Ramsuratkumar appeared as a beggar dressed in rags, sitting out on the streets or up in the Theradi Mandapam, on the porch of the tiny house at Sannadhi Street or later at Sudama House, there was a very definite protocol around him. It was absolutely necessary to bring sensitivity to that protocol if one wanted to participate in his *lila* and receive what the teaching he had to offer.

Once a Russian-Jewish woman came to see him. She had been at Amritananda Mayi's ashram, and when she came to Yogi Ramsuratkumar's darshan at Sudhama House, he said, "Please sit here," pointing right to the spot. She sat there, but then she got up and walked assertively over to Ma Devaki.

"I want to ask Swami a question," she said. She was asked again to sit down and return to her seat, which she did. A few minutes later, she got up, walked over to Ma Devaki and asserted again that she had a question to ask. When that happened Yogi Ramsuratkumar said, "This beggar will be leaving you now," which meant that it was time for her to go, in no uncertain terms.

Yogi Ramsuratkumar always orchestrated the space he was in, and part of that included instructing people in where to sit. At the Theradi Mandapam and in Sannadhi Street, there was usually just a candle burning at night; all that could be seen was the glow of his cigarette when he said to people, "You sit here." Often he would guide them by walking over and actually putting them where he wanted them to be: "You sit here. You sit here. You sit here, and you sit here." Nevertheless, people still wanted to get up, move around or completely change their seat. Then he would get up and put them back in their seat, saying, "This is your seat. Right here. Please don't leave it."

Will spoke about the necessity for honoring this kind of instruction and protocol around a saint, which he learned from his years with Yogi Ramsuratkumar:

> Swami did give us good training, just to be around him every day and to be always thinking of how could we serve him: What exactly is he going to need next? How are we going to respond? There was always an anticipation of what would be the next thing he would want.
>
> Hilda used to say, "Will and Joan are the only ones who show me the proper respect. They know what the proper respect is, and the rest of you don't have a clue." They argued with her. They had differences of opinion. I always said what I thought but I never challenged her, like, "You're wrong." But people did that all the time. They just didn't have any idea that when you were around somebody who has that wisdom and intelligence—that level of awareness—you're not in a position to argue with them. You shouldn't be in a position to argue with them, anyway; it shows your stupidity, your egotism, your grossness. It's not something you should be proud of! You should be really humble about your own stupidity, you know. I found that quite the contrary with some people's actions around saints.

If one was willing to pay attention and bring some humility and sensitivity to the situation, Yogi Ramsuratkumar would train people in how to serve him and how to participate in his *lila*, or to serve his work. Lee Lozowick spoke about how any small request from Yogi Ramsuratkumar was an opportunity to serve his work, but he often made it crystal clear by actually saying, "Would you like to do some work for this beggar?" So often people want to be given glorious jobs by the master—something prestigious that will bring accolades and acknowledgments, feed one's sense of self-importance. But for the master, all work was the same. Lee said in a talk during Yogi Ramsuratkumar's darshan in 1998:

> Yogi Ramsuratkumar's entire life—every movement, every gesture and word—is work for God. We have our personal needs, but then there is what God needs of us. Each of us is unique—not separate from God, but individual also. Each of us has specific work to do for Father in heaven. The blessings of Yogi Ramsuratkumar can allow us to do the work of Father in heaven in our lives, the work that we have come here to do. We each have a unique service that we are to do for Father in heaven. Maybe the unique service of the man in the tea stall was just to give tea to Yogi Ramsuratkumar once a month. Maybe that was his work for Father in heaven in this life. Maybe our unique work for Father in heaven is not to change the world, to feed everyone, but just to bring tea to a great being like Yogi Ramsuratkumar.

Yogi Ramsuratkumar put a tremendous amount of energy into every action; the smallest acts were meaningful, saturated with his power to bless, and it was a force that could be tangibly felt. For example, the beggar once told Will and Joan that he always put something—a blessing of some kind—into the letters he wrote. People who corresponded with him over the years realized that the letter itself carried such "joy and happiness" it would just "come over you," as Will described it.

The importance of something like a letter to Yogi Ramsuratkumar was demonstrated once when Joan was taking a letter to be mailed for him. It was during the mid-seventies, and they were out in the fields with him. He had just received a letter from Sri Raman, an elderly Westerner who knew the yogi well and corresponded with him.

"Could I carry it back?" Joan asked, after Yogi Ramsuratkumar had finished writing the letter.

"Yes, but keep it in a newspaper," he cautioned.

"No, no, it'll be all right. I'm just going to keep it in my hand," Joan insisted. It was a long walk from where they were to the post office in town—perhaps half an hour—and it was very hot. Joan's fingers were sweaty, and it made a hole in the envelope. When Swami saw that, he was very angry.

"What? You spoiled this!" he almost shouted. Then he said that he had to make an energetic adjustment, so he drew a circle around the hole and held the letter, but he told Joan it would never be the same. It could never be the same.

On another occasion the yogi sent Joan and Will to the post office to mail something for him. They took off walking and after three or four steps they turned back to ask him how he wanted the letter sent. He was furious with them, saying, "Once this beggar sends you, you don't turn back. You don't break the momentum of what this beggar is doing." He was extremely sensitive to the energetic matrix of the work he was conducting, and very strict in protecting that work.

A similar example occurred when Chandra Swami sent Yogi Ramsuratkumar a gift of a shawl on his *jayanthi* in 1997. Yogi Ramsuratkumar wrote a letter to him immediately, and asked Lee in darshan to have one of his students take it to the post office. Lee gave the letter to Tom Lennon, saying, "Don't do anything else. Don't stop for anything. Just take this and go right there as fast as you can and come back here." With one of Yogi Ramsuratkumar's attendants with him, Tom ran to the ashram gate. He recounted:

> It took awhile to get through town in the jitney, and one of Yogi Ramsuratkumar's attendants went with me, so we went through the post office and I did exactly what the attendant told me to do. This was an internal letter, and somehow the clerks demanded that we go to the international letter table, and I paid eleven rupees to send this half-rupee letter. We were on the way back and the man stops the jitney, and I said, "No, no, no," and he said, "One minute." He jumped out and he went to do some personal business. So I got back to the ashram and it must have been over half an hour.
>
> I went running into the temple, and I could feel that something was going on. Lee said, "All Yogi's been doing is asking 'Where is he?' ever since you left."
>
> Yogi Ramsuratkumar had stopped everything until I got back and he knew that the letter had been mailed. I never realized how important it was. I felt bad because I didn't know that Yogi Ramsuratkumar was asking about the letter. When I realized how he had waited and kept asking, "Where is he? He should be back by now," really made an impact on me. And we really hustled, but it wasn't fast enough.
>
> Lee explained later that Yogi's mind was focused on getting that letter where it needed to go, and until I came back, that was unfinished business for him. For him, that letter had to get out right away, so there was a great lesson for me. We take things casually, but for him everything is very serious. Timing is everything. I learned a big lesson about paying attention and doing exactly what you're told.
>
> But that wasn't the end of it. After I got back, I went up to the dais and Yogi Ramsuratkumar said, "How did it go?" I said, "Fine."
>
> "Ask him how much he paid," he said to Ma Devaki. She asked me.
>
> "Eleven rupees," I said.
>
> "Ohhh!" Yogi Ramsuratkumar said, then he started laughing and

> slapping his leg, and everybody was laughing along. He whacked me on the back.
>
> There was no way for me to explain it—I wasn't looking good, let me tell you that! It was eleven rupees to mail that letter! But, to see him laugh and laugh as heartily as he did . . . that was worth it.

The beggar dressed in rags was meticulous in many ways; he always wanted things done in a crisp and timely manner, and he was a perfectionist about being on time. Also a stickler for being on time and efficient energy management, Lee had a natural radar for what Yogi Ramsuratkumar wanted in this regard.

Lee and company—thirty-five people—planned to leave the ashram at midnight on December 10, 1998 to go to northern India where they would travel for two weeks. Earlier that day, when Yogi Ramsuratkumar had asked Lee what time he planned to leave, Lee said, "Twelve o'clock, midnight."

At fifteen minutes till midnight, about twelve people waited with Lee in the dark, wet van for the other two vans that were parked at the ashram gate, waiting to be loaded with luggage and people. Outside a drenching rainstorm raged, and several people were straggling behind. As midnight drew closer there still seemed to be some confusion with the other vans. Lee turned to Tom Lennon and said, "Go tell Purna that we leave at midnight whether the other vans are ready or not. We leave at *exactly* midnight! They can catch up with us later, at the airport, if they need to." Not even a slow-moving, unwieldy or unresponsive group of thirty-five people would prevent Lee from keeping his word to his Father, or from staying in alignment with the blessing force that Yogi Ramsuratkumar was unquestionably pouring his way.

A similar teaching lesson had been made just the day before, when Dan Fitz had left to accompany Alain de Rosenbo to the airport to catch his plane back to France. Lee had instructed Dan, "You leave at two-thirty and two-thiry *exactly*—not 2:31, but two-thirty," because that was the time of departure Alain had given to Yogi Ramsuratkumar in the morning darshan, when Yogi Ramsuratkumar said that he would come from Sudama House to the ashram to see Alain off. Lee was determined that the master would not have to wait for even one minute for late devotees.

Yogi Ramsuratkumar's expectation of his devotees was a radical one. Because his way of working was both universal and highly individual, each devotee seemed to understand a facet of the diamond that was Yogi Ramsuratkumar. The closer one came to him, however, the greater the demand was to not only understand his context of life and surrender to the will of God, but to come to embody the example of his life and teaching.

Yogi Ramsuratkumar gave everyone opportunities to work for him as a way of teaching and as a way of offering transformational blessings. Lee Lozowick commented:

> Whenever Yogi Ramsuratkumar was sitting with devotees and he needed something done, some task, he would always say to one or another of the people there, "Would you like to do some work for this beggar?"

> We were there one day and he turned to one of his Indian devotees and he said, "Would you like to do some work for this beggar?" The man said, "Yes," and Yogi Ramsuratkumar said, "Go and bring some tea for these friends."
>
> When Mr. Mani came to Yogi Ramsuratkumar and he was asked if he wanted to "work for this Beggar," and he said yes, the result was an ashram, a temple, an entire sanctuary. But Yogi Ramsuratkumar was just as grateful for the tea as he was for the temple, because everybody has their particular work for Father. What makes us all equal, exactly equal, is that we do Father's work with faith, with confidence and with integrity.
>
> There were some people in Tiruvannamalai who felt that Yogi Ramsuratkumar had a bias towards Westerners, towards rich people and so on. No! No! There was never any question of caste! No question of class! No question of skin color, religion! No question! As Pon Kamaraj said when Yogi Ramsuratkumar asked, "Do you want to do some work for this beggar?" only one thing mattered—absolute obedience. Money did not build Yogi Ramsuratkumar's ashram in Tiruvannamalai; faith and obedience did.
>
> Every single devotee is equal. When you come to the true guru there is no question of big work and little work—it's all just work. You can't expect a cook to be an engineer and you can't expect a man who is an engineer or a lawyer to be a mother. Everybody has their work, so I would like everybody to feel that they are absolutely equal in the eyes of the guru and in the heart of the guru.[15]

In the mid- and late seventies Yogi Ramsuratkumar had a particular *lila* that he played out with the women devotees. Going against strict social convention, he would often gently touch these devotees, ask them to light his cigarettes or to serve him in some other small task. In India there is a strict protocol of relationship between the sexes; it is not considered proper for a man of any age to engage intimate friendships or physical interactions of even the most innocent kind with women. Even husbands and wives do not show physical affection for each other in public. These women devotees had their entire attention focused on Yogi Ramsuratkumar, and it was a very intense and challenging time for them, in which they had to stretch themselves to understand the master's paradoxical behavior.

Parthasarathy said, "Swamiji would touch those ladies, and he would ask those ladies to light cigarettes, just to drive away the unserious people." Those who allowed their societal conditioning or conservative prejudices rule were nonplussed or insulted by such an unconventional holy man: "This Swami smokes? Then he can't be a swami! This swami never takes baths? Then how can he be a swami?" By enacting this shocking and

15 Lee Lozowick, December 7, 2001, Mayamma Mayamma Samajan, Kanya Kumari.

provocative relationship with his women devotees, and by many other actions such as his unpredictable moods, actions and fits of ecstasy, or his smoking, Yogi Ramsuratkumar effectively drove away about half of his would be "devotees." These were the people who weren't serious enough to look at things more deeply. Parthasarathy remembered how radical the master's actions were during this time:

> But Swamiji is not a male or a female. He remains a mystery. No, no one would approve, for a lady to light a cigarette! Particularly in Indian culture it is not proper. Whenever I would come to Swami, I would come alone, without my family. Even if my mother saw me lighting a cigarette for Swami, my mother would not understand! So I would not force my guru on them. If they wanted a guru, they could go on their own. I would never induce people to go to Swami.
>
> He would not obey any laws, rules. He was violating every rule. Whatever he says *is* the rule, *is* the law! He was totally revolutionary—totally revolutionary! Many years ago in Ramanashram [in 1959], a very close devotee of Ramana came to Swami and started instructing him. He said, "Whenever you come to the ashram you should take a bath and you should come neat and clean." Swami said, "Don't try to teach this beggar. If you want to know anything from this beggar, you come and touch this beggar's feet, and you will be knowing everything." But there was another disciple of Ramana, Sundareshan, who knew about Swami, and he started saying to people, "He is a great yogi."
>
> Swami told me, "Sundareshan first called this beggar 'yogi.' " Very few people know about that. It was Sundareshan.

Parthasarathy, who has been a devotee of Yogi Ramsuratkumar since 1976, spoke about his guru's radical way of living the highest dharma. Parthasarathy's observation was that devotees could only remain very close to Yogi Ramsuratkumar for a limited number of years before they were expected to live in resonance with the guru without the help—or the "crutch," in some cases—of the guru's physical presence. In short, although guru yoga remained the path, Yogi Ramsuratkumar did not want people to be dependent upon his form, but to begin to contemplate the guru within themselves. One could not go on relying upon the guru's physical presence indefinitely, or else be driven away or parted from him in one way or another.

Perhaps in a similar vein, Caylor Wadlington spoke about how many countless lives were touched by Yogi Ramsuratkumar, people who were close to the beggar at different times of his life and particularly in the early years, who would remain unknown. These are the people who "faded away" and went on with their lives, but the experience of being in the company of Yogi Ramsuratkumar remained unforgettable—they found themselves forever changed. Caylor reflected in January, 2003:

There were dozens of people like me who had some duration of ongoing contact with Yogi Ramsuratkumar, where there were teachings and *lilas*—all of them were Indian people. I never met them; they were there in the 1960s, in the 1950s. I don't know any of them, but I know that they existed. Every now and then I would encounter someone, like an Ayurvedic doctor in Madras, who knew Yogi Ramsuratkumar from years ago, long before I'd been in India. So there was a big block of time where there were people involved in his life and his work who are forgotten. He had unbelievable meetings with people; he met some of India's greatest people, some of the greatest sages and seers, and all of that's forgotten!

He was the center of my universe and my guru, my all and all. He was an enormous heart teacher—he exists inside of me. There were all these interactions between us and all kinds of creativity happened as a result of us connecting, but then years passed and he only heard from me once a year, and then once every few years, when Will would bring back a little letter or something. So there was a time when our connection together created all kinds of sparks and changes in me and in him. There was a lot of interaction and a dynamic effect in me, at least, and an effect of bringing other people to know about him. But now there are other people who are really the catalyst for that.

What remains for me is just him within me . . . . His expression in my outer world is fading out till what is left is just he and I, in my heart. It's not about me; it's about him, so if I fade out, like so many of those people who once knew him and had been impacted by him but are forgotten, it's alright.

Yogi Ramsuratkumar often said that when people—this guru or that master—attained nirvana or samadhi, the great attainment was to end the cycle of rebirth. But he said, "This beggar doesn't know about those kind of things. This beggar only wants to be reborn here forever." He would often say, "This beggar will be coming back forever." And so for him, certainly from his point of view, [his time with me was] just a little chapter. I'm certainly not enlightened or liberated from the cycle of rebirth, but even if I were, I have the same sentiment as him: if I had something to give or offer, a capacity to serve or save others from suffering, I would always come back.

He's influenced me a lot even in that one remark, that one sentiment. It used to shock me when I would hear him say that, because I would ask him, "Are you liberated?" or use some word like that. He'd go, "Hah!" and he'd come around to this remark about always coming back. I must have heard him say it three or four times over the years, and it always used to amaze me because it came from such a huge heart place—just a humongous, giant heart place. Somehow he was trivializing it to such a

> degree in the manner in which he said it, that it was stunning and shocking. You realized that he had just said something that was really big, in a very off-the-cuff manner. So I often thought about that. Even that single memory of him saying that, who knows how much it has affected me? It's hard to measure, but it's a huge, huge impression.

Obedience

Yogi Ramsuratkumar often trained his devotees by giving them opportunities to learn lessons the hard way—through personal experience—knowing that there were times when this was the only way that an individual could mature. A striking example of this occurred when a young woman appeared in the street outside Sudama House. She was in her early thirties, but she looked much younger. She had serious emotional problems, and she would sit or sleep in the street outside Sudama House near the gutter where there were snakes, centipedes and scorpions. She seemed ill, and her coughing and generally poor condition attracted the sympathy of the Sudama sisters. Finally they approached Bhagawan about her.

"Take pity on her," Devaki pleaded with Bhagawan. "Why don't we call her and help her, Bhagawan? Such a young girl sleeping all alone in the dead of the night—do you see her?" Yogi Ramsuratkumar said nothing, but his silence spoke volumes, and in his wisdom, he did not invite the unfortunate women into the house.

Nonetheless, the pathos of the young woman's plight touched the hearts of the Sudama sisters. At night the woman would come at eight or nine o'clock, lay some newspapers down on the ground and then lie down in the street outside the garden wall. Devaki and the Sudama sisters were afraid she would be bitten by snakes or centipedes, and they saw that she had one sari to cover herself. The household servants tried to drive the woman away, saying that she was a mad person and she ought not be encouraged. They warned, "She will make trouble."

Yogi Ramsuratkumar understood dimensions of the situation that the women could not see, and recognized the way of real compassion. He knew the psychology of the young woman and recognized that she had serious mental problems. He also knew that showing her pity would ultimately not be of any benefit to her, and would only land Devaki and the Sudama sisters in trouble. Ma Devaki recounted:

> So, he knew the whole picture even then; in his wisdom, he was keeping quiet, but stupid me wouldn't let him. And I kept on asking, begging him, "Bhagawan! Why can't we call her? At least we can give her a sari, Bhagawan, she doesn't have anything. She's very young."
>
> "All right. You call her," he said, in that way that he knows something

> will happen. She came inside and she was very nice. She spoke excellent English and she spoke very, very sensibly.
>
> When he gave her a new sari, she said, "No, I don't want a new sari. What will I do with a new sari in the street? It will only bring me trouble." She said, "Give me used clothes, that would do for me." And it sounded perfect; it sounded very reasonable. So, we were very impressed with her and we were wondering why Bhagawan should take it up like that.

Things went along for a short while, but soon the woman began to make demands. As long as they gave her everything she wanted, all was fine, but then she demanded a place to stay on the ashram. Bhagawan said, "We don't have that kind of place here in the ashram." In a few days she was making more demands, and a family gave her shelter. She began to throw tantrums, and although the family was willing to give her a room for a few days because of Bhagawan, they were unable to handle her.

Her demands became greater and greater. She wanted to see her mother, and she expected Bhagawan and the Sudama sisters to give her whatever she wanted. Soon she became outright abusive; she was screaming and yelling at Bhagawan, cursing and calling people names. One night at nine o'clock she came to the street outside Sudama House and started screaming in the quiet of the night.

"Devaki! Prostitute! You are a prostitute!" she screamed, "Rowdy Ramsuratkumar! Come out!" She spoke in the filthiest language possible and it went on and on until eleven-thirty or twelve o'clock that night, until her throat became so hoarse that she couldn't yell any more. She was too tired to speak.

After that she sent letters of abuse, demanding money: "You have to pay me ten lakhs." That is when Devaki and Vijayalakshmi understood why Bhagawan had kept quiet when they insisted on helping her. It was a hard and bitter lesson, but one that Yogi Ramsuratkumar allowed the women to learn well, through direct experience. Devaki recounted:

> Bhagawan's every move, every gesture was pure wisdom. You see, when she was in that condition, it was we people who pitied her and invited trouble on ourselves. And when she started shouting we could not stand it; I was getting all worked up and tense. Whenever I heard somebody mention her name, or I saw her at the corner of the street, something would be crawling over me. I used to get that kind of feeling. But Bhagawan took it all very quietly—very, very quietly—and he would still work Father's blessings on her. He helped her with whatever money she demanded—except in *lakhs*, of course, we couldn't afford it. But thousands [of rupees] we always gave, and hundreds. Six hundred, five hundred. Once she wanted two thousand, and the money was given to her. We arranged for food for her. When she was staying in the ashram, she was still very abusive but still Bhagawan used to send the gardeners with

> food to the ashram where she was residing and she would be fed there. Imagine, it was such royal treatment for her, for someone who abuses so much! The ashram paid the rent for her room and arranged food. You need a lot of patience to live with a saint!
>
> He listened to us, and we learned the hard way. I was the one mostly hit by that. Somehow she chose Bhagawan and me as targets, and it was I who invited the trouble in the first place also. (Laughter) It all boomeranged on me. But he used to say, "Keep those letters safely there. They're all blessings pouring like rain from Father." He had a sense of humor also. Sometimes he would say it humorously, sometimes he would say it seriously. But always he used the word "blessing"—blessings from Father.

Obedience to the guru often demands that we listen to the guru's silences, as in this case, and this may be one of the hardest lesson of all. Slowly, through obedience, the devotee comes to know from his or her own experience to trust the wisdom of the guru, and to listen to the communication that is being made, whether it is spoken or wordless.

Obedience is crucial to the path of guru yoga, and Yogi Ramsuratkumar expected absolute obedience from those who deeply committed to the path of grace in his company. The guru builds the capacity for obedience in the disciple, because it is implicitly necessary in becoming resonant with the guru's state of being.

Lee Lozowick frequently says that his relationship with his master was one of obedience. He is fond of telling stories about how Yogi Ramsuratkumar worked directly with him to craft obedience, including the following one, when he was obedient to Yogi Ramsuratkumar, even when he didn't want to be—with an amazing outcome.

> Yogi Ramsuratkumar was always asking me to do things like, "Go speak to these Westerners and see what they want." So I would go and talk to them. Sometimes he would say, "Go sit over there in the corner and talk to them." He was always networking, putting me together with people, and I really didn't like it, but I always did exactly what he said, to the best of my ability. So I would be sitting over in the corner and He would look over every few minutes, because when He said, "Talk to them," He meant, "Talk to them," not, "Sit together and look at me."
>
> If I've ever had one big problem, it is being social. So, Yogi Ramsuratkumar is always putting me in these social situations. I am his man though, so he says, "Organize these things, handle these people, talk to them, figure things out."
>
> One time he called me up and said that he wanted me to meet an American man whose name I'd heard, but I had no idea who he was, where he lived or if he was even alive anymore. I was really thinking, "How am I going to find this guy in two hundred millions Americans?" So with a voice that was somewhat tainted with the belief that I was going to fail, I

> said, "I'll try."
>
> Yogi Ramsuratkumar was in a fabulous mood on this day, and He was laughing! He hit me on the back and said, "Lee won't try—he *will*!"
>
> I went back to America and said to one of my students, "I've got to find this guy." She said, "Well, I'm on the Internet. Let's just plug his name in and see what happens." Wonder of wonders! The guy specialized in Oriental medicine and he had a website! So she plugged his name in and poof! It popped out. As I found out later, he had been writing to Yogi Ramsuratkumar all along. Yogi Ramsuratkumar had his address, and He didn't tell me where he was! He let me find out myself because it was my task and I was mature enough not to need a little push to get rolling.
>
> So I called the guy up and said, "Yogi Ramsuratkumar gave me your name and asked if I would get together with you." The guy was very surprised and said, "Okay, why not?" This was not like being in India on the ashram and going up and speaking with someone at Yogi Ramsuratkumar's request. This was in America; the guy lived in a different state, I had to get it together to get a plane ticket, had to take time from my life to fly to where this guy was living. He wasn't going to fly to me, that's for sure. He was willing to meet me, but he wasn't going to change his schedule for it, so I had to fit into his schedule. It all depended on me to make the thing happen.
>
> I made it happen, eventually. I met the guy and discovered that he had this tremendous treasure of thirty-year-old photographs of Yogi Ramsuratkumar and all this kind of thing. I was being very covetous, you know. I wanted the photos, so I said, "Ah, this is really nice," and he said, "I don't really want it. I don't want to have anything to do with it. I offered to give it to Yogi Ramsuratkumar, to give it all to him, since he gave it all to me to begin with. He said, 'No, you just keep it, and one day you'll know what to do with it.' This was twenty years ago. If you want it, you can have it." Of course, I took it! This whole process took a couple of months—two or three months—and I had no idea how it was going to turn out.[16]

The "guy" turned out to be Truman Caylor Wadlington, and the connection between Lee and Caylor resulted in the opening of a whole new possibility in documenting and archiving the life of Yogi Ramsuratkumar, but in the most delightful way. In this *lila* it seems that Yogi Ramsuratkumar linked Lee and Caylor in a way that would play a major role in future biographical projects about the beggar saint.

Obedience does not come easily to most people of the East or West, and lessons in obedience from Yogi Ramsuratkumar were often the most difficult, at times bringing out

16 Lee Lozowick, *Hohm Sahaj Mandir Study Manual* Volume IV, pp. 281-282.

the beggar's rarely shown wrathful side. Janarthanan relayed the following story of a teaching lesson that Yogi Ramsuratkumar made to him about following the guru's instructions:

> Once in the early eighties when we had gone to Swami, he expressed the need for photos and asked us to bring some during the next visit. When we went to Sivakasi, we found the photos were exhausted. I informed him by post.
>
> The next time I went to meet Swami at Sannadhi Street house, while opening the door itself, Swami said angrily, "Due to your negligence, you allowed this beggar's photographs to get exhausted." He took me inside and we spent more than three hours tallying the account. He said, "Normally those who commit such a great blunder will be stopped from coming here. Exemption is given because it is Janarthanan who did this blunder." Saying this, Swami took 1000 Rs. from his bag, gave it to Shivashankara and asked him to give it to Premkumar for buying paper and printing the photos. Again he said, "Last time you didn't take any money to print this. That is why you were careless to check the stock. This time you will be aware."
>
> When we printed the first lot, we had printed Swami's name as "Yogi Ram Surat Kumar, the God Child, Tiruvannamalai." This time Swami brought out the book by Truman Caylor Wadlington and said, "This time you have to print 'Yogi Ramsuratkumar, The Godchild Tiruvannamalai,' as printed in this book." (Yogi is one word; Ramsuratkumar is one word; Godchild is one word and Tiruvannamalai is one word.) Swami gave me a paper and asked me to write the name and address correctly, and then show it to him.[17]

Under the careful supervision of Janarthanan, the photos were reprinted, with the name printed as "His Holiness Yogi Ramsuratkumar, The Godchild, Tiruvannamalai," because it was Janarthanan's habit to address Yogi Ramsuratkumar in this way in his letters to him. He took the two hundred photos and offered them to the beggar, who opened the packet and accepted them. The last time Yogi Ramsuratkumar had given Janarthanan sixteen hundred rupees for the printing costs, he had simply donated it to Anandashram. This time Swami went inside the inner rooms of his house, brought out fourteen hundred rupees and said, "Some shop owners of this city used to take money from this beggar and mix it in their cash box with other money. They do so for prosperity for their businesses."

On returning to his office, Janarthanan took the cue from Yogi Ramsuratkumar and mixed the fourteen hundred rupees with the cash box money for his business. Two months

17 Janarthanan, *A Life With Truth*, unpublished manuscript.

later he met Yogi Ramsuratkumar again.

"This time also you spoiled this beggar's photograph!" the beggar said, pre-empting all other considerations. Not comprehending the problem at all, Janarthanan was shocked.

"How many times did I tell you that if you want to make any changes in this beggar's photo you must take permission from this beggar? Don't you know this? How can you add the words, 'His Holiness'? I don't feel like distributing these photos. This beggar gives the photograph to everyone by his own hands. While giving like that, how can he glorify himself by stating 'His Holiness'? "

Feeling contrite about his disobedience and misunderstanding the fine points of what his master wanted, Janarthanan quickly said that he would print them again and give them to Yogi Ramsuratkumar right away, but Swami refused by saying, "Father's will."

The lesson in obedience continued: The next time Janarthanan saw his master, Yogi Ramsuratkumar said, "Janarthanan, you have to be aware when you work for this beggar. Didn't you check while printing the photos this time?" Again Janarthanan was shocked.

"How many times this beggar has told you that the name of the beggar is more important than the form! The name is not at all there in the photos you have printed," he said, pointing to the offending photo. Then it dawned on Janarthanan that he was seeing one or two of the photos where the name was cut out due to quirks in the printing process; however, the majority were alright. Swami denied this angrily, saying, "So many photos are without name!"

Yogi Ramsuratkumar called Jayarama, who was attending to him then, and went back inside to look at the photos again. After checking further, he discovered that Janarthanan was right. He came back to the porch with a bright smile and said, "You are right, friend. Only one photo doesn't contain the name."

The teaching had gone from training in obedience to how to be gracious and concede when one is wrong—which Yogi Ramsuratkumar demonstrated by his own example.

A GREAT SENSE OF HUMOR

In December 1995 Lee Lozowick was visiting Yogi Ramsuratkumar with a number of students. One night they had gone into town and eaten some ice cream. One of the students, Steve Scheel, ate a liter and a half of ice cream and had gotten violently and deliriously ill. Fortunately Doctor Ramananda, the brother of Justice Arunachalam, was visiting the ashram, and Yogi Ramsuratkumar asked him to treat the young American and keep him closely informed of his condition.

The next morning in darshan the doctor reported on Steve's condition to Yogi Ramsuratkumar. He had given Steve intravenous liquids to hydrate him along with some medication, and he was swiftly on the way to recovery. In fact, he was well enough to come to darshan that morning and receive Yogi Ramsuratkumar's blessing.

Lee and his group were leaving for the States that day, and Yogi Ramsuratkumar began to inquire about their travel plans. Yogi Ramsuratkumar always wanted to know every detail, and Mani recounted Lee's itinerary almost down to the minute, relaying that they would spend one day in Madras before their flight left. He ended with, "They will go shopping in Madras for one day, Bhagawan."

"Oh yes!" Bhagawan quipped with a sparkle in his eye, "I hear they are having a big discount on ice cream!" He threw his head back and laughed uproariously. It was a great spontaneous joke that elicited hearty and joyous laughter from the whole group—a healing laughter. Regina Ryan wrote about this moment, "How sweet this beggar's laughter. How it opens the heart, empties the mind, and captivates the body."[18]

Laughter was a big part of Yogi Ramsuratkumar's "medicine," which he amply administered to his devotees. The sound of his laughter was a healing balm in and of itself, and he loved to joke around— bringing humor to a situation in a way that was not just harmless, but that actually healed and uplifted everyone involved. He could also deliver a "teaching blow" through humor—the kind of communication that went in because it was eased with the balm of laughter.

In the early years in the brass market Yogi Ramsuratkumar often used humor to distract unwanted seekers. When someone asked him, "Swami, what is kundalini?" he would say, "Oh, what does this beggar know about kundalini? That's for scholars and fake yogis!"

Later he wanted to take a nap and told Joan Zulkowski to wake him up at five p.m. When the time arrived, she said, "Swami, it's time for all good yogis to be up."

"How about fake yogis?" he joked, rousing himself. Will reflected on this story:

> He was really, really quick. He was totally alive in that instant, and that's why he was always fun. You always felt so spontaneously alive with him because he was always so charged, and every time we were with him, we kind of floated home. He was really a ball of light, a ball of fire. But we always had a lot of fun. He liked to laugh and he always made jokes—the jokes were always about himself and how crazy he was.

Once V. Ganeshan had gone to Varanasi, which is on the Ganges, to intensify his sadhana. Yogi Ramsuratkumar told him not to have any contact with the outside world, not even to write letters to his family and closest friends. After some time a friend of Ganeshan became worried about him and came to darshan, hoping that she could voice her concerns to Yogi Ramsuratkumar.

She was sitting near Bhagawan in darshan at the same time that a couple brought some sweets as a gift to Yogi Ramsuratkumar. Ganeshan's friend had been advised by her doctor to avoid all sweets, but as she sat quietly near Bhagawan, he kept feeding her the

18 Regina Sara Ryan, *Tawagoto*, Winter 1996, p. 36.

sweets while he talked with the couple. He showered the couple with loving concern and kept asking them questions—whether the husband was happy with the way the wife was taking care of him, how the food was—all the while he fed sweets to Ganeshan's friend.

Finally he asked the man, "What is your name, my friend?" The man looked surprised, because Yogiji had known them for years, but he answered, "Ganeshan." Then Bhagawan turned to the wife and asked, "And yours, my friend?" The wife was also puzzled but she answered, "Ganga." Yogi Ramsuratkumar roared with laughter and slapped his thigh, saying over and over again, "So Ganga is taking care of Ganeshan, Ganga is taking care of Ganeshan!" The friend, who had now eaten all of the sweets, smiled to herself at this secret joke, shared with Bhagawan, who seemed as delighted at the amazing synchronicity of the interchange as Ganeshan's friend was.[19]

In 1998 Ashish Bagrodia was talking with Yogi Ramsuratkumar and proposed that he come to bless his factory. He said, "We can charter a helicopter and take you to our factory, and we'll bring you back on the same day. Unfortunately there is no airport, otherwise we could charter a plane. Or, first we'll go to Madras and then take you by plane." The beggar kept laughing as Ashish came up with better scenarios for getting him to the factory.

Finally the beggar said, "No Ashish, this beggar is very dirty. People cannot accommodate him."

It took a few moments for Ashish to realize that he was just pulling his leg.

"See Bhagawan, you're pulling my leg. You don't want to come to our factory," Ashish countered.

"No, Ashish, this beggar is very weak. He can't pull anybody's leg. Other people pull his leg!" And then he started laughing.

Yogi Ramsuratkumar freely enjoyed both the giving and receiving of humorous repartee with his devotees and friends. In the latter years on the ashram a devotee named Padmanaban was earning sufficient money to send to Yogi Ramsuratkumar. One time he sent a little more money than usual to the ashram, and the next time he came to the ashram Bhagawan said, "How are you earning money? You are sending a lot of money to this beggar."

"You are giving; I am sending," Padmanaban joked. "There is no excitement in this! You are giving and I am sending." Bhagawan laughed and laughed.

Once a group of seekers came to Tiruvannamalai and wanted to meet Yogi Ramsuratkumar. One of them wanted to mine for gold in a mountainous region in the U.S. He had many photographs of the mountain from all angles and degrees and he wanted Yogi Ramsuratkumar to go through the file of photos.

Saravanan was standing on duty nearby when Bhagawan called him, indicated the thick file of photos and said, "Saravanan, you go through it and you tell me what is there

19 Vijayalakshmi, *Waves of Love*, pp. 48-49.

in the file." Saravanan was going through it, reading every page when Bhagawan said, "He is in need of a treasure. He is in need of a treasure! Oh, he needs a lot of money to do the work; it is a big project. How can you pay all the laborers?"

Saravanan immediately replied, "Bhagawan, after he finds the treasure, then he will pay all the laborers!" Yogi Ramsuratkumar laughed with unbridled enjoyment at the witticism, then kept laughing as he repeated the little joke over and over. "Oh Saravanan said . . . " Then he told Devaki Ma and everyone, "Oh Saravanan . . . ." It was a small thing, but the fullness of enjoyment that Yogi Ramsuratkumar brought to it had a healing effect on everyone around him.

Saravanan later said of this exchange, "It was just a joke, but have you heard him laugh? When he laughs, I feel that everyone in the world is laughing! It's a formless presence. An extraordinary being! Whenever you are with Bhagawan, you can *feel* each and every second."

In darshan Yogi Ramsuratkumar heard a story about Haridas, a very pious and holy man who was quite orthodox in his religious observance. He had unexpectedly fallen in a river and drowned. Immediately Yogi Ramsuratkumar quipped, with a hint of drollery, "Devaki, that's why this beggar doesn't take bath!" Then he laughed and laughed.

Bhagawan often joked around with everyone over breakfast in the hut, where both staff members and devotees were intimately gathered around him every day. One morning a woman came to the breakfast hut, and she was writing furiously in her notebook.

"What are you writing?" he asked.

"I am writing questions to ask you, Swamiji," she answered.

"How many questions are there?"

When she answered, "Ten," a little smile stole across his face.

"Ten questions! This beggar is not so competent to answer all your questions. You find somebody else!"

Like on this occasion, he was often laughing when he made such jokes, but the teaching that was encapsulated in his words could have the effect of hammering on the ego when the point struck home with impact. The woman's questions were nothing more than an intellectual exercise, a function of curiosity. Yogi Ramsuratkumar was teaching her that the price of the guru's wisdom is paid for by the innocence, sincerity and true need of the seeker. This time the guru's arrow hit its mark and the woman left, having been given something to reflect upon.

There were times when the ashram was so low on money that the devotees humorously considered with Yogi Ramsuratkumar all kinds of wild possibilities for making money, even joking that they would buy a lottery ticket. Once Janarthanan told Yogi Ramsuratkumar a story: Nityananda Swami, the great master of Muktananda, had constructed ashrams in quite a few places, one of which was in Kanhangad. During the construction, every day the devotees needed money for some new project, but they didn't have it. In the evening they would go to Nityananda and tell him that there was a need for money, but there wasn't any. Then he would put his hands out and the money would magically appear!

"You take the money," Nityananda would say, as he gave the money to them. Each time it was the exact amount of money that they needed!

Listening to Janarthanan's story of such high magic, Yogi Ramsuratkumar smiled and said wryly, "Janarthanan, this beggar hasn't got that much power at all!"

In 1993 Yogi Ramsuratkumar asked Lee Lozowick to explain to him about rock & roll, since Lee was in the unusual situation of being a spiritual teacher who performed in a rock band with some of his students. Lee gave Yogi Ramsuratkumar cassettes and videos of his band so he could see for himself what rock & roll was, and what Lee was doing with the music. When Yogi Ramsuratkumar, Ma Devaki and the Sudama sisters saw the video, it was outrageous by traditional Indian standards, but Yogi Ramsuratkumar was delighted by it. Ma Devaki humorously recalled:

> Lee was dancing this rock & roll! There were times I almost closed my eyes, I didn't want to see! The type of shirt he was wearing—I was scandalized looking at it! It was so strange, and Bhagawan was there laughing, laughing, laughing, "Oh that is Lee Lozowick!" Then Bhagawan would begin to dance like that. He would show his hand.
>
> I have seen Lee sitting still, speaking very little or not at all and then he opens his mouth freely only when he stands before people to make a certain point. Otherwise he just sits still and does not speak much. I've seen him instructing [his students] sometimes like the teacher, like a disciplinarian, very strict, but it was a totally different man on the stage. But he drew Bhagawan out and he began to dance, laughing!

Yogi Ramsuratkumar found great enjoyment in the comical remarks made by his devotees as well. Once when Bhagawan asked Lee to give a talk during darshan he started talking about a rock & roll song written and recorded by the Rolling Stones called "Under My Thumb." He used it as an example of his relationship with Yogi Ramsuratkumar. He said, "Yogi Ramsuratkumar keeps me under his thumb. I still get distracted, but if I get too far off it's like I have a chain around my neck and Yogi Ramsuratkumar pulls the chain, and back I go!" Yogi Ramsuratkumar's shoulders shook up and down as he laughed at this image. He covered his face with his hands as if he was both embarrassed and delighted. Everyone in the room laughed along with him. Lee was entertaining Yogi Ramsuratkumar. Lee concluded:

> Lee Lozowick is not very subtle. When a message comes to me I need it to be loud and clear, so Yogi Ramsuratkumar's blessings have always been loud and clear for me. They have been unmistakable! So even when I've tried to take the wrong fork in the road, the opportunity is clear, the way is clear and the signs from Yogi Ramsuratkumar are very clear. We see obstacles that seem like a mountain in the center of the road. We chant

> Yogi Ramsuratkumar's name and the obstacles clear away like morning mist under the hot sun and are gone. But we have to ask what is needed to serve him.[20]

In 1999 Will Zulkowski went to visit Yogi Ramsuratkumar. He asked, "Will, how many cigarettes are you smoking?"

"Oh, we're not smoking, Swami."

"Will, how many cigarettes again are you smoking?" he asked a few moments later.

"Swami, whenever I have the urge to smoke, I smoke through you!" The beggar loved this answer: he cracked up with laughter.

"Say a few words," Yogi Ramsuratkumar said to Lee in darshan one day in December, 1998. Lee began by saying that Yogi Ramsuratkumar only does what his Father in heaven tells him to do. Then he relayed how, a few years before, Yogi Ramsuratkumar had said to him, "Father blesses Lee with whatever he wants." Then he paused and restated it, saying, "Father blesses Lee with whatever he *needs.*"

Reflecting humorously on that moment, Lee smiled and said, "Father in heaven must have said, 'Wait a minute!' " Everyone laughed, especially Yogi Ramsuratkumar who looked up from his cigarette and laughed out loud, his shoulders shaking with mirth.

Lee has often spoken about humor being one of the most important forms of Yogi Ramsuratkumar's teaching:

> One of the things about Yogi Ramsuratkumar that was so deeply touching was his irrepressible humor. Yogi Ramsuratkumar expressed the complete range of feelings and moods and emotions; they were all just the flow of phenomena as the catalyst of the needs of his devotees or even of his environment. Whatever was demanded of him, he expressed—completely, spontaneously and naturally. It could be anger. As many people have said, when he was angry, as soon as his anger had served its purpose it was gone, absolutely gone. It was one of the most miraculous things, because we get angry when somebody does something we don't like, and we talk to the person to resolve the situation, but we stay angry. We get up the next day and we're still angry. Yogi Ramsuratkumar would be angry and then it was finished in the next instant! You'd say, "How? How did He do that?"
>
> Well, of course, the point was, he didn't do it. Yogi Ramsuratkumar's moods and emotions and feelings were like physics. When we study the science of physics we usually study very impersonal energy forces and how they interplay with reality. Well, there are also the physics of the master. It's like Yogi Ramsuratkumar's response to the circumstance was

20 Lee Lozowick, December 1998, Yogi Ramsuratkumar Ashram.

> just physics—the physics of God in human form. So he would respond as needed, and as soon as the response had had its effect there was no residual, no effect, nothing left. His mood was completely burnt up, and even if there were ashes left it was the feeling in the person who He touched of love and faith and surprise and so on.[21]

Even in his last days Yogi Ramsuratkumar could bring levity to his situation. Mani said, "Sometimes a devotee would ask Bhagawan, 'How are you?' He would answer, 'Not dead, still living!' "

THE BEGGAR AND HIS POLITICS

On August 14, 1947 India finally gained independence from the yoke of British colonization after a long, bitter and arduous struggle. It was the same year that Yogi Ramsuratkumar left his family home in Bihar to visit Sri Aurobindo, Ramana Maharshi and Swami Ramdas, beginning in earnest his search for freedom from the world of illusion and separation. During the years of the fight for independence, Yogi Ramsuratkumar was a young schoolteacher who was deeply concerned for the fate of India. He had tremendous respect and admiration for Mohandas Gandhi in particular, who was a great lover of God, a political pacifist and fierce nationalist. It meant a lot to Yogi Ramsuratkumar that Gandhi was a great practitioner of Ramnam, and that he had died saying, "Ram, Ram," the name of God. Will Zulkowski commented, "Yogi Ramsuratkumar thought Gandhi was a great guru, and that he could really benefit India. That India should have the right political people was a very great concern of his—it was always on his mind. Who was going to be the best? Who could serve India?"

Throughout his life Yogi Ramsuratkumar continued to have a profound interest in politics. He was dedicated to the potential of India as a force in world politics. He had a long-range vision that India would make a tremendous contribution toward world peace and the dawning of a new age. He sometimes expressed to Will Zulkowski that he thought the Congress Party was the most dharmic. There were times in the early years when members of the Congress Party would visit him and receive his blessing. On election nights, nobody could approach him; he absolutely would not be distracted from sitting with his hands cupped behind his ears so that he could hear the election returns on the radio.

He could discuss politics, both national and global, with tremendous knowledge and passion. Many people who knew him commented that he knew more about any subject than anybody they had ever met. When he was so moved, he could converse brilliantly on

21 Lee Lozowick, December 5, 2001, Yogi Ramsuratkumar Ashram.

many topics—mathematics, politics, geography, literature. Will commented:

> I had three years of graduate work in political science, history, economics—but Swami knew more about politics than anybody I ever talked to in my life. He just knew who was behind what was going on in the world. We talked about China, we talked about everything. He knew the intricacies of all these governments, and how they worked and who was in charge, and all that. He was absolutely astounding, completely astounding in how much he really knew—there was just never any end to it.

During the 1980s Rajiv Gandhi—the popular and benevolent son of Indira Gandhi who reluctantly entered politics and became India's prime minister—came to Tiruvannamalai to give a public talk during one of his campaigns. A politician, one of many contacts that Yogi Ramsuratkumar had in politics and government service, came to Sannadhi Street and took the beggar in his car to the college where Rajiv Gandhi was speaking. Yogi Ramsuratkumar got to have a front row seat for the talk.

Yogi Ramsuratkumar once told Will that one part of his mission was to work with the politicians, because they had so much negative thinking on them—projections of dislike and hatred—that he somehow shielded them from that. His focus was to help them receive a higher energy. He said, "You see how Sri Rajiv Gandhi faces the problems of the day? He wants the country to come forward. But what are we people doing? We simply criticize him. Instead of giving moral support to Sri Rajiv Gandhi, we criticize him. But he is not bothered about that. He simply pulls the country forward, so we should all give moral support to him."[22]

In May, 1991 Rajiv Gandhi, now the former prime minister, was touring Tamil Nadu and planned a stop at Tiruvannamalai. He sent one of his top secretaries to see Yogi Ramsuratkumar at Sannadhi Street with the message, "Rajiv Gandhi would like to meet you."

"Rajiv Gandhi will never meet this beggar," Yogi Ramsuratkumar replied with tears in his eyes. Three days later, on May 21, 1991, Rajiv Gandhi was assassinated by Tamil terrorists from Sri Lanka.

The beggar saint believed deeply in the destiny of India; he was convinced that the spiritual heritage of India contained the seeds of wisdom that could transform the world at an international and global level. His vision was that India's wisdom would nourish the newly forming global community and steer humanity toward a time of greater peace and harmony on earth. Yogi Ramsuratkumar said:

> Bharata Mata (Mother India) is the loka guru, loka mata, and she alone will lead the universe. As far as this beggar is concerned, I feel that India, our country, will flourish and pave the way to the whole universe.

22 Yogi Ramsuratkumar, *Divine Message to Humanity*, 1988.

> India will lead in every aspect all other nations, and India's words will be heard by the whole universe very shortly. The time has come . . . . India will show the path, the right way in every sphere to other nations.[23]

In reference to the vision of Sri Aurobindo, the beggar once said to Caylor Wadlington:

> World unity is not a utopia. It has been realized that no longer can mankind remain separated. The world must become one indivisible whole, one brotherhood. The whole world will be united, Mr. K. Though utopias were tried so many times before on economic and social lines, never before has it been tried on the spiritual line.
>
> India is our playground—the playground of the masters, the custodians of the divine plan. It will never be divided or taken away from us. Believe me, my friend, truth shall have its way. Truth shall stand. This beggar has been assigned a great mission, and this beggar does his work in every step he walks. Please excuse him for giving some importance to this body.

At the conference held by Rajamanickam in Pondicherry in 1988 on Yogi Ramsuratkumar, there was a focus on such radical political statements that Yogi Ramsuratkumar had made over the years to various devotees. Without question, these issues were of great importance to Yogi Ramsuratkumar, especially in the earlier years of his work, when the revolutionary fervor of India's victory and subsequent independence was still fresh and alive in the minds and hearts of the people. Two hundred years of colonial subjugation would naturally become a major concern of any great being who is involved in the transformational potential of individuals whose lives are influenced by their environment. During the sixties and seventies, and most probably in the fifties as well, Yogi Ramsuratkumar was like a firebrand in his frequent cries of "Mahatma Gandhi Ki Jai! Jawaharlal Nehru Ki Jai! Bharat Mata Ki Jai!" Liberation on the national front was an accurate metaphor for the liberation of the soul. Yogi Ramsuratkumar said:

> Swami Ramdas, my master, is one among the brightest stars of the whole universe. He will guide us in the way in which he wants us to serve our nation, beloved country. Our nation will prosper in every field of activity. The greatest work in the whole universe is only to be a good instrument in the hands of the masters, the gurus. Our aim should always be in serving our masters faithfully and always thinking of Him in whatever condition we happen to serve our country.[24]

23 Ibid.

24 Ibid.

His devotees recorded many comments of this nature. But the context of this passion for politics is found in the following statement by Yogi Ramsuratkumar, whose keen interest in politics was always seen through the lens of the Divine at play in the world of form:

> To tell you the truth, the whole humanity exists only because of the Vedas, the Veda mantras and the great masters. In this ancient Holy Land, many great masters have come and always some great master or another lives here. In fact, this Holy Land, Bharata Desam—the Indian nation—is only the playground of great masters. This is our land. It will always be looked after by my Father. We are lucky to be born in this Holy Land.[25]

Yogi Ramsuratkumar called Mother India "this beggar's heart . . . . the playground of this beggar." One aspect of his deep belief in the importance of India was that India has always supported the culture and tradition of the holy beggar, the religious mendicant or renunciate sadhu, who are the backbone of the spiritual path. He believed that the great masters, the Vedas or the teaching, and the sadhus or holy beggars should always have a place of sanctuary and protection in India. He was extremely disturbed by the movement in India to get rid of the beggars, because the same culture that supported beggary is the culture that supported the religious mendicant—nourishing and sustaining them, providing food and at times shelter. But the greatest gift India provided to religious mendicants was the shelter of acceptance and a tacit understanding of their value within the fabric of a sacred culture. Yogi Ramsuratkumar once stated:

> For the last ten years, the state government has been making such attempts like harassing people reading Sanskrit and the Vedas, and who are chanting the Vedas. Oh! They cannot succeed in their attempts. As long as they try to harass, though they may try their best, they will not succeed. By my Father's blessings, these activities will increase and our land, the nation, will march onwards and it will show the path, the correct way, to the whole universe.[26]

Yogi Ramsuratkumar saw Mother India as the birthplace of the greatest philosophy and spiritual teachings in the world—the great progenitor of dharma, or cosmic law as it manifests on earth. Without adherence to dharma, chaos and cruelty reign; therefore, keeping India and its traditions alive and thriving was of utmost universal importance. If dharma was not kept alive in the world, humanity would fall into an unimaginable dark age at a global level and possibly not survive as a species. The key to protecting this precious heritage lay in maintaining a culture in which the great masters could continue

---

25 Ibid.

26 Ibid.

to incarnate. Yogi Ramsuratkumar said:

> At least one realized soul should always exist. Fortunately this Holy Land is always protected by great masters. Whatever you do, whether you run for government or business or remain in the top most position, unless you do something to protect the sadhus, the sannyasins and the realized souls, it is of no use. You should try to realize yourself, you should always try to move in the right direction, shown by the great masters. If you have one realized soul, he will show the way, the right path, to the whole universe, the whole humanity. If you do not protect the holy men, you are doing nothing for humanity. The whole humanity exists because of the sadhus. To tell you the truth, the law exists only because of the sadhus.[27]

During the seventies the beggar was vocal at times about his opinion of world politics and events. When Will Zulkowski told Yogi Ramsuratkumar that he had protested the Vietnam war in the States, had been a conscientious objector, and was in fact thrown in jail for it, the beggar said that he felt the antiwar people were very courageous and did a great service to humankind. He felt that the American government was wrong in getting involved in Vietnam, because it interfered with a peoples' own determination.

Yogi Ramsuratkumar's passionate interest in politics, like everything else, bled into his universal work. As the years passed, his work in the political domain seemed to gravitate more toward the global community, and he focused quite often on politics in the West. When Bill Clinton was elected as President of the United States, Perumal told Will that Yogi Ramsuratkumar had said Bill Clinton was a good man, which Will understood to mean that he could work with the energy around Clinton. Yogi Ramsuratkumar was attuned to everything that was going on.

When Nixon was President of the United States, Yogi Ramsuratkumar astutely told Will that he was "clever," meaning in a manipulative, scheming way. Will and Joan had told the beggar about Rudolph Steiner and the Waldorf School, and he wrote in a letter to them, "Oh, this is the best system of education this beggar has heard of." Then he said that somebody coming out of Waldorf School will never turn into another Nixon. Will remembered, "Swami never liked Nixon. He never thought Nixon was a good guy. He liked the Kennedys. He always thought there was something different there in the Kennedys—they had so much money that they couldn't be bought, so they could run on principle. Swami was always very direct, always spoke very directly."

Yogi Ramsuratkumar was deeply concerned with the flow of energies in the world at large and with the destiny of the planet. He once said:

> The Soviet Union, Japan, America—all are playing politics. They want to know who is supreme, who has supreme power . . . . Dirty politics

27 Ibid.

> are going on nowadays, but my Father will see the beauty of the play. My Father knows the beauty of present day dirty politics. In fact, he is the King of politics, and he knows how to play. He is the King of rulers. In the Bhagavad Gita, Lord Krishna says that he is the King of rulers, the King of kings.[28]

Parthasarathy remembered that during the time when Gorbachev was in power in the U.S.S.R., he was instituting many reforms that liberated the people and established alliances and bonds of trust with the West, and with the United States in particular. Yogi Ramsuratkumar was very happy about this, and heaped "lavish praise" on Gorbachev. One day he surprised Parthasarathy with an amazing consideration.

"Parthasarathy, is it possible for you to go to Russia?" Stunned by such an idea, Parthasarathy was silent for a moment. Yogi Ramsuratkumar continued, "If it is possible for you to go to Russia, you should meet Mr. Gorbachev and convey this beggar's salutations to him."

"Yes, Swami," Parthasarathy said, nonplussed by the idea. The trip never materialized.

World peace and the prosperity of all peoples were also of deep and abiding importance to Yogi Ramsuratkumar. The prayer written by the Shankaracharya of Kanchipuram for the United Nations in 1966 reflects a great deal about why the beggar focused so much concern and attention in this critical area—the worldly domain of politics. Throughout the nineties and until this day, this prayer was sung in every darshan on the ashram. The English translation is:

> Cultivate friendship that will conquer all hearts.
> Look upon others as thyself.
> Renounce war, foreswear competition.
> Give up aggressions on others, which is wrong.
> Wide mother earth, our mother is here, ready to give us all our desires.
> We have the Lord, our Father, compassionate to all.
> Thee peoples of the world, restrain yourselves, be kind.
> May all people be happy and prosperous.

Yogi Ramsuratkumar used anything and everything as a tool for his work, with which he could give blessings; newspapers played a major role in this, and he read them every day. Ma Devaki guessed that most of the accumulated burlap bags full of "stuff" were newspapers that contained all the "projects"—world events, crises, wars, natural disasters—that he had "worked" upon. During his years on the streets he almost always carried the daily newspaper with him wherever he went.

In later years at Sudama House and on the ashram he read all the news each day. Once his interest had been piqued by an event, the newspaper and everything around had

---

28 Ibid.

to remain untouched by others. He often told Ma Devaki and Vijayalakshmi that everyone had to be careful in his presence because a small change here and there would have an effect on the whole cosmos. Everyone had to bring tremendous attention and care to everything around him. Even something as innocuous as an empty cigarette box was inextricably bound up in his work. If someone came over hurriedly and moved it, he or she would change the whole scheme of things and upset the beggar deeply.

For that reason he always wanted people to just sit quietly around him. He had the newspapers arranged in an order that worked for him, and sometimes the numbers of newspapers would pile up. Then Devaki would ask, "Bhagawan, there are so many papers! Can I remove some of them from here?"

"No, wait. Let my Father say," he would reply. One or two or even several days would pass before he would perhaps say, "You can remove some of them." Then he would instruct Devaki in exactly how and how many and in what way it should be done. Nothing should be done abruptly or sharply; everything had to be done gradually, without disturbing the surrounding environment too much. Ma Devaki commented:

> He was a cosmic man. He lived as a cosmic man. And he always told me that any disturbance around him would cause a greater disturbance on a wide scale—on the cosmic scale. Similarly, if he blessed some individual in a certain situation, he used to say that blessing would go to all such individuals in similar situations. Again, it was cosmic.

Yogi Ramsuratkumar always worked toward a vaster and grander harmony—globally and universally. Wherever there was a troubled place in the world, his attention would immediately go there. Every morning Devaki read the newspaper to him. At first he would tell her what to read and what not to read, until she began to understand what he was looking for. Then she would just pick up the paper and start reading and he would start smoking, from the minute she began to read until it was finished.

Important international events captured his attention. In the early nineties, just weeks before the Berlin Wall came down, Yogi Ramsuratkumar began to talk about it to his devotees, saying, "You see, there is a Berlin Wall between this East and West Germany." A few weeks later, it was announced in the news that the Berlin Wall had been taken down. The devotees wondered about the connection, because before Bhagawan had started talking about the Wall, there was nothing in the newspapers about it at the time. When it appeared in the paper, they understood that even while Yogi Ramsuratkumar was talking about the Wall that day, he was smoking the whole time, and whenever he was smoking, there was higher work going on.

Later they heard from some visiting Germans that it was a sheer accident that the Berlin Wall was brought down—a slip of the tongue of a politician. Someone in a very high post was giving an interview to a newspaper reporter, and he somehow implied that the Wall would come down. The next morning the news was out and then the politician realized he had made a mistake—it was never meant to happen that way—but it was too late. The news began to spread and it miraculously just happened.

Yogi Ramsuratkumar himself would never make any statements about it; he didn't talk about his work at all. He would only say things like, "Father is happy with this beggar's work," but his closest devotees so often saw parallels between what captured his attention in the news and subsequent world events that they came to believe that there was an undeniable connection.

As so we see again and again that Yogi Ramsuratkumar's interest in politics and politicians was always a function of his work for humankind, the planetary being and the cosmos. In 1999 there was a problem in Kashmir; the threat of war between India and Pakistan was looming on the horizon. Yogi Ramsuratkumar looked at the newspapers and said repeatedly, "It looks as if there is going to be a war. It looks as if there is going to be a war." He made this declaration many times for three or four days and after that, the conflict somehow subsided.

Sonia Gandhi, the wife of Rajiv Gandhi, refused to get involved in politics for a long time, although many asked her to. Whenever there was news of Sonia Gandhi, Yogi Ramsuratkumar would ask Devaki to read the newspaper articles, then he would begin to smoke. Finally Sonia Gandhi began to participate actively in political events, and eventually ran for election. Yogi Ramsuratkumar used to say, "She is very good at it." He commented that the whole family was very good at this work and it would be for the good of India if she won the election. Devaki recounted:

> There were so many projects he would take up on the world level, the level of the country, and even in the street, you see. After he came to Sudama, he would go to the next house, the house opposite and he would walk the entire street, up and down, as if to clear the space, so that things and elements would be friendly with his work and there would be harmony in the street. I remember one neighbor lady was very quarrelsome, just before he came. After he walked up and down and then looked here and there and cleared the air completely, she became totally the opposite—so friendly, so sweet to me. So you could say even from the immediate person to the most complicated projects, the problems of the world, was Father's work for him. Wherever there was disharmony, it was his job to bring harmony there. It was always towards harmony.

All Kinds of Beings

His work concerned all types of beings—both incarnate and discarnate, physical and subtle, human and nonhuman. When Sudama was built the usual *garha prevasam*, the blessing of the new dwelling, was performed. That day Yogi Ramsuratkumar walked around and around the house, then he looked up on the terrace. He stopped and smoked, looking up in the direction of the terrace, then he walked again, going around and around. For years afterward he often told Devaki that he didn't want her to go to the terrace. It was forbidden. "This beggar doesn't want you to go up there to the terrace. That will be harmful to you," he said, but he gave only the slightest hints about such things.

When Yogi Ramsuratkumar was not well, toward the end of his life, a mahatma came to visit the ashram. He said, "You see this very place, this abode abounds with extraordinary beings. There are billions of them." Subtle beings from all levels of creation were drawn to the source of light and blessings that radiated from Yogi Ramsuratkumar. Some came because they were in great need, while others were drawn in praise and adoration; still others were bodhisattva spirits, which are drawn to higher work wherever it is occurring. The beggar was a magnet for all of this.

One day in darshan in 1995 Yogi Ramsuratkumar was sitting and smoking. He began to look up near the ceiling, as if he was looking at an invisible but tangible entity or force that was hovering there. For an hour he worked with this presence, and at one point he appeared to be angry. He was raising his hands and swatting them through the air as if he was banishing something. Everyone in the room was watching what he was doing, looking up to the ceiling and straining to see what he saw there. It was a pitched battle, and when it suddenly broke, Yogi Ramsuratkumar laughed and smiled, and it was all over.

On another occasion a devotee named Anuradha was living in her house alone. She kept hearing a repetitive and troublesome noise, but she could not locate the source of it. It was not an insect or an animal, nor was it the creaking of a door or window. It was inexplicable and unnerving. The sounds persisted, often shattering the silence of the night. Finally she told Yogi Ramsuratkumar about it, and he compassionately told her he would come. He walked around the outside of the house near the wall. The noises were never heard again—they had vanished along with whatever was making them.

The compassion of the beggar saint for all life extended to the animal world as well. Yogi Ramsuratkumar was very moved by his dogs. When Satya Sai Baba was taken away by the dog collector in Tiruvannamalai, the beggar was upset for a week. Over and over again he said, "He took my dog, he took Satya Sai Baba, he took him." For those around him, Yogi Ramsuratkumar was clearly suffering everything that the dog went through.

When the beggar spent a lot of time in the temple, every time the dog saw him it would bark. The Brahmins would then throw stones at the dog to get him to be quiet, so that the dog's howling for Yogi Ramsuratkumar was putting it in actual peril. Nonetheless, Sai Baba followed Yogi Ramsuratkumar around the temple and hung around wherever he was, and the beggar fed and took care of him.

Once somebody pushed the dog down the stairs of the *mandapam* where Yogi Ramsuratkumar regularly sat with devotees. They watched in amazement as he took the dog in his lap and stroked its paw for an hour, saying, "Oh, Sai Baba, you're going to be all right. You're going to be all right. You're going to be all right."

In the company of the master, animals were lifted up out of their unconscious existence; many of Yogi Ramsuratkumar's devotees believed that Sai Baba, however mangy, dirty and smelly he may have been, was conscient, in the same way that Mother Mayee's dogs had an apparent awareness. Lee Lozowick remembered:

> I've met many great masters in my life, but I've never been a disciple of anybody except Yogi Ramsuratkumar. I did go to visit Mayamma in 1988, before she passed. We got off of the bus and there were a number of us, standing there looking around, not knowing what to do. A man came up and said, "Where are you going?" We said, "Mayamma." He said, "Follow me," and he took us to the house she was in.
>
> There were several dogs there at the house where she was. We were invited into the house for darshan and the dogs came with us. When darshan was finished we left the house and the man who had showed us the way was gone and there was nobody around. We were just standing in the middle of the field—we had no idea where the bus stand was. One of the dogs came out of the house and started walking. He stopped about ten yards away and turned around and looked at us and turned around and started walking again. So it seemed we should follow the dog. The dog led us right to the bus stand and sat with us until the bus came and we got on! When the bus left, then the dog turned around and went back. So I can personally say that Mayamma had great affection for Yogi Ramsuratkumar's disciples and made sure that they got where they needed to go.[29]

Similarly, in the early seventies when Wendel Field would leave the beggar's company at night, there was always a big, strong, healthy dog that used to accompany Wendel. All the other dogs would run out and bark and snap at his heels, but this dog would appear and escort him about a half-mile, through town and the territory of the other dogs, back to his lodgings. Then the dog would disappear. Every night the dog would come just when it was time for Wendel to leave, but he never saw the dog at other times. Joan and Will Zulkowski reported having the same experience with this dog, which clearly had a special link with Yogi Ramsuratkumar.

Prasad and Gifts of All Kinds

During the late 1980s, when Vijayalakshmi had only known Yogi Ramsuratkumar a short time, she came from Salem to visit him at Sannadhi Street and brought a beautiful ashtray as a gift. She offered it to him on the street, and was then invited inside the house

29 Lee Lozowick, December 7, 2001, Mayamma Mayamma Samajan, Kanya Kumari.

to sit in one of the rows of devotees on the porch. He kept it near his old ashtray, and she sat and watched him closely, hoping that he would use it while she was there. Vijayalakshmi recounted:

> He went on smoking. He might have used it normally, but my whole concentration was on the ashtray, and I was just looking at him. A half hour passed, then one-and-a-half hours, two hours. The time had come for me to leave. I couldn't bear it anymore. I said in a begging tone, "Bhagawan, why don't you use it? Are you not using this, Bhagawan?" He kept quiet. You see, I had to push ahead: after five minutes, I said, "Bhagawan I would be so happy if you would use it, Bhagawan."
>
> "Ohhh," he said. That was a heavy warning, and I didn't realize it. Then the third time I said, "Bhagawan . . ." I only so much as raised my hand and he said, "Come here." He took the ashtray and dumped it in my hand and he said, "Take it and go!" My God, I learned the lesson of my life that day! Never again push like that.

Vijayalakshmi was visiting Sannadhi Street house another time when a similar teaching lesson was made. Yogi Ramsuratkumar was seated on the step inside the porch with two rows of people on either side of him. A man came and gave a lemon as *prasad*, then he said to Yogi Ramsuratkumar, "I want that lemon back." He wanted the lemon blessed and then given back to him. Like many people, he did not understand the protocol in the company of the master, which means that once one has given a gift, it should be released completely to the master. The devotee or supplicant does not then make demands about the gift or tell the master what to do with it. When the man continued to insist on having the lemon back, Yogi Ramsuratkumar became angry and threw it back into his hand. After that person left Yogi Ramsuratkumar himself told the following story:

> This beggar had gone to the temple once, and somebody had brought a *mala*, a flower garland. The *pujari* took the *mala* from his hand and put it on Arunachala Shiva, and the man was really happy with his offering being accepted and placed on Arunachala Shiva. Within ten minutes time, this man was still standing there, and the *pujari* took the *mala* off and gave it to another party. Sometimes they give prasad away. The man who was watching the whole thing got very wild. He got very angry with the *pujari* and he started shouting, "You see you are taking my *mala* and giving it to him." The *pujari* said, "I thought you had given it to Arunachala Shiva. Now you are saying it is your *mala*. Once you give the *mala* to Arunachala Shiva, anything can be done with it. You shouldn't bother!"

Yogi Ramsuratkumar was very strict about gifts of *prasad*. In 1993 when Lee was visiting, one of his students reached out his hand to take *prasad* from Yogi Ramsuratkumar the way one would pick something up from a table, with the palm down. Yogi Ramsuratkumar stopped him and then made a teaching demonstration for everyone present. He looked at the group, which was seated on the floor in the shrine room of Sudama House, and said, "This is how you should receive prasad." He cupped his two hands together with palms facing up in a gesture of total receptivity, so that they made a vessel. It was an unforgettable moment when the master himself instructed in such an important aspect of protocol.

Whenever *prasad* was given in the form of food Yogi Ramsuratkumar expected it all to be eaten, and this included meals that were served in his company or on the ashram. Nothing should be left on the plate or wasted in any way. Vijayalakshmi recounted:

> What is *prasad* is not ours. It is part of one's *tapas*. Later on at Sudama House, Bhagawan always insisted that I should take his leftovers. I had double meals every time. I became so fat! I had to have my meal and then he would only eat half of his meal, and the rest would come to me, and he would insist. He would take the leaf himself and put it on mine, and I would have to eat the whole thing. It was prasad. I had to mind him. I couldn't leave even a little bit. He would wait very patiently until I was finished. I had no chance of escaping!
>
> Once it happened that there was a gathering at Sudama House. That day, he ate and he asked me to serve him. He called me and said, "Will you serve me?" So I began to serve. After he finished, he had left quite a bit there. He said, "You sit here and eat." Then I began to eat, and people began to serve me also, because it was just a little bit and they wanted to serve me more. I was screaming, "Please don't, don't!" They put more on the plate, and I just couldn't finish.
>
> At one point, the mass wouldn't go in. It was too much for me. I was looking at Bhagawan and I kept saying, "Bhagawan I'm unable to eat any more." He was very annoyed, so I kept on pushing things inside, but there was so much left and I just couldn't eat anymore. He saw me struggling and he said, "I'll let you get up." He called to Jayarama, who at that time was attending on Bhagawan. He said, "Jayarama, come here. You sit here and eat her leftover." He made Jayarama eat my leftovers, because then I understood that it was all blessed food. It was all blessed by him. So it would be such a waste if I had left it there and it was thrown to the dogs. He saw to it that someone else who was serving him took the rest.

In the early seventies the farmers and their wives often brought Yogi Ramsuratkumar peanuts, rice and other foods. The village women brought cooked meals, but there were also times when there was simply nothing to eat. Because he was a beggar, Yogi Ramsuratkumar did not eat on a regular schedule. If there was food, he ate it and shared it with whoever was there. If there wasn't food, he simply didn't eat. Perumal said that in the early days when Swami didn't have any money they would buy big bags of puffed rice, which was very cheap. A small amount of puffed rice taken with a glass of water expanded in the stomach, and made the hunger go away, so that was often what they ate. Will recounted:

> I remember a lot of times we would go and buy big bags of puffed rice for Swami. It was very funny because Swami was staying at one of the little shops that closed at night, and he carried this bag of rice around. There was a little mouse that came every night to get the puffed rice, and Swami just laughed, you know. That was so cute, this little mouse. Anybody else would have freaked out with a mouse eating from their food, but he would just say, "Oh, we have a visitor now." He never made a big thing out of it. Oftentimes we brought out our little blankets and we just laid down on the concrete there with him, with just a candle going. We never fell asleep, though.

Yogi Ramsuratkumar loved to give things to the people around him—flower garlands, *prasad* in many forms like cooked food, bananas, apples, oranges, coconuts, limes, rock candy, sweets. Many people asked him to bless their prayer *malas*, used for japa or repetition of the name of God. He would take the *mala* and hold it, just going through it bead by bead, until he had been through each bead of the *mala*. Then he might just hold it for a while, hand it back and say, "You can wear it." Everything that was given was *prasad*.

At the level of daily interactions, it was not uncommon for the beggar to give the gift of his own physical substance, through means of transubstantiation, either by sipping from a cup before giving it to a devotee, or by pouring a small amount from his own cup into theirs. He often offered bites of food from his own banana leaf, or gave his leftover food and drink to others to consume, as he did with Ma Devaki, Vijayalakshmi, Jayarama and many others.

Yogi Ramsuratkumar also gave empowered gifts to his devotees at specific times over the years. On certain occasions he gave various people highly sanctified objects that had become sacred artifacts by virtue of his touch and attention. For example, when Will Zulkowski came to visit Yogi Ramsuratkumar in 1990, one year after the death of his wife Joan, he arrived at Sannadhi Street and took his seat with several others, including Kirsti, Devaki and some other friends. Yogi Ramsuratkumar walked in, looked around at everyone and said unexpectedly, "Nobody knows this beggar. Nobody knows this beggar. There's only one person who does know this beggar, and that's Will." He immediately went into the inner room of his house and brought out a rough sketch of himself holding his fan, which he offered to Will.

"Swami, it's beautiful, but I already have this huge painting from Wendel," Will responded. Yogi Ramsuratkumar went back inside, then returned to the verandah carrying two palmyra fans that he had carried for ten years, tied together with a large amount of string.

"Will, would you like these?" he asked. "Can you keep them nicely?"

"Ah, I'll keep them very nicely!" Will said, stunned at the magnitude of the blessing he had just been given; he knew only too well that Yogi Ramsuratkumar had carried those fans and worked with them for ten years. They were priceless artifacts of his work and his spiritual authority.

"Will," the beggar said, "I couldn't give you that fan before." What exactly he meant by this Will didn't ask, preferring to simply receive the gift with gratitude. Immediately Will bought a hard suitcase in which to transport the artifacts back to New York. He later commented:

> Everything that I got from Swami was always *prasad*. It was his way of sharing on a material plane—always kind of fun and very loving and giving. I never took it lightly, I just always felt this was a great blessing from him. He didn't have to do any of it, you know? We were just lucky to be there and to be on the receiving end. The fans he gave me were the greatest gift. I don't let anyone touch them. He just said, "You can have these fans. Would you like these fans?" But the greatest gift, I think, is not any of the physical *prasad* but the gift of consciousness—his blessing. That's the greatest gift.

In July 1996 Yogi Ramsuratkumar gave his turban and coconut bowl to Ma Devaki. He asked her to wear the turban, but she declined, saying, "Why would I want to wear this, Bhagawan, when you are here?"

Yogi Ramsuratkumar gave Lee Lozowick the *dhoti* that he had worn wrapped around his body for a very long time and countless shawls, many of which had been worn on his body as well. He also gave Lee the gift of having his poetry published in India; the poetry declares that Yogi Ramsuratkumar gave Lee the greatest gift of all—his divine madness.

Many years earlier the beggar had given Caylor Wadlington his coconut bowl, as well as several other gifts, such as numerous drawings and bits and pieces of writing that Yogi Ramsuratkumar made when they were together. The lemons that Yogi Ramsuratkumar gave to Caylor twenty-five years ago never rotted and are still intact. Caylor reported, "I would meditate for years holding these lemons, and finally they started to get little dark spots, but for years they dehydrated and stayed yellow and never spoiled. Now they have a few decomposition spots, but that is only from my handling them."

A month after Caylor met Yogi Ramsuratkumar, the mad beggar gave him an unusual gift. In August of 1970 Yogi Ramsuratkumar would often go to Ramaswami's shop in the bazaar to gaze lovingly at a small stone figure of Nandi bull, Shiva's mount. He seemed to be infusing it, literally, with his own self through the power of his attention.

On this particular morning, when Yogi Ramsuratkumar arrived at the shop, the sculpture of Nandi was sitting up on a shelf. He asked Ramaswami to bring it down, and he silently handed it to Caylor and asked him to keep it for some time. Caylor wrote:

> It was a hot summer morning, probably about 85 or 90° F before eight o'clock. The morning dew and mist disappeared in the span of a few minutes to make way for the oven-like heat of the summer day. It was a surprise to find the happy man, all in his rags and already brisk in his movements, sitting there on the platform-like floor of Ramaswami's stone shop. Together we shared some fruit and bread, and maybe some tea as well.
>
> This morning his attention turned mine to a subject different from that which was typical of our early relationship. Yogi Ramsuratkumar began to talk of his love for a certain stone figure of Shiva's bull, Nandi. He explained to me briefly the commonly-assigned nature of the symbol, meaning that nothing esoteric entered into his description. He almost never spoke of anything the slightest bit spiritual except my progress in meditation or the affairs of spiritual or political India.
>
> Nandi was a small, gray-toned soapstone carving created by a young man named Annamalai, Ramaswami's brother. This person was said to be an excellent artist and well-known image-carver for temples, different than many of the artists of India today. Yogi Ramsuratkumar had made Ramaswami promise not to sell the tiny figure for thirty days. The deal was that if the beggar man would bring a sum of not less than twenty-five rupees for the bull within thirty days, then the proprietor would display the Nandi bull but would not sell it.
>
> I was pleased to take the Nandi bull, except I didn't know how to love the small thing. I didn't know if I was even supposed to, and my attention was always sort of magnetized to following the movements of Yogi Ramsuratkumar, so after I had lost what little attention I had for the stone carving, its "father" gently received him back to his own lap. It was then that the Yogi began to express verbally his love for the temple image. His emotions were authentic and his movements so childlike that I began to accept the [idol] as truly something special. I understood further that what he did so often to flowers and other objects had been done in a special manner—in an intensely careful way—to this carved image so endeared and loved by Yogi Ramsuratkumar. He asked me if I would like to have it to keep in my room. He explained that he would lose this friend if he did not give it to someone he cared for. He thought I could love the thing as he had loved him.

Yogi Ramsuratkumar didn't have the rupees to pay Ramaswami for the sculpture of Nandi, and he asked Caylor to pay the twenty-five rupees. Sensing that it was a very important opportunity, and because of the awe and respect that he felt for the beggar who he considered to be a "cosmic man"—who had imbued the statue with such love and energy—the young American took Nandi, receiving it as a spiritual gift in the truest sense from Yogi Ramsuratkumar. He also sensed that paying for one's spiritual development and inner work was a lawful requirement of receiving such a gift.

Yogi Ramsuratkumar proceeded to instruct Caylor in how Nandi would be very good for him, and would accompany him as a spiritual companion for a long time. He further instructed Caylor in the care of Nandi: to never to disfigure the stone image in any way; to keep it with him whenever he traveled; and to shield Nandi from those who were not friendly to Caylor by covering the sculpture with a cloth.

Yogi Ramsuratkumar said that because he was personally unable to watch over Nandi and care for him, Caylor should try to love Nandi in the same way that he did. He explained that the sacred image of Nandi should be with one who loved its master—that is, Yogi Ramsuratkumar—and for that reason, Caylor had been entrusted with its care. It was clear that Yogi Ramsuratkumar intended Nandi to be a link between them that could also serve as a meditation for Caylor. All Caylor had to do was look at Nandi to remember his benefactor. He wrote:

> The next morning I again ambled along the village roads past the children—alive and fresh as the morning—and the bullock carts, which seemed to be alone in frequenting the streets so early in the morning. That morning I received the Nandi for twenty-five rupees, and was pleased to hold the little one in my hands. In my mind I felt a dreaded incapacity to give it my love—I knew not how to love such things—but in my heart I felt gratitude and simple liking for a man I revered as a Perfect One. I sometimes feel inadequate to be gifted with emotions and experiences so divine and beautiful in their own way. My relationship with the mad beggar man is too wonderful . . . I ask, why?

During the seventies Yogi Ramsuratkumar often made enigmatic drawings which he gave to various people. At a cursory glance these could be viewed as merely the scribbles, circles, lines and random words of a child, but he often included names, words and dates, sometimes in Hindi, Sanskrit or English, and clearly had an intention for each one. He did a whole series of drawings on paper for Caylor and at other times for Will and Wendel. The following pages of drawings done by Yogi Ramsuratkumar (circa 1971) were gifts from Yogi Ramsuratkumar to Caylor, who preserved them.

Caylor noted in his journals that on December 8, 1970 Yogi Ramsuratkumar gave him some small scraps of paper with his handwriting on them. From his pocket he also pulled out an old cigarette box, on which he drew a diagram or *yantra*. Each mark was made with visible care and intention. Caylor wrote in his journal at the time:

> The last three marks on the cigarette box were added a few moments after he had handed the card to me, after taking a final look at it and adding some peculiar forms that must have served some importance in the total force of the card, for his decision and determination were sudden and profound as he worked to make the slight addition.
>
> First went the two wavy lines, then his signature, and finally the written word, "Om," and a darkened scribbled area. It was impossible to know what these things were, or what Yogi Ramsuratkumar's intention was for them. He explained to me that neither the cards nor the writing paper on them was to be altered, cleaned up or anything else. Every mark and seeming imperfection also plays its part in the function of the whole. He further explained each mark on the white paper diagram, but made no such explanation of the cigarette box diagram.
>
> I remember how I sat working with those two cards. Gazing into them, I was asked by Yogi Ramsuratkumar in a very light, almost sarcastic way, "Does it do something for you?" We laughed together and I conceded that I didn't know, but only supposed that it did so in an invisible manner.
>
> We sat quietly together after these cards had been turned over to me. Holding in hand each of the two mementos and supposed tools for my development, I turned to Swami and said how happy I was to receive these two cards. I added, further, how for the past two or three days I had been hoping that he might write a few words on a piece of paper for me. Oh my gosh, how he laughed! We both new well enough that he had done this for that very reason. He told me that I should keep the two cards in my wooden box.

The drawings usually reflected whatever was happening in the moment—an idea the beggar had sparked upon, a conversation, a meaningful date, such as August 14, which was both the date of Indian independence and the birthday of Sri Aurobindo. They were never the product of an idle mind or sheer boredom, but contained the seeds of whatever Yogi Ramsuratkumar was working on. At the same time, Yogi Ramsuratkumar was entirely childlike and unpremeditated in his play with the drawings. Yogi Ramsuratkumar often stained his drawings with smudges of plant matter—dandelions, grass and such. Caylor commented later:

> I felt like the drawings were just for fun—he had such glee making those drawings, they were such a lark. He would get totally into them and excited and feel so proud them. He'd ask me to look at it and tell him what I saw and what I thought, and I think he was very amused that I couldn't see what he did, like it was a master work of some energy thing. He'd usually say, "Ohh, ohh yes," feigning amazement, like, "Oh, you're so insightful," but of course he was letting me know that I completely missed it!

Bhagvadgita

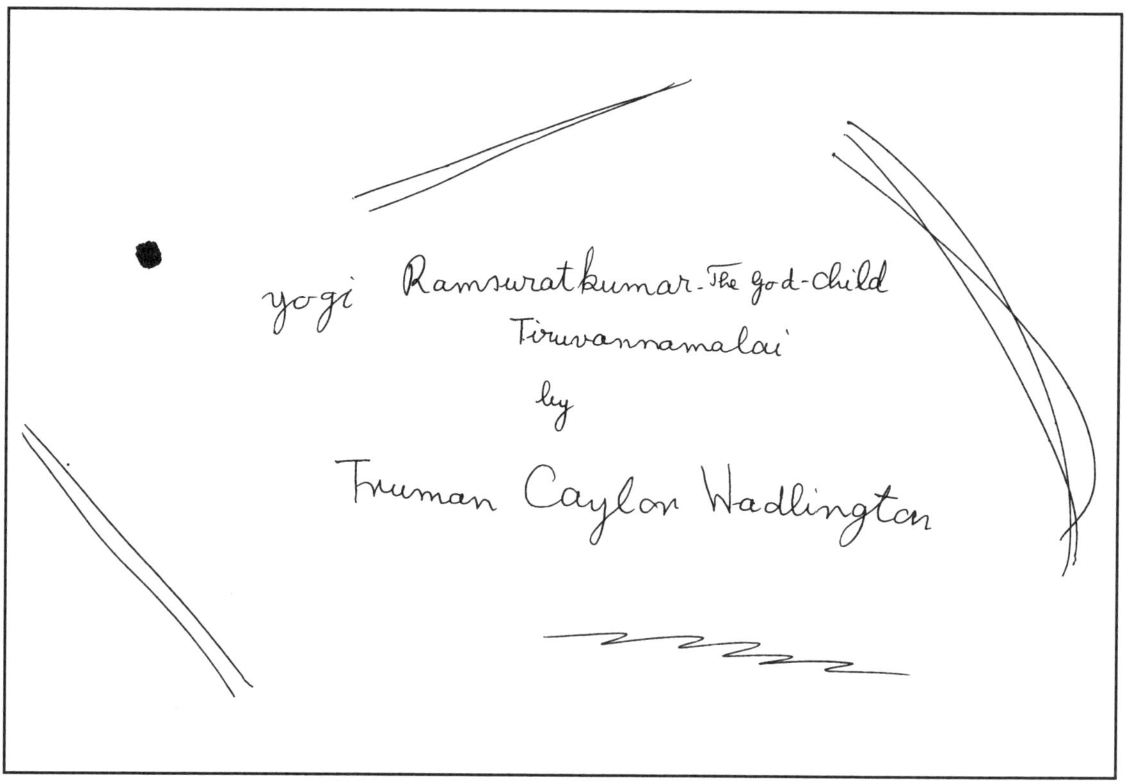
yogi Ramsuratkumar - The god-child
Tiruvannamalai
by
Truman Caylor Wadlington

Drug
The four Vedas
Max Muller
The Secret Doctrine
H. P. B
Soma

I love Hermann Hesse

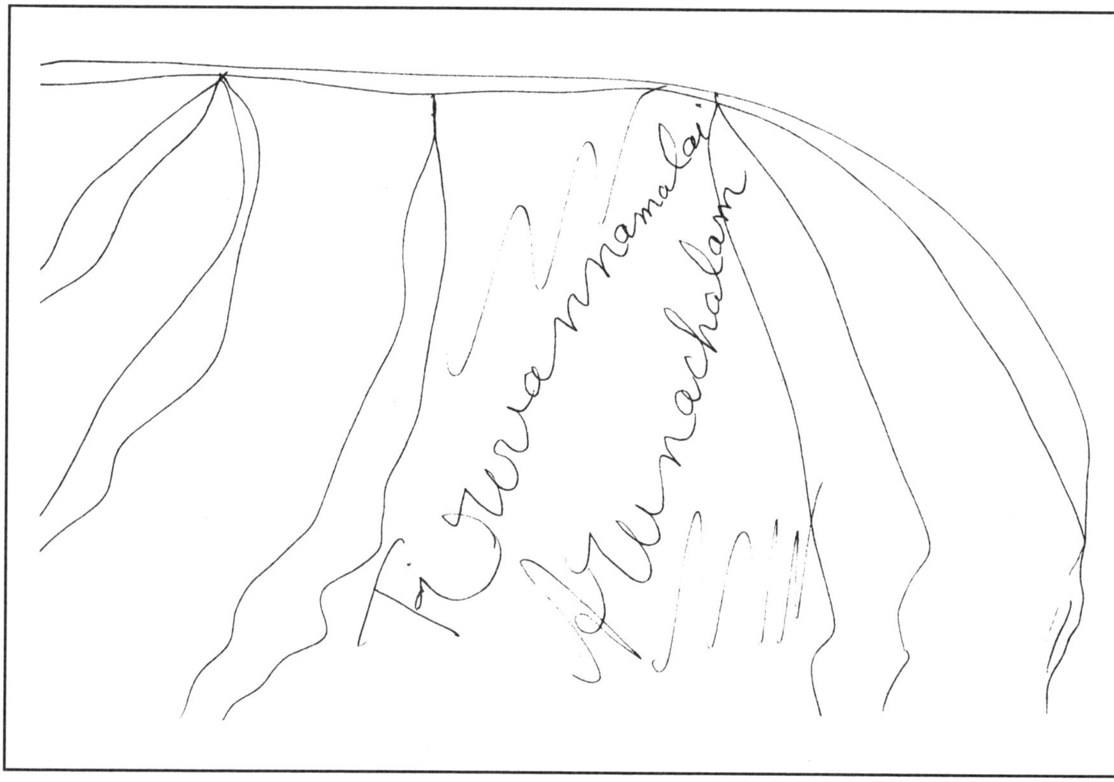
Tiruvannamalai
Arunachalam

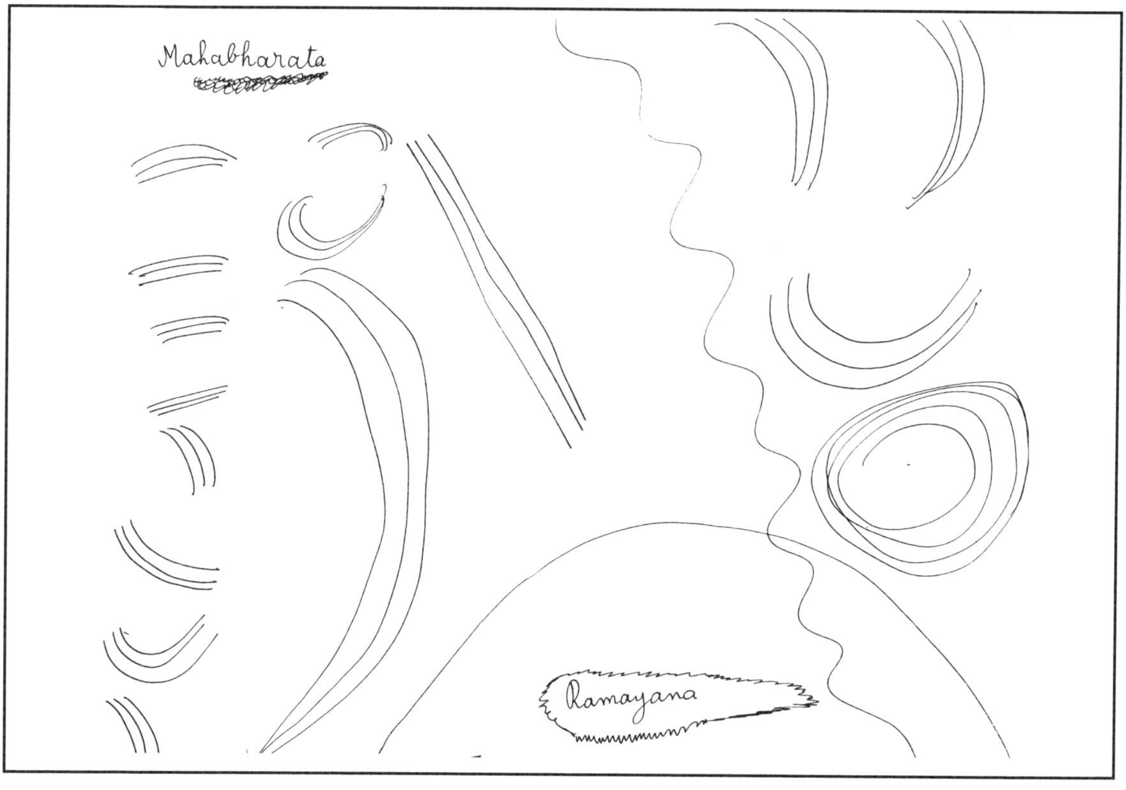
Mahabharata
Ramayana

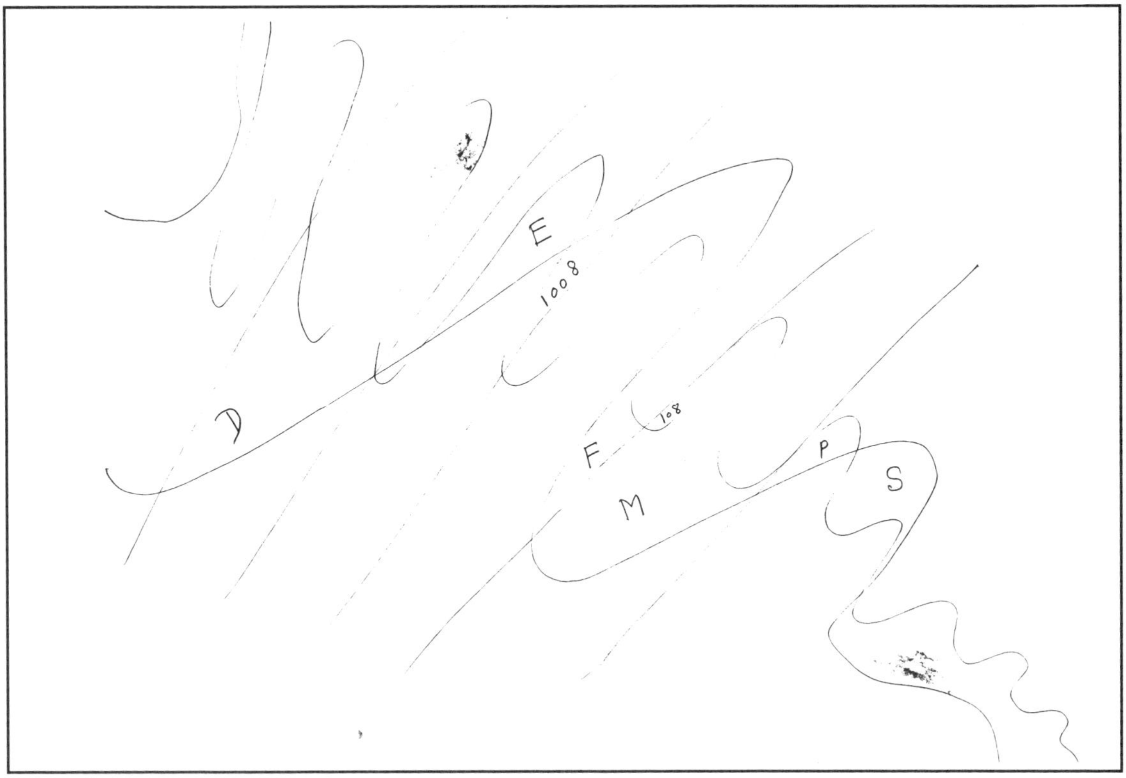
E
1008
D
108
F
P
S
M

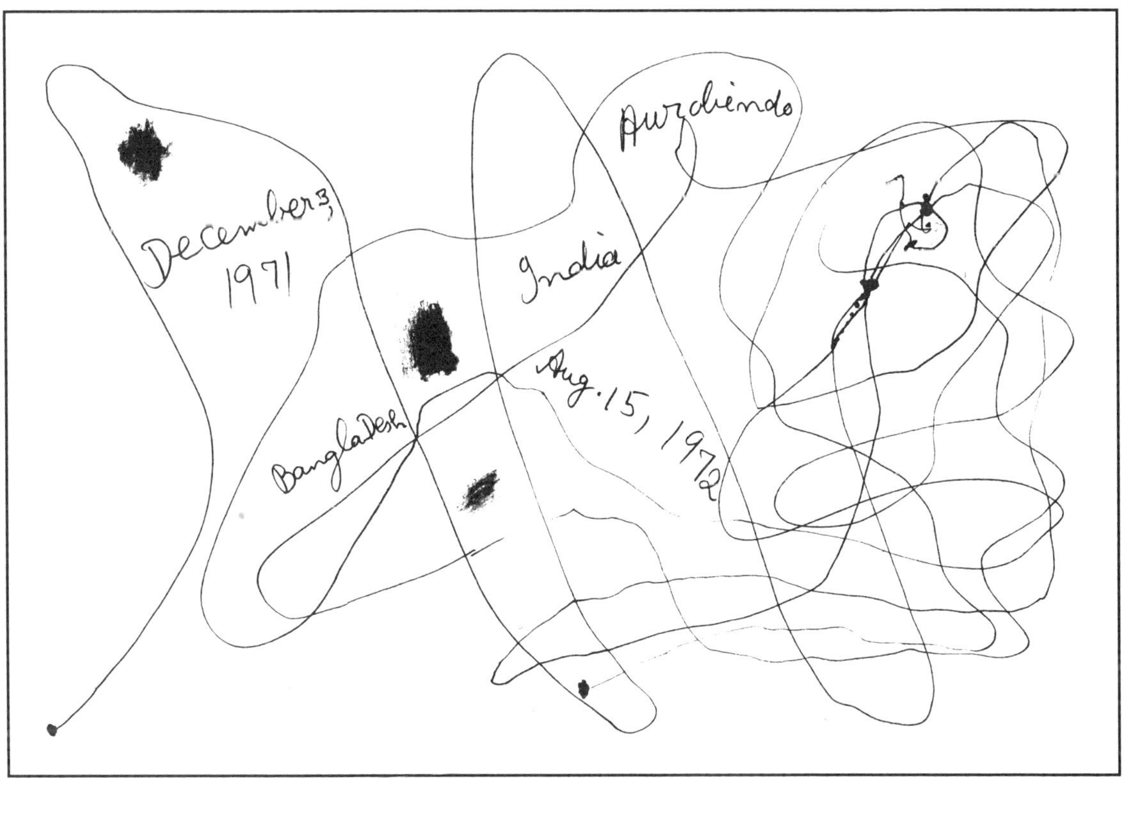
Aurobindo
December 3,
1971
India
Aug. 15, 1972
BanglaDesh

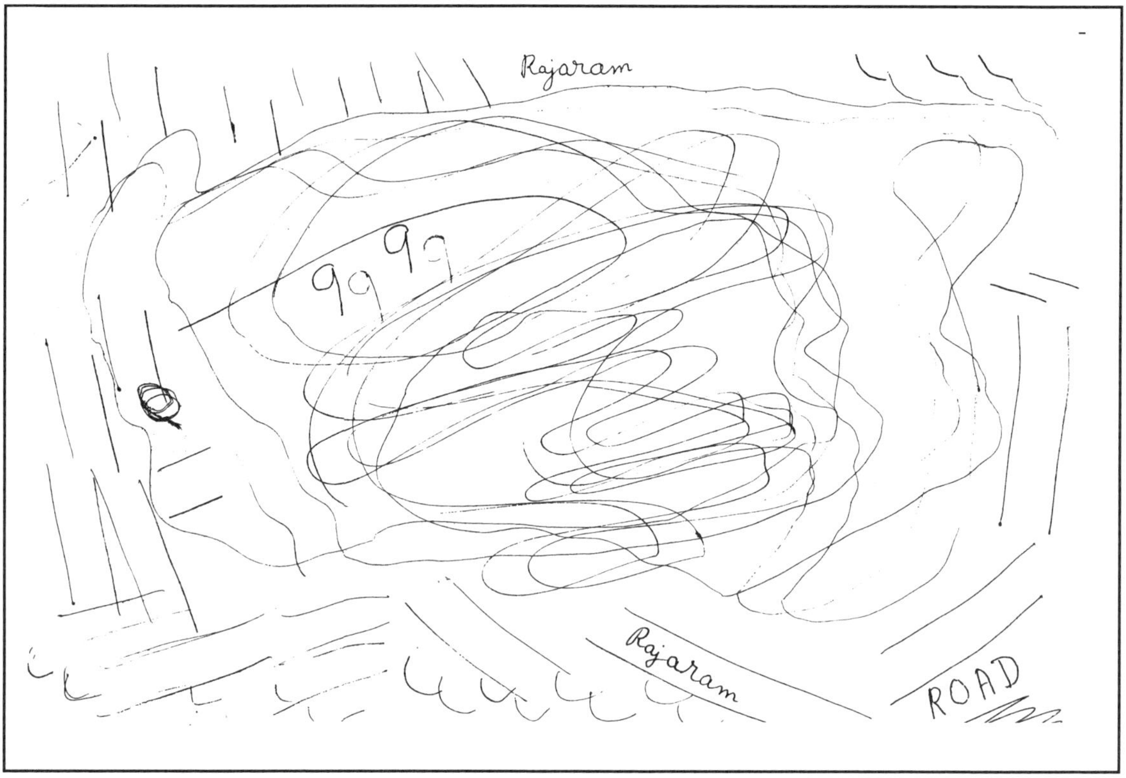
Rajaram
9999
Rajaram
ROAD

Secret Doctrine

The Use of the Name

"Swami, why do you ask all the people to remember your name?" someone once asked the beggar.

Turning to one of his devotees, Yogi Ramsuratkumar asked in all innocence, "This beggar is also wondering! Why, this beggar asks—can anybody tell? Why does this beggar ask to chant his name alone?"

"Swami, all other mantras are very old, Swami, centuries old, but your name is fresh," a young boy replied. The beggar smiled.

All mantras are equally powerful, and many are ancient, but the name of Yogi Ramsuratkumar has captured not just his closest devotees, but many people with its easy and rippling melody. Parthasarathy commented on the use of the beggar's name, "It will occupy you. I used to chant his name twenty-four hours a day. Now it is within me. It is within me. . . . . It comes automatically to me. It has become part and parcel of me. Whenever his name is there, Swami's vibrations will be there. It will protect. It will make people evolve to the highest evolution, there is no doubt about it."

Yogi Ramsuratkumar was God's gift to the world—an appearance of the Divine in human form. There are many similarities that can be drawn with other saints and great masters, but he was an exceedingly rare mixture of qualities. One minute he was sublime, lost in a *bhava* of divine intoxication, the next minute he could converse on world politics, make a joke or heal a child. His work with individuals was aimed toward transformation, and yet personal transformation was not enough. Many clairvoyants who interacted with him were stunned by the magnitude and vast implications of the spiritual influence they encountered there.

Yogi Ramsuratkumar told Will in the 1970s, during the cold war, that a day would come when his name would be chanted in even Moscow, and that a story would be written about him that would really inspire people. At the time it sounded like a ridiculous idea—he was a dirty beggar living on the streets, a hidden saint. Will said:

> At that time I didn't really believe it, but now I see that people from Russia are coming to India like crazy. Swami was kind of a visionary into the future, and now I can see that it's possible, not through him directly but through his disciples, that some change in consciousness will happen just because of his name. People have a contact, or they experience something to perpetuate who he was in the body by transforming their being around his model—not in the sense of becoming who he was, but just to take what

> he has given and add that into their mix. That would be a good key for personal transformation as well as for transforming the earth, because he said that if you're in this for personal transformation, it's not enough. That's just too limited, too selfish.
>
> The real work of devotees is to transform the earth—to take this vibration that he has given and then try to project that out. I have my own personal way of tuning to his vibration—who he was and what he was about—and then trying to project that out. Transformation, that's what the whole thing is about. It's not me personally taking liberation for myself. It's long-term meditation, long-term prayer, long-term spiritual practice. He has been the vehicle of transformation, and he always said that if people would chant "Yogi Ramsuratkumar," then they could tune in to who he was on some level, and that would be transformational—a vibrational transmission.

Hilda Charlton once said that human beings are basically all alike; it's not until one evolves to the "yogic grade" that some differences appear. It was her belief that the true masters are the hidden ones who sustain the vibration that keeps the earth in balance. Hilda felt that the masters were the salt of the earth—they didn't need any fancy shows or people bowing at their feet. Countless times Yogi Ramsuratkumar used to say to people who were *pranaming*, "That's not necessary," or simply, "Get up!" Often he would get people up by slapping them affectionately or soundly on the back and saying, "Ram, Ram!"

Yogi Ramsuratkumar sometimes talked about his earlier life to various people. He told Will Zulkowski that he had gone to Aurobindo's ashram and found that Aurobindo wasn't available, but he wrote a note to the Mother and she sent back a little packet of flowers. That was her usual dispensation, but he said that as soon as he touched the flowers, he realized that there was a much higher life that was possible, and it gave him great inspiration. Other devotees reported that Yogi Ramsuratkumar said that he was doing the work that Sri Aurobindo had begun—working with the supramental. Aurobindo once made the comment that Ramana Maharshi's realization stopped where his work began; Aurobindo's idea was to go beyond enlightenment to transform the body at a cellular and atomic level into a being of light—in other words, to divinize the body.

Will commented, "What's remarkable about these beings like Yogi Ramsuratkumar is the amount of light that their body has to sustain and can sustain without going out of consciousness—into *samadhi* or something like that—and still be functional on earth." That's where the guru's guidance and the need for purification of the chakras and various subtle systems comes into play on the spiritual path.

But for Yogi Ramsuratkumar, chanting the name of Ram—and later, specifically the name "Yogi Ramsuratkumar"—would catalyze purification, move one toward surrender, and activate any and all processes of spiritual transformation when they needed to become active. With the guru's grace, all that was needed was the divine name. He would sometimes say, "When you chant the name 'Yogi Ramsuratkumar' it not only helps your own spiritual progress, it helps this beggar's work also. It helps Father's work." He further stated, "This beggar has not built any temple. Nor has he written any books. There's nothing about this beggar's life that is inspiring, but he has left a Name for mankind. Father has given a name, 'Yogi Ramsuratkumar,' to humanity for its benefit, out of His Love."[30]

Sankara Rajulu had been practicing kriya yoga for two years and Yogi Ramsuratkumar told him to stop. He said, "This is not necessary; you repeat God's name."

He told Will Zulkowski about "etheric markers," meaning that a mantra that had been repeated millions and even billions of times by many practitioners over thousands of years was literally imprinted into the "air" or the etheric plane of existence. He once said to Will that his work was "in the air." Hilda Charlton confirmed this about Yogi Ramsuratkumar, saying, "Will, he's really not working on this plane. He's working in all the ethereal realms . . . with name and sound and energy." If one uses a mantra that has been imprinted into the world soul, then one plugs into a vast storehouse of energy and spiritual power that has accumulated over eons of time.

Yogi Ramsuratkumar himself once said, "This beggar's name is in the sky. This beggar's name can be heard in the sky. When anybody remembers this beggar, Father sends help."[31] Will commented:

> He was very adamant that the name of Ram is all you need, but he wasn't pushing anything down anybody's throat. He always said he tried to go to the path of whoever came to him. If they wanted to come and talk about Marx, he talked about Marx. He didn't divert their path, he only tried to go with what they were interested in. He was very flexible that way. Once Joan and I were out in the field with him and we were asking, "Why are saints incarnated in India, particularly?"
>
> "Well," he said, "in this yuga India has always been the playground of the saints because where else in the world, even though you're a nobody, with nothing, will they give you food and shelter and honor you and revere you? There's no other country in the world." He said that's why the saints always incarnate, take birth in India. In this country or in Russia they would have been locked up in some mental institution—treated like freaks. He also said that there was a lot of persecution of the saints, especially in the Middle Ages in Europe. He said that's why the saints love to come to India and keep incarnating there over and over and over again, because that reverence is always there for them.

Yogi Ramsuratkumar used to joke with Will and Joan, saying, "You know, chanting

---

30 Yogi Ramsuratkumar, "The Divine Beggar On Himself," *Saranagatham*, March 2003, p. 30.

31 Ibid, p. 31.

your own name is the biggest sin." After Hilda Charlton met him she said, "You know, 'Yogi Ramsuratkumar' is one of the names of God." His life was a work of art in praise of the Divine, and his work went on continuously, day and night; to sing the name of Yogi Ramsuratkumar awakens that vibration and continues his work even in perhaps an infinitesimal way. He made it clear that the name Yogi Ramsuratkumar was not a name, but a state of being that must be experienced.

In a very rare moment of self-revelation, when caught up in ecstasy, the beggar said, "Scatter this beggar's name across the length and breadth of the country, from north pole to south pole!" But he also cautioned that "Yogi Ramsuratkumar" was not the only sacred name, and that his devotees should not take a fundamentalist or dogmatic attitude about the name of Yogi Ramsuratkumar. Clearly stating his love for the *Ramayana*, the *Mahabharata*, and the names of Ram and Krishna, he once said, "Ram Nam and Krishna Nam are dear to this beggar. If anybody insists that this beggar's name alone is important, they are doing a great sin."[32]

At another level in the dimensional play of Yogi Ramsuratkumar, he placed importance on the integrity of the names of those with whom he worked, as Caylor commented:

> Names were very important to him. When he wrote to me it was usually to "Truman Caylor Wadlington." He would have me sign letters that I had written to him, and I would write "Truman Caylor Wadlington." A lot of his letters to me were signed "YogiRamsuratkumar" without any interruption—one continuous word. Those were power connections. That name existed on some level as an entity or connecting point to people. When I first met him he was called "Yogi Ramsuratkumar," although most people called him "Swami," and most children called him "Rama," but if you asked him what his name was, it was "Yogi Ramsuratkumar."

Yogi Ramsuratkumar had a very specific way of working with people's names. Names were very important to him because the name itself carried a certain vibration. He could know everything he needed to know about a person in order to bless them simply by hearing their name. Once Will and Joan got a letter from a friend in the States describing a conflict that was in progress at the Waldorf School. Yogi Ramsuratkumar simply touched the letter for an instant, and then he said, "Can I see the handwriting?" He glanced at the handwriting and asked, "What is his name?" Then he described the friend to Will and Joan perfectly, "right down to the feet."

Whenever someone came with a request for blessings for a friend or relation, he simply said, "Tell me the name." Once a young woman from Canada came to see him; she had a newborn niece that she asked blessings for. The baby had some significant health

32 Ibid.

problems, and when Yogi Ramsuratkumar heard the baby's name, the first thing he asked was, "Is it possible to change the name?"

The woman responded, "No, no, the parents will never call her anything else." He gave the baby a new name anyway and said, "You call her that."

A German man came to visit who had had a great deal of mystical experience. When Yogi Ramsuratkumar met him, he said, "That's not your given name." The man said, "You're right. I was born in Germany but we moved to Canada during World War II, so my mother didn't want the Canadians to have an association with the German name, so she started to call me Henri."

When Mani's grandchild Chandramani was born, the doctors first thought the birth would have to be by caesarian section due to complications. Because Mani's son was away on business, the in-laws wanted Mani to be there, but when he asked Yogi Ramsuratkumar's permission to leave the ashram, Bhagawan said, "This beggar doesn't like you going there. If you want, you are free—you can go—but it will be a normal, safe delivery." Mani suggested that perhaps Raji should go, but again Bhagawan insisted, "No, it is going to be a normal, safe delivery. This beggar is not worried, but if Rajalakshmi or you think you should go, you can do whatever you like." It was clear that Bhagawan did not want Mani or Raji to go, and they decided to stay at the ashram.

The baby's birth was a normal delivery with no problems. Mani and Raji went to Bhagawan to ask him to name the child, a girl. Yogi Ramsuratkumar said, "No hurry. If the child had been a boy, I would have named him Hari," he said, making a play on words.

After twenty-five days the baby still had no name. Mani had been busy with Lee's visit, and after Lee left for Arizona, Bhagawan suddenly called his attendant Selvaraj up to the dais and showed him a picture of Vivekananda.

"Do you know his name?" he asked.

"Yes, Bhagawan, it's Vivekananda," Selvaraj replied.

"Do you know his guru's name?"

"Yes, Bhagawan, it is Ramakrishna Paramahansa."

"You know Ramakrishna Paramahansa's mother's name?" he asked. Selvaraj answered no. "It's Chandramani. Chandramani is Ramakrishna Paramahansa's mother's name, and it is the name of the grandchild of Mani and Rajalakshmi. Go and tell them."

Shortly he called for Rajalakshmi. "Rajalakshmi, has Selvaraj told you the name of the child?"

"Yes, Bhagawan."

"What is the name?" he pressed.

"Chandramani."

"You know whose name that is?" he asked. She answered that she knew it was the name of Ramakrishna Paramahansa's mother. He said, "If you think that is a long name, you can call her Chandra." A message was sent to Mani's son in Malaysia, but the name was misunderstood, and the baby was called Chandramagi. When Mani's son wrote to Bhagawan thanking him for naming his daughter and spelled the name Chandramagi, Yogi Ramsuratkumar exploded.

"Rajalakshmi! What is going on here? The name is changed!" It was fairly unusual for Yogi Ramsuratkumar to name a child, which he had done on some occasions, as he had also done with Shankara Rajulu's grandchild. Again he told Mani and Raji that if they wanted to change the name, they could, but the name he had given the child was Chandramani.

Three months later when Mani's son arrived from Malaysia, someone asked him the name of his daughter, and he said, "Chandramani."

It has been a common trend in the West for people to change their names, especially to more exotic and beautiful Eastern names. Often the motive for such a change interferes in the process of working with the karma of the original name that has been given. Yogi Ramsuratkumar often said to people, "Please use your real name." If anyone came to visit who wasn't using their real name, he knew it immediately, and he would say, "That is not your correct name. Please use the name that was given."

Yogi Ramsuratkumar didn't care for the Western fetish with Indian and Sanskrit names. If a Westerner came to him with a Sanskrit name, he often asked, "Where did you get that name?" He instructed more than one person, including Lee Lozowick, to keep their Western names.

Once a Western disciple of Punjaji, an Indian guru who traces his lineage to Ramana Maharshi, introduced herself with a Sanskrit name. When Yogi Ramsuratkumar heard this name, he made a rare caustic remark, saying, "The cheapest thing in India are the names!"

Names contain seed power and are encoded with karmic influences that should be honored and acknowledged in order to reap the full benefit of the name. However, no law is written in stone, and there were always exceptions; there were times when Yogi Ramsuratkumar instructed people to change their names as well, but most of the time he expected people to abide by and respect the original name they had been given.

Yogi Ramsuratkumar changed his own name, however slightly, and the result was a profound reflection of the transformation that occurred in his life. Because of that transformation the world was left with the name of Yogi Ramsuratkumar as *taraka mantra*—the mantra that liberates from illusion. As early as 1970 Yogi Ramsuratkumar was revealing a vision of the work that had been given to him, including the use of his name as mantra, as seen in the following story.

"Victory to Truth! Victory to God! Victory to Sacrifice! Victory to Righteousness!" These were the first words that Yogi Ramsuratkumar said to Caylor after they had greeted one another at the tiny blue tea stall on December 9, 1971. For the past three days they had met regularly after Caylor's *pradakshina* of Mount Arunachala, and each time Yogi Ramsuratkumar would first give him a green fruit to eat—*amla*, a large variety of gooseberry used by yogis because of their rich nutritional value. With over three times the vitamin C of an orange, they are also said to have certain properties that cause them to effect the energies in the body in a "mystic and beneficent manner."

On this day Yogi Ramsuratkumar sat with Caylor on a bench in the Sundar Sweet Shop, owned by Dasaratha. They sat together, facing a photograph of Dasaratha's guru, Pundi Swami (the hidden swami)—a well-known swami who lived nearby. Caylor had visited Pundi Swami on three occasions previously—he was a "weird-looking figure, sitting almost motionless by the side of a village road," who paradoxically seemed to have a high level of realization. Legend had it that he had sat like this, without awareness of his physical body and without need of food or bathroom facilities, for seven years. He was also considered a "karma eater," smoked cigarettes, and oddly enough, the photograph hanging on the wall bore a remarkable resemblance to Yogi Ramsuratkumar.

Caylor had often been struck by the similarity in the two men, but never before had the beggar saint given so much attention to this picture of Pundi Swami. A number of times previously he had pointed out the photo and had mentioned that Dasaratha was his devotee. On this occasion however, Yogi Ramsuratkumar would hardly look away from it—he was working through it for hours on end. Caylor wrote:

> Yogi Ramsuratkumar sat quite still beside me. With a cigarette in hand he worked inside of me. I might add that it was quite curious to note that Pundi Swami also uses a cigarette as an instrument for (as some speculate) his work. It seems to serve these great souls as an anchor to the physical plane, while work is being done on higher planes. During the last two hours little was spoken, for throughout most of the time, Yogi Ramsuratkumar's gaze was fixed upon the aforesaid photograph. I sat quietly beside him. My forehead was pulsating with eddies and currents of energy all swirling at that point. Then whenever we stopped to talk, this pressure would cease for a time. Who can say what this great soul was doing to me? And who can say what he was doing as his attention focused on the photo of Pundi Swami?
>
> "The world begins as Spirit and ends in Spirit," the beggar began to speak. "In between there is this manifestation. But it is also Spirit, Mr. K. It is only because of some veil, some veil, that we are ignorant of the Truth." He pointed to the ceiling and spoke to me, "A spider wears his web outside of his body. Sometimes the spider drops down at the end of his thread—is it not? Then when he gets tired of this play and wants to go back up, he take the web back into his body. Do you follow my point, Mr. K?"
>
> This was the week of Deepam. Many people had come to the city so Swami and I were by no means left undisturbed to sit or work. Often we sat through the greatest commotion and noise—radios playing, children playing, the questions of inquisitive visitors or malicious political activists. I sat quietly absorbed in the activity that was carrying on in my forehead, which was often moved to contortions—not through pain, but by the pressure of the energy being manifested there. People sitting about were

obviously puzzled about the behavior of Swami and myself. It was ignored in my case but in the yogi's it was termed "madness."

Yogi Ramsuratkumar told a story: A yogi in Benares took a beautiful rose flower and held it up in his hand. When he opened his hand—here Yogi Ramsuratkumar was enthusiastically enacting the gestures of this yogi's miracle—the rose flower changed its color! He said, "If it was a white rose, he would change it to blue. If it was a blue flower, he would change it to red. He explained to this beggar that there is only one Substance. And out of this one Substance all things are created. One time a friend of this beggar picked up some ordinary leaves, and then dropped them into my hands. When they fell, they turned to coins. Do you follow my point, Mr. K? There is only one element: Spirit—that all-pervading substance."

Much was said that has been lost to my memory, but I shan't forget how he expressed himself to me. So often he would repeat the same sentences, words, or sentence fragments over and over, as if to plant thought forms that might serve him well in days to come.

"Theoretical conviction," Yogi Ramsuratkumar said, "theoretical conviction of the unity of all is a great step forward. A great step forward, Mr. K. Though it may not change altogether how we see things, intellectual conviction is a wonderful advancement! This beggar has been assigned a great mission, and this beggar does his work in every step he walks. This beggar has been assigned a great mission. His work could not be done by others. Please excuse him for giving some importance to this body."

Yogi Ramsuratkumar continued, "The name of this beggar will be left behind. When his mission is completed, this beggar will pass away. But the name, Yogi Ramsuratkumar, will remain in the history of spiritual India. And to a few chosen individuals, his name will be a source of inspiration. This beggar is working to uplift this country. He gives advice or help to those few people who come to him, but as a general rule, his real work goes unnoticed."

As I put forth a query, he said, "Please, Mr. K, do not ask about this work. It could not be understood at this time. When a building is built, tools must be brought from far away. Those people who offer food and shelter to this beggar are his tools. A yogi's work is never left unfinished. Though obstacles may come, it is certain they (the obstacles) will never succeed. That job which he had been sent to do will be completed. No obstacles can stop it. He will see to it."

As he said the very last words, he pointed with his finger to the heavens above. Whenever he spoke of God he would often tilt his head in a child-like manner and point gently to heaven above. Where are the words to capture such synchronous expressions of body and soul? This particular

> gesture I had seen a number of times. I never could fail to smile inside or to shrink in awe at the Forces he made such vivid reference to. I say he is a child.

In the end, Yogi Ramsuratkumar gave his name as the immediate entryway into his state of being, as spiritual practice and as prayer. There is a story that Yogi Ramsuratkumar once said quite enigmatically to Ma Devaki and the Sudama sisters, "This beggar will betray you." Lee Lozowick spoke one day in the beggar's darshan on this very statement, saying, " 'This beggar will betray you' means that if we look at the appearance of things and don't look at the depth of the unitive Reality underneath, then we will feel betrayed. Yogi Ramsuratkumar is not the body, not the shawls, not the cigarettes, not the crown. He is only the pure Divine, and he has given us his name. Whatever happens, his name will live on—not just beyond his lifetime, but forever."

WORK WITH OTHER SAINTS

There is a subtle connection that happens between saints and spiritual adepts of a high caliber; they do not need to be introduced in social terms, or to talk together to mull over the state of the world and the spiritual evolution of humanity. There is a natural connection of consciousness and exchange of awareness or energetic process that occurs between such beings without any effort or volition. Yogi Ramsuratkumar had such a relationship with countless individuals, including Mother Mayee and many of the swamis and adepts who lived in southern India during his time—Mouni Swami, Nyanar Swami, Gnanananda Giri Swamigal, the Shankaracharya of Kanchipuram, Krishna Premi—as well as the more popular, well-known gurus and teachers, including J. Krishnamurti, Satya Sai Baba, Swami Muktananda, Anandamayi Ma and Amritananda Mayi Ma, the popular divine mother who is known affectionately as "Ammachi."

Will visited Yogi Ramsuratkumar in February 1990 and told him that he had been to see Ammachi. The beggar was very happy to hear this, and told Will that when he met Ammachi he thought that she was the divine mother. At Ammachi's ashram Will heard the story that when Ammachi went to Tiruvannamalai, Yogi Ramsuratkumar came to see her and prostrated on the ground at her feet. As the story went, she asked him to sit on the stage with her while she gave darshan, and a photograph was taken of the two of them together.

When Will visited Yogi Ramsuratkumar again in 1993, he brought a gift from Ammachi for him:

> Swami had one love. It was lemons. He loved lemons. We call them limes. So whenever I went to the bazaar to get [*prasad* for him] it wouldn't

> be flowers, it would be lemons, because every time anybody came, he always gave them a lemon. I have so many dried-out lemons that he gave me—all gifts from him! I never ate them, I kept them and they just shrank and shrank. Any time I would bring lemons, he always had a big smile on his face, like I knew what he wanted.
>
> Once I went to Ammachi's ashram [in southern India] and I knew I was going to see Swami in Tiruvannamalai, so I bought a lemon and took it to her. Ammachi was giving darshan and I said, "Could you bless this for Yogi Ramsuratkumar?" She took the lemon, closed her hand around it, and then she gave it to me; I had never seen her do this before.
>
> Swami was at Sudama house, and I came up for darshan in a long queue. At the time Swami's hearing was really bad. For a couple years he had a hard time hearing everybody, and then it got better. His hearing became normal again. So, I brought this lemon from Ammachi and put it directly into Swami's hand. His eyes got really bright, and then he started smelling it, taking deep breaths even—just relishing it, you could tell. He didn't say a word.
>
> Then a big smile came over his face. I said to Ma Devaki, "Tell him this lemon is from Mata Amritanandamayi." She got the name wrong and Swami said, "Ammachi!" He looked over with this big smile and he said, "Oh, Will's brought this beggar something very fine." Big smile! He just kept sniffing at it, smelling it. He totally ignored everybody else and was just sniffing this lemon for a long time; every time he sniffed he had this big smile on his face. Then, he walked up and down. At that time when he was giving darshan he would pace up and down, with the people on either side. Every time he walked past me he had this beautiful, big broad smile because I'd brought him something nice.

Yogi Ramsuratkumar placed supreme importance on the guru's grace in one's life. Will Zulkowski said, "Swami's main teaching was, 'Find your master. Serve them well. Receive their grace.' " It was always Yogi Ramsuratkumar's opinion that no one could awaken their consciousness to the Divine by themselves, and it was delusional to think that one could because the ego is not going to turn on itself. Will said, "Is the thief going to turn himself into the police? Of course not, you know? The ego wants to keep stealing. The ego wants to keep surviving, so it does all this crazy stuff."

Mouni Swami, the "silent swami," wrote a book called *In the Days of Great Peace*, in which he spoke about Tiruvannamalai in the old days when Ramana Maharshi was alive, and of his experiences with him. He also wrote about going to the tomb of Haji Baba, a Muslim saint who lived in Tiruvannamalai when Ramana was alive. Haji Baba had had twelve disciples, and was known to have walked to Mecca. His tomb is situated near a small mosque, and the local Muslims often brought flower garlands as offerings to the tomb—a humble *samadhi* site with a roof on four posts. Will and Joan used to go to visit Pundi Swami, and then stop at Haji's tomb on the way back with offerings of incense and crackers or cookies for the caretaker there. The caretaker had a long peacock feather that he used to brush the tomb and then touch the seeker. When he was alive, Haji Baba used to send greetings to Ramana Maharshi. Before he died he said that if any sincere seeker came to his tomb after his death and asked anything in his name, he would intercede with God on their behalf.

Yogi Ramsuratkumar sometimes told people to go to Haji Baba's tomb. It was a place that he liked, and he told Will and Joan that it was a very powerful place. He once told Aruna not to go there too much, because it was so powerful that if she had a stray thought that she didn't really intend, it might be fulfilled. He instructed that one had to be careful what one prayed for around saints.

Yogi Ramsuratkumar knew all of the local hidden saints, many of whom lived very reclusive lives on Arunachala, and the beggar saint seemed to have relationships with them. The following story demonstrates this: Yogi Ramsuratkumar often said, "Go for a walk around the hill." Once he sent a Western man to walk around Arunachala and he somehow found his way onto one of the inner paths that was much less traveled. He ran across a cave, off the beaten trail, where someone was obviously living. When he came back to see Yogi Ramsuratkumar, he described it to him. Yogi Ramsuratkumar said, "Oh yes, there is a yogi who lives there. He's seven hundred and some years old. You know, we shouldn't bother those kinds of people."

THE BEGGAR'S WORK

"Most of this beggar's work is hidden. Only a fraction can be seen," Yogi Ramsuratkumar said at different times and in different ways. In the mid-nineties hundreds of people were coming to the temple on the ashram and Yogi Ramsuratkumar was not giving any formal darshans to anyone. People could only come and see him sitting in his chair by the statue in the big cavernous space of the temple as they circumambulated and *pranamed* in the queue with everyone else. Some people complained that things had changed; he was no longer accessible like he had been before. One day Devaki asked him directly, "Bhagawan, why don't you see the devotees personally as you used to?"

He answered by telling Devaki not to trouble herself over such matters, saying, "My Father is seeing them all. Anyone who enters this ashram is blessed by Father, whether they know it or not. Seeing people and talking to them is only a fraction of my Father's work. Most of this beggar's work is hidden." The cultivation of faith was at the core of his instruction to his devotees, the context of which was always absolute surrender to the will of God. "My Father alone exists," was the resounding phrase of his teaching. Swami Papa Ramdas called it "seeing Ram in everything."

Yogi Ramsuratkumar always told Ma Devaki, "Devaki and this beggar have to accept any situation Father puts us in and be grateful to God for it." He wanted his devotees to see God's grace in every circumstance, and he believed that "Father creates special situations for his chosen people in order to cleanse them, in the interest of Father's work." Like his spiritual father, Swami Ramdas, who saw Ram in every circumstance, no matter how difficult, dangerous or uncomfortable, Yogi Ramsuratkumar wanted his devotees to understand that "Father is everything"—even the worst of situations—and by "my Father alone" would everything be resolved, one way or another. Ma Devaki reflected:

> Bhagavan was right—things would get arranged themselves, by his grace. Wonderful in the least! There were so many miracles, which wouldn't look like miracles at all. One thing I noticed was that Bhagavan did not do any conspicuous miracle—that is, anything that would draw attention specifically as a miracle. Most of his miracles were part of the natural flow of life. You know, something very nice would happen that would fit so well with the rest of your life, with the rest of your routine, you wouldn't think that it had happened by his grace, but I knew in the heart that it was so only by his grace. Always there was some indication from him to assure me that it was only by his grace—just one word, one look, or very casually, "How is it now?" Then I would know that he knew all along and he had set it right! I was thinking it happened very naturally, when it was his hand!
>
> I saw it happening to so many people, people wouldn't even be aware that he had done it. That was something very remarkable about him. It would happen so naturally, so much part of your routine life, you wouldn't think it's by some special grace that has come upon you. I have seen some of them even boast that they had done it themselves. You can't blame them. They would claim, but all along it was his grace. That's what most of his work was, hidden. So much hidden that he would make a joke of it at times. He would say: "What does that beggar do, Devaki? He may only smoke. He eats, he sleeps, he smokes. All that he does is only this. It's my Father who is working. This beggar is not doing any work, Devaki." Then, to betray this he would laugh and laugh and laugh, so much in the special way of his, so that we would know he was making a joke. Otherwise, we may have come to think that he was serious.
>
> He could easily convince people into thinking that he was really only doing that—just smoking—because he would be silent smoking. After that he would be very tired, he would go to bed, and after waking up he would ask for something to eat. That's what you would see outwardly. So he would say: "This beggar is a very lazy beggar, he is very mad, he is very bad, all he can do is eat and sleep and smoke and buy cigarettes with the money that you people bring!" And then he would burst into laughter.

The miracle of faith was at the core of Yogi Ramsuratkumar's teaching. "Whatever happens, happens by Father's will. Whatever happens is His grace. Whatever happens is perfect, because Father is perfect. Whatever happens is a blessing. It's pure grace from Father. Whatever happens is the best that can happen. It is good for the individual, good for the whole cosmos. Father has to run the whole cosmos, so whatever suits Father's work, that alone happens."[33]

Because whatever happens is God's will, it is perfect as it is; to surrender to the will of God is to accept that every situation we find ourselves in is for our own good, and for the good of the world. In this birth, karma is enacted, and God's grace is at work underneath it all. Yogi Ramsuratkumar used to say often, "Whatever happens, happens to be God's will, and it is God's grace."

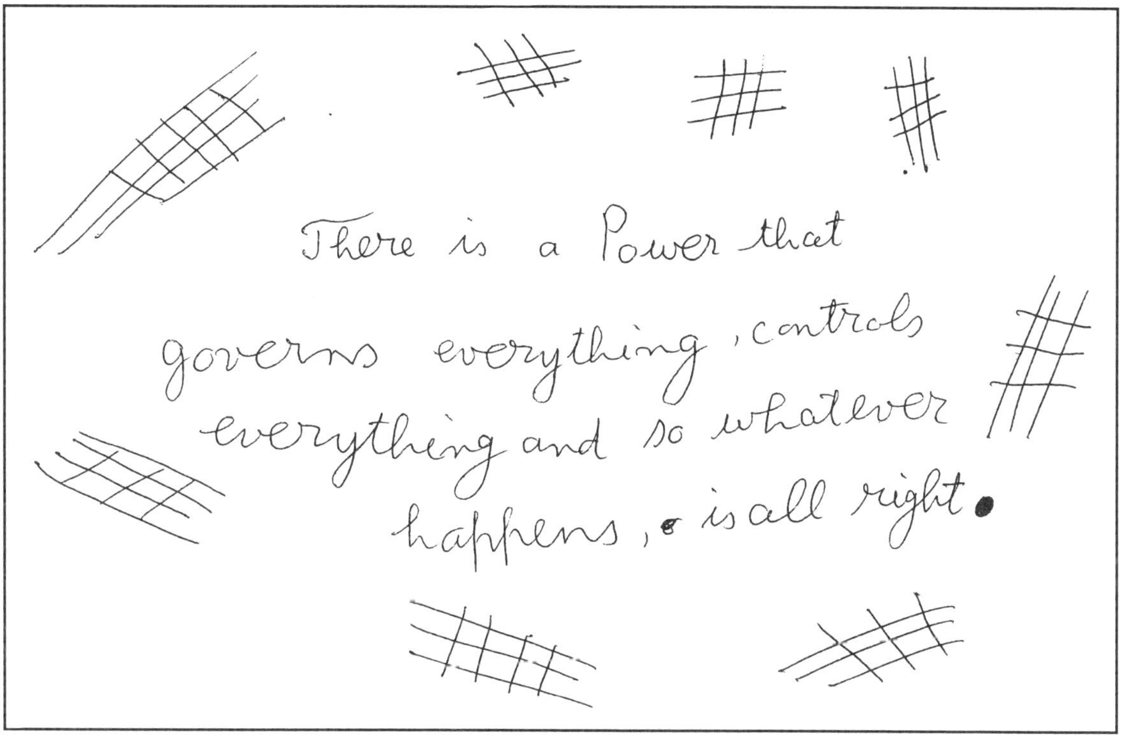

What did Yogi Ramsuratkumar mean when he said, "this beggar's work"? He once said, "Every movement, small or big, that this beggar makes is linked with Father's work. It's not a mere physical movement. Everything is linked in the cosmos. It's a totality. When this beggar rearranges things here, the atmosphere will not be the same again. This beggar has to be very careful. Every small movement is connected with the entire cosmos. This beggar prefers no changes."

The work was tacitly implied in every action that he made: "When we do everything for God, offer all our actions—every breath—then surrender comes. When God accepts this surrender, He takes possession of the body, mind and intellect. Then we become His

33 Yogi Ramsuratkumar, "The Divine Beggar On Himself," *Saranagatham*, January 2003, p. 33.

instruments. Father begins to work through us. We don't exist then. This beggar doesn't exist. Every thought, word and action of this beggar is governed by my Father, who is the cosmic controller."[34]

There were multiple levels upon which the beggar king of Tiruvannamalai "worked." In one dimension he worked with his devotees, blessing, instructing and setting a supreme example. He was a constant source of spiritual nourishment to all who came across his path. He was compelled to bless; as Hilda Charlton said of Yogi Ramsuratkumar, "He is bringing energy in from outside the universe." In this and all regards his work was multi-dimensional, spanning the spectrum from gross to subtle, from mundane to sublime and esoteric. He was as acutely attuned to the microcosm of life on planet Earth as he was to vast cosmic movements. He once said, "In this universe, everything is related. The sun, moon, the trees, this house, you and me—all are related. Any single movement of any one of them is bound to affect the entire cosmos. We should learn to look at life as a totality. It is all one life. All are related."[35]

Yogi Ramsuratkumar lived on a very delicate edge of awareness that gave him a raw sensitivity than spanned dimensions and created an acute perception of the vibrational reality of universal or archetypal principles and the interconnectedness of all things. As he once said to Swami Nityananda at Tapovanum, he was able to perceive the *rishis*—the awakened beings who wrote the *Vedas* by receiving them from subtle vibrations. It is understood that the *Vedas* and other sacred scriptures have an existence of their own on invisible planes of being; in other words, the truth—or the dharma—is alive, and communicates to those who have the awakened consciousness to be receptive to them. Yogi Ramsuratkumar spoke at times with Will Zulkowski about the impact of technology on the dharma and these subtle vibrations, not only on the planet, but in the cosmos. Will recalled:

> He told us why the scriptures were being interfered with. He said that in the old days the scriptures were in the air, and all you had to do was be silent and you could tune in to the scriptures and "hear" them. He could feel it, he could live it. But now there is electromagnetic interference from the TVs, from the radios, from the shortwaves, the cell phones, from all the static we're putting in the air electronically, and it's interfering with the scriptures—it's a big impediment [to the dharma]. He says that's why the dharma is failing, because people can no longer hear the scriptures when they are quiet.
>
> He said that, because of nationalism and the new global consciousness, there had to be a new reality, a new set of scriptures for the behavior of nations, not just for people. He thought that was a very important thing that had to be done, but he didn't ever say how, or when, or where this was

34 Ibid.

35 Yogi Ramsuratkumar, *Facets of the Diamond*, p. 157.

> going to come. Once he made a comment to somebody from Hilda's group, "Your satellites are interfering with this beggar's work." He was so sensitive that he could feel what the influence of the satellites was and what they were up to.

Sri Aurobindo said that enlightenment is only the beginning of the powerful process of transformation. Yogi Ramsuratkumar told Caylor Wadlington, "Every cell of the body goes through a transformation. Every cell of the body is transformed." One of the manifestations of the transformation that Yogi Ramsuratkumar went through after "Ramdas killed this beggar in 1952" was that he began to smoke in order to bear the intensity of his inner experience. He told various people on different occasions that he never liked smoking before "this madness came over this beggar." In fact it is known that he disliked smoking before his awakening; if anyone smoked in his presence, he felt quite sick. He told Ma Devaki, "After this beggar died at the lotus feet of Swami Ramdas, Father gave some work, and somehow this beggar began to smoke." To mitigate the effects of the smoking and the dryness of the mouth that resulted, he kept a piece of gooseberry in the corner of his mouth whenever he smoked.

Similarly, when Caylor Wadlington asked him directly why he smoked, Yogi Ramsuratkumar told him that before his awakening in 1952 he could never stand the smell of smoke, but after the changes that occurred in him by the grace of Swami Ramdas in 1952, he couldn't bear to be around humans because their vibrations were too gross; the only way he could do it was to make his body more gross, to make his aura more dense by smoking. Then he could bear the intensity that pummeled his senses. Smoking was his way of concentrating on a certain problem, of grounding himself on the earth.

There were two very unusual manifestations around his smoking: no one ever saw him exhale, and the usually strong smell of tobacco smoke was never detected around him or on his person. Many people noticed that he never exhaled, and Devaki once asked him where the smoke went. He just smiled and said, "This beggar doesn't know where it goes, Devaki. This beggar doesn't know where it goes."

Most people who came to him understood or could quickly sense that when they sat before him and he was smoking, it was the outward manifestation of a deeper work of blessing and purifying—the literal burning up of karma and *samskaras*—so that he was benefiting that person's physical, mental and spiritual welfare. It was commonly understood that, depending on one's receptivity, Yogi Ramsuratkumar smoked away one's karma, but his smoking was also an inextricable part of his universal work.

His state of consciousness and the condition of his awareness—"this beggar's madness"—was so rarified, so highly sensitized and delicate that he had to smoke in order to focus himself in the world of form in order to be able to work. This extreme sensitivity, as a delicate instrument of receiving, sending and working with energy on many different levels of creation at once, is reflected in the many stories of how he often had to leave whenever he was with a small group of people and someone else would suddenly walk up—as he said, he had to make an "adjustment."

Although this biography has sought to refrain from sensationalizing the miracles surrounding Yogi Ramsuratkumar, two stories in particular reflect how profoundly the beggar saint lived in a multidimensional world that goes far beyond the confines of consensus reality. Once a devotee and her daughter came to Sannadhi Street, bringing with them in a tiffin box some milk sweets as a gift for the beggar. When he asked the children about their school, they answered that they were studying in a Catholic school, and that the sisters there had told them that the Hindu gods were not capable of making miracles. As they relayed this to the beggar, he took a draw on his cigarette, then blew the smoke into the top of the tiffin box. Instantaneously the metal was oxidized to form a "smoke picture"—a permanent image of the beggar's face! Yogi Ramsuratkumar said, "Go and show that to the teachers. Tell the teacher that Hindu gods are also capable of making miracles!"

Once during the seventies a Westerner was visiting Yogi Ramsuratkumar. They were standing in a tea stall when the visitor asked the yogi, "What is death?" Suddenly the beggar smashed a fly on the counter. It's wings were broken, its innards spilled out. The fly was completely dead.

"Look," Yogi Ramsuratkumar said as he focused his attention intensely on the dead fly, his hands held up in blessing. The visitor watched in wonder as the fly slowly began to take shape, then twitch and move. Within seconds the fly was normal and flew away, resurrected from death. After answering the Westerner's question with this demonstration, the yogi said simply, "Death is energy."

The point of such stories is not to fascinate or distract us, but to stop the mind and give a teaching about the true nature of reality. The context for such miracles is ultimately found in a radical trust, a sublime faith, in the benevolence and transcendent intelligence of the Divine.

The beggar's universal work comes into focus around a number of stories from the seventies. Yogi Ramsuratkumar once said to Joan Zulkowski, "There is a fire on the hill. Don't worry. Don't have any fear. It won't hurt you. You're in Tiruvannamalai. All is well." Many times Yogi Ramsuratkumar said to various people, "The mountain helps us." He himself spent many years wandering on the mountain and taking shelter in its caves. When he left Ramanashram in 1960, it was Arunachala that was his first sanctuary. Looking at the difference in the photographs of Yogi Ramsuratkumar between 1960 and 1970, the change is stunning; clearly a deep process of transformation was still at work in him. Based on his own comments, this transformation seems connected in part to his subtle relationship to the divine force within Arunachala. When he made the statement, "There is a fire on the hill. Don't worry. Don't have any fear," he was also saying to Joan and Will, "God is alive in this world—all is well, have faith."

Where is the Fire?
The Fire is there on the hill there.
But I don't see it there.
You can see it if you are really bent upon seeing it

Are you afraid of being engulfed by it?
Then you can't see it
Have courage, no fear
You are sure to see it
Yogi Ramsuratkumar

The "Fire" referred to by Yogi Ramsuratkumar as poet is the mystical fire of Creation, the light that is perceived burning within Mount Arunachala as the embodiment of Shiva. The annual Deepam festival, when the top of the mountain is soaked with ghee and set on fire, is the symbolic enactment of what Yogi Ramsuratkumar experienced as a constant living reality. This holy Fire burned at the core of the beggar's absolute certainty: his faith in "a Power that governs everything, controls everything," and so, no matter what happens, everything is as it should be.

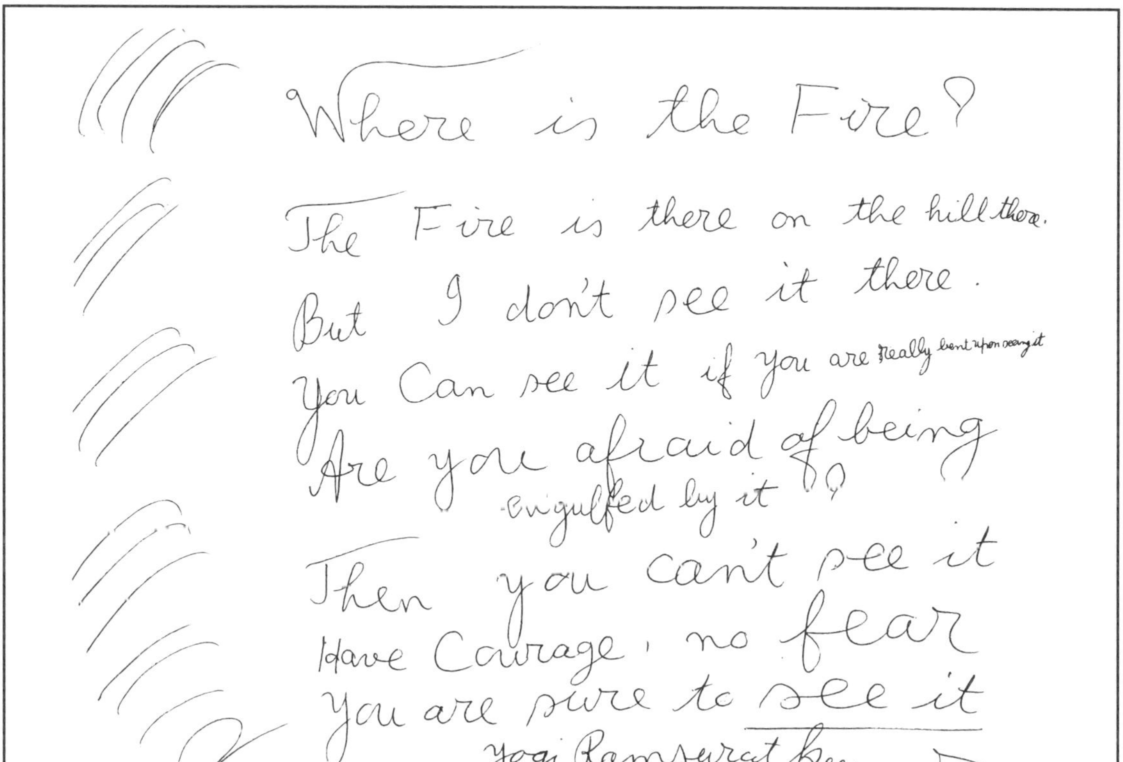
Where is the Fire?
The Fire is there on the hill there.
But I don't see it there.
You Can see it if you are Really bent upon seeing it
Are you afraid of being engulfed by it?
Then you can't see it
Have Courage, no fear
You are sure to see it
Yogi Ramsuratkumar

Yogi Ramsuratkumar also had a mysterious and transformational relationship to the cosmic fire of the Sun, the ultimate physical manifestation and symbolic representative of cosmic fire or divine light. Yogi Ramsuratkumar was very fond of the writings of Sri Jnanadeva, who wrote the following words, spoken by the supreme Lord, in his ecstatic prose poem, *Jnaneshwari*:

The radiance belonging to the Sun that illumines the entire world;

> that which is in the Moon, and in the Fire; that radiance, understand, is Mine own. All radiance that illumes the entire structure of the Universe including that of the Sun, is all My own, from the beginning to the end . . . . Permeating the Earth I sustain the beings through My vital force. I also nourish the herbs all, by becoming Soma, whose essence is the sap. I, becoming the Vaisvanara (Fire), abide within the body of animals, and, in association with the outgoing and incoming Vital Airs [breath], effect the digestion of the fourfold food.[36]

This wisdom refers specifically to what Jnanadev calls "Purusottama Yoga," through which the individual may realize the Divine Person, or the Supreme Self, residing within: "He who, freed of delusion, thus knows Me as the Purushsottam: he, having discovered the All, proffers with his whole being service unto Me, O Scion of Bharata."[37] The result of this ultimate realization is what Yogi Ramsuratkumar called "slavery, sweet slavery" to "Father in heaven" or the experience of the Divine as Ishvara, the personal God.

The relationship of the "cosmic man" with the sun as divinity—a kind of "sun yoga"—was one dimension of the master's work as heaven's servant. Yogi Ramsuratkumar wrote the following poem in praise of the sun in the mid-seventies:

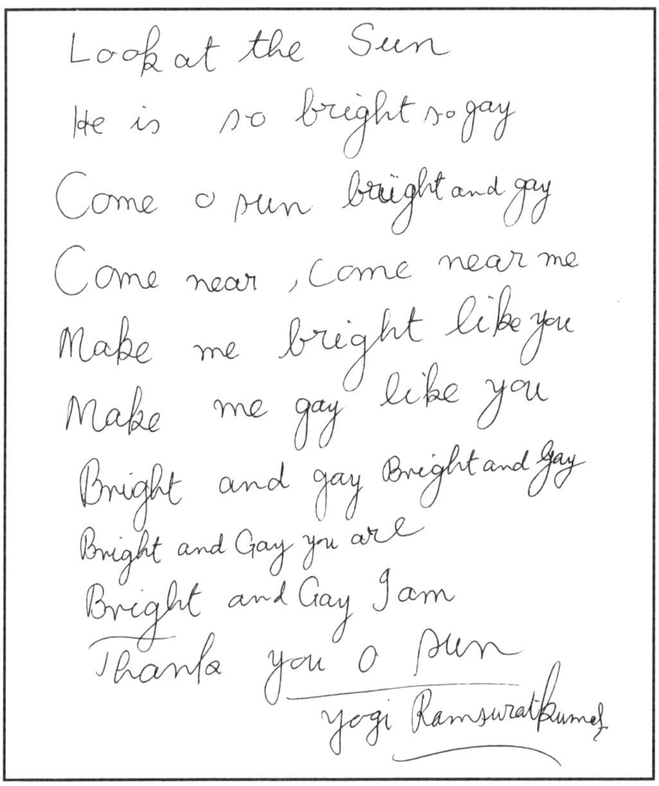

Look at the Sun
He is so bright so gay
Come o sun bright and gay
Come near, Come near me
Make me bright like you
Make me gay like you
Bright and gay Bright and gay
Bright and Gay you are
Bright and Gay I am
Thank you O sun
Yogi Ramsuratkumar

36 Jnanadeva, Jnaneshwari, Chapter XV, "Purusottama Yoga," pp. 471-472.
37 Ibid, p. 482.

Kirsti once found Yogi Ramsuratkumar comfortably resting on the stone pavement in the courtyard of the Shiva temple, peering at the sun through a crack in his fan. As she walked up, he asked, "How many *pradakshinas* have you done around the sun?" On another occasion she was on Mount Arunachala with Yogi Ramsuratkumar at the banyan tree cave. He pointed to the sun and said, "Krishna belongs to the lunar dynasty, Rama to the solar dynasty. Some people say this beggar comes from there," he mused wonderingly. It was a very hot day, and the blazing April sun that poured down on their heads was blinding to look at.

"This beggar carries the whole globe on his head," he said finally, with the virtue of a divine child.

Will Zulkowski remembered that he often found Yogi Ramsuratkumar out in the farmers' fields on the edge of town, lying on his back with his fingers interwoven, palms up and hands over his face. He was peering at the sun through a crack between his fingers.

> He would do this every day, for hours at a time. He was connected with the sun. The central Sun—the light behind the whole universe. That's the energy he worked with, for hours on end. He was murmuring, not a prayer, but repetitions—a mantra, or something. It was just like he was communicating with something.
>
> Once a devotee came back from seeing Sri Shankaracharya of Kanchipuram. He said that the Shankaracharya said, "Do you go see Yogi Ramsuratkumar?" The devotee said yes, then the Shankaracharya said, "Next time you come, you bring Yogi Ramsuratkumar," then he said, "Oh, he belongs to the sun!" The big Sun. I asked Hilda about that and she said, "That's his path— light. His whole path is just light."

The sun is the most potent and direct source of cosmic energy that is available to us; the esoteric practice of absorbing the light of the sun has been wisely used for millennia by yogis, shamans and healers for harmonizing, gathering energy, rejuvenating and purifying the human body. But further, the spiritual master, the awakened one, has become the sun through a process of radical surrender and divine alchemy.

Yogi Ramsuratkumar often spoke of other saints and masters as "the sun," making reference to a very high level of God-realization—the sun, as source of all life and light, being the symbol and literal representative of the Divine for our planet.

One year when Richard Schiffman was visiting, he asked the beggar, "Have you had the darshan of Satya Sai Baba?"

"Yes, this beggar has seen him," Yogi Ramsuratkumar replied.

"You've seen him in Puttaparthi?" Richard asked, referring to Sai Baba's ashram.

"No, this beggar has never been there," came the answer.

"Well, maybe you've seen him in Whitefield?"

"No, this beggar never went to Whitefield."

Finally Richard said, "Well, Madras. He goes to Madras occasionally."

"No, this beggar never saw him in Madras."

"Then, Swami," Richard said, "maybe you had a vision or something?"

"No, no, no. This beggar doesn't have visions."

Not willing to let go of the question, Richard went on, "Well, where did you see him?"

"I see him every day," Yogi Ramsuratkumar said.

Richard countered, "You mean, inwardly. You see him inwardly every day?"

"Yes," Yogi Ramsuratkumar said, and he pointed to the sun.

An anonymous Western seeker was traveling in India during the 1970s and decided to visit Tiruvannamalai, the home of Ramana Maharshi. He found himself in the brass bazaar with Yogi Ramsuratkumar, who he described as "a simple and majestic sadhu who had given up a university post for the beggar's bowl and staff, and who had wandered for thirty years or more, apprenticing himself at one time or another to Nityananda, Ramana and his own guru, Papa Ramdas"—or so the legend went as this particular seeker had heard it.

The Westerner spoke with Yogi Ramsuratkumar about various holy men he had visited. The beggar "roared with laughter and slapped his sides at the busy futility of my seeking." Then Yogi Ramsuratkumar asked the seeker to read a paragraph from Isherwood's translation of the *Yoga Sutras of Patanjali*, which he had found in the visitor's pockets. Many years later the same seeker wrote:

> It was a solemn enough passage, about discrimination and aspiration, but as I read it he kept bursting into laughter, and he made me read it again, many times over, as if it were a splendid comic turn, until he was holding his sides with the pain of his laughter, rocking from side to side at the hopelessness of my seeking.
>
> "How important!" he cried, poking me in the ribs. "This is such a serious matter!" And taking the book out of my hands, he was about to strike me on the head with it when a photo of Neem Karoli Baba fell out of it.
>
> His laughter was gone in an instant. He held the picture to his forehead for a long time, and then fell silent.
>
> Then he said quietly, "Oh, he is the sun! He is the sun! I am just a poor beggar, but he is the sun!" And with tears in his eyes, he grabbed my arm and held onto it tightly for long moments, pressing hard, and his body seemed to shine with an astonishing radiance. And after a while, he sent me away without a word.

All things pass. Even the stars burn out eventually, but from our finite perspective, the sun is the source of eternal light in our solar system. A bodhisattva is very much like the sun, but having realized the truth that exists beyond the physics of time and space, such a one shines eternally on all sentient beings, shedding light in the world, remaining steady, constant, life-sustaining. The *sadhaka* takes refuge in the words of such a saint as

Yogi Ramsuratkumar, who said, "This beggar will be coming back forever." The beggar said many times that if even one person benefited from his life, he would always return to this earth. He also said, "The presence of one perfect being can change the whole atmosphere; whatever he does will benefit the whole mankind, not just individuals alone. People are suffering. Where a saint lives, life becomes worth living once again. People will find life worth living again! There is only one sun, and you see how its light benefits the whole world."[38]

Many people have called Yogi Ramsuratkumar an avatar. It is a word that is often misused in the West, but if we take an avatar to mean a sudden outburst of divine energy—a being with the radiance of the sun—then the use of such an appellation becomes true. The sun shines on all alike.

It is no accident that for so many years when the beggar lived on the streets he chose the punnai tree as his shelter—the very tree that plays a significant part in the myths of Hinduism. Almost every village in south India has shrines for certain archaic goddesses, sometimes rough or unhewn stones representing the village "Amma" or "Mother" who wards off evil and propagates life. Of these deities, it is Kali and Paramesvari who are said to live in a grove of punnai trees. What is unique about these shrines is that they are available to everyone, not just to a spiritual, intellectual or material elite.[39]

But the most popular legend of the punnai tree sheds a greater light on the beggar king's choice of habitation. The punnai tree is considered sacred to Lord Krishna because he once enacted an important *lila* with the *gopis*. As the story goes, Krishna discovered the *gopis*, the love-maddened maidens of Vraja, swimming naked in the Yamuna River:

> The maidens of Vraja thought of Krishna constantly. In the first month of winter, they observed "the vow of the Goddess." Taking a bath in the waters of the river Yamuna at daybreak, they would make an image of the Goddess in sand, worshipping it with sandal paste and fragrant flowers and incense, and laying many gifts before it. As each maiden performed the worship, she repeated the same prayer, "O Goddess! O Great Maya of the Universe! Be pleased to grant the son of Nanda to me as my husband!" Once, in the course of that vow, the maidens left their garments as usual on the bank and entered the waters of the Yamuna nude, playing merrily. All the time, however, in mind, word and deed, they were with Krishna. That day Krishna, seeing them from a distance, collected all their garments and surreptitiously climbed up a kadamba tree[40] nearby, laughing to himself, and hanging the garments on the branches that now appeared "like fluttering banners from a distance."
>
> Perceiving the trick that Krishna was playing, the maidens were

38 *Facets of the Diamond*, p. 155.

39 H. Krishna Sastri, *South Indian Images of Gods and Goddesses*, pp. 223-224.

40 Punnai tree.

> simultaneously overcome with love and embarrassment. Krishna spoke to them, saying that he would give their garments back if they came to him of their own accord. Bashfully, the maidens looked at each other and smiled, but no one came out of the water. They consulted and finally said: "Dear Krishna! Do not be unjust with us. We know that you, the son of Nanda, whom the whole of Vraja adores, are our beloved. But pray, do return our clothes, for we shiver so with cold." But plead as they would, Krishna refused. His face beaming with smiles, he said they had to obey him first.[41]

Covering their bodies chastely with their hands, the gopis came shyly out of the water, but Krishna, "perceiving the purity of their hearts," told them that they had offended the gods by entering the water nude during the observance of a religious vow. "For the expiation of this sin," Krishna said, well-known for his mischievousness, "you should bow, raising joined hands to your heads. Then shall you receive your clothes."

Hearing this command that seemed "full of religious significance," the maidens tried to obey, but with one hand held up in praise, and the other covering their bodies. Krishna was relentless and said, "Respects to the Lord should be paid with both hands!" Driven to utter helplessness, the gopis realized that Krishna was asking complete surrender of them and that through their vulnerability and the baring of their bodies and souls, they would receive grace. Raising both hands in praise, and with perfect trust in the beneficence of the Lord, the *gopis* walked out of the river, cleansed of all flaws.

Satisfied at last with this act of pure love and total surrender, Krishna gave them back their clothes and smiled upon them with the radiance of a *crore* of suns. Having known all along the deepest desire of their hearts, Krishna blessed them and granted their wish to find fulfillment through the enjoyment of the Lord, saying, "You will spend your autumnal nights in enjoyment with me." Holding his promise close to their hearts, the maidens returned to Vraja, contemplating the lotus feet of the Lord.[42]

"Don't divide. Don't divide," Yogi Ramsuratkumar said. "Krishna said to Arjuna, 'Except for me not the smallest thing exists. I alone exist.' The whole cosmos and everything in it is His body. This beggar is just dust at His feet." And yet, in a *bhava* Yogi Ramsuratkumar once said, "This beggar is mad. When the madness comes, sometimes he feels he is Krishna!"

The beggar who lived under the punnai tree was himself the living example of total vulnerability, perfect trust and surrender to the Supreme Lord. His childlike innocence, sublime sweetness and crystal-like *vastu* were demonstrations of a true *prema murti*, an embodiment of love. And yet, Yogi Ramsuratkumar remains forever a mystery—a great human being who lived beneath a punnai tree and simultaneously was the One who shines with the radiance of ten million suns.

---

41 Prof. B.N. Goswamy and Prof. A.L. Dallapiccola, *Krishna, the Divine Lover*, p. 49.

42 Ibid, pp. 49-50.

दत्तात्रेय हरे कृष्ण
उन्मत्तानन्ददायक
दिगम्बर मुने बालपिशाच
ज्ञानसागर

O Dattatreya, O Hari, O Krishna
O the giver of wild joy, O sky-clothed
O the silent, O Child-like innocent,
O the one who eats within

Glossary

Abhisheka. Refers to the ceremonial act of pouring consecrated water or other substances on an empowered, ritual object such as a Shiva lingam, or on a devotee; an anointing; a direct empowerment, initiation or spiritual transmission.

Achintyarupa. The unfathomable, unknowable Divine in form.

Amla or Amlaka. The Indian gooseberry; a round, green, very sour fruit.

Arati. Traditional worship ceremony that usually includes waving a burning flame (camphor or ghee) on a tray before the image of a deity or holy figure along with offerings of incense, flowers, water and possibly other sacred substances.

Arhat. One who is worthy of reverence by virtue of having attained a state of perfection or Buddhahood.

Arunachalesvara Temple. The large ancient Shiva temple in Tiruvannamalai, Tamil Nadu, India where Yogi Ramsuratkumar spent a great deal of time from 1959 through 1993.

Asvattha. Sacred peepal or bodhi tree; a type of fig tree venerated by Indians as sacred and referred to as the "World Tree" and the "Tree of Life," the asvattha is symbolic of cosmic existence, which has its roots in the transcendent realms, while its branches extend into the world.

Avadhuta ("cast off"). A spiritual adept who has cast off all worldly things and concerns; a human being who has attained divine knowledge and has relinquished all ties to the world.

Bhagawan ("Lord"). The Supreme Lord; also used as a title of reverence indicating the divinity of the spiritual master.

Bhajans. Devotional songs of worshipful praise.

Bhiksha. The alms that the *bhikshu* receives in the form of food.

Bhikshu. A renunciate monk (usually Buddhist) who receives his or her food through begging for alms.

Crore. Ten million.

Damaru. The drum of the Hindu god, Shiva, which accompanies him as Lord of the Dance. It is shaped like an hourglass, with each half representing male and female forces; from the symmetry of the two, the cosmos is created.

Darbar. The king's royal court.

Dattatreya. A legendary sage who was elevated to the status of a deity. He was the archetypal crazy-wise adept, an *avadhuta* who was considered the incarnation of Vishnu, but who is revered by worshippers of both Vishnu and Shiva. He was credited with writing the *Avadhuta Gita, Jivan-Mukta-Gita* ("Song of Living Liberation") and the *Tripura-Rahasya* ("Tripura's Secret Teaching").

Deepam. The Festival of Light in Tiruvannamalai when the top of Mt. Arunachala—considered the embodiment of Lord Shiva—is covered with ghee and then lit; the flame can be seen for miles around and is symbolic of the infinite light of creation, or the power of Shiva.

Deva ("shining one, god"). Refers to the Divine but also to lesser deities or divine forces in nature.

Ganga. The river Ganges, sacred to Hindus.

Garha Prevasam. The ritual ceremony that is performed to enter a new house; a spiritual house-warming.

Gayatri. One of the most sacred verses of the *Rig Veda*, it is a prayer to the sun, Savitar, whose celestial splendor is the divine source of life, potency and manifestation.

Gopuram. In South Indian temple architecture, tall stone towers that are covered with sculptures of deities, celestial beings and mythological stories.

Guru Purnima. Traditional Hindu celebration of the appearance of the guru in the world, held every year on the Thursday after the first full moon in July.

Gurubhai. Brothers in the guru; those who have the same guru.

Guru-bhakti ("devotion to the teacher"). Devotion in the form of loving attachment to the teacher or guru as deity.

Gurunadhar. Writing the name of God as a practice.

Ista Devata. The chosen deity of a spiritual practitioner.

Japa mala. A chain of beads used as a helpful aid in the repetition of a sacred name or formula as a form of meditation, often made of *rudraksh* (a sacred seed), rock crystal, sandalwood, tulsi seeds or other stone beads.

Jayanthi. Birthday.

Jivatman. The personal or individual soul associated with the physical body.

Kali-Yuga ("dark age"). The present eon of spiritual decline.

Krishna. An ancient spiritual adept who was deified as an incarnation of Vishnu. The mythology of Krishna is extensive in Hindu literature; he is immortalized in the *Bhagavad Gita* and many other sacred texts.

Kripala. Grace.

Lila ("sport or play"). The spontaneous cosmic play of the creator in the manifest world; divine playfulness;

Lingam. A symbol of the universal masculine principle generally connected with Shiva, depicted as a stone in the form of a phallus.

Mahasamadhi. Physical death of a saint.

Mahasiddha. A great adept who has realized perfection or enlightenment, usually through having acquired the tantric teachings and attained great (*maha*) spiritual powers or accomplishment (*siddhis*).

Mandapam. A decorative structure over a sacred place, usually an ornate roof held up by columns.

Mandir. Hindu temple.

Mudra ("seal"). An objective hand gesture or bodily posture used to communicate or invoke primal truths or divine energy, which either express or transmit specific spiritual states or moods.

Murti ("form"). Any empowered image of the deity or guru, which can be invoked for the purpose of worship: for example, a stone or bronze sculpture or a photograph.

Mutt. An ashram, temple or place where sadhana is performed.

Nama japa. Repetition of the name of God as a spiritual practice that focuses the attention on the deity and the deity's qualities or essence, the purpose of which is to align the practitioner with the deity.

Namaskar. Respectful salutation.

Nellikkai. Indian gooseberry. *Amla* or *amlaka* in Sanskrit.

Nirvikalpi-samadhi. The state that obliterates all identifications or distinctions which lead to a sense of any separate self, which leads to liberation from illusion.

Paramatman. The supreme Spirit or Self.

Pradakshina. Hindu rite of circumambulation expressing reverence to a deity, shrine, temple, ashram or sacred object.

Prakriti ("nature"). The primal principle of Creation, or the world of form, from subtle to gross.

Pranam. A reverential bow or greeting to the Divine or a respected individual, by pressing the palms together at the level of the chest, by touching the feet of the one being greeted and then one's forehead, or by prostration.

Pranayama. A yogic discipline involving the careful regulation of the breath through specific techniques to induce higher states of consciousness for the purpose of spiritual transformation.

Prasad or Prasada ("grace"). Divine blessings in any form; usually refers to the gifts that are exchanged between guru and devotee, often in the form of food or flowers.

Prema-bhakti. Transcendent love of God.

Puja ("worship"). A ritual worship ceremony usually including the offering of flowers, incense, mantras, fire, water.

Pujari. One who performs *puja*.

Purusha ("spirit"). The transcendental Person or pure Spirit, as the cosmic opposite of Prakriti.

Rama. One of the incarnations of Vishnu and the main hero of the *Ramayana*.

Rasa ("taste"). An objective mood that has many different textures and may range from the quintessence of bliss (*ananda*) to many different moods of divine love to the fire of longing; also refers to the nectar of immortality or *amrita*—the alchemical elixir of the tantric or yogic path. Some sources say there are nine objective rasas: peace; hero (courage, nobility); wonder and awe; erotic; humorous; furious (violent passions and unrestrained energy); odious; pathos (sadness, compassion, sorrow); terrible (dread or fear).

Rishi. A specific type of ancient sage, also called seers, saints, and inspired poets, to whom the hymns of the *Vedas* were revealed. The *rishis* had the ability to "see" or perceive truth which resides in the luminosity that exists behind the veil of manifest existence.

Sadhana. The spiritual path, or way of realization or awakening.

Sadhika. A female spiritual pracitioner.

Sadhaka. A male spiritual pracitioner.

Samadhi ("ecstasy"). A powerful internal state of unification, or no separation between ego and other, in which one experiences the fundamental oneness or connectedness of all phenomena. This state can be experienced as complete absorption within, or as an open-eyed ecstasy (*sahaj samadhi*).

Sampangi. Fragrant white flower often used in garlands.

Sampanthavinayaka. A form of Ganesh.

Samskaras ("activators"). Habitual actions or volitions that form one's character and keep one enmeshed in the world of illusion.

Sarvadhikari. Chief administrator.

Sarvatmabhava. Transcendent, total love.

Satguru. Root guru.

Seva. Steadfast service, usually through action, offered to the guru or teacher as a way of sadhana, and through which one receives blessings and initiation; the idea of *seva* is that work is love made manifest.

Shakti. In general terms, the feminine aspect of the Divine; the power aspect of the Divine.

Shiva. One of the threefold deities of Hinduism that make up the Trimurti or triune Godhead: Brahma (creation), Vishnu (preservation), and Shiva (destruction.) Shiva is the god who destroys illusion and grants liberation and wisdom.

Siddha Purusha. One who has realized the Divine Person within and demonstrates the accomplishment of that through compassionate action.

Sloka. The smallest literary unit of the epics, such as the *Mahabharata*; also refers to a verse of poetry or song.

Soma. A fermented juice that was one of the primary ingredients of Vedic sacrifice (a libation or divine intoxicant); also an inner secretion produced in the body, usually through yogic means or intense spiritual practice, which confers immortality.

Sudama. Childhood friend of Krishna.

Tapas ("heat"). Asceticism or the endurance of extremes or discomforts in sadhana that produce an inner heat.

Taraka mantra. A mantra that liberates the practitioner from illusion.

Tulsi. (Also tulasi.) A plant whose leaves and flowers are sacred to Lord Vishnu, and to Krishna, an incarnation of Vishnu, in particular; also known as Holy Basil.

Vastu. A dwelling, habitation, chamber or house.

Vibhuti ("to manifest"). Any manifestation of divine power; an outpouring of divine energy, sometimes in the form of miracles.

Vigraha ("form"). The Divine represented through a manifest form; a consecrated image.

Vaikuntha. Vishnu's eternal paradise.

Vinayaka. A form of Ganesh, the elephant-headed god who removes obstacles.

Vishnu. One of the threefold deities of Hinduism that make up the Trimurti or triune Godhead: Brahma (creation), Vishnu (preservation), and Shiva (destruction.) The *lila* or play of creation is Vishnu's dream. As the great sustainer, and because of his compassion and love for creation, Vishnu took many incarnations on Earth, including as Lord Rama and Lord Krishna, wherein he enacted many *lilas*.

Bibliography

Capellini, Young & Farcet. *Facets of the Diamond.* Prescott, AZ: Hohm Press, 1994.

Caplan, Mariana. *Do You Need A Guru?* London: Thorsons, 2002.

______. *Divine Message To Humanity: H.H. Yogi Ramsuratkumar, The God Child, Tiruvannamalai.* Pondicherry, India: A.R.P.N. Rajamanickam, 1988.

______. *Divine Slave Gita.* Prescott, AZ: Hohm Press, 1986–1991.

Feuerstein, Georg. *The Yoga Tradition.* Prescott, AZ: Hohm Press, 1998.

Feuerstein, Georg. *Encyclopedic Dictionary of Yoga.* New York: Paragon House, 1990.

Goswamy, Prof. B.N. and Dallapiccola, Prof. A.L. *Krishna, the Divine Lover.* New Delhi: B.I. Publications, 1982.

Grof, Stanislav. *The Adventure of Self-Discovery.* New York: State University of New York, 1988.

_______. *Hohm Sahaj Mandir Study Manual, Vols. I–IV.* Prescott, AZ: Hohm Press, 1996–2002.

Jnanadev, Sri. *Jnaneshwari.* Translated from Marathi by Ramchandra Keshav Bhagwat. Madras: Samata Books, 1979.

Lozowick, Lee. *For the Love of God.* Mt. Tabor, NJ: Hohm Press, 1977.

Lozowick, Lee. *The Cheating Buddha.* Mt. Tabor, NJ: Hohm Press, 1980.

Lozowick, Lee. *The Only Grace Is Loving God.* Prescott, AZ: Hohm Press, 1982.

Lozowick, Lee. *Poems of a Broken Heart, Part I.* Chennai, India: Sister Nivedita Academy, 1993.

Lozowick, Lee. *Poems of a Broken Heart, Part II.* Chennai, India: Sister Nivedita Academy, 1997.

Lozowick, Lee. *Death of a Dishonest Man.* Prescott, AZ: Hohm Press, 1998.

Martin, Sita. *The Hunger of Love: Versions of the Ramayana.* Kanya Kumari, India: The Yogi Ramsurat Kumar Manthralayam Trust, 1995.

McDaniel, June. *The Madness of the Saints.* Chicago: The University of Chicago Press, 1989.

Ramani, L. "The Joyous Presence of Yogi Ramsuratkumar," *Saranagatham.* Tiruvannamalai, India: Yogi Ramsuratkumar Trust, May 2002.

Ramdas, Swami. *Ramdas Speaks.* Bombay: Bhavan's Book University, 1971.

Ramdas, Swami. *In the Vision of God.* Bombay: Bhavan's Book University, 1974.

Rangarajan, Professor V. *Glimpses of a Great Yogi.* Madras: Sister Nivedita Academy, 1987.

Redington, James D. *Vallabhacharya's Commentaries on the Love Games of Krshna.* Delhi: Motilal Banarsidass Publishers, 1990.

Sadaiyan, Perumal. *Treasures of the Heart: The Unforgettable Yogi Ramsuratkumar.* Tiruvannamalai, India: Published by Perumal Sadaiyan, 1998.

Sastri, H. Krishna. *South Indian Images of Gods and Goddesses.* Madras: Asian Education Services, 1995.

Satchidananda, Swami. *The Gospel of Swami Ramdas.* Kerala, India: Anandashram, 1990.

Sepuri, Haragopal. *Experiences With Yogi Ramsuratkumar.* Madras: Sister Nivedita Academy, 1989.

Sepuri Haragopal. *Further Experiences With Yogi Ramsuratkumar and Other Experiences.* Madras: Sister Nivedita Academy, 1994.

Srinivasan, Professor Ranganayaki. *Bhagawan Sri Yogi Ramsurat Kumar: His Divine Life and Message.* Kanya Kumari, India: Yogi Ramsurat Kumar Manthralayam Trust, 1991.

______. *Tattva Darsana.* Professor Sadhu V. Rangarajan, Editor. Chennai, India: Sister Nivedita Academy, quarterly publication, 1988–2002.

______. *Tawagoto.* Prescott, AZ: Hohm Press, quarterly publication, 1988–2002.

Tyberg, Judith. *The Language of the Gods.* Los Angeles: East-West Cultural Centre, 1970.

Vijayalakshmi. *Waves of Love.* Tiruvannamalai, India: Yogi Ramsuratkumar Ashram, 2003.

Vijayaraghavan, Sujatha. *The Spiritual Renaissance in India: 1830–1980.* Pondicherry, India: Sujatha Vijayaraghavan, Pondicherry University, 1988.

Wadlington, Truman Caylor. *Yogi Ramsuratkumar, The Godchild, Tiruvannamalai.* Madras: published by Truman Caylor Wadlington, 1972 and 1979.

______. *Yogi Ramsuratkumar Souvenir Book.* Tiruvannamalai, India: Yogi Ramsuratkumar Trust, 1995.

Interviews

Bagrodia, Ashish. Interview with author. Bombay, India, December 13, 2002.

Caplan, Mariana. Interview with author. Mahabalipuram, India, December 9, 2002; Bombay, India, December 19, 2002.

Fedorschak, Vijaya. Interview with author. Tiruvannamalai, India, November 28, 2002 and March 10, 2003.

Field, Wendel. Interview with Tom Lennon. Bloomington, Indiana, June 24, 2002.

Gogul, Dev. Interview with author. Tiruvannamalai, India. November 25, 2002.

Jairaj, C.A. Interview with author. Sivakasi, India, December 3, 2002.

Jayarama. Interview with author. Tiruvannamalai, India, November 25, 2002.

Ma Devaki and Vijayalakshmi. Interviews with Mariana Caplan. The Yogi Ramsuratkumar Ashram, Tiruvannamalai, India, December 2, 3, 4 and 5, 2002.

Mukilan, J. Interviews with author. Chennai, India, December 7 and 9, 2002.
Nateshan and Sarada. Interview with author. Trivandrum, India, December 3, 2002.
Nityananda, Swami. Interview with author. Tapovanum, India, November 24, 2002.
Pankkajam. Interviews with author. Tiruvannamalai, India, November 30 and December 1, 2002.
Paranjape, Makarand. Interview with author. Bombay, India, December 14, 2002.
Parthasarathy. Interview with author. Tiruvannamalai, India, November 26, 2002.
Pon Kamaraj, T. Interview with Mariana Caplan. Kanya Kumari, India, December 8, 2002.
Rajalakshmi. Interview with the author. Chennai, India, December 11, 2002.
Rajulu, Shankara. Interivew with Mariana Caplan. Madurai, India, December 10, 2001.
Ramamoorthy. Interview with author. Tiruvannamalai, India, November 30, 2002.
Ramanlal. Interview with author. Chennai, India, December 10, 2002.
Ravi. Interview with author. Tiruvannamalai, India, November 28, 2002.
Reddy, Dwarak Nath and Sandiya. Interview with Ute and Volker Augustyniak. Tiruvannamalai, India, January 23, 2003.
Saravanan. Interview with author. Tiruvannamalai, India, November 27, 2002.
Shakuntala. Interview with author. Tapovanum, India, November 24, 2002.
Steinitz, Purna. Interview with author. Tiruvannamalai, India, November 28, 2002.
Subramanian, N.S. (Mani). Interviews with Mariana Caplan, December 7 and 8, 2002. Interview with author, December 1, 1998; December 2002.
Vasugi. Interviews with author. Sivakasi, December 2 and 3, 2002.
Wadlington, Truman Caylor. Interviews with Tom Lennon. Denver, Colorado, June 1, 2002; June 23, 2992; November 3, 2002; January 26, 2003.
Zuccarello, Balarama. Interview with author. February 6, 2003.
Zulkowski, Will. Interviews with Tom Lennon. New York, November 8-9, 2002.

Unpublished Material

Bagrodia, Ashish. Memoirs. Bombay, India: 2002.
De Rosanbo, Alain. Untitled Memoirs. Brussels: 2003.
Janarthanan, S.P. *A Life With Truth*. English translation by K.S. Padmanabhan: India, 2002.
Kirsti. Untitled Memoirs. Tiruvannamalai, India: November, 2002.
Kirsti. "At the Gate of Yogi Ramsuratkumar". Tiruvannamalai, India.
Prakash Yogini. "Treasure of Grace," Ramji Ashram, Kanya Kumari, India: 2001.
Wadlington, Truman Caylor. "Journals of Meetings with Yogi Ramsuratkumar," June 1970 - 1976; "Book Ideas" and "Journals of Meetings with Yogi Ramsuratkumar," 1978 - 1980; India 1993.
Wadlington, Truman Caylor. "Written Accounts of Meetings by Various Hilda Devotees," from January 1974; August 1978; October 1978; May 1979.

Temples and Ashrams

The Yogi Ramsuratkumar Ashram, Tiruvannamalai, Tamil Nadu, India. Daily *bhajans* are held 10-12 noon and 4-6 p.m. in the Pradhan Mandir or main temple, which accommodates four thousand people and houses the *mahasamadhi* shrine of Yogi Ramsuratkumar. The Pradhan Mandir is open from 5:30 a.m. until 9:00 p.m. every day. Also on the property are the Darshan Mandir, library, meditation hall, dining hall and the Veda Patashala. The Veda Patashala is open to visitors 9-10 a.m. and 6-7 p.m. daily. Prasad is served in the dining hall at 8:30 (breakfast) and noon (lunch). In addition to daily *pujas* and *arati* services, at eight o'clock every morning a formal Vedic ceremony (*abhisheka*) is performed for the Shivalingam and Salagrama which have been installed at the *mahasamadhi* shrine.

In addition the ashram performs many charitable services including providing a school for children, medical services for the local community, and a program for feeding sadhus. A monthly journal, *Saranagatham*, is published by the Yogi Ramsuratkumar Trust. Sarvadhikari: Justice T.S. Arunachalam.

Yogi Ramsuratkumar Trust
Agrahara Collai
1833/1, Chengam Salai
Tiruvannamalai 606603
Tamil Nadu, India
Telephone: 04175-37567

Manthralayam, Kanimadam, Tamil Nadu. A temple complex situated near the ocean at Kanya Kumari in the small village of Kanimadam that has been functioning since 1993. A twelve-foot-high stone vigraha or statue of Yogi Ramsuratkumar is installed in the main temple where daily *bhajans* and Ramnam are chanted. Chief administrator: T. Pon Kamaraj.

Ramji Ashram, Kumarakoil, Tamil Nadu. Daily bhajans and Ramnam are conducted in the shrine room. Contact: Swamini Om Prakash Yogini.

The Yogi Ramsuratkumar Bhavan, Mauritius. Established by French devotee Krishna Carcelle in 1987, this *mandir* conducts regular *bhajans* and Ramnam and publishes a small monthly review, *RamNama*. Contact Krishna Carcelle via Internet.

Hosur. A temple that houses a stone sculpture of Yogi Ramsuratkumar in seated posture where worship ceremonies are conducted. Contact Sri Swarnanathan.

Srivilliputhur. A temple is nearing completion. Contact Sri Perumalappan.

Tuticorin. A *bhajan mandapam* is being constructed where chanting will be conducted.

Chennai. Regular satsangs and bhajans are conducted and a monthly journal, Mano Layam, is published. The Sri Yogi Ramsuratkumar Bhajan Mandali meets periodically and holds *satsang* and *bhajans*. Contact Ragahawashramam Smt. Sucheendram Rajalakshmi.

Shri Karumari Amman Peetam. Regular *satsangs*, celebration of Yogi Ramsuratkumar's *jayanthi* and a monthly journal, "Sri Navasakthi Vijayam, is published. Contact Smt. Om Bhavatharini.

Triveni (Hohm Sahaj Mandir), Prescott Arizona. This ashram was established in 1980 by Lee Lozowick. *Bhajans* and chanting the name of Yogi Ramsuratkumar are conducted and formal teachings given three times weekly. The daily ashram schedule includes morning meditation and *arati puja.* Yogi Ramsuratkumar Jayanthi and three formal Celebrations, including Guru Purnima, are held annually. Study groups are available in the U.S. and Canada: Berkeley, San Diego and Claremont, California; Vancouver, B.C.; New York City; and Boulder, Colorado. Contact: Paul.

Hohm Community
P.O. Box 31
Prescott, Arizona 86302

Ramji Association, France. An ashram established by Lee Lozowick in 1995. *Bhajans* and chanting the name of Yogi Ramsuratkumar are conducted three times weekly. Study groups are available in Europe: London, Paris, Montpellier, Rennes; Freiburg and Hamburg, Germany. Contact: Clint or Brindavan Callahan.

Ramji Association
86260 St Pierre de Maillé
France

Triveni II, Hohm Sahaj Trust, Tiruvannamalai, Tamil Nadu. Established by Lee Lozowick in 1999, this ashram is located one block from the front gate of the Yogi Ramsuratkumar Ashram. A regular schedule of events and charitable activities can be obtained by contacting Volker and Ute Augustyniak.

Hohm Sahaj Trust
Triveni II
95 Chengam Road.
Ramana Nagar
Tiruvannamalai, India 606603

Trimurti, Bozeman, Montana. An ashram established in 2000 by Purna Steinitz. Chanting and *satsang* are held regularly. Contact: Purna Steinitz

Trimurti
P.O. Box 1952
Bozeman, Montana 59771

HOHM PRESS publishes works in the fields of health, personal transformation, poetry, fine spiritual literature and children's books. If this book was of interest to you, we will be happy to send you a catalog.

Name ______________________________

Street or box number ______________________________

City ______________________________

State ____________________ Zip ____________________

Email ______________________________

☐ PLEASE DO NOT PUT MY NAME ON YOUR MAILING LIST.

HOHM PRESS publishes works in the fields of health, personal transformation, poetry, fine spiritual literature and children's books. If this book was of interest to you, we will be happy to send you a catalog.

Name ______________________________

Street or box number ______________________________

City ______________________________

State ____________________ Zip ____________________

Email ______________________________

☐ PLEASE DO NOT PUT MY NAME ON YOUR MAILING LIST.

HOHM PRESS
P.O. Box 2501
Prescott, Arizona 86302

HOHM PRESS
P.O. Box 2501
Prescott, Arizona 86302